PATTERSON SMITH REPRINT SERIES IN
CRIMINOLOGY, LAW ENFORCEMENT, AND SOCIAL PROBLEMS

REPORTS
OF THE
PRISON DISCIPLINE SOCIETY
OF BOSTON

PUBLICATION No. 155: PATTERSON SMITH REPRINT SERIES IN
CRIMINOLOGY, LAW ENFORCEMENT, AND SOCIAL PROBLEMS

REPORTS

OF THE

PRISON DISCIPLINE

SOCIETY

OF

BOSTON

The Twenty-nine Annual Reports of the Board of Managers
1826–1854
with a Memoir of Louis Dwight

Reprinted from the 1855 Edition
with the Illustrations restored
and a new Introduction
and Analytical Index added

VOLUME

4

Reports 16 to 20: 1841–1845

Montclair, N.J.
PATTERSON SMITH
1972

Annual Reports of the Prison Discipline Society, Boston
Originally published 1826 to 1854

Republished 1855 by the Society

Republished 1972 by Patterson Smith Publishing Corporation
Montclair, New Jersey 07042

New material copyright © 1972 by
Patterson Smith Publishing Corporation

ISBN: 0 87585–155–X

Library of Congress Catalog Card Number: 71–129322

SIXTEENTH

ANNUAL REPORT

OF THE

BOARD OF MANAGERS

OF THE

PRISON DISCIPLINE SOCIETY,

BOSTON, MAY, 1841.

—◆—

𝔅𝔬𝔰𝔱𝔬𝔫:

PUBLISHED AT THE SOCIETY'S ROOMS,
51 Court Street.

STEREOTYPED AT THE
BOSTON TYPE AND STEREOTYPE FOUNDERY.

1841.

CONTENTS.

———

CONSTITUTION

OF THE

Prison Discipline Society.

———◆———

ARTICLE 1. This Society shall be called the PRISON DISCIPLINE SOCIETY.

ART. 2. It shall be the *object* of this Society to promote the improvement of Public Prisons.

ART. 3. It shall be the *duty* of this Society to take measures for effecting the formation of one or more Prison Discipline Societies in each of the United States, and to co-operate with all such Societies in accomplishing the object specified in the second article of this Constitution.

ART. 4. Any Society, having the same object in view, which shall become auxiliary to this, and shall contribute to its funds, shall thereby secure for the Prisons, in the State where such Society is located, special attention from this Society.

ART. 5. Each subscriber of two dollars, annually, shall be a Member.

ART. 6. Each subscriber of thirty dollars, at one time, shall be a Member for Life.

ART. 7. Each subscriber of ten dollars, annually, shall be a Director.

ART. 8. Each subscriber of one hundred dollars, or who shall by one additional payment increase his original subscription to one hundred dollars, shall be a Director for Life.

ART. 9. The officers of this Society shall be a President, as many Vice-Presidents as shall be deemed expedient, a Treasurer, and a Secretary, to be chosen annually, and a Board of Managers, whose duty it shall be to conduct the business of the Society. This Board shall consist of six clergymen and six laymen, of whom nine shall reside in the city of Boston, and five shall constitute a quorum.

Every Minister of the Gospel, who is a member of this Society, shall be entitled to meet and deliberate with the Board of Managers.

The Managers shall call special meetings of the Society, and fill such vacancies as may occur by death or otherwise, in their own Board.

ART. 10. The President, Vice-Presidents, Treasurer, and Secretary, shall be, ex officio, Members of the Board of Managers.

ART. 11. Directors shall be entitled to meet and vote at all meetings of the Board of Managers.

ART. 12. The annual meetings of this Society shall be held in Boston, on the week of the General Election, when, besides choosing the officers as specified in the ninth article, the accounts of the Treasurer shall be presented, and the proceedings of the foregoing year reported.

ART. 13. The Managers shall meet at such time and place, in the city of Boston, as they shall appoint.

ART. 14. At the meetings of the Society, and of the Managers, the President, or, in his absence, the Vice-President first on the list then present, and in the absence of the President and of all the Vice-Presidents, such Member as shall be appointed for that purpose, shall preside.

ART. 15. The Secretary, in concurrence with two of the Managers, or, in the absence of the Secretary, any three of the Managers, may call special meetings of the Board.

ART. 16. The minutes of every meeting shall be signed by the Chairman or Secretary.

ART. 17. The Managers shall have the power of appointing such persons as have rendered essential services to the Society either Members for Life or Directors for Life.

ART. 18. No alteration shall be made in this Constitution except by the Society, at an annual meeting, on the recommendation of the Board of Managers.

ANNUAL MEETING.

—◆—

THE Sixteenth Annual Meeting of the Prison Discipline Society was held at No. 2 Marlboro' Chapel, on Monday, May 24, 1841, at 3 o'clock, P. M.   A quorum being present, the Rev. Dr. JENKS, the oldest Vice-President then present, whose duty it was, according to the Constitution, in the absence of the President, took the chair, and opened the meeting with prayer.   The Secretary read the minutes of the corresponding meeting of the last year.   At the request of the Chairman, Mr. H. M. WILLIS, one of the auditors, read the Treasurer's Report, and the certificate of its correctness by the auditors, JAMES MEANS and H. M. WILLIS.   Mr. DANIEL SAFFORD was appointed a committee to distribute, collect, and sort the votes for the officers of the ensuing year.   This being done, the officers of the preceding year were declared elected.   A vote of thanks was passed unanimously to Mr. CHARLES CLEVELAND, for his faithful and gratuitous performance of the duties of Treasurer, for many years.   The meeting then adjourned, after prayer, to meet in the large hall of the Marlboro' Chapel, on Tuesday, May 25, at 11 o'clock.   The Rev. Dr. LOWELL, at the request of the Chairman, closed the meeting with prayer.

The Public Meeting was held in the Marlboro' Chapel, according to adjournment, on Tuesday morning, at 11 o'clock.   The President, the Hon. SAMUEL T. ARMSTRONG, took the chair.   At his request, the Rev. Dr. JENKS read a part of the 25th chapter of Matthew, commencing with the 31st verse, to the close, and offered prayer.   The Secretary, Rev. LOUIS DWIGHT, read an abstract of the Annual Report.

The Rev. T. S. CLARKE, of Stockbridge, Mass., moved the acceptance of the Report, and reference of the same to the Board of Managers, to be published.   This resolution was seconded by the Rev. NEHEMIAH ADAMS, of Boston, and passed.

The Rev. EDWIN HOLT, of Portsmouth, N. H., moved the following resolution : —

Resolved, That the introduction of the improvements which have been found so valuable in Penitentiaries and State Prisons into County Prisons and Municipal Jails, — as far as they are practicable, — is loudly demanded as a work of great importance, and of indispensable necessity.

This resolution was seconded by the Rev. FRANCIS PARKMAN, D. D., of Boston, and passed.   The Rev. Dr. HOPKINS, President of Williams College, submitted the following resolution : —

Resolved, That the results of the Prison Discipline Society furnish a new and striking proof of the expediency of benevolent action.

This resolution was seconded by the Rev. President HUMPHREY, of Amherst College, and passed.

And the meeting was closed with a benediction by Rev. Dr. DANA, of Newburyport.

ANNUAL REPORT.

———◆———

THE managers of the Prison Discipline Society, in presenting their Sixteenth Annual Report, begin by acknowledging the goodness and mercy of God.

They also notice the death of the Hon. WILLIAM BARTLETT, of Newburyport, Mass., first vice-president of the Society, and a great friend and benefactor of the human race ; and the death of THOMAS VOSE and JOSEPH COOLIDGE, of Boston ; of Miss WALDO, of Worcester, and SAMUEL WARD, of New York ; — all of them worthy to be had in affectionate remembrance by this Society, for the countenance and aid which they extended to it.

Mr. Bartlett and Miss Waldo, by their last will and testament, gave liberal bequests to various objects of benevolence.

The plan of the Report is embraced in the following parts, viz. : Notice of Valuable Documents ; Lunatic Asylums ; Penitentiaries ; County Prisons ; Houses of Refuge ; Imprisonment for Debt ; and Narrative of Journeys performed.

1. NOTICE OF VALUABLE DOCUMENTS.

DOCUMENTS CONCERNING LUNATIC ASYLUMS.

First Annual Report of the Directors of the Maine Insane Hospital. December, 1840. Augusta, Me. : Severance & Dorr, State Printers. Octavo ; pages, 47.

Report of the Trustees of the New Hampshire Asylum for the Insane, made to the Legislature, at their November Session, 1840. Cyrus Barton, State Printer, Concord, N. H. Octavo : pages, 22.

Fourth Annual Report of the Trustees of the Vermont

Asylum for the Insane, presented to the Legislature, October, 1840. R. P. Walton & Son, Printers, Montpelier, Vt. Octavo; pages, 15.

Report of the Superintendent of the Boston Lunatic Hospital, and Physician of the Public Institutions at South Boston. July 1, 1840. City Document, No. 16. John H. Eastburn, City Printer. Octavo; pages, 31.

Annual Report of the Board of Trustees of the Massachusetts General Hospital, for the Year 1840. Boston: James Loring, Printer. Octavo; pages, 41.

Eighth Annual Report of the Trustees of the State Lunatic Hospital, at Worcester. December, 1840. Boston: Dutton & Wentworth, State Printers. Octavo; pages, 100.

Seventeenth Annual Report of the Directors of the Retreat for the Insane, at Hartford, Conn. Tiffany & Co., Printers, Hartford, 1841. Octavo; pages, 35.

Report of the New York Hospital and Bloomingdale Asylum, for the Year 1840. Mahlon Day & Co., Printers, Pearl Street, New York; pages, 32.

Report of the Commissioners of the State Lunatic Asylum, to the Legislature of New York. Assembly's Document, No. 26. January 13, 1841. Octavo; pages, 19.

Report of the Commissioners appointed by the Governor of New Jersey, to ascertain the Number of Lunatics and Idiots in the State, submitted to the Legislature on the 26th of February, 1840. Printed by M. S. Harrison & Co., Newark, N. J. Octavo; pages, 47.

Seventeenth Annual Report of the Managers of the Lunatic Asylum, for 1841, to the General Assembly of Kentucky. Octavo; pages, 17.

Second Annual Report of the Directors and Superintendent of the Ohio Lunatic Asylum, to the General Assembly of the State Legislature. Presented, December 20, 1840. Samuel Medary, Printer to the State, Columbus, Ohio. Octavo; pages, 45.

A Visit to Thirteen Asylums for the Insane, in Europe; to which are added, a brief Notice of similar Institutions in Transatlantic Countries, and in the United States; and an Essay on the Causes, Duration, Termination, and Moral Treatment of Insanity, with Copious Statistics; by Pliny Earle, M. D. Philadelphia: J. Dobson, Printer. Octavo; pages, 144.

Hints for the Young, in Relation to the Health of Body and Mind. Fourth Stereotype Edition. Boston: George W. Light, No. 1 Cornhill. Duodecimo; pages, 65. — This little manual is written by one of the wisest and most experienced physicians in Massachusetts, in regard to the causes of insanity, and ought to be

in the hands of every parent, and every young man and woman.

An Hour's Conference with Fathers and Sons, in Relation to
a Common and Fatal Indulgence of Youth. Boston: Whipple
and Damrell, No. 9 Cornhill, 1840. Duodecimo ; pages, 88. —
This book, also, is written by a physician of great intelligence
and experience in the treatment of insanity ; one great cause of
which is here exposed. It is proper to add, that the authors
of the books last named stand at the head of two of the most
important institutions in New England. It would be wise for
teachers of youth universally, as well as parents, to read what
they have written, and for the young themselves to search out this
cause of insanity.

DOCUMENTS CONCERNING PENITENTIARIES AND PRISONS.

Report of the Warden, Physician, and Chaplain, of the New
Hampshire State Prison, June Session, 1841. Cyrus Barton,
State Printer, Concord, N. H. Octavo ; pages, 10.

Documents relative to the State Prison at Charlestown, Massachusetts, presented to the Legislature, January, 1841. Dutton
& Wentworth, Printers, Boston. Octavo ; pages, 21.

Two Semiannual Reports of the Inspectors of Prisons for the
County of Suffolk, on the House of Correction, House of Reformation, Jail, Lunatic Hospital, and House of Industry. June
and December, 1840. John H. Eastburn, City Printer. Octavo ; pages, 48.

Report of the Directors of the Connecticut State Prison to the
General Assembly, May Session, 1841. Document No. 4.
Courant Office, Hartford, Conn. Octavo ; pages, 28.

Annual Report of the Inspectors of the Mount Pleasant State
Prison, January 13, 1841. Assembly's Document, No. 42.
Octavo ; pages, 29, with 12 tables.

Annual Report of the Inspectors of the State Prison at Auburn, to the Legislature of New York, January 13, 1841. Assembly's Document, No. 28. Octavo ; pages, 72.

Reports of the Inspectors of the State Prison, and of the Joint
Committee on State Prison Accounts, January, 1841. Printed
by Sherman & Harmon, Trenton, N. J. Octavo ; pages, 35.

Report of the Directors of the Maryland Penitentiary, made
to the Executive, and by him communicated to the Legislature,
December, 1840. James Lucas, Printer, Baltimore, Md. Octavo ; pages, 8, with 10 tables.

Twelfth Annual Report of the Inspectors of the Penitentiary

of the District of Columbia, January 30, 1841, communicated by the President to Congress. Document No. 92. Octavo; pages, 10.

Report of the Board of Directors of the Virginia Penitentiary, communicated by the Executive to the House of Delegates, December 18, 1839. Document No. 3. Quarto; pages, 21, with tables.

Annual Report of the Keeper of the Penitentiary, Frankfort, Kentucky, December 7, 1840. Octavo; pages, 5.

Report of the Superintendent of the Tennessee Penitentiary, to the General Assembly, October 12, 1839. Octavo; pages, 15.

Report of the Principal Keeper of the Georgia Penitentiary, October 29, 1840.

Report on the Penitentiary of Louisiana, to the House of Representatives, December 31, 1839.

Sixteenth Annual Report of the Managers of the Society for the Reformation of Juvenile Delinquents, to the Legislature of New York, 1841. Mahlon Day, Printer. Octavo; pages, 48.

Report on the Subject of County Prison Discipline in Common Jails, made to a Convention of Delegates at Brooklyn, Conn., December 9, 1840; by A. T. Judson. Octavo; pages, 16.

2. LUNATIC ASYLUMS.

ORDER OF TIME IN WHICH INSANE ASYLUMS WERE ESTABLISHED IN THE UNITED STATES.

The first hospital for the insane was built at Williamsburg, Virginia, before the Revolution; and the buildings were used as barracks for the troops during the revolutionary war. One department of the Pennsylvania Hospital, in Philadelphia, was used for the insane as early as 1752.

Asylum for the Insane at Frankford, Penn., May, 1817.

McLean Asylum at Charlestown, Mass., 1818.

Asylum for the Insane at Bloomingdale, N. Y., 1821.

Asylum for the Insane Poor at Lexington, Ken., 1824.

Connecticut Retreat for the Insane, opened April, 1824.

Dr. White's Private Asylum, Hudson, N. Y., 1830.

State Lunatic Hospital at Worcester, Mass., opened January, 1833.

Asylum for the Insane Poor at Brattleboro', Vt., opened December 12, 1836.

Asylum for the Insane at Nashville, Tenn., built in 1838.

Ohio Lunatic Asylum at Columbus, opened December, 1838.

Asylum for the Insane Poor of the City of New York, on Blackwell's Island, opened 1838.

Boston Lunatic Hospital at South Boston, opened December 11, 1839.

Asylum for the Insane in Baltimore, Maryland, having been used as a hospital, was improved, enlarged, and devoted to the insane, 1839.

Maine Insane Hospital at Augusta, opened October 14th, 1840.

Georgia Asylum for the Insane at Milledgeville, 1840.

New Hampshire Asylum for the Insane, being built in 1841.

Asylum for the Insane Poor, two miles west of Philadelphia, opened 1841.

State Asylum for the Insane Poor in Pennsylvania, provided for by law, 1841.

State Asylum for the Insane Poor at Utica, N. Y., located in 1837 ; building, 1840 and 1841.

Asylum for the Insane at Columbia, S. C. ; unknown.

Asylum for the Insane Poor in Connecticut ; no decisive action.

Asylum for the Insane Poor in New Jersey. Do.

Asylum for the Insane Poor in District of Columbia. Do.

From the above statement, it appears that one institution was established, and another used for the insane in the 18th century : two were established in the first twenty years of the 19th century ; three from 1820 to 1830 ; eight from 1830 to 1840 ; six are opened, provided for, or being built, in 1840 and 1841 ; besides much preparation for three others : by which it appears that about four times as much has been done, and is being done, in the two last years, for the insane, as was done in the whole of the 18th century, and about four times as much as was done in the first twenty years of the 19th century, and about four times as much now, in two years, as was done in ten years from 1820 to 1830, and about as much now, in two years, as in ten years from 1830 to 1840.

SUPERINTENDENTS AND OTHER OFFICERS OF INSANE ASYLUMS IN THE UNITED STATES.

Maine Asylum, at Augusta. BENJAMIN BROWN, REUEL WILLIAMS, WILLIAM C. LARABEE, directors ; ——————— superintendent ; CHAUNCEY BOOTH, JUN., assistant physician ; HENRY WINSLOW, steward ; CATHARINE WINSLOW, matron.

New Hampshire Asylum, at Concord. JOHN CONANT, JOSEPH

Low, CHARLES J. FOX, GEORGE W. KITTREDGE, IRA ST. CLAIR, SAMUEL SWASEY, CHARLES H. PEASLEY, trustees. Superintendent not yet appointed.

Vermont Asylum, at Brattleboro'. WILLIAM H. ROCKWELL, superintendent; CHAUNCEY BOOTH, JUN., assistant physician.

McLean Asylum, at Charlestown, Mass. EDWARD TUCKERMAN, president; JONATHAN PHILLIPS, vice-president; HENRY ANDREWS, treasurer; WILLIAM GRAY, secretary; CHARLES AMORY, WILLIAM APPLETON, GEORGE BOND, N. I. BOWDITCH, MARTIN BRIMMER, EBENEZER CHADWICK, G. M. DEXTER, HENRY EDWARDS, ROBERT HOOPER, JUN., THOMAS LAMB, FRANCIS C. LOWELL, IGNATIUS SARGEANT, trustees; LUTHER V. BELL, physician and superintendent; JOHN FOX, assistant physician; COLUMBUS TYLER, steward; MARY E. TYLER, matron; HOMER GOODHUE, male superior; RELIEF R. BARBER, female superior.

Massachusetts Asylum, at Worcester. ABRAM R. THOMPSON, A. D. FOSTER, MATURIN L. FISHER, DANIEL B. KING, HENRY GARDNER, trustees; SAMUEL B. WOODWARD, physician and superintendent; GEORGE CHANDLER, assistant physician; A. D. FOSTER, treasurer; Mr. and Mrs. ELLIS, steward and matron; GEORGE ALLEN, chaplain.

Asylum for Poor Lunatics at South Boston. JOHN S. BUTLER, superintendent; Mr. and Mrs. CROSBY, steward and matron.

Connecticut Retreat, at Hartford. THOMAS C. BROWNELL, president; DAVID WATKINSON, vice-president; JAMES WARD, treasurer; JAMES B. HOSMER, auditor; CHARLES SHELDON, secretary; AMARIAH BRIGHAM, physician and superintendent; THOMAS H. GALLAUDET, chaplain; JOEL F. ERVING, apothecary; VIRGIL CORNISH, steward; Mrs. CORNISH, housekeeper; MARY SHELDON, matron.

Connecticut Asylum for the Insane Poor. Not yet organized.

New York Asylum, at Utica. Superintendent not yet appointed.

New York Asylum, at Bloomingdale. WILLIAM WILSON, resident physician.

New York Asylum, on Blackwell's Island. Dr. McLELLAN, superintendent; Mr. and Mrs. BISHOP, steward and matron.

New York Private Asylum, at Hudson. D. S. WHITE, and his son Dr. G. H. WHITE, physicians and proprietors.

New Jersey Asylum. Not yet organized.

Pennsylvania Asylum, at Frankford. JOHN C. RICHMOND, superintendent; CHARLES EVANS, attending physician; PLINY EARLE, resident physician.

Pennsylvania Asylum, two miles west of Philadelphia. THOMAS L. KIRKBRIDE, superintendent.

Pennsylvania Asylum for Poor Lunatics.　A state institution. Superintendent not yet appointed.

Maryland Asylum, in Baltimore.　WILLIAM FISHER, superintendent.

District of Columbia Lunatic Asylum.　Superintendent not yet appointed.

Virginia Asylum, at Williamsburg.　PHILIP J. BARZIZA, superintendent.

Virginia Asylum, at Staunton.　FRANCIS T. STRIBLING, superintendent.

South Carolina Asylum, at Columbia.

Georgia Asylum, at Milledgeville.

Kentucky Asylum, in Lexington.　JOHN CATHERWOOD, keeper.

Tennessee Asylum, at Nashville.　JAMES OVERTON, M. D., superintendent.

Ohio Asylum, at Columbus.　WILLIAM M. AWL, superintendent; SAMUEL M. SMITH, assistant physician.

The names of the superintendents and physicians of these institutions, such as Rockwell, Bell, Woodward, Brigham, White, Wilson, Stribling, and Awl, we believe, as far as known, to be dear to the friends of humanity.

PROPORTION OF INSANE TO THE WHOLE POPULATION.

The following table, prepared by Dr. Brigham, superintendent of the Connecticut Retreat at Hartford, from the late census of the United States, gives the number of insane and idiotic at public and private charge, white and colored, in each of the states and territories. It furnishes the most dense and complete view on the subject which has been published.

| | WHITE. | | COLORED. | | Total. | Population. | Proportion of Insane to Pop. |
	Public.	Private.	Private.	Public.			
Maine,........	207	330	56	38	631	501,793	1 to 795
New Hampshire,	180	306	8	11	505	284,574	1 " 563
Massachusetts, ..	471	600	27	173	1271	737,699	1 " 580
Rhode Island, ..	117	86	8	5	216	108,830	1 " 503
Connecticut, ...	114	384	20	24	542	310,015	1 " 572
Vermont,......	135	252	5	2	394	291,948	1 " 740
New York, ...	683	1463	138	56	2340	2,428,921	1 " 1038
New Jersey,....	144	225	46	27	442	373,306	1 " 844
Pennsylvania,...	469	1477	132	55	2133	1,724,022	1 " 808
Delaware, ...	22	30	21	7	80	78,085	1 " 976
Maryland, ...	134	255	97	42	528	469,232	1 " 888
Virginia,......	317	731	326	58	1432	1,239,797	1 " 865

	WHITE.		COLORED.		Total.	Population.	Proportion of Insane to Pop.
	Pub-lic.	Pri-vate.	Pri-vate.	Pub-lic.			
North Carolina,.	153	408	191	28	780	753,110	1 to 965
South Carolina,.	91	285	121	16	513	594,398	1 " 1158
Georgia,*	43	200	93	16	352	677,197	1 " 1923
Alabama, ...	39	192	88	25	344	569,645	1 " 1655
Mississippi, ...	14	102	66	16	198	375,651	1 " 1892
Louisiana,†	8	45	37	8	98	351,176	1 " 3592
Tennessee, ...	103	596	124	28	851	829,210	1 " 962
Kentucky,.	276	406	110	41	833	777,397	1 " 934
Ohio, ...	363	832	62	103	1360	1,519,467	1 " 1117
Indiana, ...	110	383	46	29	568	683,314	1 " 1203
Illinois,.	25	162	32	8	227	474,404	1 " 2089
Missouri, ...	44	165	52	17	278	381,102	1 " 1370
Arkansas, ...	3	14	6	5	28	95,642	1 " 3415
Michigan,.	6	37	22	4	69	211,705	1 " 3053
Florida, ...	1	10	12		23	54,207	1 " 2356
Wisconsin, ...	3	7	3		13	30,752	1 " 2365
Iowa, ...	2	5	4		11	43,068	1 " 3915
Dist. of Columbia,	1	13	4	3	21	43,712	1 " 2081
Total,‡. . . .	4278	10001	1957	845	17,181	17,013,379	1 " 990

NUMBER OF PERSONS WHO BECOME INSANE ANNUALLY.

" In the year 1835, there were received into three of the institutions in Massachusetts, from that state alone, 124 patients who became crazy that year." — *Dr. Brigham.*

This number is estimated by the same author to be probably not more than one half who became insane, in the same state, during the same period. If this statement and opinion be made the basis of an estimate, it will give, as the number who become insane annually, in the United States, 5719.

IN WHAT EXTENT IS PROVISION MADE FOR THE INSANE IN THE UNITED STATES?

We have seen that the whole number of insane, according to the last census, is 17,181, and the number who became insane

---

* Returns from nine counties wanting, seven of which contained, in 1830, 55,881. This number is included in the population above, while only the insane and idiotic from other parts of the state are given.

† Parish of Washington not received.

‡ These returns do not, I presume, exhibit more than two thirds of the actual number. According to the census, there are but 542 in Connecticut, 138 of whom are at public charge. This we know to be considerably less than the actual number. In the state of New York, according to the census, there are but 739 supported at public charge, while, according to the late returns of the superintendents of the poor of that state, there are 1058.

annually, by estimate, 5719. According to the tabular view of
eleven asylums, contained in the Report, the whole number under treatment in these institutions, last year, was 1470; and the
number received into them during the year, 932. There are five
other asylums established, and in operation, from which returns
have not been received, which may increase the whole number
under treatment to 1800, or, possibly, to 2000; (Dr. Brigham estimates the number at 1800;) while the number received annually may be 1200. When the Asylum at Utica is completed for
the accommodation of 1000, 3000 may have provision made for
their accommodation each year, and 1500, or, possibly, 1800, for
their reception; so that the great work of making suitable provision for the 17,181 insane in the United States, and the 5719
who become insane annually, is well begun, but not more than
one fourth or fifth part accomplished.

Proportion of Recoveries in well-conducted Asylums.

The following table, from Dr. Brigham's last Report, shows
the proportion of recoveries from old and recent cases, inclusive,
in the most celebrated Hospitals for the Insane, both in Europe
and the United States.

Hospitals.	Time.	No. of Patients.	Recoveries.	Per Cent.
Bethlehem, England, ...	14 years,	2445	1124	45.56
St. Luke, "	50 "	6458	2811	43.52
Wakefield, "	17 "	2242	991	44.20
Lancaster, "	15 "	1750	697	39.82
Retreat, York, "	39 "	508	236	46.43
Cork, Ireland, ...	20 "	1431	751	52.48
Salpetriere, France, ...	12 "	3007	1625	54.04
Charenton, "	8 "	1205	516	42.82
Aversa, Italy, ...	20 "	3897	1514	38.85
Penn. Hospital, U. S.	84 "	4116	1349	32.77
Frankford, Penn.	21 "	507	214	42.21
Bloomingdale, N. Y.	20 "	2496	1145	45.88⅞
McLean, Charlestown, Mass.	22 "	1749	761	43.51
Mass. State, Worcester, . .	7 "	1196	506	42.30
Vermont, Brattleboro', . . .	3 "	239	89	37.23
Ohio, Columbus, ...	1 "	258	80	31.00
Retreat, Hartford, Ct. . . .	17 "	1068	600	56.17

Proportion of Recoveries in recent Cases, compared with old Cases.

The statistics from the Asylums the last year, as in former years, prove that the recoveries in recent cases are from 80 to 90 per cent., while in old cases they are from 15 to 35 per cent. ; showing the importance of removing the insane to an Asylum, while the disease is yet recent, instead of leaving them to become incurable by neglect.

Small Number of Persons ever recovered from Insanity in Prison.

" Of the hundreds and thousands which have been confined to Prison, nobody ever knew or heard of more than three instances of recovery from insanity during the confinement of a person to a Jail or House of Correction." — *First Report of the Trustees of the N. H. Asylum.*

This language may be too strong, and not fully authorized by facts. Still, very few persons will be found to call it in question. It is substantially correct.

Expense of supporting the Insane in Asylums.

The price, at Augusta, Me., for board, medicine, and attendance, is $2 00 a week, in ordinary cases ; and in no case can more than $3 00 be charged.

The price of board, at Brattleboro', Vt., is, for the poor of Vermont, $2 00 per week ; some patients pay $3 00 ; and those with private rooms, pay more.

At Worcester, Mass., the price of board, for several years, has been $2 50.

At South Boston, the price is fixed at $2 50.

At the McLean Asylum, at Charlestown, the lowest price is $3 00 per week, and for those belonging out of the state, $4 50 per week ; and private patients, with abundant means, pay according to their ability and accommodations.

At the Connecticut Retreat, in Hartford, for patients belonging to the state, to be accommodated in the wings, without a separate attendant, $3 50 per week ; for those with similar accommodations belonging to other states, $4 00 per week. For patients in the centre building, with separate rooms, and attendant devoted to each, from $10 00 to $12 00 per week. For indigent lunatics, belonging to the state, not exceeding ten in number, $2 00 per week.

At Nashville, Tenn., the expense is about $1 25 per week.

MEANS OF CURE IN SUITABLE ASYLUMS. — FARMS AND GARDENS OF INSANE ASYLUMS.

The trustees of the Maine Asylum say, —

" We consider the farm, connected with the Hospital, of very great importance to the interests and success of the institution. No employment is so congenial to the human constitution as agriculture. Man was made to ' till the ground.' Agriculture furnishes the most healthful exercise, and enables the operator to breathe the pure air of heaven. The farm also may be made a source of great profit. The land is of excellent quality, and the means of enriching it are abundant. When put under proper cultivation, it may furnish a large portion of the agricultural products consumed in the Hospital, and thus very considerably diminish the amount of legislative appropriation. A vegetable and flower garden would not only be a source of great profit, but would furnish a delightful exercise, in the warm season, for such of the female patients as might be disposed to pass their time in the open air. Most of the labor necessary about the premises would be voluntarily done by the patients. The spot is capable of being rendered one of the most delightful on earth. The prospect of the river, with the romantic scenery and beautiful villages, with which its banks are lined, is surpassingly beautiful. Let but the grounds about the Hospital correspond to the scenery of the neighborhood, and few spots could compare with it."

The quantity of land connected with the Maine Asylum is about 78 acres.

The trustees of the New Hampshire Asylum, before its location, said, —

" One hundred acres should be secured, if possible ; and if it should prove to be of good quality, there would be no excuse for the superintendent, with the great supply of labor he would have at his command, if it was not the pattern farm for all that region."

The trustees of the N. H. Asylum have secured, as we understand, a farm of greater size.

The trustees of the Vermont Asylum, besides the garden and grounds on which the mansion-house stands, and the natural terrace on which the new building is erected, about 50 feet above the meadow, have secured about 50 acres of meadow land ; and the only regret seems to be that they had not funds to secure 150 for the same purpose.

The trustees of the McLean Asylum, within a few years, have

added several acres to their farm, at $1000 per acre, increasing their garden and grounds to 25 acres. During the present year, several acres more have been added, at $500 per acre.

The Boston Asylum has a garden of one or two acres only, at present, under its control.

The Worcester Asylum has about 70 acres.

The Connecticut Retreat has about 14 acres.

The Blackwell's Island Asylum for the city of New York has several acres on the north end of the island.

The Bloomingdale Asylum had a beautiful garden and grounds, but has been encroached upon by the streets and lanes of the city.

Dr. White's Private Asylum has a beautiful piece of ground in the rear, of dimensions too limited.

The State Asylum at Utica has about 120 acres.

The Frankford Asylum, near Philadelphia, has 61 acres, of which 20 acres is a grove, &c. ; part of this is a park for deer.

The Pennsylvania Hospital, two miles west of Philadelphia, intended particularly for the insane of the city, has a large farm, of which 42 acres are enclosed.

The State Asylum of Pennsylvania, for which provision was made last year by act of the legislature, proposes to commence with a large farm.

The Maryland Asylum, in Baltimore, has 10 acres of land. It was proposed to enclose this land with a high wall, at an expense of $10,000. We hope this part of the plan has been abandoned, as it would be money worse than thrown away ; giving the place a Prison-like appearance, without the least utility.

The Western Lunatic Asylum, at Staunton, Virginia, has a farm containing 65 acres of fine land, on an eminence.

The Asylum at Williamsburgh, Virginia, has a narrow space, or small square, in the village.

The Ohio Asylum has 30 acres of land, beautifully situated.

We do not know how much land is connected with the Asylums in Kentucky, Tennessee, North Carolina, and Georgia.

We make a few remarks only with regard to the gardens and farms connected with Lunatic Asylums. They should be extensive: an acre to a patient would be a good general rule. They should be well watered with living springs of pure water, and running streams, if possible. They should be of varied surface and fertile soil. They should have in prospect beautiful scenery of nature and art. Every thing calculated to promote the happiness of the rational mind should be secured, to restore the insane.

MORAL EFFECTS OF LABOR ON THE INSANE.

" The farmer is pleased when he can see the Earth yielding her fruits, as she did before the dark cloud of insanity overshadowed him ; and the gardener rejoices again when he can make the tender plant, and the flower, start forth at his will."— *First Report of the New Hampshire Asylum.*

" As a moral regimen," says Dr. Knapp, of the Maine Asylum, " manual labor is of immense importance. While it improves the bodily health, it withdraws the attention from illusive fancies, which disturb and agitate the feelings, and fixes it on purposes associating the idea of utility. Thus accustomed, the mind has an opportunity to resume its natural manifestation."

Dr. Bell, of the McLean Asylum, says, —

" There is one appliance of moral treatment, which has been proved immeasurably superior to all others, as regards a large class of male patients. It is a systematic, regular employment in useful labor."

Again he says, — " The class of patients whose former avocations have been the farthest removed from mechanical employments, such as merchants, lawyers, and physicians, have been found amongst those most willingly and usefully interested. A certain class of melancholic and stupid subjects, when once thus engaged, are almost sure to recover."

" No class of our patients," says Dr. Woodward, " are so contented and happy as the laborers ; no other convalescent recovers so rapidly or favorably."

Again he says, — " It is customary for patients, who have been brought up to labor, as soon as the first excitement is over, to request employment ; it is granted, and considered by them a great favor. They sleep well after the fatigue of the day, always have a good appetite, and are cheerful and happy. The same excitement, which by others is expended in mischief and noise, they expend in useful and agreeable employments ; and they leave the Hospital better satisfied with its government, and with themselves, than those who have been unaccustomed to manual labor, or who declined to engage in it."

" The following case, from among many," says Dr. Woodward, " will show the benefit of labor : — A farmer, aged about thirty, was brought to the Hospital, in August last, so violent as to be attended by *five* stout men. He had been reduced by disease and remedies, but was considered violent and dangerous. A few days after his admission, he requested to go out and aid the farmer in his work ; he was permitted to do so. After he commenced labor, he improved in a very favorable manner ; slept well, had a good appetite, and gained flesh and strength. At the end of a month, he was well ; and before the expiration of *two* months, he returned to his home quite recovered. In such a case, it is difficult to conceive the effect of confinement ; irritation, anger, and violence, requiring restraint, might have followed, which would almost necessarily have made a protracted case, and probably an imperfect cure."

" The true value of labor," say the trustees of the State Hospital at Worcester, " is to be estimated by a higher standard than money. Labor is the health of the mind. It is that power in man which unfolds and directs his capacities, and thus reveals and secures the sources of his happiness. The man who labors shares first and largest in the fruits of his own toil ; for, in every condition of human life, useful employment is the surest enjoyment — the best security of a sound mind in a sound body. In a disordered state of mind, judicious occupation is among the best remedies, and agricultural and horticultural occupations are among the best of all. 'Grain and fruit are God's bounty ; the flowers are his smiles.'

" This beautiful thought may come over the troubled mind, when engaged in the field or the garden, in the midst of Heaven's gifts, with a divine power to dispel gloom, and infuse hope, peace, and joy."

Dr. Awl, of the Asylum at Columbus, Ohio, says, —

" Above all, and before every thing else in the world, for the substantial welfare and improvement of both mind and body, is regular and profitable labor." — " Man was made to be active ; even in Paradise, he was employed in the healthy and pleasant exercise of cultivating a garden."

PECUNIARY RESULTS OF LABOR IN INSANE ASYLUMS.

Dr. Knapp, of the Maine Asylum, says, —

" The farm may be made a source of great profit. When put under proper cultivation, it may furnish a large portion of the agricultural products consumed in the Hospital, and thus very considerably diminish the amount of legislative appropriation, annually necessary to meet the current expenses of the institution."

Again, Dr. Knapp says, —

" Most of the male patients are engaged, a short time every day, in preparing wood for the fires, and other light labor about the Hospital ; and such of the convalescents as can work with joiners' tools, are occasionally accommodated in our workshop; and several of the female patients are engaged, a portion of the time, daily, in assisting in the labor of the kitchen."

Mr. Columbus Tyler, steward of the McLean Asylum, credits the institution $1665 37 as the value received from the farm connected with the institution, and cultivated in a great degree by the patients. In four years, the produce of the farm, consisting of only 25 acres, has been worth, according to the steward's estimate, $4862 51.

Mr. Ellis, the steward of the State Hospital at Worcester, estimates the produce of the farm, connected with the Hospital, and cultivated by the patients, as being worth, last year, $1,887 89. He, also, estimates the work done in the shoe-shop as being worth $937 52 ; but a small part of this result from the shoe-shop is net profit. Besides the labor on the farm and in the shop, the superintendent, Dr. Woodward, says,—

" Many important improvements have been made upon the grounds and in the fields. The meadows have been extensively drained, and made better ; the pastures have been cleared of stones and bushes, and made more beautiful and productive; extensive walls have been made, especially a bank wall, substantial and handsome, and forty or fifty rods in length, in front of a grove, which has been much improved, laid out into walks and paths, and rendered smooth, and cleared from stone. Whatever has been done in this way, is designed to be permanently and thoroughly done, having in view both utility and beauty.

" In these various ways," says Dr. Woodward, " we are enabled to employ a great amount of labor to interest our patients in improvements and productions, which they, as well as others, see to be valuable and useful to all. We have placed upon our premises one hundred thrifty apple-trees, of the choicest varieties of ingrafted fruit, many of which begin to bear. We have, also, a great number of English cherry-trees, pear-trees, and peach-trees, all of which are growing rapidly, and many of them furnish specimens of choice varieties of fruits. Whoever comes after us will discover that, in these particulars, we have labored in prospective, and that our object has been to give permanency to the means of enjoyment, as well as to partake of them ourselves.

" In all domestic labor, we can, at a moment's warning, call together whatever help is needed; and in the kitchen, laundry, and wash-room, are every day found many individuals usefully and pleasantly employed, from whose labor important benefit is mutually derived."

Dr. Awl, of the Ohio Asylum, says,—

" Many of our male patients find useful employment, at present, in clearing up the premises, and grading and leveling the grounds, in attending to the vegetable gardens, assisting in the care and management of the stock upon the farm, and preparing all the fuel that is used. The females find constant employment within doors ; and it will be sufficient to say of them, that the making and mending of all the wearing apparel for the indigent, and all the washing and ironing for the whole household, is chiefly performed by their assistance.

" According to an accurate estimate of the male and female work done by our patients, in the last six months, we find them entitled to the credit of 3690 days' labor; so that, with all our amusements, we belong to the laboring classes, and may be considered an industrious, though crazy, community."

Moral and Religious Instruction in Insane Asylums.

Dr. Knapp, of the Maine Asylum, says,—

" Nearly all our patients attend the daily evening religious exercise conducted in the Hospital, and, almost without an exception, manifest much pleasing interest in the subject. The service consists in reading a portion of sacred Scripture, in which the officers, attendants, and many of the patients unite ; a prayer, and the singing of a hymn or psalm.

" We have recently commenced arrangements to have preaching in the Hospital, weekly, on the Sabbath, for which purpose the clergymen of different denominations, in the vicinity, will be invited to officiate in rotation.

" The remedial influence which the insane derive from a regular attendance on discreetly-conducted religious services, probably can never be too much lauded. The religion of HIM, whose advent was proclaimed by a message of peace on earth and good-will to men, can never, when appreciated, fail to soothe and calm the stormy commotions of the human mind."

Dr. Bell, of the McLean Asylum, says, —

" On the Sabbath, all such as are in a proper condition, attend some of the various churches in the vicinity, according as their preferences or early habits may dictate a selection. At one church, our average number of worshippers is from twelve to twenty, every Sabbath ; and the whole number usually abroad to public worship, is, perhaps, about thirty."

" As the motives to self-control and self-respect are augmented by such a participation in society as public worship amongst the world affords, I believe the course pursued here, especially as it has never yet caused the slightest inconvenience or disturbance to the religious societies which we attend, is superior, for our class of patients, to having a specific chapel for the insane. On Sunday evenings, we have a discourse, to which many of those whom it would not be deemed prudent to take abroad to church, are invited.

" The regulated, discriminating, and cautious attention to the exercises of religion, is so valuable an auxiliary to the moral means of treating the diseased mind, not less from its specific influence on the heart and feelings, than from its administering to the self-control of the individual, that we have rejoiced to see the experience of this institution adopted in others."

Dr. Woodward says, —

" The Rev. Julius A. Reed officiated as chaplain of the Hospital for *one* year ending the first of October. His services were well appreciated, and he left us with the good wishes of all our family. He is a plain, practical preacher, sincere and honest in his efforts to do good, and succeeded well in winning the affections and securing the confidence of his hearers. His services were always judicious and solemn, well attended to, and influential on the conduct of his audience. No disturbance ever took place in the chapel during his ministrations, and universal regret was felt in our household at his departure.

" After Mr. Reed decided to leave his charge, immediate application was made to the Rev. George Allen to supply the vacancy. He received the appointment of chaplain, and commenced the duties of his office on the first of October. From our knowledge of Mr. Allen, we were led to suppose that his good sense, experience, and practical wisdom, would qualify him for the station. In this we have not been disappointed. We consider ourselves fortunate in having obtained a chaplain of such talents and varied attainments, and have strong confidence that, under his auspices, increasing good will result from our chapel services.

"We have now had regular religious worship on the Sabbath for more than *three* years. In the course of that time, nearly 600 patients have attended meetings more or less, and less than 90 have been in the Hospital, who have failed to attend.

"Our expectations of benefit from the chapel have been more than realized. From 120 to 150 patients assemble on each Sabbath, and no congregation is more orderly and attentive. There is a solemnity visible in the countenances of those present, which clearly indicates that they know for what purpose they have come together; and even those who are at first disposed to be restless and disorderly, catch the influence which is every where prevalent around them, and become calm and sober themselves.

"The instances of self-control manifested in the chapel, by those who are often greatly excited, restless, and noisy, in the halls, are truly remarkable.

"The Sabbath previous to the day on which this sheet was written, a woman, who had been greatly excited, very profane, and noisy, requested to attend chapel. All efforts at self-control while in the halls were unavailing, except for a few moments at a time; she would promise to be quiet, but, in a moment, be as noisy and talkative as before. Knowing, however, her reverence for the Sabbath, and the strength and sincerity of her resolutions to be quiet, she was permitted to attend. The most careful observer would not have been able to detect any thing in her appearance and conduct that would distinguish her from the most dignified and rational person in the house.

"During the evening previous to the same Sabbath, a patient, furiously mad, was brought to the Hospital in the care of a sheriff. He had been considered quite dangerous, and the sheriff hesitated whether it would be safe to come with him unless he was confined in irons. He appeared calm on the following morning, and it was proposed that he should attend chapel; he seemed pleased with the privilege, attended the service all day, and conducted with the utmost propriety. These occurrences, which were of yesterday, are happening almost every Sabbath, and show most clearly the propriety and importance of religious worship on the insane.

"The truth is, that many insane persons are rational on religious subjects, and a few are insane on these subjects only. Both classes are often benefited by religious instruction.

"It is through the healthy avenues of the mind that religious truth is received and makes its impression upon the feelings. On most subjects the insane can reason, and feel the force of reasoning, as well as others, and, even if insane on religious subjects, plain and forcible illustrations of truth may weaken their confidence in insane impressions, and throw light where darkness only has been prevalent.

"The habits of New England people require order and decorum in the place and time of religious worship. The insane feel the force of this habit equally strong; they frown upon those who work or trifle upon the Sabbath, and are particularly indignant to those who are disposed to disturb the quiet of our religious assemblies. There is a feeling of pride extending over our whole household in the quiet and orderly observance of the Sabbath in the Hospital. The good counsels of the chaplain are treasured up and often repeated in the week time, as motives of self-control to themselves and as admonitions to others.

" When patients have recovered, and are about to return to their friends, they often speak of their enjoyment of chapel exercises, express their regret at leaving those interesting services, and implore the blessing of Heaven upon future ministrations.

" An excellent woman, who recovered from dreadful melancholy at the Hospital, a year or two since, writes in substance thus, after inquiring after the general welfare of the family : — ' How do you get along in your beautiful little chapel ? I shall ever feel deeply interested in your religious meetings, as I feel sensible that one of the first rays of light that entered into my benighted mind was in the solemn worship of that house.' "

Dr. Butler, of the Boston Lunatic Hospital, says, —

" Religious instruction is another influence to which we have looked for beneficial results. Considering our immediate household, and our patients, as one great family, and recognizing the family as a divine institution, your superintendent has deemed it his duty to gather as many as practicable together for family worship, at an early hour in the evening. The usual regular services of the Sabbath have been supplied to us every Sunday afternoon, with few exceptions. For this inestimable privilege, we have been indebted to the gratuitous labors of those of our clerical friends, whose hearts have been warmed towards those of their fellow-beings who are sitting in darkness. There is no more fitting place in which to express to the Rev. Messrs. Cleveland, Crowell, Abbott, Washburn, and other gentlemen who have officiated for us, our grateful sense of that benevolence, which has led them to preach to our family the soothing precepts of Him who said to the tempest, ' Peace, be still ! ' The average attendance of our patients upon these services is over 40, and it is rare that they exhibit any deviation from good order and propriety. Though it is the first time for years that many of our inmates have been thus recognized as members of the human family, their fixed attention and serious deportment is a pleasant illustration of the adaptation of the gospel to all sorts and conditions of men. The utility of these influences should be undoubted. No one can look upon our household, assembled for the instruction of the Sabbath, or for the familiar worship of the evening, and see them there, as one family, rise up silently and reverently, to pray to our Father in heaven, without realizing that some feel the solemnity of the act, without being convinced that a chord may there be struck, whose ultimate vibration may awaken some recollection of early life, and bring back upon the excited and bewildered mind some calm and solemn influences, and give him that one moment of self-control, in which the first link in the chain of diseased associations may be broken."

Dr. Brigham, of the Connecticut Retreat, says, —

" The importance of religious instruction, as part of he system of moral treatment of the insane, has not been overlooked. Those of the patients who are capable of joining in religious services, assemble every evening, when the chaplain reads a portion of the sacred Scriptures, and conducts the devotions of the family. On Sunday, he preaches to the assembled household, and often, during the week, presents the truths of Christianity, and its consolations, to those who are care-worn, anxious, and dejected. Much good has resulted from this practice, and great credit is due to the gentleman who has, with uncommon discretion and sound judgment, performed this sacred duty."

Dr. White, of the Private Asylum, Hudson, N. Y., says, —

" The quiet patients continue to enjoy the beneficial effects of family worship, as heretofore."

Dr. Earle, of the Frankford, Penn., Asylum, says, —

" There are but four institutions in this country in which there is not some religious devotional exercise; and wherever this duty has been observed, it has been accompanied by beneficial results."

Those patients whose condition will admit of it, in the institution under his own immediate care, assemble on Sabbath afternoons to hear a portion of the Scriptures. Some of them attend meeting in the village of Frankford.

Dr. Earle also says, divine worship on the Sabbath has been introduced into the Maryland Asylum with good effect.

Dr. Awl, of the Ohio Asylum, says, —

" Through the blessing of Almighty God, we have been permitted to continue our regular family worship, every evening in the week, and the reading of a short sermon on the Lord's day, not only without interruption from the patients, — who, to the number of 30 or 40, usually attend, — but with the most happy influence and positive benefit to many of our patients, and the large family of officers, attendants, and assistants, connected with the institution. At first, it is true, we had some doubts concerning the necessity and propriety of daily religious exercises for the insane mind, and the difficulty of conducting the service appropriately appeared great; but we felt constrained to make the experiment, through a strong sense of duty; and the experience of two years has abundantly satisfied our mind upon the subject. In an institution of this kind, we have an extensive family to govern, as well as to provide for the daily wants of the insane; and merely as a moral obligation, the daily worship of God is of the first consequence to inspire confidence and respect, and to harmonize the feelings; but above all this, we are fully prepared to add our testimony to the importance and value of religious exercises with the insane as a special *mean of grace*, well calculated to bring light and wisdom to the mind, relief and peace to the heart and conscience. By many of the convalescing, it is estimated as a blessed privilege; and in respect to them there can be no doubt of its propriety. We have never seen any evil effects from the practice, with the most diseased and unsteady; and when we find many of the positively deranged, who are anxious to accompany the rest, and spend half an hour in social worship, and not only conduct themselves with propriety and order, but sincerely thank us for the privilege, we are satisfied that, in many instances, the soul has been refreshed, though there may have been but an imperfect and beclouded view of a merciful Redeemer.

" When the bell rings for worship, they gather in from the different galleries, each several class accompanied by its proper attendant, and all are regularly seated, without strife or confusion, males on the right and females on the left of the superintendent's table ; and there is the most respectful attention when the blessed Bible is opened, and the words of eternal life are read. There, amid the group upon the right, is one who has been a witness to many sorrows ; upon the opposite side sparkle the wild eyes of a stronger mind in ruins ; and directly in front is the pale form of the female homicide, who with one awful stroke severed the head from the body of her sleeping husband ! — all ready and willing to unite in the praise of God, and, in a greater or less degree, enjoy the spiritual blessings of the gospel of righteousness and peace." " In the wreck of mind and loss of reason, perhaps the very last ideas which remain will be something of the reverence and respect which are due to the Maker of our frame; and it is not at all uncommon to see the aged and demented Christian reverently bend the knee, when years of darkness, to all human appearance, have shut out all correct knowledge of earth and heaven."

RESTRAINTS.

Dr. Butler, of the Boston Asylum, says, —

" We seek to avoid personal restraint as far as practicable, and apply it, when necessary, with as much gentleness and as little irritation as possible. The means of restraint that we use are, confinement to rooms in the hall with guarded windows, or the application of straps, (leather wristbands, fastened by rings to a belt, passing around the body and secured behind,) with, or, more generally, without, the mittens. These produce no pain, and effectually prevent violence to themselves, to others, or to the building. We have one strong chain, which is rarely used."

Dr. Bell, of the McLean Asylum, says, —

" An absence, in the early part of the year, of about four months, in search of health, under permission of your board, — a permission granted in a manner, and accompanied with circumstances, calling for his grateful acknowledgments, — gave your superintendent some opportunity to observe and compare, and, if occasion had offered, to improve, by the long-established and extensive insane institutions of the Old World. While surprised and gratified at the extent and magnificence of many of these establishments, there seemed little or nothing in architectural arrangements, or in modes of moral or medical treatment, of value, which has not long since been transplanted to, or discovered in, the American institutions. The only noticeable peculiarity worth communicating would seem to be, the experiment commenced recently in some of the British hospitals, of an entire disuse, as they consider it, of corporeal restraints. At the Lincoln Lunatic Asylum, it is said in the Report of the Middlesex Asylum at Hanwell for 1839, that the last personal restraint occurred in January, 1837; and at the last-mentioned institution, restraining apparatus has been thrown aside since the latter part of September, 1839. I consider one of the greatest pleasures of my visit to Europe to have been the privilege of spending the greater portion of a day at Hanwell, and the opportunity of conversing freely on this as well as other subjects relating to the insane, with Dr. Conolly, the head of this extensive establishment, whose reputation, as a medical philosopher and writer on mental alienation, is no less recognized on this side the Atlantic than at home, and whose urbanity and attention to a stranger, with no claims beyond a community of interests and pursuit, I cannot but gratefully recall. As any thing like improvement in the present system, introduced elsewhere, must soon attract attention here, and as the idea of absolutely discarding personal restraint has something so attractive in its very mention, I have been induced to bestow considerable reflection upon the expediency of adopting such a universal rule at this Asylum. Thus far, at these two great institutions referred to, — the former with about 150, and the latter with over 800 patients, — the experiment has been found so successful as to be persevered in; whether adopted beyond these hospitals, or not, I have no means of ascertaining. It is certain, however, that the attempt has been much noticed and applauded in England, and of course will soon have its praises transferred to every portion of our land.

" As regards Great Britain, the encomiums bestowed upon this innovation may be all deserved. In a country where, at this moment, *a chain* to each bed, of at least one long dormitory, may be seen at the extensive metropolitan Hospital of St. Luke, such a discovery, as puts an end to such barbarity, may well excite applause; or at the Lincoln Asylum, where the number of patients under restraint were 39, of an entire number of 72, in 1830; 54 of 92, in 1831; 40 of 70, in 1832; 55 of 81, in 1833; 44 of 87, in 1834, and so on, the change must be most gratifying to every humane heart.

" Dr. Conolly, in ' The Fifty-first Report of the Visiting Justices of the County Lunatic Asylum at Hanwell,' for the year 1839, (page 47,) remarks as follows: — ' For patients who take off or destroy their clothes, strong dresses are provided, *secured round the waist by a leathern belt, fastened by a small lock.* For some, who destroy the collar and cuffs of their dresses with their teeth, a leathern binding to those parts of the dress is found convenient. *Varied contrivances* are adopted with variable results, *for keeping clothing on* those who would otherwise expose themselves to cold at night; and warm boots *fastened round the ankles by a small lock* instead of a button or buckle, are sometimes the means of protecting the feet of those *who will not lie down.* * * * * *Those who are in the habit of striking suddenly, tearing the bed-clothes, &c.*, sometimes wear a dress of which the sleeves terminate in a *stuffed glove, without a division for the thumb and fingers.* But no form of strait waistcoat, no hand-straps, no leg-locks, nor any contrivance confining the trunk or limbs, or any of the muscles, is now in use. The coercion-chairs, about forty in number, have been altogether removed from the wards; no chair of this kind has been used for the purpose of restraint since the middle of August.'

" Any gentleman, familiar with the management of this, or, I believe, any other of the New England institutions, from their origin, will at once declare, if this is all that is meant by an absolute disuse of restraining means, — if the application of leathern mittens, waist-straps, varied contrivances for keeping on clothing, boots with locks, &c., are considered so mild and trifling measures, as not to be included under the phrase of *personal restraint*, — that this innovation, or experiment, or improvement, can never be introduced here, for the best of all reasons, that the application of the severe measures reported as discarded at Hanwell, never was heard of in our Asylums, and but a few even of the measures deemed so insignificant as to form no exception, have ever been found necessary here. If this is all that is intended in the new system, our experience for years may encourage them to go on fearlessly.

" An amount of restraint less than is intimated in these exceptions, has long proved adequate in this institution : the necessity, for example, of restraining apparatus for keeping the patient covered at night, is here obviated by the admission of heated air to the sleeping apartment, when necessary. For some years, the average number of patients under the restraint of leathern mittens, has not exceeded one per cent.; and often week after week elapses without even a single instance.

" I have no doubt that this rare use might with safety be carried to a still greater extent — to that of absolute interdiction ; but how far it may be dispensed with, or how far the best good of the sufferer demands its application, is a question of judgment to be decided in view of all the circumstances of each case. An important rule is, that no restraint, even of the slightest kind, should ever be applied or removed except under the direction of an officer. This rule has always been incorporated in our code of domestic regulations. But to lay down the broad, absolute rule of disusing all the mild forms of restraint, would not comport with the best good of an institution. I do not doubt that, with the number of active and trusty assistants we now have, it might be practicable to pursue such a system, perhaps without any results of consequence to be regretted. Yet its adoption would be cutting off the power of employing a remedial means, often of great value to the patient. A portion of the feeling in England as to restraining measures, is based on a delusion. Which is the greater restraint, to shut up a patient disposed to strike upon any sudden impulse, in his solitary dormitory, having its light admitted just below the ceiling, or to place large leathern mittens on his hands, and permit him to go into a large court-yard and to walk up and down in the open air ? The seclusion within a room is not considered *personal restraint*, in the reports referred to.

" Or, which is least oppressive, to a patient disposed to certain troublesome habits, — as, abrading the skin of the face by perpetual picking, or plucking out the hair root after root, — habits become from neglect so inveterate and involuntary, that even while the physician is dissuading or promising restraint, his hand unconsciously returns to its wonted act, — to place the hands in a muff of leather, at once simple, free from pain, and effective, or to trust to the vigilance or the eventually annoying and irritating remindings or restraints of an assistant? Who can doubt as to the comparative advantage of personal restraint from the hands of attendants, or of apparatus, in those cases of delirium-like fury, where the sufferer is constantly endeavoring to rise from his bed, and where the presence of faces around him is associated in his blind frenzy with enemies to be contended with, regardless of their numbers? The mind may be in that state where the most soothing attentions are met only with fury and suspicion. How valuable, in such a case, is the beautiful and simple apparatus, constructed, I believe, by my distinguished predecessor, Dr. Wyman, which holds the sufferer gently in his position on his bed, allowing him almost every natural and proper movement, yet prevents his wearing himself out by constant efforts to rise, and allows every person to leave his immediate apartment, (for his disordered fancy makes cruel enemies of all,) with a certainty that he is safe and comfortable!

"Again, in some highly-active forms of the suicidal propensity, where no human vigilance can prevent the consummation of the dreadful act, except accompanied by the ceaseless application of the force of several persons, a proper restraining means, such as the leathern muff, at once allays the violence of the propensity, by showing the patient that he need not be on the watch to elude his attendants, and that attempts are vain to accomplish his design by force. The best proof of the value of the occasional use of this and other means of vigilance, is manifested in the extraordinary fact, that of the more than 650 patients admitted within the last five years, amounting to more than one third of all the inmates during the 23 years of the existence of this institution, a single individual only has committed suicide! I cannot here forbear to refer to this remarkable result, as one redounding to the honor of the male and female supervisors, and entitling them in the highest degree to the obligations of the community; for to them necessarily appertains, to a great extent, the merit of a prompt detection, often no easy matter, and a successful prevention, of this sad accident. This result will be duly appreciated when it is considered that the number of those evincing this propensity has sometimes amounted to a dozen, and I have never known the period when no instance existed. I recall also from memory no less than three instances within as many years, where patients have returned home, upon partial convalescence, or from other motives, and resorted almost immediately to the fatal act successfully, although the friends and relatives were forewarned to exert their utmost vigilance by our experience."

Dr. Woodward, of the Worcester Asylum, says, —

"The British institutions are at present making an effort to surpass each other in the success of managing the insane without restraints. Some of them have abolished them almost entirely, while others have noted the hours, in the course of the year, that they have applied them. The restraints here considered are the strait waistcoat, muffs mittens, and confining chains; solitary rooms are not included.

"In this Hospital, strait waistcoats and muffs are never used, and confining chains but rarely. Mittens and wristbands are all the restraints which are here applied, and those only when absolutely necessary to the comfort of the individual, or the safety of the patients who occupy the same apartment. These restraints are made use of for two purposes for the individuals themselves, viz., to keep clothes upon them when they are disposed to take them off, and as a safeguard in case of suicidal propensity. For the more violent, such as strike, tear clothes and bedding, break furniture, &c., they are sometimes applied for a short period, but never continued for a great length of time.

"While restraints should be applied as rarely as possible, and never for the benefit of the attendant, but only for the good of the patient or the safety of those with whom he associates, yet I cannot but consider them as important auxiliaries in the treatment of the insane. It is undoubtedly true, that, with corporeal restraints judiciously applied, patients will sooner be made tranquil than by the presence of one or more attendants, who they know will watch all their movements and interfere with their mischievous designs. Their presence will often be a source of irritation which will serve to keep up the excitement; and, in most cases, restraints that are not painful are far less disagreeable to both the furious and suicidal patients, than that unceasing surveillance which is necessary as a substitute.

"Whenever a patient is under restraint, we frequently propose a release, on condition of a pledge to avoid the irregular conduct for which it was imposed. These pledges we require to be given in a solemn manner, stating to the patient the condition he will be in, if, by a forfeiture of his word, it should be necessary to re-apply them. Both his self-respect and desire of liberty are here called in requisition, to prevent him from further violation of decorum, and afterwards, in many cases, restraints cease to be necessary.

"*Pledges.* We think much of pledges with the insane, and often avoid restraints, by taking the word of a violent patient to be quiet and peaceable. Even the suicidal, who have been detected in making preparation for self-destruction, or in secreting instruments for future use, will generally, and with me have never failed to, adhere strictly to a pledge given in good faith, with feelings of solemnity.

"With most patients, ever so violent, there are times when they will make promises, which will have no inconsiderable influence. Those who are desirous to labor, are easily induced to give a pledge to be orderly and industrious, and make no effort to escape. A more quiet and regular class of patients, of which we always have more or less, are permitted to go abroad unattended, on a pledge to return with punctuality; and few, indeed, ever forfeit it.

"Advancement to a better gallery, permission to ride or walk, admission to the matron's parties, liberty to attend chapel on the Sabbath, are obtained on a pledge given or implied, and well understood, that every propriety suitable to be observed in the place is absolutely binding on them. It is sufficient, in most cases, for patients to know that privation of privileges will follow violation of a pledge, to induce them strictly and punctually to adhere to whatever is expected of them.

"Having adopted this course with respect to pledges, and the incul cation of self-respect and self-control, we have very little need of per sonal restraints; and, while this sheet is being written, but *one* individual in the Hospital has any restraint upon his person, and this only to prevent his destroying his clothes and bed; he is quiet, and entirely harmless.

"*Courts or Yards.* By relying upon the pledges of our patients, and inculcating self-respect, we have been able to dispense with the use of courts. They have a Prison-like appearance, and, while in them, our patients were constantly rolling in the dirt, or sleeping upon the ground, thus soiling their clothes and becoming sunburnt. We find that *one* attendant can take charge of the same number of patients while walking or at labor, as he could formerly in the courts, and they are more pleasantly and usefully employed. Escapes were more common while these were used, for, the wall being considered a protection, less vigilance was used by the attendants. We now dispense with them entirely, and find that not only the personal appearance of our patients is improved, but they are also more quiet, and have more self-respect."

CAUSES OF INSANITY.

" The most frequent causes of predisposition to insanity are, unrestrained indulgence, unbridled appetites and desires, pernicious mechanical restraint upon the free movement of organs essential to life, improprieties of dress, excessive effeminacy, or ill-directed education, by which the individual is not prepared to meet the vicissitudes and trials which must be encountered in the journey of life; and particularly from that *intensity* of the mind and feelings, which is too often encouraged, but which overtaxes the young brain, and excites it to morbid irritation and actual disease. If this is not counteracted, it will, most assuredly, result in that perversion of the faculties which is exhibited in mental alienation, or in organic lesion, which will sooner or later prove fatal.

" Let this subject receive the attention it should do, and insanity will lose half its victims, and hereditary predisposition be divested of most of its terrors." — *Dr. Woodward; Eighth Annual Report.*

The per cent. of cases, from the same author, from the most prominent causes, is as follows: — From intemperate drinking, 12¼ per cent.; from ill health, 25 per cent.; from the affections, such as domestic afflictions, disappointed affection, &c., 16¼ per cent.; concerning property, 4⅔ per cent.; religious, 4⅔ per cent.; masturbation, 6⅔ per cent.

In the Ohio Asylum, at Columbus, Dr. William M. Awl assigns the following as the causes of insanity in the 258, the whole number of cases admitted: —

Intemperance,	18	Matrimonial perplexities,	10
Domestic affliction,	10	Fright,	3
Ill health of various kinds,	23	Seduction,	1

Jealousy, ... 2	Intense application, ... 4
Epilepsy, ... 17	Disappointed love, ... 10
Injuries of the head, ... 5	Excessive joy, ... 1
Constitutional, ... 15	Excessive use of snuff, ... 1
Masturbation, produced or per-	Disappointment and mortifica-
petuated by the practice, . . 17	tion, ... 16
Ill treatment from parents or	Fear of want and loss of prop-
guardians, ... 6	erty, ... 7
Unknown, ... 34	Religious excitement and anx-
Puerperal, ... 22	iety, including perplexity,
Loss of friends, ... 5	exultation, enthusiasm, fa-
Indulgence of temper, ... 1	naticism, doubt, and fear of
Political excitement, ... 1	future punishment, ... 29

Mortality of Lunatic Asylums.

We find the following valuable table on this subject in Dr. Earle's book on Insanity and Insane Asylums: —

Asylum.	Time.	Number of Patients.	Deaths.	Per Cent.
Hauwell, England, ...	1832 to 1837	3327	418	12.56
Lancaster, "	1832 to 1837	2148	522	24.29
Wakefield, "	1818 to 1836	2242	709	31.64
York, "	1777 to 1814	2635	399	16.80
" "	1815 to 1837	1131	217	19.27
York Retreat, "	1796 to 1836	508	113	22.22
Charenton, France, ...	1826 to 1833	2049	546	26.64
Salpêtrière, "	1801 to 1804	1002	250	4.95
" "	1805 to 1813	2804	790	28.17
Bicêtre, "	1784 to 1794	1405	685	48.75
Aversa, Italy, ...	in 20 years	3897	1222	31.35
Amsterdam, Holland, ...	1832 to 1837	255	55	21.56
Pennsylvania Hospital, U. S.	1752 to 1836	4116	548	13.31
Bellevue, New York, "	1791 to 1821	1553	154	9.91
Bloomingdale, N. Y. "	1821 to 1835	1915	146	7.62
Frankford, Penn. "	1817 to 1838	634	90	14.19
Maryland State, "	1835 to 1839	393	34	8.65
Connecticut Retreat, "	1834 to 1839	1001	60	5.99
Massachusetts State, "	1833 to 1840	1196	90	7.50
Ohio State, "	1839 to 1840	258	22	8.52
Kentucky State, "	1824 to 1838	627	238	37.35

21 Asylums, from 1752 to 1840, 88 years, 35,096 patients; average mortality, 19 per cent.
In the British Asylums, 21 per cent.

In the French Asylums, 32 per cent.
In the American, including Kentucky, 12 per cent.
In the American, excluding Kentucky, 9 per cent.

STATISTICS OF ELEVEN LUNATIC ASYLUMS, FOR 1840.

	Whole Number under Treatment.	Number at the Commencement of the Year.	Received during the Year.	Recovered.	Much improved.	Improved.	Dead.	Remaining at the Close of the Year.	Number admitted from the First.	Whole Number of Recovered.	Time of opening the Institution.
Maine Asylum, at Augusta,.	30	...	30	1	..	1	..	28	28	1	1840
Vermont Asylum, at Brattleboro',....................	142	69	73	33	..	13	6	81	....	....	1836
McLean Asylum, at Charlestown, Mass...............	263	108	155	75	12	20	13	125	1856	802	1818
Boston Asylum, at S. Boston,	104	...	104	5	..	1	2	87	104	....	1839
State Hospital, at Worcester, Mass....................	391	229	162	82	un.	29	15	236	1196	506	1833
Connecticut Retreat, at Hartford.....................	....	...	84	50	..	...	2	...	1001	563	1824
Bloomingdale Asylum, city of New York,..............	251	118	133	68	un.	32	14	126	....	....	1821
Dr. White's Private Asylum, at Hudson, N.Y.........	84	48	36	21	10	4	5	36	1000	563	1830
Friends' Asylum, at Frankford, Penn., in 1839,......	....	...	54	25	5	9	4	un.	688	239	1817
Pennsylvania Hospital, in Philadelphia, from 1752 to 1832,.....................	....	...	...	...	..	...	..	...	3718	1289	1752
Ohio Asylum, at Columbus,.	215	114	101	53	2	un.	14	138	258	80	1838
Eleven Asylums,...........	1470	686	932	413	29	109	75	857	9849	3843	

From the table it appears that the whole number under
treatment during the year in eleven Asylums was . . . 1470
Number at the commencement of the year, ... 686
Number at the close of the year, ... 857
Increase during the year, ... 171
Number received during the year, ... 932
Number recovered, ... 413
Much improved, ... 29
Improved, ... 109
Dead, ... 75
Whole number under treatment from the first, ... 9849
Whole number recovered, ... 3843

3. PENITENTIARIES.

EFFECT OF MORAL AND RELIGIOUS INSTRUCTION IN PENITENTIARIES.

The chaplain of the Connecticut State Prison, the Rev. Josiah Brewer, says, —

"Prevailingly, its inmates have given good attention to searching the Holy Scriptures, and many of them have manifested increasing diligence in committing select portions to memory. Less progress, however, than would be desirable has been made by those who are learning to read."

"A goodly number have, *professedly*, become confirmed in virtuous resolutions, particularly on the subject of temperance. Should such, on leaving Prison, find employment where intoxicating liquors are no longer sold, or openly used as a beverage, a considerable portion will, I am persuaded, avoid that vice, which, beyond every other, was the fruitful source of their present misery and disgrace. I shall be much disappointed if a few of my unhappy flock do not continue to give evidence of a decided change."

The chaplain of the Massachusetts State Prison, the Rev. Mr. Curtis, says, —

"Results as encouraging and happy have been witnessed, from religious and moral culture, during the past year, as in almost any preceding one, since the present organization of the institution."

Again, he says, —

"There will always be some, whom no kind offices can move, and whose minds cannot be reached by any influences which can be brought to bear upon them. But, in very many instances, and, it is hoped, in a majority of the whole, an affectionate attention to their wants, sympathy in their afflictions, advice and counsel, faithfully and affectionately given, suited to their condition, and religious instruction, in conversation and the more public exercises of the Sabbath school and the sanctuary, produce, habitually, a very salutary effect. The heart is softened, the passions are brought under control, serious and salutary reflection induced, resolutions of amendment formed and strengthened; and in some cases, it is believed, genuine penitence for sin, and a cordial trust and confidence in the Savior, have been the happy result."

The physician of the same Prison, Dr. W. J. Walker, ascribes the excellent health of the institution, and the few deaths, in part, " to the great pains taken to inform the minds, to improve and elevate the moral principle, and consequently to quiet the turbulent passions of the tenants of this place."

The chaplain of the Auburn Prison, the Rev. Thomas R. Townsend, says, he is encouraged in his work by the kindness of the officers, by the blessed effects of moral and religious instruction, by the spirit manifested by prisoners on leaving the Prison, and by the good conduct of many after their discharge.

The inspectors of the Prison at Sing Sing say, the whole religious department of the Prison is in active and progressive improvement.

The chaplain of the Prison at Sing Sing, the Rev. John Luckey, says, —

"Of the female Prison I will say, there have been evident indications of the most beneficial effects of the gospel on a number of convicts, within a few months past. The matron and her assistants are of opinion, that 25, out of 72 confined in that Prison, have participated in this benignant influence, which has produced a signal change in their tempers and conduct."

He adds, in regard to the Prison for men at Sing Sing, —

"Being prepared to make all proper deductions for spurious pretensions, which the nature of their circumstances may seem to demand, I am constrained to believe that, during the last two years, not less than 150 convicts have been brought to experience the beneficial effects of gospel truth, either in its saving efficacy, or to such an extent as to induce them to seek for mercy and forgiveness."

The inspectors of the Prison in New Jersey, say, —

"The moral condition of the convicts has been less the subject of attention during the past year than any preceding time within this institution. Peculiar circumstances have occasioned this neglect." They further say, that "neglect of this important duty"—that is, of instruction—"destroys the great object of the institution."

The keeper of the New Jersey Prison, Mr. John Voorhees, says, —

"In regard to the moral character of the convicts, there are some, I believe, truly regenerate in their spirit and temper; but far the greater portion of them evince a different temperament; and yet I believe that, with regular, constant, and faithful moral and religious instruction, many even of these might be brought, if not to see their true character in view of their Maker, at least to reflect and mourn over their past evil course. And although the reverend clergy of the city of Trenton, and other preachers, have kindly ministered to the spiritual necessities of the prisoners, yet the interruptions to a regular ministration have been frequent, and therefore less effective."

There is no resident chaplain.

The inspectors of the new Penitentiary in Philadelphia say,—

"The experience of another year confirms our opinion of the importance of the labors of the moral instructor, in the preservation and development of the true design of the separate system. We refer to his interesting report annexed. It exhibits such a view of the causes of crime, as must convince every candid mind, that no otner remedy can be successfully applied to the mass of moral disease, than that which sound moral and religious instruction, under the blessing of Heaven, affords."

The warden of the new Penitentiary in Philadelphia, Mr. George Thompson, says,—

"I appreciate highly the benefits rendered the convicts by the labors of the moral instructor, during week days, and his services, with those of the clergymen who volunteer, on the Sabbath."

The physician of the same Prison, Dr. Wm. Darrach, says, —

"More constant moral influence and official supervision on the colored prisoners would, likely, diminish sickness in this institution."

The moral instructor, Thomas Larcombe, says, —

"No particular excitement has been visible through the past year, but an encouraging attention and general good deportment, with repeated instances of apparent usefulness, has encouraged the prosecution of this department of my labor ; and I indulge the hope, that, although, in many instances, the prisoner may be discharged unreformed, the germinating principle of truth may be lodged in his bosom, which, in after time, will produce the desired fruit."

"Among the number of deaths which have occurred, I have been occasionally called to witness the sustaining influence of religion. The careless have been aroused to timely concern ; the unbeliever has relinquished his false hope, and turned to the true and sure refuge ; the broken-hearted have been healed, and, trusting in the love and grace of the Lord Jesus, have smiled in death. At least five have inspired the hope that God had wrought in them the requisite preparation."

The warden of the Penitentiary in the District of Columbia, Isaac Clarke, Esq., says,—

"Religious and moral instruction, by means of preaching and the Sabbath school, is still pursued, and with like results. Enough has been demonstrated, to show, even under our worst circumstances, that no point in our system is more necessary and useful than this."

The chaplain of the same Penitentiary, Rev. John B. Ferguson, says,—

"During the period (the last eight months) in which I have discharged the duties of chaplain in the Penitentiary, I am pleased to have it to say, that the conduct of the prisoners, during the time of those services, has been serious, attentive, and respectful ; and have no doubt but the influences of those services, the former part of the year, contributed mainly to the decorum thus exemplified, and to the hope that much will be accomplished in the reclaiming of the hearts of many of the convicts."

The directors of the Maryland Penitentiary say, —

"The moral instruction of the convicts is confided to the care of the chaplain ; and the religious exercises performed by him on the

Sabbath are attended with apparent interest by all the inmates of the Prison. In addition to this means of improvement, the institution possesses, as it has enjoyed through a long series of years past, the voluntary and frequently-repeated visits of the Rev. Dr. Wyatt. Attracted by the bland, yet dignified and impressive manner of that gentleman, many of the convicts have sought, and are in the constant habit of receiving, his kindly and beneficent ministrations. And surely the exertion of abilities of so refined and exalted an order, so directed and continued with such unwearied assiduity, cannot but be productive of the happiest and most salutary effects."

The annual report of the institution contains nothing from the chaplain himself or the Rev. Dr. Wyatt.

In the report of the Virginia Penitentiary we find nothing on the subject of moral and religious instruction.

The committee of the legislature on the Penitentiary in Louisiana say, —

"Nor can your committee close this report without again adverting, in the most emphatic manner, to the great advantage to be attained to the institution, in its discipline, and in the moral improvement of its inmates, by the introduction within its walls of a judicious and zealous Christian minister." The committee add, "It is believed, that no Penitentiary in the Union is without its chaplain, or without some equivalent provision for the religious and moral improvement of this erring portion of our race. It is yet a cherished portion of the Penitentiary system, that the elements of reform and amelioration exist in the moral organization of every human creature, however abandoned, and that no reasonable means should be denied, which would give a fair trial of the experiment."

SABBATH SCHOOLS IN PRISON.

The inspectors of the Prison at Sing Sing say, —

"The report of the Rev. John Luckey shows a very minute and detailed history of labors performed and services rendered as chaplain of the Prison. The experience of this gentleman in his department, his faithfulness and unwearied exertions for the dearest interests of those committed to his care, have been hitherto subject of remark to the legislature. Assisted by the agent in the various religious duties of the Prison, the same are carried on, in conjunction with the Sunday school, in both Prisons with much zeal, combining the aid of several benevolent individuals of both sexes."

The reverend chaplain of the Prison above named says, —

"As an instance of the beneficial results of Sabbath school and other instructions in this (i. e. the female) department, it has been ascertained, that only about two in ten of all the convicts could read, at the time of their being committed; and at the time of their discharge, eight out of ten have been able to read the New Testament with comparative ease."

Again he says, — " Our Sabbath school, which commenced on the 10th of May last, with 114 scholars, is in a prosperous condition, and is found to be a powerful auxiliary in promoting the intellectual and moral well-being of the convict. The institution, which is attended to immediately after service in the male Prison, while the chaplain is preaching in the female Prison, is solely under the care and superintendence of the agent and principal keeper."

The chaplain of the Prison at Auburn says, —

" I am happy in being able to report that the Sabbath school in connection with this institution (embracing about 300 of its inmates) has been in successful operation during the past year, excepting the ordinary semi-annual vacations, occasioned by the dispersion of the young gentlemen of the seminary, upon whom we depend for instructors. A sense of propriety, no less than the promptings of gratitude, constrains me to refer to their voluntary, assiduous, and effective labors in this department. Sure I am that the gratitude of all the officers of this institution, of the numerous and afflicted friends of those here taught, and also of all the friends of good order and virtue, *is their due.*

" I cannot doubt that the blessing of many ready to perish will be their reward. Thanksgiving should also be unceasingly rendered to the *all-wise* Director and Disposer of all events, for the juxtaposition of these two institutions. Our Sabbath school is made up, first, of the ignorant ; *second,* of the young ; *third,* of those who appear most highly to prize its precious privileges. Here many are taught the first principles of education, and also of religion. None but a heart incapable of emotion, can contemplate the scene it presents with indifference ; nor is the scene more affecting than its fruits are precious. It has repeatedly been my happiness to see young men, and even husbands and fathers, leave these walls with the Bible in their hands, able to read, understandingly, its heavenly truths, who, at the time of entering, were ignorant even of the letters of the alphabet. Indeed, the familiarity obtained by many with the doctrines and precepts, the promises and threatenings, of the word of God, is such as nearly to exceed the credulity of any but eye-witnesses. And what is more than all, is their practical effects upon their hearts, as witnessed by their lives."

The warden of the Penitentiary in the District of Columbia says, —

" Moral and religious instruction, as imparted to the prisoners by means of preaching and the Sabbath school, for several years past, is still pursued, and with like results. Of the prisoners, 31 could read when admitted, and 23 have since learned to read through the instrumentality of the school."

COMMON DAY OR EVENING SCHOOLS IN PENITENTIARIES AND PRISONS.

In the House of Correction at South Boston, a day school has been taught by the clerk, two hours each day, during several years past, for a class of young convicts, in the common branches of knowledge, in a room carefully fitted up for that purpose, and great good has resulted from it.

The governor of the state of New York, in his last message, says,—

" I would have the school-room, in the Prison, fitted as carefully as the solitary cell and the workshop; and although attendance there cannot be so frequent, I would have it quite as regular."

The chaplain of the Prison at Wethersfield, in his last report to the legislature, urges the importance of this mode of instruction in Prison.

Modes of Punishment for Misdemeanor in Penitentiaries.

The keeper of the State Prison at Charlestown, Charles Lincoln, Esq., says,—

" There has been no relaxation of effort, on the part of the officers, to keep the convicts under strict discipline, and to promote habits of order and industry among them.   But with a view to comply with the wishes of the board of inspectors, and also of the public generally, some change has been made with respect to the means used of enforcing an observance of the rules and regulations of the institution.

" The old method of punishment, by solitary confinement, on a diet of bread and water, has again been tested, and found to answer no better purpose in subduing stubborn offenders, than was accomplished by it in the earlier years of this establishment.   Some other and more effectual means became necessary to maintain order and to secure prompt obedience.   To avoid, therefore, if possible, the necessity of again resorting to corporal punishment, the ' shower bath' has been introduced, and is now in a course of experiment.   At present, it seems to answer, to a good degree, our wishes and anticipations; but it is, at least, doubtful if it proves sufficiently effective to restrain the bold and hardened offender ; and it is most probable that cases will arise which will render it necessary to inflict a moderate amount of corporal chastisement — a mode of punishment which seldom fails of producing the most decisive and salutary results."

The inspectors of the Auburn Prison say, —

" So far as our own investigations and frequent observations have enabled us to judge of the state and condition of the discipline of the Prison, we feel warranted in saying, that the police has seldom, if ever, been excelled at any period since its establishment.   The present keeper combines with his other, or constitutional fitness, the advantages of several years' experience as an assistant-keeper in this Prison. Under his administration of the police and discipline, we have not the remotest apprehension of any unnecessary severities being either practised or allowed.   We are also much gratified at witnessing the unusual degree of harmony and good feeling existing among the officers and guards, so essential to the reputation, as well as the best interests, of the institution."

The inspectors of the Prison at Sing Sing say, —

" In carrying out the views of the legislature, and in accordance with public feeling, it was resolved by the board, at an early period of its labors, that the assistant keepers report to the principal keeper, in every case of breach of discipline of the convicts, previous to inflicting punishment ; and that the principal keeper determine the amount of punishment, and report the name of the convict, the offence, and by whom inflicted, at every monthly meeting of the board. This duty has been performed, and with most gratifying results; the extreme severity of punishment is essentially done away with, and no greater rigor is used than is deemed necessary for the safe-keeping of the convicts, and the enforcement of the rules of the Prison. While the condition of the convicts is thus ameliorated, the labor performed is equal in amount, if not superior, to what it has hitherto been ; it is done with apparent cheerfulness and good feeling, unaccompanied by complaints for want of food ; and under this relaxation no attempt at insurrection has ever been made, no escape, and but one attempt at escape. The firm and persevering efforts in carrying out the views of the board, have mainly contributed to this desirable state of police ; and the acknowledgment of intelligent convicts discharged, and otherwise, strengthen the belief that a most salutary change in the police department of the Prison has been effected for the benefit of the convicts in every respect."

The chaplain confirms the statement of the inspectors, as follows : —

" I cannot forbear to mention here another thing, which has tended greatly to facilitate our operations in this (i. e., the moral) department. It is the effect upon the spirit and conduct of the prisoners of the resolution passed by your honorable board, requiring the assistant keepers to report to the principal keeper every case of the breach of discipline or insubordination in the convicts, *previous* to inflicting punishment, and referring to the principal keeper the *determination* of the *amount* of punishment and the *time when* it shall be inflicted. As this procedure brings every offender directly before the chief officer, and exposes his delinquency to one whose good opinion he is naturally desirous to retain, it is a more powerful restraint against disorderly conduct by the convicts, than the severest castigation inflicted under other circumstances would be, while, at the same time, it is far less injurious to their moral feelings. It affords, too, the advantage to this responsible officer, to administer such admonition and impart such counsel to offenders as the nature of the case may require, and as will convince them that he is not influenced by malice or ill-will in causing them to be punished, but does it in discharge of his duty, for the purpose of preserving order.

" The effect of this mode of discipline upon the convicts is, that it disarms them of all that virulence of feeling, which a less paternal mode is calculated to produce, and thus prepares them to receive the benefits of moral and religious instruction with the same docility from the officers of the Prison as children do from their parents or teachers, who *govern* at the same time that they teach and admonish them. A neighboring clergyman, a short time ago, after having spent some time assisting me in giving instructions to the convicts, remarked, that he was not surprised at the amount of moral and religious feeling he had witnessed while thus employed, after hearing, as he had, the unanimous expressions of affectionate regard among the prisoners for the officers of the institution; and then, addressing himself to the agent and principal keeper, he added, ' Your property and lives would, I believe, be perfectly safe in the hands of the vilest of them.' The same favorable opinion, as to the state of moral feeling among the prisoners, has been expressed by the different clergymen of various denominations who have visited us, and occasionally preached in the chapel. These remarks apply as well to the convicts in the female as in the male Prison."

Does the Auburn System of Prison Discipline depend on Stripes?

Preliminary Remarks.

The discussion of this question demands candor, patience, and frankness, without fear or favor.

The officers and prisoners have both sacred and inviolable rights.

The officers have the right to govern with humanity, firmness, and authority.

The prisoners have a right to live, (if they do not attempt to kill,) to breathe, to eat, to be clothed, to be taken care of when they are sick.

The government of a Prison, however, is delegated and committed, by higher powers, to elected officers, who have no right to transcend the powers committed to them; and the prisoners have no right to resist the authority of the officers, when exercised according to law.

Absolute power, unlimited power, despotic power, are entirely inadmissible in the American Penitentiary system.

All the Prisons are, or should be, regulated by law, and nothing is more important, than that it should be seen and known by competent, unprejudiced, and disinterested inspectors, that the laws are faithfully executed, and no more.

The very beginning of assumption in regard to powers not delegated, should be crushed on the threshold. When an elected officer of a Prison begins to say, "I shall do as I please; I care not for the law, or the inspectors; if they know it, and like it, well; if not, well; my will shall govern, and no question shall be asked or answered ; " — you have despotism and tyranny, which the legislative and appointing powers should crush at once. It is the government of a tyrant over men, which the prisoners hate, which the laws do not sanction, which the ignorance of the inspectors cannot excuse, and which sets the hearts of the prisoners at enmity against society, because they are not treated according to law.

So important was this matter, in the view of the immortal Howard, that he always contended, that there should not only be laws for the government of a Prison, but they should be printed and published, and suspended upon the interior walls of the Prison, that every inmate might understand the laws by which he was to be governed, and that every officer and inspector might frequently be reminded of the laws by which alone the Prison could be governed, without trampling upon the rights of the prisoners or neglecting his own duties.

The fundamental principles laid down in these preliminary remarks, it is believed, are so obvious and self-evident, as to require neither proof nor illustration.

We proceed, therefore, to discuss a question of fundamental importance, which may need discussion and illustration.

It has been said that terror, and not moral improvement, is the great end of the Auburn system ; that the lash, and not moral means, will keep men out of Prison. It has been said, and a pamphlet has been written to prove it, that the Auburn system depends for its existence on the lash, and cannot be carried on without it.

If this were true, it would be a deadly blow against the system.

But it is not true, in the sense here intended. That the lash has generally been used at Auburn and Sing Sing is true. But to what extent the system depends for its existence and success upon the lash, is a question of vast importance, and deserving most grave and impartial consideration. We think it can be proved that it does not depend for its success upon the lash.

What, then, is the Auburn system of Prison discipline ? It is not one thing ; it is many things. It is a great improvement of the nineteenth century in a very important science.

In the first place, it is solitary confinement at night.

The importance and effect of this one feature of the system cannot readily be conceived by those who have not been familiar with the dreadful evils of the crowded night-rooms of the old Prisons.

Where old thieves taught young thieves, in companies of fifteen or twenty, how to pick pockets and pick locks ; how to burn houses and break stores ; how to make and set the matches ; how to make the false keys ; where were the most exposed places, and the richest plunder ; who kept money in their houses ; in what part of the house it was kept; when the men of the house were away from home ; whether the houses were guarded by dogs, and in what manner the doors were fastened ; and, moreover, how the old corrupted the young, by practising the sin of Sodom ; it was well said, " *Better that the laws were written in blood, than thus executed in sin.*"

Pickpockets had a language of their own, which was taught in these rooms. Picklocks had moulds and models of false keys, which would go through all the locks of the city, and would furnish a key to unlock the door, by having the impression of a key-hole on a piece of wax. A key, furnished many years ago, by one of the old teachers, in an old Prison, has been preserved, which would probably unlock 5000 locks in the city of Boston ; and another false key, with six or eight variations, which would probably unlock half the stocklocks in the commonwealth. Instruction in these arts was the business of the old night-rooms. " *They were committee-rooms of mischief.*" " *Nature and humanity cried aloud* for redemption from this dreadful degradation."

It was done, and done effectually, by the first great feature of the Auburn system of Prison discipline, viz., solitary confinement at night.

The second great feature of the system is silence by day and by night.

This is scarcely less important than the other ; for, although men might be removed from personal contact with each other, and from the dreadful degradation of the old night-rooms, still, if they were permitted, by word of mouth, to teach the arts of mischief, but half the evil was prevented. Hence the importance of the second great law of the system — silence by day and by night. Persons, who did not know why the law was made, might think it severe ; but those who have stood, night after night, unperceived by the prisoners, alongside of the old night-rooms, and heard the conversation of the old and experienced convict with the novice in crime, would almost choose that the tongue should cleave to the roof of the mouth, rather than that it should not cease to make such communications. Silence by day and by night, therefore, became the second great feature of the Auburn system.

How completely this object has been effected, is illustrated by the anecdote of a prisoner who requested a sheriff, when conducting him from Wethersfield to New Haven, to put him a night in the County Jail with *another man;* because, he said, it made his tongue feel so good to talk, and added further, "One man is as good as five newspapers."

The third great feature of the Auburn system is moral and religious instruction. The evil communication being cut off, the good instruction is communicated. The morning and evening prayers; the private visits, conversation, advice, and sympathy of the chaplain; the kind and faithful admonitions, instructions, and prayers of the Sabbath school teachers; the appropriate and pungent preaching; and, not unfrequently, the paternal advice and counsel of the warden, in the chapel, on the Sabbath, in the presence of all the officers and visitors; — this is the third great feature of the Auburn system.

In the chapel of the Auburn Prison, the late Judge Powers addressed a few words of kindness and affectionate regard to the prisoners, and about one half the whole number were in tears. How admirably this combination of the great features of the system is calculated to bring men to reflection! A prisoner was asked in the new Prison at Wethersfield, Conn., which is built and conducted, substantially, on the Auburn plan, "How do you like the new Prison, compared with the old Prison, where they were lodged seventy feet under ground, in large night-rooms?" He said, " *There, it is, Hail, fellows, well met;* but *here,* it is prayers the first thing in the morning, and the last thing at night, and silence by day and by night; *we see our comrades, and say nothing;* but think, think, think. I do not like this so well as the other."

Several other important features of the system, although not, perhaps, as important as those which have been mentioned, are essential to its completion, and distinguish it from any system ever introduced previous to the present century.

The building is a Prison within a Prison, greatly diminishing the chances of escape, and preventing the ceaseless anxiety, calculation, craft, and cunning, of the old Prisons, in regard to escapes.

Moreover, the construction gives a place, in the area, around the block of cells, for a sentinel to be always on duty, during the night. If the prisoner gets out of his cell into the area, he is exposed to the fire of the sentinel on duty. This is a very distinct and important feature of the Auburn system, greatly distinguishing it from the old system of Prison discipline, where plots to escape, combinations for the purpose, insurrections, and rebellion, were the order of the day. We have scarcely heard of such a thing since the Auburn system was introduced.

There are still other features of the system, too important not to be mentioned, going to show that it is no one thing, but many things, that make the Auburn system.

The same relative position, to a vast extent, is preserved among the men. My neighbor to-day is my neighbor to-morrow and the whole year. The names, faces, crimes, sentences, of prisoners, *in different shops*, and, to some extent, in the same shops, are not known to fellow-prisoners. The extent to which this remark is true, owing to preserving the same relative position, would surprise any critical examiner.

And then the same relative position is preserved, by the lock-step, from the shops to the night-rooms, from the night-rooms to the chapel, and from the chapel again to the shops; and thus the jostling, bustle, and confusion of the old system is done away.

Again, to prevent evil communication by signs, the men are extensively arranged, on the Auburn system, improved to the highest degree, back to face, and not face to face; so that the thing signified by signs, what does it signify, if it is not seen?

This is an imperfect outline of the Auburn system. There is evidently much in it to subdue, to silence, to instruct, to restrain, to render submissive and pliable, to keep in safety, before a word is said about stripes. The stripes are as the drop to the ocean, compared with the whole. It is not true, that it depends on stripes. Its *efficiency* does not depend upon them; its success does not depend upon them; the preventing evil communication does not depend upon them; the good instruction does not depend upon them; the construction of the Prison does not depend upon them; its reformatory character does not depend upon them; the keeping down insurrections, and the preventing escapes, do not depend upon them; keeping the convicts ignorant of each other does not depend upon them. In short, stripes ought to be, if they are not, either a very small part, or no part, of the system.

What becomes, now, of the principle, which we set out to discuss, that terror, and not moral improvement, is the great end of the Auburn system of Prison discipline. We have seen that all the great features of the system aim at moral improvement, by preventing evil and communicating good.

The solitary confinement at night; the silence by day and by night; the moral and religious instruction; the very construction of the Prison; the chapel, the solemn assembly, the morning and evening devotions; the Sabbath school; the paternal advice of the warden; the sympathetic and affectionate visits of the chaplain; the night watch; the preserving the same relative position; the cutting off the language of signs; — all, all is designed to prevent evil communication, and, in the place of it, to pour upon the mind good instruction. The man who says it depends altogether upon the lash, does not understand the system. It is a powerful system without stripes. We are now prepared to show that it can be conducted, and has been conducted, as well, if not better, without stripes. In the House of Correction, at South Boston, with 300 inmates, it has been in successful operation six years without stripes. The Auburn system, in all its great features, can nowhere be seen in more successful operation.

IMPROVEMENT AND ENLARGEMENT OF WORKSHOPS IN PENITENTIARIES.

The warden of the Massachusetts State Prison, in his last report, speaks of the necessity of some additions to the workshops.

The warden of the Connecticut State Prison, in expending the moneys appropriated by the last legislature for repairs, has greatly enlarged and improved the workshops, so that the whole range of shops in this Prison is now very ample, well adapted, and complete. Probably no Penitentiary in the United States is now provided with better workshops.

The inspectors of the Auburn Prison, in their last report, call the attention of the legislature to this subject, as follows : —

" We fully concur in the opinion of the agent, in his report, in reference to the pressing necessity of the erection of at least one new shop, at as early a period as practicable, for the accommodation of the several contractors by him therein named. At present, the respective contractors for the employment of the hame-makers and tailors, are suffering much inconvenience, and the state a pecuniary loss, for the want of proper and sufficient shop-room. Should the agent continue to be exempted from the payment of sheriff fees for the transportation of convicts hither, we have no good reason to doubt that the resources of the Prison will be ample for constructing such shops, and for completing such other necessary improvements and repairs as he has suggested."

The agent of the Auburn Prison says, —

" Most of the workshops are in a leaky and very dilapidated condition."

The physician of the same Prison proposes to the board of inspectors

" The propriety of establishing an invalid department, separate and wholly distinct from the hospital, the object of which should be the reception and employment of all the convicts after being discharged from the hospital, while yet in a feeble state, and unable to do duty in the shops; also all weak, enfeebled, and broken-down subjects, who are unable to labor in the shops, but still able to do something towards paying for their keeping. At present, there is no stopping-place between the hospital and the workshop; and, although the hospital is the proper place for the sick, it is frequently the wrong place for the convalescent. Men will frequently recover their strength tardily while in the hospital; the consequence is, they are sometimes sent back to the shops before they have recovered sufficient strength; hence ensue relapses, and perhaps the confirmation of some latent disease, which ultimately destroys the subject. Such an improvement would have an important bearing upon the health of the convicts, lessen the amount of mortality in the Prison, and more fully comport with the humane principles of Prison discipline of the present day."

BAD CONSTRUCTION AND VENTILATION.

The physician of the new Penitentiary in New Jersey, on the Pennsylvania plan, says, in his last report, —

" The evils of bad ventilation ought to be seriously considered. One of the worst systems of heating is adopted in this Prison, — that of radiation from pipes. If a plan were devised for warming without purifying an apartment, a more effectual mode could not be conceived. The same air may remain for days, excepting the occasional entry and escape from apertures, that have not been made for the purpose; for, owing to a deficiency of heat from the pipes, the ventilators are kept closed, in winter, by the convicts, or they suffer from cold. Heated air, as they cannot have fireplaces, or stoves, in their cells, is the only plan, that ought to be resorted to. . . . The first breath that a stranger inhales, is felt instinctively to be unwholesome. The emanations from the prisoners and the outlet pipes, are floating through the interior of the building, when there ought to be a strong current of air, driving them out of doors."

A correspondent in Louisville, Kentucky, concerning the Indiana Penitentiary at Jeffersonville, says, —

" On each side of a central wall is arranged a row of forty cells. These cells are back to back, and open into two passages, which are on each side between them and the outer wall. The cells are $7\frac{1}{2}$ feet long and 4 feet wide, ventilated by an aperture 2 feet long through the outer wall; but are perfectly dark when closed," i. e., when the cell doors are shut.

The Rev. Mr. Barrett, in a letter dated May 12, 1841, concerning the same Prison, writes that —

" It ought not to be spoken of with any kind of patience. It is a disgrace to the state. A few years ago, a new building for cells was erected within the narrow walls. A worse place for human beings to sleep in can scarcely be contrived. It professes to be on the Auburn plan; but the blocks of cells are entirely of wood; the doors of wood, with a single small hole through them, without grating. The cells are only 5 or 6 feet from the external wall; and a tight floor at each story goes from the cells to the outer wall, and thus precludes fresh air. The cells cannot be entered without low stooping. Reading in the cells is entirely out of the question; and how a man can breathe there long, with any comfort, 'tis hard to understand."

Length of Sentences in Penitentiaries.

Average sentence of 322, the whole number in the Massachusetts State Prison, Sept. 30, 1840, ... 5 yrs. 9 mos.

Average sentence of 189, in the Connecticut State Prison, March 31, 1841, ... 7 yrs. 3 mos.

Average sentence of 152, in the New Jersey State Prison, Sept. 30, 1840, ... 4 yrs. 7 mos.

Average sentence of 129, in the new Penitentiary in Philadelphia, received during the year 1840, 2 yrs. 5 mos.

Average sentence of 104, in the Baltimore Penitentiary, received during the year ending Nov. 30, 1840, ... 3 yrs.

Average sentence of 79, in the Penitentiary in the District of Columbia, during the year 1840, . 3 yrs. 8 mos.

Average sentence of 181, in the Virginia Penitentiary, Sept. 30, 1839, ... 6 yrs. 10 mos.

Average sentence of 162, in the Kentucky Penitentiary, Nov. 30, 1840, ... 4 yrs.

Average sentence of 68, received in the Louisiana Penitentiary, during the year 1839, ... 5 yrs. 1 mo.

Causes of Crime.

The chaplain of the Massachusetts State Prison says, —

" Intemperance ever has been, and still continues to be, the fruitful source of more vice and crime than all other known causes combined."

The chaplain of the Prison at Sing Sing says, —

" About one third of all the convicts now in your Prison were confirmed drunkards at the time of their conviction; another third were habitual drinkers of ardent spirits; and a large portion of the residue were in the constant use of cider, strong beer, &c., and *occasionally* drank ardent spirits. And all these have freely declared their convictions that, but for these habits, and the associations to which this dissipation led, they would not have been here."

The chaplain of the new Penitentiary in Philadelphia says, —

" In examining the causes which have impelled to the earliest commission of crime, I have been led, after a careful investigation, to the following results," (in four hundred cases:)

Propensity, independent of external temptation,	116
Temptation of evil companions, chiefly in early life,	70
Intemperance,	61
Licentiousness,	115
Gaming, 9; circus shows, 2; domestic trouble, 1,	12
Pecuniary difficulties, 4; revenge, 17; lotteries, 3,	24
Malicious mischief,	2
	400

IMPRISONMENT OF LUNATICS IN PENITENTIARIES.

The physician of the Connecticut State Prison, Dr. Archibald Welch, says, —

" There are, at the present time, six insane convicts. Robello, from Portugal, and De Wire, from Ireland, are the most prominent cases. The first was committed in 1836 for safe-keeping, having been previously tried for murder, but was acquitted on the ground of insanity. The second received a wound, and probably a fracture of the skull, in a fit of intoxication, at the time of his arrest; and from that time, he has occasionally been insane, refusing to take food except by the use of a stomach tube. He is now in the hospital, in a state of mental derangement, with diseased lungs, which preclude all hope of recovery. The others have mental disease of less severe character, which does not ordinarily interfere with their regular employment in the shops. Some of them are, however, in the opinion of those who have an opportunity of judging, more fit subjects for an Asylum for the Insane, than for a Penitentiary."

The inspectors of the State Prison at Charlestown, William Minot, Samuel Greele, and Bradford Sumner, say, in their last report, —

" Among the prisoners are several idiots or lunatics, and some who have passed the age of labor, and for whom no employment can be provided. The Prison has no accommodations for the safe-keeping or relief of persons who are destitute of reason. While here, they are a source of expense to the government, and can derive no possible benefit from a residence in the Prison. Those who, from age or bodily infirmity, are incapable of labor, are necessarily permitted to sit in idleness in the workshops, and in some measure interfere with the labor of the working men."

The warden of the same Prison, Charles Lincoln, Esq., says, —

"There are in confinement several convicts, who are either deranged, or so far deficient with respect to their mental faculties, as to render it very difficult, if not actually impossible, to keep them under the restraints required by a rigid discipline. They are a constant tax upon the institution; for, if they are put to labor, their earnings amount to little or nothing; and several are in a condition which renders them very unsafe persons to be at large in the yard. For the latter class, we have no suitable accommodations; consequently, they are very likely to be made worse, rather than improved in mind, by a continuance in this place. It would seem but the dictate of humanity, that such persons should be placed in circumstances more favorable to the restoration of their reason, or at least in circumstances better adapted to their unfortunate condition, than are the confinement and restraints of a Penitentiary. It may not be improper to remark, that of the five convicts who are suffering under the effect of deranged intellects, to an extent which requires them to be kept in close confinement, but one of the number became reduced to this situation since his commitment to this place. The others were deranged before they came here. This fact has suggested to my mind the expediency of some legislative enactment, providing for the relief of this institution, in the cases of all convicts who, at the time of their commitment here, should be manifestly insane or *non compos mentis.*"

The physician of the Auburn Prison, Dr. Erastus Humphreys, says, —

"There have been two cases of insanity, since my connection with the hospital, — one a strongly-marked case, produced by masturbation. This one has recovered. The other was evidently insane on his admission. He has been subjected to medical treatment, at different periods, and has also recovered."

The inspectors of the New Jersey Penitentiary say, in their last report, —

"According to the physician's report, there are twelve deranged persons in the Prison," (i. e., more than $\frac{1}{13}$ part of the whole number) "and more than half fit subjects for a Lunatic Asylum when they were received. The board feel that the admission of these persons into an institution that requires solitary confinement, quiet, and orderly discipline, is subversive of all system, and that it is an evil that calls for redress. Our Prison is no Asylum for the Insane. Solitary imprisonment, instead of affording relief, is of a character to confirm the malady."

The inspectors of the new Penitentiary in Philadelphia, of whom Thomas Bradford, Esq. is chairman, say, —

"We cannot omit to bear our testimony, with the thousands of our fellow-citizens who are petitioners before the legislature, in favor of a State Lunatic Asylum. Every year some of this unhappy class of men become unjustly the inmates of this Penitentiary, where they cannot receive that peculiar care and treatment which their melancholy condition requires."

The late warden, Samuel R. Hood, says, —

" I have alluded to three deranged persons having been received from the crime of murder in the second degree. That these men were so deranged, at the time the murder was perpetrated, there is no doubt; and these are not the only cases of deranged persons having been sent to the Eastern Penitentiary. Many have been clearly and decidedly proven to be so at the time of their conviction. They were, however, ill-disposed and mischievous, and the judges ask, What can be done with them? Until the legislature of Pennsylvania shall provide a suitable Asylum for the indigent deranged, (a measure which every motive of policy, of economy, and humanity, imperiously demands,) we must expect that such will be sent to the Penitentiary."

" In a future age, it will scarcely be believed, that, in the nineteenth century, in a Christian land, in a state containing, throughout its extent, innumerable monuments of piety, of intelligence, and benevolence, that those whom Providence, in its mysterious dispensations, had visited with the most grievous, the most appalling calamity, the deprivation of reason, and consequently of responsibility; that indigent lunatics should be deprived of all sympathy, of all justice, by the cruelty or negligence of their fellow-men, — should be consigned to a Prison appropriated only to felons of the vilest degree, where no friend or relative could visit them, or alleviate their distress, and where almost every surrounding circumstance is hostile to their repose, their comfort, and their restoration to reason."

ENCOURAGEMENT TO EFFORT FOR DISCHARGED CONVICTS.

The governor of New York, in his last message to the legislature, in speaking of the Female Penitentiary at Sing Sing, says, —

" The chief obstacle to a reformation of this class of offenders, is the inflexibility with which society rejects them after their season of penance is past. While the cause of public morals requires their exclusion, at least until they have given satisfactory evidence of reformation, humanity and expediency unite in recommending proper efforts to sustain those who are truly reformed. It has been suggested, that a Retreat might be provided for them at Mount Pleasant, where, under the care of benevolent females, they might maintain themselves by labor, until, by good conduct, they should become entitled to employment elsewhere. Such a plan must necessarily be left to private liberality; and I am informed that such liberality is awakened to the undertaking, and ready to engage in it, if a proper edifice can be obtained. There is a building which belongs to the state, situated near the Prison, and now of very little use, which might be devoted to this humane purpose, at least until the experiment can be tested. The whole number of male convicts in the State Prisons is 1423; of females, 74. The sex has a just claim to extraordinary effort for the reformation of the small number of persons it furnishes to our State Prisons."

The house or building here spoken of by the governor, we suppose to be the same as that spoken of by the agent in the following manner: —

" When your agent came, he found the house on the farm, known as the State-House, unoccupied, and he took the liberty of allowing the chaplain to move in, and use two or three rooms without any charge, provided he looked after the rest of the building and premises, to see that it took no damage. He would suggest the propriety of asking the legislature to pass a law allowing the chaplain to occupy as much of the house as is necessary for his family, and land enough for a garden. His is the home for all discharged convicts that are willing to call on him, and it appears but reasonable that the state should allow him to live in the house rent free."

The chaplain (the Rev. John Luckey) of the Female Prison, of which Governor Seward here speaks, says, —

" Great pains have been taken by the matron to procure for the convicts which have been discharged, places of employment, where they would be encouraged in a virtuous course of life; and success in this benevolent work may be inferred from the fact, that, of the entire number of those who have gone out of the Prison from the commencement, two only have been recommitted."

Among the 200 men and women discharged the last year, he says, —

" There were some 18 or 20 whom I had noted as having given satisfactory evidence of a gospel change, exhibiting the fruits of it in their lives."

" A majority of these, residing in New York and the vicinity, we have visited, and conversed freely with both them and their friends, and hence have the best evidence that they observe a correct course of conduct; and I correspond with others or their friends, so that I am constantly advised of their conduct and prospects; and I know not an instance of one who, having made a profession of piety while in the Prison, has dishonored that profession by returning to his former corrupt practices. A few of them have so far secured the confidence of the Christian community, as to be admitted into different churches, in which they now occupy a respectable standing."

" The honorable testimony which individuals have borne to the upright character and correct moral deportment of reformed convicts, whom they have taken into their employ after their discharge from Prison, is truly gratifying."

" Not long since, I met a gentleman in New York, who had employed one who was in his service at the time he was arrested.

" With feelings of interest of which I cannot divest myself when the case of any of these unfortunate men is introduced, I inquired after his welfare. The gentleman promptly replied, ' My dear sir, I had been so vexed and disgusted with the conduct of that young man for some months before his arrest, and so exceedingly mortified by the developments showing his criminality at his trial, that I determined to abandon him forever. But when I first saw him after his return from Prison, his very appearance disarmed me of all my former prejudice against him. There he stood, bathed in tears, confessing his crimes, and begging for pardon and protection; and he appeared so sincere and deeply affected, that I almost involuntarily said, " Yes, come back, and I will be your friend and guardian." And, sir, such has been his conduct ever since he has been with me, that my confidence in the sincerity of his professions of a change has increased every day.'

" Of another reformed convict, a very worthy Christian gentleman, under whose care the convict had been employed since his discharge, said to me a few days since, ' Why, sir, I have that confidence in the genuineness of the moral and religious change wrought in that man, and the integrity of his principles, that I should not be afraid to trust my property or my life in his hands.'

" Many similar testimonials of the uniformly good conduct of this class of discharged convicts, after their leaving the Prison, might be given, but it is not necessary. These instances of radical reform are sufficient to convince the most skeptical that even the convicts of the State Prison — those who acknowledge their guilt and the justness of their punishment — are not beyond the remedial influences of the gospel ; and that God, who declares himself to be ' merciful and gracious, forgiving iniquity, transgression, and sin,' does, in the plenitude of his compassion, condescend to grant pardon to the contrite among men, ' even to the rebellious.' "

The chaplain of the Prison at Auburn, the Rev. Thomas R. Townsend, says, —

" I am greatly encouraged by the cheering reports received from many, who have returned from these walls to their families and firesides. Some have gone away as they came; others have returned ' as the dog to his vomit; ' but the greater proportion have become better husbands, better fathers, better sons, better citizens, and, through the abounding grace of God in Christ, consistent, devoted Christians, adorning their profession by a holy walk and godly conversation."

" Many heart-broken wives and mothers have had their sorrows turned into joy, their tears and lamentations into songs of praise ; many poor, neglected children have now a kind and affectionate father to provide for all their temporal necessities; to instruct them in the principles of industry, honesty, and religion ; to lead them to the domestic altar and to the house of God."

The moral instructor, Thomas Larcombe, of the new Penitentiary in Philadelphia, says, —

" Here are persons who have possessed character and respectability at home, until, in some surprisal of passion, or unguarded moment of inebriety, they have violated the laws of their country. After some years of confinement, by which they have expiated the offence, they return to the circle of former acquaintanceship, and to their welcoming homes, not degraded and vitiated by intercourse with the vilest felons, but prepared to enjoy those friends and homes with a zest that will fortify them against future temptations to transgress."

The warden of the new Penitentiary, in the District of Columbia, Isaac Clarke, Esq., says, —

" Of the number discharged the last year, two are known to have become respected and esteemed members of a Christian church; and there is good reason to hope that others have come to a knowledge of their lost estate, and now rely, with Christian hope and confidence, upon a Savior's merits. That every case of professed reform is not genuine, there is good reason to know ; but that many of them are, is attested by a refusal to return to the society of old accomplices, and a changed life and conversation."

USE OF SURPLUS EARNINGS IN PENITENTIARIES.

The legislature of Connecticut, at its last session, passed a resolution authorizing the directors of the State Prison to pay $9000 of the surplus earnings of that institution, $1000 to each county, as a bonus, to encourage the counties to build County Prisons on the plan of that at Hartford, — when they should obtain satisfactory evidence of its being done. The directors say, in their report just published, that they have personally visited the Jails in Hartford, New London, and New Haven, and found that these buildings are constructed according to the terms specified in the resolution.

" We have accordingly authorized the warden to pay the treasurer of each of these counties the sum of $1000. This money has been paid. The same officer has moreover deposited with the treasurer of the state the sum of $5000 to meet the appropriation made by the general assembly, whenever the other counties comply with the condition of the resolution referred to above."

This is not all. The warden has expended $5000 of surplus earnings, the last year, in most valuable and important improvements of the State Prison itself; particularly in the improvement of the shops and cells. Moreover, he has $14,529 40 on hand, in notes and book accounts, and $2263 22 in cash. The whole amount of surplus earnings, above all expenses, since the Prison went into operation, is $72,203 02. The warden now proposes to the government to pay from their surplus earnings, if the legislature will sanction it, from $3000 to $5000 a year for 10 years, for the purpose of building an Asylum for the Insane Poor.

Statistics of Fifteen Penitentiaries, from Reports of 1840 and 1841.

Penitentiary	Prisoners at Commencement	Prisoners at Close	Increase of Prisoners	Diminution of Prisoners	Discharged	Pardoned	Recommitted	Escaped	Dead	Per Cent. of Deaths	Became lunatic	Lunatics	Expenses above Earnings	Earnings above Expenses
New Hampshire	78	84	6	·	13	7	18	·	·	1 in 160 [a]	·	5	·	$460 62
Massachusetts	318	322	2	·	83	14	·	·	·	·	·	6	·	8,282 90
Connecticut	169	205	36	·	34	2	·	·	2	1 in 92	·	2	·	3,427 25
Auburn, N. Y.	670	695	25	·	146	33	·	1	14	1 in 50	·	13 [f]	·	6,044 14
Sing Sing, N. Y.	762	827	65	·	192	22	7	8	17	1 in 48	9 [d]	12	unknown [g]	·
New Jersey	160	152	·	8	43	24	13	6	2	1 in 79	·	·	512 45 [e]	·
Pennsylva. Philad.	434	376	·	58	154	20	27 [b]	·	22	1 in 18	5 [c]	·	10,325 40	·
District Columbia	62	54	·	8	21	3	·	·	1	1 in 58	·	·	179 43	·
Maryland, Baltim.	328	329	1	·	103	20	·	·	14	1 in 23	·	·	3,239 26	·
Frankfort, Ky.	157	162	5	·	28	24	·	·	3	1 in 53	·	·	·	6,345 83
Columbus, Ohio	485	483	·	2	·	6	·	·	4	1 in 120	·	5	·	26,000 43
Indiana	179	181	2	·	33	·	·	·	·	·	·	·	·	3,600 00
Virginia	158	182	24	·	38	·	4	·	17	1 in 10	1	·	·	3,390 57
Louisiana	155	155	·	·	29	·	·	2	3 [h]	1 in 55	·	·	·	6,086 79
Georgia	·	·	·	·	·	·	·	·	5	1 in 31	·	·	587 48	·
15 Penitentiaries	4115	4306	166	76	904	175	69	17	104	·	·	43	$14,844 02	$63,638 53

[a] The warden says, "This result has not been produced by a discharge from Prison, of any of the sick or infirm through the interposition of executive clemency."

[b] It does not appear from the official report how many of this number had been in this Prison since it was rebuilt on the Pennsylvania plan.

[c] The physician says, "Some have been pardoned, on account of the inroads made upon health by the system here adopted," i. e., the Pennsylvania system, "who have died soon after they left the Prison."

[d] The physician says, more than half the whole number of lunatics became so last year.

[e] Not including salary of officer, paid from the state treasury.

[f] The inspectors and physician agree in saying that the instances of mental disorder have been about half those of the previous year. The previous year they were 26.

[g] As nearly as we could ascertain, not less than $15,000 above earnings.

[h] One other was killed.

From this table it appears, that the whole number of prisoners, in
15 Penitentiaries, at the commencement of the year, was 4,115
Number of prisoners at the close of the year, . . .   4,306
Increase in one year, ...   *166
Diminution of this increase for the Indiana Penitentiary, ...   99
Positive increase in 14 Penitentiaries, ...   †67
Number discharged by expiration of sentence, . . .   904
"   pardoned,.   175
"   recommitted, (returns imperfect,)   69
"   escaped, (from 9 Penitentiaries, 0,)   17
"   dead, (of whom 22 from new Penitentiary
in Philadelphia,). . . . .   ‡104
Proportion of deaths in Prisons on the Auburn plan,   1 in 45
Proportion of deaths in Prisons on the Pennsylvania
plan,. . . . .   1 in 23
Number of lunatics, (of whom 25§ are in the two
Prisons on the Pennsylvania plan,)   43
Expenses above earnings in 5 Penitentiaries, . . . $14,844 02
Expenses above earnings in the new Penitentiary in
Philadelphia, as nearly as we can ascertain, . . $15,000 00
Earnings above expenses in 9 Penitentiaries on the
Auburn plan, ... $63,638 53

4. COUNTY PRISONS.

The improvement of County Prisons is a subject of more importance than is generally supposed. The number of County
Prisons in the United States is not far from 420. The number
of persons annually confined in the County Prisons of Boston,
New York, and Philadelphia, is about 10,000 ; in the cities of
Albany and Troy, about 2700 ; in the Prisons of the state of
New York, about 18,000 ; in all the County Prisons in the land,
probably not less than 75,000. Not that so great a number are in
the County Prisons at one and the same time, but are committed to
them annually. Important practical questions arise on these facts.

---

* This number should be diminished 99, the number in the Indiana Peniten-
tiary at the close of the year, because the number at the commencement is not
stated.
  † This rate of increase would require 44 years to double the number of prisoners,
while the population doubles in 23 years.
  ‡ If the mortality had been as great in the other Penitentiaries as in that in
Philadelphia, it would have been 228, instead of 104.
  § Most of them became lunatic in Prison, viz., 14 out of 25.

Shall the County Prisons be schools of vice, or reform ? Shall they be places of labor, or idleness ? Shall they support themselves, or shall the public support them ? The answer to this last question makes a difference to the country of about $1,260,000 annually. Whether this sum is earned in neat, and orderly, and silent workshops, by 75,000 inmates of County Prisons, after the model of that in the Hartford County Prison, or whether it is paid to support them in idleness, filth, obscenity, gambling, and instruction in the arts of mischief — these are the questions. What answer shall be given to them ? In political economy, they are important. In the moral government of the world, how are they ? In preparing the way to fulfil the dying command of Christ, " Go preach the gospel to every creature," have they any bearing ?

The question is answered, and the whole matter illustrated, by example, in Hartford, Conn. There the County Prison supports itself, and yielded surplus earnings of $600 last year. There the school of vice has become the place of reformation. There the gospel is preached, and there it has taken effect upon the hearts of the subordinate keeper, a master mechanic, who, of his own accord, introduced morning and evening prayers, and conducts the worship himself ; and there a number of the prisoners have yielded their hearts to this heavenly influence. Moreover, this new County Prison, this good place of reformation, was built, in part, by the surplus earnings of the State Prison ; and other Prisons, on the same plan, during the last year, have been built in the same manner in Norwich and New Haven, and $5000 more, from the same source, deposited in the state treasury, to extend the same system through the state ; and now the warden of the State Prison offers to the legislature from $3000 to $5000 a year for 10 years, from the surplus earnings of the State Prison, to build an Asylum for Poor Lunatics. Such facts are worthy to be repeated.

" Surely the wrath of man shall praise the Lord." Why not make the 75,000 convicts in County Prisons earn $1,260,000 annually, and apply it to public improvement ? Why not apply the surplus earnings of State Prisons to encourage the counties to build County Prisons on the plan of that in Hartford, Conn. ? To show that this plan is both important and practicable, take the case of Ohio. Its Penitentiary earned, last year, above all expenses, $26,000 43. This amount of money, offered to the different counties, $1000 to a county, for this purpose, would greatly encourage them to build County Prisons, on the plan of that in Hartford, Conn. The average cost of County Prisons, sufficiently large for the interior counties of Ohio, on this plan, would probably not

exceed $6000. The importance and necessity of such a move-
ment is apparent from the following communication : —

"OHIO COUNTY PRISONS.
" *A Letter from E. Lane to W. H. Channing and J. H. Perkins.*
"NORWALK, HURON COUNTY, }
November 20, 1840.   }

" GENTLEMEN : — I have endeavored to carry into execution the plan
you suggested, of visiting such of the County Jails of Ohio as fell
within my ride. I have examined the Prisons of twenty-three counties,
and have made the inquiries relating to their management, which were
permitted by the time I could command, and by my inexperience. I
have preserved rough plans of these places of confinement, and notes
of the several matters which fell under my observation.

" My present object is to communicate the results; for the details, at
present, would be of little use. It is strange that the condition of our
County Prisons has attracted so little the notice of benevolent men.
Most other fields of philanthropy have been more or less explored; our
Penitentiary system has been remodeled and reformed, so as nearly
to meet the expectations of its friends; but our Common Jails have
almost escaped the eyes of Christian charity, and the members of our
faith have mostly forgotten the promises of our Master to those who
visit the prisoner in Prison. Yet the number of persons in confinement is not too inconsiderable to deserve notice. In the 23 counties,
it amounts to 383 persons accused of crime during the past year, and
the aggrega.e time spent is 1301 weeks. Nor is it because there is
no need of good officers; for I have been informed, that lately, in one
of our principal towns, a respectable stranger, arrested for debt, was
enclosed, for several days, in the same cell with an insane black woman; and I have seen the unwashed blanket, which wrapped the
limbs of a prisoner, while recovering from exposure in an attempt to
escape two years ago, retained in ordinary prison use, of which more
than a square yard was stiffened with blood and corrupted matter; and
I have heard and believe, that, not many years since, the feet of
another were frozen while in confinement in his cell, in spite of his
efforts to preserve them.

" Since the last law relating to imprisonment for debt, the number
of debtors in Jail has become very small. Our penal system does not
rely much upon imprisonment as a punishment, and confinements for
this purpose are not numerous. The prisoners in our County Jails
are mostly untried criminals. The only demands of society upon these
are for safe-keeping. They ought to be subjected to no harshness or
restrictions, except those necessary to this object; and they are entitled to wholesome food, pure air, exercise, and other means for the
preservation of health, and to the ordinary accommodations and conveniences which tend to mitigate the sufferings of confinement, and
are not inconsistent with secure custody.

" In all the counties of our state, except Hamilton and Cuyahoga,
the number of prisoners rarely exceeds two or three at a time, and

the rules applicable to large Prisons, as to separation, &c., are hardly applicable. With the Jail of Hamilton county I am not acquainted. The average number confined in the Cleveland Prison is 14 ; but the accumulation at each term of the court is considerable. These are distributed in three cells, each about 10 feet by 15, and two rooms above, each about 18 feet square. The rooms are regarded somewhat insecure, and the cells are filled until they will contain no more. The walls of the cells are of squared stone, two feet thick. There is neither window nor fireplace. The aperture of the door-way is closed by two grated doors, which admit the only air, light, or heat, which the apartment receives from without. There are two single bunks below, and two double ones above, filled with loose straw, changed about once in two months. There are no beds. Blankets are used in the bunks, benches for seats, and a large tub, emptied when full, or about once a week. The upper rooms are provided with vaults, which are offensive, except when cleansed by rain. This Jail is kept as cleanly and as well as its construction admits, but it is a grossly improper place of confinement. It is unhealthy from its crowded condition and the impossibility of ventilation. It is so dark, that when the cell door is closed, reading would be difficult in the outer, and impossible in the centre cell ; and it admits of no separation of prisoners, of young and old, the hardened and the novice. The people of that county should never rest until these evils are cured.

" The other County Jails may be divided into two classes — those provided by the newly-organized counties, as temporary, designed to serve until the finances of the county admit a larger expenditure, and those intended to be permanent. Among the counties I have visited, 9 are of the first, and 14 of the last class. The temporary Jails are built of squared logs, generally unplastered, heated by stoves, and rarely provided with a yard ; the large rooms cold, the small, ill ventilated and unhealthy ; and the whole insecure, without the use of fetters.

" A description of one of this class will answer as a specimen : —
" No. 10 — built about 15 years ago. It is a log building, 24 feet square, two stories high, standing alone in a lot, without a yard. The lower story is made of two thicknesses of logs, each a foot square, with an interval between them of six inches, filled with stones. The outside door is double, and opens into a lobby 8 feet wide, extending across the whole front of 24 feet. Opposite to the outside door is the door of the first cell, which occupies half the remaining space, or 16 feet by 9. This cell is lighted and ventilated by a diamond in the door, 6 inches square, and by a window in the side, 10 inches by 8, before which stand a few palisades, which exclude all view without. The two walls have settled unequally, so that the opening for the window in one does not correspond with the opening in the other wall, and little light can penetrate. I think a person could not read in this cell, unless by the diamond while the outer door was open. Within this first cell, a close door opens to the second cell, of the same size, but having no light except what shines through a circular window. In the second story is a large room, above these cells, 16 feet by 24, with two grated and sashed windows, and a stove ; but the open cracks

above and beneath, and on every side, forbid all hope of a comfortable temperature in cold weather. There is another small room above, from the end of the lobby, 6 feet by 6, with a bed on the floor, and no light except what streams through the chinking. In the room up stairs is a bed, a coarse bedstead, and some chairs : below there is no furniture, except a bed on the floor, and a broken door. This Jail has been often broken, and fetters are constantly used, there being no safety without, and little with them.

"I will describe a Jail of a more permanent kind : —

"No. 17 — a well-constructed house, built of brick, except the lower story of the Jail side is of cut stone. The north half is devoted to prisoners, and is separated from the family apartments by a passage through the house. In the centre of the passage, a double door, one grated and one close, opens to another passage, 18 feet long and 5 feet wide, which gives access to four cells, two on each side, each 12 feet by 9. Each cell has a window about seven feet from the floor, large enough to admit three panes of 7 by 9 glass. Each cell has a stove, and a straw bed on a bedstead made by stretching coarse canvass on a frame, and laying it in trestles. The division in the second story is similar, except that each cell contains a common-sized grated window. The whole interior is whitewashed, and looks cleanly. The only fault I discover in its construction is, the absence of a yard, and the want of ventilation in its lower story.

"I believe there is no reason for complaint of the food of prisoners, at any of our County Jails in this state. It is ordinarily furnished from the table of the jailer, and in most cases thrice a day.

"A considerable difference is found in our Jails, as to personal cleanliness. In most cases, water for washing, and a towel, are provided every morning, and shaving and changing of linen once a week. In most cases, the weekly washing of clothes is done in the jailer's family, without additional charge ; but in some counties, such a charge is paid by the county. I believe that necessary clothing and medical attendance for destitute prisoners are provided by the county. But I find in some counties, that no regard is paid by the jailer to the weekly change of clothing. In one county, the jailer informed me he did not furnish water for daily ablutions, because the statute did not direct it to be done.

"It is the general usage of our county jailers to admit the counsel of the prisoners at all reasonable times, without restraint ; and to permit the visits of prisoners' friends, at convenient times, in the presence of the jailer.

"The interests of humanity must excuse plain speaking upon another subject. Various means are adopted of providing for the prisoners' necessities. In a few of the permanent Jails are vaults within the house. I am informed the use of these is abandoned in the best-constructed Prisons, from the difficulty of suppressing bad smells, and preserving them clean without chloride of lime, or other precautions not likely to be used. In some of our Jails, large tubs are employed, and emptied when full ; these infect the whole house, and are always objectionable. In others, smaller vessels, sometimes covered, and sometimes open, and daily cleaned. There is much room for reform in this respect, by providing a night-bucket for each prisoner, partly filled with water, to be emptied by him daily, or oftener.

" The ordinary use of fetters, as a security from escape, is general in the poorer Jails, and not unfrequent in all. They may be permitted to enforce the observance of Prison rules, and perhaps in some extraordinary cases; but to subject all persons to their annoyance, adds greatly and unnecessarily to the evils of confinement.

" There is not much *complaint* of vermin, yet traces of them are found in most of them. In the old log Jails, bed-bugs seem to be the natural inhabitants; fleas are found in most places; and in one I heard of lice. Most of the permanent Jails, however, are washed and scrubbed at convenient intervals, and kept in tolerable tidiness. There is no regular whitewashing; in most cases it is neglected too much; some have been left without this means of purification for a dozen years. No one reform is more needed than a law requiring it, at least twice a year.

" I believe that, in none of our County Prisons, lights are furnished in the evening, unless at the expense of the prisoner.

" The beds are filled with straw; sheets are not usual; beds are found in about half the Jails.

" In the 23 Jails I have visited, I found Bibles in five only. In four of them, I find that books, tracts, and newspapers are provided, with some degree of system; and in some others, their keepers have assured me, that such would be furnished, if asked for. In seven only have I found that clergymen and religious people have visited prisoners. When capital offences are committed, the clergy of the neighborhood, especially of the denomination in which the criminal has been educated, usually give their attention; in other cases, the prisoner is left to himself.

" I cannot refrain from again expressing my surprise at the neglect of this benevolence by good men. The opportunity of rendering a thousand good offices to the destitute, — the rapturous delight and earnest gratitude with which the prisoner accepts every thing which diversifies the monotony of confinement, — would be a rich reward for the trouble. But humanity demands that the community should maintain such an oversight of the Prison-house as will insure to the destitute a supply for his common wants, and prevent the infliction of unnecessary suffering, and repress the disposition, which unwatched men often feel, to tyrannize over those within their power. Besides, Christian duty rarely presents itself in a more pressing form; for the poor outcast, friendless and humiliated, frequently possesses susceptibilities which may be ripened into permanent reform; and the youthful offender, or the novice in crime, may be restored to society a good man, under judicious Christian effort.

" You ask me to name such evils as I conceive admit of correction. I have so little knowledge or experience upon this subject, that I cannot rely much upon any plan of reform which I can frame. At the risk of being deemed officious, I will venture to propose, —

" 1st. That the commissioners be required to provide, in each county, a Prison, safe without the use of fetters; capable of being warmed and ventilated; large enough to admit classification, by separating young from old, the untried from the convict; with a yard, to prevent unauthorized visits, and to admit some degree of exercise.

"2d. That the legislature frame (or cause to be prepared) a plan of treatment of prisoners in County Jails, embracing the points of food, drink, clothing, and medicine, for the destitute, and all matters relating to cleanliness and internal management.

"3d. That the grand jury of each county, at each term of the court, be required to visit the Jail.

"If a good design of a Prison-house, embracing modern improvements, and costing between $6,000 and $10,000, could be prepared, I think it would be often adopted in our counties.

"Our County Jails are likewise used as places of confinement for the insane. I find, in seven counties, 18 insane persons have been kept during this year, whose collective time is 107 weeks. It is hoped that the State Lunatic Asylum will soon be in readiness to receive all such patients ; for they can receive no proper medical aid in Jail, and I fear cruelties are sometimes inflicted upon them, both in neglect, and in more active forms, under the name of correction, such as is little suspected by the public.

"With my most earnest wishes for the success of the plan you have undertaken, and my thanks for the opportunity you have given me of contributing to it,

"I am, with great respect, your ob't serv't,

E. LANE

"Messrs. W. H. CHANNING,
        JAS. H. PERKINS,
                Cincinnati."

5. HOUSES OF REFUGE.

In addition to those now in operation in Boston, New York, and Philadelphia, in which about 500 youth and children are in a constant course of education and training for apprenticeship, the following extracts show that something more is contemplated. The governor of New York, in his last message, says, —

"The success which has crowned the benevolent efforts of the founders of the House of Refuge, has induced an opinion that it would be profitable to establish a similar institution in the western part of the state, where the subjects of its discipline could be maintained at much less expense than in the city of New York."

Dr. Collins, of Baltimore, also, who distinguished himself so much in the legislature of Maryland, in behalf of the insane poor of Maryland, appeared again in an able speech before the citizens of Baltimore, on the evening of the 30th of November last, in favor of a Manual Labor School for Indigent Boys. The following extract from an article in the Baltimore Patriot of December 8, 1840, shows the design of the movement : —

" After the Charter of the institution was read, Dr. COLLINS offered the following resolution, —

" *Resolved*, That the effort now being made to establish, in the vicinity of Baltimore, a Manual Labor School for Indigent Boys has, in an eminent degree, claims on the consideration and coöperation of the Christian, the Philanthropist, and the Patriot;

" And supported the resolution with an address : —

" MR. PRESIDENT : — Your kind partiality, with that of the other benevolent gentlemen engaged in this noble charity, has selected me as an advocate of the orphan and the indigent. Conscious of my inability to do justice to the subject, I respectfully ask this audience not to allow the feebleness of my advocacy to prejudice my cause.

" On the 16th December, 1839, a number of gentlemen met and appointed a committee to report on this subject. The committee made their report to a public meeting on the 17th of March, 1840 — ' That it is expedient to establish, in the neighborhood of Baltimore, a Manual Labor School for Indigent Boys.'

" Since then, the public mind has been intensely excited by the political questions which have agitated this country from the St. John to the Sabine; and it was not deemed expedient to jeopard the success of the plan, by calling for public aid during the existence of those all-absorbing political discussions. But now, sir, the storm has ceased to agitate the bosom of the ocean, which has subsided into its wonted repose; and this large and highly-respectable assemblage of citizens of Baltimore has convened, this evening, for the purpose of hearing the claims of this institution enforced; and then, if it receives their approbation, to contribute for its establishment.

" The design of the board of directors is, to purchase a farm in the vicinity of the city, where they will be able to accommodate indigent boys, who are exposed to all the evils arising from want of culture and from vicious associations; and, by combining mental cultivation with manual labor, cause them to contribute to their own support, while, at the same time, they will become qualified to obtain a future subsistence. The charities of the institution will first be extended to *indigent orphans;* and then, as far as their means will avail, to other destitute boys, whose parents cannot, or will not, extend them the protection and care which belong to the relation. The principal expense to the community will exist in the organization of the institution, and during the first year. After that period, the proceeds of the labor of the beneficiaries will nearly, if not altogether, support the establishment."

6. IMPRISONMENT FOR DEBT.

New Hampshire, Vermont, New York, and Tennessee, have abolished it. In other states the business has been curtailed ; in Massachusetts, for instance, about two thirds, or 2000 annually ; and in Pennsylvania a man cannot now be found imprisoned a month for two cents, the least sum for which it can be done being limited to $5 33. About 10,000 less are imprisoned, annually, for debt, in the state of New York alone, and probably 20,000 less in the other states. The law of the state of New York is a thoroughly abolishing act, with perhaps two slight exceptions. The governor says, in his last message to the legislature, —

"The law which authorized the imprisonment of non-resident debtors, against whom no fraud was alleged, was repealed at the last session, upon the ground that the practice operated injuriously to trade, and was inconsistent with the benign spirit of our code. There remains now only one relic of that usage in this state. Imprisonment for debt is allowed in actions brought in the federal courts; and, by the laws of this state, our Jails, designed only for the custody of criminals, are permitted to be used as Prisons for the confinement of debtors, under process issued by the authority of the United States. If you shall be of opinion that no principle of the Federal Union requires us to extend our courtesy so far, we shall no longer witness the imprisonment of honest but unfortunate debtors, with the sanction of this state."

Besides the exception here mentioned, there is an exception in practice, if not in law, by which debtors are imprisoned for fees, in the state of New York. Cases of this kind are sometimes, though not frequently, found in the Prisons; and in answer to the inquiry why they are there, the reply is, for fees. The following extract from an article in the Auburn Journal and Advertiser, dated November 4, 1840, shows that an oppressive case, of the class above named, occurred in that village, during the last year. We know, from personal observation, that similar cases have occurred in other counties under the present law : —

"MESSRS. OLIPHANT & SKINNER : — Owing to a report in circulation, that a person was confined in our County Jail for debt, and such cases being very rare at the present time, the writer was induced to visit the keeper, and make inquiries relative to the subject that now occupies the minds of several individuals.

"The facts, as related by the jailer, are these, viz. : Mr. Garret Wafle, of the town of Victory, was, on the 18th or 20th of April last, committed to the Jail of our county, on a debt due for attorney's costs of a suit at law in which he had been engaged. He further stated that the man is entirely destitute of property; that he has a wife and seven children residing in the town of Victory; that they are almost wholly dependent upon him for support, and, further, that he bears the reputation of an honest and industrious citizen. His family are in part supported, from necessity, by charity. The expenses already accrued to the county for his support and cost of sickness amount to about $15 more than the debt for which he is confined, (which is about $80;) and the debt is of that nature, (being for cost due to an attorney,) that the creditor may hold him there for life."

7. NARRATIVE OF JOURNEYS PERFORMED.

Journeys have been performed, and Lunatic Asylums, Penitentiaries, and County Prisons examined, in Vermont, Massachusetts, Connecticut, New York, New Jersey, Pennsylvania, District of Columbia, Virginia, North Carolina, South Carolina, Georgia, Alabama, Louisiana, Missouri, Tennessee, Kentucky, Indiana, and Ohio. Mr. Barrett's agency and journey in the Middle, Southern, and Western States have been crowned with the goodness of God, in regard to funds collected, Prisons examined, information communicated and received, correspondence opened, &c. We are happy in his safe return and presence.

Extracts from the Journal of Mr. Barrett.

" *December* 8, 1840. In company with two members of the legislature, visited the Virginia Penitentiary, Richmond. This Penitentiary was built some 40 years ago, on a peculiar plan, which was suggested by a French gentleman. It embraces 176 cells, in two stories, built of brick, forming an arc of a circle, with doors opening towards the centre, and has now 180 inmates. The number committed to this Penitentiary since its establishment, is 2097; pardoned, 368; died, 385; escaped, 10. Health of prisoners good, only one in the hospital. Chief business, weaving, wagon and shoe-making. Workshops not well arranged for inspection. The old law, requiring convicts to be kept, the first six months of their sentence, in solitary cells, was cruel and deadly, and has been repealed. The dark and cheerless cells in which they used so severely to suffer, are no longer to be seen. Felt thankful to Col. Morgan, the keeper, for his polite attention. Was sorry to find that this institution, in the metropolis of so noble a state, had no chapel, nor chaplain, nor Sunday school, nor regular preaching.

" Spent part of two days at the Richmond Jail. It is not what it should be. The same night that I arrived in the city, a man died in his cell in the Jail from cold and neglect. The verdict of the jury of inquest was, ' that Shepherd came to his death by neglect of not having sufficient heat in his cell, and sufficient bedding to keep him warm during the present inclement season.' It is not easy for one who looks at the facts in the case, to doubt as to the truth of this verdict. There are 12 cells in the Jail for male criminals and vagrants. These cells, about 6 feet wide and 10 long, are in the same range, on the ground floor. An iron, grated door leads from each room to the open atmosphere. There is nothing, in any season of the year, to keep the elements from driving into the cells through the grated doors. Even in the coldest weather, but little artificial heat comes to the prisoners. In a kitchen, 6 feet from the nearest cell, is a furnace, where coal is consumed. Springing from this furnace, a 9 inch stove-pipe passes through the upper part of each cell in the range. What heat the prisoners get from the furnace radiates from that portion of the stove-pipe which passes over their heads through their cells. Shepherd was in the eleventh cell, about 70 feet distant from the furnace. He was alone. The wind blew with violence; the cold was piercing; the sleet and snow fell fast, and drove through the grating of his door. The bed-clothes which the prisoner had, were less than a single good blanket. He said he was freezing, and plead for more covering, but plead in vain. Before morning Shepherd was dead.

" A public meeting was called, at which statements were made concerning the Jail. The governor, members of the legislature, and chief citizens, were present. Next morning, called on the governor. He showed that he had a heart to feel for the suffering prisoner, and spoke about my making examination of all the Jails in the state. The same day, a respectable citizen of Richmond said, ' I was at the meeting last night, and heard the statements about our Jail, and I must confess with shame, that though I have lived in this city more than 20 years, I have never entered our Jail, and had no idea that the description of the cells had reference to our Jail, till you were more than three quarters through.'

" It is a relief to know that an investigation in respect to the Jail has been made by the civil authorities, that a change of government has taken place; so that there is good ground to hope for future improvement, and the absence of unnecessary suffering.

" *December* 10. With my old friend Dr. P., went to the Capitol to meet the committee of the legislature on Lunatic Asylums. Free remarks were invited, and indulged, concerning the condition and treatment of poor lunatics. It was pleasant to see such general interest taken in the subject as was there manifested. It was stated that, during the past year, more than 50 poor lunatics had been confined in the County Jails in Virginia, at an expense to the state of more than $9000, because the Asylums at Williamsburg and Staunton had no room to receive them. Virginia is liberal in her provisions for this class of sufferers.

"*December* 18. Found the Jail at Petersburg, Va., in good condition, — cleanly, secure, and without tenants, except three runaway negroes.

" Petersburg Poor-House, two miles from the city, has 50 inmates, and is under excellent regulations. Annual expense above earnings about $1000. Connected with the institution is a large and well-cultivated farm. Much attention is paid to the comfort and instruction of the paupers.

" *December* 24. At Raleigh, N. C. The Jail here is old, insecure, and badly ventilated. It contains four rooms for criminals, and one for debtors. In the four rooms 13 persons are confined on charge of crime, two of whom are murderers. A female is confined in the same room with several males. In one room is an insane man, who has been a respectable merchant. His shrieks at times disturb the whole neighborhood. Two are in Jail for debt.

" No State Penitentiary, nor Insane Hospital in North Carolina. The legislature has just had the subject, in reference to both, under consideration. The question concerning a Penitentiary has been submitted to the people, to be decided by their votes at the polls. Gave a lecture this evening in reference to the insane, at which some of the members of the legislature now in session were present. North Carolina, as a state, stands almost alone in not making provision for the insane, although inquiry has shown that there are, in a part of the state only, 249 insane persons.

"*December* 27. At the Jail in Fayetteville found an intoxicated jailer in charge with 6 prisoners. The building is more secure, and the rooms are better arranged, than the Jail at Raleigh. Descending the Cape Fear River, arrived at Wilmington in two days and a night after leaving Fayetteville.

" *Wilmington, December* 31. Went with friend D. to see the Jail. It is probably the best in the state. The construction is peculiar. It is three stories high. The first story is occupied by the jailer and his family, the second by debtors, and the third by criminals. Access from the second story to the third is up a flight of stairs, and through a trap door. This door is made fast by a padlock on the lower side. The cells in the third story are about four feet from the external wall, in two ranges, with a passage in the centre between. The security is manifold and complete. If one should break out of his strong cell, and penetrate the outer wall, his distance from the ground would be so great, he could not escape. There is a want of sufficient light and pure air in the cells. Twelve persons are now confined in this Jail, one of whom is deranged, and the son of a clergyman. No labor performed, nor instruction given.

"*January* 1, 1841. The market place in Wilmington was filled today with negroes of both sexes, young and old, who had been sent there by their owners in order to have their services for the coming year sold by the public auctioneers to the highest bidder. The services for a year, of a little girl 12 or 13 years old, were purchased for 37 dollars, and those of adults in proportion. Besides the $37, the buyer pays for the girl $2 tax, and finds her in food, raiment, and medicine. At the north, the services of a girl of that age are not deemed more than an equivalent for her board and clothing.

" This afternoon, left Wilmington for Charleston. Came near being wrecked while crossing the sand-bar at the mouth of the river. The chain attached to the tiller rope got fast, so that the rudder could not be moved, and all command of the boat was lost. The wind blew towards the shore with great force. The foaming waves carried the boat out of the channel, and dashed it like a plaything on the sand-bank. For some time the boat continued to strike with violence, and the danger of being dashed to pieces was great. At length she was got off with difficulty, taken some distance back up the river, and anchored for the night.

"*January* 4. In Charleston, S. C. Called at the mayor's office with Mr. H. The mayor politely presented me with a paper signed by himself, to serve as a passport to any of the public institutions of the city. Went to the City Prison. It is quite secure, and neatly kept. In the main building are a large number of commodious rooms, ranged on each side of a wide passage, that goes lengthwise through the centre of the building. A back wing contains 16 small cells, on the

Auburn plan. There are about 50 persons in Prison, of whom four are for debt. Some are under sentence of death, and others are to be tried for their lives. The laws of South Carolina are sanguinary. Forgery and horse-stealing are here made capital crimes. Saw a fine-looking man, scarcely 21 years old, under sentence of death for forging an order of some ten or twelve dollars. Public flogging in the market place is much practised in Charleston, as a punishment for crime. I saw a man who had just returned from taking the last ten of 'forty stripes save one.' He was a queer mortal, and in quite good humor. He told me where he had been, and said he blacked his face before he left his room, that he might pass for a negro, when he was whipped in public, and thought it quite hard that he should be compelled to wash his face clean before the stripes were inflicted. This man had been in Prison a year. He was a painter by trade, and pursued his profession for his own amusement, while in Prison. Over the door of each cell, at his end of the passage, he had painted, in glaring capitals, some such motto as these — ' Mansion of Reformation ' —' Place for Reflection.'

" One room was filled with a family of blacks — father, mother, and ten children. They interested me much. They were well dressed, modest, good-looking, and intelligent. A free black man attempted to sell this family for debt. They claimed that they were free, and were remaining in Jail till they could have a chance of proving their freedom.

" Close by the City Prison is an establishment, very much resembling a Prison, called the Sugar-House. Here such gangs of slaves as are sent to the city to be sold, are kept till the time of their sale. Here, too, refractory and disobedient slaves are sent from all parts of the city to be flogged, and to receive different kinds of punishment. Owners pay a certain fee for having each slave flogged, and $18\frac{3}{4}$ cents per day during the time they are kept in confinement. There are now about 100 persons confined in this place. The tread-wheel was here in operation. Six or eight slaves, male and female, were upon it, as a part of their punishment. The labor did not seem to be very severe. When the wheel performs a certain number of revolutions, it rings a bell, as a signal for the one, who has been on the longest, to get off, and another to get on. In another part of the yard, I saw three negroes turning a hand-mill for grinding corn, much after the manner of the ancient Hebrews.

" Charleston Orphan Asylum is an honor to the city. The main building is a noble edifice, and stands several rods back from the street. In the rear are, a neat chapel, school-rooms, play-grounds, out-houses, and gardens, all in fine order. About 100 orphan children are now enjoying the benefits of this institution. As I saw the children in their school-rooms, they seemed healthy and cheerful. Several bright lads were pointed out, who are almost fitted for college. Two orphan boys, who went from this institution, are now members of the college in this city, and two others are members of the college at Columbia. One of the most respectable lawyers in the city of Charleston, was once a poor orphan boy. This Asylum took him in, dried up his tears, fed him, clothed him, taught him, and was the blessed instrument, under Heaven, of making him what he is.

" The Charleston Poor-House contains about 50 inmates, including 10 or 12 idiots and lunatics, and seems to be well managed.

"*January* 9.   Called on Dr. B.   Found him quite intelligent on the subject of Prison discipline.   He has made the tour of Europe, and looked into the condition of Prisons there.   He says, in all parts of Europe, where he has been, with scarcely an exception, Prisons are in a bad condition.   When in Paris, he heard a lecture before a literary society on Prison discipline, in which the lecturer advocated the Auburn system before all others.   The doctor thinks there ought to be a State Penitentiary in South Carolina, and believes there will be one before many years.   It would go far, he thinks, towards relaxing the unreasonable rigor of some of their present laws.

" Went from Charleston to Savannah by what is called the inland steamboat route.

" The Jail at Savannah, Ga., is old and insecure.   Saw where prisoners had broken out through the walls.   One room was filled with blacks taken from the different vessels in the harbor.   Most of them were cooks or stewards to these vessels.   Free blacks belonging to any vessel that enters a harbor of a southern state, are taken ashore and kept in confinement during their stay in the place.   In Savannah they talk about having a new Jail.   They have now about 20 persons in Jail, and, as they have ample room in their yard, it seems a pity that some of them, at least, should not be required to labor.

"*Augusta, Ga., Jan.* 23.   Found 16 persons in the Jail at Augusta, Ga., — 10 blacks, 6 whites.   No chair, nor stool, nor bed, nor bunk, nor straw; nor fire nor fireplace, and nothing but a filthy floor to lie on, and a scanty covering of blankets, in any of the rooms.   The air in the rooms is sickening.   There is no such thing attempted among the prisoners as instruction, classification, or labor.   Only 3 out of the 16 can read.   Those who can read have no books; 300 persons are annually confined in this Jail; and for board in such a horrible place as this, the jailer receives 47 cents per day for whites, and 16 cents per day for blacks.   It was some relief not to find any confined here for debt.   Here, as in the yard of most of the Jails at the south, was an apparatus for making fast the head, and hands, and feet of such as they wish to flog.   As a matter of experiment, I allowed my neck, and wrists, and ankles, to be inserted in the grooves cut in the timbers of the frame, but was quite willing to dispense with what were the usual subsequent steps in the process.

"*January* 27.   At Milledgeville, Ga.   Went to the Penitentiary, and saw where Worcester and Butler once worked in convicts' garb, and slept in solitary cells.   This institution, established 23 years ago, stands in the suburbs of the town, on ground too low, and has 150 cells, occupied by 160 prisoners, among whom are four females, one mulatto, no negroes.   The cells are after the Baltimore plan, but smaller, and the space between the two ranges is entirely floored over at each story.   The cell doors are of wood, without grating, and fastened with a padlock.   In one of the cells saw a convict in effigy.   He was kneeling on the foot of his bunk, and looking out of his window into the yard.   His back was towards the door, his hat on, one hand in his pocket, the other, with his fore arm, resting on the window-

sill. By means of this effigy the living occupant had made his escape.
He left it in his cell in the position described, when he went out
to work. At evening he did not come in with the other prisoners,
but hid himself in the workshop. The keeper, coming to the door,
which was closed as usual, looked through a small aperture, and,
seeing in the image what he took to be the real man, made proper ad-
justment of the lock, supposing all was safe, and retired. The deception was not discovered till the next morning. During the night, the
prisoner crept from his hiding-place, scaled the wall, and has not been
heard of since.

"There has been but one insane person in this Penitentiary in the
space of four years. Received during the last year, 48; discharged
by expiration of sentence, 24; by pardon, 21; died, 5; now in the
hospital, 6. Chief business, shoe, harness, and wagon-making. Lacked
of supporting itself last year, $2511 19; year before last, $6000.
This year considerable income is anticipated. The last legislature
appropriated $20,000 to pay debts against the Penitentiary, contracted
in former years. No ardent spirits, nor tobacco, are allowed to be
used in the Penitentiary. Twenty-five officers are connected with the
establishment, whose aggregate pay amounts to about $12,000. 30
out of the 160 prisoners cannot read, and 52 cannot write. None but
their fellow-convicts do any thing towards teaching the ignorant to
read. There is preaching once a week in the Penitentiary, by a minister, who has a charge in the town. He receives $150 per annum
for his services. Punishment by stripes has been prohibited by law,
as being too severe; but that by the paddle, which is probably more
severe, has been substituted without law. The paddle consists of a
piece of wood 4 feet long, 2 or 3 inches in diameter, one end of
which is wider than the rest, flattened, and filled with holes. With
the flat end from 5 to 30 blows at a time are applied to the bare
skin of a prisoner, while he is held over a block, or a barrel. The
wall about the Prison yard is of brick, too low, and so weak, that the
keeper says a man could dig through it with a shoe-knife in a few
minutes.

"An Insane Hospital, two miles from Milledgeville, on rising
ground, amid lofty pines, is being erected. It is designed to accommodate 160 persons. One four-story building, of brick, with convenient rooms, will be ready for the reception of patients this year.
The state have granted $37,000 for the erection of the Hospital. It
is not designed exclusively for the insane poor.

"Before leaving Milledgeville, had an interview with Governor
McDonald, at the Capitol. He seemed to take an interest in my mission, kindly furnished me with public documents, statistics, &c., and
invited me to call at his house, and take tea in the evening. I accepted the invitation, met an interesting family, and profited by the
governor's conversation.

"*January* 30. Found seven male prisoners in the Jail at Macon,
Ga.; one under sentence of death. The Jail building has been lately
improved, and, though its construction is not the best, the establishment seems to be in tolerable good condition.

"*February* 3, 1841. To-day, after much wearisome travel by land,

arrived at Montgomery, a town on the Alabama River, 400 miles above
Mobile, and 50 miles below Wetampke.   At the last-named place, a
State Penitentiary is being built on the Auburn plan.

"*February* 8.   In Mobile.   Went with Rev. Mr. H. to examine
the Jail.   Could not help smiling, as we were entering, to see Mr.
H. put his watch-guard out of sight, and carefully secure his watch.
' I do not wish to offer temptation to the fellows,' said he.   So bad a
Jail, with so many inmates, I never saw before.   Of the 41 persons
now in Jail, 27 are confined in three rooms, each 8 feet wide, and 16
feet long, on the ground floor.   But little dependence can be placed
on the walls of this Jail for security.   Hence, in the centre of each
room, is a large iron ring, made fast to a strong and well-secured staple.   From this ring, as a centre, go out, as so many radii, nine
chains, as large as ox chains, which are attached to the ankles of an
equal number of prisoners.   The prisoners' bed is the floor ; their
covering the clothes they wear.   Nine, the present number in each
room, can just lie down together on the floor, without crowd-
ing ; but sometimes there are 15 in one of these rooms.   Four,
of the 27 in these rooms, are in Jail for capital offences.   Of these
four, two are sentenced to be hung next Friday, one is sentenced to
be hung next April, and the other is waiting his trial.   The two who
are to be hung next Friday are slaves.   Their crime was an attempt
to break into a store.   They were tried and condemned without jury.
According to law, they must be executed within 10 days after conviction.   A white man, convicted of a similar offence, would receive but
39 lashes for his punishment.

" Went into the cell with Mr. H. to converse and pray with the
condemned blacks.   They were attentive, seemed to take our services
kindly, and showed some feeling.   The air in the room was so offensive, that, to make it tolerable, while we were there, some of the prisoners kept the end of a tarred rope burning.   For this kind office I
am sure we were grateful.

" On going alone, the second time, to the Jail, I went in silence to
the grated door of the middle room, and looked in upon its inmates,
unperceived.   They were sitting on the floor, and employed in the
following manner :   A white man sat in front of the condemned negroes, reading to them, in a loud voice, the parable of the prodigal
son.   Next to them were two men playing checkers on a board, which
they had marked on the floor between their feet.   At the farther end
of the room, four, in loud talk and boisterous mirth, were playing
cards.   If still further variety were wanting, it might have been found
in the loud voices and clanking chains of the prisoners in the two adjacent rooms.   Verily, here is a poor place for men who have less
than a week to live, to prepare for eternity.   How specially horrible
must it be thus to fill these rooms with human beings in such a
climate as this in the heat of summer !

" At a public meeting, which was numerously attended by the most
intelligent and influential citizens of Mobile, statements were made
concerning the condition of the Jail.   Rev. Mr. H. not only corroborated the statements that had been offered, but made a peculiarly
bold and powerful appeal to the men of office, wealth, and influence

in the city; calling upon them, by many moving considerations, to arouse, and have a speedy remedy applied to the crying evil.

"The distance from Mobile to New Orleans, by steamboat route, through Lakes Borgne and Ponchartrain, thence a short distance by railroad, is 160 miles. The large fleet of vessels through which we passed, as they lay at anchor, some 20 miles below Mobile, waiting for freights of cotton, was a noble sight.

"*February* 13. In New Orleans. Went to the City Prison. This Prison stands a little way out of the city, has been lately built, and numbers between 300 and 400 inmates. After the keeper, who is a Frenchman, had shown me round the Prison, with that politeness which is peculiar to his countrymen, I asked him if I might be allowed to preach to the prisoners, if I should come there on Sunday. 'Do no good, sir,' said he. 'Such men as these rather drink rum than hear preaching. They not hear you. They insult you, and throw things at you.' 'No fear of that,' said I. 'O well, sir,' said he; 'if you willing to try, if you run the risk, come and welcome; I have no objection.'

"Sunday morning found me at the Prison. The turnkey opened the large iron door, and let me in alone among the prisoners. Where could I arrange my audience so as to address them? was the question. I asked the first man I came to. He said he had been in Prison nine months, but had never known any one come there to preach before, and, as the pavement was wet, he did not know where they could be placed, so as to hear. Concluded to have them seated on a long gallery and staircase, and went from cell to cell to invite the men to come out. In one cell found a dozen, or more, sitting in a circle on the floor, playing cards. When spoken to, they dropped their cards, saying, 'O yes; come, let us go out.' My hearers, who were of all ages and colors, and from all quarters of the earth, gave good attention. At the close of the service, they flocked around me like so many bees, expressed their thanks, and urged me to repeat my visits. I was surprised to find so large a proportion of the criminals from the Northern States. One man, 60 years old, tall and good looking, said he was from Windham county, Conn. 'Had you a pious mother?' said I. 'Yes, sir.' Didn't she use to take your hand in hers, and lead you to church?' 'Yes, sir, she did;' and as he spake, his lips quivered, and his eyes filled with tears. Saw some of the good people of New Orleans in reference to their Prison, and there is good reason to hope that they will not allow it to remain neglected as it has been.

"*February* 23. Spent part of the day at the Jail in Natchez, Mississippi. This Jail is unfit for use; and yet, within the last four years, not less than 1164 persons have been sent to it. Saw three or four different places, through which escapes had been made. Four had broken out but a few nights previously, among whom was a murderer. The jailer is down the river after them now, and a large reward is offered for their apprehension. Sixteen men are herded together in one room, and most of them heavily loaded with iron, to prevent their escape. Such Jails as this lead to much unnecessary suffering. Their insecurity makes it necessary, in order to prevent the escape of the prisoners, to have them chained, as at Mobile, or to have huge bars of iron attached to their legs, as here; or to have them kept in some way specially injurious to health.

"There are many kind hearts and noble spirits among the citizens of Natchez, and it is only necessary that they should know all the truth about their Jail, to have it abandoned, and a good one built in its stead. They have already begun to move in the matter.

"The Jail at Vicksburg is still worse than the one at Natchez, but has fewer persons in it. Such as are charged with high crimes are not sent to this Jail, on account of its insecurity. One reason why the Vicksburg gamblers were hung, as they were, without judge or jury, is to be found in the miserable condition of their Jail. The gamblers were numerous, bold, and daring. They had threatened, and grossly insulted, the citizens. They had shot Dr. Bodley, a respectable physician, dead in the street. They were seized. The Jail, a mere shell, rickety, and ready to crumble to pieces, would not have kept them till the time of trial. There was no place in the city where the murderers could have been securely kept. There should have been. There will be soon. The foundation for a new Jail has lately been laid.

"*February* 26. Went by railroad, about 40 miles, from Vicksburg to Jackson, the capital of Mississippi. The directors of this road showed their respect for clergymen, by allowing them a seat in their cars without any charge.

"One of the best Penitentiaries in the Southern States has just been built at Jackson, at an expense of about $100,000. It was first occupied last April, and has now 31 inmates. Col. Hart, the keeper, seems admirably fitted for his station. When completed, this Prison will contain 300 cells. Here are embraced features peculiar both to the Auburn and Philadelphia Prisons. They have the cells here arranged much like those of the latter, and require the prisoners to leave their cells, and work together in the shops, in silence, by day, and to remain in their cells in solitude and silence at night, after the manner of the former. The wing now occupied contains 150 cells, 3 stories high, in two ranges, facing each other, with 19 feet space between them. Each cell is $7\frac{1}{2}$ feet long, 4 feet wide, and 8 feet high, arched at the top. The doors are iron, grated all the way down. Each cell has a window at the farther end, too small for a man to creep through, defended by cross bars of iron, and cased with plates of cast iron. The ventilation is perfect. The bedsteads are of iron. The bedclothes are kept clean, and aired every day. The prisoners rarely perform the offices of nature in their cells. Each cell is furnished with a Bible. The open space between the cells furnishes a light and airy chapel, into which the prisoners are brought every Sunday, to hear preaching. The entire dress of the prisoners is changed once a week in winter, and twice a week in summer. If things continue to go on as they have commenced, here will be a Prison worthy of being imitated by other states in the south.

"The Penitentiary of Illinois is pleasantly situated on a bluff, at Lower Alton, on the margin of the Mississippi River. It was first occupied in 1833. It has a high, well-built, stone wall, which embraces three acres of ground. Within the walls, at one corner, stand the keeper's house, Prison cells, &c. The cells, 56 in number, were designed to be on the Auburn plan, but are a miserable failure. They are without ventilators, and yet two men are often crowded into one cell, 7 feet long, 7 feet high, and $3\frac{1}{2}$ feet wide. The cell doors open inward. The galleries are clumsy and tottering. The area between the cells and outer wall is too narrow, (about eight feet in width,) and cluttered with sacks of salt, boxes of muskets belonging to the state, &c. There is neither chapel nor hospital. What is used for a hospital, and where several lie sick, is a cellar-kitchen with a stone floor. In the yard one sees hogs and horses, cows and convicts, all moving about amidst the filth and rubbish. The workshops are poorly built and badly arranged. One shop has its roof leaning directly against the Prison wall, so as to furnish strong temptation to escape in that direction. Present number of prisoners, 81, of whom 2 blacks and 1 female are for life. Received last year, 56; discharged, 50; pardoned, 14; died, 5.

"This Penitentiary is under the direction of three persons, appointed by the legislature, one of whom is physician to the Prison. These directors have, by agreement, committed the care and management of the Prison to two individuals, who act in the different capacities of warden, deputy-warden, contractor, &c. They have all they can make from the prisoners after supporting them, the state paying for their conviction and transportation to Prison.

"The great aim, as might be expected under these circumstances, is to make money. Hence the peculiar condition of the Prison, as has been described. Hence no instruction, except occasional preaching, is allowed to be given to the prisoners, though one out of every seven can neither read nor write. The good people of Alton stand ready to go and teach the prisoners, either in a Sunday school, or in their cells, but are not permitted. The reason which the warden gave, why he could not allow the prisoners to be taught, even in their cells, was, if he did, he should have to give his guard higher wages, on account of the extra trouble it would give them.

"Prisoners do not leave the Penitentiary reformed. The warden told me that, of the last 50 that had left Prison, all but one or two had gone back to strong drink or bad conduct again.

"Overstints are allowed here. Punishment is by stripes on the naked back. Prisoners take their food in the cook-room, in a standing posture. Chief business is coopering.

"The following is a specimen of the printed rules that are posted up in different parts of the Prison for the prisoners to read: —

"'If a prisoner complains of being unwell soon after he has eaten a meal, he is to be kept without food for 24 hours after.'

"'If a prisoner is seen behind the warden or guard, without some manifest reason, he is to be severely punished.'"

"*March* 14, 1841. Visited the Jail at St. Louis. Present number of prisoners, 27, among whom are 7 negroes, 1 Indian, and 2 debtors. One of the negroes had suffered castration in Jail, the penalty in Missouri for committing a rape. 864 persons were sent to this Jail last year. The Jail is one of the best on the Mississippi River, yet it is too small and insecure. Six made their escape from it last July.   The jailer is much devoted to his duties.   A new Jail is talked of.

"*March* 29.   At Nashville, Tenn.   Busy in examining the Jail, Insane Hospital, and Penitentiary.   The Jail is an old, miserable concern.   Last year, 245 persons were sent to it, of whom 7 were lunatics. Now in Jail, 7 criminals, and 1 lunatic.   The Insane Hospital is a little way out of the city.   A high wall of stone, laid in mortar, enclosing seven acres, is a great and needless expense.   The Hospital building, near the centre of the enclosed space, is four stories high, and has well-arranged rooms sufficient to accommodate 100 patients. It has been occupied about a year, and has now 15 patients, 10 males, and 5 females.   It is designed both for pay patients and for such as are paupers. $50,000 have been expended on the Hospital.

"The Tennessee Penitentiary stands half a mile from the city of Nashville.   It contains 200 cells, on the Auburn plan, 100 in four stories, at each end of a long building, whose centre is occupied by the keeper and his family, &c.   Cell doors of wood, grating small, ventilation imperfect, area 25 feet wide, gallery resting on cast-iron arms inserted in the brick work of the cells.   Number of prisoners, 181; of whom 173 white males, 6 black males, and 2 females.   Before the Penitentiary system was introduced into the state, in 1833, criminals were punished by whipping, cropping, hanging, &c.   The change in the mode of punishment is much approved by the most intelligent gentlemen in the state.   Saw among the convicts the notorious negro stealer, or 'land pirate,' Murrell, about whom Virgil Stewart has written a pamphlet.   Nothing very peculiar in his appearance.   Most of the convicts are employed in hatting, stone-cutting, or blacksmithing.   Articles are manufactured and sold on the state's account.   Gains, biennially, above all expenses, as follows: (1835,) $9,214; (1837,) $14,430; (1839,) $8,111.

"Punishment consists of solitary confinement on spare diet, during which time five days are added to the term of one's sentence, for each day spent in punishment.   As a motive for good conduct, a deduction of two days from every month is made from the term of the sentence, to such as behave well.

"In respect to instruction, there is a deficiency.   No chaplain, nor Sunday school.   Preaching each Sunday to one half of the prisoners, (those who are in the same end of the Prison,) by different ministers from the city.

"Never any deranged person in this Penitentiary.   No deaths for nearly two years.   Mr. Anderson, the keeper, appears to be a valuable officer.

"*April* 3, 1841.   Examined the Indiana Penitentiary, at Jeffersonville.   It contains 104 prisoners.   The establishment has been leased by the state for five years ending next June.   The two contractors have the use of the building and property belonging to the Prison, the control and labor of the prisoners, in consideration of their paying all the expenses of the Prison, and $3,520 per annum into the treasury of the state.

"About all that seems to be required of the prisoners is, that they shall work, and not run away; yet four or five made their escape last year.   No order, silence, nor discipline, is imposed upon them.   They are taken from the Prison all over town to work, making gardens, building houses, &c. There is no chapel nor hospital here, nor instruction given, except by occasional preaching. The sick were in the tailor's shop, lying about on the floor, tables, &c., without beds. The night-rooms are horrible places. I have never seen the like before. Hewn logs are placed in the interior of a large brick building, so as to form several stories of small cells, something on the Auburn plan. The area between the cells and the outer wall is about four feet wide, floored over tight at each story, and so dark that the keeper often has to carry a light to guide him when he goes to lock the cell doors. The cells are lathed and plastered inside. A small tube running from each cell horizontally to the open air, is a mere apology for a ventilator. The entrance into the cells is so low, that one must stoop to get in. The cell doors are of wood, without grating, with a single small aperture at the top. In the lightest day, the cells are almost perfectly dark. It is enough to make one shudder to think of spending a hot summer's night in one of these cells. Every consideration of humanity calls upon Indiana to provide a different place for her prisoners.

"*April* 6. With Rev. Mr. H., visited the Jail at Louisville, Ky. Found 15 miserable creatures huddled together in one room, and about a dozen in another — half clad, and without labor or instruction. Went to the room of White, the murderer. He was alone. His looks were bad. He declared he was not guilty; said he had never been much troubled in his mind on account of sin; did not think he was a great sinner; and was prepared to die. We tried plainly to show him his danger and duty, prayed with him, selected several passages in the Bible for him to read, and took our final leave. Poor man! we afterward heard that he made a frightful mock of our attempts to do him good, and showed a fiendlike spirit shortly before he was hung.

"The citizens of Louisville are not satisfied with their Jail, and are determined soon to have a new one. They need a new one.

"*April* 14. At Cincinnati, I got a permit from the sheriff to examine the Jail. A new Jail, just back of the old one, has lately been built, on the plan of the Auburn Prison, safe and convenient. In 1840, 498 persons were sent to this Jail, of whom 22 were taken to State Prison. Some of the prisoners are taken out to work on the streets. All could not find employment in the Jail. The Jails, generally, in the state of Ohio, are in bad condition."

Extracts from the Journal of the Secretary.

Wednesday, September 9, 1840. Commenced a journey from Stockbridge, in the business of the Prison Discipline Society, through the states of New York, Vermont, New Hampshire, and Massachusetts. Arrived in Albany at 8 o'clock, P. M. Thursday morning, at 10 o'clock, called on Governor Seward. He received me with great kindness; entered into familiar con-

versation concerning the Prisons at Auburn and Sing Sing,
County Prisons generally, the House of Refuge in New York,
imprisonment for debt, Lunatic Asylums, the Prison Discipline
Society, &c. &c. The governor says the amendments of the
last winter to the Penitentiary law, dividing the duties, responsi-
bilities, and pay of the agents of the Prisons at Auburn and
Sing Sing, creating in each Prison two officers, instead of one,
charging one with the financial duties, and the other with the
police duties, have been very useful. In Prisons so large, this
measure may be necessary; but in Prisons of 200 or 300 convicts, instead of 600 or 700, it is not necessary. Even in these
large Prisons, divided counsels, jarring interests, and selfish con-
troversies, may grow out of it, between the agent and keeper.
Time and experience may show it to be a good change in the
law, or, on the other hand, may show it to be a bad one.

The reform in the Prisons at Auburn and Sing Sing, by which
the old officers were ejected, and new officers appointed, has
thus far resulted favorably ; and although, by law, the power of
inflicting stripes has not been taken away, in practice it has been
greatly diminished ; and the public mind at Auburn is now perfectly tranquil in regard to the administration of the Prison, and
at Sing Sing there is scarcely the shadow of complaint. The
officers in the different Prisons, since the change, are as follows:
—At *Sing Sing*, — inspectors, WILLIAM NEWTON, of Albany,
EDWARD KENNYS, ISAAC NELSON, JUN., ISAAC G. GRAHAM, JUN. ;
agent, D. L. SEYMOUR ; keeper, ANGUS MCDUFFEE. At *Auburn*, — inspectors, BENJAMIN ASHBY, HENRY IRESON, JUN., PE-
TER G. FOSDICK, all of Auburn, HARVEY LYON, of Leverett, and
C. A. HOWLAND, of Venice ; agent, HENRY POLHEMUS ; keeper,
ROBERT COOK.

In regard to County Prisons, the governor renewed the as-
surance of his interest in their improvement, and said the next
winter would be a more favorable time than the last for a movement on the subject in the legislature. He expressed himself
as being much pleased that a full narrative was to be given, in
the Fifteenth Report, of a journey in the state of New York, in
the autumn of 1839, for the purpose of visiting the County Prisons, and asked for the Report as soon as published.

In regard to the House of Refuge in the city of New York,
he expressed himself as being well satisfied.

In regard to imprisonment for debt, he said the action of the
legislature last winter was without opposition to repeal the exception in the general law, by which transient persons were liable to
imprisonment for debt, and place them on the same ground with
resident citizens. The general law, thus amended, is acceptable
to a vast majority of the people.

The north front of the State Lunatic Hospital at Utica, i. e., one of the four buildings for the accommodation of 1000, will be ready to receive patients next season.

After spending an hour with the governor, I visited the Jail in Albany, and found between 40 and 50 prisoners, in idleness and a state of great disorder and filth. The jailer said it was necessarily so, when they were cleaning. The men were ordered to form a line in the area, in front of the cells, and number themselves. The line was formed, and they began to number themselves; but it did not go right, and when they got about half through, the jailer told them to begin again. This they did, and still went wrong, and began once more. After much confusion and disorder, and some scolding, they got through. Then the jailer moved about, and made some changes in the location of several prisoners in the cells, and directed one to sweep here, and another to clean there, till the dinner came in, which consisted of soup in a large tin pail, and a quantity of coarse meal, in a very large vessel, which a prisoner took out of the vessel with his hands, and distributed, in small tin pans, which another prisoner covered with soup from the tin pail, till as many small pans were filled as there were prisoners, when each prisoner took one. It was altogether a dirty job, done with much disorder and confusion. While the food was preparing for the men, the jailer went above with me, and opened the female apartment, where were about 10 females, shut up in idleness, without supervision, without employment, and with no other restraint than being locked up. Their place of sleeping was on the floor, with few beds or blankets. The general disorder of this apartment was all that might be expected among such women, without employment and without restraint. After visiting the male and female apartments, we visited a room where a man was confined for murder, and saw a man under arrest, the father of 13 children, for killing his wife. He had not yet had his trial. He denied his guilt as a wilful murderer; said the death was occasioned by the accidental discharge of his gun, while he was holding it in his hand, and his wife sat by him. He acknowledged his guilt as a drunkard, and attributed all his troubles to that besetting sin; seemed to feel that he had many sins to confess as a drunkard, but persisted in denying his guilt as the murderer of his wife. He had a large Bible open before him, a part of which he had evidently been reading with attention; for when I referred him to the 51st psalm, and told him the story of Jacob Hodges, who committed this psalm to memory, in his solitary cell, at Auburn, and found great benefit and comfort from it, he said, "I have just learned that psalm;" and although he could not read very well, he recited nearly the whole of it to me from his memory.   I asked this unhappy man if I should pray with him, to which he gratefully assented, and after prayer seemed both grateful and affectionate.   He has since been tried, condemned, and executed.

Thursday, September 10, 1840.   Visited the Jail in Troy, and found it in a better condition than the Jail in Albany, though not essentially improved, or altered, from the condition in which I found it, as described in the Fifteenth Report of the Prison Discipline Society, page 49. — The number of prisoners confined in this Jail, annually, varies from 1000 to 1700.

Friday, September 11.   Visited the Jail in Ballston.   The Jail is under the same roof with the Court-House.   There are three rooms on the first floor, and this is the whole number of rooms in this Jail.   The number of prisoners was but two ; no female or debtor.   The rooms are large and airy, and, in a good degree, clean.   The jailer was polite and attentive.

Caldwell, Tuesday, September 15, 1840.   Visited the Jail, at sunrise.   It has three rooms on the first floor, and on the north side of the keeper's house.   The rooms are sufficiently large, but not well lighted and aired.   The defect in regard to light and air was in a degree remedied, in two of the rooms, by having an open grate two or three feet in width, surrounding the doors of the rooms, and extending into the hall.   Into the space enclosed by this open grate, the prisoners are admitted, and permitted to spend the day.   The other room (not provided with such an airing-place) is unused, except as a lumber room.   There were but two prisoners.   They were in one room, which was very dark when the door was shut.   There was no female or debtor in this Prison.

Middlebury, Vt., Wednesday, September 16, 1840.   Visited the Jail, which consists of four rooms, under the same roof with the keeper's house.   The two west rooms in this Jail are totally unfit to be used at any time, and under any circumstances, for the confinement of human beings.   They too nearly resemble dark dungeons ever to be used.   If they were in a heathen land, Christian people would cry out against them, for such barbarity as would be indicated by confining MEN in such places.   At the time of this visit, they were not used.   At the time of a former visit, they were used.   It is very nearly impossible for a man to read a single word, in one of these rooms, in any position in which he can place himself.   In the lower room, which I entered to examine, I could see nothing of its present state without a lamp, which the keeper brought me, at my request, that I might examine it.

The two east rooms are far better; and if the number of prisoners is never to exceed two, which, so far as I have seen or learned, is not far from the average number, then this Jail will answer a very good purpose. If, therefore, the people of Middlebury, and of the county, are so virtuous as not to have an average of more than two persons in Jail, or if efforts can be made to keep vice and crime in check, so as thus to limit the average number of prisoners, then this Prison is an honor to the place, or, rather, the people are an honor to themselves; but if the Jail is to have an average of five or six prisoners, as is common in places of equal population, then this Jail ought to be condemned as a nuisance, in its present construction; for the moment it becomes necessary to place a man in one of those west rooms, and confine him there for a single day and night, that moment the town and county are disgraced.

It ought to be said, however, in honor of Vermont, that this Jail, as well as others in the state, indicates a near approach to that state of society in which Jails can be dispensed with altogether, and if the good people would make a united and persevering effort to raise the low and vicious a little higher, and restrain them a little more, the present Jails, few and far between, and very small, as they are, might answer all needful purposes, and become one of the strongest proofs of the excellent moral character of the people. In no part of the United States is the reflection more impressed upon the mind than in Vermont, that the time may not be distant, when there shall be less use than at present for Prisons. May the Lord hasten the happy day!

Vergennes, Vt., Thursday, September 17, 1840. Visited the Jail, which is one quarter of a mile from the keeper's house; not kept under lock and key; no prisoner in confinement; no debtor for two years; seldom any criminal, except now and then a drunkard, till he gets sober; one such about three weeks ago. He was confined without legal process, in obedience to the public sentiment — a dangerous precedent; not likely to be often abused in Vergennes. This Jail is a stone building, about 20 feet square, and two stories high; the lower room only finished; the upper room never wanted. This is the Jail of the only *city* of Vermont. The mayor and aldermen are a court to try cases, but they seldom have any business of this kind. They hold a court four times in a year. The jailer was working on his farm; told me I might visit the Jail alone; it was not locked; there was no one in it; he had no pay for keeping it, and nothing to do; but would change his clothes, and accompany me to see the Jail, if he was not so busy.

Burlington, Saturday, September 19, 1841. Visited the Jail in company with the Rev. Mr. Converse. It is kept by a humane and careful man. It consists of one room only fit for use. When there is a female prisoner, she is confined in a chamber in the keeper's house. In the one room fit for use were seven prisoners.; and in this one room it is necessary to confine old and young, black and white, debtors and criminals, condemned and uncondemned. This room is about 18 feet square, and has but two small windows. It was, at this time, in a tolerably neat and cleanly condition; as much so as could have been expected, while occupied, day and night, by such a number of prisoners, without employment or supervision. There were beneath this room, in the lower story, two rooms, nearly dungeons, in a condition of great neglect and disorder. The pipe of the vault from the upper room passes through one of the lower rooms, and renders it exceedingly loathsome. In this room a man was confined a few months, and he had nearly worked his way through the wall, when he was discovered. The stone which he dug from the wall remained in a heap in the room, and the hole which he dug in the wall was partially filled with timber. The jailer apologized for the filthy and neglected condition of the lower part of the Jail, by saying that the court would not allow his accounts for repairs and improvements. He had once expended thirty-five dollars, and his account was not allowed; and he could not afford to pay more money in this way. It was apparent that there was great neglect and fault somewhere, in the care and management of this Jail; and the jailer's statement, without reservation, cast it upon the court. If it be admitted that one room, of the size and construction above described, is sufficient for this town and county, the jailer is entitled to much credit for keeping it as well as he does. When a chamber in his house was used, not long since, for the confinement of a female, she escaped by jumping out of the window in the second story.

Montpelier, Tuesday, September 22, 1840. Visited the Jail, a stone building, two stories high, two rooms on the lower floor, and one on the upper; the former condemned by custom as unfit for use, except in extreme cases; the latter, the upper room, only being used. In the common upper room of the Jail, 18 feet by 20, were four prisoners, of whom two were debtors; and one of them a non-resident, who came to Vermont, not expecting an arrest; but he had found what he did not expect, and knew not when he should be liberated. Both the debtors appeared to bear their imprisonment very well;* especially as

---

* The new law of Vermont, abolishing imprisonment for debt, is supposed **not** to be retrospective, nor applicable to non-resident citizens.

they were confined with criminals, in an apartment which, at best, was a bad place of confinement for criminals. The air of the whole Jail was rendered offensive by a permanent vault, which had a wood pipe, conducting filthy fluids through one of the lower rooms. The lower rooms and the rear of the jailer's house were offensive from this cause.

Danville, Vt., Wednesday, September 23, 1840. Visited the Jail, and found a young man, by the name of Amariah Sabin, from Walden, who had been in Jail since the Friday preceding, and was liable to remain in Jail six months longer, for a military fine of $2; on which the costs had amounted to $3; and his board already to $2; making, in all, $7. I told the tavern-keeper, who had been deputy-sheriff, and went with me to the Jail, that I would buy the young man's watch, at the highest price the watchmaker would prize it, if he and others around would raise the remaining sum, to procure the young man's freedom, and let him go home. He said he would give his share; the sheriff and a lawyer of the village said the same. The watchmaker prized the watch at $5, which was paid, and the sheriff and others supplied the deficiency; and the sheriff took the money, and brought out the young man, in the presence of all, and set him at liberty, with the advice, from us, not to get into Jail again for military fine.

The Jail is a stone building, two stories high, with two rooms on a floor, each room about 12 by 15 feet. The lower rooms are so nearly dark dungeons, that a prisoner cannot see to read at any orifice about the room. There is an orifice in the side of the room, through the thick wall; but it is made angular, so that it answers no purpose for light. There is also an orifice in the door; but this is so small, and the door is so thick, and the passage into which it opens so dark, that printed letters cannot be seen on the inner edge, when the door is shut. There was also an orifice for a stove-pipe, in the ceiling; but if the room is used, this must be filled with stove-pipe, and cannot be left open to admit a ray of light. Practically, therefore, these rooms in the lower story are rendered useless by construction.

The rooms above have comfortable light, and one of them, which was the only one occupied, was in good condition, except the permanent vault, which was filthy, as all permanent vaults are, with scarcely an exception, in Common Jails. — In one of these upper rooms were two prisoners, of whom one was the young man for military fine, whose case has been mentioned. He was about 21 years of age, of respectable appearance and connections, of industrious habits; but his neighbors, he said, a good many of them, advised him to go to Jail rather than pay

the fine.   After he was committed, he attempted to escape by
breaking Jail, and had well nigh succeeded, when he was discovered.   Had he succeeded, he would have been guilty of a
State Prison offence ; for which, if he had been prosecuted and
sentenced, he might have been ruined for life.   Such is the public sentiment, however, in that part of Vermont, in regard to
imprisonment for military fine, that, if he had succeeded, he
probably would not have been prosecuted.   The man in the
same room with him, the only other prisoner in the Jail, said, in
the town where he lived, about twenty men were fined for not
doing military duty, and one of them was brought to Prison, and
the others paid their fines.   My own reflection on the whole
matter was, that all the good results of all the military trainings
we had seen on the journey (which were several) would not
compensate for the evil of the imprisonment of this one young
man.

   Windsor, Vt., Wednesday, September 30, 1840.   Visited the
State Prison.   Mr. Brown, the keeper, was at home, and treated
me with much politeness and attention.   He is a good-looking,
gentlemanly man, about 45 years of age, and appears, in many
respects, well qualified for his station.   He went with me through
the dormitory building and the shops.   The cells of the former,
and the bedding, are not in prime order.   The area, too, around
the cells, is not perfectly white and sweet.   The shops appear
better than the dormitory building.   The construction of the
dormitory building is very good, and there is no good reason
why it should not be kept perfectly white and sweet.   The
number of prisoners is about 80 — a diminished number from the
average for many years.   Crime appears to have been steadily
diminishing in Vermont for a considerable time.   The branches
of business pursued in the Prison are gun, shoe, and carriage
making ; partly for the state, and partly for contractors.   The
old contract system, by which one man took the Prison, had its
earnings, and supported it, has been done away, as injurious to
the best interests of the institution.

   The superintendent sent for Mr. Harvey, the chaplain, to
meet me at the Prison.   He did so ; and told me that there was
no unusual interest, at this time, among the prisoners, concerning their souls' concerns ; that the usual services of the Sabbath
and the Sabbath school were continued ; that the attention to
preaching was good ; and that much progress had been made by
the prisoners of the Sabbath school, in committing the Scriptures
to memory.

   After we got through the examination of the Prison, Mr.
Brown very kindly asked me for my opinion and advice concern-

ing the institution; and I told him as kindly, and with perfect frankness, that the first effort should be to cleanse it, and that this was particularly needful in the dormitory building; that the cells, bedding, area, &c., were not in prime order. He apparently received the communication, as he had asked it, kindly, and as it was given. It was new business to him; he had not been long in office; and had probably never seen a Prison like the House of Correction at South Boston.

Brattleboro', Vt., Thursday, October 1, 1840. Visited the Asylum for the Insane, in company with Mrs. D., and Mr. and Mrs. B. Saw Dr. and Mrs. Rockwell, who received us with great kindness, and were pleased to show us the institution. The new building is finished, in the centre and west wing, on the general plan of the Asylum at Worcester. The hall between the sleeping rooms appears to be about two feet wider. If so, it is so much better. The class of patients occupying the hall into which Dr. Rockwell took us, appeared tolerably well, and the hall and rooms in tolerably good condition. One female patient from Stockbridge was brought out from her apartment to see us in the parlor. Perhaps she appeared as well as she could be expected to appear. The case is one of long standing and difficult management. Her condition is said to be improved by being at Brattleboro'.

We were shown many curious specimens of painting and mechanical ingenuity by one of the patients; among other things, a complete model, in wood, of the Asylum, with its out-buildings, as it should be when completed. We saw, also, some beautiful paintings by a female patient, and heard some fine music on the piano from the same lady. She is very accomplished in both music and painting. She is a melancholy victim to overwork, in teaching a school of young ladies, to support herself and family in misfortune.

The institution, as a whole, appeared tolerably well. The location is exceedingly beautiful; the plan of building is according to the most approved model; the cleanliness and order did not appear to me to be No. 1. The health has not been as good the last as in some former years. The economy is very rigid and thorough; the pay of the patients supporting the establishment. The grounds owned by the institution are beautifully fertile and cultivated. The quantity of ground owned by the institution is about one third what it should be. It is now about 50 acres. It ought to be 150. There are other grounds, south, east, and north of the Asylum, not now belonging to it, which naturally belong to it, beautifully located, and created for its convenience, which ought to be immediately purchased, and which can now be purchased at the rate of $80 per acre. If the purchase is long delayed, it will probably cost twice that sum. Here, then, is a most favorable opportunity to invest $8000 for the permanent benefit of this institution. If no individual is found to give it, and the state will not make the purchase, the trustees ought to raise the money by private solicitation among the resident and native citizens of Vermont, if it can only be obtained in sums of 25 cents.

Dr. Rockwell showed us the dining room, in which his own family, with the better class of patients, take their meals together, and said he wished himself and family to have no better fare than the patients had. On the whole, I was much pleased and interested in the Vermont Asylum.

Greenfield, Friday, October 2, 1840. Visited the Jail. No person in it, of any description. Eleven criminals only committed within the last year; of whom two were sent to the State Prison — one for adultery, and one for theft; five to the House of Correction — four for drunkenness, and one for assault. Nine debtors the last year; of whom seven on execution, and two on writ; — four by Court of Common Pleas, and five by justices' process. Ten years ago, seventy-one were committed for debt in a year.

There is a difference of about one half, too, in the number of criminals committed in ten years.

The bills for support of prisoners indicate the change. They amounted, at that period, (i. e., ten years ago,) to about $900 a year; and now they amount to $150, and there has been no essential change in the law to make this difference. Mr. Jones, the present keeper, has been in office eleven years, and attributes the change to the progress of TEMPERANCE.

Northampton, Saturday, October 3, 1840. Visited the Jail early in the morning. Found the same old gentleman keeper, who has been there twenty-four years. I never have seen this Jail in so good condition. The use of whitewash, as a purifier, applied to the floor, as well as to the ceiling and walls, appears to be well understood by Mr. Clapp and his assistant. I was pained to find, however, within the walls of the Jail, in Northampton, an increase in the number of prisoners. For many years the most remarkable thing about this Jail has been the small number of prisoners, when any have been found in it. Now it has an unusual number, and the old gentleman says it has been so all summer. The prisoners were more numerous than the apartments; consequently he was obliged, in some cases, to place two in a room. Of course, this did not appear an oversight or fault in the keeper, as he could not do otherwise. It is not uncommon, in the Jails of Massachusetts, to find two or three in a room, contrary to law, when there are rooms enough, and more than enough, to separate the prisoners ; and the only reason sometimes alleged is, that they had rather be together, or it is more convenient. The only explanation or apology for such violation of law, and breach of trust, is, that the keepers are ignorant of the evils of unrestrained communication in the night-rooms of Prisons, and do not understand the reason why the law was made. Mr. Clapp would not thus violate law, if he *did not* understand why the law was made ; and any keeper who will do it ought to be displaced.

The number of *debtors* committed to the Northampton Jail in the lapse of a year is very small, — not more than eight or ten, — and seldom is one found locked up.

In the progress of this journey, so far as Vermont was concerned, the most remarkable thing to witness was the diminution, rather than the increase of crime; the smallness of the Jails, and their comparative emptiness ; the effect of the Temperance Reformation on this department of human affairs ; the almost total exemption of the citizens from imprisonment for debt, and the evils resulting from military trainings and imprisonment for military fines. The trainings had better be dispensed with, as in Massachusetts, rather than kept up as in New York and Vermont. Besides the evils as seen at the Jails, almost the only annoyance we had on the whole journey was from military trainings.

New York City, October 17, 1840. Visited this day, in company with Mr. Fairbanks, of New York, and Mr. Chamberlain, of Cambridge, Mass., the Halls of Justice, falsely so called, in the city of New York. They should be called, as at present managed, the Halls of Filth. I have been fifteen years engaged in visiting Prisons, and I have never seen human beings in a more filthy, neglected, and insufferable condition, than in the Halls of Justice, in the city of New York, this day. Well may they be called, as they have often been in the daily papers, Egyptian Tombs. They were built at an immense expense, (of at least $200,000,) within a few years, on a plan recommended by Haviland the architect, as the best ever designed ; and yet what is said above is true. Where are the philanthropists of the city ? where the intelligent and humane editors ? where the Christian ministers ? " *I was in Prison, and ye visited me not.*" The most filthy of all places in this filthy establishment, are in the lower story of the House of Detention. The double cells, on the lower floor, in the north end of the building, are crowded with prisoners. Although originally designed each for one, they frequently contain eight or nine; without beds, chairs, blankets, or benches, almost without windows; with permanent vaults overflowing in the rooms; prisoners more than half naked, sick, diseased, covered with vermin. In one apartment, into which I attempted to put my head, I could not continue it one minute. I had almost vomited from inhaling a single breath. Col. Stone, Park Benjamin, Hallock and Hale, where are ye? Missionary men, Bible men, tract distributors, friends of Africa and the slave, where are ye? If there could be found in the islands of the sea, or on the coasts of Africa, or in the middle passage, scenes of such horror as in the Halls of Justice, on Leonard Street, within half a mile of the City Hall, and fifty rods of Broadway, thousands could be raised to change the scene. No great expense of time or trouble is required to do it in this case. Say not that you are in no danger yourselves from suffering this nuisance to be unabated. It may breed a Jail fever, which shall extend to the bar and the court, and thence to the city.

New York City, October 18, 1840. Visited this day (it being the Sabbath) Blackwell's Island. Rode on horseback to the East River Ferry, or Fifty-first Street, about three miles from the City Hall. Blew the horn for the boatman, who soon came, and put my horse in the stable belonging to the city. Met at the ferry an exhorter of the Methodist Episcopal Church, who was on his way to the chapel of the Penitentiary. We crossed the ferry together. Learning my name, he invited me to preach for him. I consented to assist him in the services. Mr. Howell, the keeper of the Penitentiary, received us very kindly; gave us pleasant seats in the parlor, while the prisoners were assembling; and, after they were assembled, conducted us to the chapel. About 400 prisoners, male and female, were in their seats. The chapel is a large, airy, and convenient room, in the third story of the centre building, occupying the whole of this story, being sufficiently high, and lighted with numerous and large windows, on the east and west sides, having seats facing the east, for men on the south side and women on the north, being separated by a partition, in the centre of the room, a little higher than a man's head, and extending from the west side of the room to a point on the east side near the speaker's desk. The prisoners were all silently seated when we entered the chapel, under the care of officers, on elevated seats in different parts of the room. The order and neatness of the chapel, furniture, prisoners, and dress, were very good. The air was as pleasant as in ordinary churches. My friend and brother of the Methodist church commenced the service by reading and prayer. The prisoners sung a hymn, and listened to preaching from the text, "These words, which I command thee this day, shall be in thine heart." The object of the discourse was to show that the law of the Lord should be in their hearts, and govern their lives, and then there would be no trouble. The attention to preaching was solemn and good. It was a privilege to magnify the law. My friend thanked me for the assistance and encouragement afforded him, and we left the chapel in good fellowship, having enjoyed together this opportunity of usefulness. The prisoners retired in silence and perfect order, the men to their cells, and the women to their day-room. Mr. Howell, the keeper, politely invited us to dine with him. I accepted the invitation, but my friend and brother declined, for the purpose of going before dinner to the farms across the East River, about three quarters of a mile, to conduct a religious service among 750 or 800 children, at the Nursery, so called, on Long Island. After dinner, I visited the Insane Asylum, about half a mile distant from the Penitentiary, on the northern extremity of the island. On my way thither, I called at the door of the superintendent of the whole island, but he was not at home. I found the Insane Asylum, which had been finished and occupied since I was last on the island, about two years ago, a most beautiful establishment. The location, material, and finish, are not surpassed, in the whole country, in any similar institution ; — all plain, simple, durable, appropriate, complete, and exceedingly beautiful. It was now occupied by more than 200 patients, and the management, *in the main building*, appeared as good as the location, construction, and finish. They had had public worship in the morning, conducted by Dr. Proudfit, when 70 or 80 patients were assembled in one of the halls. Here, as elsewhere, religious worship among the insane is exerting its salutary influence. The steward, Mr. Bishop, and his lady, treated me with attention and kindness. The physician, Dr. McLellan, I did not see. I passed through the halls with Mr. Bishop, and found them, and the rooms adjoining, in perfect order, and the patients, as we passed, all quiet and well-behaved. The mode of heating is by steam, and appeared to answer a good purpose. It was tried the last winter in the coldest weather, and was found entirely sufficient. I was on the whole agreeably disappointed in the good management of this new Asylum for the pauper lunatics of the city of New York. I knew the location, material, and finish were of the best kind ; but I feared it would fail in management. My opinion is, that it does not fail in management, so far as the main building is concerned ; but there is a building, erected for a lodge, on the verge of the island, a little distant from the main building, intended for the worst class of patients, in regard to which my mind is in doubt. Without special care, this part of the institution will be too much out of sight and out of mind. The physician, steward, and matron, must have a vigilant eye to this part of the establishment, or it will but poorly correspond with the main building The grounds and gardens about the whole were in fine condition, and occupy the whole of the north end of the island. Efforts are making to carry forward the main building, according to the original design. The north wing only, three stories high, ex-tending about 200 feet from east to west, is now completed. The original design was to extend the centre building from the east end of the north wing, about 600 feet southerly, and a south wing from the southern extremity of the centre building 200 feet westerly. This being done, as well as begun, New York will have an Asylum for its pauper lunatics of great beauty and admirable adaptation. I left the place with a heart full of grati-tude to the great Author of all good designs.

As I returned to the ferry to leave the island, I called again on the superintendent of the whole island, but did not find him at home. As I came near the ferry, I looked in upon the females of the Penitentiary, where they were assembled in their day-room, and where they had been since they left the chapel in the morning, and where a religious teacher might have had every opportunity and facility for reading, singing, instruction, and prayer, for several hours.

I left the island with a deep conviction of the importance of it, as a place of usefulness for a resident chaplain.

I was much pleased to hear various and strong expressions of affection and gratitude from Mr. Howell, the keeper of the Peniten-tiary, and the boatman and his family at the ferry, towards the Rev. Edwin W. Dwight, since deceased, who spent several months, about two years since, as a chaplain in the employment of the Prison Discipline Society, among the criminal and humane insti-tutions in the city of New York. Col. Vanderbilt and his family, before they left the island, expressed the same strong af-fection for him.

Monday, October 19, 1840. Visited the House of Refuge of the city of New York for Juvenile Delinquents. The number of in-mates, as usual for several years, was about 200, of whom about 40 were girls. The superintendent, Mr. David Tenny, was not at home ; I found his assistant in charge of the boys, who were assem-bled in the dining-room, which appeared to be in good condition, in regard to fixtures and neatness, but not well lighted. The boys were decently clad, and under good discipline. They retired from the room in good order, in single file, and spent about fif-teen minutes in a large, open court, in active, athletic exercise and sport. When the time of play was over, they assembled, at the sound of a whistle, in two rows, in front of the workshop, and marched to their work. This is performed in a separate building from their dining-room, and consists in chair, shoe, and razor-strop making. The two former branches appear to be well adapted to the house, and likely to be permanent, as the articles are always necessary and in good demand.

The superintendent, Mr. Tenny, returned from the city, and accompanied me through the workshops. It is beautiful to see the places of useful labor, the employment, industry, and skill of the boys, who appear more cheerful in spending the hours allotted to labor every day, thus usefully, than they ever appeared in their paths of wickedness. The proceeds of their labor amounts to about $2000 annually. The females are employed about six hours every day, in another building, with equal industry, in making, mending, and washing garments for the boys.

About four hours of each day are devoted to common-school instruction, in a room neatly fitted up, on the Lancasterian plan, in the same building with the dining-room. The progress here made, in the common branches of education, is probably equal to that made by any equal number of boys, who are not usefully employed in labor six or eight hours of each day. Boys are not made to study all the time, nor to work all the time, but to get knowledge and make themselves useful; and both these objects are kept in view daily in the House of Refuge. In this respect, it is an example for families.

In another respect, also, it is worthy of imitation. A given time, daily, is devoted, by the rules of the institution, to play. All work and no play is not the thing for children. There is a time and place, daily, in the House of Refuge, for play; and all the boys know where it is, and when it is, and they go to it with all their hearts; and there is no scolding because they are so full of it. No matter how hard they play, in the proper place and time, if they play pleasantly. The master looks, and smiles, and likes them all the better for being wide awake. The play being over, they go to work, as they went to play, with a good heart. Their limbs have been exercised, their muscles brought into play, and the whole body put in pleasant action, and their minds and hearts too; and now they are prepared for usefulness.

The whole man is regarded in the House of Refuge. They are treated morally as well as physically. There is a chapel for public worship on the Sabbath, neat and appropriate, where they all assemble, morning and evening, to worship God. There are also places and seasons for family prayer and secret prayer; and they always implore audibly the blessing of God at their meals. There is much to be learnt in the House of Refuge in regard to the proper management and training of children; for a way has been discovered, in which very bad children can have, in a good degree, undone the evil which has been done, and, by a proper course of moral, intellectual, and physical instruction, fitted, in a few years, for useful and honorable apprenticeship. Surely, then, there is a way in which other children, who have never been exposed to evil example, can be trained in the nurture and admonition of the Lord. No doubt much more can be done than is done, in the House of Refuge, to train up children for usefulness and heaven; but much is done to prepare them for usefulness, and much more is done, than in many private families, to fit them for heaven.

There is a comfortable place of rest in solitude, after the labors, studies, amusements, and religious services, are all over The sleeping-rooms are neat, comfortable, well adapted, and well furnished; so that every boy can enjoy his rest undisturbed; and if vicious indulgence exists in the night season, it must be solitary vice, which none but the eye of God can see. To what extent such vice exists in this institution, should be a subject of careful inquiry; and a little book entitled " Hints to the Young," and another entitled " An Hour's Conference with Fathers and Sons," should be put in every sleeping-room.

On leaving the Refuge, Mr. Tenny presented two copies of the Fifteenth Annual Report of the House of Refuge, — a very important document, — and accompanied me in a walk some distance from the House, when we parted and wished each other well in our different pursuits.

Tuesday, October 20, 1840. I visited New Haven. Called, in the afternoon, on my old friend Charles Robinson, Esq., who rendered essential service to the Prison Discipline Society, two years ago, in getting up the public meeting, in that city, in favor of a new Jail. I found him at home, glad to see me, and very polite. He left his business, and went immediately with me to see the new Jail, now building. It is on the most approved plan, after the model of the Hartford County Jail. There is a slight variation in the length of the windows of the external wall; but this is an injury rather than a benefit. It would be better that they should be one foot longer, than one foot shorter. The building had progressed so far, however, that it was too late to change without incurring more expense than the committee were willing to incur. Besides, there are so many windows in the external wall, (five on each side, and two at the end,) and they are so large, (6 feet by 4,) though diminished, that they will give a good degree of light.   Still it would have been better, in my opinion, to adhere more closely to the model.   When a plan has been studied as long, and perfected as well, as that of the County Prison at Hartford, and is pronounced by a most experienced Prison keeper to be ' *as neat as a pin, and he does not see how it can be improved,*' people ought to be slow to depart from this model.

In another particular it was in contemplation to depart from the model, i. e., in raising the external walls higher than they are in Hartford, before the windows were put in.   In this respect, my visit was seasonable, and prevented the variation contemplated, and caused them to put in the windows, so low down, as to be, at the sill, a little above the head of a tall man.   This is high enough for prison purposes.

In still another and more important particular, it was proposed to depart from the model, viz., in opening a communication, or sluice, between a permanent vault, in the rear of the Prison, and the area of the Prison around the cells ; thinking in this way, by an oblique tube, to convey all the filth of the Prison into the vault ; the consequence of which would be, that the foul air would have been driven, with every wind, through the whole area, into all the cells, and through the keeper's house.   The committee reconsidered the matter of this proposed improvement, and ordered that the model should be followed, and this improvement (falsely so called) dispensed with.

On the whole, notwithstanding these contemplated changes, some of which were prevented, I was agreeably disappointed to find New Haven so closely imitating Hartford in its excellent model County Prison ; pleased with the progress already made in the building ; not sorry, but rather glad, that they had fixed the location on the east side of the public square, on the estate owned by the county, and occupied formerly by the old County House and Jail.   If the new Prison shall be, in its management, like the Hartford County Prison, it will not be a nuisance, but an honor, in the midst of the city so long as it shall be necessary to restrain and punish vice and crime.

Thursday, October 22, 1840.   I visited the County Prison in Hartford, Conn.   I found Mr. N. H. Morgan, the keeper, at home.   He treated me with much kindness, cordiality, and attention.   Mr. Morgan appears to be a good man, acting in his official capacity, so far as I could judge, in the fear of God and love of man.   The number of prisoners was about twelve.   They were all (except one, accused of murdering his wife) in their places of labor, in the east area of the Prison building, alongside of the cells, industriously employed in making shoes.   The business of making a shoe is here divided into five or six parts; so that each prisoner, old and young, with or without experience, can be at once employed, and in three or four days profitably. So much per day is paid by the contractor for their time, and the proceeds of the business, last year, was $600 more than enough to support the establishment. It was pleasant to see the prisoners in this Jail, with one exception, industriously employed. It was equally pleasant to see the neatness and order of the place, and the supervision and discipline. The supervisor is a mechanic, who can not only exercise supervision, and preserve order and silence, but teach them their trade ; and, having these useful qualifications, he is employed at a price as reasonable, as if he did not possess the useful qualities of a good keeper and master mechanic. Besides, it is important that he should be a mechanic, because he can then have employment himself, in the presence of the prisoners, and thus become an example to them, while he keeps himself out of idleness, which is as irksome to a good mind as it is injurious to others by way of example. Should it be said that the superintendent or supervisor of a shoe-shop in a County Prison, must have as much as he can do, to keep the men under his care out of idleness and mischief, and keep them industriously employed, — the answer is, that this depends, in a great measure, on the construction of the shop and its fixtures, the kind of discipline introduced, and the post of observation for the keeper. If the shop is an oblong building, and has in it but one open space from side to side and from end to end ; if it is lofty, so that the keeper can have an elevated position, and easily overlook the whole; if the prisoners are placed facing one way, with their backs to the keeper, and in relation to each other back to face ; — then they do not know whether the keeper is looking at them or not, but suppose that he is looking at each of them, every moment of time, even if he is not. This construction and arrangement of a Prison workshop and its fixtures, and the arrangement of the prisoners, enables a keeper to do more to preserve order and promote industry, a hundred to one, than a shop with partitions and hiding-places, or even an open space with fixtures and prisoners scattered about, some looking one way and some another, with the keeper in the midst of them, with his face to some and his back to others. There is no Prison or Penitentiary where the importance of this construction and arrangement is better illustrated than in the shoe and chair-shops of the Connecticut State Prison at Wethersfield. It is well illustrated in the Hartford County Prison, but not quite as well as in the State Prison ; for, in the former, a prisoner may sometimes be seen facing the wrong way, or with a side view. This should never be while seated at their work, because it breaks in upon a most important rule of Prison discipline, by which the admirable order, industry, and silence of the reformed prisons are secured with simple means. It is in a good degree done at Hartford, but not quite as well as at Wethersfield ; better, however, than in any County Prison in the land.

The dormitories or cells of this Prison are larger, more airy, and better constructed, than the cells of the reformed State Prisons generally, on the Auburn plan. If there is any difference, it *should be* in favor of the County Prison, because persons untried and uncondemned are found in it. The doors of the cells, in the Hartford County Prison, are better constructed, to admit light, heat, and air, than those of any State Prison in the land, unless the doors of the cells in the Connecticut State Prison have been made to conform to this very perfect model door, since the date of this visit. They are of round iron, with orifices as large as they can be with safety, open from top to bottom, with as little solid matter as consists with strength and security. It is on many little things, which may appear in themselves very small, to a person not familiar with the subject, that the character of the Hartford County Prison depends for its acknowledged superiority to all County Prisons previously erected.

The cells of the Prison, at the time of this visit, were in tolerably good order ; but I was not strongly impressed with the peculiar neatness, purity, and whiteness of the floors and walls, nor with the peculiar cleanliness, sweetness of the furniture, beds, and bedding. Something may be learnt, in these respects, in the House of Correction at South Boston, by all the Prisons I have ever seen. Comparisons are said to be invidious ; but they ought not to be so, when the object is simply to promote the improvement of Prisons. They have formerly been places of so much wretchedness, and it is so difficult to make them, in all respects, what they ought to be, and keep them so, that any one, who has any thing to do with Prisons, should hail every suggestion, fact, and comparison, which may lead to improvement.

After examining carefully all the cells, taking the dimensions of the doors, windows, grates, &c., I left the Prison part of the building with a growing conviction that it will not soon be surpassed, as a model County Prison. There may be a departure from the model, in sundry particulars, by way of experiment ; but let him who makes the departure be well advised before he comes to the conclusion that it will be an improvement; for he may find, after it is done, that it is any thing but an improvement. They thought to make some of these improvements in New Haven, but, before they had gone too far to retreat, they were convinced that they were mistaken, and adopted the plan of the model.

In passing from the Prison part of the building to the keeper's dwelling-house, through the office, the keeper showed me the facilities which he had for inspection at night, from his bed-room, and in the daytime, from the kitchen, all going to show the excellence of the plan of this building with reference to the great principle of supervision day and night. We passed, also, through the family apartments, where he introduced me to the matron, his wife, a lady-like woman and a tidy housekeeper, who sees that all things are done well in her department of the establishment. The house and kitchen were as neat as any private dwelling; more so than many with which no Prison is connected.

On the whole, my previous impressions, which were exceedingly favorable to the construction and management of this Jail, were more than sustained. I could not but rejoice, as I left the place, that the world has at length been furnished with such a model County Prison.

Thursday, October 22, 1840. Visited, in the morning, the State Prison at Wethersfield. Found my old friend Amos Pilsbury, the warden, at home, and glad to see me. He put out my horse, introduced me to his wife and children, and accompanied me about the Prison. We visited, I believe, all its parts, shops, chapel, dormitories, lunatic apartments, bathing-room, hospital, kitchen, and female apartments. The neatness, order, industry, and discipline of the *shops*, are, on the whole, nowhere surpassed. I think, however, that there ought to be a little more attention and expense in the clothing of the convicts, and an economy, in this respect, not quite so rigid. Their clothing should be better while at work, and they should be allowed an extra suit for the Sabbath. I noticed nothing else demanding improvement in the shops, except the crowded condition of some of them, which will be entirely obviated, as soon as the new shops are done, which are now nearly completed. About $1500 of the $5000 appropriated by the last legislature for the improvement of the State Prison, from its surplus earnings, have been expended in improving and enlarging the shops. It is a great and necessary improvement, and will essentially conduce to the improvement of the discipline, appearance, and moral good of the institution. When the shops, thus enlarged, shall be occupied, and a little more attention have been given to the clothing of the prisoners, visitors will look in vain for a Prison where the *workshops* are in a better condition than in this. The tool, chair, shoe, and smiths' shop, appeared, at the time of this visit, in admirable condition. I went not only to the places in the rear of the railing, where visitors usually go, but within the railing, and among the prisoners; and from one end of the shop to the other, and have never seen better discipline and order. These things, too, were evidently there as a matter of habit, and not put on for the occasion. It was something attained by long-continued subjection, application, and industry, and not assumed. I was never so much pleased before with the shops of this Prison. There was no flurry, no assumed authority, not a word spoken; but quiet, silent, active industry, among two hundred convicts, with the regularity and uniformity of a clock, each man having his place, and keeping his place, each one understanding his business, and attending to it without diversion.

The apartments for lunatics, which we visited after leaving the shops, are well enough, if there must be any such apartments in a State Prison; but there should be none, because it is not the appropriate place for the treatment of this dreadful malady. It is bad enough to be lunatic, without being confined in the solitary cell of a State Prison, and punished with felons for the greatest of all afflictions. It is devoutly to be desired that the State of Connecticut would build an Asylum for the Insane Poor, and remove this suffering class from the State Prison. Let the members of the legislature visit the Prison, and see Rabello, the homicide, and hear him gnash his teeth, as he looks at them through the grate of his solitary cell, and then visit the institution at Worcester, and see nine cases of homicide, in themselves equally hopeless, as gentle and docile as lambs, and hear Dr. Woodward speak to them, and see them look up in his face, and smile upon him, and pat him on his shoulder, or his side, as their physician and father, and it appears impossible for the members of the legislature, as rational beings, any longer, under the responsibility of their oaths of office, to confine lunatics in the State Prison. The State Prison is not the place for lunatics. They cannot be treated in a proper manner. There is nothing in the system appropriate to the cure of the disease. It is little better than *insanity in the government*, to allow it, after the light which experience has thrown upon the subject.

After leaving poor, suffering Rabello, in his solitary cell, to gnash his teeth with pain, we visited the bathing-room, which is in the rear of the cells for lunatics. It is supplied abundantly with water, cold and hot, from an adjoining apartment, where there is a steam engine. It is a large bathing-place, containing a large quantity of water, is much used on entering the Prison, and during the period of imprisonment, and is of great value to health, cleanliness, and comfort, far beyond what was anticipated before it was built.

Every Prison should be supplied with a bathing-room equally spacious and convenient ; but very few are thus supplied.

The dormitory, or cell building, we next examined thoroughly, in all the stories and ranges of cells. These are now undergoing important changes and improvements in regard to fixtures and furniture. The old plank doors are being removed, and open doors, grated with round iron, after the model of the improved door of the Hartford County Prison, are being substituted for them. This is a great and important improvement in regard to security, light, and air, and consequently health and life. The old wood-frame and canvass bedsteads are being removed, and the round iron bed frame, with canvass bottom, substituted. This, also, is a great and necessary improvement. With the old plank doors, and the old frame bedsteads, it was very difficult to keep out fleas, bugs, and other vermin ; not so with these substitutes. When these changes are effected, the cells will be in good condition ; while they are being done, of course, they do not appear so. At the House of Refuge in New York city, in a late visit, Mr. Pilsbury was quoted as authority for saying that it is impossible to keep a Prison without fleas. I asked him whether he said so. He said, Not in general and unqualified terms, so far as he recollected ; but he had not been able to do it at Wethersfield. While I admitted with these old frame plank doors and bed-frames, it might be impossible, I denied that it is impossible with proper fixtures and furniture. I never saw and never heard of a flea in the House of Correction at South Boston ; nor do I believe, if there was one, 24 hours would pass without his destruction. If, however, there were such doors and such bedsteads at the House of Correction, as were formerly used at Wethersfield, and as are still used in many Prisons, it might be impossible to prevent this nuisance.

The posts and railings of the dormitory building in the Connecticut State Prison are painted *black*, instead of being white-washed or painted white. I do not like the appearance of these dark, funeral pall galleries. A Prison is never more likely to reform men by being made dark, gloomy, and dismal. The confinement is punishment enough, without adding to it by darkness and blackness. The lighter, the whiter, and the purer, the more likely to answer the benevolent purpose of a Penitentiary. When the changes and improvements here suggested are made, then I should say of the *dormitory buildings* in the Connecticut State Prison, as of the shops, a visitor may look in vain to find any thing better ; but not so now. He may find better dormitory buildings, and fixtures, and furniture, at South Boston, Mass., and in the Hartford County Prison.

The female apartments and the kitchen were in fine condition, under the superintendence and care of Miss Pilsbury, sister of the warden, and daughter of old Captain Pilsbury, who has raised so many sons and daughters to be greatly useful in the superintendence and care of Penitentiaries. The number of females in the Prison is reduced to nine ; it has formerly been about twice that number. They are mostly employed in cooking, washing, and mending, for the other prisoners.

The hospital was, also, in good condition, with only three inmates ; one the nurse, another for a slight cause, and the third with consumption. The health of the Prison is very good at this time, and has generally been very good.

As we passed through the Prison, and around it, in the rear of the yard wall, we saw the various improvements which are in progress, all in consequence of the appropriation by the legislature of $5000 of surplus earnings for this object. These improvements, when completed, will be very great, and will give to the Prison a new aspect. It is right that so large a portion of surplus earnings should be appropriated for the improvement of the Prison itself. The legislature probably never did a wiser act than to appropriate $5000 of surplus earnings for the improvement of the Prison itself, and $9000 from the same source to encourage the counties to build County Prisons on the plan of that at Hartford.

On the whole, I left the Prison more impressed than ever before with its favorable character, results, and prospects.

Thursday, October 22, 1840 ; 3 o'clock, P. M. The Rev. Thomas H. Gallaudet, chaplain of the Retreat for the Insane in Hartford, Conn., called for me to visit the Retreat with him. Dr. Brigham, the superintendent, kindly sent the carriage for us. When we arrived at the institution, it was apparent, at the first glance of the eye, that the spirit of improvement had been there since my last visit. Much had been done in the way of painting, cleaning house, &c., to give every thing the appearance of neatness and comfort. We entered first the superintendent's office, where he has a library for the institution, mostly presented by himself, and in an adjoining room, opening into the office, his private library. Opening into the same room, also, was the apothecary's shop, in good order, and convenient.

We visited next the apartments of the men ; saw and saluted many of them, as we passed through the halls, who appeared cheerful and courteous, and even glad to see us. The patients were in good condition with respect to their persons and dress ; the attendants polite, intelligent, and kind ; the furniture, beds, and bedding, all clean and sweet. The order of the establish-

ment, thus far, was strongly in favor of improvement and progress towards a high standard. The superintendent showed
much taste and skill, as well as urbanity, kindness, and controlling influence over mind, as we proceeded. We visited the
lowest places and the most unpromising subjects, but did not
find any very low places, bad subjects, or deep and unmitigated
misery. In an institution of 100 insane patients, there are, of
course, difficult cases to be managed. If these are managed as
well as they can be, what more can be asked or expected? That
this was pretty nearly the case, at the Retreat, at the time of this
visit, according to the present state of knowledge, I believe.
During the whole visit, in all parts of the institution, it was apparent that the chaplain delightfully fills an important place of
usefulness among all connected with it. The superintendent
says of him, in his last report, "His experience with the sick
and insane, his accurate observation and knowledge of the human mind, deservedly entitle his remarks to great attention."
The following are the remarks of the chaplain alluded to by the
superintendent : —

"The usual religious exercises on the Sabbath, and the evenings
of the other days of the week, have been regularly continued during
the past year. A large proportion of the patients have been in the
habit of attending these exercises, and have evinced the benefit derived from them by the good order and becoming deportment which,
with very few exceptions, have prevailed. The religious sensibilities
are, in this way, often rekindled. Self-control is aided in regaining
its dominion; and peace, at least for a season, visits the most agitated
breast. May we not hope and pray that the Spirit of grace and consolation will here, as well as elsewhere, shed down its hallowed influences to enlighten, to purify, and to bless the soul? Our Savior, before
he left the world, promised *the Comforter* to his disciples; and will he
not delight to fulfil this promise among such as are kindred sufferers
with those who shared so largely in his compassion while on earth.
Among these sufferers we often find some of his most faithful followers.

"Cases frequently occur which, in the opinion of the physician, require the services of the chaplain, in the way of personal intercourse
with the patients; when the hope-inspiring views and promises of the
gospel may be addressed to the desponding mind with great benefit.
Such services have been promptly and cheerfully rendered.

"Death sometimes enters the walls of the institution; and it has
more than once happened, that the spirit, about to take its flight to
another world, and in full possession of its reasoning powers, finds its
faith and hope invigorated by the consolations which are administered,
and the prayers which are offered up, at this trying hour. It is a solace, too, to the friends of the deceased, to know that the funeral
solemnities are conducted with appropriate religious exercises. They
have themselves often been present at these exercises.

"There are other occasions, also, when feeble and convalescent patients express a wish to have the chaplain visit them, that they may enjoy the privilege of religious counsels, and of uniting in supplication at the throne of grace. With the advice and approbation of the physician, such visits are made, and evidently with very beneficial results.

"In addition to this, it has been the custom of the chaplain to visit the patients throughout the institution, from time to time; to exchange civilities and pleasant conversation with them, and to let them see that he takes a personal interest in their welfare. The respect and kindness with which they uniformly treat him, is no less grateful to his feelings than indicative of the advantages which such intercourse, wisely conducted, is capable of affording. The insane know well how to appreciate acts of sympathy, and among others those of a minister of the gospel.

"The other inmates of the establishment, including the attendants and nurses, all of whom are usually present at the religious exercises, it is not to be forgotten, come in for their share of the benefits which these exercises afford. Every day they hear truths and precepts from the Word of God, which, if cherished and obeyed, will tend to make them more faithful in the discharge of duty; and they have the gospel preached to them, from Sabbath to Sabbath, which they would otherwise be but seldom permitted to hear, as their constant attendance on the patients is one essential feature of the management of the institution.

"Commending it, with its various interests and concerns, to the guidance, protection, and blessing of Almighty God, the chaplain cannot conclude this report of his labors, without acknowledging the respectful kindness which has always been shown him, in the discharge of his official duties, by the physician and all the other officers and inmates of the Retreat.

T. H. GALLAUDET.

"*May 12th*, 1841."

On the whole, the institution is among the best in the land.

CONCLUSION.

In view of the whole matter of this Report, we remark — It is the glory of the Son of God "to bring good out of evil."

And again — "If we possess not his spirit, we are not his."

And finally (it is a standing text for the society) — "Blessed is he that considereth the poor: the LORD will deliver him in time of trouble."

"The LORD will preserve him, and keep him alive; and he shall be blessed upon the earth; and thou wilt not deliver him unto the will of his enemies."

"The LORD will strengthen him upon the bed of languishing: thou wilt make all his bed in his sickness."

OFFICERS.

PRESIDENT.

*GEORGE BLISS,
SAMUEL T. ARMSTRONG.

VICE-PRESIDENTS.

*WILLIAM BARTLETT,	LUTHER F. DIMMICK,
*WILLIAM REED,	EDWARD BEECHER,
LEONARD WOODS,	SIMON GREENLEAF,
WILLIAM JENKS,	DANIEL SHARP,
ELIJAH HEDDING,	J. S. STONE,
*EBENEZER PORTER,	LUCIUS BOLLES,
*BENJAMIN B. WISNER,	JOHN C. WARREN,
*JEREMIAH EVARTS,	HENRY J. RIPLEY,
S. V. S. WILDER,	CHARLES LOWELL,
JOHN TAPPAN,	JOHN S. PETERS,
SAMUEL H. WALLEY,	ROGER MINOT SHERMAN,
BROWN EMERSON,	THOMAS H. GALLAUDET,
ALEXANDER HENRY,	JOEL HAWES,
CHARLES CHAUNCEY,	JEREMIAH DAY,
*STEPHEN VAN RENSSELAER,	BENJAMIN SILLIMAN,
ALEXANDER FRIDGE,	ELEAZER LORD,
*ROBERT RALSTON,	JOHN M. MATHEWS,
*EDWARD D. GRIFFIN,	WILLIAM JAY,
HEMAN HUMPHREY,	THEODORE FRELINGHUYSEN,
*SAMUEL GREEN,	SAMUEL SOUTHARD,
FRANCIS WAYLAND,	SAMUEL MILLER,
JUSTIN EDWARDS,	ARCHIBALD ALEXANDER,
ALONZO POTTER,	HOWARD MALCOM,
PETER O. THACHER,	FRANCIS PARKMAN,
FRANCIS C GRAY,	ABBOTT LAWRENCE.
EDWARD TUCKERMAN,	

CORRESPONDING MEMBERS.

THOMAS BRADFORD, Jr., *Philadelphia.*	THOMAS PADDOCK, *St. John, N. B.*
JOEL SCOTT, *Frankfort, Kentucky.*	J. M'AULEY, *Toronto, U. C.*
SAMUEL HOARE, *of London.*	M. S. BIDWELL, *New York City.*
DR. JULIUS, *of Hamburgh.*	WM. H. ROCKWELL, *Brattleboro', Vt.*
G. DE BEAUMONT, } *of Paris.*	LUTHER V. BELL, *Charlestown, Mass.*
A. DE TOCQUEVILLE, }	WM. SAM'L JOHNSON, *New York City.*
SAMUEL L. DAVIS, *Augusta, Georgia.*	P. D. VROOM, *Somerville, N. J.*
REUEL WILLIAMS, *Hallowell, Me.*	S. F. M'CRACKEN, } *Columbus, Ohio.*
S. E COUES, *Portsmouth, N. H.*	WM. M. AWL, }
J. C. HOLBROOK, *Brattleboro', Vt.*	W. H. BURTON, } *New South Wales.*
*THOMAS G. LEE, *Charlestown, Mass.*	DR. LANG, }
SAM'L B. WOODWARD, *Worcester, Ms.*	JACOB BEESON, *Niles, Michigan.*

MANAGERS.

R. S. STORRS,	SAMUEL A. ELIOT,
RUFUS ANDERSON,	HENRY HILL,
JAMES MEANS,	SAMUEL LAWRENCE,
DANIEL SAFFORD,	H. M. WILLIS,
JARED CURTIS,	SILAS AIKEN,
DAVID GREEN,	W. M. ROGERS.

CHARLES CLEVELAND, TREASURER.
LOUIS DWIGHT, SECRETARY.

LIFE DIRECTORS,

BY THE PAYMENT OF ONE HUNDRED DOLLARS AND UPWARD.

Albany, N. Y.
*Van Rensselaer, Stephen

Boston.
Appleton, Samuel
Armstrong, Samuel T.
Bussey, Benjamin
*Chamberlain, Richard
*Cobb, Nathaniel R.
Coolidge, Joseph
Dwight, Edmund
Eliot, Samuel A.
Gray, Francis C.
Greenleaf, Jonathan, by a
Homes, Henry   [Friend
Hubbard, Samuel
Jackson, Charles
Jackson, James
Jackson, Patrick T.

Lawrence, Amos
Lowell, Charles
*Lowell, John
Munson, Israel
Parkman, Francis
Phillips, Jonathan
*Phillips, William
Prescott, William
Shattuck, George C.
Shaw, Robert G.
Tappan, John
Ticknor, George
Tuckerman, Edward
Ward, Artemas
Wells, Charles
White, Stephen
Willis, Nathaniel
Dedham, Mass.
Burgess, Ebenezer

Geneva, N. Y.
Dwight, Henry
Norwich, Conn.
Greene, William P.
Peterboro', N. Y.
Smith, Peter
Portsmouth, N. H.
Coues, S. E.
Rochester, N. Y.
*Bissell, Josiah
Salem, Mass.
Peabody, Joseph
Worcester, Mass.
Abbott, J. S. C.
Foster, Alfred Dwight
Salisbury, Stephen
Sweetser, Seth, by 3 sisters
Waldo, Daniel

LIFE MEMBERS,

BY THE PAYMENT OF THIRTY DOLLARS AND UPWARDS.

Albany, N. Y.
Delavan, Edward C.
*Hopkins, Samuel M.
M'Intire, Archibald
Norton, John C.

Andover, Mass.
*Cornelius, Elias
Edwards, Justin
*Porter, Ebenezer
Woods, Leonard

Auburn, N. Y.
Lewis, Levi, by Officers of
the Prison
Seymour, James S.
Smith, B. C., by Officers of
the Prison

Baltimore, Md.
Backus, John A.
M'Kim, W. D.

Bath, N. H.
Sutherland, David, by Ira
Goodale

Bedford, N. Y.
*Jay, John
Jay, William

Beverly.
Oliphant, David

Boston.
Adams, Nehemiah
Amory, John
Beecher, Edward
Beecher, Lyman
Blake, George

*Bowdoin, James
Brooks, Peter C.
Brooks, Peter C., Jr.
Chadwick, Ebenezer
Clapp, Joshua
Cobb, Richard
*Codman, Catharine
Codman, Elizabeth
Codman, Charles R.
Codman, Henry
Cogswell, William
Cushing, John P.
Dana, Nathaniel
Dorr, Samuel
Eckley, David
Edwards, Henry
*Eliot, William H.
Frothingham, N. L.
Gray, Horace
Gray, John C.
*Green, Samuel
*Greene, Gardiner
Greenwood, F. W. P.
Hill, Henry
Homer, George J.
Jones, Anna P.
*Jones, John Coffin
Lawrence, Abbott
Lawrence, Samuel
Lawrence, William
*Lyman, Theodore
Lyman, Theodore, Jr.
Marvin, T. R.
*M'Lean, Ann
Munroe, Edmund
Newhall, Cheever
Otis, Harrison Gray
Parker, Daniel P.
Parker, Ebenezer
Parker, John

Parkman, Francis
Potter, Alonzo
Rand, Asa
Randall, John
Reed, Benjamin T.
Rice, Henry
Ropes, William
Safford, Daniel
Sears, David
Stoddard, Charles
Thorndike, Israel
Vose, Thomas
Wales, Thomas B.
Warren, John C.
Wigglesworth, Thomas
Williams, John D.
Winthrop, Thomas L.
*Wisner, Benjamin B.
Worthington, William

Brooklyn, N. Y.
Carrol, D. L.

Cambridge, Mass.
Donnison, C. L.
Farwell, Levi
Greenleaf, Simon
Holland, Frederic West
Quincy, Josiah

Canandaigua, N. Y.
Eddy, Ansel G.

Catskill, N. Y.
Cooke, Thomas B.
Day, Orrin

Charleston, S. C.
Corning, Jasper

Charlestown, Mass.
Curtis, Jared
Walker, William J., Jr.

Coxackie, N. Y.
Van Dyck, Abraham

Danvers, Mass.
Braman, Milton P.
*Cowles, George
*Oakes, Caleb

Douglass Farm, L. I.
Douglass, George, by the hand of Mrs. Joanna Bethune

Dorchester, Mass.
Codman, John

Edinburgh, Scotland.
Dunlop, John

Fairfield, Conn.
Sherman, Roger M.

Geneva, N. Y.
*Axtell, Henry

Gloucester, Mass.
Jewett, David, by a Lady

Hampton, N. H.
Harris, Roswell

Hartford, Conn.
Hawes, Joel
Spring, Samuel

Haverhill, Mass.
Keeley, George
Phelps, Dudley

Ipswich, Mass.
Kimball, David

Jamaica, L. I.
Crane, Elias W.

Marblehead, Mass.
Hooper, Nathaniel
*Reed, William

Middletown, Conn.
Crane, John B.

Milton, Mass.
*Tucker, Nathaniel

Newark, N. J.
Hamilton, W. T.

Newbury, Mass.
Wright, Henry C.

Newburyport, Mass.
Banister, William B.
Bartlett, William
*Brown, Moses
Dimmick, Luther F.

Proudfit, John
By a donation in books from Charles Whipple, to constitute the following persons Life Members:
Davis, Mary A.
Greenleaf, Mary C.
Hodge, Mary D.
Thompson, Sarah

New Haven, Conn.
Bacon, Leonard
Brewster, James
Fitch, Eleazer T.
Robinson, Charles, by his sister Elizabeth
Salisbury, Abby

New York City.
Adams, William
Allen, Stephen
Astor, John Jacob
Averill, Heman
Bethune, G. W.
Boorman, J.
Brewster, Joseph
Broadhead, Dr.
*Chambers, William
Cox, Samuel H.
Crosby, W. B.
Eastborn, Manton
*Falconer, Archibald
Hedges, Timothy
How, Fisher
Johnson, William Samuel
Lenox, Robert
Mason, Cyrus W.
Mathews, John M.
M'Auley, Thomas
Milnor, James
Patton, William
Perrit, Pelatiah
*Post, Joel
Proudfit, Alexander
Phillips, W. W.
*Rutgers, Henry
Schrœder, J. F.
Shatzel, Jacob
Spring, Gardiner
Starr, Philemon R.
Stephens, J. C.
Tappan, Arthur
*Varick, Richard
Ward, Samuel
Woolsey, William W.

Peterboro', N. Y.
Smith, Gerrit

Portsmouth, N. H.
Coues, Lucy Louisa
Goodwin, Ichabod
Peabody, Andrew P., by Ladies of his Society

Philadelphia, Penn.
Allen, Solomon
Carey, Matthew
Elmes, Thomas

Ely, Ezra Stiles
Henry, Alexander
Livingston, Gilbert R.
Skinner, Thomas H.

Pittsfield, Mass.
Newton, Edward A.

Plymouth, Mass.
Robbins, Josiah

Portland, Me.
Tyler, Bennett
Dwight, William T.

Poughkeepsie, N. Y.
Cuyler, Cornelius

Providence, R. I.
*Ives, Thomas P.
Wayland, Francis

Rahway, N. J.
Squier, Job

Salem, Mass.
Cleveland, J. P.
Emerson, Brown
Phillips, Stephen C.
Williams, William
Worcester, Zervia F.

Schenectady, N. Y.
*Smith, Peter

Springfield, Mass.
Osgood, Samuel

Thomaston, Me.
*Rose, Daniel

Troy, N. Y.
Tucker, Mark

Utica, N. Y.
Lansing, D. C.
Stocking, Samuel
Varick, Abraham

West Haverhill, Mass.
Cross, Abijah

Wethersfield, Conn.
Barrett, Gerrish
Pilsbury, Amos

Williamstown, Mass.
*Griffin, Edward D.

Wiscasset, Me.
Hooker, Edward W.

Worcester, Mass.
Foster, Alfred Dwight
Lincoln, John W.
Waldo, E. S. & R.
Waldo, Daniel
Salisbury, Stephen

TREASURER'S REPORT.

PRISON DISCIPLINE SOCIETY, *in Account with* CHARLES CLEVELAND.

DR.

1841.

Balance from old account, ...	1,449 64½
May 21.—To cash paid for incidental and travelling expenses, ...	290 17
To do. paid Boston Type and Stereotype Foundry, ...	144 43
To do. paid Grant & Daniell, for paper, ...	200 00
To do. paid Abraham Jackson, for office rent, ...	175 00
To do. paid for binding books and use of chapel, ...	88 92
To do. paid agency in Middle, Southern, and Western States, ...	924 93
To do. paid balance of interest account, ...	106 51
To do. paid salary of secretary, ...	1,700 00
	$5,079 60½

CR.

1841.

May 21.—By cash received of the Legislature of Massachusetts, for 500 copies of the Fifteenth Annual Report, ...	125 00
By do. received of the Legislature of New York, for 400 do., ...	100 00
By do. received for one year's dividend on 9 shares in New England Bank stock, purchased with the legacy of the late Nathaniel Tucker, of Milton, ...	54 00
By do. received second dividend on $1,000, legacy of Captain Thomas S. Winslow, by Benjamin P. Winslow, executor, ...	164 38
By do. collected by Rev. G. Barrett, in the Middle, Southern, and Western States, ...	1,218 93
By do. received sundry subscriptions, donations, and contributions, ...	2,292 38
Balance carried to new account, ...	1,124 91½
	$5,079 60½

Permanent Fund, by direction of the late Nathaniel Tucker, of Milton, who gave it as a legacy:—

Nine shares in New England Bank stock, ...	$936 75
Deposit in Tremont Savings Bank, on account of the Society, ...	63 00
Cash, ...	25
	$1,000 00

BOSTON, 22d MAY, 1841.   Errors excepted,

CHARLES CLEVELAND, *Treasurer.*

MAY 21, 1841.—We certify that we have examined the foregoing account, and find the same correctly cast and properly vouched.

JAMES MEANS, } *Auditors.*
H. M. WILLIS, }

SUBSCRIPTIONS AND DONATIONS,

From May 23, 1840, *to May* 25, 1841.

Albany, N. Y.		Amory, Charles	20 00	Channing, Walter	2 00
Cash from a Lady	3 00	Appleton, Samuel	30 00	Chandler, Daniel	2 00
Cobb, Sandford	2 00	Appleton, William	10 00	Chandler, Abiel	2 00
Dale, Wm. A. Tweed	2 00	Armstrong, Samuel T.	20 00	Chickering, J.	5 00
Platt, Ananias	2 00	Appleton, Nathan	10 00	Choate, Rufus	3 00
Wood, Bradford R.	2 00	Amadon, Homes	2 00	Cotton, Joseph	10 00
		Andrews, J. W.	2 00	Cummings, Daniel	2 00
Amsterdam, N. Y.		Atkins, Benj.	2 00	Curtis, T. B.	2 00
Bartlett, Chandler	1 00	Bacon, Daniel C.	3 00	Cushing, T. P.	2 00
Coll. in Pres. Church	7 36	Baker, T.	1 00	Crocker, Uriel	2 00
Dean, J.	1 00	Bates, Stephen	1 00	Colby, J. & G.	4 00
Miller, C.	1 00	Bacon, J. V.	3 00	Callender, G.	3 00
Sandford, J.	1 00	Blanchard, F. H.	1 00	Campbell, J.	1 00
		Bent, Ann	2 00	Callender, W. B.	3 00
Augusta, Ga.		Bates, William	1 00	Chamberlain, N. B.	2 00
Bostwick, Wm.	5 00	Bacon, Joseph V.	3 00	Chase, Th.	5 00
Cash	1 00	Barnes, D. W.	2 00	Chadwick, Eb.	20 00
Cash	1 00	Barnard, Charles	5 00	Chapman, Jon.	20 00
Cash	3 00	Barnes, S. H.	2 00	Cleveland, Charles	2 00
Cash	2 00	Bancroft, Jacob	2 00	Coolidge, Thos. B.	10 00
Cash	5 00	B. A. E.	5 00	Coleman, H.	1 00
Cash	3 00	Bird, S. J.	2 00	Cushing, J. P.	20 00
Cash	2 00	Blagden, George W.	2 00	Choate, Rufus	3 00
Cash	2 00	Blanchard, Joshua	2 00	Cash	1 00
Dearing, Wm. E.	2 00	Bond, Wm.	2 00	Cash	1 00
Haines, Wm., Jun.	3 00	Bowditch, N. I.	5 00	Cash, N. D.	5 00
Riley, H. W.	3 00	Brewer, W. A.	2 00	Cash	1 00
Richmond, H. A.	2 00	Brewer, Nathaniel	2 00	Cash	1 00
Scranton, J. H.	3 00	Brewer, Samuel N.	2 00	Cash	1 00
Scranton, P. A.	2 00	Brown, Charles	2 00	Cash, A. E. B.	5 00
Woodbury, Wm., Jun.	2 00	Briggs, Billings	5 00	Danforth, Samuel A.	2 00
		Boardman, Wm. H.	5 00	Dana, Ephraim	2 00
Binghampton, N. Y.		Brooks, Edward	10 00	Dana, Nathaniel	5 00
Gregory, Henry	5 00	Brooks, Peter C.	20 00	Daniell, Otis	2 00
Hall, S. H. P.	3 00	Bumstead, John	5 00	Davis, Samuel	2 00
McKenney, Charles	2 00	Bumstead, Josiah	6 00	Dearborn, Nathaniel	2 00
Murdock, Cary	2 00	Bumstead, Josiah F.	5 00	Denny, Daniel	2 00
Pearce, H.	2 00	Butler, Dr. J. S.	5 00	Devens, Richard	2 00
Pope & Tucker	2 00	Burgess, Benj., & Sons	5 00	Doane, John	2 00
Stevens, U. C.	3 00	Bird, Wm.	2 00	Dorr, Samuel	10 00
Thorp, Curtis	2 00	Boyden, A.	1 00	Dwight, Edmund	20 00
Whiting, M., Jun.	1 00	Babcock, S. H.	3 00	Darracott, George	2 00
		Ballister, J.	2 00	Dodge, W. A.	2 00
Boston, Mass.		Balch, Joseph	2 00	D. P. L.	2 00
Abbot, S. L.	2 00	Bird, F. W.	1 00	Dana, Luther	2 00
Adams, Charles B. L.	1 00	Bradford, J.	2 00	Danforth, Samuel A.	2 00
Adams, Abel	5 00	Baker, Joseph	3 00	Davis, James	20 00
Adams, Chester	2 00	Ballard, Joseph	3 00	Doane, George B.	5 00
Adams, James	2 00	Bartol, C. A.	10 00	Doane, H. S.	2 00
Adams, Wm.	2 00	Beal, Samuel	2 00	Dole & Hallet	2 00
Adan, John R.	5 00	Blake, G. B.	5 00	Eaton, John	2 00
Aiken, Silas	3 00	Brewer, Geo. A.	2 00	Edmands, J. W.	5 00
Allen, F.	2 00	Bradley, Abm.	2 00	Everetts, Moses	2 00
Almy, Patterson, & Co.	5 00	Bradley, Benj.	2 00	Eustis, W. T.	2 00
Anderson, Rufus	2 00	Brown, Charles	5 00	Everett, Edward	5 00
Alger, Cyrus, & Co.	5 00	Brooks, P. C., Jun.	30 00	Eliot, Samuel A.	50 00
Amory, Wm.	5 00	Brinley, Edward	3 00	Eckley, David	30 00
Andrews, Eben. T.	2 00	Carlton, Wm.	2 00	Foster, James H.	4 00
Andrews, W. T.	2 00	Capen, Nahum	2 00	Fairbanks, Stephen	2 00

Fearing, Albert	2 00	Hooper, Robert, Jun.	5 00	Manning, Chs.	2 00
Francis, David	2 00	Howard, Abram	2 00	Mann, Horace	2 00
Friend, J. C. P.	20 00	Horton, H. K.	2 00	Macomber, I.	5 00
Faxon, George N.	2 00	Holbrook, Ed.	1 00	Meriam, S. P.	2 00
Fearing, A. C.	2 00	Huse, Joseph	5 00	Minot, Wm.	5 00
Fisk, E. P.	2 00	Humphrey, Wm.	2 00	Merrill, James C.	3 00
French, Jonathan	5 00	Ingersoll, James	5 00	Munson, Israel	20 00
Friend, L. B.	10 00	Inches, Misses	5 00	McBurney, Chs.	2 00
Friend	5 00	Inches, Henderson	5 00	Mayer, P. S.	2 00
Forbush	5 00	Inches, Henderson, Jun.	2 00	Morse, R. M.	1 00
Friend	1 00	Jackson, Charles	20 00	Manning, I. C.	1 00
Friend	3 00	Jackson, Ward	2 00	Moore, Thomas	1 00
Friend	3 00	Johnson, Samuel	2 00	Newman, Henry	2 00
Gay, P. E.	2 00	Jacobs, Benj.	1 00	Newhall, Cheever	32 00
Gilbert, Samuel	2 00	Johnson, W. P.	2 00	New York State for Re-	
Gilbert, Timothy	2 00	Jones, G. B.	2 00	ports, by Act of the	
Gilbert, Lemuel	2 00	Jones, Eliphalet	2 00	Legislature	100 00
Gordon, G. W.	2 00	Keep, I. C.	3 00	Newhall, Cheever	32 00
Gray, Frederick T.	2 00	Keep, N. C.	3 00	Newhall, George	2 00
Grant, Moses	2 00	Kendall, A.	2 00	Newhall, E. F.	1 00
Greene, Charles G.	2 00	Kittredge, Alvah	2 00	Nicholls, L. W.	1 00
Grosvenor, L. P.	2 00	Kuhn, George	5 00	Oakes, James	2 00
Gurney, Nathan	2 00	Kimball, Jewett, & Co.	10 00	Osgood, Isaac	2 00
Greene, David	3 00	Kendall, G. A.	2 00	Otis, H. G.	20 00
Greene, B. D.	5 00	Kimball, John	1 00	Parkman, Francis	10 00
Gray, John C.	20 00	Kimball, David	2 00	Paige, J. W.	2 00
Gray, Francis C.	30 00	Lincoln, R. B.	1 00	Parker, M. S.	2 00
Grant & Daniell	10 00	Lincoln, Wm.	1 00	Phelps, Sewell	2 00
Gardner, John D.	2 00	Lawrence, Amos	20 00	Porter, Royal L.	2 00
Gage, J.	5 00	Lawrence, William	10 00	Perkins, Thomas H., Jr.	5 00
Gardner, S. P.	5 00	Leach, James	2 00	Parker, Isaac	3 00
Gardner, John L.	5 00	Lothrop, Samuel K.	2 00	Parker, John	4 00
Gilbert, John	1 00	Leland, Sherman	2 00	P. O., Mrs.	2 00
Gassett, Henry	10 00	Little, Charles C.	2 00	Parker, James	5 00
Gray, Horace	20 00	Lincoln, Heman	2 00	Perkins, Thomas H.	25 00
Goodwin, Ozias	25 00	Lobdell, Thomas J.	2 00	Pratt, George	5 00
Greenleaf, Samuel	5 00	Lombard, A. C.	2 00	Prescott, William	20 00
Gove, Watson	2 00	Loring, C. G.	2 00	Parkman, George	2 50
Glover, Henry R	2 00	Loring, Henry	2 00	Palmer, Simeon	2 00
Gray, George H.	2 00	Low, J. J.	2 00	Parker, Isaac	5 00
Greele, P., Jun.	3 00	Low, Francis	2 00	Park, Luther	3 00
Harrington, A.	2 00	Lowell, John A.	10 00	Perrin, A.	5 00
Hicks, James H.	2 00	Lyman, Theodore	50 00	Perkins, Mrs. J.	5 00
Harvey, Peter	5 00	Lyman, George W.	10 00	Peters, E. D.	5 00
Hale, Moses L.	2 00	Lampson, Edwin	3 00	Phelps, Abel	5 00
Hayden, J. C.	2 00	Langdon, J. W.	2 00	Pond, Moses	2 00
Hallet, George	5 00	Lamb, Thomas	5 00	Phipps, W. & S.	2 00
Hersey, Cornelius	2 00	Lawrence, Samuel	20 00	Phillips, Willard	2 00
Hill, Henry	3 00	Lawrence, Abbott	20 00	Putnam, A.	2 00
Hill, Jeremiah	2 00	Leeds, La Fayette	2 00	Quincy, Josiah, Jr.	10 00
Hill, Jeremiah	2 00	Lewis, Winslow, Jun.	2 00	Rhoades, A. H.	1 00
Howe, S. G.	2 00	Livermore, Isaac, & Co.	5 00	Rhoades, Eb.	2 00
Howard, Benjamin	2 00	Lincoln, M. S.	5 00	Reports	50
How, Hall J.	2 00	Lowell, F. C.	5 00	Reports	50
Howe, J. C.	2 00	Loring, Elijah	5 00	Reports	1 00
Hubbard, Wm. J.	2 00	Loring, James	2 00	Reed, Benjamin T.	5 00
Homes & Homer	10 00	Long, E. J.	2 00	Rice & Thaxter	5 00
Hurd, John	5 00	Lyford, G. C.	2 00	Rice, John P.	5 00
Hilliard, Gray, & Co.	5 00	Massachusetts, By or-		Robbins, Charles	2 00
Hayden, George	1 00	der of the Legisla-		Rogers, J. G.	2 00
Hay, Joseph	2 00	ture, for 500 copies of		Rogers, W. A.	2 00
Haven, Calvin	3 00	the 15th Report, by		Rogers, W. M.	2 00
Haywood & Norton	2 00	the hand of J. P.		Ropes, Hardy	2 00
Hall, Henry	2 00	Bigelow	125 00	Read, J.	3 00
Hall, J. P., Jun.	2 00	Melledge, James	2 00	Rice, J. P.	3 00
Haughton, J.	2 00	Mellen, Moses	2 00	Raymond, Emmons	3 00
Hall, A. T.	3 00	Means, James	2 00	Raymond, Z. L.	2 00
Hallet, George	5 00	Metcalf, Nathan	2 00	Reed, G. P.	1 00
Hawes, Gray, & Co.	5 00	Mills, J. K.	10 00	Reed, James	2 00
Hovey, G. O.	2 00	Morse, R. M.	1 00	Richardson, Charles	2 00

Richardson,G.B.,& Co.	2 00	
Robbins, E. H.	2 00	
Rogers, John H.	2 00	
Rogers, John Gray	2 00	
Safford, Daniel	10 00	
Safford, Henry	2 00	
Salisbury, Samuel	2 00	
Stimpson, M. H.	5 00	
Stevenson, Wm.	2 00	
Scudder, Charles	2 00	
Stimpson, F. H.	2 00	
Stimpson, W. C.	2 00	
Stodder, R. H.	2 00	
Stone, J. S.	2 00	
Sumner, Bradford	2 00	
Swett, Samuel	2 00	
Stone, Wm. W.	5 00	
Simonds, Artemas		
Sigourney, Henry	10 00	
Shaw, Robert G.	30 00	
Stoddard, Charles	6 00	
Shimmin, Wm.	2 00	
Shorey, Jno.	2 00	
Shurtleff, Benj.	3 00	
Slocumb, Thomas	3 00	
Sears, Willard	2 00	
Sargent, B.	2 00	
Searle & Upham	5 00	
Skinner, Francis	5 00	
Shaw, Blake, & Co.	5 00	
Sprague, Phineas	5 00	
Sullivan, John	2 00	
Sullivan, Richard	20 00	
Shipley, S. G.	2 00	
Southwick, J.	2 00	
Smyth, Henry	2 00	
Storer, R. B.	2 00	
Steele, Robert	2 00	
Stone, S. S.	1 00	
Tilden, Joseph	2 00	
Tarbell, Thomas	2 00	
Tenney, Samuel	2 00	
Ticknor, George	10 00	
Townsend, H. B.	2 00	
Twombly, Alex. H	2 00	
Train, Samuel	10 00	
Train, Enoch	5 00	
Tappan, Lewis W.	3 00	
Tappan, S.	2 00	
Tolman, Josh. A.	2 00	
Timmens, Henry	5 00	
Tucker, J. L.	5 00	
Trott, George	5 00	
Train, Samuel F.	2 00	
Tufts, James	2 00	
Thatcher, Peter	2 00	
Thayer, B. W.	2 00	
Upham, Henry	2 00	
Upham, Phinehas	10 00	
Van Wart, W.	5 00	
Warren, John C.	10 00	
Wells, Charles A.	2 00	
Wetmore, Thomas	10 00	
White, Joseph	2 00	
Wigglesworth, Edward	2 00	
Wigglesworth, Thomas	5 00	
Williams, Timothy	2 00	
Woodcock, Joseph	2 00	
Waterston, Robert	2 00	
Whittemore, George	2 00	
White, Charles	3 00	

Whitney, Paul	5 00	
Wolcott, J. H.	5 00	
Willis, Nathaniel	50 00	
Warren, Charles	2 00	
Ware, John	5 00	
Welles, John	5 00	
Williams, Moses	5 00	
White, F. E.	5 00	
Wheelwright, Lot	5 00	
Wilder, David	5 00	
Wells, John B.	2 00	
Wellington, Alfred A.	2 00	
Weld, W. F.	2 00	
Welch, Francis	3 00	
Winslow, Thomas S., 2d dividend on $1000 legacy, by B.P.Winslow, executor	164 38	

Cambridge, Mass.

Bigelow, Benjamin	5 00	
Farwell, Levi	20 00	
Norton, Andrews	10 00	
Palfrey, J. G.	2 00	
Valentine, Chas.	10 00	
Ware, Henry, Jun.	2 00	
Worcester, J. E.	2 00	

Charleston, S. C.

Adger, Wm.	5 00	
Beach, E. M.	5 00	
Bingley, C. W.	2 00	
Boinest, D.	5 00	
Burkmyer, I. C.	5 00	
Caldwell, J. M.	5 00	
Cash	2 00	
Cash	50	
Cash	2 00	
Cash	1 00	
Cash	3 00	
Cash	1 00	
Cash	5 00	
Cash	5 00	
Cash	2 00	
Cash	2 00	
Cash	2 00	
Cash	5 00	
Cash	5 00	
Chasal, P. A.	2 00	
Harwood, W. B.	5 00	
Howland, Wm.	10 00	
Huger. Mrs.	2 00	
L. L. B.	5 00	
Maies, L.	2 00	
Nelling, J. W.	2 00	
Smith & Boice,	3 00	
Smith, Thos., Rev.	5 00	
Snowden, M. E.	2 00	
Stephens. S. N.	5 00	
Stoddard, H.	2 00	
Watson, L.	2 00	

Charlestown, Mass.

Abbot, Samuel	2 00	
Abbot, William	2 00	
Bell, Luther V.	20 00	
Crosby, Daniel	2 00	
Flint, Simeon	2 00	
Frothingham, H. K.	2 00	
Goodhue, Homer	2 00	
Hunt, Enoch	2 00	

Lawrence, Edward	2 00	
Lincoln, Charles	5 00	
M'Intire, E. M. P.	2 00	
Skelton, Edward	2 00	
Skelton, Matthew	2 00	
Skelton, George	2 00	
Tyler, Columbus	2 00	
Tufts, Amos	2 00	

Cincinnati, Ohio.

Alpha, J.	2 00	
Allen, M.	2 00	
Bishop, S. P.	2 00	
Bowles, R. B., & Co.	2 00	
Cash	1 00	
Cash	1 00	
Cash	1 00	
Cash	1 00	
Cash	1 00	
Cash	1 00	
Brown, A. O.	1 00	
Clark, H.	2 00	
Cousin, D.	2 00	
Cash	2 00	
Cash	2 00	
Chase, S. P.	2 00	
Cooper, W. U.	2 00	
Goodman, Wm.	2 00	
Ellis, R.	2 00	
Cash	2 00	
Duffield, Charles	2 00	
Fisher, Charles	2 00	
Findlay, S. B.	2 00	
Fosdick, Samuel	2 00	
Gage, Edmond	2 00	
Harries, E. S.	2 00	
Hewson, B. W.	2 00	
Iglehart, N. P.	2 00	
Lange, P.	2 00	
Lucas, E.	2 00	
Luckey & Co.	2 00	
Lee, R. W.	2 00	
Manser, William	2 00	
Miller & Johnson	2 00	
Mathewson, B.	2 00	
Mitchell, R. G.	2 00	
Ogden, J. K.	2 00	
Phillips & Heaton	2 00	
Reeves, J., & Co.	2 00	
Reynolds, James	2 00	
Starr, Henry	2 00	
Smith, Joseph	2 00	
Shiletto, John	2 00	
Sheneberger, J. K.	2 00	
Thorp, John D.	1 00	
Thomas, N. W.	2 00	
Wayne, J. S.	2 00	
Whiteman, L.	2 00	
Woodworth, W., & Co.	2 00	
Yeatman, T. W.	1 00	
Yeatman, S. O.	2 00	

Courtlandville, N. Y.

Barbor, Paris	2 00	
Barbour, J.	2 00	
Boies, Rufus	1 50	
Blackfield, W.	50	
Cash	1 50	
Donnelly, Mrs.	50	
Elder, William	2 00	
Hitchcock, S. D.	1 00	

Hitchcock, Neal	2 00	Ormsby, Hite, & Co.	2 00	Du Bace, J. C.	2 00
Hobart, G.	1 00	Richardson, Wm.	5 00	Elliot, Robbins	3 00
Hubbard, Lyman	1 00	Read, T. I.	2 00	Elslava, M. D.	2 00
Lockwood, Peter	2 00	Russell, Sam'l	2 00	Friend	2 00
Munger, E.	1 00	Sample. A. B.	2 00	Gilbert, C. A.	3 00
Platt, Dennis	2 00	Smith, G. W.	1 00	Graham, T.	3 00
Smith, Noah	1 00	Wilson, J. E.	2 00	Green, S. S.	2 00
Sherman, S.	1 00			H. R.	2 00
Stevens, Henry	2 00	*Lyons, N. Y.*		Hatter, W. P.	2 00
Walrad, Peter	2 00	Taft, Howell	1 00	Johnson, W.	2 00
Woodworth, S. B.	2 00			H. J.	2 00
		Marion, Ga.		Lovely, S. J. G.	2 00
Dorchester, Mass.		Baldwin & Brothers	2 00	Lowber, D. C.	3 00
Codman, John	20 00	Bond, E.	3 00	Miller & Tomlinson	2 00
		Butler, D. B.	2 00	McZlen, W. L.	2 00
Fairfield, Conn.		Cash	1 00	Powers, W. L.	3 00
Sherman, Roger M.	30 00	Cash	50	R. S. H.	2 00
		Cash	2 00	Rassalye, G.	2 00
Fayetteville, N. C.		Cash	2 00	Reid, John, Jun.	2 00
Cash	1 00	Campbell, D. C.	2 00	Robbins, H. W.	2 00
Cash	1 00	Campbell, Charles	2 00	Russell, J. Y.	5 00
Colton, Simeon	2 00	Cowles, J.	3 00	Shaw, F., & Co.	3 00
Martine, James	2 00	Dickinson, S.	2 00	Shepherd, J. F.	2 00
McArn, John	2 00	Ellis, W. S.	2 00	Smith, W. A.	5 00
Ray, D. A.	1 00	Graves, E. & R. R.	5 00	Stewart, Wm.	2 00
		Griffin, B. J.	2 00	Tastleton, G. W.	5 00
Green, N. Y.		Herrett, E.	2 00	Vanhook. M. A.	2 00
Lott, Adrian	2 00	Logan, G. M.	2 00	W. S.	3 00
		Ray	2 00	Walker, D. L.	3 00
Hartford, Conn.		Stow, J. B.	5 00		
Morgan, H. N.	2 00	Weed, E. B.	5 00	*Nashville, Tenn.*	
				Anderson, H. J.	10 00
Ithaca, N. Y.		*Memphis, Tenn.*		Cash	2 00
Andrews, W.	2 00	Atkinson, J. C.	3 00	Cash	2 00
Bates, Daniel	2 00	Brook, J.	1 00	Cash	2 00
Camp, F. N.	2 00	Cash	3 00	Cash	2 00
Cash	2 00	Cooper, James	2 00	Cash	2 00
Esty, Joseph	2 00	Foulker	2 00	Cash	2 00
Hardy, Mrs. C.	2 00	Gwinn, Tho's., & Co.	2 00	Connor, C.	2 00
Luce, W. P.	1 00	Lofland, Charles	2 00	Eakin, W. & T.	2 00
Miller, Mrs. Sarah	2 00	McCoul, Neal	2 00	Fisher, P. W.	2 00
Sayles, H.	2 00	Nelson & Titus	2 00	Hamilton, James	2 00
Stevens, John	2 00	Robbins & Lucas	2 00	McNair, N. A.	2 00
Therrill, Augustus	2 00	Walker, R. L.	2 00	Morgan, Allen, & Co.	2 00
Williams, N. T.	2 00	White, Waldron, & Co.	2 00		
Williams, S. P.	2 00	Winchester, M. B.	2 00	*Natchez, Miss.*	
		Webb, Thomas	2 00	Baldwin, H. M.	1 00
Jackson, Miss.				Butler, W. A.	2 00
Hart, C. M.	5 00	*Milton, Mass.*		Butler, John T.	2 00
		Tucker, Nathaniel, de-		Cash	2 00
Johnstown, N. Y.		ceased, semi-annual		Cash	5 00
Collection in Presbyteri-		dividend on 9 shares		Collins, James	2 00
an Church	5 29	of New England Bank		Ernest, P.	2 00
		stock, purchased with		Ferriday, H. C.	5 00
Little Falls, N. Y.		his legacy of $1000	27 00	Fox, G. W.	2 00
Burch, Thomas	2 00	Do. do half		Gaines, R. M.	5 00
		year's dividend	27 00	Henry, W. K.	2 00
Louisville, Ky.				Holmes, F. C.	2 00
Bowles, Joshua B.	2 00	*Mobile, Ala.*		Kerr, John	2 00
Cash	2 00	Austin, H.	3 00	Lacosta, C. A.	2 00
Cash	2 00	Bigelow, I.	2 00	Lambson, S. H.	2 00
Cobb, D.	2 00	Bull, M.	2 00	Loria, Jacob	2 00
Cassady, S.	2 00	Burdsall, Richard	2 00	Merrill, A. P.	5 00
Chambers, J. S.	2 00	C. M.	2 00	McAllister, Wm.	2 00
Chentworth, J. S., & Co.	2 00	Cash	3 00	McAllister, S.	5 00
Danforth, J.	2 00	Cash	2 00	Montgomery, Alex.	5 00
Davis, B. O.	2 00	Cash	2 00	Newman. S. B.	2 00
Davis, Nathaniel	2 00	Cash from several	24 00	Tooley, H.	5 00
Fellows, W.	2 00	Cleveland, George, Jr.	5 00	Watson, H. R.	5 00
Lemon & Kendrick	2 00	D. L. B.	2 00	Waters, L.	5 00
McGinnes, E. G.	2 00	Davenport, G.	2 00	Winchester, George	5 00

Newark, N. J.

Baldwin, Isaac	2	00
McNet, C. S.	1	00
Whitehead, Asa	1	00

New Brunswick, N. J.

Stout, J. W.	2	00

Newburyport, Mass.

Contribution	17	38

New Orleans.

Cash	3	00
Cash	2	00
Cash	3	00
Cash	1	00
Cash	1	00
Franklin, S.	2	00
Gardiner, C.	2	00
Hatch, T.	5	00
Maybin, J.	5	00
Thayer, N.	2	00

Norwich, N. Y.

Bellows, Daniel C.	1	00

Owego, N. Y.

Donations	2	50
Platt, H.	1	00
Platt, Wm.	2	00
Pompelly, Wm.	2	00
Taylor, D.	2	00
Wright, S.	2	00

Oxford, N. Y.

Baldwin, Rufus	1	00
Burtis, Arthur	2	00
Coll. in Presb. Church	5	14
Hatch, John		50
Mygett, Wm.	1	00
Wilcox, Ira	3	00

Palmyra, N. Y.

Fenton, I. J.	2	00
Handy, P. W.	1	00
Hotchkiss, D.	1	00
Jessup, George	2	00

Peterborough, N. Y.

Smith Gerrit,	10	00

Petersburgh, Va.

Booth, R. H.	1	00
Cash	2	00
Cash	2	00
Cash	3	00
Cash	1	00
Cash	1	00
D. & D.	4	00
Donnar, D.	1	00
Dunlop, D.	4	00
Higginbottom	2	00
Jones, G. H.	3	00
Haldenby, A.	1	00
Meters, H. W.	2	00
Pierce, J.	2	00
Taliafero, R. H.	2	00
Winfree, W.	2	00

Philadelphia.

Demnic, Charles R.	2	00

Portland, Me.

Cross, Nathaniel	10	00

Poughkeepsie, N. Y.

Collection in Congregational Church	6	83

Richmond, Va.

Cash	2	00
Davenport, Isaac	2	00
Devereaux, P.	1	00
Dilzell & Colquiet	3	00
Dunlop, Moneure, & Co.	5	00
Fogg, J. P.	1	00
Gardiner, J. H.	2	00
Gill, Joseph	2	00
Hubbard, W. H.	2	00
Keen, Geo. A. & Co.	2	00
Kent, Kendall, & Co.	5	00
McFarland, W. A.	5	00
Myers, S. S., & Co.	6	00
Reeve, J.	1	00
Reed, Roberts, & Co.	5	00
Sizer, James	2	00
Thompson, John	2	00
Webb, Lewis	5	00
Wellen, D.	2	00

Rochester, N. Y.

Alling, Wm.	2	00
Avery, George A.	1	00
Cash	2	00
Cheeney, M. H.	2	00
Cole, D.	1	00
Ely, E.	1	00
Fenn, H. N.	1	00
Garbutt, S.	2	00
Graves. S.	1	00
Hall, F. F.	2	00
Hoyt, D.	1	00
Haight, I. M.	2	00
Nottingham & Redding	2	00
Peck, E.	2	00
Scranton, E.	1	00
Smith, E. F.	5	00
Shepherd & Strong	2	00
Ward, L.	10	00

Salem, Mass.

Contribution	14	50
Dodge, Mrs. Pickering	10	00
Peabody, Joseph	50	00
Phillips, S. C.	50	00
Pickman, D. L.	10	00
White, D. A.	10	00

Savannah, Ga.

Barstow, J.	2	00
Bayard, J. W.	2	00
Cash	2	00
Cash	2	00
Cash	2	00
Cash	2	00
Cash	5	00
Cash	3	00

Cash	1	00
Cash	1	00
Cash	1	00
Cash	2	00
Cash	10	00
Cash	2	00
Cash	2	00
Cash	2	00
Cash	2	00
Cash	5	00
Cummings, Joseph	3	00
Huntington, A.	2	00
Ives, J.	2	00
Jones, G. W	2	00
Laman, George B.	10	00
Lewis, G. A.	5	00
Lewis, John	5	00
Mallery, John	5	00
Paddleford, Ed.	5	00
Ponce, F. J.	2	00
Wallace, R. C.	2	00
Wead, A. B. & H.	5	00
Withington, E.	2	00
Woodbridge	2	00

St. Louis, Mo.

Adams, A.	2	00
Alleyne,	2	00
Bacon, H. D.	2	00
Bacon, S. J.	2	00
Blow, J.	2	00
Burnet, Isaac	2	00
Cash	2	00
Cash	1	00
Cash	2	00
Cash	2	00
Cash	1	00
Cash	1	00
Cash	1	00
Cash	1	50
Cash	2	00
Cash	1	50
Cash	2	00
Cash	1	00
Cash	2	00
Cash	2	00
Cash	2	00
Cash	1	00
Cash	2	00
Cash	1	00
Cash	1	00
Cash	3	00
Cash	2	00
Camden, John B.	2	00
Child, A.	1	00
Clapp, B.	2	00
Davis, H. N.	1	00
Davis, S. C.	2	00
Ganngle	2	00
Hackner, H. L.	2	00
Kerr, John	5	00
Lee, J.	1	00
Lockwood, J.	2	00
Lynch, W. A.	2	00
McGill, H. L.	2	00
Melody, George	2	00
Mott, J. H.	2	00
Powell, Joseph	5	00

Pratt, Bernard	2 00	Davenport, H. V., & Co.	2 00	Goodwin, Samuel	1 00
Ray, Isaiah	1 00	Doland, E.	2 00	Sundry Contributions	2 25
Risley, W.	1 00	E. M.	2 00		
Semple, C.	2 00	Gilmore, J. Q.	2 00	*Wheeling, Va.*	
Simonds, John	5 00	Hall, N. A.	2 00	Boyd, Robert	2 00
Stagg, John	3 00	Hardison, Mr.	2 00	Brown, H. D.	2 00
Wilson, S. K.	2 00	Harrison, J.	2 00	Chapline, J.	1 00
		Harper & Dickinson	2 00	Crangle, Robert	2 00
Utica, N. Y.		Hay, Wm.	2 00	Cutberton, Thomas	2 00
Aylesworth, S.	1 00	Jones & Vaill	2 00	Drakely, Thos.	2 00
Butter, H.	2 00	Kyle, John	2 00	Fisher, John	2 00
Faxton, I. V.	2 00	Limerick, T.	2 00	Jacob, Z.	2 00
Johnson, A. B.	2 00	Markham, George	2 00	Knott, John	2 00
Sherman, W. H.	2 00	McDowell, J. R.	2 00	List, J.	2 00
Walker, T.	1 00	Palmer, Job	2 00	Lowther, S.	2 00
		Pearce, J. & A.	2 00	Ott, Samuel	2 00
Vicksburgh, Miss.		Scott, T. S.	2 00	Senseney, J.	2 00
Aiken & Gwinn	2 00	Smith, J. S.	2 00	Thompson, G. W.	2 00
Aimes, W. R.	2 00	Stinson & Wells	2 00	*Winthrop, Me.*	
Ball, G. W.	2 00	Taylor, E. H.	2 00	Thurston, J., and others	2 00
Cash	2 00				
Clark, J. S.	2 00	*Waterville, N. Y.*		*Worcester, Mass.*	
Collins, J. T.	2 00	Bacon, Josiah	1 00	Waldo, Daniel	60 00
Cox, Prichard, & Co.	2 00	Bacon, Reuben	1 00	Salisbury, Stephen	50 00

SEVENTEENTH

ANNUAL REPORT

OF THE

BOARD OF MANAGERS

OF THE

PRISON DISCIPLINE SOCIETY,

BOSTON, MAY, 1842.

Boston:

PUBLISHED AT THE SOCIETY'S ROOMS,

51 Court Street.

STEREOTYPED AT THE
BOSTON TYPE AND STEREOTYPE FOUNDERY.

1842.

CONTENTS.

CONSTITUTION

OF THE

Prison Discipline Society.

———◆———

ARTICLE 1. This Society shall be called the PRISON DISCIPLINE SOCIETY.

ART. 2. It shall be the *object* of this Society to promote the improvement of Public Prisons.

ART. 3. It shall be the *duty* of this Society to take measures for effecting the formation of one or more Prison Discipline Societies in each of the United States, and to co-operate with all such Societies in accomplishing the object specified in the second article of this Constitution.

ART. 4. Any Society, having the same object in view, which shall become auxiliary to this, and shall contribute to its funds, shall thereby secure for the Prisons, in the State where such Society is located, special attention from this Society.

ART. 5. Each subscriber of two dollars, annually, shall be a Member.

ART. 6. Each subscriber of thirty dollars, at one time, shall be a Member for Life.

ART. 7. Each subscriber of ten dollars, annually, shall be a Director.

ART. 8. Each subscriber of one hundred dollars, or who shall by one additional payment increase his original subscription to one hundred dollars, shall be a Director for Life.

ART. 9. The officers of this Society shall be a President, as many Vice-Presidents as shall be deemed expedient, a Treasurer, and a Secretary, to be chosen annually, and a Board of Managers, whose duty it shall be to conduct the business of the Society. This Board shall consist of six clergymen and six laymen, of whom nine shall reside in the city of Boston, and five shall constitute a quorum.

Every Minister of the Gospel, who is a member of this Society, shall be entitled to meet and deliberate with the Board of Managers.

The Managers shall call special meetings of the Society, and fill such vacancies as may occur by death or otherwise, in their own Board.

ART. 10. The President, Vice-Presidents, Treasurer, and Secretary, shall be, ex officio, Members of the Board of Managers.

ART. 11. Directors shall be entitled to meet and vote at all meetings of the Board of Managers.

ART. 12. The annual meetings of this Society shall be held in Boston, on the week of the General Election, when, besides choosing the officers as specified in the ninth article, the accounts of the Treasurer shall be presented, and the proceedings of the foregoing year reported.

ART. 13. The Managers shall meet at such time and place, in the city of Boston, as they shall appoint.

ART. 14. At the meetings of the Society, and of the Managers, the President, or, in his absence, the Vice-President first on the list then present, and in the absence of the President and of all the Vice-Presidents, such Member as shall be appointed for that purpose, shall preside.

ART. 15. The Secretary, in concurrence with two of the Managers, or, in the absence of the Secretary, any three of the Managers, may call special meetings of the Board.

ART. 16. The minutes of every meeting shall be signed by the Chairman or Secretary.

ART. 17. The Managers shall have the power of appointing such persons as have rendered essential services to the Society either Members for Life or Directors for Life.

ART. 18. No alteration shall be made in this Constitution except by the Society, at an annual meeting, on the recommendation of the Board of Managers.

ANNUAL MEETING.

THE Seventeenth Annual Meeting of the Prison Discipline Society having been notified, according to law, at least seven days before, was held in Park Street Vestry on Monday, May 23, 1842, at 3 o'clock. The Rev. Dr. JENKS, being the oldest Vice-President then present, took the chair, and, a quorum being present, opened the meeting with prayer. The Secretary read the minutes of the corresponding meeting of the last year. The Treasurer read his Report, and the certificate of the Auditors, HENRY HILL, Esq., and JAMES MEANS, Esq., which Report was accepted. Mr. DANIEL SAFFORD was appointed a committee to distribute, collect, and sort the votes for the officers of the coming year. All the officers of the previous year were reëlected, except Rev. RUFUS ANDERSON, D. D., and Rev. WM. M. ROGERS, who declined reelection on the ground that numerous other avocations had prevented them from attending the meetings of the Board. In their places the Rev. SAMUEL K. LOTHROP and Rev. GORHAM D. ABBOTT were elected as members of the Board of Managers. The following gentlemen were elected Directors, in consideration of important services rendered: — Hon. JOHN R. ADAN, GEORGE B. EMERSON, Esq., and Rev. JACOB ABBOTT.

A vote of thanks was passed to the Rev. CHARLES CLEVELAND for his faithful and gratuitous services as Treasurer another year.

It was then voted to adjourn, after prayer, to meet in the Park Street Church on Tuesday morning, May 24, at 11 o'clock, to hear the Report and addresses. The meeting was closed with prayer by the Rev. GORHAM D. ABBOTT.

The Public Meeting was held, according to adjournment, in Park Street Church, on Tuesday morning, May 24, 1842, at 11 o'clock, A. M. The President of the Society, the Hon. SAMUEL T. ARMSTRONG, took the chair, and, at his request, the Rev. SILAS AIKEN opened the meeting by reading the 35th chapter of Isaiah, and by prayer. " The wilderness and the solitary place shall be glad for them ; and the desert shall rejoice, and blossom as the rose." The Rev. CHARLES CLEVELAND read the Treasurer's Report. The Secretary read an abstract of the Seventeenth Annual Report.

The Rev. GEORGE ALLEN, chaplain of the State Hospital at Worcester, offered the resolution for the acceptance of the Report. Dr. WALTER CHANNING seconded the resolution, and Rev. ANSEL D. EDDY, of New Jersey, still further sustained it. These gentlemen all addressed the meeting in a most encouraging manner.

The Rev. GORHAM D. ABBOTT offered the second resolution, which was seconded by the Rev. Mr. KIRK: —

Resolved, That this institution, whose object it emphatically is, to bring relief and consolation to suffering humanity; to instruct the ignorant; to reclaim the vicious; to bring the guilty to repentance, and all the blessings of mercy and peace to the condemned and lost, — has a peculiar claim upon every professed disciple of the Savior of the world.

These gentlemen, also, both addressed the meeting in such a manner that, on the whole, it was considered one of the most encouraging anniversary meetings which the Society had ever held.

ANNUAL REPORT.

WITH gratitude to God for his mercies, and earnest prayer, in the name of our Lord and Savior Jesus Christ, for the out-pouring of his holy spirit on all Prisons, and on all the Insane Poor, whether remaining in Prison, or already removed to suitable Asylums, the managers of the Prison Discipline Society present their Seventeenth Annual Report.

"Blessed is he that considereth the poor : the Lord will preserve him, and keep him *alive.*" In looking over the large list of principal friends and benefactors of the Society, we notice the death of but *two,* during the last year. It is a source of grateful feeling, that so large a proportion of our friends have been kept *alive.*

Among those, however, who have been benefited by the Society's labors, we have lost a friend, in the person of a re-formed convict, who, perhaps, did more for the cause while liv-ing, and may continue to do more though dead, than any other man. We shall notice him at length in the

PLAN OF THE REPORT.

1. Jacob Hodges.
2. Diminution of Crime.
3. Penitentiaries and Prisons.
4. Pennsylvania System of Prison Discipline.
5. Asylums for Lunatics.

---

1. JACOB HODGES.

EXTRACT OF A LETTER CONCERNING HIM FROM THE REV. ANSEL D. EDDY, OF NEWARK, N. J.

Mr. Eddy was formerly pastor of the Congregational church in Canandaigua, with which Jacob united when he went there to live. He remained in Canandaigua several years after Jacob joined the church under his care, and had frequent and favorable opportunities of observation upon his conduct. After Jacob's death, in February, 1842, Mr. Eddy was requested by the Committee of arrangements for the seventeenth anniversary of the Prison Discipline Society, to be present at the annual meeting in Boston, and testify before the friends of the Society, what he knew concerning the conduct and character of Jacob Hodges, a reformed convict, who had long been a cherished object of care and affection with the Society. Mr. Eddy wrote, in reply to the letter of invitation, as follows : —

" NEWARK, N. J., *May* 11, 1842.

" I will try to be with you. The object is one near my heart. I have written his history, and offered it to the Sabbath School Committee for publication. It is about the extent of three sermons. I wish I could give you a brief of it. I think it would add interest to your meeting to have his whole life and death before you.

" He was born in Lancaster, Penn., of poor free parents. At ten years of age, he entered a seafaring life, — a boy waiter to every body on board; continued at sea till some time during the last war, visiting every part of Europe. Thrown upon shore, in his poverty, ignorance, and guilt, he wandered into Orange county, where his crime was perpetrated. If you can lay your hand on a book called the 'Criminal Calendar,' you will find the detail of his trial. This, with his own story, and Abbott's 'Young Christian,' with what I knew of him myself, furnished me the data from which I made up my account of him.

" Mrs. Martin, with whom he lived in Canandaigua, who is now at our house, is enthusiastic in her admiration of him.

" In addition to the notice of Jacob in the 'New York Observer,' I would state that Jacob's Bible may have a story with it. There was one wretched white family in Canandaigua, forsaken of all; — too low and bad to call forth help or hope. He went to see, and urge them to rise and live. He spent night after night with them; *took his Bible,* and read to them. The son came to Jacob for instruction. His mother soon followed; the father also. The two first mentioned have joined the church; the old man is reformed. This is one specimen of his usefulness."

Mr. Eddy was present at the meeting, and gave his testimony concerning Jacob.

The secretary of the Prison Discipline Society had several conversations with him at different periods, both in Prison and after his discharge, embracing a period of thirteen years of his life, and made, at the time, a record, from his lips, of his conversation, which has been carefully preserved, and is now given to the public. Mr. Abbott's notice of Jacob, published some years since in the " Young Christian," was taken from the second conversation, as here published. It was given in that book without a name, as the Second Convict's Story, with the initial W. because the person to whom it related was then alive. The following is a record of the first conversation : —

October 12, 1826.

My First Conversation with a Black Man, called Jack Hodges, in the Auburn Prison.

" How old are you ? "

" I don't know exactly ; but I judge myself to be about fifty-two."

" Have you been a great sinner ? "

" I have, sir — a very great sinner."

" What have you done that is so wicked ? "

" I have done every thing that is abominable in the sight of God ; — cursing, and swearing, and getting drunk, and murder at last."

" Do you know that no murderer can enter the kingdom of God ? "

" I thought, first, that there could be no hope ; but as I read further, I found that, if I repented and believed in the Lord Jesus Christ, I might be saved."

" If you get to heaven, how do you expect to get there ? "

" Through the mercies of the Lord Jesus Christ. In my prayers I cast myself on him."

Said Mr. Curtis,

" In the providence of God, you have a long sentence ; here you must live, and here you may die. Can you say, ' Thy will be done ' ? "

" That is my prayer."

Again, I said to him,

" Do you feel any gratitude ? "

" Yes, sir ; I feel grateful that I was brought here. When Mr. Curtis had been here about five months, he preached his last sermon, and said he was going away. I thought my all was lost, — that I should die ; but when he came back, I was so lifted up, I cannot tell how I felt. My happiness is in hearing the word of God."

" What has the Lord Jesus Christ done for your soul ? "

" I don't know that he has done any thing for my soul yet ; for when I think heaven is such a good place, I think that such a sinner as I am cannot go there ; but then I hear some words — ' Come, cheer up! you may be saved.' "

Mr. Curtis said,

" I preached last Sabbath for the purpose of showing you how you might know whether you are a child of God."

" I said, as I examined myself, I could find no holiness in me."

" Do you feel that you are growing better ? "

" I feel worse and worse every day. My guilt appears worse and worse."

" Do you think sin is any less sinful because it is repented of ? "

" No, sir, I should think not. The more I love God, the more I hate myself."

" Do you think you love God ? "

" I do."

" What makes you think you love God ? "

" Because I don't love to see any thing that is bad ; and because, when I go to hear his word, it kindles up in me, and I love it."

" Did you not always have such feelings towards God ? "

" No, sir. When I first came to this place, I loved every thing else."

" How long since you began to love God ? "

" About four months ago, I was thinking upon my past life, and I felt a weight in my heart, and I thought I should sink, and then the love of God was shed abroad in my heart."

" Do you love to read the WORD OF GOD ? "

" Yes, sir, — more than my victuals and my drink."

" Do you remember what is said concerning ' my Beloved ' ? "

" I feel love to him who gave himself for my justification."

" Do you believe there is any Holy Ghost ? "

" I read it."

" What do you understand by it ? "

" I do not know."

" You believe something has been done in your heart."

" I believe my heart has been changed."

He seemed pleased with the views which were given him of the Holy Ghost.

" Where would you have been if you had not been arrested ? "

" I should have been this day in torment ; for I was going swift to destruction."

He was asked if he loved Mr. Curtis. He said he poured out his whole heart in prayer for Mr. Curtis. He finished this interview in language expressive of so much humility and brokenness of heart, and, at the same time, of so much spirituality and Christian affection, and in a manner so endearing, that I did not attempt to write, or stop him that I might take the words from his mouth, lest I should break the beautiful flow of his language and thought. When he took my hand, with a giant's grasp, to bid me " Good-by," the great tears rolled down his cheeks, and he turned and walked away from us with great gravity and humility. As he shut the door, Mr. Curtis said, "I have not a brother in the world whom I love more than that negro." I will only add to the narrative, in this place, what I have often said, that Jack Hodges was the only man that ever reminded me, by his air, his gravity, his native dignity, his step and tread, of Washington. He always did. And, as some proof that it was not my eye alone that was thus moved by seeing him, it may be stated that, when this remark was made concerning him, some years since, to the superintendent of the Baltimore Penitentiary, who had just returned to Baltimore from a visit to the Auburn Prison, he instantly said, " I saw that man when I was there, and marked him in the yard among six hundred convicts, for his air. Did he not lead one of the gangs in their daily marches through the yard?" The place allotted to him was always as a leader of one of the gangs.

AUBURN PRISON, N. Y., March 31, 1828.

Made preparations with Mr. Curtis, the chaplain, for personal conversation and examination of serious convicts.

My Second Conversation with Jack Hodges.

He is familiarly called *Old Jack.* He is a black man, aged about fifty-four; was born in Lancaster, Penn. "Does not know his age accurately; is ignorant; could not read the Bible when he came to this Prison. Since he came here, has studied in his cell, and learnt to read. The crime for which he was sentenced for twenty-one years was, killing a man. He was led away to commit this crime by the man he lived with, who had been at him five or six months to do it, before he would; and then he would not; but he was first made drunk, and then he committed the horrible crime for which he was sentenced. The man who was killed was a very bad man — so counted by all Orange county."

"But, bad as he was," said Jack, "it was no cloak for me: I had no business with him. I shot at him," said Jack, "and then Dunning took the gun, and beat him over the head till he was dead."

"You was drunk, was you?"

"I was not very drunk, at the time that I shot; but I had been stupid, and the rum had got out of me. It was in the skirts of the woods. I had been asleep there, and Dunning came and woke me up, and said, if we meant to do any thing, we had better do it then. It hurts my heart to talk about it," said Jack, turning to me with a look of anguish, and laying his hand on his heaving bosom.

"Canning was hung, and James Tid was hung. Concklin, who was the instigator, was sent for life, and Jack was sent for twenty-one years."

"Jack, how does this, and all your other sins appear?"

"Very great," said Jack; "but this does not appear so great as all my other sins against God — cursing, and swearing, and getting drunk." Jack said, "When I first began to reflect, I saw my sins, in my cell, so great, that I felt, if God should not, for Christ's sake, have mercy on me, I must go down to the lowest hell. I was sitting down at my work, in the north wing. Mr. Curtis came along, and asked me my crime. I told him. He said that was one of the greatest crimes; but then he told me I might remember David's sin, and he was forgiven. Before that, I had thought my crime was so great that I could not be forgiven. A little while after, Mr. Brown came along, and asked Mr. Curtis if he had been talking with me any thing about my crime. Mr. Curtis told him yes, he was just talking with me. The keeper then passed on. Mr. Curtis then said, 'Let your crime be as great as it will, pray to God, and put your trust in him, and you shall find rest to your soul;' which I shall ever love him for while God gives me breath. I shall love Mr. Curtis, for he put me in the way to save my soul. He made me promise him, faithfully, that I would go to God, and try to find mercy. And yet, master, I had a doubt, in my heart, my sins were so heavy, whether I should be forgiven. Mr. Curtis left me, and I went into my cell, and poured out my heart to God to have mercy on me. He told me, 'If you can't read, I will visit you, at your cell, and put you in the way.' The more I prayed, the worse I grew; heavier and heavier, the worse my sins grew. The next day, Mr. Brown came along, and I asked him to read a chapter to me. Mr. Brown, as God would have it, turned over a chapter, the fifty-fifth chapter of Isaiah, which says, 'Every one that thirsteth, come ye to the waters, and he that hath no money; come ye, and buy wine and milk without money and without price.' He read along till he came to where the prophet says, 'My thoughts are not your thoughts, nor my ways your ways, saith the Lord. For as the heavens are higher than the earth, so are my ways higher than your ways, and my thoughts than your thoughts. For as the rain cometh down, and the snow from heaven, and returneth not thither, but watereth the earth, and maketh it bring forth, and bud, that it may give seed to the sower and bread to the eater, so shall my word be, that goeth forth out of my mouth : it shall not return unto me void, but it shall accomplish that which I please, and it shall prosper in the thing whereto I sent it. For ye shall go out with joy, and be led forth with peace ; the mountains and the hills shall break forth before you into singing, and all the trees of the field shall clap their hands. Instead of the thorn shall come up the fir-tree, and instead of the brier shall come up the myrtle-tree ; and it shall be to the Lord for a name ; for an everlasting sign that shall not be cut off.'

" I found it give me great encouragement to go on to pray to see if I could find relief from all my troubles — the load of sin that was on my heart. I thought, and prayed ; and the more I prayed, the worse I growed ; the heavier my sins appeared to be.

" A night or two after that, Mr. Curtis came to my cell, and asked me how I felt. I told him my sins were greater than I could bear — so guilty, so heavy. He asked me if I thought praying would make my sins any less. I give Mr. Curtis no answer. He left me, and I went to prayer. I was almost fit to expire. In all my sorrows, I had not a right sorrow. My sorrow was because I had sinned against man. The Sunday following, just after I had carried my dinner into my cell, I put down my dinner, and I went to prayer. I rose, and just as I rose from my prayer, Mr. Curtis was at the door. Says he, ' We are all guilty creatures, and we cannot be saved, except God, for Christ's sake, will save us. If we pray and go to God, we must go in the name of Jesus Christ. If we expect to be saved, we must be saved through the blood and righteousness of Jesus Christ.' Then I plucked up encouragement. Says he, ' The sins which you have committed are against your fellow-creatures, but especially against God.' Now, I never knew before that they were against God. Mr. Curtis left me, and I went to prayer again. I could eat no victuals that day. I did not eat a mouthful.

" It struck me that Mr. Fiske, a minister of Goshen, told me, whenever I had a chapter read, to have the Fifty-first Psalm read. I could not see any body to get to read it, and how to find it I did not know ; and the Sunday following, before the keepers unlocked the door, I rose up, and went to prayer ; and I prayed, ' O Lord, thou knowest I am ignorant — brought up in ignorance ; thou knowest my bringing up. Nothing is too hard for thee to do. May it please thee, O Lord, to show me that chapter, that I may read it with understanding.' I rose from prayer, and went to my

Bible, and turned over, and counted every psalm, and it appeared to me that God was with me, and I counted right to the Fifty-first Psalm. I marked it, and then the door was opened, and we went to empty our pails. When we came back, I opened the Bible again, and looked at that psalm, and it come to me just as plain as if I had had learning. I could read a little, and began to spell, ' H-a-v-e m-e-r-c-y,' &c. I"looked over it, and spelt it, and read it, and put the Bible down, and fell upon my knees. ' Have mercy upon me, O God, according to thy loving-kindness : according unto the multitude of thy tender mercies, blot out my transgression. Wash me thoroughly from mine iniquities, and cleanse me from my sins ; for my sin is ever before me. Against thee, thee only, have I sinned, and done this evil in thy sight ; that thou mightest be justified when thou speakest, and be clear when thou judgest. Behold, I was shapen in iniquity, and in sin did my mother conceive me. Behold, thou desirest truth in the inward part ; and in the hidden part thou shalt make me to know wisdom. Purge me with hyssop, and I shall be clean ; wash me, and I shall be whiter than snow. Make me to hear joy and gladness; that the bones which thou hast broken may rejoice. Hide thy face from my sins, and blot out all mine iniquities. Create in me a clean heart, O God, and renew a right spirit within me. Restore unto me the joys of thy salvation, and uphold me with thy free spirit. Then will I teach transgressors thy ways, and sinners shall be converted unto thee. Deliver me from blood-guiltiness, O God, thou God of my salvation ; and my tongue shall sing aloud of thy righteousness. O Lord, open thou my lips, and my mouth shall show forth thy praise. For thou desirest not sacrifice ; else would I give it. Thou delightest not in burnt-offering. The sacrifices of God are a broken spirit ; a broken and a contrite heart, O God, thou wilt not despise. Do good in thy good pleasure unto Zion ; build thou the walls of Jerusalem. Then shalt thou be pleased with the sacrifices of burnt-offering and whole burnt-offering. Then shall they offer bullocks on thine altar.' That is the last of the psalm," said Jack.

"Now, master, when I came to the words, ' *Deliver me from blood-guiltiness,*' I was struck dumb. I could not say any more at that time. I fell upon my knees, and prayed to God to have mercy upon me for Christ's sake. I grew worse and worse. I went on that way, praying, striving, and fighting, against sin and Satan, and growing worse and worse, before I found any relief from my misery. I recollect something gnawing in my breast, and telling me it was no use to pray ; but when I saw Mr. Curtis, he would give me encouragement. As I prayed, I recollected I used to hear old people say, that when a sinner sets out to serve God, Satan sets out to keep him off from his watch. I concluded it was Satan. I went to prayer, and I prayed to God to keep Satan away from me : ' Suffer no evil to approach my poor, feeble heart. Thou knowest my frame and my weakness. Thou knowest that I am nothing but dust. O, deliver me from my distresses, and keep the evil One from me ! '

" I fought on so till about the 15th of June. I was in my cell, and cried to God to have mercy upon me, and I grew worse and worse. All my sins, and all that ever I had done come plain and open in my sight, and I was led to see that I must perish, and drop down into hell. There was no help for me ; all my sin was upon my head. I went upon my knees, and I went to the same psalm, and I repeated it all over, — ' Deliver me from blood-guiltiness, O God.' And I fell down upon the floor, and was struggling, like a man ignorant of every thing — no sense in me at all. I felt a relief from my load of sin. I rose up on my knees, and turned round, and Mr. Doxtater was at the door. He heard me struggling. He asked me, ' What is the matter, Jack ? ' ' Lord, master,' said I, ' I don't know.' ' Do you feel happy there, Jack ? ' ' Lord, master,' said I, ' how can I feel happy, — a poor sinner ? " He went away, and I fell down upon my knees again, and went to prayer. And in my prayer, my sins were moved from me, and I was lightened, and I thought I could fly. I felt as though I could fly. I looked around me, and my cell appeared to be as big as two such cells, and all appeared to be as light as noon ; just the same as if I was in a palace. I looked around me, and it appeared to me that I could see my Savior upon his cross, bleeding for poor sinners. I could see the blood gushing out from his side. I rose up, and I began to bless his holy name. My sins, my load of sins, moved away from me, and I felt light, as though I could fly. I stood upon my knees, and all I could say was, ' Glory to God ! Glory to God ! ' Mr. Doxtater came again, and said he, ' Don't make such a noise.' Said I, ' Mr. Doxtater, I can't help it, sir. If you was to bring a gun, and point at me, I must pray to God now.' He asked me, said he, ' Shall I call Mr. Curtis ? ' ' It is no use,' said I. ' O, no ; don't call Mr. Curtis.' He left me, and I continued praising my God all that whole day. Whether he told Mr. Curtis, I don't know. I said to myself, ' I will take notice of this day.' I did not know the day of the month. Monday morning, I went to Captain Cobb, and I asked him the day of the month. He laughed at me, and would not tell me for some time. At last, he told me it was the 15th of June. And ever since that, master, the place where I am confined has been more to me like a palace than a prison ; every thing goes agreeable. And I, once and a while, I find a deceitful heart ; but Jesus tells, if I lack knowledge, he will always lend ; if I cast my care on Jesus, and not forget to pray."

Mr. Curtis said, " Do you not remember that Mr. Dwight conversed with you last year."

" Yes, but I was so borne down with sin then ! but thanks be to God, who has brought me into his marvellous light ! "

Mr. Curtis remarked, " Some expect to get to heaven on account of their own righteousness."

" O, yes ; I might have thought so, too ; but now I see there is no heaven without a glorious God and his Son Jesus Christ. I remember," said Jack, " Mr. Markam come to the cell, about three or four weeks ago. I was praying, just before church, begging God to give me an ear to hear, and a heart to receive. And in my prayer, some how or other, something come out about Mr. Curtis. And Mr. Markam heard it, and said, ' Do you love Mr. Curtis ? ' I did not answer for some time. At last said I, ' Mr. Markam, I want to ask you one question, and I hope you won't be offended.' ' No,' said he, ' I won't ; say what you are a mind to.' ' Now,' said I, ' Mr. Markam, if you was standing over a great large fire, and ready to fall down in it, and any man at all — I don't say Mr. Curtis — was to come and haul you out of the fire, and keep you from being burnt up, wouldn't you love him ? ' Said he, ' I don't know but I should.' ' Well,' said I, ' this is the very reason that I love Mr. Curtis. I was falling down into hell headlong, and he hauled me out. That is the reason I love Mr. Curtis."

Mr. Curtis said, " You know, Jack, a State Prison is considered a dreadful place. You have a long and dreary sentence, and you may die here. What have you to say to that ? "

" I have considered all that, and I am willing. I have considered, Mr. Curtis, let me die where I will, if I may die in peace, if I may have that sure and well-grounded hope, I don't care where I die."

" Do you consider," said Mr. Curtis, " that God's will is the best ? "

" I do."

" Will you tell me how the Savior appears to you ? "

"The Savior appears to me now, in my daily walk, glorious."

"After all," said Mr. Curtis, "would you rather get to heaven through your own righteousness?"

"No, I would not. I know there is no righteousness, in any man, to carry him to heaven. It must be by the righteousness of Christ."

Mr. Curtis said, "We read of Christ's coming to judgment. Do you never feel afraid that he will overlook poor Jack?"

"I have often felt so," he replied; "but I do not feel so now. He has opened his arms, and received me; and, I have no doubt, I am one of his poor servants. I have awaked in the night, and found my Savior in my arms."

Mr. Curtis said, "Is it any comfort to you to carry your fellow-prisoners to the throne of grace?"

"Yes," said Jack, "a great comfort. It appears to me that I could grasp them all in my arms, and fly to a bleeding Savior."

"Have you any desire that he should bring them all to him, and not let any one go out, and go back to his wickedness?"

"It is my prayer, morning and evening," said Jack, "that I may hold on, and hold out. If I die here, let me die, O Lord, in thine arms! I have great reason to bless this institution, and every stone in it."

In the autumn of 1837, as I was travelling in the Western District of New York, in company with some family friends, and two young gentlemen from Boston, we lodged in Canandaigua. I think I had not seen Jack Hodges since my conversation with him, in the Auburn Prison, on the 31st of March, 1828; but I had heard that he lived in Canandaigua. In the morning, before sunrise, I inquired at the inn if any such man lived in the place. They told me yes, and the place where. I sought the residence of the lady with whom he lived, and found it a beautiful place, on the hill, overlooking the fine country around, just as the morning sun was coming out of his chambers. I met Jacob at the gate, with his hoe and spade. He did not know me at first, for I did not appear to know him; but when I smiled for joy to meet my venerable friend, he grasped my hand like a giant, and said,

"Mr. Doit! Thank God, my friends will come to see me! And where is Master Curtis?"

"I saw him three weeks ago, and he was well."

"I never goes on my knees," said Jacob, "before my heavenly Father, but what I see that man standing before me just like that tree ; " raising his arm from his shoulder, and pointing to a tall elm standing near us. Mr. Curtis is a tall man, somewhat like it.

We were glad to meet again. I said, " Where is that Bible, Jacob ? " He said, " It is on my pillow." I told him I had some friends with me, who had heard me speak of him, and we all wished to see him. He said, " My mistress has gone from home, into the western country ; but the whole house is left open, in my care. Will you come, with your friends, and see me ? " I went for them, and in a few minutes returned with a company of six. He received us at the front door, and gave my friends a hearty welcome. He opened for us a beautiful parlor, into which we entered ; and, when we had taken our seats, I asked Jacob to bring that old Prison Bible from his chamber. When he had done so, I asked him to read the Fifty-first Psalm. He did so ; and I would give more to hear him read it again, than to hear Garrick or Whitefield. I have never heard such reading of the Scriptures from any man. When he came to the words, " Deliver me from blood-guiltiness, O God ! " it seemed, as it always did, when he came to those words, that he would sink beneath the heavy weight of his transgressions. After he had done reading, I asked him if he would pray with us. He fell upon his knees ; and such an offering of thankfulness, that his friends would come to see him, such a poor old sinner ; that God had spared his life, and had mercy on his soul ; such fervent petitions for his friends, — it is not the common lot of travellers to meet with on a journey. A prayer was offered for him. After prayer, I told him I had one favor to ask, — that he would give me that Bible, and I would give him, for it, a new one, of larger print, for his old eyes.

" O, no, master ! I can never part with that Bible."

" But I can make great use of it, as the Bible which has done you so much good."

" No, master, I cannot part with it ; you must not ask me. It is my Prison Bible. It has always been with me." I think he said, " I always sleep with it on my pillow. I can never part with that Bible, while I live."

" Well, Jacob, if you cannot part with it while you live, if I live longer than you, will you give it to me when you are dead ? "

" O, yes, master ! I will write your name in it, and it shall be yours when I am gone."

We bade him farewell with great affection, and returned to

our breakfast at the inn, while the old man followed us to the gate, and kept his eyes upon us as long as he could.   Blessed man !

———

In the autumn of 1839, as I was travelling, with my family, in the Western District of New York, we reached Canandaigua about 12 o'clock at noon, stopped at the inn, and I went immediately to see my old friend Jacob.   The lady with whom he lived met me at the door, and told me he had gone into the woods for a load of chips ; but he would soon be home, and asked me to walk in, and wait till he came.   I told her my wife and children were with me, and I must return to them, but would call again.   When I mentioned my name and object, she insisted on my coming there, and making that my home while we remained in the place, that we might see her servant Jacob as much as we desired.   Mrs. M. not only urged it, but went herself to the inn to effect it.

After we had been at the house a short time, we saw Jacob coming with his wagon-load of chips.   He was walking in all his gravity, dignity, and humbleness of mind, by his horse's side.   As he came up to the back door, I went with my little child to meet him.   The child was full of play.   Jacob was very serious and devout.   I approached him, and took his hand without *appearing* to know *him*.   He was old, his eye was dim, and he did not know me.   After a respectful salutation, he was about leaving me to resume his work, when I smiled with joy to meet him, and he recognized his old friend, took my hand, and uttered himself in a strain of thought which I had no means of catching or preserving, indicative of a heavenly mind and great communion with God.   I told him I had seen his mistress, and she had invited us to spend the day there, and in the evening I wanted an opportunity to sit down with him and have a good long talk.   " Well, master," he said, and went to unload his chips, while we went to dinner.   After dinner, he came to the door of the dining-room, with his broad-brimmed hat, having changed his dress, and put on his Sunday clothes, and his clean calf-skin shoes, and signified that he was ready to walk with me.

CANANDAIGUA, *October* 2, 1839.

My Last Conversation with Jacob Hodges.

I visited the Jail in this place, in company with my aged and venerable friend from the Auburn Prison, who is a wonderful monument of redeeming love.   His Christian character and example are much admired by all who know him. The testimony of the pious lady with whom he lives, and has lived for seven years, is most decidedly in favor of his faithfulness and piety. My interview with him, a record of which was made at the time, in my note-book, will be found below, and will speak for itself.

As we proceeded to the Jail, from the house where he lived, and came upon the sidewalk in that beautiful village, and every thing above and below appeared bright and lovely, and our hearts burned within us towards the God of providence and grace, Jacob said, " O, Mr. Doit, little did I think, when I saw you at my cell in the Auburn Prison, that I should ever walk by your side in the streets of Canandaigua."

After we returned from the Prison, and had taken tea, and he had attended to his duties in the garden and at the barn, and had eaten his supper, and every thing was set in order at the fireside, in his comfortable apartment, where he spent his evenings at home, Jacob came to the parlor door, and said, " Mr. Doit, will you come and see Jacob now." I gladly accepted the invitation, and took my seat by his side, and made the following record of his conversation : —

" Well, Jacob, do you think you love the Lord Jesus Christ ? "

" I do, sir. I think I have no other object, in this world or in the world to come, but my blessed Lord and Savior."

" How does he appear to you, Jacob ? "

" He appears to me, in my daily walk and conversation, the chief among ten thousands, and the one altogether lovely."

" *Why* does he appear so to you ? "

" Because he plucked me as a brand from the burning, as I hope."

" What do you mean by that ? "

" Why, sir, I mean that I was a very great sinner, and he appeared to me as a deliverer from sin. O the mercy ! "

" How could he be a deliverer ? "

" It is because he was the Son of God, that came into the world to seek and save that which was lost."

Here he drew nigh to me, and rested his arm upon my knee.

" Do you ever have any affecting views of his character ? "

" Very often, very often. And it is my daily desire and striving, to know more and more of his character."

" What *are* the views that you have of *him* ? "

" He appears to me daily as the Savior of the world, and he appears to me able and willing to save all who come to God by him."

" How do others appear to you in comparison with him ? "

" Nothing but chaff before the wind ; and the things of the earth appear as dust compared with the glory of the Son of God."

" How can he bear to be seen by such a sinner as you are, and I ? "

" Because he bears with us a long time. He is long-suffering, and not willing that any should perish. He came to seek and save that which was lost."

" Where is he ? "

" He is in heaven, and every where present. He is omniscient, and every where."

" How do you know ? "

" I feel his Spirit moving upon my soul, every once in a while, especially when I forget him."

" When you forget him ? "

" When I let the things of the world get between my soul and him, it is not long before I miss him, and strive to find him again."

" Did you ever form any conception of his appearance ? "

" His appearance ? "

" Yes, of his person."

" No, sir. He appears to me sometimes, by an eye of faith, as the Lamb of God, that taketh away the sin of the world. This I saw this day."

" Where were you when you saw it this day ? "

" In the woods, in picking up chips."

" How came you to think of him ? "

" Why, sir, I am always thinking of him; but the thoughts have been stronger lately. I was stooping down, picking up chips, and I thought, by an eye of faith, that I could see him as a lamb. And, all at once, he appeared like a man, dressed in white, beautiful and glorious."

" What did you do ? "

" The first that I knew, tears came into my eyes, and I went and fell down on my knees, and every thing appeared joyful and glorious, even the trees of the field."

" Then what next ? "

" Why, sir, I got my load, and came home, and it appeared to me that I was comforted all the way home, till I got into the gate here, and saw you."

" Well, how did you feel after you saw me ? "

" After I saw you, the thoughts of my Savior vanished from my mind, and I did not know you; but your countenance seemed to be familiar. When I came to find you out, I went to the barn, and fell down on my knees, and blessed God for the privilege of seeing you again.   And I believe the Savior was there with me.   I am led to be astonished, Mr. Doit, many a time, that God has had compassion on me, and sent his Son to raise me from the depths of sin and degradation; and, many a time, I look upon myself, and see my own heart, and I feel that I deserve to be banished from his presence, and the glory of his power."

" Why don't he banish you?"

" Because he desires that all should be saved."

" What gives you this feeling of unworthiness?"

" Looking back upon my past life, and feeling my hell desert — deserving nothing but the bottomless pit; and this brings me to feel that nothing but the grace of God has kept me till this day."

" You often speak of feeling so heavy, Jacob.   What do you mean by that?"

" So heavy?"

" You spoke of it this morning, — as having that feeling before you went into the woods."

" O, yes !   It is that feeling that Mr. Hubbel told me I ought not to have more than I could help.   When I look back, and see my sins, — when the Lord takes away his Spirit from me, and leaves me to myself, — then I feel very heavy and depressed by my sin and guilt, till the Savior appears to me again by his Spirit, and I feel like a new man.   And I feel that my Savior has come to me, and raises me up, and puts joy and gladness into my heart, and causes me to feel life, and joyful.   I have often felt that if I was left to myself, — if it was not for the grace of God, and his Spirit, — I should go into despair, and sink in despair."

" How do you get rid of these feelings of despondency, Jacob?"

" Fall down at his feet, and never give him rest till he gives me rest by his Spirit."

" Fall down at his feet?"

" Fall down at the foot of the cross, and pray for his mercy, and the enlightening influence of his Spirit."

" Fall down, you say?"

" Kneel down, I mean by falling down."

" Do you commonly do that when you pray?"

" Yes; but then I am always looking to God, when I am working on any thing."

" Does it do you good to kneel down to pray?"

" It does.   I have found, along back, that I have let the

world and business stop me, when I have been pressed by the Spirit to go and pray; and I have found out lately, that the only way I can obtain the Spirit of God, at all times, is to pray often."

" How often? "

" That is to say, set apart three times a day, and let nothing prevent."

" Three times a day?   Any particular place? "

" In the barn, when I am about home; if not, in the woods. No worldly object shall stop me, when I am pressed by the Spirit of God; and if I cannot go this moment, the Lord will make a way for me to go the next."

" You speak much of the Spirit of God pressing you."

" Yes; driving me to do my duty to my Master."

" What measures do you use to have the movings of the Spirit upon your soul? "

" When I feel that I am left alone by the Spirit, I pray for the Spirit, and the Lord, according to the promise, sends his Spirit to comfort the mourning, weeping sinner."

" Does the Bible help you any about this? "

" O, yes! the Bible is my guide and my chart.   It is a light to my feet, and a lamp to my path."

" Now, about that Bible, that I have asked you so often to give me."

" Well, master, that Bible is as dear to me as my own soul, almost; because the Bible always shows me my duty to God, and shows to me the Lamb of God that takes away the sin of the world."

" Well, but *that* Bible, in particular; *that old* Bible."

" Well, I don't know about any other Bible.   I never read any other.   It always reminds me of my friends, and it shows me what I am by nature, and what I must be by grace, before I am fitted for the kingdom of God."

" But any other Bible shows you the same."

" Yes, sir, it does; but because it was given to me in the Prison, I seem to be more touched with it; because out of it, I found relief from my sin, and rest to my soul — out of that very same Bible."

" So you cannot let me have it? "

" No, master.   I would let you have it, if I could go with you, so that I could read it every night and every morning. But even if I would give it to you, you would not have it; you would not take it from me? "

" If I left you a new one, and a better one, and a larger print."

" It would not answer.   Mr. Curtis led me on by *that* Bible. Mr. Curtis led me to the feet of Jesus out of that same Bible; and by Mr. Curtis' leading me by *that* Bible, I saw by the Fifty-first Psalm and the Fifty-fifth Chapter of Isaiah; — the Fifty-first Psalm condemned me to eternal death, and there was no help for me; and by the Fifty-fifth Chapter of Isaiah, I found relief to my soul."

EXTRACT OF A LETTER FROM ONE OF THE TEACHERS IN THE FEMALE HIGH SCHOOL.

CANANDAIGUA, *March* 3, 1842.

" An old colored man, by the name of *Jacob*, died here within a few weeks. His death is considered a great loss by the church.   Mr. Abbott alludes to him in the ' Young Christian.'   He was in Auburn State Prison, where he was sentenced to pass a great part of his life, on account of murder.   He was converted while there.   Mr. A. describes his conversion, and speaks of him as W.   The account is on the 153d page, the ' Second Convict's Story.'   If you will read it, you will be glad to hear that he was pardoned; that his conduct has been most exemplary; that his piety has been of a very high order; and that, having lived here ten or twelve years, a blessing by his example, his prayers, and his exhortations, — exhibiting a striking illustration of the mighty power of Christianity, — he has at length passed to his rest, universally deplored.   Mr. Thompson preached a most interesting funeral sermon."

EXTRACTS FROM REV. MR. THOMPSON'S FUNERAL SERMON.

[Furnished for the New York Observer.]

" *Black Jacob, or Jack Hodges.*

" This is a very humble name, yet not unknown.   In one form or the other, it will seem a familiar one to many readers of the Observer.   I cannot help imagining with what different emotions it will be recognized by different persons.   To some, it will be associated with all that is revolting in depravity and horrible in crime; and to others, with all that is attractive in virtue and lovely in religion.

" ' *Jack Hodges!* ' will one exclaim; ' why, this is that wicked, drunken old negro, who, many years ago, was concerned in a murder that was committed in Orange county, in this state.   I was young then; but so strong was the impression which the circumstances made upon me at the time of their occurrence, that I remember them as though it were yesterday.   Three white men were Jack's accomplices.   It appeared in the investigation, that they had made him their tool.   They brutalized him with rum, and tempted him with promises of reward, until, in an evil hour, he consented to shoot their victim; and his promise was fearfully kept.   All the four were found guilty, and condemned to be executed; two suffered, and Jack, with the other, under a commutation of the sentence, was sent to the State Prison for twenty-one years.'

" ' *Black Jacob!* ' another will say; ' why, this must be that pious old colored man at Canandaigua, of whom I have heard so often; said to be a wonderful Christian, and one of the brightest ornaments of the church in that village.'

" Perhaps the name will meet the eye of Jacob Abbott.   I know not what he will say; but I am greatly deceived if his heart will not throb with unusual excitement when he reads it. He cannot have forgotten Jack, or lost any of the interest which he once felt in his history. If the reader of this article has at hand Abbott's 'Young Christian,' 1 would request him, before looking farther, to turn to the seventh chapter of that book, and read what the author calls the 'Second Convict's Story.' The person whose conversion is there described was Black Jacob, or Jacob Hodges, the subject of this sketch.

"Jacob died in this place, (Canandaigua, N. Y.,) on Wednesday, the 16th of February, 1842. He is supposed to have been about eighty years of age.

"The following consists of extracts from a discourse preached by the writer, in the Brick Church, on the morning of the Sabbath which succeeded his death : —

"When he was very young, Jacob was indentured to a sea-captain, and was employed on shipboard in such services as he was then able to perform. After several years passed as a cabin-boy, he became at length an ordinary sailor, and in that capacity followed the sea under various masters for more than half his life. In describing himself, during this part of his career, he has told me that he was distinguished for his wickedness, and for the excess to which he indulged in all the bad habits of the class to which he belonged. He was terribly profane at all times, and, when on shore, addicted to the constant practice of licentiousness and intoxication. He has often said of himself, — and I cannot doubt the literal truth of his representations, — for, besides what the well-known facts of his history testify, the big tears, that frequently stood in his eyes when speaking of this subject, were evidence enough that he had no desire to magnify his faults, — that, among all his companions, there was not another so vicious, so ill-tempered, ungovernable, and devoted to all sorts of mischief, as himself. To use his own words on one occasion, he said with an expression of self-abhorrence which I shall not readily forget, 'Why, master, I was a sarpent ; it does seem as though the wicked one possessed me, and I wonder that the Lord suffered me to live.'

"Why he abandoned the sea, I am not able certainly to say, though I have a decided impression that he once told me, it was owing to the unwillingness of shipmasters to employ him, on account of the notorious badness of his character.

"After wandering for some time from place to place, with no particular home, or any regular occupation, he seems at last to have gained some permanence in Orange county. What his character was there, may be easily inferred from the events which there transpired.

"The gracious change which took place in Jacob in the Prison at Auburn, became very soon so manifestly a reality, that his friends, and among them, as most active, the superintendent, interested themselves in his behalf, and procured his pardon and release. Now, as you may well suppose, came a severe trial of his religious character, and he was followed from his cell out into the world, by many a watchful and anxious eye. All hoped for him, but none could tell what the result would be. Would his old and inveterate habits draw him back again into sin, or would grace triumph ? It was a doubtful and a most deeply-interesting question. But, as Jacob has said to me, 'I went out of Prison, believing that, if I tried to live right, and prayed to the Lord to keep me, and trusted in him with all my heart, I *should be preserved.*' He had hold of the true strength, and he *was preserved.* Never but once, and that was during the first year of his liberation, did he seem to waver. On one solitary occasion, he was known to have tasted the intoxicating cup ; and the horror of mind and deep repentance which it occasioned him, were perhaps better evidences of the genuineness of his piety, than if he had never fallen.

"He remained more than two years in Auburn, growing constantly in the confidence and affections of all who knew him. It is about ten years since he came to this place ; and, during this period, his life has been before you. Two weeks ago to-morrow, Jacob spent not less than two hours with me in my study. We had much conversation in relation to himself. Among other things he said, — and, from the connection in which he said it, I know that it was not in a spirit of boasting, — 'I have now lived ten years in Canandaigua. Every body knows Black Jacob, at least by sight; and I challenge all, men, women, and children, to say if I have ever injured any body, or done any thing inconsistent with my profession, except that I have not been as humble, and as much like my blessed Master, as I ought to have been; and this I know better than any body can tell me, and I am ashamed and mourn for it.' This was saying much, — more, I fear, than many of us dare say. But, we must all confess, it was a safe challenge for Jacob.

" Some things I would particularly say of him; and I would ask your attention to them, as furnishing examples well worthy of imitation.

" *He was a man of prayer.* This he must have been, or he could not have been what he was in other respects. He began his Christian course with a strong sense of his dependence on God. Perhaps there was something in the peculiar difficulties which he had to overcome, that led him in a peculiar manner to realize this truth. Certain it is that he did realize it more than almost any other Christian that I ever knew, and, as a necessary consequence, he prayed more than most other Christians. Those of you who have heard his eloquent pleadings with God in the prayer-meeting, need no other evidence that the exercise was a familiar one. How often has the remark been made, that one of Jacob's prayers was always enough to change the character of an otherwise dull and spiritless meeting! How full and fervent were his petitions! How near to the throne he always seemed to get! Think, that it was not until he was in Prison that he learned to read; then remember how chosen was his language, how exceedingly *fine* it was sometimes; how apt and abundant were his quotations from Scripture, how well he could adapt himself in prayer to the peculiar circumstances of the time; and you must be convinced that he was thoroughly practised in the duty.

" *Jacob was a very humble Christian.* You may say that he had much reason to be humble. So had he many temptations to be proud. You know with what marked respect he has always been treated among us; and he was the object of very general interest, so that strangers, visiting the place, have frequently sought to be introduced to him. Many times I have been apprehensive that he would be injured by the attentions which he received, but I never discovered that he was. He did not seem disposed, on any occasion, to put himself improperly forward, or anxious to attract notice. The memory of what he had been, seemed always to be present with him. Many of you well remember that thrilling scene in our lecture-room, a year ago, just previous to the commencement of our precious revival; when, just as we were about to separate under most disheartening circumstances, Jacob was invited to address us. You have not forgotten that truly eloquent and overwhelming appeal, which seemed to shake the very house in which we were assembled, while the whole congregation was convulsed with weeping.

" Do you remember the words with which he began? 'My masters and mistresses — for I dare not call you my brethren and sisters.' There was breathed the spirit of the man; and I never knew him to appear to cherish any other. There was a peculiarity in his prayers which you must have noticed. In that part of them which consisted of confession, he always used the 'first person singular.' He seemed to think that *his* confession of sin could only be appropriate for himself. He often alluded to the past with expressions of the most profound abhorrence and shame. Sometimes he spoke of his *crime*, but it was always with so much evident pain, that it was distressing even to hear him. I have seen him seized with violent trembling at the bare mention of that subject. He has said to me, 'Master, I do believe that my heavenly Father loves me; but how wonderful it is that he should love *me!* I cannot love myself; it seems to me that nobody ever sinned against him as I have done.'

"*Jacob was an earnest Christian.* This was true of him in every sense, but I speak now with especial reference to the work of his own salvation. He was constantly examining himself. Every sermon he heard he sought to apply in some way as a test of his own character; and he was never satisfied unless he saw evidence that he was growing in grace. To this end he was diligent in his use of all the *means* of grace. Until his health began to fail, during the present season, he was very rarely absent from any religious meeting; and his familiarity with the Scriptures, acquired by the constant perusal of them, was truly wonderful. When I have met him, and inquired casually after his health, nothing was more common than for him to reply in some such terms as these, showing the channel in which his thoughts habitually flowed —'Very well, master, in body; but, O, this wicked heart! I want a great deal more grace.' He complained much of a disposition of *worldliness.* His little matters of business engrossed so much of his attention, he was compelled, he said, to be praying constantly against it. He wondered how rich Christians *could* keep along.

"*Jacob was a useful Christian.* Such a Christian could hardly be otherwise. I do believe that it may be said of him, 'He hath done what he could.' I attribute the last revival of religion in this church, in no small degree, to the influence of his prayers, and to his direct instrumentality. There are not a few in this village who owe their conversion, under God, to his faithfulness; and I doubt not there are some now listening to my voice, who are ready to rise up and call him blessed. His uniform and consistent life of piety cannot but have had a happy influence on all who have observed him; and I doubt not there are those before me, yet impenitent, who would confess, if asked, that they have felt religion to be strongly commended to them by his holy example. He loved and longed to do good. I once asked him why he was so anxious to be rendering services to me, for he was constantly inquiring if he could not do something for me. His reply was, that it seemed almost the same as if he was preaching the gospel, when he was helping his minister.

"There is an anecdote of him, highly illustrative of his character, which, though a proper place has not seemed to occur for it in this hurried sketch, I am unwilling to omit, because it shows so strikingly his feelings on a subject, in relation to which every Christian needs constantly to examine himself. Some two years ago, he had a violent attack of the same disorder (inflammation of the lungs) of which he died; and it was supposed then that he could not recover. In one of the many delightful interviews which I had with him, I recollect to have asked him this question: 'Are you quite sure, Jacob, that you hate sin?' I never can forget the earnestness of his manner, and the peculiar expression of his eye, as he rose up quick in the bed, and, stretching out his arms, exclaimed, 'Master, I do hate my very flesh on account of sin!'

"His death, at the time it occurred, was anticipated but a very few hours. I saw him on Monday, and had much conversation with him, though without any suspicion of the nearness of his end. He referred to the lectures which I have been delivering weekly for some months past, on Christian experience, and said they had been greatly serviceable to him. He told me that he had been led by them to go over the whole ground again, and to examine himself — to use his own language — 'all over anew, from beginning to end, to see whether he was on the sure foundation.' 'Well, Jacob,' I said, 'and what is your conclusion?' 'I think,' he replied, 'it is all right, master.' 'Then you think,' I continued, 'that you are running no risk if you die now?' 'Not any,' was his prompt reply; 'Christ is able and faithful.'

"To one who went into his room the last morning of his life, to ask how he felt, and if he needed any thing, he simply said, 'O, I want more grace in my heart!' His last hours were passed in a state of unconscious stupor, and at six o'clock in the evening he expired — a liberated prisoner indeed! — not sent forth into this world of sin and trial, where we must follow him with trembling solicitude, but caught up by angels when the door of his dark cell was opened, to wear the conqueror's everlasting crown, and rejoice forever in the fadeless inheritance of the just."

2. DIMINUTION OF CRIME.

PROOF THAT THERE IS A DIMINUTION OF CRIME.

In the Maine State Prison, at Thomaston, the average number of prisoners, for 13 years previous to 1837, was 80. According to the warden's last report, for 1841, the average number, for ten months and a half last past, has been 42 — a diminution of almost one half.

In the Vermont State Prison, the warden said, in 1840, " Our number of prisoners is constantly diminishing. The average number, for 25 years previous to 1839, has been 100. It is now reduced, according to a letter recently received from the chaplain, to 79. The number has formerly been as high as 138, from which number it is ..ow reduced 59.

In Worcester, Mass., where the number of prisoners, in the House of Correction alone, was, for many years, 35 and 40, and among them many common drunkards, the Jail is now united with the House of Correction, and the number of prisoners in both is reduced to 20, and among them was recently found but one common drunkard.

In the House of Correction in New Bedford, Mass., where the number of prisoners has been as high as 80, it is now reduced to about one half that number. The following information is furnished by an esteemed friend, who has done much in promoting the cause of temperance, and the diminishing of crime in New Bedford : —

" The New Bedford Washington Total Abstinence Society was organized about the 15th of July last. In a statement of the effect of said society on the prospects of the town, contained in an appeal to the public on their behalf, made about the 5th of October, and published in the New Bedford Mercury, the following facts were given, viz. : —

Commitments to the House of Correction in said Town, from the 4th of July to the 4th of October, 1841.

		1840.	1841.		Reduction.
From the whole county,	}	{ 57 { 36	.... 48 33	.... all offences, ... drunkenness,	.... 16 .... 8½
From New Bedford alone,	}	{ 38 { 22	.... 28 18	.... all offences, ... drunkenness,	.... 26½ 18

Commitments to the Jail in said Town for same Period.

	1840.	1841.		Reduction
From the whole county,	87 .... 59	67 .... 22	all offences, drunkenness,	23 22
From New Bedford alone,	81 .... 55	62 .... 45	all offences, drunkenness,	23 18

" The cases of arraignment for drunkenness, as informed by the judge of the Police Court, from his *general impression* on the subject, have diminished nine tenths, since the formation of the Washington Total Abstinence Society.

" 10 mo., 5, 1841."

" It may be remarked, that part of the good results above noted may be ascribed to the action of the committee appointed to suppress the illegal traffic in spirituous liquors, which had lessened the number of tippling shops, and induced more care in the venders than heretofore. A comparison of the same period for 1842, I think, would give *more* encouraging results.

" S. R. — 4 mo., 18, '42."

In the House of Correction at South Boston, the number of prisoners is reduced about one fourth. The number of females is reduced nearly one half.

In the Massachusetts State Prison at Charlestown, the number of prisoners, at the close of the year before last, was 322 ; at the commencement of that year, it was 318. It is now reduced to 293. The average number, for 8 years ending 1828, was 298. The number at the present time is less than the average number during that period. The number committed last year, from September 30, to April 25, was 79 ; this year, in the same time, it was 43.

In Providence, R. I., where, three years ago, the State Prison was thought to be too small, and it was in contemplation to build a large House of Correction, it is found that the State Prison is more than sufficient to accommodate the present small number of about 25 convicts, and it is much less in contemplation to build a House of Correction of any description, because it is much less necessary.

In the New York State Prison at Auburn, the number of prisoners, contrary to the general rule of the present year, has increased from 695 to 707. It ought to be stated, however, that the number pardoned has been 6 less than the average for 6 years previous to 1837 ; and the number of deaths was only 9, which is 4 less than the average number of deaths for 14 years. If there had been an average number of pardons and deaths, the increase of prisoners would have been but 2, which is a very small increase, considering the great growth of the Western District of New York.

In the New York State Prison at Sing Sing, the inspectors reported, on the 30th of September, 1831, that the number of prisoners at one time, during the year then passed, had exceeded 1000 ; and that it might be fairly estimated that the number would not fall short, in the course of the year then following, of 1200. In this prediction they were entirely mistaken. The number diminished rather than increased ; and the number at the present time is less than the average, at that period, for the space of 6 years. The average then was 814. It is now reduced to 811, although all the female convicts in the state are now sent to Sing Sing, many of whom were formerly sent to Auburn.

Whole number committed in 11 months of 1831, ... 338
Whole number committed in all of 1832, ... 289
Whole number committed in the year 1837, ... 261
Whole number committed, including the females formerly
    sent to Auburn, in 1841, ... 241
Average number committed annually in the three first-
    named periods, ... 296
Whole number committed last year, including females as
    above, ... 241
Diminution in the number committed annually, ...   55

In the new Penitentiary in Philadelphia, the number of prisoners, in 1838, was 387 ; in 1839, 417; in 1840, 434; in 1841, 376; in 1842, 335.

Average number for 4 years preceding the last, ... 403
Number at the close of the last year, ... 335
A diminution, from the average number, of   68

In the Penitentiary in Baltimore, the number of prisoners, in 1833, was 363; in 1834, 377; in 1835, 404; in 1836, 396 ; in 1837, 387; in 1838, 353; in 1839, 328; in 1840, 329; in 1841, 284.

Average number, in 8 years preceding the last, ... 367
Number at the close of the last year, ... 284
Diminution from the average number, ... 83

In the State Prison at Columbus, Ohio, the number of prisoners, at the commencement of the last year, was 483 ; the number at the close of the year, 480. The number of convictions during the past year has been 121, being a decrease of 16 from the number of convictions in 1840, and a diminution of 23 from the average number of convictions annually for the 4 preceding years.

We think it is proved, by the foregoing induction of particulars, that there is a diminution of crime in the United States.

CAUSES OF THE DIMINUTION OF CRIME.

1. *Washington Temperance Societies.* As intemperance is a great cause of crime, so the Washington Temperance · Societies are a great cause of the diminution of crime.

2. *Reformed Prisons.* As the old Penitentiaries and Prisons were schools of vice, so reformed Prisons, with pious officers, mild punishments, faithful chaplains, devoted Sabbath school teachers, solitude at night, labor by day, evil communication prevented, good instruction communicated, the Bible in every cell — Houses of Refuge for Juvenile Delinquents — systematic and benevolent effort for discharged convicts — a spirit of prayer for Prisons — and, above all, in answer to prayer, the Spirit of God poured out upon officers and prisoners ; — these are good and sufficient causes for the diminution of crime.

---

3. PENITENTIARIES AND PRISONS.

PENITENTIARIES AND PRISONS WHICH HAVE ATTAINED A HIGH DEGREE OF EXCELLENCE.

State Prison in New Hampshire.
State Prison at Charlestown, Mass.
House of Correction at South Boston, Mass.
State Prison at Wethersfield, Conn.
County Prison in Hartford, Conn.
County Prison in New Haven, Conn.
State Prison at Sing Sing, N. Y.
State Prison at Auburn, N. Y.
County Prison in Philadelphia.
State Prison in Baltimore, Md.
State Prison at Frankfort, Ken.
State Prison at Columbus, Ohio, with a great abatement in the latter for want of more systematic and thorough moral and religious instruction.

It is not intended, in presenting this list, under the above head, to convey the idea that there is not room for improvement in these institutions. One general remark is applicable to all, — less perhaps, during the last winter, to the State Prison at Charlestown, than any other, — i. e., there is want of increased moral power and of the outpouring of the Spirit of God. This is the great attainment, to which all connected with them, and all Christians, should look forward, and for which they should earnestly pray. This is that which will diminish crime, perfect our institutions, and raise the fallen.

There are minor points, also, of improvement, which are worthy of particular notice. So far as our information extends, there is only one of the above institutions, viz., the State Prison at Charlestown, where the prisoners are provided with *an extra suit of clothes for the Sabbath.* We deem this unjust, especially where the prisoners more than support the Prison, from the proceeds of their own industry. It is immoral in its tendency, and it is debasing. It is not the dictate of humanity, wisdom, or religion.

Again; all windows, in the external walls of Prisons on the Auburn plan, should be large, like the windows of dwelling-houses; better still, like the windows of churches, and for the same reason, — to give light and air. Darkness and bad air are not reformatory in their tendency. Prisons require, above all other places, good light and pure air. This general rule has been well observed in nearly all the Prisons above named; but in the dormitory buildings in the Prisons at Charlestown and Sing Sing, the windows in the side walls are more like the port-holes of a man-of-war, than like windows. The walls being very thick, and the orifices very small, they answer a very poor purpose to admit light and air. The author of these port-hole windows called them an improvement, at the time ; but they are now, so far as we know, universally disapproved.

Once more ; all grated windows and grated doors, in Prisons, should be made of round iron; the orifices being as large as they can be consistently with security. The light and air are comparatively but little intercepted by the bars of a round iron grate. A person not much accustomed to observation on Prisons, would scarcely believe it possible that so much of the comfort and improvement of Prisons depends on this simple provision of round iron in all the grated windows and doors. The cell, for instance, of a Prison on the Auburn plan, which has a grated door of round iron from top to bottom, with orifices as large as they can be, consistently with security, is almost as light and airy, as the area of the Prison, or a common room in a dwelling-house ; but where the grate is but a small part of the door, and that of square bars, as at Charlestown, with small orifices, it makes the cell gloomy and uncomfortable.

The work-shops, also, in several of the most highly improved Prisons, require enlargement of space and facilities for inspection, by improving or rebuilding, to perfect the system. This has been admirably done at the House of Correction in South Boston, at Wethersfield, Conn., and in Baltimore, Md.; is being done at Auburn, N. Y., and is greatly needed at Charlestown, Mass. The inspectors of the Prison at Charlestown, in their last report, urge this matter upon the government.

There are other matters, of minor importance, admitting of improvement, in the most highly improved Prisons; but we are confident, from the history of the past, that they will be attained in time, by patient continuance in well-doing.

It may excite surprise, that the new County Prison in Philadelphia should be included in the above list of Prisons which have attained a high degree of excellence. It should be borne in mind, that it is done notwithstanding our decided opinion against the plan of building, for the purpose of approving of many other things which are excellent, in neatness, order, *industry*, and general government.

We close the notice of this class of Prisons, with the testimony of the venerable Quaker chemist, John Griscom, concerning the *House of Correction at South Boston*, on the Auburn plan. He is a Friend, extensively known in the cause of education and human improvement, who resides in Burlington, near Philadelphia. The testimony of no one individual would probably be more valuable : —

" Having received an introduction to Captain Robbins, master of the House of Correction in South Boston, I was obligingly conducted by him through the different departments of that institution, and received explanations of the system of management pursued by him in it. In relation to the government of Prisons, I hesitate not to confess, that, of the numerous institutions designed for penal infliction, and the moral reformation of adult prisoners, which I have visited in this country and in Europe, I have never witnessed any thing better than was here presented to my notice. The perfect external order and neatness, and the quiet, subdued, and yet contented aspect of the prisoners, were striking features of the establishment; and to learn that all this order, quiet, industry, and submissiveness, were effected with a resort to no other instrument of punishment whatever than the shower-bath, produced at once an opinion of the superior efficacy of purely moral treatment, and the remarkable adaption of the man to the avocation.

JN. GRISCOM.

" Boston, 5 mo., 19, 1842."

PENITENTIARIES AND PRISONS WHICH ARE DEFECTIVE IN VERY IMPORTANT POINTS.

State Prison in Maine, very defective in construction
State Prison in Windsor, Vt.

State Prison in Rhode Island, without work-shops, without a chapel, without a Sabbath school, without a chaplain, and, in proportion to the number of prisoners, very expensive in construction and management.

Penitentiary on Blackwell's Island, very defective in profitable employment, and in moral and religious instruction.

State Prison at Trenton, N. J., very defective in construction, and in moral and religious instruction.

New Penitentiary in Philadelphia, very defective in construction.

Penitentiary in Richmond, Vir., very defective in moral and religious instruction.

Penitentiary at Milledgeville, Geo.

New Penitentiary in Jackson, Miss., very defective in government, and in moral and religious instruction.

PENITENTIARIES AND PRISONS REMAINING VERY BAD.

County Jail at Lechmere Point, Cambridge. In consequence of the number of lunatics confined in this Jail, it is impossible that it should be otherwise than revolting to every feeling of humanity.

Jail on Leverett Street, Boston ; bad in construction, without employment, and injurious to morals.

County Prison on Lombard Street, New York city ; the same.

Jail in Baltimore ; the same.

Old Jail in Washington city ; the same.

Jail in Richmond, Vir. ; the same.

Jail in Savannah, Ga. ; the same.

Jail in Augusta, Ga. ; the same.

Jail in Mobile ; the same.

Jail in New Orleans ; the same.

Jail in Natchez, Miss. ; the same.

Jail in Nashville, Tenn. ; the same.

Jail in Louisville, Ken. ; the same.

Old Jail, Adams county, Miss.

Penitentiary in Indiana ; the same, except that the prisoners are employed.

In regard to the improvement of this class of Prisons, hope deferred makes the heart sick. After visiting the new Jails in Hartford and New Haven, Conn., and finding them as neat as a pin, to be obliged to make such a list of very bad Jails is hard work.

The following item of intelligence from the Natchez Courier is very pleasant, with reference to its bearing on the Western country : —

"*Adams County Jail.* — We take pleasure in announcing that the Board of Police of this county have ordered the erection of a *New Jail*, the necessity for which cannot be questioned, after the report of the committee of citizens on that subject, and the recommendation of the grand jury.

" The board have appointed a committee, consisting of Dr. A. P. Merrill, Dr. John Ker, Dr. Wm. Dunbar, Thos. Henderson, and Peter Little, Esqrs., to select a site, to contract for, and superintend, the building of a Jail, on the plan of the Hartford (Connecticut) County Prison, to contain fifty cells. They are also authorized to sell the present County Jail, and the lot on which it stands, and are requested to report on the whole subject at the next regular term of the board."

MORAL AND RELIGIOUS INSTRUCTION IN PRISONS AND PENITENTIARIES.

The warden of the *Maine Prison*, Mr. John O'Brien, says, in his last report to the legislature, in January, 1842, —

" Two discourses are preached on every Sabbath, in the Prison chapel, by the Rev. Job Washburn, besides other religious instruction, in which he is assisted by the clerk and other overseers. Many of the convicts seem apparently interested in these exercises on the Sabbath. The library attached to the chapel, for the use of the prisoners, is somewhat reduced, and should be replenished, by a new selection of books, early in the spring. They have, for the last season, been weekly furnished with temperance papers, and many of them appear to be much interested in the cause." — *Pages 9 and 10 of Report to the Legislature.*

The annual report from this Prison contains nothing from the inspectors or the chaplain in regard to the condition of the Prison. As they hold offices of important trust and great usefulness, in a State Penitentiary, there can be no doubt that the people of Maine, as well as others, would be highly pleased to hear from them on the subject of moral and religious instruction.

A letter was received from the chaplain, dated Thomaston, April 5, 1842, in which he says, —

" I received your letter, dated March 18, 1842, giving an account of the good work of the Lord in the Prison at Charlestown, Mass. Surely it is matter of joy, and cannot fail in producing many thanksgivings to God. It has revived some new hopes and desires in my mind, that God will yet remember this Prison in mercy.

" You requested me to give you an account of the religious state of things among the convicts and officers of our Prison. O that I could give you such intelligence as would, in some good degree, compare with the contents of your letter!

" The convicts appear (as a general thing) very attentive, and sometimes *solemn*, under preaching; and my hopes are raised, that good will result, but I am often disappointed. When I converse with them, I often find them tender in their minds, and many of them assure me that they are determined, whenever they obtain their liberty again, to live a new life. If I tell them, '*Now is the time to commence*,' I find the impression quite general, that the Prison is no place to be religious; that it would bring upon themselves the scorn and persecution of their fellow-prisoners.

" The largest number of convicts, at any one time, has never exceeded 110; for some years past, the number has gradually been lessening; some few months past, the number was reduced to 40; at the present time, the number is 46 or 47.

" Our Sabbath school consists of about 20, who are divided into two classes. I have charge of one class, and the clerk of the Prison, the other. The classes use the Union Questions. I have before my class a large map of Asia Minor and the adjacent countries, and whenever a place is mentioned in the lesson, it is pointed out to them on the map. Most of them appear interested in the exercises.

" I request an interest in your prayers in our behalf, and also wish our case to be remembered in the prayer meeting established in the Prison at Charlestown.

" Be assured, any communication from you, regarding the welfare of this or any other Prison, will be thankfully received.

" Your sincere though unworthy brother in Christ,
" JOB WASHBURN,
" *Chaplain of the Maine State Prison.*"

The last report of the *New Hampshire Prison* contains a short but interesting and useful report from the chaplain, the Rev. Edmund Worth, to which respectful reference is made by the warden, Mr. Coolidge. The annual report of this Prison contains nothing from the directors on the subject of moral and religious instruction. We think the public are always interested to hear the testimony of the directors and warden on the subject of moral and religious instruction.

The chaplain says, —

" While our penal laws are intended to inflict a just punishment on the criminal, it is no less gratifying to every philanthropic mind to contemplate the fact that they are also designed to reclaim and reform the transgressor. Punishment due to crime is one object — reform, another; and while justice requires the first, every moral principle of man cheerfully sustains the second.

" In relation to the unhappy class of men under your watch, it is undoubtedly true, that unjust opinions have been entertained by the community. The inmates of our Prisons are generally looked upon as being so hardened and abandoned, as not to be within the reach of moral effort, and that their reformation is altogether hopeless. But why should it be so? They are still men, and they possess the feeling and sympathies of men. Many of them are but youth, in whom the affections and sensibilities of our nature are tender and easily moved. Nearly one half of the convicts in our Prison committed their crimes through the influence of intoxicating liquor; others were led from the path of virtue by vicious companions; while another class were neglected in childhood, grew up destitute of all moral, religious, and even intellectual training, and were made an easy prey to alluring vice; — while yet another class have been the subjects of early moral culture, have virtuous connections, and have moved in respectable circles. All these have now the advantages of seclusion from the scenes and temptations of the world, for serious reflection; and are favorably situated for receiving instruction, and for being profited by the plain and faithful exhibition of divine truth. Under such circumstances, why may there not be a reasonable expectation, that many of the prisoners will be induced, by the powerful incentives placed before them, to forsake their evil ways, and pursue a moral and virtuous course?

" During the past year, I have preached in the chapel once on the Sabbath, and the attention to the word has been such as to encourage the hope that its influence would not be lost. I have passed from cell to cell several times, and endeavored to impart suitable instruction to each individual, verbally, and by means of moral and religious tracts. These interviews with the prisoners have been of the most pleasing character. Instead of a single instance of opposition or disrespect, these visits have been earnestly solicited and thankfully received. My own heart has been much affected, and a deep sympathy has been enlisted in their behalf, as I have listened to the tale of the past, the frank acknowledgments of guilt, and seen the tears trickling down and falling from the cheek of those who manifested signs of deep contrition. There is reason to believe that, after making all due allowances for deceptions, there are several in whose hearts the principles of our holy religion have been implanted, and which will be evinced, in future time, by fruits meet for repentance.

" In conclusion, it is ardently to be hoped that this class of men will not be forgotten as subjects of moral improvement, but, while they may deservedly endure penal inflictions for their past misdeeds, they may also enjoy those means of moral and religious instruction, which, by the blessing of God, will affect their hearts, and produce a thorough reformation of character.

" Respectfully submitted,
" EDMUND WORTH. Chaplain.

"CONCORD, June 1, 1841."

The chaplain of the Vermont State Prison, Rev. Rufus L. Harvey, in a letter, dated March 21, 1842, says, —

" In answer to your first interrogatory, ' What is the present state of religious feeling in the Prison?' I will say there does appear to be a more deep and solemn attention to religious instruction, of late, among the convicts, than I have witnessed before since I renewed my labors among them. In my last course of visits at the cells, I found a number who appeared quite serious, and requested an interest in my prayers. Yesterday we buried one of the convicts. During our services, the convicts were unusually serious, and many of them wept. Our Sabbath school is very interesting. Many of the convicts seem to delight in committing to memory, and reciting, portions of the Holy Scriptures. But I doubt not that our Sabbath school would be far more interesting, if Christian persons from without should volunteer their services, and come in on the Sabbath, and act as teachers. But, for want of such help, some of the most confidential convicts are chosen to perform this duty. I think, however, that our school is prosperous, and doing much good."

The inspectors of the Massachusetts State Prison, William Minot, Samuel Greele, and Bradford Sumner, say, in their last report, concerning the moral and religious instruction of the prisoners, —

" They are provided with religious instruction by the daily performance of public worship, and the chaplain is always ready to teach the ignorant and encourage the penitent."

The warden says nothing, in the annual report, on the subject of moral and religious instruction. It is well known that he is deeply interested in it, and we are confident that the public wish to hear his testimony on this part of the subject, from year to year. The chaplain, the Rev. Jared Curtis, says, —

"The chaplain of the State Prison, in presenting his report for the year ending September 30, 1841, is happy in being able to speak of the great goodness and watchful kindness of the sovereign Lord of all to the institution in which he is called to labor. By His smiles general health has been enjoyed. Quiet, order, industry, and submission to wholesome authority, have prevailed. The means of religious instruction and improvement have been daily and sedulously applied to the minds and hearts of the prisoners, and, it is believed, with marked and happy success. The Sabbath school has also been in operation during that portion of the year allotted to its continuance, and its influence has been most decidedly favorable. A new, and, it is believed, much improved, organization has recently taken place in this school, by which competent teachers have been secured to take charge of the several classes, steadily and for the season. By this arrangement a change from Sabbath to Sabbath is avoided. The teachers will now become acquainted with the members of their classes ; know, better than they otherwise could, how to adapt their instructions to their capacities and wants ; and be made to feel a deep interest in the spiritual and moral improvement of those intrusted to their charge ; while, at the same time, the members of these classes become strongly attached to those whose Christian benevolence brings them, from Sabbath to Sabbath, to their Prison-House, in performance of their labor of love and compassion. The appearance of the school has never exhibited so much of cheering promise as at the present time. The state and the institution owe much to these teachers for their multiplied and self-denying labors in behalf of this unhappy class of their fellow-men ; but their reward is in their own bosoms, and will, ultimately, be perfected in heaven, in the enjoyment of the presence and smiles of Him, who will say to them, 'I was in Prison, and ye came unto me.'

"It is cheering to be able to state, that a lively, and, it is hoped, a very salutary, influence has been exerted on the minds of a large portion of the prisoners, in relation to the interesting and peculiarly important subject of temperance ; and no community can more need the renovating power of such an influence. The spirit of the 'Washingtonians' has found its way within our walls ; and it can hardly be conceived how deep an interest has been awakened in relation to that deadly evil, to which most of the inmates of the institution owe their degradation and their downfall. They have, during the past season, enjoyed the benefit of repeated lectures on this subject, from some of the ablest and best lecturers in the country. In this number might be named several reformed inebriates, whose experience, as developed in their most thrilling and heart-stirring statements, came home to the minds of their hearers with a power, in many cases, almost overwhelming. Every prudent effort will be continued to keep alive and to increase this interest. Only let the fountains of intemperance be dried up, and what a change would come over the face of society! At least three fourths of the poverty, and degradation, and suffering, and crime, over which the philanthropist and the Christian are now constrained to weep, would be banished from our commonwealth. Let, then, a cheering voice go out from our Prisons and Alms-Houses, and the abodes of poverty and suffering, to greet the ears of the embattled host who are contending in this holy cause, and to animate them in their great and good work. Let their watchword be, ' Onward,' until the conquest aimed at shall be achieved, and victory shall crown all their efforts."

The chaplain of the *House of Correction at South Boston,* the Rev. Charles Cleveland, in his last report, says to the board of overseers, —

"Having, through your appointment, officiated as chaplain at the House of Correction, from November 1, 1840, and it being proper that you be furnished with an account of my stewardship, I proceed herewith to present it.

" On the Sabbath, divine worship has been attended through the day. My dependence for success, while striving to emancipate the soul from the strong grasp of an ever-watchful and subtle adversary, has been fastened upon the omnipotent power of the Holy Spirit.

" In connection with chapel instructions, my people have been invited to commit to memory portions of Scripture, and recite to their chaplain between meetings. My heart has been ofttimes refreshed, and I have thanked God, and taken courage, when attending these recitations. One man recited at a hearing, 173 verses, and another, 138 — a female, 176; another, 127, and another, 88. From the commencement of the exercises, 24th January, the total number of verses committed was 5857.

" *In the female Sabbath school,* the number of pupils in attendance has averaged 100. Ladies, members of various city churches, have been conveyed over, at the expense of the city, to engage in the good work of instruction. Sixteen of the last eighteen Sabbaths, the same eleven teachers, the requisite number, were present. Experience has proved that the system of dependence on *permanent* teachers has several and important advantages over that of *alternation.*

" This arrangement has, most clearly, conduced to the maintenance of order. The officer presiding is always consulted, in reference to the character of individuals whose time of discharge may be near, touching their several tempers and propensities, as also their qualifications for service as domestics. Those of *fair,* and those of even tolerable promise, are sent to families in the country, on handing from the chaplain a card of introduction to the *Secretary* of the society of ' *The Friends of Virtue,*' Chapel Place. Through the maternal care of this lady, and the Treasurer, of kindred spirit, the women are supplied with whatever may appear deficient in their apparel, so that none pass from their hands, but are decently clad. Of *seventeen* individuals thus highly favored, *four* only have, within the knowledge of the ladies, forfeited their solemn pledge, and returned to their former wretched course.

" *Visits in the Week.* I have passed fifty-nine evenings in visiting the prisoners from cell to cell. Have endeavored to understand their individual cases; to sympathize with them in their sorrows; to mitigate their woes; to bear their burdens; and, above all, to direct the heart to Him, who ' is the Rock; whose work is perfect; whose ways are judgment; a God of truth, and without iniquity.'

" *The men, on their discharge, have taken from the chaplain an introductory card, to the Washington Total Abstinence Society,* with a view to enlist the sympathies of its members in behalf of their suffering brethren. Three of those thus discharged, have become zealous and successful lecturers on the security and blessings of *temperance.*

" *I have visited the work-shop of the females every day, Saturday excepted, that, at its close, we might bow in prayer.*

" It has been my desire to furnish prisoners with a *practical* comment on principles advanced from the pulpit, by regard to their individual requests. In accordance with this object, I have visited all parts of the city, taking messages, inquiring after the welfare of connections and friends, and returning answers.

" *I have given forty-six visits to the hospitals.* At these seasons, have endeavored to ascertain, gently, the state of mind of the patient, that appropriate counsel might be imparted. Have avoided protracted conversation, lest the sick should suffer disquietude, to the increase of his disease; yet I have felt the importance of faithful dealing, in view of that solemn tribunal, at the bar of which we must all, ere long, stand.

" In my visits to the Prison, I have uniformly been favored with the cordial coöperating influence of the master and his officers.

" With adoring gratitude to the Most High, will we make mention of his wise and gracious care over us all, giving unanimity of feeling and harmony of action, in reference to the great objects of an institution, to which our hearts are alike attached, — for blessings upon which we are bound to offer up our earnest and devout supplications, with thanksgiving.

"CHARLES CLEVELAND, *Chaplain.*"

A committee of the general assembly of Connecticut, on the *Connecticut State Prison,* in their report at the May session, 1842, signed by Clark Bissel, Alfred Smith, Jeffery O. Phelps, and Richard Hine, say, —

" The statute provides for a chaplain to the Prison, and requires him to devote his whole time to the religious instruction and moral improvement of the prisoners; also that suitable apartments shall be provided for the introduction of a system of Sabbath school instruction, to be conducted under the superintendence of the warden and chaplain, in such manner as may be prescribed by the by-laws.

" The chaplain performs religious services in the morning of each Sabbath, at which most of the male prisoners attend, and in the afternoon with the female convicts. There has been no Sabbath school for some years past. The principal reason assigned by the warden for the omission, is the difficulty of obtaining teachers. The chaplain instructs some of the prisoners from cell door to cell door, especially on the Sabbath, but the amount of instruction is small, to each prisoner. The opportunities for giving instruction on week days are not considerable, and most of the prisoners, on the Sabbath, prefer resting from labor rather than attending to moral or religious teaching. The committee would recommend that the prisoners, in small divisions, might, in rotation, have time and opportunity of receiving instruction from the chaplain. If half of each day, or from three to four hours, were allowed among two or three such small divisions of prisoners, the whole number might have an hour and a half or two hours once in a fortnight, which would not take much from the earnings of each prisoner. Better still, if each division could be tried faithfully, with an hour and a half or two hours of instruction, once in each week, in addition to the opportunities now afforded them.

" Out of 805 of the male convicts heretofore or now in the State Prison, and whose ages are recorded, 171 were from 12 to 20 years of age inclusive, being more than one fifth of those whose ages are recorded. Probably about one fifth of the whole number of prisoners received at the Wethersfield Prison, have been from 12 to 20 years of age, when first received there.

" Of the 211 convicts in the State Prison, on the 31st of March, 1842, the ages of 163 are recorded. The number from the age of 12 to 20 is 43, or one fourth of the whole number of those whose ages are given. 28 of these were of the ages of 16, 17, 18, and 19, viz., seven of each of those ages.

" The committee earnestly recommend that greater opportunities for instruction be allowed and provided for a class of young prisoners. In other states, Houses of Refuge or Reformation have been established for young offenders, where they not only work and receive instruction, but care is used to find them places for earning a living, after their discharge, removed from old associates, haunts, and temptations, instead of leaving them to their own unaided resources and resolutions. Such an institution would offer to young offenders many more chances and means of reformation than the State Prison.

But even without waiting for a new institution, it appears to the committee, that, by selecting the more youthful and docile prisoners, requiring them to work by themselves, and allowing the afternoon or some part of every day for instruction, and caring for them when they leave the Prison, some part of them might be reformed, and become useful, instead of vicious and dangerous, members of the body politic "

The directors of the Connecticut State Prison, Walter Booth, Oliver H. King, and Henry Barnard, adopted the following rules and regulations concerning the " Duties of the Chaplain " in said Prison : —

" The chaplain shall, as required by law, devote his whole time to the religious instruction and moral improvement of the prisoners.

" He shall perform morning and evening service daily with the convicts, who shall be assembled for that purpose. He shall perform divine service in the chapel every Sunday. He shall have the care and management of the Sabbath school, with the coöperation and concurrence of the warden.

" He shall see that every convict is furnished with a Bible, and may apply to the warden for a proper supply. He shall have the privilege, and it shall be his province, to visit the convicts at all times when in their cells, or in the hospital, and administer to them such instruction and consolation as he may deem best calculated to promote their subordination, reformation, spiritual and eternal welfare ; and, at all proper times, endeavor to impress upon their minds the *justice of their punishment,* the *necessity of amendment,* and a *strict conformity to the rules of the Prison.*

" He shall not furnish them with any information or intelligence, other than relates to their duty, without permission of the warden.

" He shall use his utmost endeavors to instruct, through the grating of the cell doors, all who are unable to read.

" He shall conform, in all cases, to the general rules and regulations of the institution."

The inspectors of the *Prison at Sing Sing,* Edward Kemeys, William Newton, Hudson McFarlan, Isaac G. Graham, Jun., and Thomas Bailey, say, in their last report, —

" The report of the Rev. John Luckey, chaplain of the Prison, marked C, exhibits a highly favorable account of the moral and religious condition of the convicts. The unwearied industry of the chaplain in his department, his devotion to the welfare of the convicts, and his incessant labors for their reformation, entitle him to our warmest commendation. He does not appear to have labored in vain ; many of the convicts, under his lessons of instruction, exhibit evidence of a radical moral and religious reformation.

" The Sunday school for the convicts is still continued with evident benefit, and the convicts are furnished from the library of the Prison with books of a moral and religious character.

" We consider the library of great importance to the convicts, occupying in useful reading that portion of their time which would otherwise be spent in idleness, and furnishing them with opportunities for intellectual and moral improvement."

The agent, Mr. David L. Seymour, who is known to be exceedingly devoted to the moral and religious instruction of the prisoners, in the Sabbath school, in the Bible class, and in personal conversation, says nothing, in the annual report, on this important branch of the subject.   We suppose it is because he considers himself the financial agent, and that what he does in the moral and religious department, is incidental, and gratuitous, and therefore he will let it pass unnoticed.   If Mr. Seymour will deem our opinion, on this point, of any importance, we have no hesitation in expressing it, that there is no part of his labors and duties, in regard to which the public at large would be more glad to hear his testimony, than concerning the effect on the Prison of moral and religious instruction.   It would be entirely within his province to show what effect it has upon the financial department.   Are cheerful obedience, submission to authority, contentment, industry, and good-will, produced?   Are escapes, insurrections, punishment, and loss of time for misdemeanor, prevented by moral and religious instruction?   If so, how far are the favorable pecuniary results connected with moral and religious instruction? This may be all as plain as day to Mr. Seymour; but there are Prisons, and places, and persons, looking for evidence, on these important points, to the financial agents of Prisons.

The chaplain, the Rev. John Luckey, says, in his report, —

"It is with the deepest gratitude to the Divine Dispenser of all good, that I am permitted to make a favorable report in relation to the moral and religious condition of the prisoners under your supervision.   Making due allowance for the many and peculiar temptations to hypocrisy on the part of the convict, and which arise directly out of the relation he sustains to the officers, I am, nevertheless, confident in the opinion that an unusual degree of good moral and religious feeling prevails among the prisoners.

"The Sabbath school has more than doubled its numbers during the past year; and, as the attendance is *voluntary,* and the chief employment of a decidedly moral and religious character, an increase of numbers argues an increase of good moral feeling.   There were only 114 in the Sabbath school at the close of the last year, but now there are 337 industriously, and, as we hope, profitably, employed in it.   One half are learning to read, and the other half belong to Bible classes.

"Twenty-five of those who had been discharged during the past year had learned to read in the Sabbath school.   There are ten or twelve who, having learned to read in the Sabbath school *proper,* are transferred to the Bible classes.

"The undivided and serious attention manifested by each in the prosecution of his studies, has frequently called forth the public gratulations of visitors.

"I venture the opinion that no patriot, no philanthropist, and surely no *Christian,* can witness these operations for one Sabbath, without being fully satisfied of their powerful influence in reforming the convict.   Other and paramount indications of reform might be given; such as the great reduction of stripes, with as much or more labor performed than formerly; the apparent cheerfulness with which the prisoners toil; the ready and willing obedience they render; and the affectionate regard with which they uniformly speak of their keepers in general, and the principal keeper and agent in particular.

"Of these facts there is no one, perhaps, who has a better opportunity of speaking from *knowledge* than their chaplain, who is with them constantly, and to whom the officers have given them to understand, that they may open their minds freely on these subjects."

"It is true that our confidence in the professions of reform made by convicts while in Prison, has been somewhat shaken, within the last two years, by the return of two or three of this class to their former *criminal course* since their discharge. But, we ask, are there more, in proportion to the twenty of whose professions we reported favorably last year, than usually fall away out of the same number who make similar professions at our altars *out* of Prison? I think not.

"Why, then, are we accustomed to indulge such unusual suspicions respecting convict professions? It will be seen that I speak advisedly on this subject, when I say, through the generosity of Captains Odell and Haywood, who have conveyed me, *free of cost*, to and from New York, I have been permitted to visit a majority of the convicts above alluded to, several times since their discharge; and was happy to learn, both from themselves and their friends, that, like *men* and *Christians*, they had met and overcome the various cruel, and, in many instances, unlooked-for, temptations and rebukes, which naturally fall to the lot of such men; and, for the space of one or two years, had been demonstrating the superior advantage of a reform predicated on *principle* over that of impulse.

"I am, therefore, prepared, if needs be, to give the names and residence of nearly, if not quite, a score of this description, who are living in and near the cities of Brooklyn and New York.

"Besides, I have on file a number of letters from others of this class, living in various parts of the country, as also from their friends, advising me of their continued reform.

"I mention these facts solely for the purpose of encouraging the efforts which are now making in behalf of those unfortunate men, and, if possible, to contravene the opinion, *far too prevalent*, that, when a man is once detected in crime, there is little or no hope in his case, and that he should therefore be uniformly treated with *austerity* or *neglect*.

"The favorable moral condition of the prisoners is only what might be expected to result from the means made use of."

"Another source of great benefit to the prisoners, and which has a direct tendency to cultivate their moral feelings, is the intercourse allowed, under certain restrictions, between the convict and his relatives. The parents, wife, brothers, and sisters, are, in the presence of an officer, permitted to see their unfortunate friend, at least once during his confinement, and converse freely with him, when, as their conversation is restricted to social and moral subjects, the most wholesome and salutary advice and admonitions are generally given. These, coming, as they do, from the dearest of friends, have usually a peculiar and lasting effect.

"The same may be said of the scores of letters written for and received by them.

"As this duty generally devolves on me, and consequently the contents of the letters are known to me, I am prepared to say, that nine of them out of ten contain the best moral lecture that these men ever listened to, and which, being the production of an *injured* and *faithful friend*, produces the most lively impressions."

"As to the *decidedly religious* feeling among the convicts, I am conscious that it is on the increase. Four or five in the Prison, and about the same number who were discharged during the last year, have died under the pleasing prospects of obtaining 'the inheritance of the just,' through the forgiving mercy and abounding grace of our heavenly Father. Two of those who died at their homes, *thus happy*, had received a pardon from His Excellency, on account of their illness, only a few weeks before their death. I can, at this moment, call to mind the cases of about 20 individuals, who are now in good standing in the various churches, but whose convictions of sin and conversion to God were experienced during their confinement here. This not only encourages me to persevere in my labors with ardor, but causes me also to esteem *vital piety* as the *surest*, if not the only, antidote for vice and crime.

" Respecting the Female Prison, I would say that, under the supervision of the excellent matron and her assistants, it continues to prosper. From the visitors, both domestic and foreign, I have heard no expressions respecting it but those of approbation. From the fact that there are nearly, if not quite, as many females as there are males in the state, and yet we have 14 or 15 male prisoners to one female, our inference can be no other than that the courts and jury of our country will not, as doubtless they ought not, consent to send any female to the State Prison save the *vilest of the vile.* In view of this fact, what can be more evident than that the moral improvement of these women is *very great?* and although it may be thought by some that more of the females, in proportion, who leave the Prison with professions of reform, return to their former habits of pollution and sin, than those of the males who make a similar profession, yet it would seem, from the fact that only two of the former ever returned to this Prison, that they are no more, if as much, disposed to return to a *criminal* course, than are the males.

" The professions of piety among the females are about the same, both in number and character, as was reported last year.

" One or two of those who have died this year, left strong hope of having died in peace.

" The Sabbath school in this department is doing much towards preparing these unfortunate females to regain a respectable standing in the community, and much credit is due those ladies, who, through great sacrifice, render their assistance in promoting the interests of the school."

The chaplain of the *Prison at Auburn,* the Rev. Thomas R. Townsend, in the last annual report of that institution, says, —

" The general attention given to the gospel preached, has been such as to excite the hope that, to many, it might prove the power of God unto salvation. Indeed, I cannot doubt that, to some, already the word of life has been ' as cold water to the thirsty soul.' My personal visits to the cells of the convicts have met, almost invariably, with their warmest reception. As a general rule, they are perfectly accessible, and exhibit, contrary to impressions usually received, a degree of sensibility nowise inferior to that of men in other and more favored circumstances. Flowing tears and a heaving breast are often the index to the big emotion struggling within, at the mention of home, parents, wives, and children. Here, excluded from many of the exciting causes of dissipation and debauchery, they emerge from their debasing and benumbing influence. The tender sympathies of our common nature, which had been so nearly blotted out, are revived. Reason, so long perverted and enslaved, is reënthroned, the slumbering conscience is reawakened, and thus are they rendered peculiarly susceptible of moral and religious impressions.

" Our Sabbath school, embracing about 300 of the younger and more ignorant class of convicts, has been in successful operation during the past year. The Christian sympathy of the young gentlemen of the Auburn Theological Seminary is, as heretofore, deeply enlisted in the religious training of these outcasts from society, and I fear, too much from the thoughts and prayers of the Christian public. Their strong desire, I doubt not, is to do good to their unfortunate and guilty fellow-men. They neither expect nor wish remuneration from men; but He who has promised to reward a cup of cold water, given for His sake, will not fail to remember them in their self-denying and philanthropic efforts. Permit me, gentlemen, through you, to express to them my warmest thanks ; my prayers also shall be with and for them in all their labors, both here and elsewhere.

" It has been satisfactorily ascertained, that, of the whole number committed to this Prison, who are unable to read the Bible intelligently, the proportion is about as one to four or five. Through the criminal, and, I had almost said, unpardonable, neglect of parents and guardians, they have been allowed to grow up in the most abject ignorance ; they not only are unable to read or write, but, in some cases, cannot even count *ten* correctly. In this state of extreme ignorance, who cannot see their lamentable exposure to become the dupes of crafty and designing men ? Their history is brief. Beset with temptations, they are made the easy prey of their seducers, fall into crime, and are cast into Prison. The question suggests itself forcibly to my mind, Cannot something more be done for this truly pitiable class of our fellow-men, than has hitherto been done ? I rejoice to know that it is the policy of this state to extend the means of education just as far as the interests of the whole population will allow. For this purpose large appropriations from the public treasury are annually made. But here is a class of men whose last hope of instruction (as a general remark) is circumscribed within these walls, but for which nothing like an adequate provision has as yet been made. Here, or nowhere, these neglected and unfortunate youth must be instructed in the first principles of education, their minds elevated, and they thus prepared to become better sons, better husbands, better parents, better citizens. It is true, our Sabbath school, and the public services of the sanctuary, do something towards meeting their necessities, but are quite inadequate, as must appear to every reflecting mind. An hour or two in seven days, however well employed, can do but little, comparatively, towards securing for them that moral and intellectual culture which is absolutely necessary in order to the achievement of one of the most important ends of our Prison discipline. Is it not equally the dictate of philanthropy and sound policy, that larger provision should be made for the education of these young men, and such as is adapted to meet the extreme exigency of their condition ? Let but one or two hours of each day be devoted to their intellectual improvement, and what might we not anticipate as the blessed results, not only in the way of direct influence upon themselves, but also indirectly upon their families and society, and, further still, as an example to other kindred institutions ? "

The inspectors of the *Penitentiary in New Jersey* say, in their report, October 28, 1841, —

" We believe there is a deficiency of moral and religious books in the Prison, and are of the opinion that, if the number and variety of them were increased, it might have a salutary effect.

" It is very difficult to arrive at any certainty about the religious and moral character of the convicts, there being so great a difference in their professions while here, and their practices after their discharge from the walls of the Prison.

" The board would be extremely remiss, were they to neglect to notice the voluntary and constant attention of the clergy of Trenton and its vicinity, and the zeal and interest they have manifested at all times, in endeavoring to inculcate principles of religion and morality among the prisoners, and the readiness they have shown to point out and lead them in the paths of religion and virtue."

The legislative committee of council and assembly say, —

" It is with great pleasure that your committee respond to that part of said report which recommends an increased supply of moral and religious books for the use of said Prison, believing they would have a tendency to exercise the otherwise dormant energies of the minds of the convicts, and improve their morals. Your committee recommend that a small appropriation be made for the purpose of furnishing a library for the benefit of the prisoners, and herewith report the accompanying resolution.

" *Resolved*, That the committee of ways and means be and they are hereby directed to bring in a bill making an appropriation of a sum not exceeding one hundred dollars, for the purpose of furnishing a library for the use of the prisoners, to be placed under the control and direction of the keeper."

The inspectors of the *Eastern Penitentiary*, Thomas Bradford, John Bacon, Matthew L. Bevan, Robert Patterson, and Richard Vaux, say, in their last report, —

" The efforts of the moral instructor have been useful and fruitful of good. His desire has been to reform, and instil sound morals, without cant or sectarianism."

The moral instructor, Mr. Thomas Larcombe, in the last report of the Eastern Penitentiary, says, —

" It would be highly gratifying to me to be able to present undoubted proofs of much good having been done through the instrumentality of my visits and instructions, during the year just closed; but, from the very peculiar nature of the service, such attestations are not often possible.

" The influence of entire seclusion, upon the minds of many persons, by calling up before them their past turpitude, awakens remorse, and naturally leads them to religion as the sovereign antidote for all their guilt and grief; and, too often mistaking that remorse for repentance, they resort to reading the Scriptures and daily prayer, and on this slight foundation rest their hope of an assured and permanent change having been effected, until, after the lapse of a few weeks or months, the sad mistake becomes evident. In addition to this, a considerable proportion are so depraved as to take pleasure in deceiving, or hope to compass some private or selfish purpose by false professions. These, and other causes, often produce doubt where there are appearances of real good having been effected. My position, therefore, is like that of a husbandman who cultivates a sterile soil, in the hope of a future and distant reward.

" The effects of moral and religious instruction have not been so encouraging during the past year as in the two years preceding: at least, an equal amount of good impression has not been observable. The year, however, has not closed upon us without some pleasing indications of the usefulness of religious instruction. Its influence is visible in promoting quietness and order, and the general good deportment of the prisoners. Of the number of those discharged during the year, I entertain the hope that eighteen are morally benefited, and that seven others have given as satisfactory evidence of an entire change of heart and life, as, in their peculiar circumstances, could reasonably be expected. I am encouraged to express the hope of their future good conduct, by the fact, that, of a private record of such as I have ventured to consider the subjects of reform, during more than three years, not one has yet returned; and of the general propriety of their conduct, so far as information has been received, there is no cause for doubt. It has given me much satisfaction to have received, within the year, certain information of the entire reform of twelve persons, formerly inmates of this Penitentiary, who are now engaged in honest occupations, and respected in society. The history of one of these, a young man, has been distinguished by severe and distressing trials during six months of great privation, from which, sustained by the grace of God, he has come forth unharmed by temptation; and, during an equal portion of time since, he has given encouraging evidence of a steadfast adherence to Christian principle.

"From another prisoner, whose crime was occasioned by intemperance, a very satisfactory letter has recently been received, from which is given the following extract: — 'I have been idle only three days, and have my choice of a full winter's work in three places. I am strictly temperate, and intend to remain so as long as I live. I formed that resolution on my knees, on the morning in which I left my cell; for I concluded that, as I had been kept from spirit three years, I could keep from it all my life; and, if it please God to continue my health, I hope to do better than I have ever yet done.'

"One, who formerly occupied a cell in this Prison, closed his earthly career in the early part of the past year. He learned while in this place the deep pollution of his nature, and, in the fountain opened for sin, obtained cleansing. Having a good education, he became, after his release, a messenger of mercy to others, and, as a minister of the gospel, endeavored, with zeal and fidelity, to turn many to righteousness. His last end was peace.

"I have reason to hope that two of the number of those who died in Prison, were prepared for that solemn event by a well-founded trust in the mercy of a gracious God.

"During the past year, I have been aided in the Sabbath exercises, as usual, by ministers of the gospel, of various denominations. One hundred and sixty-five addresses have been delivered to the prisoners, who are now distributed through six corridors; and on each alternate Sabbath, all have heard the gospel; and as the result of these services, some twelve or more appear to have received impressions which, I hope, will prove to be permanent and salutary.

"Of the number discharged, 74 could read and write, 9 of whom learned in Prison; 69 could read, 28 of whom learned in Prison; and 22 could not read.

"Of 126 committed in the same period, 2 had a good education, 67 could read and write, 26 could read only, and 31 could not read."

The directors of the *Penitentiary in Baltimore,* in their last report, signed by Jacob G. Davies, president, dated December, 1841, say, —

"The discipline of the several departments under the direction of the warden has been marked during the past year by an exactness and uniformity of operation, which prove that the laws and regulations have been duly administered, and that these were happily devised to secure a well-ordered system. In so far as reformation may be effected by the means of silence and non-intercourse, we believe that its accomplishment is much and steadily aided by the established economy of the Prison. The observance of silence during the day is, by the strictest regulations, required of the convicts; and their separation in the cells at night completes the solitude in which the period of their imprisonment is passed.

"Under the influence of these circumstances, an evident deep contrition is developed in very many cases, in which a purpose of permanent reform is earnestly professed, and, we have no doubt, is, for the time, sincerely entertained. To strengthen the impressions that are thus produced, and confirm the amended inclinations arising from them, — to rescue from the ills and degradation of vice, and teach the excellence and the advantages, in all respects, of its opposite, — are the especial objects of the religious exercises of the Sabbath, and of the moral and religious instructions long since commenced, and still continued with unabated interest by a clerical gentleman to whom we alluded in our report of last year.

"We have no means of judging, with any probable accuracy, of the amount of enduring reformation that has been produced, — aware, as we are, that professions of amendment made during the term of confinement, are too often but the result of circumstances incidental to it, which are influential only during the period of restraint. Such professions it would be futile to confide in, as proof, in all cases, of established change of character; but the almost total absence of recommitments since the introduction of the improved discipline into the Prison, affords a reasonable ground for belief that much of real good has been effected.

" The nature of the discipline is certainly such as to prevent a further deterioration; and in this it has relieved the institution from an opprobrium which, until latterly, it shared in common with all unimproved Prisons, — that of aggravating the vicious qualities of its inmates, by leaving them to unrestricted intercommunication. Under present arrangements, such an effect is wholly precluded. The period of admission is, to all, one at which the progress of demoralizing tendencies is arrested, — the term of confinement one of continued moral coercion, peremptory in its restrictive requirements, yet acting in association with all the milder methods of conducting to good. The lessons that are so inculcated are not inefficacious; and although, in some instances, they may leave but a transient impression, yet, in the less corrupt, and in those who are not irreclaimable, they do not fail to produce a permanent amelioration. To those who are hopelessly abandoned to crime, — and our experience has taught us to believe that such there are, — a class addicted to habitual theft, but not unmindful of the chances of detection, — to those the system is of sufficient dread to divert them to other states, as yet imperfect in penal discipline, in which a conviction of the infraction of laws would consign them to imprisonment less rigorously irksome, and not without the solace of congenial companionship."

The keeper of the *Georgia Penitentiary*, Charles H. Nelson, Esq., in his last report, dated November, 1841, says, —

" While we have used all the means in our control, to bring this institution within the pale of others, in the states, of highest reputation, we have not been unheedful of those moral influences, thought best calculated to cause the return of the prodigal son. Sunday schools have this year been instituted, and directed by charitable individuals, without cost, other than such books as were required of me, which were promptly furnished, under a ready hope that their labors would bring the returning sinner home."

" When added to the duties of the official clergyman, whose labors have been uniform, we have a hope (although delayed) that there may be realized a goodly repentance with many; and may the God of mercies so direct it to the minds of all, that, rather than make the Penitentiary the school of crime, it may be made one of virtuous and lasting repentance."

The joint select committee of the Mississippi Legislature appointed to examine the *Penitentiary at Jackson, Mississippi*, say, in their report to the legislature in February, 1842, —

" If a system of education on the Sunday school plan were introduced, it would, no doubt, be productive of beneficial results. Many of the convicts might be taught reading, and the useful branches of literature and sciences, in addition to moral and religious instruction; and the Christian and the benevolent portion of the community of Jackson and its vicinity, would, no doubt, cheerfully lend their gratuitous assistance in the promotion of so laudable an object. If a small sum, say one hundred dollars, were appropriated in the purchase of suitable school books, or histories, for the use of the institution, such a library would, no doubt, soon be greatly augmented by the voluntary contributions of the humane and the benevolent.

" Those who deny the practicability of the reformation of Penitentiary convicts in this manner, only evince the want of a proper knowledge of human nature. Those who engage in the high and laudable object of inculcating the principles of religion, morality, and virtue, where they are enforced by exemplary conduct, will command the respect of all men; and to deny the possibility, and even probability, of a reformation and improvement, to some extent, at least, in the convicts, would be to deny that man is impressed with the image of his Creator: nor ought we necessarily to suppose that all who may be sent to the Penitentiary, are to be regarded as having lost all character or sense of propriety."

Mr. C. D. Learned, president of the board of inspectors of the Mississippi Penitentiary, thus answers the following question, from the committee of the legislature, on the subject of moral and religious instruction : —

" Do you not believe that, if a system of Sunday school instruction was introduced among them, so as to permit those who are disposed to improve themselves, to spend the Sabbath day in receiving literary, and religious, and moral instruction, that it would be productive of good, in improving the morals of the convicts, and at the same time render their situation more comfortable ?

" *Answer.* I have no doubt but a moral instructor would be productive of much good, and the report of the chaplain will show the manner they are taught at this time."

The report of the chaplain, here referred to by the president of the board of inspectors, we regret to say, is not published with the official document, which contains the above testimony in favor of the Sabbath school and other moral and religious instruction.

The inspectors of the *Penitentiary in Nashville*, R. C. Foster, John Harding, and William Carrol, in their report to the legislature, dated October 11, 1841, say nothing on the subject of moral and religious instruction.

The keeper also, Mr. H. J. Anderson, spoken of as a valuable man, says nothing, in his report, on the subject of moral and religious instruction. Last year, there was preaching each Sabbath, to one half the prisoners, by ministers from the city — but no Sabbath school — no chaplain.

The keeper of the *Kentucky Penitentiary*, Thomas S. Theobald, in his last report, dated January 3, 1842, says, —

" In regard to the morals of the convicts, they have had every incentive set before them to promote their reformation of heart. The gospel is regularly preached to them, every Sabbath, by pious ministers, and other means of moral instruction are employed. While, as it regards a large number of the prisoners, I cannot profess any confidence in their moral reformation, there are unquestionable examples of moral improvement, if not regeneration, which should greatly encourage the efforts and prayers of the Christian philanthropist in their behalf."

The inspectors of the *Ohio Penitentiary*, William Spencer, Samuel Spangler, and John McElvain, in their report to the legislature, dated December 25, 1841, say, —

" In our report of December, 1840, we called the attention of the legislature to the fact, that we had dispensed with the services of a chaplain at the Prison.

Since that time, none has been employed. We have received a communication from the Rev. Samuel F. Mills on that subject. Mr. M. has, for some time past, been gratuitously officiating as chaplain. We have, however, made an appropriation of one hundred dollars, since the performance of the services by him, being unwilling that they should go entirely unrewarded. We refrain from giving any opinion as to the propriety of employing an individual in that capacity. We consider it a matter entirely with the legislature, and that we have no discretion, and we are not disposed to make any appointment without being expressly directed by law."

The warden, Mr. William B. Van Hook, says nothing, in his last report, on the subject of moral and religious instruction.

MILD PUNISHMENTS IN PENITENTIARIES.

The keeper of the *Maine Prison*, John O'Brien, in his last report, page 9, says, concerning the prisoners under his care, —

" Their conduct has been much better than at any preceding period. I expressed to them a wish that their deportment should be such as to cause no complaint from any of the subordinate officers; and I feel gratified to state that but very few have been reported as delinquent, and that a gentle reprimand for misbehavior has proved to be far more salutary than severer punishment."

The inspectors of the *Massachusetts State Prison* say, in their last report, page 4, —

" The discipline of the Prison has been effectually preserved without resort to stripes, except in a very few instances, by the use of mild punishments."

The inspectors of the *Prison at Sing Sing* say, in their last report, page 9, —

" The discipline of the Prison requires implicit obedience on the part of the convict to the orders of the keepers, and no violation of the rules of the Prison is suffered to pass with impunity. The discipline, while necessarily strict, is tempered with humanity. The convict is treated as a rational being, and made to feel that he is such, and that though, degraded by crime, he must necessarily submit to the penalties of the law, yet still there is justice and mercy for him notwithstanding his degradation."

The chaplain of the Prison at Sing Sing, in his last report, page 25, says, —

" I still regard the influence of the resolution which refers all the punishment to be awarded, and the time when it should be inflicted, to the decision of the principal keeper, as being exceedingly friendly to the moral feelings of the convicts.

" These favorable results flow as much, perhaps, from the prudent and faithful manner in which the designs of this resolution have been executed, as from the designs themselves."

And again, page 26 and 27, —

" That *mildness* connected with *firmness* in government, exerts a powerful influence upon the moral feelings, is evident from many facts, which have, during my chaplaincy, come to my knowledge. Permit me here to introduce one example. An individual who was, through executive clemency, liberated some two years since, came to visit me the other day, and, while in conversation on Prison affairs, observed that, although he had been for several years an inmate of this Prison, his moral feelings remained unaffected to any extent, until a few weeks before his release, when the agent came to the door of his cell, and, giving him some friendly advice of a moral and religious kind, put a tract in his hand, and passed on to the next cell. While this act of attention was softening his heart — perhaps the very next day — the principal keeper passed through his shop, and, on recognizing a convict whom he had brought to Prison a few years previously, stepped up to him, and, in a friendly manner, shook hands with him. These kindnesses, he said, so thrilled his soul, that he determined instanter to *die* rather than to mortify and disgrace *such officers* by a *future course of crime ;* and he observed, ' These are the feelings of my heart at this moment.'

" I speak from *knowledge* when I say that better evidence of having conducted with great moral integrity since his liberation than this man produced cannot be given."

The keeper, A. McDuffee, in his last report, says, pages 29 and 30, —

" A resolution was adopted, at the meeting of the board on the 3d of June, 1840, requiring that the assistant keepers report to the principal keeper every breach of discipline, or insubordination of the convicts, previous to inflicting punishment, and that the principal keeper shall determine the amount of punishment inflicted, and the time when such shall be inflicted. In my opinion, the above resolution has had a tendency to produce a very beneficial and gratifying result. I find that unsubdued human nature is the same here as any where, and that it is a true maxim that ' soft words turn away anger.' The management of our Prison has been a subject of much excitement, and great feeling has shown itself amongst all classes of the community, and perhaps not without a cause. I am fully aware that many of the convicts are of the most abandoned and desperate character, and that some of them need very severe restrictions to keep them in subordination. But there is a chord, even in the most corrupt heart, that vibrates to kindness, and a sense of justice which knows when it has been rightly dealt with. I am persuaded that much evil has emanated from those who preceded me in the administration of the Prison ; and by the mode of punishment to which they resorted to inflict chastisement upon convicts, men are aroused to hatred and fiendish revenge. I find that by mild treatment and rational punishment, the convicts behave in a more discreet and uniform manner, and accomplish more work.

" It is thought by the keepers who have had long experience, that the present mode of management is far the best. The convict seems more mild and pleasant, and some say that not one tenth part of the punishment is inflicted ; and they further say that cruel treatment and oppression is done away, and the convicts are much easier managed than ever before."

The inspectors of the *Eastern Penitentiary, in Philadelphia,* say, in their last report, page 4, —

" During the past year, the conduct and deportment of a very large majority of the prisoners have been good. Few cases have required any other than humane treatment, and where any such cases have occurred, the mildest form of punishment the inspectors could adopt, has been resorted to.

" The inspectors can never forget that the persons committed to their charge are men ; and, although fallen, debased, and convict, yet they possess feelings susceptible to kindness, and minds capable of improvement."

The warden of the Eastern Penitentiary says, in his last report, page 8, —

" During the past year, the deportment of a great majority of the prisoners has been good. Few cases have occurred in which punishment has been necessary; and, when resorted to, the most severe inflicted has been confinement on bread and water, without work, and for a period not in any case exceeding a week."

EVILS IN PENITENTIARIES REMAINING TO BE CORRECTED.

In the *Maine State Prison, at Thomaston*, the warden says, in his last report, pages 8 and 9, —

" For several years past, the attention of the legislature has been called to the bad construction of the cells of this Prison; and I trust that the subject will, at this time, receive your particular notice. I would state that these cells were originally designed to test the efficacy of solitary confinement without labor. They seem to have been formed exclusively with a view to inflict a great degree of punishment in a short time, and at the least expense. A few months' experience, however, fully satisfied its most sanguine advocates, that this mode should be totally abandoned. There are real and unavoidable evils imposed upon the convicts, by their confinement in these cells, which claim consideration. No light can be reflected into the cells, so that the prisoners may be enabled to read, or engage in any study to improve their minds or morals. Neither can their cells be warmed; therefore they are obliged to remain constantly in their beds, in cold weather, from sunset until near sunrise, which has a tendency to weaken and debilitate both mind and body. Besides, a large sum is annually expended for the purchase of bed-clothes, which, from dampness or other causes, soon go to destruction. A thorough inspection cannot be had; therefore that degree of cleanliness which should be rigidly enforced, can never be maintained in this Prison. Have we any right thus to inflict unnecessary sufferings on our fellow-creatures? Is it creditable to our state to have an institution so constructed as to render such evils unavoidable? I trust that the liberal and enlightened policy of other states in the Union, as exercised in the construction of convenient and comfortable Prisons for the confinement of that unfortunate class who may from time to time require the restraints of the Penitentiary, will not be disregarded by the legislature of Maine. Other states, as well as our own, were unsuccessful in their first structures; but they have long since corrected their error by the erection of suitable ones, which in every instance has produced its desired effects, both in a moral and pecuniary point of view."

INSUFFICIENT AND IMPERFECT WORK-SHOPS.

In the *Massachusetts State Prison, at Charlestown*, the inspectors, Messrs. Minot, Greele, and Sumner, say, in their last report, —

" The enlargement of some of the work-shops is practicable, and very desirable for the health and comfort of the prisoners. Several of the shops are much crowded, and do not afford sufficient room for the work performed in them, or for preventing communication between the prisoners."

IMPRISONMENT OF LUNATICS.

The inspectors of the *State Prison in Massachusetts* presented a memorial to the last legislature to have the lunatics, of whom there were several, removed to the State Hospital at Worcester; but without success.

The physician of the *State Prison in New Hampshire* says, —

"I would beg leave to state the fact to the board, that several persons are confined in this Prison who are so unequivocally *insane,* as to be rendered more fit subjects for the *moral training* of a Lunatic Asylum than the *penal discipline* of a Penitentiary. One in particular is at this time confined to his cell, laboring under a severe paroxysm of the disease. Through the kindness and attention of the officers, he is rendered as comfortable as the circumstances of the case will admit, but cannot, of course, have the advantages of an institution expressly adapted to the wants of the insane."

The physician of the *Ohio Penitentiary* says, in his last report, page 27, —

"There is, at present, one individual laboring under mental derangement; but, such is the situation of the hospital, that he cannot receive that treatment that would be necessary to restore him to reason.

"It is well known to all who have charge of the insane, that the most mild and gentle means should be made use of toward persons laboring under mental derangement; and any thing like severity or coercion only tends to aggravate, rather than alleviate, their sufferings.

"It therefore appears to me indispensably necessary that some place should be provided, for the treatment of those who may become insane in this institution."

CHARACTER OF OFFICERS.

A committee of the legislature of *Mississippi* summoned witnesses before them, last winter, in regard to the character and habits of the officers of the Prison, when the following testimony was given : —

P. Duzett's Testimony.

"Philemon Duzett, being sworn, says, that he acted as guard, from May 1 to December 31, and that he saw No. 10 hung up to a post by one arm, without a cap, for four or more hours, in the hot sun, and frequently in the stocks by head and hands, for half a day at a time. Saw Hart pull him down by the hair, and push him about, and curse him, (when he complained of being sick, and was then under the care of the doctor.) Saw Hart step behind him, and heard No. 10 say frequently, 'Don't kick me;' and Hart pushed him along before him. Has seen prisoners kept in the pillory on Sunday, ten hours, or all day, and not allowed to go to church; make them always turn up the side of the head shaved, and cap pulled off when in the stocks. Says 28 has been kept in the dark cell seven days, on bread and water. Says No. 12 has been kept also six or seven days, and in the pillory all day. Says Hart is generally very severe; that he is partial; treats No. 15 with more kindness than others; that he treats No. 27 very severe, who is unable to undergo hard labor; that the stocks spoken of is really a pillory, so fixed as to compel the convict to stand on a small pole, with the hands and head confined; that the pole can be moved up or down, so as to suit the length of the man confined. And further this deponent saith not."

H. J. White's Testimony.

"H. J. White, being sworn, says, that he commenced working as a master workman, (wheelwright,) September, 1840, and continues yet. That he saw

Hart, on a cold morning, pull off the shirt of No. 17, who was sickly; left convict with nothing on but a roundabout. 27 was then faithfully at work; witness directed convict to place his bench near the fire to work, but Hart came and made him remove again. Saw No. 10 fastened with one arm to the post extended on his feet, so as hardly to be able to stand. Says he has seen Major Hart frequently intoxicated, but seldom comes out among the convicts when in that situation; says, when sober, and in a good humor, he is very kind, but when angry with a prisoner, is very severe, and uses partiality among the convicts."

James Duncan's Testimony, to whom Men were reported, and who kept a Record of Punishments.

"*Question.* Have you ever seen Major Hart, the keeper, intoxicated; and if so, what was his conduct towards the prisoners and others connected with the Penitentiary?

"*Answer.* I have seen him in a drinking way, but I cannot say that he was much intoxicated. I have never seen him troublesome at such times. It appears to have the effect more of making him good-humored. I believe he seldom or ever keeps spirits about the Penitentiary, and does not come about it if he is in that way."

President of the Board of Inspectors, C. D. Learned's Testimony.

"State what are the habits of the keeper and inferior officers, in regard to the use of ardent spirits. Have you seen him or them, on duty, under the influence of ardent spirits?

"*Answer.* The use of ardent spirits, within the institution, is prohibited. I have seen the superintendent and the clerk under the influence of spirituous liquors, out of the Penitentiary, but not, as I recollect, when upon duty."

DIMINISHING THE LENGTH OF SENTENCES FOR CRIME, IN MASSACHUSETTS, CONNECTICUT, AND VIRGINIA.

The average length of sentence in the State Prisons is about two or three times as long, in the states just mentioned, as in Pennsylvania. The following statements sustain this general fact : —

LENGTH OF SENTENCES IN PENITENTIARIES.

Average sentence of 322, the whole number in the Massachusetts State Prison, Sept. 30, 1840, ...   5 yrs. 9 mos.

Average sentence of 189, in the Connecticut State Prison, March 31, 1841, ...   7 yrs. 3 mos.

Average sentence of 152, in the New Jersey State Prison, Sept. 30, 1840, ...   4 yrs. 7 mos.

Average sentence of 129, in the New Penitentiary in Philadelphia, received during the year 1840, ...   2 yrs. 5 mos.

Average sentence of 104, in the Baltimore Penitentiary, received during the year ending Nov. 30, 1840, ...   3 yrs.

Average sentence of 79, in the Penitentiary
in the District of Columbia, during the
year 1840, ... 3 yrs. 8 mos.
Average sentence of 181, in the Virginia Penitentiary, Sept. 30, 1839, ... 6 yrs. 10 mos.
Average sentence of 162, in the Kentucky
Penitentiary, Nov. 30, 1840, ... 4 yrs.
Average sentence of 68, received in the Louisiana Penitentiary, during the year 1839, . 5 yrs. 1 mo.

The joint standing committee on Prisons, in the legislature
of *Massachusetts*, submitted a report to the legislature, March
16, 1840, in which they recommend a diminution ˙ in the
length of sentences for certain crimes, and give the following
reasons in its favor. They quote from the report of the
inspectors of the Prison at Charlestown, as follows : —

" The time is not very distant, when, from the increasing population of the
commonwealth, an addition to the accommodations of the Prison will be required. The new Prison contains only 304 cells, and there have been, at one
time during the past year, 330 convicts within the walls. The old Prison
contains only 28 cells which are safe and convenient places of confinement,
the residue of the building being required for the hospital, and as a place of
deposit of the public property."

The committee go on to say, —

" It is alleged, that it ought not to be the policy of the state to multiply
Prisons beyond the most absolute wants of society ; that the objects of the
Prison are twofold — to protect society, and reform the offenders. One class
of offenders, who have forfeited all their claims to personal freedom, and the
enormity of whose offences can only be expiated by a life of incarceration
and toil, within walls of stone and iron, are sentenced during natural life.
This class is small, and it is not thought that the safety of the community
would admit of any change in relation to them. But, with regard to the
other class, who are sentenced for a term of years, for the double purpose of
expiation and reformation, it is believed that a beneficial change may be made.
The term of imprisonment allowed by law is much longer in this, than in
most of the other states, for the same offence, and is thought, by those who
have investigated the subject, to be much longer than serves any useful purpose, as a reformative measure. Besides, in most cases, now, there is a
strong hope of pardon, and the applications for the exercise of executive
clemency have become numerous and incessant. Let the period for which
they are sentenced be shortened, according to the provisions of the accompanying bill, and, at the same time, let it be understood that the punishment
will be certain, and not terminated or cut short by a pardon, and its effect in
deterring from the commission of crime, it is believed, will be quite as great
as it now is. This measure will greatly relieve the Prison, by lessening the
number of its inmates, and thus it will do away the necessity of building
another for many years. It will also reduce the labors of the executive, by
abolishing the hope of pardon ; it will consequently diminish the applications
for it. It is understood that the labors of the committee of the executive
council on pardons, are exceedingly onerous, from the multiplicity of applications. Were the term of imprisonment shortened, the cases really demanding

an exercise of the power would be so infrequent as not to hold out an inducement for frequent and repeated petitions for it by the friends of convicts. By
this statement, however, the committee would not be understood as expressing
an opinion, even by implication, that the pardoning power has been, heretofore, too freely or too frequently exercised, so as to invite applications for it;
for they entertain no such opinion. They only say, that the circumstances
calling for its exercise will be so changed by the proposed measure, that the
necessity of resorting to it will, to a great extent, be abolished. With these
views, the committee report the annexed bill.

" All which is respectfully submitted.

" FOSTER HOOPER, per order.

" <i>March</i> 16, 1840."

" An Act to reduce the Term of Time for the Punishment of certain
Crimes.

" Be it enacted by the Senate and House of Representatives, in General
Court assembled, and by the authority of the same, as follows: —
" That the Revised Statutes, chapters one hundred and twenty-five to one
hundred and thirty-three, inclusive, be so amended as to read, <i>five years,</i> for
' <i>twenty years ; ' four years,</i> for ' <i>ten years ; ' three and a half years,</i> for ' <i>seven
years,</i>' and <i>three years,</i> for ' <i>five years,</i>' wherever the terms of years above
quoted occur in said chapters."

The chaplain of the State Prison at Charlestown, in his
last report, makes the following remarks, founded on the experience and observations of years, on this subject : —

" The undersigned hopes he may not be thought to be going out of his appropriate limits, if he ventures to make a few suggestions in relation to a subject which he is aware belongs more directly to the consideration and action
of those who enact our laws. He refers to the <i>length of sentences</i> to hard
labor in the State Prison, where such sentences are for <i>a term of years,</i> and
not for life. This is a subject to which he has given much thought, and in
regard to which he has studied to come to a correct result. He has carefully
watched the operation of confinement and wholesome discipline on the minds
and hearts of those subjected to their influence, as the term of their sentences
has progressed, and he is free to say, that the conviction has been strengthening in his mind, from year to year, that many of the sentences are unnecessarily and injuriously severe. These sentences were originally fixed when a
system of confinement and discipline was in operation in our State Prison
altogether different from that which at present exists. And, furthermore,
when our statutes, a few years since, were revised, this fact, it is presumed,
did not strike the minds of those to whom this revision was intrusted, nor of
our legislators, to whom this revision was submitted, and by whom it was
approved. It is believed that the cause of humanity would be subserved, and
the authority of the laws at the same time maintained, by a very material
change in most, or even all, the longer sentences, <i>for a term of years,</i> as at
present established by our criminal statutes.
" Correct principles of Prison discipline aim to reform as well as to punish
the offender. When discharged from his confinement, they would send him
back into society with a renovated character, prepared to bless his friends,
and the community of which he may be a member; and, whilst our laws
should be so framed as to be a 'terror to evil-doers,' they should never lose
sight of ultimate benefit, and the best practical results, to all those whom they
may subject to Penitentiary discipline. The undersigned cherishes a confident belief, that it is neither the duration nor the severity of punishment, to
which we are to look for those results which are designed to be produced by

our present improved system of Prison discipline, but rather to its nature or kind, and the manner of its infliction. He is furthermore satisfied, from long and careful observation, that, in a great majority of instances, whatever may be the length of the sentence to which the convict is subjected, where a hopeful reformation or change of character takes place, the work is accomplished within a comparatively short period of time after his commitment to the Prison. If the first two or three years pass away without any sensible and hopeful transformation of character, the anticipations for the future are always painful. It is true there are occasional exceptions, but they are comparatively few. By long confinement the mind becomes accustomed to its condition, and ordinarily becomes more and more insensible, and consequently less and less impressible, whatever means or motives may be applied to waken its sensibilities or move it to penitence.

" It is true that the good of the convict is not the only thing which claims attention. The public good is, and must be, a paramount consideration. The authority of the laws must be sustained. The public welfare demands it. Still, as has been already remarked, it is believed that both these objects may be secured, and yet the terms of confinement, as they now exist in our statute books, in many instances, be greatly shortened.

" It needs only that a person have an intimate acquaintance with the operation of the system of confinement and discipline, as at present existing in this Prison, when compared with the same as they existed in former times, — with crowded night-rooms, with an intercourse between the convicts almost unrestrained by day and by night, and with the means of procuring all sorts of indulgences and practising all the arts of villany, — to be satisfied that the confinement of a single year, with its silence and solitude, and subjection to wholesome discipline, as they now exist, is productive to the prisoner of more real, and heartfelt, and salutary suffering, than he would experience in twice that length of time under the ancient system. Then, he could enjoy the society of his fellows; amusements of various kinds were at his command; and, by the various ways which ingenious villany can devise, he could contrive to stifle conscience, to banish reflection, and make the mind callous to all those sensibilities and recollections, which, in his present situation, throng upon him, and torture and harrow up his spirit.

" In connection with these remarks, the undersigned would suggest, whether the penalties of 20, 14, 10, 7, and 5 years, may not, wisely and safely, be changed to 10, 7, 5, 4, and 3 years, or to something not varying materially from that ratio, — leaving sentences for life, and those for confinement for 1 and 2 years, to stand as they now are. Such a step would, it is believed, very soon materially lessen the number of convicts in our Prison, and furthermore greatly reduce the multiplied applications now made to the executive department of the government for pardon and remission of sentences. In fact, very few, whatever may be their term of sentence, are retained in Prison beyond the period of 7 or 10 years. Would it not be better, then, to lessen by statute the term of confinement, than to burden the executive with the labor of exercising the pardoning power as frequently as it is now considered a duty to do it, in consequence of the severe operation of laws framed to meet a state of things very different from that which now exists, and which existing circumstances do not seem to call for ?

" These suggestions are made with diffidence ; but, as the code of our criminal laws is, it is understood, now undergoing the process of correction and revision, it has been thought, yet perhaps presumptuously, that some remarks of this character might not be altogether inappropriate or useless.

" Some objection may possibly exist in the minds of some to the foregoing suggestions, in regard to the propriety of reducing the terms of sentence, that such reduction would injuriously affect the pecuniary results of the institution. This might, perhaps, be the case, to some small extent ; and, should it be so, who is prepared to maintain that the claims of humanity and justice, and public policy, are to be sacrificed to the accumulation of a few dollars and cents? '*Fiat justitia, ruat cœlum!*'

"All which is respectfully submitted.

"JARED CURTIS,
"*Chaplain of the Mass. State Prison.*

"CHARLESTOWN, *Dec.* 15, 1841."

EFFORT FOR DISCHARGED CONVICTS.

The chaplain of the *Massachusetts State Prison*, in his last report, pages 21 and 22, says, —

"It will doubtless be gratifying to your Excellency and Honors to learn, that very many, who have been discharged from this institution in years past, are now sober, industrious, and respectable members of the community; and some, in regular and good standing in our Christian churches; and it is thought that, of those who have been discharged the past year, a greater number than usual seemed honestly and resolutely determined, with the help of God, to live lives of sobriety, industry, and virtue. Some, it cannot be doubted, will return to their old habits and evil courses; yet, while this is to be deplored, gratitude should, notwithstanding, be cherished for the good which, by the divine blessing, the institution has been destined to accomplish.

"It is highly important, and it is hoped that the feeling will prevail more and more extensively in the community, that this unhappy class of men, when they shall be discharged from their confinement, and shall manifest a disposition to make amends for the past, — shall be seeking for employment, and manifest a desire to regain a reputable standing in society, — be taken by the hand, and, by all appropriate acts of kindness, be patronized and encouraged to persevere in the ways of well-doing. Let them not, by frowns and chilling repulses, be disheartened, and, from unkind treatment, be forced to draw the conclusion that they are doomed to be outcasts, and thus driven, in despair, back upon their former vicious and ruinous courses of life. There is a wonderful charm in Christian sympathy and kindness, to win back to virtue the wayward and the wandering. The Redeemer of the world came to seek and to save that which was lost; and while the self-righteous and the proud complained that he companied with publicans and sinners, he was never diverted for a moment from the accomplishment of the errand which brought him into the world. Only let his benevolent spirit be cherished, and his example followed, and many a parent and desolate wife shall be made to rejoice over prodigals who were once dead, but now are alive again — were lost, but now are found. Repentance, when heartfelt and genuine, though it be found in those who may have been the vilest of the vile, should never be met but with kindness. A kind hand extended, a look of compassion, or a smile of approval and encouragement, will do more to allure to, and secure in, the path of virtue and peace, than all the frowns, and rebuffs, and reproachful epithets, with which some may be disposed to treat them. But, as in all other things, so in the treatment of those who are discharged from our Prisons, 'wisdom is profitable to direct.' But it is better to err on the side of humanity and kindness, than in the other extreme."

The agent of the *Prison at Sing Sing*, David L. Seymour, Esq., says, in his last report, pages 21 and 22, —

"Has the state done all its duty towards the unfortunate prisoners, when they are discharged, by giving them the bare pittance the statute allows — the average of three dollars to carry them back to the places of their conviction, and not to exceed ten dollars' worth of clothing? Now, suppose they do go back to the places they were sent from; they have the mark of Cain upon them, and are hunted down or shunned as would be some ferocious beast, (with few exceptions, I am happy to say, friends have received them, as did the father his prodigal and erring son:) or suppose they remain in this neighborhood, to look for employment, as is often the case; they meet, at almost every inquiry, the cold and withering reply, ' Ah, ah! you have been in the State Prison:' or we will suppose they go far away, where they are not known, or attempt, with the pittance they have allowed them, to seek employment among strangers; their little is soon gone, and they are forced to live on the cold charities of strangers. Their clothes become filthy and ragged; and who of us, I would ask, would take a person into our houses under such circumstances? we might possibly give him something that was left from our table to eat, such as we are in the habit of throwing to our dogs, and bid him seek shelter some where else: or suppose they find some person in want of help, and who, for the sake of griping those in necessity, will hire them at less wages than others are getting; and even then a thorough catechizing is gone into, as to where they are from — for even these heartless men, that would *grind the face of the poor*, and get the labor of his fellow for nought, are very suspicious of the honesty of *others*, and would not employ them, if they knew they had ever been convicted of crime; here you see the great temptation for falsehood; the only alternative seems to be starvation or dishonest gain. The men who refuse to employ them may be as guilty in the eyes of the Judge of all the world; yet they have not laid themselves open to the laws of their country, and suffered the penalty of their violation, as have these degraded men.

" I would ask, Cannot something be done to better their condition, and elevate their character, and fit them for respectable places in the society from which they have fallen, and, if possible, lead them to the *sinner's Friend?*

" Allow me to suggest the propriety of employing a suitable man to take charge of and carry on the state farm, for and on account of the state; allow him to occupy the 'state house,' or other suitable buildings, and employ, at a fixed rate of wages, such discharged convicts as are disposed to work, and such as have no friends willing to receive them. Here they can learn the art of husbandry and gardening, and, in a well-regulated family, under religious and moral instruction, may establish a character that will recommend them to such as are in want of help, and save them from the contaminating influence of their vicious associates. I am aware that your board cannot authorize such a measure; but a recommendation from you, I am confident, would influence the legislature."

The chaplain of the same Prison, the Rev. John Luckey, says, on the same subject, in his last report, pages 27 and 28, —

" The suggestions contained in the agent's report, concerning the employment of discharged convicts on the state farm, &c., receive my hearty approbation.

" That this should be done, or that a society should be formed, consisting of benevolent individuals, living in different parts of the state, who should, in an *unostentatious manner*, take the supervision of the morals and employment of such of these men as can be recommended, when discharged, appears to me to be very important. Several individuals have lately acted in this capacity with great success. It is well known that a majority of our convicts, having been convicted in the city of New York and its vicinity, must, according to the present statute, ' made and provided' on this subject, (I refer to that section of the law which directs that the convict, when discharged, shall receive money enough *merely* to defray his expenses ' back to the *place* of his conviction,') return to seek employment in that city, where reside their former companions in vice and crime; and this, those of them who have formed resolutions of reform, dread almost as much as they dread perdition itself.

"I know, gentlemen, that I speak in *strong* language, but no stronger, I think, than the case warrants. I not unfrequently accompany those of this class to the city, for the express purpose of defending them from the attacks of their former associates, as also to assist them in procuring employment, and a proper boarding-house.

"On these occasions, we have sometimes found these 'stool pigeons' of darkness on the boat which conveyed us to the city; sometimes on the wharf, at the city; and sometimes on the corners of the streets, in the city; waiting for their prey, and always ready to *bribe* to crime, when their object was most in need of the bribe. How few have the moral courage to withstand such temptations, and especially when their very souls within them are withering under the sad tokens of a misguided public proscription! It is not, therefore, surprising to me that there should, under the present economy, be so many here for the second and even third time."

It will be seen by those who have carefully read the reports of the Prison Discipline Society, in former years, how well the opinions here expressed by the chaplain of the Prison at Charlestown, and the agent and chaplain of the Prison at Sing Sing, correspond with the opinions of Dr. Tuckerman, late of Boston, and the keeper of the new County Prison in Hartford, Conn., in regard to the solemn and imperious duty of Christians, and all good citizens, to befriend discharged convicts. The teachers of the female Sabbath school in the House of Correction at South Boston, and Mrs. Beard, the matron of the female Prison at Sing Sing, with her associates, have had much encouragement in their efforts to provide homes for the discharged who have been under their care.

TABULAR VIEW OF TEN PENITENTIARIES, IN 1841.

Penitentiaries.	Number of Prisoners at Commencement.	Number of Prisoners at the Close.	Increase of Prisoners.	Diminution of Prisoners.	Number Discharged.	Number Pardoned.	Number Escaped.	Number Dead.	Number Recommitted.	Expenses above Earnings.	Earnings above Expenses.
Maine,...............	68	42		26							
New Hampshire,........	78	84	6		13	7		2			460 62
Massachusetts,..........	322	331	9		131	26		8		1,015 92	
Rhode Island,...........	14	21	7		3					6,458 86	
Auburn, N. Y............	695	707	12		168	35		9			17,076 76
Sing Sing, N. Y.........	827	811		16	216	19	2	18			9,640 10
Peniten. at Philadelphia, .	376	335		41	134	15		17	27		
Maryland,..............	329	284		45	84	25		16		6,493 13	
Frankfort, Ken..........	162	162			51	16	5				11,718 53
Columbus, Ohio,........	483	480		3	62	46	4	13			21,897 32½
	3354	3257	34	131	862	188	11	83	27	13,967 91	60,793 33
Connecticut, rec'd after the above was made up,	205	211	6		38	3		10			8,065 29

Diminution of prisoners in ten Penitentiaries, 97.   There is an increase of 34 in New Hampshire, Massachusetts, Rhode Island, and at Auburn, N. Y.; and a diminution of 131 in Maine, New York, (at Sing Sing,) Pennsylvania, Maryland, and Ohio. But, since the returns were made, there is a diminution in Massachusetts, equal to the whole increase of the previous year.

Discharged by expiration of sentence from ten Penitentiaries, ... 862
Discharged by pardon from the same, ... 188

Total number discharged last year, ... 1040

How important that the Penitentiaries should be reformatory!

Escaped from ten Penitentiaries, 11.   These were all in Kentucky and Ohio, except 2 from Sing Sing.   From seven Penitentiaries there was no escape.   The American Penitentiary system is very secure.

Number of deaths in ten Penitentiaries, out of an average of 3305 prisoners, 83, or less than 1 in 39.   Deaths in the new Penitentiary in Philadelphia, out of an average of 360 prisoners, 17, or 1 in 21.   Deaths in all the Penitentiaries, except the new Penitentiary in Philadelphia, out of an average of 2945 prisoners, 66, or 1 in 44.

Deaths in the new Penitentiary in Philadelphia, 1 in 21.

Expenses above earnings, in three Penitentiaries, $13,967,91.

Earnings above expenses, in five Penitentiaries, $60,793,33.

4. PENNSYLVANIA SYSTEM OF PRISON DISCIPLINE, THAT IS, SOLITARY CONFINEMENT DAY AND NIGHT WITH SOLITARY LABOR.

A letter from Bissett Hawkins, M. D., one of the inspectors of Prisons for the Southern and Western District of *Great Britain*, dated London, March 12, 1842, says, —

"I am no friend to confining prisoners to labor in the cell.   In the year 1841, we have had several cases of insanity in the Penitentiary at Millbank, where prisoners are confined to labor in their cells, but have daily exercise in their yards in company.   This *separate system*, as it has been denominated, has made but little progress here as yet."

The inspectors of the new *Penitentiary in Rhode Island,* where this system was introduced about four years since, say, in their report to the legislature, in October, 1841, that

"The experiment of solitary confinement has not, since the Prison has been in operation, proved perfectly satisfactory. They fear the effect is to injure strong minds, and to produce imbecility or insanity in those that are weak. They recommend your honorable body to consider if you ought not to direct the erection of work-shops, in which the convicts may be compelled to labor under constant supervision."

This report is signed by seven inspectors — Thomas M. Burgess, Roger M. Potter, Barzillai Cranston, George Rice, Martin Stoddard, Christ. Rhodes, Amherst Everett.

The physician of the same Prison, in his report to the legislature, which is printed in the same Legislative Document, says, —

"No. 6 and 22 are laboring under mental derangement, and it is feared No. 24 will be a case of the same character."

This document is signed by Richmond Brownell, and published on the 31st page of Legislative Document, for October, 1841.

The physician of the new *Penitentiary in New Jersey,* which is built on the Pennsylvania plan, says, in his last report, October, 1841, —

" The opinions expressed heretofore on the effects of solitary confinement, are strengthened by every year's experience. The more rigidly the plan is carried out, the more the spirit of the law is observed, the more its effects are visible upon the health of the convicts. A little more intercourse with each other, and a little more air in the yard, have the effect upon mind and body, that warmth has upon the thermometer, almost every degree of indulgence showing a corresponding rise in health of the individual. That an opinion to the contrary should have been advocated at this time, when the influences that control the animal functions are so well understood, seems like a determination to disregard science in the support of a mistaken but favorite policy."

The physician of the *new Penitentiary in Philadelphia,* in the Thirteenth Annual Report of that institution, submitted to the legislature in February, 1842, says that the cases of mental disorder in the Eastern Penitentiary, in 1839, were 26 ; in 1840, 21 ; in 1841, 11.

The disorder, he says, " is now designated *Erotic Enervation,* a term demanded by the necessity of the case." " The instances of mental disorder and of erotic enervation, are in inverse proportion to each other, the former becoming fewer with the more frequent detection of the latter."

COMPARATIVE MORTALITY OF PRISONS.

In *New Hampshire,* the average number of prisoners, for 13 years, has been 76. The number of deaths, in the whole time, has been 8, giving a mortality of less than 1 in 100, annually.

In *Connecticut*, the average number of prisoners, for 12 years, has been 183. The average number of deaths, each year, has been $3\frac{1}{6}$, giving a mortality of less than 1 in 50.

In *Massachusetts*, the average number of prisoners, for 14 years, has been 282 ; the number of deaths, 76 ; the average number of deaths annually, $5\frac{3}{7}$, or less than 1 in 50.

In *New York, at Auburn*, the average number of prisoners, for 14 years, has been 657 ; the number of deaths, 175 ; the average number of deaths, $12\frac{1}{2}$ annually, or less than 1 in 50.

In *Pennsylvania*, in the new *Penitentiary in Philadelphia*, the average number of prisoners, for 12 years, has been 256 ; the whole number of deaths, 127 ; the average number of deaths, $10\frac{7}{12}$, or more than 1 in 25.

In all the Prisons and states here named, except the last, the Prisons are built and managed on the Auburn plan of solitude at night, and labor in shops by day. In the last, the Prison is built and managed on the Pennsylvania plan of solitude day and night with labor. It has always been urged against this plan, that it was injurious to health, and destructive of life. We see in the above results, from the experience of all the years since it went into operation, that the bill of mortality is unfavorable. In no one of the Prisons mentioned, on the Auburn plan, is the mortality 1 in 50, or 2 per cent. In the new Penitentiary in Philadelphia, it is more than 1 in 25, or more than 4 per cent. ; making the difference of more than *two* lives, annually, in every hundred prisoners. The average number of prisoners, in the five Penitentiaries from which the above results of experience are drawn, is 1454. It makes a difference, therefore, of TWENTY-NINE lives, annually, on this average number of prisoners, between the Auburn and Pennsylvania systems.

There is another aspect, not less important, in which to view the facts in the table from which the above conclusions are drawn. The number of deaths, in the four Prisons on the Auburn plan, exhibited in the table, for the term of years mentioned, was 297. If the deaths had been in the same proportion as in the new Penitentiary in Philadelphia, the number of deaths would have been 685, instead of 297, making a difference, in the term of time mentioned, of THREE HUNDRED AND EIGHTY-EIGHT LIVES.

The following table is the one from which the above results are drawn : —

Time when.	Solitude at Night. AUBURN PLAN. New Hamp.		Solitude at Night. AUBURN PLAN. Vermont.		Solitude at Night. AUBURN PLAN. Wethersfield, Conn.		Solitude at Night. AUBURN PLAN. Charlestown, Mass.		Solitude at Night. AUBURN PLAN. Auburn, N. Y.		Solitude Day and Night. PENNSYLVANIA PLAN. Philadelphia new Penitent'ry.	
	Pris.	Deaths.	Pris.	Deaths.	Pris.	Deaths.	Pris.	Deaths.	Pris.	Deaths.	Pris.	Deaths.
1828	..	.	...	2	...	1	290	4	571	9	..	.
1829	48	1	...	.	134	.	262	6	639	5	..	.
1830	54	.	...	1	167	4	290	5	620	18	31	1
1831	82	.	...	.	182	4	256	7	647	14	67	4
1832	89	1	...	1	192	2	227	11	683	12	91	4
1833	87	.	108	1	186	3	250	6	679	11	123	1
1834	86	.	...	1	189	1	277	4	679	11	183	5
1835	90	1	125	2	197	4	279	3	654	10	266	7
1836	82	1	120	2	204	8	278	4	648	18	360	12
1837	72	1	101	2	204	1	284	5	678	19	386	17
1838	73	.	95	1	187	9	302	6	660	15	402	26
1839	78	1	...	.	170	.	309	5	670	10	418	11
1840	81	.	...	.	187	2	320	2	682	14	405	22
1841	81	1	...	.	...	.	326	8	701	9	356	17
	993	8	...	.	2199	38	3950	76	9211	175	3088	127

PRESENTMENT OF THE GRAND JURY OF PHILADELPHIA.

SEPTEMBER TERM, 1841.

The following extract from the presentment of the grand jury of the city and county of Philadelphia contains weighty and important statements : —

" The Grand Inquest, in closing their labors for the September term of the Court, do report:

" As a matter of courtesy to the Grand Jury, we visited the Eastern Penitentiary ; but having no legal right so to do, we deem it improper to make any comments on the manner in which the institution is conducted, or the treatment of the prisoners. By the 3d section of the Act of Assembly passed the 23d of April, 1829, the Grand Jury of the City and County of Philadelphia were allowed to visit the prisoners therein confined ; but by the 5th section of the Act of Assembly passed the 27th day of February, 1833, the right was taken away. The reasons for so doing do not appear obvious to us, and we would earnestly recommend to the legislature, at its next session, to restore this right, as it may be productive of much good, and have a tendency, if not to correct abuses, at least to bring them legitimately before the public, so that proper measures can be taken to secure the requisite inquiry."

Signed by sixteen jurors and the secretary.

5. ASYLUMS FOR LUNATICS.

ASYLUMS WHICH HAVE ATTAINED A HIGH DEGREE OF EXCELLENCE.

Maine Insane Hospital, at Augusta.
New Hampshire State Lunatic Asylum, at Concord ; in location, construction, and opening prospects.
Vermont Asylum for the Insane, at Brattleboro'.
McLean Asylum, at Charlestown, Mass.
State Lunatic Hospital, at Worcester, Mass.
Boston Lunatic Hospital, at South Boston, Mass.
Connecticut Retreat for the Insane, at Hartford.
Bloomingdale Asylum, N. Y., seven miles from the city of New York.
Asylum for the Insane Poor of the City of New York, on Blackwell's Island.
Pennsylvania Hospital for the Insane, two miles west of Philadelphia.
Asylum at Frankford, Penn., five miles north of Philadelphia.
Maryland Hospital for the Insane, in Baltimore.
Western Lunatic Asylum, at Staunton, Virginia.
Ohio Lunatic Asylum, at Columbus.

These Asylums are, without exception, beautifully located. They are all supplied with good gardens ; most of them, with many acres of fertile and cultivated land ; a considerable number, with large and productive farms.   They are constructed of good materials, — stone or brick, — on the general plan of a centre building with wings.   They are under the superintendence of very superior men.   This remark scarcely admits of an exception.   The assistant physicians, stewards, matrons, and attendants, have been chosen with great care, and are, many of them, the very salt of the earth.   The principles of government and conduct are religious and Christian to an admirable degree.   The employments, recreations, amusements, instructions, and influences, are very various, and well fitted to soothe the excited, cheer the desponding, guide the erring, check the. vicious, raise the fallen, and restore the insane.   The restraints are very few.   Who can look upon these institutions, without gratitude to the God of heaven, and the Savior of the world, for what has been done, in a few years, to provide such Asylums for the Insane, in the United States; many of whom, in former years, have been confined in cellars, cages, dungeons, and Prisons?

"*Her wilderness shall become like Eden, and her desert like the garden of the Lord.*"

ASYLUMS IN PROGRESS, BUT NOT YET COMPLETED.

In *Rhode Island,* the Hon. Nicholas Brown, deceased, has bequeathed 30,000 dollars for the establishment of an Asylum for the Insane in Rhode Island. He enjoins it upon his executors, J. Carter Brown, Moses B. Ives, and Robert H. Ives, men of great public spirit and philanthropy, to proceed in the execution of his design as soon as it can be done consistently with a wise settlement of his estate. The deceased was one of America's great men. This act of his last will is only one among many proofs of it.

The following is an extract from one of the codicils, dated July, 1841 : —

" Whereas it has long been deeply impressed on my mind, that an Insane or Lunatic Hospital, or Retreat for the Insane, should be established upon a firm and permanent basis, under an act of the legislature, where that unhappy portion of our fellow-citizens who are, by the visitation of Providence, deprived of their reason, may find a safe retreat, and be provided with whatever may be most conducive to their comfort, and to their restoration of a sound state of mind; Therefore, for the purpose of aiding an object so desirable, and in the hope that such an establishment may soon be commenced, I do hereby set apart and give, devise and bequeath, the sum of thirty thousand dollars towards the erection or endowment of an Insane or Lunatic Hospital, or Retreat for the Insane, or by whatever other name it may be called, to be located in Providence, or its vicinity ; and I do hereby order and direct my said executors to pay the said sum of thirty thousand dollars in the promotion and advancement of an institution for that object ; trusting and fully confiding in my executors, that they will carefully examine and be satisfied that the establishment is placed on a firm and legal basis, and that the payment of the above amount be made at such times, and in such sums, as will best promote the desired object, and be least prejudicial to the settlement of my own estate ; hoping that my sons and other friends will coöperate in the humane and benevolent design, that the benefits of the institution may soon be realized."

In *Connecticut,* the legislature, at the last session, in 1842, authorized the governor to expend 2000 dollars a year for the support of the insane poor of the state at the Retreat in Hartford. Dr. Brigham, the superintendent of the Retreat, after the passing of this act, writes as follows : —

" This sum, with such aid from towns and friends as they will be able and willing to afford, will probably maintain from 20 to 30 at the Retreat constantly, and, if they are judiciously selected, (and no doubt they will be,) great good will result. We have not, at present, accommodations for this number; but I trust the directors of the Retreat will make the requisite additions. I hope to get a new kitchen, dining-room, chapel, and perhaps a house for the superintendent, in one building, and two separate mansions, one for each sex, in each of which from 10 to 20 quiet patients and convalescents can be accommodated, as in the best private establishments."

In *Utica, N. Y.*, one of the four large buildings for the accommodation of 1000 patients, is finished, and ready for the reception of patients, and the government of the institution is about being organized.

In *New Jersey*, commissioners are appointed to fix the location of a State Asylum, ascertain the cost of the same, determine what buildings will be necessary, and report to the next legislature.

In *Pennsylvania*, a good law is enacted, and commissioners were appointed to carry it into effect; but we learn by a private letter from a well-informed gentleman in Philadelphia, that there have been strange doings in the premises, and that no desirable progress has, in his opinion, been made. We are not at liberty to publish the letter. It is sad that such an object should be deferred by such means.

ASYLUMS FROM WHICH WE HAVE RECEIVED NO REPORTS

From the Williamsburg Asylum, *Virginia*, we have received no information, and seen no report. So far as our information extends, the annual reports of this institution are not published. If we mistake not, there is no one thing more calculated to promote the improvement and usefulness of an Insane Asylum, than the publication of an annual report. This is well illustrated at the other Asylum in Virginia. Dr. Stribling's reports are of great value, not only to the Asylum at Staunton, but to the world. We hope another year will secure the publication of a valuable report from the Asylum at Williamsburg — the oldest Asylum exclusively for the Insane in the United States.

In *South Carolina*, also, so far as we know, the annual reports concerning the Asylum at Columbia are not published. Dr. Earle says of it, —

"The state has appropriated 100,000 dollars to this institution. Nothing further than this can be said of it for want of data."

We have written expressly to obtain information, but have not been able to obtain it. We sincerely hope that this public institution, which has been so liberally patronized, will fall into the good way of almost all the rest, in publishing an annual report.

From *Georgia*, too, no information comes in the form of annual reports, concerning the Asylum at Milledgeville. Dr. Earle says, —

" We can say nothing in regard to its extent, organization, or success."

The Rev. Mr. Barrett, the agent of this Society for the Middle and Southern States, visited it last year, and says, —

" An Insane Hospital, two miles from Milledgeville, on rising ground, amid lofty pines, is being erected. It is designed to accommodate 160 patients. One four-story building, of brick, with convenient rooms, will be ready for the reception of patients this year, i. e. in 1841. The state has granted $37,000 for the erection of the Hospital. It is not designed exclusively for the insane poor."

In *Louisiana*, concerning the Insane Asylum at New Orleans, Dr. Edward Jarvis, of Louisville, Kenn., in his invaluable pamphlet, *"What shall we do for the Insane?"* published in February, 1842, says, —

" The *Insane Asylum* at New Orleans is simply a building in the yard of that noble institution the Charity Hospital, of which it is a branch. It is built well, strong, and perhaps convenient; certainly it will answer the purpose of security. But there is such a small extent of grounds, so little room for exercise, so little preparation for labor, amusement, or other occupation, that surely they have not the usual, and, what is elsewhere supposed, the necessary facilities for curing the insane, and we ought not to expect as much from them as from others. This Asylum, however, has as yet hardly gone into operation, and we leave it to develop its powers, and to manifest its results. By these shall it be judged hereafter."

In *Tennessee*, the Insane Asylum at Nashville has furnished no report. Dr. Jarvis says, it is " richly endowed by the state, and can accommodate about 100 patients. Farther than this we are not informed." The Rev. Mr. Barrett says, —

" It is a little way out of the city of Nashville. A high wall of stone, laid in mortar, enclosing seven acres, is a great and needless expense. The Hospital building, near the centre of the enclosed space, is four stories high, and has well-arranged rooms sufficient to accommodate 100 patients."

It had been occupied, at the time of his visit, in 1841, about one year, and had 15 patients, of whom five were females. It is designed both for pay patients and poor lunatics. 50,000 dollars had been expended on it.

In *Kentucky*, Dr. Jarvis, of Louisville, says, at the close of his pamphlet, —

" We are happy to give testimony here, to the great improvement of the Kentucky Asylum within the last year, under the faithful care of Dr. Bush. The report for 1841 is more satisfactory than any that preceded it, and shows a greater success than in any former year. This account is corroborated by other and independent sources of information.

" We are informed that there is no doubt that the legislature will grant to the Asylum all the facilities that its warmest friends desire — a well-paid physician, a sufficient corps of attendants, and lands and shops for the occupation of the patients. When this shall be done, our own Asylum will be second to none in the country."

DR. WHITE'S PRIVATE ASYLUM IN HUDSON, N. Y.

It is located in the city of Hudson, on the east bank of Hudson River, on an eminence overlooking the river, about three fourths of a mile from it, in full view of the Catskill Mountains and other grand and beautiful objects of nature. The quantity of land is too limited, not much exceeding one acre. The building accommodates about 60 patients. The institution has been in operation many years; is under the care of men highly esteemed — Dr. White and son; has received from its commencement about 600 patients, and has restored about 250, and greatly improved many more.

CAUSES OF INSANITY IN SEVEN ASYLUMS.

Causes of Insanity.	Total in seven Asylums	Massachusetts Lunatic Hospital, at Worcester.	Bloomingdale Asylum, N. Y	Frankford, Penn.	Pennsylvania Hospital.	Western Lunatic Asylum, Vir.	Ohio Lunatic Asylum, for one Year.	Ohio Asylum, for three Years.
Intemperance,	301	204	26	9	16	14	7	25
Ill health,	360	208	34	7	32	24	16	39
Masturbation,	155	113	12	2	2	3	3	20
Domestic affliction and loss of friends,	230	145	10	4	16	12	9	34
Religious,	188	100	16	3	8	9	11	41
Loss of property and pecuniary embarrassments,	133	77	13	4	15	9	4	11
Disappointed affection,	98	58	15	3	4	4	2	12
Disappointed ambition,	49	28	..	2	1	..	1	17
Epilepsy,	68	40	..	2	..	3	3	20
Puerperal,	86	36	10	..	6	2	5	27
Wounds of the head or injury,	31	17	3	1	3	2	..	5
Abuse of snuff,	8	8	..	..	..	..	..	..
Hereditary of having insane ancestors,	..	388	35	24	..	..	6	21
Fright,	14	...	1	1	2	1	3.	6
Remorse,	2	...	2	..	..	..	..	..
Litigation,	2	...	2	..	..	..	..	..
Political excitement,	11	...	2	..	..	..	3	6
Jealousy,	7	...	1	..	..	2	1	3
Over-exertion of mind,	19	...	3	..	5	7	..	4
Unknown,	168	...	22	14	50	24	12	46

Important lessons in favor of temperance, care of health, purity, submission, faith in Christ, supreme love to God, and against all inordinate affection and ambition, are taught in this table.

TABULAR VIEW OF ELEVEN LUNATIC ASYLUMS, IN 1841.

Lunatic Asylums, in 1841.	Number under Treatment.	Number at the Commencement of the Year.	Received during the Year.	Recovered.	Much improved.	Improved.	Died.	Remaining at the Close of the Year.	Number admitted from the first.	Whole Number recovered.	Time of opening the Institution.
Maine Asylum, at Augusta,....	133	28	105	33	..	20	3	54	135	34	1840
Vermont Asylum, at Brattleboro',......................	165	81	84	41	..	....	4	95	323	130	1836
McLean Asylum, at Charlestown, ...	283	126	157	75	11	13	11	142	2013	877	1818
Boston Asylum, at South Boston,	136	87	49	14	..	2	7	108	153	19	1839
State Hospital at Worcester,...	399	236	163	82	..	36	12	232	1353	884	1833
Connecticut Retreat, at Hartford,	146	79	67	38	4	6	9	83	1068	600	1824
Bloomingdale Asylum, City of New York,.................	233	131	102	55	..	14	18	133	2698	1200	1821
Friends' Asylum at Frankford, Penn.,......................	97	58	39	13	4	10	3	58	784	263	1817
Pennsylvania Hospital, two miles west of the City,............	176	....	176	30	5	6	9	115	176	306	1841
Old Hospital in the City,.......	....	....	....	..	..	....	..	....	3718	1289	1752
Western Asylum, at Staunton, Vir.,......................	122	69	53	15	..	....	6	100	....	....	1828
Ohio Asylum, at Columbus,....	223	138	85	44	..	5	14	142	343	124	1838
Eleven Asylums, in 1841,......	2113	1033	1080	440	24	112	96	1262	12664	5450	....

From this table it appears that the whole number under treatment during the year was 2,113

Number at the commencement of the year, ... 1,033

Number received during the year, ... 1,080

Number recovered, ... 440

Number much improved, ... 24

Number improved, ... 112

Number dead, ... 96

Number remaining at the close of the year, ... 1,262

Whole number under treatment from the first, ... 12,664

Whole number recovered, ... 5,440

Average number during the year, ... 1,147

Number of deaths during the year, ... 96

Proportion of deaths, 1 in 11.

Proportion recovered, 40 per cent. of all received.

PREMATURE REMOVAL OF PATIENTS FROM INSANE HOSPITALS, AND THE INDISCREET VISITS OF FRIENDS.

Dr. Ray, of the *Insane Hospital in Maine,* says, —

" In many instances, towns have determined to give their insane poor the benefits of a few months' residence with us. This is certainly a most commendable measure ; but it is neither just to the institution, nor to the patient, to place him here, with the calculation of removing him at the end of a certain time, whatever may be the result of the experiment. The most that can be done, in so short a time, in the greater portion of cases, is to render the patient more comfortable, and improve his personal habits, all which is generally lost soon after his removal from the Hospital. ' Three, and even twelve months,' says Dr. Woodward, ' are considered too short a period to make a decided impression upon some chronic cases, that, by a persevering application of medical, moral, and intellectual means, will ultimately be restored.' In a pecuniary point of view, it certainly must be more economical to give such cases a fair trial of Hospital treatment, than to fix them at once, and forever, as a life-charge upon the town or their friends. We have had to witness the removal of some who were greatly improving, and would probably have recovered, merely because the time had expired for which the towns had voted to keep them here. An additional outlay of fifty or a hundred dollars would probably have restored them to health, and enabled them to support themselves; whereas, now, the most of them will become a yearly burden, that will accumulate, before they die, to thousands of dollars. Table 8, in which we have compared the expenses of some of our old cases with those of an equal number of our last-discharged recent cases, while in the Hospital, should be pondered well by those who look at this matter solely in an economical point of view. It must be recollected, too, that these old cases are yet to be supported as long as they live, and some of them may be expected to live many years. In view of these facts, then, we would say to towns, ' If you conclude to send us your insane poor, let not their term of residence be fixed beforehand, but be governed by the circumstances of each particular case, remembering that, so long as there continues to be any improvement, we may hope for a final cure.'

" But it is in regard to recent cases, that we have most to deplore this impatience of friends, which leads to a premature removal of the patient; because perseverance is so generally crowned with success. The signs of improvement are mistaken for those of recovery, and the fact of the strong tendency of insanity to relapse when the patient is prematurely exposed to causes of excitement, is but little known or heeded. Because the reason is no longer disturbed by delusions, and the patient craves employment; because the affections have revived, and memory fondly reverts to home, with all its endearments ; it by no means follows that the mind is fully restored. These, it is true, are favorable symptoms ; but they are symptoms of improvement merely, not of recovery, as the result of removal generally proves. They indicate the approach of convalescence, — or that stage of the disease in which seclusion and quiet are more necessary even than in any other, and that, too, in which injudicious management is more injurious than in any other. Instances of the lamentable consequences of the mistake in question have been painfully frequent with us during the past year. A notice of some of these cases may serve to deepen the impression we are desirous of making on this point. — A man, who had been six weeks insane before admission, had so far improved at the end of a month, that he became interested in whatever was going on around him, and worked the greater part of the day. At this time, he was visited by his wife, who found him raking hay. She concluded that he had staid long enough, and accordingly removed him. In a few days, he became so excited and violent, as to frighten his family, and at the end of three weeks he was brought to us again. He improved for a season, then became stationary, and he seems now to be sinking into an incurable form of insanity. — A young man was brought to the Hospital in a state of high maniacal excitement, which gradually passed off, and in three months' time, he had become perfectly quiet, docile, and disposed to labor. His friends, visiting him about this time, and finding him at work, came to the conclusion that, if he were well enough to work, he was well enough to go home, and obtained his discharge. In ten days, he was returned, having been so excited and wild, that he was caged the greater part of the time he was absent; and, although he finally recovered, it was full three months before he had regained the ground he lost. — Another, admitted shortly after the latter, and in a similar condition, was removed under similar circumstances. His friends could not comprehend why he might not work as well, and improve as fast, at home, as with us, and he too was removed. In about a month, he was returned worse than when he entered at first, having been caged most of the time ; and now, five months afterwards, he has but slightly improved.

"If minor degrees of improvement are so much misapprehended, it is not strange that convalescence should often be mistaken for entire and permanent cure. In the course of a single short interview, the patient manifests no sign of mental aberration, nor undue exhilaration of spirits, and in every respect appears like himself when well. It is impossible to convince the friends that the mind, though sound, is not strong, and cannot be exposed to causes of excitement without great danger of a relapse. Relying with presumptuous confidence on their own sagacity, our advice is listened to like a tale that is told, and forthwith the patient is removed. For a few days, or weeks, they rejoice in the course they have taken; but, in a large portion of cases, the sight of old friends, exciting conversation, and the revival of old associations, prove too much for the mind, in its weakened condition, and soon the derangement returns in all its original severity. If we are entitled to any confidence at all, we claim it in regard to our opinions on this point. If the friends are better judges than we are as to the most proper time for removing a patient, then are they also more competent to direct the management of the case in its previous stages. Since, however, the latter are immediately intrusted to our management, what can be more inconsistent and absurd, than the idea that, in the latter stage of the disease, no further dependence need be placed on our judgment ? The fact is, that the convalescent stage is that in which there is most liability to mistake ; and in nothing is the judgment of the physician more closely exercised, than in determining when convalescence ends, and perfect recovery is established. On a point so important and delicate as this, we conceive that our ampler means of information render our opinion worthy of some consideration. If incorrect, it can, at the worst, merely occasion a few days' or weeks' unnecessary detention; and every one must know how much less an evil it is, to keep a patient too long, than to remove him too soon.

"We would take the opportunity of saying a few words on a subject somewhat akin to the latter in its consequences, — we mean the visits of friends to patients. On no point have we found so little disposition to acquiesce in our views as this. With amazing confidence, the friends persist in declaring how sure they are that their visits cannot hurt the patient; and many a time have we been obliged to permit an interview under the painful conviction, that, in all probability, it would aggravate the mental disorder. We certainly do not covet the trouble of objecting to such visits; but since we so frequently see their mischievous effects, it becomes our duty to prevent them, if possible, by plainly stating our reasons therefor, though at the risk of giving offence. In old cases, where we have no hope of cure, we have never discouraged them ; and in recent cases, before the period of high maniacal excitement is finished, or symptoms of improvement have appeared, we have not thought it worth while to offer much opposition; for though they may sometimes temporarily increase the excitement, yet the patient is too much under the influence of disease to be deeply affected. But from the period when the cloud that obscures the mental vision begins to disperse, and the mind is struggling into a dim consciousness of its true condition, to that when the stage of convalescence is firmly established, any intercourse with friends is liable to be followed by injurious effects. It would seem as if, while the mind is in this transition state, if we may so call it, emerging from the darkness and confusion of disease into the clear atmosphere of health, the sight of near friends, by suddenly recalling a crowd of painful associations, or too rudely awakening the domestic affections, produced a degree of nervous excitement, that the brain, in its weakened, irritable condition, is unable to bear. None but those engaged in the care of the insane, can conceive how seriously they may sometimes be affected by the slightest circumstance that acts upon the moral affections. If the mention of a familiar name can agitate the whole frame, and the sight of a bundle of old clothes from home give rise to the most distressing emotions, it may be easily conceived, if one will but consider the matter, how much risk is run by interviews with friends. I do not mean that they always prove injurious; but, as they do so in the larger proportion of cases, and we have not always the means of distinguishing between them beforehand, it becomes our duty to discountenance them in all. It must be considered, too, that the evil is greatly aggravated by the conversation of the friends who, instead of cheering and encouraging the patient by inspiring him with hopes of a seasonable recovery, and representing things as going on smoothly at home, oftentimes, by some strange obliquity of judgment, talk of nothing but misfortunes and grievances, and such like disagreeable subjects, that should be kept as far as possible from his thoughts. This is a matter we cannot control, and the general promises of friends to abstain from all topics that might unpleasantly affect the feelings, we have found, by painful experience, are little to be relied on. If it is as much as a patient can bear to meet his friends, and hear only cheerful intelligence, it may well be conceived that, when their communications awaken the most painful emotions, the mind must inevitably stagger under the shock. The letters of friends are liable to the same objections, unless they are of a cheering character; and, even then, there are cases where they had better be withheld. When judiciously written, however, they often prove highly beneficial — sometimes, even, in cases where a personal interview might have been hazardous."

MORAL AND RELIGIOUS INSTRUCTION IN INSANE ASYLUMS.

Dr. Ray, superintendent of the *Insane Hospital in Maine,* says, in his report. dated December 31, 1841, —

"In pleasant weather, a number of our male patients have attended church in the village; and on Sabbath evenings, we have had a religious service, which has generally been conducted by some clergyman in the vicinity. About three fourths of our patients have usually attended; and though some of them, no doubt, have been little improved thereby, yet I have no hesitation in saying that, on the whole, the effect of the service has been highly beneficial. It is well to permit the insane to continue their usual customs, duties, and modes of life, just so far as they are compatible with the police of the institution, and with the means made use of for their recovery. Generally speaking, the more they are suffered to act like other men, the more they will strive to become like them. To attend divine service on the Sabbath, is one of those observances of ordinary life which a large portion of them are anxious to maintain, and to some it is a source of heartfelt joy.   Many attend merely to change the scene, without caring for the religious influences of the occasion; but, even with such, it is not without its benefits.   It serves as a powerful motive to self-control; and it is curious how admirably some control themselves there who never do it any where else.   This is something gained; and if it constituted the principal benefit of religious services, this would be a sufficient inducement for continuing them.   To that class of patients to whom the ' earth seems a sterile promontory, and this brave o'erhanging firmament to be nothing but a foul and pestilent congregation of vapors,' the services of the Sabbath are sometimes directly beneficial.   Cheering views of divine Providence, and exhibitions of the parental character of God, are, in some instances, as efficient as any means we have to encourage and confirm the desponding spirit.   Convalescent patients, softened by sickness, and penetrated by a sense of divine goodness, are in just that condition of mind to be favorably affected by the truths of religion.   To the clergymen of this vicinity, Doctor Tappan, Messrs. Warren, Barnard, Jenne, and Freeman, of Augusta; Cole, Thurston, Butler, Gunnison, and Adlam, of Hallowell; Messrs. Adams of Portland, and Sewall of Baltimore, Md., our thanks are due for the cheerfulness and promptness with which they have always complied with our request to officiate for us."

Dr. Rockwell, superintendent of the *Vermont Asylum for the Insane*, says, in his report, dated October 1, 1841, —

" The effects of our religious exercises have been very beneficial.   All who are in a proper condition attend them, and to many they are a source of the greatest comfort.   We have had religious exercises from the commencement of our operations.   In no instance do we recollect of their being injurious to any individual; and to many they have been of great benefit."

Dr. Woodward, superintendent of the *State Hospital at Worcester*, says, in his report, dated November 30, 1841, —

" In November, 1837, the Hospital chapel was dedicated for religious worship.   Since that time, there have been in the Hospital 845 patients, of whom 797 have attended religious worship on the Sabbath, more or less, and 48 have failed to attend.

" Of the 399 patients who have been in the Hospital the past year, 373 have attended these exercises, and 26 have not attended.

" Of the 232 patients that are now in the Hospital, 214 have attended the religious services, and 18 have not attended.   In this number are included 6 recent cases, that will probably all attend when they shall be able to exercise sufficient self-control, leaving but 12 old cases that are not in a condition to attend the chapel.   Some of these remain in the house in consequence of their liability to epilepsy, some from continued excitement, and some from habits of negligence and want of regard to personal decency.

" There have been regular services in the chapel every Sabbath of the past year, and all parts of the service have been performed which are customary in the New England churches.

" A respectable choir of singers has always been in attendance, consisting of persons employed in the institution, and patients, accompanied by from two to four musical instruments.   Their performance has been good at all times, and has never been interrupted by disturbance or discord.   Much credit is due to those members of the family who have assisted in this pleasant and very desirable part of religious worship.

" Sacred music is one of the safest and most salutary exercises for the insane.   Its influence on the feelings is soothing.   It awakens attention, diverts the mind from its reveries, and prepares for the accompanying duties of the place.

" During the last year, the Rev. George Allen has officiated as chaplain of the Hospital. The services of the house have always been conducted by him with solemnity and discretion, and the influence of religious teaching has never been better. He is judicious in the selection of his subjects, and appropriate and solemn in the application of religious truth, and has never failed to interest his hearers, while he has been sufficiently guarded not to offend them.

" His mode of preaching has shown that any topic, discussed with prudence, is as suitable for our congregation as for others, and that the insane bear instruction and reproof as well as other religious assemblies. With few exceptions, they are attentive listeners, always wide awake, and they carry much of the influence of the Sabbath into the ensuing week. They often recollect the texts of both services, and will repeat many of the leading thoughts of the sermon many days after.

" On the day following the last Sabbath, as an experiment, I inquired the place of the text, chapter, verse, &c., of eight or ten patients, some of whom are generally so much excited, and others so much abstracted, that I would not have believed that they gave the least attention to the services ; yet, to my surprise, all knew the place of the texts and the subjects of the discourses. One woman, who had recently come into the Hospital, had not only recollected the place of the text, but, after her return to her room, had surrounded with the mark of a pen, the portion of the verses principally used in the discourse ; another had turned down the leaf of her Bible to the text.

" The good order and solemnity of our chapel exercises have been the subjects of frequent remark and commendation by strangers and visitors ; and all who witness them cannot fail to be impressed with the propriety and peculiar fitness and value of religious services for the insane.

" These exercises are very acceptable to a large proportion of the inmates of the Hospital. They generally attend voluntarily ; and those who are required to attend are of that class who are equally opposed to any thing else that requires an effort.

" The preparation for attendance in the chapel, the assembling together, the music before service, the solemn exercises of the place, and the topics of conversation to which all these operations lead, with the variety they afford, and the pleasure they give, make the Sabbath, to many, the most interesting day of the week. Instead of the dread with which its dull monotony was formerly contemplated, it is hailed as a day of gratification and delight by many members of our family.

" Besides the religious services of the Sabbath, there is a prayer-meeting on Saturday evening, and a Bible class on the Sabbath, which many of the patients attend.

" The change of public sentiment with regard to religious instruction for the insane, has been great for the last few years. When this Hospital was erected, it was not contemplated, and no provision was made for assembling together for this purpose. This is the only institution of the kind in the country, so far as my knowledge extends, which has a chapel set apart for religious worship.

" In many of the institutions, religious meetings are regularly held on the Sabbath, and this practice is being extended through most of the Asylums in the country.

" For four years we have tried this experiment fairly, admitting to the exercise all patients who were in a situation to attend. Here are collected the excited maniac, the gloomy melancholic, the anxious inquirer after truth, those who imagine themselves guilty of the unpardonable sin, the gods, saviors, and prophets, the infidel, the scoffer, — and yet we have found no injury arise from such attendance, and no disposition to disturb the quiet and solemnity of the place.

" By our whole moral treatment, as well as by our religious services, we inculcate all the habits and obligations of rational society. We think the insane should never be deceived; all their delusions and false impressions of character should be discouraged by removing, in the kindest manner, every badge of honor and distinction which they are disposed to assume, and by directing their attention to other subjects of interest. They may be held responsible for their conduct so far as they are capable of regulating it. By encouraging self-control, and respect for themselves and others, we make them better men, more orderly and reasonable, before any impression is made upon their delusions. To aid this, it is easy to see how useful must be that religious instruction which points out their duty to themselves and to their fellow-men, and their responsibility to God.

" The evils that we at first anticipated do not accompany these salutary influences. There is certainly a choice of subjects for their consideration, but the range is much wider than we at first supposed; and, whatever is the topic of discourse, the service is seldom objectionable to any one, and usually acceptable to all."

Dr. Bell, of the *McLean Asylum at Charlestown, Mass.*, conducts a religious service himself, every evening in the week, Sundays excepted, when he sometimes gets the assistance of a clergyman from the neighborhood. Besides, many of the patients attend worship, every Sabbath, in churches of their own choice, in Cambridge, Charlestown, and Boston. Dr. Bell speaks, in his last report, of " a proper participation in the services of religion " as being among the moral means of the highest utility to the insane.

Dr. Butler, superintendent of the *Lunatic Asylum at South Boston*, conducts a religious service himself, every evening, for the benefit of his household and the patients, assembled together ; and he is generally able to obtain the assistance, on the Sabbath, of some one of the many ministers in Boston. Dr. Butler says, in his last report, —

"The extended experience of the year has abundantly confirmed all that was stated in the last report, in respect to the influence of religious services. Simply considered as remedial and disciplinary measures, I would on no consideration dispense with their assistance. We trust they have a higher and more extensive influence. The expression of grateful obligation which has come to us from many of our inmates, is due to those clergymen to whose acceptable services, gratuitously performed, we have owed the privilege of listening, for nearly every Sabbath of the year, to the preaching of the gospel.

" The spacious room in the third story of the east building, which has been vacant, is now being prepared for a chapel — an excellent accommodation, that the increased number of our attendants on public worship renders very desirable."

Dr. Brigham, superintendent of the *Retreat at Hartford, Conn.*, says, in his report for 1841, —

" Religious services have been continued during the past as in preceding years. Every evening, the patients and attendants assemble, when a hymn is sung, and a portion of Scripture read, and prayer offered by the chaplain. On Sunday, he preaches to the assembled household. On these occasions, from *two thirds* to *three fourths* of our patients assemble, and several assist us in singing. Rarely is there any disturbance. I have frequently witnessed, with pleasure and surprise, those who were constantly in motion and noisy elsewhere, remain quiet, and conduct with the utmost propriety, during religious services.

" I have no doubt these services are beneficial to our patients. Permission to attend them is solicited by nearly all, and many are induced to exercise their self-control, in order to enjoy this privilege.

" The Sabbath is now looked forward to by our patients with pleasurable anticipations ; but I apprehend it would be to them the most melancholy day of the week, and the one in which they would make the least improvement, were it not for our religious exercises.

" The chaplain frequently visits and freely converses with the patients at their apartments. Good has resulted from this practice, conducted, as it has been, with discretion and good judgment. Not unfrequently his timely and judicious remarks have given hope and encouragement to the melancholy and desponding, and essentially aided us in the moral treatment of our patients.

" Annexed to this report are some interesting observations by the distinguished gentleman who officiates as chaplain. His experience with the sick and insane, his accurate observation, and knowledge of the human mind, deservedly entitle his remarks to great attention."

The chaplain's report is as follows : —

" The usual religious exercises on the Sabbath, and the evenings of the other days of the week, have been regularly continued during the past year. A large proportion of the patients have been in the habit of attending these exercises, and have evinced the benefit derived from them by the good order and becoming deportment which, with very few exceptions, have prevailed. The religious sensibilities are, in this way, often rekindled. Self-control is aided in regaining its dominion ; and peace, at least for a season, visits the most agitated breast. May we not hope and pray, that the Spirit of grace and consolation will here, as well as elsewhere, shed down its hallowed influences, to enlighten, to purify, and to bless the soul ? Our Savior, before he left the world, promised *the Comforter* to his disciples ; and will he not delight to fulfil this promise among such as are kindred sufferers with those who shared so largely in his compassion while on earth ? Among these sufferers we often find some of his most faithful followers.

" Cases frequently occur which, in the opinion of the physician, require the services of the chaplain, in the way of personal intercourse with the patients ; when the hope-inspiring views and promises of the gospel may be addressed to the desponding mind with great benefit. Such services have been promptly and cheerfully rendered.

" Death sometimes enters the walls of the institution ; and it has more than once happened, that the spirit, about to take its flight to another world, and in full possession of its reasoning powers, finds its faith and hope invigorated by the consolations which are administered, and the prayers which are offered up, at this trying hour. It is a solace, too, to the friends of the deceased, to know that the funeral solemnities are conducted with appropriate religious exercises. They have themselves often been present at these exercises.

" There are other occasions, also, when feeble and convalescent patients express a wish to have the chaplain visit them, that they may enjoy the privilege of religious counsels, and of uniting in supplication at the throne of grace. With the advice and approbation of the physician, such visits are made, and evidently with very beneficial results.

" In addition to this, it has been the custom of the chaplain to visit the patients throughout the institution, from time to time ; to exchange civilities and pleasant conversation with them ; and to let them see that he takes a personal interest in their welfare. The respect and kindness with which they uniformly treat him, is no less grateful to his feelings than indicative of the advantages which such intercourse, wisely conducted, is capable of affording.

The insane know well how to appreciate acts of sympathy, and among others those of a minister of the gospel.

"The other inmates of the establishment, including the attendants and nurses, all of whom are usually present at the religious exercises, it is not to be forgotten, come in for their share of the benefits which these exercises afford. Every day, they hear truths and precepts from the Word of God, which, if cherished and obeyed, will tend to make them more faithful in the discharge of duty; and they have the gospel preached to them, from Sabbath to Sabbath, which they would otherwise be but seldom permitted to hear, as their constant attendance on the patients is one essential feature of the management of the institution.

"Commending it, with its various interests and concerns, to the guidance, protection, and blessing of Almighty God, the chaplain cannot conclude this report of his labors, without acknowledging the respectful kindness which has always been shown him, in the discharge of his official duties, by the physician, and all the other officers and inmates of the Retreat.

"T. H. GALLAUDET.

"*May* 12, 1841."

Dr. William Wilson, resident physician of the *Bloomingdale Asylum, New York,* says, in his report, dated January 29, 1842, —

"To the benefits resulting from the observance of public worship in the institution, I add my willing testimony. It is to the patients a source of pleasure, and, I trust, to some, at least, not without a profitable tendency in maintaining in their minds the kindly influences of religion on the heart, as well as the habits and associations of their former lives. This observance of public worship, and its beneficial influence on the insane, (no longer a problem, it having been introduced successfully into this Asylum for the last ten years, and I believe in almost all others in the United States,*) is another advantage afforded to patients, from which, if at home, they would be most assuredly debarred."

Dr. Kirkbride, superintendent of the *Pennsylvania Hospital for the Insane*, says, in his report for the year 1841, —

"It has been a source of gratification to find the Sabbath, in this institution, almost invariably the day of greatest comfort and quiet among the patients; and we have never, in any situation, felt more sensibly the favorable influence of a respect for the day, than in the household with which we have been connected during the past year. Visitors are not admitted to the Hospital on that day, — the usual employments and amusements of the patients are voluntarily laid aside, — they remain in the parlors or halls, engaged in reading and conversation, or, in fine weather, walk through the extensive garden and grounds within the enclosure.

"A portion of the patients, either alone, or accompanied by some of the officers or attendants, are allowed to attend service, either in the city, or at some of the numerous places of worship in our immediate vicinity.

"Early in the evening, those patients who are not violently excited, and are so disposed, assemble in the large rooms on the first floor of the centre building, where the steward and matron read to them portions of the Scriptures. This reading occupies from thirty to forty minutes, and is preceded and followed by a short period of silence.

* "The regular observance of public worship was first introduced into this Asylum during the winter of 1831–2, whilst under the charge of Guy C. Bayley, M. D., the Rev. John M. Forbes, at present rector of St. Luke's Church, N. Y., officiating as chaplain."

"From eighty to ninety per cent. of all our patients have voluntarily attended; and the uniform good order, the respectful attention with which most have listened to the pages of the inspired volume, and the quiet manner in which they have passed to and from the room, have been highly gratifying at each return of the day. We have never had any serious disturbance at these readings; many have asked to attend, as a favor; some, who, in the halls, were noisy and profane, after giving a pledge of good behavior, have conducted in the most exemplary manner. Simple as is this observance of the Sabbath, we believe its effects have been of no little value — not only from the habit of self-restraint which it imposes, but from the consolations of the blessed truths which have been heard by an afflicted community, comprising members of almost every religious denomination. All the officers, with any of their friends who may be with them, join the patients in one or other of the rooms."

Dr. Stribling, superintendent of the *Western Lunatic Asylum in Virginia*, says, in his last report, dated January 1, 1842, —

"It will probably be recollected that, in a former report, I urged with some zeal upon the court of directors, the necessity of employing a chaplain, and establishing in the institution religious services at regular and stated periods; but, for reasons which they doubtless deemed sufficient, action upon the subject was deferred until a more propitious season. From subsequent intercourse with the insane, and on further reflection, I became more and more convinced, that it was of the utmost importance to the contentment and happiness of many of our inmates, that they should be permitted sometimes to enjoy the advantages of public worship; and as, for obvious reasons, very few of them could, with safety or propriety, attend such ministrations in the neighboring churches, we resolved, in the early part of the past year, to convene those of them who might be disposed to attend, on each Sabbath afternoon, for the purpose of reading to them a sermon, selected with care from the writings of some judicious divine, and that, with one heart and one voice, we might unite in offering praise, thanksgiving, and supplication to Him, who, when on earth, 'delighted to behold the wild maniac at his feet, sitting and clothed, in his right mind,' and who so affectionately invites all, whatever the character of their affliction, to come to him, that they may be healed. These meetings were commenced on the 21st day of February last, and have been held, without intermission, on each succeeding Sabbath. And, from the good effect already produced, as well as the growing interest daily manifested in regard to them, we can but mark their introduction as an epoch in the history of our institution. The officers and attendants are punctual in being present, and the patients consider it so valued a privilege to attend, that a fear of its forfeiture often secures a degree of self-control which no other influence could effect. It is by no means unusual for individuals who are excited and noisy, when the sound of the bell is heard summoning them to service, to become instantly calm and quiet, and afterwards conduct themselves throughout the ceremonies with the utmost propriety and decorum. Some, who cannot be controlled elsewhere, are, at such times, calm and composed, and it has several times happened, that those who have been brought to us bound with chains, owing to the supposed violence of their insanity, have, within three days after their arrival, been permitted to attend these meetings, without the least excitement, restlessness, or impatience, being manifested. It is indeed most gratifying to behold the solemn stillness which pervades these assemblies, the respectful attention exhibited on such occasions, and the deep interest depicted in the countenances of the audience. Before us sits usually 'lord Primat,' whose empire extends over the whole church militant; on our right appears the 'Virgin Mary;' to the left of us is to be seen the fallen angel 'Apollyon;' and immediately at our elbow sits the 'Mother of the ten tribes of Israel;' all, for the time, seeming to forget their peculiar hallucinations, whilst their thoughts are engrossed in rational meditation upon the simple and sober truths of divine revelation.

" Many of our patients, although laboring under mental delusions in regard to some subjects, are nevertheless entire masters of their own conduct, retain a correct sense of right and wrong, and appreciate with such accuracy the relation which they sustain to a Supreme Being, that they can but be considered as moral agents, 'equally responsible with ourselves for their thoughts and actions; and hence we can but feel happy at being enabled to afford them even such opportunities for religious enjoyment and spiritual improvement; and in regard to those whose minds may be so far impaired as to exempt them from such responsibility, still the setting apart one day in seven for this purpose, has the effect, if it does nothing more, of breaking in upon the monotony of their existence, and thus relieving them from that *ennui* which uninterrupted sameness is so certain to produce.

" The singing is executed by a choir composed of attendants and patients, who meet on certain evenings during the week, with a view to improvement in this respect; and, besides the social pleasures derived from these associations, (which seem to be highly prized,) our music on the Sabbath is thereby greatly benefited.

" Out of the whole number in the institution during the year, *one hundred* have attended these services more or less regularly, being about four fifths; and the average number present upon such occasions, exclusive of officers and attendants, has, for a short time past, been about *seventy*.

" I shall be pardoned, doubtless, for again calling the attention of the directors to the importance of employing a suitable chaplain. This has been done, in several of the best institutions in this country, with the most beneficial effects, and its advantages over the system pursued by us, must be so apparent to the board as to render comment unnecessary. I do not, of course, apprehend for a moment, that a motive of selfishness will be attributed to me in urging this recommendation; as my past course must surely afford ample evidence, that no labor, effort, or sacrifice, would be shunned, which by possibility could add to the happiness or well-being of those intrusted to my charge. Nor is it necessary to add, that if, from pecuniary or other obstacles, the directors should now deem it inexpedient to comply with this suggestion, although I may regret the necessity which impels to such a decision, still with cheerfulness will I continue to perform the duty heretofore assumed."

Dr. William M. Awl, superintendent of the *Ohio Lunatic Asylum*, says, in his last report, dated November 15, 1841, —

" Religious services have been regularly continued, as heretofore, during the past year, and, so far as we have been able to understand their effects upon the insane mind, with decidedly beneficial results. Religious feelings have a deep root in the heart of man. They are, in fact, a part of his very constitution and nature; and so connected and interwoven with all the hopes and fears which actuate him in life, that no change of condition, or circumstance of disease in his bodily organs, can entirely obliterate and remove their influence from his memory. And the gospel of Jesus Christ, as it accommodates itself with great tenderness and mercy to every painful and distressed condition of the mind, is peculiarly worthy of serious attention, in the moral treatment of those who are intellectually deranged. Our patients, indeed, in most cases, esteem this service as a privilege, and their applications for permission to attend are frequently urged in the most pressing and interesting manner. We are, of course, not unwilling to grant their request; but, as we like to take advantage of this, and every other occurrence, to encourage self-restraint, the terms, of *good behavior, strict attention*, &c., are sometimes considered to be sufficiently extravagant. It is a fact, that many, who are restless and uneasy, and even noisy, in the halls, will enter the place of prayer with sufficient self-control not only to remain quiet, and give audience, but to regard the place, and unite in the service of OUR FATHER IN HEAVEN.

" And, in respect to the government of a public institution of this description, our judgment and experience still continue to view these periods of devotion as highly important and interesting. Though brief and simple in themselves, they certainly add solemnity to moral virtue, and while they cherish and give encouragement to piety, they have a strong tendency to strengthen the social connections in life, and produce a happy influence upon that friendly intercourse which is necessary among those who find employment in the same line of duty."

WHAT REMAINS TO BE DONE FOR POOR LUNATICS?

Some may suppose that the agency of this Society in relieving poor lunatics from their distresses in Prisons, and causing them to be provided for in Asylums, is at an end. Would that it were so! But the facts in the case demand a different conclusion. In proof of this, we begin at a distance from home, and return by a circuitous route.

Dr. Madden, in his " Travels in Turkey," says, concerning the *Asylum at Grand Cairo, in Egypt,* —

" I believe that no eye hath witnessed, elsewhere, such a melancholy spectacle as this place affords. The keeper made many objections to my admission. He said no Frank was suffered to go in; but the name of the *hakkim* of the English consul, and the sight of half a dozen piastres to boot, removed his scruples.

" I was led from one passage to another; door after door was unbarred; the keeper armed himself with a *courbash*, (a whip made of one solid thong of the hippopotamus,) and we at length got into an open court, round which the dungeons of the lunatics were situated. Some, who were not violent, were walking, unfettered; but the poor wretches in the cells were chained, by the neck, to the bars of the grated windows. The keeper went round, as he would in a menagerie of wild beasts, rattling the chain at the window, to rouse the inmates, and dragging them by it when they were tardy in approaching. One madman, who spat at me as I passed his cell, I saw the keeper pull by his chain, and knock his head against the bars, till the blood issued from his nose. I forced him to desist. Each of them, as we passed, called out for food. I inquired about their allowance, and, to my horror, I heard that there was none, except what charitable people were pleased to afford, from day to day. It was now noon, and they had had no food from the preceding morning. Two well-dressed Turkish women brought in, while I was there, a large watermelon and two cakes of bread; this was broken in pieces, and thrown to the famished creatures. I never saw nature subdued to such lowliness. They devoured what they got like hungry tigers, some of them thrusting their tongues through the bars, others screaming for more bread. I sent for a few piastres' worth of bread, dates, and sour milk; its arrival was hailed with a yell of ecstasy that pierced the very soul. I thought that they would have torn down the iron bars to get at the provisions; and, in spite of the courbash, their eagerness to get their portions rendered it a difficult matter to get our hands out of their clutches. It was humiliating to humanity to see these poor wretches tearing their food with their filthy fingers. Some of their nails were so long as to resemble the talons of a hawk."

" A black man, who followed the trade of a butcher, had been confined there many years ago. He had been allowed the range of the house, with two or three others, whose derangement was attended with no violence. One night, the black butcher secreted a knife ; he induced another man to enter his cell, prevailed on him to lie down, and then cut his throat; he calmly cut him in quarters, and distributed the joints around his cell, as he was in the habit of arranging his meat in his shop. He solicited the custom of his comrades, and to those who were chained, he carried such portions as they desired. The keeper was disturbed by the cannibal rejoicings ; it was the first full meal they had had for many a long day. On examining the cells, he found one man missing. He asked the black butcher if he had seen him, and he replied that he had sold the last joint of him. ' Since that time,' said the keeper, ' we look out better, otherwise they would eat one every day.' "

Dr. Ray, superintendent of the *Insane Hospital at Augusta, Maine,* in his last report, dated December 31, 1841, page 27, says, —

" The first point that arrests our attention, is the comparatively small number of the insane that have been received into the Hospital. By the United States census of 1840, it appears that there are in this state 631 insane persons. A large portion, no doubt, are idiots and other incurables, who can hardly be considered as fit subjects of medical or moral treatment, and who are as well off, wherever they are kindly treated, as they would be with us. Still, after making all reasonable deductions of this kind, there are unquestionably more than 134, who would be either completely restored, or greatly improved, mentally and bodily, by a residence in the Hospital."

The trustees of the same institution, in the report of the previous year, say, —

" There are in this state many insane paupers. Several of the towns, acting under an enlightened and liberal policy, that is truly commendable, have provided for the insane poor in the Hospital. There are, however, many of the towns, which, under a mistaken policy of *selfishness,* — a policy too often influencing those bodies which are said 'to have no souls,' — have adopted the practice of selling the keeping of their poor at auction. What kind of treatment insane paupers, thus sold to the lowest bidder, would be likely to receive, may be readily conjectured. If any constitutional measures for the protection of insane paupers could be adopted by the legislature, humanity would rejoice at the result."

Dr. Stribling, of the *Western Lunatic Asylum of Virginia,* in his last report, dated January 1, 1842, says, —

" The fact, however, as developed by this table, in which we are most interested, is, that there are in Virginia *one thousand and forty-eight* white lunatics and idiots, — a statement which, astounding as it may at first seem, is doubtless far below the truth. It is scarcely probable that, in any instance, an individual was registered as insane, who was not so; but it is absolutely certain that many were omitted, who should have been included under this head. A number of such cases are within my knowledge, which, if necessary, could be here cited; but it will suffice to establish at least the plausibility of my remark, for me to state, that, in the county of Frederick, there is only one individual reported by the census as being insane, and at public expense, when there were certainly *seven,* if not eight, such in the jail of said county, at that date. But, even on the supposition that the number has been correctly reported, who is there that can refrain from inquiring, Where are these *one thousand* and *more* poor creatures, who have been deprived of the God-like attribute of reason? and what is their present condition? We know that but about *two hundred and fifty* of them are in the Asylums of the commonwealth, and are of course left to conjecture as to the location and circumstances of the remainder. Many are doubtless with their friends, receiving all the attention which affection can bestow, and surrounded by every comfort, which, in their unhappy state, they can appreciate; but their disease is doubtless becoming more firmly riveted by every day's duration, and many of them may be already doomed to continue its victims during life. Others are wretched wanderers, traversing the highways or by-paths of the commonwealth, unprotected and uncared for, suffering with cold and hunger, and exhibiting, wherever they go, an exterior but too well harmonizing with a 'mind in ruins.' Whilst a third and most hapless class are immured in the gloomy Prisons of the country, degraded to a level with the criminal who has violated the laws both of God and man; chained like wild beasts to the floors of their grated cells; but half fed, and altogether naked; often writhing, too, under the lash of their cruel keeper; and in this state are cut off from intercourse with all other living creatures, save, indeed, the creeping vermin which feed upon the filth in which their bodies are incased. Would that this picture was the result of fancy, or was even a reality somewhat exaggerated; but — alas for the honor of Virginia! — it is too faithful a representation of what many of this class of unfortunates are now suffering within her borders; and whilst no one could be more unwilling than myself to do aught by which her fair fame might be tarnished, it would surely seem, in this particular, a false delicacy to disguise the truth, if its disclosure could, by possibility, lead to the rescue of a single one of these unhappy sufferers. Not to dwell upon the cases of some four or five individuals, who, within a few weeks past, have been brought to this institution, (from the Jails in which they had been lying, some of them, for many years,) bound with chains, and marked with stripes, as evidencing the cruelty and inhumanity which are so commonly practised, — I feel it a duty to relate the circumstances of a visit, made in person, during the last summer, to one of these receptacles for the insane, not a hundred miles distant from this Asylum; and it is to be seriously apprehended that the scenes there exhibited afford too striking a criterion by which to judge the condition of most of those confined to the Jails throughout the state. — Being accidentally at the place just alluded to, and understanding that a number of insane persons were confined in the Jail, I was induced to visit it; but more especially to see one of these individuals, in whose fate my sympathies had become particularly enlisted, from hearing him represented as a genteel young foreigner, of industrious habits and fine moral character, who had within a very short period lost his reason. On arriving at the Prison, and informing the keeper of my object, he readily tendered his services to conduct me to the several apartments, in which were confined the unhappy beings for whom my visit was designed. It is probably due to the old man, whose head seemed frosted by at least threescore winters, that I should premise, that his appearance and conversation prepossessed me favorably as to his goodness of heart, and a disposition to do, in behalf of his *prisoners*, whatever his judgment could sanction as being proper; although, as will appear from the sequel, he must have indulged the antiquated and superstitious idea, that the 'insane are possessed with demons,' and hence that it was more important to confine and restrain them, than to minister to their comfort, or attempt an alleviation of their affliction.

" The first cell to which I was introduced was dark, and imperfectly ventilated, and contained, 'solitary and alone,' the young man in whom I had felt most interested. He sat in a remote corner of the apartment, on a dirty bag, partly filled with straw, having a strong chain riveted to his ankle, and binding him to the floor. His features were almost concealed by the long beard which had grown in unchecked luxuriance, and, together with his profuse and dishevelled locks, gave to him an appearance somewhat savage and repulsive.

His body and limbs were uncovered, save that he wore on his shoulders part of an old, filthy, cloth coat, which badly concealed his nakedness. On my first approach, he hung his head, as if conscious of his apparent degradation; but, in a short time, seeming to be actuated by a desire for release, he elevated and fixed upon me an eye expressive only of anxiety and distress, and, without uttering a syllable, by a significant gesture directed my attention to the chain upon his ankle. Finding him any thing else than a maniac, I turned to the keeper with surprise, and inquired why it was he had him thus fettered; nor was this astonishment allayed by the reply, that it was in consequence of his tearing his clothes and destroying his furniture; for if he had been as poorly provided with either when free, as in his then condition, he could surely have indulged his destructive propensities to the utmost, without any *serious* damage resulting. After learning from the keeper that he was never dangerous or violent, I endeavored to prevail upon him to be satisfied with merely confining his hands, and proposed to direct him how to make a muff, which would effectually prevent his doing mischief, whilst he could be permitted to wear his clothes, and walk about his room; but the old man seemed wedded to his chain, and no persuasion could induce him to abandon it. I, of course, left the apartment deeply pained at the spectacle presented, and regretting most sincerely that the poor sufferer could not be admitted into this Asylum, where his comfort would have been secured, and the disease, which was fast becoming more firmly riveted than the chain which bound him, could almost certainly have been removed.

"The next cell to which I was conducted, contained an object the most forbidding that it had been my lot to behold in human form. Like the poor German above described, his long and profuse hair and beard seemed not to have been cut or combed for a great while. He was covered with filthy rags, and the heavy chain which fastened him to the floor was only long enough to admit of his lying down on his comfortless bed of boards and blankets. The appearance of the poor creature, indicating that he had drunk a twofold portion of the cup of affliction, suffering the horrors of mental disease, aggravated by physical neglect and torture, and the effluvia which issued from his filthy abode, alike operated to prevent my tarrying long with him. On retiring, I was shocked still further to learn that he had been in this condition, chained to the floor, for more than *three* years. This individual has been since admitted into our Asylum; nor was I surprised to find, that, from his long confinement to a particular position, his lower extremities had become entirely paralyzed. He is now, from this cruel treatment, a helpless cripple, unable to walk or stand, and will, in all probability, so continue during life.

"A third apartment, which opened into a narrow passage, was, if possible, still more revolting than either of the former, not because it appeared more uncomfortable or cheerless, — for such could not well have been the case, — but because it was the abode of *five* insane females, three of whom were white, and two black. One of each color was chained in opposite corners of the room, whilst the remaining three were permitted during the day to exercise or labor in the adjoining passage. A further description of their appearance and circumstances, horrible as it might be, could not surely aggravate the deep loathing which must be produced in the mind of every humane and intelligent individual, by this simple statement as to their number, sex, color, and condition. There was one other male confined elsewhere in the establishment; but, having witnessed enough of the degradation and sufferings of my fellow-beings, I did not impose upon the *goodness* of the old man to conduct me farther.

"This jailer received annually, from the public treasury, within a fraction of *two thousand dollars,* for the manner in which he thus treated these unfortunates, — a sum which, had there been apartments here for their reception, would have supported comfortably and genteelly, for the same period, these *eight* and *five* others, making in all *thirteen.* As before remarked, is there not too much reason to fear, as this exhibition has occurred in one of the most wealthy, intelligent, and populous counties of the state, that it but represents the condition of many others, throughout our country ?   And does it not call, with a loud voice, upon the Christian, the philanthropist, and the statesman, to be up and doing, not only to alleviate the privations and sufferings of this ill-fated class of fellow-immortals, but to erase this humiliating stain from the escutcheon of our beloved Virginia.   Surely the apathy which has existed in regard to this subject, thus far, must have resulted from the fact, that both legislators and their constituents have been ignorant of the hapless condition to which so many of this class of our unfortunate fellow-citizens are consigned; and hence it is all-important that these and similar facts (of which it is to be regretted there are such a number) should be made public. The press, that mighty engine of weal or woe to the destinies of our state and the welfare of her citizens, should be made to teem with the shrieks and groans of the ill-fated lunatics, until the comfort of every domestic fireside in the commonwealth is disturbed, and the now dormant sympathies of a whole people be aroused to a just appreciation of their sufferings and degradation.   The humane and talented editor of the Charlestown (Va.) Free Press, has lately spoken with emphasis and power upon this subject ; and we will doubtless be pardoned for quoting here his eloquent and touching remarks : — ' It is our fate,' says he, ' to be located opposite the County Prison, in which are now confined four miserable creatures, bereft of the God-like attribute of reason, — two of them females, — and our feelings are daily excited by sounds of woe, that would harrow up the flintiest soul in creation.   Oh ! it is horrible, that, for the sake of a few thousand dollars, the wailings of the wretched should be suffered to issue from the gloomy walls of our Prisons without pity and without relief.   Would that our law-makers were doomed to listen, but for a single hour each day, to the clanking chains and the piercing shrieks of these forlorn wretches !   Relief would surely follow, and the character of our state be rescued from the foul blot which now dishonors it.'   Let the press echo and re-echo the cries of the suffering lunatic, until the hearts of the hardest are melted ; and let no public man be trusted who listens not to the demands of humanity."

The Rev. G. Barrett, an agent of the Prison Discipline Society, in a letter, dated *Wilmington, Delaware*, April, 19, 1842, says, —

" The Poor-House in this place has received, last year, 35 insane persons, which, according to the census, is half the whole number in the state.   There are now about 20 insane in the Poor-House.   Their condition is not as it should be.   Each is placed in a dark, illy-ventilated room, — their bed a bunk of straw, or straw on the floor, and an old blanket.   *A chain fastens each to a ring in the centre of the room.*   Among them was a good-looking girl of sixteen.   The physician does not think there is much hope of restoring the patients to reason in such a place as this.   I mean to tell the people something about their insane this evening."

In the last report, page 6, of the *Friends' Asylum near Frankford, Penn.*, signed by Dr. Evans and Dr. Earle, they say, —

" It is cause of regret, that, within our own as well as other yearly meetings, there are Friends, laboring under different forms of mental disease, who are not partakers of the benefits which our Asylum offers ; and it is greatly to be desired that the relatives of such, or others interested in their welfare, would adopt measures for placing them within the benign influence of the institution."

A committee of the legislature of *Pennsylvania* say, in their report to the legislature, dated March 11, 1839, (and no State Asylum has yet been built, and we shall see in the sequel that these things must remain as they were while this is the case,) —

" What, then, is the present condition of the insane and idiotic persons now dwelling in the Poor-Houses, Jails, and Penitentiaries of our commonwealth ?

" From one county we have the following statement : — ' We have two places only for the reception of the insane poor — the common Poor-House, and the County Jail. In the latter place are generally males who are too violent and dangerous to be kept in a common Poor-House. For the public peace and protection of the community, they were charged with breaches of the peace, or petty misdemeanors, that were made the pretence for confinement, and, being unable to give bonds, were committed. Here their society is chiefly convicts, or, if kept in solitary confinement, so ill are the accommodations for this, that they suffer more than the rigor of Penitentiary discipline ; and thus are they kept, from year to year, with the same treatment that is meted out to those convicted of high crimes.'

" From another county we have the following information : — ' The accommodations for the insane in the County Poor-House consist of a single room, in which the furious and violent are confined, male and female in the same apartment, separated only by the length and restraint of their chains. Their hands being at liberty, they frequently strip themselves of all covering. The condition of these furious and violent maniacs, confined in the same room, destitute of all comforts, and with every thing around calculated to aggravate their madness, is degrading and deplorable in the extreme. Bad as is the condition of poor insane lunatics, dwelling in private hovels of poverty, yet the condition of the violent is better there, with more comfort and hope of alleviation and relief, than in the mad apartment of the public Poor-House, chained with others as mad as themselves. Though they may not have as regular an allowance of bread and meat in the humble cabin, yet there they may have eyes to pity, hands to afford relief, or voices to utter some comfort and consolation.'

" Another report states as follows : — ' We have no special accommodation for the insane, and such as we have is wretched. They are kept in an old, dilapidated building, scarcely tenantable. Five or six are chained in so many small, separate compartments on the same floor. In a word, the insane of this county, whether in or out of the Poor-House, are, we are sorry to say, scarcely considered proper objects of medical attention, and still less of moral discipline.'

" In another county, a memorial was addressed to the board of directors of the poor, by the attending physicians, setting forth that they have, ' for a long time, regretted the defectiveness of the present arrangements for the treatment of insane patients. The only apartments now used,' they say, ' are in a damp, confined, ill-ventilated, and comfortless situation ; calculated more to increase both the physical and mental derangement of such patients, than to coöperate with the sanative influence of medical treatment.' And again, ' That we are not disposed to exaggerate the deficiencies and inconveniences of the present arrangement, it is only necessary to state that, since the erection of the present buildings, several LIVES HAVE BEEN LOST, from the imperfect construction of the cells for the insane, and where no possible blame could attach to the keepers.' This memorial was made part of the report of the grand jury to the court of quarter sessions, in August of 1838. At the November sessions following, the presiding judge called the particular attention of the grand jury to the hospital, and they were induced to visit the premises, accompanied by the attending physician. After a full and fair examination of their condition, the grand jury say, 'These unfortunate individuals (the insane) are now placed in confined, damp, and illy-ventilated apartments on the ground floor, resembling more the cells of a Prison than any thing else. When permitted to take exercise and recreation in the open air, they are loaded like convicts with hobbles and chains, and exposed in summer to the hot sun without the protection of a single shady tree. In this situation they associate, in the same yard with the other paupers, who, though more rational, unfeelingly provoke them with jeers and scoffs, and thus aggravate the violence of their disease. Under these circumstances, the grand jury believe it impossible to render them such medical and moral assistance as their peculiar diseases require, and which are curable only by a proper combination of physical, medical, and moral treatment.' 'Distressing as it is to the feelings of humanity, it is notwithstanding true, that this class of patients, which call loudest for our sympathy and our aid, and whose disease, we are informed, requires the nicest and most exact kind of treatment, are here placed in a situation wholly unfit for the successful treatment of *any* disease, and particularly for that of *insanity*. These unfortunate beings are deprived of even the ordinary comforts of the pauper, and their derangement, instead of being cured, becomes confirmed.'

" 'From two to four physicians are annually elected to attend *all* the inmates of the hospital. The year is then divided into sections, and each physician attends singly his own section. During this period, the physician seldom visits the insane regularly, and seldom prescribes for them. This is owing to the imperfect and uncomfortable arrangements made for them, and the impossibility of combining proper moral and physical treatment with the medical.'

" 'In consequence, therefore, of the imperfect construction of the building, the medical treatment of the insane at our hospital is more neglected than that of any class of individuals in the house.'

" In the Poor-House of another county are found 8 sufferers, whose average term of insanity is 19 years. One of them, 89 years of age, has been bereaved of reason 40 years, and another, of 64, has been in the like condition 34 years.

" Your committee have also been furnished from an unquestionable source with the following facts : — In one of our Poor-Houses, an insane white female was found naked from the hips upwards, while the lower part of her body was confined in a sack or bag filled with straw. She was wallowing about the floor in her own filth, and, from the stench of the room, it would seem she could not be cleansed oftener than once a week.

" A cold, comfortless place, scarcely fit for a cow stable, is the habitation of a decent woman who has seen good days.

" The principal object is *security;* and while they are generally confined behind iron bars, in narrow cells, some, who are only partially deranged, are chained to trees and logs, when the weather permits.

" In one county, of 40 persons more or less deranged, 7 are confined in cells, which are nearly if not quite under ground. They may be seen from without, through iron bars in the cellar windows. Among them is a German girl, 20 years old, seemingly in perfect health of body, with beautiful teeth and hair, and without any symptoms of malignity, who has been in such a cell 5 months, and considered as incurable. This interesting case, under treatment for a few months, in a proper Insane Hospital, would probably result in a complete restoration to reason and liberty.

" A man 50 years old, who has been in this state 5 years, presented a picture of settled, hopeless wretchedness.

" Several other like cases are described; and all these, we are told, 'are shut up, under bolts and bars, neglected, and almost forgotten, with no friendly voice to break the silence of their solitude, and presenting, one and all, the same revolting picture of suffering.'

" In another county, ' A man, 35 years old, had been confined for years in a miserable shed. When the bolt was drawn, and the door opened, he was lying on the floor among straw; no bed was to be seen, though it was cold weather; and we had to plunge through snow, which had fallen the day previous, to get to his wretched abode.'

" ' In another county, a woman of 35 was confined in like manner till she raved herself to death.'

" While decided testimony is given to the good keeping and kind treatment of paupers generally, 'the poor lunatics are found with the feet chained together, or chained by the body to iron weights, logs of wood, or to the trunks of trees, or, what is more common, under ground, without light or ventilation, and breathing an air loaded with intolerable stench.'

" In the report from another county, we have the following remarks: — 'Our poor are bound out, at so much a year, to those who will take them at the cheapest rate. From this you may infer how far their situation is comfortable, or how far their unfortunate condition is likely to be ameliorated.'

" And the report of another states 'that their insane poor receive all the medical attendance that can possibly be rendered, but, in consequence of the want of sufficient apparatus and the superintendence of prudent and judicious persons, the recoveries are few, — not more than two or three per year, and those confined to recent cases where the exciting cause is fully understood.'

" In one of the only two counties in which a serious doubt is raised as to the expediency of the contemplated Asylum, we find, as we think, a forcible argument for the prompt action of the legislature. It is said that their insane paupers are indispensable, as the steward could not well get along without their assistance; they are made to serve the old, and sick, and crippled. These services are often of a very disagreeable character, such as the sane are unwilling to render, and such as hirelings will not do without very large pay.

" Why should the poor lunatic be thus humbled and degraded? Is it not enough that his light is turned into darkness, and his joy into sorrow? Must he be made the outcast and offscouring of the earth?

" That there is nothing singular in the state of things presented by these reports we need hardly remark. Until within a few years, the idea that insanity is a curable disease, seems never to have been practically entertained in any part of the world. The insane were considered as doomed to hopeless, remediless suffering; and the only inquiry was, Where can they be most securely confined? Hence resort was had to the cells and dungeons of Prisons, under special contract with the keeper for their support.

" The vilest criminal could not be made to suffer what the poor maniac, though incapable of crime, has often endured.

" We are told that the cases in which the early symptoms of this disease are most violent, most easily yield to seasonable and proper treatment; and it is in these severe paroxysms, that outrages upon life and property are generally committed, and of consequence those who might have been most easily relieved have suffered most severely from the absence of the means.

" It has been well said, that, were a system now to be devised, whose express object it should be to drive every victim of insanity beyond the limits of hope, it would scarcely be in the power of a perverse ingenuity to suggest one more infallible than that which, for so many years, has been in practical operation among us.

" To say nothing of the amount of human suffering it has caused, it cannot be doubted, that, with appropriate treatment, one half, at least, of all the lunatics whose support must now continue to be a burden upon the state, while they live, might have been restored; and this half might have added as much to the resources of the state as the other would have subtracted from them."

" Although there are at least two charitable institutions in our state, which provide, partially or exclusively, for the sufferings of the insane, it is well known that their accommodations are private.   Unless, therefore, suitable provision is made at once by public munificence, the mass of wretchedness we have been contemplating must remain unrelieved, and be constantly increasing."

The commissioners appointed by the governor of *New Jersey* to examine the condition of lunatics in that state, say, —

" It is believed that cases have existed in each county, of lunatics confined in Jail, either because they were believed to be dangerous to the community when at large, or because of some flagrant outrage.   Some have remained in confinement for years, and some of them *in chains.*   There are now in Newark Jail two lunatics ; in New Brunswick, two in chains ; and one in Gloucester Poor-House, one in Cumberland, and one in Salem, all in chains.   The individual in chains, in Gloucester Poor-House, is confined by hand and leg irons, with a chain extending from each to the floor.   He is neither vicious nor violent, and would harm no one, unless, indirectly, by some mischievous prank.   He is so restless and uneasy, that, when not confined in this way, he is constantly engaged in tearing his cell and his clothes to pieces.   It is highly probable that this man might be rendered useful to the community, instead of being a burden, were he in a well-regulated institution.   In this same county, also, there is a female who, though but 28 years of age, has been chained by the ankle 12 years.

" In the 4th district, Dr. McChesney says, ' I find scenes of misery and wretchedness that the citizens of New Jersey have never dreamed of — enough to melt the heart of the most obdurate.'   He has been able to trace 14 of these cases to intemperance, 6 to religious excitement, and 4 to the influence of love.   The greater part arose from causes unknown.   Some were said to have been *confined in cells upwards of* 20 *years.*

" If the state shall determine to erect an Institution for its Insane, we presume it will be intended principally for that class of unfortunates, who, for the want of such an establishment, are committed to Jails because the community is unsafe when they are at large.   They are wandering at all hours, break into dwelling-houses at night, and greatly disturb the repose of families.   In many instances, they pilfer for hunger — make violent assaults upon the defenceless — set fire to dwellings — and sometimes commit horrid murders — yet, in the eye of the law, they are not *criminals,* because they are *insane.* The peace and safety of society demand their confinement; and of necessity they are shut up with felons and criminals in County Jails, where every thing around them tends but to confirm their insanity, and to render recovery hopeless."

Dr. Awl, superintendent of the *Ohio Lunatic Asylum, at Columbus,* in his last report, dated November 15, 1841, says, —

" Amidst all its " (i. e., the Asylum's) "favorable results and blessings, it is still matter of sincere and painful regret, that we are compelled, for want of room, to deny its comforts and privileges to so many unfortunate and afflicted citizens in the different counties of the state.

" Over 100 formal and informal applications for admission, from our own people, have, on this account, been refused during the past year ; and of those received, we have, in most cases, been compelled to postpone their admission for six, nine, and even twelve months after date.   This, by depriving us, in many instances, of the recent and curable cases as they have occurred, has had a very important and unfavorable influence upon our success, and is the chief reason why the actual number of recoveries is less than was reported last year.   Besides, the necessity of postponing the reception of many applicants, has occasioned disappointment and grief to the friends of the afflicted, and, we may say, the public at large ; for a maniac is not only the cause of extraordinary trouble and distress to his own immediate connections, but he very frequently disturbs a large circle of friends, and is sometimes the source of anxiety, if not alarm, to an extensive section of country.

" The board of directors are acquainted with these facts, and they have been faithful in carrying out the provisions of the statute in relation to such lunatics as have been found, ' *after the expiration of sufficient time, to be incurable, and not dangerous to go at large,*' in order to extend the usefulness of the institution, and make it accomplish the greatest amount of good that circumstances would allow. But this unpleasant application of the law is comparatively of small importance, as experience proves it to be unpopular, and the relief which is in this manner obtained is not unmixed with distress ; for some of these forlorn and helpless children of affliction and misfortune, having lived with us long enough to become fixed in their habits, and attached to the comfortable home which the hand of public benevolence has provided, have been filled with sorrow on receiving the unwelcome intelligence, and have left with a reluctance alike painful to us and them."

" In connection with the subject, we cannot refrain, upon this occasion, from inviting the attention of the Christian philanthropist to the necessities which exist for a corporate or private Asylum for the Insane, in the immense region watered by the navigable rivers flowing south and west. According to our computation upon the census returns for 1840, there are in the states of Alabama, Mississippi, Louisiana, Tennessee, Kentucky, Ohio, Indiana, Illinois, Missouri, Arkansas, and the teritories Wiskonsan and Iowa, *two thousand one hundred and sixty-seven insane persons*, exclusive of idiots and imbeciles ; and, with the exception of the three state institutions in Kentucky, Tennessee, and Ohio, which, it will be seen, can, unitedly, admit but *three hundred and eighty persons*, we are not aware of any suitable accommodations, public or private, for the medical and moral treatment of the insane, in all this enterprising, wealthy, and extensive region of country. Two or three flourishing cities might be named as favorable locations ; and, considering the deep solicitude which must exist under such extraordinary and very peculiar circumstances of distress, there could not be a single doubt as to the support which a private or corporate Asylum of high character, and undoubted moral reputation, would immediately receive.

" Such an institution would greatly relieve the pauper Asylums of the several states, and might be made a desirable and profitable retreat for the restoration of a certain class of inebriates, who frequently require as much treatment and restraint as the insane."

Dr. Edward Jarvis, of Louisville, Kentucky, in his able pamphlet of February, 1842, entitled " *What shall we do with the* Insane ?" says, —

" What shall we do with our insane ? This is a question that must come home to all of us, whether physicians or citizens, and sometimes appeal with fearful earnestness to our hearts and understandings for answer. And are we ready to give it ? Every one of us is liable to find insanity, in some form or other, in his own family. Every physician may be called, at any time, to see it among his friends. His advice is then pressingly asked, — ' What shall be done with the patient suffering from moral or intellectual derangement ? '

" This is a question, — not, indeed, of life or death ; for insanity is not a dangerous disease ; comparatively few need die of it ; — but it is a question of future soundness of reason and of correct feelings, or of permanent insanity. And whether our patients or our friends shall be brought back to mental life and all its enjoyments, to usefulness, society, and to happiness ; or whether the incubus of lunacy shall weigh forever upon their understandings, their feelings and affections be enchained or perverted, and they become a burden upon their families, a terror to society, or, perhaps, sinking into fatuity, a mockery to the unthinking and the heartless, — which of these shall happen, depends upon us, and our answer to the question, 'What shall be done with the insane?'

"Nor is this a rare question. It has been asked, or it ought to be asked, frequently; for there were, at the last national census, taken in the year 1840, 833 lunatics and idiots in Kentucky; 851 in Tennessee; 568 in Indiana; 227 in Illinois; 278 in Missouri; and 1360 in Ohio.* And their claims press, with an irresistible importunity, upon our professional skill and upon our humanity, to tell them what they shall do. And though our fathers, and we, hitherto, have not told them, and these insane patients have got no relief, and a large portion of them have become incurable maniacs, or have sunk into hopeless imbecility, yet we can no longer be silent; we must tell what shall be done with the 4441 lunatics and idiots that live in the valleys of the Ohio and the Mississippi. The present state of medical science will not suffer these any longer to be neglected, and still less will it permit that those, who hereafter shall become insane, shall have their disease permanently fixed upon them."

"Within a few years, the states of New Hampshire, Connecticut, New Jersey, Pennsylvania, and Maryland, have appointed commissioners to investigate the condition of the insane poor in their limits. These commissioners have made reports, and all give melancholy proof of our position. They show that, of all the pauper lunatics, at their homes, or confined in Jails, Houses of Correction, or Poor-Houses, none are cured, few alleviated, but most become confirmed in chronic insanity. The Reports of the Prison Discipline Society confirm this opinion. And that Society has used its influence to persuade sane men to give their insane brethren the earliest, and therefore the best, chance of relief in the institutions especially built and set apart for them."

"In the United States, there are 19 public and 2 private Asylums for the Insane. 4 of the former are in the Western Country, — at New Orleans, Nashville, Tenn., Lexington, Ky., and Columbus, Ohio. All others are beyond the Alleghany Mountains, and can be reached by us only through a long and tedious journey."

"The above-named 4 are all the institutions of the West, and they cannot contain a fifth of the lunatics of the West who ought to be in them. All the

---

* " *Statement of the Number of Insane in the Western States, — taken from the last National Census, — and how supported.*

States.	WHITES.		COLORED.		Total.	Population.	Proportion of Insane to Population.
	Public.	Private.	Private.	Public.			
Mississippi, ...	14	102	66	16	198	375,651	1 in 1,892
Louisiana, ...	8	45	37	8	98	351,176	1 " 3,592
Tennessee, ...	103	596	124	28	851	829,210	1 " 974
Kentucky, ...	276	406	110	41	833	777,397	1 " 934
Ohio, ...	363	832	62	103	1360	1,519,467	1 " 1,117
Indiana, ...	110	383	46	29	568	683,314	1 " 1,203
Illinois, ...	25	162	32	8	227	474,404	1 " 2,089
Missouri, ...	44	165	52	17	278	381,102	1 " 1,370
Arkansas, ...	3	14	6	5	28	95,642	1 " 3,415
	946	2705	535	255	4441	5,487,363	1 " 1,235

The average for all the United States is 1 to 990."

other hospitals are beyond the mountains, and patients have often been carried from this valley to be healed in those Eastern Asylums."

"From this examination we are led to the melancholy confession of the want of due provision for the comfort and the cure of the insane sufferers of the Western Country. In this broad and rich valley, from the lakes to the Gulf of Mexico, — from the Alleghanies to the Rocky Mountains, — embracing a sane population of more than 5,000,000, and a lunatic population of more than 4000, with no deficiency of wealth, skill, or benevolence, we have but 4 Asylums for the Insane. And these could not contain a tithe of all who might be subjected to their influence, and not a fourth of those who could be benefited by them.

"Even these Hospitals, however excellent some of them may be, are intended primarily for the poor, and are therefore prepared and conducted in a style necessarily more economical, than the richer classes would willingly pay for, or could enjoy, with advantage. And our pauper lunatics are sufficiently numerous to exclude all others. To accommodate this unfortunate class, we ought to have public Asylums in Indiana, Illinois, Missouri, Arkansas, and Mississippi. And, beside these, we want then another Asylum in the West, one of more elegant accommodations than ought to be expected in any state intitution. The rich and the luxurious, the refined and the cultivated, are as liable to be bereft of their reason as their less fortunate brethren. There is a manifest propriety in providing for them, in their sickness, buildings and comforts somewhat corresponding to what they enjoy in health. And we have no doubt that an Asylum of elegance and convenience, similar to the private institutions in the Eastern States, if established near the great navigable thoroughfare of the Western Country, would soon be filled with patients, and do an immense service to society, and save many valuable citizens from irretrievable loss.

"We want a Hospital in the West, to be planned and constructed, furnished and administered, according to the best ideas of the present age. From its very inception to its final operation, nothing should be overlooked or spared, that could, directly or indirectly, bear upon the comfort or the cure of the insane. Such an Asylum should be situated near to the great thoroughfare of the West, near to the Ohio or the Mississippi River."

The trustees of the *New Hampshire Asylum,* in their report for 1840, say, —

"Where now are the insane of New Hampshire? The strong rooms, the cages, and the Jails, will answer for at least 81 of the number; and others of them are perhaps as badly off, wandering at large, irritated and insulted by the idle and vicious, and often refusing, through fear or jealousy, the proffered boon from the cold hand of charity. Many will not keep themselves comfortably clad, and they *must* suffer. A few of the insane will not complain of the cold, if in tolerable health, and will apparently bear the severity of the weather better than persons of sane minds. This state of the system arises from some peculiarity of their disease. But this number is extremely small; for as many as 9 in 10 are in feeble health, with great susceptibility in the nervous system, and suffer keenly from the cold. They need more clothing and warmer atmosphere than persons in health, and yet the falling of the thermometer with many is not a sufficient admonition of danger, to make them draw more closely around them their tattered garments. These afflicted beings should have, for the winter season, at least, a habitation like the comfortable quarters in the best Insane Hospital in New England; made strong and tight, but well ventilated, light and cheerful, and heated throughout by a constant current of pure air thrown in by furnaces, so that all parts of the establishment shall have a warm and temperate atmosphere. In no other place can many of our neighbors and friends, who are insane, be made as well off as we should wish to be were we in their stead."

The State Asylum is just opened at Concord, New Hampshire, and we shall see, during the coming year, to what extent the proper remedy is applied for the relief of the insane.

In *Massachusetts*, the State Hospital at Worcester has been constantly full from its opening, — so much so, that a law was early passed, authorizing the trustees to return incurable and hopeless cases to the Jails and Houses of Correction whence they came, to make room, if necessary, for recent cases. The consequence has been, that many such, and many other poor lunatics, are now in the Jails and Houses of Correction of our good old commonwealth. Does any one doubt it, let him visit, this day, the common Jail, at Lechmere Point, Cambridge, Middlesex county, within two miles of the State House, and one mile from the monument on Bunker Hill, and examine the condition of 22 lunatics in that establishment, most of them in close Jail. We almost fear having our heads cut off by one class of men for saying it, and by another for not saying it sooner and louder. So it is. Go and see.

Boston, Boston has triumphed gloriously. Her insane poor are all provided for. A victory has been won completely. There is no unalleviated and unmitigated misery among this class of persons in Boston. The Hospital at South Boston, erected at the expense of the city, by the inmates of the House of Correction, for the insane poor of the city, is large enough to accommodate all who need its accommodations, and its numbers are beginning to diminish by the number recovered, while the population of the city is rapidly increasing. Of what other spot on earth can the same be said? The Jail and House of Correction are no longer the home of lunatics in Boston. May the same soon be true of Cambridge, and all the other Jails and Houses of Correction in the commonwealth! There is almost as much necessity for the enlargement of the Hospital at Worcester as there was originally for its erection. This can be done advantageously, in the opinion of Dr. Woodward, by an extension of the wings of the front building, in a direct line north and south, beyond the veranda corners, about 100 feet on each wing. 100 more patients would thus be accommodated. There might then be a Jail delivery of lunatics throughout the state. May the Lord hasten it!

" *He that goeth forth and weepeth, bearing precious seed, shall doubtless come again with rejoicing, bringing his sheaves with him.*" — Psalm cxxvi. 6.

OFFICERS.

PRESIDENT.
*GEORGE BLISS,
SAMUEL T. ARMSTRONG.

VICE-PRESIDENTS.

*WILLIAM BARTLETT,
*WILLIAM REED,
LEONARD WOODS,
WILLIAM JENKS,
ELIJAH HEDDING,
*EBENEZER PORTER,
*BENJAMIN B. WISNER,
*JEREMIAH EVARTS,
S. V. S. WILDER,
JOHN TAPPAN,
SAMUEL H. WALLEY,
BROWN EMERSON,
ALEXANDER HENRY,
CHARLES CHAUNCEY,
*STEPHEN VAN RENSSELAER,
*ALEXANDER FRIDGE,
*ROBERT RALSTON,
*EDWARD D. GRIFFIN,
HEMAN HUMPHREY,
*SAMUEL GREEN,
FRANCIS WAYLAND,
JUSTIN EDWARDS,
ALONZO POTTER,
PETER O. THACHER,
FRANCIS C. GRAY,
EDWARD TUCKERMAN,

LUTHER F. DIMMICK,
EDWARD BEECHER,
SIMON GREENLEAF,
DANIEL SHARP,
J. S. STONE,
LUCIUS BOLLES,
JOHN C. WARREN,
HENRY J. RIPLEY,
CHARLES LOWELL,
JOHN S. PETERS,
ROGER MINOT SHERMAN,
THOMAS H. GALLAUDET,
JOEL HAWES,
JEREMIAH DAY,
BENJAMIN SILLIMAN,
ELEAZER LORD,
JOHN M. MATHEWS,
WILLIAM JAY,
THEODORE FRELINGHUYSEN,
*SAMUEL L. SOUTHARD,
SAMUEL MILLER,
ARCHIBALD ALEXANDER,
HOWARD MALCOM,
FRANCIS PARKMAN,
ABBOTT LAWRENCE.

CORRESPONDING MEMBERS.

THOMAS BRADFORD, Jr., *Philadelphia.*
JOEL SCOTT, *Frankfort, Kentucky.*
SAMUEL HOARE, *of London.*
DR. JULIUS, *of Hamburgh.*
G. DE BEAUMONT, *of Paris.*
A. DE TOCQUEVILLE, *of Paris.*
SAMUEL L. DAVIS, *Augusta, Georgia.*
REUEL WILLIAMS, *Hallowell, Me.*
S. E. COUES, *Portsmouth, N. H.*
J. C. HOLBROOK, *Brattleboro', Vt.*
*THOMAS G. LEE, *Charlestown, Mass.*
SAM'L B. WOODWARD, *Worcester, Ms.*

THOMAS PADDOCK, *St. John, N. B.*
J. McAULEY, *Toronto, U. C.*
M. S. BIDWELL, *New York City.*
WM. H. ROCKWELL, *Brattleboro', Vt.*
LUTHER V. BELL, *Charlestown, Mass.*
WM. SAM'L JOHNSON, *New York City.*
P. D. VROOM, *Somerville, N. J.*
S. F. McCRACKEN, *Columbus, Ohio.*
WM. M. AWL, *Columbus, Ohio.*
W. H. BURTON, *New South Wales.*
DR. LANG, *New South Wales.*
JACOB BEESON, *Niles, Michigan.*

MANAGERS.

R. S. STORRS,
SAMUEL A. ELIOT,
JAMES MEANS,
DANIEL SAFFORD,
JARED CURTIS,
DAVID GREEN,

HENRY HILL,
SAMUEL LAWRENCE,
H. M. WILLIS,
SILAS AIKEN,
SAMUEL K. LOTHROP,
GORHAM D. ABBOTT.

CHARLES CLEVELAND, TREASURER.
LOUIS DWIGHT, SECRETARY.

LIFE DIRECTORS,

BY THE PAYMENT OF ONE HUNDRED DOLLARS AND UPWARDS.

Albany, N. Y.
*Van Rensselaer, Stephen
Boston.
Appleton, Samuel
Armstrong, Samuel T.
*Bussey, Benjamin
*Chamberlain, Richard
*Cobb, Nathaniel R.
*Coolidge, Joseph
Dwight, Edmund
Eliot, Samuel A.
Gray, Francis C.
Greenleaf, Jonathan
Homes, Henry
Hubbard, Samuel
Jackson, Charles
Jackson, James
Jackson, Patrick T.
Lawrence, Amos

Lowell, Charles
*Lowell, John
Lyman, Theodore, Jr.
Munson, Israel
Parkman, Francis
Phillips, Jonathan
*Phillips, William
Prescott, William
Shattuck, George C.
Shaw, Robert G.
Tappan, John
Ticknor, George
Tuckerman, Edward
Ward, Artemas
Wells, Charles
White, Stephen
Willis, Nathaniel
Dedham, Mass.
Burgess, Ebenezer

Geneva, N. Y.
Dwight, Henry
Norwich, Conn.
Greene, William P.
Peterboro', N. Y.
Smith, Peter
Portsmouth, N. H.
Coues, S. E.
Rochester, N. Y.
*Bissell, Josiah
Salem, Mass.
Peabody, Joseph
Worcester, Mass.
Abbott, J. S. C.
Foster, Alfred Dwight
Salisbury, Stephen
Sweetser, Seth, by 3 sisters
Waldo, Daniel

LIFE MEMBERS,

BY THE PAYMENT OF THIRTY DOLLARS AND UPWARDS.

Albany, N. Y.
Delavan, Edward C.
*Hopkins, Samuel M.
McIntire, Archibald
Norton, John C.

Andover, Mass.
*Cornelius, Elias
Edwards, Justin
*Porter, Ebenezer
Woods, Leonard

Auburn, N. Y.
Lewis, Levi, by Officers of
   the Prison
Seymour, James S.
Smith, B. C., by Officers of
   the Prison

Baltimore, Md.
Backus, John A.
*McKim, W. D.

Bath, N. H.
Sutherland, David, by Ira
   Goodale

Bedford, N. Y.
*Jay, John
Jay, William

Beverly.
Oliphant, David

Boston.
Adams, Nehemiah
*Amory, John
Beecher, Edward
Beecher, Lyman
*Blake, George

*Bowdoin, James
Brooks, Peter C.
Brooks, Peter C., Jr.
Chadwick, Ebenezer
Clapp, Joshua
Cobb, Richard
*Codman, Catharine
Codman, Elizabeth
Codman, Charles R.
Codman, Henry
Cogswell, William
Cushing, John P.
Dana, Nathaniel
Dorr, Samuel
Eckley, David
Edwards, Henry
*Eliot, William H.
Frothingham, N. L.
Gray, Horace
Gray, John C.
*Green, Samuel
*Greene, Gardiner
Greenwood, F. W. P.
Hill, Henry
Homer, George J.
Jones, Anna P.
*Jones, John Coffin
Lawrence, Abbott
Lawrence, Samuel
Lawrence, William
*Lyman, Theodore
Lyman, Theodore, Jr.
Marvin, T. R.
*McLean, Ann
Munroe, Edmund
Newhall, Cheever
Otis, Harrison Gray
Parker, Daniel P.
Parker, Ebenezer
*Parker, John

Parkman, Francis
Potter, Alonzo
Rand, Asa
Randall, John
Reed, Benjamin T.
Rice, Henry
Ropes, William
Safford, Daniel
Sears, David
Stoddard, Charles
Thorndike, Israel
Vose, Thomas
Wales, Thomas B.
Warren, John C.
Wigglesworth, Thomas
Williams, John D.
Winthrop, Thomas L.
*Wisner, Benjamin B.
Worthington, William

Brooklyn, N. Y.
Carrol, D. L.

Cambridge, Mass.
Donnison, C. L.
Farwell, Levi
Greenleaf, Simon
Holland, Frederic West
Quincy, Josiah

Canandaigua, N. Y.
Eddy, Ansel G.

Catskill, N. Y.
Cooke, Thomas B.
Day, Orrin

Charleston, S. C.
Corning, Jasper

Charlestown, Mass.
Curtis, Jared
Walker, William J., Jr

Coxackie, N. Y.
*Van Dyck, Abraham

Danvers, Mass.
Braman, Milton P.
*Cowles, George
*Oakes, Caleb

Dorchester, Mass.
Codman, John

Douglass Farm, L. I.
Douglass, George, by the hand of Mrs. Joanna Bethune

Edinburgh, Scotland.
Dunlop, John

Fairfield, Conn.
Sherman, Roger M.

Geneva, N. Y.
*Axtell, Henry

Gloucester, Mass.
Jewett, David, by a Lady

Hampton, N. H.
Harris, Roswell

Hartford, Conn.
Hawes, Joel
Spring, Samuel

Haverhill, Mass.
Keeley, George
Phelps, Dudley

Ipswich, Mass.
Kimball, David

Jamaica, L. I.
*Crane, Elias W.

Marblehead, Mass.
Hooper, Nathaniel
*Reed, William

Middletown, Conn.
Crane, John B.

Milton, Mass.
*Tucker, Nathaniel

Newark, N. J.
Hamilton, W. T.

Newbury, Mass.
Wright, Henry C.

Newburyport, Mass.
Banister, William B.
Bartlett, William

*Brown, Moses
Dimmick, Luther F.
Proudfit, John
By a donation in books from Charles Whipple, to constitute the following persons Life Members:
Davis, Mary A.
Greenleaf, Mary C.
Hodge, Mary D.
Thompson, Sarah

New Haven, Conn.
Bacon, Leonard
Brewster, James
Fitch, Eleazer T.
Robinson, Charles, by his sister Elizabeth
Salisbury, Abby

New York City.
Adams, William
Allen, Stephen
Astor, John Jacob
Averill, Heman
Bethune, G. W.
Boorman, J.
Brewster, Joseph
Broadhead, Dr.
*Chambers, William
Cox, Samuel H.
Crosby, W. B.
Eastborn, Manton
*Falconer, Archibald
Hedges, Timothy
How, Fisher
Johnson, William Samuel
Lenox, Robert
Mason, Cyrus W.
Mathews, John M.
McAuley, Thomas
Milnor, James
Patton, William
Perrit, Pelatiah
*Post, Joel
Proudfit, Alexander
Phillips, W. W.
*Rutgers, Henry
Schroeder, J. F.
Shatzel, Jacob
Spring, Gardiner
Starr, Philemon R.
Stephens, J. C.
Tappan, Arthur
*Varick, Richard
*Ward, Samuel
Woolsey, William W.

Peterboro', N. Y.
Smith, Gerrit

Philadelphia, Penn.
Allen, Solomon
*Carey, Matthew
Elmes, Thomas
Ely, Ezra Stiles
Henry, Alexander
*Livingston, Gilbert R.
Skinner, Thomas H.

Pittsfield, Mass.
Newton, Edward A.

Plymouth, Mass.
Robbins, Josiah

Portland, Me.
Dwight, William T.
Tyler, Bennett

Portsmouth, N. H.
Coues, Lucy Louisa
Goodwin, Ichabod
Peabody, Andrew P., by Ladies of his Society

Poughkeepsie, N. Y.
Cuyler, Cornelius

Providence, R. I.
*Ives, Thomas P.
Wayland, Francis

Rahway, N. J.
Squier, Job

Salem, Mass.
Cleveland, J. P.
Emerson, Brown
Phillips, Stephen C.
Williams, William
Worcester, Zervia F.

Schenectady, N. Y.
*Smith, Peter

Springfield, Mass.
Osgood, Samuel

Thomaston, Me.
*Rose, Daniel

Troy, N. Y.
Tucker, Mark

Utica, N. Y.
Lansing, D. C.
Stocking, Samuel
Varick, Abraham

West Haverhill, Mass.
Cross, Abijah

Wethersfield, Conn.
Barrett, Gerrish
Pilsbury, Amos

Williamstown, Mass.
*Griffin, Edward D.

Wiscasset, Me.
Hooker, Edward W.

Worcester, Mass.
Foster, Alfred Dwight
Lincoln, John W.
Salisbury, Stephen
Waldo, E. S. & R.
Waldo, Daniel

TREASURER'S REPORT.

PRISON DISCIPLINE SOCIETY, *in Account with* CHARLES CLEVELAND.

Dr.			Cr.	
1842.			1842.	
May 23.—To cash from last account,... Balance from last account,...	1,194 91½		May 23.—By cash received of the Legislature of Massachusetts, for 500 copies of the Sixteenth Annual Report,...	125 00
To cash for incidental and travelling expenses,...	214 61¼		By do. received of the Legislature of New York, for 400 do.,...	100 00
To do. paid Boston Type and Stereotype Foundry,...	147 83		By do. received one year's dividend on 9 shares in stock of New England Bank,...	
To do. paid Grant & Daniell, for paper,...	110 00		By do. legacy of Nathaniel Tucker, of Milton, deceased,...	54 00
To do. paid S. N. Dickinson, for printing,...	224 45		By do. collected by Rev. G. Barrett, in the Middle States,...	540 25
To do. paid for binding, collecting, &c....	58 00		By do. from subscribers and donors,...	2,928 05
To do. paid rent of office, and expenses at do....	236 75		Balance to new account,...	995 77¼
To do. paid balance of interest account,...	94 56			
To do. paid expenditures of agent in the Middle States,...	831 96			
To do. paid salary of the secretary,...	1,700 00			
	$4,743 07¼			$4,743 07¼.

Permanent Fund, by direction of the late Nathaniel Tucker, of Milton, who gave it as a legacy: —

Nine shares in the capital stock of New England Bank,...	$936 75
Deposit in Tremont Savings Bank,...	63 00
Cash,...	25
	$1,000 00

Boston, May 23d, 1842.   Errors excepted,
CHARLES CLEVELAND, *Treasurer P. D. S.*

Boston, May 23, 1842.—We certify that we have examined the foregoing account and find the same correctly cast and properly vouched.

JAMES MEANS, } *Auditors*
HENRY HILL,

SUBSCRIPTIONS AND DONATIONS,

From May 25, 1841, to May 23, 1842.

Albany, N. Y.
By the Legislature, for the 15th Report, for the use of the members 100 00
Batchelder, Galen 2 00
Boyd, R. 2 00
Fowler, W. 2 00
Marvin, A. 2 00
Seward, William H. 5 00
Treadwell, G. C. 2 00
Webb, H. L. 2 00
Wilder, J. N. 2 00

Alexandria, D. C.
Hallowell, Benjamin 2 00

Andover, Mass.
Abbott, Henry 1 00
Cash 2 00
Coleman, Lyman 2 00
Derby, John 1 00
Edwards, Justin 3 00
Gould, A. J. 2 00
Green, Aaron 2 00
Pierce, William 2 00
Stone, T. D. P. 2 00
Stuart, Moses 5 00
Taylor, S. H. 2 00
Taylor, J. L. 2 00

Auburn, N. Y.
Cook, Robert 2 00

Baltimore, Md.
Albert & Co. 2 00
Barker, R. J. 2 00
Brown, R. P. 2 00
Brune, F. W. 2 00
Bigham, John & Sam'l 2 00
Cash 2 00
Cash 2 00
Cash 2 00
Cash 2 00
Carrol, H. D. G. 2 00
Carrol, James 2 00
Cushing, Joseph 2 00
Fisher, William 2 00
Gable, John 2 00
Gillet & Co. 2 00
Jenkins, Mark W. 2 00
Jones, T. & Co. 2 00
J. W. & Co. 2 00
Kyser, Charles M. 2 00
Lynch, Edmond 2 00
McDonnel, William 2 00
McKim, W. & H. 5 00
Norris, George S. 2 00
Smith, John 2 00

Sterling, A. 2 00
Schermacher, H. & Co. 2 00
Wilson, Wm. & Sons 5 00

Bedford, Westchester Co., N. Y.
Jay, William 25 00

Beverly, Mass.
Hooper, Mrs. Nathaniel 10 00

Boston, Mass.
Adams, William 2 00
Adams, James 2 00
Adams, Abel 5 00
Aiken, Silas, by sundry subscribers, by Mrs. C. & Miss Q. 3 75
Aiken, Silas 3 00
Almy, Patterson, & Co. 5 00
Amory, Charles 20 00
Andrews, W. T. 2 00
Andrews, E. T. 2 00
Appleton, Nathan 10 00
Appleton, William 10 00
Armstrong, Samuel T. 10 00
Bacon, J. V. 3 00
Bailey, Calvin 1 00
Ballard, Joseph 3 00
Balance, from sundry subscribers, by Rev. G. Barrett 11 97
Barrett, Rev. Gerrish 50 00
Bancroft, Jacob 2 00
Baylies, C. F. 1 00
Barnard, Charles 5 00
Barnes, D. W. 2 00
Barnes, H. S. 2 00
Bartoll, C. A. 5 00
Bates, Stephen 1 00
Bates, William 1 00
Beal, Samuel 2 00
Bent, Ann 2 00
Bird, S. J. 2 00
B. J. W. 5 00
Bond, William 2 00
Bradford, John 2 00
Blanchard, Joshua P. 2 00
Blake, C. B. 5 00
Blagdon, George W. 2 00
Blake, Charles 2 00
Bradley, Benjamin 2 00
Bradshaw, Jesse 1 00
Bradshaw, Andrew 5 00
Brigham, A. 2 00
Brooks, Edward 10 00
Brewer, George A. 2 00
Brewer, Nathaniel 2 00
Brewer, S. N. 2 00

Brewer, W. A. 2 00
Briggs, Billings 5 00
Brooks, Peter C. 20 00
Brown, Mr. 5 00
Bowditch, N. J. 5 00
Butler, John S. 5 00
Bumstead, Josiah F. 5 00
Bumstead, John 5 00
Bumstead, Josiah 6 00
Burgess, Benj. & Sons 5 00
Callender, G. 2 00
Carlton, William 2 00
Cary, T. G. 5 00
Cash 2 00
Cash, a Friend 7 00
Cash 1 00
Cash, a Friend 5 00
Cash 1 00
Cleveland, Charles 2 00
Clement, J. S. 2 00
Chamberlain, N. B. 2 00
Chandler, Abiel 2 00
Channing, Walter 2 00
Chapman, Jonathan 20 00
Chilson, Gardner 2 00
Chickering, Jonas 5 00
Colby, Gardner 2 00
Codman, Henry 10 00
Codman, Charles R. 5 00
Colby, Josiah 2 00
Cordin, Thomas 5 00
Cotton, N. D. 2 00
Couch, Edward 1 00
Cotton, Joseph 10 00
Cotton, Joseph H. 2 00
Crocker, Uriel 2 00
Curtiss, Samuel 2 00
Curtis, T. B. 2 00
Cushing, T. P. 2 00
Cummings, David 2 00
Daniell, Otis 2 00
Dana, Ephraim 2 00
Dana, Luther 2 00
Dana, Nathaniel 5 00
Darracott, George 2 00
Denny, Daniel 2 00
Dixwell, J. J. 10 00
Doane, Bradstreet, & Co. 2 00
Doane, G. B. 2 00
Doggett, Samuel 5 00
Dole & Hallet 2 00
Dorr, Samuel 10 00
Eaton, John 2 00
Edmands, J. W. 5 00
Ellis, Baxter 2 00
Ellis, Jonathan 2 00
Eliot, Samuel A. 50 00
Eustis, W. T. 2 00
Everett, Moses 5 00

Fairbanks, Stephen	2 00	Hooper, Robert	5 00	Mellen, Moses	2 00
Fales, D. N.	2 00	How, H. J.	2 00	Metcalf, Nathan	2 00
Fales, Thomas B.	20 00	Howard, Benjamin	2 00	Mills, C. H.	5 00
Faxon, Nathaniel	2 00	Howe, S. G.	2 00	Mills, James K.	10 00
Fearing, Albert	2 00	Horton, H. K.	5 00	Minot, William	3 00
Faxon, George N.	1 00	Humphrey, William	3 00	Morse, R. M.	1 00
Fearing, A. C.	2 00	Huse, Joseph	2 00	Munson, Israel	20 00
Fletcher, Richard	2 00	Hubbard, W. J.	2 00	Newman, Henry	2 00
Fisk, E. P.	2 00	Inches, E. & S.	5 00	Newhall, George	2 00
Fiske & Rice	2 00	Inches, Henderson	5 00	Norton, Joshua, Jr.	2 00
Fisk & Leland	2 00	Inches, Henderson, Jr.	3 00	Notts, J.	1 00
Fisk, William	1 00	Jacobs, Benjamin	1 00	Osgood, Isaac	2 00
Forbush, Jonathan	5 00	Jackson, Charles	20 00	Otis, Harrison G.	10 00
Forbes, R. B.	10 00	Jackson, Patrick T.	10 00	Paige, J. W.	2 00
Francis, David	2 00	Jackson, Ward	2 00	Palfrey, J. G.	2 00
Francis, Ebenezer	10 00	Johnson, James	5 00	Palmer, Simeon	2 00
French, Jonathan	5 00	Johnson, W. P.	2 00	Parker, M. S.	2 00
French, Moses, Jr.	5 00	Jones, Frederick	2 00	Parker, James	5 00
Friend	2 00	Jones, A. P.	10 00	Parker, Jonathan	1 00
Friend	5 00	Jones, Eliphalet	2 00	Parkman, Francis	10 00
Friend	2 00	Jones, W.	2 00	Payson, S. R.	2 00
Friend	5 00	Johnson, Samuel	2 00	Peck, A. G.	5 00
Friend	1 00	Kendall, A.	2 00	Peirce, C. H.	1 00
Friend	2 00	Kuhn, George H.	5 00	Perkins, Thomas H.	25 00
Friend	3 00	Kimball, Daniel	4 00	Perkins, T.	5 00
Friend	1 00	Kimball, Jewett, & Co.	10 00	Perkins, E. H.	5 00
Friend	2 00	Kimball, John	1 00	Pickman, Benjamin	5 00
Friend	1 00	Kimball, J. Merrill	2 00	P. G.	2 50
Gassett, Henry	5 00	Kittredge, Alvah	2 00	P. O.	2 00
Gardner, John L.	5 00	Lamb, Thomas	5 00	Phelps, Sewell	2 00
Gardner, Samuel P.	5 00	Lawrence, Abbott	20 00	Phelps, A.	5 00
Gardner, John D.	2 00	Lawrence, Amos	50 00	Phipps & Co.	2 00
Gilbert, Timothy	2 00	Lawrence, William	10 00	Porter, R. S.	1 00
Gilbert, Samuel	2 00	Lampson, Edwin	2 00	Prescott, William	20 00
Gilbert, Lemuel	2 00	Lamson, L., & Co.	2 00	Quincy, T. D.	5 00
Gore, Watson	3 00	Langdon, J. W.	1 00	Reed, James	5 00
Gray, George H.	2 00	Lawrence, A. A.	5 00	Reed, B. T.	5 00
Gilbert, John, Jr.	2 00	Leach, James	2 00	Reports sold	50
Gordon, George W.	2 00	Leland, Sherman	2 00	Reports and balance	3 88
Gray, F. C.	50 00	Leeds, Jos. La Fayette	2 00	Reports and balance	3 50
Gray, Frederick T.	2 00	Lincoln, W. S.	2 00	Rice, J. P.	5 00
Gray, John C.	30 00	Lincoln, W. G.	2 00	Rhoades, Asa H.	1 00
Glover, Henry R.	1 00	Lincoln, Heman	2 00	Rhoades, Eben	1 00
Grant, Moses	2 00	Lincoln, Levi	5 00	Rice & Thaxter	5 00
Grant & Daniell	10 00	Little, C. C.	2 00	Richards, Reuben	5 00
Greele, P., Jr.	3 00	Littlehale, S. S.	5 00	Rogers, John Gray	2 00
Grew, Henry	2 00	Livermore, Isaac	5 00	Rogers, John H.	2 00
Greenleaf, Samuel	3 00	Lobdell, T. J.	2 00	Rogers, Henry B.	10 00
Green, David	3 00	Long, E. J.	2 00	Rotch, William	2 00
Greene, Charles G.	2 00	Lowell, John A.	10 00	Ropes, Hardy	2 00
Green, Benjamin D.	5 00	Lothrop, S. K.	2 00	Reports sold	3 45
Gridley, William	2 00	Low, J. J.	2 00	Rogers, W. A.	2 00
Grosvenor, Lemuel P.	1 00	Lowell, F. C.	5 00	Rogers, W. M.	2 00
Gutterson, William	5 00	Low, Isaac	2 00	Robbins, E. N.	2 00
Gurney, Nathan	2 00	Loring, C. C.	2 00	Rogers, J. G.	2 00
Hale, M. L.	2 00	Loring, Henry	2 00	Russell, N. P.	5 00
Hall, Andrew T.	3 00	Loring, James	2 00	Safford, Daniel	5 00
Hall, J. P.	2 00	Lyford, G. C.	4 00	Sawyer, C. B.	1 00
Hall, Henry	5 00	Lyman, Theodore	50 00	Salisbury, Samuel	2 00
Hardy, A.	1 00	Means, James	2 00	Scudder, Charles	2 00
Harvey, Peter	10 00	Mayer, P. J.	2 00	Sears, David	20 00
Hawes, Gray, & Co.	5 00	Manning, F. C.	1 00	Sears, Joshua	1 00
Hayden, J. C.	2 00	McBurney, C.	2 00	Sears, Willard	1 00
Hayward, George	5 00	Metcalf, Theodore	2 00	Shaw, Robert G.	30 00
Hicks, J. H.	2 00	Merriam, S. P.	1 00	Shimmin, William	3 00
Hill, Henry	5 00	Massachusetts, by Act		Shorey, John, & Co.	2 00
Hill, Jeremiah	2 00	of the Legislature, for		Skilton, George	5 00
Hobert, Peter, Jr.	2 00	500 copies of the 16th		Slocumb, Thomas	2 00
Hobart, Albert	2 00	Annual Report, for		Sigourney, Henry	10 00
Homes & Homer	10 00	use of the members	125 00	Smith & Sumner	3 00

Smith, Henry	2 00
Simpson, M. H.	5 00
Southwick, J.	2 00
Sprague, P. & S.	5 00
Stevenson, William	2 00
Stimpson, W. C.	2 00
Stone, John S.	2 00
Steele, Robert	3 00
Stone, W. W.	5 00
Stoddard, Charles	10 00
Storer, Robert B.	2 00
Stone, S. S.	1 00
South Boston Iron Co.	5 00
Sumner, Bradford	2 00
Swett, Samuel	2 00
Simonds, Artemas	2 00
Tappan, L. W.	3 00
Tarbell, Thomas	2 00
Tenney, Samuel	2 00
Thomas, William	2 00
Ticknor, George	10 00
Tilden, Joseph	2 00
Timmens, Henry	5 00
Train, Samuel F.	2 00
Train, Samuel	5 00
Trott, George	5 00
Tolman, Joseph A.	2 00
Townsend, S. D.	3 00
Townsend, Elmer	2 00
Townsend, H. B.	2 00
Turner, J. N.	1 00
Tucker, John L.	5 00
Tufts, James	2 00
Tufts, Quincy	1 00
Upham, Henry	2 00
Van Wart	5 00
Wales, Thomas B.	20 00
Walley, Samuel H.	10 00
Warren, Charles	4 00
Warren, John C.	10 00
Ware, John	5 00
Waterston, Robert	2 00
Welles, John	10 00
Wells, Charles A.	2 00
Wells, John B.	2 00
Welch, Francis	3 00
White, Charles	3 00
White, Joseph	2 00
Wetmore, Thomas	10 00
White, Robert	2 00
Wilder & Brownell	1 00
White, F. E.	5 00
Whitney, J.	2 00
Whitney, Paul	5 00
Whiton, James M.	2 00
Whitmore, George	3 00
Wigglesworth, Thomas	5 00
Wigglesworth, Edward	2 00
Wilkins, John H., &	
Carter, R. B.	2 00
Williams, John D.	10 00
Williams, E., & Co.	2 00
Williams, Moses	2 00
Willis, Nathaniel	50 00
Winslow, B. T.	5 00
Winchester, E.A.& W.	10 00
Wolcott, J. H.	5 00

Cambridge Mass.

Farwell, Levi	20 00

Norton, Andrews	10 00
Ware, Henry	2 00
Watson, Nathaniel	10 00
Worcester, Joseph E.	2 00

Catskill, N. Y.

Cooke, T. B.	2 00
Cooke, J. W.	1 00
Day, E. B.	1 00
Hill, H., Jr.	2 00
Lockie, J. J.	1 00
Willard, J.	2 00

Cazenovia, N. Y.

Hough, W. J.	1 00
Lathrop, W. K.	1 00
Litchfield, E. B.	1 00

Charlestown, Mass.

Abbot, Samuel	2 00
Adams, Chester	2 00
Bell, Luther V.	10 00
Braman, Bayles	2 00
Brown, A. N	2 00
Brown, John	2 00
Corey, Isaac	2 00
Crowninshield, A. W.	2 00
Crosby, Daniel	2 00
Curtis, Jared	5 00
Dana, James	2 00
Doane, John	2 00
Ellis, George E.	2 00
Eddy, George R.	2 00
Forster, Henry	5 00
Forster, Charles	2 00
Francis, James M.	2 00
Gardner, James M.	2 00
Goodhue, Homer	2 00
Hill, H. & S. P.	5 00
Hoadley, Rev. L. J., by	
two Sisters in Wor-	
cester	100 00
Hunt, Enoch	2 00
Hurd, John	5 00
Kidder, Samuel	10 00
Lawrence, Francis	2 00
Little, George W.	2 00
Lincoln, Charles	5 00
Marshall, Albert	2 00
McIntire, E. P.	1 00
Parker, Warren B.	2 00
Perkins, John	2 00
Russell, Daniel	2 00
Russell, Thomas	2 00
Skilton, John	2 00
Skelton, M.	2 00
Stetson, Sarah	2 00
Tyler, Columbus	2 00
Tufts, James F.	3 00
Vinal, Otis	2 00
White, Daniel	3 00

Clinton, N. Y.

Catlin, W.	2 00
Cash	1 00
Davis, Henry	2 00
Gridley, O.	2 00
McNeil, H.	2 00
North, S.	2 00

Dorchester, Mass.

Codman, John	10 00

Dover, N. H.

Whitehouse, James, Jr.	1 00

East Needham, Mass.

Whitaker, Edgar K.	2 00

Fairhaven, Mass.

Borden, Samuel	10 00

Frederick, Md.

Birely, V.	1 00
Baltzell, John	2 00
Bantz, G.	2 00
Harkey, Rev. S. W.	2 00
Hanson, A. B.	2 00
Haack, Henry	2 00
Markell, John	2 00
Marshall, Richard H.	2 00
Nixdorff, Henry	2 00
Page, Calvin	2 00
Potts, R.	2 00
Quynn, Casper	2 00
Ross, H.	2 00
Tyler, W. B.	2 00
Waters, William	2 00

Hartford, Conn.

Morgan, H. N.	2 00
Wadsworth, Daniel	10 00

Jamaica, L. I.

Shelton, Nathan	2 00

Jordan, N. Y.

Otis, Isaac	2 00

Lexington, Mass.

Chandler, Samuel	5 00

Lowell, Mass.

Blanchard, Amos	2 00
Bixby, Daniel	2 00
Clark, John	5 00
Cook, James	2 00
French, B. F.	5 00
Lawrence, Samuel	20 00
Means, Robert	10 00

Manlius, N. Y.

Bayley, C. C.	1 00
Fleming, Robert	2 00
May, F. & E.	2 00
Smith, A.	2 00

Marblehead, Mass.

Reed, Mrs. William	10 00

Maryland.

McIntire, Rev. James,	
by a Friend in New-	
buryport, Mass.	30 00

Milton, Mass.

Semiannual dividend
on 9 shares of New
England Bank stock,
legacy of Nathaniel

Tucker, deceased	27 00
Do. do.	27 00

New Bedford, Mass

Arnold, James	20 00
Barker, Abraham	5 00
Cash	3 00
Cash	10 00
Cash	5 00
Coffin, Timothy G.	5 00
Coggershall, John, Jr.	5 00
Congdon, James B.	10 00
Eddy, Job	5 00
Greene, D. R.	10 00
Gibbs, Alfred	2 00
Howland, George	20 00
Leonard, N.	2 00
Merrihew, S.	2 00
Morgan, C. W.	10 00
M. R.	3 00
Parker, J. A.	10 00
Perkins, John	2 00
Rodman, Elizabeth	20 00
Rodman, William	5 00
Rodman, Benjamin	10 00
Rodman, Samuel	10 00
Robeson, Andrew	10 00
Rotch, William, Jr.	20 00
Warren, Charles H.	5 00

Newburyport, Mass.

Dimmick, Mrs. L. F., by a Friend	30 00
Dimmick, Luther F.	2 00
Greenleaf, Mary	30 00
Simpson, Paul	2 00
Smith, Nathaniel	10 00

New York City.

Adams, Benjamin	2 00
Appleton, D.	2 00
Aldrich, H. D.	2 00
Belnap,	2 00
Bowers & McNamee	2 00
Buckhalter, S.	2 00
Bliss, James C.	2 00
Brower, John L.	2 00
Bowne. William	2 00
B. E. T.	1 00
Brooks, J.	3 00
Bridges, L. K	2 00
Bull, W. G.	3 00
C.	1 00
Cash	1 00
Cash	1 00
Cash	2 00
Cash	5 00
Cash	1 00
Cash	5 00
Cash	5 00
Cash	3 00
Cash	2 00
Cash	1 00
Cash	1 00
Cash	2 00
Cash	2 00
Cash	2 00
Cash	3 00
Cash	3 00
Cash	2 00

Campbell, Samuel	2 00
Collins, J. B.	2 00
C. B.	1 00
Caldwell, Ebenezer	2 00
Chardon, A.	2 00
Center, R.	1 00
Cock, Thomas	2 00
Collam & Iselin	2 00
Caswell, S.	2 00
Day, Mahlon	2 00
Dorr, A. H.	2 00
Draper, S.	2 00
D. C. P.	2 00
Engs, P. W.	2 00
Ely, C.	2 00
Elliot, D.	2 00
Ernsenpatch, J. C.	2 00
Fairbanks, Dexter	15 00
Few, Mrs. Catharine	10 00
Franklin, W. H.	2 00
Grosvenor, S.	2 00
Gordon, O. H.	2 00
Gilson, J.	2 00
Hosmer, O. E.	2 00
Holden, Horace	2 00
Hinsdale, Henry	2 00
Hurd, J. R.	2 00
Hall, Charles	2 00
Hallock, Gerard	2 00
Herdman, John	2 00
Hoe, R.	1 00
Hale, J. L.	2 00
Hadden, D.	2 00
Halsted, W. M.	2 00
Harper, S. B.	2 00
Hoffman, P. V.	2 00
Hoyt, E.	2 00
Jones, S. T.	2 00
J. H.	2 00
J. D.	2 00
Kinsdale, Henry	2 00
King, J. G.	2 00
Kip, L. W.	2 00
Kelly, William	2 00
Laight, H. Church	10 00
Leeds, Samuel, Jr.	2 00
Lee, O. H.	2 00
Lefferts, J.	2 00
Lovatt, James	2 00
Murray, Lindley	2 00
M.	1 00
Merle, G.	2 00
Mills, F., & Co.	2 00
Mills, Zophar	2 00
Nevins, R. H.	2 00
Nichols, R.	2 00
Painter, W. P.	2 00
Patten, J. T.	2 00
Phyfe, John	2 00
P. S.	1 00
Parsons, A. M.	2 00
Parker, W. S.	2 00
Peck, H. N.	2 00
Rankin, John	2 00
Rand, C. H.	2 00
Rowland, H. A., from Ladies of Pearl Street Church to constitute him a Life Member	30 00

Roche & Brothers	2 00
Robinson, Nelson	2 00
R. E.	1 00
R. H. N.	2 00
Sand, C. H.	2 00
Stuart, R. L. & A.	3 00
Stuart, J. & J.	2 00
Sampson, Jacob	2 00
Stoddard, A. N.	3 00
Sheffelin, H. H.	2 00
Tapscott, W. & J.	2 00
Tracy, George M.	3 00
T. T. & Sons	2 00
Taylor, J. R.	2 00
Van Nest, John	2 00
Ward, Sill, & Thomas	2 00
W. C.	2 00
Walker, W.	1 00
Wendell, John D.	2 00
Wolcott, F. H.	2 00
W. W.	1 00
W. H. R.	2 00

New York Mills, N. Y.

Smith, Anson	2 00
Torrey, N.	1 00
Walcott, B. S.	2 00
Walcott, W. D.	2 00
Yourp, W. R.	2 00

Northampton, Mass.

Williston, S. P.	10 00

Otis Co., N. Y.

Sundry contributors	11 25

Oxford, N. Y.

Dwight, Joseph H.	1 00

Peterboro', N. Y.

Smith, Gerrit, Esq.	10 00

Plainfield, N. J.

Ayres, Mr.	1 00
Bond, Lewis, Rev.	2 00
Craig, J. W.	2 00

Plymouth, Mass

Robbins, Josiah	5 00

Portland, Maine.

Cross, Nathaniel, from his Daughter, after his decease, at his request	8 00

Portsmouth, N. H.

Burroughs, Charles	5 00
Foster, J. W.	2 00
Haven, A. W.	10 00
H., Mrs. E. W.	4 00
Haven, E. G. W.	5 00
Halliburton, Andrew	6 00
Jones, W.	10 00
Knowlton, John	2 00
Ladd, Alexander	10 00
Ladd, Chs. H. & A. W.	5 00
Peabody, Andrew P.	2 00
Peabody, Miss M. R.	1 00
Rogers, D. R.	10 00
Treadwell, Mrs. Anna	30 00

Providence, R. I.		Cushman, J. P.	2 00			*Wethersfield, Conn.*	
Brown, J. Parker	10 00	Gates, Elias	2 00		Pilsbury, Amos		5 00
Cash	5 00	Grant, Gurdon	2 00				
Goddard, W. G.	10 00	Hart, J. C.	2 00			*Whitesboro', N. Y.*	
Ives, Robert H.	10 00	Haight, W. D.	2 00		Dexter, S. Newton		2 00
Ives, Moses B.	10 00	Hubbel, H. R.	2 00				
Wayland, Francis	10 00	Lockwood, H. N.	2 00			*Wilmington, Del.*	
		Loveland, A.	2 00		Bush, D. & George		2 00
Salem, Mass.		Merritt, C. H. & J. J.	2 00		Bullock, John		5 00
Merrill, B.	3 00	Meneely, A.	2 00		Cash		1 00
Peabody, Joseph	20 00	Mallory & Doughty	2 00		Cash		1 00
Phillips, Stephen C.	10 00	Marvin, V.	2 00		Hall, Willard		2 00
White, D. A.	2 00	Norton, S.	2 00		Hall, Mrs.		2 00
		Rosseter, H. C.	2 00		Janvier, B. A.		2 00
Syracuse, N. Y.		Slason, A.	2 00		Knight, Dubre		3 00
Cash	1 00	Schoonhoven, J.	1 00		Tatnall, Edward		5 00
Dana, D. & M.	5 00	Silliman, R. D.	2 00		Wilson, David C.		2 00
Wheaton, C. A., & Co.	2 00	Stow, S. K.	2 00				
		Thompson, John L.	2 00			*Worcester, Mass.*	
Troy, N. Y.		Wicks, J.	2 00		Davis, John		5 00
Blatchford, S. M.	1 00	Wicks, V. W.	2 00		Foster, A. D.		5 00
Cash	1 00	Wicks, Eliphalet	2 00		Waldo, Daniel		60 00
Cash	1 00				Two Sisters		100 00
Coffin, C. M.	2 00	*Watertown, Mass.*			Woodward, Samuel B.		10 00
		J. C. P.	20 00				

NOTE.

Typographical Errors corrected in last Year's Acknowledgment.

CURTIS THORP, of *Binghampton*, should have been *five* dollars, instead of *two ;* and F. SHAW & Co., of *Mobile, Ala.*, should have been *ten* dollars instead of *three.*

APPENDIX.

" 1842. *March* 15—20. Visited the MARYLAND PENITENTIARY. Saw the prisoners in their work-shops; prayed with and addressed them in the chapel; conversed with them alone in their cells, and visited and prayed with the sick in the hospital.

" Hospital in an upper story, not sufficiently easy of access. Work-shops newly built, spacious, well-ventilated, and conveniently arranged. A narrow passage is attached to each shop. In each of these passages a keeper is stationed, so that, through small apertures, he can observe any of the prisoners who are at work in the shop, without their being able to see him. Chief business, weaving and shoemaking. Sorry to find the prisoners not as well provided with instruction as formerly. No Sunday school nor chaplain; no singing in the chapel at the religious service on Sunday. Never before so sensibly felt the want of that soft-ening and soothing effect, which music produces on the heart, as during the last religious service which I attended here. Formerly 200 or 300 dollars a year were paid to secure regular preaching at the Penitentiary. That grant is now withheld.

" That ' murder will out,' strikingly illustrated in the case of a man here in Prison, who, 15 years after he killed a man, was, by a remarka-ble concurrence of circumstances, found a pauper in the Alms-House in Philadelphia, and brought to punishment.

" Present number of prisoners in the Penitentiary, 284, which is less, by 24, than it was a year ago. Last year, 16 died, 25 were pardoned, 80 received, (of whom 50 were natives of Maryland,) 84 discharged.

" Expenses above earnings, $6493 13.

" BALTIMORE JAIL repeatedly visited. Found about 50 inmates, of whom 15 were blacks, and 9 debtors. 11 of the blacks were in the same room. Of these but 1 could write, and but 2 could read. 6 of the 11 had lately been sold as a punishment for their crimes, and were every day expecting to be sent south. They had been sold for periods varying from 3 to 15 years, and for prices from $15 to $ 90.

" By a law of the state, free blacks in Maryland, who repeat a Peni-tentiary offence, must be sold at auction, and taken out of the state. The bearing of this law is specially severe, because, how short soever the time may be, for which one is sold, it is conceded by those who know, that it is a rare thing for him ever to get his liberty, or to return to the state again. One of the best-looking blacks in the room had just been sold for 5 years for $25. Feeble health was one cause of his being sold at so low a price. His crime was stealing a wood-saw. He was freeborn in the city of Baltimore, and about 25 years old. He has living a mother, grandmother, father, 3 brothers, and 2 sisters. 5 weeks ago he was married. In a plaintive voice he said, 'I am sold, and in a few days expect to be sent south to a cotton plantation; and as sure as I go there, I shall never come back. Mentioned this man's case to some friends in B., and was glad to know that efforts were made to keep him from being sent away.

" The room in which the blacks were, was remarkable for its cleanliness. Being at a loss how to account for it, I asked how they managed, among so many, to keep their floor so white, and every thing about the room so very neat. 'By our laws, sir,' one replied. 'Your laws! what are they?' 'Why, sir, one law is, that any one who spits on the floor shall receive 2 blows of the paddle.' 'Any other?' 'Yes, sir. Another is, that whoever uses profane language shall receive 5 blows of the paddle.' They then explained the instrument of punishment, the manner of its application, and the grades of the different officers by whose authority transgressors were tried, and punishment inflicted. ' Verily,' thought I, 'here is an instructive lesson for our no-government men to read.'

" Last year there were 1646 commitments to the Baltimore Jail, of whom 1028 were white persons, and 618 black. Of this number of commitments, 365 were for debt. That imprisonment for debt is rarely followed by payment of the debt, may be seen from the fact, that, out of 360 debtors discharged from the Baltimore Jail last year, only 25 paid the debt for which they were imprisoned. It is surprising to see how few, compared with the whole number committed, are convicted on trial, they being, last year, only 38 out of 1281. Whites seem to be more disposed to acts of violence than blacks. Of 19 persons sent to the Baltimore Jail, last year, on charge of murder, all but 1 were white; of 10 sent for assault with intent to kill, 6 were white; of 9 sent for piracy, all were white; of 6 sent for mutiny, all were white.

" Found in Jail painful evidence that the Fire Engine Companies in Baltimore are any thing but schools of morals. 4 young men, each about 18 years, specially reckless and dangerous, now here in Jail, were all members of the same Fire Company. They used to make the engine-house their place of rendezvous. Here they met on Sunday; here they would collect at evening to carouse, and plan iniquity; and here spend the night, when out too late to be received at their homes. One of the number confesses that he has frequently gone at night, and with his own hands set fire to buildings in Baltimore. In execution of one of their plans, these young men attacked Mr. Nickerson, a broker, as he was returning home from his office in the evening, knocked him down, nearly killed him, and robbed him of $12,000 in money. For this atrocious deed, they are now in Jail, waiting their trial. Seldom ever saw persons show less compunction for their evil deeds.

" The Jail here seems to be well kept. It would be an improvement if fewer persons were placed in the same room, and if productive labor were required from the prisoners.

" *March* 27. Preached to the insane at the MARYLAND HOSPITAL. About 50 inmates present, some of whom united in singing very correctly. Attention good ; pleasant season. This Hospital, embracing 10 acres of land, has a beautiful location, about a mile from the city ; is under the care of Dr. Fisher ; can accommodate 120 patients, has now 81. Provision is here made for 50 pauper lunatics, on condition the counties whence they come pay $100 per annum for their support. Religious service is held with the inmates every Sunday by some clergyman from the city. The institution seems to be well managed. Just as I was stepping into the carriage to return to the city, one of the inmates, a nephew of John Randolph of Roanoke, who stood by, signified a desire to ride with me. Dr. Fisher allowed him to do so. Though deaf and dumb, as well as insane, he is good looking, and proved to be a polite and agreeable companion. He seemed greatly interested with what he saw on the way, and on our taking leave of each other, he requested me to write my name in his prayer book, and in a beautiful hand wrote his name on a blank leaf in my pocket Testament.

" BALTIMORE FARM SCHOOL FOR BOYS is 6 miles from the city, has 30 boys, and is in a prosperous condition. The boys are either bound out to a trade when of proper age, or retained on the farm till they are 21. Its friends hope to make it a self-supporting institution, and productive of much good.

" *April* 2. Examined the JAIL AT FREDERICK, MD. This Jail is an old, stone building, half a mile from the town, and contains 5 large rooms for prisoners,— 1 on the first floor, 4 on the second floor, — which are occupied by 14 prisoners, 2 white and 9 black males, 1 white and 4 black females. None of the blacks can read. One of the white men has been 14 years a schoolmaster, and deems himself to be of no small importance to the world. He says he has in manuscript all the sums in Pike's Arithmetic completely worked out by himself, which he means to have printed as soon as he gets out of Jail. He thinks it will be a noble help to schoolmasters, and expects to reap a rich pecuniary harvest from its sale. A mother, a good-looking black woman, had just come to the Jail to see her son, a bright lad, 14 years old, who was soon to be sold. She showed strong affection for her son. ' It makes me feel mighty bad,' said she, ' to think that my boy is to be sold, and carried off, I don't know where. I am afraid he'll never come back, and that I shall never see him again.' One of the black women had an infant, which she wished to have baptized. Last year there were 334 commitments to this Jail. Cost per day, for keeping a prisoner here, 25 cents. Prisoners remain without labor or classification. They need here a Jail of better construction.

" PENITENTIARY AT WASHINGTON, D. C., on the Auburn plan ; admirable in construction, and a model of neatness. No vermin in the cells ; no impure air perceived about the establishment ; not an invalid in the hospital. Number of prisoners, 80, of whom 4 are females. Chief business, shoemaking. Hospital spacious, airy, and easy of access and inspection. Chapel convenient, where the chaplain has a religious service every Sunday. Punishment mild. A record is made, in a book kept for the purpose, of the name of each prisoner who commits an offence, of the offence committed, and of the punishment inflicted. It is pleasant to see a Penitentiary, of such a character as this seems to be, at the seat of government.

"THE OLD AND NEW JAIL AT WASHINGTON, D. C., stand near together, just back of the City Hall. The old one will soon be vacated, and the sooner the better. There are 23 rooms in the old Jail, 6 feet wide by 8 feet long. It was painful to learn that from 100 to 150 human beings have, at the same time, been crowded into these 23 rooms, and there left, in indolence, to suffer, as they must, and to make each other worse and worse by their corrupt communications.

"There are now, April 6, 1842, 25 persons confined in the old Jail. In one room saw two mothers holding each an infant in her arms. One of the infants was sick and drooping. Last night 6 women and these 2 infants were huddled together in the same room. No wonder the poor child looked so feeble. Where so many found air to breathe or room to sleep, 'twas difficult to see.

"The new Jail, nearly completed, is 4 stories high, built of brick, and surrounded on 3 sides by a brick wall. Its interior construction is quite peculiar. A passage, some 6 or 8 feet wide, runs lengthwise, in each story, through the centre of the building. On the south side of this passage, at each story, are spacious rooms for the keeper's family, debtors, &c., with windows overlooking the city. On the other side, in each story, the space is occupied by small cells, whose backs make one of the side walls of the centre passage, and whose iron grated doors open into a narrow space, which lies between the cells and the northern external wall. Each of these spaces has the height of a single story, is half the length of the building, is secured by a grated door at its entrance, and is lighted by glazed and grated windows in the outer wall. The security seems to be complete, but whether sufficient ventilation will be obtained admits of a doubt. The arrangement of the rooms, and the style of finish, are such, as to give to the building, taken all together, very little the appearance of a Jail.

"JAIL AT ALEXANDRIA, D. C.; built by act of congress, in 1828, at an expense of $16,000, and contains apartments for the keeper and his family, and 13 cells for prisoners. The cells are 2 stories high, and built on the Auburn plan, except that they are larger, and arched overhead, and have in front a narrow area, floored over at each story. Now, April 9, 1842, there are 17 persons confined here, of whom 1 is a criminal, 2 are debtors, and 4 vagrants. 2 insane persons were lately taken from this Jail, and carried to the Maryland Insane Hospital, congress having lately made provision for their support there. Last year, 120 commitments. A large yard, enclosed by a high brick wall, affords convenient space for work-shops, should any be wanted.

"WILMINGTON POOR-HOUSE, DEL., stands about a mile from the city; main building of stone; location good; connected with 60 acres of good land, under high state of cultivation. Number of persons received last year, 340; average number in the house through the year, 170. Annual expense, $9922 55, — equal to about $58 per annum for each individual. Value of products from the farm, $616 44.

"According to the last census, there were 80 insane persons in the state of Delaware. According to the records of the Wilmington Poor-House, 35 insane persons were its inmates during the year ending January 1, 1842. Now, in April, there are about 20 insane persons confined here. Never saw so many, in one place, in such miserable condition, before. They do not occupy apartments in the Poor-House proper, but have their lonely abode in 2 small out-houses. One of these houses is but one story high, without either window or chimney, or any arrangement for warming, and so low and contracted, that no one, on seeing it, would be likely to suspect that it was ever designed for human beings to live in. The rooms are small, dark, and badly ventilated. The doors open outward, like barn doors, and the effluvium which issues when a door is opened, is horribly sickening. The light which entered when the door was opened, revealed what was within. It was a squalid human being bereft of his reason. He lay in the corner, on some loose straw. Not a vessel of any kind was to be seen in the room. The poor creature seemed to have scarcely strength enough left to hurt a child; still he was fastened to the floor by a chain. Even the females here are chained. I saw a good-looking girl, scarcely 16 years old, recently deranged, not violent, alone in a strong room, chained fast to the floor; and another, in the same condition, who was the sister of one of our most distinguished naval officers. Every insane person here, I believe, is chained; not, as I understood, because they were generally refractory, or dangerous, if not chained, but because, being thus confined, a poor old woman, who is paid one dollar a week for her services, can go round among them, and, without any fear open their doors, and give them their food. It is some comfort to find that the attending physician is not at all satisfied with this state of things. He has no hope of success in using means for restoration of reason with such as are placed as they are here. He thinks a State Hospital for the Insane is loudly called for without delay. Were all the good people of Delaware to see what may be seen at the Poor-House in Wilmington, I am sure they would be of the same opinion.

" Delaware has no State Penitentiary. It is quite observable, that the criminal code, in those states of the Union which have no Penitentiary, is specially severe and sanguinary. Such is the case in Delaware, though the laws here are milder than they were a few years ago. In this state, murder, arson, rape, and kidnapping, (second offence,) are crimes punishable by death. Burglary is punishable by fine of from $100 to $1000, 1 hour in the pillory, by being publicly whipped from 20 to 60 lashes on the bare back, and imprisoned in the County Jail from 1 to 12 months. For larceny, free negroes are punished by being whipped from 12 to 39 lashes, and sold from 2 to 7 years.

" Imprisonment for debt was abolished in Delaware in 1841.

" It is affirmed, on good authority, that one half of the criminals, and one third of the paupers, in the state of Delaware, are blacks, though the whites in the state are more than four times as numerous as the blacks. Nor need this be wondered at, if facts in the case are considered. The blacks are kept in ignorance. Though there are in the state 15,000 blacks who are free, or will be free, no provision is made for their education. The school fund of the state gives, each year, to every white child, from 5 to 15 years old, $1 for his education; but no black child can go to a school where the white children are taught, and the former have no schools of their own. Besides, the blacks are kept in poverty and dependence on public charity more than the whites. One of the most intelligent gentlemen of the state gave it as his belief, that not over 1000, out of the 16,000 blacks in the state, are permanent slaves. By law, owners of slaves are allowed to set them free after a certain age, and in doing so they are released from all legal obligation to provide for them in after life, when sick, old, or infirm. This may well account for the small proportion of permanent slaves, and the large proportion of black paupers.

" Crime in the state of Delaware does not seem to be of frequent occurrence. The grand jury, who met at New Castle, May 9, 1842, after inquiring into the crimes and misdemeanors that had been committed during the last 6 months, in a population of 33,000 souls, say that ' they found but 10 bills of indictment, and 5 of them were for mere misdemeanors, and closed their session in two days.' In their presentment, ' the grand jury respectfully inform the court, that they have examined into the condition of the Jail, and inquired into the treatment of the prisoners. They report, with great satisfaction, that the apartments are kept in the best possible order, as regards cleanliness and ventilation, two important considerations in reference to the preservation of the health of prisoners.'

" PHILADELPHIA, *May* 1. Preached twice to prisoners in the EASTERN PENITENTIARY. Only the prisoners in one range of cells can hear at the same time. The speaker, while he is speaking, does not see a single individual whom he addresses. During the service, the outer door of all the cells of both stories, on each side of the corridor, is left partly open, that the words spoken may pass to the hearing of the prisoners through the opening in the inner door. A loud echo entirely prevents free and impassioned speaking. In order to be understood, it is necessary to speak in a low tone, and make a painful pause after every word that is uttered. Here the influence of the speaking eye and countenance, the expressive gesture, natural voice, and mutual sympathy, is lost. It takes the chaplain three weeks to address all the prisoners once, provided he preaches twice, or a sermon in two ranges, each Sabbath. After preaching, went into several cells to converse with the prisoners. In most of the cells, though the day was windy, the air was confined, and unpleasant to breathe. In some cells, it was sickening. In one of the cells, saw a man who had been 11 years and 5 months in prison. His health was not good. Sorry to learn that, even now, after so long a time, he breathes out threatening and slaughter towards the judge who sentenced him.

" About 300 now in Prison, of whom the chaplain considers 12 or 15 radically reformed. Mortality greater here than in most other Prisons, and greater among the blacks than among the whites. Prisoners first sent here in 1825. Labor of its inmates has never been sufficient to support the institution. Up to January 1, 1842, 1677 criminals had been committed, of whom 108 had died, 97 had been pardoned, 1 escaped, 1 was hung, 1 committed suicide, and 1145 had been discharged on expiration of sentence, leaving in Prison 324 prisoners, of whom 23 were females.

" Some peculiar advantages may be connected with a Prison built on the plan of the Eastern Penitentiary, such as, 1st, greater safety to the keepers; 2d, prisoners less liable to raise rebellion, or escape; 3d, less number of guards and keepers required; 4th, communication between prisoners more effectually cut off. Advantages, perhaps, more than counterbalanced by disadvantages, such as, 1st, greater expense in building; 2d, labor of prisoners not sufficient for their support; 3d, prisoners not so well prepared, from the habits which they form, and the trades which they learn, to provide for themselves when they leave Prison; 4th, less healthy; 5th, causes more mental derangement; 6th, denies the most efficient means of instruction and reformation, viz., the Sunday school and appeals to a collected, visible congregation. If this system does not work well here, it will work well nowhere. Perhaps no city in the country can furnish a larger number of persons whose hearts dispose them to do good to the prisoner, than Philadelphia. Officers of higher character, or more inclined to put forth their best efforts for the health, instruction, and reformation of prisoners, than those who have the management of the Eastern Penitentiary, can scarcely be any where found. If unfavorable results appear in the operations of this Penitentiary, they may, in some measure at least, be ascribed to the peculiar construction of the building.

"PHILADELPHIA COUNTY PRISON, AT MOYAMENSING, is a very complete and costly establishment, built on the same general plan as the Eastern Penitentiary, and embraces 3 long ranges, radiating from a common centre. These ranges form 3 distinct departments, 1st, for male vagrants, and such as are waiting their trial; 2d, for males who have been convicted; 3d, for vagrant and convicted females, and those who are waiting their trial. Spent part of two days in examining the different departments.

" In the female department, there are 111 vagrant and untried women, occupying 50 cells, and 30 convicted females in separate cells, all under charge of a matron. One of the females is under sentence of death. She had killed a woman in a spirit of jealousy. Had conversation and prayer with her. She seemed to be intelligent and serious, but did not think she was prepared to die.

" The department for convicted males is the middle range, and contains 204 cells, arranged, like the cells of the other departments, in 2 stories, on each side of a spacious area, which is lighted from windows above. The inmates of this department are all required to work. Most of them work in their cells, but some are allowed to go and labor in the work-shops, which have been erected in the Prison yard. Health is promoted by going out of their cells to work. Formerly the law did not allow criminals to be sent to the County Prison for more than 2 years; now, they may be sent there for any time, at discretion of court.

" The southern range of cells is for vagrants and unconvicted. Here the inmates are not required to labor. Saw a young man, in this department, under sentence of death for murdering his wife. He confessed the deed, but justified it on the ground of her want of fidelity to him. He says his parents died before he was 12 years old; that he has been intemperate, profane, and a Sabbath-breaker, and that he got no good from being a member of a Fire Engine Company. He is strongly opposed to capital punishment, even in theory, and holds that all punishment which has any thing but the reformation for its object, is revenge; that all are punished according to their deserts as they go along; is sure that *he* has been; and though he has no heart to pray, has no fear of any punishment beyond the grave, and expects to go to heaven when he dies. He was willing to listen to the reading of the Scriptures and to counsel, and, when prayer was offered, he kneeled by the side of his chair, and seemed somewhat affected. May the Lord lead him to that repentance that needeth not to be repented of!

"Each cell in this vast establishment has hydrant water conveyed to it; and 16 coal-heaters, consuming 350 tons of coal in a year, furnish the requisite heat. Lights burn all night in the corridors, and a sentinel in each range is on duty. Preaching in two departments each Sunday, but no attempts to teach the ignorant to read, and but little private conversation with the prisoners. The records of this Prison show, that, out of the last 298 persons committed, 107 cannot read, and 196 cannot write; so that only 108, out of 298, can both read and write.

"In the month of December, 1841, 420 persons were sent to this Prison, which is 180 more than were sent in the corresponding month of the preceding year. During the year ending March 1, 1842, there were committed to this Prison 2123 white males, and 915 white females; 1042 colored males, and 930 colored females; making, in all, 5010 human beings committed to a single County Prison in 1 year! Average cost of each sent to the department of convicted criminals, about $13.

"It does not appear that shutting men up in solitary cells, and leaving them without much instruction, leads to reformation. Out of the last 110 persons that have been sent to the convicts' department of the Moyamensing Prison, the records show that 36 had been committed twice, 2 three times, 5 four times, 1 five times, and 1 seven times!

"Debtor's Prison stands near the Moyamensing Prison, contains 20 cells, and, April 23, had in confinement 40 debtors, and has had as many as 50 in confinement at the same time. Rarely does any one go here to give instruction, or help to make the poor inmates in the best sense rich. Lately a converted sailor has shown the spirit of his Savior by going, of a Sunday, to these imprisoned debtors, and urging them to lay up treasure in heaven.

"House of Refuge stands not far from the Eastern Penitentiary, was established in 1825, and has received 1498 youth, of whom 1057 were boys, and 441 girls. Present number of inmates about 150, who seem to be well managed. In preaching to the dear children, urged them to be obedient and industrious; to avoid the beginnings of wrong doing; to have nothing to do with wicked companions, corrupting books, or ardent spirits; to remember the Sabbath day, read the Bible, pray, think about God, and to repent of their sins. Attention good. Religious services are held twice each Sabbath with the children here, by different clergymen from the city. On week days, the children work part of the time, and attend school part of the time. Good accounts have been heard from many after they have left the institution."

VALUABLE PRISON DOCUMENTS OF 1841 AND 1842.

Annual Report of the Warden of the State Prison at Thomaston, Maine. Senate Document No. 2 ; pages, 10.

Reports of the Warden, Physician, and Chaplain of the New Hampshire State Prison, June Session, 1841, and 1842. Octavo ; pages, 10, and 12.

Documents relating to the State Prison at Charlestown, Massachusetts, September 30, 1841. Octavo ; pages, 28.

Report of the Inspectors and Physician of the State Prison to the General Assembly of Rhode Island, October Session, 1841 ; 31st, 32d, and 33d pages of Legislative Documents.

Report of the Directors of the Connecticut State Prison to the General Assembly, May Session, 1842. Document No. 5. Octavo ; pages, 19.

Report of the Committee appointed by the General Assembly, in 1841, on the Connecticut State Prison, to the General Assembly, May Session, 1842 ; with accompanying Documents. Document No. 6. Octavo ; pages, 79.

Annual Report of the Inspectors of the Auburn State Prison to the Legislature of New York, January 12, 1842. Assembly's Document No. 31. Octavo ; pages, 109.

Annual Report of the Inspectors of the Mount Pleasant State Prison. Senate's Document No. 39. January 20, 1842. Octavo ; pages, 140.

Reports of the Inspectors of the State Prison, and of the Joint Committee on State Prison Accounts, October 29, 1841. Octavo ; pages, 27.

Thirteenth Annual Report of the Inspectors of the Eastern Penitentiary of Pennsylvania to the Legislature, February, 1842. Octavo ; pages, 23.

Report of the Directors of the Maryland Penitentiary to the Executive, December Session, 1841. Octavo ; pages, 17.

Report of the Principal Keeper of the Georgia Penitentiary to the Legislature, November, 1841. Octavo ; pages, 16.

Report of the Joint Select Committee to the Legislature, appointed to examine the Mississippi Penitentiary, presented February, 1842. Octavo ; pages, 27.

Report of the Inspectors and Agent of the Tennessee Penitentiary, October, 1841. Octavo ; pages, 19.

Annual Report of the Keeper of the Penitentiary, Frankfort, Kentucky, January 3, 1842. Octavo ; pages, 6.

Report of the Directors and Warden of the Ohio Penitentiary, December, 1841. Octavo ; pages, 32.

VALUABLE ASYLUM DOCUMENTS FOR 1841 AND 1842.

Second Annual Report of the Directors of the Maine Insane Hospital, December, 1841. Octavo ; pages, 55.

Fifth Annual Report of the Trustees of the Vermont Asylum for the

Insane, presented to the Legislature, October 25, 1841. Octavo; pages, 12.

Annual Report of the Trustees of the Massachusetts General Hospital, for the Year 1841. Octavo; pages, 40.

Ninth Annual Report of the Trustees of the State Lunatic Hospital at Worcester, December, 1841. Octavo; pages, 102.

Annual Report of the Directors of the Retreat for the Insane, at Hartford, Conn.

State of the New York Hospital and Bloomingdale Asylum, for the Year 1841. Octavo; pages, 31.

Report of the Trustees of the State Lunatic Asylum, with the Documents accompanying the same, in Senate, January 12, 1842. Octavo; pages, 231.

Twenty-fifth Annual Report of the Asylum for the Relief of Persons deprived of the Use of their Reason, Third Month, 1842. Octavo; pages, 29.

Report of the Pennsylvania Hospital for the Insane, for the Year 1841. Octavo; pages, 46.

Annual Report of the Court of Directors of the Western Lunatic Asylum to the Legislature of Virginia, with the Report of the Physician, for 1841. Octavo; pages, 70.

What shall we do with the Insane? By Edward Jarvis, M. D., of Louisville, Kentucky. February, 1842. Octavo; pages, 45.

Insanity and Insane Asylums. By Edward Jarvis, M. D. 1841. Octavo; pages, 40.

Third Annual Report of the Ohio Lunatic Asylum, December, 1841. Octavo; pages, 60.

REFUGE REPORTS FOR 1841 AND 1842.

Seventeenth Annual Report of the Managers of the Society for the Reformation of Juvenile Delinquents to the Legislature, &c., of New York, January 1, 1842. Octavo; pages, 46.

Fourteenth Annual Report of the House of Refuge in Philadelphia; with an Appendix; January 1, 1842. Octavo; pages, 31.

Charter and By-Laws of the Baltimore Manual Labor School for Indigent Boys, 1841. Octavo; pages, 15.

EIGHTEENTH

ANNUAL REPORT

OF THE

BOARD OF MANAGERS

OF THE

PRISON DISCIPLINE SOCIETY,

BOSTON, MAY, 1843.

———

Boston:

PUBLISHED AT THE SOCIETY'S ROOMS,

47 Beacon Street.

STEREOTYPED AT THE
BOSTON TYPE AND STEREOTYPE FOUNDERY.

———

1843.

CONTENTS.

———◆———

PART I.

LUNATIC ASYLUMS

PART II.

HOUSES OF REFUGE.

PART III.

COUNTY PRISONS AND HOUSES OF CORRECTION.

PART IV.

STATE PRISONS.

CONSTITUTION

OF THE

Prison Discipline Society.

———

ARTICLE 1. This Society shall be called the PRISON DISCIPLINE SOCIETY.

ART. 2. It shall be the *object* of this Society to promote the improvement of Public Prisons.

ART. 3. It shall be the *duty* of this Society to take measures for effecting the formation of one or more Prison Discipline Societies in each of the United States, and to coöperate with all such Societies in accomplishing the object specified in the second article of this Constitution.

ART. 4. Any Society, having the same object in view, which shall become auxiliary to this, and shall contribute to its funds, shall thereby secure for the Prisons, in the State where such Society is located, special attention from this Society.

ART. 5. Each subscriber of two dollars, annually, shall be a Member.

ART. 6. Each subscriber of thirty dollars, at one time, shall be a Member for Life.

ART. 7. Each subscriber of ten dollars, annually, shall be a Director.

ART. 8. Each subscriber of one hundred dollars, or who shall, by one additional payment, increase his original subscription to one hundred dollars, shall be a Director for Life.

ART. 9. The officers of this Society shall be a President, as many Vice-Presidents as shall be deemed expedient, a Treasurer, and a Secretary, to be chosen annually, and a Board of Managers, whose duty it shall be to conduct the business of the Society. This Board shall consist of six clergymen and six laymen, of whom six shall reside in the city of Boston, and five shall constitute a quorum.

Every Minister of the Gospel, who is a Member of this Society, shall be entitled to meet and deliberate with the Board of Managers.

The Managers shall call special meetings of the Society, and fill such vacancies as may occur by death or otherwise in their own Board.

ART. 10. The President, Vice-Presidents, Treasurer, and Secretary, shall be, *ex officio*, Members of the Board of Managers.

ART. 11. Directors shall be entitled to meet and vote at all meetings of the Board of Managers.

ART. 12. The annual meetings of this Society shall be held in Boston, on the week of the General Election, when, besides choosing the officers as specified in the ninth article, the accounts of the Treasurer shall be presented, and the proceedings of the foregoing year reported.

ART. 13. The Managers shall meet at such time and place, in the city of Boston, as they shall appoint.

ART. 14. At the meetings of the Society, and of the Managers, the President, or, in his absence, the Vice-President first on the list then present, and, in the absence of the President and of all the Vice-Presidents, such Member as shall be appointed for that purpose, shall preside.

ART. 15. The Secretary, in concurrence with two of the Managers, or, in the absence of the Secretary, any three of the Managers, may call special meetings of the Board.

ART. 16. The minutes of every meeting shall be signed by the Chairman or Secretary.

ART. 17. The Managers shall have the power of appointing such persons as have rendered essential services to the Society either Members for Life or Directors for Life.

ART. 18. No alteration shall be made in this Constitution except by the Society, at an annual meeting, on the recommendation of the Board of Managers.

ANNUAL MEETING.

———

THE Eighteenth Annual Meeting of the Prison Discipline Society, having been notified according to law, at least seven days previous, was held in Park Street Vestry, on Monday, May 29, 1843, at 3 o'clock, P. M.

The oldest Vice-President then present, the Rev. Dr. JENKS, took the chair, and opened the meeting with prayer. A quorum being present, the Secretary read the minutes of the corresponding meeting of the last year. The Chairman read the Treasurer's Report and the Certificate of its correctness by the Auditors, which Report, as thus audited, was accepted. Mr. EDMUND MUNROE was appointed a committee to distribute and collect the votes for the officers of the ensuing year. The Rev. FRANCIS WAYLAND was nominated as President, Rev. DANIEL SHARP and A. A. LAWRENCE, Esq., Managers, and W. W. STONE, Esq.,* as Treasurer, in the places of Hon. SAMUEL T. ARMSTRONG, HENRY HILL, Esq., Rev. DAVID GREENE, and Rev. CHARLES CLEVELAND, who declined a reëlection. The persons thus nominated to fill the vacancies, together with the officers of the preceding year, were elected.

The meeting was then closed with prayer.

The Eighteenth Annual Meeting of the Prison Discipline Society, to hear the Report and Addresses, was held in Park Street Church, Boston, on Tuesday, May 30, at 11 o'clock, A. M. In the absence of the President, the Rev. FRANCIS WAYLAND, the Hon. WILLIAM B. BANNISTER took the chair, and at his request the Rev. WILLARD CHILD, of Norwich, Conn., opened the meeting with prayer, after reading the 53d chapter of Isaiah. The Treasurer's Report was then read by the Chairman, and the Certificate of its correctness by the Auditors. An abstract of the Report of the Board of Managers was read by the Secretary.

The resolution for the acceptance of this Report, and referring it to the Managers to be printed, was moved by the Rev. O. FOWLER, of Fall River, and seconded by the Rev. Mr. TOWNE, of Boston.

The second resolution was moved by SAMUEL E. COUES, Esq., of Portsmouth, and seconded by Rev. GORHAM D. ABBOTT, of New York city, as follows: —

Resolved, That the Bible, the chapel, and the chaplain; the Sabbath school room and the Sabbath school teacher; reading the Scriptures morning and evening, accompanied with singing and prayer, in the chapel; faithful religious conversation with the prisoners, by the chaplain and others who have a heart for it; visiting the prisoners; solitary confinement at night; the constant supervision of humble, faithful, and pious officers; pure air, good light, and wholesome food; careful attention to the sick; mild punishment for misdemeanor; cleanliness, order, and obedience; intelligent superintendence, careful inspection, and full published annual reports, — are the means which we approve in Prison discipline.

This resolution was supported by addresses, and accepted, and the meeting dissolved.

---

* *Mr.* STONE *subsequently declined accepting the office of Treasurer, and Mr.* A. A. LAWRENCE *was appointed by the Board of Managers, and accepted.*

ANNUAL REPORT.

———◆———

God, in great mercy, has preserved alive the managers of the Prison Discipline Society, for which we render to him our humble and hearty thanks.

One of the vice-presidents of the Society, long known in this community in the administration of public justice, has died during the last year—the Hon. Peter O. Thatcher. Two valued members of this Society, one, living in Charlestown, Mass., the Rev. Daniel Crosby, and the other in New York, the Rev. Alexander Proudfit, D. D., whose names have long been on the list of our friends, and whose countenance and-approbation have often cheered our path, have also died. With these exceptions, we believe, we have not to record a single death among the long list of officers, life directors, and life members. While, therefore, we mourn the death of some of our friends, and are admonished of our own dissolution, we would be grateful that so many are preserved alive, and are permitted to enter upon the duties of another year, in this department of benevolence.

The Eighteenth Report, which is the Report of the last year, and which we now submit, is arranged in

FOUR PARTS.

1st. *Lunatic Asylums.*	3d. *County Prisons.*
2d. *Houses of Refuge.*	4th. *State Prisons.*

PART I.

LUNATIC ASYLUMS.

DOCUMENTS

Third Annual Report of the Directors of the Maine Hospital, December, 1842. Pages 32; duodecimo. Wm. R. Smith & Co., Printers to the State.

Reports of the Board of Visitors of the Building Committee and of the Trustees of the New Hampshire Asylum for the Insane, June Session, 1842. Pages 21; octavo. Concord: Carroll & Baker, State Printers.

Sixth Annual Report of the Trustees of the Vermont Asylum for the Insane, presented to the Legislature, October, 1842. Pages 16; octavo. Montpelier: E. P. Walton & Sons, Printers.

Annual Report of the Board of Trustees of the Massachusetts General Hospital, for the Year 1842. Pages 40; octavo. Boston: Press of James Loring. 1843.

City Document No. 17. Report of the Superintendent of the Boston Lunatic Hospital and Physician of the Public Institutions at South Boston, July 1, 1842. Pages 39; octavo. Boston: John H. Eastburn, City Printer.

Rules and Regulations of the Boston Lunatic Hospital. Duodecimo; pages 12. Boston: John H. Eastburn, City Printer. 1843.

Senate of Massachusetts, Document No. 19. Tenth Annual Report of the Trustees of the State Lunatic Hospital at Worcester, December, 1842. Pages 115; octavo. Boston: Dutton & Wentworth, State Printers. 1843.

The Eighteenth Annual Report of the Officers of the Retreat for the Insane at Hartford. 1842. Pages 36; octavo. Case, Tiffany, & Burnham, Printers.

Brief Report, in the Republican and Advertiser, Hudson, N. Y., of Dr. White's Private Lunatic Asylum, Hudson, N. Y. One half column, in a weekly newspaper.

An Act to organize the State Lunatic Asylum at Utica, New York, and more effectually to provide for the Care, Maintenance, and Recovery of the Insane. Passed April 7, 1842.

Annual Report of the Bloomingdale Asylum, for the Year 1842. Pages 15; octavo. New York: Press of Mahlon Day & Co. 1843.

No Report from the Asylum on Blackwell's Island.

Report of the Commissioners appointed by the Governor to select a Site for a State Lunatic Asylum for the State of New Jersey. Read, November 8, 1842, and ordered to be printed. Octavo; pages 14. Trenton: Printed by Sherman & Harron. 1842.

Report of the Pennsylvania Hospital for the Insane, for the Year 1842; by Thomas S. Kirkbride, M. D., Physician to the Institution. Printed by Order of the Board of Managers. Philadelphia, 1843.

The Annual Report of the Court of Directors of the Western Lunatic Asylum to the Legislature of Virginia, with the Report of the Superintendent and Physician, for 1842. Pages 61; octavo. Staunton, Virginia: Printed by Kenton Harper. 1843.

Lunatic Asylum of South Carolina. Report of the Committee of Regents; Report of the Physician; Report of the Superintendent; Laws of the Institution. Published by Order of the Regents. Pages 42; octavo. Columbia, S. C.: Printed by J. C. Morgan. 1842.

Fourth Annual Report of the Directors and Superintendent of the Ohio Lunatic Asylum to the Forty-first General Assembly, December 9, 1842. Pages 88; octavo. Columbus: Samuel Medary, State Printer.

An Act making Provision for the Enlargement of the Lunatic Asylum at Columbus, Ohio; February 28, 1843.

CHANGES AND IMPROVEMENTS IN ASYLUMS FOR POOR LUNATICS, DURING THE LAST YEAR.

The Maine Asylum, at Augusta, has come into more general favor, and more extended usefulness.

The New Hampshire Asylum is occupied for the first time, and Dr. Chandler, formerly Dr. Woodward's assistant, is appointed superintendent.

The Vermont Asylum has been enlarged, and the enlargement brought into use.

The McLean Asylum has done much to provide for indigent persons, whose means were exhausted, and who must have left the institution, before their restoration was complete, except for the timely and generous provision of some excellent friends and benefactors of the institution.

Dr. Stedman, formerly physician of the Marine Hospital at Chelsea, has been appointed superintendent of the Asylum at South Boston.

Provision has been made for the enlargement of the Hospital at Worcester, to accommodate 150 more of the insane poor of Massachusetts, by an act of the legislature, authorizing the trustees to expend the Johonnot legacy of $42,000 for that purpose, provided the Supreme Court shall decide that it can be done legally. An article in the Christian Examiner, another in the North American Review, and the Memorial of Miss Dix to the legislature, contributed to the accomplishment of this object. Since the above was written, a decision of the question by the Supreme Court is in favor of the enlargement.

We are not apprized of any progress yet made in Rhode Island, by the executors of Mr. Brown, and other friends of the insane in Providence, towards the building of an Asylum for the Insane in Rhode Island; for which Mr. Brown, by his last will, appropriated $30,000. At the same time he expressed his confidence in his executors, that they would act with wisdom in regard to the time when this amount could be taken from his estate for this purpose.

Dr. Butler, formerly superintendent of the Insane Hospital at South Boston, has been appointed superintendent of the Retreat at Hartford, Conn. The governor of Connecticut, in his late message to the legislature, recommends an appropriation of $5000 a year for the support of the insane poor of the state in this institution.

Dr. Brigham, formerly superintendent of the Retreat in Hartford, has been appointed superintendent of the New York State Asylum at Utica, and has entered upon the duties of his appointment.

Commissioners have been appointed to select a site for the contemplated Asylum in New Jersey, and they have examined several farms, mostly near Trenton, in the vicinity of which, as it is the seat of government, they think it should be located.

We hear of no further progress in Pennsylvania towards the establishment of a State Asylum for Pauper Lunatics.

An effort is making, in the District of Columbia, to prepare the old Jail to be a receptacle for lunatics. We fear it will be a poor receptacle.

New and beautiful buildings have been erected for the enlargement of the Western Asylum in Virginia, at Staunton. We regret to learn that Dr. Stribling, the admirable superintendent of the institution, has been obliged to leave his post of usefulness, for a season, on account of ill health. The trustees, however, indulge the hope and expectation, that he will not be permanently disconnected with it.

A very favorable report has been received from the Lunatic Asylum at Columbia, South Carolina — the first published report of this institution which we have ever seen.

A law has been passed by the legislature of Ohio, for the erection of additional buildings for the better accommodation of the Asylum at Columbus, and authorizing the warden of the Penitentiary to use the labor of the convicts from the Penitentiary, as far as it can be done, to forward the work.

MAINE INSANE HOSPITAL.

Benjamin Brown, Esq., Hon. Ruel Williams, and Amos Nourse, M. D., directors.

Isaac Ray, M. D., superintendent and physician.

Chauncey Booth, Jun., M. D., assistant physician.

Mr. Joshua S. Turner, steward, and Mrs. Betsey Bartlet, matron.

The directors report to the governor and council, that the Hospital has undergone an improvement quite beyond what they were prepared to expect at the beginning of the year.

The number of patients has been greater than at any former period, ranging from 65 to 73. Last year, the average number was 61$\frac{5}{6}$.

The directors feel themselves fully authorized to attest that it is faithfully and ably conducted. The numerous cures, as well as the great improvement of the incurables, are the evidence on which they rely.

This institution is the receptacle of every class, and the directors hope it will be, until separate provision is made for accommodating a portion of the incurable cases.

" All who have applied have been received, and yet there is room." The directors ask, why it is that an institution so well adapted and commodious, in a state containing more than 600 insane, should seldom contain more than 70 inmates. The directors believe that the want of ability is the cause, more than all others. They are therefore of opinion that legal provision ought to be made for furnishing to persons of this class such aid as their circumstances may require; and they believe that the best plan is to require the towns to support their own insane poor at the institution.

The directors concur with a committee of the legislature in recommending that a board of trustees be appointed, who shall appoint the officers, and superintend the affairs of the Hospital.

The directors also recommend some further provisions by law, which shall authorize a legal tribunal to decide the question in regard to the insanity of an individual.

The directors say, the supply of water has proved insufficient, and they recommend the laying of an aqueduct, one mile in length, by which an abundant supply can be brought to every elevation of the building ; this can be done at an expense of $1000.

Much improvement has been made, during the year, in the grounds, fences, and out-buildings.

The farm, also, has been much improved, and has produced, under the skilful management of the steward, $710 worth of produce.

The directors have been obliged to borrow a carriage, in consequence of their limited means. They recommend the purchase of one for the benefit of the patients.

An increased number of attendants, also, is required.

The expenditures are thus stated : —

Total amount last year, ...	$8,817 73
Probable amount next year, ...	8,254 72
To meet this they have debts due, ...	2,220 65
Estimated payments by next year's patients, . . .	4,970 04
Leaving a deficit, to be made up, of	1,064 03
Add expense of carriage, ...	250 00
Purchase of spring, and expense of aqueduct, ...	1,100 00
Total appropriation required, ...	$2,414 03

The directors recommend that the proceeds of the legacy of the late Hon. Bryce McLellan be expended to purchase books for the use of the patients.

The steward gives, in his report, a detailed statement of expenditures, amounting to $9,151 04 : receipts from state treasury, $2,981 00 ; from towns and individuals, for support of patients, $6,170 04.

The superintendent says,

"We cannot be too grateful to the Great Disposer of all events, that we have had so much reason to be gratified and encouraged. The number of patients has increased ; the relative number of recent cases has been greater ; and we have had no more than the ordinary allotment of sickness."

	Males.	Females.	Total.
Number of patients, December 31, 1841, ...	36	18	54
Admitted during the year, ...	50	37	87
Whole number receiving benefit, ...	86	55	141

Discharged during the year,

	Males.	Females.	Total.
Recovered,	21	15	36
Improved,	6	10	16
Not improved,	7	11	18
Died,	4	2	6
Total discharged,	38	38	76

	Males.	Females.	Total.
Remaining in the Hospital, 31st of Dec. 1842,	47	18	65
Greatest number of patients at any one time,			73
Smallest number,			50
Average number last six months			67

The superintendent's report contains much valuable information on statistics of Lunatic Asylums, causes of insanity, &c.

NEW HAMPSHIRE ASYLUM FOR THE INSANE.

This new Asylum has been finished and occupied during the last year. Dr. Chandler has been appointed superintendent, and has entered upon the duties of his appointment. The prospects of the institution equal the expectations of its most sanguine friends.

We have received a brief synopsis from our obliging correspondent, Charles J. Fox, Esq., one of the trustees, of the First Report, just submitted. The Hospital was opened for the reception of patients, October 28, 1842.

Number of admissions — males, 39 ; females, 37 ; total, 76
Recent cases — males, 20 ; females, 18 ; . . . . . . total, 38
Old cases — males, 19 ; females, 19 ; . . . . total, 38
Number remaining, May 31, 1843 — males, 27 ; } total, 47
   females, 20 ; . . . . }
Discharged — males, 12 ; females, 17 ; . . . . . . total, 29
Recovered — males, 6 ; females, 6 ; . . . . total, 12
Improved — males, 5 ; females, 5 ; . . . . total, 10
Not improved — males, 1 ; females, 5 ; . . . . . . total, 6
Died, ... total, 1

Sent by friends, 53 ; by towns, 22 ; by a county, 1. Those by towns and county were pauper patients.

" The Hospital," says Mr. Fox, " has been more fortunate than we anticipated. Dr. Chandler is a most excellent man, and, under his judicious conduct, the institution is rapidly becoming popular."

It is delightful to see this good beginning in New Hampshire.

ASYLUM IN VERMONT.

This institution has gone on, during the last year, with steady progress, in improving its buildings and grounds; securing more and more the confidence of the state where it is located, as well as the confidence of many in other states; and accomplishing its object at a very moderate expense. Dr. Rockwell is a very discreet, practical, experienced, and successful superintendent; the location, buildings, and grounds, are very good; and the mountain air and scenery do much for the restoration of patients. The legislature appreciates the institution, and makes the necessary appropriations for its enlargement.

The Sixth Report, in October last, says, since the last annual report, the new wing has been completed. During six years, 424 insane persons have been received, 311 discharged, 179 restored to reason; 113 remain in the institution, many of whom now partake of the comforts of life, who have been confined in cages and chains. During the last year, 101 have been received, 83 discharged, 49 recovered. No serious accident has ever happened to patient or attendant. There has been no case of suicide. The mortality has been a little less than 5 per cent. A most benevolent provision was made by the legislature of 1842, for persons in the state suffering the double affliction of poverty and insanity. The trustees believe it will be adequate to give a fair trial to every recent case that may be offered for admission. They regret that the law was not so framed that application could be immediately made for every recent case, instead of its being necessary to wait, as the case may be, from February or March, nearly a year before the application can be made. The superintendent's report shows that the expenses of the establishment have been $12,615 54; the income from board of patients, $12,935 36. The patients have come from eleven states and territories, and one of the West India Islands. The terms of admission are, for indigent patients of Vermont, $2 00 per week, or $100 a year; for all others, $2 50 per week for the first six months; after that time, $2 00 per week. No charge is made for damages in any case. The means of cure in this institution are abundant, and well adapted to the end. Its whole history is one of success, with as little variation as can be found in almost any thing human.

McLEAN ASYLUM AT CHARLESTOWN.

A quarter of a century has now elapsed since this institution went into operation. The number of patients, which was from 40 to 60 in 1818 and 19, varies from 130 to 150 in 1841 and 42. The number received annually has changed, in the same time, from 30 and 40 to 130 and 140; the whole number receiving its benefits annually, from 50 and 60 to 270 and 280; the recoveries, from 10 and 11 annually to 75 and 80. A tabular view, touching all these points, and others scarcely less important, is presented in the last report of the superintendent, going to show the steady progress of this noble charity, with scarcely the shadow of variation, from its commencement to the present time. And although institutions have been opened in Maine, New Hampshire, and Vermont, within a few years, of a similar character, besides the Hospitals at South Boston and Worcester, Mass., the Asylum at Charlestown had 133 patients at the close of the last year — a greater number than at the close of any previous year, except one, since its commencement.

The accommodations furnished at Charlestown are such as can only be furnished by an immense outlay of funds.

The whole cost of the land and buildings at the McLean Asylum amounts to $245,845 98. The executors of Mr. McLean and Miss Belknap paid from the estates of these great benefactors from 90 to $100,000 each. The invested capital of the institution is debited on the books of the treasurer at $110,056 72, not including the grounds and buildings. The income is derived from the following sources; — the annual profits of its invested capital; a right to one third of the yearly profits of the Hospital Life Insurance Company; the board of its patients; and annual subscriptions for free beds at the Hospital.

Receipts last year: —

Profits from invested capital, ...	6,727	78
Profits of the Hospital Life Insurance Company, . .	5,000	00
Ten annual subscribers, ...	1,400	00
Total, ...	$13,127	78

Received for board of patients at the Hospital, . . .	2,650	10
do. do. do. at the Asylum, . . .	30,000	00
Receipts exceed expenses, ...	5,153	16

The trustees express the hope that, in future years, the Asylum will be able to defray its expenses; but they do not suppose it will be able to do much more than that.

In regard to its management, the trustees say, " that, in general health and peace, in freedom from every painful accident, and in its curative results, the year now completed will compare favorably with any former period."

The average number of patients has been 132; the number under treatment, 271; received during the year, 129; discharged, 138; remaining in the house, 133; — recovered, 80; much improved, 8; improved, 12; not improved, 20; died, 15. The number of entire recoveries is larger than that of any previous year.

The committee commend Dr. Bell for his bold and discriminating views in regard to the statistics of Insane Asylums. They notice the lamented death of the chairman of their board, George Bond, Esq. "A man of sterling integrity, sound judgment, and generous impulses, his memory is entitled to the respect of all who honor virtue, or love practical benevolence."

Dr. Bell, in his report, cherishes the memory of Dr. Rufus Wyman, the first superintendent of the McLean Asylum, as a great public benefactor. He says, " What is due to his memory can never be realized or appreciated, except by the small number whose opportunities and duties enable them to judge of the difficulties he encountered and the means he projected to meet them."

Dr. Bell also pays a well-deserved tribute to the memory of Dr. Lee, the second head of the institution, "who was removed from the most brilliant prospects of success, and the affectionate esteem of all who knew him, in October, 1836."

Under Dr. Wyman's care, ... 1152 patients were received;
Under Dr. Lee's care, ... 150 do. do. do.
And under Dr. Bell's, ... 841 do. do. do.

Making a total of 2142

The extent of the operations of the institution during its entire existence, may be seen in the following table : —

Year.	Admitted.	Discharged.	Whole Number under Care.	Unfit.	Eloped.	Dead.	Not improved.	Improved.	Much improved.	Recovered.	Remaining at End of Year
1818 ⎱ 1819 ⎰	58	35	58	1	0	5	5	9	4	11	23
1820	44	40	67	1	4	1	11	8	4	11	27
1821	47	46	74	1	2	3	10	8	12	10	28
1822	64	50	92	0	0	5	17	8	6	14	42
1823	73	61	115	1	2	2	19	11	6	20	54
1824	53	56	107	0	1	5	14	5	8	23	51
1825	59	56	110	2	4	8	8	3	10	21	54
1826	47	46	101	0	1	5	14	5	1	20	55
1827	58	56	113	1	0	5	6	2	8	34	57
1828	77	65	134	3	0	5	12	12	10	23	69
1829	73	77	142	1	1	9	19	12	9	26	65
1830	82	78	147	0	2	10	6	8	18	34	69
1831	83	84	152	0	2	8	16	15	13	30	68
1832	94	98	162	1	0	10	14	9	21	43	64
1833	103	100	167	0	2	8	10	25	13	42	67
1834	107	95	174	0	0	7	6	15	26	41	80
1835	83	84	163	1	0	11	7	11	9	45	77
1836	106	112	183	0	0	10	24	5	9	64	71
1837	120	105	191	3	0	8	8	4	10	72	86
1838	138	131	224	2	0	12	13	7	23	74	93
1839	132	117	225	3	0	10	13	11	11	69	108
1840	155	138	263	0	0	13	18	20	12	75	125
1841	157	141	283	2	0	11	29	13	11	75	142
1842	129	138	271	3	0	15	20	12	8	80	133
	2142	2009		26	21	186	299	238	262	957	

The total amount of expenses of the McLean Asylum, for the year ending January 1, 1843, was $26,755 03

Receipts for board of patients, ... $30,000 00

BOSTON LUNATIC HOSPITAL.

Number of patients, during the year ending June 30, 1842, 148, of whom 74 were males, and 74 females; of less duration than 1 year, 44; of longer duration than 1 year, 104.

Number remaining at the end of the year, 95; of less duration than 1 year, 16; of longer duration, 79.

Number discharged, 53; recovered, 17; improved, 9; not improved, 10; died, 17.

Number recovered, of less duration than 1 year, 17; improved, 5; not improved, 1; dead, 5.

Number recovered, of greater duration than 1 year, 0; improved, 4; not improved, 9; dead, 12.

Average number of patients, about 100.

Of those remaining in the Hospital, of less duration than 1 year, 10 ; from 1 to 2 years, 6 ; from 2 to 3 years, 5 ; from 5 to 10 years, 34 ; from 10 to 15 years, 13 ; over 15 years, 9 ; unknown, 18.

Under 20 years of age, 1 ; from 20 to 30, 9 ; from 30 to 40, 21 ; from 40 to 50, 20 ; from 50 to 60, 17 ; from 60 to 70, 2 ; over 70, 2 ; unknown, 18.

Causes of insanity : — amenorrhea, 1 ; congenital, 5 ; disappointed affection, 7 ; disappointed ambition, 1 ; domestic afflictions, 11 ; epilepsy, 8 ; fear of poverty, 1 ; injury to the head, 5 ; indulgence of temper, 1 ; intemperance, 28 ; ill health, 8 ; jealousy, 2 ; loss of property, 6 ; masturbation, 7 ; puerperal, 3 ; religious excitement, 6 ; vicious indulgences, 1 ; paralysis, 1 ; unknown, 90.

The statistics of this institution, from December 11, 1839, to June 30, 1842, are as follows : —

Whole number admitted, ... 193
Of less duration than one year, ... 66
Of longer duration than one year, ... 127
Whole number discharged, ... 98

Recovered, 36 ; improved, 13 ; not improved, 22 ; died, 26 ; eloped, 1.

Whole number of old cases admitted, 126 ; old cases recovered, 2 ; improved, 7 ; not improved, 20 ; died, 17 ; eloped, 1 ; remaining, 79.

Whole number of recent cases admitted, 67 ; recovered, 34 ; improved, 6 ; not improved, 2 ; died, 9 ; remaining, 16.

STATE LUNATIC HOSPITAL AT WORCESTER, MASS.

The Tenth Annual Report is before us — an octavo pamphlet of 115 pages.

The trustees begin by returning their thanks to the Supreme Being. They anticipate the establishment of an Asylum, in ten years more, in every state in the Union, — since so much has been done for the insane poor in ten years past.

Number of patients from the first, ... 1557
Committed by the courts, ... 1157
Private boarders, or committed by the overseers of ⎱ 400
   the poor, ... ⎰
Discharged in ten years, ... 1319
Recovered, of the whole number, ... 676

Received the benefits during the last year, ... 429
Number at the commencement of the year, ... 231
  do.   do.   close of the year, ... 238
Discharged during the year, ... 191
Recovered   do.   do.   98
Died, ... 12
Sent away as incurable and harmless, ... 52
Sent to Jails and Houses of Correction in the counties ⎱
   from which they came, for want of room, ... ⎰ 12
Discharged, improved, ... 25
   Do.   as incurable, ... 2
Recent cases recovered, (of less than one year,) 70
Old cases recovered, (of more than one year,) 18

The trustees have made their monthly visits, and found all things well. Dr. Chandler has left, and gone to Concord, N. H., to be superintendent of the New Hampshire Asylum. Dr. John R. Lee has been appointed assistant physician in his place. Mr. and Mrs. Ellis, the steward and matron, have left, and Mr. Charles P. Hitchcock, the former steward, has been reappointed. Dr. Woodward has not been removed to Utica, but remains at his post.

A new barn has been built, at an expense, including the fitting up of the old barn for workshops, of $2000. The receipts of the institution, from all sources, amounted to $31,320 67; the expenditures to $27,546 87. The great source of income has been for board of patients, at $2 50 a week, which has been the standing price from the commencement. It is now reduced to $2 30. There have always been between 30 and 40 state paupers in the Hospital, for whom nothing has been paid, except when the board of the other patients was insufficient to support the institution. Then the state has made an appropriation. The sum total of these appropriations may have been equal to the regular price of board for patients. The trustees recommend that, hereafter, the accounts against this class of patients, in the treasurer's books, be audited and paid from the state treasury, in the same manner as other state pauper accounts are paid. The trustees have experienced much inconvenience, in regard to a supply of water from the aqueduct; one of the neighbors of the institution having cut off the pipes, where they crossed his land, because his demands for compensation for the water, which he claimed a right to have pass over his land, were considered unreasonable. Much expense of time and trouble has been the consequence; and an injunction from the Supreme Court, for the time being, was obtained.

What will be the final result, we do not know. We hope the insane will be supplied with good water, and enough of it, notwithstanding the fact that what they might drink, and use for washing, should diminish the quantity of water in a mill-pond, 40 or 50 hogsheads a day.

The last subject of notice and attention in the trustees' report, is the enlargement of the Hospital. There are 229 rooms for the accommodation of patients; there have been, most of the time, more patients than rooms; and at all times, the rooms have been full. The trustees are obliged to receive all committed by the courts, and to make room for them, if they have no room, by sending some to Poor-Houses, and others to Jails. Thus the very object of the institution is defeated. Seventy-six incurable patients have been removed for want of room. They have even been compelled to send many to the Jails, to make room for those committed by the courts. One of the strongest motives for building the Hospital was, to afford relief to the wretched maniacs confined in Prisons and dungeons; yet at this moment, say the trustees, there are more lunatics confined in the Prisons of the state than there were when the Hospital was built. There have been, during the past year, 157 applications in behalf of persons who were not admitted at the time when the applications were made, and 119 of them were not admitted at all. The 119 rejected applications, and the 76 removed for want of room, make 189, who have been deprived of the benefit of the Hospital for want of room. By the last census of the United States, it appears that there are 1271 insane persons in Massachusetts: 650 of them, at least, ought to be provided for in Asylums. The three Asylums at Worcester, Charlestown, and South Boston, cannot accommodate, advantageously, more than 480, leaving 170 unprovided for. The trustees, therefore, are of opinion that 150 more should be provided for at Worcester. They propose to do this by extending the west front north and south about 100 feet each way, and thus not only provide for 150 more patients, but reduce the price of board on those already in the Hospital. They ask that the Johonnot legacy of $42,000 may be appropriated to this object. The legislature, in accordance with this request, passed a law authorizing such an appropriation of the fund, provided the Supreme Court should decide that it could be done consistently with the provisions of the will.*

The treasurer's accounts exhibit an expenditure for the sup-

---

* *The decision of the court is in favor of the act.*

port of the institution, of \$27,546 87 ; and receipts, including balance on hand at the close of the last year, \$31,320 67.

The balance on hand was	2,446 11
Receipts from cities, towns, and individuals, . . .	28,299 96
Bills for shoes, oxen, cows, &c.	574 60
Total amount of receipts, ...	\$31,320 67

Leaving a balance of cash on hand of \$3,773 80. The treasurer received so much more money from other sources than he anticipated, that it has not been necessary to draw from the state treasury the sum last appropriated for current expenses, and no appropriation was required for the ensuing year.

We notice among the items of expense in the treasurer's account, the following, which show how much the expenses of such an establishment may be diminished by the productions of a large farm and the labor of the patients : —

Apples, pears, peaches, berries, ...	\$520 03
Soap, \$350 22; vinegar and cider, \$46 25 ;	396 47
Milk, \$39 45; butter, \$1,729 46 ;	1,768 91
Cheese, \$599 34 ; eggs, \$72 93 ;	672 27
Lard, \$4 55 ; beans, \$70 60 ;	75 15
Peas, \$10 03 ; honey, \$9 88 ;	19 91
Corn, \$676 30 ; rye, \$260 36 ; oats, \$79 30 ; . . .	815 96
Biscuit, \$130 31 ; flour, \$1,583 81 ;	1,714 12
Turnips, \$12 50 ; potatoes, \$513 90 ;	526 40
Poultry, \$84 18 ; ham, \$170 42 ;	155 60
Mutton and lamb, \$110 48 ; pork, \$108 70 ;	219 18
Beef, \$1,402 82 ; salt pork, \$81 08 ;	1,483 90
Veal, \$223 72 ; tripe, \$26 88 ;	250 60
Sausages, \$59 88 ; wood, \$2,289 25 ;	2,349 13
Total value of articles of this kind, ...	\$10,967 63

An amount equal to more than one third of the whole expense.

The above are articles consumed, as we understand the accounts, for which money was paid out, in addition to similar articles produced on the farm, which were used for the benefit of the institution, of which we find a full account in the superintendent's report, showing the amount and value of the produce of the farm.

The farm consists of about 70 acres, which was not in a high state of cultivation when purchased. The following is the steward's statement of the quantity and value of the produce of the farm, as approved by Dr. Woodward, and incorporated in his report for the last year : —

Produce of the Farm, seventy Acres, at the Worcester Hospital, in 1842; *a large Proportion of the Labor being performed by the Patients.*

50 tons of hay, of which 15 tons were the second crop,	$500 00
50 bushels of tomatoes,	25 00
100 bushels of onions, $50 00; 60 bushels of green peas, $60 00;	110 00
243 bushels of potatoes, $60 75; 302 bushels of corn, $226 50;	287 25
100 cabbages, $5 00; 28 bushels of soft corn, $10 50;	15 50
275 bushels of beets, $68 75; 180 of ruta baga, $45 00;	113 75
100 bushels of turnips, $25 00; 680 bushels of carrots, $170 00;	195 00
405 pounds of broom-corn brush, $20 25; 6 loads of pumpkins, $9 00;	29 25
5 cwt. winter squashes, $7 50; garden vegetables, $100;	107 50
Corn fodder, $35 00; pasturing 10 cows, $140;	175 00
Poultry raised, $15 00; 29,200 quarts of milk, $1,186 00;	1,201 00
7114 pounds of pork, $355 70; 4816 pounds of beef, $240 80;	596 50
Small pigs sold,	52 00

Total value of produce raised on the farm, ... $3,507 75

The Worcester Hospital farm will compare very favorably with any farm in the commonwealth, and is a beautiful illustration of the economy and value of a farm attached to an Insane Asylum. We have given the above in detail, that it may be clearly seen how much the insane can do towards supporting themselves. It illustrates the importance of having good land, and enough of it, connected with every Insane Asylum. It greatly diminishes the expense of supporting the institution; it furnishes many articles for consumption, of the best kind, in the best manner.

"There is no employment," says Dr. Woodward, "in which they so cheerfully engage as in hay-making. From 20 to 30 workmen were often in the field at one time, all busily employed. At one of my daily visits to the hay-field, I found *four homicides* mowing together, performing their work in the best manner, and all cheerful and happy. Of the 50 tons of hay gathered this season, 75 per cent. of it was probably mowed, made, and gathered in, by patients; and the arrangement and beauty of their hay-mows challenge competition any where."

The importance of increasing the quantity of land connected with this institution appears to us obvious from the facts stated above ; and, as a general rule, we think there may well be an acre of land for every patient.

A class of facts, stated in the superintendent's report, shows most clearly how great the evils which have arisen from want of larger accommodations.

There have been discharged by the trustees, mostly as harmless and incurable, for want of room, in 10 years,   247

Sent to Jails by the trustees as incurable and dangerous, ...   38

Discharged by the Probate Court, as incurable and dangerous, ...   23

If they had room to retain all whose residence in the Hospital is desirable, there would be few discharges, except those who recover or those who die. But the trustees often meet to send away incurable cases, to make room for recent cases.

"It is with great reluctance that the trustees ever send patients to the Jails ; but the crowded state of the Hospital, the last year, has compelled them to do so, in an unusual number of instances. The trustees do not discharge the *dangerous* and *incurable* in any other way ; but the judge of probate, on application of the friends, does occasionally discharge some of this class."

How important, that the accommodations should be such as to prevent the necessity of ever doing it.

The results of the superintendent's 3d table, and his remarks connected with it, are important.

The number of patients has been greater than in any former year ; the admissions and discharges more numerous. The changes have been 389 ; the number of residents, 430.

"Formerly there was much difficulty in keeping patients as long as was desirable ; now, there is a strong desire, on the part of friends, to continue the residence of patients in the Hospital for a longer period ; and it is not uncommon for patients themselves to desire to remain, and to wish to return, on the recurrence of the slightest indisposition."

"Towns sometimes unreasonably urge the discharge of paupers, to save a small sum, and place them in Poor-Houses, where the difference in expense can hardly be fifty dollars a year, in any case."

The results of the 4th table are, that the vigor of manhood, from 25 to 50, is emphatically the age of insanity, 159 cases out of 238 being between these periods.

"It is when the mind is most vigorous, and the cares and burdens of life most heavy, that the brain becomes diseased, and the mind most frequently loses its balance and becomes insane."

The 8th table shows the causes of insanity : — intemper-

ance, 225; ill health, 244; masturbation, 126; domestic affliction, 168; religious, 120; property, 83; disappointed affection,
60; disappointed ambition, 28; epilepsy, 40; puerperal, 41;
wounds on the head, 18; snuff and tobacco, 8; hereditary, 465;
periodical, 308; homicidal, 20; having committed homicides,
15; suicidal, 167; physical causes, 703; moral causes, 459.
Many not classed.

Of the first 778 cases received, 135 were caused by intemperance. Of the last 778 cases received, only 90 were caused
by intemperance. *This is a great fact in favor of the temperance reform.*

Most of the other causes of insanity named, have produced
about the same proportion of cases of insanity of late, as
formerly.

Dr. Woodward remarks that

"Some new views of religious truth have recently disturbed many persons,
who have deep solicitude for their future well-being, and have brought a
number of patients under our care. Some of these views are greatly calculated to alarm those who entertain them, and I greatly fear that, for some
months to come, this agitation of the public mind may, in this and other
communities, add many to the list of the insane."

Dr. Woodward expresses the opinion that

"Hereditary predisposition alone is never the cause of insanity, in any
case." "It is with insanity as with other predispositions to disease;— a
slighter cause produces effects to which the individual is liable in consequence
of this predisposition." Still he says, "Congenital insanity is hardly less frequent than congenital idiocy."

There has been no case of suicide in the Hospital in the last
eighteen months, although many have a strong propensity to
suicide. "In some families there is a strong natural propensity
to suicide." One patient in the Worcester Hospital had twenty
male relatives who had committed suicide.

The 9th table shows the occupation of those received. The
principal were farmers, 181; laborers, 132; shoemakers, 62;
seamen, 55; merchants, 59; carpenters, 41; manufacturers,
32; teachers, 26; students, 22.

The 10th table shows the principal diseases which have
proved fatal in the Hospital :— marasmus, 25; epilepsy, 14;
consumption, 10; apoplexy and palsy, 10; suicide, 7; disease
of the heart, 7.

The 11th table shows the comparative expense of supporting
old and recent cases.

The average expense of 25 old cases, each, ... $2,020 00
Whole expense of 25 old cases, ... 50,611 00
Average expense of 25 recent cases, ...   45 20
Whole expense of 25 recent cases till recovered, . 1,130 00

"The last 25 recent cases, which have recovered and been discharged, have cost, before and after admission, an average of $45 20; while the 25 first on the list, who now remain in the Hospital, have cost on an average $2,020 00."

The 12th table shows the duration of insanity, age, civil state, &c.

An unusual number of recent cases, and a less number of old cases, have been admitted during the last year. And the number of cases favorable to recovery remaining at the close of the year, has never been greater.

The 13th table shows the comparative curability of insanity at different periods of disease. Of 699 cases committed during the first year of insanity, 622 have recovered, or are considered curable ; 40 only remain in the Hospital, most of which will probably recover. Of the 500 which have been insane from 1 to 5 years, 237 have recovered, or are considered curable ; and of the 250 which have been insane from 5 to 15 years, only 27 have recovered, or are supposed to be curable.

The 5th table is a very full and complete summary of the statistics of the institution, from its opening, in January, 1833, to November 30, 1842 : —

	1833	1834	1835	1836	1837	1838	1839	1840	1841	1842
Admitted,.........	153	119	113	125	168	177	179	162	163	198
Discharged, including deaths and elopements, ...	39	115	112	106	121	144	168	155	167	191
Recovered,........	25	64	52	58	69	76	80	82	82	88
Improved, ...	7	22	23	17	23	24	23	29	36	25
Not improved,.....	2	20	28	22	20	28	37	29	37	66
Died,.............	4	8	8	8	9	16	22	15	12	12
Eloped,...........	1	1	1	1	..	..	..	..	..	..
Enjoying the benefits, ...	153	233	241	245	306	362	397	391	399	430
Sent by courts,....	109	55	90	117	129	123	123	106	110	157
Private patients,...	44	64	23	8	39	54	56	56	53	41
Average number,..	107	117	120	127	163	211	223	229	233	238

The first four years, the Hospital accommodated 120 patients. In 1837, another wing was added, when the number was increased to 163. Since that time, a fourth wing has been added, and the patients have increased to an average number of 238.

There are other valuable and important tables in the Tenth Report of the Worcester Hospital, from the 14th to the 19th inclusive, which we have not space to notice at length. The 19th table, on recommittals, with the remarks upon it, by the superintendent, is important to all, and might do much good, if generally circulated, to guard persons constitutionally liable to insanity from its attacks. The report contains, also, a very full account of all the cases of homicidal insanity which have been and are in the Hospital. The information under this head is of great importance.

On the whole, the Tenth Report of the Trustees and Superintendent of the Worcester Hospital, is, in our estimation, one of the best ever published.

BLOOMINGDALE ASYLUM, NEW YORK.

Whole number under treatment last year, 219; number at the commencement of the year, 133; number at the close of the year, 110; number received during the year, 86; number recovered during the year, 55; number improved, 15; deaths, 7; — whole number admitted from the first, 2,784; whole number recovered, 1,255; 76 per cent. of recent cases were cured last year, and 40 per cent. of cases of longer duration than one year.

The insane patients were removed from the Hospital in the city to the new building at Bloomingdale, in 1821. The whole expense of the new establishment, thus opened and prepared for insane patients exclusively, was about $180,000. Previous to their removal from the New York Hospital, in the city, 1,553 insane patients were admitted; 704 recovered, and 52 were removed to Bloomingdale.

The whole expense of the Bloomingdale Asylum, last year, was $29,393 17. The report does not state from what sources this amount was received.

The means of cure, in this institution, are stated in the last report, and the statistical tables contained in the appendix are very good.

DR. WHITE'S PRIVATE ASYLUM AT HUDSON, NEW YORK.

It has been in operation $12\frac{1}{2}$ years, during which time 580 patients have been received. During the last year, 71 patients have received the benefits of the institution; 38 have been received during the year. Of 12 recent cases, 10 have been cured, and 2 are recovering. Of 22 chronic cases, 4 have been cured, and 2 are recovering; 15 have been improved, and 1 has died. Of the intemperate cases, 4 left with their systems renovated, and resolving to abstain from all intoxicating drinks. There remained under treatment, at the close of the year, 33 patients. The board of supervisors of the county paid an official visit to the institution in November last, and passed upon it high commendation, which was signed by the chairman and clerk, furnished to the proprietors, and published. Thus the board of supervisors act, in some measure, the part of directors or trustees, in recommending the institution to the public.

NEW YORK STATE LUNATIC ASYLUM.

"Dear sir,   "UTICA, *June* 9, 1843.

"We are now fairly under way, and thus far have had fair weather. As you are aware, we opened the institution about the middle of January, 1843;—have since received 145 patients; 50 of them came the last month, and others are arriving daily. We shall probably be full in a short time, and, next winter, ask for additional buildings. I am pleased to be able to tell you that our arrangements prove better than I anticipated, and the whole forms an *exceedingly comfortable* home for the insane. Our large halls, each 220 feet by 13, and each connected with a dining-room, and large, open veranda, enable patients to amuse and exercise themselves to as great an extent as is desirable, and will prove useful to the excited and the melancholic ;— but our large, fine farm (125 acres) is our best remedy, and on which you may daily see 20, 30, or more patients voluntarily engaged in various kinds of labor; and our ladies assist us in furnishing the house, as we make all our mattresses, beds, &c., ourselves. On the whole, we think we are doing very well; *but do come and see.* 19 have been discharged cured. My object in writing you now is to invite you to the *dedication of our chapel, July* 12, at 3, P. M. Dr. Nott is expected to preach, and the neighboring .clergy to be present. The latter we expect to invite to preach for us for a few weeks, until we find a good chaplain.

"In haste, but with very great respect,
"Your obedient servant,
"A. BRIGHAM."

NEW JERSEY LUNATIC ASYLUM.

The commissioners for selecting a site, in their report, submitted to the legislature November 8, 1842, describe several farms, in the vicinity of Trenton and Princeton, which may be bought for about $100 an acre. They do not select, but deem an appropriation of $10,000 necessary to purchase a suitable one. They propose to erect a building, with a front of 240 feet, on the general plan of the Worcester Asylum, which may accommodate about 100 patients. For this purpose, they think $24,000 will be necessary ; and afterwards lateral wings may be erected, at an expense of $18,000, for the accommodation of 100 more inmates. The whole expense of site and building, with wings for the accommodation of 200 patients, with furniture, the commissioners estimate at $75,000. Here the matter is left in the report, all argument, to show the expediency or necessity of such an institution in New Jersey, being deemed superfluous.

PENNSYLVANIA HOSPITAL FOR THE INSANE.

The report of this institution, by Thomas S. Kirkbride, M. D., for 1842, is a most important and interesting document. At the date of the previous report, there were 115 patients, since which 123 have been admitted, 120 have been discharged or died, leaving 118 under care, at the close of the year. The whole number receiving the benefits of the institution, in 1842, was 238. Of those discharged, 60 were cured, 11 much improved, 19 improved, 18 stationary, and 12 died. Of those discharged cured last year, 37 were residents of the Hospital not exceeding three months. The report contains 13 valuable statistical tables. The arrangements for warming the building by heated air, answer well the purpose designed. The supply of water has been abundant at all times. The farm is large, beautiful, and productive. The location proves healthy. Dr. Kirkbride's remarks upon the importance and economy of early treatment, the visits of friends, and the avoidance of deception with the insane, are all good. There is a paragraph or two in the report, concerning the mode of treatment, which we quote at length : —

"Writing, drawing, painting, the study of the mathematics, and other branches of learning, have tended to beguile many tedious hours. Several gentlemen have been usefully engaged in imparting instruction to others in the same ward, and two have been improved by giving regular lessons, for a short time, in one of the modern languages.

"In this way, several patients have been strikingly benefited, by associating with others in the Hospital. The conversation and peculiarities of his neighbor have often tended to withdraw a monomaniac's attention from himself; and, in a few instances, I have seen striking good effected by asking one patient to take special notice and care of another. To two or three, who have been under treatment this year, I can most truly, and do cheerfully, award a very considerable share of the credit of restoring more than one patient; and the most pleasant part of these cases was, that, while benefiting their neighbors, their own delusions were found to have vanished."

The whole report and institution are worthy of admiration and praise.

STATE ASYLUM FOR THE INSANE POOR IN PENNSYLVANIA

We find in a June number of the Sabbath School Journal, published in Philadelphia by the American Sunday School Union, the following article on this subject : —

"THE CONDITION OF THE INSANE.

" It is to be regretted that, after all the labor and expense bestowed on the preliminary measures, the project of a State Lunatic Asylum for Pennsylvania, should have been so ignominiously defeated. Several hundred dollars, and many months of valuable time, were freely contributed to bring the subject properly before the public and the legislature. The necessary act was passed with gratifying unanimity ; and every thing but the times promised an early and liberal provision for the suffering maniacs in Jails, Alms-Houses, and private custody. It would seem, however, as if there was nothing too sacred or pure for a selfish spirit to crawl over and cover with its filthy slime; and, without going into the offensive details of the matter, it may suffice to say that, for some cause, it was judged proper to arrest the proceedings under the act, and to suspend all further measures in relation to an Asylum. When, or under what auspices, it may be revived, is quite uncertain. In the mean time, it must be a source of deep sorrow to any compassionate mind, that the suffering which such a Hospital would unquestionably have alleviated, (if not prevented,) must still be endured ; and that the ancient and proverbially benevolent state of Pennsylvania must still be destitute of an institution, which so large a proportion of her sister states have provided.

" It is no consolation to be told that the necessary funds could not have been obtained, if all things else had been properly managed. We have reason to believe that persons would have been found disposed to take the stock which was authorized by the act, without any view to profit, and even with the certainty of considerable loss. A single individual was found ready, in a neighboring state, to appropriate to a like object, from his private funds, an amount equal to the whole sum contemplated by the Pennsylvania act ; and who knows what some opulent citizens among us might have been prompted to do, had not the fiendish spirit of self-aggrandizement, or political favoritism, clothed the whole project with suspicion and dishonor ? The subject has been presented to our minds within a short time with fresh interest, by two facts communicated to us by an intelligent friend, as within his personal knowledge. A young man in Bucks county was confined in the mad apartment of a Poor-House. He was seized with the small-pox. This so alarmed the inmates and guardians of the house, that they favored his escape. He hastened to his home. His appearance threw the neighborhood into a perfect consternation, and all avoided him. He found a resting-place, at last, with a relation, in a poor, miserable house, where he soon after died from sheer neglect. What cruelty of savage or pagan can exceed this? The other case is that of a young man, a school-mate of our informant, who is, and has been for four and a half years, confined in chains in his father's house, notwithstanding his derangement is of the mildest form, and by no means requiring restraint. Both these unhappy cases, and many scores like them, would have been provided for at once in the proposed Hospital; and life would have been preserved, reason restored, families blessed, and the community be decidedly the gainers.

" And must the sufferings of so many hundreds of our fellow-citizens be endured, and aggravated, and rendered irremediable, by long delay ? Is there not some form of relief for at least a portion of them ?

" In the county of Philadelphia alone, there are at least 230 lunatic paupers, for whom no suitable provision is now made. This is as many, perhaps, as it would be desirable to have collected in one place, under the supervision of one physician or governor. Might it not be wise, as well as humane policy, to erect forthwith a plain, substantial Hospital, with suitable out-grounds, on a spot easy of access from the city, and yet so far removed from it as to be obtained at a low price? Such sites, in these times, are not difficult to be obtained ; and perhaps one might be found, the buildings of which would suffice for the purpose of a Hospital, at least for a few years, without material expensive alterations or additions, except for repairs and fences; for it is one of the prominent advantages of the improved system of treating the insane, that much less expense is necessary in providing against escapes, &c., than in former times. It is not our province to enlarge on this suggestion; our chief object in adverting to this topic at all, is to recall the attention of benevolent people to the condition of the lunatic paupers of our community, and to inquire whether some more general relief cannot be afforded, in the absence of public provision, for their restoration or comfort."

WESTERN LUNATIC ASYLUM OF VIRGINIA.

The report of this institution by the court of directors and Dr. Stribling, is a very fine document. The legislature appropriated, last year, $22,000 for current expenses; $9,060 44, to pay off the balance of a debt contracted some time since for additional buildings; and $24,000, for new buildings. With this appropriation, a large three-story building, to accommodate 45 females, and two large buildings for noisy patients, are to be erected and completed by the first day of July, 1844. The directors have been successful in supplying the institution with an inexhaustible supply of good water, conducted from a fountain two miles distant, through three-inch iron pipes, and distributed most conveniently about the grounds and buildings. The directors confidently hope that Dr. Stribling will not be obliged permanently to retire from the institution, on account of ill health, as he fears he may be obliged to do.

The superintendent, in his report, gives the number of patients, during the last year, as being 152; number at the commencement of the year, 99; at the close of the year, 110; received during the year, 53. In no year have so many been received and benefited, and yet in no year have there been so many applicants who could not be admitted. Of the discharged, 42 in number, 19 were recovered, 7 improved and unimproved, 15 died, and 1 eloped. The unusually-large number of deaths, Dr. Stribling says, was not owing to its locality, construction, or general management. The first suicide since the institution was opened, took place during the last year, by a patient's striking his head against the walls of his room. Dr. Stribling's report contains 9 valuable statistical tables, with useful and important remarks, and many important practical observations on medication, moral means, classification, diet, amusements, books and periodicals for the library, labor and employment, religious services, early application of remedies, discharged cases, and simulated insanity. Altogether, the report is more full and important than any which have preceded it.

LUNATIC ASYLUM AT COLUMBIA, SOUTH CAROLINA.

The first published report, which we have ever seen from this institution, we have received during the last year. It is a valuable document, prepared with much labor. It contains a report of a committee of the regents, which lays down the general principles on which all good Asylums are conducted, and gives a brief history of the efforts which have been made in this country for the insane; — also, the report of the physician, by which it appears that the Asylum in South Carolina was at first rendered unpopular by the improper conduct of those employed in planning and erecting the buildings. He says large sums of money were uselessly expended, so that the Asylum became a by-word and reproach. He suggests many improvements of modern times, by which all unfavorable early impressions may be removed. The number of patients, since Dr. Trezevant took charge of the institution, has been 206, of which number 83 have been cured, and removed much improved, and 54 have died, and 6 have committed suicide. If the improvements suggested by the physician should be made, more favorable results may hereafter be expected.

The superintendent, Mr. Parker, says, —

" Although many of the unfortunate inmates of this institution were brought here in chains, and represented as being exceedingly dangerous, we have invariably, on their admission, released them from their shackles, and in no case have we had cause to regret the experiment. A persuasive and conciliatory manner, on the part of the keeper, has greater influence with the most insane, than any punishment which can be enforced.

" There is sometimes a difficulty among the patients. On such occasions, the cause may be traced to my own mismanagement, or that of some one of the keepers. Hence the great importance of selecting suitable persons for taking charge of them; they aid much in the recovery of the patients; while an improper person may effectually counteract every prescription of the physician."

There is great good sense in these remarks, and, if we do not entirely misinterpret the language of this report from the regents, the physician, and the superintendent, of the South Carolina Lunatic Asylum, a new day has dawned upon that institution.

OHIO LUNATIC ASYLUM.

The Fourth Report of this institution is more full and important than any which have preceded it. They have all been very good, but this appears to us to be the best. Dr. Awl is an admirable superintendent; and this and all the other humane and criminal institutions at Columbus, speak well for the future as well as the past, in this new and growing state.

It is remarkable that an example is set to every other western state, at Columbus, Ohio, in regard to suitable provision for the insane, the blind, and the criminal and vicious. Not that the institutions here are perfect, (for instance, the Penitentiary has no religious teacher provided by law, and supported by the state,) but it is surprising and delightful to see such noble foundations laid, in a state so new, for so many important and humane institutions.

"Institutions of benevolence," says Dr. Awl, "belong to God. They are the fruit of that spirit which breathes peace upon earth, and the durable pyramids which mark the triumphant progress of the Christian world.

"Since the date of our last report, we have been blessed with general health, comfort, and safety. No serious accident has occurred, either in the house, or with the numerous patients, who have almost constantly been employed in the open air.

"We still continue to have a crowded house at all times; the average number of inmates accommodated, in the past year, being 145, which is greater than at any former period; whilst the number waiting for places, in different parts of the state, is increased rather than diminished."

Dr. Awl's report contains 22 statistical tables, with remarks which we deem of great value. We have space for only the results of the Ohio Asylum from its commencement : —

	1839.	1840.	1841.	1842.	Total.
Admitted,	157	101	85	65	408
Discharged,	42	78	81	65	266
Recovered,	27	53	44	41	165
Died,	8	14	14	11	47
Eloped,	1	2	2	1	6

Per cent. of recoveries on all the recent cases discharged in three complete years, 86.05.

Average per cent. of recoveries on all the old cases discharged in three complete years, 35.63.

The expenditures the last year have been $15,877 44; the receipts, $19,357 85; of which $17,000 was from the state treasury, $2,304 67, from patients, and $53 18, from an individual.

Dr. Awl has a few remarks upon moral treatment and restraints, which we cannot deny ourselves the pleasure of quoting : —

"Our system of discipline depends upon neither secret arts nor physical force. It is entirely based upon the plainest and most simple principles of parental kindness and common sense, with such tact and ingenuity as necessity may suggest, or occasion require. A cheerful, encouraging, friendly address; kind but firm manners; to be patient to hear, but cautiously prudent in answering; never making a promise that cannot safely be performed, and when made never to break it; to be vigilant and decided; prompt to control, when necessary, and willing, but cautious, in removing it, when once imposed; — these are qualities which will command the respect, and gratitude, and attention of the misguided lunatic, when they could never be attained by force.

" The great points are,— a kind heart, pure motives, and sound judgment. " We allow no one in our employ to insult, taunt, ridicule, abuse, strike, whip, chain, or iron a patient, under any circumstances whatever. There never was a man or woman chained or put in irons of any kind, since the Asylum received a patient; and we never had a strait jacket in our possession."

The simple leather wrist-bands; the waist-belt, fastened to the back of a chair; the leather mitten or muff; the arm-chair, and the strong-room for seclusion, are the restraints named by Dr. Awl as sometimes, but seldom, in use at Columbus.

" At the moment we are engaged in the composition of this paragraph," he says, " with 148 insane persons under charge in the Asylum, there is not a single individual under any other restraint than the walls of the Asylum; and this is frequently the case for weeks together. They talk in England and on the continent of their *recent improvements* in these respects; of the value of mild treatment, and the disuse of all harsh means and cruel restraints, describing at the same time the means which their experience has proved to be sufficient. It is well. We are thankful that the things which they have laid aside have never been in service with us. What they call mild restraints have always been our strongest measures, and their conclusions our point of beginning."

Dr. Awl and the Ohio Lunatic Asylum have our best wishes for their continued prosperity.

We close this notice of Lunatic Asylums, and this part of our Report, with a tabular view of fourteen Asylums, for the year 1842 : —

Fourteen Lunatic Asylums in 1842.	Number under Treatment during the last Year.	Number at the Commencement of the Year.	Number at the Close of the Year.	Number received during the Year.	Number recovered during the Year.	Number much improved.	Number improved.	Number of Deaths during the Year.	Number admitted from the First.	Whole Number recovered.	Not improved.	Whole Number discharged.	Time of opening the Institution.
Maine Asylum, at Augusta, ...	141	54	65	87	36	..	16	6	222	69	18	....	1840
New Hampshire Asylum, at Concord,	76	....	47	76	12	..	10	1	76	12	6	29	1842
Vermont Asylum, at Brattleboro', ...	196	95	113	101	49	..	...	6	424	179	..	311	1836
McLean Asylum, at Charlestown,...	271	142	133	129	80	8	12	15	2142	957	20	....	1818
Boston Asylum, at South Boston,....	148	108	95	40	17	..	9	17	193	36	10	....	1839
Massachusetts Asylum, at Worcester,	429	231	238	198	88	..	25	12	1557	676	*66	1319	1833
Connecticut Retreat, at Hartford,....	179	83	90	96	56	..	16	8	1164	656	9	....	1824
New York Asylum, at Utica,........	145	....	126	145	19	..	...	...	145	....	..	....	1843
————, at Bloomingdale,	219	133	110	86	55	..	15	7	2784	1255	..	....	1821
Dr. White's Asylum, at Hudson, N. Y.	71	38	33	33	14	..	23	1	....	580	..	....	1830
Pennsylvania Asylum,† two miles west of Philadelphia,.............	238	115	118	123	60	11	19	12	299	90	18	....	1841
Friends' Asylum at Frankford, seven miles north of Philadelphia, ...	†97	58	58	39	13	4	10	3	784	263	...	....	1817
Virginia Asylum, at Staunton, ...	152	99	110	53	19	..	...	15	....	....	...	....	1828
South Carolina Asylum, at Columbia,§ Ohio Asylum, at Columbus,.........	207	142	142	65	41	..	...	11	408	165	13	....	1838
Total in fourteen Asylums,..........	2569	1298	1478	1271	559	23	155	114	7694	4938			

* Sent away as incurable, 12; to Jails and Houses of Correction, 52.
† The Pennsylvania Hospital was founded in 1752; has received 40,000 patients, of whom 4336 were insane; of these 1493 were entirely recovered, and 913 improved.
‡ Year 1842, ending third month.
§ In 1836, 53; in 1842, 65; in 7 years, under treatment, 206; cured and much improved during the time, 83; died, 54.

PART II.

HOUSES OF REFUGE.

DOCUMENTS.

The House of Reformation for Juvenile Delinquents, at South Boston, publishes no report itself; but a committee of the city government, through their chairman, Moses Grant, Esq., has for six years made a report on the institutions, including this at South Boston, and the inspectors of Prisons for the county of Suffolk have made a report semiannually. These documents are very valuable. So few of them, however, are published, that very few persons ever see them, and, after a little time, they cannot be obtained.

Eighteenth Annual Report of the Managers of the Society for the Reformation of Juvenile Delinquents, to the Legislature of the State, and Corporation of the City of New York. Octavo; pages 42. Mahlon Day, Printer.

The Fifteenth Annual Report of the House of Refuge of Philadelphia; with an Appendix. Octavo; pages 28. E. G. Dorsey, Printer.

HOUSE OF REFORMATION AT SOUTH BOSTON.

Daniel Chandler, superintendent.
William R. Lincoln, assistant superintendent and teacher.
Samuel Fisk, assistant.
No other officers.
Number of inmates, 56, of whom 6 are colored; no females. Work of the house done mostly by the boys. Rise early, — at 5 o'clock, in summer, — make their own beds, sweep their own rooms, and get ready for prayers, reading the Scriptures, and singing, at a quarter before 6 o'clock. Nearly all sing, and those who do not, at first, with a very few exceptions, soon learn. Breakfast at 7. Play in a yard, about 100 feet by 80, from breakfast till 7 o'clock. Work from 7 to 10; attend school from 10 to 3, with an hour's intermission for dinner and play. Work from 3 till 6. Sup at 6. Play till dark. Settle accounts for good or bad behavior every evening; the remainder of the evening being spent in intellectual exercises for recreation and amusement. Retire at half past 8 o'clock.

Although the number of children is not large, in this institution, if it is large enough to take all from the city who need its benefits, what more could be desired? unless it be that the benefits of it should be extended to other parts of the state, by opening its doors, as in the House of Refuge in New York, for juvenile delinquents from all parts of the state, whose waywardness might be corrected in this institution. It will be difficult to find a place, in this or any other state, where this class of boys can with more certainty receive benefit. The labor is wholesome and abundant, at certain hours ; the school is of the first order for any place ; food, recreation, and play, are all well provided; the chapel, school-room, work-shop, play-grounds, and garden, are all good, well arranged, and beautiful. The Sabbath is observed as in the best-regulated Christian communities and families. Public worship twice a day, Sabbath school instruction and reading. The health is almost perfect. There has been no death for 18 months. The opportunity for bad boys, when reformed, to be well apprenticed, is very good.

We greatly lament that this institution itself does not furnish and publish an annual report, which might be preserved as the published and authorized record of its important results.

HOUSE OF REFUGE IN NEW YORK.

This is an institution like that in Boston, for the benefit of juvenile delinquents. It has been in operation 18 years. The number of boys and girls received from the commencement to January 1, 1843, was 3,128, of whom 897 were girls. Of the whole number, 2,817 have been bound as apprentices.

" If there is one fact," say the managers, " which shows forth the utility and beneficial effects of this institution, it is the large number of youths, of both sexes, who have been rescued from a life of vice and degradation, and thus assisted in their progress to virtue and usefulness."

Number of children in the house, January 1, 1842, . . . 275
Number received during the year, ... 284
Number enjoying its benefits in 1842, ... 559
Number remaining January 1, 1843, ... 306
Number apprenticed during the year, ... 253

The great cause of delinquency is idleness.
Time is divided, in this institution for reformation, between the work-shop, school-room, play-ground, dining-room, and dormitory ; about 8 hours to labor, about 8 hours to study and recreation, and about 8 hours to rest.

The great lessons inculcated are, 1st, cleanliness in person, habitation, and dress; 2d, early rising; 3d, order and regularity; 4th, truth; 5th, industry; 6th, moral and religious observances.

A library of 576 volumes of good books is provided for their instruction and amusement.

The Sabbath is observed in the manner most common in very well regulated Christian communities and families : — public worship twice, Sabbath school instruction, reading, rest from labor, &c. &c.

The health is indicated by the bill of mortality; 2 deaths only last year, among nearly 300 inmates.

The receipts have been $21,350 42; the disbursements, $21,228 62; leaving a balance, in favor of the institution, of $121 80.

Receipts from following sources : —

Balance from last year's account, ...	$ 135 50
Labor of the children, ...	4,212 69
Marine Hospital fund, ...	8,000 00
Licenses of theatres and circuses, ...	2,800 00
Corporation of the city of New York, from excise fund, ...	4,000 00
Legacy from the estate of Archibald Campbell, . .	1,202 23
Finance committee, ...	300 00
	$21,350 42

A new stone building has been erected, during the year, 89½ feet by 34½, 2 stories high, to enlarge the accommodations.

The benefits of the institution are extended to colored (about one sixth part of the whole) as well as to white children. It is the same in Boston. But it is not so in Philadelphia. Very just and severe remarks have been made on Philadelphia, for such a distinction. But as colored children were not received in either of the three cities for several years, possibly, since they are now received in two of them, it may soon be done in Philadelphia.

The annual report contains, in the appendix, the reports of the ladies' committee, physician, teacher, and matron, — all important and interesting documents.

Although the deaths have been but 2, and two thirds of the year there was very little sickness, still, in the other four months, there were many hospital cases, mostly from sore eyes; 75 were thus afflicted. In no case has the sight been lost, and in only two or three cases has the eye been at all injured.

An abstract of the daily journal, and extracts from 19 or 20 letters of a very encouraging character, concerning the good behavior of children who have been apprenticed, close this report.

May this institution, so rich in blessings to poor children, continue its great usefulness!

HOUSE OF REFUGE IN PHILADELPHIA.

This institution, like the House of Reformation in Boston, and the House of Refuge in New York, is for the benefit of juvenile delinquents. It has been in operation 15 years; has received 1119 boys, and 485 girls; total, 1604. On the 1st of January, 1842, there were 150 inmates; during the year, 109 were received, and 109 discharged, leaving 150 at the close of the year. Of those received, 100 were sent by magistrates and courts, 5 were returned by their masters, and 4 returned voluntarily. Of those discharged, 54 were indentured as apprentices, 7 were sent to sea, 22 were returned to their friends, 11 became of age to be free, 11 were not proper subjects, 3 died, 1 escaped; total discharged, 109.

Expenditures, $18,013 36; receipts, $23,060 48. Of the receipts, $2,269 10 were for labor of boys; $9,000 from county commissioners, by legislative appropriation; and $5,000 from the state treasury, by legislative appropriation.

The annual report contains very full accounts, from the superintendent, of the work done by the boys, and of the expenses of the institution; — also from the ladies' visiting committee, and from the teachers of both the boys' and girls' schools.

The appendix contains extracts from 30 letters, concerning the good conduct, with few exceptions, of boys and girls who have been apprenticed.

SUMMARY.

Total number of children and youth, in the three institutions, at the close of the last year, 512.

Total number received last year, in New York and Philadelphia, 393.

Total number apprenticed, in New York and Philadelphia, last year, 307.

Total number received from the commencement, in New York and Philadelphia, 4,732.

Total number apprenticed, in New York alone, 2,817.

Total number of deaths, in the three institutions, during the last year, 5, or less than 1 in 100.

PART III.

COUNTY PRISONS AND HOUSES OF CORRECTION.

The best model County Prisons known to us, in the whole world, are in Connecticut; and the best model House of Correction is at South Boston, Mass. Captain Robbins, the master of the House of Correction at South Boston, is quoted in Germany as a master of his art, although he has been spoken of very contemptuously in Philadelphia, where he has visited the institutions for solitary confinement, and exposed some of their weak points. If any one doubts his character or ability in this department of human affairs, let him go and see the institution under his care. It has often been described in the reports of this Society. It speaks for itself.

In Hartford, New Haven, and Norwich, Conn., are well and cheaply-constructed, well-managed, and reformatory County Prisons. The plan of building (the *working* plan) is attached to the cover of this Report, and will be, till something as good or better is devised. It is substantially the Auburn plan, — a Prison within a Prison, — almost perfectly secure, — as light as day, — cool in summer, and easily warmed in winter, — as neat as a pin, — easily inspected, — well arranged for classification, labor, solitary confinement at night, instruction, supervision, and government. Let it be imitated till it is surpassed.

As a specimen of the manner of doing things, so new, strange, and important, in a common Jail, we give an extract from a letter recently received from the keeper of the Hartford County Prison : —

"HARTFORD, *February* 22, 1843.

"On my return yesterday from a short absence, I found your letter, in answer to mine of the 15th inst.; and to your very kind inquiries I cannot refuse an answer, although brief. Our ordinary means of religious instruction, here, are, preaching, by Rev. Mr. Gallaudet, on the Sabbath ; reading a chapter of Divine Truth, and invoking the Divine blessing in prayer, every morning, with the prisoners, at the commencement of the day's labor. Every Saturday evening, and sometimes on other evenings, I take my whole family into the hall, assemble the prisoners, and spend the evening in giving them the best counsel, admonitions, and religious instruction, that I am capable of; with prayer, and singing, in which all who can sing join with my family. Sometimes, by way of variety, my wife reads some interesting religious book. We try to make it, in short, a simple, unassuming family devotional circle ; and it would do your heart good to look in upon us, on these occasions, and witness the interest manifested by these misguided and unhappy beings, to many of whom these are new and strange scenes. The effect of all this is, on all occasions, to produce that subdued, chastened tone of temper and spirit, which is more efficacious by far, in *mere discipline*, than *stripes*. But in the early part of the present winter, an increasing interest was evident, and personal conversation upon those things which pertain to their everlasting peace was not only welcome to, but strongly solicited by, many of the prisoners. Such conversations were had; our evening meetings were held oftener; exercises took a more earnest, fervent cast; and we have now pretty good evidence that these poor outcasts, abandoned, as they have been almost, by their fellow-men, and cut off from their society and their sympathies, have not been abandoned by their God; but that he has visited them in Prison by his Spirit, and, in some five or six cases at least, by his pardoning grace; thus showing them that 'his ways are higher than our ways,' and his government more merciful than man's; for while man exacts the full penalty, to the uttermost farthing, for a violated law, God offers a full, free pardon to the contrite offender. The interest still continues, though, perhaps, a very little abated. I ought to add, perhaps, that my assistant, a very devoted man, an ecclesiastical student, who designs himself for the missionary service eventually, and who lives to do good, has engaged heartily in all our efforts here. He is the overseer of the work-shop, — a practical mechanic, and works at his trade."

The above extract shows the means and results of moral instruction and improvement in a Jail.

How are the prisoners made to work in a Jail, before trial and after trial, old and young, men and women, vagabonds, and all others? Simply by giving them a place, an opportunity, and a little care, supervision, and instruction, in the presence of the jailer or his assistant, who devote themselves, conscientiously and kindly, to their important trust.

What influence is exerted over them, morning and evening, and on the Sabbath, to favor such results of labor? This question is answered in the extract of the letter from N. H. Morgan, inserted above. It speaks volumes.

It will be matter of pleasing intelligence to the citizens of Massachusetts, that a County Prison is building in Lenox, Berkshire county, on the same general plan as the improved Prisons in Connecticut.

And it will cause sorrow and pain to the citizens of Boston, that, while we have so much reason for congratulation in regard to the criminal and humane institutions of the city, at South Boston, we still have a Jail, on Leverett Street, which has been presented as a nuisance by the grand jury; which has had proceedings instituted against it, year after year, by the city government; which the present faithful mayor of the city exposed with so much truth and labor in his speech in January last; and yet there is no final action for its removal or change.

The following extract from the mayor's address on the subject, is just, and will remain a proof of his truth and faithfulness, before and after the new Prison is built.

LEVERETT STREET JAIL.

" The first subject to which I feel it my duty to draw your attention, is the situation and construction of the County Prison. The Jail for the county of Suffolk stood, within the recollection of most of us, in the immediate vicinity of this place. The increase of population demanded a new erection, farther from the centre of business, and more in conformity with the improvements of the age. In the year 1819, the county determined to erect a new Prison, and a commission was appointed, who brought to the subject all the information and experience which the times possessed, and all the devotion which the subject required. The Jail, when built, was doubtless considered the model Prison of the times. It is as unreasonable to demand of them the improvements of later years, as to complain of the navigator of forty years since, that he did not navigate the ocean by steam. But, gentlemen, the times are changed, and we must conform to the advancements of the age. The great merit of the present construction was supposed to be its strength, but *recent events* have shown that this supposition is without foundation. Within the Jail yard are two Prisons; one was erected for a House of Correction, the other for a common Jail, and both so far removed from the jailer's house, as to render an immediate supervision over either impossible.

" The leading objections to the mode of construction are, —

" 1st, That, from their remote position, the jailer can have no supervision over the prisoners at night, and they are necessarily left to their own machinations, without the possibility of detection;

" 2d, That there is no mode of preventing the inmates from having communication with each other, and any prisoner may communicate with any other, in cells on the same floor or on any other;

" 3d, That the mode of warming the cells is defective in the extreme; the common entries being made the *hot-air chambers*, from which, and from which only, the cells are but imperfectly warmed;

" 4th, That, the cells being built contiguous to the outside walls of the Prison, and communicating with the yard by grated windows, there is no mode of preventing persons from without scaling the Jail yard wall, and furnishing the inmates with means of escape, or instruments of self-destruction.

" 5th, The impossibility, on the present construction, of properly classifying the prisoners. This is now done, under the direction of the intelligent and benevolent sheriff of the county, as far as the malconstruction of the Prison will allow. But the classification is far, very far, from what it should be. Shall the poor debtor, whose only crime, perhaps, is his misfortune, — or the suspected prisoner, detained for trial and acquittal, — the youth, new in the paths of crime, — be mixed up with the indecent, the blasphemer, the scorner, the hardened in infamy and crime? Shall females, innocent or abandoned, be mixed together, corrupted by, or corrupting, each other? Shall our brave and hardy mariners, detained by the government as witnesses, liberally paid, but illy requited if they are to acquire in our Prison a finished education in vice, be brought into contact with the hardened criminal? The dictates of reason and humanity forbid. The untried prisoner should be separated from the convict — the young should not be subject to the contamination of the old offender — and the poor debtor should be separated from both. Apartments entirely disconnected should be provided for females, and all intercourse, of every kind, with other prisoners, be prevented; and, above all, a fit place should be provided where any and all *may* receive religious instruction.

"The quantity of land within the outer walls of the County Jail, affords ample room for the construction of a new Prison, and leaves, if strict economy is to be consulted, a valuable portion of land for sale. The cost of a new Prison, on the most approved plan, has been variously estimated at from 30 to $40,000, subject to a deduction of such land as may be sold, and of such old material of the present buildings as may be used; — an expense, divided, as it should and probably would be, among the expenditures of two years, which would not, in the present state of our finances, be of serious consideration.

"This subject has been repeatedly presented for your consideration by my two immediate predecessors. Three times, within the last four years, has the County Jail been presented by the grand jurors, selected from among our own fellow-citizens, for its malconstruction. In the year 1833, a commission was appointed by the legislature, to examine and report upon the several Jails and Houses of Correction in this commonwealth. In a very able report, made in February, 1834, are the following remarks in reference to the Suffolk County Jail: 'Its construction is about as bad as that of the old State Prison at Charlestown, the rooms being of similar size, form, &c.; and the arrangement such as to *bar all inspection.* In this building, too, many debtors are confined, and it is impossible to prevent evil communication from the apartments of pirates, highwaymen, and murderers, with debtors, as the case may be, of pure minds and heavy misfortunes. In addition to this, females may be, and are often, confined in this building, and sometimes of such a character, that one of them, in the language of the sub-jailer, makes a *hell of the whole establishment.* And it is not impossible that females and males of pure minds should be confined in this Prison; because we have seen, that, during the year ending September, 1833, more than a seventh part were females, and more than a fourth part were discharged by the court, *as not guilty.* On the whole, considering the number of persons committed to this Prison annually — its construction and management — we think it is the heaviest weight upon the public morals which we have seen or heard of in the commonwealth.' It must be recollected that this statement refers to the year 1833; and if there is any complaint of its present management, it is entirely referable to its bad construction, which remains the same. The great objects of a Prison are, first, the safe keeping of the criminal, and, second, as far as may be, his reform. The offended majesty of the law demands not revenge, but correction; not only punishment, but prevention. The present erection answers none of these objects, and it does not compare with the other buildings in the county devoted to similar purposes.

"I do not ask you, gentlemen, to adopt my opinions, or even the opinions of any committee which may happen to be appointed on this subject; but I do ask each member of the city council to visit the County Prison, and judge for himself, fully satisfied that a subject in which the well-being and the credit of the city are so intimately connected, may with great confidence be left in your hands, for your disposal."

PART IV.

STATE PRISONS.

DOCUMENTS.

Senate Document No. 42. Annual Report of the Warden of the Maine State Prison, containing also the Report of the Inspectors. Duodecimo; pages 21.

Annual Report of the Warden, Physician, and Chaplain, of the New Hampshire State Prison, June Session, 1843. Pages 14; octavo. Concord: Carroll & Baker, State Printers.

Senate Document No. 17. Documents relating to the State Prison at Charlestown, Mass.; containing Annual Reports of Inspectors, Warden, and Chaplain. Octavo; pages 24.

Annual Reports to the General Assembly of Rhode Island, at the October Session, 1842, in Relation to the State Prison and Providence County Jail. Octavo; pages 8.

Document No. 3. Report of the Directors of the Connecticut State Prison; together with the Report of the Warden, Physician, and Chaplain; May Session, 1843. Printed by Order of the Assembly. Octavo; pages 28. Hartford: Alfred E. Burr, Printer.

State of New York. No. 10. In Senate, January 13, 1843. Annual Report of the Inspectors of the Mount Pleasant State Prison; containing also the Reports of the Agent, Keeper, Chaplain, and Physician. Octavo; pages 47.

State of New York. No. 9. In Senate, January 16, 1843. Annual Report of the Inspectors of the State Prison at Auburn; containing also Reports of Agent, Chaplain, and Physician. Octavo; pages 79.

Report of the Condition of the New Jersey State Prison, embracing the Reports of the Inspectors, Physician, and Joint Committee of State Prison Accounts. Read November 5, 1842. Octavo; pages 30. Trenton: Printed by Sherman & Harron.

Fourteenth Annual Report of the Inspectors of the Eastern Penitentiary of Pennsylvania; read in the Senate and House of Representatives, March, 1843; containing Reports of Inspectors, Warden, Chaplain, and Physician. Octavo; pages 22. Philadelphia: Printed by Joseph & William Kite.

Report of the Inspectors of the Western Penitentiary of

Pennsylvania, for the Year 1842, with the accompanying Documents ; containing also the Reports of the Warden, Physician, and Moral Instructor. Octavo ; pages 20.

Charge to the Grand Jury, delivered by Judge Harrington, at the Opening of the Court of General Sessions of the State of Delaware, Spring Sessions, 1843. Published by the Grand Jury. Wilmington, Del. Octavo ; pages 8.

Report of the Directors of the Maryland Penitentiary, made to the Executive, and communicated by his Excellency Governor Thomas to the Legislature, December Session, 1842. Octavo ; pages 16. Baltimore : Printed by James Lucas.

Annual Report of the Keeper of the Penitentiary at Frankfort, December Session, 1842. Octavo ; pages 8.

Also Report of Legislative Committee on the Penitentiary at Frankfort, Ken. Octavo ; pages 7.

And Report of the Keeper and Clerk of the Kentucky Penitentiary, in Answer to a Call from the House of Representatives. Octavo ; pages 3.

Report of the Principal Keeper of the Georgia Penitentiary to the Legislature of the State, in November, 1842. Octavo ; pages 14.

Annual Report of the Directors and Warden of the Ohio Penitentiary, relative to its Condition, January 4, 1843. Columbus : Samuel Medary, Printer. Octavo ; pages 34.

CHANGES AND IMPROVEMENTS IN PENITENTIARIES DURING THE LAST YEAR.

The legislature of Maine has authorized the erection of a dormitory building, as a substitute for the wretched old cells or pit-holes always used as sleeping-rooms for the convicts in that institution. The inspectors have examined the subject, and commenced a building on the Auburn plan.

The cold shower-bath is used as a punishment for misdemeanor in the State Prison in New Hampshire. It is of simple construction, in regard to the shower, and is said by the officers to answer a good purpose in most cases.

A new chaplain and a new warden have been appointed, without their own seeking for office, by the legislature of Vermont, at the State Prison in Windsor. The present chaplain is the Rev. Ebenezer Tracy, long and favorably known as an able editor of the Vermont Chronicle.

Permanent teachers have been fixed upon at the State Prison at Charlestown, as more useful than a constant alternation of teachers; and with this new arrangement of the Sabbath School, and unusual effort of the subordinate officers, all under the direction of the experienced chaplain, an amount of moral power has been exerted upon the prisoners, such as we most earnestly desire to see increased and extended to all Prisons.

In Rhode Island, the Pennsylvania system of Prison Discipline has been abandoned, and the Auburn system introduced.

At Wethersfield, Conn., the new chaplain appears to be devoted to his work; a Sabbath school has been established for young convicts, taught by the warden, chaplain, and clerk; and the moral power of the Prison appears to be very great.

In the Prison at Sing Sing, there has been an entire change of the officers of both the male and female Prisons. Capt. Lynds and Mrs. Beard have been reappointed to the offices of keeper and matron. These persons have both extraordinary powers in discipline. Cleanliness, order, obedience, and industry, always prevail where they are; and the matron is deeply and thoroughly impressed with the value and importance of moral means in the government of a Prison. Capt. Lynds's troubles and difficulties have always arisen from his modes of punishment. If he should, in this respect, change, and give a due prominence to moral means, and adopt the more lenient and mild modes of punishment, where punishment is necessary, he would stand among the first Prison keepers in the land. With his great experience, decision, promptitude, firmness, and love of order, we most earnestly wish he would adopt the moral means of government, so far as they will answer the purpose. We do not know that he has not already altered his views in regard to the best modes of punishment, and the value and importance of moral means in the government of a Prison. In the female Prison, we learn from one of the inspectors, that stripes are prohibited. In the Prison for men, the great trial will be made. If it is to depend wholly or principally upon stripes, there will be bloody work.

In the change of government, the chaplain, the Rev. Mr. Luckey, was not removed. He had the confidence and good-will of all parties.

In the Prison at Auburn, the mode of punishment by the cold shower-bath has been introduced, and is thought, by the keeper and physician, to be an excellent substitute for stripes. The cold shower-bath, however, which is in use at Auburn, is not constructed as it is generally. It is rather a bolt-bath than a shower-bath, and ought, in our opinion, to be immediately discontinued. It consists of a column of water, of varied diameter, and length, and degree of coldness, let down upon a single point of the head, and may be made, if it is not, an instrument of torture, and a most dangerous one ; while the simple shower-bath answers the same purpose, with comparatively little risk to life and health.

Another change at Auburn is in the enlargement of the yard, the erection of new, airy, and very extensive and lofty brick work-shops, 2 stories high, 6 or 700 feet in length, 12 feet high in each story, with numerous large windows on both sides. These, being substituted for the low, confined, and illy-lighted and ventilated shops, under the wall, and close to it, must make a vast difference in the appearance, order, supervision, and health, of the Prison.

The present chaplain of the Prison proves a most excellent man for the important trust ; the Sabbath school teachers hold an increasingly-high character in the public mind with respect to usefulness ; and the moral power of the Prison appears to have been very great during the past year.

In the new Penitentiary in New Jersey, the Pennsylvania system, which was first adopted, has been so far changed as, by direction of the physician, to put the men together, when their minds are in danger, and, if this does not answer, let them out to work in the yard.

In the new Penitentiary in Philadelphia, we are not told, in the official report, that any important changes have been made in the system ; but we believe that the twelve or thirteen acre lot, within the walls, is mostly cultivated as a vegetable garden, and we have seen convicts at work in it in the autumn. But to what extent the convicts are released from their solitary confinement, to engage in this work ; how much of it is done by them ; how they are prevented from seeing each other when engaged in it ; who are the favored ones, and how many are allowed the privilege ; and what has been the effect of it upon erotic enervation, the mental disease which the physician says is peculiar to the Prison ; what substitute is used for it in the winter season ; and whether the cap, with which the convicts used to be led blindfold into the Prison, is dispensed with since it has been found necessary to let them out to work in the open air, and in the garden, — we are left in ignorance by the official reports. It is not long since the inspectors expressed the idea in their report, that the danger was, that they should depart from the Pennsylvania system of solitary confinement, day and night, for the whole period of their confinement.

NEW PENITENTIARY IN PHILADELPHIA.

Number of Prisoners, January 1, 1843, 331; which is 4 less than at the commencement of the year, and 57 less than the average number for 6 years preceding.

Number received, 142, which is 18 less than the number received in each of the 7 years preceding the last.

Number recommitted, not stated in the body of the Fourteenth Report of the institution; but in the Appendix it is stated that, on first conviction, there were 102; on second, 29; on third, 7; on fourth, 2, and on sixth, 2; making 40 cases, in all, of conviction for second, third, fifth, or sixth time. This is a large proportion of old convicts, considerably more than one fourth of the whole number.

Number of Pardons, 23, — the largest number ever pardoned in 1 year, and twice the average number pardoned during the preceding 8 years. The reason of this departure from the usual policy of the institution in regard to pardons, is not stated. We are sorry to see it, and especially without explanation. It is the settled policy of nearly all the states, to exercise the pardoning power but seldom; and in favor of this policy Pennsylvania has, in former years, urged many and strong reasons, and set a very good example. We hope Pennsylvania will not suddenly abandon her former policy in regard to a cautious exercise of the pardoning power.

Number of Deaths last year, 9; which is a great improvement on the average number for the preceding 5 years, which was 18. The deaths, however, are still 1 in 37 : they ought not to be more than 1 to 50. Whether they have been diminished by pardoning those who were likely to die, as has been done in New Jersey, we are not informed.

The inspectors impute the fixed opinion of some against their system of solitary confinement to the "ripening of a favorite prejudice," and say, "*if* it be permitted to develop itself fully, the time is not far distant when the Penitentiary system of our state will be regarded among the proudest monuments of the wisdom of her people."

They say that "14 years' experience has convinced them that the bodily health of the prisoner is improved by it." This they say notwithstanding the fact that the mortality has been 1 in 21, for 5 years preceding the last, while the average mortality of many improved Prisons, on the Auburn plan, has been less than 2 per cent., or 1 in 50.

In regard to its Effect on the Mind, the inspectors say

nothing; and in that part of the physician's report which has usually been occupied with the mental diseases of the Institution, showing that there have been 90 cases of derangement in 6 years, most of which became so in the solitary cells, the report of the physician, this year, instead of giving the information as usual, has a long line of asterisks. To us, these stars mean, *dead minds*.

Escapes, none.

Expenses above Earnings, we know not how much. The report, as usual, contrary to the practice of nearly every improved Prison in the United States, gives no account of its expenses and earnings; but says, in general terms, "that the annual expenses have been very much reduced, during the past year." It does not say how much, nor from what amount; and concludes with this saying, — "The inspectors hope that, from the light of experience, increased reductions may be effected, and thus place the pecuniary department of this Penitentiary second to no other Prison in a just economy." Vain hope! always promised, never fulfilled.

Moral and Religious Instruction. The inspectors say, "it is known to them, that many instances of a return to the pleasures and advantages of an honest life have taken place, and they can point to those who acknowledge their restoration to society has been altogether owing to the moral and religious influences exerted in their behalf within the walls of this Penitentiary."

The warden speaks, in his report, of the improvement in the conduct and deportment of the prisoners; of the faithfulness and kindness of the officers; of the usefulness of the moral instructor, and other professors of religion, whose labors, he is confident, have been blessed; of the kind attentions, weekly, of the Ladies' Prison Society. This looks as if the stern severity of the Pennsylvania system was yielding a little to the dictates of humanity and the sympathies of Christian brotherhood; as if common sense was taking the law into its own hands, and admitting good persons, not recognized by the law as official visitors, to visit the prisoner for pious purposes, in obedience to the law of Christ. It is time it were done to a much greater extent. It was nine years before a moral instructor was provided, and now, with all the help he can get from others, it takes more than a fortnight to give all the convicts one discourse, as the Prison is constructed; and no Sabbath school system of instruction is yet formed, or, so far as we see, ever can be. He says, "There has been paid, the last year, for overwork, the sum of $955 54, which has enabled many, on leaving the Prison, to provide themselves with good clothing," &c. This overwork proved a very mischievous system at Charlestown many years ago, and was abandoned, therefore, as tending to mutual bribery and corruption of officers and prisoners; and at Charlestown, all convicts, on their discharge, are now furnished with a good new suit of clothes, and from 3 to 5 dollars in money, from the Prison funds. The new warden in Philadelphia has adopted the same system as the old one, of publishing no account of earnings, expenses, and net proceeds or deficit, — a mode of doing business which is submitted to in Pennsylvania, in regard to a public institution, but not adopted generally in the new and improved Prisons out of that state, because by it knowledge is not increased. The warden's report contains valuable tables on the nativity, crimes, education, relations, age, frequency of conviction, habits, color, and sentences, of those received during the last year, and of the whole number committed.

Some of the important results from the tables are, first, in regard to *nativity*. 72, out of 142, are natives of Pennsylvania, and 43 of the remainder were natives of New Jersey, New York, Ireland, and Germany; while only 16 were from slave states and districts. This does not look as though all the evils, or any considerable part of the evils, such as sickness, loss of mind, expensiveness, and recommitments of the new Penitentiary in Philadelphia, were owing to the location of the Prison in a city bordering on the slave states, which received an unusual proportion of the miserable and outcast of the slave population. This reason has been assigned for years, in official documents, as the great reason why this Prison has failed to answer the expectations and promises of its early friends, in regard to its effect on body and mind, moral character, and expensiveness.

Another important result from the tables is in regard to the *number of reconvictions*. 42, out of 142, are on second, third, fifth, and sixth convictions; i. e., more than one fourth part of the whole. This is for the last year; for the whole term of time, the proportion is nearly the same. 499, out of 1622, have been old convicts for second, third, fourth, fifth, sixth, seventh, and ninth convictions.

It is difficult to find, in the records of any Prison, under even the old and corrupt system of Prison discipline, a stronger proof than this of the corrupting and demoralizing tendencies of the system. It is more like the old Walnut Street Prison, the old Prison at Greenwich, and the old Prison at Charlestown, in their worst days, than like the reformed Prisons generally on the Auburn plan.

Another important result from the tables is in regard to *education*. 30, out of 142, could not read, and 61, out of 142, could not write; — a large proportion of the whole number, neglected and wretched in their early education, now arrested for crime, and confined in solitary cells day and night. Is this all of man's humanity to man?

Another important result from the tables is in regard to *age*. 203, out of 1622, were under 20 years of age, and a proportion of them, of course, of neglected education. The moral instructor says, of those now in Prison, 22 were orphans at 12 years old and under, 8 had a father only, 28 had a mother only, 120 received no religious instruction in early life. They need a House of Refuge, rather than a solitary cell.

Another important result of the tables is, that 78, out of 142, were *drunkards*, and only four of the whole number, persons of sobriety, in regard to the use of intoxicating drinks. The modern mode of reforming such persons is by kindness rather than severity. The enervated and trembling system of the inebriate, even if he be criminal, requires something very unlike a solitary cell to restore its vigor, so that he can once more gain an honest livelihood.

Another important result of the tables is, that 40, out of 142, or more than one fourth part of all, are *colored people*. This is no reason, especially taken in connection with the fact that a very large proportion of them have been entirely neglected in their early education; we say, their being black or copper-colored, and not white, is no reason why they should be punished for crime in a solitary cell, day and night; and then have the annual reports give it as the great reason why so large a proportion die under the infliction, that they are colored, and not white. This has been the standing apology, for years, of the inspectors and physician, for the dreadful mortality of the Prisoners, that so large a proportion of them are colored. It is the strongest reason against the system, instead of being an apology for it. Their color indicates that they have been neglected and down-trodden. Why adopt a system of punishment for their crimes, which is so destructive of human life to persons of their color? Is this humane? or are not colored people human? Is patience a virtue, in the endurance of such wrongs? Above all, is it reasonable and good for official magistrates of great institutions of justice and humanity to apologize for their own chosen system, in destroying the lives of so many, that they who die in the greatest proportion are colored people?

Another important result of the tables is in regard to the *mortality*. Out of 1622, the whole number received, 134, nearly 1 in 12, have died. We know no parallel to this among all the reformed Prisons in the United States. It is necessary to go back almost an age, and search among the records of Prisons before the reformation began, to find the parallel.

Another important result of the tables is, that the *crimes* for which this terrible punishment of solitary confinement day and night, so destructive of human life, is inflicted, are crimes against property, in so large a proportion, and not against the person. More than three fourths of all the crimes for which the 1622 were committed were crimes against property.

Are not the milder punishments — loss of liberty, loss of civil rights, separation from the world and from friends, incarceration, solitary confinement at night, and hard labor by day, in silence — sufficiently severe punishments for crimes against property ?

The physician's report is entirely silent on the great point, in regard to which all persons, well informed concerning the past history of the Prison, will look to it with most interest, i. e. *the effect of the system on the mind.* Whether this is because the facts in the case are too bad to be stated, or because there is nothing worthy of notice, we cannot tell. If the former, it is a reason above all others why they should be stated ; if the latter, we should suppose it would be the strongest possible reason, with the physician himself, for making the statement, because the history of the Prison for the last 6 years has been so bad, in regard to its effect on the mind, that any improvement in this respect would be hailed by all the friends of the system. When a Prison has had 90 cases of derangement of mind, in 6 years, among 400 prisoners, if a year has come which is exempt from such mournful results, it should be announced as a year of jubilee. The history of the new disease, first known by the name of *erotic enervation*, in the new Penitentiary in Philadelphia, should be continued ; or, if it has ceased to be, the year of its termination, and the manner of preventing it, should be distinctly announced.

The moral instructor says, " The condition and prospects of the prisoners, in reference to moral and religious influence, appear to me at present to be rather favorable than otherwise. The general quietness and good order is equal to that of any previous year since the commencement of my services in this institution." Then follows a long line of stars : —

" *   *   *   *   *   *   *   *   * "

" With this generally-improved state of mind " . . . . . .
What generally-improved state of mind ? What was it before ?

What is it now? If these questions were answered in the part omitted, it is the part of all others which should have been retained.

He says, " Occasional instances are occurring in which good impressions are more clearly developed."

He has heard from some who left last year, and " the intelligence is satisfactory." He has " received credible information that 2 prisoners, discharged in July and November, 1840, are in their former homes, restored to society and respectability."

" Through the aid of ministers of different denominations, there have been 165 sermons and lectures delivered, which has supplied religious exercises to all the corridors nearly each alternate Sabbath."

" Tracts have been circulated." " The library has been replenished." " The Bible has been liberally supplied." " 11 learned to read and write in Prison, of those discharged last year; 30 learned to read."

There is a valuable table in regard to the *causes of crime*, at the close of the moral instructor's report: — Intemperance, 28; licentiousness, 13; propensity, 54; passion and revenge, 8; bad company, 23; gaming, 4; unknown, 12.

In regard to *condition in early life*, — orphans at 12 years old or under, 22; had a father only, 8; had a mother only, 28; had parents, but placed out very early, 15; received religious instruction in early life, 15; received none, 120; attended Sunday schools, 11; did not attend, 116; hired at taverns, 58; frequently intoxicated, 49; occasionally intoxicated, 54; temperate, 12; unknown, 27.

On the whole, the report is favorable in regard to a diminution of crime in the Eastern District of Pennsylvania. It is unfavorable, compared with the general average of other Prisons, in regard to the bill of mortality, although far less unfavorable during the last than the 5 preceding years. It is very unfavorable in regard to reconvictions, and gives no satisfactory information in regard to expenses and earnings, and the effect of the system on the mind.

On the system generally we remark, —

1. *The Pennsylvania system fails to answer the expectations and designs of its early friends in dispensing with labor.*

Solitary confinement without labor was the original design.

The president and commissioners appointed to superintend the erection of the Eastern Penitentiary, adapted and modelled to the system of solitary confinement, say, in their letter and report on the penal code, which were read in the senate of Pennsylvania, January 8, 1828, page 25, "*It never was the design of the legislature who passed the law, or of those who planned and built the Prison, to introduce labor into the system.*" This report is signed by Thomas Sparks, Thomas Bradford, Jun., James Shasara, Roberts Vaux, Michael Baker, Caleb Carmalt, John Bacon, William Davidson.

How far was this part of the original design carried into execution?

In the second report, for 1830, page 9, the inspectors say, —

"Absolute solitude for years, without labor or moral and religious instruction, probably does bear too severely upon a social being like man; and were such the mode of punishment in this institution, the board would feel little hesitation in recommending its repeal, as cruel, because calculated to undermine the moral and physical powers of the prisoner, and to disqualify him from earning his bread at the expiration of his sentence; as impolitic, because, when persisted in beyond a very limited time, it tends to harden rather than reform the offender, while it produces great expense to the public, the prisoner in no way contributing by his labor to his support. An opportunity of witnessing the effect of absolute solitude without labor, has been presented, when, as a punishment to a sturdy and disorderly convict, the warden has ordered the light of his cell to be closed. Little time has elapsed, with the most hardy, before the prisoner has been found broken down in spirit, and begging for his work and his Bible, to beguile the tedium of absolute idleness in solitude.

"When a convict first arrives, he is placed in a cell, and left alone, without work, and without any book. His mind can only operate on itself. Generally, but few hours elapse before he petitions for something to do, and for a Bible. No instance has occurred in which such a petition has been delayed beyond a day or two."

From and after this period, solitary confinement without labor found few advocates, and the idea was practically abandoned in the Eastern Penitentiary.

2. *The Pennsylvania system fails to answer the expectations and promises of its early friends in preventing evil communication.*

Did they expect and promise that evil communication would be prevented?

They did so expect and promise.

In 1829 and 1830, the warden of the new Penitentiary in Philadelphia, in his first report to the inspectors, says, —

"To effect the great objects of Penitentiary discipline, it is indispensable to prevent all intercourse among the prisoners. I feel, therefore, much pleasure in adding, that experience has convinced me that the structure and discipline of this Penitentiary have completely accomplished this great desideratum. Conversation and acquaintance are physically impracticable to its inmates." — *Page 14 of First and Second Reports, in one pamphlet.*

1830, 31. Warden's second report: —

"It has been said that the prisoners could, and therefore would, be likely to communicate from cell to cell. I believe it possible for a prisoner to hollow so loud that he may be heard. The keeper, however, has by far the best opportunity of hearing. But we have never known an instance of their thus communicating; nor do I believe that any prisoner in the establishment knows who is in the next cell to him. Those who have been discharged have gone out unacquainted with those who have been inmates with them." — *Page* 18 *of First and Second Reports, in one pamphlet.*

The message of Governor Wolf to the legislature of Pennsylvania in December, 1832, contains the following declaration : —

" The prisoners work to more advantage. Having no opportunity for conversation or amusement, they eagerly desire employment. Here all communication is cut off; no one knows his fellow-prisoner; no acquaintance is formed; no contamination takes place; the convict sees no one, holds communion with no one, except such as will give him good advice." — *Page* 372 *of Hazard's Register of Pennsylvania.*

The Prison Society in Philadelphia, in 1833, published a pamphlet which contains the following declaration : —

" It has been suggested that intercourse by means of conversation will prevail in our Penitentiary ; that the prisoners will be enabled to effect this by means of the tubes conveying heated air into their cells. The experiment of an attempted conversation by two parties in adjoining cells has been repeatedly tried. It was utterly impracticable." — *Page* 82 *of Smith's Defence, &c.*

Thus we see that the early friends of the system did expect and promise that evil communication would be prevented.

Does the Pennsylvania system fail to answer the expectations and promises of its early friends in preventing evil communication ?

In 1835, a minority report of a committee of the legislature of Pennsylvania, read in the house of representatives, March 26, 1835, contains the following declaration : —

" In the course of the investigation," [an investigation of abuses in the Eastern Penitentiary, which lasted 53 days, and extended to the examination of 64 witnesses,] " the committee observed an important defect in the construction of the sewer or privy pipes, by means of which the convicts were enabled to communicate with each other. This defect was well nigh proving fatal to the institution, inasmuch as a general insurrection had been concerted by the convicts, and was on the point of breaking out, when discovered by the vigilance of the warden, and frustrated by his energy and decision."

A report of a committee of the legislature of Pennsylvania, of which Samuel F. Reed was chairman, read in the house of representatives, January 23, 1837, relative to the Western Penitentiary at Pittsburg, which had been recently rebuilt, at an immense expense, to conform to the Eastern Penitentiary in Philadelphia, discloses the following important facts, in regard to the entire prevention of evil communication in the Pennsylvania system of Prison discipline. The extract is as follows, from the report signed by Messrs. Reed, Trego, and Hopkins : —

" A perusal of the report of the inspectors of the Western Penitentiary, made to the legislature, March 4, 1836, first informed the committee of the existence of evils in that institution, which, in the opinion of the inspectors themselves, went far to destroy the boasted system of Prison discipline, which had its origin in, and was, at much cost and trouble, carefully nurtured by, Pennsylvania. The committee were not a little surprised to learn from that report, that it was the serious belief of the inspectors, that the system could not be carried into successful operation in the Penitentiary under their control, and that their hopes and expectations of success had been utterly disappointed. With the most anxious regard for its complete triumph, and for the purpose of remedying, if possible, the great and overwhelming difficulties by which it appeared to be surrounded, they made a protracted and scrutinizing inquiry; and take great pleasure in submitting, in as few words as possible, the result of their researches.

" The inspectors, warden, assistants, and prisoners, generally, concurred in their statements, upon the subjects of inquiry; and it was evident, from information received from them, that the defects of the construction of the Prison prevent, in a great measure, the possibility of strict solitary confinement, and admit of almost unlimited communication between the inmates of adjoining cells.

" Prisoners were in no instance , when the committee asked the question) ignorant of the name, crime, sentence, time of liberation, &c., and, in some instances, even able to give other information, which appeared highly improper for them to possess, because it should only appropriately be known to the officers of the institution." — *Page* 4.

Again, an author of great respectability, whose knowledge and opinion on this subject is of practical importance, says, —

" I was an officer in the Western Penitentiary at Pittsburg, connected with the reconstruction of the cells, from April, 1833, to August, 1835, and had an opportunity of becoming acquainted with the whole plan, both in its construction and practical operation. Having daily intercourse with the warden, there was rarely any thing of moment transpired in the Prison, which did not come to my knowledge. Until the convicts were introduced into their cells, every one connected with the Prison esteemed the new system as approaching to perfection; but the experiment proved, I believe, to the satisfaction of all, that the attempt to prevent communication of sound, was a complete failure. For myself, I consider it a *physical impossibility* so to construct a range of cells, as to answer the purpose of *constant confinement*, with suitable apparatus for ventilation, heating, and cleanliness, without affording facilities for conversation between the prisoners; and I believe this to have been the opinion of the warden and overseers, at the time I was connected with that Prison. For ventilation, there must be an opportunity for the air to pass into the cells, and to escape; and where air will pass, sound will pass. The prisoners in the Western Penitentiary were in the habit of conversing through the ventilators; and this could not be discovered by the overseers, unless they were watching *outside of the cells*, as the sound would not communicate to the observatory or the hall, where the overseers are stationed. An amusing incident happened, on one occasion, which will serve to illustrate the many ways of communication which the ingenuity of men thus situated will contrive. A rat or mouse had been domesticated by a prisoner in one of the cells in the lower story. He was allowed to amuse himself in this way, as no harm was likely to result from it; but, very much to the surprise of the overseers, the rat or mouse was found in the upper cell. It was afterwards ascertained that the prisoner in the upper cell had attached a weight to a string, and thrown it into the pipe which is placed in the top of the cell to carry off foul air. This pipe communicates with the one that goes out of the lower cell ; and the weight dropped down below.   The prisoner in the lower cell tied the string to the rat, and thus he was drawn up to the second story.

"Again, for cleanliness, there must be some contrivance for carrying off filth; and this furnishes another medium for communicating sound.   In this Prison, large water-pipes run through the whole range of cells.   These are designed to be kept full of water, and discharged once in twenty-four hours.   But it is scarcely possible to keep a stop-cock so tight as to prevent a little leakage.   If there is any sand in the water, it will prevent it from shutting close.   The consequence is, that the pipes are never kept quite full of water ; and thus a free communication for sound is left, through a whole range of cells.   But, if this could be obviated, the prisoners will converse during the letting off of the water.

"Again, there must be some arrangement for communicating heat to all the cells from a common source ; and wherever heat can pass, sound will pass.   Here the cells are warmed by steam, which passes in pipes through the whole range.   The expansion created by heat opens a crevice, where the pipe passes through the wall, sufficient to admit of the passage of sound.   Convicts have been known to place a tin basin upon this pipe, and to hold the opposite end in their teeth, standing near the wall, in adjoining cells, and thus converse with comparative ease.   It has been attempted to prevent this, in the last block that has been built, by wrapping the pipes in cloth, where they pass through the wall ; but it is probable the heat will soon destroy the elasticity of the cloth, and leave the evil worse than before."

The warden himself, of the new Penitentiary in Philadelphia, in his report for 1839, says, —

"The alteration in the hot-water pipes, made in one of the blocks during the past summer, has effectually accomplished the object desired.   An agreeable temperature has been obtained, and there is no possibility of the prisoners communicating, as they formerly did, through the small crevice by the side of the pipe.   An alteration in the other blocks should be effected, so soon as the weather will permit." — *Page* 11.

It might be inferred by some, that it is asserted in this extract, that evil communication is *now* effectually prevented ; and yet a careful examination of the language shows that evidence is afforded, by this extract itself, that there are facilities for communication from cell to cell, throughout the Prison, in all the other ranges or corridors.   The warden says, — "An alteration should be effected in the other blocks as soon as the weather will permit."   Why?   Not only because a better mode of heating will be obtained, but because there will be no possibility of the prisoners' communicating through the small orifice by the side of the pipe.   It is a fair inference from the language, that there remained free and easy communication from cell to cell, through all the corridors except one, through the small crevice by the side of the pipe conveying hot water.   If not, why make the change in the other blocks?

Further evidence is afforded, concerning this failure to prevent evil communication, by the master of the House of Correction at South Boston, who visited the new Penitentiary in Philadelphia in June, 1838. On his return, he held the following conversation with a friend concerning the various modes of communicating from cell to cell : —

" There is no difficulty in their communicating.

" *How ?*

" Through their pipes.

" *What pipes ?*

" The pipes from which they let off the water. When the water is let off, the prisoners have every opportunity to talk, and the keepers cannot know whether they talk or not.

" *How long does it take to let off this water ?*

" I do not know precisely.

" *Had you any evidence that they avail themselves of this opportunity of talking ?*

" Yes. I was informed by one of the keepers, that they talk in this way frequently.

" *What other mode of talking ?*

" By removing the plastering around the heating pipes through the partition walls.

" *By removing the plastering, you say ?*

" Yes. They make a little hole around the pipe.

" *Did you see places where this had been done ?*

" Yes.

" *Where ?*

" In the Philadelphia Prison.

" *Don't they punish for such things ?*

" Yes, sir.

" *How ?*

" They are deprived of their rations, and put in a dark cell.

" *Any other mode of talking ?*

" Yes ; from ventilator to ventilator.

" *Outward, or inward ?*

" Outward.

" *Can the talk in this way be heard by the keeper ?*

" Not unless the keeper is on the outside.

" *Do they have a keeper on the outside ?*

" Occasionally a keeper walks round ; but I saw none.

" *How many keepers would it take to prevent talking in this way ?*

" I should say it would take one man, at least, on each side of each block ; and then I doubt whether he could tell where it proceeded from.

" *How many, then, would be necessary to prevent talking through the ventilators ?*

" At least, 10 ; or, if there are 7 blocks, as in Philadelphia, 14. I can conceive nothing to prevent their communicating from yard to yard, and they have communicated in that way.

" *Do they use those yards now ?*

" Yes, sir.

" *Is there any other mode of communicating ?*

" The keeper says not ; but I have not the least doubt, that they can communicate from door to door.

" *Why have you not ?*

" Because they can put their face down to the door, and, speaking to the prisoner in the next room, they can be heard easy enough.

" *Down to the cracks of the door, do you mean ?*

" Yes, sir.

" *Any other mode ?*

"They can communicate by tapping on the wall. The least tap can be heard; and, after getting acquainted, they can understand each other.

"*Have you any reason to think they do understand each other in this way?*

"I have not the least doubt of it. By all my experience in Prison, if they cannot communicate in one way, they will in another; and they will do it in that way which is least likely to be detected.

"*Is there the same opportunity to detect them in that Prison, as in Prisons on the Auburn plan?*

"No, sir.

"*Why not?*

"Because they can talk through their pipes; then nobody can detect them, unless they have an officer at every door.

"*How much more can one officer do in detecting on the Auburn plan than on the Philadelphia plan?*

"I think one officer can do more in detecting on the Auburn plan, in a Prison of 180 prisoners, than ten on the Philadelphia. The sound is conveyed so through those pipes, and the sound reverberates so, that an officer told me it was almost impossible to detect them."

We think it evident from the above, that Prisons built on the Pennsylvania plan have failed to prevent evil communication.

3. *The Pennsylvania system fails to answer the expectations and promises of its early friends in deterring from crime and preventing recommitments.*

Did the early friends expect and promise that the Pennsylvania system of solitary confinement would have a great effect in deterring from crime and preventing recommitments?

They did so expect and promise.

The inspectors of the Eastern Penitentiary say, in their first report, for 1829, —

"The extraordinary fact, that but 9 convicts have been sent from the counties composing the Eastern District, containing so large a majority of this populous state, demands and deserves great consideration from all interested in our penal code; but the inspectors refrain from the expression of any sentiment resulting therefrom, as they cannot consider themselves justified in expressing a judgment, the result of their experience after so short a trial of the system."

The inspectors, in their second report, for 1830, say, —

"Great terror is known to have been impressed upon the minds of the convict community by this institution; and the small number of prisoners sent from the Eastern District, including a vast majority of the population of the state, together with the careful manner in which it has been ascertained that the most knowing rogues avoid committing those offences which would subject them to its discipline, may be regarded as powerful reasons for extending its operations to those Penitentiary offences not at present comprehended within the statute."

The warden of the Prison, in his report for 1831, says, —

"Of the whole number discharged," (there had been then but 15 discharged,) "from the commencement of the establishment, we have received an unfavorable account of but 1. This was an old convict, who has been passing from one Prison to another for 15 years. He has, however, shown a decided disposition to avoid this Prison hereafter."

The governor of Pennsylvania, in his message for December, 1832, says, —

" One fact, in reference to this institution," (i. e. the Eastern Penitentiary,) "bears strong testimony in favor of its discipline. It appears that not a single convict discharged from this Prison has ever been returned to it, which would seem to prove pretty clearly, either that a thorough reformation has been produced, or that a dread of repetition of the unsocial manner of life, which had proved so irksome before, has deterred from the commission of crimes within those limits of the state in which a conviction would insure a sentence to the Eastern Penitentiary."

The inspectors, in their fourth report, for 1832, say, concerning the discharged, —

" There may be some on whom no change has been wrought, but of such we would say, that the term which they spent in their lonely cell has made such an impression as to induce them to bid a long farewell to the state where legislators have provided a penal code involving so many privations."

The warden says, in his fourth report, for 1832, —

" Many reasons may be assigned for the diminution of this class of prisoners, but I believe that it may be attributed mainly to the knowledge that the community of thieves have of the nature and discipline of our establishment."

Thus we see that the early friends of the system did expect and promise, that it would greatly deter from crime and prevent recommitments.

Have their expectations and promises been realized?

In the warden's fourth report, for 1832, it appears that, of 142, the whole number received from the first, 32 " were known to be old offenders." There were, however, none yet recommitted, of those discharged from the Eastern Penitentiary.

In the warden's fifth report, for 1833, he says, that " 77 were received last year," of whom 9 were on second conviction, 5 on third, and 2 on sixth; none previously to that Prison.

In the warden's sixth report, for 1834, he says, " 118 were received; " — on second conviction, " 20; on third conviction, 4; and on the fifth, 1."

Now begin the reconvictions from among those discharged from the new Penitentiary.

The warden says, in his sixth report, " 3 have returned to this Prison reconvicted."

The inspectors say, in their seventh report, of those who had " served out their time, 16 have been recommitted in the course of the last two years."

The warden says, in his seventh report, — " Of 217 prisoners received in 1835, 57 were for second, 19 for third, 9 for fourth, 1 for fifth, 1 for sixth, and 1 for ninth conviction."

The warden says, in his eighth report, — "Of those received in 1836, 100 came in on first conviction, 32 on the second, 10 on the third, and 1 on the fourth. With the exception of 6, who had been in this Prison once before, all the prior convictions had been to other Prisons."

The inspectors say, in their ninth report, — "The number of prisoners reconvicted to this institution during the past year, was greater than in any former year." "11 of the 19, who were reconvicted, have been repeatedly inmates of the Walnut Street Prison."

The inspectors, in their tenth report, for 1838, say, — "There have been 23 reconvictions during the year. 15 of them are known to have been old offenders, the tenants of other Prisons."

The inspectors, in their eleventh report, for the year 1839, say, — "There have been 35 recommitments during the year, 3 of whom have been sentenced the third time. This is a greater number than any previous year." "Of these recommitments 26 are ascertained to have been old convicts." "Some of them served sentences four or five times in the Walnut Street and other Prisons."

Thirteen were reconvicted in 1840, of those discharged from the Eastern Penitentiary.

The inspectors say, in their thirteenth report, for the year ending January 1, 1842, —

"It may not be irrelevant here to state that, of the whole number of prisoners admitted in the Eastern Penitentiary since its organization, but 27 have been convicted a second time, and sent back to it, during the last year. Of these, 19 were white, and 8 colored. 11, out of the 27, were on their first conviction sent to this Penitentiary; of these, 9 were white, and 2 colored; and the other 16 were old convicts, who, by the contaminating influence of the former system of Prison discipline, are, it is feared, beyond the benefit of the improved plan. This fact, as connected with the operation, and benefits upon society, of the Pennsylvania system of solitary confinement with labor, speaks conclusively in its favor, as one not only reformatory upon the prisoner, but a preventive of crime."

In the appendix of the same report which contains this language of congratulation from the inspectors, in regard to the effects of the system in preventing crime and reforming the prisoner, we find the following facts, on an inch or two of paper, in a tabular form: —

Of 1480 prisoners, the whole number received in that Penitentiary from the commencement, 278 had been twice sent to that or other Prisons, 108 three times, 45 four times, 13 five times, 12 six times, 1 seven times, and 2 nine times.

It also appears, from the annual reports of the institution, that, of those discharged from the Eastern Penitentiary, amounting to 1045, 139 had been recommitted to it two or more times, making the proportion of recommitments 1 to 7½, nearly, of all discharged; and of 1480, the whole number received, 460 had before been tenants of that or other Prisons, from two to nine times. Such were the facts in January, 1842. How, then, are the expectations and promises of the early friends of the Pennsylvania system realized?

"Many reasons," says the warden, "may be assigned for the diminution of this class of offenders." — *Report for* 1832.

"The term which they spent in their lonely cell has made such an impression," say the inspectors, "as to induce them to bid a long farewell to the state where legislators have provided a penal code involving so many privations." — *Report for* 1832.

"One fact," says the governor, "in reference to this institution, bears strong testimony in favor of its discipline. It appears that not a single convict discharged from this Prison has ever been returned to it." — *Message for December,* 1832.

"Of all discharged," says the warden, "we have received an unfavorable account of but one." — *Report for* 1831.

"Great terror," say the inspectors, "is known to have been impressed upon the minds of the convict community by this institution." — *Report for* 1830.

How are these expectations and promises of the early friends of the Pennsylvania system to be regarded, after ten years' experience of the results of this system? *One* out of *seven and a half,* of all discharged, recommitted, and 460, out of 1480, the whole number committed, who had been in that and other Prisons, from two to nine times.

4. *The Pennsylvania system fails to answer the expectations and promises of its early friends in regard to its effects on health and life.*

Did they expect and promise that it would not prove injurious to health and destructive of life?

They did so expect and promise.

The warden says, in his report for 1830, —

"In relation to the supposed injurious effects of the discipline on the minds and bodies of the prisoners, I can safely assert, that the reverse has been the case in every instance."

Again he says, in the same report, —

"I am inclined to believe that those who have most vehemently condemned its severity will, before many years, censure its mildness."

The inspectors, in their report for 1831, say, —

"The opinion heretofore expressed, that the practical operation of this institution is not injurious to the physical powers of the prisoners, has been confirmed by another year's experience and observation."

The warden says, in his report for the year 1831, —

" The proportion of deaths is large for the number of prisoners, but can in no respect be attributed to the system of confinement."

The governor of Pennsylvania says, in his message, December, 1832, —

" The experiment made in the Eastern Penitentiary has demonstrated the fact that solitary confinement with labor does not impair the health."

The physician says, in his report for 1832, —

" The deaths which have taken place are not of a character to throw a doubt on the propriety or humanity of the system."

The inspectors say, in their fifth report, for 1833, —

" The general health of the prisoners, as the physician will fully establish, has equalled the most sanguine hopes of the early friends of the system."

The physician says, in his report for 1833, —

" Upon the whole, it may be safely asserted, as the result of more than four years' experience of the operations of this Penitentiary, that the peculiar mode of confinement, so far from being injurious to the health of the convicts, is generally beneficial, and forms a decided improvement, in this particular, over the modes of incarceration pursued in other Prisons."

Thus we see what the early friends expected and promised in regard to health.

Have their expectations and promises been realized ?

The physician says, in his report for 1836, —

" The prisoners have experienced, this year, an average share of health."

In a tabular view, he shows that the deaths, for the year 1836, were $3\frac{3}{10}$ per cent., and then he says, —

" The average annual mortality, deduced from the results of the seven years given in the above table, will be found, on calculation, to be 3 per cent. Upon the whole, this is a low mortality for a Prison. All confinement and restraint are necessarily unhealthy, and especially in criminals, in whom, for the most part, the vicious and depressing passions are constantly operating as remote causes of disease ; and whenever confinement improves the health of convicts, it is but substituting less unhealthy influences for those to which the criminal subjects himself by his vicious courses."

The inspectors say, in their ninth report, for 1837, — " There have been more deaths in the past than in any preceding year." They then refer for particulars to the report of the physician; and the physician says, in his report, that " The general health of the prisoners has been favorable." " 17 deaths have occurred the last year among an average of 387 prisoners." He afterwards shows, in a tabular form, that the deaths among the white prisoners were 3 per cent., " and among the colored prisoners between 6 and 7 per cent.," although he had previously said that the general health had been favorable

The inspectors, in their report for 1838, say, —

"The mortality has been greater during the past than in any preceding year. Of the 26 deaths which occurred, 7 were white, and 19 colored prisoners."

The inspectors, however, say, in the same report, that it is not correct to charge the system of solitary confinement with the amount of mortality which has taken place during the two last years.

From the period of 1836, the official reports of the institution begin to abound with apologies for the unusual mortality. Sometimes they were colored people who died; sometimes they came in diseased; and sometimes the mortality is compared with that of the old Walnut Street Prison, where the mortality, in its worst condition, was from 6 to 10 per cent. Without giving a detailed statement of the mortality of the last few years, suffice it to say, that the deaths in the Eastern Penitentiary, during five years, from 1837 to 1841, inclusive, were 1 in 21, or 5 per cent. nearly, while the average mortality of the reformed Prisons on the Auburn plan, for many years, has been 2 per cent., or 1 in 50. The latter class of Prisons are steadily improving in their bills of mortality, while the new Penitentiary in Philadelphia is waxing worse and worse.

Thus we have proved that the Pennsylvania system of solitary confinement has failed to answer the expectations of its early friends in regard to its effects on health and life.

5. *The Pennsylvania system fails to answer the expectations and promises of its early friends in regard to its effects on the mind.*

Did they expect and promise that it would not injure the mind?

They did so expect and promise.

The warden says, in his report for 1830, —

"It was said that the punishment was so severe that men could not endure it, and that it would destroy them mentally." "The report of the physician completely refutes these allegations."

A pamphlet, republished in 1833, by order of the Philadelphia Society for alleviating the Miseries of Public Prisons, entitled "A Defence of the System of Solitary Confinement," says, —

"We have evidence in our favor, which proves most incontrovertibly, that solitary confinement, when administered in suitable buildings, and accompanied by careful instruction and employment for the mind and body, is not injurious to the health or intellects of those who are thus confined."

We do not find such an amount of evidence as we expected, in the early documents, from the friends of the solitary system, that they expected and promised that it would not injure the mind. In fact, we find so little expectation and promise, on this point, from the early friends, and so strong a note of remonstrance from others, that we are inclined to believe that the earliest and warmest friends of the system were not without fearful misgivings on this most important point. The warden of the Prison, however, and the author of the pamphlet above mentioned, unhesitatingly declared their convictions and expectations as above; and the Philadelphia Society sanctioned the declaration by publishing the pamphlet.

How are the expectations and promises contained in the declarations answered by experience?

The physician's report for December 31, 1832, when the average number of prisoners was 91, gives the case of No. 10, as insane when admitted, and insane when discharged; No. 75, as idiotic when admitted, and idiotic when discharged; No. 48, as insane when admitted, and insane when discharged; No. 112, as predisposed to insanity when admitted, and maniacal when discharged; No. 49, as insane when admitted — death by suicide.

These cases, however, although they seemed to stand very thick, in a list of 24 persons, which comprehended the whole number who had died or were discharged during the year, did not do more than excite apprehension and confirm fears in regard to the effect of solitary confinement on the mind.

It was not till 1837, that the evidence began to be published in the official documents of the Prison, in such a quantity, and of such a character, concerning mania, hallucination, dementia, &c., as to show such a state of things, in these respects, as had never before been heard of in the United States, among an equal number of prisoners. The physician says, in his report for 1837, —

"The effects of this last-noticed cause (i. e. mst.) are presented in an annexed table, showing that two thirds of its influence is on the colored prisoners, and that the 14 cases of dementia reported in the medical table are referable to this cause. These cases of dementia have all been discharged cured except one only relieved and another yet on the list."

The table of demented cases for that year was not published, and we have never seen it.

The physician's report in January, 1839, contains a statement of cases of diseased mind, in 1838, to wit : —

No. 661, aged 20, born in Pennsylvania, in good health on admission, became deranged with monomania, caused by masturbation; was relieved in some degree; subsequently died of consumption, having been deranged 6 months and 10 days. He became deranged 10 months and 3 days after admission to the Prison.

No. 342, aged 22, from Ireland, scrofula on admission, became deranged with monomania caused by scrofula; was subsequently relieved, and went to work. He became deranged after 2 months' confinement.

No. 776, aged 27, from Ireland, mind disturbed on admission, became deranged with acute dementia, from cause unknown; was subsequently cured, but occasionally peculiar; remained in a state of derangement 2 months and 6 days; became deranged 8 months and 5 days after imprisonment.

No. 835, aged 22, from New York, in good health on admission, became deranged with acute dementia, caused by masturbation; was cured; duration of attack 1 month and 1 day; became deranged 3 months and 9 days after admission.

No. 675, aged 60, from Ireland, with imperfect health and disturbed mind on admission, became deranged with acute dementia, caused by disturbed mind; was cured; remained deranged 4 months and 18 days; became deranged 2 years 3 months and 7 days after admission.

No. 546, aged 31, from Pennsylvania, with imperfect health and troubled mind on admission, became deranged with hallucinations about a pistol presented at his wicket from cause unknown; afterwards cured; yet he says it was so; remained in a deranged state 14 days. He became deranged 2 years 5 months and 4 days after admission.

No. 859, aged 55, from Pennsylvania, with good health on admission, became deranged with hallucinations, from unknown cause, and was cured; remained so 9 days, and became deranged 6 months and 1 day after admission.

No. 842, aged 27, from Holland, with good health, but a disturbed mind, on admission, became deranged with mania from unknown cause, which continued at the time the report was made, after 5 months and 20 days. He became deranged 7 months and 12 days after admission.

All the above cases of derangement in 1838 were white prisoners.

No. 556, aged 22, from Africa, with good health, and mind doubtful, on admission, became deranged with acute dementia, caused by masturbation; was cured; continued in a deranged state 16 days. He became deranged 2 years 3 months and 5 days after admission.

No. 322, aged 22, from Pennsylvania, with good health on admission, but sorry, became deranged with acute dementia, caused by masturbation; was cured in 7 days, and was attacked 3 years 2 months and 10 days after admission.

No. 812, aged 21, from Delaware, with imperfect health on admission, became deranged with acute dementia caused by masturbation; was cured in 11 days, and was attacked 5 months and 17 days after admission.

No. 800, aged 18, from Pennsylvania, with imperfect health on admission, became deranged with acute dementia, caused by masturbation; was cured; remained deranged 2 months and 8 days, and was attacked 7 months and 20 days after admission.

No. 744, aged 72, from Pennsylvania, with good health on admission, became deranged with acute dementia caused by masturbation; afterwards relieved, but left with hallucinations; remained deranged 7 days; attacked 1 year and 19 days after admission.

No. 888, aged 32, from Baltimore, with chronic disease and gonorrhea, became deranged with acute dementia, caused by masturbation; afterwards cured; duration of attack, 1 month and 5 days; commencement of attack, 3 months and 24 days after admission.

No. 927, aged 17, from Maryland, health imperfect from masturbation and gonorrhea on admission, became deranged with acute dementia, caused by masturbation; duration of attack, 4 days; commencement of attack, 1 month and 8 days after admission.

No. 921, aged 23, from Delaware, syphilitic and asthmatic, became deranged with acute dementia, caused by masturbation; afterwards cured; derangement continued 19 days, and commenced 2 months and 27 days after admission.

No. 632, aged 24, from Pennsylvania, health good, mind indifferent, became deranged with acute dementia, caused by masturbation; afterwards cured; duration of attack, 1 month; commencement of attack, 1 month and 6 days after admission.

No. 721, aged 24, from Delaware, emaciated and sickly, became deranged with acute dementia, caused by masturbation; afterwards cured; duration of attack, 2 months and six days; commencement of attack, 1 month and six days after admission.

The physician's report, in January, 1840, for 1839, contains a still more alarming table of diseased mind, exhibiting 26 cases, 1 of mania, 1 of monomania, 7 of hallucination, 9 of dementia, and 8 of other forms of diseased mind. Of the whole number of cases, 15 were caused by the secret vice; 15 were said to be cured, 6 relieved only, 3 continued. This number of cases of mental disorder occurred among 402 prisoners. It is the same as if 6467 cases had occurred in Philadelphia in a single year, when the city contained 100,000 inhabitants. [*See table on the other side of this leaf.*]

The physician's report in January, 1841, is not in our possession. The inspectors and physician agree in saying that the cases of mental disorder were about half as great in 1840 as in 1839. In 1839, they were, as we have already seen, 26. But the physician says, in his report in January, 1842, that the number of cases of mental disorder in 1840 were 21, which is only 5 less than in 1839. We do not know how to reconcile this statement with that of the preceding year, that they were only about *half* as many as in 1840.

The physician says, in his report, January, 1842, for the preceding year.

" What is the nature and cause of mental disorders in the Eastern Penitentiary, and how frequently do they occur? Answer: In 1839, there were 26 such cases; in 1840, 21 cases; and in 1841, only 11 cases. This decrease is owing to the detection of the cause, and the timely application of remedies in the forming stage of the disorder, which is now designated *erotic enervation,* a term demanded by the necessity of the case. The instances of mental disorder and erotic enervation are in inverse proportion to each other, the former becoming fewer with the more frequent detection of the latter, and occur both more frequently among the colored than among the white prisoners."

The result for 5 years, therefore, is as follows: — Cases of mental disorder in 1837, 14; in 1838, 18; in 1839, 26; in 1840, 21; in 1841, 11. Total cases of mental disorder in 5 years, the average number of prisoners being 393, NINETY.

Does the report of the physician, after 13 years' experience, completely refute the allegation that the punishment would destroy the prisoners mentally?

Table of the Mental Disorders in the Eastern Penitentiary, during 1839.

WHITE PRISONERS.

Prisoners.	Age.	Country.	Health on Admission.	Diseases.	Causes.	Effects of Treatment.	Duration of Attack. y. m. d.	After Imprisonment. y. m. d.	Present State of each Prisoner, January 1, 1840.
No. 947.	46 yrs.	Pennsylva.	Asthma and pleuritic pain.	Hypochondria.	Unknown.	Cured.			Discharged from Eastern Penitentiary, Sept. 17, 1839, in sound mind and health.
867.	30	New York.	Dysentery and gleet.	do.	do.	Relieved.	22	1 0 21	do. do. April 13, do.
784.	21	England.	Good mind and health.	do.	Masturbation.	Cured.	10	1 7 5	do. do. July 3, do.
926.	39	Germany.	Plethora and pain of chest and abdomen.	do.	Unknown.	Relieved.	24	1 1 16	do. do. May 3, in sound mind, imperfect health.
988.	40	Ireland.	Hallucinations, from mania a potu.	Hallucinations.	Intemperance.	Continues.	. .	1	A worthless prisoner, subject to violent fits of anger.
975.	26	Pennsylva.	Imperfect health, and mind disturbed.	do.	Unknown.	Cured.	18	10 24	Discharged from Eastern Penitentiary, September 8, 1839, in sound mind and health.
1128.	55	Delaware.	Good, but hard drinker, and distressed.	do.	Intemperance.	Relieved.	16	7 19	At work at knitting, and continues distressed.
1069.	40	Pennsylva.	Monomania.	Monomania.	do.	Pardoned.	. .	1	Pardoned, and sent to the Alms-House.
1039.	26	Germany.	Eccentricity of mind.	Eccentricity of mind.	do.	Relieved.	16	1 16	In third block of cells, picking wool, and in sound mind and health.
1055.	21	. .	Scrofula.	Dementia, acute.	Masturbation.	Cured.	11	1 3 0	In seventh block, at weaving, and in sound mind and health.
1062.	29	. .	Good health.	do.	do.	do.	5	1 2 0	In fourth block, at shoemaking, and in sound mind and health.
673.	59	Pennsylva.	Imperfect, and mind troubled.	do.	Unknown.	do.	11	7 12	In third block, at making hickory brooms; in sound mind and health.
842.	27	Holland.	Good health, disturbed mind.	Mania.	do.	Pardoned, July, '39.	1 23	7 12	Sent to the Alms-House.

COLORED PRISONERS.

Prisoners.	Age.	Country.	Health on Admission.	Diseases.	Causes.	Effects of Treatment.	Duration of Attack. (y. m. 7d.)	After imprisonment. (3y. 3m. 10d.)	Present State of each Prisoner, January 1, 1840.
No. 492.	28 yrs.	Pennsylva.	Good; mind discontented.	Hypochondria.	Masturbation.	Relieved.	1 9	3 3 22	In fourth block, (infirmary;) good health, self-willed, and malicious.
531.	21	Maryland.	Good.	do.	do.	Cured.	13	25	In fifth block, at shoemaking; in sound mind and health.
1107.	19	Delaware.	do.	Hallucination.	do.	do.	7	6 10	In infirmary, and wishes to go to work.
924.	19	Maryland.	Gonorrhea, wilful.	do.	do.	do.	17	6 17	do.; has been at spooling, but is too workless to be continued at work.
1096.	18	Pennsylva.	Good.	do.	do.	Relieved.	9	1 4 2	Is again in infirmary for hallucination.
746.	23	do.	Subject to vertigo.	do.	do.	Cured.			In fourth block, weaving; in sound mind and health.
845.	21	N. Carolina.	Good.	Dementia, acute.	do.	do.	2 20	1 4 3	Discharged from Eastern Penitentiary, August 30, 1839, in sound mind and health.
588.	29	N. Jersey.	Typhus pneumonia, from Arch St. Prison.	do.	do.	do	2	2 8 28	Discharged April 19, 1839, in sound mind and improved health.
1021.	26	Va. a run. slave; mur.	Rheumatic; destructive disposition.	Deviltry.	Unknown.	Continues.		1 17	Continues to be very destructive; otherwise reasonable.
569.	29	Pennsylva.	Good.	Dementia.	Masturbation.	do.		2 10 5	In good health, and mind much restored, and disposed to be at work in his own way; very pleasant and mild.
921.	23	Delaware.	Syphilis.	do.	do.	Cured.	1	9 6	He died, August 24, 1839, of chronic pleurisy and scrofula.
632.	26	Pennsylva.	Health good; revengeful.	do.	do.	do.	1 6	2 6 14	Discharged from Eastern Penitentiary, August 19, 1839; sent to Moyamensing Prison.
984.	18	Philadel.	Good.	do.	do.	do.	27	8 22	In third block, picking wool; in sound mind and health.

Does the evidence prove most incontrovertibly that solitary confinement is not injurious to the intellect ?

6. *The Pennsylvania system fails to answer the expectations and promises of its early friends in regard to self-support.*

Did the early friends thus expect and promise?

They did so expect and promise.

The warden, in his first report, for 1829, page 14, says, —

" I am sanguine in the belief, that, if the proper machinery, &c., were provided, the Penitentiary would not only produce the great good which we all so ardently desire to the unfortunate inmates, but would, also, relieve the several counties who send them of the great burden, which they have hitherto borne, in the support of the convicts."

The warden, in his second report, for 1830, says, page 16, —

" The short time we have been in operation induces me to believe, that the net profits of a Prison conducted on the plan of separate confinement, will be greater than those which might result from joint labor."

The governor of Pennsylvania says, in his message, December 6, 1832, —

" It is not doubted, that, as soon as the Prison shall have been fully organized, the entire expenses will be defrayed out of the proceeds of the establishment." — *Hazard's Register, page 372.*

The inspectors of the Prison, in their fourth report, say, —

" We entertain the belief, heretofore expressed, that, when the entire plan shall be completed, and the Prison fully occupied, a revenue will arise from the labor of the convicts."

Thus we see that the early friends of the system did expect and promise that it would support itself.

Does the Pennsylvania system fail to answer the expectations and promises of its early friends in regard to self-support?

The inspectors say, in their seventh report, for 1835, —

" The profitable employment of the prisoners has ever been a subject of deep interest with the board, and we regret to state that, owing to circumstances not under our control, the avails of their labor for the past year have not been equal to their support."

In their ninth report, for 1837, —

" The inspectors regret to say that the manufacturing operations of the institution, during the past year, have been attended with considerable loss."

The inspectors, in their tenth report, for 1838, say, —

" The unproductiveness of the institution, compared with other institutions, is referred to and explained by the warden, in a manner entirely consistent with our knowledge of the course of labor and the expense of the Penitentiary."

The National Gazette, for January, 1839, contains the auditor-general's account, which has among the items of payment from the treasury of the state, for the year 1838, $34,308 to the

Eastern Penitentiary; and the account of the same public officer, for 1839, shows $18,378 76 paid to the Eastern Penitentiary, i. e. $52,686 76, paid from the treasury of the state, in two years, to the Eastern Penitentiary. It is an admitted fact, that the salary of the officers has always been paid from the state treasury, which is altogether contrary to the common rule in the United States.

The Pennsylvania system, therefore, fails to answer the expectations and promises of its early friends in regard to self-support.

The gloomy fears and predictions of the early friends of the solitary system in Pennsylvania, in regard to the Auburn system, that it would not support itself, have not been realized.

Did they thus fear and predict, that the Auburn system would not support itself?

They did.

In a pamphlet, already alluded to, republished in 1833, by the Philadelphia Society for alleviating the Miseries of Public Prisons, entitled, " A Defence of the System of Solitary Confinement," they say, —

" Our opponents refer to the productive labors of Auburn, Wethersfield, and Sing Sing, as indicative of their superiority to our system."

To this objection they reply, —

" Such success has, however, been always transient, never constant. The *new* Prison at Wethersfield is stated as an instance of self-support, if not of profit. Peculiar efforts have been made to render this Prison productive for *this, the first year of its existence.* Can we imagine that this condition will *continue ?* "

In the above declaration, the words " *new,*" and " *this, the first year of its existence,*" and " *continue,*" are Italicized by the friends of the Pennsylvania system ; as though it was out of the question that the new Prison at Wethersfield would continue to be productive.

Of Sing Sing they say, —

" It is productive only in the future tense: it has not yet been tested ; the mere prophecy of its conductor is no demonstration.

" Auburn has, heretofore, been unable to support itself. The last year has been the *most productive ;* but, notwithstanding the apparent assertion of Mr. Powers to the contrary, it has not constituted an exception to our remarks."

Have these fears and predictions of the early friends of the solitary system in Pennsylvania, that the Auburn Prisons would not support themselves, been realized ?

We have prepared a table of results of earnings above expenses, so far as we have been able to do it from authentic documents in our possession, in answer to this question ; by which it appears that the following are the great results of the experience of years in regard to the Auburn system supporting itself :

The Auburn Prison, from 1828 to 1841, supported itself, and paid the salary of the officers, with the exception of two years, the years 1837 and 1838.

Not only so; but the Auburn Prison produced, above all expenses, including the salary of the officers, from 1828 to 1841, inclusive, sixty-nine thousand four hundred and sixty dollars and fifty-nine cents.

The new Prison at Wethersfield, on the Auburn plan, supported itself every year, from 1827, when its operations commenced, to 1842, with the exception of six months in 1833.

Not only so ; but the new Prison in Wethersfield produced, above all expenses, including the salary of the officers, from 1827 to 1842, seventy-eight thousand six hundred and ninety-nine dollars and eighty-seven cents.

The Prison at Sing Sing, on the Auburn plan, supported itself every year except one, from 1833 to 1842.

Not only so ; but it produced, from 1833 to 1842, above all expenses, including the salary of the officers, one hundred and nineteen thousand five hundred and twenty-seven dollars and twenty-four cents.

The Prison at Charlestown, Massachusetts, on the Auburn plan, supported itself every year except two, from 1831 to 1842.

Not only so ; but it produced, from 1831 to 1842, above all expenses, including the salary of the officers and the expense of transporting prisoners, forty-five thousand five hundred and ninety-three dollars and seventy-four cents.

The Prison at Columbus, Ohio, which was rebuilt and finished on the Auburn plan in 1835 and 1836, has supported itself every year from 1835 to 1842.

Not only so ; but it has produced, above all expenses, including the salary of the officers, in six years, from 1835 to 1842, one hundred and twenty-four thousand nine hundred and sixty-three dollars and seventy-eight cents.

The gloomy fears, and forebodings, and predictions, of the early friends of the Pennsylvania system, in regard to the Auburn system not supporting itself, have not been realized.

Table showing the Net Proceeds of several Penitentiaries.

Year.	AUBURN.	WETHERSFIELD.	SING SING.	MASSACHUSETTS.	OHIO.
1821					
1822					
1823					
1824	*8,306 66	....	....	1,212 78	
1825	*6,879 25	....	....	10,051 32	
1826	*7,168 16	....	....	4,197 37	
1827	*2,609 12	{ New Prison } finished.	....	*6,392 56	
1828	4,029 22	1,017 16	....	*12,167 07	
1829	1,732 65	3,229 41	....	*7,599 70	
1830	4,319 26	5,008 94	....	*6,897 02	
1831	3,333 08	7,804 02	....	*477 31	
1832	3,528 16	8,713 53	....	4,192 32	
1833	8,225 05	*1,608 44	....	6,995 57	
1834	....	4,758 87	....	....	
1835	5,494 53	5,268 83	21,000 00	7,296 28	
1836	7,388 38	6,505 49	18,803 36	7,000 00	{ New Prison } finished.
1837	2,415 90	7,438 94	22,473 81	13,428 25	17,770 80½
1838	*25,000 00	5,015 02	17,760 17	806 81	12,557 96½
1839	*5,000 00	3,060 28	23,559 19	56 94	26,657 62½
1840	8,490 25	4,511 19	*246 47	4,623 27	20,037 06½
1841	3,427 25	8,282 90	6,044 14	*179 43	26,043 00
1842	17,076 76	8,065 29	9,640 10	*1,015 92	21,897 32½
	69,460 59	78,699 87	119,527 24	45,593 74	124,963 78½

* The sums thus marked are loss.

The Prisons above named, on the Auburn plan of solitary confinement at night, and labor in work-shops, in silence, by day, — i. e. the Prisons at Auburn and Sing Sing, N. Y., Wethersfield, Conn., Charlestown, Mass., and Columbus, Ohio, — have earned, above all expenses, including the salary of the officers, since 1827, four hundred and thirty-eight thousand two hundred and forty-five dollars and twenty-two cents.

How is the declaration of the early friends of the solitary system realized, then, " that such success as was promised concerning the Auburn system has been always transient, never constant " ?

In contrast to these great and important results for a long course of years, showing that five Prisons on the Auburn plan have earned $438,245 22, above all expenses, we think we could show, if we had access to the accounts of the Prison in the new Penitentiary in Philadelphia, that that Prison has been a consumer to the state treasury and the county treasuries, in fourteen years, the whole time of its operation, to the amount of four hundred and twenty thousand dollars, for current expenses, to support less than five hundred convicts. We think so, because we know that in two years of this time, the only two years in regard to which we have been able to obtain authentic information, the auditor-general's accounts show $52,686 76, paid to the Eastern Penitentiary.

7. *The Pennsylvania system has not answered the expectations and promises of its early friends by dispensing with severe punishments for misdemeanor in Prison.*

The president and commissioners appointed to superintend the erection of the Eastern Penitentiary, in their letter and report on the penal code, adapting the one to the other, and read in the senate of Pennsylvania, January 8, 1828, say, —

"Imprisonment in the solitary cells, on bread and water, has always produced a spirit of submission and obedience. It requires no resort to such a system of terror and cruelty," (referring to the Auburn system) "to preserve order and enforce obedience."

How have these expectations and promises been answered, in those Prisons where the Pennsylvania system has been introduced?

The inspectors of the new Penitentiary in Rhode Island say, in their report to the legislature in 1841, page 32, —

"The little variety of punishment permitted by law, makes it difficult to compel order and obedience. Deprivation of food and furniture are almost the only punishments that can be inflicted; and the want of food has, in some cases, been endured until great weakness resulted. In one case of very gross insubordination, the inspectors directed that the convict should be placed in irons, which have been worn for several weeks without producing the desired effect of prompt obedience. A majority of the undersigned feel compelled to recommend a modification of the law, so as to authorize the infliction of corporal punishments." They add, — "The punishments now in use are not sufficient to produce so strict a discipline as ought to be maintained."

According to the recommendation of the inspectors of the new Penitentiary in Rhode Island, a law was passed by the legislature authorizing the infliction of corporal punishment in the Prison, to secure order and enforce obedience in the solitary cells. In their report for 1842, page 1, the inspectors say, —

"Since the passage of the law authorizing corporal punishment, no case has occurred to require its infliction; but the advantage of possessing the authority is apparent. The discipline and order of the Prison are good."

In the new Penitentiary in New Jersey, on the same plan, the master of the House of Correction at South Boston learned, in his visit to that institution, in June, 1838, that the modes of punishment there for misdemeanor were, "to stop the ration — put in a dark cell — that generally subdues them : when it does not, fasten a chain around their ankle, and the other end fast to the wall."

In the Prison at Pittsburg, also on the same plan, Mr. Robbins received the following information concerning the modes of punishment for misdemeanor: — " Keeper says it is impossible to build a cell but what they can communicate." Punished for it " by being deprived of their meals — put in a dark cell — a strait jacket — put in a box just large enough to put a man in — box stands upon the end, and so fixed that a man cannot lean one way or the other.   To prevent their kneeling down, there is a piece of hard wood or iron put through the box, so as to strike their shins."   " The box is shut up tight."   Whether it had any ventilation Mr. Robbins did not know, for he did not see it.   This mode of punishment was a contrivance of the keeper having charge of the Prison in the spring of 1838.   Mr. Robbins says he asked the keeper if he had any corporal punishment.

" He said, No; but some young lads he had there, when other punishments did not answer so well, he tied their wrists and their feet, and put their hands over their knees, and shoved a stick through, back of their knees, and over their arms, and turned them over, and pulled down their pantaloons, took a piece of leather, and cut it in strips, and flogged them, and found it had a very good effect."

These are all the State Prisons on the Pennsylvania plan, except the new Penitentiary in Philadelphia ; and these are, or have been, some of the various modes of punishment.   How has it been in the new Penitentiary in Philadelphia ?

A member of the legislative committee, appointed December 6, 1834, for the purpose of examining the Eastern Penitentiary, says, —

" That punishments not known to our penal code have been inflicted on helpless convicts in the Eastern Penitentiary, is fully proved by the testimony taken before the committee of the legislature, which is published *in extenso* in this volume.   I proceed to classify and describe those punishments which were inflicted at the mere motion of the stipendiary of the commonwealth.   I shall note them in conformity to the degree of pain inflicted by each upon the sufferer.   It does not appear, by any published document, that the board of inspectors regulated the degree of punishment, or justified its infliction by their sanction.

" PUNITIVE DISCIPLINE.

" No. 1.   DEPRIVATION OF EXERCISE.
" No. 2.   MODERATE DEPRIVATION OF FOOD.
" No. 3.   THE DUNGEON, AND EXCESSIVE DEPRIVATION OF FOOD.
" *Dark Cell.* — This is a common cell, from which the light is excluded. The prisoner is locked up in total darkness, with nothing but a blanket to cover him, and in some cases he is even deprived of that covering.   No bed is allowed him; — he reposes on the floor of his cell.   He is allowed eight ounces of bread, and some water, every 24 hours.   His sufferings are intense, particularly in cold weather; and when relieved, he is the victim of rheumatism and the severity of his treatment.   Fears are entertained, that, in some

instances, the physical and moral man sunk under the rigors of this illegal punitive discipline. It is said, one man, remarkably active, athletic, and vigorous, was taken out of the dark cell little removed from an idiot — his nervous system unstrung — and in a few months, his sorrows and his crimes found a common grave. One convict was kept in this situation for 42 days. On the evening of that day, one of the keepers was attracted to the cell of this miserable wretch by repeated knockings at his wicket. On looking into the cell, the convict, a yellow boy, exhibited every symptom of delirium produced by starvation; he was on his knees, his eyes rolling in frenzy, and his frame reduced to a skeleton by the severity of his punishment. On the keeper inquiring why he had knocked, the miserable boy held out his little tin cup in his hand, with which he had been furnished to drink his water, and exclaimed, ' My father told me to knock to get a little mush.' The keeper, in violation of discipline, gave him some bread, and next morning reported his case to the physician, who entered on his journal, ' No. 132, weak from starvation.' Notwithstanding this entry, the prisoner was not released; and, on the second day after, the keeper again reported the case to the physician, who entered on his journal, after examining the prisoner's health, ' Suffering from starvation.' He was then released by order of the warden, in so emaciated a state, that he had to be supported from the dungeon to his cell by two men.

" No. 4. DEPRIVATION OF FOOD.

" This mode of punishment was an absolute deprivation of food. It is said that one prisoner, named Kyser, No. 66, experienced this deprivation for 6 successive days!!! This, however, was an extreme case, and 3 days is the limit of this species of torture, in usual cases.

" No. 5. DUCKING.

" This punishment is inflicted by suspending the offender from the yard wall by the wrists, and drenching him with water poured on his head from buckets, in nature of a shower-bath. The degree of this punishment depended on the state of the atmosphere. If temperate, the inconvenience was moderate. The pain was increased in proportion to the frigidity. Thus, in the case of Seneca Plumly, the weather was intensely cold, he was in a state of nudity, and icicles formed on his hair, and his person was incrusted with ice.

" No. 6. MAD OR TRANQUILLIZING CHAIR.

" The mad-chair was a large box-chair, constructed of plank. The prisoner was placed in this chair. His arms, above his elbows, were fastened by straps to the back of the chair. His hands were linked together by handcuffs. Straps were passed round the ankles, and firmly fastened to the lower part of the chair. He had no resting place for his feet, there being no footboard. It was impossible for an individual thus manacled to move any part of his body or limbs. The pain must have been intense; and yet prisoners have been beaten while in this painful and helpless posture. When released, the arms and legs are swelled to a frightful extent.

" No. 7. STRAIT JACKET.

" The strait jacket consisted of a piece of sack or bagging-cloth of three thicknesses, with pocket holes for the admission of the hands in the front part of the inside. In the back part rows of eyelet holes were worked. The jacket was forced over the head of the prisoner, and his hands inserted in the pockets. It was then laced tightly behind with a cord half an inch in diameter. The collar fitted about the neck, but the head was left free. It was kept on the culprit from four to eight or nine hours. They have been so tightly laced in this machine, that their necks and faces were black with congealed blood. Their hands became numbed by reason of the suppressed circulation, and in one instance a convict lost the use of his hand.

" No. 8. THE IRON GAG.

" This was a rough, iron instrument, resembling the stiff bit of a blind bridle, having an iron pallet in the centre, about an inch square, and chains at each end to pass round the neck, and fasten behind. This instrument was placed in the prisoner's mouth, the iron pallet over his tongue, the bit forced in as far as possible, the chains brought round the jaws to the back of the neck. The end of one chain was passed through the ring, in the end of the other chain, drawn tight to the fourth link, and fastened with a lock. His hands were then forced into leather gloves, in which were iron staples, and crossed behind his back. Leather straps were passed through the staples, and from thence round the chains of the gag, between his neck and the chains. The straps were drawn tight, the hands forced up toward the head, and the pressure consequently acting on the chains which press on the jaws and jugular veins, producing excruciating pain, and a hazardous suffusion of blood to the head. By the application of this Macumsey was deprived of life, and many others tortured beyond human endurance. It ought to be forever abolished."

It *was* abolished, after Macumsey died under its application; and it ought to be mentioned, that, although Macumsey's death took place while the instrument was on him, and he was suffering from its application, it was the opinion of a majority of the examining committee, that his death was not wholly owing to this cause.

"The Spanish inquisition cannot exhibit a more fearful mode of torture; and I, for one," says the member of the committee of the legislature who wrote the book containing the above description, "enter my unqualified protest against its repetition." "The annexed engraving exhibits a convict in the position of undergoing this illegal torture, as described by Leonard Phlegar, S. S. Steele, and others, in the testimony which is embraced in this volume. One of the prisoners was suffered to bleed to death. For two days, he bled at the nose, without medical attendance. On the third, the physician was called in, but too late: he died in an hour or two.

"The means by which men were tortured and put to death by the inquisition were at least sanctified by the law of the land; but in the Eastern Penitentiary, those things were perpetrated in defiance of law and legislative enactments."

"*The excellence of solitary confinement over every other mode of punishment is undeniable.*

"The tortures inflicted on refractory convicts should be abolished, and strict solitary confinement adopted in its stead. The experiment has been tried, and found effectual. The following is the result of an experiment made by William Griffith, late principal keeper in the Eastern Penitentiary. William Napier, No. 50, was a notorious robber. He had been several years a man-of-war's-man; was upwards of six feet high, robust, and athletic, and of remarkable fierce and stubborn temper. He affected to become religious, prayed, &c., and attracted the attention of the inspectors. He now became careless of his work, and would spoil it, and alleged that, inasmuch as he was blind in one eye, the other was getting sore, and he could not see to work, and ought to be put on the sick-list. He was frequently remonstrated with by Mr. Griffith without effect, who at length reported him to the warden, who permitted Griffith to manage him in his own way. Griffith immediately removed his tools and books, and restricted his visits to those of necessity. Before a week had elapsed, he gave evidence of great uneasiness, by sighs, and groans, and the rapidity with which he walked his cell, and humbly begged that he might have his work back again—'that he had been playing old soldier' about his eye, and could see well enough. No attention, however, was paid to his request.

"Before the expiration of three weeks, he exhibited strong symptoms of ennui, misery, and despair. He would pace his cell with a hurried step; at other times, he would suddenly turn round, and utter imprecations on his own folly; at others again, he would sigh, and gaze about his apartment with a vacant air, as if he wanted relief, and knew not how to obtain it; and when his cell-door was opened, he would exclaim to the keeper, 'Give me back my work, or 1 will go crazy,' . . . . 'Give me a book, or some work, or I shall die.' At the expiration of three weeks, Mr. Griffith, by permission of the warden, restored his tools and materials; he pursued his work with unusual industry, and never after gave cause of complaint.

" One of the British commissioners, who examined the Penitentiaries of the United States, says, in speaking of the Eastern State Penitentiary, — 'The only offences, which the prisoner can commit, are idleness and wilful damage to the materials on which he is at work. On such occasions, he is punished by the loss of employment, the diminution of his food, or close confinement in a dark cell. The necessity of correction is very rare. There is not a whip, nor are there any fire-arms, within the walls of the Prison.' This quotation contains many errors. Were the assertions contained in it accurate, the necessity for legislative interference would have been obviated. The picture is ideal. . . . . The above-described modes of punishment, and the blows inflicted on Macumsey in the corridor, will perhaps cause the British commissioner, (we omit his name,) should these pages ever meet his eye, to search for truth at greater labor, and not to place too much reliance on the statements of those whose interest will not permit them to disclose the unvarnished truth.

" It is in vain for men to form an opinion of an institution so interesting to mankind, on a mere cursory glance, a hasty visit of an hour or a day; and it is unjust to publish those opinions to the world, endorsed by an honorable name; because they are calculated to deceive the people, and the philanthropist reposes in security, while the object of his solicitude is writhing under barbarian tortures inflicted by a modern inquisitor. On such occasion, that of scientific or official visits, notice of a day or more is usually given, and matters arranged in holiday trim. The inmates of the cells are placed on good behavior; they are apprized of the expected visit. No reliance can be placed on the statements of the convicts, whose minds are unceasingly haunted with the apprehension of undergoing inflictions not sanctified by law, at the arbitrary will of their keepers. They dare not express a complaint, lest it should reach the ear of the warden; for how does the tenant of a solitary cell know to whom he converses? It is true you may tell him you are an official visitor, a member of the legislature, or a commissioner from England to examine the state of the Penitentiaries in the United States; but, excluded from intercourse with mankind, he knows you not; you may be a spy, an agent of the warden or inspectors, sent to him to elicit his real opinions, the expression of which will subject him to reproof. If he complains, and condemns the conduct of the warden and inspectors, he is probably not believed, and put on the black list. His interest and his fears prompt him to applaud with his lips, while his unsubdued spirit and lacerated heart condemns." . . . . " Little reliance is to be placed on the report of superficial visitors."

The expectations and promises of the early friends of the Pennsylvania system have not been realized by dispensing with severe punishments for misdemeanor in Prison.

8. *The Pennsylvania system fails to answer the expectations of its early friends in regard to its extension in America.*

The early friends of the system did expect and promise, that it would extend and fill the land. They say, in their defence of the system, in 1833, —

" After speaking of it as the most effectual, the most economical, which the wisdom of man has hitherto discovered for the prevention of crime and the reformation of offenders," they say, " the eyes of the Union are upon us; the great experiment of Penitentiary reform was commenced in our commonwealth, whence it has extended to other lands."

It is evident, from this extract, what were the expectations of the early friends in regard to its extension, not only in this but in other lands. Such were not only their expectations, but the impression has in some way gone abroad that these expectations have been realized in regard to America. H. A. Frazier, an able advocate of what he calls the French system of Prison discipline, wrote a prize essay, in 1838, in which he speaks of the principle of solitary confinement as adopted in the greater number of the American Prisons. He was not speaking of solitary confinement at night, and labor in shops by day, but of separate confinement day and night, as adopted in Pennsylvania. This is almost a total misapprehension. When H. A. Frazier wrote, in 1838, there were but three *State Prisons* in the United States, viz., two in Pennsylvania, one in Philadelphia and one at Pittsburg, and one in New Jersey, at Trenton, on the Pennsylvania plan; while, within a few years previous, the Auburn plan had been adopted in New Hampshire, Vermont, Massachusetts, Connecticut, New York, (at Auburn and Sing Sing,) in Maryland, the District of Columbia, Virginia, Georgia, Tennessee, Illinois, Ohio, and Upper Canada.

Since 1838, a small State Prison for the state of Rhode Island has gone into operation, on the Pennsylvania system, which has been in operation four years, and which the inspectors of it, in January, 1843, recommend to the legislature to appoint a committee to examine, that they may learn its injurious effects upon the mind, and its expensiveness, with a view to its abandonment, 6 out of 37 of the prisoners having been deranged since its establishment. With this solitary exception, no other state in America has adopted the separate system since 1838; while Louisiana, Mississippi, Alabama, Kentucky, Indiana, Michigan, and Maine, have adopted the Auburn system.

In regard to County Prisons and Houses of Correction, a few have been built in Pennsylvania and New Jersey, one in New York city, and one is projected in Louisville, Kentucky, on the Pennsylvania plan; while the Auburn plan has been extended, and is extending, to County Prisons and Houses of Correction more generally in the Northern, Middle, Southern, and Western States, after the model of their own State Prisons.

The Houses of Refuge for Juvenile Delinquents in America,

are all on the plan of solitary confinement at night, (or sleeping in separate beds under constant supervision,) and labor in shops by day. A great advocate of the Pennsylvania system, in 1833, in his defence of that system, expressed his regret "that the principle of solitary confinement should not have been made the basis of these otherwise excellent establishments, the Houses of Refuge." The pamphlet containing this sentiment, which appears so strange in America in 1843, had the sanction of the Philadelphia Prison Society. It is doubtful whether any person in America could now be found willing to extend the principle of solitary confinement to children and youth in Houses of Refuge.

The above statement is sufficient to correct the great misapprehension of H. A. Frazier in regard to the fact, as he supposed it to be, that the principle of solitary confinement has been adopted in the greater number of American Prisons, and to show that the expectations of the early friends of the system have not been realized in regard to its extension in this country.

What will be done in other countries is evidently suspended, in a great degree, on the results of more experience in regard to the effects of the system. All nations are looking with intense interest for the proofs in regard to the most humane, the most effectual, the most economical system of Prison discipline, for the prevention of crime and the reformation of offenders. The decision of a vast majority of the American states, on the subject, up to the present time, is in favor of the Auburn system. The expectations of the early friends of the Pennsylvania system, therefore, have not been realized in regard to its extension in America.

HISTORY OF THE NEW JERSEY PENITENTIARY, THE SECOND PENITENTIARY IN AMERICA, OUT OF PENNSYLVANIA, ON THE PENNSYLVANIA PLAN.

The joint committee of council and assembly, consisting of seven gentlemen, members of the legislature, say, in the first report after the new Penitentiary was occupied, —

"The committee, in their investigation of the affairs of the new Penitentiary during its first year's operations, feel great satisfaction in calling the attention of the legislature to the pleasing fact of the net gain, over the last year's balance, of $6,348 70, and a clear surplus in favor of the Prison, after paying all its expenses, and the salary of the several officers, of $1,741 41.

"This favorable result cannot but satisfy the most skeptical of the great pecuniary gain to the state by the adoption of the present improved plan of

Prison discipline. It is, however, the moral condition of the convicts, and the efficiency of the punishment, which afford to the friends of humanity and lovers of social order the principal recommendation of the system, and this cannot but be peculiarly gratifying to those liberal philanthropists who, through evil as well as good report, firmly sustained their onward and unwavering course in promoting their benevolent object."

" After the most minute examination into the situation of the prisoners, and the mode of treatment and discipline which has been observed, the committee find nothing to condemn."

" While there is great cause of mutual congratulation in the satisfactory results which have been produced in the infant operations of the establishment," the committee say, they " feel it a duty to guard the public against too large anticipations of such increase, i. e. an increased balance in favor of the state."

The committee conclude their report by recommending an appropriation, without delay, of $4,000, to finish and furnish the unfinished cells.

The physician says, in his report for the first year, the whole of which is comprehended in seven lines, —

" I do not know, as yet, whether the cell confinement may not be as healthy as a more free and open space was formerly ; in corroboration of which I have only to state that no death has taken place within the walls since the removal to the new Prison."

This report is signed by James T. Clarke.

The average number of prisoners had been 127, and the length of time for which the report was made, was from October, 1836, to November, 1837.

This was very favorable.

The warden says, in his report for the same year, —

" As it respects the health of the prisoners, we have cause to be grateful to a kind and gracious Providence. We have had but little sickness, and no death."

" In respect to the discipline," he adds, " it is mild and humane. We find that the milder punishments, such as depriving the convicts of light, of work, and of food, have the best effect, and seldom fail to bring the most refractory to submission."

Respecting the moral and religious instruction, he says that

" Every convict is supplied with the Bible, and almost every Sabbath they have preaching by the clergy of the city of Trenton." " Other pious persons, particularly members of the Friends' society, have manifested a concern for them by visiting and speaking, to their manifest comfort." " It is believed," he adds, " that it would improve the morals of the convicts, if they had a greater variety of religious books to read."

This favorable report is signed by Joseph A. Yard, keeper.

The inspectors, in their first report, say, on the 24th of October, 1836, the 113 convicts from the old Prison were removed to the new State Penitentiary, placed immediately in separate confinement, and put to labor, with the exception of 17, employed in building, and a few cooks, bakers, &c. There had been no final escape during the first year, and no death.

And notwithstanding all the embarrassments and difficulties of removing the convicts, and commencing operations in the new Prison, they had paid all expenses, including salary of officers, and had over one thousand seven hundred dollars left, and with a milder system of treatment than could possibly be introduced into the old Prison.

"It will be naturally inquired," say the inspectors, "*How* has this been accomplished? We answer, By the conscientious fidelity (as we believe) with which the principal keeper has discharged his duty to the state; in the judicious and systematic arrangement and employment of the convicts, aided by experienced and intelligent mechanics as assistant keepers — men who know their duty, and have performed it faithfully."

Again they say, —

"We feel peculiar pleasure in having it in our power, even in the infant state of the new Penitentiary, to bear testimony to the beneficial effects of the Pennsylvania system upon the minds and morals of many of the convicts."

They then mention the great change which had taken place in the minds of many old convicts, who were removed from the old Prison, and say, with very few exceptions, every convict removed here, who can read, bears unequivocal evidence of their improved condition, and, almost to a man, regret that they were ever placed at social labor; dreading to meet again with their old associates in crime after the expiration of their sentence.

"This simple fact alone speaks volumes as to the vast superiority of separate confinement, with labor and instruction, in ameliorating the condition of the convict, over every other system of Prison discipline that we have any knowledge of."

"In solitary confinement, every prisoner who can read has placed within his reach the Word of Life, and we have good reason to believe that not a few of these unfortunate men peruse it daily to advantage — as their orderly conduct abundantly testifies."

"We have watched with great solicitude the conduct of those who have been committed to the new Penitentiary within the past year for the first offence, *who can read;* and, thus far, both from the report of the principal and assistant keepers, and our own personal observation, we are inclined to think favorably."

"But when we turn to the moral degradation, too glaring in those cells, where the miserable inmate has never been blessed with even the rudiments of moral culture, would you witness the stern severity of the Pennsylvania system of separate confinement with labor in its most appalling form, you will find it there; where the unfortunate victim of neglected education is placed, by his violation of a law, of which, perchance, he is ignorant; without one ray of hope glimmering upon his benighted mind, save the occasional instruction he receives from a keeper, the casual official visitors who may chance to call upon him, or the distant voice of the minister of the gospel, in his labor of love on Sabbath afternoon. All else to him is one vast vacuum; the mind has nothing else to rest on for relief; labor and sleep are his only comforters; and, in his distress of mind, he either sinks down into stupidity, an object more of pity than of punishment, or, reckless of life, in his narrow cell, he sets the majesty of the law at defiance, resists the authority of his keepers, and subjects himself to the salutary restraints necessary to sustain good order in the institution."

"Convinced, as we are, of the superiority of the Pennsylvania system of separate confinement, with labor, on the minds of the more enlightened convicts, we are well satisfied that it cannot be considered as complete, until moral and religious instruction is carried daily into every cell in the new Penitentiary. We consider that the most benevolent feature in the system is the moral reformation of the convict. But this cannot be effected without the means to accomplish that end. And as, from the favorable operations of the institution for the past year, we have reason to hope that (if prudently managed) it will hereafter sustain itself, we would respectfully suggest the appointment (either by the honorable the legislature or the board of inspectors) of a suitable person, with a reasonable compensation, *as a teacher*, to give daily instruction to those of the convicts who cannot read, and also to the whole of the convicts, in the duties which they owe to their Creator, to society, and to themselves ; one who would lay sectarian feelings at the threshold of the Prison, and enter upon his duties in this moral wilderness with a persevering determination to impart, as far as in his power, useful instruction to those ignorant beings ; nor consider his labors as completed, until he has taught each convict to read for himself the glad tidings of salvation. We believe that instruction of this nature, and carried out in this way, would do more towards reclaiming and reforming the convict, than the most polished and eloquent discourses, delivered publicly at stated periods.

" If you would reach those benighted and abandoned immortals, effectually, it must be done in their cells."

The inspectors recommend the purchase of moral and religious books for the use of the convicts, and express an opinion adverse to the frequent granting of pardons. On the whole, this first report of the New Jersey Penitentiary is so favorable, that, if followed by others of a like character, and indicative of progressive improvement, it would speak volumes in favor of the Pennsylvania system. As the only motive is, or should be, to ascertain the truth, let us pursue the inquiry from year to year, and obtain the information from the official documents, the annual reports of the institution.

The second report afforded no evidence of the tendency of the system to diminish crime, either from the number of prisoners in confinement, or the number of commitments during the year. The former had increased from 141 to 163, and the latter from 63 to 78. A private letter announced the fact, that there had been 3 recommitments already from those discharged. The effect on life and health was not favorable, 5 having died, which is at least 3 per cent., 1 per cent. more than it ought to be, and many having been sick. The effect on the body, as well as the mind, is thus stated by the physician, James B. Coleman, in the second annual report : —

" The close confinement of prisoners in the New Jersey Penitentiary, so different from that of the old Prison, must give rise to the question, whether being debarred from open air, sunlight, and suitable exercise, does not produce derangements of the system of a peculiar character. From the observations of the past year, I am convinced that there are diseases peculiar to the Prison, and which will make the report less favorable to the health in the institution than what is expected.

" The tendency to glandular obstruction is seen in almost every prisoner who has been confined in the cells for more than a year, when he is in the least degree indisposed. The complexion is pale, of a dropsical hue, such as continued shade almost always produces, and the symptoms of disease of the internal organs are of the character that mark the languid action which prevails under such circumstances. Some *post mortem* examinations have been made, and in all of them the lymphatic glands were enlarged to an enormous degree, indurated and obstructed. There is reason to believe, had these deaths occurred in out-of-door practice, the same state of this important part of the system would not have been found. The obscure pains and dyspeptic symptoms that trouble many of the prisoners, are owing, no doubt, to similar obstructions, which must be regarded as the effect of solitary confinement, such as obtains in the New Jersey Penitentiary. The ranges of cells that have a southern exposure, and into which a small portion of direct sunlight is admitted, are the most healthy. In them there is less disease than in the others.

" The effect of solitary confinement upon the mind deserves some notice. In many instances there is remarked that weakness of intellect which results from an unexercised mind. The nervous system must suffer with the other parts of the body, from the causes already mentioned. If the prisoner's mind, on his admission into the cell, has not been of a reflective character, and capable of exercising itself on abstract subjects, imbecility is soon manifested, which leads him to amuse himself in the most childlike employments. If this confinement were continued for many years, such individuals would, no doubt, become permanently injured in their faculties.

" There is a practice in which many of the prisoners indulge, to which I must here call your attention, and which, under existing circumstances, it seems almost impossible to prevent. I allude to Onanism. This, as far as I have been informed, is not confined to our Penitentiary. It is the vice of solitary confinement. Apart from observation, they give up to their depraved propensities, and in a short time produce a very obvious effect upon the system. But it is then too late to warn them against the consequences; the mind has lost its control over their passions, and they become maniacal or imbecile. Of the cases of mental derangement now in the Prison, almost all of them can be traced to this abuse."

The inspectors seem inclined not to coincide in opinion with Dr. Coleman entirely. They say, —

" The influence of close confinement, and the expulsion of the sun's rays on the health of the prisoners, is a subject which has particularly engaged the attention of the physician, and to his report we respectfully refer you for the result of his observation. On this subject we will remark, however, that we have seen no evidence of the ruinous effects on the constitutions of the convicts, which have been ascribed to this mode of imprisonment. The prisoners generally present a pale and rather unhealthy appearance; but this, we believe, is in consequence of living entirely in the shade, and not an effect of disease. In corroboration of this, we have observed that some who present this appearance most strongly, enjoy uninterrupted health."

The number of deaths is palliated, both by the physician and inspectors, as being cases of men diseased when they came into the Prison.

With respect to earnings this year, the inspectors say they were \$1,541 74, above expenses; but they were obliged to draw on the treasury for the payment of officers' salaries, amounting to $6,192 49, owing, they say, to the failure of one of the contractors. Still the inspectors and the keeper express confident expectations that they shall be able, here-after, to support the institution without calling upon the treasury.

The editor of the State Gazette, published at Trenton, N. J., February 1, 1839, says, —

" For our own part, we confess that the two years' experience of this state in the system of solitary confinement has not fully answered our expec-tations."

A correspondent of the same paper, of the same date, one of the most intelligent, influential, and candid men in New Jersey, since, we believe, elevated to the bench of the Supreme Court, says, —

" I am one of those who had the most sanguine expectations from the faith-ful application of the system of separate confinement. But I do nevertheless confess, that your own reports " (addressing the inspectors) " have occasioned many misgivings."

" Among the fondest anticipations, one of the most prominent was, that it would prove such a terror to rogues, as greatly to lessen the number in con-finement. This anticipation, it cannot be denied, has failed to be realized. Your keeper, in his report, candidly admits this. The number of recommit-ments are quite as great in this state and in Pennsylvania as in New York, Connecticut, and Massachusetts.

" That the separate confinement plan would prove detrimental to the bodily and mental health of the prisoners was, from the first, one of the strongest objections to it. What have been the results of a few years' experience ? The report of your own physician says, ' I am convinced there are diseases peculiar to the Prison.' No one can read his report without feeling the most painful apprehensions. The case is the same in regard to the new Peniten-tiary in Philadelphia. The proportional number of deaths has been greater than in other Prisons ; and the number of cases of insanity so great, as to be truly alarming ; at least so it appears to me, although I am aware that the in spectors express a different opinion.

" In regard to the expense of the two systems, the friends of solitary con-finement did not expect so much. It must be allowed, however, that, in this particular, the other system is the best. After the immense expense incurred in the Philadelphia prison, it comes greatly short of supporting itself. Ours has done better. Nominally, it has earned something ; but in reality, it has been a tax on the treasury. It cost about $200,000, the interest of which is $12,000. The Connecticut State Prison cost only about $45,000, accommo-dating 200 prisoners, and in 10 years has paid for itself, and earned a surplus exceeding $10,000.

" There are, no doubt, some things in which the New Jersey system of im-prisonment is superior to that practised in Massachusetts and several other states. But there are others in which those systems are superior to ours. Theirs, I think, are superior, besides the particulars above noticed, in the facilities they afford for religious and moral instruction."

On the whole, the aspect of the second year's results is far less favorable than the first.

The third year's report shows a diminution of 3 prisoners ;

but 37 were pardoned — a very large number. The commitments were 1 less than the previous year. The deaths 2 — a favorable bill of mortality. Expenses above earnings, $5,584 16.

Effect of the System on the Mind. — The physician says, —

"The report of this year, if it merely embraced the number of sick and the deaths, would be very brief — an unusual degree of health, with but few aggravated cases of disease, and but 1 death. But, gentlemen, this is not all that is expected from an office that gives such opportunities to investigate the effects of solitary confinement.

"In the last report, it was stated that there was a tendency among the convicts to glandular obstructions. The experience of the year now ended has confirmed what was then reported. In this region, the past year has been one of almost unprecedented health; and no disease has prevailed within the Prison, which may not be expected during the most favored seasons. It has been the best opportunity to observe the sole influence of solitary confinement on the health of the prisoners. The enervating influence that has been felt during the past year is what will ever be experienced.

"There are some among the convicts who came from the old Prison. While there, they were in strong health, and, for the first two years, in this Penitentiary, complained but little. Now, they have become debilitated, are languid, and exhibit decided symptoms of a decline of their physical powers.

"Among the prisoners are many cases of insanity. Some, on their admission, showed symptoms of derangement, and since then have continued in the same state. Almost all the cases that have occurred in the Prison can be traced to Onanism. Among the prisoners there are many who exhibit a child-like simplicity, which shows them to be less acute than when they entered. In all who have been more than a year in the Prison, some of these effects have been observed. Continue the confinement for a longer time, and give them no other exercise of the mental faculties than this kind of imprisonment affords, and the most accomplished rogue will lose his capacity for depredating with success upon the community. The same influence that injures the other organs will soften the brain. Withhold its proper exercise, and, as sure as the bandaged limb loses its power, will the prisoner's faculties be weakened by solitary confinement."

After stating how much attention is paid to the prisoners by the warden and other officers, to interest their minds and improve their character, he says, —

"Were another course pursued in this institution, and the superintendent possessed of no sympathy with the convict, nor desire for his reformation, feeling satisfied if he tasked him to the full amount of his ability to labor, and gave him food at the appointed times, in less than a year, the New Jersey Penitentiary would be a Bedlam.

"The practice alluded to in the last report, and which seems to be an evil hard to prevent, is perhaps not so general as it was at that time. The derangements and deaths that have resulted from the practice have become a warning to many, and caused a partial relinquishment of the habit. As may be expected where so many are confined, there is still much of the solitary vice.

"There are generally from 10 to 20 on the sick list: some of them are predisposed to consumption, and 2 or 3 have the disease in a confirmed state, and will die in Prison, unless they are pardoned out. Of all the cases that occur, those disposed to consumption are most unmanageable in solitary confinement.

"These observations have been made with no predilections for any kind of Prison discipline." Signed by James B. Coleman.

The fourth report shows a decrease in the number of prisoners of 8 from the beginning to the close of the year. Number pardoned, 24. Number for second, third, or fourth time, 27 — whether to this Prison is not stated. Number of deaths, 2. Very favorable in appearance ; but the physician says, "Some have been pardoned on account of inroads made upon health by the system, who have died soon after they left the Prison." He does not say how many. Expenses above earnings, $512 45, officers' salaries not included, having been paid from the state treasury.

The inspectors say, —

" For the particulars of the prisoners' health, we refer you to the physician's report, believing that there are evils peculiar to solitary confinement as it is here applied, and that the principal derangement of health is owing to insufficient warmth and bad ventilation — conditions in punishment that ought to be avoided.

" From the keeper's report it will be perceived, that the money operations have not been as favorable as could be wished.

" On the subject of solitary confinement, viewed in a moral light, the board have to report but a few changes for the better, among the convicts. The board undoubtingly believe that the solitary system is the best of all others.

" According to the physician's report, there are 12 deranged persons in the Prison, and more than half fit subjects for a Lunatic Asylum when received.

" The moral condition of the convicts has been less the subject of attention, during the past year, than any preceding time within this institution.

" The board acknowledge their obligations to the clergy of Trenton, no chaplain or moral instructor having been appointed."

The physician says, in his fourth report, —

" The effect of solitary confinement on the prisoners in this institution is well determined, however different it may seem from what is reported of other similar establishments. As the punishment is carried out in this place, the result upon the convict is a diminished force of his organs generally ; and particularly a weakening of the muscular fibre ; obstruction of lymphatic glands, and vitiated nervous action. The mind suffers, in this state of the organs, when absolute derangement does not take place."

" In this Prison, as much attention is paid to the health of the convicts as the nature of their confinement will admit. Wholesome food, abundantly supplied, sufficient clothing, cleanliness, kind treatment, all tend to make their situation as comfortable as possible. When sickness requires a departure from the law, the convict has a nurse in his cell, or he has the privilege of taking the air in the yard. As far, then, as this mode of treatment extends, every opportunity is afforded to make the system of punishment tolerable. But still the injurious effects are a constant cause of complaint among the prisoners ; and as they are making applications for pardon on this ground more than any other, the physician is constantly solicited for certificates of health, under the belief that his statements will go far to induce the court to suppose a further confinement will destroy the life of the petitioner. Some have been pardoned for this reason, who have died soon after they left the Prison."

" As the tendency of the present system is injurious to the health of the convict, such alterations ought to be made in the arrangements of the Prison as will insure the greatest degree of health, consistently with the plan of solitary confinement. Some change ought to be made in heating and ventilating the cells. This is imperiously demanded. Confinement in a small, unventilated room will produce any where, and on almost any animal, the very effects which have been observed in our Penitentiary. Some pathologists have lately been trying experiments on animals to prove the defects of a sufficiency of air and light, and the results of all their trials have been a development of tubercles in the lungs, and glandular obstructions — the very state of the organs that is produced in our Prison. It was said in a former report, that *post mortem* examinations had shown excessive glandular obstructions; and also, that of all diseases, those of the chest were the most unmanageable."

"There are now, amongst the 152 prisoners, 12 deranged men. More than half of these were fit for a Lunatic Asylum when they were received. Instead of receiving any benefit from their confinement, they became confirmed in their malady. The other cases of derangement have occurred in the Prison from masturbation and from the nature of the confinement."

In the sixth and last report of the New Jersey Prison, it appears that the number received the last year is 15 less than the year before; and the number in confinement at the close of the year, 14 less than at the commencement. The number of pardons was but 13, and there had been no death. The number of recommitments the last year is not stated, although it appears from a table in the annual report, that, of the whole number of prisoners, 112, 25 were for second, third, or fourth offences. It does not appear from the report how many of these had been in the new Penitentiary more than once. The warden's account shows, that the earnings above *total* expenses are $4,178 22. This is the language of the account. Total expenses, however, do not include officers' salaries, paid from the state treasury, amounting, in the second year, to $6,192 41. The warden states how much money he paid into the treasury from surplus earnings, but he does not state how much was drawn out for the salary of the officers. In what sense this is earnings above total expenses is not easily seen. Notwithstanding this, the sixth and last report of the new Penitentiary in New Jersey is the most favorable ever submitted since the institution went into operation. The inspectors say there has been no death. By this they mean, of a prisoner. A child, born in the Prison within three months after the mother's commitment, they say, survived but a few hours, and they add, "We believe its premature death was occasioned by the close confinement of the mother." It would seem as if the sternness and severity of solitary confinement itself might give way in such circumstances, and spare the life of the infant child whose birthplace is a Prison. The inspectors immediately go on to say, that the health of the Prison is much better than in any previous year; that the business operations are in a prosperous condition; that 1,600 dollars have been paid into the state treasury; that 2,848 dollars and 6 cents remain cash in hand. They say nothing of the money drawn from the treasury for the support of the officers, and no allusion is made, in any part of the report, to the fact. The new heating apparatus answers a better purpose than the old. They do not tell in what the difference consists. We believe the old was by hot-water pipes, and the new by heated air. The library has been wisely increased with the 100 dollars appropriated by the legislature for this purpose. And the inspectors say, in conclusion, —

" In our intercourse with the prisoners, we have no reason to recommend a change from the present system of solitary confinement, but are still better satisfied of its efficiency as a mode of punishment, and better calculated to produce a reformation than one more social."

What does the physician say, on these great points, in regard to the present system of solitary confinement, and the importance of changing it ? He says, —

" Knowing the circumstances under which mind and body suffer most, care is taken to avoid all such evils as far as practicable. And now, while we admit the enervating tendency of solitary confinement, we can report for the last year no death amongst an average of 141 prisoners. There have been but a few on the sick list at any time during the year, and no case of insanity has originated in the house during this time."

Why is this? we ask. How is this change effected ? The same physician, who has been writing for years concerning the ruinous effects, on body and mind, of solitary confinement, now suddenly changes the tone of his communication to the public. The inspectors say, —

" We have no reason to recommend a change from the present system of solitary confinement."

Again we ask, What does the physician say ? He says, —

" These very favorable results are to be attributed to the constant employment furnished the convicts, *and also to the treatment the prisoner receives on the first appearance of disease. If his mind begin to fail, and he shows symptoms of derangement,* ANOTHER CONVICT IS PUT WITH HIM IN HIS CELL. *This invariably restores the patient.* When that state of the system is induced, which experience has taught us is peculiar to close confinement, and with it symptoms of an aggravated character are beginning to appear, the patient is suffered to go into the yard a portion of each day, or has employment found him out of his cell. This likewise is prompt in arresting disease. Attention to these points make the system much less objectionable than when a less reasonable course is pursued.

" *If* the present plan be continued," he adds, " leaving it to the judgment of those in the management of the Prison how to proportion the exercise of the convicts to their actual wants ; when to give them *society* for mental relief; when to indulge them with the air of the yard for sickness, making a separate rather than a solitary system, — our institution will stand first in point of excellence."

What, then, is the *present* system of *solitary confinement* spoken of by the inspectors in the New Jersey Penitentiary, which needs no change ? It is putting the convicts together two in a cell, to prevent derangement of mind, when the fatal effects are seen to be approaching, and letting them out into the open air and yard, — how many together we are not told, nor whether under any supervision, — and giving them society for mental relief. If men can be saved from death, and their minds from derangement, by such means, why not do it? Whether it is worth while to wait "till the *mind* begin to fail," before the convicts are put together in an open work-shop, under constant supervision, instead of being put together in a cell by themselves, — and still more whether it is worth while to wait till "that state of the system is induced which is peculiar to close confinement, and with it symptoms of an *aggravated* character are beginning to appear," before they are put to work in open and airy shops, in silence, under constant supervision, instead of letting them out into the yard, debilitated and sick, to do no one knows what, to remain there in idleness, no one knows how many together, nor for what sort of evil communication, — are questions of moment, after the Pennsylvania system of solitary confinement is so far abandoned, as it is at the present time in New Jersey.

HISTORY OF THE RHODE ISLAND PRISON, THE THIRD AND LAST STATE PRISON IN AMERICA ON THE PENNSYLVANIA PLAN.

In August, 1838, the first warden was appointed. He was instructed by the inspectors, before entering upon the duties of his appointment, to visit the Penitentiaries in Pennsylvania and New Jersey, of which this was in imitation, for the purpose of obtaining information. The first 4 convicts to the solitary cells in this Prison were received on the 16th of November, 1838. Ten, in all, were in Prison when the inspectors made their second report, in October, 1839.

The inspectors' first report contains nothing in regard to the operation of the system upon the body, mind, or morals of the prisoners.

The inspectors say, in their second report, 1839, —

" It is as yet but the very commencement of an experiment in this state to diminish crime and reform criminals. There is good reason to anticipate successful results, and to believe that it may be carried on without pecuniary loss to the state for the support of its convicts."

Again they say, at this early period in the history of the institution, —

" Of the effect of the discipline and regimen of the State Prison upon the convicts, the inspectors have a very favorable opinion. Experience shows it to be beneficial, rather than injurious to health." " The effect of idleness and solitude upon them," (i. e. before labor was introduced,) " greatly aggravated their discontent and wretchedness." "Sufficient time has not elapsed to form an estimate of the result in this state as to its expenses." "How far it is reasonable to expect success from efforts to reform adult criminals, it is a difficult matter to determine." "Perhaps no condition can be imagined, in which they could be placed, all circumstances considered, more advantageously for society and for themselves." "The cells were constructed with a view to prevent all communication between the prisoners; but they only partially effect that object."

The physician, Dr. Hartshorn, expresses no opinion, in his second report, in regard to the effects of the system. The number of prisoners was 10. He says, "There have been 12 cases of sickness." The convicts being known only by number, those reported sick were, "No. 3, four times; No. 4, twice; No. 5, twice; No. 6, twice; No. 7, once; No. 9, once."

The physician, in his third report, October, 1840, says, —

" During the year ending with the present month, there have occurred in the Prison 29 cases requiring his professional services."

Again he says, —

" Considering the small number of prisoners, not averaging over 10 or 12, there has been a great amount of sickness. It may reasonably be doubted whether any 50 men, taken promiscuously, would be found to have the same amount of sickness in the same period of time. As to the causes, one has unquestionably been bad or imperfect ventilation; on the plea of choking the ventilators, that thereby the heat of the cells was retained."

Once more he says, —

" A great variety of medicines have been administered, with only partial and temporary benefit. Air and exercise, the obvious remedies, although recommended, could not, it seems, consistent with Prison discipline, be allowed to any advantageous extent."

No. 7 was taken out of his cell.

" The privilege," says the physician, " of fixing his eyes upon new objects, and of breathing a better atmosphere, drove the hectic flush from his cheek, and gave a new impulse to his system." — *Extracts from Physician's Report; Assembly's Documents, pages 46, 47, and 48.*

The warden says, in the same document, —

" The experience of two years has convinced the warden, that little or no profit can be realized from the labor of men committed to solitary confinement for the term of one year. And I find it to be the opinion of those of longer experience, that it is too short a time to produce any good moral effect upon minds long bent on mischief."
" Several gentlemen have devoted considerable time, during the year, to the moral and religious instruction of the convicts, which has been kindly and profitably received by them; and several of them are anxious to receive instruction in such branches of learning as would be advantageous to them in after life; feeling, as they do, that their confinement will prove to them a lasting blessing."

We find no report from the inspectors among the public documents for the third year.

The physician's report for the fourth year is comprehended in ten lines. Dr. Richmond Brownell says, —

"The undersigned, having been appointed physician to the State Prison on the 14th of July last," (the report was presented to the legislature in October; the physician therefore had held the office about three months,) "would report, that he has attended to the duties of that office. He has visited the Prison 55 times since his appointment. Most of the prisoners have been troubled with bowel complaints; there have been several cases of dysentery; but few of them, however, have given much alarm. Nos. 6 and 22 are laboring under mental derangement, and it is feared No. 24 will be a case of the same character."

The inspectors say, in their fourth report, —

"The general management of the Prison has been on the same principles as during the preceding year. Since July last, attempts have been made to enforce a more strict discipline. The little variety of punishment permitted by law, makes it difficult to compel order and obedience. Deprivation of food and furniture are almost the only punishments that can be inflicted; and the want of food has, in some cases, been endured until great weakness resulted. In one case of very gross insubordination, the inspectors directed that the convict should be placed in irons, which have been worn for several weeks without producing the desired effect of prompt obedience. The punishments now in use are not sufficient to produce so strict a discipline as ought to be maintained."

"By the warden's report, it will be perceived that the labor done in the Prison is not a source of profit to the state. This results partly from the fact that separate confinement prevents constant inspection. Many are inclined to be idle, and the undersigned believe that the cases in which the taking away of labor would be considered by the convicts to be a hardship, are very rare."

"The inspectors recommend that a law be enacted forbidding persons outside of the Prison from communicating with the convicts at all, and that it should be made highly penal for a convict to attempt to escape, or to assault an officer of the Prison. The attention of the inspectors has been drawn to this subject by the discovery of a well-arranged plan of insurrection, which, had it not been detected, might (for aught we can see) have been carried into effect."

"The inspectors further report, that the experiment of solitary confinement has not, since the Prison has been in operation, proved perfectly satisfactory. They fear the effect is to injure strong minds, and to produce imbecility or insanity in those that are weak. They recommend your honorable body to consider if you ought not to direct the erection of work-shops, in which the convicts may be compelled to labor, under constant supervision."

Signed,
"THOMAS M. BURGESS,
ROGER W. POTTER,
BARZILLAI CRANSTON,
GEORGE RICE, } Inspectors."
MARTIN STODDARD,
CHRIS. RHODES,
AMHERST EVERETT,

The inspectors, in their fifth report, October session of the legislature, 1842, say, —

"The affairs of the Prison have been conducted on the same plan as during the previous year. Since the passage of the law authorizing corporal punishment, no case has occurred to require its infliction; but the advantage of possessing the authority is apparent. The undersigned respectfully renew their recommendation that you would cause a full examination to be made both of the State Prison and County Jail, with a view to deciding whether the present mode of separate confinement is not expensive to the state, and injurious to the minds of the convicts."

"Of the 37 convicts who have been committed to the State Prison, 6 have become insane, of whom 4 now remain in Prison; 1 has been cured, and 1 discharged. Several others have at times exhibited slight symptoms of derangement."

This report is signed by the same inspectors as the last. The physician says, in his fifth report, —

"Nos. 6, 19, 22, and 23, are in a state of mental derangement. No. 20 was deranged for several weeks previous to the expiration of the time for which he was committed; but immediately improved in health on being set at liberty, and is believed at this time to be of sane mind.   RICHARD BROWNELL."

Since the above was written, the Pennsylvania system has been abandoned in Rhode Island, and the convicts removed from their solitary cells into the spacious corridor of the Prison, which is now used as a work-shop by day, while the convicts are lodged in their solitary cells at night.

THE EXPERIMENT OF SOLITARY CONFINEMENT TRIED AND ABANDONED IN MAINE.

[From the Second Report, 1827.]

"In the Maine Prison, which has been in operation about three years, a large number of the convicts have been sentenced to six months' solitary confinement day and night, and to a period of time afterwards of solitary confinement at night and hard labor by day. A considerable number more have been sentenced to solitary confinement day and night, for the whole term of their imprisonment. This Prison is under the management of a gentleman who has been a member of the senate in the state of Maine, and who is also a skilful physician. He has therefore been intrusted with discretionary power, by the executive, to remove the men from the cells to the hospital, when their health and life required it. The former governor of the state informed the secretary of this society, that it would not have been thought safe to inflict sentences of so long continuance in solitary confinement, if great confidence had not been placed in the discretion of the superintendent. The judges, however, and the executive, when the Prison was built, were strongly in favor of solitary confinement day and night, and they wished to make a fair experiment. What, then, is the testimony of the superintendent of this Prison, on this vastly important and interesting subject? And what is the testimony of the records of the Prison? The following statement is collected from the records and the superintendent. It exhibits the names of several convicts; the length of time they were sentenced to solitary confinement; the length of time they were able to endure it before they were removed to the hospital; the length of time they remained in the hospital before they returned to the cells; the alternation between the cells and the hospital to fulfil the whole term of solitary confinement; and the suicide of two convicts in the cells. These are the only convicts who have died since the Prison was organized.

Name and Sentence.	*In Solitary.*	*In Hospital.*	*In Solitary.*
"Joseph Bubier,	June 18.	July 1.	12 days.
62 days' solitary,	July 3.	July 8.	5 days.
and 1 year	July 11.	July 23.	12 days.
hard labor.	July 28.	Aug. 24.	27 days.

"In this case, it was necessary to remove the man to the hospital 4 times, to enable him to endure 56 days' solitary. The secretary saw him when he was removed from the cell the last time. He shivered like an aspen leaf; his pulse was very feeble; his articulation could scarcely be heard from his bed to the grate of his cell, 8 feet; and when he was taken out, he could with difficulty stand alone.

Name and Sentence.	*Solitary.*	*Suicide.*	*In Solitary.*
"Simeon Record,	Dec. 5.	Dec. 8.	4 days.
70 days' solitary, and			
4 years' hard labor.			

"At half past seven o'clock, on Wednesday morning, he was found dead, having hung himself to the grate of the cell with a piece of the lashing of his hammock.

Name and Sentence.	*Solitary.*	*At Labor.*	*In Solitary.*
"Isaac Martin,	March 27.	April 20.	24 days.
60 days' solitary, and	July 1.	July 26.	25 days.
3 months' hard labor.			

"Isaac Martin cut his throat in his cell July 26, when he was removed to the hospital, where he remained nine days, and died.

Name and Sentence.	*Solitary.*	*Hospital.*	*Solitary.*
"Elisha Cole,	Nov. 6.	Dec. 28.	52 days.
100 days' solitary.	Jan. 4.	Feb. 22.	48 days.

Name and Sentence.	*Solitary.*	*Hospital.*	*Solitary.*
"Socrates Howe,	July 4.	Sept. 7.	66 days.
6 months' solitary.	Sept. 21.	Nov. 7.	47 days.
	Dec. 2.	Jan. 16.	44 days.
	Jan. 19.	Feb. 12.	23 days.

Name and Sentence.	*Solitary.*	*Hospital.*	*Solitary.*
"Nathaniel Parsons,	July 3.	Aug. 16.	43 days.
6 months' solitary.	Aug. 19.	Aug. 27.	8 days.
	Aug. 28.	Sept. 17.	20 days.

"This man remained in the hospital, after his discharge from the cell the last time, from September 17 till December 3, when he was pardoned on account of ill health.

Name and Sentence.	*Solitary.*	*Hospital.*	*Solitary.*
"Edmund Eastman,	Sept. 9.	Jan. 9.	4 months.
4 months' solitary.			

"This man endured the whole period without leaving the cell.

"Asa Allen was sentenced to 6 months' solitary and 2 years 3 months and 14 days' hard labor. He went immediately into solitary, and remained 74 days without interruption. At the end of this period, he came out in good health, and performed a good day's labor in the quarry. Dr. Rose expresses the opinion, that this man would live in solitary confinement about as well and as long as any where else. He has been a *soldier*, and has been accustomed to the hardships of a camp. He has been a wanderer in the world, without a home. It is not material to him where he is. The keeper thinks that 6 months' solitary to this man would not be a greater punishment than 15 days' to a convict who had been accustomed to the comforts of life ; also, that he would rather endure 6 months' solitary confinement than 10 stripes.

" John Stevens and John Cain both entered the Prison at the same time, under sentence of 3 months' solitary, and both endured the whole period without interruption, having received nothing except the usual allowance of bread and water, and a little camphor to rub on their heads.

" Benjamin Williams, also, endured 3 months' solitary without interruption.

" But, in general, the superintendent states, that nearly as much time is necessary in the hospital to fulfil long solitary sentences, as in the cells. He also expresses an opinion, in his last report to the legislature, that long periods of solitary imprisonment inflicted on convicts, are worse than useless as a means of reformation. The character of the superintendent of this Prison is such, that the opinions expressed by him on this subject, as the results of his experience, will be thought worthy of particular consideration. He says, ' The great diversity of character, as it respects habits and temperament of body and mind, renders solitary imprisonment a very unequal punishment. Some persons will endure solitary confinement without appearing to be much debilitated, either in body or mind, while others sink under much less, and, if the punishment was unremittingly continued, would die, or become incurably insane.

" ' However persons of strong minds, who suffer in what they deem a righteous cause, may be able to endure solitary confinement, and retain their bodily and mental vigor, yet it is not to be expected of criminals, with minds discouraged by conviction and disgrace.

" ' Those persons who shudder at the cruelty of inflicting stripes as a punishment, but can contemplate the case of a fellow-being, suffering a long period of solitary imprisonment, without emotion, must be grossly ignorant of the mental and bodily suffering endured by a long confinement in solitude.

" ' As far as the experience in our State Prison proves any thing respecting the efficacy of solitary imprisonment in preventing crimes by reforming convicts, it will induce us to believe that it is not more effectual than confinement to hard labor. Seven of the convicts now in the State Prison are committed a second time, for crimes perpetrated after having been discharged from this Prison ; three of these had been punished by solitary imprisonment without labor, and the others by solitary imprisonment and confinement to hard labor.

" ' The keeper of the Auburn State Prison, in the state of New York, very justly observes, " that a degree of mental distress and anguish may be necessary to humble and reform an offender ; but carry it too far, and he will become a savage in his temper and feelings, or he will sink in despair. There is no doubt, that uninterrupted solitude tends to sour the feelings, destroy the affections, harden the heart, and induce men to cultivate a spirit of revenge, or drive them to despair."

" ' I would not wish to be understood to express an opinion, that solitary imprisonment ought not, in any case, to be inflicted. On the contrary, there can be no doubt that it is a proper punishment for Prison discipline in many cases ; but for that purpose, short periods only will be necessary ; seldom, if ever, to exceed 10 days. In the cases of juvenile offenders, it may also be very useful and proper, in periods of 20 or 30 days, but never to exceed 60 days. If repentance and amendment are not effected by 30 days of strict solitary confinement, it can rarely be expected to be obtained by a longer period.'

" The legislature of Maine, in consideration of the opinions and facts above stated, passed a law, in February, 1827, in the words following : ' *Be it enacted,* that all punishments, by imprisonment in the State Prison, shall be by confinement to hard labor, and not by solitary imprisonment: provided, that nothing herein contained shall preclude the use of solitary confinement as a Prison discipline for the government and good order of the prisoners.' "

THE EXPERIMENT OF SOLITARY CONFINEMENT TRIED AND ABANDONED IN NEW YORK.

" At Auburn, N. Y., the experiment was tried in 1822, by the friends of solitary confinement day and night, on 80 convicts, for a period of 10 months. The experiment was conducted with great care, and the observations made appear to have been impartial. As it was done by the friends of the system, it may be supposed that the results were as favorable as they could make them. In the report of the commissioners to the legislature, in January, 1825, these results are stated with philosophical accuracy. Concerning these results, it is sufficient to say, that they were unfavorable to this mode of punishment, and it was accordingly abandoned in that Prison. It was found, in many instances, to injure the health ; to impair the reason ; to endanger the life ; to leave the men enfeebled and unable to work when they left the Prison, and as ignorant of any useful business as when they were committed ; and, consequently, more productive of recommitments, and less of reformation, than solitary confinement at night and hard labor by day."

The commissioners' report was as follows : —

" From a pretty close examination of the prisoners, as to the effects of solitary confinement upon their constitutions and general health, we were led to the conclusion, that, upon most of them, the effects were injurious ; particularly upon those who had been in confinement 1 year and upwards. They generally complained of excessive weakness and debility ; some of violent, and others of slight affections of the lungs ; some of rheumatic pains, numbness, and swelling of their limbs, which they described as paralyzed, or frequently falling asleep. One stated that he was ruptured, which he attributed to weakness brought on by his confinement ; and another that he was frequently attacked by convulsions, which left him much debilitated ; several, that they had lost much flesh since their confinement ; that their appetite was poor, and their sleep much disturbed. They generally declared that they would prefer the hardest labor and coarsest food to their present condition, and two of them begged that they might have work in their cells, in order to make the time pass off less irksome. It was the opinion of the inspectors, that, in many cases, confinement in solitude, for a year or more, produces nervous affections or extensive debility, and that, in a few instances, diseases of the lungs have been contracted in solitude, which have proved fatal. Some of the convicts, they observed, would sink under this mode of punishment, unless they were permitted to go into the yard for a few weeks, where fresh air and light labor invigorates their constitutions, and generally restores them to health ; and it was the opinion of the physician, that solitary confinement had an effect, on some constitutions, to accelerate the progress of consumption. The quiet and submissive demeanor of the Auburn prisoners, before mentioned, is strong proof of the power of solitary confinement to subdue the perverse tempers of bad men. But, unfortunately, we have been furnished with no evidence, proving that those who have been released from this punishment by pardon have been made good by the operation. On the contrary, the instances furnished tend to prove the reverse ; for we find that three, who had experienced a long confinement in the cells before they were pardoned, returned to their Prison a few months after their liberation. If any conclusion can be relied on, founded upon a comparison of those who have been in solitude, and those who have not, previous to their pardon, taking into consideration the time they were at large before their second commitment, it would appear that the punishment by labor, with the discipline of the Prison, had been more effectual in retarding the commission of crime than solitude."

With the statement of a majority of the commissioners, the official reports of the Prison entirely coincide. From the report of the physician, for 1823, it appears that there had been 10 deaths, 7 of them by consumption, 5 of whom were from among the solitary convicts. The patients who came into the hospital from the cells were affected with difficulty of respiration and pain in the breast. The following are his words : —

" It is a generally received and acknowledged opinion, that sedentary life — no matter in what form — disposes to debility, and consequently to local diseases. If we review the mental causes of disease, we shall probably find the sedentary life in the Prison, as it calls into aid the debilitating passions of melancholy, grief, &c., rapidly hastens the progress of pulmonary disease."

The report of 1824 stated that, of 9 deaths, 5 were persons who had been in solitary confinement, and who died with consumption, accompanied with effusions of water ; that a number were pardoned by reason of disease, which, by continued confinement, would have terminated in consumption and death, and in fact some cases did so terminate after pardon.

" A number of these convicts became insane while in solitude ; one so desperate, that he sprang from his cell, when the door was opened, and threw himself from the gallery upon the pavement, which nearly killed him, and undoubtedly would have destroyed his life instantly, had not an intervening stove-pipe broken the force of his fall. Another beat and mangled his head against the walls of his cell until he destroyed one of his eyes." — *G. Powers's Account of the Auburn Prison, page* 36.

The result, as before stated, was the abandonment of solitary confinement without labor at Auburn, and the introduction of the system of separate dormitories with joint labor.

THE EXPERIMENT OF SOLITARY CONFINEMENT TRIED AND ABANDONED IN VIRGINIA.

The physician of the Penitentiary, in his report for 1825, says, —

"I believe it to be a duty I owe to my country and to humanity to remark, that, whatever may have been anticipated from the effect of solitary confinement under the present arrangement, the practical operation is not in accordance with the principles upon which the Penitentiary system of punishment was established. Whether it is the climate, the construction and ventilation of our cells, or from what other cause, I am unable to say ; but, from a fair experiment, nothing has presented itself to my observation, since I have had charge of this institution, more destructive to the health and constitution of the convicts, than the 6 months' close and uninterrupted solitary confinement upon their first reception into the Prison. The scurvy and the dropsy are the diseases most prevalent. A demonstration of this fact is known to you, from the frequent application to the proper authorities for their removal from the cells to the hospital, and the length of time remaining there debilitated and emaciated by these distressing maladies, before they are in a condition either to be returned to the cells or put to any regular business." — *Physician's Report for 1825.*

The superintendent of the same Penitentiary says, —

" There is perhaps no punishment that can be •devised, better calculated to keep vice in check, than solitary confinement; but how far this should be extended, consistently with the principles upon which the Penitentiary system was originally established, is a subject which has called forth a variety of opinions. To be close and uninterrupted, (as far as my experience goes,) *it will destroy the constitution of seven tenths of those on whom it is inflicted, and kill many.* To confine for limited periods, and then associate them together, will destroy all the moral effect the confinement has had on the convict. To confine separate, and to work at the same time, (by which the health is preserved,) is perhaps the best plan; but the kind of work that can be done would be unprofitable, and I doubt if any would pay the cost of materials, except shoemaking, which, in a close room, would aid the confinement in destroying the constitution of the prisoner. One of the great objects of the Penitentiary system of punishment, is to put the offender in a condition that may enable him to be useful to himself. If this is not desired at the present day, and the only object sought is to place him where he has no power to injure society, then the close and uninterrupted solitude is the plan. While in this condition, society is as safe as if the offender were dead. Upon being discharged, society would in a great degree be secure; few would have the strength to do much injury, because of their broken-down constitutions; the public would have them generally to maintain. I have not seen but one that stood close solitude 12 months, that was able to get a living from his own labor. It strikes me very forcibly, that the experiment of close solitary confinement (so far as it relates to our climate) would turn loose on society a mass of emaciated human beings, without trade, money, or friends, to be supported by the public, thereby increasing pauperism instead of diminishing it."

THE EXPERIMENT OF SOLITARY CONFINEMENT TRIED AND ABANDONED IN NEW JERSEY.

" The experiment in New Jersey was continued 4 years, previous to 1827, upon an average number of 12 convicts, some of whom have been 18 months, and some 2 years, in the cells, without intermission; but in this case, though the men were in separate cells, still the cells were so arranged, that several men could converse as freely as if they had been in the same room, and no attempt was made to prevent it. This, therefore, is to be regarded no farther as an experiment on solitary confinement day and night, than as keeping the men from seeing or coming in contact with each other, but not from evil communication and corrupt society. In the opinion of the keeper of that Prison, this mode of punishment was useful in preventing recommitments, and not permanently injurious to health or reason."

At the session of the legislature of New Jersey of 1826 and 1827, a joint committee was appointed to examine into the condition of the Prison, who made a report recommending the abandonment of solitary confinement in the following words : —

" They consider solitary confinement as not answering the purposes expected in improving the morals of the prisoners, any more than hard labor, if so much ; and they recommend confinement to hard labor in future as the best mode of punishment, and most productive to the state."

The system was accordingly abandoned in the old Prison till the new Prison was built, when it was again introduced, and is still under experiment, with various modifications.

MR. ROSCOE'S OPINION OF THE PENNSYLVANIA SYSTEM.

Mr. Roscoe, of Liverpool, said, before the new Penitentiary was built, —

" At Philadelphia, as has before been observed, it is intended to adopt the plan of 'solitary confinement in all cases,' *'the duration of the punishment to be fixed,'* and *'the whole term of the sentence to be exacted,'* except in cases where it shall be made to appear, to the satisfaction of the governor, that the party convicted was innocent of the charge.

" By the establishment of a general system of solitary confinement, a greater number of individuals, imprisoned for *minor offences, will probably be put to death,* by the superinduction of diseases inseparable from such a mode of treatment, than will be executed through the whole state, for the *perpetration of the most atrocious crimes ;* with this remarkable difference, that the law has provided for the heinous offender a brief, and perhaps an unconscious fate, whilst the solitary victim passes through every variety of misery, and terminates his days by an *accumulation of sufferings which human nature can no longer bear."*

GENERAL LAFAYETTE'S OPINION OF THE PENNSYLVANIA SYSTEM.

" As to Philadelphia," says the general, in a letter to Mr. Roscoe, " I had already, on my visit of the last year, expressed my regret that the great expenses of the new Penitentiary building had been chiefly calculated on the plan of solitary confinement. This matter has lately become an object of discussion ; a copy of your letter, and my own observations, have been requested ; and as both opinions are actuated by equally honest and good feelings, as solitary confinement has never been considered but with a view to reformation, I believe our ideas will have their weight with men who have been discouraged by late failures of success in the reformation plan. It seems to me, two of the inconveniences most complained of might be obviated, in making use of the solitary cells to separate the prisoners at night, and multiplying the rooms of common labor, so as to reduce the number of each room to what it was when the population was less dense — an arrangement which would enable the managers to keep distinctions among the men to be reclaimed, according to the state of their morals, and their behavior." " In these sentiments," says Mr. Roscoe, " I have the pleasure most fully to concur ; and I hold it to be impossible to give a more clear, correct, and impartial decision on the subject."

" The people of Pennsylvania think," said Lafayette, " that the system of solitary confinement is a new idea, a new discovery. Not so ; — it is only the revival of the system of the Bastile. The state of Pennsylvania, which has given to the world an example of humanity, and whose code of philanthropy has been quoted and canvassed by all Europe, is now about to proclaim to the world the inefficacy of the system, and to revive and restore the cruel code of the most barbarous and unenlightened age. I hope my friends of Pennsylvania will consider the effect this system had on the poor prisoners of the Bastile. I repaired to the scene," said he, " on the second day of the demolition, and found that all the prisoners had been deranged by their solitary confinement, except one. He had been a prisoner twenty-five years, and was led forth during the height of the tumultuous riot of the people, whilst engaged in tearing down the building. He looked around with amazement, for he had seen nobody for that space of time, and before night he was so much affected, that he became a confirmed maniac, from which situation he has never recovered."

DR. COMBE'S OPINION OF THE PENNSYLVANIA SYSTEM.

" In regard to the effect of the discipline in the Eastern Penitentiary, l observe, that the system of entire solitude, even when combined with labor and the use of books, and an occasional visit from a religious instructor, leaves the moral faculties still in a passive state, and without the means of vigorous, active exertion. According to my view of the laws of physiology, this discipline reduces the tone of the *whole* nervous system to the level which is in harmony with solitude. The passions are weakened and subdued, but so are all the moral and intellectual powers. The susceptibility of the nervous system is increased, because organs become susceptible of impression in proportion to their feebleness. A weak eye is pained by a degree of light which is agreeable to a sound one. Hence it may be quite true, that religious admonitions will be more deeply felt by prisoners living in solitude than by those enjoying society ; just as such instruction, when addressed to a patient recovering from a severe and debilitating illness, makes a more vivid impression than when delivered to the same individual in health ; but the appearances of reformation founded on such impressions are deceitful. When the sentence has expired, the convict will return to society, with all his mental powers, animal, moral, and intellectual, increased in *susceptibility*, but lowered in *strength*. The excitements that will then assail him will have their influence doubled, by operating on an enfeebled system. If he meet old associates, and return to drinking and profanity, the animal propensities will be fearfully excited by the force of these stimulants, while his enfeebled moral and intellectual will scarcely be capable of offering any resistance. If he be placed amidst virtuous men, his higher faculties will feel acutely, but be still feeble in executing their own resolves. Convicts, after long confinement in solitude, shudder to encounter the turmoil of the world ; they become excited as the day of liberation approaches, and feel bewildered when set at liberty. In short, this system is not founded on, nor in harmony with, a sound knowledge of the physiology of the brain, although it appeared to me to be well administered."

Again ; " The Auburn system of social labor is better, in my opinion, than that of Pennsylvania, in so far as it allows of a little more stimulus to the social faculties, and does not weaken the nervous system to so great an extent."

Once more ; " Phrenologists have long proclaimed, that the great cause of the incorrigibility of criminals is the excessive predominance of the organs of the animal propensities over those of the moral and intellectual faculties, and that this class of persons is really composed of moral patients, who should be restrained, but not otherwise punished, during life. As Nature is constant in her operations, the truth will in time force itself on the conviction of society ;

and after injustice and severity shall have been perpetrated for ages, by the free and fortunate, towards the ill-constituted and unhappy, a better system of treatment will probably be adopted. Why are the clergy, those guardians of the poor and ministers of mercy, silent on this subject?"—*Notes on America*, *pages* 221, 223, and 224.

"A democracy which refuses moral and religious instruction to convicts, is a greater foe to freedom than the most ruthless despot of Europe."—*Ib.* *page* 220.

DICKENS'S OPINION OF SOLITARY CONFINEMENT, OR THE NEW PENITENTIARY IN PHILADELPHIA.

"In the outskirts stands a great Prison, called the Eastern Penitentiary, conducted on a plan peculiar to the state of Pennsylvania. The system here is rigid, strict, and hopeless solitary confinement. I believe it, in its effects, to be cruel and wrong.

"In its intention, I am well convinced that it is kind, humane, and meant for reformation; but I am persuaded that those who devised this system of Prison discipline, and those benevolent gentlemen who carry it into execution, do not know what it is that they are doing. I believe that very few men are capable of estimating the immense amount of torture and agony which this dreadful punishment, prolonged for years, inflicts upon the sufferers; and in guessing at it myself, and in reasoning from what I have seen written upon their faces, and what, to my certain knowledge, they feel within, I am only the more convinced that there is a depth of terrible endurance in it which none but the sufferers themselves can fathom, and which no man has a right to inflict upon his fellow-creature.

"I hold this slow and daily tampering with the mysteries of the brain, to be immeasurably worse than any torture of the body: and because its ghastly signs and tokens are not so palpable to the eye and sense of touch as scars upon the flesh; because its wounds are not upon the surface, and it extorts few cries that human ears can hear; therefore I the more denounce it, as a secret punishment which slumbering humanity is not roused up to stay. I hesitated once, debating with myself, whether, if I had the power of saying 'Yes' or 'No,' I would allow it to be tried in certain cases, where the terms of imprisonment were short; but now I solemnly declare, that with no rewards or honors could I walk a happy man, beneath the open sky by day, or lie me down upon my bed at night, with the consciousness that one human creature, for any length of time, no matter what, lay suffering this unknown punishment in his silent cell, and I the cause, or I consenting to it in the least degree.

"I was accompanied to this Prison by two gentlemen officially connected with its management, and passed the day in going from cell to cell, and talking with the inmates. Every facility was afforded me that the utmost courtesy could suggest. Nothing was concealed or hidden from my view, and every piece of information that I sought, was openly and frankly given. The perfect order of the building cannot be praised too highly; and of the excellent motives of all who are immediately concerned in the administration of the system, there can be no kind of question.

"Between the body of the Prison and the outer wall there is a spacious garden. Entering it, by a wicket in the massive gate, we pursued the path before us to its other termination, and passed into a large chamber, from which seven long passages radiate.

"On either side of each is a long, long row of low cell doors, with a certain number over every one; above, a gallery of cells like those below, except that they have no narrow yard attached, (as those in the ground tier have,) and are somewhat smaller. The possession of two of these is supposed to compensate for the absence of so much air and exercise as can be had in the dull strip attached to each of the others, in an hour's time, every day; and therefore every prisoner in this upper story has two cells, adjoining and communicating with each other.

"Standing at the central point, and looking down these dreary passages, the dull repose and quiet that prevails is awful. Occasionally, there is a drowsy sound from some lone weaver's shuttle, or shoemaker's last, but it is stifled by the thick walls and heavy dungeon door, and only serves to make the general stillness more profound. Over the head and face of every prisoner who comes into this melancholy house, a black hood is drawn; and in this dark shroud, an emblem of the curtain dropped between him and the living world, he is led to the cell from which he never again comes forth until his whole term of imprisonment has expired. He never hears of wife or children, home or friends, the life or death of any single creature. He sees the Prison officers; but, with that exception, he never looks upon a human countenance, or hears a human voice. He is a man buried alive, to be dug out in the slow round of years, and in the mean time dead to every thing but torturing anxieties and horrible despair.

"His name, and crime, and term of suffering, are unknown, even to the officer who delivers him his daily food. There is a number over his cell door, and in a book, of which the governor of the prison has one copy, and the moral instructor another. This is the index to his history. Beyond these pages the Prison has no record of his existence; and though he live to be in the same cell ten weary years, he has no means of knowing, down to the very last hour, in what part of the building it is situated; what kind of men there are about him; whether, in the long winter nights, there are living people near, or he is in some lonely corner of the great Jail, with walls, and passages, and iron doors, between him and the nearest sharer in its solitary horrors.

"Every cell has double doors; the outer one of sturdy oak, the other of grated iron, wherein there is a trap, through which his food is handed. He has a Bible and a slate and pencil, and, under certain restrictions, has sometimes other books, provided for the purpose, and pen, and ink, and paper. His razor, plate, and can, and basin, hang upon the wall, or shine upon the little shelf. Fresh water is laid on in every cell, and he can draw it at his pleasure. During the day, his bedstead turns up against the wall, and leaves more space for him to work in. His loom, or bench, or wheel, is there; and there he labors, sleeps, and wakes, and counts the seasons as they change, and grows old.

"The first man I saw was seated at his loom, at work. He had been there six years, and was to remain, I think, three more. He had been convicted as a receiver of stolen goods, but, even after this long imprisonment, denied his guilt, and said he had been hardly dealt by. It was his second offence.

"He stopped his work when we went in, took off his spectacles, and answered freely to every thing that was said to him, but always with a strange kind of pause first, in a low, thoughtful voice. He wore a paper hat of his own making, and was pleased to have it noticed and commended. He had very ingeniously manufactured a sort of Dutch clock from some disregarded odds and ends; and his vinegar-bottle served for the pendulum. Seeing me interested in this contrivance, he looked up at it with a great deal of pride, and said that he had been thinking of improving it, and that he hoped the hammer and a little piece of broken glass beside it 'would play music before long.' He had extracted some colors from the yarn with which he worked, and painted a few poor figures on the wall. One, of a female, over the door, he called 'The Lady of the Lake.'

"He smiled as I looked at these contrivances to wile away the time; but when I looked from them to him, I saw that his lip trembled, and could have counted the beating of his heart. I forget how it came about, but some allusion was made to his having a wife. He shook his head at the word, turned aside, and covered his face with his hands.

"'But you are resigned now!' said one of the gentlemen, after a short pause, during which he had resumed his former manner. He answered with a sigh that seemed quite reckless in his hopelessness. 'O yes, O yes! I am resigned to it.' 'And are a better man, you think?' 'Well, I hope so: I'm sure I hope I may be.' 'And time goes pretty quickly?' 'Time is very long, gentlemen, within these four walls!'

"He gazed about him—Heaven only knows how wearily—as he said these words, and, in the act of doing so, fell into a strange stare, as if he had forgotten something. A moment afterwards, he sighed heavily, put on his spectacles, and went about his work again.

"In another cell, there was a German, sentenced to five years' imprisonment for larceny, two of which had just expired. With colors procured in the same manner, he had painted every inch of the walls and ceiling quite beautifully. He had laid out the few feet of ground, behind, with exquisite neatness, and had made a little bed in the centre, that looked, by the by, like a grave. The taste and ingenuity he had displayed in every thing were most extraordinary; and yet a more dejected, heart-broken, wretched creature, it would be difficult to imagine. I never saw such a picture of forlorn affliction and distress of mind. My heart bled for him; and when the tears ran down his cheeks, and he took one of the visitors aside, to ask, with his trembling hands nervously clutching at his coat to detain him, whether there was no hope of his dismal sentence being commuted, the spectacle was really too painful to witness. I never saw or heard of any kind of misery that impressed me more than the wretchedness of this man.

"In a third cell was a tall, strong black, a burglar, working at his proper trade of making screws and the like. His time was nearly out. He was not only a very dexterous thief, but was notorious for his boldness and hardihood, and for the number of his previous convictions. He entertained us with a long account of his achievements, which he related with such infinite relish, that he actually seemed to lick his lips as he told us racy anecdotes of stolen plate, and of old ladies whom he had watched as they sat at windows in silver spectacles, (he had plainly had an eye to their metal even from the other side of the street,) and had afterwards robbed. This fellow, upon the slightest encouragement, would have mingled with his professional recollections the most detestable cant; but I am very much mistaken if he could have surpassed the unmitigated hypocrisy with which he declared that he blessed the day on which he came into that Prison, and that he never would commit another robbery as long as he lived.

"There was one man who was allowed, as an indulgence, to keep rabbits. His room having rather a close smell in consequence, they called to him at the door to come out in the passage. He complied, of course, and stood shading his haggard face in the unwonted sunlight of the great window, looking as wan and unearthly as if he had been summoned from the grave. He had a white rabbit in his breast; and when the little creature, getting down upon the ground, stole back into the cell, and he, being dismissed, crept timidly after it, I thought it would have been very hard to say in what respect the man was the nobler animal of the two.

"There was an English thief, who had been there but a few days out of seven years; a villanous, low-browed, thin-lipped fellow, with a white face, who had as yet no relish for visitors, and who, but for the additional penalty, would have gladly stabbed me with his shoemaker's knife.

"There was another German, who had entered the Jail but yesterday, and who started from his bed when we looked in, and pleaded, in his broken English, very hard for work. There was a poet, who, after doing two days work in every four-and-twenty hours, one for himself and one for the Prison, wrote verses about ships, (he was by trade a mariner,) and 'the maddening wine-cup,' and his friends at home. There were very many of them. Some reddened at the sight of visitors, and some turned very pale. Some two or three had prisoner nurses with them, for they were very sick; and one fat old negro, whose leg had been taken off within the Jail, had for his attendant a classical scholar and an accomplished surgeon, himself a prisoner likewise. Sitting upon the stairs, engaged in some slight work, was a pretty colored boy. 'Is there no refuge for young criminals in Philadelphia, then?' said I. ' Yes, but only for white children.' Noble aristocracy in crime!

" There was a sailor, who had been there upwards of eleven years, and who in a few months' time would be free. Eleven years of solitary confinement!

" 'I am very glad to hear your time is nearly out.' What does he say? Nothing. Why does he stare at his hands, and pick the flesh upon his fingers, and raise his eyes for an instant, every now and then, to those bare walls, which have seen his head turn gray? It is a way he has sometimes.

" Does he never look men in the face, and does he always pluck at those hands of his, as though he were bent on parting skin and bone? It is his humor: nothing more.

" It is his humor, too, to say that he does not look forward to going out; that he is not glad the time is drawing near; that he did look forward to it once, but that was very long ago; that he has lost all care for every thing. It is his humor to be a helpless, crushed, and broken man. And Heaven be his witness that he has his humor thoroughly gratified!

" There were three young women in adjoining cells, all convicted at the same time of a conspiracy to rob their prosecutor. In the silence and solitude of their lives, they had grown to be quite beautiful. Their looks were very sad, and might have moved the sternest visitor to tears, but not to that kind of sorrow which the contemplation of the men awakens. One was a young girl, not twenty, as I recollect, whose snow-white room was hung with the work of some former prisoner, and upon whose downcast face the sun in all its splendor shone down through the high chink in the wall, where one narrow strip of bright blue sky was visible. She was very penitent and quiet; had come to be resigned, she said, (and I believe her;) and had a mind at peace. ' In a word, you are happy here?' said one of my companions. She struggled — she did struggle very hard — to answer, Yes; but, raising her eyes, and meeting that glimpse of freedom overhead, she burst into tears, and said, ' She tried to be; she uttered no complaint; but it was natural that she should sometimes long to go out of that one cell; she could not help *that*,' she sobbed, poor thing!

" I went from cell to cell that day; and every face I saw, or word I heard, or incident I noted, is present to my mind in all its painfulness. But let me pass them by, for one, more pleasant, glance of a Prison on the same plan, which I afterwards saw at Pittsburg.

" When I had gone over that, in the same manner, I asked the governor if he had any person in his charge who was shortly going out. He had one, he said, whose time was up next day; but he had only been a prisoner two years.

" Two years! I looked back through two years in my own life — out of Jail, prosperous, happy, surrounded by blessings, comforts, and good fortune — and thought how wide a gap it was, and how long those two years passed in solitary captivity would have been. I have the face of this man, who was going to be released next day, before me now. It is almost more memorable in its happiness than the other faces in their misery. How easy and how natural it was for him to say that the system was a good one; and that the time went " pretty quick — considering;' and that, when a man once felt he had offended the law, and must satisfy it, ' he got along, somehow;' and so forth!

" 'What did he call you back to say to you, in that strange flutter?' I asked of my conductor, when he had locked the door and joined me in the passage.

" 'O! that he was afraid that the soles of his boots were not fit for walking, as they were a good deal worn when he came in; and that he would thank me very much to have them mended, ready.'

"These boots had been taken off his feet, and put away with the rest of his clothes, two years before!

"I took that opportunity of inquiring how they conducted themselves immediately before going out; adding that I presumed they trembled very much.

"'Well, it's not so much a trembling,' was the answer—'though they do quiver—as a complete derangement of the nervous system. They can't sign their names to the book; sometimes can't even hold the pen; look about 'em without appearing to know why, or where they are; and sometimes get up and sit down again, twenty times in a minute. This is when they're in the office where they are taken with the hood on, as they were brought in. When they get outside the gate, they stop, and look first one way, and then the other; not knowing which to take. Sometimes they stagger as if they were drunk, and sometimes are forced to lean against the fence, they're so bad;—but they clear off in course of time.'

"On the haggard face of every man among these prisoners, the same expression sat. I know not what to liken it to. It had something of that strained attention which we see upon the faces of the blind and deaf, mingled with a kind of horror, as though they had all been secretly terrified.

"In every little chamber that I entered, and at every grate through which I looked, I seemed to see the same appalling countenance. It lives in my memory, with the fascination of a remarkable picture. Parade before my eyes a hundred men, with one among them newly released from this solitary suffering, and I would point him out.

"The faces of the women, as I have said, it humanizes and refines. Whether this be because of their better nature, which is elicited in solitude, or because of their being gentler creatures, of greater patience, and longer suffering, I do not know; but so it is. That the punishment is, nevertheless, to my thinking, fully as cruel and as wrong in their case as in that of the men, I need scarcely add.

"My firm conviction is, that, independent of the mental anguish it occasions, —an anguish so acute and so tremendous, that all imagination of it must fall far short of the reality,—it wears the mind into a morbid state, which renders it unfit for the rough contact and busy action of the world. It is my fixed opinion, that those who have undergone this punishment, MUST pass into society again morally unhealthy and diseased. There are many instances on record, of men who have chosen, or have been condemned, to lives of perfect solitude; but I scarcely remember one, even among sages of strong and vigorous intellect, where its effect has not become apparent, in some disordered train of thought, or some gloomy hallucination. What monstrous phantoms, bred of despondency and doubt, and born and reared in solitude, have stalked upon the earth, making creation ugly, and darkening the face of heaven!

"Suicides are rare among these prisoners; are almost, indeed, unknown. But no argument in favor of the system can reasonably be deduced from this circumstance, although it is very often urged. All men who have made diseases of the mind their study, know perfectly well, that such extreme depression and despair as will change the whole character, and beat down all its powers of elasticity and self-resistance, may be at work within a man, and yet stop short of self-destruction. This is a common case.

"That it makes the senses dull, and by degrees impairs the bodily faculties, I am quite sure. I remarked to those who were with me in this very establishment at Philadelphia, that the criminals who had been there long were deaf. They who were in the habit of seeing these men constantly, were perfectly amazed at the idea, which they regarded as groundless and fanciful. And yet the very first prisoner to whom they appealed—one of their own selection— confirmed my impression (which was unknown to him) instantly, and said, with a genuine air it was impossible to doubt, that he couldn't think how it happened, but he *was* growing very dull of hearing.

"That it is a singularly unequal punishment, and affects the worst man least, there is no doubt. In its superior efficiency as a means of reformation, compared with that other code of regulations which allows the prisoners to work in company, without communicating together, I have not the smallest faith. All the instances of reformation that were mentioned to me, were of a kind that might have been — and I have no doubt whatever, in my own mind, would have been — equally well brought about by the silent system. With regard to such men as the negro burglar and the·English thief, even the most enthusiastic have scarcely any hope of their conversion.

"It seems to me that the objection that nothing wholesome or good has ever had its growth in such unnatural solitude, and that even a dog, or any of the more intelligent among beasts, would pine, and mope, and rust away, beneath its influence, would be in itself a sufficient argument against this system. But when we recollect, in addition, how very cruel and severe it is, and that a solitary life is always liable to peculiar and distinct objections of a most deplorable nature, which have arisen here; and call to mind, moreover, that the choice is not between this system and a bad or ill-considered one, but between it and another which has worked well, and is, in its whole design and practice, excellent; there is surely more than sufficient reason for abandoning a mode of punishment attended by so little hope of promise, and fraught, beyond dispute, with such a host of evils."

STATISTICS OF THE NEW PENITENTIARY IN PHILADELPHIA DURING ITS WHOLE HISTORY, FROM 1829 TO 1841.

Year.	Received.	Discharged.	Average Number.	Pardoned.	Died.	Recommitted.	Old Convicts.	Deranged.	Money from State Treasury.
1829	9	...	4½	..	..	..	..	..	
1830	49	3	31	..	1	..	..	..	
1831	50	12	67	1	4	..	..	..	
1832	34	20	91	..	*4	..	†32	..	
1833	77	17	123	2	1	..	16	..	
1834	118	41	183	8	5	3	25	..	
1835	217	70	266	15	7	13	88	..	4,998 91
1836	143	87	360	3	12	6	43	..	
1837	161	159	386	10	17	19	59	14	
1838	178	133	402	10	26	23	..	18	34,308 00
1839	179	138	418	13	11	‡35	65	26	18,378 00
1840	139	154	405	20	22	13	§93	21	
1841	126	134	356	15	17	27	38	11	
	1480	968	3092	97	127	139	459	90	

* One suicide.   † Old convicts to this time.   ‡ Three of these third time.
§ This is equal to the whole number of old convicts sent to Prison in 1838 and 1840.

Important general results from the table : — DEATHS in the first five years, 1 in 36 ; DEATHS in the second five years, 1 in 23; DEATHS in the last five years, 1 in 21; DEATHS of all received, 1 in 10; DEATHS to all discharged by remission of sentence, 1 in 8.

DERANGED, of all received, 1 in 16; DERANGED of all received in the last five years, 1 in 8; nearly all became so in Prison.

RECOMMITTED in the first five years, 00; RECOMMITTED in the second five years, 1 in 5; RECOMMITTED of all discharged, 1 in 7. OLD CONVICTS to all received, 1 to 3, nearly.

TABULAR VIEW OF FIFTEEN PENITENTIARIES IN 1842.

Penitentiaries in 1842.	Number at the Commencement.	Number at the Close.	Increase.	Diminution.	Received.	Discharged.	Pardoned.	Died.	Escaped.	Recommitted.	Earnings above Expenses.	Expenses above Earnings.
Maine,..............	42	57	15	...	31	10	6	..	...	...	*838 13	
New Hampshire,....	92	99	7	...	28	17	4	..	...	...	*758 36	
Charlestown, Mass.,.	331	287	..	44	85	112	9	†2	..	7	931 36	
Rhode Island,.......	21	23	2	...	9	5	2	..	...	...	....	5,526 23
Wethersfield, Conn.,.	211	203	..	8	54	51	3	8	...	...	6,069 25	
Auburn, N. Y.,......	707	712	5	...	244	187	38	7	2	..	13,478 36	
Sing Sing, N. Y.,....	811	785	..	26	269	219	38	37	...	...	1,374 31	
New Jersey,........	151	137	..	14	44	45	13	..	...	...	‡4,178 22	
Philadelphia,........	335	331	..	4	142	114	23	9				
Pittsburg, Penn.,....	161	163	3	...	69	46	16	5	...	...	‡4,449 86	
Baltimore, Md.,......	284	290	6	...	100	62	18	14				
Richmond, Vir.,.....	186	205	19	...	63	44	8	10				
Georgia, ...	159	167	8	...	42	26	6	3	..	...	....	111 69
Frankfort, Ken.,.....	162	163	1	...	76	36	36	2	9	..	28,684 24	
Columbus, Ohio,....	480	461	..	19	137	79	66	8	..	13	21,679 05	
Fifteen Penitentiaries,	4133	4083	66	115	1393	1053	286	105	11	20	82,441 14	5,637 92

DEATHS ONE IN THIRTY-NINE.

* Not including warden's salary.   † One suicide at Charlestown.
‡ Not including the salary of the officers.

We had prepared an abstract of an article, written by Prof.
Mittemaier, of Heidelberg, and translated for the American Ju-
rist for October and January, 1842, showing the chaotic state
of public opinion, in other countries, on the great questions
connected with the best mode of Prison discipline ; but, having
already exceeded the limits usually assigned to our Reports, we
are obliged to omit it ; with the notice of several Penitentiaries,
on the Auburn plan, which have been distinguished for their
excellence, for a course of years, and particularly for the last
year ; such as the Prisons at Auburn, N. Y., Charlestown, Mass.,
Wethersfield, Conn., and we should add Columbus, Ohio, were
not moral and religious instruction so much neglected in that
institution. We are obliged, also, to omit, partly for the same
reason, and partly because it came so late to our hands, a very
valuable Report of the Rev. Gerrish Barrett, on the Penitentiaries and Prisons which he visited during the last year, in the
Western States. By the omission in this Report, however, it
will not be lost.

Having thus noticed, as proposed, Lunatic Asylums, Houses
of Refuge, County Prisons, and Penitentiaries, —

WE CLOSE BY SAYING, CHERISH HOPE. THE WILDERNESS
SHALL BECOME LIKE EDEN, AND THE DESERT LIKE THE GAR-
DEN OF THE LORD.

OFFICERS.

PRESIDENT.
*GEORGE BLISS,
FRANCIS WAYLAND.

VICE-PRESIDENTS.

*WILLIAM BARTLETT,	LUTHER F. DIMMICK,
*WILLIAM REED,	EDWARD BEECHER,
LEONARD WOODS,	SIMON GREENLEAF,
WILLIAM JENKS,	DANIEL SHARP,
ELIJAH HEDDING,	J. S. STONE,
*EBENEZER PORTER,	LUCIUS BOLLES,
*BENJAMIN B. WISNER,	JOHN C. WARREN,
*JEREMIAH EVARTS,	HENRY J. RIPLEY,
S. V. S. WILDER,	CHARLES LOWELL,
JOHN TAPPAN,	JOHN S. PETERS,
SAMUEL H. WALLEY,	ROGER MINOT SHERMAN,
BROWN EMERSON,	THOMAS H. GALLAUDET,
ALEXANDER HENRY,	JOEL HAWES,
CHARLES CHAUNCEY,	JEREMIAH DAY,
*STEPHEN VAN RENSSELAER,	BENJAMIN SILLIMAN,
*ALEXANDER FRIDGE,	ELEAZER LORD,
*ROBERT RALSTON,	JOHN M. MATHEWS,
*EDWARD D. GRIFFIN,	WILLIAM JAY,
HEMAN HUMPHREY,	THEODORE FRELINGHUYSEN,
*SAMUEL GREEN,	*SAMUEL L. SOUTHARD,
JUSTIN EDWARDS,	SAMUEL MILLER,
ALONZO POTTER,	ARCHIBALD ALEXANDER,
*PETER O. THACHER,	HOWARD MALCOM,
FRANCIS C. GRAY,	FRANCIS PARKMAN,
EDWARD TUCKERMAN,	ABBOTT LAWRENCE.

CORRESPONDING MEMBERS.

THOMAS BRADFORD, Jr., *Philadelphia.* THOMAS PADDOCK, *St. John, N. B.*
JOEL SCOTT, *Frankfort, Kentucky.* J. McAULEY, *Toronto, U. C.*
SAMUEL HOARE, *of London.* M. S. BIDWELL, *New York City.*
DR. JULIUS, *of Hamburgh.* WM. H. ROCKWELL, *Brattleboro', Vt.*
G. DE BEAUMONT, } *of Paris.* LUTHER V. BELL, *Charlestown, Mass.*
A. DE TOCQUEVILLE, } WM. SAM'L JOHNSON, *New York City.*
SAMUEL L. DAVIS, *Augusta, Georgia.* P. D. VROOM, *Somerville, N. J.*
REUEL WILLIAMS, *Hallowell, Me.* S. F. McCRACKEN, } *Columbus, Ohio.*
S. E. COUES, *Portsmouth, N. H.* WM. M. AWL, }
J. C. HOLBROOK, *Brattleboro', Vt.* W. H. BURTON, } *New South Wales.*
*THOMAS G. LEE, *Charlestown, Mass.* DR. LANG, }
SAM'L B. WOODWARD, *Worcester, Ms.* JACOB BEESON, *Niles, Michigan.*

MANAGERS.

R. S. STORRS,	SAMUEL LAWRENCE,
SAMUEL A. ELIOT,	H. M. WILLIS,
JAMES MEANS,	SILAS AIKEN,
DANIEL SAFFORD,	SAMUEL K. LOTHROP,
JARED CURTIS,	GORHAM D. ABBOTT.
DANIEL SHARP,	

A. A. LAWRENCE, TREASURER.
LOUIS DWIGHT, SECRETARY.

LIFE DIRECTORS,

BY THE PAYMENT OF ONE HUNDRED DOLLARS AND UPWARDS.

Albany, N. Y.
*Van Rensselaer, Stephen
Boston.
Appleton, Samuel
Armstrong, Samuel T.
*Bussey, Benjamin
*Chamberlain, Richard
*Cobb, Nathaniel R.
*Coolidge, Joseph
Dwight, Edmund
Eliot, Samuel A.
Gray, Francis C.
Greenleaf, Jonathan
Homes, Henry
Hubbard, Samuel
Jackson, Charles
Jackson, James
Jackson, Patrick T.
Lawrence, Amos

Lowell, Charles
*Lowell, John
Lyman, Theodore, Jr.
Munson, Israel
Parkman, Francis
Phillips, Jonathan
*Phillips, William
Prescott, William
Shattuck, George C.
Shaw, Robert G.
Tappan, John
Ticknor, George
Tuckerman, Edward
Ward, Artemas
Wells, Charles
White, Stephen
Willis, Nathaniel
Dedham, Mass.
Burgess, Ebenezer

Geneva, N Y.
Dwight, Henry
Norwich, Conn.
Greene, William P.
Peterboro', N. Y.
Smith, Peter
Portsmouth, N. H.
Coues, S. E.
Rochester, N. Y.
*Bissell, Josiah
Salem, Mass.
Peabody, Joseph
Worcester, Mass.
Abbott, J. S. C.
Foster, Alfred Dwight
Salisbury, Stephen
Sweetser, Seth, by 3 sisters
Waldo, Daniel

LIFE MEMBERS,

BY THE PAYMENT OF THIRTY DOLLARS AND UPWARDS.

Albany, N. Y.
Delavan, Edward C.
*Hopkins, Samuel M.
McIntire, Archibald
Norton, John C.

Andover, Mass.
*Cornelius, Elias
Edwards, Justin
*Porter, Ebenezer
Woods, Leonard

Auburn, N. Y.
Lewis, Levi, by Officers of
  the Prison
Seymour, James S.
Smith, B. C., by Officers of
  the Prison

Baltimore, Md.
Backus, John A.
*McKim, W. D.

Bath, N. H.
Sutherland, David, by Ira
  Goodale

Bedford, N. Y.
*Jay, John
Jay, William

Beverly.
Oliphant, David

Boston.
Adams, Nehemiah
*Amory, John
Beecher, Edward
Beecher, Lyman
*Blake, George

*Bowdoin, James
Brooks, Peter C.
Brooks, Peter C., Jr.
Chadwick, Ebenezer
Clapp, Joshua
Cobb, Richard
*Codman, Catharine
Codman, Elizabeth
Codman, Charles R.
Codman, Henry
Cogswell, William
Cushing, John P.
Dana, Nathaniel
Dorr, Samuel
Eckley, David
Edwards, Henry
*Eliot, William H.
Frothingham, N. L.
Gray, Horace
Gray, John C.
*Green, Samuel
*Greene, Gardiner
*Greenwood, F. W. P.
Hill, Henry
Homer, George J.
Jones, Anna P.
*Jones, John Coffin
Lawrence, Abbott
Lawrence, Samuel
Lawrence, William
*Lyman, Theodore
Lyman, Theodore, Jr.
Marvin, T. R.
*McLean, Ann
Munroe, Edmund
Newhall, Cheever
Otis, Harrison Gray
Parker, Daniel P.
Parker, Ebenezer
*Parker, John

Parkman, Francis
Potter, Alonzo
Rand, Asa
Randall, John
Reed, Benjamin T.
Rice, Henry
Ropes, William
Safford, Daniel
Sears, David
Stoddard, Charles
Thorndike, Israel
Vose, Thomas
Wales, Thomas B.
Warren, John C.
Wigglesworth, Thomas
Williams, John D.
Winthrop, Thomas L.
*Wisner, Benjamin B.
Worthington, William

Brooklyn, N. Y.
Carrol, D. L.

Cambridge, Mass.
Donnison, C. L.
Farwell, Levi
Greenleaf, Simon
Holland, Frederic West
Quincy, Josiah

Canandaigua, N. Y.
Eddy, Ansel G.

Catskill, N. Y.
Cooke, Thomas B.
Day, Orrin

Charleston, S. C.
Corning, Jasper

Charlestown, Mass.
Curtis. Jared
Walker, William J., Jr.

Coxackie, N. Y.
*Van Dyck, Abraham

Danvers, Mass.
Braman, Milton P.
*Cowles, George
*Oakes, Caleb

Dorchester, Mass.
Codman, John

Douglass Farm, L. I.
Douglass, George, by the hand of Mrs. Joanna Bethune

Edinburgh, Scotland.
Dunlop, John

Fairfield, Conn.
Sherman, Roger M.

Geneva, N. Y.
*Axtell, Henry

Gloucester, Mass.
Jewett, David, by a Lady

Hampton, N. H.
Harris, Roswell

Hartford, Conn.
Hawes, Joel
Spring, Samuel

Haverhill, Mass.
Keeley, George
Phelps, Dudley

Ipswich, Mass.
Kimball, David

Jamaica, L. I.
*Crane, Elias W.

Marblehead, Mass.
Hooper, Nathaniel
*Reed, William

Middletown, Conn.
Crane, John B.

Milton, Mass.
*Tucker, Nathaniel

Newark, N. J.
Hamilton, W. T.

Newbury, Mass.
Wright, Henry C.

Newburyport, Mass.
Banister. William B.
Bartlett, William

*Brown, Moses
Dimmick, Luther F.
Proudfit, John
By a donation in books from
  Charles Whipple, to consti-
  tute the following persons
  Life Members :
Davis, Mary A.
Greenleaf, Mary C.
Hodge, Mary D.
Thompson, Sarah

New Haven, Conn.
Bacon, Leonard
Brewster, James
Fitch, Eleazer T.
Robinson, Charles, by his
  sister Elizabeth
Salisbury, Abby

New York City.
Adams, William
Allen, Stephen
Astor, John Jacob
Averill, Heman
Bethune, G. W.
Boorman, J.
Brewster, Joseph
Broadhead, Dr.
*Chambers, William
Cox, Samuel H.
Crosby, W. B.
Eastborn, Manton
*Falconer, Archibald
Hedges, Timothy
How, Fisher
Johnson, William Samuel
*Lenox, Robert
Mason, Cyrus W.
Mathews, John M.
McAuley, Thomas
Milnor, James
Patton, William
Perrit, Pelatiah
*Post, Joel
Proudfit, Alexander
Phillips, W. W.
*Rutgers, Henry
Schroeder, J. F.
Shatzel, Jacob
Spring, Gardiner
Starr, Philemon R.
Stephens, J. C.
Tappan, Arthur
*Varick, Richard
*Ward, Samuel
*Woolsey, William W.

Peterboro', N. Y.
Smith, Gerrit

Philadelphia, Penn.
Allen, Solomon
*Carey, Matthew
Elmes, Thomas
Ely, Ezra Stiles
Henry, Alexander
*Livingston, Gilbert R.
Skinner, Thomas H.

Pittsfield, Mass.
Newton, Edward A.

Plymouth, Mass.
Robbins, Josiah

Portland, Me.
Dwight, William T.
Tyler, Bennett

Portsmouth, N. H.
Coues, Lucy Louisa
Goodwin, Ichabod
Peabody, Andrew P., by La-
  dies of his Society

Poughkeepsie, N. Y.
Cuyler, Cornelius

Providence, R. I.
*Ives, Thomas P.
Wayland, Francis

Rahway, N. J.
Squier, Job

Salem, Mass.
Cleveland, J. P.
Emerson, Brown
Phillips, Stephen C.
Williams, William
Worcester, Zervia F.

Schenectady, N. Y.
*Smith, Peter

Springfield, Mass.
Osgood, Samuel

Thomaston, Me.
*Rose, Daniel

Troy, N. Y.
Tucker, Mark

Utica, N. Y.
Lansing, D. C.
Stocking, Samuel
Varick, Abraham

West Haverhill, Mass.
Cross, Abijah

Wethersfield, Conn.
Barrett, Gerrish
Pilsbury, Amos

Williamstown, Mass.
*Griffin, Edward D.

Wiscasset, Me.
Hooker, Edward W.

Worcester, Mass.
Foster, Alfred Dwight
Lincoln, John W.
Salisbury, Stephen
Waldo, E. S. & R.
Waldo, Daniel

TREASURER'S REPORT.

Dr.   PRISON DISCIPLINE SOCIETY, *in Account with* CHARLES CLEVELAND.   **Cr.**

Dr.	
1843.	
May 25.— To cash paid A. Beadley, for binding, stitching, and folding Reports,..........	995 77
To do. paid Marcus Latham, for collecting bills and distributing Reports,..........	38 19
To do. paid Abraham Jackson, office rent,....	61 78
To do. paid J. G. Rogers, Boston Type and Stereotype Foundry,..........	43 75
To do. paid incidental and travelling expenses,..........	158 11
To do. paid balance of interest account,..........	174 29
To do. paid Rev. G. Barrett for his agency in the Middle, Southern, and Western States,..........	54 32
To do. paid agency in the Northern and Eastern States, salary of the secretary,..........	785 48
	1,700 00
	$4,011 61

Cr.		
1843.		
May 25.— By cash received of the Legislature of New York for Reports,..........		100 00
By do. dividend received on nine shares of New England Bank stock, purchased with the legacy of Nathaniel Tucker, late of Milton, deceased,..........		54 00
By do. collected in the Middle, Southern, and Western States, by Rev. G. Barrett,..........		785 48
By do. dividend, received on Thomas S. Winslow's legacy, by B. P. Winslow, executor,..........		170 63
By do. subscriptions and donations, in the Northern and Eastern States,..........	2,046 37	
Balance to new account,..........		855 13
		$4,011 61

Permanent Fund, by direction of the late Nathaniel Tucker, of Milton, who gave it as a legacy:—

Nine shares in the capital stock of New England Bank,....	$936 75	
Deposit in Tremont Savings Bank,..........	63 00	
Cash,..........	25	
	$1,000 00	

BOSTON, MAY 25, 1843.   Errors excepted,

CHARLES CLEVELAND, *Treasurer P. D. S.*

BOSTON, MAY 26, 1843.— We certify that we have examined the foregoing account and find the same correctly cast and properly vouched.

JAMES MEANS, } *Auditors.*
HENRY HILL, }

SUBSCRIPTIONS AND DONATIONS,

From May 23, 1842, to May 25, 1843.

Adrian, Michigan.		Cash	2 00	Forbush, Jonathan	5 00
Baker, Harris, & Millard		Cash, a Friend	2 00	Forbes, R. B.	10 00
	2 00	Cash	1 00	Foster, J. H.	2 00
Berry, L. G.	2 00	Cash	5 00	Francis, Ebenezer	10 00
Field, I.	2 00	Cash	25	Francis, David	2 00
T. A.	1 00	Cash, A. E. B.	5 00	French, Jonathan	5 00
		Cash, D. L. A.	3 00	Friend	10 00
Bennington, Vt.		Cash, B. D. G.	1 00	Friend	10 00
Hooker, Edward W.	2 00	Cash, Mr. M.	1 00	Friend, G. C. P.	5 00
		Cash, a Friend	1 00	Friend	2 00
Berlin, Conn.		Cash, a Friend	1 00	Friend	1 00
Porter, Norman	2 00	Cash, a Friend	1 00	Friend, A. B.	2 00
		Cash for Reports	50	Friend, Mr. W.	2 00
Boston, Mass.		Cash for Reports	25	Friend	2 00
Abbot, Miss S.	50	Callender, G.	2 00	Friend	2 00
Adams, Chester	2 00	Cabot, Samuel	10 00	Gassett, Henry	5 00
Adams, James	2 00	Cary, T. G.	5 00	Gilbert, Lemuel	2 00
Adams, William	2 00	Carlton, William	2 00	Gilbert, Samuel	2 00
Adan, John R.	5 00	Chickering, Jonas	5 00	Gilbert, Timothy	2 00
Akerman, Mrs.	50	Chandler, Abiel	2 00	Gordon, George W.	2 00
Almy, Patterson, & Co.	5 00	Clap, James	2 00	Gray, William	2 00
Amory, Charles	20 00	Clarke, T. M.	2 00	Gray, George H.	2 00
Amory, William	5 00	Clark, Ab.	2 00	Gray, John C.	20 00
Anderson, Rufus	2 00	Channing, Walter	2 00	Gray, F. C.	30 00
Andrews, S. W.	2 00	Chapman, Jonathan	10 00	Gray, Frederick T.	2 00
Andrews, E. T.	2 00	Cotton, Joseph H.	2 00	Gray, George H.	2 00
Ammedown, Holmes	2 00	Crocker, Uriel	2 00	Green, David	2 00
Appleton, William	10 00	Cushing, T. P.	2 00	Greene, Charles G.	2 00
Ballard, Joseph	3 00	Curtis, T. B.	2 00	Greenleaf, Samuel	3 00
Bartoll, C. A.	5 00	Curtiss, Samuel	2 00	Gridley, William	2 00
Baker, Joseph	3 00	Codman, Henry	10 00	Hale, Moses L.	2 00
Barnard, Charles	5 00	Chamberlain, N. B.	3 00	Hall, Henry	3 00
Bartlett, Sidney	2 00	Colby, Gardner	2 00	Hall, J. P.	2 00
Bailey, Calvin	2 00	Davis, I. P.	2 00	Hallet, George	5 00
Barnes, D. W.	2 00	Dana, A. W.	1 00	Hallet, James H.	2 00
Barnes, S. H.	2 00	Dana, Luther	2 00	Harraden, Andrew	3 00
Bent, Ann	2 00	Dana, Ephraim	2 00	Harvey, Peter	5 00
Bancroft, Jacob	2 00	Darracott, George	2 00	Hawes, Gray, & Co.	5 00
Blanchard, Joshua	2 00	Dearborn, Nathaniel	1 00	Hayden, J. C.	2 00
Blake, James	2 00	Denny, Daniel	1 00	Hayward, George	5 00
Bird, S. J.	2 00	Dexter, George M.	5 00	H. A. P.	3 00
Bliss, S.	2 00	Dixwell, J. J.	10 00	Hill, Jeremiah	2 00
Bond, William	2 00	Dorr, Samuel	10 00	Hollis, Thomas	1 00
Bowditch, N. I.	5 00	Eaton, John	2 00	Homans, John	5 00
Brewer, Nathaniel	2 00	Edmands, J. W.	5 00	Homes & Homer	10 00
Brewer, S. N.	2 00	Eliot, Samuel A.	50 00	Howard, Benjamin	2 00
Brewer, W. A.	2 00	Ellis, George	2 00	Howe, Samuel G.	2 00
Brooks, Peter C.	20 00	Emerson, E. C.	2 00	How, Hall J.	2 00
Bowditch, W. I.	2 00	Emmons, H. N.	2 00	Howe, Jabez C.	2 00
Brewster, Osmyn	2 00	Er. bal.	9 87	Hubbard, W. J.	2 00
Brimmer, E.	10 00	Eustis, W. T.	2 00	Humphrey, William	2 00
Brimmer, Martin	10 00	Eveleth, Joseph	2 00	Hurd, John	2 00
Brooks, Edward	10 00	Everett, Moses	5 00	Inches, Misses	5 00
Bumstead, John	5 00	Fairbanks, Stephen	2 00	Inches, Henderson	5 00
Bumstead, Josiah	6 00	Faxon, George N.	2 00	Inches, Henderson, Jr.	2 00
Bumstead, Josiah F.	5 00	Falkner, Hamilton	2 00	Jacobs, Benjamin	1 00
Burgess, Benj., & Son	5 00	Fearing, Albert	2 00	Jackson, P. T.	10 00
Brigham, A.	1 00	Fiske & Rice	2 00	Jackson, Ward	2 00
Bradford, John	2 00	Fletcher, Richard	2 00	Johnson, James	5 00

Johnson, Samuel	2 00	Quincy, Josiah, Jr.	10 00	Whitney, Paul	5 00
Jones, Anna P.	10 00	Quincy, Samuel	2 00	Whiton, James M.	2 00
Jones, Eliphalet	2 00	Rhodes, A. H.	1 00	Wigglesworth, Thomas	5 00
Kendall, A.	2 00	Rice, F.	1 00	Wigglesworth, Edward	2 00
Keep, N. C.	9 00	Rice, J. P.	5 00	Wilkins & Carter	5 00
Kuhn, George H.	5 00	Rice & Thaxter	5 00	Willis, Nathaniel	25 00
Kimball, J. Merrill	1 00	Richards, Reuben	5 00	Willis, H. M	2 00
Kimball, Jewett, & Co.	5 00	Reed, Benjamin T.	5 00	Williams, Mrs. E. W.	1 00
Kimball, A. P.	1 00	Robbins, E. H.	2 50	Williams, John D.	5 00
Kimball, J.	1 00	Robbins, Charles	5 00	Winchester, W. P.	10 00
Kirk, Edward N.	100 00	Rogers, H. B.	5 00	Winslow, Thomas S.,	
Kitredge, Alvah	2 00	Rogers, Warren A.	2 00	deceased, 17½ per	
Lamson, Edwin	2 00	Rogers, William M.	2 00	cent. on legacy, by	
Lane, Susan	2 00	Rogers, John G.	2 00	B. P. Winslow, his	
Lang, W. B.	2 00	Rogers, J. G.	2 00	executor	170 63
Langdon, J. W.	1 00	Rogers, J. H.	2 00	Wolcott, J. H.	5 00
Lawrence, Abbott	20 00	Rollins, William	5 00		
Lawrence, Amos	50 00	Ropes, Hardy	2 00	*Bowling Green, Ken.*	
Lawrence, William	10 00	Ropes, William	10 00	Goodwin, Baker, &	
Lawrence, A. A.	5 00	Russell, N. P.	5 00	Hooper	2 00
Leland, Sherman	2 00	Salisbury, Samuel	2 00	Graham, John H.	2 00
Lewis, William G.	2 00	Sears, David	20 00	Smith, Zachariah	1 00
Lincoln, W. S.	2 00	Shaw, Robert G.	30 00	Stebbins, Samuel	2 00
Lincoln, Heman	2 00	Sigourney, Henry	10 00		
Little, C. C.	2 00	Simpson, M. H.	5 00	*Buffalo, N. Y.*	
Littlehale, S. S.	5 00	Skinner, Francis	5 00	Bull, J. B.	1 00
Livermore, Isaac, & Co.	2 00	Slocumb, Thomas	2 00	Clarey, Mrs. Joseph	2 00
L. L.	3 00	Smith & Sumner	3 00	Fillmore, M.	2 00
Lloyd, Anna	10 00	South Boston Iron Co.	5 00	Lee, John R.	2 00
Long, E. J.	1 00	Stedman, C. H.	5 00	Rumsey & Howard	2 00
Loring, Charles G.	2 00	Stevenson, William	2 00	Seibold, Jacob	1 00
Loring, Elijah	5 00	Stimpson, W. C.	2 00	Seymour, H. R.	2 00
Loring, Henry	2 00	Stoddard, Charles	5 00	Sprague, N. B.	2 00
Loring, James	2 00	Stone, W. W.	5 00	Walden, E.	2 00
Lothrop, Samuel R.	2 00	Storer, Robert B.	2 00	Walbridge, G. B.	2 00
Lowe, J. J.	2 00	Storer, S. S.	1 00	Wilkins, R. P.	2 00
Lowe, Francis	2 00	Sullivan, Richard	10 00		
Lowell, John A.	10 00	Sumner, W. H.	10 00	*Cambridge, Mass.*	
Lowell, Francis C.	5 00	Sumner, Bradford	2 00	Farwell, Levi	15 00
Lyman, Joseph, Jr.	5 00	Sumner, Charles	2 00	Norton, Andrews	10 00
Lyman, Theodore	50 00	Swett, Samuel	2 00	Worcester, Joseph E.	2 00
Mathews, Asa	2 00	Symonds, Artemas	2 00		
Mayer, P. J.	2 00	Tappan, L. W.	3 00	*Charlestown, Mass.*	
McBurney, C.	2 00	Tarbell, Thomas	2 00	Bell, Luther F.	10 00
Means, James	2 00	Tenney, Samuel	2 00	Goodhue, Homer	2 00
Mellen, Moses	2 00	Tilden, Joseph	2 00	Crosby, Daniel	2 00
Metcalf, Theron	2 00	Timmins, Henry	5 00	Hunt, Enoch	2 00
Metcalf, Nathan	2 00	Townsend, Henry B.	2 00	Lincoln, Charles	5 00
Munson, Israel	20 00	Townsend, E.	2 00	McIntire, E. P.	2 00
Neale, R. K.	2 00	Train, Samuel	5 00	Skelton, M.	2 00
Newman, Henry	2 00	Trott, George	5 00	Tyler, Columbus	2 00
Norcross, Otis	2 00	Tucker, Thomas	2 00		
Nott, James, & Son	2 00	Tucker, J. L.	2 00	*Chilicothe, Ohio.*	
Osgood, Isaac	2 00	Tufts, Quincy	1 00	Alston, J. R.	1 00
Osgood, J. P.	2 00	Valentine, Charles	5 00	Atwood, J. S.	2 00
Paige, James W.	2 00	Vinton, Alexander	2 00	Campbell, I. D.	1 00
Palfrey, John G.	2 00	Welch, Francis	3 00	Campbell, I. P.	1 00
Parker, Jonathan	1 00	Wales, Thomas B., Jr.	2 00	Cash	50
Parker, M. S.	2 00	Walley, Samuel H.	10 00	Cash	50
Parker, Isaac	3 00	Ware, Henry	2 00	Deming, R. W.	1 00
Parkman, Francis	10 00	Ware, John	5 00	Ghormby, Thomas	1 00
Parkman, George	2 00	Warren, John C.	10 00	Leiggett	1 00
Payson, S. R.	2 00	Waterston, Robert	2 00	McFarland, I.	1 00
Perkins, Thomas H.	25 00	Wells, Charles A.	2 00	Miller, William	1 00
Perkins, H. G.	1 00	Wells, John B.	2 00	Ott, W.	1 00
Phelps, Sewall	2 00	Wells, John	10 00	Sproat, A. D.	1 00
Phipps & Co.	2 00	Wetmore, Thomas	10 00	Wilcox, L.	5 00
Pickman, Benjamin	5 00	White, Charles	3 00		
Prescott, William	20 00	White, Joseph	2 00	*Cincinnati, Ohio.*	
Quincy, J. D.	5 00	White, F. E.	3 00	Allen, Manton	2 00

Bates, J. C. & Co.	2 00	Fay, Cyrus	2 00	Baldwin, J. W.	1 00
Blackley, J. W.	2 00	Gere, George	2 00	Perry, H.	1 00
Bowler, R. S.	2 00	Goodale, L.	2 00	Ryder, O. R.	2 00
Burrows, J. D.	2 00	Gynnes & Samson	2 00		
Cash	1 00	Hubbel, H. N.	2 00	*Frankfort, Ken.*	
Cash	1 00	Hubbard, Willard	2 00	Davidson, J.	2 00
Candley, J. M.	2 00	Kimball & Jones	2 00	Hodges, A. G.	2 00
Calhoun, I.	2 00	Moodie, Thomas	2 00	Letcher, R. P.	2 00
Carlisle, G.	1 00	Pinney, A. H.	2 00	Lindsey, Thos. N.	2 00
Carran, I. R.	2 00	Smith, Samuel M.	2 00	Page, Thomas	2 00
Clark, Henry	2 00	Stanton, L. B.	1 00	Parker, A. S.	2 00
Davis, P.	1 00	Starling, L.	2 00	Stevenson, Thos. B.	2 00
Davis, Henry F.	2 00	Stone, A. P.	2 00	Swyert	2 00
Elliot, S. B.	2 00	Swan, J. R.	2 00	Taylor, E. H.	2 00
Ellis, Rowland	2 00	Swayne, M. H.	2 00	Theobald, Thomas S.	2 00
Fisher, Charles	2 00	Whiting, J. N.	2 00		
Goldthwait, H.	2 00	Wheaton, J. B.	2 00	*Hartford, Conn.*	
Groesbeck, I. H.	2 00	Wilcox, P. B.	10 00	Morgan, N. H.	2 00
Haines, E. S.	2 00			Wadsworth, Daniel	10 00
Hall, James	2 00	*Dayton, Ohio.*			
Hartshorn, W.	2 00	Bomberger, J.	2 00	*Haverhill, Mass.*	
Kellogg, S.	2 00	Brown, Samuel B.	2 00	Morse, Hazen	1 00
Kellogg, H. S.	2 00	Claflin, L. F.	2 00		
Lawrence, J.	2 00	Crawford, Z.	2 00	*Holly, N. Y.*	
Manser, W.	1 00	Davis, E. W.	2 00	Taft, George W.	1 00
Mathews, J. J.	2 00	Decker, S.	2 00		
Moore, J. B.	1 50	Ellis, B. F.	2 00	*Lexington, Ken.*	
Mussey, R. D.	2 00	Este, D. K.	2 00	Berkley, B. S.	2 00
Robbins, E.	2 00	Estabrook, F. C.	2 00	Bush, J. M.	2 00
Sampson, N.	2 00	Haines, Job	2 00	Carter, H. H.	2 00
Shillette, John	2 00	Odlin, P.	2 00	Cochran, J. W.	2 00
Spencer, H. E.	2 00	Perrine, James	2 00	Collins, Thomas	2 00
Starr, H.	2 00	Sayre, J.	2 00	Dudley, B. W.	2 00
Taylor, H. H.	2 00	Stoddard, H.	2 00	Dunham, T.	1 00
Taylor, A. M.	2 00			Huggins, Thomas	1 00
Thornbergen, E. K.	2 00	*Detroit, Michigan.*		Leary, W. A.	2 00
Walbridge, J. D.	2 00	Armstrong & Sibley	2 00	Logan, A.	2 00
Wayne, J. S.	2 00	Baldwin, H. P.	2 00	Mitchell, J. D.	2 00
		Beecher, Luther	2 00	Pendell, R.	2 00
Cleveland, Ohio.		Brooks, E.	2 00	Richardson, W. H.	2 00
Barney, N.	2 00	Brown, H. H.	2 00	Scott, J. W.	2 00
Brayton, H. T.	2 00	Bush, F.	1 00	Scott, M. T.	2 00
Cash	1 00	Burchard, W.	2 00	Sloan, J. R.	2 00
Cash	50	Davenport, Dennis	3 00	Tilford, J.	2 00
Crittendon, J. H.	2 00	Dow, J. R.	2 00	Wheeler, Leonard	2 00
Gaylord, C. F.	1 00	Drigg, W. S.	2 00		
Gillet & Hecox	1 00	Eaton, T. H.	2 00	*London, Eng.*	
Hardy, T. P.	1 00	Elared, E.	2 00	Hawkins, Bissett, M. D.,	
Haskell, J.	2 00	Hand, G. E.	2 00	Inspector of Prisons	8 00
Hubby, L. M.	2 00	Hastings, E. P.	2 00		
Kirkland, I. T	2 00	Larned, B. F.	2 50	*Louisville, Ken.*	
Lamb & Dwight	2 00	Moore, Franklin	2 00	Anderson, J.	2 00
Morgan, Eli	2 00	Newbold, A. H	2 00	Bassett, J. C.	2 00
Otis, William A.	1 00	Owen, I.	2 00	Beatty, D. L.	2 00
Redington, J. A.	1 00	Platt, Z.	1 00	Cash	2 00
Richmond, Thomas	2 00	Rowland, Thomas	2 00	Cash	2 00
Seymour, A.	1 00	Watson, J.	1 00	Cassady, Samuel	2 00
Servance, I. C.	2 00			Chenworth, S. R.	2 00
Weatherby, J. L.	2 00	*East Hampton, Mass.*		Clifton, W. B.	1 00
Whitaker, Stephen	2 00	Williston, Samuel	5 00	Clarke, Charles I.	2 00
Wittlesey, F.	2 00			Cobb, Daniel	2 00
Woolson, C. I., & Co.	2 00	*Elizabethtown, N. J.*		Culver, W. E.	2 00
		Friend, in full to consti-		Curren, P.	2 00
Columbus, Ohio.		tute Rev. Nicholas		Curtis, J. V.	2 00
Andrews, I. W.	2 00	Murray a Life Mem-		Cutter, B. C., & Co.	1 00
Awl. William M.	5 00	ber, $28 00 having		Danforth, J.	2 00
Bunson, B. R.	2 00	been before received	2 00	Fellows, W. C., & Co.	2 00
Chapin, W.	2 00			Gowdy, A.	1 00
Clarke, Sumner	2 00	*Elyria, Ohio.*		Gwathney, George C.	2 00
Comstock, B., & Co.	2 00	Beebe, A.	2 00	Holbert, A. G.	1 00

Humphrey, E. P.	2 00	
Lees, James	2 00	
Low, J., & Co	2 00	
Masby, L. H.	2 00	
Morris, J. L.	1 00	
Nock, S. L.	2 00	
Pope, E. P.	1 00	
Reed, Thomas J.	2 00	
Richardson, Wm.	2 00	
Russell, Samuel	2 00	
Russell, W.	2 00	
Temple, A. B.	2 00	

Lowell, Mass.
Lawrence, Samuel — 100 00

Madison, Indiana.

Cash	50
Cooper, S.	2 00
Flint, A. W.	2 00
Paine, Thomas L.	2 00
Park, Moody	2 00
Stephens, S. C.	1 00
Sullivan, Jeremiah	2 00

Madison, N. J.
Collection — 3 98

Maine.
State Library, for Reports, by S. D. Harris — 3 00

Manchester, England.
Holden, James P., for Reports — 4 25

Marblehead, Mass.
Reed, Mrs. William — 5 00

Marietta, Ohio.

Cotton, John	2 00
Cash	1 00
Cash	50
Guitteau, A. E.	2 00
Hildreth, S. P.	2 00
Nye, A. S.	1 00

Marshall, Michigan.

Comstock, O. C.	2 00
Fitch, I. S.	2 00
Parsons, I. M.	2 00
Taylor, H. W.	1 00
Wetmore, Frederic	2 00

Maysville, Ken.

Collins, Gen.	2 00
Dwees, J. C.	2 00
Grundy, R. C.	5 00
Miner & Crittendon	2 00
Reed, J. C.	2 00

Mendon, N. Y.
Contribution — 1 50

Milton, Mass.
Nathl. Tucker, deceased, semi-annual dividend on 9 shares of New England Bank stock — 27 00
do.   do.   do. — 27 00

Nantucket, Mass.
Sprague, N. A. — 25

Nashville, Tenn.

Anderson, H. J.	5 00
Armstrong	2 00
Bass, J. M.	2 00
Cassaday	2 00
Castleman	2 00
Conner, C.	2 00
Eichbaum	2 00
Fleming, F.	2 00
Hains, M., & Co.	2 00
Hamilton, James	2 00
Jennings, Thomas R.	2 00
McAlister, J. A.	2 00
McIntosh	2 00
McWairy, N. A.	2 00
Norwill, C. C.	1 00
Perry & Fanuahill	2 00
Robertson, F.	2 00
Thompson, G. T.	2 00
Walker, J. W.	2 00
Wells, Thomas	2 00
Woods, James	2 00
Yeatman, J.	2 00
Young, John S.	2 00

New Albany, Indiana.

Austin, John	2 00
Benton, E. W.	2 00
Cash	50
Connor, J.	1 00
Howe, F. S.	2 00
McBride, John	2 00
Shields, I. R.	2 00
Smith, H. W.	2 00

Newark, N. J.

Brinsmade, H. N.	2 00
Burnet, J. B.	2 00
Eddy, Ansel D.	50 00
Nichols, David	2 00
Van Wagener, J.	2 00

New York.
By Act of the Legislature, for 16th Report, William H. Seward, Governor — 100 00
Frelinghuysen, T. — 5 00

Paris, Ken.

Brace, Thomas Y.	2 00
Marshall, J. K.	2 00
Spears, Abraham	2 00
Smith, Thomas P.	2 00
Talbut, Charles	1 00
Thornton, J. R	2 00
Wright, A. H.	2 00

Philadelphia, Penn.
Sundry subscribers, by the hand of G. Barrett — 104 00

Pittsburg, Penn.
Abree, W. T. — 2 00
Avery, Charles — 2 00

Bagaley, W.	2 00
Baker, T., & Co.	2 00
Bickley, C. G.	1 00
Burbridge, J. W.	2 00
Carter, Thomas	2 00
Cash	1 00
Cash	1 00
Cash	50
Cash	50
Cash	1 00
Cash	1 00
Cash	1 00
Cash	1 00
Cash	1 00
Childs, H.	2 00
Church, S.	2 00
Cooper, J. M.	2 00
Dickey, N., Jr.	2 00
Drucker, L.	2 00
Fahnestock, B. A., & Co.	2 00
Higby, Henry	2 00
Holmes, N.	2 00
Jones, Morris	2 00
Kay, C. W.	2 00
Kidd, J.	1 00
King, Josiah	2 00
Leach, M.	2 00
Leach, A.	2 00
Lewis, Hutchinson	2 00
Little, John, Jr.	2 00
McCatchen, W. R.	2 00
McCormick, P.	2 00
McCully, J.	2 00
Morgan, L. E.	2 00
Murphy & Brothers	2 00
Park, J., Jr. & Co.	2 00
Searfe, W. B.	2 00

Putnam, Ohio.

Buckingham, A.	2 00
Guthrie, J. C.	2 00
Guthrie, A. A.	2 00
Guthrie, S. H.	50
Mathews, H.	1 00
Mathews, Increase	2 00
Reed, Mrs.	1 00
Safford, H.	1 00

Rochester, N. Y.

Allen, John	2 00
Cash	1 00
Cash	50
Cash	50
Cash	50
Cash	50
Cole, D.	1 00
Ely, E.	2 00
Fenn, H. N.	50
Graves, J.	1 00
Kidd, W.	2 00
Parden, C. L	2 00
Peek, E.	1 00
Pitkin, W.	2 00
Reynolds, A.	2 00
Sampson, Ashley	2 00
Strong & Dawson	1 00
Tolman, J. T.	2 00
Ward, A. S.	2 00

Springfield, N. Y.		Means, James	2 00	*Worcester, Mass.*	
Barrett, Gerrish	20 00	Wilson, H.	2 00	Foster, A. D.	5 00
				Friend	3 00
Springfield, Ohio.		*Watertown, Mass.*		Hitchcock, C. P.	2 00
Crain, J. A.	1 00	Boyden, Dwight	10 00	Salsbury, Stephen	20 00
Halsey, J. S.	1 00	J. C. P.	20 00	Two Sisters	100 00
Nottinger & Co.	1 00			Woodward, Samuel B.	10 00
Murdock, J.	2 00	*Wheeling, Virginia.*			
Rogers, W. A.	2 00	Brady, S.	2 00		
Rumyon, William	1 00	Cash	1 00	*Zanesville, Ohio.*	
Spencer, W. M.	2 00	Jacob, Z.	2 00	Ball, Edward	2 00
Torbot, J. S.	2 00	Laidly, A. T.	2 00	Cowers, C. C.	2 00
Warden, Jeremiah	2 00	Lest, J.	1 00	Howe, A. E.	1 00
		Zane, D.	2 00	James, George	2 00
Steubenville, Ohio.				Paguet, I.	2 00
Cash	1 00	*Winthrop, Me.*		Moneyping	2 00
Cash	1 00	Thurston, David	1 00		

NINETEENTH

ANNUAL REPORT

OF THE

BOARD OF MANAGERS

OF THE

PRISON DISCIPLINE SOCIETY,

BOSTON, MAY, 1844.

———◆———

𝔅𝔬𝔰𝔱𝔬𝔫:

PUBLISHED AT 63 ATKINSON STREET.

STEREOTYPED AT THE
BOSTON TYPE AND STEREOTYPE FOUNDERY.

———

1844

CONTENTS.

———

PART I

PROVISION FOR POOR LUNATICS.

PART II.

COUNTY PRISONS.

PART III.

PENITENTIARIES.

PART IV.

HOUSES OF REFUGE.

APPENDIX.

CONSTITUTION

OF THE

Prison Discipline Society.

———◆———

ARTICLE 1.   This Society shall be called the PRISON DISCIPLINE SOCIETY.

ART. 2.   It shall be the *object* of this Society to promote the improvement of Public Prisons.

ART. 3.   It shall be the *duty* of this Society to take measures for effecting the formation of one or more Prison Discipline Societies in each of the United States, and to co-operate with all such Societies in accomplishing the object specified in the second article of this Constitution.

ART. 4.   Any Society, having the same object in view, which shall become auxiliary to this, and shall contribute to its funds, shall thereby secure for the Prisons, in the State where such Society is located, special attention from this Society.

ART. 5.   Each subscriber of two dollars, annually, shall be a Member.

ART. 6.   Each subscriber of thirty dollars, at one time, shall be a Member for Life.

ART. 7.   Each subscriber of ten dollars, annually, shall be a Director.

ART. 8.   Each subscriber of one hundred dollars, or who shall by one additional payment increase his original subscription to one hundred dollars, shall be a Director for Life.

ART. 9.   The officers of this Society shall be a President, as many Vice-Presidents as shall be deemed expedient, a Treasurer, and a Secretary, to be chosen annually, and a Board of Managers, whose duty it shall be to conduct the business of the Society.   This Board shall consist of six clergymen and six laymen, of whom nine shall reside in the city of Boston, and five shall constitute a quorum.

Every Minister of the Gospel, who is a member of this Society, shall be entitled to meet and deliberate with the Board of Managers.

The Managers shall call special meetings of the Society, and fill such vacancies as may occur by death or otherwise, in their own Board.

ART. 10.   The President, Vice-Presidents, Treasurer, and Secretary, shall be, ex officio, Members of the Board of Managers.

ART. 11.   Directors shall be entitled to meet and vote at all meetings of the Board of Managers.

ART. 12.   The annual meetings of this Society shall be held in Boston, on the week of the General Election, when, besides choosing the officers as specified in the ninth article, the accounts of the Treasurer shall be presented, and the proceedings of the foregoing year reported.

ART. 13.   The Managers shall meet at such time and place, in the city of Boston, as they shall appoint.

ART. 14.   At the meetings of the Society, and of the Managers, the President, or, in his absence, the Vice-President first on the list then present, and in the absence of the President and of all the Vice-Presidents, such Member as shall be appointed for that purpose, shall preside.

ART. 15.   The Secretary, in concurrence with two of the Managers, or, in the absence of the Secretary, any three of the Managers, may call special meetings of the Board.

ART. 16.   The minutes of every meeting shall be signed by the Chairman or Secretary.

ART. 17.   The Managers shall have the power of appointing such persons as have rendered essential services to the Society either Members for Life or Directors for Life.

ART. 18.   No alteration shall be made in this Constitution except by the Society, at an annual meeting, on the recommendation of the Board of Managers.

ANNUAL MEETING.

THE Nineteenth Annual Meeting of the Prison Discipline Society, having been previously notified according to law, was held in Park Street Vestry, on Monday, May 27, 1844, at 3 o'clock, P. M

A quorum being present, the Rev. Dr. JENKS, the oldest Vice-President then present, took the chair, and opened the meeting with prayer.

The Chairman, in the absence of the Treasurer, AMOS A. LAWRENCE, Esq., read the Treasurer's Report, and the certificate of its correctness by the Auditors, JAMES MEANS, Esq. and WILLIAM W. STONE, Esq., which Report, as thus audited, was accepted.

Mr. DANIEL SAFFORD was appointed a committee to distribute and collect the votes for the officers of the ensuing year.

Before collecting the votes, a letter was received from Mr. LAWRENCE, the Treasurer, resigning his office; which resignation was accepted, and the Hon. SAMUEL A. ELIOT was nominated to fill the vacancy.

The committee then proceeded to collect the votes for the officers of the ensuing year, when it was found that the officers of the previous year were reëlected, together with the Hon. SAMUEL A. ELIOT, as Treasurer, AMOS A. LAWRENCE, Esq. and Rev. CHARLES A. BARTOL, as Managers. Mr. BARTOL subsequently declined.

The meeting then adjourned, to meet in Park Street Church, on Tuesday, May 28, at 11 o'clock, A. M., to hear the Report and Addresses, after prayer by the Rev. Mr. Aiken.

The Nineteenth Public Annual Meeting of the Prison Discipline Society was held in Park Street Church, according to adjournment, at 11 o'clock, on Tuesday, May 28.

The Rev. FRANCIS WAYLAND, D. D., President of the Society, took the chair, sustained by Rev. Dr. JENKS and JOHN TAPPAN, Esq., Vice-Presidents.

At the request of the President, the Rev. ANSEL D. EDDY, of Newark, N. J., opened the meeting by reading the Scriptures and prayer.

The Rev. Mr. AIKEN, of Boston, read the Report of the Treasurer, and the Certificate of the Auditors.

The Secretary read the Annual Report of the Board of Managers.

The first resolution, for the acceptance of the Report, and referring it to the Managers to be printed, was offered by SAMUEL GREELE, Esq., accompanied by a speech, and seconded by the Rev. Mr. PERKINS, Chaplain of the McLean Asylum.

The second resolution, namely, " Resolved, That lunatics in Penitentiaries claim the earnest attention of the Government," was offered by Rev. ROBERT C. WATERSTON, of Boston, and seconded by the Rev. FREDERIC W. HOLLAND, of Rochester, N. Y.

The third resolution, namely, " Resolved, That, in the present state of Prison Discipline, we regard the employment of humane, intelligent, exemplary, and moral assistants, under-keepers, and attendants, of all kinds, as the most efficient of reformatory means," was offered by the Hon. HORACE MANN, accompanied by a speech.

The fourth resolution, namely, " Resolved, That a Committee be appointed to present a Memorial to the City Government of Boston, on the condition of the Prison in Leverett Street," was offered by WALTER CHANNING, M. D., and seconded by Rev. Dr. JENKS.

A Committee to prepare the Memorial was then appointed, namely, the Hon. SAMUEL T. ARMSTRONG, Hon. SAMUEL A. ELIOT, LOUIS DWIGHT, SAMUEL GREELE, Esq., and Dr. WALTER CHANNING. Mr. ARMSTRONG subsequently declined serving as Chairman, and Mr. ELIOT performed the duty in a most effective manner.

The meeting then adjourned.

ANNUAL REPORT.

THE managers of the Prison Discipline Society present their Nineteenth Annual Report, in humble acknowledgment of their dependence on God, and in grateful praise for his care and goodness. At the same time, they have to record the death, on the 15th of June last, of their esteemed friend and fellow-citizen, CHARLES LINCOLN, warden of the Massachusetts State Prison, by a most sudden and awful act of homicide ; by which the Prison was deprived of its head, society of a most useful man, and his wife and 11 children of a husband and father. The benevolent of this city and vicinity testified their regard for his memory, by depositing $2,700 in the Life Insurance Office for the benefit of his family, and the government of the state appropriated, during the last session of the legislature, $1,500 more for a similar purpose. The unhappy convict, who perpetrated this dreadful act, was acquitted of guilt, before the Supreme Court of Massachusetts, by a jury of his country, on the plea of insanity, and was mercifully committed by the court to the care of the State Hospital at Worcester, where, after recovering so far from his delusions, as to work quietly at his trade, in solitude, for several months, his delusions returned, his labor was given up, and, at evening prayers, just before the close of the service, he suddenly thrust himself through a window of the chapel, fell 15 or 16 feet upon the ground, was taken up senseless, and soon died.

In contrast to this awful scene, we also have to record the death, in a good old age, after a few days' sickness, of a friend and benefactor of this Society, of whom it has been said with equal taste and justice, " ISRAEL MUNSON, a wealthy merchant of Boston,— another name for truth and honor."

Although it was not known at the time of the annual meeting, it is true, that another most excellent friend and benefactor of this Society was dead, but not yet buried, at the very time when the meeting was held. We refer to the Hon. LEVI FARWELL, of Cambridge. We can never forget his cheerful countenance in our cause, and his liberal support.

We mourn over a great loss, in the three friends here named. We must leave them, however, for they are gone, and proceed to the

PLAN OF THE REPORT.

PART I. — PROVISION FOR POOR LUNATICS.

States in which Asylums for the Insane are established.
States in which Asylums for the Insane are not established.
Efforts making in States where no Asylums are yet established.
Number of Lunatics in Penitentiaries, and Necessity of Legislative Action in their Favor.
Legislative Action in Favor of Lunatics in Penitentiaries and elsewhere.
Improvement and Enlargement of Insane Asylums.
Notice of particular Insane Asylums.
Tabular View of Insane Asylums.

PART II. — COUNTY PRISONS.

Smallness of Prisons, and Number of Prisoners in the New England States, in Proportion to the Population.
Neglect of Moral and Religious Instruction in County Prisons.
Diminution of Crime.

PART III. — PENITENTIARIES.

General Conduct of Prisoners, Mode of Treatment, and Mode of Punishment in Penitentiaries.
Moral and Religious Instruction, Public Worship, and Sabbath Schools, in Penitentiaries.
Changes in the Pennsylvania System of Solitary Confinement.
Tabular View of Penitentiaries.

PART IV. — HOUSES OF REFUGE.

FUNDS OF THE SOCIETY.

PART I.

PROVISION FOR POOR LUNATICS.

STATES IN WHICH ASYLUMS FOR THE INSANE ARE ESTAB-
LISHED:

Maine, New Hampshire, Vermont, Massachusetts, Connecticut, New York, Pennsylvania, Maryland, Virginia, South
Carolina, Georgia, Louisiana, Tennessee, Kentucky, and Ohio.

STATES IN WHICH ASYLUMS FOR THE INSANE ARE NOT
YET ESTABLISHED:

Rhode Island, New Jersey, Delaware, District of Columbia,
North Carolina, Alabama, Mississippi, Missouri, Illinois, Indiana, and Michigan.

EFFORTS MAKING IN STATES WHERE ASYLUMS ARE NOT
YET ESTABLISHED.

In *Rhode Island,* the Hon. Nicholas Brown bequeathed
$30,000 for the establishment of an Asylum for the Insane.
Mr. Cyrus Butler has now offered $40,000 more, provided
the citizens of the state will raise $40,000 more ; provided,
also, that, when the lands are purchased, and the buildings
finished and furnished, $50,000 of the $110,000 raised, shall
remain untouched, to be invested as a permanent fund, the
interest of which, only, shall be expended for the support of
the institution.   Intelligent citizens of Providence say, the
conditions of Mr. Butler will be complied with.

In *Delaware,* Rev. G. Barrett, in a letter dated Wilmington,
Del., April 21, 1844, says, —

"You will rejoice and give thanks with me, to learn that commendable improvements have taken place in the Insane Department of the Poor-House.
Not a single insane person is chained.   In almost every room, a chain is fastened to a ring and staple; but it fetters no limb, and helps to show the contrast between the present and past.   The filthy, loose straw, in one corner, on
the floor, has given place to comfortable beds ; and, instead of an imbecile old
woman, to attend on the inmates, are a respectable matron and her husband.
A room has been fitted up, in which some of the inmates assemble each day
to sew, &c.   With the present buildings, it would be difficult to make the
condition of the insane more comfortable.   I know you will rejoice to hear of

the change that has taken place within the last two years ; and take courage when you know, that the Reports of the Prison Discipline Society, more than any other instrumentality, have been productive of the improvement."

In a letter, dated April 19, 1842, Mr. Barrett thus describes the same establishment : —

" The Poor-House in this place has received, last year, 35 insane persons, which, according to the census, is half the whole number in the state. There are now about 20 insane in the Poor-House. Their condition is not as it should be. Each is placed in a dark, illy-ventilated room ; their bed a bunk of straw, or straw on the floor, and an old blanket. *A chain fastens each to a ring in the centre of the room :* among them was a good-looking girl of sixteen. *The physician does not think there is much hope of restoring patients to reason in such a place as this.*"

In *Indiana*, Dr. Evans, of Attica, delivered an address on insanity, before the committee on education, in the legislature, on the 25th of December, 1843. It was a very able address, occupying five closely-printed columns in the State Sentinel, and shows Dr. Evans to be thoroughly possessed of the subject. He treats the subject under the following heads : —

1st. The history of the disease.

2d. The condition of pauper lunatics in Indiana.

3d. The benefits and cost of an Asylum.

Under the first head, he shows how the insane were regarded and treated in the last century, and how they are now treated in the Improved Asylums ; laying down, clearly and concisely, all the great and good principles of action which govern the treatment of the insane in this age.

Under the second head, he states that Indiana has, within her borders, near 250 insane, in a deplorable condition ; between 75 and 100 of whom are at public charge.

Under the third head, he shows the economy of an Asylum in *curing* the insane, above the system which neglects them till they become *in*curable, and then that a tax, for 3 years, of 1 cent on every $100 00 valuation, which is equivalent to 1 cent out of 10,000, would build the needful Asylum.

In conclusion he says, —

" While the state has nobly commenced the discharge of her duty to the deaf and dumb, by raising a fund for their education, I have been an attentive observer of the effects of the measure upon public sentiment ; and, after extensive inquiry, in different parts of the state, I have not heard a voice on the subject but that of unqualified approbation. If, then, as certainly is the case, the lunatics are far more imperious in their demands for relief, by the greater number of sufferers, by their more deplorable condition, and by the more forcible call for immediate action lest all be lost, how gladly would the public of Indiana respond to the appeals of the lunatic too! My inquiries upon the subject enable me to say most positively they would.

" Where, I ask, is to be found the citizen of Indiana, who would not willingly spare one cent out of ten thousand, for so noble an enterprise ? "

NECESSITY FOR LEGISLATIVE ACTION IN FAVOR OF LUNATICS IN PENITENTIARIES.

The inspectors of the *State Prison at Charlestown, Mass.*, say, in their last report, —

"There is a subject which we deem important, and to which we beg leave respectfully to ask the attention of the government, and that is, the case of a number of insane convicts, now confined within the walls of the Prison, some of whom, we have reason to apprehend, were insane at the time of committing the offence of which they were convicted, and have been so during the whole period of their confinement. These unfortunate individuals are little other than a mere expense to the government. From the very malady under which they are suffering, they are unfit for duty themselves, nor is it safe for them to be at large, and to mingle with the other convicts, at their different places of labor. They are, therefore, from necessity, placed in the solitary cell, shut out from the world, and from the air and light of heaven, until the expiration of their sentence.

"A Penitentiary is doubtless a very fit place to punish crime, but not to cure a malady of body or mind. This the maniac himself knows, as well as the man who has never been deprived of his reason. The insane man is rational on many subjects. He is conscious of his own insanity, and often strives to conceal it. He is peculiarly jealous of his rights, and is feelingly alive to a sense of injustice, when he supposes himself to suffer wrongfully; and such must be his feeling when he finds himself immured in the solitary cell of a Prison, suffering as a criminal for that which should call forth from every one sympathy and commiseration. Such a residence as this, with the mode of treatment inseparable from it, whatever else it may do, can never effect the return of reason to its wonted seat and power.

"Ernest A. Erving was committed to the Prison in September, 1836, for the crime of larceny, having been sentenced to three days' solitary imprisonment and ten years' hard labor; and in the month of August, 1837, he was placed in one of the cells in the old Prison, where he has been confined till the present time, being considered a dangerous man to be at large, on account of insanity.

"Could this unfortunate man, at the time he entered the cell at the Prison, so many years ago, have been placed in either of the Asylums for the Insane in our commonwealth, or in some other situation affording like advantages, he might, without doubt, under the kind and successful treatment there adopted, long ago have been cured of his malady, and restored to the bosom of his family, 'clothed and in his right mind.' Other cases, less aggravated than the one here mentioned, exist, and might be named.

"BRADFORD SUMNER,
"SAMUEL GREELE."

The warden of the Prison says, in the same report, —

"There are four convicts in this Prison wholly or partially deranged, and consequently very unsafe persons to be at large in the Prison yard. No suitable accommodations are provided for insane persons in this Prison. The only thing that can be done for them, is to shut them up in solitary cells, where the diseases of the mind, instead of being healed, are aggravated and confirmed. One man has been confined in this way constantly several years, and two others, shorter periods of time. It would seem but the dictate of humanity, that such persons should be placed in circumstances more comfortable, and more favorable to the restoration of reason, than constant confinement in solitary cells — a discipline more apt to deprive sane men of reason, than to restore reason to the insane. Some legislation, it seems to me, is necessary for the relief of insane persons in Prison."

The directors of the *Connecticut State Prison* say, in their report for May, 1843, that

" They cannot but express their regret, that nothing has been done by the legislature to relieve the unfortunate Rabello — a subject which has been before presented for their consideration. This poor lunatic was committed to the State Prison in 1837, for safe keeping ; having previously been arraigned for the murder of a boy, but acquitted in consequence of insanity so fully proved as not to admit of a doubt.

" We believe that such means as have been in the power of the warden have been extended for the comfort of this pitiable being. Yet it would seem due from humanity, that he should be placed in circumstances more favorable to the restoration of his reason, and better adapted to his melancholy condition, than the limited space afforded within a solitary cell. To be bereft of reason is a calamity which should enlist our sympathy, instead of incarcerating such subjects in a Penitentiary, appropriated to felons, where bolting of bars, and every movement in connection with the discipline, being averse to their repose, tends consequently to increase the malady, and prevent their recovery.

" This case, in the opinion of the directors, calls for some special act, by which the subject may participate in the relief extended in aid of the indigent insane, passed May session, 1842. Although, by the efforts of the active and indefatigable warden, a large surplus, over and above the expenses of the Prison, has frequently been paid in to the treasury of the state, yet, in the opinion of the directors, both the nature and design of the institution forbid its being considered as a regular and legitimate source of public revenue."

It might have been added, that the warden had offered to build a State Asylum for the Insane Poor, including Rabello, from the surplus earnings of the institution ; but this offer had been declined, and by some treated with contempt, while the money had been paid into the state treasury, and poor Rabello left to grate and gnash his teeth with anguish. What work the day of judgment will make with such neglect of suffering! " I was in Prison, and ye visited me not." " Inasmuch as ye did it not to one of the least of these, ye did it not to me."

The chaplain says, —

" 20, out of 183, are so deficient in mental powers, that, with our limited means, but little can be done for their improvement. There are quite a number, who are under the influence of greater or less degrees of mental aberration, from various causes. For this class of the convicts my sympathies are deeply enlisted, and I can but indulge the hope, that the day is not far distant, when the humane, intelligent, and Christian philanthropists of this renowned state will *devise* and *provide* the means and place adapted to their real wants."

The physician of the *New Jersey Prison* says, in his last report, page 12, —

" There are a few cases to which your attention must be again called. These are convicts suffering under the evils of solitary imprisonment, who are in reality not accountable for their actions. Insanity ought to have some other Asylum. The arrangements of this Prison do not permit the necessary attendance on such cases, and render the cures hopeless; and, besides the great wrong to the sufferer himself, the outcries of these maniacs are subversive of the order that ought to prevail in the institution."

The inspectors of the *Prison at Sing Sing* say, in their last report, —

" No suitable provision is made for convicts who become deranged. There is always a number of these in the Prison. Some are so when they arrive, having doubtless committed their offences while partially insane. Others become so while in confinement, being reduced to that condition either by disease or mental suffering.

" In every recent case, it is well known that the disease of insanity yields as readily as any other to the proper remedy. No provision being made at the Prison for this class of convicts, they are confined and treated as others are, until they become so outrageous and violent as to disturb their associates, when they are sent to a Lunatic Asylum. By that time they become confirmed maniacs, and the disease, which, in its early stage, would have yielded to proper treatment, has become incurable.

" It is difficult to avoid this result; for insanity is so frequently feigned among the convicts, that it would by no means be safe to remove them to an Asylum until they give incontrovertible proof of the reality of the disease. The time elapsing during this period is precisely that when the disease is most susceptible to remedies.

" The erection of a suitable building, where such patients might be properly treated if truly afflicted, or where they might be punished if feigning, and where, in either event, they would neither disturb nor be disturbed by their fellow-convicts, is a measure dictated by every principle of humanity.

" Of the convicts belonging to the Prison, 7 are now confined in the Lunatic Asylum at Bloomingdale, at an expense of $3 a week, each, to the Prison. The law does not allow of their being sent to the State Asylum; and the inspectors respectfully suggest such an alteration in the law, as will permit them to use that institution for these purposes.

" There is another defect in the law relating to this class of convicts. If insane at the expiration of their sentence, and unable to support themselves, there is no provision made for them. The officers of the Prison cannot any longer retain them in custody, nor can they any longer expend any money on their account. If they are discharged from the Prison, they become chargeable to the county of Westchester. If discharged from the Asylum, they become chargeable to New York. All power of the officers of the Prison over them has ceased, and they run the hazard of perishing from want.

" It is respectfully suggested, that, in such cases, it should be made the duty of the agent to take care of them until they could be returned to their friends, or to the charge of the proper authorities in the county where they were convicted.

" The importance of this suggestion will be manifest to all who, like the undersigned, become aware how much more frequently crime is the fruit of alienation of mind, than the world at large is willing to believe or admit.

" The number of insane among the convicts is 17."

The inspectors of the *new Penitentiary in Philadelphia* say, in their last report, —

" It not unfrequently happens, that there are received in our institution very improper subjects for the operation of Penitentiary reform.

" Of the whole number of prisoners under sentence during the year 1843, 6 were unable to acquire knowledge on account of their advanced age, 12 from indifference, *and 27 by reason of mental incapacity.*

" Thus, during the last year, about 5 per cent. of prisoners were unable to receive instruction in reading and writing, owing to mental disqualification, and this existing, it is believed, at the time of conviction."

The physician says, in the same document, page 34, —

" At least 19 undoubted cases of defective intellect, consisting of imbecility, idiocy, dementia, and mania, have been received in the past year. Besides the subjects of these, others have entered in a state of mind that was at least doubtful, and several have come in with their reason unsettled, from great mental anguish."

Again, —

" We have had under treatment, during the year, 5 recent cases of mental derangement, of which 3 existed, to a greater or less degree, before imprisonment."

And again, —

" The total number of cases, old and new, (i. e., of mental derangement,) is 14; in addition to which, we have had 3 old cases dismissed by expiration of sentence, — making an aggregate of 17 cases, in the house some time in the course of the year. 6 of these 14 were more or less affected before committal.

" I feel bound respectfully to bespeak your consideration for some alteration, which, after further reflection, I shall take an opportunity to propose, in the treatment of lunatics who may hereafter come within your jurisdiction.

" As long, however, as the necessity arising from the want of a State Hospital continues, indigent idiots and lunatics, addicted to disorderly conduct, will be convicted of penal offences and sent to the Penitentiary.

" It behoves us, therefore, to consider the feasibility of adopting some means of mitigating the character of their confinement here."

LEGISLATIVE ACTION IN FAVOR OF LUNATICS IN PENITEN-TIARIES AND ELSEWHERE.

In the state of *Maine*, a lunatic, who has been in the Prison in Paris, Me., 3 years, indicted for murdering his wife and two children, acquitted by the jury on the plea and proof of insanity, by an act of the last legislature, is to be sent to the Asylum at Augusta, and, after his own property is expended, is to be supported at the expense of the state.

The legislature of *Vermont* passed the following resolution at the October session, 1843 : —

" *Resolved, by the Senate and House of Representatives*, That the governor be requested to appoint a committee to devise the best means of alleviating the unfortunate condition of the insane who are deemed incurable, and to report to the next General Assembly by bill or otherwise."

The legislature of *Connecticut*, at the May session, 1843, made the following appropriation in favor of the insane poor : —

" Whereas, at the session of the General Assembly, held in May, 1842, an appropriation of at least $2000 per annum was made in aid of the insane poor ;

and whereas the Retreat for the Insane, at Hartford, has not, at present, suitable buildings for the accommodation of the insane poor, nor has said Retreat
the present means of erecting such buildings ; —
　" Now, therefore, in order to encourage said Retreat to erect such buildings,
it is hereby resolved, that the governor of this state, as commissioner under
said resolution of May, 1842, be, and he hereby is, authorized to advance, to
said Retreat, said annual appropriation of $2000 per annum for the ensuing
five years ; that is, to advance to said Retreat $10,000, instead and in lieu of
the next five years' annual appropriation of $2000.　And the comptroller of
public accounts is hereby authorized and directed to draw, under the authority
and direction of the governor of this state, an order on the treasurer of the
state, in favor of said commissioner, for said sum of $10,000, in lieu of the
annual sum of $2000 for the ensuing five years, as now directed ; provided,
that said commissioner, on advancing said sum of $10,000, shall take proper
contracts, on the part of said Retreat, to support the insane poor at said Retreat on such terms as may be agreed upon between said commissioner and
the officers of said Retreat ; and provided, further, that the relief to be furnished to the insane poor, under this resolution, shall be extended through
said period of the ensuing five years, and be as nearly equal in each year as
can conveniently be made."

　In *Massachusetts*, Governor Briggs brought the condition
of the lunatics in the State Prison before the legislature, by
special message, and proposed that a commission be instituted, consisting of the physician of the Prison and the superintendents of the McLean Asylum and the State Hospital at
Worcester, who should examine the cases, and, if in their
opinion insane, they should be removed to the Hospital at
Worcester.　A law was passed in accordance with the suggestions in the message, and three lunatics have since been
examined by the commissioners, pronounced insane, and
removed to Worcester.　Of these, one had been confined in a
solitary cell between 6 and 7 years.　Two others have been
examined by the commissioners, whose cases are not yet
decided. — See the message of the governor, and the law of
the commonwealth consequent upon it.

" MESSAGE.
" *To the Senate :*
　" In the report of the warden of the State Prison, made to the governor,
in November last, he says, ' There are four convicts in the Prison, wholly or
partially deranged, and consequently unsafe persons to be at large in the
Prison yard.　No suitable accommodations are provided for insane persons.
The only thing that can be done for them is to shut them up in solitary cells,
where the diseases of the mind, instead of being healed, are aggravated and
confirmed.　One man has been confined in this way for several years, two
others for shorter periods of time.'
　" The inspectors of the Prison, in their report, call the attention of government to the fact, that there are several insane persons in the Prison, for whom
no suitable provision is made.　They further say, ' they have reason to apprehend, that some of these persons were insane at the time of committing the
offences of which they were convicted, and have been so during the whole
period of their confinement.'　I have seen those unfortunate men, and witnessed the cheerless and gloomy cells, in which, from necessity, under exist-

ing laws, they are shut up. With no one to look after them, capable of administering to minds diseased, they are left alone to the workings of their disordered brain. There is reason to believe that cases, which, in their early stages, would yield to proper treatment, if neglected as these persons now are, will end in hopeless insanity.

"It seems inhuman and cruel, that persons bereft of their reason, upon whom punishment can produce no useful effect, should be made to suffer more severely than those who are conscious they are paying the just penalty of violated law.

"Existing laws make provisions for sending persons, in County Jails, under sentence, who may become insane, to the State Lunatic Hospital at Worcester. And if, on the trial for an offence before the courts, a jury find the prisoner not guilty, by reason of insanity, the court have power to send him to the Lunatic Hospital. This has been done in the case of the miserable man who killed the late warden of the State Prison, whilst his fellow-prisoners are shut up in their cells.

"I recommend the enactment of a law, directing that convicts in the State Prison, who shall be found to be insane, shall be removed to the State Lunatic Hospital at Worcester, until their reason shall be restored, or the time for which they are committed to Prison shall have expired.

"To ascertain the fact of insanity, the cases of those convicts who appear to be insane might be submitted to the examination of persons whose education and professional experience qualify them to be judges. Perhaps a commission, consisting of the superintendents of the State Lunatic Hospital at Worcester and at the McLean Asylum, and the physician of the State Prison, would constitute a safe and useful board for such a purpose. Whether the persons to make such examinations should be named in the law, or left to be appointed in some other mode, will be for the legislature to decide, if they shall see fit to act on the subject.

"It appears to me, that the condition of the present lunatic inmates of our State Prison, calls for prompt action on the part of the legislature.

"I deem it my duty to direct your attention to their situation, and respectfully but urgently to invite you to make immediate provision for their relief.

"GEO. N. BRIGGS.

"*Council Chamber, February 10th, 1844.*"

"AN ACT ENTITLED AN ACT FOR THE REMOVAL OF INSANE CONVICTS FROM THE STATE PRISON.

"*Be it enacted by the Senate and House of Representatives, in General Court assembled, and by the authority of the same, as follows:* —

"SECT. 1. Whenever a convict confined in the State Prison shall become deranged, it shall be the duty of the warden or the inspectors of the Prison to communicate notice of the fact to the chairman of the commission for examining insane convicts in the State Prison. The said chairman, upon receiving said notice, shall forthwith call together the members of said commission, at the Prison aforesaid, who shall proceed to investigate, and, after due examination, report upon, the supposed case of insanity, if any report be necessary.

"SECT. 2. If, in the opinion of said commission, or the majority of them, the convict has become insane, and, in their opinion, his removal would be expedient, they shall report the same, together with their reasons, to the judge of the Municipal Court of the City of Boston, who, on receiving said report, shall issue his warrant, under the seal of the court, directed to the warden, and authorizing him to remove said convict to the State Lunatic Hospital at Worcester, there to be kept till, in the opinion of the superintendent and trustees thereof, he may be recommitted to the State Prison consistent with health. And said superintendent, when so satisfied as aforesaid, shall certify the fact of such restoration upon the warrant aforesaid, and give notice thereof to the warden, who shall thereupon cause the convict to be reconveyed to the State Prison, there to suffer the residue of his sentence pursuant to his original commitment.

" Sect. 3.   The physician of the State Prison, who shall also be chairman, together with the superintendents for the time being of the State Lunatic Hospital and of the McLean Asylum at Somerville, shall constitute the commission for the examination of convicts in the State Prison aforesaid, alleged to be insane ; and each of said commissioners shall receive, for his services in such capacity, three dollars per day, for each and every day he may be so employed, and be remunerated for all his travelling expenses ; the same to be an expense chargeable to the Prison.

" Sect. 4.   This act shall take effect from and after its passage.

[*Approved by the governor, March* 15, 1844.] "

In the state of *New York*, Miss Dix says, in her Memorial to the legislature, —

" She is spared the pain of describing the Jails of New York, as containing, like those of Massachusetts, receptacles for the insane — or dungeons occupied not by criminals, but by those whom misfortune, not guilt, has brought low.   Against that monstrous abuse your just laws have effectually guarded."

The law of New York provides that

" No lunatic, or mad person, or person disordered in his senses, shall be confined in the same room with any person charged with or convicted of any crime ; nor shall such person be confined in any Jail more than four weeks ; and if he continue furiously mad, or dangerous, he shall be sent to the Asylum in New York, or to the County Poor-House or Alms-House, or other place provided for the reception of lunatics, by the county superintendents." — *Revised Statutes*, Vol. I., chap. xx., sect. 7.

" The county superintendents of the poor of any county, and any overseers of the poor of any town, to which any person shall be chargeable who shall be or become a lunatic, may send such person to the Lunatic Asylum in the city of New York, by an order under their hands." — Vol. I., chap. xx., sect. 9.

" Any overseer of the poor, constable, keeper of a Jail, or other person, who shall confine any lunatic or mad person in any other manner, or in any other place, than such as are herein prescribed, shall be deemed guilty of a misdemeanor, and, on conviction, shall be liable to a fine not exceeding two hundred and fifty dollars, or to imprisonment not exceeding one year, or to both, in the discretion of the court before which the conviction shall be had." — Sect. 11.

In *New Jersey*, the legislature passed the following law in February, 1843 : —

" An Act respecting Poor Lunatics and Idiots.

" Sect. 1.   *Be it enacted, by the Council and General Assembly in this state, and it is hereby enacted by authority of the same,* That it shall be the duty of the overseers of the poor of the several townships in each and every county in this state, to make out and furnish to the board of chosen freeholders of the county in which said townships are situated, a list of all the poor lunatics and idiots within the bounds of their townships, stating the age of such lunatics or idiots, when such lunacy commenced, what means, if any, they have for support, with all other facts connected with each case, calculated to give information of their actual state and condition.

" SECT. 2. *And be it enacted*, That the said board of chosen freeholders shall, at their annual meeting, cause an examination to be made into the condition and circumstances of such idiots and lunatics ; and, if it shall appear to them that there is reasonable ground to believe that any of such persons can be restored to their right mind, it shall be their duty to cause such persons, under a warrant signed by direction of the board, to be taken to a Lunatic Asylum, in one of the adjoining states of New York or Pennsylvania, and there supported, at the expense of such county, for such time as they may deem necessary and expedient for a fair trial to recover such persons ; provided they can be maintained at such Asylums at the same rates at which they respectively maintain the pauper lunatics of the several states in which they are situated."

In *Delaware*, the legislature passed the following resolution at the last session : —

" *Resolved, by the Senate and House of Representatives of the state of Delaware, in General Assembly met,* That Willard Hall, James W. Thompson, Lewis P. Bush, Robert B. Porter, and Henry F. Askew, be a committee, who are requested to communicate to the legislature, at its next session, a report upon the condition of the insane in this state, what alteration should be made in their treatment, an estimate of the probable cost of erecting an Asylum, and the probable yearly cost of the same, and such other information as they may deem proper to communicate.

" Adopted at Dover, February 28, 1843."

In *Virginia,* a law was passed during the session of 1842 and 3, concerning lunatics in the Jails of that commonwealth, which compels the jailers to apply to the Asylums every six months for their reception. There had been previously a constant neglect of any measure of the kind. Application has been made, under the operation of this law, to the Eastern Asylum, at Williamsburg, (the Western Asylum, at Staunton, being full,) from Jails throughout the state, and a large number of cases, which had been confined in the Jails for years, nearly all of them utterly incurable, have been received into that excellent Asylum, now under the care of Dr. John M. Gault, a most accomplished superintendent.

" The action of the law," says Dr. Gault, " has a very beneficial tendency, in all respects. The expense to the state of each patient yet admitted, is very much decreased. An ulterior consequence of the law is attended with greater benefits even than its present effects ; for, henceforth, no recent case can remain in Jail till it becomes incurable. The jailers having to apply to the Asylums every six months, patients will be sent in the early stage of the disease. Thus, on account of their comparative recency, a large number will be cured ; and this will happen, too, generally, to the most destitute class of patients — those who could not easily procure medical means, who had few friends, and who would, for these reasons, be otherwise kept in Jail until they had become hopelessly incurable. Thus, instead of being retained in Jail till they become incurable, and a burden to the state for years, they are sent to an Asylum, and restored to reason, and the cost to the state through a long life, either in Jail or in an Asylum, is entirely saved."

In *Ohio,* the law provides, that a poor lunatic, if found lunatic by a competent tribunal, may be sent to the Asylum ;

but, if he is found incurable, he may be returned or sent to the Common Jail. — *Laws of Ohio*, 72d chapter, 2d and 4th sections.

IMPROVEMENTS AND ENLARGEMENTS OF INSANE ASYLUMS.

The *Maine Asylum* has laid an aqueduct.

The *New Hampshire Asylum* proposes, as an important improvement, a separate building for noisy and violent patients.

The *Vermont Asylum* proposes an extension of the right wing of the building 23 feet, to correspond with the west wing, and for the accommodation of the increasing number of patients.

The *McLean Asylum*, " over more than half the galleries, has introduced carpets, paper-hangings, curtains, time-pieces, looking-glasses, toilet-tables, wash-stands, and articles of mahogany furniture, and table furnishings, customary in genteel families. The results of this experiment justify the assertion, that the amount of damage is less than would occur in an ordinary hotel. In two or three years' use, not one article has been intentionally destroyed."

The Rev. Mr. Perkins, of East Cambridge, has officiated as chaplain during the year, and is the regular chaplain of the institution.

The *Boston Lunatic Hospital* is expending about $4,500, an appropriation from the city, for a lodge-building and work-shops. Its garden, grounds, and outhouses, have also been improved.

The *State Lunatic Hospital, at Worcester*, has enlarged the chapel ; opened a beautiful library and office for the superintendent ; procured the passing of a law to lay an aqueduct ; laid the foundations, and made considerable progress in the erection, of new north and south wings, on a line with the west front, for the accommodation of 150 more patients, at an expense of about $42,000, the amount of the Johonot legacy. Its grounds, also, are much improved.

Dr. White's Private Asylum, at Hudson, has received patronage from the legislature of the state of New York.

The *New York State Lunatic Asylum* has expended, from April, 1842, to December, 1843, $16,241, in finishing rooms and other improvements within the building ; $2,579 86, for obtaining a supply of water ; $7,955 95, for furniture ; $1,164 20, for improvement of grounds, &c. ; $2,761 54, for a stone barn, 100 feet by 40; and has obtained a grant of $70,000, from the last legislature, for an enlargement of the building with wings. The chapel was dedicated on the 12th of July last; sermon by Dr. Nott. Three schools for the insane — two for men, and one for women — have been established, which exceed the highest expectations of their founders.

The *Pennsylvania Hospital for the Insane*, 2½ miles west of the Schuylkill, opposite Philadelphia, was very complete at the close of the last year, in all its parts — farm, garden and grounds, main building, outhouses, lodges, circular railway, &c. &c. More than 300,000 dollars having been expended upon it, we could not expect that much need be said or done about improvements.

On the *Western Asylum of Virginia, at Staunton*, $1,806 have been expended in substituting a tin roof for one of shingles, which improvement, the directors say,

"had become essential to the safety of the patients, and the preservation of the Asylum from entire destruction by fire; the importance of which had been impressed on our minds by repeated accidents, (particularly during the last year,) which threatened an enormous loss of the public property, and inevitable and horrible death to a large proportion of the inmates."

The water lately introduced upon the premises has also been distributed about the buildings, at an expense of $1,337 40. Two small buildings, for the accommodation of 30 patients, were to be finished on the 1st of April, 1844; and one, for the accommodation of 50 patients, on the 1st of August, 1844. For finishing and furnishing them, and the support of patients, the directors asked an appropriation from the legislature of $30,000. Dr. Stribling says, although they have no chapel, and no chaplain, they have religious services every Sabbath.

The *Eastern Asylum of Virginia* has a fine chapter, in the last report, on improvements. The board has commenced publishing annual reports of the institution; and if the first, by Dr. Gault, is a specimen of what they are to be hereafter, the world will be benefited by this measure. The facts presented by Dr. Gault, in his report, led to the passing of a law, by the legislature, for a Jail-delivery of lunatics, and their removal to the Asylum, once in six months. Better clothing has been furnished to the patients; a proper organization has been adopted; religious services have been added as a permanent provision, and a chaplain appointed; the old gratings, with their Prison-like appearance, have been replaced by modern and greatly improved castings, like window-frames. The rooms have been provided with iron bedsteads, from

Utica, N. Y., of an excellent kind; arrangements have been made to secure good attendants, in the place of ordinary colored servants, who were formerly employed. No institution of the kind, in the country, affords evidence of more cheering progress, during the last year, than the Eastern Asylum at Williamsburg, under the care of Dr. Gault.

The *Lunatic Asylum at Frankfort, Kentucky,* is not second in improvements, during the last year, to the Eastern Asylum in Virginia. The present physicians, three in number, having charge of the institution, (T. B. Pinckard, S. M. Letcher, and I. S. Price,) say, —

" The officers of the institution are not now required to enforce its laws by chains, stripes, and box-houses, but by kind and affectionate treatment. Insane persons are not now treated as malefactors, nor fed in cages like wild beasts, in their own filth; their personal cleanliness is most carefully attended to, and they are seated, in perfect order, at as fine a table as any hotel in Kentucky can furnish."

Again say they, —

" Among the patients, we found but few who did not use tobacco habitually and intemperately; whose brain and nervous system had been so powerfully impressed by this peculiar poison, that, had they been examined by the most astute physician beyond the walls of a Lunatic Asylum, they would have been pronounced the certain subjects of *delirium tremens.* This practice was therefore interdicted. The result of this law was truly remarkable. There are now those, who, a few months since, were pale, emaciated, and tottering about as confirmed debauchees, who are comparatively ruddy and robust."

" Again there were many, who, from disease, and general physical exhaustion, were incapacitated from taking exercise on foot in the open air; but had been cloistered for years within the narrow walls of the Asylum. The evils arising from this source were so palpable, that we at once made application to the board of commissioners, to supply the institution with carriages. This was most cheerfully granted. Again, as we ourselves are fond of good living, we directed the patients generally to be well fed on the best beef and mutton the market affords."

What was the effect on the per centage of cures, and the bill of mortality, of these and other changes and improvements?

" The per centage of cures," say the three physicians, in their report, " during the 11 months that we have been connected with the institution, is greater by 20 per cent. than it has ever been since its organization. Since the year 1824, up to 1843, the average per cent. of deaths, per annum, has a little exceeded 39. During the last year, the per cent. of deaths has been 4 and a small fraction, from which number should be deducted 4 deaths, 3 of which occurred in 10 days from the time of our appointment. The difference, then, between the per cent. of deaths for 1843, and the average per cent. for the last 19 years, is more than 36 — a remarkable difference."

NOTICE OF PARTICULAR INSANE ASYLUMS.

MAINE INSANE HOSPITAL.

This institution was opened in 1840. It has had some difficulties to contend with, from changes of officers, and jealousies, which are yielding to kindness, benevolence, public confidence, and increased usefulness. Dr. Ray is its intelligent superintendent. Its last report is a printed document of 38 pages. It embraces the reports of the trustees, steward, and superintendent; by which it appears that the number of patients under treatment has been 147

Number at the commencement of the year, ... 65
Number at the close of the year, ... 68
Number recovered during the year, ... 31
Number improved, ... 27
Number of deaths, ... 4
Whole number under treatment, from the first, ... 304
Whole number recovered, from the first, ... 100
Number not improved, ... 17

The officers of the institution have been appointed under the new law of 1843; their salaries have been fixed; they hold their offices during the pleasure of the trustees. The trustees have settled the treasurer's accounts; made a schedule of all the property belonging to the institution, and taken a bond from the treasurer and steward; made monthly visits to the Hospital, and found it in good order; laid an aqueduct for conducting excellent spring water to every elevation of the building; purchased a carriage for the use of the patients; reduced the price of board, in certain cases, for females, to $1 50 per week; and they urge the importance of having all the wards filled, which are now but a little more than half filled, — its number of patients being 68, and its capacity great enough for the accommodation of 108. The receipts of the institution, from all sources, have been $8,792 38; the expenditures, $8,999 68. The bills for the support of patients have been cheerfully and punctually paid by towns and individuals; the farm has yielded $787 in produce; the labor having been performed by the patients. The whole report indicates steadily-increasing prosperity.

NEW HAMPSHIRE ASYLUM FOR THE INSANE.

The first report of this institution has appeared during the last year. It is a printed document, of 23 pages octavo, and contains the report of the board of visitors, trustees, and superintendent. The board of visitors say, " they do not perceive that any thing is wanting, to carry into full effect the design of this humane institution, except a separate building for noisy patients." This they recommend.

The trustees say, the expenditures for finishing and furnishing the building, and for the aqueduct, have been $9,866 56 ; which, together with other expenses for provisions, fuel, officers' salaries, &c., amount to $12,633 74. The receipts have been $9,248 56 ; of which $1,124 63 have been from the board of patients. The indebtedness of the Asylum was $3,386 28. The available funds would liquidate this debt, and leave a balance, in favor of the institution, of $161 93.

The number of patients admitted in 7 months was . . . 76
Number *recovered* and discharged, ... 12
Number improved, ... 10
Number of deaths, ... 1
Number discharged, ... 26
Number not improved, ... 6

The trustees say, " The large number of patients admitted within seven months, (i. e. 76,) proves its necessity and importance. Within this period, it has removed from the hands and feet of the insane many a manacle and chain; it has furnished for many, who were previously suffering all that it was possible for human beings to suffer, a pleasant retreat, where they have enjoyed all the liberty and comfort which their condition would admit ; and it has restored husbands to wives, wives to husbands, children to parents, and parents to children, who might otherwise have dragged out a miserable existence in incurable insanity."

Expense per week, for patients from abroad, $2 50 ; patients in the state, $2 25.

Dr. Chandler's report is modest and sensible, highly creditable to his good sense and judgment ; and we unite with him very truly in saying, this Asylum has made a successful beginning.

Since the above was written, the second report of the New Hampshire Asylum has been received. It is a handsomely-printed document, of 32 pages octavo, and contains the reports of the visitors, trustees, and superintendent. It speaks only of prosperity and success, no adverse circumstances having occurred to cast a gloom over the institution. The only thing regretted by all is, that the measure proposed last year, of erecting a lodge-building for violent and noisy patients, has not yet been carried into execution. All agree in opinion in regard to its importance, and urge importunately upon the legislature to make immediate provision for it.

The whole number of patients admitted during the second year, was 104
    Number enjoying the benefits during the year, ... 151
    Number at the commencement of the year, ... 47
    Number at the close of the year, ... 70
    Whole number admitted from the beginning, ... 180
    Whole number discharged, ... 110
    Whole number recovered and discharged, ... 49
    Whole number otherwise discharged, ... 61
    Per cent. of recoveries in recent cases ; males, ... $76\frac{8}{22}$
                                   females, . . . $77\frac{14}{18}$
    "   "   "   "   "chronic cases ; males, ... 20
                                     females, . . . $9\frac{11}{21}$

Dr. Chandler notices, with regret, that successful treatment in particular cases has been prevented by premature removals. He says, 20 have left partially restored, many of whom, by longer perseverance in remedies, would have been entirely restored. The principal reason of premature removals, he says, is pecuniary inability — showing the value and importance of charitable provision for this class of cases.

Among the supposed *causes of insanity*, of those received last year, Dr. Chandler gives the following : — Ill health, 20 ; religion, (false religion, we suppose,) 10 ; pecuniary embarrassment, 7 ; taking cold, 6 ; disappointed ambition, 5 ; intemperance, 4 ; watching with and care of the sick, 3 ; hard work, 3 ; domestic affliction, 3 ; unknown, 43.

In regard to the *occupation* of the patients before they came to the Asylum, out of 104, 19 were farmers, 23 were housekeepers, and 29 were daughters of farmers, living mostly at home.

In regard to the *civil condition* of patients, 44 were married, 53 unmarried, and 7 were widowers and widows.

Dr. Chandler says, —

"It is admitted to be true, that there are more insane in single life than in the married life." "The disproportion," he says, "arises mainly, in his apprehension, from the fact that many become insane previous to the time when age and other circumstances would have favored a matrimonial connection. Quite a large share of all become insane before the age of 20 or 25. The

additional cares which a family imposes upon an individual, bring with them
a fixedness of purpose, that conduces to serenity of mind; while the loneli-
ness of celibacy unsettles the purposes of life, which renders the mind un-
stable."

The same principles govern Dr. Chandler now as when he
was at Worcester.

The farm has yielded produce valued at $558 92. Much
labor has been performed both by male and female patients.
Many of the patients are fond of reading, and very acceptable
donations of pamphlets, papers, and books, are gratefully acknowledged. House plants are cultivated. Occasional religious services are attended on the afternoon of the Sabbath,
which some of the clergy of the village have been kind enough
to conduct ; and more than 50 of the patients have attended
the meetings at some of the churches in the village, without
disturbance to others, and with great benefit to themselves.

On the whole, the New Hampshire Asylum, at the end of
the second year, appears to be a most worthy member of the
family of Asylums.

VERMONT ASYLUM FOR THE INSANE.

The seventh annual report of this institution has been
received, and is a closely-printed document of 12 pages octavo, and embraces the reports of the trustees and superintendent. It speaks only of success.

Whole number of patients enjoying its benefits last year, 224
Number at the commencement of the year, ... 113
Number at the close of the year, ... 136
Number received during the year, ... 111
Number recovered, ... 51
Number of deaths, ... 11
Whole number received from the first, ... 535
Whole number recovered, ... 230
Whole number discharged, ... 399
Institution opened in 1836

A commissioner has been appointed, to receive applications,
which is a measure of excellent utility. To him the selectmen of towns can make application *at all times.* The state
is small, many are received annually, many are cured, the
expense is moderate of each patient, and the institution supports itself; so that we see how benevolence and enterprise
have gained an important ascendency in Vermont, in the management of this alarming disease of insanity.

Expense of patients, $2 a week, or $100 a year. Total

expense, $13,050 15; total income, $13,493 61; balance in favor of the institution, $448 46.

For employment, they have a farm and garden, a shoe shop, a joiner's shop, and an editor's table. Whether the printing of the Weekly Journal, in the Vermont Asylum, is done within the walls of the establishment, we are not informed. It is a novel and very useful appendage to an Insane Asylum. We wish Dr. Rockwell great success in all his economical, practical, and useful designs for the benefit of the insane. The history of the institution under his care has been one of uninterrupted prosperity.

McLEAN ASYLUM AT CHARLESTOWN, MASS.

This noble institution, under the care of Dr. Bell, sustains its high character. The class of patients sent to this institution, on account of its excellent accommodations, is of a high order.

Whole number receiving its benefits last year, ... 260
Number at the commencement of the year, ... 131
Number at the close of the year, ... 134
Number received during the year, ... 127
Number recovered during the year, ... 63
Much improved, 8; improved, 17, ... 25
Number of deaths, ... 18
Whole number admitted from the first, ... 2,269
Whole number recovered from the first, ... 1,020
Number not improved, last year, ... 15
Institution opened in 1818

"The number admitted, the average of the house, and the number at the close of the year, are almost exactly the same as during the previous year." The institution "has never yet been obliged to refuse an application." Notwithstanding the successful operation of the institutions in Maine and New Hampshire, there has been no falling off in the average household at the McLean Asylum. Patients "are seldom prematurely removed, which was formerly one of the greatest trials;" because "the means for their support are now permanently secured by the understandingly adapted benefaction of a late member of the board" of trustees. "No considerable change has been made in the general care and mode of treatment. The guiding star of our system," says Dr. Bell, "has, as far as possible, been kindness and occupation." Dr. Bell "is still satisfied that no amount of human aid will always render the entire disuse of personal restraints advisable." His report abounds in important results of observation and experience, in the care of more than 1000 patients, to which we refer all who wish for instruction on the subject.

By the steward's statement, it appears that the expenses of the institution have been $22,257 55.

BOSTON LUNATIC HOSPITAL.

The report of the superintendent, Dr. Stedman, was presented to the city government on the 1st of July. It was published as City Document No. 27, in an octavo pamphlet of 28 pages.

Whole number of patients admitted, ... 259
Number receiving the benefits last year, ... 157
Number admitted last year, ... 62
Number admitted from October to July, ... 40
Number under treatment   "   "   "   147
Number discharged,   "   "   "   38
Number restored,   "   "   "   . . . . •22
Improved, 2 ; unimproved, 5 ; died, ... 9
Of 157, in the Hospital last year, there were aliens . . 85
Natives of Massachusetts and other states, ... 20
Native citizens of Boston, ... 52
Of those received in 8 months, married, 21 ; unmarried, 19, ... 40
Of those in the Hospital who could not read or write, . 32
Capacity for hard labor, 30 ; light ditto, ... 30
Could not be induced to labor, 15 ; unable, ... 33
Received from July, 1840, to July, 1841, ... 49
   "   "   "   1841, "   "   1842, ... 44
   "   "   "   1842, "   "   1843, ... 62

Of the 108 patients remaining July 1, 1843, "probably not more than 10 will ever recover ; " — such is the opinion of the superintendent ; still, many of them have capacity for labor, and, as the superintendent says, it is much to be regretted that so little opportunity is afforded the patients for labor. The institution has only five acres of land, and of this "three fifths are occupied with buildings, yard, paths, and wharf." The want of work-shops, and a lodge-building, mentioned in the report, has been provided for by the city. " The general treatment, both moral and medicinal," the superintendent says, " has been the same as in other establishments of the kind. No concealment, no artifice, no form of tyranny, no display of brute force, nothing, in short, will control them like the conviction, that, in our attempts to govern them, we are practising the precept, 'Whatsoever ye would that men should do to you, do ye even so to them.'"

Favors of many friends in performing religious services, in supplying literary and religious papers and books, and making friendly visits, are gratefully acknowledged. The institution is an honor and blessing to the city.

STATE LUNATIC HOSPITAL AT WORCESTER.

This institution has been established 11 years. "From the laying of the foundation stone to this day, Heaven seems to have directed the undertaking, and to have crowned with its mercies the entire work."

Number of patients at the commencement of the last year, ... 238
Number received during the year, ... 220
Number remaining at the close of the year, ... 255
Number receiving its benefits during the year, ... 475
Number recovered during the year, ... 116
Discharged improved, 32; ditto, harmless and incurable, 24, ... 56
Sent to House of Correction, for want of room, by trustees, ... 2
Discharged by courts, 6; by trustees, (private patient,) 1, 7
Average number of patients, ... 244
Deaths, ... 22
Recovered cases of less duration than one year, ... 84
   "   "   " greater duration than one year, . . . 32

Applications have been made for the admission of 157 patients who were not received at the time, and of 98 who have not been received at any time, for want of room.

The expenses of the Hospital have been $27,914 12
Receipts from cities, towns, and individuals, . . $26,930 83
Cash on hand, balance to new account, ... $3,108 68

Amount appropriated for current expenses, by the legislature, March 3, 1842, remains in the state treasury, and no additional appropriation was required for the present year.

We might occupy a large space in our report from the rich pages of knowledge and experience in the last report of the Worcester Hospital; but we must refer to the report itself, as one of the most valuable ever published; and only add the two following tables, showing the causes of insanity : —

Causes of Insanity, and Circumstances connected with Causes and Predisposition to Insanity.

Intemperance,	239	Fright,	11
Ill health,	279	Hereditary, or having insane ancestors or kindred,	503
Masturbation,	133	Periodical,	356
Domestic afflictions,	179	Homicidal,	20
Religious,	148	Have committed homicide,	15
Property,	98	Suicidal,	188
Disappointed affection,	64	Have committed suicide,	8
Disappointed ambition,	33		
Epilepsy,	45		
Puerperal,	47	Have dark hair, eyes, and complexion,	589
Wounds on the head,	21		
Abuse of snuff and tobacco,	8	Have light hair, eyes, and complexion,	608
Jealousy,	5		

Arising from physical causes, ... 722
Arising from moral causes, ... 538
Many not classed.

Per Cent. of Cases from the most prominent Causes each Year.

	1833	1834	1835	1836	1837	1838	1839	1840	1841	1842	1843
Ill health,	8½	17½	21½	22½	21½	28	26¾	25	21½	17⅔	$15\frac{10}{11}$
Religious,	8½	6½	7½	6½	6½	9	4½	4¾	3½	9½	12¾
The affections,	13¾	11½	17½	16	16	14¾	25	16¾	12¾	14¾	9
Concerning property,	6½	10¾	8¾	5½	6½	10½	5½	4¾	3½	3½	7
Intemperance,	24¾	24	22¾	14½	10½	16¾	7½	12½	12¼	7½	6¼
Masturbation,	5	5¾	7¾	16½	21½	5½	8¾	6¾	6	3½	3

STATE LUNATIC ASYLUM AT UTICA, N. Y.

This Asylum was opened, under the care of Dr. Brigham, on the 16th of January, 1843. The first annual report is the Assembly's printed Document No. 21, containing report of the managers, treasurer, and superintendent, in an octavo pamphlet of 66 pages.

In ten and a half months, there were admitted to the Asylum 276; of whom 53 recovered, and were discharged, 14 were improved, 6 were unimproved, and 7 died. "The institution has been entirely exempt from fevers, dysentery, or other serious affections of the bowels, and from catarrhal complaints." This is attributed, by Dr. Brigham, to the thick walls of the building, and the great space enclosed by them, which preserves a large body of air of nearly the same temperature. "We were not," he says, "at all oppressed by the heat of summer, and we know nothing of the severity of winter." Evidence of good health is found in the following : — Total weight of 276 patients, on admission, 34,856; increase in weight of all received, 1,029 pounds. With the exception of 2, all discharged cured had gained flesh, some of them from 10 to 18 pounds, one 37 pounds.

Of the *civil condition*, Dr. Brigham gives 140 married, and 125 single ; 7 widowers, and 4 widows. This is a different result from what is commonly seen in reports of Insane Asylums.

The supposed *causes of insanity* at this Asylum are, religious anxiety, 50; ill health, 46; unknown, 40; puerperal, 20; loss of property, 17; doubtful, 15; excessive study, 12; intemperance, 10; death of kindred, 10; fright, 7; Millerism, 7; abuse of husband, 5; perplexity of business, 5; disappointed ambition, 3; epilepsy, 3; seduction, 3; blows on the head, 3; disappointment in love, 4; masturbation, 3; political excitement, 2; jealousy, 2. — Dr. Brigham says, "We find no advice so useful, to those who are predisposed to insanity, or to those who have recovered from an attack, as carefully to avoid every thing likely to cause loss of sleep ; to pass their evenings tranquilly at home, and to retire early to rest." He says, also, that " it is an excellent rule for every person to follow, that, when the mind is found constantly dwelling on one subject, to strive to withdraw it, and to become interested in some other, for a part of the time at least, and to let no one subject, however important, wholly engross the thoughts." We refer the reader to six pages of important remarks on the causes of insanity, and the means of preventing it, in Dr. Brigham's report, beginning on the top of the 30th page.

PENNSYLVANIA HOSPITAL FOR THE INSANE.

Thomas S. Kirkbride, superintendent. Last report, a beautifully-printed octavo pamphlet of 38 pages, having before the title-page an elegant copperplate engraving of the buildings. The pamphlet contains only the very able report of the superintendent. Both the lodges and the main building have been occupied regularly during the year.

There have been restored to their families, in the full enjoyment of health, ... 68

Many others have been materially improved.

Number in the Hospital at the commencement of the last year, ... 118

Number in the Hospital at the close of the year, ... 132
In 1841, there were admitted 83 patients; in 1842,
    111 ; in 1843, 140.
Total number under care, in 1841, 176 ; in 1842, 238;
    in 1843, 258.
Of 126 discharged in 1843, cured, ... 68
    "   "   "   "   " much improved, ... 7
    "   "   "   "   " improved, ... 14
    "   "   "   "   " stationary, ... 20
    "   "   "   "   " died, ... 17
    The report contains 13 valuable tables, showing the sex,
age, occupation, civil condition, nativity, causes of disease, &c.
The report is a rich and instructive document.

MARYLAND HOSPITAL.

The first published report of this institution has been received the last year.   It is a handsome octavo pamphlet of 24
pages.   It consists of the report of the president of the board
of visitors; the report of the physician, Dr. Fisher; and the
report of the chaplain.   As the institution has now commenced
publishing its reports, we hope it will never fail to publish them.
Publicity is the life of correction and improvement.   Although
reports have been annually presented to the board of visitors,
there has never been one published till the present time.   The
report of Dr. Fisher, the superintendent, is a valuable document.
    The institution was at first designed for the benefit of the
sick generally, as well as the insane, and, while devoted to general purposes, up to the year 1816, $154,000 had been raised
for its benefit.   By an act of the legislature of 1834, $30,000
were granted for its enlargement, and its benefits were confined to lunatics.   The whole amount expended, up to the
present time, is nearly $200,000.   The grounds are about 10
acres, handsomely laid off in gardens and pleasure walks.
    The health of the institution has been good.   The deaths
have been 5½ per cent. only.   The recoveries have been, in
cases of less duration than 12 months, 82 per cent.   " The
institution continues to be furnished with such means and
appliances as are now generally employed."   Religious exercises in the chapel are regularly attended on the Sabbath.
" Occupation, exercise, and amusement, are varied according to
the taste and inclination of the patients."   A carpenter's shop,
gardening, and various household duties, afford requisite em-

ployment for those who are willing to work. A select library, with daily papers and periodicals, is furnished. A school, on a small scale, as an experiment, has been introduced, and is spoken of very favorably by Dr. Fisher. "Music, instrumental and vocal, is much practised." Dr. Fisher thinks that nothing but absolute necessity should justify absolute restraint. "Punishment is totally repudiated." "If," says Dr. Fisher, with Esquirol, "you wish to benefit the insane person, you must love him and devote yourself to him." Excellent attendants have been secured. "The diet of the patients is substantial and abundant." "Nearly all the inmates eat at table." "The bedrooms are large and well ventilated, and warmed in winter with heated air." Grateful acknowledgments are made to 24 clergymen, of four different denominations, by name, for their acceptable services. Our good old friend, Stephen Williams, is honored in the report as the man who commenced this labor of love in 1840, and continued his gratuitous services for many months. May he long live to lead all denominations of Christians in Baltimore in good works, where they might not think of going except for him! The Rev. J. N. McTilton, of the Episcopal church, and the Rev. Mr. Hamilton, of the Methodist church, now officiate with much regularity in the morning and afternoon.

Number of patients, January, 1843, 80; admitted during the year, 62; whole number under care, 142. Recovered, 45; improved, 3; not improved, 5; died, 8; remaining at the end of the year, 81. Of 45 recent cases, 37 recovered; of 98 old cases, only 8 recovered. Of all the patients in the house, 93 were single, 25 married, 14 were widows, and 8 were widowers. The principal causes of disease, as far as known, were, 26 from intemperance, 18 from ill health, 10 from masturbation, 7 from constitutional infirmity, 7 from domestic trouble, 6 from religious excitement, 6 from pecuniary losses, 5 from want of employment.

Whole number admitted in 10 years,					649
"	"	recovered	"	"	276
"	"	discharged	"	"	568
"	"	died	"	"	60
Per cent. of recoveries		"	"		48.7
"	"	" deaths	"	"	10.5
Suicide in 10 years					1

EASTERN ASYLUM OF VIRGINIA.

This institution, located in the city of Williamsburg, has published, the last year, for the first time, a report, wholly prepared by Dr. Gault, the intelligent superintendent, in an octavo pamphlet of 43 pages. As we have had, and shall have, occasion to allude to this report elsewhere, we must be brief in our notice of it here.

Whole number of patients receiving benefit, ... 135
Six of the male patients, and nine of the females, were
  colored persons.
Number of patients on the 1st of January, 1843, . . 93
Number received during the year, ... 42
Number discharged, ... 12
Number of deaths, 14, or 10⅓ per cent.
Number of patients at the close of the year, ... 109

Civil Condition. Unmarried, 77; married, 47; widows, 5; widowers, 5.

Causes of Insanity. Domestic troubles, 9; domestic affliction, 8; jealousy, 2; disappointed affection, 9; religious feelings, 8; fright, 2; anxiety of mind, 10; loss of fortune, 1; excessive attention to business, 1; intemperance, 11; use of opium, 1; ill health, 16; exposure to the sun, 1.

Occupation before Committal. Farmers, 24; laborers, 11; mechanics, 22.

In the moral management, according to Dr. Gault, every thing may be comprehended under kindness and occupation. Religious services are established, and the Rev. Joseph R. S. Clarke is the chaplain. A summary of various and important improvements, introduced in the Eastern Asylum by Dr. Gault, during the last year, is given in another part of this report. It may be doubted whether any institution in the land has made greater improvements.

WESTERN LUNATIC ASYLUM OF VIRGINIA.

The sixteenth annual report, for 1843, of this institution, located at Staunton, is a printed pamphlet of 42 pages, octavo. It contains the report of the board of directors, and the report of the superintendent. It is, like former reports, since the institution has been under the care of Dr. Stribling, a very valuable document.

Number of patients at the commencement of the year, 109
Admitted during the year, ... 46
Remaining at the end of the year, ... 119
Receiving the benefits in the course of the year, ... 155
Recovered, 23 ; improved, 2 ; unimproved, 1 ; died, 7 ;
    eloped, 3.
Number admitted in 7 years, ... 258
Number discharged in 7 years, ... 162
Cured, in 7 years, ... 94
Civil Condition of Patients. Single, 96; married, 42;
widowers, 8 ; widows, 6 ; unknown, 3.
Principal Causes of Insanity. Ill health, 31 ; intemper-
ance, 16 ; masturbation, 5 ; epilepsy, 8 ; injury to the head, 5 ;
dissipation, 3 ; religious causes of all kinds, 11 ; domestic
trouble, 7 ; domestic afflictions, 6 ; hard study, 6 ; disappointed love, 5 ; death of friends, 3 ; loss of property, 3 ; pecuniary
embarrassment, 3 ; ungoverned temper, 2.

OHIO LUNATIC ASYLUM.

The fifth annual report of this noble institution, located
at Columbus, in the great and growing state of Ohio, under
the care of Dr. William M. Awl, is an octavo pamphlet of 78
pages. It contains the report of the directors, and the very
able report of the superintendent. Two additional wings are
building for the accommodation of 100 patients. When finished, the institution will accommodate 345 patients, and be
among the largest in the country.

Number of patients in 5 years, ... 473
    of whom, 259 were old cases, and 214, new cases ;
    349 were paupers, and 124, pay patients ; 226 were
    single, 203 married ; 33 widows, and 11 widowers.
Whole number discharged in 5 years, ... 325
    of whom, 203 recovered, 18 were improved, 51 were
    incurable, 2 were idiotic, and 51 died.
Of 175 recent cases, 154 recovered, 4 were incurable,
    and 17 died. Of 325 old cases, 49 recovered, 67 were
    incurable, and 34 died.
Number in the Asylum at the end of the last year . . . 142
Number admitted during the year, ... 130
Number discharged during the year, ... 59
Per cent. of recoveries of all discharged, ... 64.40
Per cent. of recoveries of recent cases discharged, . . 100.

Per cent. of deaths the last year, ...2.72

Number at the close of the year, ... 148

The history of the institution is one of great prosperity. Dr. Awl says, —

" Our exemption from physical suffering has been extraordinary, and is, no doubt, in a great degree, attributable to our excellent arrangements for warming and ventilating the buildings, in every part; the wholesome practice of starting fires early in the season, and at all times in chilly and damp weather; thorough cleanliness and regular whitewashing, in all the apartments; the completion of the drainage, in all directions, upon the premises; constant vigilance in regard to the detection and immediate removal of all noxious and unpleasant matters; together with a careful and systematic attention to the diet, clothing, and person of every patient under charge."

" With an average number of 147 inmates, there was a full period of twelve months without a single death. Consequently," says Dr. Awl, " the Asylum has been crowded with patients from the first period of its existence; and we have constantly been pressed with applications for admission far beyond our means of accommodation."

The legislature of Ohio, "ever prompt in the cause of humanity," passed an act at the last session, appropriating $20,000 in cash, and $25,000 in convict labor, for the accommodation of 200 incurable patients.

Dr. Awl's report, as usual, contains a large number of valuable tables, from which we give the following results : —

Aggregate cost of supporting 25 old cases, ... $35,464

Aggregate cost of 25 recent cases, ... $1,608

Average number of years for each old case before admission to the Asylum, ...   13

Average number of weeks spent in the Asylum by each recent case, ...   21

Average cost of each old case, before admission to the Asylum, ... $1,418 56

Average cost of each recent case recovered in the Asylum, ... $64 32

Civil Condition of the Patients. Single, 226; married, 203; widows, 33; widowers, 11.

Supposed remote and exciting Causes of Insanity. Intemperance, 35; ill health, 79; puerperal, 32; constitutional, 28; intense application, 5; injuries of the head, 6; excessive joy, 1; domestic trouble, 28; domestic afflictions, 18; disappointed love, 16; jealousy, 6; ill treatment, 7; seduction, 1; fear of want, 4; loss of property, 12; religious, of all kinds, 57; disappointment, mortification, &c. 14; masturbation, 27; unknown, 63; fright, 6; indulgence of temper, 3.

TABULAR VIEW OF FIFTEEN ASYLUMS.

Fifteen Asylums.	Number under Treatment.	Number at the Commencement of the Year.	Number at the Close of the Year.	Number received during the Year.	Number recovered during the Year.	Number much improved.	Number improved.	Number of Deaths during the Year.	Number admitted from the First.	Whole Number recovered.	Number not improved.	Number discharged.	Whole Number discharged.	Time of opening the Institution.
Maine Asylum, at Augusta, ...	147	465	68	82	31	..	27	4	304	100	17	79	....	1840
New Hampshire Asylum, at Concord, ...	151	47	70	106	49	..	10	5	180	49	..	110	....	1842
Vermont Asylum, at Brattleboro', ...	224	113	136	111	51	..	..	11	535	230	..	88	399	1836
McLean Asylum, Massachusetts, ...	260	131	134	127	63	8	17	18	2269	1020	15	126	2135	1818
Boston Lunatic Hospital, ...	157	9	108	62	22	..	2	9	233	58	5	38	....	1839
State Lunatic Hospital, at Worcester, ...	458	238	255	220	116	..	32	22	1777	792	33	203	1522	1833
Connecticut Asylum, at Hartford, ...	...	...	...	...	...	..	..	..	....	....	..	...	....	1824
New York Asylum, at Utica, ...	276	...	196	270	53	..	14	7	276	53	6	80	80	1843
————, at Bloomingdale, ...	195	110	100	85	49	..	23	14	2769	1304	..	94	....	1821
Dr. White's Asylum, Hudson, N. Y., ...	48	38	28	10	6	..	13	1	594	....	..	20	....	1830
New York Asylum, on Blackwell's Island,	...	...	...	...	...	..	..	..	....	....	..	...	....	1838
Pennsylvania Asylum, at Frankford, ...	...	...	...	...	...	..	..	..	....	....	..	...	....	1817
Pennsylvania Asylum, two miles west of Philadelphia, ...	258	118	132	140	68	7	14	17	334	158	..	126	....	1841
Maryland Asylum, in Baltimore, ...	142	80	81	62	45	3	5	8	*649	*276	..	....	588	1839
Western Asylum, at Staunton, Virginia, ..	155	109	119	46	23	..	2	7	....	....	..	29	....	1828
Eastern Asylum, Williamsburg, Virginia, .	135	93	109	42	†24	..	..	14	....	....	..	12	....	....
Georgia Asylum, at Milledgeville, ...	...	...	...	...	...	..	..	..	....	....	..	...	....	1840
Kentucky Asylum, at Lexington, ...	230	156	170	74	33	..	..	15	....	....	..	...	....	1824
Ohio Asylum, at Columbus, ...	207	142	148	65	38	..	..	4	473	203	..	59	....	1838
South Carolina Asylum, at Columbia, ...	...	...	...	...	...	..	..	..	....	....	..	...	....	1838
Tennessee Asylum, at Nashville, ...	...	...	...	...	...	..	..	..	....	....	..	...	....	1838

* In ten years.   † In the last two years.

PART II.

COUNTY PRISONS.

NUMBER OF PRISONERS, IN THE NEW ENGLAND STATES, IN PROPORTION TO THE POPULATION.

In *Oxford county, Maine,* with a population, in 1837, of 40,637, there were but 5 persons, of all descriptions, in Prison on the 24th of April, 1844. Only 19, including debtors, had been committed to Prison during the year. There were no debtors, females, colored people, or juvenile delinquents, in Jail at the date above mentioned. There had been only 6 debtors committed during the year. So seldom was any youth under 16 years of age committed, that the jailer deems a House of Refuge for this class uncalled for. There was 1 poor lunatic in Jail, who had been there three years, who was acquitted of crime, on the plea of insanity, in killing his wife and two children. During all, or nearly all, this time, there had been an Asylum in the state, where he should have been placed. After so long delay, the legislature provided by law, at the last session, that he should be sent to the Asylum, and supported there at public expense, after his own means were exhausted.

In *Kennebec county, Maine,* with a population, in 1837, of 62,377, there were in Prison at *Augusta,* the only shire town, on the 20th of April, 1844, only 12; 58 criminals, and 19 debtors, during the year. 1 debtor, only, in Prison at the above date; 2 females, no colored person, and only 1 youth under 16 years of age. In the opinion of the jailer, no House of Refuge was required for juvenile delinquents. There were 2 lunatics, of whom 1 is blind, and has been in Prison since July 30, 1835, almost 9 years; and the other since July 19, 1839, almost 5 years. The keeper, Mr. Moore, says, he has tried to get them into the Asylum, but could not succeed. Being incurable cases, and having no residence in the state, they are supported at the expense of the state. The last-mentioned lunatic, who has been in the Prison almost 5 years, is noisy and very troublesome; the first, who has been in the Prison almost 9 years, is idiotic and blind.

In *Dover,* one of the four county towns of *Strafford county,*

N. H., with a population of 5,449 in the town, and 58,910 in the county, there were but 6 persons in Prison, of all classes, on the 23d of April, 1844; between 30 and 40, for all offences, during the past year. 3 debtors, only, in the same time, and only 5 since 1841; and these because fears of absconding were entertained. No female, or colored person, or juvenile delinquent under 16 years of age. Here, too, our satisfaction is marred by the imprisonment of 1 poor lunatic, subject to fits of insanity of from 1 to 6 weeks' duration, and who has been imprisoned for debt more than 2 years.

In *Newport, Sullivan county, N. H.*, the only county town in a county containing, in 1830, 19,669 inhabitants, on the 27th of April, 1844, there was only 1 person in Jail; no debtor, female, colored person, youth under 16 years, or lunatic; 19 only, of all classes, during the year, of whom 12 were debtors. Of the debtors, 3 only remained in Jail one night.

In *Rutland, Vt.*, the only county town in *Rutland county*, containing a population, in 1830, of 31,294, 10 persons were in Jail, on the 26th of April, 1844, of whom 1 was a debtor. No female, colored person, youth under 16, or lunatic; no House of Refuge required; 20 or 25 criminals of all classes, during the year, and from 10 to 20 debtors.

In *Newfane, Vt.*, the only county town in *Windham county*, containing a population, in 1830, of 28,746, there was no person in Jail on the 19th of April, 1844. There had been, during the year, 15 criminals of all classes, and 13 debtors; but no debtor had remained in Jail one night. No House of Refuge required for juvenile delinquents; no poor lunatic in Prison, no female, or colored person.

In *Chelsea, Vt.*, the only county town in *Orange county*, containing a population, in 1830, of 27,285, there were 3 persons in Jail, of all classes, on the 24th of April, 1844; no female, colored person, or juvenile delinquent. No House of Refuge required. 35 criminals, and 28 debtors, committed since December, 1843. 2 debtors in Prison on the 24th of April; 5 debtors in Prison one night during the year. 1 poor lunatic, who has been 5½ years in Prison, insane at times, but most of the time rational; can only be sent to the Asylum under direction of the court; remains in Prison.

In *Montpelier, Vt.*, the only county town in *Washington county*, containing a population, in 1830, of 21,378, there were 5 persons in Jail on the 20th of April, 1844, of whom 1 was a debtor. There was no female, colored person, youth, or lunatic. No House of Refuge required for juvenile delinquents. About 100 criminals, of all classes, committed during the year; about 75 debtors; but the debtors usually give bonds, and leave the same day; they are committed without remaining in Prison one night.

In *Middlebury, Vt.*, the only county town of *Addison county*, containing a population, in 1830, of 24,940, there were 4 persons in Jail, of all classes, on the 20th of April, 1844.

In *Barnstable, Mass.*, the only county town in the county of the same name, containing, in 1837, a population of 31,109, there were 3 persons in Jail on the 21st of April, 1844; there was no debtor, female, colored person, juvenile delinquent, or poor lunatic. No House of Refuge is required. One debtor only has been committed during the past year, and this one remained in Jail only one night. 16 persons, of all classes, had been committed, including the 1 debtor, for all offences, during the year.

In *Duke's county*, at *Edgartown, Mass.*, with a population of 3,785, there was no person in Jail on the 2d of May, 1844. There were only 5 persons committed during the year, for all offences, and no debtor. No female, colored person, youth, or poor lunatic. No House of Refuge required.

In *Newburyport, Mass.*, one of the three county towns in *Essex county*, containing a population, in 1837, of 93,689, and the town itself containing a population, in 1837, of 6,741, there was but 1 person in Jail at the date of the returns in April, 1844. No debtor, female, colored person, or juvenile delinquent; the only person in Jail, a poor lunatic, who had been in Jail 3 years, on the 9th of December last. He is thought, by his friends, unsafe to be at large. He has been at the Asylum at Worcester, and has been returned as incurable.

In *Nantucket, Mass.*, the only county town in the county of the same name, containing a population of 9,048, in 1837, on the 19th of April, 1844, there was only 1 person in Jail; during the last year, only 5 criminals, and 2 debtors. At the above date, no debtor, female, colored person, youth, or poor lunatic.

In *Plymouth*, the only county town of *Plymouth county, Mass.*, containing a population, in 1837, of 46,253, there were 2 persons in Jail on the 19th of April, 1844. 24 persons committed for crime during the past year; only 2 debtors during the same time; and on the 19th of April, no debtor, female, colored person, juvenile delinquent, or poor lunatic, in Prison. No House of Refuge for Juvenile Delinquents required.

In *Dedham, Mass.*, the only county town of *Norfolk county*, containing a population, in 1837, of 50,399, on the

19th of April, there were 3 persons in Jail. During the year, there had been 35 persons, for all offences, and 19 debtors. At the date above mentioned, there was no debtor, female, colored person, youth, or poor lunatic, in Prison.

In *Greenfield, Mass.*, the only county town in *Franklin county*, containing, in 1837, a population of 28,655, on the 22d of April, 1844, there was only 1 person in Prison; during the last year, 36 persons, for all offences, and 14 debtors. At the above date, no debtor, female, colored person, juvenile delinquent, or poor lunatic, in Prison. "Not much use for a House of Refuge for Juvenile Delinquents." 8 of the debtors committed last year remained in Jail one night.

In *Northampton, Mass.*, the only county town of *Hampshire county*, containing a population, in 1837, of 30,413, on the 7th of May, 1844, there were 3 persons in Jail. During the year, there were 50 prisoners confined in Jail, of whom 8 were debtors. At the date above mentioned, there was no debtor, female, colored person, juvenile delinquent, or poor lunatic, in Prison. No House of Refuge required for Juvenile Delinquents.

In *Litchfield, Conn.*, the only county town in the county of the same name, containing a population, in 1830, of 42,858, on the 19th of April, 1844, there was only 1 person in Prison. Whole number of commitments, from April 21, 1843, to April 21, 1844, 46. No debtor, female, colored person, or poor lunatic, remained in Jail on the 19th of April; the only prisoner was a youth of 14 years. There is no House of Refuge for Juvenile Delinquents in Connecticut. The subject of establishing one is before the legislature. During the past year, no debtor, for debt on contract, has been committed to Prison in Litchfield county; 8 have been committed for military fines.

In *Danbury, Conn.*, a half-shire town in *Fairfield county*, containing a population, in 1830, of 47,010, there were 3 persons in Jail on the 20th of April, 1844. 20 persons had been committed during the year. No debtor, female, colored person, or poor lunatic, was in Jail on the 20th of April last; 1 juvenile delinquent, under 16 years of age. The jailer thinks no House of Refuge is required for this class.

In *Brooklyn, Conn.*, the only county town in *Windham county*, containing a population of 27,082, on the 18th of April, 1844, there were 9 persons in Prison. Whole number committed during the year, 55. There was no debtor, female, youth under 16, or poor lunatic, in Jail, on the 18th of April last. No person had been committed during the year for debt on contract, but 2 had been committed for military fines.

TABULAR VIEW OF TWENTY COUNTY PRISONS.

Diminution of Crime.	County Prisons.	Bible in every Room.	Population.	Prisoners.	During the Year.	Debtors.	Females.	Colored.	Juvenile Delinquents.	Poor Lunatics.	Religious Service and Sabbath School.
Yes.	Paris, Oxford county, Maine, ...	Yes.	40,637	5	19	0	0	0	0	1	00
Yes.	Augusta, Kennebec county, Maine, ...	Yes.	62,377	12	77	1	2	0	1	2	00
Yes.	Dover, Strafford county, New Hampshire, . .	Yes.	14,727	6	38	1	0	0	0	1	00
Yes.	Newport, Sullivan county, New Hampshire, .	Yes.	19,669	1	19	0	0	0	0	0	00
Yes.	Rutland, Rutland county, Vermont, ...	Yes.	31,294	10	40	1	0	0	0	0	00
Yes.	Newfane, Windham county, Vermont, ...	Yes.	28,746	0	28	0	0	0	0	0	00
Increases; cause, Temperance!	Chelsea, Orange county, Vermont, ...	Yes.	27,285	3	63	2	0	0	0	1	00
Yes.	Montpelier, Washington county, Vermont, . .	Yes.	21,378	5	175	1	0	0	0	0	00
Yes.	Middlebury, Addison county, Vermont, ...	Yes.	24,940	4	00	0	0	0	0	0	00
Yes.	Barnstable, Barnstable county, Massachusetts,	Yes.	31,109	3	16	0	0	0	0	0	00
Yes.	Edgartown, Duke's county, Massachusetts, .	Yes.	3,785	0	5	0	0	0	0	0	00
Yes.	Newburyport, Essex county, Massachusetts, .	Yes.	31,229	1	54	0	0	0	0	1	00
Yes.	Nantucket, Nantucket county, Massachusetts,	No.	9,048	1	7	0	0	0	0	0	00
Yes.	Plymouth, Plymouth county, Massachusetts,		46,253	2	26	0	0	0	0	0	00
Unknown.	Dedham, Norfolk county, Massachusetts, . .	Yes.	50,399	3	54	0	0	0	0	0	00
Yes.	Greenfield, Franklin county, Massachusetts,	Yes.	28,655	1	50	0	0	0	0	0	00
Yes.	Northampton, Hampshire county, Mass., . . .	Yes.	30,413	3	50	0	0	0	0	0	00
Yes.	Litchfield, Litchfield county, Connecticut, . .	Yes.	42,858	1	46	0	0	0	0	0	00
Yes.	Danbury, Fairfield county, Connecticut, ...	Yes.	23,500	3	20	0	0	0	1	0	00
Increases.	Brooklyn, Windham county, Connecticut, . .	Yes.	27,082	9	55	0	0	1	0	0	00
	Twenty County Prisons, April and May, 1844,		601,384	73	842	6	2	1	2	6	00

1 prisoner . . . . . to   8,238 souls, in April, 1844.
1 prisoner . . . . . "   714   "   " the whole year.
1 debtor   . . . . . " 100,230   "   " April, 1844.
1 female   . . . . . " 300,692   "   "   "   "
1 youth under 16 " 200,461   "   "   "   "
1 poor lunatic . . . " 100,290   "   "   "   "

NEGLECT OF MORAL AND RELIGIOUS INSTRUCTION IN COMMON JAILS.

The keeper of the Prison in *Oxford county, Paris, Me.,* under date April 24, 1844, says, every room is supplied with a Bible, but there is no religious service on the Sabbath, and no Sabbath school.

The keeper of the Prison in *Kennebec county,* at *Augusta, Me.,* under date April 20, 1844, says, every room is supplied with a Bible; but there is no religious service on the Sabbath, and no Sabbath school.

The keeper of the Prison in *Strafford county*, at *Dover,* *N. H.*, under date April 17, 1844, says, every room is supplied with a Bible ; but there never has been a religious service on the Sabbath, and there is no Sabbath school.

The keeper of the Prison in *Sullivan county*, at *Newport,* *N. H.*, says, every room is supplied with a Bible ; but there is no religious service on the Sabbath, and no Sabbath school.

The keeper of the Prison in *Rutland county*, at *Rutland,* *Vt.*, under date April 26, 1844, says, every room is supplied with a Bible ; but there is no religious service on the Sabbath, and no Sabbath school.

The keeper of the Prison in *Windham county, Vt.*, says, every room is supplied with a Bible ; but there is no religious service on the Sabbath, and no Sabbath school.

The keeper of the Prison in *Orange county, Vt.*, under date April 24, 1844, says, every room is supplied with a Bible ; but there is no religious service on the Sabbath, and no Sabbath school.

The keeper of the Prison in *Washington county, Mont-* *pelier, Vt.*, under date April 20, 1844, says, every room is not supplied with a Bible, and there is no religious service on the Sabbath, and no Sabbath school.

The keeper of the Prison in *Addison county, Middlebury,* *Vt.*, under date April 20, 1844, says, every room is supplied with a Bible ; but there is no religious service on the Sabbath, and no Sabbath school.

The keeper of the Prison in *Barnstable county, Barnstable,* *Mass.*, under date April 21, 1844, says, every room is supplied with a Bible ; but there is no religious service on the Sabbath, and no Sabbath school.

The keeper of the Prison in *Duke's county*, at *Edgartown,* *Mass.*, under date May 2, 1844, says, every room is supplied with a Bible ; but there is no religious service on the Sabbath, and no Sabbath school.

The keeper of the Prison at *Newburyport, Mass.*, under date April, 1844, says, every room has a Bible ; but there is no religious service on the Sabbath, and no Sabbath school.

The keeper of the Prison at *Nantucket, Mass.*, under date April 19, 1844, says, every room is not supplied with a Bible ; it is unknown to him whether prisoners are supplied with a Bible when in their rooms ; and there is no religious service on the Sabbath, and no Sabbath school.

The keeper of the Prison in *Plymouth county, Mass.*, under date April 19, 1844, says, the prisoners are supplied with the

Bible when in their rooms ; but there is no religious service on the Sabbath, and no Sabbath school.

The keeper of the Prison in *Norfolk county*, at *Dedham, Mass.*, under date April 19, 1844, says, every room is supplied with a Bible, and, when a number are in Prison, persons frequently call, on the Sabbath, to distribute tracts, and hold religious conversation with the prisoners ; but no regular service — no Sabbath school. The Jail is frequently empty.

The keeper of the Prison in *Franklin county, Greenfield, Mass.*, under date April 22, 1844, says, every room has a Bible ; but there is no religious service on the Sabbath, except occasionally, and no Sabbath school.

The keeper of the Prison in *Hampshire county*, at *Northampton, Mass.*, under date May 7, 1844, says, every room is supplied with a Bible ; but there is no religious service on the Sabbath, and no Sabbath school.

The keeper of the Prison in *Litchfield county*, at *Litchfield, Conn.*, under date April 23, 1844, says, every room is supplied with a Bible ; but there is no religious service on the Sabbath, and no Sabbath school.

The keeper of the Prison at *Danbury, Conn.*, under date April 20, 1844, says, not quite every room is supplied with a Bible ; the prisoners are not supplied with the Bible when in their rooms ; and there is no religious service on the Sabbath, and no Sabbath school.

The keeper of the Prison at *Brooklyn, Conn.*, under date April 23, 1844, says, every room is supplied with a Bible ; there is a religious service on the Sabbath, in the summer once in two weeks, in the winter not so often ; there are three clergymen in town, who take their turns, — Mr. Huntington, Mr. Camp, and Mr. Celitson ; but there is no Sabbath school.

In 18 County Prisons, out of 20, there is no religious service on the Sabbath, and no Sabbath school. In 1 of the 20, persons frequently call to hold religious conversation, and distribute tracts. In another of the 20, three clergymen alternate in performing a religious service.

In 1 out of 20, every room is not supplied with a Bible, and the keeper does not know whether the prisoners are supplied when in their rooms.

In 1 out of 20, every room is not supplied, but the prisoners are supplied when in their rooms.

Thus we see the neglect of moral and religious instruction in County Prisons.

DIMINUTION OF CRIME.

In *Maine*, the keeper of the Prison, Eleazer C. Shaw, in *Oxford county*, at *Paris*, in answer to the question, "What has been the effect of the temperance reformation on crime?" under date April 24, 1844, says, "Crime has greatly diminished."

The keeper of the Prison, Lewis D. Moore, in *Kennebec county*, at *Augusta, Me.*, in answer to the question, "Does crime increase, or diminish?" under date April 20, 1844, says, judging from the number of prisoners committed for the last two or three years, and previous to that, "I should think crime was diminishing." And in answer to the question, "What are the causes of this diminution?" he says, "A better state of society in all respects, particularly caused by the temperance reform."

In *New Hampshire*, the keeper of the Prison, James Hanson, in *Strafford county*, at *Dover*, in answer to the question, "Does crime increase, or diminish?" says, under date April 23, 1844, "Crime decreases;" and in answer to the question, "What are the causes of this diminution?" he says, "The Washingtonian movement," and adds, "petty larceny, committed while intoxicated, diminishes since the glorious reform in favor of temperance — the effect is 99 per cent. diminution."

The keeper of the Prison, David Harris, in *Sullivan county, Newport, N. H.*, under date April 29, 1844, says, "Crime diminishes," and assigns as the cause, the "temperance reformation."

In *Vermont*, the keeper of the Prison and sheriff in *Rutland county*, under date April 26, 1844, says, "Crime probably diminishes," and assigns, as one cause, the "temperance reformation."

The keeper of the Prison in *Windham county, Vt.*, William H. Osgood, under date April 19, 1844, says, "Crime diminishes; the effect of the temperance reformation on crime is good." "As this is a mere Jail, the business, as I am proud to say is the case throughout our state, is very small. Present number of prisoners, none. No debtor in Jail a single night during the year."

The keeper of the Prison, Charles Howes, in *Orange county, Chelsea, Vt.*, under date April 24, 1844, says, "Crime increases ; and assigns the temperance reformation as one of the causes " ! !!

The keeper of the Prison, Gamaliel Washburn, in *Washington county, Montpelier, Vt.*, under date April 20, 1844, says, " Crime diminishes ; " thinks " temperance is the cause ; " and says, " the temperance reformation has done much for the prevention of crime."

The keeper of the Prison, J. Dorrance, in *Addison county, Vt.*, under date April 16, 1844, says, " Crime diminishes ; " " the reason is, the cause of temperance prevails ; " and says, " The effect of the temperance reformation on crime has been great."

In *Massachusetts*, the keeper of the Prison, Charles Lewis, in *Barnstable*, writes, under date April 21, 1844, that he "thinks crime diminishes ; " that " one cause of this diminution is the temperance reform."

The keeper of the Prison, Josiah D. Pease, in *Duke's county, Edgartown, Mass.*, under date May 2, 1844, says, " Crime has diminished ; " assigns " temperance as the cause." " The effect of the temperance reformation on crime has been very great." Number of prisoners at the present time, none ; whole number, of all classes, during the year, 5 ; debtors and females in Prison during the whole of the past year, none.

The keeper of the Prison, Elisha Starbuck, in *Nantucket, Mass.*, under date April 18, 1844, says, " As a matter of opinion, crime diminishes." Present number of prisoners, 1 ; whole number during the year, 5.

The keeper of the Prison in *Plymouth, Mass.*, under date April 19, 1844, says, " Crime diminishes ; the temperance reformation diminishes the number of prisoners." Present number of prisoners, 2 ; number of debtors and females in Prison during the year, none.

The keeper of the Prison, John Akerman, in *Newburyport, Mass.*, under date April, 1844, is " happy to answer, Crime diminishes ; " assigns as the cause, " the Washingtonian movement ; " and says, " There has been no commitment to the Jail in Newburyport for the crime of drunkenness since December 4, 1843." Present number of prisoners, 1.

The keeper of the Prison, D. M. Carpenter, in *Greenfield, Mass.*, under date April 22, 1844, says, " I think crime diminishes ; the records so show." The causes of this diminution are " temperance and education." Present number of prisoners, only 1.

The keeper of the Prison at *Northampton, Mass.*, under

date May 7, 1844, says, "Crime diminishes, and the effect of the temperance reformation on crime has been favorable."

In *Connecticut*, the keeper of the Prison, A. C. Smith, in *Litchfield county*, under date April 23, 1844, directs a letter to be written, which says, "Crime diminishes;" assigns as the cause of this diminution, "temperance societies;" and says the present number of prisoners is only 1.

The keeper of the Prison, D. A. Hoyt, in *Danbury, Conn.*, under date April 20, 1844, says, "Crime diminishes;" assigns as the cause, "the temperance reform."

The keeper of the Prison, Clark Hill, *Windham county, Brooklyn, Conn.*, under date April 23, 1844, says, crime increases; assigns as the cause, intemperance; but still says the temperance reformation has been the cause of preventing a great deal of crime.

DIMINUTION OF CRIME, AS INDICATED BY THE NUMBER OF PRISONERS IN PENITENTIARIES.

Maine State Prison. Number of prisoners in 1843, 63; in 1842, 57; in 1841, 42; in 1840, 68; in 1837, 77; — average number, for 13 years previous to 1837, 80; — so that the number of prisoners has diminished nearly one fourth, while the population has increased at least one fourth.

The number of persons committed to the State Prison in 1843 was 27; in 1842, 31; — the average number committed in 13 years previous to 1837, was 44; — showing a decrease of more than one third in the number of commitments, while the population has increased in nearly the same proportion.

Vermont State Prison. The number of prisoners in 1843 was 65; in 1842, 73; in 1837, 92, which was the smallest number in 25 years, the average number for that period having been about 100, and the highest number, 138; showing a diminution of more than one third, from the average for a long period of years. At the same time, the population increased about one third.

The number of persons committed to the State Prison in Vermont indicates, also, a diminution of crime. In 1843, 23; in 1837, 30; — average number for 20 years preceding, 36; — a diminution in the number of commitments of one third, and at the same time an increase in population of about one third.

The chaplain of the Prison, Rev. E. C. Tracy, says in his last report, —

" It is worthy of remark, that the number of inmates in the Prison is rapidly diminishing. Other causes may have influence in producing this result; but it must be attributed mainly to the diminution of crime among us. While our population is increasing, the number of convicts, instead of keeping pace with it, diminishes; showing a greater actual diminution, than a mere comparison of the actual State Prison returns would suggest."

In *New Hampshire State Prison,* number of prisoners in 1843, 99; in 1842, 92; in 1841, 84; in 1840, 78; in 1839, 78; in 1837, 72; — average number for 10 years, 73; — showing an increase of the number of prisoners of about one fourth, which increase corresponds nearly with the increase of population.

The number of commitments to the State Prison also increased in similar proportion.

In *Massachusetts State Prison,* number of prisoners in 1843, 265; in 1842, 287; in 1841, 331; in 1840, 322; in 1839, 318; in 1837, 291; — average number in 10 years preceding 1837, 270; and average number in 10 years preceding 1827, 298; — showing a diminution of 33 from the average number 25 years ago. During this time, the population has increased about one half.

The number committed last year was 97; the average number committed for 10 years previous to 1837 was 99; — showing, in this regard, a small diminution, while the population greatly increased.

In *Connecticut State Prison,* number of prisoners in 1843, 203; in 1842, 211; in 1841, 205; — average number for 9 years previous to 1838, 191. Here is a small increase of prisoners, but not in proportion to the increase of population.

Number committed to Prison year ending 1843, 54; — average number committed for 10 years preceding 1837, 61; — showing a diminution in the number of commitments, notwithstanding the increase of population.

In *Rhode Island State Prison,* number of prisoners in 1843, 22; in 1842, 23; in 1841, 21; in 1840, 14; this was very soon after the commencement of the Prison's operations.

The number committed last year was 10; the year before, 9; and the year before that, 6; showing a small increase; but the whole number committed, from November, 1838, to October, 1843, was only 47.

In the *New York State Prison at Sing Sing,* the number of prisoners in 1843, 763; average number for 6 years previous to 1837, 814. The Prison contains 1000 cells, and on the 30th of September, 1831, the inspectors reported to the governor, that the number of convicts at one time, during the year then past, had exceeded 1000, and that it might be fairly estimated that the number would not fall short, in the course of the following year, of 1200. Instead of this, it diminished, and, in September last, it was 763; — showing a very considerable diminution, notwithstanding the vast increase of population in the state and city of New York. These remarks apply only to the Prison for men, the Prison for women at Sing Sing having been established comparatively a short time.

In the *New York State Prison at Auburn*, the number of prisoners in 1843 was 771; in 1842, 712; in 1841, 707; in 1840, 695; in 1839, 670; in 1837, 678; — average number for 10 years previous to 1837, 641; — showing a very gradual increase in a period of nearly 20 years, of about one sixth part, while the population of New York has increased in that period more than 1,000,000, or nearly one half; — showing, therefore, not a diminution in the number of prisoners, but an increase in a far less ratio than the increase of population.

In *New Jersey State Prison*, the number of prisoners, in 1843, was 155; in 1842, 137; in 1841, 151; in 1840, 152; in 1839, 160; in 1838, 163; — showing a diminution, rather than an increase, in the number of prisoners during the last 6 years. It is true that the population of New Jersey has not increased as rapidly as that of many other states. It doubles in about 40 years, while, in some of the other states, it doubles in 20 and 25 years. The diminution in the number of prisoners, therefore, in New Jersey, is not in so strong contrast to the increase of population, as in some of the other states; although there is and has been a positive diminution in the number of prisoners.

In the *Pennsylvania State Prison*, in Philadelphia, the number of prisoners in 1844 was 359; in 1843, 356; in 1842, 331; — average number in 6 years preceding 1842, 387; — showing, on the whole, a diminution in the number of prisoners; while the population of Pennsylvania has increased about 300,000, or one third, in each period of 10 years.

In the *Maryland State Prison*, at Baltimore, the number of prisoners in 1843 was 287; in 1842, 290; in 1841, 284; in 1840, 329; in 1839, 328; in 1838, 353; — in 5 years preceding 1838, an average of 381; — showing a diminution in the number of prisoners of one fourth; which the inspectors, in their last report, attributed in part to the law of 1836, by which negroes, convicted of felonies a second time, shall be sold out of the state; partly to the custom of judges of the city court, in apprenticing youths convicted of crimes, as sailors, instead of sending them to the State Prison; and partly to the reformatory character of the Prison discipline; they might with propriety add, partly to the temperance reformation, which has been great in Baltimore. But, from whatever cause, the diminution of prisoners is great, while the population has increased at the rate of about one eighth in ten years.

In the *Virginia Penitentiary*, at Richmond, the number of prisoners received last year was 52. The average number for 43 years was 55, and the average number for 10 years preceding 1823, was 72;—showing a diminution of 3 from the average number each year, since 1800, and a diminution of 20 from the average of 10 years preceding 1823.

Thus we see, that crime not only does not increase in proportion to the population, but—so far as can be learned from the opinion of Prison keepers, here expressed, and the records of Penitentiaries—that it actually diminishes; and the principal cause assigned is the Temperance Reformation.

PART III.

PENITENTIARIES.

GENERAL CONDUCT OF PRISONERS, MODE OF TREATMENT, AND MODE OF PUNISHMENT IN PENITENTIARIES.

Maine State Prison. The warden, Benjamin Carr, Esq., says, the conduct of the prisoners, for the past year, has been uncommonly good, and but slight punishments have been inflicted.

The inspectors, John Merrill, George A. Starr, and Benjamin F. Buxton, say, " The discipline in this Prison is perhaps as perfect as any in the country. The punishments are almost universally mild and merciful, and the calendar of punishments, for the past year, shows them to be fewer in number, and milder in degree, than in almost any former year. Corporal punishment seems to be almost obsolete; it has not been inflicted for several years past in this Prison. The mode of punishment almost invariably adopted is, solitary confinement in a cell for a few days, which is always found sufficient

to subdue even the most stubborn.   Experience has fully
shown, that the old mode of inflicting corporal punishment,
although it may subdue, will never reform, the criminal; but
will enkindle, and keep alive, the blighting spirit of revenge.
The right spirit now seems to prevail upon this subject.   The
convict is now treated as a reasoning being; and he sees that
justice and mercy may be united even in punishments; and
that the officer, under whose care he is placed, is governed by
the laws of kindness and humanity.   It is sufficient punishment for a convict, to know that he is deprived of his liberty,
as a punishment for his crimes, without being subjected to
corporal punishment, or any unnecessary suffering." — *Annual Report*, p. 5.

Such are the opinions and practices of the principal officers
in the Maine State Prison.

The warden of the *State Prison in Vermont* says, in his
last report, p. 1, —

"The conduct of the convicts generally has been good, rendering frequent
and severe punishment unnecessary, to enforce obedience and establish good
discipline.   The mode of punishment, however, has been varied according to
the nature of the offence and the disposition of the offender, as, in my humble
judgment, would best effect his reformation.   In pursuance of this object, I
have erected an apparatus to punish with cold water, on the plan of the Auburn Prison, which has exerted a very salutary influence in subduing the
refractory, saving time, and the loss of health, caused by the former mode of
confinement."

If the superintendent means that a shower-bath, like the
one used at Auburn, which has been abandoned there, has
been constructed and used in Vermont, we have no doubt it
should be abandoned in Vermont.   It was a *bolt*-bath, instead
of a shower-bath — capable of having a solid column of water,
extended in length, enlarged in size, let down upon the top
of a man's head, secured in one position.   This was abandoned
at Auburn, as injurious to health, and will be, we doubt not,
in Vermont, if this is the construction.

The inspectors of the *Massachusetts State Prison*, Bradford
Sumner and Samuel Greele, make a favorable report on the
discipline of the Prison under the present warden.

The warden of the Prison, the Hon. Frederick Robinson, late
president of the senate of Massachusetts, says, —

"I entered upon the discharge of the duties of warden of this Prison on the
22d day of last July, after the tragical and lamentable death of the late warden, Charles Lincoln, jun., Esq.; and, as the successor of so competent and
experienced an officer, I could not but feel the weight of the responsibleness
assumed; for I could not hope to be able to discharge the various, arduous,
and sometimes dangerous duties, every way so successfully, at first, as my able
and accomplished predecessor.   But, having consented to accept the office, I
resolved to endeavor to let assiduity answer for experience, and such knowl-

edge of human nature as I have been able to acquire in my intercourse with mankind, serve me instead of an acquaintance with criminals, Penitentiaries, and punishments. I came here with the most liberal views concerning the human race — with a heart of kindness towards all men. I have long looked upon a man as a man, whether he be the occupant of a palace or a Prison, and, in whatever situation he may be, entitled to human sympathy, kindness, and respect. He is my brother, wherever he may be, whatever of wrong or of crime he may have been tempted to commit. The more he has erred, and strayed from the path of right and virtue, the more he is to be pitied, and the louder is his call upon our commiseration, our sympathy for his sufferings, and our efforts for his reformation, for his restoration to rectitude, to usefulness and happiness. We are all liable to fall into temptation; if it were not so, we should not have all been taught to beseech our Father in heaven to 'lead us not into temptation.' I felt my own frailties and imperfections, and was resolved to do by others as I should wish to be done by, if I were in their situation. It seemed to me, therefore, in entering upon the duties of this office, if I erred at all, I should prefer rather to err on the side of kindness, clemency, and humanity, than on that of severity of punishments. I knew that the laws, rules, regulations, and discipline of the Prison must be enforced. But I wished, if possible, to enforce them without recourse to corporal punishment or physical suffering. And I have succeeded, thus far, as well as I could have expected. With the exception of three cases, and those soon after I took charge, the government of the Prison has been administered without corporal punishment. The shower-bath has not been used. And yet I think I can safely say, that the convicts are as orderly, as industrious, and obedient, as heretofore, and more contented, docile, and happy. A feeling of mutual respect, kindness, and friendship, seems to be growing up between us. I am sure I experience these affections towards the convicts, and every day gives evidence that the same affections are being excited in their breasts towards me. I have long believed that what comes from the heart will reach the heart; and I am happy to learn that this will apply to convicts in Prison as well as others; that there is no sane convict that cannot be reached by sincere and persevering affection. Men may be governed by severity, but not reformed. It takes but little trouble or labor to let men know, that every violation of a rule shall be visited upon them with an ample measure of bodily pain. Fear of punishment will keep men in subjection; but the tiger is only chained, not tamed, and, when released, only the more excited to evil by the severities to which he is obliged to submit. It requires more time, patience, perseverance, and labor, to govern by appeals to the affections, to reason, and conscience; yet, when the heart can be reached in this way, a change of character may reasonably be expected. Excessive severity always tends to harden the heart, and make the convicts look upon society as their enemies, and nourish a desire of vengeance and retaliation, which leads them to re-commit depredations, and wage war upon society, with a good conscience. Some have confessed to me, that they have experienced feelings of this kind. But when I told them, I hoped a better disposition was growing up in society with respect to them; that the duty was beginning to be felt, of receiving them back again into the bosom of society, after they had faithfully and industriously worked out the penalty inflicted upon them for the violation of the law; again to afford them encouragement, employments, and friendships, according to their deserts; — that there are now many in society who begin to regard those who have fallen into temptation as men to be pitied and reformed as well as to be punished; that there is less of the priest and Levite, and more of the good Samaritan feeling with regard to this class of our fellowmen, than heretofore; — such sentiments seemed to touch their feelings, soften their hearts, and give them new motives to submission, industry, and virtue."

The directors of the *Connecticut State Prison*, Richard

Niles, John Cotton Smith, jun., and Edwin Stearns, say, in their last report, dated April 1, 1844, —

"that they have, during the year, visited the Prison regularly, in conformity to the act establishing this institution, and, having carefully watched every part of its affairs, can state with satisfaction, that nothing, in their opinion, has occurred, during the time, calculated to impair the uniform confidence heretofore expressed in this system of discipline, nor in the least to detract from the well-known reputation of its keeper.

"Every prisoner enjoys, and knows that he enjoys, the privilege of applying to the directors, at all proper times, for relief; and the directors observe with satisfaction, that very few cases have occurred since their connection with the Prison, requiring any correction from them."

They further add, —

"that the government and discipline of the Prison have been strict, firm, consistent, systematic, and humane; and the conduct of the convicts has been good, with few exceptions.

"It is fully believed," say they, "that the uniform success and prosperity of the Connecticut Prison, for so long a series of years, have been mainly owing to the systematic and uniform course with which the institution has been conducted by the warden, and to his successful exertions in keeping its management entirely aloof and independent of all local or party influences of the vicinity where it is located, as well as to the fact, that, while the friends of the two political parties, for the last ten years, have had the direction and supervision of the establishment for about an equal length of time, no change or alterations have been made in its policy or government."

The inspectors of the *Auburn Prison*, S. A. Goodwin, William H. Noble, M. S. Myers, Samuel Brown, and Elijah Wheeler, say, in their last report to the legislature, dated Auburn, January 4, 1844, —

"We may be permitted to congratulate your honorable body on the eminent success (notwithstanding occasional shocks) which the system of Prison discipline, originated in New York, and fostered under wise and philanthropic council, has attained. Having reformation for its object, it seeks the end by kind treatment and wholesome moral instruction, separate confinement, nonintercourse, and the silent and social labor required for health of body and mind, and which may reimburse to the community the expenses of necessary imprisonment."

The warden of the Prison, U. F. Doubleday, in the same document, says, —

"The convicts generally attend strictly to their business, are submissive to their officers, and seldom show a disposition to spoil their work, or damage the property of the state, or of the contractors. They seem to be sensible, that those who have charge of them desire their welfare, and inflict on them no more pain than is necessary for the preservation of order. Care is taken, that they be provided with a sufficiency of food of good quality, that they be comfortably warm in their cells and in their shops, and that they be well provided for and nursed when sick."

"Soon after the present keeper came into office, he became satisfied, from observation and from the representation of the physician, that showering with cold water, in the way it has been practised here, and when continued long enough, and in the mode, to make it an efficient punishment, was injurious to health; and he has, therefore, with the approbation of the inspectors, caused it to be discontinued."

The physician of the Prison, Theodore Dinion, also, says, —

"Immediately after entering upon the duties of physician, I made the subject of punishment with cold water a matter of thorough investigation, and came to the conclusion, that, when managed so as to form an efficient means of punishment, it would be dangerous to health and life."

With regard to the shower-bath in use at Auburn, the last Report of the Prison Discipline Society has the following paragraph : —

"The cold shower-bath which is in use at Auburn, is not constructed as it is generally. It is rather a bolt-bath than a shower-bath, and ought, in our opinion, to be immediately discontinued. It consists of a column of water, of varied diameter, and length, and degree of coldness, let down upon a single point of the head, and may be made, if it is not, an instrument of torture, and a most dangerous one."

The inspectors of the *Prison at Sing Sing*, S. W. Edmonds, T. M. Niven, Henry Romer, Isaac Birdsall, and Henry Harris, say, in their report, dated December 23, 1843, —

"One object of a Penitentiary, that of punishment, is very well provided for here; the other object, and one equally important, that of reformation, is not. All this array of officers and guards, and all this liberal expenditure of money, seem to have the former object mainly in view ; for, except $500 a year, in a salary to the chaplain, and the expense of a few Bibles and Prayer-Books, not a dollar of the many thousands expended on the Prisons, is devoted to purposes of moral instruction ; and moral suasion, as a means of arriving at either of the objects of a Penitentiary, is almost entirely neglected.

"The keepers are specially instructed to have themselves, and permit to others, no intercourse with the convicts, except such as will enable them to perform their duty ; and that duty, under our system, is confined to the safe keeping of the convicts, and the performance of their allotted labor. This occupies all their time.

"It is regarded as a standing rule of our system, that no offence of a convict in the Prison shall go unpunished ; the certainty of punishment being deemed of essential consequence in securing obedience.

"The board believe in the propriety of the rule requiring certainty of punishment ; but they do not believe, that the mode of punishment ought, in all instances, to be by stripes. With some, the only effective punishment is doubtless the lash ; but there are many, to whom it does more hurt than good, and it falls principally on those whose transgressions, outside and in, are mainly owing to the misfortune of early neglect, and of never having been taught the salutary lesson of self-control, while the cunning and adroit escape the infliction. Hundreds of the latter pass their whole term of imprisonment without ever receiving any chastisement, and without giving any evidence that they entertain the slightest aspiration for reformation ; while there are very many, who are continually struggling against the infirmity of their natures, and who repent as sincerely as they transgress suddenly, and who often entertain sincere intentions of repentance, yet who are the most frequent objects of the lash. The board are persuaded, that, with many of this class, moral instruction, kindness, and persuasion, would do as much as stripes in producing obedience, and infinitely more in working reformation.

"This is a matter, however, which the inspectors cannot entirely control. It must of necessity rest with the keeper and his assistants, whose business is the daily supervision of the convicts. Hence it was that, in appointing their principal keeper, the board disregarded all local and other claims, and selected a gentleman for many years connected with our Penitentiary system, and from whose experience they hoped to obtain valuable assistance. So far as regards order, obedience, subordination, industry, and cleanliness among the convicts, the board have reason to be satisfied with his government. But they differ with him in opinion as to the means of attaining these ends.

" His method is the most easy and convenient to him and his keepers, and, with some of the convicts, it is doubtless the only mode ; but the board are persuaded, that, with the great mass of the convicts, the same ends might be attained, with more labor to the keepers perhaps, but with infinitely greater advantage to the prisoners, by producing lasting and salutary impressions upon their minds.

" In the view of the inspectors, he is not the best keeper, who punishes most ; but he who, with the least punishment, keeps the best order. This is a matter which the board cannot regulate, because it must depend mainly upon the peculiar character and temper of mind of the persons employed as keepers.

" From a reference to the chaplain's report, herewith submitted, and which the board have perused with great satisfaction, it will be seen how much has been done, even with the restricted means of the Prison, towards the reclamation of its inmates. From this exhibition of what has been already effected, the board are admonished that, with the power of increasing the means of moral instruction, the advantages would be more than commensurate."

The last Report of the Prison Discipline Society has the following paragraph on this subject : —

" In the Prison at Sing Sing, there has been an entire change of the officers, both of the male and female Prisons. Captain Lynds and Mrs. Beard have been re-appointed to the offices of keeper and matron. These persons have both extraordinary powers in discipline. Cleanliness, order, obedience, and industry, always prevail where they are ; and the matron is deeply and strongly impressed with the value and importance of moral means in the government of a Prison. Captain Lynds's troubles and difficulties have always arisen from his modes of punishment. If he should, in this respect, change, and give a due prominence to moral means, and adopt the more lenient and mild modes of punishment, where punishment is necessary, he would stand among the first Prison keepers in the land. With his great experience, decision, promptitude, firmness, and love of order, we most earnestly wish he would adopt the moral means of government, so far as they will answer the purpose. We do not know that he has not already altered his views in regard to the best modes of punishment, and the value and importance of moral means in the government of a Prison. In the female Prison, we learn from one of the inspectors, that stripes are prohibited. In the Prison for men, the great trial will be made. If it is to depend wholly or principally on stripes, there will be bloody work."

Since the above paragraph was written, the great trial has been made. It was made to depend principally on stripes. And in a few months it failed, and Captain Lynds was discharged.

The inspectors of the *New Jersey Prison* say, under date September 30, 1843, —

" During the past year, the board have adopted the shower-bath as a mode of punishment, in place of the dungeon and a short allowance, and are satisfied it is more effectual in the prevention of offences, without any injurious effect on the health of the offender.

" There has been a decided improvement in the discipline of the institution, although punishment of any kind has rarely been necessary. The bath has been adopted in other Prisons, and we believe uniformly with good effect."

The physician of the Prison, Dr. Coleman, in his last report, says, —

" Until the last year, the infliction of punishment for breaches of the rules of the House, had a bad effect upon the health of the prisoners. The system adopted was the ordinary dungeon and short-allowance punishment. In proportion to the obstinacy of the subject was the time required to bring him to terms of submission; and in many cases, the offender, at the termination of his punishment, had more the appearance of a person suffering from consumption, than from correction for a breach of the discipline of the House. A hint was taken from the practice of another Prison, and under your sanction, a cold-water bath was substituted as a mode of punishment. A cell was fitted for its application, and the first experiments were made with great caution. It was found efficient as a mode of punishment, and not in the least degree injurious to the health of the prisoners ; taking care, in all cases, not to subject any individual to the shock of the cold water, who had symptoms of diseased lungs or other important organs. Thus far, as a mode of punishment, it is found superior to all others that have been tried. It is expeditious and effectual ; for seldom does the same convict require the second application ; while the old plan had to be frequently repeated, to the great loss of time as well as health. As physician to the House, I have approved of this mode of punishment, believing it to be the most humane that can be adopted."

It must depend entirely upon the construction of the shower-bath, and the mode of application. It is used successfully by some, and abandoned by others, of equal experience, judgment, and humanity.

The inspectors of the *New Penitentiary in Philadelphia* say, in their last report, dated February 28, 1844, —

"How are you to benefit the convict ? By causing him to reflect on his condition, review his life and conduct ; show him the evil of crime, the disadvantages of evil, the hardships of the transgressor's ways — the moral, mental, social miseries gathering around his days spent in wrong, — teaching him to think, to reflect that he is a man, that his wicked course of life can do him no good, nor society, of which he is a member, any good ; — show him the contrast between a happy day of frugal honesty, compared with the dreadful hours of a night of lawlessness and crime. Reason with the convict ; do not whip him : condole with him ; don't aggravate him : bring him back to the standard of integrity ; don't debase him below the degree of a felon.

" Teach him to read, to write ; give him a trade ; direct his thoughts in a proper current ; give him the advice of the benevolent, the kind, not the precept and example of those worse than himself ; uproot his evil tendencies ; don't strengthen and nourish the seeds of vice.

" Can it be possible that society glories in the utter depravity of any of its members ? In this our day, are there to be found those who hope to make a convict a demon, by depriving him, cutting him off from all aspirations of reform, branding him, paralyzing his efforts to improve, and precluding him from an opportunity of returning to honest life ? Why, such a course makes him either a convict or a pauper for life ! This is not punishment ; no ! this is destruction. Such a discipline destroys the heart, depraves the mind, stultifies the understanding, deadens the moral character, and turns from your Prison doors an engine of destruction against man, laws, society, moral government, and God."

" The inspectors are gratified in stating that the conduct and demeanor of the prisoners has been such, during the past year, as to give increased satisfaction."

The warden of the Prison, in the same document, says, —

"The conduct of the prisoners, during the past year, has been good, with very few exceptions. Few punishments have been necessary to maintain discipline, and only those of the mildest kind have been resorted to."

The inspectors of the *Maryland Penitentiary*, in Baltimore, in their last report, say, —

"The discipline of the Prison, directed by the warden, continues to obtain the approval and commendation of observers, official and private, as it comes under their inspection. A pervading silence, unbroken except by sounds of active industry, is established." [The Auburn system was introduced in 1837.] "Whether Prison discipline, thus organized and directed, may essentially contribute to the public good, is no longer a subject of mere speculation. The excellence of the plan over former irregular and exclusively vindictive punishments, is now universally acknowledged; its freedom from any tendency to cause a further depravity of convicts is apparent; and that it has a just adaptation to the great object of reform, has been manifested in ascertained changes of moral character effected by it, in instances sufficiently numerous to serve for demonstration of the fact.

"The more extended favorable influence of the system, as established in this state, is evidenced, we think, in the large diminution of the number of convicts which has taken place since it has been fully in operation."

The warden of the *Penitentiary in the District of Columbia* says, in his last report, dated January, 1844, —

"The general deportment of the prisoners has been such as to meet my approbation; and it affords me much pleasure in stating, that there has not been discovered a single instance of disorder or disturbance; which must be attributed to the evident improvement in their morals and tempers, as also to the assiduous and faithful discharge, by the several officers, of their duties."

The warden has previously paid a well-merited tribute of respect to moral means, by saying, —

"The chaplain has discharged his duties with his usual zeal; from which, I have every reason to believe, much good has resulted, and will result."

The directors of the *Virginia Penitentiary*, in their report for December, 1843, —

"regret to be constrained to say, that a spirit of insubordination and rebellion has manifested itself in the Prison, in the past year, of a character so serious as to demand the most decisive correction. One prisoner has openly assaulted, in the daytime, and in the presence of all the convicts, one of the officers, with a weapon calculated to destroy life, with the declared design to kill him."

The warden of the Prison, Charles S. Morgan, says, in the same report, —

"It is a subject of pain to me, after the many efforts I have made for the improvement of the condition of the convicts, and for the mitigation of their sufferings, to say, that their conduct, during the past year, has not been as good as usual. This result is attributable to the gradual effects of a general increase of prisoners within the last three years; the inadequacy of the Prison to accommodate them in separate cells, and the particular increase of men rendered desperate from the commission of high crimes, and the infliction of long sentences. In very many cases, two persons have necessarily to be lodged together, where they can converse, in violation of all the restrictions of law, and no vigilance of the guard can prevent it. Thus situated, they have learned and felt their strength. No less than from twelve to fifteen attempts have been made, within three years, to escape, by cutting, breaking, or burning the Prison, and several of them coupled with the design of assassination and murder. Indeed, human life is in peril in every such attempt. These various attempts have been detected from time to time, and prevented. Open rebellion was strongly urged about eighteen months ago, as I have been recently informed, and again contemplated, during the last summer. Finally, on the 15th day of May last, open resistance was made by one of the prisoners (who was delinquent) to the authorized punishment of the institution, and an attempt by him to assassinate his officer, which, however, was fortunately prevented by the fidelity and timely interposition of other prisoners ; but not until several wounds had been inflicted with a large hatchet. This was followed by assaults on two other officers by the same convict."

The warden then gives a minute statement of the manner in which two convicts escaped, from whom nothing has since been heard.

The warden assigns some of the true and great causes of these difficulties, viz., *the inadequacy of the Prison to separate the convicts at night ; the necessity of putting them together, two and two, in their night cells ; the impossibility of preventing all sorts of evil communication among them, as they are thus placed together, and as the Prison is constructed ; and he might have added, with immense truth and importance, the neglect of the state to provide the means of moral and religious instruction and education, and of the Christian community in Richmond, to visit the institution, for religious purposes.* We read in the reports of this institution, for many years, of no chapel, no chaplain, no morning and evening prayers, no Sabbath school, no particular interest or attention to the Prison from the Christian community.

What right has a Christian community to construct Prisons, and shut up men, and keep them shut up on the Sabbath ; and do nothing, year after year, about having the gospel preached to them ? If they have a right to shut them up, and it is necessary to do it, for the protection of society, they are bound by the laws of Christ to furnish them the means of grace. They have no right to destroy the great moral law of love to man, and the observance of the Sabbath ; nor to shut out by bars and bolts the glad tidings of the gospel. If it is done, they must expect just such consequences as they see in the Virginia Prison.

MORAL AND RELIGIOUS INSTRUCTION, PUBLIC WORSHIP, SABBATH SCHOOLS, &c., IN PENITENTIARIES.

The chaplain of the *Maine State Prison* says, in his last report, —

"As to the Sabbath school, or Bible class, some few attend with interest and delight; but we find it hard to engage a majority of them in the work of searching the Holy Scriptures."

Is this the fault principally of the prisoners? The chaplain says, in the very next paragraph, —

"It would be very desirable to procure some Bibles of a large and fair type, as most of those now used, when new, were unfit for such a place."

He also says, —

"Some addition, also, to the library is needed; but, considering the dampness of the cells, which soon renders books unfit for use, together with the want of light to read, there may be sufficient reason to delay the purchase, until these evils are removed."

What does this mean? It means that the men in the Maine State Prison are placed in pit-holes, about ten feet deep, entered by a trap-door from the top, without windows for light, without fires or stoves for heat; and that, consequently, the cells are so dark, damp, and cold, that the prisoners can scarcely be seen themselves, much less can they see the small, poor print of their Bibles, and give their attention to reading.

And the cold chills and dampness of spring and autumn gather around them, and the ice of winter freezes in their dark pit-holes, — pit-holes above ground, — worse than good cellars; because good cellars will not freeze; and here, the chaplain says, in another place, "human beings, of flesh and blood like us, are shut up in cold, damp cells, during a long winter night of between fifteen and sixteen hours."

Is it, then, principally the fault of the prisoners that the religious teacher should "find it hard to engage a majority of them in the work of searching the Holy Scriptures"?

To the praise of Dr. Buxton, one of the inspectors, be it known that this gentleman attended the legislature, at its session winter before last, and procured the appointment of a committee of that body, to visit the prisoners in these cold, dark, damp, and icy cells, during the session of the legislature, that they might see for themselves, and thus be made to feel, in what condition the prisoners of that state were placed in winter. It so happened that the committee made their visit in a very favorable time, on a very cold day. They felt the cold, they saw the ice. They went into the pit-holes, —

and the argument was sufficient. If they could have had the trap-door sprung over them, and only remained one night, or sixteen hours, without a fire, and with little clothing, and poor bed and blankets, as the prisoners did all winter, it would have been found very difficult, no doubt, to engage a majority of them, for the time being, in the work of searching the Holy Scriptures.   Instead of this, they would have been thinking of nothing but getting out of these pit-holes.   So it was ; and they returned to Augusta, and procured, with the help of Dr. Buxton, the passing of a law for building a new Prison, on a plan admitting good light, heat, and air.   This was done, and the new Prison is now in a state of forwardness, and, when finished and occupied, it will be much less difficult to engage a majority of the men in searching the Scriptures.

The evils above mentioned have been minutely and particularly stated, and promulgated for many years, by the Prison Discipline Society, in its Annual Reports, which have been furnished to the legislature ; and yet these evils have remained, until the passing of the law above alluded to, for building a new Prison, without any legislative action to remove the evil. Many times it has been attempted — never before accomplished.

In the *New Hampshire State Prison,* a new chaplain has been appointed during the last year ; more liberal provision has been made for his support by the legislature, which appropriated $300, instead of $50, as a permanent salary ; and the new chaplain devotes his Sabbaths, and many of his evenings, to the prisoners.   The legislature has recently made provision for fitting up a new chapel.

We learn, from an esteemed correspondent, that the new chaplain, "the Rev. Mr. Atwood, is laboring with benevolence and zeal for the reformation of the convicts.   He has acquired the respect and confidence of the prisoners.   The discharged convicts (17 in number, the last year) have generally left with right feelings.   They frequently call at his office for advice. Some of them are now settled down to respectable courses of life ; and from none yet has there been any established complaint of crime.   The feelings with which they now leave the Prison have thus proved to be the best security of the public against a future course of crime."

In the *Vermont State Prison,* the warden, assisted by his sons, and the officers of the Prison, devotes considerable time, on the afternoon of the Sabbath, to the instruction of the prisoners.

In the *State Prison at Charlestown, Mass.*, the chaplain says, in his last report, —

" During the past year, the results of moral and religious instruction have not been so marked and cheering as during the year next preceding ; still, they will compare with those of most years since his connection with the Prison. A good degree of interest has been manifested, on the part of the prisoners, in the instructions, both private and public, which have been given.

" The Sabbath school has continued to be an important auxiliary in favorably impressing the minds and hearts of those who have enjoyed its instructions ; and he cannot but feel that both the institution and the commonwealth owe a debt of gratitude to the numerous teachers who, from Sabbath to Sabbath, voluntarily and cheerfully perform the arduous duties connected with such service."

In the *State Prison in Rhode Island*, the inspectors say, in their last report, —

" The undersigned respectfully recommend that provision be made by law for the employment of a suitable religious instructor, to be compensated by the state. The present mode of leaving the instruction of the convicts to the benevolence of individuals, is not satisfactory in its results, and, it is feared, may have an unfavorable effect on the discipline of the Prison."

The chaplain of the *Connecticut State Prison* says, in his last report, dated April 1, 1844, —

" We feel that we have abundant reason to be thankful for so many gracious as well as providential indications of divine favor as have been granted us.

" There has been good order, with strict discipline, in connection with the most precise and vigilant *police* that can probably be found in this country. No disposition has evinced itself in insurrectionary acts, and no flagrant cases of individual outbreak have come to my knowledge.

" We have formed three classes, which are assembled every Sabbath for intellectual and religious training. Two of these classes are males, from the juvenile department ; the other includes all the females. The latter have made as great improvement, especially in reading and spelling, considering their opportunities, as could possibly have been expected.

" They can all read quite well, with the exception of two, who have recently come here. Thirty-eight could not read at all when they came here. Most of those who have been here any length of time have learned to read, some of them quite fluently."

The following account is given by the chaplain, of the system and effects of religious instruction pursued in this Prison, to which allusion is made in the report : —

" The males are met every Sabbath morning in the chapel, where are held with them the usual services of public religious worship. The attention is good, with scarcely a fault. There is a very deep interest manifested in these means of grace, by a majority of the convicts. After they retire to their cells, I pass around and converse with them separately at their doors. In the afternoon, the females are assembled in their work-room for intellectual and religious improvement. I usually preach a short discourse, hear them read, and correct them, and subjoin such remarks as appear to be appropriate to the occasion. At other times, I change the exercises into a Bible class, and close the whole by singing and prayer. They have made decided improvement in learning to read. Every morning and evening, the males are assembled in the hall for reading the Scriptures (sometimes singing) and prayer. I meet the females in the evening only.

"Of the religious state of the institution, during the last nine months, the report is quite favorable. There have been many cases of the deepest anguish of spirit and sorrow of heart, on account of their sins, that I have rarely ever witnessed. Some of them are cases of peculiar interest. Many of them have at times been so anxious to receive instruction, that it has been necessary to break away from them, leaving them in tears both of joy and distress. There have been quite a number, who have, during the last half- of this fiscal year, professed to be reformed, and trust they are regenerated in heart, and consequently in their lives. I have carefully and personally examined every one of the 183 who form the basis of the foregoing calculations repeatedly. They have freely expressed their minds to me on the subject of experimental religion, and 66 of that number assure me that they have good evidence, to their minds, that they have been renewed, through the operations of the Holy Spirit. Some of them, by their fruits, indicate the *incorrectness* of their conclusions. However, many of them do, to my mind, give pleasing evidence both of the correctness of their belief, and the genuineness of the good they profess to have received."

The keeper of the *Auburn Prison* says, in his last report, —

"Nearly 300 convicts have received instruction weekly in the Sabbath school. About 100 are taught to read, and the remainder are instructed in the knowledge of the Scriptures, and of their moral and religious obligations. All the convicts, except the sick, attend religious service on Sunday; and an audience more orderly or attentive is not to be found in any religious congregation."

The chaplain says, —

"Among the convicts, I find a warm and hearty reception. — They embrace me as an old friend, though a stranger, and listen with intense anxiety and interest to such instructions as I think best suited to their present condition and future happiness. My private visits are deeply interesting to myself, and highly satisfactory to them, so far as I have the means of knowing.

"Our Sabbath school progresses finely. It is a delightful scene to see more than 260 of those men, selected from the vast multitude here, as the most illiterate and needy, snugly seated, in some 40 companies, either learning to read, repeating portions of the sacred volume, or listening with profound attention to the pious instructions of their teachers, who are mostly supplied from the Theological Seminary in this town, and whose Christian kindness to me, and devotedness to the present and everlasting good of these men, is worthy of public acknowledgment.

"Our meetings of worship are enjoyed with increasing interest. Great attention pervades the whole concourse, (with but few exceptions,) and many a weeping eye is but an index to sorrowful and repenting hearts. There is also an increasing anxiety manifested by quite a number of them on the subject of religious reformation, and I have good reason to believe, that several have become truly pious within the last year.

"Our singers have done honor to themselves, and rendered material assistance in our devotional exercises.

"The Bible is the standard work for the perusal of these men, and some of them read no other book. I very much regret that some of them are compelled to use the old, worn-out books, unfit for further use in any place, especially in the dark cells in the Prison, for the want of new ones with which to supply an exchange.

"The Book of Common Prayer is frequently sought after by the convicts; but I have distributed all that were on hand, and frequent applications are made for more.

"The agent has recently furnished two dozen of Colburn's Mental Arithmetic, which are very useful to men deprived of the use of slates. These are all taken up, and more called for. There is a lack of library books for those who wish to read them. We have a tolerable supply of tracts on hand. If we had a few thousand pages more, of a *new variety*, it would add much to the reading interest of the place.

" If we had 100 or even 50 volumes of Watts's, Blair's, or Clough's Sermons, or some other approved works upon practical piety and religious devotion, I do think they would be read with deep interest.

" Notwithstanding the necessary rules of discipline must be rigidly enforced in such a place as this, for the good and safety of all, — consequently occasional corrections are necessary, — yet the law of kindness is the mighty lever with which to move the human mind.

" They are furnished with convenient shops for labor, and clean, healthy apartments for study, retirement, and sleep. With wholesome food, and enough of it; with warm clothing by day, and comfortable lodgings by night; with the word of God to peruse, and a rich variety of other reading matter; they have the benefit of a well-conducted Sabbath school, and the pleasure of a good choir of singers. They attend a religious meeting of worship every Sabbath, and have frequent evening visits by the chaplain, to encourage, instruct, enlighten, and reform them. When sick, they have the attention of an eminent physician, and the best of care by day and by night. And notwithstanding I find in almost every man a high sense of mortified pride, which is seldom felt outside, yet a great majority of them go to their work, and pursue it with diligence, and appear as cheerful and happy, as most men in the common circles of life."

The chaplain of the *Prison at Sing Sing*, the Rev. John Lucky, in his last report, dated October 31, 1843, says, —

" My own convictions are, that the present moral and religious condition of the convicts is, on the whole, favorable. These convictions are founded principally upon the general and uniform attention to the word preached, the personal interest manifested in the truths advanced, and the quiet and orderly demeanor among the prisoners. I would merely add, that a higher, and, in my opinion, a better tone of moral and religious feeling would be discovered among the convicts, had the resolution of the inspectors, inviting competent teachers to conduct the Sabbath school, been responded to. I cannot but hope that the call will be heard and answered by those to whom it was addressed, or by some other class of humane and benevolent citizens.

" My Sabbath labors consist, briefly, of a sermon in each Prison, services in the hospital, and private interviews at the cells of those convicts who send for me. These generally occupy six hours successively, and are therefore exceedingly exhausting.

" The labors of the week (for I am at the Prison daily) are made up of visits to the sick, both in the hospitals and without; attending funerals, inquiring of the keepers concerning the character and conduct of those convicts with whom I had conversed on the Sabbath, and making diligent inquiries of sheriffs and other visitors concerning the character and habits of convicts previous to their coming here, as well as after their discharge. I also consume some time in visiting the families and friends of those convicts who are now in Prison, as well as those who have left; and as the families, &c. of nearly one half of our men live in and near the city of New York, much can be accomplished in a short time.

" Now, all this diligence of inquiry may by some be deemed not merely unimportant, but absolutely impertinent. When, however, the *exclusive* object and beneficial results of this solicitude shall be fully developed, it will be duly appreciated.

" Through the aid of my note-books, (now seven or eight in number,) I have been able to test the silent or Auburn system, in this respect, (i. e. in regard to its reformatory effects,) by keeping an eye upon, and searching out, discharged convicts.

" I have, during the last three years, made every effort to collect and concentrate all the statistics which had a bearing on this question. These statistics include a few months over three years, which is the average term of commitments. Not far from 800 is the average number of convicts in Prison, during this time, (i. e. three years,) while the same number have been discharged during the same time, by death or otherwise. Of course, our Prison is filled and emptied once in three years. The statistics of three years, therefore, will afford *criteria* from which unequivocal decisions may be had in reference to the comparative utility of the Auburn system.

" The first item in the accompanying list of statistics, includes the names, addresses, and references of 100 convicts, who have been discharged, since the spring of 1840, and who, when last heard from, were doing well.

" A considerable number of these 100 men are in church fellowship with the different denominations of Christians.

" Most of them signed the temperance pledge when they left the Prison.

" Permit me here, gentlemen, to suggest the importance of not exposing these men, when inquiry at their several addresses may be made for them.

" The names of more than a score of discharged convicts, whom I have casually seen or heard from, and am confident, therefore, that they are doing well, might, and in justice ought to, be added to the list; but as no other reference could be offered than my own treacherous recollection, it was deemed injudicious to present them.

" The second item of statistics which accompanies this report, contains all the names of those convicts who have died during the period already specified. They are, as will be seen, 74 in number.

" Those who gave any reasonable hope in their death, are designated by the term ' well,' which is connected with 22 of their names.

" It will be seen by the third item of statistics, that, of the 854 who have been discharged since the spring of 1840, 43 only have returned to Prison. Hence not far from 1 in 19 are what is familiarly called ' second comers,' [or have been recommitted.]

" From item fourth, the inspectors will learn, that, of the 95 who have been the favored subjects of executive clemency, during the above-specified period, only *four* have returned to this Prison, which furnishes an unsophisticated argument in favor of a judicious exercise of the pardoning power.

" It has been stated, that 854 criminals, after having tested the Auburn system of Penitentiary discipline, for some three years, have been discharged.

" Now, the question of greatest possible interest to this institution is, ' Where are these men?' The statistics which accompany this report answer this question only in part. They state that 74 of the 854 died in Prison, leaving 780. Deduct from this number the 43 who have returned to Prison, and the 100 whom the statistics represent as doing well, still 637 remain unaccounted for.

" Again the important question revolves, ' Where are they?' My own opinion is, gentlemen, that at least one half of them ought to be added to the list of those 100 who are represented as doing well. My reasons for this opinion are these : —

" 1. I should know most of these men, let me see them where I might; but in none of the Prisons which I have visited, have I seen altogether, during the three years, more than 6 of them; nor have I heard from those who had a personal knowledge of the facts ; and I have made diligent inquiry.

" 2. The arrest of those who have once been in Prison, is generally announced in the papers ; but I have read all which came to hand, with this object constantly in view, and, up to this hour, I have failed of seeing more than one half a dozen of the names or descriptions of persons, which would apply to the men we are inquiring after, nor have I heard any person say he had *seen* more or *knew* of more.

" 3. Although the population of this state was less, by one third, in the winter of 1830 and 31, than it now is, yet there were 200 convicts more then (i. e. in Prison at Sing Sing) than there now are. Under these circumstances, gentlemen, what charitable or even reasonable conjecture is left for us, other than that a majority of these men have found an asylum in some sequestered spot, where, far from the withering and proscriptive ire of their more fortunate fellow-men, they may consummate the good resolutions they formed while under your wholesome discipline ? "

The inspectors of the *New Jersey Prison* say, —

" The books lately procured by direction of the legislature are generally read with interest, and we hope not without profit to many of the convicts.

" Our renewed thanks are due to the clergy of Trenton and vicinity, of the different denominations, for their continued voluntary exertions in behalf of the unfortunate and depraved inmates of the Prison.

"Public worship on the Sabbath is generally performed, and, we hope, in some cases, with a salutary effect."

The chaplain of the new *Penitentiary in Philadelphia* says, —

" The past year has been marked by the general good deportment of the prisoners, quietness, industry, order, and contentment. There are very few who do not feel grateful for attention to their religious interests, and receive respectfully any suggestions relating to their moral and religious welfare.

" Of the prisoners discharged in 1843, a considerable portion excited the hope of reform. I have seen or heard from a number of them, who appeared to be restored to the confidence of their friends and society, and are engaged in various, and some in trustful, occupations. Others remain in Prison, who, during the past year, have yielded satisfactory evidence of being benefited by the discipline and instruction of the institution.

" Aided by the valuable services of several gentlemen, the usual religious services have been maintained as heretofore. Sermons have been delivered, tracts circulated, and additions made to the library of the Philadelphia Prison Discipline Society. Copies of the Holy Scriptures have been supplied by the Young Men's Bible Society of Philadelphia ; and, through the kind interposition of Mr. Frederic A. Packard, the American Sunday School Union have contributed a large number of their hymn books for the use of the prisoners.

" Of those who were discharged last year, 42 entered the institution unable to read and write. Of these, 19 were taught to read, and 14 to read and write ; while 9 were unable to read, 6 of them disqualified by age or indifference, and 3 refused to receive instruction. Others, who were able to read only, on their admission, were taught to write during their confinement. Of 156 committed, 99 read and write, 26 can read, and 31 cannot read."

The chaplain, John B. Ferguson, of the *Penitentiary in Washington, D. C.*, says, under date January 1, 1844, —

" It affords me pleasure to report to you the good conduct of the prisoners during the past year. I cannot speak too highly of their deportment during religious services. Not in a single instance have I been interrupted in the discharge of my official duty. I also have the pleasure of stating that the Sunday school is in successful operation, and, with the aid of some of the prisoners, (who act as teachers,) much may be expected from it in improving the minds of many whose education has been neglected. Some have, during the past year, progressed from their letters to a knowledge of reading. We now have the evidence in this institution of its fitness as a place of correction, to those unfortunate individuals, many of whom, I doubt not, will hereafter make useful members of society.

" I think it due to Mr. Dale, the warden, and the officers under him, to state, that much of the good effected has been brought about by their good discipline, which is well adapted to the wants and condition of the prisoners."

The inspectors of the *State Prison at Jackson, Michigan,* say, in their report, dated October 31, 1843, —

" The advantages of moral and religious instruction, commonly enjoyed by the inmates of similar institutions, have been impartially extended to all the convicts ; and the result has been, without doubt, highly beneficial to the good order and discipline of the Prison, and the mental and moral condition of the convicts ; many of whom, by having their attention directed to spiritual things, have exhibited dispositions and impulses in their daily deportment, which do not generally characterize the self-abandoned and criminal."

CHANGES IN THE PENNSYLVANIA SYSTEM OF SOLITARY CONFINEMENT, AND EFFECTS OF THESE CHANGES ON THE BODY AND THE MIND OF THE CONVICT.

The inspectors of the *State Prison in Rhode Island* say, in their report dated October 24, 1843, —

" The results of the discipline and management of the Prison, are more satisfactory than at the time of any previous report. After the passage of the act (i. e. of the legislature) giving them authority, the inspectors so modified the regulations of the Prison, that a portion of the convicts work together. The confinement in the cells, when there is no work, continues to be separate, excepting in cases of sickness. The symptoms of insanity have disappeared from the Prison, since the modification of the system of confinement, and the general health of the prisoners is good."

The physician, Dr. Brownell, says, October 24, 1843, —

" The undersigned is happy to report, that the general health of the prisoners in the State Prison has been good during the past year. There has been no case of alarming sickness, nor has there been any case of insanity in the Prison, since the abolishment of solitary confinement." — *Annual Report,* p. 4.

The physician of the *New Jersey Prison,* Dr. Coleman, says, in his report for the year ending September 30, 1843, — presented to the legislature, November 2, 1843, (page 11 of printed documents,) —

" The opinions that have been advanced on the influence of solitary confinement upon health, are too well established, by this time, to need new facts, or any further repetition. So well is the effect of this peculiar treatment understood, that every indulgence that comes within the law is offered to the prisoners, and, instead of carrying the system as far as its zealous advocates demand, it is found now in accordance with good sense to stop as far short of that point, as a liberal construction of the law will admit. By taking this course, better health, sounder minds, and better discipline, are secured, and the great interests of the establishment promoted."

The warden of the *New Penitentiary in Philadelphia,* Mr. George Thompson, says, in his report submitted to the legislature in March, 1844, —

" The prisoners, during the past year, have enjoyed an improved degree of health. The manifest improvement in the health and general condition of the inmates, I consider due to the good effects of the change made last year in the medical department, viz. the appointment of a resident physician to the entire charge of that department. While it has enabled me, with the aid of professional suggestion, to carry out more successfully measures necessary for securing the health of the prisoners, it has also secured to the helpless occupant of the cells more ample and constant medical attention. The presence of the physician at all times on the spot, relieves the mind from embarrassment, as to the treatment of sick prisoners, (formerly unavoidably great to an unprofessional officer,) while it enables him promptly to distinguish the impostor, endeavoring to avoid work, from the real sufferer, in need of the succor which is now more speedily afforded him.

"Among the advantages of having the physician's advice always within reach, is the increased facility of procuring needful exercise, in the open air, for the infirm convicts, whom the familiarity of that officer with the whole number enables him to select as the most proper recipients of such a privilege. In this way, I am happy to say, a number have been employed, (under the provision of the law,) one at a time, in the separate enclosures, recruiting their health, and cultivating large supplies of wholesome vegetables for the Prison mess." — pp. 12 and 13.

At the *Pentonville Prison*, two and a half miles northwest of London, the Manchester Guardian says, on the authority of Mr. Ashmead, the entire routine of the discipline of the Prison is as follows : —

"On entering the Prison early in the morning, he found nearly 100 of the convicts engaged in cleaning the corridors, on the ground floor and in the galleries. The convicts thus work, at certain distances from each other, face and back ; the peaks of their caps, in which are small holes, being brought over their eyes, to prevent their recognizing each other. This employment occupies one hour, and, not being laborious, is excellent exercise, previous to the commencement of the cell occupations of the day. Half an hour is then given to the convicts to wash themselves, and to put their apartments in order, when breakfast is served, at half past 7, consisting of bread and chocolate. This meal is supplied to the whole of the convicts in less than ten minutes. At 8 o'clock, the bell rings for prayers, and the convicts are seen proceeding in their companies, at about eight paces from each other, under their respective wardens. On their return to their apartments, the daily employments of the convicts commence in their different branches of trade, consisting of carpentering, joinering, shoemaking, tailoring, rug-weaving, mat-making, weaving, &c. Those working as shoemakers and tailors are daily employed for one hour at the crank machine for pumping, to supply the institution with water. It is raised from the Artesian well, the cisterns being on the roofs of the different corridors, from which the convicts are furnished with water in their cells. Four days in the week, only, are required of the convicts to work at their trades, from 8 A. M. to 8 P. M., with the exception of one hour for chapel; one hour for dinner, from 1 o'clock till 2; half an hour for supper, half past 5 to 6; one hour in the exercising yard. In addition to this, the convicts may be moved to attend to the periodical claims of the corridors before dinner; to bathers, (every prisoner has the bath once a fortnight,) or is taken to the trade's instructor's shop, to be taught to cut out his work, or to receive such instructions as cannot be imparted in his cell, only one prisoner at a time being so taught. The day's labor closes at 8 o'clock, P. M. One hour after is allowed for reading, and the gas in all the apartments is extinguished at 9 o'clock. By the regulations of the Prison, cell labor commences at 8 o'clock, A. M. and closes at 8 o'clock, P. M. Of these twelve hours, two are allotted to meals, one to exercise, and one to chapel; so that the working-hours are eight hours per day, four days in the week, and the average is even lessened with those who work at the pump and other occasional out-of-the-cell engagements, reducing it to an estimate of about seven hours per diem, or twenty-eight hours per week cell labor of the convicts. The other two days are occupied in moral and religious instruction, and opportunities for general intellectual improvement. The Sabbath is devoted to religious worship, instruction, and reading. The educational part of the discipline is under the direction of the reverend chaplain, under whom are a principal teacher and three assistants, and is conducted within the chapel of the institution. The convicts are divided into three classes. The lowest class is composed of those who are wholly ignorant, or cannot read with any fluency. In the second class are those who can read pretty well, several of whom can also write a little, and have some knowledge of accounts. The first or highest class is made up of those who have received a tolerable education, and each of these classes attends school in the following order: — third class, Mondays and Thursdays; second class, Tuesdays and Fridays; first class, Wednesdays and Saturdays. The school hours are four each day, and the remainder of their respective school days is allowed to the convicts for further moral and intellectual improvement; making a break between the days assigned for convict labor, which must be a consequent physical relaxation. The course of instruction imparted to the convicts under the probationary discipline, embraces reading, writing, and accounts. Scripture, geography, English grammar, mensuration, some knowledge of the elements of natural philosophy and sacred music; and the teacher stated that there were not more than about 20 convicts, out of 436, the number then in confinement, who could not read the Scriptures, — a much larger proportion of educational acquirement than will be found in any other penal institution in the United Kingdom, and must, in a great measure, be the result of the instructions received in the Prison. In the eighteen months' probationary discipline before transportation, the convicts are allowed to see their friends every three months, and to write to their friends once in three months; so that a convict may keep up communication with relatives or friends, once every six weeks."

TABULAR VIEW OF FIFTEEN PENITENTIARIES, IN 1843.

Penitentiaries.	Number at the Commencement.	Number at the Close.	Increase.	Diminution.	Received.	Discharged.	Pardoned.	Died.	Escaped.	Recommitted.	Earnings above Expenses.	Expenses above Earnings.
Maine,	57	63	6	..	27	13	6	2	..			
New Hampshire,	92	99	7	..	28	17	4	..	..	..		
Vermont.,	73	65	...	8	23	18	*9	1	1	..		2,737 65
Massachusetts,	287	265	...	22	97	84	23	2	1	..		4,492 75
Rhode Island,	23	22	...	1	10	6	3	2	..			5,801 02
Connecticut,	203	192	...	11	50	44	4	12	..	..	6,808 92	
Auburn, N. Y.,	712	771	59	..	263	152	38	11	1	21	3,379 21	
Sing Sing, N. Y.,	720	763	43	..	306	181	38	33	9			
New Jersey,	137	155	18	..	88	48	19	3				
Philadelphia, Penn.,	331	359	28	..	156	102	15	11				
Pittsburg, Penn.												
Maryland,	290	287	...	3	97	100	12	21	..	..	483 66	
District of Columbia,	62	63	1	..	31	26	4					
Virginia,	209	213	4	..	52	36	6	6	2			
Michigan, at Jackson,	87	94	7	..	43	36	...	1	3		2,346 56	
Fifteen Penitentiaries,	3393	3558	173	45	1271	827	186	105	17	21	13,018 35	13,031 42

* 8 by the governor.   † 10 by pardon, and 13 by remission of sentence, = 23.
‡ Of whom 2 by fine and costs remitted, and 1 by *habeas corpus*.

PART IV.

HOUSES OF REFUGE.

DOCUMENTS.

House of Reformation at South Boston. The last official report of the inspectors of this institution, is contained in City Document No. 2, a periodical published semi-annually, containing, in the last number, 32 pages octavo.

House of Refuge, New York City. The nineteenth and last annual report of this institution is a printed document of 46 pages octavo, presented to the legislature of the state, and the corporation of the city of New York, for the year ending January 1, 1844.

House of Refuge in Philadelphia. The sixteenth and last annual report of this institution is a printed document of 24 pages, octavo, presented to the house of representatives of Pennsylvania, and to the contributors to the House of Refuge, for the year ending January 1, 1844.

HOUSE OF REFORMATION AT SOUTH BOSTON.

Captain Daniel Chandler, superintendent; Mr. William R. Lincoln, teacher. This institution is located two and a half miles south-east of the state-house in Boston, and occupies that part of the beautiful public grounds, within the stockade fence, at the right hand of the gate of entrance. The inmates occupy the west end of the building on the right, near the entrance ; their work-shop in the basement, their school-room in the second, and their lodging-rooms in the third story ; their garden in front of the House, and their play-ground in the rear. 8 hours are devoted to sleep ; 6 hours to labor ; 4 hours to instruction ; 2½ hours to recreation ; 3½ hours to taking their meals, sweeping their rooms, making their beds, and keeping the House in order. The number of inmates, last December, at the time of the official inspection, was 64 ; it is now, May 22, 1844, diminished to 53. The females, only 4 in number, belonging to this department, occupy a building attached to the House of Industry, and were under the care of Miss Whitney at the time of the last inspection.

The causes of commitment were as follows, of those in the House in December last : — stubbornness, 23 ; idleness, 12 ; larceny, 33 ; common drunkards, 2 ; passing counterfeit money, 1 ; vagabonds, 6 ; pilfering, 4 ; total, 81.

The number receiving the benefits of this House, last year, was 81 ; the number indentured, 8 ; discharged by order of court, 5 ; died, none. The health of the institution is, as it always has been, nearly perfect. There is seldom a death in the House, or one sick in the hospital. This is explained mostly by the division of time, order, cleanliness, industry, a proper observance of the Sabbath, and generally good behavior. The inspectors say, at the date of the last official report, — "The boys attend Sabbath school, and are instructed by teachers from the city, every Sabbath morning." "After school, they attend divine service at the House of Industry. Prayers are attended morning and evening. A blessing is asked before each meal. All are furnished with Bibles, and are required to read them before and after meeting." Thus the Sabbath is spent. In school, during the week, four hours every day, they are regularly taught reading, arithmetic, grammar, geography, writing, and spelling. In December last, 50 wrote a small, and 11 a large hand. In the hours of labor, 40 boys are employed on contract, at shoemaking, 6 hours daily ; and in the hours of recreation, they play in sober earnest. After a suitable time, the boys are apprenticed mostly to farmers in the country ; and, if they obtain good places, in quiet agricultural districts, away from the temptations of cities and villages, they generally do well. The institution is well named the "House of Reformation."

HOUSE OF REFUGE IN NEW YORK CITY.

The number of children in this House, on the 1st of January, 1843, was 306
Number received during the year, ... 224
Number remaining in the House, January 1, 1844, . . 321
Number disposed of during the year, ... 209
Apprenticed to farmers, — white, 82 ; colored, 23 ; total, 105
Hatters, 3 ; blacksmiths, 3 ; sea-service, 3 ; bookbinders, 2 ; shoemakers, 2 ; chairmaker, 1 ; painter, 1 ; miller, 1 ; saddler, 1 ; cabinet-maker, 1 ; confectioner, 1 ; mason, 1 ; cooper, 1 ; Britannia manufacturer, 1 ; — all white boys ; — total as above, not including the farmers, ... 22

Housewifery, — white girls, 43; colored do. 8; total,   51
Total apprenticed, boys and girls, ... 178
Discharged, given up to friends, or sent to Alms-House,   25
Escaped, 1; deceased, 5; total, ...   6
Total disposed of from the Refuge in 1843, ... 209
Whole number of children received into this House from January 1, 1825, 3320, of whom 953 were girls. Whole number apprenticed during the same period, 2995.

The average age of 197 received in this House during the year, was 13 years, 9 months, and 3 days.

The parentage of 169 white children, received during the year 1843, was, Irish, 92; American, 47; English, 22; Scotch, 5; German, 2; French, 1; total, . . . 169

The places from whence 224 children were received, were, from New York city Police Office, 95; from Court of Sessions, 54; from Commissioners of Alms-House, 9; from different counties in the state of New York, 39; returned to the House after having been given to friends or indentured, 27; total, . . . 224

The boys of the House were employed in getting out, from the rough plank, chair-seat frames, then filling them with cane prepared on the premises by the children for that purpose; also in manufacturing razor-strops; pocket-books; paper-cases; making and mending shoes; washing, making, and mending, for the whole establishment.

The girls are employed in needle-work mostly, and perform a great amount of labor.

The health of the House does not appear to have been as good as formerly. The physician's report shows five deaths. There are a number of cases of inflamed eyes under treatment in the hospital, and six or eight patients with other diseases. The number of scrofulous cases has increased. The physician attributes this to the imperfect ventilation of the school-rooms and work-shops; because, he says, "soon after means were taken to correct this evil, a decided improvement took place among the boys, both in their health and general appearance." The introduction of the Croton water, also, into the Refuge, which has been done during the past year, he says, has been another means of checking the increase of that formidable disease, i. e. scrofula. The physician then has some general remarks on the *healthful* treatment of juvenile delinquents, which are worthy of being written in letters of gold: —

"The frequent ablution of the body, to which the children are subjected, greatly invigorates the strength, and renders more cheerful and active the mental faculties. Every thing which tends to make the children clean, cheerful, and contented, not only improves and confirms their general health, but is also a powerful means in effecting their reformation. Every kind attention and tender treatment, which they may properly receive from their keepers, whether in sickness or health, strikes a chord in their hearts, which calls into action their better feelings, and renders them more susceptible of receiving and retaining the good counsel of their benefactors. The mind must be administered to as well as the body; and hence the necessity of giving it that kind of medicine which will bring it under the control of reason. Then your object and wishes are accomplished — the reformation of the delinquent."

Dr. Carter's mode of treatment in regard to ventilation, cleanliness, and kind treatment, together with good food, and enough of it, will cure sore eyes, scrofula, incipient consumption, and a host of other diseases, both of body and mind, in juvenile delinquents.

We close this notice of the House of Refuge in New York, with a letter, contained in the Appendix of the Report from the master of one of the boys, on a western prairie, so full of illustration and amusement, that we copy it for the instruction of all, who wish to know how to bring up bad children, and make them healthy and useful : —

" B. J., November 11th, 1843.

"DEAR SIR,

"Agreeably to request, (of circular addressed me, and accompanying the indenture of Sandy,) I address the institution; and be assured it affords me a great pleasure to be able to give so good an account of Sandy. He has the general work of a farm to attend to, viz.: we milk six cows, and feed and fodder them and the cattle and calves, clean a span of almost white horses, and feed before breakfast; and, much to Sandy's credit, he takes delight in keeping and making his horses look a little better than any other team in the neighborhood. He feels quite proud when I am detained in town over night, and come back with the horses all stained up from under the charge of professed hostlers, who do not clean the team as well as he does. After breakfast, there is wood to chop and split, water to draw from the spring, &c., for all of which Sandy is as good as I am. Of our farm-work, he can hoe potatoes and corn, or dig potatoes, pull beets, turnips, husk corn, &c., as well as I can, as also he can most other work, except it be beyond his strength.

"Next summer he thinks he can cut as much grass as I can. I shall give him a scythe, and let him try. He expects to make considerable next harvest as raker and binder; (last harvest, he was hardly strong enough, except to bind some very light oats.)

"In hunting cattle, (and we have had a great deal of it to do, our pasture is so large, being nothing more nor less than a large prairie,) Sandy beats me all to pieces, for he is an excellent horseman; (we ride bareback.) He delights to get his cattle up when no other boy in the neighborhood can, which he has frequently done in very dark nights. I have sometimes feared he was lost, but he says there is no danger of that, for you can't lose the horses, and he can stick to the horse, he knows.

"When we arrived here, Sandy was very sullen and saucy, and I was obliged to flog him; and after about six months he. in company with one of my neighbor's boys, ran away. We however found them at night about 9 o'clock, camped in the woods, with a good fire, probably left by some travellers. Brought them home, gave Sandy a severe flogging, and then resolved never to do the like again, and have taken an entire different course to bring him up.

"I commenced by appealing to his feelings, and talking to him and giving him encouragement in various ways, making him to have confidence in himself. In hurrying times, such as haying, harvesting, and cleaning up grain, I made a bargain with him, and he has earned enough in that way, by extra work, to pay for part of his winter clothing, and he has also a fine calf. It is my intention to turn his earnings into stock, and in course of a few years he will have quite a smart chance of cattle. Don't think I shall ever flog again — I am well convinced it does no good. Sandy now has a regard for me, and takes an interest in things. Flogging would only make him do what he was compelled to, through fear. One cheerful hand is worth a dozen grouty ones. You would hardly recognize Sandy, he has grown so. I should think he would weigh full one half more than when he left the Refuge. He is about as large as I am, except in height, and is healthy and strong as a young giant. In fact, I hardly know what or how I should do without Sandy, and feel under many and lasting obligations to you for your kindness and selection of such a good boy as Sandy. We'commence our school again in a few days, and I intend Sandy shall write you before spring, perhaps about new-year's. My long delay in writing has been to give a good account of the boy, which I am now able to do. In hopes to hear from you occasionally, particularly if you could communicate any thing to the interest of the boy,

I remain yours,
E. P. D.

"To DAVID TERRY, Jr. Esq.
Superintendent House of Refuge, N. Y.

"P. S. Sandy wishes to be remembered to you, and says he will write you as I have promised above."

HOUSE OF REFUGE IN PHILADELPHIA.

Number of inmates, December 31, 1843, 110 boys, and 58 girls. It does not yet extend its benefits to colored children. Average age of boys, 13¾; girls, 14½. Whole number enjoying the benefits of the institution during the year, 256.

Received during the year, 74 boys, and 34 girls. All except 8, from as many different counties, were from Philadelphia. All American children, whose birthplace could be ascertained, except 21. Committed by magistrates, 87; by courts, 15. Committed at the request of their parents and near relations, 37 boys, and 23 girls.

Discharged during the year, 56 boys, and 34 girls. Apprenticed, 24 to farmers; 5 to shoemakers; 6 to as many mechanical arts; 19 to housewifery.

The health of the institution has been excellent; not one death has occurred. Government is parental; punishment, rare and mild. Religious exercises daily, morning and evening. Clergy of the city officiate in the Sabbath school. Common school instruction, as in former years, excellent;

Sabbath school instruction conducted with great benevolence and zeal, and productive of much good. Effects produced on the minds of the inmates very gratifying to the managers and patrons. Funds in an improved condition ; debt diminished. One legacy of $3000, from Mr. Grandom, and another of $1000, from Mr. Blenon, have been paid. No donations of books have been made to the library. The matron, who has been fifteen years in the establishment, Mrs. Wheelock, whose faithful services the ladies' visiting committee commend, and the loss of which they deplore, has retired, — cause not assigned, — and Miss Elizabeth Morgan has been appointed to fill the vacancy. Mr. Edwin Young continues to be the superintendent, and the venerable Alexander Henry, president of the society. Since the institution was established, 1712 children and youth have enjoyed the benefits of the House ; of whom 519 were girls. Eight pages of the Appendix of the report are occupied with 32 short letters from masters of apprentices, giving favorable accounts of the discharged who have been committed to their care.

SUMMARY OF THE HOUSES OF REFUGE.

Total number of children and youth in the three
  Houses, ...   543
Whole number enjoying the benefits of the three
  Houses during the year, ...   865
Whole number enjoying the benefits of the Houses
  in New York and Philadelphia, from the beginning,   5032
Deaths last year, in Boston and Philadelphia, 0 ; in
  New York, 5, ...   5
Annual expenses of the three Houses, about $30,000,
  or for every 100 children, about $4000
Whole number received in New York, ... 3,320
Whole number apprenticed, ... 2,995
Is not this a good use of money ? " There is that scattereth, and yet increaseth ; there is that withholdeth, and it tendeth to poverty."

FUNDS OF THE SOCIETY.

Receipts, ... $3820 60
Payments, ... 3714 01
Balance to new account, ... $106 59

In conclusion, the managers of the Prison Discipline Society would take courage, because so many states have already established Asylums for poor lunatics. All except three have been established since the Prison Discipline Society was formed. With regard to the establishment of most of them, the Society has had a direct agency. The consequence has been a very general and extensive Jail delivery of this class of sufferers ; and laws of many states have permanently secured their support in Asylums, and prohibited their imprisonment. In other states, where no Asylums are yet established, the people and the government are moving on the subject. In some, liberal provision is already made ; in others, information is disseminated ; and in others still, there are individual minds, of great power, actively engaged in promoting the object. Twenty Asylums, at least, are built ; their doors are open ; their wards are filled ; their accommodations are being enlarged ; their principles are right ; their physicians are good ; their attendants kind ; their employments, amusements, and instructions, restorative and soothing to the insane. About 3000, annually, are receiving the benefits ; about 2000 are enjoying these benefits at this time ; about 1500 are received each year ; and nearly 1000, annually, are restored. Why should not this Society take courage, by what has already been done for the Jail delivery, and proper care and restoration of poor lunatics?

Again, we are encouraged by the smallness of the number of prisoners in County Prisons, particularly in New England ; (in April, 1844, 1 prisoner to 8238 souls ; 1 debtor to 100,000 ; 1 female to 300,000 ; 1 juvenile delinquent to 200,000 ; 1 poor lunatic to 100,000 ;) and the diminution of crime, as shown by the opinion of Prison keepers, and the statistics of Penitentiaries ; the causes assigned by them for this diminution of crime, — the progress of temperance, and the general improvements in society. It looks like the dawn of a better day.

The Penitentiaries, too, are no longer schools of vice. They are places of discipline, of separation, of industry, to a great extent of self-support, and instruction ; where public worship on the Sabbath, and Sabbath schools, devoted chaplains, and faithful officers, are at work. The convicts are kindly treated, and their conduct is generally good. They are objects of great solicitude and care while in Prison, and, to some extent, after their discharge. The severity of solitary confinement is yielding to the dictates of humanity ; and such modifications are adopted as to prevent the destruction of the body and the mind.

The Houses of Refuge are nipping crime in the bud, and qualifying juvenile delinquents for honorable apprenticeship. Nearly 3000 children and youth have been thus rescued by one of these Houses of Refuge, and by all of them, nearly 5000.

Imprisonment for debt, which incarcerated annually, by estimate, 75,000, 12 or 15 years ago, is extensively abolished; and seldom is an individual in Prison, for a single night, who is poor, and cannot pay, and shows no disposition to defraud his creditors.

Prison scenes are greatly changed from those which were revolting to those on which the Christian can look with some degree of approbation.

The funds of the Society are in an improved condition. We are encouraged.

OFFICERS.

PRESIDENT.
*GEORGE BLISS,
FRANCIS WAYLAND.

VICE-PRESIDENTS.

*WILLIAM BARTLETT,
*WILLIAM REED,
LEONARD WOODS,
WILLIAM JENKS,
ELIJAH HEDDING,
*EBENEZER PORTER,
*BENJAMIN B. WISNER,
*JEREMIAH EVARTS,
S. V. S. WILDER,
JOHN TAPPAN,
SAMUEL H. WALLEY,
BROWN EMERSON,
ALEXANDER HENRY,
CHARLES CHAUNCEY,
*STEPHEN VAN RENSSELAER,
*ALEXANDER FRIDGE,
*ROBERT RALSTON,
*EDWARD D. GRIFFIN
HEMAN HUMPHREY,
*SAMUEL GREEN,
JUSTIN EDWARDS,
ALONZO POTTER,
*PETER O. THACHER,
FRANCIS C. GRAY,
EDWARD TUCKERMAN,
LUTHER F. DIMMICK,
EDWARD BEECHER,
SIMON GREENLEAF,
DANIEL SHARP,
J. S. STONE,
LUCIUS BOLLES,
JOHN C. WARREN,
HENRY J. RIPLEY,
CHARLES LOWELL,
JOHN S. PETERS,
ROGER MINOT SHERMAN,
THOMAS H. GALLAUDET,
JOEL HAWES,
JEREMIAH DAY,
BENJAMIN SILLIMAN,
ELEAZER LORD,
JOHN M. MATHEWS,
WILLIAM JAY,
THEODORE FRELINGHUYSEN,
*SAMUEL L. SOUTHARD,
SAMUEL MILLER,
ARCHIBALD ALEXANDER,
HOWARD MALCOM,
FRANCIS PARKMAN,
ABBOTT LAWRENCE.

CORRESPONDING MEMBERS.

THOMAS BRADFORD, Jr., *Philadelphia.*
JOEL SCOTT, *Frankfort, Kentucky.*
SAMUEL HOARE, *of London.*
DR. JULIUS, *of Hamburgh.*
G. DE BEAUMONT, } *of Paris.*
A. DE TOCQUEVILLE, }
SAMUEL L. DAVIS, *Augusta, Georgia.*
REUEL WILLIAMS, *Hallowell, Me.*
S. E. COUES, *Portsmouth, N. H.*
J. C. HOLBROOK, *Brattleboro', Vt.*
*THOMAS G. LEE, *Charlestown, Mass.*
SAM'L B. WOODWARD, *Worcester, Ms.*
THOMAS PADDOCK, *St. John, N. B.*
J. McAULEY, *Toronto, U. C.*
M. S. BIDWELL, *New York City.*
WM. H. ROCKWELL, *Brattleboro', Vt.*
LUTHER V. BELL, *Charlestown, Mass.*
WM. SAM'L JOHNSON, *New York City.*
P. D. VROOM, *Somerville, N. J.*
S. F. McCRACKEN, } *Columbus, Ohio.*
WM. M. AWL, }
W. H. BURTON, } *New South Wales.*
DR. LANG, }
JACOB BEESON, *Niles, Michigan.*

MANAGERS.

R. S. STORRS,
CHARLES A. BARTOL,
JAMES MEANS,
DANIEL SAFFORD,
JARED CURTIS,
DANIEL SHARP,
SAMUEL LAWRENCE,
H. M. WILLIS,
SILAS AIKEN,
SAMUEL K. LOTHROP,
GORHAM D. ABBOTT,
A. A. LAWRENCE.

SAMUEL A. ELIOT, TREASURER.
LOUIS DWIGHT, SECRETARY.

LIFE DIRECTORS,

BY THE PAYMENT OF ONE HUNDRED DOLLARS AND UPWARDS.

Albany, N. Y.
*Van Rensselaer, Stephen
Boston.
Appleton, Samuel
Armstrong, Samuel T.
*Bussey, Benjamin
*Chamberlain, Richard
*Cobb, Nathaniel R.
*Coolidge, Joseph
Dwight, Edmund
Eliot, Samuel A.
Gray, Francis C.
Greenleaf, Jonathan
Homes, Henry
Hubbard, Samuel
Jackson, Charles
Jackson, James
Jackson, Patrick T.
Lawrence, Amos
Lawrence, Abbott
Lowell, Charles

*Lowell, John
Lyman, Theodore, Jr.
Munson, Israel
Parkman, Francis
Phillips, Jonathan
*Phillips, William
Prescott, William
Shattuck, George C.
Shaw, Robert G.
Tappan, John
Ticknor, George
Tuckerman, Edward
Ward, Artemas
Wells, Charles
White, Stephen
Willis, Nathaniel

Dedham, Mass
Burgess, Ebenezer

Geneva, N. Y.
Dwight, Henry

Lowell, Mass.
Lawrence, Samuel
Newark, N. J.
Eddy, Ansel D.
Norwich, Conn.
Greene, William P.
Peterboro', N. Y.
Smith, Peter
Portsmouth, N. H.
Coues, S. E.
Rochester, N. Y.
*Bissell, Josiah
Salem, Mass.
Peabody, Joseph
Worcester, Mass.
Abbott, J. S. C.
Foster, Alfred Dwight
Salisbury, Stephen
Sweetser, Seth, by 3 sisters
Waldo, Daniel

LIFE MEMBERS,

BY THE PAYMENT OF THIRTY DOLLARS AND UPWARDS.

Albany, N. Y.
Delavan, Edward C.
*Hopkins, Samuel M.
McIntire, Archibald
Norton, John C.

Andover, Mass.
*Cornelius, Elias
Edwards, Justin
*Porter, Ebenezer
Woods, Leonard

Auburn, N. Y.
Lewis, Levi, by Officers of
the Prison
Seymour, James S.
Smith, B. C., by Officers of
the Prison

Baltimore, Md.
Backus, John A.
*McKim, W. D.

Bath, N. H.
Sutherland, David, by Ira
Goodale

Bedford, N. Y.
*Jay, John
Jay, William

Beverly.
Oliphant, David

Boston.
Adams, Nehemiah
*Amory, John
Beecher, Edward
Beecher, Lyman
*Blake, George
*Bowdoin, James
Brimmer, Martin

Brooks, Peter C.
Brooks, Peter C., Jr.
Chadwick, Ebenezer
Clapp, Joshua
Cobb, Richard
*Codman, Catharine
Codman, Elizabeth
Codman, Charles R.
Codman, Henry
Cogswell, William
Cushing, John P.
Dana, Nathaniel
Dorr, Samuel
Eckley, David
Edwards, Henry
*Eliot, William H.
Forbush, Jonathan
Frothingham, N. L.
Gray, Horace
Gray, John C.
*Green, Samuel
*Greene, Gardiner
*Greenwood, F. W. P.
Hill, Henry
Homer, George J.
Jones, Anna P.
*Jones, John Coffin
Lawrence, Abbott
Lawrence, Samuel
Lawrence, William
*Lyman, Theodore
Lyman, Theodore, Jr.
Marvin, T. R.
*McLean, Ann
Munroe, Edmund
Newhall, Cheever
Otis, Harrison Gray
Parker, Daniel P.

Parker, Ebenezer
*Parker, John
Parkman, Francis
Potter, Alonzo
Rand, Asa
Randall, John
Rantoul, Robert
Reed, Benjamin T.
Rice, Henry
Ropes, William
Safford, Daniel
Sears, David
Stoddard, Charles
Thorndike, Israel
Vose, Thomas
Wales, Thomas B.
Warren, John C.
Wigglesworth, Thomas
Williams, John D.
Winthrop, Thomas L.
*Wisner, Benjamin B.
Worthington, William

Brooklyn, N. Y.
Carrol, D. L.

Cambridge, Mass.
Donnison, C. L.
*Farwell, Levi
Greenleaf, Simon
Holland, Frederic West
Quincy, Josiah

Canandaigua, N. Y.
Eddy, Ansel G.

Catskill, N. Y.
Cooke, Thomas B.
Day, Orrin

Charleston, S. C.
Corning, Jasper

Charlestown, Mass.
Curtis, Jared
Walker, William J., Jr.

Coxackie, N. Y.
*Van Dyck, Abraham

Danvers, Mass.
Braman, Milton P.
*Cowles, George
*Oakes, Caleb

Dorchester, Mass.
Codman, John

Douglass Farm, L. I.
Douglass, George, by the hand
of Mrs. Joanna Bethune

Edinburgh, Scotland.
Dunlop, John

Fairfield, Conn.
Sherman, Roger M.

Geneva, N. Y.
*Axtell, Henry

Gloucester, Mass.
Jewett, David, by a Lady

Hampton, N. H.
Harris, Roswell

Hartford, Conn.
Hawes, Joel
Spring, Samuel

Haverhill, Mass.
Keeley, George
Phelps, Dudley

Ipswich, Mass.
Kimball, David

Jamaica, L. I.
*Crane, Elias W.

Marblehead, Mass.
Hooper, Nathaniel
*Reed, William

Middletown, Conn.
Crane, John B.

Milton, Mass.
*Tucker, Nathaniel

Newark, N. J.
Hamilton, W. T.

Newbury, Mass.
Wright, Henry C.

Newburyport, Mass.
Banister, William B.
Bartlett, William

*Brown, Moses
Dimmick, Luther F.
Proudfit, John
By a donation in books from
Charles Whipple, to consti-
tute the following persons
Life Members:
Davis, Mary A.
Greenleaf, Mary C.
Hodge, Mary D.
Thompson, Sarah

New Haven, Conn.
Bacon, Leonard
Brewster, James
Fitch, Eleazer T.
Robinson, Charles, by his
sister Elizabeth
Salisbury, Abby

New York City.
Adams, William
Allen, Stephen
Astor, John Jacob
Averill, Heman
Bethune, G. W.
Boorman, J.
Brewster, Joseph
Broadhead, Dr.
*Chambers, William
Cheever, George B.
Cox, Samuel H.
Crosby, W. B.
Eastborn, Manton
*Falconer, Archibald
Hedges, Timothy
How, Fisher
Johnson, William Samuel
*Lenox, Robert
Mason, Cyrus W.
Mathews, John M.
McAuley, Thomas
Milnor, James
Patton, William
Perrit, Pelatiah
*Post, Joel
Proudfit, Alexander
Phillips, W. W.
*Rutgers, Henry
Schrœder, J. F.
Shatzel, Jacob
Spring, Gardiner
Starr, Philemon R.
Stephens, J. C.
Tappan, Arthur
*Varick, Richard
*Ward, Samuel
*Woolsey, William W.

Peterboro', N. Y.
Smith, Gerrit

Philadelphia, Penn.
Allen, Solomon
*Carey, Matthew
Elmes, Thomas
Ely, Ezra Stiles
Henry, Alexander
*Livingston, Gilbert R.
Skinner, Thomas H.

Pittsfield, Mass.
Newton, Edward A.

Plymouth, Mass.
Robbins, Josiah

Portland, Me.
Dwight, William T.
Tyler, Bennett

Portsmouth, N. H.
Coues, Lucy Louisa
Goodwin, Ichabod
Peabody, Andrew P., by La
dies of his Society

Poughkeepsie, N. Y.
Cuyler, Cornelius

Providence, R. I.
*Ives, Thomas P.
Wayland, Francis

Rahway, N. J.
Squier, Job

Salem, Mass.
Cleveland, J. P.
Emerson, Brown
Phillips, Stephen C.
Williams, William
Worcester, Zervia F.

Schenectady, N. Y.
*Smith, Peter

Springfield, Mass.
Osgood, Samuel

Thomaston, Me.
*Rose, Daniel

Troy, N. Y.
Tucker, Mark

Utica, N. Y.
Lansing, D. C.
Stocking, Samuel
Varick, Abraham

West Haverhill, Mass.
Cross, Abijah

Wethersfield, Conn.
Barrett, Gerrish
Pilsbury, Amos

Williamstown, Mass.
*Griffin, Edward D.

Wiscasset, Me.
Hooker, Edward W.

Worcester, Mass.
Foster, Alfred Dwight
Lincoln, John W.
Salisbury, Stephen
Waldo, E. S. & R.
Waldo, Daniel

TREASURER'S REPORT.

PRISON DISCIPLINE SOCIETY, in *Account with* AMOS A. LAWRENCE, Treasurer.

Dr.

1844.		
May 21. — Balance from last account,..............		855 13
Balance of subscriptions entered as cash last year, paid only in part, and remainder paid this year,...............		279 00
Cash paid Benjamin Bradley, for binding, &c.,		105 25
do. do. M. Latham, for collecting bills and distributing Reports,............		21 50
do. do. A. Jackson, office rent,............		22 76
do. do. Incidental, and travelling expenses, postage, &c.,............		87 50
do. do. Carter & Wilkins, for paper,.....		87 09
do. do. for use of Park Street Church, at anniversary,............		80 00
do. do. balance of interest on debt,.....		25 00
do. do. Grant, Daniell, & Co., for paper, ...		51 30
do. do. salary of the secretary,.........		506 07
do. do. Rev. Gerrish Barrett, chaplain and agent in Middle and Western States,		1,700 00
		$3,820 60

Cr.

1844.		
May 21. — By cash, dividend on nine shares New England Bank stock, purchased with legacy of Nathaniel Tucker, of Milton,..............		49 50
Cash collected by Rev. Gerrish Barrett, chaplain, and agent for Middle and Western States,		548 00
Cash from B. P. Winslow, executor of Thomas S. Winslow, in part of his legacy of $1000,.		180 00
Subscriptions, donations, &c., in the Eastern States,............		2,936 51
Balance to new account,............		106 59
		$3,820 60

Boston, May 21, 1844.

E. E.

Permanent Fund, by direction of the late Nathaniel Tucker, of Milton, who gave it as a legacy : —

Nine shares in the capital stock of New England Bank,.....	$936 75
Deposit in Tremont Savings Bank,......	63 00
Cash,.................	25
	$1,000 00

AMOS A. LAWRENCE, *Treasurer P. D. S.*

Boston, May 22, 1844. — We certify that we have examined the foregoing account and find the same correctly cast and properly vouched.

JAMES MEANS,   Wm. W. STONE, } *Auditors.*

SUBSCRIPTIONS AND DONATIONS,

From May 25, 1843, to May 21, 1844.

Baltimore, Md.		Wilson & Ker,	2 00	Carey, T. G.	5 00
Baughman, G., & Co.	2 00	Wilson, Thomas	2 00	Cash	1 00
Bigham, John	2 00	Wilson, Wm., & Sons,	5 00	Cash	1 00
Boggs, John, & Co.	2 00	Yates, J. R.	2 00	Cash	5 00
Brace, F. W.	5 00			Cash	1 00
Brown, G.	5 00	**Boston, Mass.**		Cash	1 00
Brown, R. P.	2 00	Abbott, G. W.	2 00	Cash	1 75
Camper & Bruff	2 00	Adams, Chester	2 00	Cash, W. G.	3 00
Canfield & Brothers,	2 00	Adams, Williams	2 00	Cash, W. S.	2 00
Cash	1 00	Adan, John R.	2 00	Chamberlain, N. B.	3 00
Cash	1 00	Aiken, Silas	3 00	Chandler, Abiel	2 00
Cash	1 00	Albree, John	10 00	Chapman, Jonathan	10 00
Cash	1 00	Allen, F.	2 00	Chase, Theodore	2 00
Cash	1 00	Almy, Patterson, & Co.	10 00	Chickering, J.	5 00
Cash	1 00	Amory, Charles	20 00	Clapp, James	1 00
Cash	1 00	Amory, William	5 00	Codman, Henry	10 00
Cash	1 00	Anderson, Rufus	2 00	Colby, Gardner	2 00
Cash	2 00	Andrews, C.	1 00	Cordis, Thomas	5 00
Cash	2 00	Andrews, Ebenezer T.	2 00	Cotton, Hill, & Co.	10 00
Cash	1 00	Appleton, Nathan	20 00	Cummings, Daniel	2 00
Cash	1 00	Appleton, Samuel	25 00	Curtis, Samuel	2 00
Chase, K., & Co.	3 00	Appleton, William	10 00	Curtis, T. B.	2 00
Conner, J. & Sons,	2 00	B. A. E.	5 00	Cushing, T. P.	2 00
Crook, Walter	2 00	Bailey, Calvin	2 00	Cushman, R. M.	2 00
Duncan, Joseph	2 00	Baker, E.	2 00	Dana, A. W.	1 00
Duval & Co.	2 00	Balch, Joseph	5 00	Dana, Ephraim	2 00
Fisher, Charles, & Co.	2 00	Ballard, Joseph	5 00	Dana, Luther	2 00
Fisher, W.	2 00	Ballister, Joseph	2 00	Daniel & Co.	2 00
Gardener, F.	1 00	Bancroft, Jacob	2 00	Darracott, George	2 00
Goldsborough, N. W.	2 00	Barnard, Charles	5 00	Davis, I. P.	2 00
Griffith, R. R.	2 00	Barnes, D. W.	2 00	Denny, Daniel	2 00
Harrison, B.	2 00	Barnes, S. H.	2 00	Dexter, George M.	5 00
Hoffman, W. H.	2 00	Bartoll, C. A.	10 00	Dorr, Samuel	10 00
Hopkins, John	2 00	Bent, Ann	2 00	D. J. J.	10 00
J. C.	2 00	Bigelow, George T.	5 00	Eaton, John	2 00
Jones, W., & Co.	2 00	Blake, James	2 00	Eckley, David	10 00
Keyser, Charles M.	2 00	Bond, George W.	2 00	Edmands, J. W.	10 00
Kroesen & Spear	1 00	Bond, William	2 00	Eliot, Samuel A.	50 00
Lemmon, W. P.	2 00	Booth, George H.	2 00	Emmons, N. H.	30 00
McDonald, William	5 00	Bowditch, N. I.	20 00	Error from last Report,	50
McKim, W.	2 00	Bradford, John	2 00	Eustis, W. T.	2 00
Norris & Beatty	2 00	Brewer, Nathaniel	2 00	Everett, Moses	5 00
Peche, D.	2 00	Brewer, S. N.	2 00	Fairbanks, Stephen	2 00
Pendexter & Alden	1 00	Brewer, William A.	2 00	Faxon, George N.	2 00
Pratt, E., & Brothers	2 00	Briggs, Mrs.	1 00	Fay, F. B.	5 00
Reynolds, William	2 00	Brimmer, E.	20 00	Fearing, A. C.	2 00
Rodewald, F., & Dieder,	3 00	Brimmer, Martin	30 00	Fearing, Albert	2 00
Schaefer, A. C.	2 00	Brooks, Edward	10 00	Fletcher, Richard	2 00
Schumaker, A.	2 00	Brooks, Peter C.	20 00	Forbes, R. B.	10 00
Sewell & Ernest	2 00	Brown, William A.	1 00	Forbush, Jonathan	30 00
Sterling, Archibald	2 00	Buck, Charles	1 00	Francis, David	2 00
Sumner, Robert	5 00	Buffington, Jonathan	2 00	Francis, Ebenezer	10 00
Talbot, Jones, & Co.	2 00	Bullard, W. S.	2 00	French, Jonathan	5 00
Tiffany, O. C.	2 00	Bumstead, Josiah	6 00	Friend, by W. L.	10 00
Turner, Wheelwright,		Bumstead, Josiah F.	5 00	Friend	06
& Mudge	2 00	Burgess, Benj., & Sons	5 00	Friend	2 00
Voss, B. F.	2 00	Burrage, I. C.	1 00	Gardner, John D.	2 00
Whitridge, Thomas	2 00	Callender, George	2 00	Gates, James W.	2 00
Williams, J. R.	1 00	Carlton, William	2 00	Gilbert, John & Co.	3 00

Gilbert, Lemuel	2 00	Lee, Henry, Jr.	2 00	Rice, J. P.	20 00
Gilbert, Samuel	2 00	Leeds, Joseph La Fay-		Rice & Thaxter	5 00
Gilbert, Timothy	2 00	ette	2 00	Richards, Reuben	3 00
Gordon, George W.	2 00	Leeds, Timothy C., &		Robbins, Edward H.	5 00
Gossler, E.	5 00	Co.	5 00	Rogers, Henry G.	10 00
Grant, Daniell, & Co.	50 00	Leland, Sherman	2 00	Rogers, J. G.	2 00
Gray, Francis C.	30 00	Lincoln, Heman	2 00	Rogers, John H.	2 00
Gray, Frederick T.	2 00	Lincoln, M. S.	2 00	Rogers, Nathaniel	2 00
Gray, George H.	2 00	Little & Brown	5 00	Rollins, William	5 00
Gray, Horace	20 00	Little, C. C.	2 00	Ropes, Hardy	2 00
Gray, J. C.	25 00	Littlehale, S. S.	5 00	Ropes, William	10 00
Green, David	2 00	Livermore, I., & Co.	2 00	Russell, N. P.	10 00
Green, T.	5 00	Lloyd, Mrs.	5 00	Salisbury, Samuel	2 00
Greene, Benjamin D.	5 00	Lobdell, T. J.	2 00	Sayles, W.	5 00
Greene, Charles G.	2 00	Lodge, I. E.	2 00	Scudder, Charles	2 00
Greene, I. S. Copley	20 00	Loring, Charles G.	2 00	Sears, David	50 00
Greenleaf, Samuel	2 00	Loring, Henry	2 00	Seaver, Benjamin	2 00
Gridley, William	2 00	Loring, James	2 00	Shaw, Blake, & Co.	5 00
Hale, Moses L.	2 00	Lothrop, Samuel K.	2 00	Shaw, Robert G.	30 00
Hall, A. S.	1 00	Lowe, Francis	2 00	Sigourney, Henry	10 00
Hall, A. T.	3 00	Lowe, J. J.	2 00	Simonds, Artemas	2 00
Hall, Henry	3 00	Lowell, Francis C.	10 00	Simpson, M. H.	5 00
Hall, I. Jr.	2 00	Lowell, John A.	20 00	Skinner, Francis	10 00
Hall, J. P.	2 00	Lyman, Joseph, Jr.	5 00	Smith & Sumner	3 00
Hallet, George	5 00	Lyman, Theodore	100 00	South Boston Iron Co.	5 00
Hallet, J. H.	2 00	Mayer, P. J.	2 00	Sprague, P.	5 00
Hardy, Alpheus	2 00	McBurney, Charles	2 00	S. S. R.	2 00
Harrington, Andrew	1 00	Mellen, Moses	2 00	Steele, Robert	2 00
Hawes, Gray, & Co.	5 00	Meriam, S. P.	1 00	Stevenson, William	2 00
Hayden, J. C.	2 00	Mills, C. H.	5 00	Stimpson, W. C.	2 00
Hayward, George	5 00	Mills, J. K.	10 00	Stoddard, Charles	5 00
Hicks, James H.	2 00	Morse, R. M.	1 00	Stone, W. W.	25 00
Hill, Jeremiah	2 00	Munson, Israel	50 00	Sumner, Bradford	2 00
Homans, John	5 00	Newman, Henry	2 00	Sumner, William	5 00
Homer, George J.	5 00	Osgood, Isaac	2 00	Swett, Samuel	2 00
Hooper, Robert	5 00	Otis, Harrison G.	10 00	Tappan, Lewis W.	2 00
Horton, H. K.	3 00	Paige, James W.	2 00	Tarbell, Thomas	2 00
Howe, George	10 00	Palfrey, John G.	2 00	Tenney, Samuel	2 00
Howe, Jabez C.	2 00	Parker, Isaac	3 00	Ticknor, George	10 00
Howe, J. C.	5 00	Parker, James	10 00	Tilden, Joseph	2 00
Howard, Benjamin	2 00	Parker, John	5 00	Trott, George	5 00
Hubbard, William J.	2 00	Parker, M. S.	2 00	Tucker, J. L.	3 00
Humphrey, William	2 00	Parker, Samuel D.	2 00	Tucker, Nathaniel, late	
Hurd, John	3 00	Parkman, Francis	5 00	of Milton, semi-an-	
Inches, Henderson	5 00	Parsons, S.	1 00	nual dividend on	
Inches, Henderson, Jr.	2 00	Payson, S. R.	2 00	New England Bank	
Inches, Misses	10 00	Peck, A. G.	5 00	stock purchased with	
Jackson, Charles,	20 00	Perkins, Thomas H.	25 00	his legacy	27 00
Jackson, Patrick T	15 00	Phelps, Abel, & Co.	5 00	Do. do.	22 50
Jackson, Ward	2 00	Phelps, Sewell	2 00	Tufts, James	2 00
Jellison,	2 00	Phipps, Samuel, & Co.	5 00	Twing, J. C.	1 00
Johnson, James	5 00	Pond, Moses	2 00	Upham, Appleton, &	
Johnson, Samuel	2 00	Pratt, George	5 00	Co.	10 00
Johnson, Samuel	5 00	Pray, Isaac C.	5 00	Valentine, Charles	5 00
Jones, Anna P.	20 00	Prescott, William	25 00	Wainwright & Tappan	3 00
Jones, Eliphalet	2 00	Quincy, J. D.	5 00	Wales, T. B.	10 00
Kendall, A.	10 00	Quincy, Josiah	10 00	Walley, Samuel H.	10 00
Kendall, A.	2 00	Rand, E. S.	2 00	Ware, John	3 00
Kimball, Daniel	2 00	Rantoul, Robert	30 00	Warren, George W.	5 00
Kimball, Jewett, & Co.	10 00	Reed, B. T.	5 00	Warren, J. C.	10 00
Kimball, John	1 00	Reports sold,	1 50	Waterston, Robert	2 00
Kitredge, Alvah	2 00	Reports sold,	1 50	Welch, Francis	3 00
Knott, James, & Son	2 00	Reports sold,	1 08	Weld, W. F.	2 00
Kuhn, George H.	5 00	Reports sold,	50	Wells, Charles A.	2 00
Lane, Lamson, & Co.	2 00	Reports sold,	50	Wells, John	10 00
Lawrence, A. A.	15 00	Reports sold to Mr. B.		Wells, John B.	2 00
Lawrence, Abbott	100 00	of N. Y.	1 25	Wetmore, Thomas	10 00
Lawrence, Amos	100 00	Reports sold T. & D.	18 18	Whiston, F. C.	2 00
Lawrence, William	25 00	Reports sold B. P.	25	White, Benjamin C.	3 00
Lee, Henry	3 00	Reynolds, Edward	5 00	White, Charles	3 00

White, F. E.	3 00	*Morristown, N. J.*		Brigham, John	2 00
Whitney, Paul	5 00	Canfield, B. O.	1 00	Brown, James	5 00
Whiton, James M.	2 00	Johnson, Silas	1 00	Buckhalter, T	2 00
Wigglesworth, Edward	2 00	Voorhees, J. F.	2 00	Bull, W. G.	2 00
Wigglesworth, Thomas	5 00	Whitehead, Ira C.	2 00	Butler, J.	2 00
Wilder, Marshall P.	5 00			Carlwell, J.	2 00
Wilkins, Charles, & Co.	2 44	*Newark, N. J.*		Cash	2 00
Wilkinson, Arthur	2 00	Baldwin, Isaac	2 00	Cash	1 00
Williams, John	2 00	Baldwin, W. A.	1 00	Cash	2 00
Williams, John D.	5 00	Brinsmade, H. N.	2 00	Cash	2 00
Williams, Moses	2 00	Cash	1 00	Cash	2 00
Willis, Nathaniel	10 00	Conger, E.	1 00	Cash	2 00
Winslow, Thomas S.,		Day, Mathias W.	2 00	Cash	1 00
by B. P. Winslow,		Eddy, Ansel D.	50 00	Cash	2 00
his executor, part of		Frelinghuysen, F. S.	1 00	Cash	2 00
$1000 legacy,	180 00	Halsey, J. H.	1 00	Cash	1 00
Wolcott, J. H.	5 00	Hubbel, S. H.	1 00	Cash	1 00
Wyman, Edward	2 00	Ingraham, H. K.	50	Cash	1 00
		Jacobus, P.	1 00	Cash	1 00
Cambridge, Mass.		Jaquith, N. C.	1 00	Cash	1 00
Austin, Daniel	2 00	McNet, C. S.	1 00	Cash	1 00
Beck, Charles	5 00	Price, Daniel	1 00	Cash	1 00
Carpenter, Mrs.	10 00	Quimby, J. M.	1 00	Cash	1 00
Donnison, Catharine	10 00	S. G. C.	1 00	Cash	1 00
Farrar, John	5 00	Smith, S. P.	2 00	Cash	2 00
Farwell, Levi	20 00	Stevens, J. H.	2 00	Cash	2 00
Hodges, Richard M.	5 00	Taylor, John	2 00	Cash	2 00
Longfellow, Henry W.	10 00	Van Wagener, J.	2 00	Cash	1 00
Norton, Andrews	10 00	Vermilyie, J. D.	2 00	Cash	1 00
Pomeroy, William	10 00	Ward, Aaron	2 00	Cash	1 00
Sparks, Jared	10 00	Whitehead, Asa	1 00	Cash	1 00
Story, Joseph	10 00			Cash	2 00
Worcester, Joseph E.	2 00	*New Bedford, Mass.*		Cash	1 00
		Coggeshall, John	5 00	Cash	50
Charlestown, Mass.		Friend	12 00	Cash	2 00
Bell, Luther F.	10 00	Friend	5 00	Cash	1 00
Crowningshield, A. W.	2 00	Green, Thomas A.	5 00	Cash	1 00
Eddy, George R.	2 00	Greene, D. R.	5 00	Cash	2 00
Goodhue, Homer	2 00	Howland, George	25 00	Chambers, James	2 00
Marshall, Albert	2 00	Morgan, C. W.	10 00	Charity	2 00
Tyler, Columbus	3 00	Randall, S. G.	5 00	Chauncey, W.	2 00
Vinal, Otis	2 00	Robeson, Andrew	25 00	Cheever, George B.,	
White, Dr.	2 00	Rodman, Samuel	10 00	from Ladies of Allen	
		Rodman, S. W.	5 00	Street Church, to	
Elizabethtown, N. J.		Rodman, W. R.	20 00	constitute him a Life	
Crane, James	1 00	Rotch, William, Jr.	20 00	Member,	30 00
Pruden, Keen	2 00			Clark & Wilson	2 00
		New Brunswick, N. J.		Clearman, G. W.	2 00
Frederick, Md.		Bishop, James	2 00	Cock, Thomas	2 00
Battsell, J.	2 00	Cash	1 00	Collins, S. B.	2 00
Birclay, Valentine	1 00	Nelson, N. S.	2 00	Cooledge, G. F.	2 00
Markell, J.	2 00	Stout, John W.	2 00	Day, Mahlon	2 00
Morgan, T. H.	2 00			Dean, N.	2 00
Potts, R.	1 00	*Newton, Mass.*		Denney, Thomas	2 00
Quynn, C.	2 00	Ripley, Henry J.	2 00	Dennison, L.	2 00
Ross, W. J.	1 00			Dibble, A. E.	2 00
Waters, William	2 00	*New York City.*		D. S. K.	2 00
		Adams, Charles	2 00	Dunham, E. W.	2 00
Hudson, Ohio.		Adee, G. S.	2 00	E. D. & Co.	2 00
Day, H. N.	1 00	Aldrich, H. D.	2 00	Edwards, Alfred	2 00
Ellsworth & Baft	1 00	Arnold, D. H.	2 00	Elliot, H. H.	2 00
Hickcock, L. P.	2 00	Baker, H.	2 00	Ely, C.	2 00
Seymour, N. P.	1 00	B. & Co.	2 00	Engs, P. W.	2 00
		Benjamin, W.	2 00	Fisher, W.	2 00
Lowell, Mass.		Bethune, Joanna	5 00	Foster, C. W.	2 00
Lawrence, Samuel	100 00	Bond, T.	2 00	Franeia, P.	2 00
		Booth, W. A.	2 00	Franklin, W. H.	2 00
Madison, N. J.		Bower, John	2 00	Frelinghuysen, Theo-	
Arms, Clifford	1 00	Bowen, McNare	2 00	dore	5 00
		Bridges, L. K.	2 00	Gillespie, W.	2 00

Gould, W. R.	2 00	Nichols	2 00	Cash	2 00
Hall, W.	2 00	N. T. & Co.	2 00	Cash	2 00
Halstead, W. M.	2 00	Partridge, William	2 00	Cash	1 00
Herriman, W. G.	2 00	P. D. & Co.	3 00	Cash	1 00
H. H. J.	2 00	Persell, Edward	2 00	Cash	50
Hinsdale, H.	2 00	Phyfe, John	2 00	Cash	50
H. J. S.	2 00	Rankin, John	2 00	Denny, C.	5 00
Hoffman, P. V.	2 00	Robertson, J. A.	2 00	Farnham, J.	2 00
How, C. W.	2 00	Rogers, J. Smith	2 00	McCanahan, S.	2 00
Howell, S. S.	2 00	Rogers & Starr	2 00	Mercer, S. A.	2 00
Hunt, John, & Co.	2 00	Russell, Israel	2 00	Weaver, George J.	2 00
Hutchinson, R. J.	2 00	Sampson, J.	2 00		
J. A. J.	2 00	S. & A.	2 00	*Providence, R. I.*	
Jenkins, Edward	2 00	S. B. C.	2 00	Arnold, F. R.	10 00
Jennings, Charles	5 00	Seaver & Dunbar	2 00	Goddard, William G.	10 00
J. J.	2 00	Spees, Christ, & Co.	2 00	Hallet, E. W.	5 00
J. S. & Co.	2 00	Spillman & Frazer	2 00	Ives, Hope	15 00
J. W. & Co.	2 00	Straban, John	2 00	Ives, Moses B.	10 00
Kelly, R.	2 00	S. S. & Co.	2 00	Ives, Robert H.	15 00
King, J. G.	2 00	Stuart, R. L. & A.	2 00	Manton, Amasa	10 00
Kirby, L. & V.	2 00	Theriot & Co.	2 00	Wayland, Francis	20 00
Lathrop, F. S.	2 00	Tonnell & Hall	2 00		
Lawrence, A. W.	2 00	T. & S.	1 00	*Springfield, N. Y.*	
Leeds, Samuel	2 00	Tucker, W. K.	2 00	Barrett, Gerrish	30 00
Lee & Brewster	2 00	Underhill, W.	2 00		
Lee, O. H.	2 00	Warren, Richard	2 00	*Watertown, Mass.*	
Leeschigh, W.	2 00	Watt, W.	1 00	A Friend	20 00
Lefferett, J.	1 00	Wells, L. W.	2 00		
Little, C. S.	2 00	Wetmore, A. R.	2 00	*Williamstown, Mass.*	
Little, E. W.	2 00	Wetmore, O. & A.	2 00	Hopkins, Mark	20 00
Lowell, Holbrook	2 00	W. H. & Co.	2 00		
Marshall, C. H.	1 00	W. H. R.	2 00	*Wilmington, Del.*	
May, John	2 00	White, Eli	2 00	Bush, D.	1 00
Maynard, L.	2 00	Whitney, W. E.	2 00	Hall, Willard	3 00
McConnelly, Charles	2 00	Whittemore, C. R.	2 00	Hogarth, W.	2 00
Merle, G.	2 00	Wilson, D. M. & Co.	2 00	Janvier, B. A.	1 00
Messinger & Brothers	2 00	Wisner & Gale	2 00	Wilson, D. C.	2 00
Mills, E.	2 00	Wolcott, Frederic H.	2 00		
Mintern, R. B.	2 00	Wood, S. S.	1 00	*Worcester Mass.*	
Moore, W.	2 00			Foster, A. D.	10 00
Morgan & Co.	2 00	*Philadelphia, Penn.*		Two Sisters	100 00
Murray, Lindley	2 00	Cash	2 00	Waldo, Daniel	50 00
Nelson, W.	2 00	Cash	1 00		

APPENDIX.

———◆———

MR. BARRETT'S JOURNAL.

————

PRISONS IN MICHIGAN.

November 18, 1842. Arrived at DETROIT last evening, at 8 o'clock, just as that terrible gale began to sweep over the western lakes, which caused the wreck of not less than 50 vessels, and the loss of more than 100 human lives. Yesterday, weather mild; to-day, thermometer stood at 8° above zero.

To-day, visited the JAIL. It is a large 2-story stone building, surmounted by a cupola; contains 32 cells, which have been homes for transgressors for nearly a quarter of a century. 8 cells on each story are ranged on opposite sides of a narrow passage, which runs lengthwise through the centre of the building.

These cells are insecure, and without windows or ventilators. A small opening, at the top of a clumsy wooden door, looking out into the narrow passage, admits what of light, heat, and air, the prisoners receive in their cells.

About 20 persons are now here in confinement, in regard to whom there is neither discipline, classification, nor labor. By day, they are let out of their cells, and allowed to congregate in the centre passage, where they spend their time in mutually corrupting each other. By night, they blackguard each other from cell to cell, and shout and sing to their hearts' content.

Out of the 206 persons committed to this Jail last year, 5 made their escape, and 12 were sent to the State Prison.

November 22. Called on the governor at the capitol. He honored me with the large, cushioned arm-chair, while he took a common one himself, and entered freely into conversation concerning imprisonment for debt, State Lunatic Asylum, and the County Jail. The Jail he condemns, as well he may. No provision has been made for the insane poor in Michigan; but, as she has now the largest territory of any state in the Union, and much of this territory is covered with inhabitants from New England and New York, it may safely be believed that she will not be long behind her sister states in this matter. Not only is imprisonment for debt abolished in Michigan, but a certain judge told me, that, in some cases, by the present laws, property to the amount of $1650 could be exempted from execution.

While at Detroit, had an interview with a reformed prisoner. A drunkard, and a gambler, a passer of counterfeit money, vile, and abandoned, he was convicted of crime, and sent to the State Prison at A. The belief is that he became, in the best sense, a free man before his release from Prison. 4 or 5 years ago, he got his discharge, and came to Detroit. Now, he is a member of one of the largest churches in the city, has a pious wife, owns a pew, teaches in the Sabbath school, prays in his family, prospers in business, is highly respected, and stands a living witness and example of what the gospel can do towards raising the fallen, and reclaiming the abandoned.

Preached three times in Detroit on the subject of my mission; took the railroad, and, passing through Ann Arbor, arrived safely at Jackson, 80 miles from Detroit.

ANN ARBOR JAIL

is among the best in the state. It is built of brick, on the Auburn plan. Cells 3 stories high; floor thrown over the area at the second story; cells of the third story for females; inside of cells covered with sheet iron; 2 tiers of windows in outside walls; doors of iron gratings, made, as were the locks also, at Auburn Prison.

JAIL AT JACKSON,

in the basement story of the court-house; inmates few; rooms low, damp, and dark;—though lately built, has nothing about it that deserves commendation, or that ought to be imitated.

November 26. Paid my first visit to the MICHIGAN PENITENTIARY, now being built at JACKSON. Its location is half a mile from the town, on ground too low for health. A stone wall, 17 feet high, built with convict labor, of stone quarried in the yard, protects the north and east sides of the 5 acres embraced in the Prison yard, and a picket fence serves as a temporary protection of the other two sides. One half of what is designed for the entire Prison building, has its outer walls completed, and its roof on. It is 220 feet long, 60 feet wide; built of sandstone; has 2 tiers of windows; lower tier too low; faces the south, and makes a good appearance.

The block of cells, which, when completed, will embrace 382, in 4 stories, has as yet been raised but 1 story, and contains only 82 cells. A work-shop, 2 stories high, and 100 feet long, has just been built.

The whole Prison, when completed, will have an east wing corresponding with the present west wing, with the keeper's house between, on the plan of the Ohio Penitentiary, and will then contain 656 cells.

The cells are like those at Auburn, excepting that the doors are flat bar iron gratings, and set out even with the front wall of the cells.

Number of prisoners, 87, occupying 82 cells. Oldest prisoner, 75, youngest, 13 years old; 4 sentenced for life, 1 for 6 months; 8 cannot read; 65 have been persons of intemperate habits.

First prisoner committed May, 1839. Whole number committed, 187, of whom 54 were committed in 1839, 44 in 1840, 52 in 1841, and 37 up to November 28, 1842. Of all committed, 23 have been pardoned, 76 have been discharged by expiration of sentence, 1 has died, and 4 have been recommitted.

The Prison ration costs 5½ cents, and consists of

    12 oz. pork, or 20 oz. beef,
    12 oz. wheat flour,
    10 oz. Indian meal; together with
    4 qts. rye, 4 qts. salt, 2 qts. vinegar,
    4 qts. white beans, 2½ oz. black pepper, } to every 100 rations.
    ½ gill molasses, and 3 bushels potatoes,

Average receipt for the labor of each convict, invalids and all, about 37½ cents per day; chief business, coopering and shoemaking. No insane prisoner has ever been in this Penitentiary.

The agent is required by law to transport the convicts from the different counties to the Prison, on receiving notice from the district attorney. This is deemed economy. Punishment by stripes seldom inflicted. When it is, a report of each case is made to the inspectors. So it should ever be.

Officers connected with the Prison are as follows : — 3 inspectors, agent, clerk, deputy keeper, physician, chaplain, 3 under keepers, and 11 guard.

The inspectors are chosen by the legislature, and receive $2 per day for their services when employed; the services of each not to exceed 30 days in a year.

The agent is appointed by the governor, with advice of the senate, and has a salary of $750, with fuel, light, &c.

The inspectors appoint the clerk, physician, chaplain, and guards. The agent appoints the deputy and assistant keepers, the former at a salary of $500, the latter at a salary of $400.

The clerk's salary is $500, and the chaplain's $100.

The physician's pay is 75 cents for a single visit, and $1 00 when he prescribes for two patients.

The inspectors, agent, clerk, and physician, are paid from the state treasury; the assistant keepers and guard from the Prison funds, and the chaplain from moneys received at the gate for admission of visitors.

The following persons are allowed by law to visit the Prison at any time without charge, viz., the governor, lieutenant-governor, members of the legislature, chancellor, judges, attorneys, and officiating ministers of the gospel; and no others, except by permission of the agent, and under such regulations as the inspectors shall prescribe.

Last March, 14 convicts escaped from this Prison. The ringleader dug through his cell at night, and got on top of the unfinished block. 2 guards were, or *should have been*, on duty. The convict out of his cell had with him 2 keys, 1 that would unlock any of the cell doors, and another that would unlock the outside door. Unperceived by the guard, he unlocked the doors of several cells, and, heading their inmates, attacked, and overcame the guard.

The night without was dark and stormy. Every convict who wished it had his cell door unlocked. The greater part did not choose it.

Some, whose doors were unlocked, did not leave their cells. 14 left the Prison.

Alarm was soon given, and close pursuit made. The leader was overtaken in a field. He fought desperately, and would not submit to be taken alive. Just as he aimed a deadly blow at one of the pursuers, another shot him dead on the spot. 2 escaped. The others were caught, and brought back to Prison.

Sunday. Went with the chaplain to the Prison, and, at his request, preached to the prisoners in the area between the cells and outer wall. Attention was good; and when a convenient chapel shall have been provided, it will be a still more pleasant and profitable service to preach to these prisoners. At present, the chaplain resides out of town, has 2 other charges to attend to, and of consequence cannot devote as much time to the prisoners as he would otherwise do. Was glad to find that a gentleman of the legal profession frequently went to the Prison to give pious counsel and instruction to the prisoners, and that the keeper, a religious man, encourages such visits. The prisoners are furnished with Bibles. They need upon their hearts the influence of Sunday school teaching, daily prayers offered in their hearing, and faithful private counsel, in addition to preaching, in order to lay good ground for their radical reformation.

THE JAIL AT MARSHALL, CALHOUN COUNTY,

consists of 3 small rooms, in the basement story of the court-house. 2 of these rooms are condemned as unfit for use, on account of their insecurity and dampness.

To make the other room somewhat more safe and tolerable, a plank partition has been put up, a little way from the outer wall, so that the prisoners are placed in something like a tight box. This, though it almost suffocates, does prevent escapes.

Last month, a man, confined here, got an auger, bored through the plank so many holes as to let his body through, crawled out, and made his escape. The night was bitterly cold. The prisoner, thinly clad, wandered about till he froze his feet; then he crept into a hay-mow, and was found there next morning, nearly frozen to death. I saw this man, with his feet bandaged, among the invalids in the Penitentiary at Jackson, and asked him what was the matter. "O, sir," said he, "I tried to help myself to a little liberty out there in Marshall, the other night, and like to have lost my life by it."

There must be a change here. That elegant and costly court-house, which so loftily towers above these dismal dens for criminals, stands as a certain pledge, that the people, who have so shown their liberality and enterprise in one public building, will not be long satisfied with so disgraceful a contrivance for a Jail.

————

There being no public conveyance, some friends took me by sleigh, through oak openings, and dense forests, where prairie hens, wild turkeys, and deer, were plenty, about 25 miles, to Coldwater, on the Chicago turnpike Branch county.

The Jail of this county, in the town of BRANCH, is a curiosity. It is a log building. The lower story contains 5 rooms; 3 for prisoners; 1 for the post-office, and 1 for county offices. The room above, just under the roof, is used for a court-room.

Branch county contains 16 organized townships, and yet, for the last 6 months, there has been no one in the county committed to Jail. It is expected that the county seat will soon be removed to Coldwater, 3 miles from Branch; then a better Jail may be looked for, as well as ampler dimensions for court-house and offices.

HINSDALE COUNTY JAIL, AT JONESVILLE,

like such as are usually found in new countries, will give place to a better one, when they have a new court-house. The same may be said of a large number of Jails in Michigan.

LENAWEE COUNTY JAIL, AT ADRIAN,

may be reckoned among the best in the state. It is built of brick, in connection with the jailer's house. Between the family apartments and Prison runs a spacious hall. Cells, 16 in number, on the Auburn plan. Door iron gratings, flat bars; windows in external wall grated and glazed. Several inmates, 1 from Oakham, Mass.: 1 had been a soldier in the Florida war; 1 had a pious mother — ruined himself by intemperance.

Saturday, December 10. To-day, Rev. Mr. B. went with me to the Jail at Adrian. In conversing with the prisoners, they expressed to us a wish to hear preaching. It was agreed that their desires should be gratified.

Sunday came. Notice was given in the church, that there would be preaching in the Jail at 4 o'clock. It was a novel notice. At the appointed hour, citizens of the town assembled, and filled the area round the cells, except the side where the prisoners were. Ladies were present.

The speaker took his stand at one corner, so as to have a full view of the prisoners, and of as many others as were on one side of the area. The service began by singing the hymn, " Alas! and did my Savior bleed ? " The singing was good. The effect, both of sentiment and sound, seemed to be greatly heightened by the peculiar circumstances in which we were placed. Prayer was offered, in which remembrance of the prisoners was made, and the aid of the Holy Spirit plead for.

Brother B. preached. His text was, " Behold the Lamb of God, that taketh away the sins of the world ! " Both text and sermon were beautifully appropriate. On one side sat guilty violators of law, human and divine. To them the preacher said, " Come ye to the Lamb of God, and ye shall find pardon and cleansing. His blood cleanseth from all sin." On the other side were youth and beauty, intelligence and morality, which in some were not connected with piety. To such the address was, " Here you see men, who are in some degree suffering the penalty of their transgressions. It may be you look on them with scorn, and are ready to say, ' God, I thank thee that I am not as these men are.' Let me tell you, — you too are guilty; you have broken the law of God; you are condemned already, and exposed to punishment such as no human government has power to inflict. Yes, the most lovely and moral among you, who have not repented of your sins, are in danger of having your eternal abode in the prison of despair. I declare to you, that nothing can save you from this dreadful doom, but your looking with the eye of faith to the ' Lamb of God, who taketh away the sins of the world.' " Then, turning to the prisoners, his words were, " Prisoners of hope, behold the Lamb of God ! Come, you who have exposed your life in fighting the battles of your country, come, halt in your rebellion against God, and enlist under the banner of Jesus. And you, too, son of a pious mother, much counselled and prayed for, do you wish to escape the end of the ungodly, and meet your mother in heaven ? come, then, to the Lamb of God."

I have seldom listened to a sermon that seemed to produce a deeper impression. There were but few dry eyes to be seen. As for myself, I had to sit and weep like a child, to see in what wonderful harmony law and grace had here met together. Here stern Law, by its secret, silent, yet resistless power, was holding hardened transgressors in their place of punishment; here, too, Grace came, making her way even to the cell of the criminal, in search of the lost and the guilty, and with voice of love, spake peace, and pardon, and eternal salvation, to all who would " behold the Lamb of God, that taketh away the sin of the world." Never before did the gospel seem to be more emphatically " good news," than when I listened to it as it was preached to the prisoners in the Adrian Jail. On taking our leave, the prisoners thanked us, and asked that the word might be preached to them again next Sabbath.

The last Jail visited in Michigan, was in Munroe, 40 miles from Adrian. This Jail, recently built of stone, is 2 stories high, with two wings. One wing is for the jailer's kitchen, the other for his office; the lower story of the centre building for parlor, &c. On the second story of the main building are 9 cells, built of plank and timbers, 10 feet long, 10 feet high, and 5 feet wide, badly lighted and ventilated, with an area round them 12 feet wide. The prisoners are kept without classification, labor, or instruction, and by day are let out together in the open area. Among them is a deranged man, once a Catholic priest in Canada. He has a well-shaped head, great urbanity in his manners, and conversed with me in Latin. What sight more sad than a human being with a mind in ruins! Michigan needs an Asylum for this class of persons.

PRISONS IN OHIO.

After leaving Michigan, the first Jail visited was at TOLEDO, Lucas county, Ohio. Judge P. went with me. We visited it by candle-light. I thought it well that a judge was with me, that he might see for himself, and testify, as to the real condition of the Jail. We came to a small, low, single-story log building. "This," said the judge, "is our Jail."

The entrance at the end is into a narrow passage, on one side of which are 3 small and dismally dark cells, without either windows, ventilators, or means of warming; and on the other side, 2 or 3 small grated apertures, which serve to remind one of windows. Through the thick plank door of each cell is a diamond 4 inches square. This hole is the medium through which light, air, and heat, enter the cells. In the narrow passage we found a small stove, and two prisoners shivering by its side. They had been permitted to go out of their cells to get at the fire. The night was cold, there was but little fire, and the prisoners complained for want of wood. One of the prisoners had been sick, and looked pale and feeble. His offence was throwing a stone at another. He had 6 months yet to remain in Jail before trial. Verily the way of transgressors is hard.

Lucas county will surely have a better Jail, when it shall have been decided, as it probably will be this winter, where the county seat is to be.

WOOD COUNTY JAIL, AT PERRYSBURGH,

is somewhat larger, but not much better, than the one at Toledo. It contains 4 rooms, in 2 stories, destitute of furniture, and without so much as a single *biped* for an inmate. Rotten logs, rings and staples, hand-cuffs and manacles, are the prominent things here to be seen.

A Jail like this, built of logs 15 or 20 years ago, standing in a town named after a distinguished naval officer, and in sight of a new and elegant court-house, and among a humane people, is surely destined soon to be only among the things that were.

THE JAIL AT SANDUSKY CITY

has a good appearance and location, is 2 stories high, and newly built of stone; contains jailer's apartments, and 16 cells for prisoners, with grated doors, on Auburn plan; and the whole is surrounded by a stone wall except in front.

JAIL AT ELYRIA,

without inmates, November, 1843. Building of stone; good external appearance; embracing jailer's apartments, and 22 cells, on Auburn plan, in 2 stories, all new. Had the walls of the cells been made of other materials than wood, and had the doors been iron grating instead of plank, it would have been very much better. 'Tis not too late now to make the improvement.

CUYAHOGA COUNTY JAIL, AT CLEVELAND,

stands in the heart of a beautiful city. Streets are wide, handsome, and well laid out; business prosperous, citizens intelligent and benevolent, and views of Erie's blue waters grand and beautiful. But to think of the Jail makes the heart sicken. It is an old, uncouth structure, partly of stone, and partly of wood, with no fence nor wall round it. But 2 rooms are used for prisoners, and these are so insecure, that 15 escapes have been effected within the last 3 months. Both these rooms are horrible places. Neither has either fireplace or stove, window or ventilator. At mid-day the jailer had to carry a lamp to show me what was within. Rough flat stones make the floor. In the centre is a huge staple and ring. At the sides are bunks filled with straw, several tiers one above another. In the middle of the room, with his back towards the door, one cannot see his hand before him at noon-day. In one of the dark receptacles was a good-looking man, 50 years old, who had been there more than a year. A lovely little daughter, 10 or 12 years old, had just come to see him. The prisoner was taken out into the passage that ran in front of his cell, that there might be light enough for the child to see her father's face. It was an affecting sight, to see the old man, with tears in his eyes, holding the hand of his little girl, and to see her stand by her father's knee, looking up into his face, as he talked to her.

The doors of the 2 cells look out into the narrow passage that has been referred to. Near the centre of this passage stands a stove. At the end of this passage, which is next the street, is a window with a lattice outside; so that even the passage itself receives but little light or air; yet all the light, heat, or air, that reaches the prisoners in their dens of gloom, has to go to them from this passage, through their grated doors.

One hundred and ninety-six human beings, during the last year, had to breathe the vitiated air, and grope in the darkness, of these abominable cells.

LAKE COUNTY, lately a part of Geauga county, has a new court-house, at PAINSVILLE, but no Jail. Had an interview with the building committee; tried to dissuade them from building the diminutive wooden Jail which they had in contemplation, and put in their hands a plan of the Hartford Jail, to imitate if they chose.

SENECA COUNTY JAIL, AT TIFFIN,

contains 2 rooms, in a single-story log building, and stands near a handsome and costly new court-house. The rooms are separated by a narrow passage, and have no prisoners in them. The room next the street was occupied as a school-room, and was filled with bright and smiling children, who were taught by a pretty-looking lady. Though it is more pleasant to prevent than to punish crime, yet it did not seem quite right, even for the purpose of instruction, thus to put children in the place of criminals.

MARION JAIL

is built of logs, a story and a half high; has 2 rooms, but no inmates, December 20, 1842.

THE JAIL AT DELAWARE

has 2 small rooms back of the jailer's apartments, built of logs, both without tenants. The jailers say that the prevalence of the temperance cause is the true reason why there is such a paucity of prisoners in the County Prisons.

BUTLER COUNTY JAIL

is a 2-story stone building; rooms large, badly lighted and ventilated, and insecure; and has annually about 70 inmates.

PREBLE COUNTY

has a new stone Jail, 30 by 50 feet; cost $7,000; rooms on second story ; doors iron gratings.

TRUMBULL COUNTY JAIL,

built in 1826, and connected with the jailer's house, has 3 insecure, badly-ventilated, and damp rooms, for the reception of prisoners.

ASHTABULA COUNTY JAIL

consists of an old log building, with 2 rooms for prisoners, one of which is not used, and the other, being insecure, dark, and illy ventilated, is not fit for use.

RICHLAND COUNTY JAIL

is a 2-story brick building, 6 years old, containing 7 rooms.

ATHENS COUNTY

is disgraced with an old, dilapidated building for a Jail, without either cleanliness or security, and which the grand jury of last October term presented to the court as a public nuisance.

THE JAIL AT GALIOPOLIS

is a 2-story brick building, with 2 rooms for criminals, from which frequent escapes have been made.

LAWRENCE COUNTY JAIL

is a small log building, one end of which is for the jailer, the other end, embracing 2 rooms, for prisoners.

THE JAIL IN MEIGS COUNTY

is a single-story stone building, containing 2 strong, badly-ventilated rooms.

BELMONT COUNTY JAIL,

an old concern, containing 2 miserable rooms. A contract for a new Jail has been entered into.

PICKAWAY COUNTY

has a Jail, a 2-story stone building, with 4 large, insecure rooms for prisoners, occupied in the course of last year by 20 or 30 inmates, among whom were 2 lunatics, and 8 or 10 debtors.

MUNROE COUNTY JAIL

is an old, wooden building, 2 stories high, embracing, under the same roof, 2 badly-ventilated rooms for prisoners, 1 room for debtors, a court-room, and the jailer's residence.

STARK COUNTY

has a Jail, built 15 years ago; rooms cold, dark, damp, and smoky.

JAIL AT LANCASTER;

miserable old brick building, lined with hewn timber, and containing 2 dark, dirty rooms for criminals, 1 for females, and 1 for debtors.

MUSKINGUM COUNTY JAIL;

an old, 2-story building, with 2 rooms for criminals, connected with privies from which comes an odor neither healthful nor pleasant.

THE JAIL AT MARIETTA,

built in 1798, is the oldest in the state, and, though of wood, has such security, that no inmate has ever left it except through the door.

In the upper story is the old court-room, where some of the first men in the state have displayed their wit, their learning, and their eloquence. Above, in the cupola, still hangs the old bell, cast in Norwich, Conn., nearly half a century ago, dragged over the mountains, and through the woods, at a large expense of time, strength, and money, and whose peculiarly sweet tones now daily salute the ears of the good people of the town, at the hours of 9 and 12, calling children to school, lawyers to court, and all to make preparation for dinner. As the court-room has been abandoned for a new one, so ought the Jail to be.

ROSS COUNTY JAIL, AT CHILLICOTHE,

has a good exterior, and contains a block of 8 cells, on the Auburn plan; only the rooms are twice as large, and are filled with sickening air from the vile privies which are under them.

JAIL AT CINCINNATI

consists of a front building, containing the jailer's apartments, and large rooms, on the old plan, and a back building, containing 40 cells, on the Auburn plan, except that the doors open inwards, the partition walls are wood, plastered over, and there are no ventilators. Within the last 12 months, 660 persons charged with offences against state laws, and 400 charged with offences against city laws, were sent to this Jail.

Sorry to see some 20 males, boys and old men, the veteran and the novice in crime, all let out together in the area, with no labor nor inspection, there to curse and swear, to quarrel and gamble, and to instruct each other in the works of iniquity.

Such prisoners as are sentenced to remain here for slight offences, have chain and ball attached to their legs, and are sent into the highways to pound stone by day, and are crowded in large numbers in the same room by night, in the old Prison.

Had conversation alone with a man who was yesterday sentenced to be hung for the crime of murder. He seemed much dejected, and said he was drunk when he did the deed.

Saw an officer bring to the Jail a good-looking, well-dressed young man, who was perfectly sober. His offence was, "not having visible means of support." To get this man to Jail, where he is kept in indolence, and at expense, the city must be taxed to pay the justice, the constable, and the jailer, their fees; and, after all, who is the better for it? Why not have a Work-House for the lazy loungers?

CLARK COUNTY JAIL, AT SPRINGFIELD,

was built a quarter of a century ago, and has 2 rooms for the jailer, and 2 rooms for prisoners. In the first room I entered, found 7 prisoners. At the farther end sat 2 men on the floor, with a candle burning, at mid-day, playing cards. As soon as they saw me, they blew out their light, saying, "We can't afford to burn candles in the daytime." All the light we then had (and it was what, in some parts of the country, they would call "mighty little") came through a single opening through the logs and brick, about a foot in diameter. As I was taking the measure of this aperture, 2 fellows stepped up slyly behind me, and were about to make free with my coat pockets. I was alone, and locked in the same dark room with rogues, and the best I could do, while using my pencil, was to stand with my back against the wall, and watch their movements. While doing so, one who had been sent to Jail for stealing, came to me with a complaint. He said, the night before, while he was asleep, $1 60 in silver had been taken from his coat pocket, though his coat was all the time snugly rolled up, and laid under his head. "Do you suppose," said I, "that any of these men here took it?" "O," said he, with a significant look, (and no doubt feeling that it was somewhat incongruous for one thief to charge another with stealing,) "it will not do, you know, for one to suspect his companions." "Could the rats have got your money?" "I don't know what rats could do with *silver* money," said he, rather dryly; "but here, sir, is my coat; you can look at it, and judge whether a rat could have torn such a hole." A rent had been made through several thicknesses of stout cloth, to get at the pocket.

"Some one here," said I, "has got your money. May be I can see it in the eyes of some one,"—giving a glance at each as I spoke. As I did so, the countenance of one of the men fell, and he showed marked signs of guilt. "My advice," said I, "is, that the one who took the money put it where the owner can find it between this and to-morrow morning; for if it is not found, no one will be allowed to leave the room without being thoroughly searched." The advice seemed to be well received; but I did not afterwards go to see, and learn the result.

This miserable old Jail will soon be abandoned, as it ought to be. Some plans for a new Jail were shown me, one of which, with a slight alteration, will be very good.

FRANKLIN COUNTY JAIL, AT COLUMBUS,

is the basement story of the new and elegant court-house. In the outer wall, 15 feet from the block of cells, are glazed and strongly-grated windows, through which comes abundance of light. There are 14 cells, 12 feet long by 7 wide, whose doors are flat bar-iron gratings, containing 10 inmates, 7 males, 3 females. In a room by himself is the wretched man, Clark, who, a year ago, killed one of the keepers of the Ohio Penitentiary, by nearly severing his head from his body with a single blow of an axe. He is now waiting his trial, and pretends to be crazy. He lay on his bed, at the farther end of his cell, and would not come to the door, nor get up. "Do you want a book to read?" "What book?" "Any book," said I. "Yes, I want a newspaper, and a law book." "Would you like a nice Testament?" "Who printed it?" was his reply.

This Jail is neatly kept, and seems secure; but Judge Lane, who presides at the present court in Bank, expresses a fear that the air, in the rooms above, is vitiated from the cells below, and therefore thinks it not well to speak of it as one which deserves to be imitated.

JAIL AT DAYTON

consists of an old building, in which are some rooms for prisoners, and apartments for the jailer. Back of this, more recently built, is a single-story stone building, containing 2 large rooms, arched overhead, which have been divided into smaller ones by wooden partitions. Taken all together, the Jail is a poor concern, and there are too many noble spirits in Dayton to let it have much longer any standing on the earth. Already the public mind is awake in the matter, and the grand jury have presented it, in a report that has been printed, as a nuisance that ought to be abated. Both the Jail and court-house, which is close by, are illy in keeping with the other improvements of this beautiful and prosperous town, in the centre of which they are placed. The land on which they stand is exceedingly valuable. It would seem good policy for the county to sell this land, and with the avails build a new court-house a little removed from the centre.

Two of the best Jails in Ohio, probably, are at Norwalk and Ravenna, both on the Auburn plan. — Have neither seen nor heard of any Jail in the state in which either systematic labor or instruction has been introduced. Very little attention, in any of the counties, seems to be paid to classification or reformation of prisoners. A large proportion of the Jails are log buildings. Judge Swan, of Columbus, says, that 4 out of the 7 counties embraced in his circuit, have log Jails.

While in Columbus, addressed letters of inquiry touching the condition of County Prisons to members of both branches of the legislature. These letters were promptly responded to. The facts thus obtained were submitted to the chairman of the committee on Jails. After this, the whole subject relating to County Prisons underwent discussion in the legislature. As the result, the following law was passed, entitled,

"An Act for the Regulation of County Jails.

"Sec. 1. *Be it enacted by the General Assembly of the State of Ohio*, That the president judges of the Courts of Common Pleas of the several judicial circuits of this state, shall, immediately after the passage of this act, and from time to time thereafter, as they may deem necessary, prescribe in writing rules for the regulation and government of the Jails in the several counties within their respective circuits, upon the following subjects, viz. : *First* — the cleanliness of the Prison and prisoners : *Second* — the classification of prisoners in regard to sex, age, and crime, and also persons insane, idiots, and lunatics : *Third* — beds and clothing : *Fourth* — warming, lighting, and ventilation of the Prison : *Fifth* — the employment of medical or surgical aid when necessary : *Sixth* — employment, temperance, and instruction of the prisoners : *Seventh* — the supplying of each prisoner with a copy of the Bible : *Eighth* — the intercourse between prisoners and their counsel and other persons : *Ninth* — the punishment of prisoners for violation of the rules of the Prison : *Tenth* — such other regulations as said judges may deem necessary to promote the welfare of said prisoners : *Provided*, that said rules shall not be contrary to the laws of this state.

"Sec. 2. That said judges shall, as soon as may be, cause a copy of said rules to be delivered to the county commissioners in the several counties in their respective judicial circuits ; and it shall be the duty of said commissioners forthwith to cause the same to be printed, and to furnish the sheriff of their county with a copy of said rules for each and every room or cell of said Jail, and also, to forward a copy of said rules by mail to the auditor of state, who shall carefully file away and preserve the same.

"Sec. 3. That the said sheriff shall, immediately on the receipt of said rules, cause a copy thereof to be posted up and continued in some conspicuous place in each and every room or cell of said Jail.

" SEC. 4.   That the said judges may, from time to time, as they may deem necessary, revise, alter, or amend said rules ; and such revised, altered, or amended rules shall be printed and disposed of by said commissioners and sheriff in the same manner as is directed by the second and third sections of this act.

" SEC. 5.   That the sheriff, or, in case of his death, removal, or disability, the person by law appointed to supply his place, shall have charge of the County Jail of his proper county, and of all prisoners by law confined therein ; and such sheriff or other officer is hereby required to conform in all respects to the rules and directions of said president judge above specified, or which may from time to time be by said judge made and communicated to him by said commissioners.

" SEC. 6.   That the sheriff, or other officer performing the duties of sheriff, of each county in this state, shall, as soon as may be after the passage of this act, procure, at the expense of the proper county, a suitable book, to be called the Jail Register, in which the sheriff, by himself or his jailer, shall enter, *First* — the name of each prisoner, with the date and cause of his or her commitment : *Second* — the date and manner of his or her discharge : *Third* — what sickness, if any, prevailed in the Jail during the year, and, if known, what were the causes of such diseases : *Fourth* — whether any or what labor has been performed by the prisoners, and the value thereof : *Fifth* — the practice observed during the year of whitewashing and cleansing the occupied cells or apartments, and the times and seasons of so doing : *Sixth* — the habits of the prisoners as to personal cleanliness, diet, and order : *Seventh* — the operation of the rule, and directions prescribed by the president judge : *Eighth* — the means furnished prisoners, of literary, moral, and religious instruction, and of labor : *Ninth* — all other matters required by said rules, or in the discretion of such sheriff deemed proper.   That the said sheriff, or officer performing the duties of sheriff, shall carefully keep and preserve the said Jail Register, in the office of the jailer of his proper county, and, at the expiration of said office, shall deliver the same to his successor in office.

" SEC. 7.   That the sheriff, or other officer performing the duties of sheriff, shall, on or before the 1st day of November, in each year, make out in writing, from said Jail Register, a Jail report, one copy of which said report he shall forthwith file in the office of the clerk of the Court of Common Pleas of the proper county ; one copy with the auditor of the county, for the use of the commissioners thereof ; and one copy of said report he shall transmit to the secretary of state ; and it shall be the duty of the secretary of state to communicate the reports of the several sheriffs of this state to the General Assembly, on or before the 1st day of January annually.

" SEC. 8.   That it shall be the duty of the Court of Common Pleas to give this act in charge to the grand jury once each term of said court, and lay before them any and all rules, plans, or regulations established by said president judge, relating to County Jails and Prison discipline, which shall then be in force.

" SEC. 9.   That the grand jury of each county in this state shall, once at each term of the Court of Common Pleas, while in attendance, visit the Jail, examine its state and condition, examine and inquire into the condition and treatment of prisoners, their habits and accommodations ; and it shall be their duty to report to said court in writing whether the said rules of the said president judge have been faithfully kept and observed, or whether any of the provisions of this act have been violated, pointing out particularly in what said violation, if any, consists.   It shall also be the duty of the county commissioners of each county of this state to visit the Jail of their proper county once during each of their sessions, in March, June, and December of each year.

" SEC. 10.   That it shall be the duty of the county commissioners, at the expense of their respective counties, to provide suitable means for warming the Jail and its cells or apartments, to provide frames and sacks for beds, night-buckets, and such permanent fixtures and repairs as may be prescribed by said president judge. Said commissioners shall also have power to appoint a physician to the Jail, when they may deem it necessary, and pay him such annual or other salary as they may think reasonable and proper, which salary shall be drawn out of the county treasury, on the order of the auditor ; and said medical officer, or any physician or surgeon who may be employed in the Jail, shall make a report in writing whenever required by the said commissioners, president judge, or grand jury.

"Sec. 11. That it shall be the duty of the sheriff of each county to provide fuel, beds, clothing, washing, nursing, (when required,) and board generally, and all other such necessaries for the comfort and welfare of said prisoners, as the said judge by his said rules shall designate, for all such persons confined by law; and he shall be allowed such compensation for services required by the provisions of this act as may be prescribed by said commissioners : *Provided*, that this section shall not be so construed as to give the sheriff a claim on the county for board or necessaries furnished any prisoner confined for debt only.

"Sec. 12. That the sheriff shall visit the Jail in person, and examine into the condition of each prisoner, at least once each month, and once during each term of the Court of Common Pleas; and it is hereby made his duty to cause all the cells and rooms used for the confinement of prisoners to be thoroughly white-washed at least three times each year.

"Sec. 13. That the jailer or keeper of the Jail shall, unless the sheriff shall elect to act as jailer in person, be a deputy appointed by the sheriff, and approved by the Court of Common Pleas, as in the case of other deputies; and such jailer shall take the necessary oaths before entering on the duties of his office : *Provided*, that, during the vacations of said court, in case of death, removal, or other disability, or refusal to act, or for misconduct, the sheriff should have discharged such jailer, he may appoint one for the time, who shall discharge the same duties, and incur the same liabilities, as if regularly appointed; and *provided also*, that the sheriff shall, in all cases, be liable for the negligence and misconduct of the jailer as of other deputies.

"Sec. 14. That if the sheriff or jailer, having charge of any County Jail, shall neglect or refuse to conform to all or either of the rules and regulations established by said judge, or to any other duty or duties required of him by this act, he shall, on conviction thereof by indictment for each case of such failure or neglect of duty as aforesaid, pay into the county treasury of the proper county, for the use of such county, a fine not less than five dollars, nor more than one hundred dollars, to be assessed by the Court of Common Pleas of the proper county.

"Sec. 15. That all acts and parts of acts which conflict with or are inconsistent with the provisions of this act, be and the same are hereby repealed.

"*March* 13, 1843."

Columbus, Ohio, *December* 29, 1842. Busy in examining the Penitentiary. It stands half a mile from the capitol, fronting south; entrance something like the one at Auburn. The gate-keeper's lodge; the flower-garden, with gravel-walks; the front door; the passage, with parlor and sitting rooms on the right, offices on the left; guard-room, from which, turning to the right, went into the east wing, where were 350 cells, on the Auburn plan, 5 stories high, in 1 block. Area 12 feet wide, well warmed by 6 stoves, and well lighted by 2 tiers of windows, from both sides of the external wall. Four galleries surround the block, sustained by cast-iron brackets without upright posts. Cell doors iron gratings, flat bars, set back a foot into the wall. Ventilators in the front, instead of the middle cell wall.

A door from the east end of this wing leads to the female apartment, which contains 36 cells and 9 inmates, 6 white and 3 black women, without matron to govern them, all idle, and some looking as fiendlike * as any human beings that I have ever beheld. 500 men, under proper discipline, would scarcely give as much trouble as these few women. They fight, scratch, and pull hair, curse, swear, and yell; and to

---

* A few days after my visit, a fiendlike *spirit* was acted out by one of the black women here, who killed a white woman in the same room with her, by beating her brains out with a pair of tongs.

bring them to order, a keeper has frequently to go among them with a horsewhip. This female apartment, as it now exists, is an excrescence upon the establishment, which ought without delay to be removed.

On the north side of the east wing is a door, which leads up a pair of stairs, into one of the best-planned hospitals that I ever saw. First is a spacious room, for a summer hospital, or to be used in case of the prevalence of contagious disease. Next is a winter hospital, of convenient size, well warmed and lighted, kept perfectly neat, in which are 10 or 12 invalids. Farther on are 2 small rooms for medicines, &c.

Under the hospital is a dining-room, where the prisoners sit at long tables to take their food, adjoining which is the cook-room; and then comes a grist-mill, driven by steam power, where grain for the prisoners' use is ground.

On opposite sides of the Prison yard are 2 steam engines, one 30, the other 50 horse power, which move various machinery, and 1 pumps vast quantities of water from the Scioto River into a large reservoir in the middle of the yard.

Over the cook-room is a work-shop, in which about 50 convicts are employed weaving lace, plating silver, &c., and farther on a room where iron castings are done.

First room in the building for shops, on the north side of the yard, contains 40 or 50 convicts, all, by profession, sons of Vulcan, whose clanking hammers, and dust and smoke, make the visitor rather unwilling to linger. A large new building, also on the north side of the yard, has a very spacious cooper's-shop in the lower story, and a room large enough for 2 or 3 chapels in the upper story, where the prisoners assemble on the Sabbath to hear preaching. Last, on the north side, is the stone-cutter's shop, now nearly deserted.

On the west side of the yard is a cabinet-maker's shop, in which some 20 prisoners are employed; tailor's and shoemaker's shop, with 62 prisoners; tool-maker's shop, with 20; broom-maker's, with 23; buckle shop, 12 prisoners.

Thus the labyrinth is threaded, the tour through the east wing, hospital, dining-room, and work-shops completed, and we come to the west wing, which is an exact counterpart of the east wing. Both wings are secure, and of easy inspection from windows in each story of the keeper's apartments.

This Prison was first occupied October 28, 1834, when 189 prisoners were brought here from the old Prison. Since that time, 1148 prisoners have been received, among whom were 43 colored, and 9 females. During the year ending November 30, 1842, there were 137 prisoners received, 79 discharged by expiration of sentence, 3 by writ of error, 66 pardoned, 8 died; remaining in Prison, 461, 41 less than the greatest number that have been in Prison at the same time before.

No one sent here for a less term than 1 year, and no increase of punishment in this state for 2d or 3d offences. No overstint. No ardent spirits nor tobacco allowed the prisoners. No escape ever made from the cells, and but 1 from the yard. But one insane person in Prison, and he was sent here insane.

The warden, deputy-warden, physician, 19 assistant-keepers, and 4 guards, constitute the Prison officers, whose annual pay amounts to between 10 and 11,000 dollars.

A large number of the prisoners are unable to read, and no provision is made for their instruction!

Within the space of 8 years, the earnings from the labor of the prisoners have been more than enough to meet all the expenses of the institution, and to pay for the first cost of the buildings. Last year, there was a net gain to the institution of $28,794 96¾, of which $945 80 was money received at the gate for admission of visitors. Costly buildings, comfortable cells, convenient hospitals, excellent work-shops, provision for the body, large income, liberal salaries; but no provision for enlightening the minds or purifying the hearts of the prisoners! Here is a dark spot resting on this Prison. No library, no teacher, no chaplain, for nearly 500 human beings! For a state like Ohio not to make suitable compensation to that worthy minister of the gospel, who has now for 2 or 3 years performed weekly gratuitous ministrations in this Prison for the highest good of its inmates, while she charges each visitor 25 cents for the sight, and receives large revenue from the labor of these inmates, is truly a matter not to be looked upon without pain and surprise.

Sheriffs in Ohio receive for carrying convicts to Prison, 10 cents per mile for themselves, and 10 cents per mile for each guard, going and coming, and 6 cents per mile going for each convict, payable from the state treasury; — a fine speculation, where several convicts go in company, since the guard can be hired for 75 cents or 1 dollar per day. Not long ago, a sheriff from one of the counties started for Columbus with 19 prisoners, guarded by 12 men, to each of whom the state paid 10 cents for each mile travelled, and after all 2 of the prisoners escaped to Kentucky. The Prison records show that about $100 are sometimes paid for transporting a single convict to Prison.

January 1, 1843. Began the year in Columbus by preaching once in the Prison and twice in the town. The day was cold, and the room used for chapel twice as large as need be. Two outside doors, left wide open, let in a constant current of cold air. A small stove, in the middle of the room, scarcely made any perceptible change in the state of the atmosphere. The prisoners, thinly clad, sat on loose benches without backs. With overshoes and wadded surtout kept constantly on, I shivered with cold. Whether the preaching of Paul, under such circumstances, would do much good, demands a doubt.

With proper improvement in the female department and chapel, with a well-selected library for the use of the prisoners, and suitable provision for their instruction, and with the absence of evils likely to attend the frequent change of wardens,* the Ohio Penitentiary would stand among the very best in the land.

---

* Within 12 months, 3 different wardens have had charge of the Ohio Penitentiary.

STATE LUNATIC ASYLUM AT COLUMBUS

stands a mile from the capitol, and is under the superintendence of Dr. Awl, assisted by Dr. Smith.

The main building, brick, facing south, 4 stories high, with east and west wings 3 stories, was built 4 years ago by convicts from the Penitentiary, (who were marched a mile each day, under guard, to their place of labor,) and contains 132 rooms for the accommodation of patients. 30 rods back of the main building are brick lodges for the worst class of patients, containing 14 rooms. The east wing, arranged very much like the apartments for patients in the Worcester Hospital, is occupied exclusively by females, who are classified so that the most deranged are lodged on the lower story, the less deranged on the second story, and the convalescent on the third story. On each story is a dining-room for the patients, and a room for the overseer.

The west wing is of similar construction, and is occupied by males.

Dr. A. was kind enough to accompany me while I made careful survey of the different departments. Every thing seemed to be in admirable order.

In the female convalescent department, was introduced to an inmate, a lady of dignified deportment and pleasant manners, born near Boston, Mass., descended from one of the first families of the state, and the wife of a distinguished clergyman. Her reason was nearly restored. As I was taking leave, she said, " I hope, sir, that Christians remember us in their prayers. We are a greatly afflicted class, and need an interest in the prayers of all praying people." I think I shall remember her remark as long as I live.

In the male department, saw a man who was carrying his arm in a sling, and asked him what was the matter. " Some time ago," said he, " I thought I had a call to preach ; so I set up preaching in my own house. My family and friends thought I had not a call, and proposed that I should go with some one to Columbus, and let Dr. Awl decide whether I had a call or not. I agreed to this, and came here, not doubting but the doctor would examine me, and say at once that I had a call to preach. Instead of that, no special examination was made, and I was put in here among the crazy people. After staying a week or two, I got out of patience, and thought I would leave ; so I removed that window-sash, tied my bed-clothes together, and, by taking hold of them, was going to let myself down to the ground. I did not get down far before the blanket I had hold of separated, and let me fall 20 feet, on to the frozen ground ; and, sir, just as soon as I found that my arm was broken, I was convinced that I had no call to preach ; for," said he with an emphatic gesture, " it stands to reason, that if the Lord had called me to preach, he would not have allowed my arm to be broken. I am now willing to stay here just as long as the doctor thinks it is best."

In the evening, attended religious service with the inmates. The service consisted of reading the Scriptures, singing, and prayer. About three fourths of the whole number were present. All behaved with great propriety, and seemed interested in the exercises.

Present number of inmates, 145, which is as many as can be accommodated. An enlargement of the building is much needed, and no doubt will soon be made. (Provision has since been made for the enlargement.) 98 applications, made last year for admission of citizens of Ohio into the institution, were rejected for want of room. About $16,000 are required annually for supporting the institution.

Recoveries are about 86 per cent. in recent cases, and about 35 per cent. in chronic cases.

Whole number of patients admitted to the Asylum, up to November 15, 1842, is 408; of whom 266 have been discharged, 165 recovered, 47 died, and 6 eloped. 165 were between the ages of 20 and 30; only 16 under 20, and but 169 were married persons. 216 males and 192 females.

From the Lunatic Asylum went to the ASYLUM FOR THE BLIND, not far distant. Contrast between the inmates of the two quite striking. There, 'twas painful to see the mind in ruins. Here, 'twas pleasing to see the mind making wonderful manifestations of its powers. Two blind boys sat at the same piano, and played different parts in sweetest harmony, their fingers touching none but the right keys, and moving as if controlled by the same volitions. Little Ellen Shaw ran her delicate fingers over raised letters and words, and, soon as touched, pronounced them correctly. In a recitation room were several boys, who, in time of recess, were lingering at their desks, and reading aloud to themselves " The History of Animals," " Pilgrim's Progress," &c.

It was curious to observe how the souls of these children employed their finger ends instead of eyes. Words brought to their minds through the medium of their fingers were pronounced as rapidly, and with quite as correct intonations of voice, as I recollect ever to have heard in good readers, who had perfect use of the eyes. When it was told me that it was from the earnings of the criminals in the State Penitentiary, that benevolence was thus permitted so kindly to " minister to minds diseased," at the Lunatic Asylum; and here, to give to the blind a substitute for sight; as well as to give instruction to the inmates of the Asylum for the Deaf and Dumb, which I afterwards visited; I saw, as I never did before, an illustration of the fact, that transgressors, condemned, and in a state of punishment, may be made to answer an important purpose.

KENTUCKY PRISONS.

February 7, 1843. Cold day. Rode with Rev. Mr. G. on horseback from Maysville to WASHINGTON, to visit the COUNTY JAIL. The building is of stone, 2 stories high, having 2 partially-lighted rooms and a dark dungeon on the second story for prisoners, and the jailer's apartments below.

In one room we found 2 white men, and a little black boy, 2 years old. The impress of villany was deep on the countenances of the white men. One was a thief, the other a counterfeiter. Both were heavily chained, because, as the jailer said, " they had been trying to help themselves to a door." I saw where they had burnt off thick plank at one end of the room, and come near effecting their escape. The black boy was a little fellow, bright and artless. He was a slave. His master's insolvency was the cause of the boy's imprisonment. He had been attached by his master's creditors, and sent to Jail for safe keeping. Here, night and day, he must listen to the profaneness and corrupting conversation of thorough-paced villains. After having been schooled in this den of pollution, he will be fully prepared for giving instruction in the ways of iniquity to other slaves, and even to the children of some future master.

In another room, found a black, sentenced to be hung next Friday week. She was about 20 years old, and showed in her countenance no marks of peculiar depravity. Her crime was being associated with a black man, who stole from, and set fire to, a building in which no one lived. The man had been sentenced to the same doom with the woman, but made his escape from Jail in a remarkable manner. We sat down, and spoke to the woman about her being prepared to leave the world. She listened with serious attention. By her side sat her child on the floor, 6 months old, born in Prison. As I was conversing with its mother, the little creature fixed its glistening black eyes full on my face, and then put on one of the sweetest smiles I ever beheld. That look went to my heart. It seemed an eloquent appeal in behalf of its mother. We kneeled down, and offered prayer to Him " who made of one blood all nations," in behalf both of mother and child.

BOURBON COUNTY JAIL, AT PARIS,

built of stone 2 years ago, is somewhat on the plan of Moyamensing Prison. A semicircular wall, 18 feet high, without any window or door, is 10 feet from the building containing the cells, and surrounds it on three sides.

Entered front door of jailer's house; by stooping, passed through a door on the right side of the passage, and found myself in an open space, 10 by 25 feet square. In this open space, the only inmate of the Jail was a black man. Here he had been for more than a year, not for any wrong doing on his part, but because his master had the misfortune to owe more debts than he could pay, and it was left for the voice of law to declare, in due time, which creditor might claim this black man as his own. He was a shrewd fellow, seemed to take his confinement in good part, and was quite inclined to be witty at the expense of his master.

Access from this to 3 cells, 8 feet long, 5 feet wide, arched at top, and lighted from the farther end. From the arch overhead goes a ventilator, unseen and unapproached by the inmate of the cell, to which is attached a tube, that, like another Dionysius' ear, conveys even a whisper that is uttered in the cell, so as to make it audible to a listener in one of the jailer's apartments. The second story contains

2 cells like those below. Only 16 persons, charged with crime, were sent from the whole county to this Jail, last year. The Jail building is strong and expensive. The prisoners are left without labor or instruction.

THE JAIL AT LEXINGTON

a stranger would hardly find without a guide. Its brick front presents the appearance of a handsome private residence. Instead of Prison walls and grated windows, to meet the eye, there is on the front a conspicuous sign, having on it, in large capitals, these words —

" PRIVATE ENTERTAINMENT."

The building is used as a sort of boarding-house, except 2 rooms in one corner, which are reserved for the use of criminals. During the last 12 months, but 11 persons, charged with crime, from the large and populous county, have been the inmates of these 2 rooms.

KENTUCKY STATE LUNATIC ASYLUM

stands one mile from the city of Lexington, and has a beautiful location. Its origin was this. About the year 1820, some medical gentlemen in Lexington projected a hospital for such of the poor as needed any kind of medical treatment. In furtherance of their benevolent design, they caused to be built what is now the centre building of the Lunatic Asylum. Not finding encouragement sufficient for perfecting their plan, they offered to give the state their building, on condition that it should be converted into an Asylum for the Insane. The offer was accepted, and the insane patients were first received here in the year 1822. Nineteen Annual Reports concerning the Asylum have been made to the legislature, but the facts which they contain are not of great value.

Thirty acres of land are connected with the institution, which have of late been surrounded by a board fence, 10 feet high, painted white, and all the grounds have been improved by gravel walks, and ornamented with shrubbery.

The centre building of the Asylum is 3 stories high, besides the basement, containing 13 rooms. To this have been added, on opposite sides, two projecting wings, each connected with a retreating wing, containing, all together, about 100 convenient rooms for patients. The centre building and the wings are now occupied exclusively by female patients, the superintendent's family, and assistants.

A hundred rods back from the main building are 2 plain, badly-located, brick buildings, 3 stories high, containing 84 rooms, exclusively for male patients. Besides, there are connected with the establishment a dead-house, a work-house, a covered spring of water, an engine-house, barn, stables, &c. Lately, a large dining hall has been added, where the better class of patients, of both sexes, sit at tables to take their food at meal times, and where, also, on Sundays, they assemble to hear preaching.

Number of patients at present, February 11, 1843, is 159 — about an equal number of each sex.

The mortality among the patients here has been truly appalling. Out of 841 insane persons admitted to the Asylum during a period of 17 years, 337 have died — something over 40 per cent. Elopements have been frequent; sometimes as many as 20 in a single year.

The government of the Asylum is usually in the hands of 5 commissioners, chosen by the legislature, though at present there are but 3. These commissioners appoint not only the superintendent, physician, and chaplain, but also all the assistants. More than this, they have been accustomed to make the purchases for the supplies of the Asylum, and to determine when an applicant is crazy enough to be admitted as an inmate, and when he is well enough to be discharged.

Evils grow out of such a system. A worthy gentleman, once superintendent of the Asylum, told me that he often had persons sent to the Asylum as assistants, who were intemperate, profane, and entirely unfit for the stations they were sent to fill.

There is no resident physician. The attending physician resides a mile from the Asylum, and pays to it occasional visits. The present superintendent, a worthy shoemaker, makes no pretension to knowledge in medicine, nor to skill in ministering to minds diseased, and probably never thought of laying claim to any peculiar fitness for his office.

There is no well-arranged work-shop, no library, no instruments of music, nor proper means for rational amusement about the Asylum.

Sufficient pains do not seem to be taken here to cherish kind feelings towards the unhappy inmates, and to treat them with attention and politeness. I was sorry to have so much proof of the truth of the last statement as I had. Going, with one who had charge of the patients, into a room where were 15 or 20 deranged females, busily engaged in sewing, a tall, good-looking woman rose from the circle as we entered, and, addressing me, said, weeping, " You put me in mind, sir, of my family." Tears ran down her cheeks as she spoke. It seemed to me, taken all together, a beautiful expression of maternal affection. But, to my grief and surprise, my conductor stepped quickly forward, and, with angry looks, and harsh tones of voice, said, " No more of that — no more of that; sit down, sit down, I say ! "

The state has shown great liberality in supporting this Asylum. Not less than $161,817 19 have been given by the state to this institution within the space of 12 years. Praiseworthy improvements have lately been made. Three years ago, the patients were not suffered to sit at table, nor use knife and fork. Now, a large proportion do both. Additions have been made to the buildings, and the grounds around have been enlarged and adorned. A chaplain is employed, who preaches one sermon a week, and receives $100 salary.

After all, the Kentucky Lunatic Asylum is not what it ought to be, and never will be so, till a resident physician, of suitable qualifications, intrusted with proper powers, and bearing a due share of responsibility, shall have been appointed, and placed at the head of the institution. Every citizen of the state has an interest in this matter. Members of the first families in the country are already inmates of the Asylum. No one can tell how soon he, or the friend of his bosom, may need the benefits which a well-regulated Asylum of this kind can afford.

Kentucky has shown a noble liberality in making annually such large pecuniary grants to this institution, as she has. Let her see to it that its internal management is such as to place it among the first of the kind in the land.*

February 17, 1843. Arrived early this morning, after a cold night's ride, at FRANKFORT, capital of the state.

Took the earliest opportunity of calling on the governor. Spoke to him about the object of my visit to the state, and called his attention to the case of the black woman now under sentence of death in Jail at Washington. The governor was pleased to say, that his own feelings sometimes prompted him to visit the prisoner, and, without being solicited, handed me a note of introduction to the keeper of the Penitentiary. In regard to the condemned black woman, he was willing to grant her a respite for one month; and in the mean time, in view of further facts that might be presented, he would determine whether he could give her a full pardon. As no one, that I could hear of, wants the woman hung, except her owner, and he chiefly because, in the event of her being hung, he will be freed from one whom he dislikes, and will get pay for her from the state, I am strongly in hopes that her life may be spared.

Went from the governor's to the PENITENTIARY, which stands about half a mile from the capitol. A stone wall, 300 feet square, and about 20 feet high, surrounds the work-shops and yard. No guard are stationed on the wall. In their stead are round, loose stones, as many as can lie on the top of the wall, ready to roll down upon any who should attempt to scale it. The keeper's house stands outside of the wall.

Entrance to the yard is from the street, through a covered way, surmounted by a tower. Passing in, you leave the guard-room and keeper's office on the right. In the yard is the want of convenient walks, and of appearance of neatness. The first building entered contains a steam engine, by whose movements corn is ground, wool carded, boards sawed, and hemp twisted. Next, the blacksmith's shop; then a room in which are 17 looms for weaving hemp bagging, at each of which it is a convict's daily task to weave $55\frac{1}{2}$ yards. Hemp is spun in the room above, threads of which are drawn out from 30 to 60 yards, and suspended on pegs at full length. Besides these there is a small harness and paint shop. The shops are neither large nor good-looking.

This Penitentiary was first built in 1798. The building which contained the cells first built has been torn down, and a new one, containing 252 cells, has lately been erected, at an expense of about $57,000. The new building is just outside of the yard, north, so as to make the yard wall on the north side answer for the entire south side of the new Prison.

No light comes into the new Prison from either end. The whole side, on the south, has but a single window, and that a small one. The north side has but one tier of windows, and these are small, and as high up as the third story of cells; so that the area round the cells, and

* Since the above was written, the necessary changes have been made

of course the cells themselves, are dark and gloomy enough. Cells on the Auburn plan. Doors flat bar gratings, with peculiar fastening. The doors, when closed, leave a recess of about six inches. A lock is attached to the front wall of the cells, between the doors, which, when locked, throws its bolt into a socket made in the end of a small bar of iron. This bar is 9 inches long, hung on a pivot near its centre, so that, as the door shuts, the lower end rises, and then falls against a projecting horizontal bar in the door. The bolt of the lock is then thrown into the socket in the upper end of the bar, whose lower end presses against a projecting bar in the door, and all is secure.

The area round the cells is 10 feet wide, and derives light at night from the burning of crude lard. The galleries are supported by brackets projecting from the cell walls, and, owing to the position of the stairs, are not easy of access.

The hospital is a small, triangular apartment, separated from the area round the cells by a grated door, and lighted by a single window.

Number of prisoners, 170, representing 18 states, of whom 129 have never been married, and 82 have no education, or a very poor one.

But 2 deaths have occurred in this Prison in 2 years.

Last year, 76 prisoners received, 72 discharged by expiration of sentence and pardon, and 9 escaped. No insane person in Prison. Three are in prison for 40 years each, but no one for life, according to the letter of his sentence.

No chapel, nor Sabbath school, nor library, nor chaplain. Prisoners hear preaching once a week from some minister in town.

No complaint from mechanics on account of the labor of the prisoners.

The government of the Kentucky Penitentiary is peculiar. There are no directors or inspectors. The state treasurer, register, and attorney-general, are visitors *ex officio;* but they are vested with no authority, make no reports, do not recognize their obligation to attend to the concerns of the Penitentiary, and of late have discontinued their visits. The principal keeper and clerk are chosen by joint ballot of the legislature for 3 years.

Years past, the arrangement has been, that the keeper should guaranty to the state an income of $5000 per annum, and take to himself one half of all the earnings from the labor of the prisoners after supporting the institution. It might be expected, under these circumstances, every thing would be made to bend to the single point of pecuniary gain. The most rigid economy is practised. No expense is incurred in attempts to enlighten and reform the inmates. Six persons, besides the head keeper, are all that are employed in guarding, providing for, and directing the labor of, 170 prisoners. One prisoner is required to superintend the labor of others. Much work, in the way of building, repairs, &c., is done for the state. The annual profits are shown to be enormous. The annual report made to the legislature January 3, 1843, presents the aggregate profits from the labor of the prisoners, over and above all expenses, from March, 1839, to November, 1842, to be $100,494 56. No other office in the state is as lucrative as that of the keeper of the Penitentiary. Hence the hard scrambling to obtain it. Not less than 20 candidates for this office are this winter zealously engaged in pressing their respective claims upon the legislature.

***

Sunday, February 19. Delivered a lecture this afternoon in reference to the insane, at the capitol, in the representatives' chamber. Did not feel quite at home in the speaker's chair, nor find his table quite high enough for a convenient pulpit; yet the large number, respectability, and good attention of the audience, made up for all the rest. The governor, members of the legislature, and chief men of the town, were present, and seemed to take an interest in the subject.

***

THE JAIL AT FRANKFORT

stands within a stone's throw of the capitol. It deserves a particular description. It is a low, 2-story building, 20 feet square, outside of brick, inside lined with four layers of hewn timber, and contains 2 rooms, 12 feet square, one above the other. There is no access to the lower room except through a trap-door in the upper room, and no way of getting to the upper room but up a crazy flight of stairs outside the building.

I got a young friend to guide me to the Jail, and there we found a black man to open the doors for us. The trap-door in the centre of the room above was made fast by passing a large chain across it, and fastening the chain with a padlock. This chain was removed, the door raised, and a ladder let down, which penetrated the total darkness below. Having descended the rickety ladder, my feet rested on the log floor below, while my head touched the timbers above. I could not see my hand before me. I called out to my friend to follow, but he looked down and declined.

I had been told that a white man was confined in this room, but I could not see or hear him. I called to him, but he did not answer. I groped my way to a rug, which had been hung over a small, double-grated, and unglazed window, and, on removing it, enough light entered to enable me to distinguish objects in the room. A human being stood shivering in one corner, with a blanket over his shoulders. His name was William Connelly, a native of Kentucky, and his father, he said, had been a soldier under Washington. The son boasted of this, and thought it very hard that he could not have liberty, seeing his father had fought for it. William *had* been a white man, but could not well lay claim to that complexion now.

The bituminous coal, with which his little grate in his stove had been scarcely supplied, had been thrown upon the small recess outside of the 2 rows of iron gratings; and to get this coal he had to reach his arm through both gratings, and draw it in, piece after piece, with his hand. It was the dust, got from collecting his coal in this manner, that gave this man his ebony hue.

" Why didn't you answer me when I called you ? " " I looked so, sir, I did not want to be seen," was his reply. He had been in this room 2 months, and expected to remain in it for months to come.

I looked about the room.   In the centre was a large staple and ring, to which a huge chain was attached.   " William," said I, " what is that chain there for ? "   With a quizzical look, he promptly replied, " To hitch cattle to, sir, I reckon."

On one side of the room lay a large pile of ashes.   On another side was half of a barrel, that had been sawed in two, which had been used for necessary purposes, probably all winter, without having been emptied.   William said he kept it as sweet as he could by putting ashes in it.   On the third side was a small stove, with a grate in it.   On the fourth side was a straw bed, with scanty covering.

Had some serious conversation with William.   He was affected, and wept.   Would gladly have protracted my stay; but, feeling sick, I hastened to get into the pure air.   Was shocked, afterwards, to learn that half a dozen persons have sometimes been confined in this room at the same time.

As the negro was shutting the trap-door, I asked him if prisoners did not sometimes refuse to go down there.   " O yes, sir."   " How do you get them down then ? "   " Men enough to put them down ; and a powerful dog, that will scare any man down right quick."

This Jail, at the capital of a rich state, and in full view of her halls of legislation, for a quarter of a century has been used as a place of confinement, but with what unnecessary accumulation of human suffering, it were painful even to attempt to conceive.   Let it be for rejoicing that its end is near.   The foundation for a new Jail has already been laid.

_____

From information obtained from members of the legislature, as well as from personal observation, there is reason to believe that there is no state in the Union, of equal age, wealth, and population, in which County Prisons are worse constructed, or less used, than in Kentucky.

_____

JAIL AT SHELBYVILLE

stands a little way out of town ; — appearance mean ; construction like the one at Frankfort ; — inmate, February 23, a solitary female.

_____

February 25, 1843.   Paid a visit to the old stone JAIL AT LOUISVILLE. It shows no improvement since my visit to it 2 years ago; and 'tis too miserable a concern ever to attempt to improve it.

Present number of prisoners, 10; whole number during last 12 months, 76; of whom 42 were sent to the Penitentiary, 3 for 40 years each; aggregate term of the whole, 238 years.

More convicts sent from this Jail to the Penitentiary, than from all the other Jails in the state taken together.

February 26, *Sunday.*   At 9 o'clock, went to the Jail to have a religious service with the prisoners.   Such service had not been common.   Doubt was expressed whether the prisoners would be willing to listen.   'Twas agreed to submit the question to the prisoners themselves.   Went to their room.   Every inmate in favor of it.   No Bible in the room. Got one from the office, and was locked in alone among the prisoners. They gave me their best chair, and seated themselves, some on the window-sill, and some on the floor. During prayer, the silence was remarkable. Read and remarked upon the 51st Psalm. Attention good. The eyes of some were filled with tears. Pleasant season. Had personal conversation with several. A large proportion were from the north. One was from Vermont; one from Troy, N. Y.; and one from Boston, Mass. Some had been employed on the river boats. Rum had been their ruin. On taking leave, was heartily thanked by my audience for my visit.

February 27. Called at the mayor's office. He received me very kindly, and showed me several plans for a new Jail which he had procured. One was a drawing of the Hartford Jail, for which both the mayor and sheriff expressed a preference; but the county commissioners had chosen another.

The plan adopted by the commissioners is somewhat peculiar, and does not seem to embrace either the simplicity, security, or cheapness of the Hartford plan. According to a drawing of it which I saw, and had explained to me by the mayor, a wall, from different parts of which lofty turrets are to rise, 124 feet long on two sides, and 90 feet on the other two sides, is to surround the Prison. At the front entrance, outside of the wall, is to be a 1-story building, with passage through the centre, leading to the Prison, on one side of which are to be 2 lock-up rooms, for the safe keeping of such as are apprehended at night, and on the other side of the passage, 2 rooms, for the use of the jailer, guard, &c. Beyond these, on opposite sides of the passage, is to be a kitchen on the right hand, and on the left hand a cook-room. Farther on is the Prison, to contain 52 cells, 2 stories high, on opposite sides of a wide area, lighted from the outside by windows 5½ feet high by only 4 inches wide. Cell doors single, of sheet iron; hole at the top, for passing food through.

A well is to be sunk in the area, from which water is to be pumped into reservoirs placed on the galleries. Location to be near the court-house, in the heart of the city. Foundation now being laid. Estimated cost, $30,000.

With a letter from the mayor, went a mile from the Jail, to visit the LOUISVILLE WORK-HOUSE. This is a place for the punishment of such as are convicted of minor offences, and might be made to occupy an important intermediate position between the County Jail and the State Penitentiary. Back of the keeper's house stands the Prison building, in the centre of a small yard, surrounded by a low brick wall. It embraces 38 cells, 3 stories high, facing each other, on opposite sides of a narrow passage. The cells are lined with timbers, have wooden doors, with a hole in the top, through which the inmates of different cells see each other, and carry on through the night the most profane, obscene, and corrupting conversation, with entire freedom. 43 inmates have nightly lodgings in these cells, among whom black and white, young and old, male and female, parents and children. Some of the men are heavily loaded with chains, and such as work are employed in sawing and breaking stone. Whatever of direction, inspection, or control, they have, is from a man who stands unarmed on the top of the yard wall.

Brazen-faced white women sat by the side of hardened men, with large, long-handled hammers, breaking stone. A simple woman was strolling about the yard among the men, begging, and chewing tobacco. Even little children are allowed to follow and be with their mothers in this place. One mother, whom I saw, had three children with her. She had been guilty of crime; and as no one would take her children, they were sent, with their mother, to this horrible place, to be thoroughly schooled in the dialect of the pit!

800 human beings are yearly sent here. It cannot be that the good people of Louisville are aware of the wretched influence which this Work-House, with its present arrangements, must have on the population of their city. Blame does not appear to attach to the keeper. He has to take things as he finds them. He has to keep the inmates as well as he can, in a contracted yard by day, in cells of wrong construction by night, and with assistants too few to maintain proper discipline under any circumstances. The keeper is aware of the evils, and declared to me that there was not only no hope of the inmates being reformed in the present state of things, but, let him do the best he could, they were sure to grow worse and worse the longer they staid there.

The strangest sight of all was to see slaves, male and female, sent here by their owners, not for wrong doing, but merely to stay till their masters could find some one to hire them. I saw these slaves working, and freely conversing with the most corrupt and abandoned characters, who had lately come from the brothel and State Prison.

Can it be that the owners of these slaves know, when they send them for cheap and safe keeping to the Work-House, that they are making them the daily companions of convicted thieves and prostitutes?

It does, indeed, seem an outrage on all decency and humanity, thus to place these blacks where they must be polluted by the association with felons, who have made sin and crime their trade, and then to seek for them a situation in some respectable family, where they may have opportunity to ruin other servants, and to poison the minds and corrupt the morals of lovely and promising children.

This establishment is a great expense to the city; and no wonder. Half the inmates who are able to work are most of the time idle, and such as work bring but little to pass.

I could not help thinking what a delightful change would here be accomplished, were the sexes separated, and a matron in charge of the females; were the yard properly enlarged, and the night-rooms rightly constructed; were there work-shops for the adults, and a school-room and teacher for the children; were there a well-selected library for the use of the inmates, and guard and keepers enough to enforce rigid discipline, and exact productive labor; and were all sweetly blended with the voice of the daily morning and evening prayer, and the proclamation each Sabbath of God's love, through his Son, for the lost and the guilty.

March 11. At Nashville, Tenn. Visited the Penitentiary. Number of inmates, 180; among whom were no insane persons. 3 colored females, 3 colored males, 1 prisoner 14 years old; 1, 80 years old; 80 between 20 and 30 years old; 2 sentenced for life, 14 for murder of the second degree, 40 for horse-stealing, 7 for negro-stealing. Prisoners chiefly employed at hatting, shoemaking, blacksmithing, and stone-cutting.

First cost of the Penitentiary, including land, yard wall, shops, keeper's house, and 200 cells, &c., about $70,000. Inmates first received in 1831. Before that time, no Penitentiary in the state. Earnings from labor of prisoners since that time, above expenses, more than enough to meet first cost of the Penitentiary.

Health of prisoners good. But 2 deaths in 2 years.

New work-shop, a fine one. More yard room needed. It is in contemplation to employ the prisoners at the bagging and rope business.

In the hospital saw Murrel, the noted "land pirate," as he is called. When he told me he did not think he had repented of his sins, I remarked to him, "Then you are in bondage in a double sense." "Yes, sir," said he, "in a threefold sense." "How so?" "From sin, from sickness, and from imprisonment."

This Prison seems to be well managed. No punishment by stripes. Defective in regard to moral and religious instruction. No Sunday school teacher nor chaplain, and, at present, there is reason to fear that no one can preach the gospel to the prisoners with much hope of success. The reason is this : — Within the last six months, more than half of all the prisoners here, without showing any sorrow for sin, or signs of reformation, have been baptized. By merely professing to yield the cold assent of their understanding to two or three historical propositions, these men, whose word, it is supposed, even the baptizers themselves would be slow to take on any other subject, have been immersed by scores, and taught to believe that, by this ceremony, all their sins, crimes, and moral pollution, are washed away. One of the inspectors of the Penitentiary, a preacher of this doctrine, has been the most active in the use of this summary means of freeing the criminal from his crimes!

Examination of 177 convicts here, shows a close connection between ignorance, intemperance, bad bringing up, and acts of crime ; e. g.

a. 84 out of 177, when at liberty, were constantly intoxicated, when they could get the means: had no moral nor religious instruction, and were almost without education.

b. 30 others were common drunkards, without moral or religious instruction ; tolerable education.

c. 20 could read and write; morally brought up, but were very intemperate.

d. 24 were constant dram-drinkers, occasionally drunk, badly brought up, without any education.

e. 4 others same as the 24 last named, except they had some education.

f. 13 had always been temperate, without education ; badly brought up ; — thus leaving but 2 individuals, out of the 177, that were temperate, morally brought up, and had good education.

NASHVILLE JAIL ;

somewhat improved within the last 2 years, new cells having been added. Present number of inmates, 15. Number received during last 12 months, 243, of whom 10 were murderers, or manslayers, — 9 white men and 1 black man. 2 of these whites are now in Jail waiting their trial. They are brothers, confess the deed, but plead extenuating circumstances. 4 of the 10 were sent to Jail for killing negroes, but were let go without further punishment. The other 4, 1 a slave, and 3 white men, were, one day last month, taken from this Jail and hung. The black man had killed his master by stabbing, at the time of being flogged. One of the white men killed a Methodist minister for his money; another killed a young man for the same cause; and the third shot a widow lady, as she sat in her house, that he and others might inherit her estate.

Last week, a young man was released from this Jail, whom I saw, and had conversation with, when here 2 years ago. He has been in confinement ever since. Of good health, personal appearance, and capacity, living at ease, respected, and happy, in an evil hour he yielded to temptation, became dishonest, and lost his liberty and character. From a high position in society, he sunk himself to the dark depths of a criminal. All the waters of the Cumberland cannot wash away his stains. A beautiful and interesting wife feels deep and lasting agony in consequence, and a lovely child may, to the day of its death, suffer from its father's wrong doings.

TENNESSEE LUNATIC ASYLUM

stands half a mile from the city, and received its first patients about 3 years ago. A stone wall, laid in mortar, 14 feet high, strengthened at intervals by buttresses, surrounds seven acres of land. Near the centre stands the Asylum, a stone building facing west, whose centre is 4 stories high, including the basement, surmounted by a cupola, with north and south wings 3 stories high, including the basement, centre, and wings, showing a front of 207 feet in length. At right angles with the north and south wings, are east and west wings, 31 feet long.

A passage, 8 feet wide, runs through the centre of the main building and all the wings, on each story, on both sides of which are rooms for the patients, 12 by 14 feet square, well lighted, secure, and quite comfortable, sufficient for the accommodation of 100 persons.

Present number of patients 29, of whom 11 are females. 11 are pay patients, and 18 are paupers, as many as the state has as yet furnished the means of supporting. Greater liberality from the state is confidently looked for. Pay patients are charged $2 50 per week.

The physician to the Asylum resides in the city, receives $500 per annum salary, regularly visits the patients twice a week, and not oftener unless sent for.

But little labor is performed by the patients. Religious service is sometimes held with them.

The institution needs a better supply of water. $2500 would furnish an abundant and lasting supply from the Nashville water-works. This will be secured as soon as pecuniary means are obtained.

In visiting the inmates, I met with one, a young physician, late graduate of the University. He stepped up to me in great haste, and, with rapid motion, put a package in my hand, saying, "I wish you to hand this to the foreman of the grand jury in Nashville." "May I not look at it first?" said I. "O no; hand it directly to the foreman of the grand jury."

What he handed me was two sheets of paper written over on all sides, so that there was scarcely room for the insertion of another word. A more melancholy picture of the movements of a mind in ruins, than this writing presented, I never saw before. There was constant flow of thought, expressed in good language, without the least connection. The following is a specimen: —

"Saint Paul's finger. I am Saint Paul on horseback. Bear the goddess up. Distant things that I have seen. Remember I taught Philip Lindsley to chew tobacco. Question, Where is the mourner? The image of a ship. The illumination of hope. The darkness thereof taken away. General Andrew Jackson. 12 miles. His wife. Question, How many more curiosities do you want to send to the house of Athens? Ink, ashes, fire, color, stove. The seed of tomato in Jail. The fruit thereof eat plenty. Love is yet a stranger to my heart. She knew there was no love in it. Why did Eliza mourn after my answer was read. I saw her dressed in red." Then follows this singular algebraic expression, " $\frac{1}{2}$ Eliza $= 2$."

IMPRISONMENT FOR DEBT

was abolished in Tennessee by the last legislature, by the passage of the following law, which, though rather remarkable for its brevity, is said by lawyers fully to effect the object designed : —

"*Be it enacted by the General Assembly of Tennessee*, That all laws now in force in this state, authorizing the issuance of writ of *capias ad satisfaciendum*, (commonly called an execution against the body of a debtor,) be, and the same are hereby repealed."

CLARKSVILLE JAIL,

on the bank of the Cumberland River, some 60 miles below Nashville, has 2 or 3 dark and dirty rooms for prisoners, and, March 20, 5 inmates — a white man, for shooting a merchant, to get his money; a slave, for setting fire to his master's grist-mill, causing him a loss of $15,000; another slave, for knocking a man down on board a flatboat, and robbing him of his pocket-book and money, being urged, as he says, by his owner, to whom he gave the pocket-book, to do the deed; and still another, that it may be decided whose property he is.

JAIL AT NEW ALBANY, INDIANA,

contains but 1 room for criminals; ring and staple in centre; lighted by 2 small unglazed windows.

INDIANA PENITENTIARY, AT JEFFERSONVILLE,

visited *March* 30. Number of inmates, 108, of whom 1 female, 1 for life, 12 blacks; ages from 15 to 75 years. Last year, no deaths; 40 discharged by expiration of sentence, 40 by pardon. Pardoning power seems to be very generally exercised, whenever a petition comes to the governor from a majority of the judges concerned in the trial.

Glad to find such marked improvement since my visit 2 years ago. A new and comfortable office has been built for the keeper; the huge, tempting gateway walled up; filth carried from the yard; pavement laid; work-shops enlarged; books procured, and a worthy chaplain appointed. But there, in one corner of the yard, still stood those horrible night-rooms. Again I went into one, and had the door closed upon me. The darkness was like midnight, and breathing difficult. 'Tis too bad to force living flesh and blood into these coffins, night after night.

Let there be rejoicing at what Indiana has concluded to do. A new Prison, mainly on the Auburn plan, is being built by labor of prisoners, half a mile from the old one. Its external wall, of brick, now 17 feet high, to be 30 feet, surrounding 5 acres of ground.

The Prison building, to contain 252 cells in 4 stories, is to extend at right angles from the middle of the wall, on the south side, 217 feet, towards the centre of the yard. The foundation has been laid, leaving the area round the cells 15 feet wide.

The plan for the work-shops is such that an overseer, from a single stand-point, can inspect three shops. Receiving-room, guard-room, offices, &c., to be between the cells and the external wall on the south. Keeper's house to stand by itself outside the wall.

Surprised to find that the plan did not embrace any place for a chapel. Mentioned the fact to the building agent. He said it was an oversight, and should certainly be attended to.

Indiana has adopted the Kentucky plan of leasing out her prisoners for a term of years, on condition of receiving a bonus and a certain proportion of their earnings. The present lease is for five years, the state to receive $4000, and one half of the earnings of the prisoners above their support, besides.

There is a single case of the small-pox among the prisoners here; but, as the subject is kept by himself, no apprehensions are felt of its spreading. The practice of shaving the hair close to the head from some of the convicts, is followed here as a matter of punishment. Pity that some other mode could not be substituted.

No guards on the wall, nor are overseers constantly in the different shops. The prisoners take their food all together in the same room. Preaching every Sabbath by the chaplain, whose salary is $250. No Sunday school; but it is expected that one will soon go into operation, to be taught by young gentlemen from the Theological Seminary at

New Albany.   Nearly half of the present inmates of the Penitentiary cannot read.

There is 1 insane person among the convicts.   Indiana needs a State Asylum for the Insane Poor.   If the same feeling prevails throughout this young and enterprising state, as was manifested the other day at New Albany, where I delivered a lecture on the subject of lunacy, a long time will not pass before Indiana shall have made abundant provision for poor lunatics.

JAIL AT WHEELING, VIRGINIA,

is a large stone building, close by the court-house, containing jailer's apartments, and 22 cells for prisoners.   The cells, some quite large, are 3 stories high, with a passage on each story running between them, and, though built at great expense, are scarcely secure.   One of the inmates lately came near making his escape, and in consequence wears heavy irons on his wrists and ankles.

In one room, its inmate had beguiled the tardy hours by hanging his cot round with festoons and curtains made from old newspapers.

In one of the passages between the cells, was a negro, kept there to be sold for his master's taxes.   He was very active and talkative, and served as a constant medium of communication between the prisoners in the different cells.

It costs $160 to convey a convict from this Jail to the State Penitentiary at Richmond.

Prisoners are kept in this Jail without labor or instruction, and under discipline so miserably lax, that they sing and yell, greatly to the annoyance of the citizens in the neighborhood.   The yard surrounding 3 sides of the Jail, too small, and without proper sewers for carrying off water and filth, is the place in which 4 huge, fierce bull-dogs are kept ready to seize on the prisoner who may adventure the sole of his foot on the ground.

JAIL AT PITTSBURG, PENNSYLVANIA,

is one of the most costly County Prisons west of the Alleghany Mountains.

May 8th, 1843, paid a visit to it, in company with the mayor of the city.   It stands on elevated ground, just back of the splendid court-house, and was built 6 years ago, at an expense of $90,000.   Outer walls hewn stone, partition walls brick.   Cells on Moyamensing plan, 60 in number, 3 stories high, between which runs a passage leading one way into the court-house, the other way into the jailer's apartments.

Size of the cells, on lower story, 9 feet wide by 16 feet long ; on the second story, the width of the gallery shorter than the cells on the first story ; and on the third story, width of the gallery shorter than the cells on the second story.   Ventilation not such as to keep the air in the cells pure and sweet.

Commitments during the year ending April, 1842, were 1437, of whom 319 were for debt, and 1118 on charges of crime and vagrancy

The law abolishing imprisonment for debt took effect last July, and the temperance cause has made good progress last year. These two causes combined, it is believed, have had the effect to diminish the number of annual commitments 460; there having been, during the year ending April, 1843, 141 fewer commitments for crime and vagrancy, and 320 fewer for debt, than there were the year before.

Prisoners kept without labor or instruction. No books but such as are furnished by the benevolent of the city.

Daily diet, bread and water, unless something more luxurious is furnished by friends of the prisoners. I asked the jailer if men could live a year in health on nothing but bread and water. " O yes," said he, " and grow fat."

It is a sore evil, that the inmates of a place like this should not be required to labor. Here are old and young, the tried and the untried, black and white, male and female, the veteran and the novice in crime, hailing from all quarters of the country. Health requires that they should have better air than they get in their close, badly-ventilated cells. Hence large numbers are allowed daily to range the passage and galleries in company, with none to oversee or prevent corrupt communications.

O! it was a sad sight to see those thorough-paced villains, whose trade, through the whole length of the vast water-courses of the west, is known to have been crime, walking arm in arm, up and down the area, with artless young men, who have just been committed on charge of trivial offences, instilling into their minds, in one short hour, lessons in knavery and crime, which they would not have learned in a lifetime, if left to themselves.

But the saddest sight of all in this Jail was the poor lunatics. I took the liberty to call the attention of the mayor especially to this class of inmates, as I knew that one poor lunatic, by name of Bates, had died last night alone in his cell, and that the mayor, from his office, was frequently obliged to send the insane to Jail, for want of any other place where they could be kept.

It is a lamentable fact, that thieves and robbers, here, fare better than the unfortunate man whose affliction it is to be bereft of his reason; for the former may, in the daytime, leave his cell, and get fresh air in the passage, while the latter is kept, day and night, in entirely close confinement.

The first room having a lunatic, which we visited, contained a young man, pale and alone, his tall form wasted to a skeleton, and naked. He came to the opening in the inner door, and, in a piteous manner, plead for a drink of water. Not a drop was in his room, nor was there any vessel for holding any. One of the prisoners in the passage took a tin cup, filled it with water, and handed it to the suffering lunatic. He seized the cup, exhausted the contents without taking it from his mouth, and handed it back with looks and expressions indicating the sincerest thankfulness.

The sight affected our hearts. Turning to me, the mayor said, " I'll never commit another lunatic to this place, if I can help it."

The condition of poor lunatics, both east and west of the mountains, is such as to call upon Pennsylvania, like the voice of many waters, to make suitable provision for poor lunatics.

THE WESTERN PENITENTIARY OF PENNSYLVANIA

has a pleasant location in Alleghany Town, about one eighth of a mile from the river. The front presents a handsome 3-story stone house, in which are store-rooms, office, and apartments for the warden's family. Before the house are pleasant grounds, handsomely laid out, and ornamented with shrubbery.

From the house back, as from a centre, go 2 ranges of cells, 2 stories high, one range containing 104, the other 76 cells. The foundation for a third range is laid, which occupies all the spare room that remains in the yard.

Around the ranges of cells, a little distance off, is an octagonal stone wall, 25 feet high, enclosing three and a quarter acres of ground. At each alternate angle in this wall rises a high circular tower, 15 feet in diameter, lighted by several tiers of windows, entrance to which is from the yard, through a door at the bottom, and access to the top by means of circular stairs. When the external wall was built, in 1822, these towers were added at great expense, with the expectation that they would serve a good purpose as watch-towers, from which the prisoners in the yard might be kept under inspection and control.

It would seem that the guard might have felt pretty secure, after having locked and bolted the strong door below, and then clambered, with his weapons of war, some 40 or 50 feet above the heads of the convicts. Eight years ago, the old cells were demolished, and the first range of cells on the present plan of the Philadelphia Prison put in their place; so now the towers are of no use, and might be taken by strangers as rather extravagant ornaments. Light and air come to these cells through windows and openings at one end. Cast-iron pipes, 6 inches in diameter, filled with hot water or steam, and passing the shortest way across the bottom of each cell, radiate to each solitary inmate whatever of artificial heat he has at any time in winter.

Present number of prisoners, 145, being less by 31 than has sometimes been in Prison. The warden ascribes this diminution to the prevalence of the temperance cause.

During the year ending January 1, 1843, 69 prisoners were received, of whom 18 could not read; 67 discharged, viz., 46 by expiration of sentence, 16 by pardon, 5 by death.

The physician says, 2 cases of mental derangement came to his notice last year, 1 of which he suspects to have been feigned.

Earnings from labor of the prisoners, above expense of their food, clothing, &c., $4449 86. Officers' salaries paid from the state treasury. If the prisoners do not support themselves by their labor, the deficiency is charged to the respective counties from which they come.

Power of appointing officers of the Penitentiary lies in the Supreme Court, who appoint the warden, physician, clerk, and moral instructor. The warden appoints his assistant keepers, of whom he has at present 6.

Of 163 inmates, at the beginning of the year, 91 were unmarried, 137 intemperate, 26 blacks, and 4 females. Number of inmates since the establishment of the Penitentiary, 915.

Chief business, at present, shoemaking and weaving.

TWENTIETH

ANNUAL REPORT

OF THE

BOARD OF MANAGERS

OF THE

PRISON DISCIPLINE SOCIETY,

BOSTON, MAY, 1845.

Boston:

PUBLISHED AT NO. 1 ASHBURTON PLACE.

1847.

CONTENTS.

CONSTITUTION

OF THE

Prison Discipline Society.

ART. 1. This Society shall be called the PRISON DISCIPLINE SOCIETY.

ART. 2. It shall be the *object* of this Society to promote the improvement of Public Prisons.

ART. 3. It shall be the *duty* of this Society to take measures for effecting the formation of one or more Prison Discipline Societies in each of the United States, and to co-operate with all such Societies in accomplishing the object specified in the second article of this Constitution.

ART. 4. Any Society, having the same object in view, which shall become auxiliary to this, and shall contribute to its funds, shall thereby secure for the Prisons, in the State where such Society is located, special attention from this Society.

ART. 5. Each subscriber of two dollars, annually, shall be a Member.

ART. 6. Each subscriber of thirty dollars, at one time, shall be a Member for Life.

ART. 7. Each subscriber of ten dollars, annually, shall be a Director.

ART. 8. Each subscriber of one hundred dollars, or who shall by one additional payment increase his original subscription to one hundred dollars, shall be a Director for Life.

ART. 9. The Officers of this Society shall be, a President, as many Vice-Presidents as shall be deemed expedient, a Treasurer, and a Secretary, to be chosen annually, and a Board of Managers, whose duty it shall be to conduct the business of the Society. This Board shall consist of six clergymen and six laymen, of whom nine shall reside in the city of Boston, and five shall constitute a quorum. One fourth part of the whole number, in the order of appointment, shall go out of office at the expiration of each year, but shall be re-eligible.

Every Minister of the Gospel, who is a member of this Society, shall be entitled to meet and deliberate with th ; Board of Managers.

The Managers shall call special meetings of the Society, and fill such vacancies as may occur, by death or otherwise, in their own Board.

ART. 10. The President, Vice-Presidents, Treasurer, and Secretary, shall be, ex officio, members of the Board of Managers.

ART. 11. Directors shall be entitled to meet and vote at all meetings of the Board of Managers.

ART. 12. The annual meetings of this Society shall be held in Boston, on the Friday succeeding the General Election, when, besides choosing the officers as specified in the ninth article, the accounts of the Treasurer shall be presented, and the proceedings of the foregoing year reported.

ART. 13. The Managers shall meet, once in two months, or oftener if necessary, at such place, in the city of Boston, as they shall appoint.

ART. 14. At the meetings of the Society, and of the Managers, the President, or, in his absence, the Vice-President first on the list then present, and in the absence of the President and of all the Vice-Presidents, such member as shall be appointed for that purpose, shall preside.

ART. 15. The Secretary, in concurrence with two of the Managers, or, in the absence of the Secretary, any three of the Managers, may call special meetings of the Board.

ART. 16. The minutes of every meeting shall be signed by the Chairman.

ART. 17. The Managers shall have the power of appointing such persons as have rendered essential services to the Society either Members for Life or Directors for Life.

ART. 18. No alteration shall be made in this Constitution except by the Society, at an annual meeting, on the recommendation of the Board of Managers.

ANNUAL MEETING.

THE Twentieth Annual Business Meeting of the Prison Discipline Society was held in Park-street vestry, on Monday, May 26, 1845, at 3 o'clock, P. M.

A quorum being present, the oldest Vice-President then present, the Rev. Dr. Jenks, took the chair, and opened the meeting with prayer.

The Chairman then read the Report of the Treasurer, Hon. Samuel A. Eliot, who was absent from the city, and the certificate of its correctness by the Auditors, W. W. Stone, Esq. and Amos A. Lawrence, Esq. The report, thus audited, was accepted.

The election of the officers was then made, and the officers of the preceding year were re-elected, with the following changes and additions : The names of William Lawrence, Esq., Amos Lawrence, Esq., and Rev. Jared Curtis, were added to the list of Vice-Presidents ; and to the list of Managers, in the place of Rev. Mr. Bartol, the Rev. Robert C. Waterston ; in the place of the Rev. Jared Curtis, the Rev. Baron Stow ; and in the place of Rev. Gorham D. Abbot, Hon. John R. Adan.

The meeting was closed with prayer by Mr. Rogers.

Mr. Waterston, on being notified of his election, asked to be excused, on the ground of numerous and pressing engagements.

The Twentieth Annual Public Meeting of the Prison Discipline Society was held in Park-street church, at 11 o'clock on Tuesday, May 27, 1845.

The Rev. Francis Wayland, D. D., President, took the chair ; and, at .his request, the Rev. Noah Porter, D. D., of Farmington, Conn., read the Scriptures, and opened the meeting with prayer.

Amos A. Lawrence, Esq., one of the managers, read the Report of the Treasurer, Hon. Samuel A. Eliot, who was absent from the city, and the certificate of the Auditors, W. W. Stone, Esq. and Amos A. Lawrence, Esq.

The Report of the Board of Managers was read by the Secretary.

The first Resolution for the acceptance of this Report was offered by George T. Bigelow, Esq.

Charles Sumner, Esq., offered a "Resolution, that the Report be committed to a Committee of —— members with instructions to inquire whether any modifications of the same be necessary, previous to its publication ; and that the Committee be authorized, in the name of the Society, to request permission to examine the Philadelphia and other prisons, and to incorporate a Report of their proceedings in the Annual Report of the Society." This resolution was sustained by Charles Sumner, Esq. and Dr. S. G. Howe, and passed.

Before the Committee was appointed, the Hon. J. W. Edmonds, of New York, late the Chairman of the Board of Inspectors, at Sing Sing, was introduced to the meeting, as a delegate and representative from the Prison Association in New York City, and extended to this Society, in his introduction, friendly salutations, as to an elder sister, from that Infant Institution. Mr. Edmonds continued his speech, and showed the great benefits which had flowed in the prison at Sing Sing from introducing a more mild and humane system of punishment for misdemeanor, and conducting the whole discipline of the Institution by the law of love, and not of terror.

The Committee was then filled, under the previous Resolution, with the following names :—Dr. S. G. Howe, Charles Sumner, Esq., Rev. Louis Dwight, Hon. Samuel A. Eliot, George T. Bigelow, Esq., Hon. J. W. Edmonds, Dr. Walter Channing, and Hon. Horace Mann.

The meeting was then adjourned.

ANNUAL REPORT.

INTRODUCTION.

THE Managers of the Prison Discipline Society present their Twentieth Annual Report, with many thanks to a merciful God. And while they thus acknowledge his preserving mercy to those of us who remain, they have, as ever, to notice the death of friends and benefactors.

JOHN DAMON, of Reading, Massachusetts, a good old New England farmer, who used to attend this anniversary, and stand at the door afterwards, and there, having his eyes moistened with tears, hand to the secretary his annual subscription of three dollars, has notified us, through his executor,—who came to pay the principal, as a legacy, the interest of which the good old man used to pay himself annually as a donation,—that we shall see his face no more.

The REV. JOSEPH CHICKERING, of Phillipston, Massachusetts, in the same way, through his executor, by a small legacy, has given us a token of his last remembrance on earth.

SAMUEL DORR, also, of Boston, a few days before he died, entered his name upon our records, with his usual approbation.

The HON. WILLIAM PRESCOTT, at the good old age of 82, wrote his name with a firm hand in our books six days before he died—an autograph worth a great deal to this Society, oft repeated as it has been, and connected as it is with intelligence, candor, knowledge, great age and experience, with a mind unruffled, and a hand which never trembled in doing good. At no period of his life did he hear with more patience or interest, or act with more promptitude and decision, than six days before he died, in favor of our cause.

The death of the REV. JAMES MILNOR, of New York, filled our hearts with sadness. As he was one of the earliest, so he has been among the most tried, faithful, and steadfast friends of this Society.

If a society is known by the character of its friends and benefactors, the above names are vouchers. " They rest from their labors, and their works do follow them." It is hard to live when such men die. But God lives.

The Twentieth Report, which we now propose to submit, will be arranged under the following heads :—

I.
FURTHER PROVISION FOR LUNATICS AND IDIOTS.

II.
BENEVOLENT EFFORT FOR PERSONS UNDER ARREST.

III.
HOUSES OF REFUGE FOR JUVENILE DELINQUENTS.

IV.
REFORMED PRISONERS, WITH REFERENCE FOR CHARACTER.

V.
AN ABSTRACT OF PROFESSOR MITTERMAIER'S REVIEW ON PRISON DISCIPLINE.

VI.
STATE PRISON IN MAINE.

VII.
STATE PRISON IN NEW HAMPSHIRE.

VIII.
STATE PRISON IN VERMONT.

IX.
STATE PRISON IN MASSACHUSETTS.

X.
STATE PRISON IN AUBURN, N. Y.

XI.
STATE PRISON AT SING SING, N. Y.

XII.
STATE PRISON IN OHIO.

XIII.
SIXTEENTH ANNUAL REPORT OF THE NEW PENITENTIARY IN PHILADELPHIA.

XIV.
CHANGES AND IMPROVEMENTS IN PENITENTIARIES AND PRISONS.

I. — IS FURTHER PROVISION FOR LUNATICS AND IDIOTS NECESSARY?

Is the great work accomplished of making suitable provision for lunatics in the United States?

In the United States are *twenty thousand* lunatics.

In 18 states and 26 Asylums, provision has been made for about 4,125 lunatics.

Even in this admission three Asylums are included, viz., the State Asylums in Rhode Island, New Jersey, and Pennsylvania, for which provision has been made, but they are not yet built; and others are extended to their utmost capacity, when finished as they are being built; but they are not all of them yet finished.

Massachusetts alone, containing less than one twentieth part of the population, has made provision for more than one sixth part of all the lunatics who have been provided for.

Massachusetts has less than 1,000,000 of inhabitants, and she has made provision for 700 lunatics. The United States have 20,000,000 of inhabitants, and have made provision for less than 4,200 lunatics. Massachusetts has no more than adequate provision for its own lunatics, not including the idiots. The United States have, therefore, more than 15,800 to provide for, to do as well as Massachusetts has done.

The following is an approximation to the provision already made :—

	Lunatics
Maine has one Asylum for	100·
New Hampshire, one Asylum for	100
Vermont, one Asylum for	150
Massachusetts has three Asylums for	700
New Jersey will have one Asylum for	*75
Pennsylvania will have three Asylums for	500
Maryland has an Asylum for	150
District of Columbia has an Asylum for	50
Virginia has two Asylums for	350
South Carolina has one Asylum for	100
Georgia has one Asylum for	100
Louisiana has one Asylum for	50
Kentucky has one Asylum for	150
Tennessee has one Asylum for	100
Ohio has an Asylum for	400

* New Jersey may provide for 100 more.

Lunatics.

Rhode Island will have one Asylum for 150
Connecticut has one Asylum for 200
New York has four Asylums for 700

Eighteen states have 26 Asylums for . . . 4,125

The states above named have done well for the time they have been engaged in the good work ; but the *United States* as a whole, have not yet made provision for one quarter of the poor lunatics. 4,125 are, or will soon be, provided for in Asylums ; while 15,875 will remain without provision for their relief.

This statement may seem unauthorized, by those who have given little attention to the subject ; but let us see, by sundry particulars, on the highest authority, whether it is not more than probable.

In the state of *Maine*, letters were addressed, by one of the trustees of the Maine Hospital, early in the season of 1844, to the overseers of the poor in all the cities and towns of the state, asking information as to the number of the insane persons and idiots in their respective cities and towns. Answers were received from 153 out of 357 towns, and the result is as follows :—

12 towns in	York county,	. .	48 insane,	46 idiots.
10 "	Cumberland,	. .	33 "	36 "
19 "	Lincoln,	. .	51 "	61 "
15 "	Oxford,	. .	15 "	26 "
7 "	Somerset,	. .	9 "	4 "
5 "	Aroostook,	. .	2 "	3 "
14 "	Kennebeck,	. .	45 "	29 "
4 "	Waldo,	. .	9 "	2 "
14 "	Penobscot,	. .	9 "	13 "
7 "	Franklin,	. .	6 "	8 "
16 "	Piscataquis,	. .	7 "	7 "
16 "	Hancock,	. .	21 "	28 "
14 "	Washington,	. .	8 "	6 "
153 towns in 13 counties,		. .	263 insane,	269 idiots.

If the number of insane persons and idiots in towns not heard from, say the trustees, should be, according to their population, as in the towns above stated, there would be 613 insane, and 627 idiots, in the whole state.

In the state of *Massachusetts*, it is stated, in a legislative document of the House of Representatives, No. 38, 1843, signed by S. G. Howe, on the memorial of Miss Dix and Robert Rantoul, that

" The number of insane and idiotic persons in the commonwealth was at least 1,700."

The report further states, that

" It appears by the Pauper Abstract of the same year that 958 of them are paupers, and wards of the commonwealth. Abandoned by their friends, and deserted by their own reason, they are, by the providence of God, thrown in trust upon the public. Your committee have anxiously inquired how this solemn trust has been discharged."

" The returns from Jails and Houses of Correction show that there are 80 insane persons confined in those establishments. The following extract of a letter from Dr. Woodward, of the Massachusetts Hospital, will show what is sometimes their condition:—

" ' In the Jails, the insane are crowded together in apartments badly warmed and ventilated, or they are secluded in some solitary room,—cold, dirty, ragged, without society, with bad air to breathe, and scanty and bad food to eat.' A jailer, giving an account of one of the insane, sent to this Hospital, thus writes:—

" ' While in the Jail, he was in the most pitiable and filthy state, covered with vermin. His beard was so long, it would reach his knees when he sat down. He was an old man, and his hair and beard were very gray. During the whole period of his confinement, he would not be prevailed upon to wash or shave himself, or change his clothes. He changed his Prison, and afterwards it was his practice to shave every three or four weeks, and *to wash him and change his whole bed and clothing* every spring and fall!' Yet the day after he came to the Hospital, this man washed himself willingly, and made no objection to being shaved and changing his clothes.

" The effect of confinement in a Jail is exemplified as stated by another. ' Elizabeth Stephens, aged about 40 years, was formerly confined as a lunatic in a Jail, and was as wretched, wild and ungovernable, as such persons usually are in such places. Five years ago she was sent to Worcester, where she was quiet and comfortable, decent and happy. She kept her room and her person tidy, was never violent, would employ herself in knitting, attended church regularly, and up to the 9th of October last, behaved with propriety. On the 12th, she was removed to make way for others, and carried to the Jail of the town of Concord. The sight of this roused her fury, and she refused to enter; but she was carried in by force, and became again a raving maniac. Since then she has been furious; has broken up her bucket, burned her straw bed, smashed her bedstead and her windows, stripped off her clothes, attacked the keeper with an iron grate, and committed every possible outrage. The result probably will be, that she must be chained up, or confined in a cage.'

" In answer to the questions in regard to the insane and idiotic in Alms-Houses, Dr. Woodward writes : ' On this subject, my experience is ample. No class of the poor, and no class of prisoners, are so badly provided for as the insane. In the Poor-Houses, they occupy the coldest, darkest, worst-ventilated apartments ; are dirty, filthy, covered with vermin, and neglected in many ways. This is by no means generally the case ; there are many exceptions ; but the rule is too true.'

" ' In private families,' says Dr. Woodward, ' this class of the insane are scarcely less wretched. They are in cages, cellars, garrets, and cold chambers, in rags, and without fire, suitable bedding, sustenance, or care.

" ' One man came to us, within two years, who had not felt the influence of a fire for four winters, nor taken food in a more decent manner than the dogs of the same establishment. A benevolent neighbor urged upon his friend the propriety of sending him to the Hospital, that a trial might be made to enable him, at least, to observe the decencies of society and enjoy some of the comforts of life. In *one week* after he was admitted he was able to labor ; and in six months he was restored to health and a sound mind.'

" 'I do not know,' says Miss Dix, 'how it is argued that mad persons and idiots may be dealt with as if no spark of recollection ever lights up the mind.'

" 'A poor idiotic young man, a year or two since, used to follow me at times through the prison, as I was distributing books and papers. At first he appeared totally stupid; but cheerful expressions, a smile, a trifling gift, seemed gradually to light up the void temple of the intellect, and by slow degrees some faint images of thought passed before the mental vision. He would ask for books, though he could not read, indulged his fancy, and he would appear to experience delight in examining them, and kept them with a singular care. If I read the Bible, he was reverently and wonderfully attentive. If I talked, he listened with a half-conscious aspect. One morning I passed more hurriedly than usual, and did not speak particularly to him. " Me, me, me! a book!" I returned; "Good morning, Jemmy; so you will have a book to-day? Well, keep it carefully." Suddenly turning aside, he took the bread brought for his breakfast, and passing it with a hurried earnestness through the bars of his iron door — "Here's bread! aint you hungry?" Never may I forget the tone, and grateful, affectionate aspect, of that poor idiot. How much might we do to bring back or restore the mind, if we knew how to touch the instrument with a skillful hand!' "

It is true that the Martha Johonnot legacy, amounting to $42,000, has been appropriated to the enlargement of the Hospital at Worcester; so that its capacity, when thus enlarged, will accomodate about 400 patients; but still, it should be remembered that our insane and idiotic, in Massachusetts, are 1,700; that 958 of these are the wards of the commonwealth; that 80 of these are in Jails and Houses of Correction; that Jails and Houses of Correction cannot be improved as they should be while they remain; that they cannot be properly treated in Prison; that the utmost capacity of all the Asylums in the commonwealth for the insane does not exceed 700, leaving 1,000 insane and idiotic, in the commonwealth of Massachusetts, not suitably provided for. No Asylum for the *Idiotic* yet exists in the United States. France has nobly led the way in this new science of philanthropy.

Massachusetts and Boston will not ignobly linger behind. Prisons in Massachusetts were not built for lunatics and idiots. We have good Asylums for the Insane, and, according to the population, the most capacious in the United States, and so far as we know, in the world. Still, if there is not a Jail delivery of lunatics when the Martha Johonnot legacy is expended at Worcester; if there is not sufficient room for all; and the incurably insane must be returned to Prisons and Houses of Correction, to make room for recent cases; then let there be another Asylum, in the western counties, for the Insane, and an Asylum for Idiots in the vicinity of Boston.

In *Connecticut*, the secretary of state was directed to send circulars, in 1840, to the selectmen of each town, to ascertain the condition of the insane and idiotic poor in the state, and also to astertain the number that would probably be sent to a public institution.

" Returns were received from 54 towns, in which there are 315 insane and idiotic, 179 of whom are reported as insane, and 136 as idiotic. 120 are reported by the towns, and 194 by their friends. If the proportion is the same in the remaining towns as in the 54 from which returns have been received, we have," say the committee of the legislature, " 465 insane, and 353 idiotic ; whole number, 818, of which 312 are supported by the towns, and 506 by their friends."—*Legislative Document, No. 8, of the House of Rep's.*

By returns made two years previously, in answer to legislative inquiry, it appeared that there were 707 insane and idiotic in 118 towns. Of these, 59 were confined by manacles or cages, 3 were found in Jails, and 7 in the State Prison.

In the State of *New York*, the trustees of the State Lunatic Asylum say, in their report for January, 1844,—

" Our predecessors, who planned and commenced the building of this institution, were convinced, after very full investigation, that the number for whom provision should be made was at least 1000, and their plan contemplated accommodation for that number. By the census of 1840, there were reported in the State 2340 idiots and lunatics. In 1841, the Secretary of State reported that there were 803 lunatics in the State supported at the public charge. In 1842, the trustees of this institution, from information received from circulars addressed to different counties, estimated that there were 430 lunatic paupers in the State then confined in *Jails and Poor-Houses.*"

The trustees, with diffidence in their own judgment, recommended the abandonment of the original design of building for the accommodation of 1,000, and recommended a further enlargement of the institution by which accommodation would be furnished for 500. Their recommendation was adopted ; so that it is perfectly apparent, when the enlargement is effected, that only a small number of the insane, in the State of New York, can receive the benefit of the State Asylum. In view, therefore, of the 2,340 insane and idiotic in the State in 1840 ; the rapidly increasing population ; the 803 pauper lunatics in 1841 ; the 403 in Poor-Houses and Jails in 1842 ; the contracting the plan of the State Lunatic Asylum ; it will be quite as apparent, in 1846, as it was in 1844, that the Alms-Houses and the Prisons will contain their hundreds of insane. We look to Rochester for one step in the redemption from this dreadful degradation.

In *Virginia*, Dr. Stribling, of the Western Asylum of Virginia, says in his last report, dated December 31, 1844,—

" There is one other subject in every respect worthy of the attention of the legislature. We allude to the importance of some provision being made for the proper care and treatment of the insane colored persons. The last census shows that, including the insane and idiots, there were in Virginia 384, of whom 58 were free. Where they are, or what is their condition, we have had little opportunity to learn, but know enough to convince us that many of them much need the sympathy and aid of the legislature. Should it be the pleasure of the legislature, at any time, to make suitable provision for such, in connection with the Asylum, we will most cheerfully devote our energies to promote their comfort and effect their cure."

The whole number of insane and idiotic in Virginia, according to the census of 1840, was 1,432. The Asylum at Staunton, in Williamsburg, will accommodate about 300. Where are the 1,132?

At the convention of medical superintendents of Insane Asylums in Philadelphia, in October, 1844, the subject of an Asylum for Idiots was referred to a committee for consideration, whose duty it will be to report at a future meeting in May, 1846. In the mean time, the following interesting and important articles have appeared in the Boston Daily Advertiser, by Dr. Samuel G. Howe.

"HOSPITAL OR TRAINING SCHOOL FOR INSANE AND IDIOTIC CHILDREN.

"No. I.

" Our country does pretty well by most of those unfortunate classes which God, in his providence, makes dependent upon others. Our State does nobly indeed by some of them, and is perhaps the only community in the world which provides ample means for the education of *all* the deaf mutes and *all* the blind, and for the cure or care of nearly all the insane.

" But all is not yet done, nor indeed will it ever be done on earth; for every step in the path of civilization and humanity brings to light new objects for the exercise of our sympathy and our benevolence.

" I wish to bring before the public the situation and the claims of a class of our fellow-citizens who are more wretched, and less cared for, than any who have yet occupied its attention and received the proofs of its sympathy: I mean the idiotic and the insane children who abound amongst us.

" I shall do this in a few short articles; and shall first describe one or two cases which I have recently seen, so as to give an idea of the class to which I refer. In order, however, to present at once the importance of the subject, let me state, that it is probable there are, in our commonwealth alone, over 500 creatures in human shape, who can hardly be called men and women, because their intellect has not been developed, and who are set down as hopeless idiots, and doomed to mere vegetative life in the Alms-Houses. Of this class, at least one half are capable of receiving such intellectual instruction and physical training as will raise them from the rank of animals to that of men, and make them comparatively useful and happy.

" Not long ago, I saw M—— R——, aged 15, the child of most respectable parents. She was a handsome girl, with a full black eye, which flashed with light, and rolled about in such a way as to show that there was too much, rather than too little activity of brain.

" She was not deaf; she had no malformation of the organs of speech; but she had never spoken a word—never even said, ' Mother!'

" She was as full of life and action as the young animals, but had less power of controlling her will and actions than they have. She had the rudiments of the moral feelings; but, undeveloped as they were, she had not the slightest idea of right and wrong.

" In my neighborhood is a fine healthy boy, 9 years of age, in the same condition. He has never spoken an articulate word; yet he hears, and might be made to speak. He is as restless as an eel, is never still a moment when awake, and is utterly incapable of controlling his action.

"He has evidently the germs of intellect, and of the affections, which might be developed, though he is now only a restless, howling animal, disturbing the neighbors with his cries, and causing constant anxiety and grief to his poor mother, who, with woman's just partiality, loves him all the more for his misfortunes.

" Now, both these children will probably grow up to be drivelling idiots, or hopeless maniacs, unless they can be placed under the charge of persons who, by study and experience, have prepared themselves for the task of training such children, in an establishment fitted for the purpose. They are types of a class for which we should have a hospital or training school. France has such an establishment, and Massachusetts must not be behind any nation on earth in good works. H."

" No II.

" Mr. Editor :—I stated in my first article, that ' there are, in our commonwealth alone, over 500 beings in human shape, who can hardly be called men and women, because their intellect has not been developed, and who are set down as hopeless idiots.'

" Dr. Woodward, of the State Asylum at Worcester, says, in a letter dated February 16, ' There cannot be less than SIX HUNDRED IDIOTS, of all classes, in Massachusetts. Half of these, at least, are of an age at which they can be instructed, their minds improved, and more or less useful knowledge imparted to them.'

" And where are these, our younger brothers in intellect,—these children of a larger growth,—who hardly know enough to keep out of fire and water ? What do we do with these poor creatures, whom God has made in our likeness, perhaps for the very purpose of calling out and strengthening our better feelings ? They are left, during youth, in the care of parents who are usually poor and ignorant, and utterly unqualified to instruct them. We open schools at the public expense, for those who have two, five, and ten talents; but the poor idiot, boy or girl, who has but one, must bury that one in intellectual sloth, and receive no other care or attention than that which contributes to the body's growth.

" When they grow to be adults, and it becomes expensive to keep them, or when their parents die, they are sent to vegetate in the Alms-House. In almost every country ' Poor-House' there will be found one or more of these harmless creatures, whose form is human, but whose meaningless eyes and lack-lustre faces make them resemble the monkey ; and who lie basking listlessly in the sun, or hang shivering over the fire, or are occupied in some simple drudgery.

" They are seldom ferocious ; and their simple, pleading looks, and utter helplessness, secure for them, among some half civilized nations, an attention which we call superstition, but which is better than the treatment we often give them.

" There was, a short time ago, a poor benighted boy of this class in the Boston Alms-House ; and in that establishment (one of the best of its kind in the country) he was treated in a way which was the best they knew how to adopt, but which showed how little they knew of the proper treatment. This poor creature had, marked upon his clothes, so as to be visible by every one, the words 'IDIOT BOY!' Were it not for the well-known benevolence of those about him, it might have seemed that they wished to prevent any one from mistaking him for a human being, and addressing him in a way which might call into action his latent human faculties; for what more certain method of preventing even the poor paupers about him from holding useful communion with him, than thus labelling him—an IDIOT ?

"If, in such an establishment as the Boston House of Industry, such ill-judged treatment was adopted, how much worse treatment is to be expected in those Alms-Houses where there is not a tithe of the intelligence or the humanity that characterize ours!

"Alas for the character of Puritan, civilized New England! The treatment of some of these poor creatures makes one blush and weep. It is still common, in country towns, to have them put up at public auction, and knocked off to the bidder who offers to board and clothe them for a year at the lowest rate per head. He makes them do all the drudgery and work that he can ; he is their master for a year, and he keeps them in life upon the smallest allowance of food and clothing. If he can underbid others the next year, he retains them ; if not, they are transferred to a neighbor, who thinks he can make money by keeping them at a lower rate.

"A few years ago, there were in an Alms-House in Massachusetts two poor idiots, brother and sister, who were so very low in the scale of humanity as to furnish a gratifying spectacle to that morbid curiosity which loves to look on human woe and degradation, even when the sight causes pain, and calls out tears. A keen Yankee offered to take them off the town's hands, and even pay a premium for them, if he could be allowed to carry them about for a show. His offer was considered by some as a good one, and no objection was at first raised ; and it was only when it reached the ears of more humane, or more reflecting people, that the proposition excited that indignation that it should have awakened the instant it was made.

"But I have no disposition to cite extreme cases, or draw harrowing pictures of Alms-House life, and of the neglect and ill-treatment which idiots sometimes receive. Such cases might be cited ; and pictures might be drawn, which, without any violation of truth, would shock the reader. The journal of Miss Dix, and of others who have followed or preceded her footsteps among the purlieus of society, would furnish abundant materials. As a general thing, idiots are treated in this state with kindness, and with as much judgment and discretion as can be expected from those who have the care of them.

"I close this article with the assertion that, as a class, they receive no intellectual culture, and no moral training ; and that they go down to the grave as beasts do, without having made any addition to the poor talent which they brought into the world,—without having received from society a helping hand to raise them a step higher towards the platform which we occupy.

"I shall afterwards show how much may be done to elevate and improve them.   H."

"No. III.

"Mr. Editor:—In my first two articles, I alluded to the number and condition of the idiots in our commonwealth. I showed them to be numerous, and to be unprovided for, and uncared for, except as far as their mere animal natures are concerned.

"This ought not so to be. Humanity demands that every creature in human shape should command our respect ; we should recognize as a brother every being upon whom God has stamped the human impress. No one can say with justifiable pride, ' *Homo sum!* ' unless he can add too, ' *Nihil humani alienum a me puto.*"

" Christianity demands that, in the great march of civilization, the rear rank should not be left too far behind; that none should be allowed to perish in their helplessness ; but that the strong should help the weak, so that the whole should advance as a band of brethren.

" Let us see what can be done to bring forward those whose powers are so limited that they are called idiots. One of the best authorities on the subject is Dr. Conolly, the distinguished head of the great Lunatic Asylum at Hanwell, in England.

" He says, 'The healthy infant is placed in a world calculated to exercise its senses, and to evoke and perfect all its muscular powers, and, to a certain extent, all its intellectual faculties. The imperfect or idiotic infant is in the same world, but its senses are, to a great extent, closed to these natural influences, and its powers of muscular motion are incomplete ; its intellectual faculties are not evoked by these means, and are even incapable of being fully evoked by any means whatever. The attention is vague, the memory feeble, the imagination futile, comparison is most limited, judgment most imperfect, and all the affections, sentiments, and moral qualities, are disordered and perverted. The interesting question is, To what extent can careful and judicious instruction make up for these natural deficiencies, and—as already done for the deaf, the dumb, and the blind—reclaim for these unfinished creatures the powers and privileges of life ? The exertions of future philanthropists will answer this question. Improvement must not be looked for beyond what is strictly relative to the imperfect individual in each case ; but it would seem to be true of idiots, as of the insane in general, that there is NO CASE INCAPABLE OF SOME AMENDMENT ; that every case may be improved or cured up to a certain point,—a principle of great importance in reference to treatment.'

" Now all, and even more than Dr. Conolly here supposes could be done, has been done in France; and the great hospital of *Bicêtre* presents a picture of truly Christian virtue, such as no country—no Catholic, or even no Protestant—can show. There is a sight to have made even the good Samaritan blush for his short-comings ; there drowning humanity 'is plucked up by the locks ;' there is a monument to the true civilization of France, more beautiful than any that her galleries can show ; there man, recognizing his obligations to God for the fire of intellect, strives to discharge part of it by kindling into a flame the feeble sparks of it which slumber on the altar of his brother's bosom. Young persons who, with us, are left to their own filthy habits, and to the blindness of their animal natures, or who, at best, have their bodily wants provided for, and who grow up to be drivelling idiots,—are there collected in classes, most carefully treated by kind attendants, and taught, as far as they can be taught, by some of the brightest minds of the country. Genius and science unite to save the poor wretches of humanity, and their success is most gratifying.

" A most careful register is kept in every case, and the improvement in most of them is very great. Dr. Conolly, a most impartial eye-witness, gives the following *résumé* of one of the most unfavorable ones:—

" ' The age of Charles Emile is 15. He was admitted to the school in June, 1843. He is described as being of a nervous and sanguine temperament, and in an almost complete state of idiocy ; the faculties which remain being in a state of extraordinary activity, and rendering him dangerous to himself and to others; but still idiotic in his inclinations, sentiments, perceptions, faculties of perception and understanding, and also of his senses, of which some were obtuse, and others too excitable. He was consequently unfit, to use the words of M. Voisin, " to harmonize with the world without." As regards his *inclinations,* he was signalized by a voracious, indiscriminate, gluttonous appetite, " *un érotisime hideux,*" and a blind and terrible instinct of destruction. He was wholly an animal. He was without attachment; overturned every thing in his way, but without courage or intent ; possessed no tact, intelligence, power of dissimulation, nor sense of propriety; and was awkward to excess. His *moral sentiments* are described as *null*, except the love of approbation, and a noisy, instinctive gayety, independent of the external world. As to his *senses*, his eyes were never fixed, and seemed to act without his will; his taste was depraved; his touch obtuse; his ear recognized sounds, but was not attracted by any one in particular; and he scarcely seemed to be possessed of the sense of smell. Devouring every thing, however disgusting; brutally sensual; passionate,—breaking, tearing, and burning, whatever he could lay his hands upon; and, if prevented from doing so, pinching, biting, scratching, and tearing himself, until he was covered with blood.

" 'He had the peculiarity of being so attracted by the eyes of his brothers, sisters, and play-fellows, as to make the most persevering efforts to push them out with his fingers. He walked very imperfectly, and could neither run, leap, nor exert the act of throwing; sometimes he sprang like a leopard; and his delight was to strike one sonorous body against another. When any attempt was made to associate him with the other patients, he would start away with a sharp cry, and then come back to them hastily.

" 'M. Voisin's description concludes with these expressions: " All the faculties of perception in this youth are in a rudimentary state ; and if I may venture so to express myself, it is incredibly difficult to draw him out of his individuality, to place him before exterior objects, and to make him take any notice of them. It would not be far from the truth to say, that for him all nature is almost completely veiled."

" 'This description not only exemplifies M. Voisin's careful mode of observation, but shows that an example of idiocy less favorable to culture could scarcely have been presented to the instructor. The same poor idiot boy is now docile in his manners, decent in his habits, and capable, though not without some visible effort, of directing his vague senses and wandering attention, so as to have developed his memory, to have acquired a limited instruction concerning various objects, and to have become affectionately conscious of the presence of his instructors and friends. His general appearance is still that of an idiot. His countenance, mode of walking, all that he does, declare his very limited faculties. Nature has placed limits to the exercise of his powers which no art can remove. But he is redeemed from the constant dominion of the lowest animal propensities ; several of his intellectual faculties are cultivated, some have even been called into life, and his better feelings have acquired some objects and some exercise. In such a case as this, we are not so much to regard what is merely accomplished for the individual. A great principle is established by it in favor of thousands of defective organizations. After witnessing the general effects of this school of the most imbecile human beings, and hearing the particulars of Charles Emile's history, it was really affecting to see him come forward when called, and essay to sing a little solo when requested; his attempt at first not being quite successful, but amended by his attention being more roused to it. His copy-book was then shown to me ; his writing was steady, and as good as that of most youths of his station in life. The schoolmaster, who seemed to take great pleasure in the improvement of this poor fellow, then showed us how he had taught Charles to count, by means of marbles and small pieces of wood, or marks made on a board, arranged in lines, the first containing an O, the second OO, the third OOO, and so on. Charles was sometimes out in his first calculations, but then made an effort and rectified himself. He distinguished one figure from another, naming their value. Large pieces of strong card, of various shapes, were placed in succession in his hands, and he named the figure of each, as square, triangle, &c., and afterwards drew their outlines with chalk on a blackboard, and, according to the desire of M. Seguin, drew a perpendicular, or horizontal, or oblique line ; so effectually attending to what he was doing, that if any line was drawn incorrectly, he rubbed it out and began anew. He also wrote several words on the board, and the name of the director of the Bicêtre, without the name being spoken to him.'

" Now, there is little doubt that had Charles Emile been born in Massachusetts, he would have been left a prey to the terrible strength of that animal nature which burned so furiously within him; he would have perished, or perhaps been confined in a cage, an object of fear and disgust.

" This is not a solitary case ; there are many like it ; and in all, as Dr. Conolly says, ' the crowning glory of the attempt is, that while the senses, the muscular power, and the intellect, have received some cultivation, the habits have been improved, the propensities regulated, and some play given to the affections ; so that a wild, ungovernable animal, calculated to excite fear, aversion, or disgust, has been transformed into the manner and likeness of a man.'

" Here is a lesson for us at home. We are too apt to think that as a people, we perform our religious and moral duties ; we fast and pay tithes, and thank God that we are not as other men, especially as the Frenchman ; but even he sets us an example of what is no less a religious duty than is fasting or prayer.   H."

" No. IV.

" Mr. HALE :—In my last was some account of the benevolent and successful attempts to meliorate the condition of idiots in France.

" If success attend this attempt, then, *a fortiori*, would it attend the attempt to train those who are insane from birth. Indeed, the adult insane are taught trades in our Asylums, and become very clever workmen. Why not, then, the congenitally insane ?

" It was stated, in the first article, that the number of these cases in our commonwealth is large ; and that they pass through this life, poor imbeciles or helpless maniacs, without having had the benefit of any scientific attempt at their relief. Dr. Woodward, in his last report, says of this class, ' They are far more numerous than I had formerly supposed, and much more interesting than idiots.' ' These little patients have intelligent faces, well-formed bodies, good developments of the head, and active minds.' They are generally dumb, but not deaf ; and their dumbness arises, in those cases which I have seen, from no malformation of the organs of the voice, but apparently from want of sufficient power of attention to associate names with things.

" Dr. Woodward says further,—' Their movements are free, easy, and graceful. Many of them are sprightly, even handsome. They are generally restless, irritable, and extremely mischievous, and are rarely able to speak. In some cases, as soon as there is any mental development, the peculiar characteristics begin to appear, without any known cause.

" ' No person, familiar with these cases, would be likely to mistake them for idiots ; they look differently, walk differently, and have different developments of body and mind.

" ' Like other insane persons, there is difficulty in fixing the attention ; they move with great rapidity from one thing to another, and are impatient of restraint.

" ' In some such persons, particular faculties seem much more active than others. One lad, in whose case I was consulted, was not able to articulate, and of course had never learned to read, but was observing of many things, particularly of mechanical operations, drawing, &c. He has left many traces of his skill on the buildings and fences of his former residence, which are yet to be seen. He has now arrived at manhood, but I have no knowledge of his present condition or of his progress in improvement for the last few years. When a lad, he was extremely mischievous, but sprightly and interesting.'

" He says, moreover,—' What has struck me as particularly worthy of remark, in all these cases, is, that while some of the faculties of the mind are active, and many of them capable of improvement, others are torpid or perverted ; bearing, in this particular, much resemblance to certain cases of insanity.' Again :—

" ' The subject of educating demented persons is new. It is at present exciting much attention, and the results are looked for with deep interest. The brain, in such cases, may not be affected with organic changes, but only be in an extremely torpid or inactive state. Some such cases, after a long torpor, in which all hope of recovery has been lost, have spontaneously come out of apparently the most forlorn condition, and been restored to health and mental soundness. So the idiot and congenital insane may have a brain capable of greater or less improvement, if persevering efforts are made to excite it to activity.'

" The number of congenitally insane persons in our commonwealth may be safely set down as almost 100 ; and Dr. Woodward remarks of them,—

" ' If one old case of insanity in ten can be restored to soundness of mind by the appliances of Insane Hospitals, should not all of this class have the benefits of such a trial ?   In a large proportion of these cases, the physical health can be improved, perverted habits can be changed, and the mind be made to enjoy, in some degree, what it has been deprived of under the influence of long-continued and neglected disease.'

" The number of idiots is much greater. We have the best authority for putting it down as between FIVE and SIX HUNDRED ; and Dr. Woodward remarks of them,—

" ' If one idiotic or demented person can have his powers of mind rendered active by effort, and some degree of knowledge imparted to him, by which his enjoyment and usefulness can be increased, even if ten fail of improvement, it will be worth the effort in all. But the case is more favorable than this supposition allows. I have no doubt that nearly all can be improved physically and mentally, and that the experiment will be productive of much good. It is certainly worthy of the consideration of the Christian and the philanthropist.'

" Most certainly it is ; and the Christian and philanthropist of Massachusetts should at once do more than consider. Suppose that only one fourth of each class are fit subjects for instruction and improvement, here are over ONE HUNDRED AND FIFTY human beings, who are thrown upon us by Providence, and who demand at our hands the gift of reason, conscience, and the moral sense ; and how can we answer to that Providence for the use of our present prosperity, if we neglect them ?

" Suppose we knew that there were hundreds of our fellow-creatures whose souls had, by some fiendish magic, been transformed into animals, and were going about amongst us in the shape of horses, cows, pigs, &c. ; should we not immediately set about contriving some potent spell by which to disinthrall them ?   Well, here we have them,—hundreds of them,—whose latent reason and moral sense are as much locked up in the animal as though they ran on four legs, and brandished horns ; and we have the spell, too, by which we may disenchant them ; nor can we be held blameless if we neglect to use it.

" The subject is one which demands the attention of the legislature, and of the people ; but in order to secure this, humane and influential individuals must first take it up ; and it is earnestly hoped they will do so. The particular course to be adopted in the case, whether there should be a branch establishment of our great Asylum at Worcester, or whether there shall be a separate Hospital or Training School—as also the details of the treatment —are subjects for future discussion.   H."

NUMBER OF THE INSANE AND IDIOTIC, WITH BRIEF NOTICES OF THE LUNATIC ASYLUMS IN THE UNITED STATES.

States and Territories.	Whites.		Colored.		Total.	Number provided for in Insane Asylums—Proximate.	Population.	Proportion of Insane and Idiots to the Population.
	Supported at		Supported at					
	Public charge.	Private charge.	Private charge.	Public charge.				
Maine..	207	330	56	38	631	100	501,793	1 to 795
New Hampshire,	180	306	8	11	505	100	284,574	1 to 563
Massachusetts, .	471	600	27	173	1,271	700	737,699	1 to 580
Rhode Island, .	117	86	8	5	216	150	108,830	1 to 503
Connecticut, . .	114	384	20	24	542	200	309,978	1 to 572
Vermont, . . .	144	254	9	4	411	150	291,948	1 to 710
New York, . .	683	1,463	138	56	2,340	700	2,428,921	1 to 1038
New Jersey,. .	144	225	46	27	442	75	373,306	1 to 844
Pennsylvania, .	469	1,477	132	55	2,133	500	1,724,033	1 to 808
Delaware, . .	22	30	21	7	80	00	78,085	1 to 976
Maryland, . .	137	263	108	42	550	150	470,019	1 to 852
Virginia, . . .	317	735	327	54	1,433	350	1,239,797	1 to 866
North Carolina,.	152	—	192	29	801	00	753,419	1 to 940
South Carolina,.	91	—	121	16	513	100	594,398	1 to 1158
Georgia, . . .	51	—	108	26	428	100	691,392	1 to 1615
Alabama, . .	39	—	100	25	357	—	590,756	1 to 1665
Mississippi, . .	14	—	66	16	198	—	375,651	1 to 1897
Louisiana, . .	6	—	38	7	100	50	352,411	1 to 3524
Tennessee, . .	103	—	124	28	851	100	829,210	1 to 974
Kentucky, . .	305	490	132	48	975	150	779,828	1 to 799
Ohio, ...	363	832	103	62	1,360	400	1,519,467	1 to 1117
Indiana, . . .	110	377	47	28	562	—	685,866	1 to 1220
Illinois, . . .	36	177	65	14	292	—	476,183	1 to 1630
Missouri, . . .	42	160	50	18	270	—	383,702	1 to 1421
Arkansas,· . .	9	36	13	8	66	—	97,574	1 to 1478
Michigan,. . .	2	37	21	5	65	—	212,267	1 to 3265
Florida Territory	1	9	12	0	22	—	54,477	1 to 2476
Wisconsin Ter.,	1	7	3	0	11	—	30,945	1 to 2813
Iowa Territory,.	2	5	4	0	11	—	43,112	1 to 3919
District of Col.,	1	13	4	3	21	50	43,712	1 to 2081
Total, ...	4333	10,192	2103	829	17,457	4125	17,069,453	1 to 977

This table was prepared from the census of 1840, mostly by Dr. Brigham. Since that time the population has increased, in all probability, to 20,000,000, and the insane and idiotic, it is supposed, have increased in nearly the same ratio. Some gross errors have been detected and exposed in the census of the United States, concerning the insane among the colored population ; but they do not show that the whole number of insane and idiotic is exaggerated.

We here rest the question whether further provision for lunatics and idiots is necessary.

IMPROVEMENTS AND CHANGES OF INSANE ASYLUMS.

Vermont has enlarged the Asylum at Brattleboro', so as to accommodate about 200 patients.

Massachusetts has nearly finished the enlargement of the Worcester Hospital, by the expenditure of the Johonnot legacy of $42,000, so that the capacity of the institution will admit about 400 patients.

Boston has added a very perfect lodge-building to the Hospital at South Boston, for the accommodation of noisy patients, at an expense of about $6,000.

Rhode Island has raised a subscription of $127,000, including Mr. Brown's legacy of $30,000, Mr. Butler's donation of $40,000, and the subscriptions of citizens $57,000 ; and Dr. Bell, with the consent of the trustees of the McLean Asylum, has been sent to Europe, to observe improvements and make the best possible plan of building. Dr. Ray is appointed superintendent, and a farm for the contemplated institution has been purchased, about 2½ miles north-east of Providence. The gentlemen in Rhode Island intend to advance a little on what the world has ever seen, in their Asylum ; and the trustees of the McLean Asylum intend, if possible, to assist them to do it. Mr. Butler seems to renew his youth in this good work of his old age.

The *State of Connecticut* has erected additional buildings at the Retreat in Hartford, for the accommodation of about 100 patients ; making the accommodations about twice as great as before.

The *State of New York* is enlarging the State Lunatic Asylum at Utica, so that it will accommodate, when finished, about 500 patients.

The *City of New York* has talked about enlarging the Insane Asylum on Blackwell's Island. There is a great need of it ; and it would have been done long ago, except for that policy which changes the managers of such institutions, in the city of New York, with every change of politics.

The *State of New Jersey* has made provision for building an Insane Asylum, and commissioners have been appointed to fix the location.

Pennsylvania, also, has done the same. Miss Dix has had a great and important agency, both in New Jersey and Pennsylvania, during the last winter, in accomplishing these objects.

In *Baltimore*, Dr. Collins is still looking after the insane poor, and has very recently made an effort to have the insane, who have been in chains in the Alms-House, removed to the Insane Hospital.

Virginia has done nobly in both the institutions at Williamsburg and Staunton, in enlarging their accommodations for nearly twice the former number of patients.

Ohio is erecting two additional buildings, for the accommodation of 100 patients each, in the Asylum at Columbus, which will give it capacity for the accommodation of about 350. *Indiana* has employed Dr. Evans to travel, examine institutions, procure plans, and make all needful preparation in knowledge, for the purpose of building an Insane Asylum in that State.

Perhaps this general statement shows as much progress in the good work of making suitable provision for the insane as in any former year.

TABULAR VIEW OF INSANE ASYLUMS FOR 1844.

	Number under Treatment.	Number at the Commencement of the Year.	Number at the Close of the Year.	Number received during the Year.	Number recovered during the Year.	Number not improved.	Number improved.	Number of Deaths during the Year.	Number admitted from First.	Number recovered from First.	Whole number of Deaths.	Not Improved.	Number discharged.	Time of opening the Institution.
Maine Asylum,	151	68	76	83	32	22	18	3	305	101	.	.	..	1840
New Hampshire Asylum, at Concord,	151	47	70	104	37	.	.	5	.	.	.	.	81	1842
Vermont Asylum, at Brattleboro',	222	136	158	96	51	.	.	7	.	.	.	.	74	1837
McLean Asylum, at Charlestown,	292	134	152	158	68	29	20	19	2142	1025	.	.	..	1818
Boston Lunatic Hospital,	137	108	108	29	9	.	.	5	.	288	.	.	180	1839
Massachusetts Asylum at Worcester,	491	255	263	236	124	49	40	15	2063	916	151	307	1749	1833
Connecticut Retreat, at Hartford,	188	83	103	105	45	9	20	11	1432	791	.	.	..	1824
New York Asylum, at Utica,	471	196	260	275	132	16	47	16	551	151	.	.	..	1843
———, at Bloomingdale,	206	100	104	106	50	.	27	13	2875	1354	.	.	..	1821
———, on Blackwell's Island,	565	291	359	274	.	.	.	.	.	.	.	.	206	1839
———, Dr. White's Private Asylum, at Hudson,	.	.	20	.	.	.	.	.	.	.	.	.	..	1830
Pennsylvania Hospital for the Insane,	285	132	151	153	75	9	38	12	592	233	50	.	..	1841
Friends' Asylum, Frankford, Penn.,														
Baltimore Asylum, Maryland,														
Virginia Asylum, at Staunton,	185	119	143	66	27	4	4	5	403	.	.	.	..	1828
———, at Williamsburg,	150	109	132	41	10	.	.	6	.	.	.	.	..	1843
South Carolina Asylum, at Columbia,	93	70	92	23	14	.	.	5	.	.	.	.	21	1827
Georgia Asylum, at Milledgeville,	33	4	29	29	.	.	.	1	.	.	.	.	4	1843
Ohio Asylum, at Columbus,	216	148	146	68	40	54	.	7	541	243	.	.	395	1838
Kentucky Asylum, at Lexington,	236	163	183	73	68	.	.	16	1128	404	416	.	..	1824

II.—BENEVOLENT EFFORT FOR PERSONS UNDER ARREST.

"Did Christian sentiments pervade our hearts and control our actions, the precincts of a criminal court would be besieged by troops of men and women, assembled to ransom their fellow brothers and sisters of the race. Men would gather around the terrible spot, where the guilty are brought to be exposed and condemned, as eagerly as they gather along the fatal shore of the sea when a storm is dashing a brave ship upon the rocks. The shame and remorse of the criminal would send out a cry more piercing than the shrieks of drowning mariners. To be lost in the abyss of guilt, would be regarded as a fate ten thousand times more dreadful than to be sunk in the depths of the ocean. The loss of character and of innocence would be deemed to be, as it is, infinitely greater than the loss of all worldly goods, and of life itself. By what efforts to save, by what kindness to solace, by what generosity to ransom and to restore, these things would task the wisdom and benevolence of man."

These are the sentiments of the Hon. Horace Mann.

A shipping merchant on Commercial Wharf said, some months ago, to the Secretary of this Society, " There is one man in Boston for whom I will head a subscription to raise an annuity for life, in consideration of what he has done for the benefit of mariners." Who is the man? And what has he done? JOHN AUGUSTUS is the man; and here follows a list of 234 men and women, for whom he has become bail, with the approbation of the judges in our criminal courts, paid their fines and costs from his own pocket, until they were able to repay, which they have done in almost all cases. The unhappy men and women have been saved from prison, restored to their families and occupations, admonished of their danger, acknowledged their benefactor; and John Augustus, the worthy shoemaker, in the narrow lane opposite the Court-house, on the north, has not suffered in his business, which is carried on, under his superintendence, by his son, with apprentices; and the good man now rides with his horse and chaise for the pleasure of carrying with him to the temporary refuge, or other place of innocence and protection, some one for whose appearance and good behavior he has become surety, and paid the fine and costs. Where is another John Augustus? *

* *List of Men and Women bailed from the Municipal and Police Courts, and saved from the House of Correction, by* MR. JOHN AUGUSTUS. *Amount of bail in each case,* $30.

No.	Date.	Names.	Residences.	No. of Court Record	When to appear.	Fine and Costs.
1	1841.					
2	August,					
3	August 3,	— N.	East Boston,	. .	. . . .	$3 62
4	" 4,	J. D.	Congress Street,	. .	. . . .	6 87
5	" 5,	— O.	Bedford Street,	. .	. . . .	3 26
6	" 6,	— B.	Union Street,	. .	. . . .	3 30
7	" 7,	J. B. C.	Dean Street,	. .	. . . .	3 94
8	" 8,	C. A.	Hay-Market,	. .	. . . .	3 62
9	Septem. 9,	O. B.	Hanover Street,	. .	. . . .	3 70
10	" 10,	— B.	East Boston,	. .	. . . .	3 16
11	Novem. 9,	J. A.	Essex Street,	. .	Novem. 30,	5 09
12	" 12,	— N.	Church Street,	. .	Decem. 3,	4 34
13	" "	J. H.	Hancock Row,	. .	" "	2 76
14	" 27,	J. G.	South Boston,	. .	" 14,	4 45

This is a new field of benevolent effort, and so far as it can be improved without a sacrifice of public justice, under the direction and with the approbation of the judges of our criminal courts, so far it will promote the great object of this Society, namely, the improvement of Prisons by keeping men out of them.

No.	Date.	Names.	Residence.	No. of Court Record	When to appear.	Fine and Costs.
15	Novem. 27,	C. R.	Chardon Street,	. .	Decem. 14,	$3 94
16	" 29,	— H.	Pleasant Street,	. .	" "	2 65
17	" "	— E.	New Hampshire,	. .	" "	2 65
18	Decem. "	— M.	Down East,	. .	" 31,	3 76
19	" "	— R.	With John Taylor,	. .	January 8,	3 17
20	" "	— R.	Lyman Place,	. .	" 24,	3 31
21	January 19,	— F.	Leverett Street,	. .	" "	3 31
22	" 24,	— D.	Poplar Street,	. .	" "	3 10
23	March 10,	C. A.	Corner of Newton Street,	. .	Febr'ry 19,	2 90
24	" 20,	M. B.	54 Warrren Street,	. .	" "	4 16
25	" "	M. F.	100 Ann Street,	. .	April . . 20,	4 54
26	" "	— M.	88 Eliot Street,	. .	" "	3 16
27	" "	— L.	38 Bedford Street,	. .	" 24,	2 77
28	" "	— O.	8 Jackson Avenue,	. .	" "	3 00
29	" "	Miss C.	106 Sea Street,	. .	" "	3 50
30	May . 10,	— C.	New Exchange,	. .	" "	2 50
31	June . . 2,	— L.	. . . .	. .	" "	2 77
32	" "	— R.*	North Market Street,	. .	June . . 2,	2 77
33	" "	B. O. T.	Union Street,	. .	May . . 11,	3 99
34	" "	C. A.	With Brother,	. .	" "	3 30
35	" "	Mrs. H.	Pleasant Street,	. .	" "	3 70
36	" "	— M.	Washington Street,	. .	June . . 2,	5 25
37	" "	— R.	Hatters' Square,	. .	" "	3 41
38	" 10,	W. M.	South Street,	. .	" 10,	4 04
39	" "	W. D.	Green Street,	. .	" 30,	4 45
40	" "	— G.	Theatre Alley,	. .	" "	3 90
41	" "	M. W.	. . . .	. .	" "	4 15
42	" "	H. H. H.	Union Street,	. .	" "	4 96
43	" "	M. C.	Hawkins Alley,	. .	July . . 8,	3 40
44	July . . 11,	— T.	Bangor House,	. .	" 11,	4 17
45	" "	— S.	Cambridge,	. .	" "	3 65
46	August 2,	— G.	83 Charter Street,	. .	August . 2,	3 40
47	" "	— S.	—— Street,	. .	" 15,	3 40
48	" "	S. H.	Eliot Street,	. .	" "	6 42
49	" "	Mrs. D.	Washington Street,	. .	" "	3 17
50	" "	— O.	Front Street,	. .	" "	2 88
51	Septem. 9,	— R.	Washington Street,	. .	Septem. 7,	3 41
52	" "	— F.	North Square,	. .	" 28,	3 40
53	" "	— R.	Union Street,	. .	" "	5 03
54	" "	T. G.	Poplar Street,	. .	October 10,	3 16
55	" "	— S.	Merrimack Street,	. .	" "	3 70
56	" 11,	— E.	Hull Street,	. .	" "	3 90
57	" "	— H.	Harrison Avenue,	. .	" 18,	4 31
58	" "	Miss P.	Cambridge Street,	. .	" 24,	3 80
59	" "	— S.	" "	. .	" "	2 86
60	" "	— R.	Corner of Milk Street,	. .	" "	4 04
61	" 24,	Mr. M.	Charlestown Street,	. .	Novem. 24,	3 50
62	Novem. 4,	N. A.	Poplar Street,	. .	" 16,	2 80
63	" "	— T.	Salem Street,	. .	" "	3 08
64	" "	— R.	Court Square,	. .	" "	3 82
65	1843-Feb.3,	M G.	Broad Street,	. .	" "	4 80
66	" "	Mr. K.	1 Lancaster Street,	. .	January 3,	4 16
67	March 15,	— L.	. . . .	. .	" 15,	5 43
68	" "	Mrs. D.	Warren Street,	. .	" "	4 16
69	" "	— B.	Tremont Street,	. .	April . . 4,	2 77

* Dead.

From the Boston Courier.

" ☞ A memorial was presented to the legislature, during its late session, asking that an institution may be founded for the reception and humane treatment of those criminals who have been made so by intemperance. No definite action was had on the memorial, and we do not recollect now whether it was indefinitely postponed, or referred to the next General Court, or whether the petitioners had *leave to withdraw.* A friend has just presented

No.	Date.	Names.	Residence.	No. of Court Record	When to appear.	Fine and Costs.
70	April . . 8,	— G.	. . . .	476	April . . 8,	$2 22
71	" 15,	— D.	South Cedar Street,	526	" 15,	2 76
72	" "	— W.	Atkinson Street,	400	" "	3 95
73	" 26,	— C.	Southack Street,	565	" 26,	4 40
74	" "	H. S.	Arbootle Street,	568	" "	2 76
75	" 15,	Mr. D.	Poplar Street,	526	" "	2 76
76	" 19,	G. B.	West Cedar Street,	563	" "	3 91
77	May . 20,	J. M.	. . . .	691	" "	2 61
78	" "	— M'l.	——— Street,	672	May . . 20,	3 20
79	" "	J. S.	Butolph Street,	705	" "	3 40
80	" "	— L.	. . . .	689	" "	5 31
81	" "	Miss D.	Corner Hanover Street,	703	" "	4 54
82	" "	— M'C.	Broad Street,	764	" 26,	2 39
83	" "	— D.	Hamilton Street,	821	" "	4 40
84	" "	— M.	Charles Street,	629	" "	2 73
85	" "	" "	" "	811	" "	3 78
86	" 26,	— G.	Merrimack Street,	790	" "	3 01
87	" "	— S.	Charter Street,	863	" "	3 36
88	June . 15,	— R.	" "	925	June . . 15,	4 44
89	" "	— H.	Lowell Street,	969	" "	3 66
90	" "	Mrs. C.	Copp's Hill,	860	" "	2 46
91	" "	S. H.	" "	860	" "	2 46
92	" "	S. H.	" "	. .	" "	. .
93	" "	M. J. W.	" "	860	" "	2 46
94	" "	— C.	Hamilton Street,	1201	" "	4 31
95	" "	— G.	Southack Street,	. .	July . . 5,	. .
96	July . . 11	H. S.	Reading,	1111	" 11,	4 78
97	" 15,	— G.	. . . .	1147	" 15,	2 63
98	" "	— H.	Lowell Street,	969	" "	3 69
99	" "	— G.	. . . .	1203	" 20,	3 16
100	" 21,	— R.	Gravel Alley,	1222	August . 5,	4 45
101	" 31,	— W.	Charles Street,	1350	" "	2 47
102	August 1,	— W.	Blackstone Street,	1581	Septem. 4,	4 55
103	" 25,	Mrs. D.	8¼ Blackstone Street,	1517	" 15,	3 17
104	" 26,	— N.	Ann Street,	1561	" "	3 26
105	Septem.15,	E. R.	. . . .	1712	" "	3 26
106	" "	A. D.	Belknap Street,	1772	" 22,	2 97
107	" 28,	Mrs. M.	Tremont Row,	1844	" 28,	2 87
108	" 29,	— C.	School Street,	1894	" 29,	3 44
109	October 4,	Mrs. H.	Oyster S. Alley,	1809	October 4,	2 98
110	" "	— M.	Charlestown B.,	1746	" "	4 15
111	" 10,	— O.	Sea Street,	. .	" 10,	4 05
112	" "	J. A.	Salem Street,	2537	" "	3 90
113	" "	R. M.	3 Aiken Street,	2313	" "	3 40
114	Decem. 5,	— D.	Poplar Street,	. .	" 5,	3 50
115	" "	— H.	Went to Sea,	2290	" 24,	3 90
116	" 19,	— L.	3 Hancock Row,	2458	" "	4 30
117	" "	T. W.	Hamilton Street,	2552	Decem. 18,	3 80
118	" 20,	— A.	Brattle Street,	2624	January 10,	3 02
119	" "	W. A.	Brighton Street,	2918	" "	3 66
120	January 8,	P. A.	South Margin Street,	. .	" 30,	4 20
121	" 9,	— P.	77 Pine Street,	67	" "	4 21
122	" 12,	W. J. M.	Church Street,	46	February 3,	3 74
123	Feb'ry 13,	W. D. B.	Stillman Street,	147	" 13,	2 72
124	" 23,	F. B.	70 Atkinson Street,	. .	" 23,	3 80

to us the following extract from the memorial, which we take pleasure in publishing—as it brings distinctly before the public a character which is deserving of their grateful admiration:—

"'In the summer of 1841, JOHN AUGUSTUS, a man in humble life, now well known to the friends of temperance in Boston, and who deserves to be, throughout the state, visited the Police Court in Boston, and being very much interested in the case of a poor man who, for the vice of drunkenness, had been sentenced to the House of Correction, stepped forward and offered

No.	Date.	Names.	Residence.	No. of Court Record	When to appear.		Fine and Costs.
125	Feb'ry 23,	Mrs. Y.	Grave Alley,	221	February	4,	$3 80
126	" "	M. S.	176 Ann Street,	225	"	"	3 40
127	March . 1,	Mrs. O.	199 " "	103	March .	. 1,	3 30
128	Febr'y . 9,	C B.	Cross Street,	250	Febr'ry	23,	3 40
129	" "	C. M'C.	Atkinson Street,	225	"	"	3 80
130	" 16,	R. C.	Hamilton Street,	310	March .	. 2,	3 81
131	" 19,	F. F.	Cambridge Street,	151	"	4,	3 81
132	" "	E. O'B	16 Cross Street,	326	"	"	3 76
133	" 21,	P. D.	53 Cambridge Street,	336	"	8,	6 26
134	" 23,	Mr. H J.	64 Cornhill,	348	"	"	2 62
135	" "	J. L. K.	Harrison Avenue,	347	"	"	5 69
136	March . 7,	Mrs. C. M'C	88 Broad Street,	425	"	"	3 90
137	" "	P. B.	Castle Street,	519	"	"	3 90
138	April . . 1,	Mrs. H. E.	Hudson Street,	593	April . .	22,	4 68
139	" "	— W.	. . . .	554	"	"	4 68
140	" 4,	J R.	East Street,	598	"	"	3 59
141	" "	M. T.	Broad Street Place,	627	"	"	3 76
142	" "	D N.	Kneeland Street,	636	"	"	3 90
143	" 15,	— M.	Warren Street,	683	'.	"	4 04
144	" "	Mrs. C.	Andover Street,	694	"	"	4 04
145	" 16,	A. W.	Gone to Hanover,	697	"	"	3 26
146	" 17,	Miss D. D.	May Street,	707	May . .	7,	4 30
147	" 22,	J. M	Cambridge Street,	731	"	14,	2 76
148	" "	E. M.	10 Cross Street,	732	"	"	3 80
149	" 24,	J. C.	. . . .	761	"	"	2 76
150	" 27,	S. C.	Washington Street,	799	"	"	4 62
151	" 29,	J. H. B.	Silver Street,	795	"	"	2 76
152	" "	S. C.	Hamilton Street,	789	"	"	2 76
153	" "	P. K.	94 Sea Street,	829	"	28,	2 80
154	May . . 7,	T. S.	Corner of London Street,	743	"	"	3 01
155	" 9,	A. F.	East Boston,	851	"	"	2 48
156	" 10,	J. P.	Commercial Street,	864	"	"	2 48
157	" 13,	Mrs. P.	East Street,	882	"	"	2 18
158	" "	— J.	Milk Street,	885	"	"	3 40
159	" "	T. A.	Church Street.	883	"	"	3 40
160	" 27,	B. H.	4th Street, S. Boston,	991	June . .	8,	2 76
161	" 28,	T. A.	Distil House Square,	883	"	"	4 28
162	" 30,	M. M.	Canton Street,	2016	"	"	3 40
163	" 28,	L. G.	. . . .		"	"	3 72
164	" 31,	L. G.	East Street Place,	1025	"	"	4 90
165	June . . 3,	A. H.	Brighton Street,	1028	"	"	2 62
166	" "	— P.	Broad Street,	1030	"	"	3 95
167	" "	J. P.	Cross Street,		"	"	3 95
168	" "	— H.	Broad Street,	1030	"	18,	3 95
169	" 6,	P. M.	Southack Street,	1045	"	'.	3 16
170	" 8,	J. W. T.	44 Lowell Street,	1098	"	"	2 87
171	" 12,	N. A.	Deacon Street,	1124	"	"	2 66
172	" 15,	— G.	Merrimack Street,	1152	"	25,	2 76
173	" 18,	L. B. E.	Colling Street,	1199	"	"	3 16
174	July . . 1,	T. M.	Canton Street,	1256	"	"	4 39
175	" 3,	D. N.	Hudson Street,	1236	"	"	3 72
176	" 8,	A. S.	Codman's Buildings,	1355	"	"	4 54
177	" 9,	A. P.	Battery March Street,	2362	"	"	2 92
178	" 11,	J. A	Doolan Street.	1383	"	"	5 50
179	" 18,	D. N.	South Dover Street,	1286	August . 7,		3 50

to become bail for him. His proposal was accepted. He paid, out of his own pocket, the fees of court, amounting to a few dollars, and took the condemned man with him out of the court-room. He persuaded him to sign the pledge, furnished him with food and lodgings, and at last secured employment for him; and from henceforth the rescued drunkard became an industrious and sober citizen.

" 'Mr. Augustus, inspired by the success of his first attempt, and impelled by the yearnings of his noble heart, continued his visits to the Police Court;

No.	Date.		Names.	Residence.	No. of Court Record	When to appear.		Fine and Costs.
180	July	22,	A. N.	Salutation Street,	1499	August. . 7,		$4 04
181	"	"	G C.	Portland Street,	. .	" 13,		4 80
182	"	25,	F. A. C.	Charles Street,	1530	"	"	3 96
183	"	27,	A M	Beverly Street,	1552	"	"	3 90
184	"	"	A. J. L.	77 Warren Street,	1554	May . .	13,	3 40
185	"	29,	B. G.	Roxbury,	1585	"	20,	6 12
186	"	"	T. M.	104 Warren Street,	1589	"	"	4 54
187	"	30,	J. M.	133 Hancock Street,	1620	"	"	2 76
188	"	"	J. A W.	Carney Place,	1617	"	"	2 86
189	"	31,	M. C.	137 Broad Street,	1581	"	"	2 76
190	"	"	E. H.	Bridge Street Place,	1666	"	"	5 42
191	August . 8,		J. C.	Warren Street,	1724	"	"	2 47
192	"	"	M. C., wife,	" "	1724	August . 20,		2 47
193	"	13,	C. S. W.	Portland Street,	1668	"	"	5 42
194	"	24,	J. M'N.	Ann Street,	1890	"	28,	4 94
195	"	"	M. C.	" "	1903	"	"	4 24
196	Septem. 9,		W. G.	2 Church Street,	1623	"	"	3 50
197	"	12,	W. M'L.	3 Hillman Street,	2073	Septem. 23,		3 80
198	"	14,	M. A.	24 South Cedar Street,	2080	"	"	3 50
199	"	23,	B. K.	South Boston,	2076	"	"	5 08
200	"	"	M. L.	Mrs. Garnar,	2196	October 8,		2 76
201	"	"	M. A. K.	85 Warren Street,	1447	"	"	2 08
202	"	24,	Mrs. B.	Cross Street,	2201	"	"	3 16
203	"	28,	J. M. R.	South Boston,	2237	"	"	2 99
204	October 5,		M. A.	" Cedar Street,	. .	"	"	1 85
205	"	11,	R. S.	Charles Street,	2369	"	29,	1 62
206	"	17,	R. G.	Carney Place,	2418	"	"	2 25
207	"	"	— W.	South Boston,	2463	"	"	3 26
208	Novem. 4,		— D.	Hamilton Street,	. .	"	"	5 76
209	"	"	— J.	Medford Street,	2370	"	"	2 08
210	"	10,	— F.	Broad Street,	2639	"	"	4 56
211	"	"	— S.	Pleasant Street,	2846	"	"	2 76
212	"	19,	Mrs. K.	Howard Place,	2633	"	"	3 50
213	"	"	— C.	Congress Street,	2798	"	17,	3 40
214	"	"	T. G.	Gower Street,	2864	"	"	3 06
215	"	"	J. W.	Kneeland Street,	2888	"	"	3 40
216	"	"	J. W.	" "	2888	Novem. 17,		3 40
217	Decem. 2,		F. H.	Morton Place,	2889	"	24,	2 18
218	"	"	E. G.	East Street Place,	. .	"	"	4 29
219	"	"	M. R.	Broad Street,	. .	"	"	
220	"	10,	J. T.	Stillman Street,	2923	"	"	5 42
221	"	"	T. G.	Chambers Street,	2864	"	28,	2 52
222	"	"	W. M.	School Street,	2966	"	"	3 90
223	"	"	Mrs H.	Cross Street,	2968	"	"	4 28
224	"	"	P. R.	East Street,	2998	"	"	2 62
225	"	14,	J. P.	South Cedar Street,	3012	"	"	5 18
226	"	"	H. M.	Church Street,	3013	"	"	4 78
227	"	"	M. T.	Washington Street,	2196	1845–Jan. 5,		2 76
228	"	"	M. L.	78 Federal Street,	2887	" 21,		2 76
229	1845–Jan. 1,		L. C	Market Street,	3098	" "		2 32
230	" 2,		A. B.	Broad Street,	2968	" "		3 41
231	" 7,		P. L.	28 Federal Street,	. .	" "		2 82
232	" 17,		— W.	Court Avenue,	110	Febr'ry 11,		2 82
233	" 22,		H B	3 Sea St. Place,	159	" "		2 32
234	" 23,		E H.	Cambridge Street,	148	" "		3 22

and from August, in the year 1841, to February of the present year, has rescued from the jaws of the House of Correction, and from the fellowship of convicted felons, one hundred and seventy-six men and fifty-six women,—in all, *two hundred and thirty-two human beings,*— a large portion of whom, but for the vice of intemperance, would have enjoyed an unquestionable right to the general regard of society. Fortunately for this benevolent attempt to stand between the drunkard and the customary course of law, Mr. Augustus has preserved a careful record of every case in which he has interested himself, and he is thus enabled to furnish an intelligent account of a large portion of the persons who, by his means, have been saved from confinement at South Boston. Full three fourths of the number, or about one hundred and seventy-five, are now temperate and orderly citizens, and are gaining a respectable livelihood. Above one half of the whole number were residents of Boston, and the other half were temporary visitors to the city from the country and from neighboring states. The proportion of foreigners was much larger of the men than the women. The amount of costs paid by Mr. Augustus, for the release of these persons, is $976 61. This amount has nearly all been paid back to him by the persons thus rescued. Of course this amount of costs has been saved to the towns liable for it. It will be readily seen, however, that a much larger sum has been saved, by so many intemperate persons having become useful citizens, instead of being shut up in Prison at the public charge. To those towns in the country which occasionally receive large bills for the support of drunkards in the House of Correction at South Boston, this point is not unworthy of notice. These considerations are glanced at, because, indeed, they should not be overlooked; but they are of little moment in comparison with the hearts which have been healed, and the families which have been made happy, by the restoration of so large a number of the great human brotherhood to temperance, usefulness and respectability. By the minute and unquestionable records kept by Mr. Augustus, rising eight tenths of all the persons sent to the House of Correction, are sent there for drunkenness. Through his Samaritan efforts, the number of commitments for this dreadful vice has been largely reduced ; and besides the diminished expense, consequent upon such reduction, the community has been incalculably blessed by the change.

" ' The following statement will show the actual reduction in the commitments to the House of Correction, for drunkenness, since the Washingtonian reform commenced in Boston, but especially as resulting from the efforts of Mr. Augustus. In 1841, they were 605 ; in 1842, they were 541 ; in 1843, 456 ; in 1844, 407. On the first of January of the present year, the number of persons remaining in the House of Correction, committed by the Police Court, was only 123 ; of which number 110 were committed for drunkenness, viz., 47 males and 63 females ; all other offences being but 13. During the last year Mr. Augustus has saved 120 persons from the House of Correction ; 20 of whom have since been sentenced to the House of Correction; the remaining 100 are doing well. It would be easy to show the actual amount in dollars and cents, saved to the state by a result like this ; but not as easy to exhibit the blessings resulting to the rescued men, or to their families, many of the members of which would, doubtless, otherwise have become outcasts, or have found their way to the Alms-Houses. But your petitioners forbear further developments in relation to the House of Correction, having, it is believed, a momentous bearing upon the subject of this petition. They believe by going nicely into facts, it would be in their power to demonstrate, conclusively, that the commonwealth will be largely benefited by an entire change of the present method of commitments to the House of Correction at South Boston.

" ' It is impossible to enter, in detail, into the formidable difficulties which a mechanic, like Mr. Augustus, has had to encounter, in order to proceed in his beneficent work. To say nothing of the formalities and liabilities which belong alike to all courts of law, he has, in most cases, provided a temporary home for his fallen brother, and allowed no rest to his head until he has done his utmost to procure for him employment. It should be added that, within a few months, a number of the " merchant princes," and other eminent philanthropists, of Boston, have given Mr. Augustus a substantial testimonial of their respect for his unwearied and invaluable services. Previous to this liberal act, Mr. Augustus had relied upon his own scanty resources, and had found it exceedingly difficult to carry into effect his praiseworthy labors.' "

III.—HOUSES OF REFUGE FOR JUVENILE DELINQUENTS.

1. *Reports of the Inspectors of Prisons for the County of Suffolk, on the Jail, Boston Lunatic Hospital, House of Correction, Houses of Reformation and Industry : December, 1844. Boston : John H. Eastburn, City Printer, No. 18 State Street.* 1845.
2. *Twentieth Annual Report of the Managers of the Society for the Reformation of Juvenile Delinquents, to the Legislature of the State and the Corporation of the City of New York. 46 pages, octavo. New York : Egbert, Honey & King, Printers,* 374 *Pearl Street.*
3. *The Seventeenth Annual Report of the House of Refuge of Philadelphia ; with an Appendix. Octavo, pages* 23. *Published by order of the Contributors. E. G. Dorsey, Printer, Library Street.* 1845.

HOUSE OF REFORMATION IN BOSTON.

The inspectors of Prisons for the county of Suffolk, commonwealth of Massachusetts, visited this institution on the 6th of December, 1844, and found it " in excellent condition, in all respects.

" Under the superintendence of Mr. Daniel Chandler, assisted by Mr. Lincoln, this House continues to be a scene of order, decorum, neatness, active industry, cheerful obedience, religious observances, successful instruction in the branches of education taught in the public common schools of the commonwealth, some cultivation of the art of vocal music, and due recreation. This institution has a most salutary influence in withdrawing children from the haunts of vice and crime, and reclaiming them, and putting them in the way of becoming respectable men and useful citizens ; and it is matter of regret that many more of the children, who are permitted to spend their time in the streets in idleness, in learning and practicing mischief, vices, and petty offences, are not brought within its beneficent discipline, instead of being left to qualify themselves, by degrees, for the House of Correction."

" The inspectors were informed that the first step of the superintendent, on the introduction of a new pupil into this school of reform, is to learn from him in what way he has been led into the fault which he has committed, and obtain a minute history of his downward progress. This preliminary information is deemed to be essential, in order to ascertain the reformatory treatment, or discipline, best adapted to the pupil's particular case. Some of the children state their cases readily and frankly ; others are reluctant, shy, and slow to yield their confidence."

"These examinations disclose the fact, that many different pupils are drawn into their errors by the same companions. It seems that there is a considerable number of youths in the city whose regular employment is to initiate others in vice and petty offences."

"The proficiency of the inmates of the House in spelling, reading, writing, elementary arithmetic, geography, and English grammar, is a striking and very gratifying feature of this institution : it does not prevent them from performing a great deal of work, leaving ample time, also, for recreation."

"The present principal employment is shoemaking ; and since the introduction of this branch of industry into the school, the inspectors have observed, with some attention, what the effect of employing so many, from the ages of 11 to 16, in one room in this labor might be upon their health and spirits ; but they have not been able to discover any indications of its being prejudicial. The boys exhibit as much vivacity and cheerfulness as usual with others of their age. Some of them were asked if they found any difficulty in drawing the thread, and if they were ever subject to any pains or weakness in the arms or chest ; and they all promptly replied that they experienced no such difficulty, pains, or weakness. The superintendent is decidedly of opinion that the occupation is not attended with any injurious effect."

"The health of the inmates has been very good, only a few instances of sickness having occurred, and those slight. The hospital has been occupied but about one week during the last preceding six months.'

"The punishments inflicted have been black marks, deprivation of play, loss of grade, and, in extreme cases, confinement ; and, as a last resort, the ferule applied to the palm of the hand. The superintendent says, in his return, that he places the greatest reliance upon mild, persuasive measures, appeals to the feelings, and encouragement to right conduct. If a boy is inclined to go astray, much pains are taken to divert his inclination into a right channel, and to point out to him the evils that are sure to follow crime. At an appointed hour in the evening, the cases of misdemeanors of the day are investigated and settled in the presence of all the boys."

"There were in this institution at the last inspection, June 6, 1844, boys, 47. Since that time to the 6th of December, 1844, there have been committed—boys, 7 ; girls, 2 : total, 56.

"Causes of commitment: stubbornness, 18 ; idleness and dissoluteness, 9 ; larceny, 26 ; vagrancy, 3 : total, 56.

"Indentured since last inspection, 4 : James M. Luardis to a bootmaker, October 3, 1844 ; Thomas Hogan to a house-carpenter, September 18, 1844 ; Henry Francis to a baker, September 28, 1844 ; Patrick Granville to a coppersmith, August 2, 1844.

"Discharged, by order of Police Court, John H. Court, September 10, 1844, to go to Lagrange, Maine, to a farmer ; James Dalton, November 21, 1844, to go to Vermont, to a farmer ; James O'Neal, August 16, 1844, to go to his father ; Richard Ryan, November 30, 1844, to go to his mother ; John Kiefe, June 28, 1844, to go to his father in Providence ; James Hayes, June 6, 1844, to go to his father ; Daniel Midger, June 6, 1844, to go to sea with his father.

"Escaped, John M'Adams and Robert H. Haley, July 6, 1844, while at work in the field. John M'Grath committed to House of Correction, by order of the Municipal Court.

"In the House, at the time of inspection, December 6, 1844, boys, 40 ; girls, 2 ; total, 42."

This report is a semi-annual document, by the inspectors of Prisons for the county of Suffolk, who are, *ex officio*, inspectors, being judges of the Probate, Municipal, and Police Courts. The present report is signed by Willard Phillips, judge of Probate ; John Gray Rogers, and James C. Merrill, judges of the Police Court ; and Luther S. Cushing, judge of the Municipal Court.

HOUSE OF REFUGE, NEW YORK CITY.

Number of children at the commencement of the year, . 321
Number received during the year, ... 262

Number receiving the benefits during the year, . . 583
Number remaining January 1, 1845, ... 307
Number disposed of during the year, ... 276

Number indentured to farmers and gardeners, . . . 118
To hatters, 4 ; shipbuilders, 3 ; shoemakers, 14, . . 21
To whaling and other sea service, ... 12
To milkmen, 3 ; tanners and cabinet makers, 2 ; carters, 2, 7
To carpenters, 2 ; to each of 19 branches of mechanics, 1, 21
Girls to housewifery, 68, of whom 6 were colored, . . 68
Discharged, given up to friends, or sent to Alms-House, 24
Escaped, ... 1
Died, out of an average of 314 children, . . . 4

Total disposed of during the year, ... 276

Of these there were, white boys, ... 165
      white girls, ... 67
      colored boys, ... 38
      colored girls, ... 6

Total of every color, ... 276

Average age of children received last year, 13 years 11 months.

Nativity of 177 white children :
Recorded Americans, ... 47
Irish, 88 ; English, 22 ; German, 14 ; Scotch, 5 ;
French, 1, ... 130

Of 262 children,
Received from Police Court, New York City, . . 114
     New York City Sessions, . . . 55
     Commissioners of Alms-House, . . 18
     Thirteen counties throughout the State, 29

Returned after having been given up to friends or
indentured, ... 46

Total number, ... 262

The employment of the children has been—making chair-
bottoms, razor-strops, pocket-books, paper cases of various
patterns; making and mending shoes for the household;
washing, making and mending, for the institution.

The treasurer's report shows a balance due him, Janu-
ary 1, 1844, ... $1,109 55
Receipts to January 1, 1845, ... 22,797 99
Disbursements, ... 22,484 00

Leaving a balance due to treasurer, ... 796 34

Of the disbursements, there were for fixtures and per-
manent improvements, ... $6,885 00
For clothing of children, ... 1,924 09
For provisions and groceries, ... 6,371 33
For furniture, beds, and bedding, ... 1,067 42
For coal, wood, oil, and stoves, ... 815 97
For school expenses, books, and stationery, . . 226 14
For hospital expenses, medicines, &c., . . . 115 69
For salaries of officers and attendants, . . . 3,923 41
Premium of insurance against fire, ... 115 61
Of the receipts, for labor of children, . . . 7,030 84
From the state treasury, a part of the surplus fund
arising from the state tax on foreign passengers, . 8,000 00
Licenses of theatres and circuses for 1844, . . 3,194 00
City of New York, from excise fund, . . . 4,000 00
Finance Committee, ... 573 15

According to the division of time, 8 hours are devoted to
labor, about 4 hours to instruction, about 4 hours to eating,
recreation and amusements, and about 8 hours to sleep.

The appendix to the last annual report is filled with short
and pithy extracts of letters, and other credentials, of children
who have been apprenticed, concerning their improvement and
good behavior. See from whence they were taken, when they
came to the Refuge. Of those received last year,

34 have been accustomed to attend school regularly;
97 have attended school irregularly, many only a few weeks
altogether;
35 say they never attended school in their life;
43 have never attended Sabbath school;
82 profess to have attended irregularly; while only
41 pretend to say they have been regular attendants;

24 were able to repeat a verse of Scripture;
75 had received some little instruction, but had never learned a verse.
67 appeared entirely ignorant of the nature, design, and contents of the Bible.

To take such children, and train them for an honorable apprenticeship, is the object of the Refuge. The managers say, page 8,—

"Very soon after entering on the discipline of the Refuge, they become reconciled to the restraints which are necessarily thrown around them, and perform without reluctance the various duties of their new condition in life. The school and the chapel afford to their minds an agreeable and profitable change from the labors of the work-shop; and their religious and intellectual cultivation opens to them new sources of enjoyment, such as they have never before experienced.

"The religious instruction of the Sabbath school is salutary in its influence.

"The school, under the superintendence of Mr. M'Kenna, is conducted with good order and success; and although a large number enter the Refuge even unacquainted with their letters, all of them leave its walls with sufficient instruction for the ordinary purposes of life.

"While every means are adopted to strengthen them and confirm them in good habits of industry, sufficient time is allowed to them, daily, for such recreation as is deemed necessary to promote their health.

"The subject of improving the ventilation, not only of the work-shops, but also of the dormitories, has attracted the attention of the managers, and they have made some experiments, which, if found to answer the purpose, will be more extensively adopted."

"The introduction of Croton water throughout the establishment has fully realized the expectations of the board of managers." "The importance is clearly seen in its moral and physical effects upon the children."

"A large bath has been erected, capable of containing nearly five thousand gallons of water; and here the children enjoy, in proper seasons, the healthful and agreeable recreation of bathing."

"The inmates of the Female House perform all the domestic work of the establishment. The washing and mending of the clothing of the children are done by them, under the supervision of the matron. They attend school daily for instruction in the various branches of a plain education."

"The health of the children, during the past year, has been good, and but *four* deaths have occurred out of an average of 314 children. Scrofula and sore eyes—diseases to which the children have been subject—have been greatly diminished in consequence of more attention to personal cleanliness in the use of the Croton water and the bath, more attention to ventilation in the domitories and work-shops, and more attention to diet, substituting more solid food, as occasion required, for that which was deemed less nutritious, to the manifest improvement of the health of all the scrofulous and sore-eyed children."

The whole number of children who have enjoyed the benefits of this blessed charity, since January 1st, 1825, is .   . 3,582
Of whom there were females, ... 1,007
The whole number apprenticed, ... 3,222

HOUSE OF REFUGE, PHILADELPHIA.

Number of children at the commencement of the year, . 168
Of whom there were 110 girls, 58 boys, . 168
Number received during the year, ... 106
Of whom there were, boys, 69; girls, 37, . 106
Number receiving the benefit of the House, . . . 274

Number discharged, of whom 69 were boys, and 44 girls, 113
Number of escapes, 2 ; deaths, 1, ... 3

Total discharged during the year, ... 116
Remaining in the House, of whom 107 were boys, . . 158
The nativity of those received during the year, Americans, 79
Of the remainder, unknown, except foreigners, . . 11
Of the Americans, there were from Philadelphia county, . 90
From six other counties of Pennsylvania, . . . 9
Returned, having escaped, 2; having been indentured, 5, 7
The authority by which committed was magisterial, at
courts, 12; returned, 7, ... 19
There were disposed of, by indenture to farmers, . . 16
To shoemakers, 12 ; to blacksmiths and storekeepers, each,
2, ... 16
To cabinet-makers and four other mechanics, each, 1, . 5
Girls to housewifery, ... 23
     The average age of boys, received in 1844, was 14½ years;
girls, 14 years.
Of the boys admitted last year, ... 69
There were ignorant of the alphabet, ... 18
Those who could read a little, ... 32
Of girls admitted last year, ... 29
There were ignorant of the alphabet, ... 8
There were who could read a little, ... 12
     Of the whole number of boys and girls discharged, 102, there
were none who could not read.
     The applications for apprentices continue numerous, and the
committee select the best places.

"During the year, many of the former pupils visited the House, and met
with a hearty welcome. Among them was one who was placed with a
highly-respectable family more than 6 years ago. She remains in the same
place, though she has been free more than 4 years. After spending a few
days at the Refuge, she returned to the family with whom she had so long
resided, and who speak of her in the highest terms.
"A manager, on a visit some time since to a Sunday school, found a
former inmate instructing a class, and was informed by the superintendent
that the young man was highly respectable and industrious, and was one of
the best teachers in the school.

"The writer of a letter, recently received, thus speaks of another inmate: 'She has been a most excellent girl, and we felt towards her and treated her as a daughter. She has continued in my family until the present time, although she has been free more than 3 years. She is a member of the church, and attends divine service every Sabbath. I have also the pleasure to inform you that she is engaged to one of the first young men in the vicinity, and will be married before this letter reaches you. Her intended husband is a professor of religion, and the owner of a farm in the neighborhood. We are, of course, glad to see her doing well; but we shall feel her loss as that of a child.' "

"The managers do not hold the expectation that reformation can be accomplished in every case; but in some of these cases, where their exertions have been apparently unsuccessful, time has shown that they have not been entirely lost.

"The board of managers urge upon parents and guardians, as well as upon magistrates, the importance of placing in the Refuge those who have just entered on a career of vice, and of not waiting until wild habits, by long indulgence, have become in a great degree fixed."

The appendix of the report is filled with letters and brief extracts, concerning the good behavior of the apprentices, both boys and girls.

The treasurer's report shows, on the credit side, $20,808 99; and on the debtor, $20,568 39.

The sources of income were, from labor of children,	$2,211 90
From county commissioners, for legislative appropriation,	9,000 00
From State treasurer,	4,000 00
From executors of Dr. P. A. Blenden,	300 00
From life and annual subscribers,	100 00
From money loaned on interest,	3,000 00
From donation-box in House of Refuge,	11 96
From articles sold,	24 00
These items, with the balance from last year's account, amounting to	2,161 13
Make up the whole amount of receipts,	$20,808 99

The expenditures were, for provisions, clothing, fuel, salaries, stationery, and repairs to buildings,	11,641 77
Pennsylvania Company, on account of mortgage,	4,000 00
For one year's interest on " " "	363 33
Improvements,	528 69
Collecting commissions, &c.,	34 60
Loans on interest,	4,000 00
Balance on hand,	240 60
Amount of disbursements,	$20,808 99

The whole number of children received into the House of Refuge, from 1828 to 1844 inclusive, was 1796, of whom 556 were girls. The whole number apprenticed is not stated, nor the proportion of apprentices who are doing well.

SUMMARY OF THE HOUSES OF REFUGE.

Total number of children and youth in the three Houses
in Boston, New York, and Philadelphia,   . . .   508
Whole number receiving the benefits during the last year,
at least   900
Whole number of deaths in the three Houses, during the
last year, out of an average of at least 500 children,
only   6
Whole number of children who have enjoyed the benefits of
this blessed charity from the first, in New York and
Philadelphia, ...   5,378
Whole number of girls who have received the benefits, . 1,563
Whole number apprenticed from the New York House
alone, ...   3,222
Annual expenses of the three Houses, about . $30,000 00
Or annual expense of each child, ...   60 00

This sum, however, is diminished by the earnings of the
children, and actual receipts for the same, more than $10,000,
or more than one third of the expense of these institutions,
although the average age of the inmates is about 14 years. In
Boston and New York, colored children, as well as white,
receive the benefits. Not so in Philadelphia. Surely they
need it as much.

THE FARM SCHOOL ON THOMPSON'S ISLAND.

" On Tuesday we accepted an invitation, from one of the directors of this
institution, to visit the island, and be present at an examination of the boys
attached to the institution. We accordingly stepped on board the well-
known Hingham steam-packet General Lincoln, and in a few moments found
ourself, under a full head of steam, ploughing our way through the water
toward Thompson's Island. This was the day on which the parents and
friends of the pupils at the island were allowed to visit the boys; and there
were many who availed themselves of this opportunity, and on board the boat
were a number of family groups, consisting of an anxious mother, and some
happy looking children, anticipating a joyful meeting with a son or a brother
from whom they had been separated for weeks or months.

" Thompson's Island is situated in the harbor, about four miles from
Boston. It contains one hundred and forty acres of land, a considerable
portion of which is under cultivation. A large brick edifice has been erected
on the highest part of the island, which serves as a habitation for the boys,
for the superintendent, matron, and instructor of the school. It is designed
and arranged in a manner admirably calculated to promote the health and
comfort of the inmates, and commands a magnificent prospect of the whole
harbor of Boston, and of the beautiful villages and country on the southern
shore.   *   *   *   *   *   *   *   *   The main object of
the institution is the education and reformation of boys, who, from the loss

of their parents or other causes, are exposed to extraordinary temptations, and are in danger of becoming vicious and dangerous, or useless members of society. The pupils are received at an early age, and are regularly and carefully instructed in their moral and religious duties, and in the elementary knowledge usually communicated in our common town schools. They are employed in a regular course of labor suited to their ages and strength, and instructed in gardening, agriculture, or such useful arts as contribute to their health and support, and tend at the same time to form in them habits of industry and order, and prepare them to earn their own livelihood.

" When we reached the island, the visitors proceeded up the gravel-walk to the institution, and found the boys all seated in the school-room, awaiting the arrival of the visitors. They numbered sixty-seven, all told, and were a fine, healthy-looking set of little fellows, as one will meet with any where on a summer's day. Their costume was remarkably neat and appropriate; their countenances were intelligent; and they looked contented and happy. They were examined by the superintendent, Mr. Morrison, a gentleman admirably qualified for the responsible situation, and Deacon Grant, who has taken a deep and constant interest in this institution, ever since it was established, in reading, spelling, geography, writing, &c., and the result was highly satisfactory. Indeed, the education they receive at this institution, and the habits of industry they acquire, and the moral precepts which are constantly inculcated on their youthful minds, qualify them, when they leave this peaceful and comfortable abode, and mingle in the busy world, to become useful citizens, reflecting honor on themselves and the country which gave them birth.

" As a school of reform, this institution is deserving of the favor of the public; indeed, similar institutions should be established in all our large towns and cities. This will be seen from the following extract from a report of the directors of the institution, describing the classes of boys who are inmates of that establishment:—

" 'They consist of truants from our public schools, and idlers in our streets and on our wharves, where they pass a large part of their time in vagrancy. Some of them are orphans, in whom little interest is felt by the poor and miserable connections, on whom they hang as a heavy burden. Some are children of widows, whose time is so filled with labor to procure a mere subsistence, that their sons, still more than their daughters, are unavoidably neglected, and at an early age become unmanageable. Some, having lost their mothers, are left to the care of fathers, whose means and opportunities for domestic control are yet less effectual than those of widows. Some have intemperate or profligate parents, and suffer, of course, from the disorder and misery to which they were born. And some are children of the ignorant, inefficient, and helpless, who seem, almost from nature, incapable of fulfilling discreetly the most common duties of life. But all of them, from these and other causes, are daily and hourly exposed to the contagion of vice, and growing up in idle and pernicious habits, from which perhaps, a few may, by fortunate circumstances, be reclaimed before they arrive at manhood; while by far the greater part will be hurried to an early death, the victims of intemperance and want, or live on, only to prey upon the community, fill our Alms-Houses and Prisons, and increase the burdens and crimes of the state.'

" Such, says the report, are the situations and exposures of hundreds of boys in our city at the present moment, for a portion of whom the Farm School affords a safe and appropriate Asylum. And surely the requirements not only of Christian philanthropy, but even of a just regard to the general welfare of the city, imperiously demand for it an adequate and liberal support. It would be well for the city and for the happiness of many individuals, if instead of sixty-seven, some *hundreds* of boys, growing up in idleness, and becoming early inducted into all the mysteries of vice, could be accommodated and taken care of at the Farm School on Thompson's Island."—*Mercantile Journal.*

IV.—REFORMED PRISONERS, WITH REFERENCE FOR CHARACTER.

A valued friend of this Society, and one of its long-tried and liberal patrons, not long since asked the Secretary how many prisoners, within his knowledge, were discharged and reformed. He could not answer, but promised a chapter in this Report, partly in answer to the inquiry. A little time, and but a little, has been taken to gather up authentic information concerning discharged prisoners, mostly from the House of Correction at Worcester, the House of Correction at South Boston, and the State Prison at Charlestown, Massachusetts. The result is an alphabetical list of about 150 individuals, designated by the initials of their names, with references to persons who have been or are acquainted with their character, and keeping out of view their specific residence, lest the feelings of honorable men, and thriving and respectable families, should be wounded by publishing the names of persons and places. The history is often vastly more interesting than fiction can be.

A.

A., F. W. Sentence, 1 year and 6 months in the Mass. State Prison. Discharged August, 1830, on expiration of sentence. Has been, so far as known, since his discharge, a good and useful citizen. Resident, when last heard from, in Norfolk county, Mass. Reference, Rev. Jared Curtis, chaplain Mass. State Prison.

A., G. W. Sentence, 3 years and 2 months in the Mass. State Prison. Pardoned out March, 1840. Subsequent conduct exemplary. Resident at W., when last heard from. Reference, Rev. J. Curtis, chaplain, &c.

A., J. M. Confined for 1 year and 9 months in the Mass. State Prison. Discharged by pardon, Dec., 1840. Has since, so far as known, led an honest and useful life at R. Reference, Rev. Jared Curtis, chaplain, &c.

A., A. J. Term of confinement, 4 years in Mass. State Prison. Discharged on expiration of sentence, March, 1841. When last heard from, was an industrious and useful citizen of N. O. Reference, Rev. J. Curtis, chaplain, &c.

A., J. M. Sentence, 1 year in Mass. State Prison. Term expired Feb., 1842. Has since been an industrious and useful inhabitant of B. Reference, Rev. J. Curtis, chaplain, &c.

A., W. Confined 5 years in the Mass. State Prison. Discharged, Nov., 1835, by expiration of sentence. So far as known, since discharge, industrious and useful. Residence, when last heard from, B. Reference, Rev. Jared Curtis, chaplain, &c.

A., J., Jr. Imprisoned 10 years and 8 months in Mass. State Prison. Pardoned and discharged, May, 1844; since which, has been, so far as known, industrious and useful. Residence in Barnstable county. Reference, Rev. Jared Curtis, chaplain, &c.

B.

B., S. D. Confined in the Mass. State Prison 8 years and 4 months. Discharged Sept., 1834, by pardon. Since his discharge, has been, so far as known, an industrious and useful citizen. Resident, when last heard from, in Illinois. Reference, Rev. Jared Curtis, chaplain, &c.

B., C. Committed to Mass. State Prison for 2 years and 8 months. Pardoned Feb., 1837. So far as known, has since led an exemplary life in the vicinity of Springfield. Reference, Rev. Jared Curtis, chaplain, &c.

B., J. C., aged 40 years, was committed to the House of Correction in Worcester, Sept. 3, 1839. Had inherited property, but had spent it all. He had become so intemperate that he would go out in the night time, without dressing himself, and roam about after rum. He was arrested and committed for 6 months. When his time had half expired, he made an unsuccessful effort to get out; but his application was refused, and he afterwards told the jailer that it would have been his ruin if his application had prevailed at that time. His longer continuance, he thought, cured him. He went home, spent most of the time, for two or three years, in promoting the cause of temperance, and died. Mr. Mathews, the jailer, says the physicians advised him, in his last sickness, to take stimulating drinks; but he had rather die.

B., E. Sentence, 2 years and 3 months in the Mass. State Prison. Discharged, by pardon, March, 1837. Has since lived an industrious and useful life. When last heard from, resided in W. Reference, Rev. J. Curtis, chaplain, &c.

B., J. B. Term of imprisonment, 2 years and 1 month in Mass. State Prison. Pardoned out Dec., 1842. Since his discharge, so far as known, has led an honest and useful life. Resides in Ohio. Reference, Rev. Jared Curtis, chaplain, &c.

B., N. Confined 1 year in Mass. State Prison. Discharged, on expiration of sentence, Oct., 1842 ; since which, he has been industrious and useful. Resided, when last heard from, at W. Reference, Rev. J. Curtis, chaplain, &c.

B., W. In Mass. State Prison 4 years and 2 months. Released, by order of court, Nov., 1843. Has since pursued an upright course of life, in B. Reference, Rev. J. Curtis, chaplain, &c.

B., L. S., cabinet-maker, 2 years in Mass. State Prison. Discharged on expiration of sentence, Oct., 1843. Has been since industrious and useful. Lives in C. Reference, Mr. Crowninshield, and Rev. J. Curtis, chaplain, &c.

B., D. Confined 3 years in Mass. State Prison. Discharged March, 1844, on expiration of sentence. So far as known, subsequent course exemplary. Resides at B. Reference to the chaplain.

B., W. V. 2 years and 9 months in Mass. State Prison. Pardoned and discharged March, 1844. So far as known, has since led an industrious and useful life, in T. Reference, Rev. J. Curtis, chaplain, &c.

C.

C., J. R. Sentence, 2 years in Mass. State Prison. Pardoned and discharged June, 1831. Industrious and useful citizen of B. References, Rev. Mr. Lord, Mariners' Church, and Rev. Jared Curtis, chaplain, &c.

C., E. Confined 2 years and 3 months in the Mass. State Prison. Discharged Sept., 1833, on expiration of sentence. So far as known, an industrious and useful citizen. Resident, when last heard from, in the vicinity of B. Reference, Rev. Jared Curtis, chaplain, &c.

C., E. Confined 1 year and 1 month in the Mass. State Prison. Discharged June, 1833, by pardon. So far as known, an industrious and useful citizen. Resident, when last heard from, in Barnstable county.

C., A. Confined 3 years and 7 months in the Mass. State Prison. Discharged Oct., 1836, by expiration of sentence. Since discharge, so far as known, an industrious and useful citizen. Resided, when last heard from, in B. Reference, Rev. Jared Curtis, chaplain, &c.

C., J. W. 18 months in Mass. State Prison. Pardoned and discharged April, 1838. Has since, so far as known, been industrious and upright. When last heard from, resided in G. Reference, Rev. Jared Curtis, chaplain, &c.

C., C. L. 5 years in Mass. State Prison. Pardoned and discharged, March, 1840. Resided in N. Dead.

C., S. Confined 5 years and 1 month in Mass. State Prison. Discharged, by pardon, Dec., 1841. Since his release, has been industrious and useful, so far as known. When last heard from, resided in A., Me. Reference, Rev. Jared Curtis, chaplain, &c.

C., J. Imprisoned in Mass. State Prison 3 years. Discharged, on expiration of sentence, Oct., 1843. So far as known, has been an industrious and useful citizen of B. Reference, Rev. J. Curtis, chaplain, &c.

C., al. W. C. Confined 3 years and 1 month. Discharged, Dec., 1843, on expiration of sentence. Has since been industrious and useful, so far as known. When last heard from, resided in C. Reference, Rev. Jared Curtis, chaplain, &c.

D.

D., W. Confined 6 years in the Mass. State Prison. Discharged April, 1834, by pardon. So far as known, an industrious and useful citizen. Resident, when last heard from, in B., Mass. Reference, Rev. Jared Curtis, chaplain, &c.

D., T. Nurse in the hospital. 27 years in Prison. Reference, officers in Mass. State Prison.

————. Was in one of the Prisons of New York for stealing; so says the representative in the General Court from ————. The representative says this gentleman stands, politically, at the head of society in ————. The whig banner was presented to him at the last election, and he delivered a speech on the occasion. He is man of property, supports his family handsomely, and practices medicine. He received a pardon, on the petition of the people of the neighborhood of ————, where he was born.

D., E. Sentence, 3 years to the Mass. State Prison. Discharged June, 1831, by expiration of sentence. So far as known, an industrious and useful citizen. Resident in Bristol county, Mass., when last heard from. Reference, Rev. Jared Curtis, chaplain, &c.

D., E. Sentence, 1 year and 3 months to Mass. State Prison. Discharged, August, 1831, on expiration of sentence. So far as known, since his discharge, an industrious and useful citizen. Residence, when last heard from, P., R. I. Reference, Rev. Jared Curtis, chaplain, &c.

D., W. Colored. Confined 3 years in Mass. State Prison. Discharged, on expiration of sentence, Aug., 1843. Has since been, so far as known, an industrious and useful citizen of B. Reference, Rev. J. Curtis, chaplain, &c.

D., W. T. Confined 2 years in Mass. State Prison. Discharged, June, 1832, on expiration of sentence. Has been, so far as known, an industrious and useful citizen. Resident, when last heard from, in P., R. I. Reference, Rev. Jared Curtis, chaplain, &c.

D., J. In Prison at Charlestown 4 years. On expiration of sentence, Dec., 1839, was discharged. Became a good citizen. While he lived, resided at S. B.

D., E. D. 3 years in Mass. State Prison. Discharged on expiration of sentence, Oct., 1839. So far as known, has since been an industrious and useful man. When last heard from, resided at A., Mass. Reference, the chaplain of the Prison.

D., H. Confined 3 years in Mass. State Prison. On expiration of sentence, discharged, Aug., 1839. Subsequent conduct believed to have been exemplary. B. Reference, Rev. J. Curtis, chaplain, &c.

D., P. Imprisoned 3 years at Charlestown, Mass. Discharged on expiration of sentence, March, 1841. So far as known, he is industrious and upright. Resident in B. Reference, Rev. Jared Curtis, chaplain, &c.

D., L. In Mass. State Prison 3 years. Pardoned out Oct., 1842. Since, as far as known, a good citizen. When last heard from, was at W. Reference, Rev. Jared Curtis, chaplain, &c.

E.

E., Seminary, T., N. Y. Reference, officers of Yale College and Louis Dwight.

E., C., a shoemaker by trade. Confined in Mass. State Prison 3 years. Discharged, on expiration of sentence, Feb., 1836. Has since, it is believed, been industrious and upright. Resident, when last heard from, in N , Conn. Reference, Deacon John Sullivan, Boston, and the Rev. J. Curtis, chaplain, &c.

E., H. 4 years in Mass. State Prison. Pardoned April, 1838. Industrious and exemplary, so far as known. When last heard from, was at S., Mass. Reference, Rev. Jared Curtis, chaplain, &c.

E., C. Confined 8 years and 8 months in Mass. State Prison. Pardoned and discharged Jan., 1841. So far as known, has since been industrious and useful. When last heard from, resided in M. Reference, the chaplain of the Prison.

E., E. 10 years in Mass. State Prison. Discharged, on expiration of sentence, April, 1842. Conduct since release, so far as known, commendable. When last heard from, was in New Hampshire. Reference, Rev. Jared Curtis, chaplain, &c.

E., C. In Mass. State Prison 8 years and 4 months. Pardoned and discharged April, 1843. Has, so far as known, been industrious aud useful since leaving Prison. Resided, when last heard from, in B. Reference, Rev. Jared Curtis, chaplain, &c.

E., D. P. Confined 2 years and 9 months in Mass. State Prison. Discharged, by pardon, Jan., 1843. Has since been upright and industrious, so far as known. When last heard from, resided at L., Mass. Reference, Rev. Jared Curtis, chaplain, &c.

E., D. In Mass. State Prison 5 months. Pardoned Feb., 1843. So far as known, has since been industrious and useful. Resided in Plymouth county. Reference, Rev. J. Curtis, chaplain, &c.

F.

F., H. Confined 4 years and 4 months in Mass. State Prison. Discharged by pardon, Sept., 1842. A young man of respectable appearance. Was at the Prison in Charlestown, on the 4th of March, 1845, with his wife, where L. D. saw him, and the officers testified to his good character and former imprisonment. Then living in Charlestown.

G.

G., M. A. Portsmouth, N. H. Reference to S. E. Coues, Esq.

G., S. Sentence, 2 years. Discharged May, 1832, on expiration of sentence. Resident, when last heard from, in I., Mass. So far as known, an industrious and useful citizen. Reference, Rev. Jared Curtis, chaplain, &c.

G., S. S. Confined 5 years and 10 months in Mass. State Prison. Pardoned March, 1841. Industrious and useful since discharge, so far as known. When last heard from, was in Norfolk county. Reference, Rev. J. Curtis, chaplain, &c.

G., L. 5 years in Mass. State Prison. Discharged on expiration of sentence, Jan., 1839. Conduct since, commendable, as far as known. In State of Maine, when last heard from. Reference, Rev. Jared Curtis, chaplain, &c.

G., N. In Mass. State Prison 20 months. Released by pardon, Aug., 1844. When last heard from, lived in G., Mass.

So far as known, an industrious and useful man. Reference, Rev. Jared Curtis, chaplain, &c.

H.

Hodges, Jacob, African servant, Canandaigua. Reference, Mrs. Martin, and Rev. Ansel D. Eddy.

H., H. W., Mass. Reference all the citizens of W. Universally known as highly respectable and useful.

H., A. Confined 3 years and 2 months in the Mass. State Prison. Discharged by pardon, May, 1834. Since then an industrious and useful citizen. Resident in B. Reference, Rev. Jared Curtis, chaplain, &c.

H., E. Imprisoned 15 months, at Charlestown, Mass. Left on expiration of sentence, June, 1841. So far as known, has since been industrious and useful. When last heard from, was at C., Mass. Reference, Rev. J. Curtis, chaplain, &c.

H., S. A. Confined in Mass. State Prison 9 months. Pardoned and released, March, 1841. Has since proved industrious and useful, so far as known. When last heard from, was at B., Mass. Reference, Rev. J. Curtis, chaplain, &c.

H., J. H., by trade a barber. In Mass. State Prison 6 years and 9 months. Discharged, by pardon, July, 1841. Has since sustained a good character, so far as known. When last heard from, resided in B. References, Mr. Charles Foster, and Rev. Jared Curtis, chaplain, &c.

H., C. T. Confined in Mass. State Prison 3 years. Was discharged, on expiration of sentence, July, 1842. So far as known, his course has since been one of industry and usefulness. When last heard from, was at S. Reference, Rev. J. Curtis, chaplain, &c.

H., F. 1 year in Charlestown Prison. Discharged, Oct., 1842, on expiration of sentence. Subsequent life correct, as far as known. Residing at W., when last heard from. Reference, Rev. Jared Curtis, chaplain, &c.

H., W. Imprisoned in Mass. State Prison 5 years and 9 months. Pardoned and discharged from confinement, July, 1843. Since industrious and useful, so far as known. When last heard from, was at N., N. H. Reference, Rev. J. Curtis, chaplain, &c.

H., L. Confined in Mass. State Prison 3 years and 3 months. Discharged by pardon, Jan., 1843. When last heard from, was at L., Mass., pursuing an honest and industrious life. Reference, Rev. J. Curtis, chaplain, &c.

H., R. 3 years and 4 months in Mass. State Prison. Pardoned Dec., 1843. Industrious and upright, so far as known. Residence when last heard from, N. Reference, Rev. J. Curtis, chaplain, &c.

H., G. J. Confined 6 years and 3 months in Mass. State Prison. Pardoned and released Feb., 1844. Upright and useful, since discharge, so far as known. When last heard from, was dwelling in Q., Mass. Reference, Rev. J. Curtis, chaplain, &c.

I.

I., J. D. In Mass. State Prison 2 years and 9 months. Pardoned and discharged, March, 1841. When last heard from, at G., was industrious, upright, and useful. Reference, Rev. Jared Curtis, chaplain, &c.

J.

J., P., 60 years of age, from B., Mass. Committed to House of Correction at Worcester, for 2 months, for intemperance, April 28, 1841. Discharged 27th of May, 1841, by Col. Lincoln and Gen. Heard, overseers, because he was a man of truth, and always had been, and they were convinced he would drink no more intoxicating drink. He was a man of property, had two farms, and 60 head of cattle. He had had 2 wives, and brought up 19 children. He was a hardworking man, and the jailer says he had averaged 1 pint of rum and 1 gallon of cider per day, for 30 years. He signed the pledge when he left the House of Correction, in the presence of L. D., and he has never violated it. He was one of the men who bought up all the rum in B. and had it burned on the public green, at a temperance celebration. He is one of the leading men in the town in the cause of temperance. References, Hon. J. W. Lincoln and Mr. Mathews.

J., H. C. Sentence, 1 year and 10 months. Discharged May, 1831, on expiration of sentence. Has been, since his discharge, so far as known, an industrious and useful citizen. Resident, when last heard from, in N., Mass. Reference, Rev. Jared Curtis, chaplain, &c.

J., A. L. 1 year and 6 months in State Prison at Charlestown. Discharged by pardon Oct., 1840. So far as known, has since been industrious and useful. Living in C., when last heard from. Reference, Rev. J. Curtis, chaplain, &c.

J., S. Confined in Mass. State Prison 6 years and 3 months. Pardoned and released March, 1844. His subsequent life exemplary, so far as known. When last heard from, was in B. Reference, Rev. J. Curtis, chaplain, &c.

K.

K., J. H., from W., aged 35. Committed to ——— House of Correction, 15th of August, 1832. Discharged, Oct. 1, 1832, by pardon from the overseers, for cause. Again committed in 1834, and remained till his time expired. Again committed in 1834, and again remained till his time expired, in 1835. He was then employed, after his discharge, as a turnkey. He was faithful and good. Then he obtained a situation as clerk in a store, and continued in that kind of employment, well esteemed, till he was engaged at ———, in ———, as superintendent of the business. He has a family of his own, very respectable and well brought up. He has a place of trust in the church, lives an exemplary life, and is a very useful citizen. Reference, keeper of the Prison.

K., W. G. Confined in Mass. State Prison 7 years. Was discharged, on expiration of sentence, Sept., 1841. Since, industrious, and of correct deportment, so far as known. When last heard from, was in Norfolk county. Reference, Rev. Jared Curtis, chaplain, &c.

K., L. In Prison at Charlestown 1 year. On expiration of sentence, April, 1841, discharged. When last heard from, resided in H. An industrious man. Reference, Rev. J. Curtis, chaplain, &c.

K., G. 1 year in confinement in Mass. State Prison. Discharged, on expiration of sentence, April, 1841. Lives in H. Industrious and useful, so far as known. Reference, Rev. J. Curtis, chaplain, &c.

K., J. Confined 7 years. Discharged Sept., 1843, on expiration of sentence. Has since, so far as known, lived in H., Mass. An industrious and useful man. Reference, Rev. Jared Curtis, chaplain, &c.

L.

L., W. Committed to the State Prison for stealing, for 3 years. Discharged, at the expiration of 2 years, by pardon, March, 1831. Has been in the employment of Mr. C., in the manufacture of ladies' shoes, 8 years. Supports his family honorably, and is very conscientious; jealous of himself, in regard to truth, honesty, and honor, and will not suffer his good name to lie under any suspicion, if he can avoid it. Formerly at A. Reference, Hon. Charles Choate, of South Reading.

M.

M'N., F. Confined 1 year in the Mass. State Prison. Discharged, May, 1833, on expiration of sentence. So far as known, an industrious and useful citizen. Resident, when last heard from, in Barnstable county, Mass. Reference, Rev. Jared Curtis, chaplain, &c.

M., G. C. In Mass. State Prison 1 year and 6 months. Pardoned and discharged Dec., 1837. An industrious and useful man, since leaving Prison, so far as known. When last heard from, was at A., in Mass. Reference, Rev. J. Curtis, chaplain, &c.

M., F. Term of confinement, 3 years and 1 month. Discharged, by pardon, July, 1840. So far as known, has since been industrious and exemplary. When last heard from, was in N. Reference, Rev. Jared Curtis, chaplain, &c.

M., D. 2 years in Prison. Oct., 1841, discharged, on expiration of sentence. When last heard from, resident in Hampden county. An industrious and useful man, so far as known. Reference, Rev. J. Curtis, chaplain, &c.

M., J. Confined 3 years in Mass. State Prison. Oct., 1843, was discharged on expiration of his sentence. Subsequent life commendable, so far as known. Resides in C. Reference, Rev. J. Curtis, chaplain, &c.

N.

N., A. In Maine. A man of property. Worked for Richards & Newcomb 7 years, and accumulated, during that time, $1,200 or $1,400, with which he bought a farm. Reference, Hon. Mr. Richards, of the Senate of Mass.

N., C. Minister in Methodist Episcopal Church. Reference, L. D.

O.

O., Mrs., wife of J. O., Boston. Reformed in the House of Correction at South Boston, about 5 years since. Visited by L. D., in 1845, who learned from her husband her good character and behavior, her usefulness and piety. Reference. Rev. N. A., pastor of Essex Street church, Boston.

O., H. G. Confined in Mass. State Prison 7 years. Discharged, on expiration of sentence, Jan. 1844. Subsequent deportment correct, so far as known. In B., when last heard from. Reference, Rev. J. Curtis, chaplain, &c.

P.

P., M. O. Confined in Mass. State Prison 2 years and 7 months. Discharged, Aug. 1835, by pardon. So far as known, since discharge, industrious and useful. Residence, when last heard from, B., Mass. Reference, Rev. Jared Curtis, chaplain, &c.

P., M. In Mass. State Prison 12 years. Pardoned and discharged Jan., 1837. Formerly at L. Respectable while he lived.

P., W. Imprisoned at Charlestown, Mass., 13 years. Discharged, by pardon, Jan., 1838. Since then, so far as known, industrious and useful. At L., when last heard from. Reference, Rev. J. Curtis, chaplain, &c.

P., D. 2 years and 3 months in Mass. State Prison. Pardoned Jan., 1838. When last heard from, was at R. ; useful and upright, so far as known. Reference, Rev. J. Curtis, chaplain, &c.

P., T., Jr. Confined in Mass. State Prison 6 years and 7 months. Discharged, by pardon, Sept., 1842. Has since been industrious and useful, so far as known, in C., Ill. Reference, Rev. Jared Curtis, chaplain, &c.

P., T. In confinement 5 years in Mass. State Prison. Was discharged Feb., 1842, on expiration of sentence. Industrious and useful, so far as known. When last heard from, was at Long Island or New York. Reference, Rev. J. Curtis, chaplain, &c.

P., G. In Mass. State Prison 4 years. Discharged, on expiration of sentence, Dec., 1842. Has been, so far as known, since his discharge, industrious and useful. When last heard from, was in B. or vicinity. Reference, Rev. J. Curtis, chaplain, &c.

P., J. Confined 11 years in Mass. State Prison. Discharged, by expiration of sentence, May, 1843. Since then, conduct believed to be upright. When last heard from, resident at B. Reference, Rev. J. Curtis, chaplain, &c.

P., C. In Mass. State Prison 3 years and 5 months. Pardoned July, 1844. When last heard from, was at G., Mass., and, so far as known, is habitually industrious and useful. Reference, Rev. J. Curtis, chaplain, &c.

P., C. In Mass. State Prison 2 years. Discharged on expiration of sentence, May, 1844. Subsequent conduct, so far as known, commendable. Residence, when last heard from, in B. Reference, Rev. Jared Curtis, chaplain, &c.

R.

R., colored man. Sentence commuted. Exemplary and useful. Reference, Governor Briggs and Mr. Bemis.

R., machinist, Andover, Mass. Reference, W. S. Eustis, Jr.

R., R., barber, Portland, Me. Reference, his widow, and L. D.

R., E. D. Confined 3 years and 9 months, in Mass. State Prison. Discharged, by pardon, March, 1840. Has since been industrious and useful, so far as known. When last heard from, resided in W. Reference, Rev. J. Curtis, chaplain, &c.

R., W., colored man. Sentence, 12 years. Pardoned and discharged Sept., 1844. Conduct since, circumspect, so far as known. When last heard from, in B. Reference, Rev. Jared Curtis, chaplain, &c.

S.

S., H. Confined in Mass. State Prison 2 years. Discharged April, 1835, by expiration of sentence. So far as known, since discharged, an industrious and useful citizen. Residence, when last heard from, N., Mass. Reference, Rev. J. Curtis, chaplain, &c.

S., W. In Mass. State Prison 2 years and 3 months. Was pardoned and discharged March, 1837. When last heard from, in Plymouth county. Industrious and useful, so far as known. Reference, Rev. J. Curtis, chaplain, &c.

S., I. Period of confinement, 2 years and 5 months. Discharged, by pardon, March, 1837. In Plymouth county, when last heard from ; and, so far as known, is industrious and useful. Reference, Rev. Jared Curtis, chaplain, &c.

S., E. 3 years in Mass. State Prison. Discharged on expiration of sentence, June, 1839. Conduct since discharge, commendable, so far as known. When last heard from, resided in B. Reference, Rev. J. Curtis, chaplain, &c.

S., R. Confined 2 years and 4 months in Mass. State Prison. Pardoned and discharged Dec., 1842. An industrious and useful citizen, so far as known. When last heard from, was at W., Mass. Reference, Rev. J. Curtis, chaplain, &c.

S., G. H. Mate in P. line of packets. Very respectable. Reference, Peter Hobart, Jr., Avery Place.

S., J., aged 51, committed to the House of Correction, at Worcester, Dec. 23, 1839. Discharged April 7, 1840 ; sentence, 6 months. Pardoned. Had been in the House twice before. A tailor by trade ; had 5 children ; an Irishman by birth. He was miserably poor ; married a native American, and did not support his family. Her relatives would do nothing to support the family unless she would abandon her husband. This she would not do. The jailer sent her meat, meal, butter, cheese, and wood, to keep the family alive while he was in Prison. Since his discharge, he has purchased a lot of land in W., built a small but convenient house, which is painted, furnished with blinds, and paid for.* He is now temperate, supports his family by his industry, has offered to pay Mr. Mathews, the jailer, for what he did for the family when he was in Prison ; but the benevolent jailer told him he would never take a cent so long as he behaved well. Mr. Mathews, the jailer, went to his brother-in-law, when he was in Prison, to get him to sign a petition for his pardon. He replied, that he would sign one to have him confined for life. Reference, Hon. John W. Lincoln and Mr. Mathews.

S., J. Confined 5 years in the Mass. State Prison. Discharged Nov., 1833, by pardon. So far as known, an industrious and useful citizen. Resident, when last heard from, in the State of Maine. Reference, Rev. Jared Curtis, chaplain, &c.

S., A. Confined 4 years in the Mass. State Prison. Discharged April, 1844, by pardon. So far as known since discharge, industrious and useful. Residence, when last heard from, H., Mass. Reference Rev. Jared Curtis, chaplain, &c.

S., O. Confined 2 years in Mass. State Prison. Discharged, on expiration of sentence, Aug., 1842. Has since been industrious and useful, so far as known. When last heard from, resided in B. Reference, Rev. Jared Curtis, chaplain, &c.

T.

T., M. Sentence, 6 years and 8 months in Mass. State Prison. Discharged Jan., 1832, by pardon. So far as known, an industrious and useful citizen. Residence, when last heard from, A. or C., Berkshire county, Mass. Reference, Rev. Jared Curtis, chaplain, &c.

T., A. Confined 5 years. Discharged, on expiration of sentence, Jan., 1836. Industrious and useful since then, so far

---

* He has also purchased a piece of land from the town, in addition to the former lot, and the first payment became due on the 1st of April, 1845.

as known. When last heard from, resided in vicinity of L. Reference, Rev. J. Curtis, chaplain, &c.

U.

1. Name untold. Pardoned. Mass. State Prison. Residence, A. Reference, Mr. Badger, representative from Adams.

2. Untold. Pardoned. Mass. State Prison. Residence, J., Mass. Reference, Mr. Jenks, Jr.

3. Untold. Pardoned. Mass. State Prison. Residence, Andover. Reference, Hon. Mr. Choate, Senate of Mass.

4. Untold. Tailor. House of Correction, South Boston. Residence, Boston, W. Street. Reference, L. D. and his father, J. W.

5. Untold. Farmer. House of Correction at Worcester. Reference, Barre.

6. Untold. Chambermaid. Residence, Hartford, Conn. Reference, matrons at the Refuge.

7. Untold. Young man. Residence, New York city. Reference, Capt. Robbins.

8. Untold.* Residence, Berkley, Mass. Reference, S. French, rep. 1836.

9. Untold.* Residence, Andover, Mass. Reference, Hon. Amos Abbot. 1836.

10. Untold.* Residence, Andover, Mass. Reference, Hon. Amos Abbot. 1836.

11. Untold.* Residence, Fitchburg, Mass. Reference, J. Putnam, rep. 1836.

12. Untold.* Residence, Brimfield, Mass. Reference, John Foster, rep. 1836.

13. Untold.* Residence, Leominster, Mass. Reference, Carter Gates, rep. 1836.

14. Untold.* Residence, Boylston, Mass. Reference, Russell Moon, rep. 1836.

15. Untold.* Residence, Watertown, Mass. Reference, J. Robbins, rep. 1836.

16. Untold.* Residence, Granville, Mass. Reference, Alf. Bancroft and Dennison Parsons, reps. 1836.

17. Untold.* Residence, Granville, Mass. Reference, Alf. Bancroft and Dennison Parsons, reps. 1836.

V.

V., G. Confined 2 years and 3 months in the Mass. State Prison. Discharged, by pardon, March, 1835. So far as

---

* Eleventh Report of Prison Discipline Society, page 50.

known, since discharge, an industrious and useful citizen. Residence, when last heard from, Q., Mass. Reference, Rev. Jared Curtis, chaplain, &c.

W.

W., J. Confined in Mass. State Prison 2 years. Handcartman. Discharged, on expiration of sentence, April, 1831. Subsequent conduct exemplary, so far as known. When last heard from, was in B. Reference, Rev. J. Curtis, chaplain, &c.

W., E. 5 years in Mass. State Prison at Charlestown. Discharged, on expiration of sentence, Oct., 1839. Industrious and useful, so far as known. In B., when last heard from. Reference, Rev. Jared Curtis, chaplain, &c.

W., F. G. 2 years and 3 months in Mass. State Prison. Pardoned and discharged Dec., 1840. Of correct deportment, since discharged, so far as known. At N. O., when last heard from. Reference, Rev. Jared Curtis, chaplain, &c.

W., S. Confined 4 years and 4 months in Mass. State Prison. Pardoned and discharged May, 1842. Industrious and upright, so far as known. When last heard from, was resident in A., Mass. Reference, Rev. Jared Curtis, chaplain, &c.

W., G. C. Imprisoned 2 years and 1 month in Mass. State Prison. Pardoned out Jan., 1841. When last heard from, was at N., pursuing an industrious life, so far as known. Reference, Rev. J. Curtis, chaplain, &c.

W., matron of Temporary Refuge. Reference, Misses Fellows, 446 Washington Street ; also, L. D.

W., C., merchant, representative from B. Reference, citizens of B., and Moses Grant.

W., O. B., a native of W., where he lives. Married after he left the Prison at Charlestown ; has several children ; supports his family ; sustains a good character, and always has sustained a good character since he left the Prison. Reference, Hon. John W. Lincoln.

W., N., aged 49 years, from H., Mass. Committed to the House of Correction in Worcester, Aug. 19, 1840. Discharged Oct. 24, 1840, by pardon from the overseers, under the impression that the imprisonment had had the desired effect. He signed the pledge on leaving the Prison. The jailer says he has always been faithful in keeping it, and has become a very useful man. He is a man of property, worth from 4 to $5,000. Reference, Hon. John W. Lincoln and Mr. Mathews.

W., J., of W., aged 55. Committed to House of Correction in Worcester, May 28, 1841, for intemperance. Discharged July 10, 1841, by pardon. He had been a selectman. Shortly after he was committed, the selectmen and others came forward, and were very anxious to have him discharged. The overseers refused, for cause. When he was discharged, he thanked the overseers for not discharging him before. He signed the temperance pledge when he was discharged, and common report says he has always kept it. He is a man of property, and a good citizen. Reference, Hon. John W. Lincoln and Mr. Mathews.

Y.

Y., J. Confined 7 years in Mass. State Prison. Discharged, on expiration of sentence, March, 1844. When last heard from, resided in P., Me. So far as known, an industrious and useful man. Reference, Rev. Jared Curtis, chaplain, &c.

The chaplain of the Massachusetts State Prison says,—

" It is fairly to be presumed, that very many who go from this Prison into different parts of the country, and of whom we receive no information, are doing well. The character they sustained while in Prison will warrant this conclusion.

" In regard to the foregoing list, [that part of it which relates to persons discharged from the Massachusetts Prison,] with many I have had personal acquaintance since their discharge. In respect to most of the others, I have received information from persons either personally acquainted with them, or living in their vicinity. In regard to numbers, I have heard nothing very recently, and some of them may have run into vice and crime, who for a time gave fair promise of a different course. I cannot therefore vouch for its perfect accuracy at this time." Dated March, 1845.

V. — AN ABSTRACT OF PROFESSOR MITTER-MAIER'S REVIEW ON PRISON DISCIPLINE.

TRANSLATED FROM THE GERMAN, FOR THE "LAW REPORTER," AND CONDENSED FROM THAT WORK.

An Abridgment of an Article on Penitentiary Improvement in Europe and North America, by Professor Mittermaier, of Heidelberg.

We regret that we cannot announce the views in regard to the most appropriate system of Prison discipline as yet settled. Even those who revise penal codes, or who deliberate upon them, are not clear among themselves, but propose punishments which have an entirely different signification, according as the system of *absolute isolation*,—that *heretofore* in use,—or the *Geneva* plan, is taken for a basis.

We would first make our readers acquainted with the contents of publications on Prisons, collected since 1838, and then make some deductions from them.

The most valuable intelligence comes from the English Prison inspectors, who make a report every year, in regard to their experience upon the efficacy of the laws, and offer suggestions for their improvement. The views of the inspector-general, Mr. Crawford, especially deserve attention. *Reports of the English Prison inspectors.*

In the second report, 1837, the inspectors express a preference for the *solitary* system, that of absolute isolation, by day and night, over the *silent* system, which enjoins the strictest silence upon the convicts. We consider as important the opinion of the governor of the Coldbathfields House of Correction, on the effects of the silent system introduced there since 1834. He complains of the difficulty of finding suitable sub-overseers, and of the necessity of inflicting frequent punishment for breaches of discipline. In the second part of the second report, Mr. William, the inspector-general of the northern and eastern district, declares himself in favor of the silent system, which he thinks easily administered. *Mr. Crawford in favor of isolation. Mr. William opposed to isolation.*

The third report of the general inspectors, Messrs. Crawford and Russell, for 1838, still defends the system of absolute isolation, and attempts to answer the objections made against this system, especially the hinderance to religious instruction it presents, (the refutation of which appears to us very unsatisfactory.) *Third report of the English Prison inspectors.*

The fourth report, for the year 1839, contains an accurate description of the Penitentiary of Millbank. The reports of the officers show that the stricter system has had many good effects, though much is yet left to be wished for. It appears, from the table, that they are often compelled to inflict disciplinary punishments upon prisoners. The same remark applies to convicts in other Prisons. *Fourth report of the English Prison inspectors.*

To this report is appended a very minute catalogue of all the prisoners in England, and a table of the relapsed offenders.

Juvenile Offenders.

Men, ...14,638		Boys, ...11,444	12 years old and younger, 1,039; over 12 years
Women, ... 6,237	In 1838.	Girls,......... 2,156	
Whole number, 20,875		Whole number, 13,600	and under 14, 2,075.

Mr. Hawkins opposes isolation.

Mr. Hill favors isolation.

France.
Christophe favors isolation.
Lucas opposes isolation.

Question submitted to the *conseils.*

Montalivet favors isolation.

Answers of the *conseils.*

Reports of the French travellers.

The third report, by the inspector-general on the southern and western district, Mr. Hawkins. opposes the solitary system, and shows its disadvantages. On the other hand, Mr. Hill, the inspector-general of the Scotch Prisons, declares himself in favor of the system of isolation.

In France, there also exists a great diversity of opinion on this subject. Whilst Moreau-Christophe is warmly in favor of the solitary system, the indefatigable Lucas remains true to his opinion that this system cannot be introduced as the general rule. The minister, Montalivet, issued, on the 1st of August, 1838, a circular to the prefects, containing the following questions, which were to be laid before the assembled *conseils généraux:* Whether persons accused and charged with crimes should be isolated as well by day as by night? whether this isolation should take place with convicts? to what persons should the privilege be allowed of enjoying a part of their earnings? The minister plainly indicates a preference for the Philadelphia over the Auburn system, by saying that it affords more "*chances d'intimidation et de reforme.*"

We should hesitate to lay much stress on the answers to this circular, since these are not such questions as experience can already have been collected upon in France. The result of the whole was, that 55 demanded the system of absolute isolation, 15 the Auburn system, and 15 declared themselves undecided, though many of the 55 desired at least some exceptions or modifications.

A rich collection of materials may be found in the reports of the travellers sent by the French government to examine the Prisons of various countries. Mr. Moreau-Christophe was sent to England, Scotland, Holland, Belgium, and Switzerland; Mr. Remacle, to Germany; and Mr. Cerfbeer, to Italy. It is hazardous, however, to trust travellers' accounts, since their imperfect acquaintance with the foreign language, the opportunity afforded those interested to give a wrong impression of an institution, and their own previous prejudices, all combine to deceive them, and consequently impair the credit of their reports.

Moreau-Christophe is so zealous an advocate of the system of absolute isolation, that we need not be surprised to find him, every where in his travels, setting forth the advantages of this system, and viewing with disfavor those institutions founded upon any other plan.

Holland.

Belgium.

Geneva.
Cramer-Audeoud and Adrien Picot favor isolation.
General sentiment opposes isolation.

Mr. Aubanel opposes isolation.

Lausanne.
Mr. Roud favors isolation.

Moreau-Christophe says that silence is not prescribed by law in the Prisons of Holland. Classification of prisoners is introduced every where. In regard to the Belgian Prisons, he observes that the system of classification according to the degrees of morality prevails, and laments that they have not yet reached the system of isolation. After praising the merits of the people of Geneva, he assures us that many respectable men (for instance Cramer-Audeoud and Adrien Picot) are in favor of absolute isolation, but do not dare to express it for fear of offending the general sentiment to the contrary. The author of the present article doubts this. Mr. Moreau praises Mr. Aubanel, but asserts that the pretended advantages of the silent system do not manifest themselves, because silence is not observed. The author has been twice in Geneva, and knows the institution pretty accurately, but did not observe that talking ever took place. An interesting letter from the chaplain of the Penitentiary, at Lausanne, Mr. Roud, is contained in his report, in which Mr. Roud notices the impracticability of carrying out the law of uninterrupted silence, and declares himself in favor of absolute isolation.

On German Prisons, Mr. Remacle has made a report which Germany. relates to the Prisons of Bavaria, Austria, Baden, Wurtemberg, and Nassau. When he states that the system of absolute iso- Isolation now growing into general favor. lation is growing into general favor in Germany, and that this system has already been introduced with great success into Eberbach, he is very much mistaken. The whole report is a work of too superficial observation, and innumerable corrections might be made almost everywhere throughout.

The report of Mr. Cerfbeer, on Italy, also leaves much to be Italy. wished for. Yet one dwells with interest on the Prison discipline established by Clement XI. in 1703, which is very little known, but does great honor to this pope, and breathes the spirit of Prison improvement. Here we find, in part, the system of absolute isolation. The author justly mentions a nobleman in Rome, Morichini, who is active for the improvement of Prisons.

For a knowledge of the progress made in Prison discipline, North America. it is important to consider what has been done in North America, the country where the Penitentiary system has been most perfected and extended.

The most important recent work on this subject is that of Dr. Julius. The author compares the different American sys- Dr. Julius favors isolation. tems, and declares himself distinctly in favor of the Pennsylvania system.

It is a great mistake, however, to suppose that the contest on the relative merits of the Pennsylvania and Auburn systems is by any means settled even in North America. It is true that the annual reports show that, in Pennsylvania, they praise the advantages of their system ; but the Prison Discipline Society Report of the Prison Discipline Society, Boston, opposes isolation. in Boston furnishes information calculated to raise great doubts in regard to it. In the Appendix to the Report of the Board of Managers of the Prison Discipline Society, Boston, 1838, there is found an interesting statement of Mr. Robbins, who remarks Mr. Robbins opposes isolation. that communications take place with great ease and frequency among the convicts in the Philadelphia Prison.

The *Journal des débats* of 13th February, 1840, published a Mr. Hessaut favors isolation. letter from Mr. Hessaut, the French consul in North America, in which he endeavors to refute the observations of the Boston Report to the disadvantage of the Philadelphia system.

A very spirited article is found in the North American Prof. Wayland opposes isolation. Review for July, 1839, in which the Auburn system is defended, and the Pennsylvania attacked.

A noble spirit pervades the writings of Lieber, who founds Lieber favors isolation. the Prison system on the first principles of criminal law. Mr. Lieber declares himself in favor of the Pennsylvania system.

Mr. Picot, in a letter published by Mr. Grellet-Waunny, de- Mr. Picot favors isolation. clares himself in favor of absolute isolation. These views are entirely opposed to those of Mr. Grellet, as expressed in his Mr. Grellet opposes isolation. work, *Manuel des Prisons, ou Exposition du Systéme Pénitentiare. Par Grellet-Waunny.* Tome II. Paris, 1839.

The most important work of Prison intelligence, in recent Count Petitti opposes isolation. times, is that of Count Petitti, a thoroughly scientific man. The author declares the system of Geneva, notwithstanding some of its defects, the best in Europe. Mr. Eaudi, who has Mr. Eaudi opposes isolation. been appointed by the King of Sardinia superintendent of the institution in Alexandria, has studied prisons on his travels. The author declares himself, in cases of many years' confinement, for the system by which the prisoners are isolated by night, and enjoined to silence during labor and rest. In regard to the Penitentiaries for great criminals, the author thinks the desideratum to be a reasonable severity, which is as far removed from the delusions of a mistaken philanthropy, as from a brutal ferocity, and which seeks to attain the aim of improvement, by moral and religious instruction.

France.

Turning to the progress of opinion in France, we find we can not count on the ascendency of any fixed system in that country. Foucher declares himself in favor of the Pennsylvania system, and Liancourt opposes it. Mr. Moreau-Christophe is its eloquent advocate ; Mr. Lucas is its known foe. Moreau's book has met, even in France, with many refutations — for example, by Cariere, in the *Gazette Medicale*, 1840 ; although in the same Gazette, Mr. G. Baillarger comes out on the same side.

Foucher favors isolation Liancourt opposes isolation.

Cariere opposes isolation.

Project of a law.

General attention, more than to any other publication, is due to the project of a law, laid before the French Chamber of Deputies in 1840. The government, however, announces that it cannot yet make a decision in preference either of absolute or relative isolation.

Government is undecided on isolation.

The duty of making the report on the proposed law, in the Chamber of Deputies, fell upon De Tocqueville. The commission, with whom Beaumont also was associated, go deeper into the subject than the government, in its preliminary statement of motives. The majority of the commission are in favor of absolute isolation ; yet, as the report states, not with the needless severity of Pennsylvania, and they acknowledge the difficulty of enforcing it. They wish to separate the prisoner from other criminals, but not to consign him to utter solitude. The commission is for applying solitary imprisonment for twelve years to those sentenced for long terms, and after that time the Geneva system.

Majority of the commission in favor of isolation.

Belgium.

Turning now to Belgium, to observe the progress of the Penitentiary system there, it appears that the exertions of the Belgian government have had for their object to introduce isolation by night, silence, classification of the prisoners, the system of private earnings, and the chance of shortening punishment by good behavior.

The government opposes isolation.

Holland.

There exists in Holland an estimable society for the moral improvement of prisoners. This Society, among whose most zealous members are M. Mollet and Suringer, felt the necessity of making suggestions to the government for improving the Prisons. Mr. Mollet asserts the necessity of introducing isolation by night, and abolishing infamizing punishments.

Mr. Mollet opposes isolation.

Recent publications : England.

The following are the more recent publications which have appeared on this subject. In England a fifth report of the Prison inspectors, 1840 ; a report relating to Parkhurst Prison ; and a highly important collection of regulations for English Prisons.

France.

In France, the chambers, unfortunately, have not yet found time to consider the proposed law on Prisons ; so that the matter in the mean time can only be helped out by ordinances of the ministry.

Belgium. Mr. Vishers favors isolation.

Mr. Vishers, in Belgium, declares himself unconditionally in favor of the system of absolute isolation.

One dwells also with particular pleasure upon the publication in which the illustrious heir to the throne of a great kingdom pronounces his opinion that every improvement in penal legislation is of no avail unless the improvement of Prisons is undertaken with energy. " *Ueber Strafe und Strafanstalten von Sr.*

K. Hoheit Oskar Kronprinzen von Schweden. Aus den Schwedischen übers. von Treskow mit Vorrede von Julius. Leipzig, 1841." The author is in favor of the Philadelphia system, but declares that since experience has not yet shown with certainty how far the solitary system may be applied without injury to health beyond the space of six years, the Philadelphia system must be resorted to only with criminals condemned to the three lowest degrees of punishment.

The latest penal codes in Geneva deserve attention, since none of them have adopted absolute isolation as a basis. Geneva.

The fact that, in Prussia, his majesty has engaged Dr. Julius to assist in drawing up the plan for reforming the Prisons, leaves us to infer that absolute isolation has found friends there. Mr. Von Harnier, a man of high merits, in Frankfort, has published a comparison between the Philadelphia and Auburn systems, in which the former is preferred. In an important report furnished in the name of a committee, January 19, 1841, the physician, privy counsellor Stiebel, in Frankfort, declares himself for the European or Geneva system. Prussia.
Von Harnier favors isolation.
Stiebel opposes isolation.

In the dukedoms of Sleswick and Holstein, the court preacher Lubkert, declares himself in favor of the Pennsylvania system. Falk, in his Political Magazine, declares himself also of the same opinion. But the high counsellor, Schirack, strongly recommends the introduction of the Geneva system into Holstein. Sleswick and Holstein.
Lubkert favors isolation, and Falk also.
Schirack opposes isolation.

If we draw conclusions from the previously expressed opinions and suggestions, it appears to be a general conviction that the Prison discipline, as heretofore existing, is good for nothing, and demands reform. But upon the point how this should be brought about, we seek in vain for an equally settled opinion. The writers who contend about the choice of systems put the question upon too narrow a basis, as they speak only of the Philadelphia and Auburn systems, and pay no regard to the existence of a *third*, which we have called the " European."

Under the circumstances, only one thing seems clear to us,—that the movement towards the decision of the question, whether *absolute* isolation shall be made the basis for all punishment, during the whole time, is not yet so ripe, that an impartial and practically educated statesman, who is occupied with penal legislation, would venture to answer it in the affirmative ; but that the undoubtedly established superiority of absolute isolation demands an application of the same in proper connection with the system of isolation by night.

Against the adoption of absolute isolation, when unconditionally applied to all punishments of imprisonment, after a conscientious examination, and careful consultation with Prison directors and physicians, we think the following reasons may be urged : —

1st. The infinite diversity of human nature, and the danger of producing serious injuries by making this isolation the unexceptionable rule, demand of the legislator not to make use of the *harshest* measure as the *regular* one.

2d. All intelligent advocates of absolute isolation presuppose that this solitude is properly managed by the uninterrupted attentions of the appointed overseers, and is broken in upon by the visits of clergymen, physicians, and directors. But just here lies the self-deception and danger of the system.

3d. There is no doubt that absolute isolation, for a length of time, may have a very injurious effect upon the prisoner.

4th. It is admitted that the fundamental condition of the efficacy of the Penitentiary system, is a proper religious influence. This requires especially, besides the visits of clergymen, and a religious instruction, exercises of divine worship, which, if properly conducted, may produce an elevating and improving influence on the minds of the prisoners. Absolute isolation steps in to prevent this.

5th. Absolute isolation, as Count Petitti has justly shown in his work, gives rise to hypocrisy far more than any other system.

6th. The favorable experience obtained in relation to Houses of Reformation for Juvenile Offenders, in Hamburg, Mettray, and Parkhurst, speaks also against the solitary system.

If now, finally, men of practical experience doubt whether the object can ever be attained of preventing prisoners from becoming acquainted with each other ; if experience teaches that prisoners may advantageously live together, under control, in small divisions, and that the apprehensions that silence would not be kept by them, and that they could concert their plans together, are unfounded ; if the advocates of the Pennsylvania system (who have the brief experience of foreign countries in their favor) must allow that isolation of long duration may become injurious to the body and mind of the prisoners ; and if, as we see, they are not agreed among themselves how long isolation may be applied without injury, — it must be granted that it is not yet time to make a system, that works well only under certain limitations, the absolute rule. Only a mixed system, which recognizes isolation at night, and common working together of the prisoners in small divisions, under the injunction of silence, as the general rule, answers actual wants.

Note. By *isolation*, in the magin, *absolute* isolation is always meant.

VI.— STATE PRISON IN MAINE.

Annual Report of the Inspectors of the Maine State Prison. Twenty-fifth Legislature. Senate Document, No. 3. Octavo ; pages 28.

The inspectors of the Maine State Prison say,—

" During the last year, the operations of the several departments have been carried on to advantage." " They have no hesitation in stating that its financial situation is as good, or better, than it has been at any former period."

" The amount of money received from the state treasury, during the year, is $8,692 50. Of this sum $5,000 were appropriated for the new Prison, $400 for purchase of fire-engine, and the balance is the amount of officers' salaries, for the three first quarters."

" The inspectors are of the opinion that no appropriation from the treasury will be necessary, for the ordinary expenses of the Prison."

In regard to the new Prison, the inspectors say,—

" In their almost daily inspection, as the work progressed, they have had an opportunity of seeing the character of the work and materials, and have no hesitation in expressing their opinion that it has been done in a faithful, permanent, and workmanlike manner." " The whole expense has fallen below the estimate made by the warden and inspectors, before commencing the work."

" It must be as cheering to the philanthropist to hear, as it is to the inspectors to announce, the fact that Maine has now a Prison that is not a disgrace to her ; one that is second to none in the country for convenience, comfort, and security."

The cells are neat, easily warmed, ventilated, and inspected ; and while perfectly secure, the doors are so constructed as to admit a sufficient degree of light. The inspectors, in their report of 1842, expressed the opinion that the quantity of granite in the old cells was sufficient for the construction of the new ones. This has been found to be the case, and there are still remaining 22 old cells. Some 6 or 8 of them should be kept for punishment cells, and the materials of the remainder might be used to good advantage for the construction of a new hospital, which is much needed, as the old one is wholly unfit for that purpose, being damp, dark, poorly ventilated, and difficult of entrance. When the legislature sees fit to authorize this alteration, the present hospital may be used for a cook-room to good advantage, as it is very nearly connected with the new Prison."

" In removing the materials of the old cells, to be used in the construction of the new ones, many of the convicts were necessarily crowded together, in the old cells and hospital. This gave them a good opportunity to lay plans and concoct mischief, and this they did not fail to do ; for, on several occasions, they were found to be almost in a state of open mutiny, and it required great vigilance and circumspection, on the part of the warden and subordinate officers, to detect them in their well-matured plans for escape. During the summer, two successful efforts were made by four of the convicts to escape. One of them was immediately retaken ; the others soon after, and a reward paid by the warden for their apprehension. It is but justice to the officers and guard to remark, that these escapes were not owing to any neglect on their part, but were effected wholly by reason of the operations connected with the remodelling of the Prison."

" Since the removal of the convicts into the new cells, their behavior has been good. They now dread solitary confinement, as it is inflicted by removing from the new cells and placing them in old ones, which they soon find, by the contrast, to be a terror to evil-doers. And it requires but a very short confinement in those dark, damp dungeons, to bring even the most refractory to good behavior."

" This work of reform would probably long since have been accomplished, had the legislature and the people properly understood the situation of convicts, while confined in the old cells. As the Prison has been a constant bill of expense to the state, but little interest appeared to be felt on the subject, and the reports of wardens and inspectors, for many years, seemed to be nearly unheeded."

" In the winter of 1842, the inspectors, with the warden, feeling the importance of reconstructing the Prison, not only as it regarded the situation of the convicts, but also in a pecuniary point of view, visited the legislature, and presented the whole subject to them through their committee."

" This committee entered into this matter with a laudable zeal, and introduced an order authorizing them to visit and examine the Prison. This order passed the house, and the committee, upon examination, found that not only the dictates of humanity, but the interests of the state, required an immediate and complete alteration, and recommended that an appropriation be made for that purpose."

" And now the building having been completed, the inspectors would respectfully suggest the propriety of authorizing the committee on the State Prison to visit it, in order, more fully and particularly than they have done, to inform the legislature of the manner in which the money has been expended."

" The inspectors take pleasure in recording their entire satisfaction with the manner in which the warden has performed, not only the ordinary duties of his office, but the increased and responsible duties under the resolve of the last legislature. While these additional duties have required his constant attention, his situation has been rendered much more responsible, and even dangerous, on account of the crowded situation of the convicts, during the season, which made it absolutely necessary for him to be constantly on the watch, both day and night, in order to prevent them from breaking into open mutiny. Yet, with all this increased care, he has kept all the departments of the Prison in a prosperous condition, and erected the new building at a much less expense than had been estimated, even by its warmest friends."

The warden makes his report for the year ending December 31, 1844. The number of convicts was 75. Employed as blacksmiths, 6 ; shoemakers, 33 ; cooks, 2 ; washer, 1 ; lumpers, 3 ; wheelwrights, 8 ; tailors, 6 ; lime quarry, 9 ; hospital, 5 ; waiters, 2 ; total, 75.

There was an increase of 12 convicts during the last year. The number decreased till 1841, but since that time it has increased ; the laws having been revised, so that none are now sent for a less term than one year. The warden considers this a good law, as he is now enabled to teach each one a trade. He says,—

" When they enter the Prison, they wish to be put to a trade.

" The prisoners are generally industrious and peaceable, although, situated as they were the last summer, they caused me much trouble and anxiety. While taking away the western wing of the old Prison, which constituted a part of the Prison wall, frequent plots were made by them to escape, and some of them were successful. It occupied about two months, the convicts in the mean time being crowded together, 2 in each cell, and more than 20 in the hospital, which gave them a good opportunity to plot mischief ; and it is believed they were not idle while thus situated. It is dangerous to allow more than one convict in a cell, although it could not be avoided in this case."

" The new Prison is now completed, agreeably to the directions of the legislature ; containing 108 cells, built of split granite. The building is 3 stories high, with 36 cells in each story, 2 abreast, with a longitudinal wall of bricks forming the backs of the cells. Each cell has a ventilator, carried up separately through the wall, and which empties itself into a granite trough, which passes the whole length of the building. On this trough are placed 2 chimneys, which carry off all the bad air from the cells. The cells are 7 feet long, 7 feet high, and 4 feet wide, in the clear. Each cell contains an iron bedstead, the frame of which is made of one-inch round iron, and filled with narrow hoop iron. When the convict is not in bed, this is turned up and fastened.

" The cells are made of split granite, one foot thick, dowelled together with iron bolts and clamps of iron, drilled into the front stone, and also into the partition stones. Over the doors is placed a walk of split granite, 3 feet wide and 6 inches thick, one foot of which is laid in the walls of the cells ; the wall of the cells, being laid upon this walk, holds it from canting. The same is done to both stories. At the edge of these walks are placed large round iron posts, 10 feet apart, into which holes are drilled and a screw cut, so that eyebolts are screwed in, which receive the railing, made of one-inch round iron, running the whole length of 90 feet of cells. The cell door is made of an iron frame ; the back part, near the hook or hinge, is 1½ inch square ; the front and two ends are 1½ by ⅝ inch ; and in the centre are two cross bars of 1½ by ⅝ inch. These middle cross bars are drilled with inch holes, through which pass 7 bars of inch round iron, and also pass through both end bars with the holes on the outer side, countersunk and riveted firmly. Two large bars for hinges, at equal distances from the cross bars, bolted to the large bar, and also to each bar, as it passes across the door, and are riveted to the front bar. A plate of iron, 6 inches wide, is bolted to the cross bars, to which is affixed a large lock, which locks the door in the centre. Over the doors passes a large bar of iron in a horizontal direction, which moves on rollers. This bar, at a single move of 4 inches, locks all the doors of one division of eighteen cells ; therefore each door is locked twice, and the convicts made perfectly secure. These doors are so open as to admit plenty of light and heat."

" The area between the outer prison and cells is 11 feet wide and 25 feet high, well lighted by large windows. The windows move on pulleys and weights, so that each morning the prison is aired by dropping the windows, which drives the bad air up the flues of the cells and leaves the Prison pure and clear. The whole inside of the outer Prison is plastered with three coats of lime mortar, and all the cells, both inside and outside, are well white-washed. The floor in the area is also made of split granite and whitewashed. The windows have green blinds on the inside, for the protection of the night watch. The doors, railing, &c., are painted black. The cells are warmed by four box-stoves placed in the area."

" The new Prison, as completed, has cost $13,177 44."

The warden recommends the construction of a hospital, as proposed by the directors.

" All that the Prison has drawn from the treasury is $7,000. The balance has been paid by the Prison, viz., $6,292 58, besides carrying on the operations of the Prison as usual."

" We are now nearly out of debt; stand $1,957 48 better than at the close of the last year ; and it is confidently believed that, in this Prison, for the year to come, it will not be necessary to ask for an appropriation for any thing, salaries of officers included."

" We now have as good a prison as is in the Union, and one that will not cause the officers to blush for shame while they are conducting visitors through it."

" The warden, with the advice of the inspectors, entered into contract, in August last, with Samuel Bigelow, of Boston, for a portion of the convicts to work at shoemaking, for 40 cents per day for the labor of each convict acquainted with that kind of work, and 30 cents per day each, for the first three months, for new hands, both parties agreeing."

" All the departments of the Prison are now in a prosperous condition."

" There has been received from the treasury of the state, during the last year, $8,692 50 in all, for the two appropriations and officers' salaries. The Prison has due in demands, over and above outstanding demands, $6,190 40. The Prison has more than paid its expenses by $1,900, after allowing the amount paid out for the new Prison or building and repairs, which is considered as property of the state."

The following is a schedule of expenses and earnings, as sworn to by Benjamin Carr, warden, before George A. Starr, justice of the peace, January 8, 1845, and examined and compared with vouchers, and found correct, by John Merrill, George A. Starr, and Benjamin F. Buxton, inspectors, at Lincoln, Maine, January 8, 1845 : —

December 31, 1843.

			By amount of stock and		
Amount of stock and tools on hand,	12,821	97	tools,	13,222	30
Cash paid convicts discharged,	373	32	Received of visitors,	81	72
Teams,	758	73	Received of convicts admitted into prison,	10	33
Officers' salaries, excepting warden's,	4,282	44	Received and charged for team,	860	41
Blacksmithing,	1,585	94	Blacksmithing,	4,675	37
Shoemaking,	1,436	80	Fuel and lights,	39	21
Wheelwrights,	2,021	40	Received for sundry articles charged to expense account,	42	04
Lime quarry,	772	23			
Fuel and lights,	433	60			
Transporting convicts, fire engine, and sundry incidental expenses,	1,693	96	Received and charged for lime quarry,	1,808	12
Building and repairs,	7,587	40	Shoemaking,	5,085	80
Subsistence,	2,481	80	Building and repairs,	228	68
Clothing,	755	45	Wheelwrights,	3,401	72
			Subsistence,	514	56
			Clothing,	301	25
			Officers' salaries,	159	81
			Balance,	6,573	72
	$37,005	04		$37,005	04

The chaplain of the Prison, the Reverend Job Washburn, after a grateful acknowledgment of Providence, says, —

"We have had two religious services on the Sabbath, one commencing at 8 o'clock, A. M., the other at 3 o'clock, P. M. The Sabbath school is in connection with the afternoon service, and has consisted of four classes; two are Bible classes, the other two are instructed from the spelling-book. Of those who form the classes, most of them appear much interested.

"Although some of the convicts appear totally regardless of the claims of their Maker, and insensible to the worth of their souls, yet I am happy to say that such appearances are not general, for the largest part of them are attentive to the word preached, and not unfrequently give proof of deep inward emotions.

"With all my discouragements, I cannot but indulge the hope that the word preached, and personal advice and counsel given them, together with my visits to the sick, have not only been received with ardent tokens of esteem and gratitude, but that (in some cases, at least) lasting good to the undying soul will be the result."

The chaplain recommends that some addition be made to the Prison library. He adds, —

"I take great pleasure in being able to say, that the new Prison cannot fail to meet the wishes and desires of a humane and feeling community. This spacious building reflects honor on our state, and much credit is due to those who have had the management of its construction. Those who have friends here confined, and all who have not visited the Prison, may rest assured that it is every thing—for *light, warmth, neatness,* and *comfort*—that a Prison possibly could be."

"With compassion for the unfortunates placed under me, as their spiritual guide, relying on the power and goodness of a merciful God to give success to my feeble efforts, and requesting an interest in the prayers of the godly, that I may so discharge my duties as to savingly benefit souls, and meet the approval of my God and judge."

"Thomaston, *January,* 1845."

The annual report from the Maine Prison, for January, 1845, contains no report from the physician of the Prison. We have looked it over, again and again, for the physician's report, but find none. We learn from the tables that there has been one death, and that there were five in the hospital, at a given time. We think the physician's report is an essential and important part of an annual report from a State Prison ; and not the less important if all are so well that sickness and death have not been known within the walls during the year.

From the tables it appears that the number of convicts in Prison, December 31, 1843, was 63 ; received during the year, 44 ; total, 107. Discharged on expiration of sentence, 26 ; pardoned, 5 ; died, 1 ; total, 32. Remaining, December 1, 1844, 75. Whole number received from the first, 852. Discharged on expiration of sentence, 616 ; died, 24 ; pardoned, 130 ; escaped, and not retaken, 7 ; remaining, 75 ; total, 852. Crimes of 75 in Prison, December 31, 1844 : arson, 5 ; larceny, 46 ; burglary, 3 ; adultery, 5 ; forgery, 3 ; assault with intent to kill, 1 ; assault with intent to ravish, 1 ; passing counterfeit money, 7 ; perjury, 1 ; murder, sentence commuted, 1 ; murder, awaiting sentence of death, 1 ; cheating, 1 ; total, 75. Age of 75, when committed : from 10 to 20, 11 ; from 20 to 30, 35 ; from 30 to 40, 21 ; from 40 to 50, 4 ; from 50 to 60, 3 ; from 60 to 70, 1 ; total 75. Terms of sentence : life, 6 ; 15 years, 1 ; 12 years, 1 ; 10 years, 2 ; 7 years, 1 ; 6 years, 2 ; 5 years, 8 ; 4 years, 11 ; 3 years, 7 ; 2 years, 13 ; 1 year and 6 months, 6 ; 1 year and 3 months, 4 ; 1 year, 12 ; sentenced to be hanged, 1 ; total, 75.

Officers, 12 ; namely, warden, deputy warden, clerk ; overseers, 9 ; total, 12.

Employed in the quarry, 9 ; smithshop, 6 ; shoemakers, 33 ; wheelwrights, 8 ; tailors, 6 ; cooks, 2 ; washer, 1 ; waiters, 2 ; lumpers, 3 ; sick in the hospital, 5 ; total, 75.

VII.—STATE PRISON IN NEW HAMPSHIRE.

Letter from the Chaplain to S. E. Coues, Esq.

"CONCORD, *March* 31, 1845.

" Dear Sir,

" Yours of the 25th inst. was duly received, and, so far as I have it in my power, I cheerfully give the desired information.

" The whole number of convicts discharged during the last two years is as follows : —

"Discharged by expiration of sentence, 23; by executive pardon, 21; total, 44.

"Discharged by reversal of judgment in the Superior Court, 1.

"Died of fever, 2; of consumption, 1; total deaths, 3.

"Of the 44 discharged within two years, a majority are sober, industrious men, and wholesome members of community.

"W. S. B., who was sentenced for life, for the crime of arson, and who was pardoned last November, has settled in the town of W., and is an industrious blacksmith. Formerly he was very intemperate; but no disposition to relapse has been manifested since he left the Prison.

"L. T., convicted of forgery, pardoned, and residing in the same town, is now a sober, industrious man, and gives evidence of having been reformed while in Prison.

"F. A. D. and J. D., convicted of larceny, and pardoned, are now supporting their familes and doing well.

"G. B., formerly a very intemperate man, and convicted of barn-burning, now resides with his friends, in A., N. H., a sober man, evidently reformed during his Prison life.

"J. H., convicted of burglary, and sentenced for life, but recently pardoned, is industriously engaged in the machine shop at M., N. H., a safe and useful member of community.

"O. C., a young man confined for larceny, but pardoned during the last winter, is now at school in W., N. H., where he holds a respectable standing as a young man of promise.

"I am fully confident the course pursued in the Prison has had a favorable influence on the prisoner, after leaving his confinement to mingle with society. Each convict is furnished with a weekly temperance paper, as well as some religious paper, or other periodical, together with some useful and interesting book from the library. This not only occupies the mind, in the solitude of the cell, but produces a taste for reading which continues when he leaves his gloomy abode. And the work of imparting instruction to a portion of the more uninformed, in the first rudiments of education, has also a very happy influence in softening the disposition, while here, as well as in producing a desire for further information, after the termination of their sentence. And some of the young men have assured me, that their first object should be, after obtaining a supply of clothing and a little money, to spend a portion of time at some public school.

"My dear sir, there is a 'luxury in doing good' to these unfortunate men, that cannot be described.

"I am, with respect,

"Yours truly,

"JOHN ATWOOD.

"P. S. I am happy to hear that young W. is doing well. There seemed to be a change in his conduct, much for the better, ever after his sickness in November. I think he went out with a determination to pursue a consistent course hereafter. J. A."

VIII.— STATE PRISON IN VERMONT.

Report of the Superintendent, Directors, Physician, and Chaplain, of the Vermont State Prison, for the Year 1844. *—Octavo, pages* 12.

The warden says the number of convicts at the commencement of the year was 65
Received during the year, ... 30
Discharged by expiration of sentence, 16 ; by governor, 11 ; by death, 1 ; total, ... 28
Leaving in confinement, September 1, 1844, ... 67
The convicts are employed—as shoemakers, 36 ; curriers, 2 ; wood-work of carriage-shop, 8 ; blacksmiths, 3 ; painter, trimmer, cooper, basket-maker, tailor, 1 each ; gun-shop, 1 ; cook-room, 2 ; washer, 1 ; yard waiter, 1 ; Prison waiter, 1 ; lumpers, 4 ; seamstress, 1 ; invalid, blind, 1 ; in solitary confinement, sentence of death, 1 ; total, . . 67
First sentence, 51 ; second sentence, 9 ; third sentence, 4 ; fourth sentence, 3, ... 67
Between 15 and 20 years of age, 7 ; between 20 and 30, 29 ; between 30 and 40, 17 ; between 40 and 50, 6 ; between 50 and 60, 7 ; between 70 and 80, 1, ... 67
White males, 63 ; white females, 1 ; black men, 3, . . . 67
Sentenced before 1841, 6 ; in 1841, 8 ; in 1842, 15 ; in 1843, 14 ; in 1844, 24, ... 67
From Vermont, 31 ; from Mass., 8 ; from New York, 3 ; from New Hampshire, 4, ... 46
Nativity :—Brought up in Vermont, Massachusetts, New York, New Hampshire, and Connecticut, 49 ; Georgia, 1 ; South Carolina, 1 ; total from the United States, 51. From England, 4 ; from Canada, 7 ; Ireland, 4 ; France, 1 ; total foreigners, 16, ... 67
For rape, 2 ; murder, 2 ; horse-stealing, 5 ; assault to kill, 2 ; burglary, 8 ; arson, 2 ; manslaughter, 2 ; receiving stolen goods, 1 ; forgery, 6 ; theft, 13 ; counterfeiting, 5 ; adultery, 3 ; stealing, 3 ; larceny, 8 ; obtaining goods by false pretences, 2 ; incest, 1 ; polygamy, 2, ... 67

Average length of sentence, 4 years, 3 months and 15 days.
Expenses above income, $900 less than last year.
Balance of expenditure over income, $1,867 15.
The warden says this balance against the institution is not

half as large as its annual average cost to the state from the first. The business of the carriage-shop has been most profitable ; but few men can be employed in it.

The discipline, the warden says, is energetic and prompt, avoiding every thing like cruelty. The warden adds,—

" By endeavoring to secure conformity to the rules, by appeals to the reason and judgment rather than by force, punishments have been rendered very seldom necessary."

" Aided by the other officers of the Prison, the warden has endeavored to give such instruction to the convicts as may be useful to them after leaving the Prison. In this he has made use of appr priate books. The influence has been very salutary. There is some reason to hope that some of them may, in consequence, be led to live a better life and become useful citizens."

The warden says,—

" The health of the convicts through the year has generally been good. In the fall and early part of winter, we had several cases of erysipelas, then a prevailing epidemic in this region. Since that time, there have been no cases of protracted disease ; the only death, that of Charles Ball, of influenza. His sentence was for life, for manslaughter. He had been an inmate of the Prison more than 21 years."

The warden calls the attention of the legislature to the importance of making suitable provision for a class of convicts like Clifford, now in solitary confinement, under sentence of death for murder, waiting the action of the executive. He says they have no suitable provision for this class, and, if they are to be sent to the State Prison, and to remain there, they ought to have provided for them suitable apartments, disconnected with the cells for other prisoners.

The directors make a brief report concerning the pecuniary affairs of the Prison, in which the only statement of general interest relates to the excess of expenditures above earnings, $1,867 15. The expenditures include salary of officers, and, if we understand the accounts, all other expenses.

There are four papers accompanying the directors' report, marked A, B, C, D, giving very full, clear, and simple statements of the financial affairs of the Prison, the substance of which is comprehended in the paper marked D.

The expenditures and income for the year ending Sept. 1, 1843, were as follows :—

Expenditures.		*Income.*	
Provisions,	$1,658 44	From carriage-shop,	$1,970 14
Clothing and bedding,	540 07	" shoe-shop,	2,802 69
Repairs,	187 70	" admittance fees,	99 50
Fuel and lights,	699 03	" gun-shop,	43 97
Prison department,	589 48	" contract account,	120 34
Medical account,	38 89	" balance, being loss,	1,867 15
Expense account,	3,190 18		
	$6,903 79		$6,903 79

The physician's report is very brief, as follows :—

" The physician of this institution, in reporting upon its medical affairs, would mention as a prominent thing, the construction of a new hospital room, and one which now meets the wants of the establishment.

" The want of a convenient and safe place to put the sick has long been felt; but we may now, I think, give them as good accommodations as are obtained in many hospitals disconnected with a Penitentiary.

" Within the last year, a single death has occurred amongst the convicts ; and that one was Ball, under sentence of confinement for life. He died of influenza, early in the winter. About the same time a few cases of endemic erysipelas occurred ; but since that time, we have had nothing but common cases of disease. There are no invalids that need any particular notice from me at this time.

" Respectfully submitted, by

" ED. E. PHELPS, M. D."

The chaplain's report is also brief, less than two pages : —

" His labors commenced the first of December, A. D. 1843. Since that time," he says, " I have attended prayers with the convicts at the close of each day, (with few exceptions,) and performed the religious services common in our churches, on the Sabbath. I have also visited them from time to time, at their cells, and elsewhere, in sickness and in health, as occasion has required ; and it is but just to say, that in all my intercourse with them, in public and in private, I have witnessed no indication of disrespect, nor have I been treated rudely, but in a single instance, in the case of Clifford, and he, perhaps, ought to be excused on the ground of insanity.

" At the commencement of my duties as chaplain, I announced to the convicts my wish to have them feel a perfect freedom in communicating to me their views on religious subjects, and presenting their difficulties in private.

" I am happy in being able here to add, that many have availed themselves of the privilege thus afforded them, with much pleasure to me, and in most cases with apparent satisfaction to themselves.

" The afternoon of the day of our Annual Fast was devoted to conference on the subject of temperance. A number spoke with much feeling in regard to their present degradation as connected with intemperance, and I should think, two thirds of the whole number of convicts gave their names to the pledge of total abstinence from all intoxicating drinks. Many of them, I hope, have strength of mind sufficient to carry out their resolution.

" I am happy to say that every facility which could have reasonably been expected, to make my labors pleasant and profitable, has been rendered by the superintendent and keepers.

" For the result of these labors we must look, as you are aware, to the future. There are so many motives for being religious here, that we dare not speak with much confidence concerning those who talk religiously. But the effects of keeping moral and religious truth constantly before the mind can scarcely fail of imposing a restraint which will be salutary in subsequent life.

" Many things have occurred, in connection with my labors at the Prison, which are deeply interesting to myself ; but as others cannot be expected to enter into them with the same interest, I will not impose a task by relating them here." [Mr. Kidder need not have limited his communication on these matters of interest and experience.]

" The place where we assemble for worship is not the most agreeable. It has all the gloom and dread appearance of a Prison, and for the purpose of confinement, it is well ; but when we meet to worship God, it is desirable that the place where we assemble should present a more cheerful aspect. And I would respectfully submit the question, whether a room better suited to the purposes of religious worship may not be fitted up as soon as it may be convenient.

"THOMAS KIDDER, *Chaplain.*

" WINDSOR, *September* 20, 1844."

IX.—STATE PRISON IN MASSACHUSETTS.

Documents relative to the State Prison at Charlestown, Massachusetts, (octavo, pages 27,) *containing Reports of Inspectors, Warden, Physician, and Chaplain.*

The inspectors say,—

" The different departments of labor have been diligently and successfully pursued, and the goverment will be glad to know that something beyond the current expenses of the year has been realized."

" An event which we consider one of the most interesting in the history of the Prison, during the last year, is the removal of a number of insane convicts from the solitary cells (where, from the nature of their disease and consequent incapacity to labor, they were, without imputing any fault to any one, in a great measure passed unheeded by) to those humane and invaluable institutions for the insane, which have so long blessed this commonwealth, and promise to bestow on the people the richest blessings in future."

" It is a fact now generally understood, and one which the public regard with increased interest, that the stern rules and punitive discipline of a Penitentiary, though necessary for the government of its inmates, have no curative virtues for the unhappy convict bereft of his reason ; and we cannot but hope that the feelings and views which we entertain on this important change in the treatment of insane convicts, so intimately as it is connected with the welfare of many of our fellow-men, will be approved and practised upon in every Prison in the land."

" Another subject, to which the inspectors feel it their duty to allude, is the harmony, the good order, and mild, but efficient discipline, which prevail at the present time among the convicts. No flagrant act of insubordination, or outbreak of violence, has been witnessed in the Prison for a long time."

" The doctrine, which has heretofore been so generally denied, and denounced by many as impracticable and visionary, that the inmates of a Prison can be kept in subjection without resort to corporeal punishment, is now, with few exceptions. fully established by the sure test of experience. That stern, stately, and soldier-like deportment, which is nowhere necessary to the maintenance of good government, and can never secure a steady and willing obedience to its requirements, (though sometimes assumed, apparently, from no higher motive than a display of power,) should never be seen within the walls of a Prison."

" It is a principle very generally, if not always true, that that obedience which is rendered to the law, or to those in authority, not willingly but through fear of punishment, has in itself the very element of rebellion, and waits only for an opportunity to throw off restraint."

These extracts are from the report of the directors, Bradford Sumner, Esq., Samuel Greele, Esq., and Abraham F. Howe, Esq.

The warden reports to the governor and council,—

Whole number of convicts remaining in Prison, October 1, 1843, ... 265
Whole number received during the year ending September 30, 1844, ... 105
Discharged during the year ending September 30, 1844, 65; by pardon, 1; by remission of sentence, 14; by order of court, 4; sent to the State Lunatic Hospital at Worcester, by decision of commissioners on insane convicts, 7; escaped, 1; died, 2, ... 94
Remaining in Prison, September 30, 1844, ... 276

Age of those in prison : from 15 to 20 years, 21; from 20 to 30 years, 117; from 30 to 40 years, 79; from 40 to 50 years, 37; from 50 to 60 years, 17; from 60 to 70 years, 5; total, 276.

Crimes of 276 in prison : larceny, 96; common and notorious thief, 19; burglary, 1st degree, 12; burglary, 2d degree, 10; murder, 4; assault with intent to murder, 3; manslaughter, 2; assault with intent to kill, 1; felonious assault, 2; highway robbery, 1st degree, 1; highway robbery, 2; assault with intent to rape, 10; arson, 1st degree, 4; arson, 2d degree, 3; forgery and larceny, 1; entering a shop and dwelling-house in the night-time with felonious intent, 1; breaking and entering a dwelling-douse, and stealing therefrom, 1; kidnapping, 1; lewd and lascivious cohabitation, 2; counterfeiting, 1; shop-breaking, 3; malicious burning, 2; incest, 2; shop-breaking and larceny, 13; stealing 10; cheating by false pretences, 2; bigamy, 1; breaking and entering a bank, and burglary, 1; maliciously setting fire to a manufactory, which was destroyed with its contents, 1; burglary and larceny, 6; attempting to pass counterfeit money, 1; burning a barn, 1; burning a barn in the night-time, 1; forgery, 4; having in possession counterfeit bank bills, with intent to pass the same, 6; receiving stolen goods, 2; breaking and entering a dwelling-house in the night-time, 1; subornation of perjury, 1; having a die or mould for counterfeiting coin, 1; assault with intent to rob, 6; having in possession ten or more pieces of counterfeit coin, 2; robbery, 5; felonious assault on a female child, 1; perjury, 2; cheating, 1; breaking and entering a dwelling-house, 2; breaking and entering a shop in the Prison, 1; adultery, 1; stealing from a dwelling-house, 2; stealing in a shop, 1; breaking and entering a dwelling-house in the night-time, and stealing therefrom, 1; stealing from a dwelling-house in the night-time, 2; gross lewdness, 1; breaking and entering a vessel in the night time, 2; burning a dwelling-house, 1; maliciously removing a rail from a railroad, 2; breaking and entering a shop, 1; stealing from the person, 3; breaking and entering a shop with intent to commit a larceny, 1; assault and robbery, 1; total, 276.

Average length of sentence of all in Prison, 5 years, 9 months and 26 days.

The prisoners were, natives of Massachusetts, 105; Maine, 18; New Hampshire, 20; Vermont, 14; Connecticut, 12; Rhode Island, 4; New York, 18; New Jersey, 4; Pennsylvania, 7; Maryland, 2; Virginia, 1; Ohio, 3; Kentucky, 1; North Carolina, 2; Missouri, 1; Louisiana, 1; Georgia, 1; England, 16; Ireland, 27; Scotland, 4; Canada, 2; France, 2; Malta, 1; Germany, 3; Nova Scotia, 3; Isle of Bourbon, 1; Cape de Verd, 1; Sweden, 1; Malaga, 1; total, 276.

Employment: stone-cutters, 56; carpenter, 1; tool-grinders, 4; team-hands, 9; blacksmiths, 16; whitesmiths, 6; tinworkers, 6; cabinetmakers and upholsterers. 57; brushmakers, 23; coopers, 8; hatters, 7; shoemakers, 29; tailors, 3; employed in the cookery, 14; barbers, 2; sweepers, 3; woodsawyers and lumpers, 5; waiters and messengers, 3; invalids, 4; attendants in hospital, 2; patients in hospital, 15; carpenters repairing the Prison, 3; total, 276.

Nativity of those received last year: Massachusetts, 33; Maine, 8; New Hampshire, 10; Vermont, 5; Connecticut, 5; New York, 9; New Jersey, 1; Pennsylvania, 4; North Carolina, 1; Ohio, 2; Rhode Island, 1; England, 6; Ireland, 17; Scotland, 1; Canada, 1; Nova Scotia, 1; total, 105.

The recommitments of 276 were 54; of whom 38 are second comers, 13 are third comers, 1 is a fourth comer, 1 is a fifth comer, and 1 is a sixth comer.

Of 105 received last year, 16 are recommitments, as follows: 12 are second comers, and 4 are third comers.

Of 16 recommitments last year, 7 were for larceny, 2 for stealing, 1 common and notorious thief, 1 for gross lewdness, 1 for breaking and entering a shop in the Prison, 1 for stealing from a dwelling-house, 1 for stealing from a shop, 1 for breaking a dwelling-house and stealing therefrom in the night, 1 for having a counterfeit bank bill with intent to pass the same; total, 16.

Of the 105 received, there were from Boston, 44; Worcester, 6; Springfield, 6; Lowell, 7; Lenox, 2; New Bedford, 12; Ipswich, 3; Dedham, 2; Cambridge, 4; Taunton, 4; Salem,

3 ; Northampton, 1 ; Greenfield, 2 ; Concord, 6 ; Plymouth, 3 ; total, 105.
The color of those in Prison is, 14 negroes, 15 mulattoes, and 247 whites.

"The affairs of the Prison," the warden says, "have been well and prosperous during the year; and it is truly gratifying for me to be able to say that there has been a high degree of good feeling, order, and industry among the convicts, which convinces me more and more of what I am most desirous of proving, that convicts in Prison can be governed by enforcing the law of human brotherhood and equality promulgated by the Savior, by doing unto others as we would that others should do unto us. In every instance of discipline, I have endeavored to keep this law before my mind, and have asked myself how I should reasonably wish to be dealt by, if I were in the situation of the convict; and I have found that the nearer I have been able to keep myself and others up to the true meaning of this law, the more successful has been the government of the Prison. I have often announced to the convicts my resolution to govern by this precept, and have frequently called upon them, and not without success, to live and act in conformity thereto. All that asperity of feeling which used to exist among the convicts, showing itself even in their looks, has gradually subsided, until kindness, and cheerfulness, and pleasant looks, have become almost universal. My experience has convinced me, that when all the officers of a Prison are vigilant, and have kind and brotherly feelings towards the convicts, and will all coöperate to promote their best good and effect their reformation, very little of punishment is required. I know that we are prone to the love of power, and to the exercise of authority ; and when our fellow-men are placed under our control, there is danger that power and authority may be abused. Yet I can truly say, I have endeavored to guard myself against this proclivity, and have been ever watchful over myself and others in this respect. I have felt it my duty to see that all the convicts should be treated well and kindly by the officers ; and I have reason to believe that all the officers are now convinced that these views of government are right and practicable, and promotive of the best interests of the convicts and of the Prison. I have good reason to thank them for coöperating with me so well in rendering successful a mild but firm and just system of discipline, which I am sure no one could do without their aid. There have been no instances of gross insubordination among the convicts during the year. Occasionally, there have been individual infractions of the rules. For these the punishment of short solitary confinement has usually been found sufficient and effectual. The shower-bath, as a punishment, has been discontinued ; and all other punishments have been diminished, in the aggregate, more than four-fifths. There is now a disposition among the convicts very favorable for their reformation. All that feeling of hostility against the government, revengefulness, and a desire to retaliate upon society, have subsided. Every convict discharged has left the Prison with apparently kind feelings, expressing a determination to do well and become honest men and industrious citizens. And there is reason to hope that they will generally adhere to their good resolutions."

"Seven convicts have been sent to the State Lunatic Hospital at Worcester, as insane, under the law of last year providing for their removal, and they are now receiving the benefit designed by this act of merciful and highly beneficial legislation."

"There has long been a Sunday school established in this Prison from the last of September to the 1st of June. Heretofore, during the summer months, there has been none. But a Sunday school was opened last summer for the instruction in reading of those who were unable to read ; so that now, instruction in reading is continued during the year, and many convicts who were unable to read have acquired, and are acquiring, that most useful of all branches of education."

" The business and financial concerns of the Prison have resulted quite as favorably as was anticipated. The earnings of the Prison have been enough to meet all expenses, and leave a small surplus of $268 68."

" The last legislature appropriated $4,611 to supply the deficiency of income of the Prison for the year before last; but this money has not been drawn from the treasury of the commonwealth, and has not been needed."

" The legislature, at the same time, appropriated a sum not exceeding $6,000 for repairs and improvements. More than one half of this appropriation has been expended, and the repairs are in progress."

The following schedule shows the disbursements and income for the year ending September 30, 1844 :—

Cash paid for provisions, .	7,245 83	Profits in stone department,	14,357 96
Hospital department, . . .	291 83	Profits in labor department,	16,892 96
Clothing, ...	2,777 40	Fees of admission, ...	1,395 72
Sundry expenses, fuel, &c.	2,416 64		
For prisoners discharged,	321 50		
Officers' salaries, ...	15,542 31		
Transportation of prisoners,	563 08		
Repairs of real estate, . . .	200 99		
Amount of convicts' labor, on especial repairs of the Prison, ...	238 98		
	$29,598 56		
To balance, ...	3,048 08		
	$32,646 64	. . . .	$32,646 64

To show the net profits, there should be deducted from the above balance of 3,048 08
Amount of bills for supplies received, but not paid, ... 2,779 40

Leaving the true balance of profits, ... $268 68

The late physician, Dr. Walker, says,—

" The number of patients admitted to the hospital of the Massachusetts State Prison during the year ending 30th September, 1844, is 178. The aggregate number of days' residence in the hospital is 3,756. In addition to this, 369 days' labor have been abated to invalids for a day, and 744 days of light labor have been advised by the physician.

" During the year, 2 have died ;—1844, January 6th, John Potter, aged 25 years, of phthisis pulmonalis ; 1844, May 15th, Lemuel Reniff, aged 30 years, of tubercular disease of the mesentery.

" During the current year, fever has prevailed in the Prison to a greater extent than for many years past. This disease has in no case proved fatal ; but one patient is now slowly convalescent, having suffered a partial paralyis of his left side."

The chaplain of the State Prison at Charlestown, Mass., says,—

" Although the number on the sick list has been somewhat larger than in some former years, yet a very gratifying degree of health has been enjoyed, and the number of deaths has been but 2, out of an average of about 270 convicts, a per centage of less than 8-10ths. It may further be stated, that, during the year commencing with October, 1842, there were but 2 deaths, and both these during the first month of the year ; so that from October, 1842, to the date of this report, December, 1844, there have been but 2 deaths.

" The year has also been characterized, generally, by cheerful submission to authority, laudable industry, and a gratifying attention to moral and religious instruction.

" It must be obvious to every reflecting mind, possessing a competent knowledge of human nature, that to improve and reform that class of men who are subjected to the confinement and discipline of our Penitentiaries, moral rather than physical power is to be relied on ; and although the latter, to some extent, is sometimes indispensable, still, this alone is altogether powerless in subduing the heart and bringing it into subjection to the benevolent principles of the gospel. The man may be broken down in body and in mind ; but his heart is not won. It is ordinarily hardened, and his condition becomes the more hopeless.

" Hence the government of this commonwealth has wisely and benevolently made provision for the employment of all requisite moral and religious means, on which, principally, reliance is to be placed for the moral improvement of the institution.

" These means and influences, so far as they are intrusted to the undersigned, he has habitually attempted to use in accomplishing the end for which they were designed ; and it can hardly be supposed that a constant and affectionate attention to the wants and woes of these men, the manifestation of sympathy in their afflictions,—advice and counsel faithfully and affectionately administered, and suited to their wants,—religious instruction kindly communicated in conversation,—the devotions of the daily morning and evening service in the chapel,—the preaching of the gospel on the Sabbath, and the familiar and affectionate instructions of the Sabbath school, can fail of producing the most happy results, on very many minds and hearts.

" The undersigned is very far from supposing that all the moral means and appliances for the improvement of the prisoners are placed in his hands. If good is accomplished by the instruction and labors of the chaplain, it is to be ascribed very much, under God, to the cheerful, hearty, and habitual coöperation of those in authority.

" The officers of such an institution should be men of correct morals ; men who can feel for the wants, and woes, and frailties, of those subjected to their authority, and who will cheerfully and habitually use every practicable means to promote their best good. Tyranny, on the part of those who rule, is always hateful. It is so in a prison as well as elsewhere. Still, those vested with authority in such circumstances, while they are bound to be humane and merciful, must also be fearless and prompt in maintaining a salutary discipline, and securing order and obedience on the part of the prisoners. They are to be a terror to evil-doers, and a praise to them who do well. All that sympathy and kindness can do should be done ; but when these fail in accomplishing their object, authority must be promptly exercised in the infliction of merited punishment. Obedience and order must be secured at any hazard. Personal sympathy must in no case stand in the way of the general welfare.

" And here the undersigned is happy to bear witness to the untiring efforts of the warden of this institution to make its government a paternal one, and as far as practicable, to secure order, obedience, and industry, by persuasion and kindness, rather than by punishment and severity. In some cases, it is true, he has been constrained to resort to severe measures ; but in most instances, mild punishments, tempered with wholesome counsel and admonition, have been found to secure the desired end.

" There is a charm in Christian love and kindness which nothing else possesses. The proud and stubborn heart may be, and often is, effectually nerved against the exercise of power, even in its utmost rigor, when perhaps that same heart would readily relent and soften at the voice of kindness coming warm from the heart of Christian love,—and be led, with the prodigal of the gospel to exclaim, 'Father, I have sinned!' The power of the tempest could lash the waters of the Lake of Galilee into terrific commotion; but the voice of Jesus, '*Peace! be still!*' is heard, and all is calm.

"The Sabbath school, for the present season, has been commenced and continued with many tokens of the divine favor. This school has never before been so full as at present, and it is characterized by a good degree of attention and interest on the part of those who attend it. It is supplied with a competent number of teachers, from Charlestown, Boston, and the vicinity, who come regularly every Sabbath, and, at much sacrifice of time and labor, perform the benevolent office of instructing these unhappy men in religion and morals.

" We feel that we owe them much for their labors of love, and the commonwealth owes them much.

" Of 105 convicts committed last year," the chaplain says, "only 33 were native-born citizens of Massachusetts,—a fact highly honorable to the state.

" Of the causes which lead to the commission of crime, whatever may be said of other causes, there is one which pre-eminently, and above all others, debases, impoverishes, and destroys, and which leads to the perpetration of every species of enormity. This cause stands out, in characters which none can mistake, on all our Alms-Houses, Penitentiaries, and Prisons. *It is the intoxicating cup.* Could the fountains of intemperance but be dried up, what a change would come over the face of civil society! At least three fourths of the poverty and suffering, the degradation and crime, over which the philanthropist and Christian are now constrained to weep, would be banished from the commonwealth.

" The cause of temperance has done much; it is still doing much. Multitudes have been redeemed, and saved from hopeless degradation and ruin. But much is still to be accomplished; and who can question that a most solemn obligation rests on the guardians of the public welfare and morals to countenance and sustain, in all suitable ways and by salutary legal enactments, a cause whose direct object and tendency are to lessen the evils of pauperism; to reduce the number of the degraded and guilty inmates of our prisons; to improve and elevate the character and condition of our citizens; and to spread abroad through all our communities the blessings of industry, of moral purity, and of all the virtues which adorn and perfect the human character?

" It is very gratifying to be able to state that, for several years past, the minds of the prisoners have been deeply interested in the great subject of temperance. Great pains have been taken to keep it, in all its bearings, before their minds. They have been frequently addressed by the most able and eloquent lecturers engaged in the furtherance of this cause; and approved temperance publications are monthly, and sometimes oftener, put into their hands, and, it cannot be doubted, with the happiest effect.

" Most of these men form the resolution—and it is believed sincerely—to abstain wholly from the use of intoxicating drinks after their discharge from the Prison. They generally sign the pledge of total abstinence at the time of their discharge. Some prove true to their pledge—perhaps many. But the heart sickens at the thought of the multiplied snares and temptations which beset them as they go out into the world, at almost every step of their progress; for although the laws of the State prohibit the sale of intoxicating drinks as a beverage, still the dram-shop and the dram-seller are found to tempt and to destroy all who can be enticed within their reach. Scarcely an individual returns to the Prison, after he has been discharged, but he has been the victim of strong drink.

" But enough, and perhaps too much, has been said on this sickening subject. It is always a painful one; but, considering the circumstances in which the undersigned, for many years past, has been placed, and witnessing, as he has, the appalling results of this dreadful evil, he feels that he could hardly say less."

May the chaplain long live to give the world the results of his observation and experience !

X.—STATE PRISON AT AUBURN, NEW YORK.

Annual Report of the Inspectors of the Auburn Prison, State of New York, Document No. 8. In Senate, Jan. 10, 1845. —Octavo, pages 89.

" The inspectors feel a just pride that they are able to report it prosperous and unembarrassed.

" The total amount of receipts into the treasury of the Prison, from all sources, during the year ending September 30, 1844, is, ... 72,913 52
" Total disbursements, ... 68,107 40

" Cash balance on hand, ... $4,806 12

" The earnings of the Prison, during the same period, are as follows :— Convict labor on contract, $52,389 10 ; job work, $886 10 ; earnings on Prison-building—estimate, $866 73 ; from visitors, $1,942 75 ; total earnings, $56,082 68. The expenses for the general support of the Prison amount to $51,041 04 ; orinary repairs, $2,725 16. Excess of earnings above general support and ordinary repairs, $2,316 48.

" One item of the agent's report is $9,037 40, for building purposes. The result is seen in the increased comfort of some of the shops, and in the addition of 214 feet to the two-story range of brick shops, which room was much needed for the employment of the convicts in Brussels carpet weaving and other business.

The earnings on contracts have been as follows :—

1836, $47,148 39 ;   1840, $57,322 99 ;   1843, $54,783 56
1837, 50,145 75 ;   1841, 58,750 26 ;   1844, 44,038 04
1838, 46,469 65 ;   1842, 59,091 24 ;   1845, 52,389 10
1839, 46,464 10 ;

The manufacture of silk has been discontinued by the agent, with the advice of the inspectors, owing to intrinsic difficulties.

" The health of the convicts has been generally good, their moral condition satisfactory, and the discipline improving. It has been our anxious study to foster and encourage the prominent use of moral means in the government of the convicts. And although we think it a Utopian idea, that such a body of criminals can be governed without punishment, yet we also think more can be accomplished by appealing to the conscience and self-respect, even of the most degraded, than many are willing to allow. There is sometimes danger that new and unusual modes of punishment, as substitute for stripes, may become more cruel than when stripes are rarely and temperately applied. Of this nature we believed the bolt-bath, which we found in operation when we came; and we accordingly, with the advice of the physician, and concurrence of the keeper, assented to its discontinuance in the summer of 1843; subsequent inquiries and observation have satisfied us of its inexpediency.

"We consider it an object of the highest moment to the interests of society at large, to foster, and, if possible, to improve, the system of Prison discipline adopted here. A large amount (about $600,000) has been expended by the state in the necessary erections. Experience has demonstrated that the great ends of punishment are best promoted by that humanity and benevolence which cares for the bodily and spiritual welfare of the convict, and converts his silent and social labor into a stern school of virtue and obedience."

The counties of Montgomery, Fulton, Saratoga, Washington, Warren, Essex, Clinton, and Franklin, have been set off from the Auburn Prison district to the Mount Pleasant Prison district, on account of the increased number of convicts at Auburn, (the number of cells being only 770,) and 30 prisoners have been sent from Auburn to Sing Sing.

"The increase of convicts employed upon contracts, over the last year, is 111; and the number of unproductive men reported is 104 less.

"The number of convicts now in Prison is 778, being 7 more than last year at this time. The number received during the year past is 261, being 2 less than during 1843. Of those received during this year, 44 were recommitments after discharge from this or some other State Prison.

"We deem it our duty, before closing this report, to press upon the attention of the legislature the expediency and humanity of authorizing the removal of insane convicts from this Prison to the Asylum at Utica, to be there kept by the state. The distance from the Prison is so short, that it will be easy; and, what is of great consequence, permits a removal in the early stages of insanity, when remedies may reach the disease. The Prison is without the necessary apartments and conveniences for the treatment of the insane.

"We are gratified to be able to state that the agent, keeper, and other officers of the Prison, have generally discharged their duty to the state with earnestness and discretion. Quietness and order reign within the walls; and, so far as we can observe, a healthful state of the public mind with regard to the Prison prevails without."

This report is signed by S. A. Goodwin, M. S. Myers, Samuel Brown, William H. Noble, Elijah Wheeler, inspectors, and dated February 2, 1845.

The agent, J. Beardsley, reports the inventory of state property to be $35,157 67, exceeding the inventory of the preceding year $1,150 30. This inventory, at Auburn, it is made the duty of the agent to make. At Charlestown, Massachusetts, it is made by disinterested persons.

The agent reports the Prison at Auburn to be free from debt, unless there be some

"unsettled accounts not recollected, of very trifling amount." "The finances of the Prison are in a much better condition than was anticipated." "Not a solitary instance of default on the part of any of the present contractors in the regular monthly payment of their dues for convict labor;"

while the earnings of the convicts for contract labor, during the year, amounted to $52,389 10.

The agent regrets the discontinuance of the manufacture of sewing-silk in the Prison, because

"it has, more or less, affected the interests of a considerable number of the citizens of the western part of the state, who have embarked in the culture of silk, and depended upon the Prison as a cash market for the raw material."

He says, however,—

"that he deemed it an improper and unprofitable business to be carried on by convict labor; owing to the great cost of the raw material, the inevitable waste and difficulty of manufacture,—a source of loss rather than profit."

It has, therefore, been abandoned, and will probably not be resumed.

The agent says,—

"It is now about 28 years since the building of the Prison was commenced, and the present season may properly be considered the date of its completion. Its total cost, including workshops, yards, walls, &c., has probably exceeded $600,000, a great proportion of which has been drawn directly from the treasury of the state. The amount has, however, been considerably enhanced, in consequence of extensive fires at different periods, which, under the present system of a careful and vigilant night-watch in the yards and shops, will not be likely to recur to any considerable extent. The buildings are now, generally, in a good condition, are constructed of durable materials, and will, with trifling repairs, withstand the action of time for a long period of years."

"As the entire extent of workships, agreeably to the original plan, are now completed, and constructed of the most durable materials for the accommodation of all the various branches of business carried on in this institution, I cannot foresee the necessity of any further extraordinary expenditures, with the exception of the repairs of the roofs of the main buildings, which are, and have been for some time past, in a leaky and dilapidated condition. It will require an expenditure of from $2,000 to $3,000 to put them in proper repair. These repairs should not, on any account, be delayed beyond the ensuing season, as the timbers composing the superstructure are already rapidly decaying in many places, in consequence of leakage. I am confident that the current resources of the Prison, under a prudent and economical management of its affairs, will be ample for the repairs above named, together with the general support of the same, under a strict observance of the limitations and restrictions of the act of 1842."

"There has been less than the usual time lost, during the fiscal year now terminated, in consequence of sickness among the convicts; and, so far as my observation and information enable me to judge, there has not only been an unusual degree of health enjoyed, but an uncommon degree of cheerful application to labor; and good conduct has prevailed among the convicts; and it is reasonable to infer that good and abundant rations, warm bedding and clothing, may have more or less contributed to this result."

The sources from which moneys have been received at this Prison, during the past year, are as follows:—

Balance from last account,		267 62	Tool shop,	. . . .	6,119 04
Coopers' shop,	. . . .	2,909 14	Stone shops,	. . . .	752 32
Carpet shops,	. . . .	11,800 72	Cutlers' shop,	. . . .	5,980 64
Hame shop,	. . . .	4,416 20	Tailors' shop,	. . . .	5,804 83
Shoe shop,	. . . .	6,363 46	Silk shop,	. . . .	4,168 42
Cotton weaving shop,	. . .	1,606 03	Machine shop,	. . . .	4,187 72
Pump shop,	. . . .	423 72	Button shop,	. . . .	3,578 87
Comb shop,	. . . .	162 64	State appropriation,	. . . .	5,303 80
Cabinet shop,	. . . .	5,635 04	Visitors,	. . . .	1,942 75
Convicts' cash deposits,	.	140 08			
Prison, miscellaneous,	. .	1,350 48	Total receipts,	. .	$72,913 52

The sums expended were as follows :—

Rations,	. . . .	13,878 28	Building and repairs,	. . .	11,762 56
Clothing and bedding,	. .	8,497 06	Fire-wood and oil,	. . . .	3,736 48
Silk, stock, &c.,	. . . . . .	2,475 49	Stock, coal, &c.,	. . . . .	105 58
Hay, grain, &c.,	. . . . .	51 58	Discharged convicts and		
Printing and stationery,	.	214 67	transporting ditto,	. . .	993 76
Salaries of Prison officers,		15,232 26	Inspectors,	. . . .	876 00
Pay of guard,	. . . .	7,199 51	Miscellaneous,	. . . .	2,277 21
Hospital stores,	. . . . . .	806 96	Total expenditures,		$68,107 40

The clerk, Mr. J. Hubbard, reports,—

The number of convicts remaining in Prison, December
31, 1843, ...   771
The number received during the year ending December
1, 1844, ...   261

Total number in Prison during the year, ... 1,032
Discharged by expiration of sentence, ...   172
Discharged by pardon, ...   43
Sent to Sing Sing, ...   30
Sent to the House of Refuge, ...   1
Died, ...   8
       —— 254

Remaining in Prison December 31, 1844, ... 778

The keeper, N. F. Doubleday, reports that,—

"The officers have, with few exceptions, discharged their duties with promptness, fidelity, and discretion. The convicts are generally obedient, observe the regulations, and manifest a quiet, subdued, and placable disposition, which, without moral means, could not be produced by severe and cruel treatment, and which are deemed essential to their improvement and reformation."

"Of the whole number of convicts who have been in Prison the past year, over 60 per cent. have not been punished at all; over 20 per cent. have been punished but once; and very few have been punished more than two or three times. The punishments have been usually light, varying from two to six blows, not often exceeding six, and none of the severest grade have been inflicted."

"The practice of whipping seems to be falling into disfavor; and it will be fortunate if methods of coercion be not substituted more cruel, more detrimental to health, and less efficient."

"The bolt-bath, for the affusion of cold water on the head and naked body, was discontinued in June, 1843, and no similar means of punishment have since been used. The shower-bath is recommended and used in some of the other Prisons. It is well calculated to subdue the refractory, but is, in my opinion, as cruel as the lash, and productive of more injurious consequences. Consumption is a prevailing disease in Prisons. When the lungs are weak, (which cannot be always known to the officer,) the application of cold water, with sufficient force and duration to make it a punishment, must cause a violent rush and pressure of blood to the lungs, which, I suppose, will prove generally hurtful, and often induce disease of a fatal character."

"Solitary confinement has been also recommended as a substitute for other modes of punishment. It may answer well in some cases, and is always to be tried in preference to very severe flogging. It is, however, uncertain in its effects, causes a loss of time, and, in our small cells, tends to injure the health of body and mind."

" Kindness and moral suasion are recommended by some as the principal means of enforcing discipline. They may be so when the convicts are not very depraved nor the number large. Such means have been used in this Prison with good success, especially during the latter part of the year, and it is believed may be made still more efficient. In addition to the instruction which the men receive in the Sabbath school, in the chapel, and by the chaplain visiting them at their cells, the officers appeal to their better feelings on all suitable occasions. They are made to understand that great care is taken to supply them with good and sufficient food and other necessaries ; that their officers wish them well, never punish them willingly, but only from a sense of duty, and feel proud of their good conduct when they behave with propriety ; and that the keeper feels mortified when obliged to record their names in the book of punishments."

" A good feeling now exists between the convicts and those who are placed over them. No escapes have occurred the past year. There has been no combined resistance of authority, and very seldom the slightest hesitation manifested in obeying orders. The men perform a very satisfactory amount of labor, do their work well, and do not, as at some former periods, steal, damage, or waste the property of the state or of the contractors. No amount of punishment could cause the stillness and order which reign in the wings during the night. In the north wing, one officer has charge of 550 men lodged in five tiers of extended galleries on each side. If many of them were badly disposed, they might cause a vast amount of trouble and confusion, and require very laborious efforts to preserve order. Offences of this kind are very seldom committed by them, and their conduct, in general, is much better than we could expect from so large a number, selected from the whole community on account of their crimes."

" Still we know that kindness and persuasion are not alone sufficient to govern men. If they were so, State Prisons might be dispensed with. It is a mistake, also, that whipping always produces vindictive feelings. Those who feel keenly the degradation, generally conduct so as to avoid punishment. There are men whose propensities are so strongly animal, that nothing but an appeal to their senses can fit them for instruction or moral reformation. Great care should doubtless be taken that the officers never act from caprice or passion, and that the men never suffer wrongfully, nor generally without previous admonition. They should always be treated with considerate mildness ; and when punishment is administered in moderation, as a solemn act of duty, for willful wrong, we know that the recipient does not usually harbor ill feeling towards the one who inflicts it."

"I have reason to believe that very severe floggings, such as have sometimes been inflicted in Prisons, and elsewhere, have a withering effect on the faculties of body and mind. and that in cases which seem to require such severe chastisement, other methods should be resorted to."

" Much suffering may be prevented by vigilance on the part of officers.

Men are not likely to transgress when they know that they are subject to strict observation. In March last, the number of convicts increased to 826, which was more than could be properly disposed of in this Prison. The consequence was, that the punishments were about twice the average in that month. In July last, severe sickness prevailed so generally amongst the convicts, that the usual regulations could not be strictly enforced. In August, the number of punishments was much increased. In the latter part of the year, but little punishment has been inflicted, and the discipline was never better. The men preserve strict order, and labor in silence with alacrity and cheerfulness. The emulation of most of them is excited, and they seem to strive to merit the good opinion of their officers."

"These views are submitted with a sincere desire to profit by the experience and suggestions of others."

The physician, Dr. Leander B. Bigelow, reports 8 deaths during the year ending December 31, 1844 ; 5 of diseases of the lungs, 1 of congestion of the brain, 1 of pleuritis, and 1 of aneurism. One had a feeble constitution ; 1 had been grossly intemperate, and had lues venerea when he came to Prison ; 1 had been for years afflicted with salt rheum ; 1 was predisposed to a pulmonary affection when he came to Prison ; another had poor health on admission. There were, however, but 8 deaths, out of an average of 774 patients.

The physician says,—

"The health of the convicts has been generally good during the past year, with the exception of the month of July, when they were suddenly attacked with diarrhœa and cholera morbus, which raged with extreme violence for about two weeks. Of the former complaint, there were 353 cases ; of the latter (cholera morbus) 36. All these patients ultimately recovered, and are now enjoying their usual health.

"It will be observed, by examining the hospital report for the year 1843, that the physician there gives the number of deaths at 11 for the then current year, and also states that there were 12 others pardoned, to save their lives. He there gives a table showing the whole number of pardons granted for a given number of years, and specifying the particular year in which they were issued. He further states, that it has been a long time a practice to grant pardons upon the above principle, and ends by giving it as his opinion, that the number of pardons granted for the purpose of saving life, during the years enumerated, was in the same proportion as in 1843. Now, to prevent any who may feel an interest in comparing the different systems of Prison discipline, and their influence upon the health of convicts, from adopting erroneous conclusions founded on the opinion of the physician given in the above-named report, I deem it my duty to expose, as far as my knowledge enables me, the errors of the doctor's statement.

"I was physician to the Auburn Prison during the term of four years, from 1834 to 1838. These four years are embraced in the time above referred to, and there was not one pardon obtained during the whole of that period for a sick convict, on the representation that it was indispensable for the preservation of life ; neither has there been during the year just ended. I have been induced to make these remarks, that the public might not be led to the very erroneous conclusion that there is a greater amount of sickness in the Prison than appears upon the record.

"There are now confined in the hospital 9 : 1 with consumption ; 1 with cancer ; 2 with rheumatism ; 1 with opacity of the cornea, causing total loss of sight; 1 necrosis of the tibia, with ulcerated lungs; 1 ophthalmia; 1 lues venerea, and 1 with debility."

The chaplain, the Rev. O. E. Morrill, says,—

" I am happy in saying that the means for the moral culture and religious instruction of the prisoners have been somewhat increased, ... by a better supply of books. Nearly all of them enjoy a season of religious worship every Sabbath, and their conduct in the chapel has been marked with that attention which evinces how much they prize the privilege.

" Our Sabbath school has been like a gentle shower upon a thirsty land. About 260 are all that can be accommodated as a school, in the chapel, at a time. Hence exchanges are made in selecting them, (excepting the spelling-book classes,) which divides the time among some 500 or 600 of them. From close observation for the year past, I am convinced that great good results to the discipline of the Prison from these instructive and religious interviews. Whatever changes may take place here, I hope the Sabbath school may never be abandoned.

" A short religious service in the dining-hall, twice each day, has been strictly attended to, (with few exceptions,) and affords a great opportunity for keeping up a religious influence in the place. Notwithstanding the discipline of the Prison necessarily precludes lengthy conversations with the convicts while in their workshops, yet this disadvantage has a remedy in the labors of the chaplain from cell to cell, on the galleries, after they retire for the night. It is there an opportunity presents to enter into close conversation, to draw out a confession of their crimes, to learn much of their natural disposition and their wants, and to make a personal application of that truth which, under other circumstances, they might feel disposed to cast away. In these evening visits I generally spend from two to four hours, and have been on the galleries as much as six out of every seven evenings during the past year. Although this increases the labors of the chaplain to more than twice what they used to be, yet I know that the wants of those men require it, and I am sensible that much good results to the institution from such a course.

" Judging from my personal interviews, from their devout attention in seasons of worship, and from their conduct in every respect, I have good evidence that quite a number of the convicts have become morally and religiously reformed during the past year. A great change for the better is very apparent, throughout the entire Prison, during the last few months.

" This moral improvement among the convicts is probably the result of a combination of causes.

" 1. They have good food, and enough of it, warm clothing, and comfortable lodgings.

" 2. The mutual friendship, union, and good feeling, existing among the officers of the Prison, from the principal keeper down, have had a happy effect among the convicts.

" 3. The rules of discipline have been strictly observed, and enforced without respect to persons.

" 4. Great care is taken not to punish the innocent, or to let the guilty go unpunished.

" 5. Much kindness and good feeling have been expressed by the principal keeper and his assistants, by way of encouragement for good conduct.

" 6. They have the attention of a good physician, who treats them kindly when sick, and who spares no pains to make them comfortable and contented.

" 7. They have been well supplied with such books as are calculated to interest them, and make good impressions upon their minds.

" 8. They occasionally see or hear from their relatives, which, after the excitement of the moment is passed, seems greatly to quiet the mind, and it has produced the best of consequences to the discipline of the Prison.

" The man who is permitted to have a short interview with his relatives, or to hear from them, once a year, for 5 years, in 24 cases out of 25, will go to them as soon as possible after being discharged ; while in a majority of cases, those who do not enjoy these privileges seem to lose, in a greater or less degree, that instinctive principle of our common nature, love of kindred, and, when discharged, wander off among strangers, fall into temptation and crime, and are again returned to Prison.

" Of the 778 convicts now in the Prison, there are, under 20 years of age, 83 ; between 20 and 30, 382 ; between 30 and 40, 180 ; between 40 and 50, 86 ; between 50 and 60, 32 ; between 60 and 70, 12 ; between 70 and 80, 2 ; between 80 and 90, 1. 10 are sentenced for life ; 94, for petit larceny, second offence ; 154 from the county of Erie ; 164 could not read when they came to Prison ; 353 confess intemperance to be the cause of their crime ; 252 left their parents when under 15 years of age ; 331 lost one or both parents when young ; 131 have been employed on the canal ; 298 have families · 301 say they have been gamblers ; 137 have been sailors ; 62 are negroes ; 5, Indians ; 192 profess now to be pious ; 101 are only sons ; 2 are lawyers ; 4, physicians ; 6, ministers ; 589 are here on the first conviction and sentence ; 136, on the second ; 35, on the third ; 14, on the fourth ; and 4, on the fifth.

" Allow me to express my gratitude to God for his abundant blessings upon the officers and convicts of this institution during the past year. Not an individual among the 50 officers of the Prison has been called away by death, and only 8 convicts have died during the year."

XI.—STATE PRISON AT SING SING, NEW YORK.

Annual Report of the Inspectors of the Mount Pleasant State Prison at Sing Sing, N. Y. No. 9, Senate Document. Jan. 10, 1845. Octavo ; pages 87.

The inspectors report the expenditures for the Male and Female Prisons, for the year ending September 30, 1840, $77,460 ; 1841, $78,222 46 ; 1842, $72,801 28 ; 1843, $66,658 60 ; 1844, $64,215 08. The number of convicts during this time has increased. In April, 1843, the average cost of each convict, per day, was 25 cents and 8 mills, and in September, 1844, it was 18 cents and 4 mills.

The buildings and outer wall never having been completed, improvements have been made amounting to $6,122 80. The receipts were $64,598 82, of which $19,500 were from the state treasury, and $45,098 82 obtained from the earnings. The earnings for the year were $57,481 10 ; for the previous year, $36,970 37. Increase during the year, $20,510 73.

" The average monthly expenditure being about $5,400, for the last half year, the earnings have equalled that amount. The amount drawn from the treasury for several years past has been, in the years ending September 30, 1841, $18,500; 1842, $16,000; 1843, $32,500; 1844, $19,500 ;—total, $86,500. It is believed by the inspectors that, for the current year, the earnings of the Prisons will be sufficient to defray the expenses. Much more could be done, were it not for the restrictions imposed by law upon the working in marble.

" The contracts now subsisting are, one for 150 convicts at making files, at 32 cents per day ; one for 100 at Brussels carpets, at 32 and 40 cents per day ; one for 50 at saddlery hardware, at 35 cents ; one for 40 at cutting fur, at 32 and 35 cents ; three for as many as can lawfully work at coopering, at 35 cents ; 50 shoemaking, 41 cents ; and 30 making hats, 32 cents ; and for three men at toy-making, at 35 and 50 cents.

" The disease that is most fatal among the prisoners is consumption, produced mostly by irregularities of life prior to their commitment. These irregularities cause many of them to be diseased on admission

" The supply of water is very deficient. During the month of September, the expense of supplying the Prisons was about $10 a day.

" To meet this difficulty, the inspectors applied to the common council of New York for leave to procure a supply from the Croton aqueduct which runs through the Prison farm. Their answer to the application is submitted, and the inspectors urge upon the legislature the propriety of the measure."

Of 31 subjects of mental alienation in different forms, which have been found in the Prison by careful examination, 22 were insane at the time of their commitment to the Prison : 3 are at the Asylum at Bloomingdale, 28 at the Prison.

One of those confined at the Asylum the inspectors do not know (owing to the confusion in which they found the books of the Prison) what to do with, how long they have a right to detain him, or how long they will be bound to maintain him.

" A convict, by the name of Theodore P. Whiting, had been several years in Prison, and had several times shown signs of insanity, as well on his first reception at the Prison as afterwards, and in every instance had been treated as simulating, and immediately recovered. In May last, he again exhibited the same signs, and the physician of the Prison, a gentleman of high standing in his profession, who has been 12 years connected with the Prison, pronounced it a case of simulation.

" There has been from the beginning but one uniform mode of treating such cases, viz., by the application of the lash; and it was applied in the case of Whiting. The board, in their report last year, remonstrated against a state of things which would render a resort to such a remedy either necessary or justifiable. They said, the erection of a suitable building, where such patients might be properly treated if truly afflicted, or where they might be punished if feigning, and where, in either event, they would neither disturb nor be disturbed by their fellow-convicts, is a measure dictated by every principle of humanity.

" When the case of Whiting occurred, and was pronounced by the physician to be a case of simulation, the keeper had no alternative but to apply to him the accustomed treatment. In a short time, however, his disease assumed such a form as to leave no doubt of its reality ; and he was removed to the Asylum, where in a few weeks he died.

" Immediately after his death it was charged, in the newspapers, that he was whipped to death.

" The board made a full and careful investigation, and from the testimony the falsity of the charge is apparent enough.

" To guard against the repetition of such an occurrence, the board, directly, as their funds became sufficient for that purpose, commenced the erection of an outer ward, to consist of 16 separate rooms, with exercising yards attached, in which such subjects can be confined.

" The board beg leave to repeat their suggestion, that power be given them to remove such cases to the State Asylum; because it is there, and not at the Prison, that the proper remedies can be most economically and most advantageously applied.

" There are always many such in the Prison. Some are so when received; others become so while in confinement, principally from self-abuse; thus destroying their mental and physical powers. The board are of opinion that, in every case where the insanity is undoubted, the patient should be at once removed to a Lunatic Asylum.

" The situation of this class of convicts, at the expiration of their term of imprisonment, is another subject that demands legislative action.

" The board, in their last report, took occasion to express their disapprobation of the mode of government which had long prevailed in the Prison, and particularly the universal use of the whip as the sole means of punishing offences against discipline. They believed it to be injurious alike to the officers who inflicted it and the prisoners who received it; but they were assured by those whose experience certainly gave great weight to their opinions, that it was a matter of imperious necessity. They were reluctant to believe in the existence of such necessity; and in April last they entered upon a new mode of government, and they are rejoiced to have it in their power to state, that the happiest results have attended the experiment. In the Female Prison the whip is never used; and in the Male Prison, now, only as a last resort; and the consequence of the change has been, that while, among the males, the number of lashes has diminished from 1,195 a month to about 200, and the number of offences against discipline has diminished from 130 a month to 50; and in the Female Prison, from 47 a month to 11; in the mean time, the inspectors are assured by their officers, by the contractors, (whose interest would make them particularly vigilant on the subject,) and by their own careful observation, that order, industry, and obedience, have been fully maintained among the prisoners; and they are confident in the hope, that when the outer ward shall be completed, so that solitary confinement for short periods can be resorted to as a means of punishing the refractory, the use of the whip can be dispensed with, save only perhaps as a last resort in extreme cases.

" The hope of reward is a more powerful, as well as a more beneficial incentive to good conduct, than the fear of punishment; and as far as was practicable, this principle has governed us. It would, however, be most effectual, if the Prisons were so constructed as to allow of a classification.

" In the Female Prison, where the principle of classification has been carried to a greater extent than is at present feasible among the males, the experiment has been very satisfactory.

" Of equal importance with classification would be the opportunity of affording instruction to the prisoners.

" Among the males, service in the chapel once on every Sunday, the funeral service performed in case of death, and the distribution of the books of a tolerable library, are all that has yet been done in this matter; among the females, however, the experiment has been more fully tried. In addition to the chapel and funeral services, and the library, they have the advantage of a Sunday school and daily instruction by the matrons.

" By producing in the minds of the convicts an impression that their welfare is cared for, that they are not hopelessly lost, and that their efforts at reformation will be met by a kindly and encouraging spirit, new aspirations after goodness and purity are produced in them, new thoughts awakened, and new and better lives aimed at.

"The straightened circumstances of our finances forbid any large expenditure for books; and but for the untiring exertions of a benevolent lady, Miss Robbins, the Prison would, in a measure, have been deprived of the great benefits they have derived from the use of them.

"This is, however, in the opinion of the inspectors, only the beginning of a work, which ought to be completed; and they earnestly recommend, that they be authorized to employ some competent teachers, whose whole time should be devoted to the task.

"It is vain to look for cheerful obedience to the laws of the Prison from those whose minds are uncultivated fields, filled only with rank and noxious weeds; whose present is a blank, whose past is the recollection of a life misspent, and whose future is a dread of the evil consequences flowing from it.

"The Prison for females must continue a heavy tax upon the state.

"The present earnings of this Prison do not exceed $1,000; while its expenditures amount to about $7,000.

"Although, in a financial point of view, the picture is thus dark, yet we are most happy to say that, where all was disorder and anarchy a year ago, all is now order, quiet, and good government. Great praise is due to the matron and assistant matrons of this Prison, for the accomplishment of a work, which the inspectors one year ago deemed impossible.

"The board, in their last report, alluded to the destitute condition of discharged convicts. The amount allowed to each person on leaving the Prison does not exceed $3 in money and $10 in clothing—an amount scarcely ever more than enough to take them to their homes, and frequently short of that. They are therefore sent forth into the world under every disadvantage; and to those upon whom their confinement has worked the reformation designed, the infliction is exceedingly severe. Instances have come to the knowledge of the inspectors, of discharged convicts, who have left the Prison with sincere desires to lead honest lives, and who have evinced their sincerity by enduring the severest privation for want of employment, when it has been apparent to them that by committing crimes their wants would be well supplied; and they have not been surprised to find former prisoners returning upon them with the true and ready excuse, 'We were compelled to steal to save us from starvation.'

"The inspectors, in their last report, alluded to this subject in the hope that some measures of relief would be adopted. Failing in that, they made an appeal to the benevolent in New York and its vicinity, and were gratified to find their appeal responded to in the most prompt and ready manner.

"A society has been formed in New York, in which many of our most valuable citizens are actively engaged, and which promises in a great degree to supply the deficiency complained of. But as the operations of that society must necessarily throw the burden of this measure upon a few individuals, while the whole community is interested in it, the inspectors beg leave again to commend it to the favorable consideration of the legislature.

> "J. W. EDMANDS,
> "HENRY ROMER,
> "J. M. NIVEN,
> "HENRY HARRIS,
> "ISAAC BIRDSALL.

"STATE PRISON ON MOUNT PLEASANT, *December* 23, 1844."

The agent of the Prison, Wm. H. Peck, reports the property belonging to the Prison, not including the buildings, to be, as per inventory, $40,205 63.

The number of convicts, September 30, 1843, males, 763 ; females, 76 ; total, 839 ; — September 30, 1844, males, 863 ; females, 72 ; total, 935. Received by commitment, males, 280 ; females, 30 ; by order of the governor, from Auburn Prison, 30 ; total, 340. Discharged by expiration of sentence, males, 159 ; females, 20 ; by pardon, males, 30 ; females, 12 ; by death, males, 14 ; females, 2 ;—reversal of sentence, males, 3 ; by habeas corpus, male, 1 ; sent to Bloomingdale Asylum, 3 ; total discharged, 244.

The number of males has increased 100 during the past year, which, the keeper says, is principally owing to having received 30 from the Auburn Prison, and the extension of the Sing Sing Prison district, by the executive, to embrace 8 additional counties. In the Female Prison, the number is 2 less than the previous year.

Employment of male convicts at productive labor, 593 ; employment of male convicts, unproductive, 270 ;—females, productive, 27 ; unproductive, 45 ;—total, 935. New contracts have been made for 50 shoemakers, at 41 cents per day ; for 40 coopers, at 35 cents per day ; for 30 men cutting fur, at 32 cents per day ; and for 54 convicts at saddlery and harness hardware, at 35 cents per day. 86 acres of the farm are rented for 3 years at $350 annually. Of the debts due the Prison at the close of the last year, $15,932 12 have been paid.

The agent estimates the improvements on the Prison and Prison grounds, during the year, at $6,122 80. He says,—

" There has been no want of employment during the past year ; but from a strict adherence to the act of April, 1842, it is found impossible to employ the convicts to that advantage which has been formerly enjoyed in our Prisons ; and, under existing circumstances, it will require the most rigid economy to prevent the Prison from falling in debt."

" Owing to the rapid decrease in the number who can be legally set to work in cutting stone, great embarrassment exists in fulfilling engagements made for cut stone ; and the time is fast approaching when it will become necessary, in order to work the quarries with a profit to the state, to render greater facilities in transporting blocks of stone to the dock, ... that a considerable outlay will be required, in opening the quarries to a greater depth, and nearly on a level with high-water mark. By laying railways to the wharf, large blocks of marble might be easily transported, and would find a ready sale, in a rough state, to supply city orders, and not excite angry feelings from those interested in mechanical branches. But, in order to do this, it would require legislative aid."

The keeper, Mr. Harmon Eldredge, reports to the board of inspectors that he has

" witnessed many gratifying improvements in the conduct of the convicts."

" In the month of May last, your board gave directions to the principal keeper and chaplain to collect the prison library, (which had not been used for more than a year,) authorizing them to make distribution among the convicts, at their discretion, and under such regulations as seemed to them right. The result of this experiment, thus far, has convinced us that it has done much to diminish the number of violations of our discipline ; because the convict, after partaking of his breakfast and dinner in his cell, will immediately seize his book, and spend the remaining part of his hour in its perusal."

" On the Sabbath, you can scarcely pass one cell in one hundred, without seeing its inmate ardently engaged in reading his library book."

" In the month of June last, your board passed a resolution that it shall be the duty of the keeper, as soon as practicable, to substitute for the lash other suitable punishments."

This resolution

" has since been followed and practised by *all*, with satisfactory results."

" We have recourse to the lash only when it is ascertained that every other and milder way has been resorted to without effect."

" We have in several instances, been successful after placing the convict in absolute solitude during the day and night, and have almost as often heard them ask to be released from their confinement and return to their labors ; promising, at the same time, to submit to every thing that our discipline requires."

" With another class of men, we adopt a different mode of treatment ; such as showering them, changing their employment, and taking from them a part of their food, and sometimes by depriving them of their bed."

" If, however, the convict has received either or all of the above punishments without producing the desired effect, then the whip is applied, as the most effective means of enforcing submission."

" I fully believe that every officer attached to this institution has a decided aversion to the use of the lash, where they can obtain their object by other modes of punishment.   *Yet with our present facilities for governing a Prison*, they would regret it much, and I should greatly fear that the discipline would become much *impaired*, were they deprived of the power to inflict corporeal punishments, with proper restrictions."

" By comparing the monthly reports of punishments for the last year, I find that the number of lashes has been reduced about 75 per cent. ; and the whole number of violations of our discipline has fallen off from 30 to 40 per cent. The cause of this great difference, in my opinion, is attributable, in a considerable degree, to the introduction of our library among them, as well as the milder mode of punishment which has been adopted, and not from actual infliction with the whip.   The latter is calculated to arouse all the baser passions, and lead to hatred and revenge ; whilst the former subdues without blunting the morals of the man already fallen in his own opinion."

" We have in one Prison 210 convicts who can only read indifferently, and 115 who can neither read nor write.   If the latter class of convicts could be assembled together in a school-room, for an hour or two once or twice each week, or oftener, for the purpose of teaching them to read, it would do much to elevate their minds, (or some of them, at least,) and induce them to contract habits of order and decorum, and have a beneficial influence on them after their return to society."

The chaplain of the Prison, the Rev. John Luckey, reports that,—

" Since the passage of those resolutions, by the Board, which placed a good book in the hand of each convict who could read, and permitting all the convicts to attend the funeral services of their deceased fellows, the tokens of genuine repentance have greatly increased."

" Respecting the condition of those convicts who have been discharged this year, I regret to say that circumstances over which I have no control prevent me from being as definite in my statistics, on this subject, as I was last year."

"It will be recollected that it was ascertained that, of the 800 convicts who were discharged during that time, [i. e., a period of three years,] 100 were doing well; while at the same time we had no proof but that a majority of the 700 who remained were doing equally well."

"From the statistics of this year, which I have, in despite of circumstances, collected, but not arranged, I am fully warranted in the assertion that there are as many, in proportion, doing as well as were reported last year."

"Two of the hundred above alluded to have returned. The rest, as far as I have been able to ascertain, are still sustaining themselves with credit."

"I ought here to say, that many of the discharged convicts, both male and female, owe, under Divine Providence, their escape from a second degradation to the timely interposition of benevolent individuals, who have acted the part of fathers and mothers to them."

"I record my sincere thanks to the board for the efficient course they have taken, by which public attention has been so actively directed towards this vastly important desideratum." (i. e., the necessity of aiding and assisting discharged convicts.)

"Not only religion and philanthropy, in their connection with the personal welfare of the convicts, but also the feelings of their respectable friends, the well-being of society, and even self-interest itself, combine to recommend reformation as the paramount object of Penitentiary punishment."

"I am fully aware, gentlemen, that neither with yourselves nor your subordinates is the importance of this object a question. The appropriate measures which have been adopted and carried out with so much success, on your part, justify this assumption. The most difficult question is, how this vastly important object can be attained with safety to a vigorous and impartial discipline, justice to contractors, and majesty to the laws. This, and many other embarrassing questions, arising out of the various weaknesses, biases, and deficiencies of convicts, can be duly appreciated only by those who, like yourselves, have had experience in Prison affairs."

"I regard the Sabbath school, and other instructions had in the female department, as an important auxiliary to the chaplain. The principal keeper and some of the assistant keepers are doing what they can to supply the lack of a Sabbath school in the male department, by teaching those who cannot read."

The physician, A. H. Hoffman, M. D., reports, total number of deaths at the Male Prison, 14; 1 of which was from suicide; 2 from rupture of a blood-vessel in the lungs; 9 from chronic, and only 2 from acute diseases.

Names.	Time of Death.	Disease.	Remarks.
John Baxter,	Oct. 26, 1843.	Consumption. — Diseased when he came to Prison.	
Henry Miller,	Dec. 12, 1843.	Rupture of a blood-vessel in the lungs.	
Samuel J. Fuller,	Mar. 16, 1844.	Consumption. — Incipient stage when he came to the Prison.	
Thomas Fowler,	Mar. 18, 1844.	Fistula. — Stricture of the urethra when he came to Prison, which he said had existed for seven years.	
Andrew Bodine,	Mar. 24, 1844.	Pneumonia and enlargement of heart. — Diseased when he came to Prison, and very feeble.	
Rodney Guy,	April 2, 1844.	Consumption. — Diseased when he came, and sent to the hospital.	

Names.	Time of Death.	Disease.	Remarks.
John Van Alstine,	April 8, 1844.	Congestive fever.	
Alexander Tyson,	May 15, 1844.	Enlargement of heart and liver.	
James Bailey,	June 1, 1844.	Cancer and consumption.—Had both when he came to Prison.	
William Nesbit,	June 3, 1844.	Suicide in a fit of insanity.	
Charles Fuller,	June 18, 1844.	Consumption.—Had disease when he came to Prison.	
William Thompson,	Aug. 23, 1844.	Typhus fever. — An old and infirm man.	
Charles Rowe,	Sept. 6, 1844.	Consumption.	
Andrew Dougerty,	Sept. 30, 1844.	Rupture of a blood-vessel in the lungs.	

" The inmates of the Prison for Females have been generally healthy. The average number of hospital cases during the year has been about 2½, and of daily prescriptions about 6. Two deaths occurred in the commencement of the year, viz : —

Caroline Smith,	Oct. 2, 1843.	Typhus fever.	
Eliza Van Husen,	Oct. 8, 1843.	Consumption.—She had been sick a long time.	

" Three insane convicts have been sent to the Lunatic Asylum during the year — Nicholas Azure, October 13, 1843; John Smith, March 19, 1844; Thomas P. Whitney, May 21, 1844.

" The diseases which have been common at the Prison, the past year, have not differed materially from preceding years. Colds, coughs, rheumatic complaints, and pneumonia, were frequent during the cold months. During the month of September, an unusual number have been affected with cholera morbus and diarrhœa, having for its cause the great and sudden change of temperature. From the 14th of August to September 30, some 20 convicts have had remittent and typhoid fever; all of whom have recovered, with the exception of the case above-mentioned. These latter complaints were not peculiar to the Prison. They were prevalent in the neighboring towns."

The committee on insane convicts reported, November 14, 1844, the particular condition of each of 31, as stated in the following list ; and the board say they cannot fail to feel the great impropriety, manifested in many of their cases, of sending to this Prison persons incapable of distinguishing between right and wrong.

" J. H., white, an Englishman ; sent from New York, October 3, 1843, for grand larceny. He had been here before for 2 years. Was out only 4 months. Says his mind is as good as any in the world. No man on earth could persuade him ; and if any man wants to give him advice, if they will give him some money with it, he will take one, if he does not take the other. Quiet, industrious, but incapable of taking a correct view of any thing. Was so before he came in."

" J. A. ; sent from Auburn Prison, where he was committed for an attempt to poison. He is quiet, industrious, and good-natured ; but laboring under a general delusion. Was so before he came here."

" J. C., white, an Irishman ; sent from New York for burglary. 22 years old ; a natural fool ; and committed the crime, he says, because he could not get an honest living outside, and thought if he got into Prison he could learn a trade."

"F. J., a black boy, from Hudson. Sent 9th September, 1836, for 10 years, for a rape. Decrepit in person and idiotic in mind. Says nothing unless spoken to, and is very quiet. Produced by turning a wheel, at which he was kept continually for three or four years."

"D. W., white; sent from Rensselaer, September 9, 1841, for assault and battery with intent to ravish; a native, 25 years old. A poor, simple fool by nature; cannot tell his own age, nor where the sun rises; says that is a hard question. Says he was drunk when he was taken to jail, and did not know any thing about the offence."

"J. McM., white; sent from New York, 15th October, 1836, for robbery; a native, 27 years old. Second time here. Been in Prison the last 16 years, except a few months. A simple, ignorant, inoffensive man; always so; but without mind enough to be responsible for his conduct."

"J. F. M., white; sent from Schoharie, October 27, 1841, for grand larceny, 4 years; a native; an uneducated man, but of strong and vigorous intellect, with a good deal of energy of character and enthusiasm. About two years ago he became addicted to onanism, and his mind and body have become very much shattered. In consequence of my reading in the chapel, about 2 months since, he broke off, and is now recovering. His main difficulty was great nervous excitement, and confusion of intellect."

"R. L., white, from New York, August 9, 1842, for 10 years, for forgery; 25 years old; native born. Been here before, and is a sad victim of onanism. Nervous excitement great; mental delusion; all the officers are down upon him; hears voices in his cell."

"R. A., white; sent from Schenectady, November 29, 1843, for 2 years and 6 months, for assault and battery with intent to kill; 43 years old; Englishman. At the age of 14, he was sent to the House of Correction at Sheerness, England; was there 3 years and 6 months; then 3 years and 6 months in the English army; then came to Canada, where he received a wound in his head which injured his mind. Talks very large; is very jealous of his wife, and begs me not to make his case public, because he is yet destined to be very notorious by reason of an invention, which he has in his head, to send vessels over the Atlantic in eight days."

"J. B. B., white; sent from Ulster, 5th May, 1836, for 10 years, for burglary, on 2 indictments; 25 years old, and a native. Quiet and industrious; subject to delusions; talks to himself."

"J. D. F., white; sent from New York, 24th November, 1838, for robbery, for 10 years and 5 months; 27 years old; native; been here three times; was out the last time only 17 days. He was insane then, and is now. He has all sorts of queer fancies. Is very polite and good-natured, works hard, and writes poetry. He is far too flighty to be responsible for his conduct."

"J. P., white; sent from Steuben county, for a rape; sentenced to 10 years; 27 years old, and a native. A strong, athletic man; uneducated, but with acute sensibility. He was taken sick at Auburn from his grief, and on his recovery was partially insane, and in that state sent to us."

"J. J., a black; sent from New York, 7 years and 6 months, for burglary, on the 20th February, 1838. 33 years old. He has been in the Prison 4 times. The first time, he was here 3 years. Was out 2 years; then in 2 years; then out 3 days; then in 4 years and 3 months; then out 4 months; and now in again. He is naturally of a weak intellect, good-natured, simple, and mischievous; always been so, and certainly has not intellect enough to know right from wrong."

"J. K., white; sent from Green county, for a rape, September 20, 1838, for 10 years; 30 years old; foreigner; subject to delusions; sees persons all about him. Has 4 boys and their mothers in the Prison; got his name from the royal blood of England. A chronic case; was so when he came in."

"A. F., white; sent from Duchess county, 30th October, 1844, for 4 years, for petit larceny, second offence, on 2 indictments. He has been here before.

He is now 28 years old, and is of weak, infirm intellect by nature; too weak to allow of any self-control."

"J. H. B., white; sent from Suffolk county, May 28, 1838, for 14 years, for a rape. He is native born; 24 years old. This is his second time here. Excitement pretty active. Says this is his native place; that he came from just over there; and he came here to keep out of trouble, because people are all the time bothering him. A decided case, and incurable; for he was so before his conviction.

"J. T., black; sent from Duchess, September 30, 1843, for grand larceny, for 5 years; 36 years old; native. A harmless maniac. Says he has lost his mind, and says it was owing to the medicine the doctors gave him. This is his second time here. He was the same when received at the Prison."

"P. B., white; sent from Clinton county, January 26, 1844, for 3 years and 6 months, for burglary. He is an Irishman, and about 45 years old. He labors under a good deal of excitement; talks very rapidly and incoherently; invents new words. He was in the same condition when he came in."

"W. S., white; sent from Schenectady, 20th October, 1842, for 5 years, for grand larceny. Is 22 years old, and native born. His is a very decided case of insanity. His excitement is always very high; talks very incoherently; suffers under delusions; hears voices all around him, except when at work; hence he works very hard, but is a good deal troubled with the dogs the people are all the time setting on him. Cause, onanism."

"J. L., white; sent from Queen's county, November 16, 1843, for 4 years and 11 months, for grand larceny; 20 years old, and native born. At the age of 16, he was sent to the Massachusetts State Prison, where he learned onanism of the convicts. His mind and health both became affected, and he felt a powerful inclination to take the warden's life, so that he might himself die a sudden death. He was deterred from that out of regard to the young children of the warden; and, to effect the same object, he determined to force the guard, in hopes they would shoot him. He made the attempt, and succeeded in escaping. He was in a few months sent here, and immediately fell into his old practices; and his sufferings, from his own description, have been horrible. He has made tremendous efforts to correct himself. He has sometimes abstained for days from eating; stripped himself naked, and, without covering, lay on the stone floor of his cell; but all in vain. He insisted that mutilation was the only cure, and he earnestly begged that it might be done. He suffers under mental delusions; hears voices around his cell. His case is very similar to Lundy's, and that of Abner Rogers, who murdered the warden of Massachusetts Prison."

"R. A., white; sent from Rensselaer for life, for murder, 23d November, 1835; native, and 31 years old. His mind is very confused; his memory is much impaired; has no correct view of any thing. He is much troubled about little things. He is at times cross, and almost savage. He was in the same condition when received, but has been much worse. He is now better; but there is no hope that he can ever be restored, for it is evident his disease is of long standing. He insists, however, that his mind is as sound as any one's. He appears to me to be on the high road to idiocy."

"J. C., white; sent from Franklin county, February 2, 1844, for 2 years, for burglary; foreigner; 29 years old. He is idiotic, and was so when he came here; but is better than he was then. His mind is unsteady, and has strange and childish thoughts. Says his head was hurt in a fight in Ireland. He has been 5 years in this country."

"N. S., black; sent from Otsego, 14th April, 1843, for 10 years, for arson; native; about 25 years old. She is at the Lunatic Asylum, and is occasionally subject to violent paroxysms; but she is decidedly better than she was when first committed to the Prison; yet there is very little hope that she can ever be cured."

"A. W., black; sent from New York, 24th June, 1842, for 5 years, for burglary; native; 40 years old. She is suffering under mental delusions; she insists she is white, and always keeps her hands covered. She is decidedly insane, but not more so than when first committed to this Prison."

" A. B., white ; sent from Columbia county, on the 23d September, 1842, for 5 years, for burglary; native ; about 45 years old ; a foolish, silly woman, without the power to take a just view of any thing. She was in the same condition when she came to the Prison, and committed a burglary in order to get a pipe and tobacco, to have a smoke."

" C. W., white ; sent from Albany, July 15, 1839, for arson, for 10 years ; 17 years old ; native. He is nervous and excitable, and occasionally violent; his mind never steady, or under his control ; caused by fits when he was a child."

" W. H., white ; sent from New York, 15th December, 1843, for 2 years, for grand larceny; 19 years old ; native born. Became addicted to onanism 3 or 4 years before he came here, and was in a shocking state of dementia when he came in. He is now in a fair way of being cured ; but is still very stupid and idiotic."

" T. T., white ; sent from New York, for murder, for life, August 18, 1842; foreigner; 42 years old. He is harmless, but stupid, and incapable of taking proper views of things ; defective memory."

" T. M. B., white ; sent from Albany, September 30, 1842, for 3 years, for grand larceny ; 35 years old ; a native. He was sent to the Asylum, November 6, 1842 ; was insane when he came to the Prison, and is doubtless incurable."

" J. T., white ; sent from Albany, August 21, 1839, for 9 years, on 3 indictments, for burglary ; 16 years old then, and native born ; sent to the Asylum before we were connected with the Prison, and our books do not show when he was sent there. He is a confirmed case of insanity ; but we are unable to procure any account of its cause or duration."

" J. S. A., white boy; sent to the Asylum in March, 1844. We cannot ascertain what his real name is, nor by what name he was received into the Prison, nor how long he is to continue. He is a confirmed lunatic ; brought on him by onanism."

Statistics of the State Prison at Sing Sing, November 23, 1844.—Of 816, the whole number of convicts, 536 can read and write, 210 can read only, 115 can neither read nor write. 603 had opportunities for early religious instruction ; 258 had no such opportunity ; 192 were in County Prison before this offence ; 154 were in State Prison before this offence ; 357 were temperate ; 504, intemperate ; 404 were married ; 457, single ; 241, with both parents living ; 96, father only living ; 207, mother only living ; 317, neither father nor mother living. The causes for committing the offences for which they are now in Prison, were as follows : 16, want of protection in early life ; 192, intemperance ; 6, intemperance of wife ; 9, intemperance of parents ; 112, destitution ; 1, no conscience ; 26, innate depravity ; 7, insanity ; 17, weak principles ; 40, sudden temptation ; 11, anger ; 7 refuse to answer as to the cause ; 149, innocent, as they assert ; 2, don't know the cause ; 3, for gain ; 2, in self-defence ; 1, jealousy ; 253, evil communications ; 7, imbecility of mind.

70 were under 15 years of age when they committed the first offence, and 284 more under 21 years of age when they committed the first offence. The whole number being 861, 507 were over 21 years of age when they committed the first offence. Colored, 204. Under 21 years of age, 179. Crimes; against the property, 760; perjury, 10; breaking jail, 1. Native born, 621.

XII.—STATE PRISON IN OHIO.

Report of the Directors and Warden of the Ohio Penitentiary, for the Year 1844. *Columbus, Ohio. Printed for the Directors. — Octavo, pages* 14.

The directors of the Ohio Penitentiary,
" in submitting to the legislature their annual report for the year ending on the 30th of November, 1844, have the pleasure of presenting it in a highly prosperous condition, and they cheerfully admit that much honor is due to the warden for procuring this favorable result."

" There have been numerous improvements made in this institution during the past year, which add much to its appearance, convenience and health."

" The report of the warden shows the entire earnings of the institution, for the past year, to be $41,139 58 ; the aggregate expenditure, for the same period, $22,796 83; making the net earnings, over and above the expenditures, $18,342 74. There has been paid into the treasury, as directed by law, $13,950 in cash."

" The number of prisoners in confinement, on the 30th November, 1844, was 464. Of this number, 415 are white males ; 3 white females; 1 Indian ; 42 colored males, and 3 colored females ; which shows an increase of 4 the present year. The number received into the Prison, during the same time, is 133 ; showing a decrease of 17. The number discharged was 129; being 22 less than during the foregoing year. Upon the whole, this presents the pleasing reflection that, although the population of our state is rapidly increasing, yet the commission of crime is decreasing."

" The legislature, at the last session, abolished the office of deputy warden. Cases may arise, and indeed did arise during the last summer, showing the indispensable necessity of an assistant qualified and empowered to act in his place. An illness of a few weeks put it out of his power to attend personally to the duties of his office. Such a thing may occur at any time. . . . We are not acquainted with any well-regulated Prison of this kind, in the United States, but has two officers, at least, to attend to the finance and discipline of the institution."

" The employment of the convicts in branches of mechanical labor, of those kinds which constitute a considerable part of the business of the surrounding country,—thus bringing their labor into competition with that of free citizens, —is a subject which has attracted a large share of the public attention, and the board have given the matter that consideration to which it is entitled. We are satisfied, by our observation of the management of the institution, thus far, that all just cause of complaint, on this ground, by the mechanics of the state, may be removed without the least injury to the pecuniary interests of the institution. The remedy, in our opinion, is easy: it is to employ the convicts in branches of business which will not create this injurious competition. This, the board are satisfied, can be done with as much profit to the state as can be realized from any other source."

"We take the liberty of recommending to the favorable consideration of the legislature the propriety of altering the law of the last session, enlarging the Lunatic Asylum buildings, so as to keep the convicts within the walls of the Prison, and appropriate the proceeds of their labor to the accomplishment of that work. . . . . There are many advantages in keeping the convicts within the Prison. There are less chances for escape, which has been a large item of expense the past year. They will not wear out as many clothes. There will be less provision wasted; discipline and the rules can be better enforced, and will be better observed. Besides, the prisoners will earn more for the state, which will be plain from the following calculation. The cost of guarding alone, on the labor expended on the Asylum last season, is 30 per cent. on the money earned, while the work done in the Prison only cost 11½ per cent. on an average; and when the cost of guarding and escapes is considered, this institution only realized 25 cents per day on the labor done; and when we take into the account boarding and lost time, it will reduce their wages to a mere song. And we are not only convinced that it would be a great advantage to the state to keep the convicts employed in the Prison, but that it would be an advantage to the Asylum likewise. They have to pay 40 cents per day for the prisoners, according to the agreement entered into last season, and a part of the guard hire; and when the lost time, from bad weather and other causes, is considered, cost here, and other incidental expenses, it will raise convict almost as high as free labor; especially when we consider that convicts cannot be put to work as early, kept as late, and earn as much, as free laborers. The way wood is now cutting shows a difference of nearly 100 per cent. in favor of free labor. Thus it would appear evident, we think, to every reflecting mind, that it would be better to appropriate the proceeds of their labor to said building, and keep them within the walls of the Prison."

"The contractors appear to be doing well, and have paid up their contracts promptly."

"We are well aware there has been too much indifference manifested to the subject of moral and religious instruction in this institution; but the remedy, in a great measure, depends on future legislation. In the absence of any legislative enactment authorizing the appointment of a moral instructor, moral and religious instruction has been statedly administered to the convicts during the year, and indeed for nearly the last 4 years, by the Rev. S. T. Mills, who is entitled to great praise for his disinterested benevolence and ardent zeal for the spiritual and eternal welfare of these unfortunate outcasts from society. The course of instruction has comprised a Sunday school for those convicts, 50 to 70 in number, who came to the Prison unable to read; preaching the gospel and expounding the Scriptures to the body of the prisoners assembled in the chapel, and personal conversation with them at their cells; connected with the distribution of the Bible, the Book of Common Prayer, and other religious books and tracts."

"The testimony of the instructor is, that his communications have been listened to generally by the convicts, both in public and in private, with serious attention, and, in very many instances, with apparently deep interest; and that the influence of the Bible and the Sabbath, in connection with the privations of the Prison, have, in a number of cases, resulted in hopeful, thorough reformation. Many, who entered the Sunday school entirely illiterate, are now able to read the Bible intelligently."

"The physician's report presents a full and comprehensive view of the health and disease of the Prison, as well as details, particularly the character of each fatal case that has occurred during the past year.—The amount of sickness has been very large ; 1,192 cases in all ; 10,970 days' lost time, and only 11 deaths."

" In our report of last year, we stated that the average per cent. of deaths per annum, in the Penitentiary, since the new Prison had been occupied, had been about 1 in 32 ; last year, it was little less than 1 in 38 ; while, in the present year, it has been less than 1 in 42 ; and the number of deaths to the number of cases is but 1 in 108."

The warden, John Patterson, reports that the sources of income have been as follows : —

Cash received on account of smith, hame, lace, and saddle-tree shops, ...	$15,595	52
On account of tool shop, ...	3,004	04
Coopers' shop, ...	4,568	10
Pail and rake shops, ...	2,622	47
Tailors' shop, ...	3,717	58
Engine and machinery, ...	1,743	59
Carpet shop, ...	974	36
State shoemakers, $295 09 ; Prison shops, $420 63,	715	72½
Blacksmiths' shop, $233 17 ; lumpers, $219 25,	452	42
Masons, $75 19 ; interest, $13 10, ...	88	29
Incidental, $23 09 ; visitors, $1,038 78, ...	1,061	87½
United States, $466 13 ; fuel, $28 88, ...	492	01
Convict labor on account of Lunatic Asylum, . .	4,635	40
United States prisoners' board, ...	558	38
Individuals, $268 22 ; labor of prisoners, $502 00,	770	22
Labor of prisoners in chopping wood, ...	139	60
Earnings for the year ending December 1, 1844, .	$41,139	58

Expenditures ;—salaries, exclusive of guards for Lunatic Asylum, ...	$7,873	26½
Guards for Lunatic Asylum, ...	934	72
Clothing, $2,665 99 ; provisions, $6,486 45, . .	9,152	44
Furniture, $685 60 ; fuel and light, $1,407 83, .	2,093	43
Forage, $238 08 ; hospital, $551,69, ...	789	77
Incidental, $294 10 ; discharged convicts, $327 25,	621	35
Stationery, $27 40 ; teams, $58 25, ...	85	65
Escaped convicts, ...	297	87
Engine and machinery, ...	290	98
Smiths' shop, ...	191	54½
Printing and postage, ...	66	44
Attendance on visitors, ...	300	00
Writs of error, ...	103	28
Total amount of expenditures, ...	$22,796	84

Balance of earnings above expenses, ... $18,342 74
Allowed and certified for prosecution and transpor-
  tation of convicts, ... 11,942 00
Allowed and certified, &c., from Franklin county
  in previous years, ... 813 75
Cash received out of earnings of the present year, . 35,035 98
Collected on debts due previous to this year, . . . 950 75
Amount on hand December 1, 1843, ... 12,383 94

Paid for expenses of the past year, ... $22,796 83
Paid into the state treasury, ... 10,918 71
Paid into the treasury of Franklin county, ... 1,700 00
Paid superintendent of Lunatic Asylum, ... 581 29
Paid attorneys for the prosecution of convicts, . . 300 00
Paid physician his salary, ... 450 00
Paid for materials for improvement, ... 719 97

                                $37,466 80
Leaving on hand, ... 10,903 87
Debts due the institution, ... 8,365 91

The number of prisoners 30th November, 1843, ... 460
Number received during the year ending November 30,
  1844, ... 133

Total in Prison during the year, ... 593

There have left the Prison by expiration of sentence, 42
Pardoned by Governor Shannon, ... 33
Restoration to citizenship by ditto, ... 4
Pardoned by Governor Bartley, ... 16
Restoration to citizenship by Governor Bartley, . . . 19
Pardoned by President of the United States, . . . 1
By writ of error, ... 2
Deaths from disease, ... 11
Death by suicide, ... 1
                                129

Leaving in confinement, November 30, 1844, ... 464

White males, 415 ; Indian ditto, 1 ; white females, 3, . . . 419
Colored females, 3 ; colored males, 42, ... 45
                                464

    " During the year, 6 convicts have been received, who had previously been discharged from this Prison—5 for the second time, and 1 for the third."
    " Every man able to work has been constantly employed."
    " Not a dollar remains due from any of the contractors for convict labor for the past year."

" Having, to some extent, changed the mode of enforcing obedience to the rules of the Prison, I will take this occasion to offer a few remarks on this subject."

" Availing myself of reports from most of the well-regulated Prisons in the United States, I found that, in the management of this unfortunate class of men, those who have had the greatest experience concur in the opinion that, although it is necessary to enforce strict obedience, and that, in doing so, punishment is sometimes necessary, it is not the only means of obtaining order and preserving discipline among them. Most of them feel a strong sense of gratitude for good treatment, and it is believed this feeling may be cultivated so as to operate as a strong incentive to good conduct. Besides, when the heart can be reached in this way, a change of character may reasonably be expected; reformation follows; and thus one of the principal objects of the law, in consigning the man to the Penitentiary, is effected."

" During the short time I have had charge of this Penitentiary, it has been my constant aim to avoid, as much as possible, all unnecessary severity, and especially to use the *lash* as sparingly as possible. As a substitute for this mode of punishment, I have constructed a shower-bath, which, in most cases, I have found more efficient and less severe. For the last nine months, I have suffered no punishment of any kind to be inflicted, (except in extraordinary cases,) unless, upon mature deliberation, I believed it to be indispensably necessary; nor has any been inflicted except in my presence. To be always present on such occasions I have considered to be important, not only for the purpose of directing what manner of punishment should be inflicted, but to impress upon the offender the fact, that his punishment, having been inflicted under the eye, and by the direction, of the principal officer of the institution, there can therefore be no appeal from his decision. This consideration, it is believed, has a very salutary influence upon offenders, who, had they been punished by a subordinate officer, and not in the presence of the warden, might suppose, and, under such circumstances, generally do suppose, that a greater measure of punishment is inflicted, than would be sanctioned by the warden."

" But it is not on punishment we principally rely to preserve and promote the good order and discipline of the prison. I regard vigilance as more effectual than either the lash or the shower-bath in preventing disorderly conduct. When the prisoner knows that the eye of an efficient officer is constantly upon him, he will not commit acts which he knows will subject him to punishment. Hence it is highly important that there should always be in attendance a sufficient number of guards to oversee all the shops and places where prisoners are employed, and that they should be men of discretion—those whose deportment towards prisoners should be equally free from familiarity and harshness. They should likewise be judges of character; for, in their intercourse with prisoners, they will find it necessary to be by turns indulgent and firm, mild and severe."

" It gives me great pleasure to say that, although punishment, in any form, is very seldom resorted to in this Prison, the discipline is as perfect as it ever has been. The prisoners perform as much labor as they have ever done, and are more docile and happy."

XIII.—SIXTEENTH ANNUAL REPORT OF THE NEW PENITENTIARY IN PHILADELPHIA.

Sixteenth Annual Report of the Inspectors of the Eastern State Penitentiary of Pennsylvania. Transmitted to the Senate and House of Representatives, March, 1845.—Octavo, pages 59.

The first statement, in this Report, worthy of particular notice, relates to the exercise of the pardoning power. It is stated, on the first page of the Report, that 46 prisoners were pardoned during the last year. The average number of prisoners, according to the warden's statement, page 27, was 360. More than one eighth part, therefore, of the prisoners in the Eastern Penitentiary, were pardoned last year.

This is a great departure from the former policy of this institution.

The number pardoned, from the commencement, in 15 years previous to the last, was 135. The number pardoned in the second five years was 46, the same as during the last year ; the average number of prisoners, during this period, being 319 ; nearly as large as the average number last year. The number pardoned, in five years preceding the last, was 86 ; not twice as many as the last year, although the average number of prisoners was 371. We see, therefore, that the exercise of the pardoning power, last year, in regard to the New Penitentiary in Philadelphia, is a great departure from the former policy of this institution.

It is also a great departure from the policy of other states, in regard to their Penitentiaries. The number pardoned in 14 Penitentiaries in the United States, in 1843, was 181, out of an average of 3,347 prisoners ; *i. e.* 1 in 18, instead of more than 1 in 8.—*Nineteenth Report of Prison Discipline Society*, page 65.

The only remark the inspectors make on this unusual exercise of the pardoning power is as follows, page 4 : —

" It may not be improper here to remark, that several of the prisoners discharged by pardon were cases of such peculiar hardship, on account of the length of sentence, and other circumstances attending their conviction, as induced many benevolent citizens, entirely disconnected with the Penitentiary or its administration, to apply energetically to the executive for its clemency."

On the subject of a free and indiscreet use of the pardoning power, the joint committee of the legislature of Pennsylvania,

relative to the Eastern Penitentiary at Philadelphia, in a report
by Mr. Anderson, of Delaware county, read in the House of Representatives, March 26, 1835, use the following language : —

"There is a subject of such interest, connected with our Penitentiary system, which, although not precisely within the inquiries with which your committee were charged, yet is of so much importance, that they cannot refuse
to consider it. This is the exercise of the pardoning power, by the constitution vested in the chief executive magistrate. Our system of criminal
jurisprudence is exceedingly mild, compared with that of other countries.
Your committee think that it is wisely so. There can be no question, that a
system of mild punishments, which are always certain to be enforced, is the
most effective. It is the certainty of punishment, instead of great severity,
which deters offenders from the commission of crime. If, however, punishments are not only mild, but uncertain,—or, in other words, if these mild
punishments are liable to be frequently set aside by the exercise of the pardoning power,—their effect in preventing crime must be greatly diminished.
But this exercise of the pardoning power has an injurious effect upon the
convict himself. Your committee found, among the convicts whom they
visited, many whose minds seemed to be occupied with the hope of pardon.
The committee cannot better express their views on this subject, than by
introducing, from the valuable Preface of Dr. Lieber to the work of Messrs.
De Beaumont and De Tocqueville, an extract from the report of Mr. Dermont
to the representative council of Geneva, which expresses, in strong and
convincing terms, the proper views on this subject.

"'It may be laid down as an incontestible principle in matters of penal
justice,—I was going to say in penal pharmacy,—every thing which diminishes the certainty of punishment is evil ; every punishment which is not fixed,
which floats between fear and hope, is a punishment badly contrived. The
causes of uncertainty between the law and its operation are already too
numerous. If this is an inevitable evil, it ought to be reduced to its narrowest
limits. But what shall we think of a law, the object of which is to render the
punishment uncertain ? And this is, nevertheless, the result of a tribunal of
pardon, open to the petitions of the prisoner during the whole term of his
imprisonment. We should know man very imperfectly, were we not aware
of the readiness with which he takes his wishes for hopes, and his hopes for
probabilities. I agree that a convict, wishing for pardon, will take care not
to create himself difficulties by acts of insubordination or violence ; I allow
that he will pay attention to his words and behavior ; but it is a fact that this
idea, always present to his mind, causing a disturbed feeling of anxiety and
expectation, will absorb and prevent him from being resigned to his situation,
and following his labor with reflection and calmness. He feels like an indigent person, who, having taken a lottery ticket, has his imagination absorbed
by dreams of success and fears of misfortune. It has been observed that
prisoners, after having been unsuccessful in their petitions for pardon, become
more calm, and resigned to their situation and duties, as soon as their fate
was fixed. I owe this interesting observation to our jailer. Thus, for the
double end of increasing the certainty of punishment, and of making more
subservient to moral correction, this indefinite recourse to pardon ought to be
abolished, and a fixed character be given to it.'"

Eastern Penitentiary, Vol. I. 55.

*The second statement in this Report, worthy of particular
notice, relates to the bill of mortality.*

The inspectors say, (page 4,) — "The whole number of
deaths during the year was 13. . . . The whole number of
prisoners in confinement during the year was 497." They

then make the per cent. of deaths on the whole number who have been in the Prison, distinguishing the black from the white ; and not on the average number. It should be on the average.

Ascertaining the per cent. of deaths, however, on the whole number, and not on the average number, is of small consequence, compared with what follows. The inspectors say, (page 14,) they believe " that the mortality under the separate system is not greater than that of any other system."

Compare this declaration with the following facts from the reports of last year : —

At Sing Sing, N. Y., there was
an average of . . . . . 887 prisoners and 16 deaths.
At Auburn, N. Y., an average of 774   "   " 8   "
At Charlestown, Mass.,   "   " 270   "   " 2   "
In the New Penitentiary in Phil-
adelphia, an average of . . 360   "   " 13   "
In eleven Prisons on the Au-
burn plan, ... 3,154   "   " 48   "
In two Prisons in Philadelphia
and at Pittsburg, . . . 488   "   " 19   "

That is, 1 death in 55 at Sing Sing ; 1 death in 96 at Auburn ; 1 death in 135 at Charlestown ; and 1 death in 27 in the New Penitentiary in Philadelphia ;—1 death in 65 last year in eleven Prisons on the Auburn plan, and 1 death in 25 in two Prisons on the Pennsylvania plan.

The table prepared from the official reports of the thirteen Penitentiaries of the last year is herewith presented. The information concerning the Pittsburg Penitentiary is taken from the Sixteenth Report of the New Penitentiary in Philadelphia, page 13.

And to show that it is not the result of one year's experience, but of the whole term of time during which the New Penitentiary has been in operation, we have prepared a table exhibiting the mortality of several Prisons from 1829, when the New Penitentiary in Philadelphia received its first inmates.

According to this table,

At Wethersfield, Conn., the total of the aver-
age number of prisoners for 15 years, was, 2,789; deaths, 67.
At Charlestown, Mass., the total of the aver-
age number of prisoners for 17 years, was 4,805; deaths, 82.
At Auburn, N. Y., the total of the average
number of prisoners for 17 years, was 11,436; deaths, 201.
At the New Penitentiary in Philadelphia,
the total of the average number of prisoners for 16 years, was . . . . . . 4,119; deaths, 160.

At Wethersfield, Conn., 1 death to 41 prisoners ;
At Charlestown, Mass., 1 death to 58 prisoners ;
At Auburn, N. Y., 1 death to 56 prisoners ;
In the New Penitentiary in Philadelphia, 1 death to 27 prisoners ;
In the three Prisons above named, on the Auburn plan, 1 death to 54 prisoners ; and in the New Penitentiary in Philadelphia, on the Pennsylvania plan, 1 death to 25 prisoners.

The third statement in this Report, worthy of particular notice, relates to the reformatory character of the New Penitentiary in Philadelphia, and its tendency to prevent crime and inspire the convict community with dread—a most important point, in regard to which the fairness and fullness of all statements should be equal to their importance. If it can be shown by the records to have the superiority in this respect, it will go far to remove all other objections, and raise up a multitude of friends to the system. In order to show this, the inspectors say, (page 5,) —

" Of 1,916, the whole number received, there have been but 76 second convictions."

" There were but 4 prisoners, of this whole number, a third time convicted, and none have been a fourth time in our Prison."

" The following are the reconvictions in this Prison in 1842, 1843, 1844 :—

Year.	No. received.	Second Convictions.	Third Convictions.
1842	142	11	1 = 8.45 per cent.
1843	156	10	2 = 7.69 per cent.
1844	138	10	0 = 7.24 per cent."

The great and important practical results deduced from these statements by the inspectors are as follows, (page 6 :) —

" Thus crime is prevented ; the evil-minded and wicked are deterred from violating the law ; reform is effected ; society protected ; and the great aim of Penitentiary punishment attained, and the prophecies of the friends of this system realized."

They further add, —

" The Massachusetts State Prison claims to be a model Prison of the aggregate system ; and by its reports for the year 1844, we find the following facts :—

" Of the 276 convicts now in Prison, 54 are recommitments ; viz., 38 are second comers ; 13 are third comers ; 1 is a fourth comer ; 1 is a fifth comer ; 1 is a sixth comer. Of the 105 convicts received into Prison the last year, 16 are recommitments ; viz., 12 are second comers, and 4 are third comers."

Let us carefully examine the above important statements and compare them with the tables from the records of the Eastern Penitentiary, as presented by the warden.

The inspectors say, (pages 6 and 7,) —

" Of this 1,916, the whole number received, there have been but 76 second convictions."

The warden says, (page 32,) —

Number of Convictions.

"First convictions to this Penitentiary, ... 1,360
Second convictions under the separate system, ... 76
Second convictions to this Penitentiary of those who had been in
    other Prisons previous to their first reception here, ... 103
Second convictions of those who are here for the first time, but have
    been once before in some other Prison, ... 163."

Again, the inspectors say, (page 6,) —

"There were but 4 prisoners of this whole number a third time convicted."

The warden says, (page 32,) —

"Third convictions under the separate system, ... 4
Third convictions to this Penitentiary of those who have been in other
    Prisons previous to their first reception here, ... 18
Third convictions of those who are here for the first time, but have
    been twice before in other Prisons, ... 104."

The inspectors say, too, that,

"In 1844, the number received was 138; second convictions, 10; third
convictions, 0; 7.24 per cent."

The warden says, (page 29,) in giving the number of convictions in 1844, —

"First convictions to this Penitentiary, ... 110
Second convictions, under the separate system, ... 10
Second convictions to this Penitentiary of those who had been in
    other Prisons previous to their first reception here, ... 6
Third convictions to this Penitentiary of those who had been in other
    Prisons previous to their first conviction here, ... 4."

Let the above statements of the inspectors and warden be
carefully compared.

Note.—"The table of convictions," the inspectors remark, in their Fifteenth Report, "has hitherto conveyed erroneous impressions, from the circumstance that no distinction was made between those who were the subjects
of the separate system alone (as far as could be ascertained) and such as were
known to be old convicts at the time of their first reception here."

The inspectors say, —

"Thus crime is prevented," . . . "the great aim of Penitentiary punishment
attained," . . . . "and the prophecies of the friends of this system realized."

There was a declaration, in the Fourth Report of the Eastern Penitentiary, that

"The lonely cell had made such an impression as to induce them" (*i. e.*,
the old convicts) "to bid a long farewell to the state where legislators have
provided a penal code involving so many privations."—*Fourth Report of Eastern Penitentiary for* 1832.

Compare with this declaration, the result from the records, as
exhibited in the warden's report, pages 32 and 33. See Sixteenth Report of the Eastern Penitentiary in Philadelphia.

Number of convictions for the *whole term of time.* — *Warden's report for* 1845, pages 32 and 33.

"First convictions to this Penitentiary, ... 1,360
Second convictions under the separate system, ... 76

Second convictions to this Penitentiary of those who had been in
other Prisons previous to their first reception here, ...   103
Second convictions of those who are here for the first time, but have
been once before in some other Prison, ...   163
Third convictions under the separate system, ...   4
Third convictions to this Penitentiary of those who have been in
other Prisons previous to their first reception here, ...   18
Third convictions of those who are here for the first time, but have
been twice before in other Prisons, ...   104
Fourth convictions, the first three having been to other Prisons, .   52
Fifth convictions, the first four having been to other Prisons, . .   18
Sixth convictions, the former five having been to other Prisons,. .   15
Seventh convictions, the former six having been to other Prisons, .   1
Ninth convictions, the former eight having been to other Prisons, .   2

Total, ... 1,916."

And to show that the results of the *last year* are similar to
those of the *whole course of time*, we quote from the warden's
report, page 29 : —

"Of 138 prisoners received during the year —
First convictions to this Penitentiary, ...   110
Second convictions under the separate system, ...   10
Second convictions to this Penitentiary of those who had been in
other Prisons previous to their first reception here, ...   6
Third convictions to this Penitentiary of those who had been in other
Prisons previous to their first conviction here, ...   4
Fourth convictions, the first three having been to other Prisons,. .   5
Fifth convictions, the first four having been to other Prisons, . . .   2
Sixth convictions, the former five having been to other Prisons, . .   1

138."

What is the evidence, in 1845, that "the lonely cell made
such an impression as to induce them " (*i. e.*, the old convicts)
" to bid a long farewell to the state where legislators have provided a penal code involving so many privations " ?

Of 1,916, the whole number of convictions, 556 had been
convicted two, three, four, five, six, seven, or nine times, to this
or other Prisons.

Is this a good basis for the inspectors' report, page 6, where
they say, " Of 1,916, the whole number received, there have
been but 76 second convictions " ?

There have been 179 second convictions to that Prison ; and
there were 556, which is more than one fourth part of the
whole number, who had been more than once convicted and
sent to this or some other Prison. Are these facts, furnished
in detail in the warden's report, the basis of the following conclusions, drawn by the inspectors, page 6 : — " Thus crime is
prevented ; the evil-minded and wicked are deterred from violating the law ; reform is effected ; society is protected ; and
the great aim of Penitentiary punishment attained, and the
prophecies of the friends of this system realized " ?

The fourth statement of the inspectors, in the Sixteenth Report of the New Penitentiary in Philadelphia, worthy of notice, is a comparison of the number of convicts in Pennsylvania and New York, for the purpose of showing the efficacy of the system of Prison Discipline in Pennsylvania. It is as follows, (page 9.) The inspectors say, —

"The prisons in Pennsylvania are on the Pennsylvanian or separate system. It is ascertained that the whole number of convicts in confinement in the two State Prisons, Pittsburg and Philadelphia, is 470. Add to these convicts in the Philadelphia and other County Prisons, gives, say, 650 to 700 for the state. . . . . . In the state of New York, where the opposite system of Prison discipline prevails, the whole number in confinement in the two State Prisons, (Sing Sing and Auburn,) as taken from the last reports, is over 1,600."

In view of the above facts, as a part of the basis of the conclusion, the inspectors say, they " believe that the Pennsylvania or separate system is pre-eminently a successful experiment in preventing crime."

The above basis and conclusion are made without reference to the fact that the population of New York, according to the last census, was 704,898 more than in Pennsylvania, and the more important fact that the average length of sentences to the New Penitentiary in Philadelphia, of the 138 convicts received last year, was 3 years and 15 days, or 1,110 days, while the average length of sentences of 868 convicts in Prison at Sing Sing, August 26, 1844, was 5 years and 5 months, or 1,975 days. It should be remembered, also, in making the comparison, that the governor of Pennsylvania pardoned one eighth of all the convicts in the Eastern Penitentiary, while the governor of New York pardoned 1 in 19 only. And 1 in 27 died last year in the New Penitentiary in Philadelphia, while last year only 1 in 68 died at Auburn and Sing Sing. If, then, Pennsylvania had had 704,898 more inhabitants, making the population equal to that of New York, then Pennsylvania would have had 286 more convicts, which would increase her 700 convicts to 986. And if the average length of sentence was 1,975 days, as at Sing Sing, according to the data above, instead of 1,110 days, as in Philadelphia, it would increase the number of prisoners from 986 to 1,754. And if the number pardoned in Pennsylvania were 1 in 19, as in New York, instead of 1 in 8, it would increase the whole number, 1,754, 1 in 11, which would be an increase of 159, making the whole number 1,913; and if only 1 in 68 of this number died, instead of 1 in 27, this would again increase the number 1 in 41, which is 45. So that, if these qualifying circumstances were considered, the number of prisoners in Pennsylvania would be 1,958, instead of 700, as stated by the inspectors; which number is much larger than 1,600, as in New York. It would seem, therefore, almost superfluous to remark, that, in comparing two states and systems for the purpose of ascertaining which has the best system of Prison discipline, there should be a comparison of the population of the states, of the length of sentences, of the frequency of pardons and deaths, under the two systems, as well as of the number of prisoners; otherwise the thing to be proved may not be proved satisfactorily. It is a great conclusion to be drawn from such premises, that "the Pennsylvania system is preeminently a successful experiment in preventing crime."

The fifth statement worthy of notice in the Sixteenth Report of the New Penitentiary in Philadelphia, is the language of the physicians concerning the effect of the system on the mind.

Dr. Hartshorne, says, (page 43,) —

"The medical question, the most vital in all its bearings, and the one by far the most difficult to answer, is that relating to the effect of this privation of mute association and partial change of scene upon the well-being of the mind.

" We feel no uneasiness in treating the question of physical health, because the results are clearly expressed, and within our reach; the facts are abundant and positive; they convince us, and ought to convince others."

In the Penitentiaries in Pennsylvania, in Philadelphia, and at Pittsburg, on the average number of prisoners last year, which was 488, the deaths were 19, or one in 25. For the same time, in 11 Penitentiaries in the United States, — Maine, Vermont, Massachusetts, Rhode Island, Auburn and Sing Sing, N. Y., Ohio, Kentucky, Michigan, Missouri, and Louisiana, — on the average number of prisoners, which was 3,154, the deaths were 48, or one in 65.

Are there facts abundant and positive in favor of the New Penitentiary in Philadelphia? Ought they to convince the physician and others that the system is favorable to health and life?

Again says the physician, —

" Theory would induce us to suppose that there is nothing in mere separation to cause a large amount of sickness or a great mortality." And he adds, " When the ever-varied and unfathomable mind becomes the subject of discussion, we feel at once that we are involved in doubts, which only a prolonged and faithful study can enable us to clear away."

Again: " As far as my individual opinion is concerned, all that I have seen and heard, during my fifteen months' residence, in daily contact with the unfortunate subjects of our observation, has only increased the confidence,—which a better understanding of the question soon forced upon me,—that the horrors of seclusion, as practised in the separate cells, and compared to the modified separation of the silent system, were altogether imaginary; and that the fears in respect to the effect upon the reason were equally groundless." . . . . . .

" As usual, we have received some prisoners in a state of mental derangement." (Page 45.)

As this is the case in all the Penitentiaries in the land, we would ask whether the cell is a suitable place for such.

. . . . "some others, who had been previously insane." (Same page.)

Is a cell, we would ask, calculated to confirm the reason or bring back the dreadful malady ?

. . . . " some, who were at the time on the verge of insanity."

Shall they be committed to cells while the reason is just on the verge of insanity ?

" Others, again, have exhibited so low a grade of intellect as to be but one degree above imbecility."

Is it just and merciful to put the poor imbeciles in cells ?

. . . . " while 2 or 3 were perfect idiots."

Shall their unhappy condition be rendered more so by confinement in cells?

" Of the 9 prisoners admitted more or less insane, there were 8 white and 1 colored."

The period of time in which these 9 insane, or partially insane patients were committed, was the first 6 months of the year 1844. The whole number of admissions, during the year, was only 138. If, therefore, an equal number of prisoners were admitted in each half of the year, more than one seventh part committed for crime, in the first half of the year, were insane or partially insane. We are not told whether any of these had ever been in this Prison before. Can we not have more information concerning these cases? Why should these insane poor not only be committed to Prison for crime, but to separate cells?

It is common, in all the Prisons, to find more or less of such cases, among those committed for crime.

What can teach more impressively the great lessons of pity, and compassion, and kindness in Prison discipline ?

" The new cases under treatment since January 1, 1844, were 1,690 and 1,862 ; the first a mulatto female, of excellent education, and previously respectable, — the wife of a negro clergyman, — who had become involved in a larceny, through the arts of a companion, to whose bad character she professed to be a stranger. She entered the Prison very much depressed in spirits, continued always silent and repining, complaining always of headache and inability to sleep. In the course of a few weeks, she began to manifest more marked symptoms of derangement, which increased in violence for a while, but have now almost entirely subsided."

Should this new case have been treated in an infirmary, or in a cell ? The physician of the New Penitentiary proposes this year such changes in the construction of the building, in regard to three old blocks of cells, as would enable them " to construct a more suitable infirmary for the sick." By this proposed improvement, it appears to be a fair inference, that fifteen years have passed away, in this Prison, with an average of about 400 prisoners, without a suitable infirmary for the sick. If there had been such an infirmary, and this new case of insanity had been committed to it, would she probably, in the course of a few weeks, have begun to exhibit more marked symptoms of derangement? or was the cell the proper place to treat this new case of diseased mind ?

" The second case was a young negro girl, admitted only a few days before my departure. She was carried into the Prison in a state of insensibility, from hysterical convulsions, and at once presented all the symptoms of a recent case of hysterical mania, from which she had not recovered when I left her, in the charge of Dr. Given."

" We have had, therefore, presented to us, in the course of the half year, two cases, neither of which can be attributed to the operation of the discipline ; since both were affected in their minds at the time of their entrance, and probably were indebted to the mortifications and anxieties of the trial, and the peculiar hardship of their conviction, for the painful state of mind into which they had been thrown."

Were these persons committed, on their entrance, to the cells? If so,—and nothing to the contrary appears in the report,—was it kind and humane ?

Surely they required, instead of cells, the treatment which Dr. Hartshorne suggests, as proper for confirmed lunatics— more indulgence as to conduct, and a greater attention to the nature of their occupations ; more exercise in the open air ; and, in a word, as much variety of scene *as the principles of the separate system will allow.* Perhaps the two recent cases above mentioned had it ; but we are not told.

Dr. Robert A. Given, the successor of Dr. Hartshorne, says, —

" I deem an observation of six months quite too limited to justify the expression of an opinion on a matter so momentous as the influence of the separate system on the mind."

" Since I have had charge of the medical department, three cases of mental alienation were developed within the institution, the first of which, No. 1,796, was notorious for the practice of self-abuse."

Was the cell a favorable place for removing the cause ? It is called the *secret vice.*

" The second, No. 1,730, is the son of an insane mother."

Dr. Given elsewhere says, that

" Twenty per cent. of all prisoners received since the date of my appointment had insane relatives."

Is the cell the place to guard against this constitutional infirmity ?

" The third" new case under Dr. Given " entered the institution scrofulous, but quite sane."

Are not scrofulous diseases, rather than almost all others,

developed in all their ruinous effects on body and mind in the cell ?

" On referring to the accompanying medical report, it will be found that 9 prisoners were admitted laboring under some form of mental derangement, and 3 others have since been received in the same condition, making 12 in all. No. 1,862, referred to by Dr. H., is now quite restored; but for the others I fear there is no chance of recovery, so long as they remain with us. I have to report the discharge of only one prisoner whose mind became deranged during imprisonment."

" The fact of 12 individuals, in the space of a single year, having been branded with the opprobrious epithets of *prisoner* and *felon*, and punished for crimes of which they are legally and morally innocent, cannot fail to strike the philanthropist with dismay. Yet so long as Pennsylvania remains without a state asylum for her insane poor, a number of this unfortunate class of persons must necessarily be committed to her Penitentiaries."

We add, that these should be treated in cells where " the physician fears there is no chance of recovery while they remain," and that this number in one Prison should be increased to 17 by 5 new cases, strikes us " with dismay."

Well may Dr. Given propose a more suitable infirmary than the cells themselves in the old blocks, which the physician of the Prison now pronounces as " inferior in their construction, as regards temperature, ventilation, and light."

We think it is time that the whole effective force of the Prison and the community were turned to the subject of improvement in the New Penitentiary in Philadelphia.

The sixth statement in this report, worthy of notice, is as follows, (page 12, at the top :) —

At Auburn, " 11 prisoners died last year. The physician reports, 'that it has long been a principle upon which pardons have been granted, viz., that they were necessary to save life.' ' 12 pardons were granted' during the last year ' for that reason.' So that, in fact, those who did die, and those who were pardoned out dying, make 23. The chief cause of mortality appears to be consumption."

" The report further states, that, since 1817, 229 prisoners have died at Auburn. Within the last 10 years, 398 prisoners have been pardoned; therefore it may be fairly estimated, from the above facts, that over 400 have died, or were pardoned dying, at Auburn since 1817. It is true that, while the whole number of deaths since 1817 are given, the accounts of pardons only extend 10 years back. The estimate may be much larger."

Thus far accurately quoted, and compared with the top of the 12th page of the Sixteenth Report.

Compare this with the language of the physician, Theodore Dimon, M. D., (Auburn Annual Report, No. 18. In Senate, January 12, 1844.) He says, (pages 80 and 81,) —

" The number of deaths in this Prison yearly is somewhat diminished by pardons ; and as it seems to me to be a legitimate subject for the report of your physician, inasmuch as it must form a part of the correct data upon which to ascertain the effects of Prison confinement upon the health, I am induced to mention it in this connection.   The number of pardons for the last ten years have been as follows, viz.: In 1834, 49 pardons; in 1835, 54 do. ; in 1836, 45 do. ; in 1837, 35 do. ; in 1838, 57, do. ; in 1839, 14 do. ; in 1840, 33 do. ; in 1841, 35 do.; in 1842, 38 do.; in 1843, 38 do.

" As it has long been a principle upon which pardons have been granted, viz., that they were necessary to save life, it is safe to presume, in the absence of actual information, that an equal proportion of the above pardons have been yearly granted for such reason.   The past year, the number of pardons granted for this reason has been 12.   Of these I have ascertained that 6 have perfectly recovered, and that 1 has died; and I have no doubt that 2 more are not, or would not have been, living at this date, if they had remained in the Prison.   If, then, the present year is a fair guide in this matter, there should be added to the yearly report of deaths 2 or 3, if it is desirable to compare the mortality in this Prison with that of others, for the purpose of ascertaining the safest mode of confinement for the health of convicts."

The inspectors of the New Penitentiary in Philadelphia say,

" Twelve pardons were granted during the last year, 'for that reason.'   So that, in fact, those who did die, and those who were pardoned out dying, make twenty-three."

Here is an addition to the bill of mortality, (which was 11,) for the cause assigned, of 12.

Dr. Dimon says, —

" If, then, the present year is a fair guide in this matter, there should be added to the yearly report of deaths 2 or 3."

Again, the Inspectors say, they " were pardoned dying."

It is a fair inference from what Dr. Dimon says, that they were pardoned to prevent dying.

Besides, Dr. Dimon says, —

" Six have perfectly recovered, and *one* has died; and I have no doubt that two more are not, or would not have been, living at this date, if they had remained in the Prison."

And what does Dr. Leander B. Bigelow say, the present physician of the Prison ?   (Senate Document, No. 8, January 10, 1845, Annual Report of the Auburn Prison, page 84.)

" It will be observed by examining the hospital report for the year 1843, that the physician there gives the number of deaths at 11 for the then current year, and also states that there were 12 others pardoned to save their lives. He there gives a table showing the whole number of pardons granted for a given number of years, and specifying the particular years in which they were issued.   He further states, that it has for a long time been a practice to grant pardons upon the above principle ; and ends by giving it as his opinion, that the number of pardons granted for the purpose of saving life, during the years enumerated, was in the same proportion as in 1843.   Now, to prevent any who may feel an interest in comparing the different systems of Prison discipline, and their influences upon the health of convicts, from adopting erroneous conclusions, founded on the opinion of the physician given in the above-named report, I consider it my duty to expose, as far as my knowledge enables me, the error of the doctor's statement."

" I was physician to the Auburn Prison, during the term of 4 years, from 1834 to 1838. These 4 years are embraced in the time above referred to, and there was not one pardon obtained during the whole of that period, for a sick convict, on the representation that it was indispensable for the preservation of life, neither has there been during the year just ended. I have been induced to make these remarks, that the public might not be led to the very erroneous conclusion, that there is a greater amount of sickness existing in the Prison than appears on the record."

The seventh statement in this Report, worthy of notice, relates to the expenses and earnings of the New Penitentiary.

If we understand the warden's account, the amount expended for subsistence, from January 1 to December 31, 1844, was $18,180 92
Profit and loss on the business of masonry, cordwaining, picking wool and oakum, carpentering, tailoring, &c. 17,468 64

Balance against the Prison, ...   712 28

The account current of expenses and earnings makes no mention of officers' salaries, which, in all Prisons, is one of the principal items of expense, generally the largest, and almost as commonly stated as the expense for provisions. Why not state the amount, and where paid ?

It appears from the warden's account of expenses, that the balance against the institution, if we understand correctly, is $712 28, which deficit is to be met from some source. The balance from last year's account is not given so that it can be understood either what it was or how it was met. But the warden says, (page 23,) in consequence of there being no state hospital for the poor, many idiots, epileptic, and insane, entirely unfit for our discipline, continue to be sent to this Prison. It is impossible to give proper accommodations in their cells to this class, and each year they continue confirms their malady ; causing a heavy charge against the counties whilst here, materially affecting the discipline of the Prison, and rendering them, most probably, a charge on the public for life. Whether this means that particular prisoners of these classes are an expense to the counties from which they come, and that bills are made out accordingly against said counties, or that, in the aggregate, they are a heavy expense to the institution, and the sum total of such expenses is shared by the counties in the annual deficit, we do not know. How is the institution supported? What are its annual expenses above earnings? These are important practical inquiries, which the world might be benefited by knowing, so as to see whether it is a good model Prison in this respect.

The eighth statement, worthy of notice, regards the general health of the prisoners.

The inspectors say, (page 11,)—

" From the monthly reports to the board by the physicians during this period," — i. e., the last six years, during which time "this subject," they say, "has received the careful observation of the inspectors," — " it appears that, in the year 1839, there were *seven hundred and ninety-three prisoners receiving medical care,* either in the cells, at work, or in the infirmary," (by " infirmary," we understand the tier of cells appropriated to the sick,) " if too sick to be at work. The aggregate number of sick, as thus given, constitute items of sickness, and reported on the sick list. In 1840, there were *eight hundred and seventy-two ;* in 1841, there were *seven hundred and forty-two ;* in 1842, there were *six hundred and seventy-seven ;* in 1843, there were *three hundred and seventy-seven ;* and last year, there were *two hundred and twenty.*"

" The great reduction in the number of items of sickness, within the last two years, arises from the fact, that a change in the medical department took place in 1843, by which the physician was required to reside in the Prison, and devote his entire attention to the sick, and the supervision of the hygiene of the institution."

This is most important information. If it proves that only 220, out of 360, the average number of prisoners, were under the care of the physician, and under medical treatment, last year, it proves that more than three times that number were under the care of the physician, and under medical treatment, from 1839 to 1842, inclusive.

The ninth statement worthy of notice is, that the warden hopes to see singing extended in religious worship.

Although the convicts do not leave their cells, nor see each other, or their minister, they can unite with him and each other in singing. The warden says, (page 22,) —

" In one block, containing nearly 100 prisoners, the Rev. Mr. Crawford has officiated, every Sunday, (with few exceptions.) Under his care, these convicts have improved much in singing, which is a part of the devotions ; and, during this exercise, there has been no attempt at communication between them. I confidently assert this," says the warden, " as, if such attempts were made, detection would be almost certain. Two officers, with woollen socks, are passing constantly in front of the cells during service. I am more particular in this notice, as I hope to draw the attention of the Board to its extension, as, in my opinion, the effects are calculated to produce a solemnizing influence on the mind, and prepare it to receive the truths of the gospel. The power of joining in church music (though attained in a Prison) might induce some to attend a place of worship after liberation."

The tenth statement worthy of notice in this Report, regards the increased amount of moral and religious instruction.

The moral instructor says, (page 56,)—

" The amount of public instruction has been considerably increased during the past year. Owing to the almost constant aid of Rev. Dr Crawford, and the occasional assistance of other ministers of the gospel, there have been 190 sermons and other addresses delivered."

In connection with this statement, it is important to know that this Prison is built with seven corridors, radiating, in as many directions, from a central building ; and it has been sometimes supposed that a man standing in the centre building could speak to all the prisoners in the Prison, and be heard in every cell. This is not the case. The speaker or preacher leaves the centre building, passes about 100 feet through a passage to the cell building, in one of the seven corridors ; and at a station near the entrance of the arch, on either side of which the cells are arranged, he takes his place, and there he speaks with a very slow, measured, and distinct articulation ; otherwise the reverberation and echo are such as to confuse both speaker and hearer. By this arrangement, the prisoners can hear, if the feed-hole doors, or other doors, are thrown open, and they stand near them to listen. In this way all the prisoners, in one block of cells, can hear the speaker ; but they do not see him, neither does he see them. Three of the blocks of cells are one-story buildings, and contain each about 38 or 40 cells, and four of them are two-story buildings, and contain about twice that number ; so that 360, the average number distributed throughout the building, in their separate cells, would require seven sermons and other addresses, that all the prisoners might hear one. The whole number of sermons and addresses last year having been 190, the prisoners, if distributed equally in the seven corridors, each heard, during the year, 27 sermons or addresses ; i. e., each had the benefit of a religious service once a fortnight. If they were placed in six corridors, then they had one seventh more.

The moral instructor would have performed a most acceptable service if he had stated how the Sabbath is spent by the prisoners in the cells,—about one half or one third the whole number, — who have no preaching ; whether they are kept shut up all day ; whether those who have no exercising yards to their cells are taken out for exercise one hour, and, if so, where ; whether any Sabbath school has yet been formed in this Prison, now sixteen years old. We know an earnest effort was made, several years ago, to establish a Sabbath school in this Prison, without success ; and we have never heard of a similar effort since. Whether the moral instructor spends his Sabbaths in the cells after preaching, and is assisted, if he does, in this benevolent work by Dr. Crawford, we are not informed. We hope he does ; for we can conceive of no condition, in Christian or heathen land, more pitiable than that of a poor, degraded, and ignorant convict, in a cell on the Sabbath, without preaching, without Sabbath school instruction, without Christian visitation and sympathy, some of them without exercise in the open air. Will the moral instructor inform the public whether this is not the condition, at least every other Sabbath, or every third Sabbath, of a large number of prisoners in the Eastern Penitentiary? If a change in this respect is one of the improvements contemplated in this Prison, we pray that it may be soon effected. Perhaps it will bring the public and the proper authorities to the consideration of the subject of building a chapel in this Prison. If they choose to build it with stalls, so that the prisoners cannot see one another, as at Pentonville, near London, so let it be; and if they choose to march the prisoners to the chapel with hoods over their heads, with peepholes for their eyes, so that they cannot see each other's features, so let it be. But as they have found out how to take the prisoners to the baths without any evil communication, and how to employ them in the large gardens, maintaining, at the same time, the Pennsylvania system; and if the invalid convicts can be let out of their cells into the open courts, without constituting a positive modification of the kind of discipline maintained; and if a suitable infirmary can be constructed, in one of the old blocks, for the sick, according to the recommendation of the physician; we see no good reason why there should not be a chapel to be used on the Sabbath, and at other times, for devotional purposes, morning and evening prayers every day in the week, and as a school-room for purposes of education, as at Pentonville.

The eleventh statement in the Sixteenth Report of the Eastern Penitentiary, worthy of particular notice, relates to increased facilities for education.

"In the last annual report of the inspectors, they say, that, 'Fully impressed with the necessity of a watchful care over the moral and mental improvement of the prisoners, as constituting a fundamental principle in this, as in all Penitentiary reform, [they] are endeavoring to effect some improvement in the present plan of such instruction, particularly as relates to the education in reading and writing; thereby to enlarge the number of those who obtain this knowledge while in confinement.'

"Within the last year, the moral and rudimental instruction has been divided. The former has been left, as heretofore, under the law, together with such religious teaching as each prisoner may desire, and from whatever professional teacher he may select. The latter has been intrusted to a competent person, who acts as an overseer when required. Ample time is thus given to both branches of learning; and thus a schoolmaster has been successfully introduced into the Prison, whose chief duty it is to teach the ignorant to read and write, and practical arithmetic.

"There are now 47 prisoners receiving instruction in the first class, the only one yet formed under the late regulation. Of these, 43 could not read on admission, 47 could not write, and 47 had no knowledge of arithmetic."

The twelfth statement in this Report, worthy of particular notice, in regard to which something has been done before, is the employment of prisoners in gardening.

Twelve acres of ground, nearly, are inclosed within the external yard walls of the New Penitentiary in Philadelphia. The centre building, with its radiating corridors, may occupy a quarter part of this area, leaving sufficient ground for six gardens, of probably more than an acre each.

The warden says, in the last report, (page 21,) —

" The physician has availed himself of the power granted him by law, of requiring me to employ separately the invalid prisoners in the cultivation of the large yards between the blocks. A careful officer, skilled in horticulture, has superintended those so employed, taking special care that no two should approach or recognize each other. The yards being divided by the buildings, makes this task easy ; and the prisoner, being aware that the privilege so highly valued would be lost by violating the rule, has no inducement thereto. This plan," says the warden, " is not only humane, but important in a pecuniary point of view—both in restoring health and making those productive who were formerly the contrary. Six gardens are cultivated in this manner, which, during the greater part of the year, can furnish, under the physician's orders, separate employment for twelve invalids half a day each. The produce of this labor has been valuable in the support, and conducive to preserving the health of the well prisoners. Between 400 and 500 bushels of tomatoes were one of the many descriptions of vegetables furnished during the last season."

The physician, Dr. Hartshorne, says, (page 35,) —

" The cultivated grounds between the blocks, and around the main wall, produce ample supplies of a variety of green vegetables, which are liberally furnished with the potatoes or rice in the daily dinner mess. Large quantities of tomatoes, onions, lettuce, and cabbage, are distributed uncooked, from time to time, among the men, and, with the vinegar, salt, and pepper for every cell, afford refreshing salads, which, to say the least, must abundantly protect the prisoners from the inroads of the scurvy. Vegetables of this description, as well as flowers, are also reared by many of the convicts themselves, in their airing yards, and are thus made the instruments of productive and very interesting amusements."

Again, the physician says, (page 37,) —

" We have continued to avail ourselves of the provision of the law which sanctions the exercise and restricted employment of individual invalids, in the open yards. 23 white and 6 colored have thus been exercised occasionally, and the most of these, having soon recovered their health, have enjoyed the privilege but for a short time. The practice, therefore, although more than ever resorted to, cannot be regarded as producing a material influence of any kind upon the mass ; or as constituting a positive modification of the kind of discipline professed to be maintained."

Twenty-nine " invalid prisoners " were let out of their cells " for exercise and restricted employment " " in the open yards," and " soon recovered their health ; " and yet this " cannot be regarded as producing a material influence of any kind upon the mass, or as constituting a positive modification of the kind of discipline professed to be maintained " !

The community is under great obligations to Dr. Hartshorne for a knowledge of the facts. We wish Mr. Thompson, the warden, who appears to be the main spring in these improvements, had informed the community, with all minuteness of detail, whether the gardens were cultivated with the plough or the spade ; whether 12 men were constantly employed in the gardens ; how long the invalid prisoners were able to work in the gardens without too much fatigue ; whether there were invalid prisoners enough to do all the work in the gardens, under the superintendence of one officer ; whether this one officer could exercise such supervision over all thus employed, if they were in different gardens, as to prevent their ever seeing or recognizing one another ; whether the prisoners who have no exercising yards get their allowance of one hour's exercise, in the open air, daily ; whether, in his opinion, any more difficulty would arise in taking convicts out of their cells on the Sabbath to the chapel, if they had one, or to an infirmary, if they had one, than to the baths and gardens ; whether the cap is now used over the head and face, when the prisoner is taken out of his cell, which was formerly used when he was first brought into the Prison and conducted to his cell. Answers to such inquiries might be very useful.

The thirteenth statement in this Report, worthy of notice, relates to exercise in the open air for all.

Dr. Hartshorne says, (page 37,) —

" *Regular exercise, out of the cells, for at least an hour a day, ought to be, and I believe is, regarded as an indispensable part of the Penitentiary discipline adopted here.* Sufficient recreation of this kind, however, is provided for the men, in the small yards communicating with their cells. But the female prisoners enjoy no such good fortune, since their position on the second floor obliges them to submit to the substitution of a double cell, instead of an uncovered area. The remedy for this is comparatively easy ; and I hope the day is not far distant when the long-contemplated arrangement of a block for the females on the ground floor will be put in operation."

What does this mean ? Most readers would probably understand Dr. Hartshorne to mean that, with the exception of the females, the convicts in the New Penitentiary in Philadelphia have regular exercise, out of the cells, for at least an hour a day ; and that this is an indispensable part of the system ; and that it is actually given, as a general rule, to all the convicts, with the exception of the females.

Perhaps, however, this is not what he means. He may mean it *ought to be* regarded as indispensable. He may mean it *is* regarded as indispensable by some, without designating by whom. He may mean it is regarded as indispensable, but he cannot say positively that it is yet given. If it is done, if it is done regularly and systematically, as a part of the system, and has been done as an indispensable part of the system, and as the general rule, the information is of great practical importance, and ought to be given to the public in detail. We most earnestly desire the exact information.

The fourteenth statement worthy of notice in this Report, regards the system of bathing, recently introduced.

The late physician, Dr. Hartshorne, and the warden, Mr. Thompson, considered

"a plan by which the prisoners could have the benefit of warm bathing, weekly or periodically," "a great desideratum;" "but as its execution was thought by some to be liable to possible difficulties, in maintaining the system of separate confinement, it was delayed until the last year."—*Warden's Report*, page 21.

The mode adopted is this : —

"Ten separate cells, each having a bath, receive the prisoners that are brought separately by their overseers, and are allowed fifteen minutes for bathing. By this means 40 can be bathed per hour, without any infringement of the separate system,—an officer walking in front of the grated doors of the bathing cells effectually preventing any possibility of communication."

It is not stated how often this is done. It may be done, evidently, the average number of prisoners being 360, as 40 can bathe in an hour, twice a week ; but if it is only done once a week, it is a great change. The change of scene from the cell ; the walk with the officer through the long corridors, being fifteen minutes, if no more, in a cell fitted up for bathing, and used for that purpose, and no other ; splashing the water, and being within the hearing of other persons engaged in this agreeable and refreshing recreation ; the sight of the officer walking in front of the grated door of the bathing cells ;— this is a greater change to those who have been for years tenants of cells, than the watering-place in summer to the inhabitants of a city.

None can conceive, who have not tried it, how great the change. A man who, for the first time in his life, had been committed to Prison, and had been subject to confinement in a cell by day and by night, would give more, if he had it, for this indulgence, at the end of the first, second, or third week, than the exhausted and weary inhabitant of a city, in the heat of summer, for a journey to Saratoga. Dr. Hartshorne and Mr. Thompson are entitled to great praise for this change in the system. This simple and harmless thing may save one life annually.

In the above notice of the Sixteenth Report of the Eastern Penitentiary, the object has been truth.

XIV. CHANGES AND IMPROVEMENTS IN PENITENTIARIES AND PRISONS.

The *State of Maine* has erected a new dormitory building, on the Auburn plan, containing 108 cells, in the State Prison at Thomaston. It has fine, large windows in the external wall; a wide area around the block of cells; open grated cell doors from top to bottom, of round iron; a ventilator in each cell; and is built of split granite.

The *State of New Hampshire* has fitted up a new chapel in the State Prison at Concord; introduced more books; better Sabbath school instruction; and more systematic and thorough labor for moral and religious improvement, by the chaplain.

The *State of Vermont* has fitted up a new infirmary or hospital for the sick, in the State Prison at Windsor; erected a new County Prison, on the half-way Auburn plan, at Burlington; and application has been made, by the constituted authorities, for the plan of a County Prison to be erected in Middlebury.

The *State of Massachusetts* has made an appropriation to build a new range of workshops in the State Prison at Charlestown; appropriated 100 dollars to procure new books for the benefit of the prisoners; directed the warden to increase the lights in the area of the dormitory building, to enable a greater number of the convicts, with more ease, and for a longer time, to read evenings; passed a resolution in favor of Sabbath schools in Prisons; appointed an agent, with a salary, to look after and befriend discharged convicts. All these measures were passed in the legislature of Massachusetts, in the winter session of 1845, without opposition.

In Massachusetts, the county of Berkshire has introduced and carried on the Auburn system of Prison discipline in the County Prison and House of Correction at Lenox. The building has been erected on reasonable terms, (about $8,000,) the labor of shoe-making introduced, and regularly and successfully carried on, under the constant and immediate supervision of an assistant keeper, who is a master mechanic. Moral and religious instruction has been furnished on the Sabbath, and during the week, with much more care and system than are usual in County Prisons. An evening school has been established, at the earnest request of the prisoners. Mr. Sedgwick and Mr. Tucker, the overseers, have themselves aided in the instruction and good moral and religious influence, on the Sabbath and at other times. Mr. Daughtry, a commissioner of the English government from the Island of Jamaica, sent to this country during the last year, to procure plans of a Prison, and plans of a Lunatic Asylum for that island, visited the County Prison in Lenox, and pronounced it the best Prison of this class that he had ever seen. The highly respectable gentlemen in Lenox, who have the oversight of this Prison, and the county commissioners, under whose direction it was built, are well satisfied with it. They see very little which they desire to alter, and very much to approve. One of the overseers lately said, that the only change he would make, if he had the power, would be to move the block of cells a little farther from the centre towards the north wall, so as to make the area on the south or sunny side of the building, which is used as a workshop, more spacious and airy.

The last report of the county commissioners, signed by Robert F. Barnard and Theodore Hinsdale, is an octavo pamphlet of 23 pages—a very important public document. If our County Prisons would publish a report annually of their condition and doings, it would do much to promote the improvement of Prisons. Publicity is the life of improvement. There are some very important points considered, discussed, and settled, with great good sense, in this document, particularly the matter of an evening school in a Prison and House of Correction. It is done in Lenox, Berkshire county, Massachusetts, with the best effect, at the earnest solicitation of the prisoners, with the strong approbation and coöperation of the good citizens.

Hampden county, Massachusetts, at Springfield, has built a new Prison for the purposes of a Jail and House of Correction. It consists of one half a Prison, on the Auburn plan. It was designed for an improvement on the Hartford County Prison. It is not a Prison within a Prison, having a block of cells, with a surrounding area, and an external wall with large windows, so that the light, air, and security, are easily obtained ; but it is a breastwork of cells with the backs on an external wall, with an area on one side only, and there are no ventilators in the cells. The disadvantages are, 1st. It is less secure, as it is not a Prison within a Prison, so that, if a prisoner escapes from his cell, he is still in Prison ; but the cells are built. on the external wall, so that, if a prisoner escapes from his cell, he is at large. 2d. It is not so well ventilated. There is not a ventilator in each cell, and the air cannot circulate around the block of cells, at the ends and on both sides; but when the sun lies on the only area, in front of the cells, in a hot summer's day, and the air or wind enters the windows, it can have no circulation, through the cells, into the ventilators, for there are no ventilators; nor around the block of cells, for the ends are blocked up. Therefore it is not so well ventilated. 3d. It does not admit so good classification. There is but one breastwork of cells. Therefore the men and the women; the tried and the untried; the noisy and turbulent, who require correction for misdemeanor in Prison; the quiet and industrious; the lunatic and the rational; the youth for first offence and the old offender; the witness and the debtor, are all arranged and confined in one breastwork of cells; while in the House of Correction and Jail at Lenox, there can readily be six classes. The Prison in Springfield does not admit so good classification. 4th. It is not so warm in winter, nor so cool in summer. These reasons are sufficient to show that it is an injurious change for the worse on the Hartford county plan and Berkshire county plan.

Massachusetts, in old Hampshire, Franklin, and Worcester counties, is doing nobly in regard to the very small number of persons arrested and committed to Prison for any cause. It is very pleasant to see a diminished business at the Jails, in these counties, as exhibited in the records. It appears that the Jails and jailers will have nothing to do very soon, if temperance and education continue to progress for a few years to come as they have done for a few years past. Colonel Lincoln, the high sheriff of Worcester, speaks confidently of the diminution of crime in that fine and growing town and county, and no one could have visited the Prisons in old Hampshire and Franklin for a succession of years, and examined the records, without being forced to the conclusion that crime is diminishing, instead of increasing, in these good old counties.

In Worcester county, at the Jail and House of Correction, the whole number of inmates is diminished. It is now an average of about 20, instead of 40, which was about the average number many years ago, when the population of the county and town was much less, and the Jail was separate from the House of Correction. This favorable change is attributed to the temperance reformation and the general improvements in society, particularly in education.

For the small average number who are confined, the sheriff has caused to be fitted up, out of the old apartments for debtors, a very convenient and suitable place of worship for a chapel, where the clergy of different denominations are invited to officiate alternately. This will help still further to diminish crime.

In Middlesex county, Massachusetts, at Lechmere Point, great improvements have been made. Two handsome, new, two-story brick buildings have been erected for the accommodation of the insane poor, who were described in a former report of the society as being in a state of extreme wretchedness in the Jail. Since the new houses have been built, the lunatic men have been removed to one of the new brick buildings, and placed under the care of an attendant, who was well trained to his business, as an attendant under Dr. Bell, at the McLean Asylum. He honors his instructor, in the care of 17 men, who are lunatic. It would be difficult to find an equal number of this class of poor lunatics more thoroughly cared for or better treated. The female lunatics have been removed from the Jail to the other new house ; and when they shall have placed over them a well-trained matron, which is contemplated at an early day, the improvement will be great.

The county of Essex, Massachusetts, at Ipswich, has also erected a spacious building for the accommodation of poor lunatics in the House of Correction. We cannot speak from personal observation of the care taken, and of the improvement in the condition of this unhappy class of sufferers at that place. Others speak of the change as being greatly for the better. We have always had fears of the results of provision, in each county, in connection with Jails and Houses of Correction, for poor lunatics, lest inadequate means, and inexperienced attendants, should leave these sufferers in a slightly-improved condition ; but if they are to be so happy as to have such attendants as at Lechmere Point, in such buildings, our fears will, many of them, vanish. The laws of Massachusetts provide that incurable lunatics may be returned from the State Hospital at Worcester to the Jails and Houses of Correction of the counties from which they came, to make room for recent cases, at the discretion of the trustees. We have always had great doubts of the wisdom of this provision of law, and have hoped that it would not often be necessary for the trustees to use the discretionary power granted to them, when the Hospital at Worcester shall have been enlarged by the appropriation of the Johonnot legacy for this purpose. The Hospital at Worcester was designed for, and built expressly to cause, a Jail delivery of lunatics, and, we trust, never will act on the principle of returning incurable lunatics to Jails and Houses of Correction, to make room for pay patients. If there is not room enough, let the trustees and physician say so, and the state will provide room enough ; but let them not return poor lunatics to Jails and Houses of Correction.

The city of Boston is again agitating the subject of a new Jail at South Boston, as a substitute for the old Jail on Leverett Street. The mayor has made an able report in favor of the measure, in which is incorporated the history of successive efforts by the city government, for many years, in favor of the same measure ; the presentment, of grand jurors, of the old Jail as a nuisance ; and the strong testimony of a legislative committee to the same effect. But what will be the result, time must determine. Our hopes and expectations of a favorable result have never been so strong ; especially as it can now be done, and money enough saved in the operation to build not only a Jail, at an expense of $40,000, but a schoolhouse worth $20,000 ; i. e., the property on Leverett Street will sell for enough to accomplish both purposes. Now, if a new and improved Jail, and a new school-house, are worth more to the city than the old Jail, then let the old nuisance be abated.

The *State of Rhode Island* has furnished and occupied a new and spacious workshop for the accommodation of all the prisoners in the State Prison ; and the convicts are now removed from their solitary cells, during the hours of labor, and employed in the shop. They have also provided for a similar change in the County Prison, by which the Auburn system shall be introduced there, solitary confinement at night, and labor in the workshop by day, under careful supervision, to prevent evil communication. The County Prison, thus changed and renovated, will be under the same general supervision and direction as the State Prison, Dr. Cleveland having the superintendence. Dr. Cleveland is a scientific man, more than 40 years of age, and of much experience as a physician. He commenced the trial of the Pennsylvania system with a favorable impression of its superiority. He has tried it four years ; has become satisfied that it is not right ; has recommended its abandonment, both in the State Prison and the County Jail. His recommendation, coming, as it does, from a physician,—the only physician in the land, so far as our knowledge extends, who is also superintendent and warden of a State Prison,—has had a great effect with the civil authorities, who have abandoned the Pennsylvania system, in both the State Prison and County Prison, and adopted the Auburn system.

The change has already taken place in the State Prison ; has had trial of more than a year ; is very satisfactory in its results ; and it is after a trial of both systems by this intelligent warden, who is a physician, that he has recommended the change in the County Prison. The report of Dr. Cleveland, who had withheld his opinions and his experience from the public till he had full time for trial, is now printed and published in a handsome octavo pamphlet of 38 pages, of great value.

The *State of Connecticut* has removed from office, as warden of the State Prison, Mr. Pilsbury, and appointed Mr. Johnson. A similar thing has been done once before in Connecticut ; and the result then was great injury to the Prison, and, after six months, the restoration of Mr. Pilsbury. Mr. Pilsbury and his father have had the superintendence of the State Prison at Wethersfield from its establishment, with the exception of one half year, when the younger Pilsbury was removed, and an inexperienced stranger placed in his stead. It was found unwise, and injurious to the Prison and the interests of the state, and, at the end of six months, Mr. Pilsbury was restored. We have not received any official report since the change was made in January last, and we do not know either the causes assigned or the results.

The State of Connecticut, having previously established, has had in successful operation four County Prisons, on the Auburn plan, in Hartford, New Haven, Norwich and Brooklyn.

The *State of New York* has made great changes both in the male and female Prisons at Sing Sing, through the agency of Hon. John W. Edmands, who acted in the capacity of chairman of the board of inspectors. Mr. Eldridge, keeper of the Prison ; Mrs. Farnham and Mrs. Johnson, matrons ; Rev. Mr. Luckey, chaplain, and Mrs. Luckey, his wife, have been most efficient helpers in these changes and improvements. These improvements consist in milder punishments for misdemeanor ; more kindness, humanity, and education ; greater forbearance, sympathy, and affection towards the prisoner. In the female Prison, the effort has been crowned with very great success. In the men's Prison, the work of reform is progressive under a new board of inspectors, greatly approved by Judge Edmands, who has been promoted to the office of judge of the Circuit Court in the state of New York, which is incompatible with the office of chairman of the board of inspectors. Before Judge Edmands resigned his office, he called the attention of the legislature to the condition and character of 31 lunatics and idiots in the Prison at Sing Sing, most of whom bore this character when committed. He also strongly favors the plan of more education in Prison on the Auburn plan, particularly during the long winter's evenings; and he has probably done more than any other man to move the city of New York to form, during the past season, a Prison Association, which shall have regard to persons under arrest, to prisoners while confined, and to discharged convicts. What is now wanted in the city of New York, to carry out the designs of Judge Edmands and those associated with him, is suitable men to devote themselves to the business of the Prison Association. Where shall the men be found? The labor to be performed at Sing Sing, on Blackwell's Island, at the city Prison called the *Tombs,* and in behalf of discharged convicts, is immense.

State commissioners, appointed last year by the legislature, for the purpose of locating a new Penitentiary in the Northern District of New York, have selected a site in the rear of Platts-burg, about 17 miles from Lake Champlain, on or near an iron-ore bed. The design is, to employ the convicts in the mining and manufacture of iron, which abounds, of excellent quality, in that region. Mr. Ransom Cook has been appointed agent and keeper, and has recently passed through Albany with nearly 100 prisoners, from Sing Sing, to commence operations.

Commissioners for the city and county of Albany have been employed, under an act of the legislature of New York, to examine the subject, and report a plan for a new Penitentiary for the city and county of Albany. They have done so ; and, after visiting Prisons, and comparing different systems, they have made a report in favor of the Auburn system ; and when we last heard from one of their number, they expected to pro-ceed with their work as soon as they could secure the location which they desired.

THUS we have seen, that much remains to be done for Lu-natics and Idiots in the United States, and, if it is not done, that many of them will fall into Prison, where they cannot receive that attention which their circumstances require ;— that Benevolent Effort for Persons under Arrest has saved many from being cast into Prison, and has resulted in the reformation of some of them ;—that the history of Houses of

Reformation and Refuge for Juvenile Delinquents continues to be good, and to afford encouragement to sustain and enlarge such Houses, and to increase the number of them; — that the Penitentiary System is reformatory, as shown by the long list of reformed convicts, mostly from a single Prison, who have been in society for years, and can give good reference for character; — that the subject of Prison Discipline is attracting attention throughout a large portion of the world, and although there is a difference of opinion on minor points, that it is regarded by many as an important subject, worthy of the attention of great and good minds; — that the language of reports from different Penitentiaries in the United States is generally language of congratulation and encouragement; — and that many changes and improvements have been made during the last year. All these things encourage perseverance, and show that the labor is not in vain. In humble dependence on God, and in gratitude for favors already received, we would therefore renew the consecration of ourselves to this great and good work.

STATISTICAL TABLE OF PENITENTIARIES IN 1844.

Penitentiaries.	Number at Commencement.	Number at Close of the Year.	Increase.	Diminution.	Received.	Discharged.	Pardoned.	Died.	Insane removed.	Escaped.
Maine,	63	75	12	..	44	26	5	1	.	.
Vermont,	65	67	2	..	30	16	11	1	.	·
Massachusetts,	265	276	11	..	105	65	15	2	7	1
Rhode Island,	*22	*22	..	..	...	...	..	2	.	.
Auburn, New York,	771	778	7	...	...	172	43	8	.	.
Sing Sing, New York,	839	†935	96	..	340	179	42	16	3	.
New Penitentiary, Phil.	359	340	..	19	138	98	46	13	.	.
Pittsburg, Penn.	*139	*139	..	..	...	...	..	6	.	.
Missouri,	130	178	48	..	53	15	5	2	.	.
Louisiana,	189	176	..	13	51	43	11	1	.	5
Frankfort, Kentucky,	169	151	..	18	41	24	33	0	.	1
Columbus, Ohio,	460	464	4	..	133	42	73	‡11	.	.
Jackson, Michigan,	94	122	28	..	61	26	2	4	.	1

* Average number.   † 30 from Auburn.   ‡ One suicide.

MORTALITY OF ELEVEN AUBURN PRISONS AND TWO PHILADELPHIA PRISONS IN 1844.

Mortality in eleven Prisons, in 1844, on the Auburn Plan.	Number at Commencement.	Number at Close of the Year.	Average Number.	Number of Deaths.
Maine Prison,	63	75	69	1
Vermont Prison,	65	67	66	1
Massachusetts Prison,	265	276	270	2
Rhode Island Prison,	...	...	22	2
Auburn, New York, Prison,	771	778	774	8
Sing Sing, New York, Prison,	839	935	887	16
Columbus, Ohio, Prison,	460	464	462	11
Frankfort, Kentucky, Prison,	169	151	160	0
Jackson, Michigan, Prison,	94	122	108	4
Missouri Prison,	130	178	154	2
Louisiana Prison,	189	176	182	1

One death in 65 prisoners in eleven Auburn Prisons in 1844. $48\,)\,\overline{3154}$ 48
$$\frac{}{65}$$

Mortality in two Prisons, viz., New Penitentiary in Philadelphia, and Prison at Pittsburg, Penn., on Philadelphia Plan, in 1844.	Number at Commencement.	Number at Close of the Year.	Average Number.	Number of Deaths.
New Penitentiary in Philadelphia,	359	340	349	13
Pittsburg, Penn., Prison,	...	...	139	6

One death in 25 prisoners in two Philadelphia Prisons in 1844. $19\,)\,\overline{488}$ 19

NEW PENITENTIARY IN PHILADELPHIA.

Date.	Received.	Discharged.	Average Number.	Pardoned.	Died.	Recommitted.	Old Convicts.	Deranged.	Money from State Treasury.
1829	9	....	4½	...	...	...	...	...	
1830	49	3	31	...	1	...	...	...	
1831	50	12	67	1	4	...	...	...	
1832	34	20	91	...	*4	...	†32	...	
1833	77	17	123	2	1	...	16	...	
1834	118	41	183	8	5	3	25	...	
1835	217	70	266	15	7	13	88	...	4,998 91
1836	143	87	360	3	12	6	43	...	
1837	161	159	386	10	17	19	59	14	
1838	178	133	402	10	26	23	...	18	34,308 00
1839	179	138	418	13	11	‡35	65	26	18,378 00
1840	139	154	405	20	22	13	‖93	21	
1841	126	134	356	15	17	27	38	11	
1842	142	104	333	23	9	24	40	...	
1843	156	102	360	15	11	18	29	14	
1844	138	157	349	46	13	§20	28	17	
	1916	1331	4134	181	160	201	556	121	

Pardoned in proportion to the received,...... 1 in 10; last 10 years, 1 in 9.
Pardoned in proportion to the discharged,.... 1 in 7; " " " 1 in 7.
Pardoned in proportion to the average number, } 1 in 22; " " " 1 in 21.
Died in proportion to the received,.......... 1 in 11; " " " 1 in 10.
Died in proportion to the discharged,........ 1 in 8; " " " 1 in 8.
Died in proportion to the average number,... 1 in 25; " " " 1 in 25.
Recommitted in proportion to the received, .. 1 in 9; " " " 1 in 7.
Recommitted in proportion to the discharged, 1 in 6; " " " 1 in 6.
Recommitted in proportion to the average number, } 1 in 20; " " " 1 in 18.
Old convicts in proportion to the received,... 1 in 3; " " " 1 in 3.
Old convicts in proportion to the discharged,. 1 in 2; " " " 1 in 2.
Old convicts in proportion to the average number, } 1 in 7; " " " 1 in 7.
Deranged in proportion to the received, ... 1 in 15; " " " 1 in 12.
Deranged in proportion to the discharged,.... 1 in 11; " " " 1 in 10.
Deranged in proportion to the average number, } 1 in 34; " " " 1 in 30.

* One suicide in 1832, and one in 1838.   ‖ This is equal to the whole number of old
† Old convicts.   convicts sent to Prison in 1838 and 1840.
‡ Three of these a third time.   § Four of these a third time.

MORTALITY OF PENITENTIARIES IN SUCCESSIVE YEARS.

Time when.	New Peniten. in Philadelphia, on Separate Plan.		State Prison in New Hampshire, on Auburn Plan.		New State Prison at Wethersfield, Conn., on Auburn Plan.		New State Prison at Charlestown, Mass., on Auburn Plan.		State Prison at Auburn, New York.	
	Pris.	Deaths.	Pris.	Deaths.	Pris.	Deaths.	Pris.	Deaths.	Pris.	Deaths.
1828			48	1	134	.	290	4	571	9
1829	4	.	48	1	134	.	262	6	639	5
1830	31	1	54	.	167	4	290	5	620	18
1831	67	4	82	.	182	4	256	7	647	14
1832	91	*4	89	1	192	2	227	11	683	12
1833	123	1	87	.	186	3	250	6	679	11
1834	183	5	86	.	189	1	277	4	679	11
1835	266	7	90	1	197	4	279	3	654	10
1836	360	12	82	1	204	8	278	4	648	18
1837	386	17	72	1	204	1	284	5	678	19
1838	402	26	73	.	182	4	302	6	660	15
1839	418	11	78	1	186	9	309	5	670	10
1840	405	22	81	.	175	5	320	2	682	14
1841	356	17	81	1	187	2	326	8	701	9
1842	333	9	95	.	207	8	309	2	709	7
1843	345	11	96	.	197	12	270	2	742	11
1844	349	13	..	.	...	..	276	2	774	8
	4119	160	1194	7	2789	67	4805	82	11,436	201
Deaths in 17 Years.	1 in 25.		1 in 170		1 in 41.		1 in 58.		1 in 56	

* One suicide.

OFFICERS.

LIFE DIRECTORS,

BY THE PAYMENT OF ONE HUNDRED DOLLARS AND UPWARDS.

Albany, N. Y.
*Van Rensselaer, Stephen

Boston.
Appleton, Samuel
Armstrong, Samuel T.
*Bussey, Benjamin
*Chamberlain, Richard
*Cobb, Nathaniel R.
*Coolidge. Joseph
Dwight, Edmund
Eliot, Samuel A.
Gray, Francis C.
Greenleaf. Jonathan
*Homes. Henry
Hubbard, Samuel
Jackson, Charles
Jackson, James
Jackson, Patrick T.
Kirk, Edward N.
Lawrence, Abbott
Lawrence, Amos
Lawrence, William
Lowell, Charles

*Lowell. John
Lyman. Theodore, Jr.
Munson, Israel
Parkman, Francis
Phillips, Jonathan
*Phillips, William
*Prescott, William
Shattuck. George C.
Shaw. Robert G.
Tappan, John
Ticknor, George
Tuckerman, Edward
Ward, Artemas
Wells, Charles
*White Stephen
Willis, Nathaniel

Dedham, Mass.
Burgess, Ebenezer

Geneva, N. Y.
Dwight, Henry

Lowell, Mass.
Lawrence, Samuel

Newark, N. J.
Eddy, Ansel D.

Norwich, Conn.
Greene, William P.

Peterboro', N. Y.
*Smith, Peter

Portsmouth, N. H.
Coues, S E.

Rochester, N Y.
*Bissell, Josiah

Salem, Mass.
*Peabody, Joseph

Worcester, Mass.
Abbott, J S C.
Foster, Alfred Dwight
Salisbury, Stephen
Sweetser Seth, by 3 Sisters
*Waldo, Daniel

LIFE MEMBERS,

BY THE PAYMENT OF THIRTY DOLLARS AND UPWARDS.

Albany, N. Y.
Delavan, Edward C.
*Hopkins, Samuel M.
McIntire. Archibald
Norton, John C.

Andover, Mass.
*Cornelius. Elias
Edwards, Justin
*Porter, Ebenezer
Woods, Leonard

Auburn, N. Y.
Lewis, Levi, by Officers of
the Prison
Seymour, James S.
Smith, B. C., by Officers of
the Prison

Baltimore, Md.
Backus, John A.
*McKim, W. D.

Bath, N. H.
Sutherland, David, by Ira
Goodale

Bedford, N. Y.
*Jay, John
Jay, William

Beverly.
Oliphant, David

Boston.
Adams, Nehemiah
*Amory, John
Beecher, Edward
Beecher, Lyman
*Blake, George

*Bowdoin, James
Brimmer, Martin
Brooks. Peter C.
Brooks. Peter C., Jr.
Chadwick, Ebenezer
Clapp, Joshua
Cobb, Richard
*Codman, Catharine
Codman, Elizabeth
Codman, Charles R.
Codman, Henry
Cogswell, William
Cushing, John P.
Dana, Nathaniel
Dorr, Samuel
Eckley, David
Edwards Henry
*Eliot, William H.
Emmons, N. H.
Forbush. Jonathan
Frothingham, N. L.
Gray, Horace
Gray, John C.
*Green Samuel
*Greene, Gardiner
*Greenwood, F. W. P.
Hill, Henry
*Homer, George J.
Jones, Anna P.
*Jones, John Coffin
Lawrence, Abbott
Lawrence, Samuel
Lawrence, William
*Lyman. Theodore
Lyman, Theodore, Jr.
Marvin, T. R.
*McLean, Ann
Munroe, Edmund
Newhall, Cheever
Otis, Harrison Gray

Parker, Daniel P.
Parker, Ebenezer
*Parker, John
Parkman, Francis
Potter, Alonzo
Quincy. Josiah
Rand, Asa
Randall, John
Rantoul. Robert
Reed, Benjamin T.
Rice, Henry
Ropes, William
Safford, Daniel
Sears, David
Stoddard, Charles
Thorndike, Israel
Vose, Thomas
Wales, Thomas B.
Warren. John C.
Wigglesworth, Thomas
Williams, John D.
*Winthrop, Thomas L.
*Wisner, Benjamin B.
Worthington, William

Brooklyn, N. Y.
Carrol, D. L.

Cambridge, Mass.
Donnison, C. L.
*Farwell, Levi
Greenleaf. Simon
Holland, Frederic West

Canandaigua, N. Y.
Eddy, Ansel G.

Catskill, N. Y.
Cooke, Thomas B.
Day, Orrin

Charleston, S. C.
Corning, Jasper

Charlestown, Mass.
Curtis, Jared
Walker, William J., Jr.

Coxackie, N. Y.
*Van Dyck, Abraham

Danvers, East.
Braman, Milton P.
*Cowles, George
*Oakes, Caleb

Dorchester, Mass.
Codman, John

Douglass Farm, L. I.
Douglass, George, by the hand
of Mrs. Joanna Bethune

Edinburgh, Scotland.
Dunlop, John

Fairfield, Conn.
*Sherman, Roger M.

Geneva, N. Y.
*Axtell, Henry

Gloucester, Mass.
Jewett, David, by a Lady

Hampton, N. H.
Harris, Roswell

Hartford, Conn.
Hawes, Joel
Spring, Samuel

Haverhill, Mass.
Keeley, George
Phelps, Dudley

Ipswich, Mass.
Kimball, David

Jamaica, L. I.
*Crane, Elias W.

Marblehead, Mass.
Hooper, Nathaniel
*Reed, William

Maryland.
McIntire, James, by a Friend
in Newburyport

Middletown, Conn.
Crane, John B.

Milton, Mass.
*Tucker, Nathaniel

Newark, N. J.
Hamilton, W. T.

Newbury, Mass.
Wright, Henry C.

Newburyport, Mass.
Banister, William B.

*Bartlett, William
*Brown, Moses
Dimmick, Luther F.
*Dimmick. Mrs. Luther F.
Proudfit, John
By a donation in books from
Charles Whipple, to consti-
tute the following persons
Life Members :
Davis, Mary A.
Greenleaf, Mary
Greenleaf, Mary C.
Hodge, Mary D.
Thompson, Sarah

New Haven, Conn.
Bacon, Leonard
Brewster, James
Fitch, Eleazer T.
Robinson, Charles, by his
Sister Elizabeth
Salisbury, Abby

New York City.
Adams. William
Allen, Stephen
Astor, John Jacob
Averill, Heman
Bethune, G. W.
Boorman, J.
Brewster, Joseph
Broadhead, Dr.
*Chambers, William
Cheever, George B.
Cox, Samuel H.
Crosby, W. B.
Eastburn, Manton
*Falconer. Archibald
Hedges, Timothy
How, Fisher
Johnson, William Samuel
*Lenox. Robert
Mason. Cyrus W.
Mathews, John M.
McAuley, Thomas
*Milnor, James
Patton, William
Perrit, Pelatiah
*Post, Joel
*Proudfit. Alexander
Phillips, W. W.
Rowland, Henry A.
*Rutgers, Henry
Schroeder, J F.
Shatzel, Jacob
Spring, Gardiner
Starr, Philemon R.
Stephens, J. C.
Tappan, Arthur
*Varick, Richard
*Ward, Samuel
*Woolsey, William W.

Peterboro', N. Y.
Smith, Gerrit

Philadelphia, Penn.
Allen, Solomon
*Carey, Matthew
Elmes, Thomas
Ely, Ezra Stiles
Henry, Alexander

*Livingston, Gilbert R.
Skinner, Thomas H.

Pittsfield, Mass.
Newton, Edward A.

Plymouth, Mass.
Robbins, Josiah

Portland, Me.
Dwight, William T.
Tyler, Bennett

Portsmouth, N. H.
Coues, Lucy Louisa
Goodwin, Ichabod
Peabody, Andrew P., by La-
dies of his Society
Treadwell, Mrs. Ann

Poughkeepsie, N. Y.
Cuyler, Cornelius

Providence, R. I.
*Ives, Thomas P.
Wayland, Francis

Rahway, N. J.
Squier, Job

Salem, Mass.
Cleveland. J. P.
Emerson, Brown
Phillips, Stephen C.
Williams, William
Worcester, Zervia F.

Schenectady, N. Y.
*Smith, Peter

Springfield, Mass.
Osgood, Samuel

Thomaston, Me.
*Rose, Daniel

Troy, N. Y.
Tucker, Mark

Utica, N. Y.
Lansing, D C.
Stocking. Samuel
Varick, Abraham

West Haverhill, Mass.
Cross, Abijah

Wethersfield, Conn.
Barrett, Gerrish
Pilsbury, Amos

Williamstown, Mass.
*Griffin, Edward D.

Wiscasset, Me.
Hooker, Edward W.

Worcester, Mass.
Foster, Alfred Dwight
Lincoln, John W.
Salisbury. Stephen
Waldo, Daniel
Waldo, E S. and R.

TREASURER'S REPORT.

PRISON DISCIPLINE SOCIETY, IN ACCOUNT WITH SAMUEL A. ELIOT, TREASURER.

Dr.

1845.		
May.—To balance from last account,	106	59
do. cash paid S. N. Dickinson,	150	00
do. do. office rent for two and a half years,	437	50
do. do. Wilkins and Carter for paper,	74	22
do. do. Boston Type Foundry, stereotyping Eighteenth Annual Report,	175	23
do. do. B. Bradley, for binding, &c.,	47	66
do. do. for use of Park Street Church, at anniversary,	25	00
do. do. incidental and travelling expenses,	159	11
do. do. salary of the secretary,	1,700	00
do. do. for one share New England Bank stock,	104	00
do. do. M. Latham, collecting subscriptions and distributing Reports,	19	48
do. do. Grant, Daniell, & Co, for paper,	3	00
do. do. Rev. Gerrish Barrett, agent in Middle and Western States, for collecting,	43	07
do. do. Counterfeit bill,	5	00
	$3,049	86
do. Balance to new account,	134	44
	$3,184	30

Cr.

1845.			
May.—By cash, dividends on nine shares New England Bank stock, purchased with legacy of Nathaniel Tucker, of Milton,		54	00
do. do. dividend on one share in New England Bank stock,		3	00
do. do. subscription to Permanent Fund, by Rev. Gerrish Barrett,		100	00
do. do. collected by Rev. Gerrish Barrett, agent for Middle and Western States,		86	14
do. do. legacy of Rev. Joseph Chickering, of Phillipston,	$50 00		
do. do. legacy of John Damon, of Reading,	50 00		
do. do. interest accrued on the same,	4 50 —	104	50
do. do. from B. P. Winslow, executor of Thomas S. Winslow, residue of his legacy of $1000,		24	75
do. do. of H. B. Stanton, for Reports,		2	50
do. do. Thomas Blair, Dayton, Ohio, for Reports,		2	91
do. do. from Tremont Savings Bank,		4	00
do. do. subscriptions, donations, &c., in the Eastern States,		2,802	50
		$3,184	30

BOSTON, MAY 23, 1845.

Permanent Fund, by Direction of the late Nathaniel Tucker, of Milton, who gave it as a legacy:

Ten shares in the capital stock of New England Bank,	1,040	00
Deposit in Tremont Savings Bank,	70	31
	$1,110	31

E. E.

SAMUEL A. ELIOT, *Treasurer.*

BOSTON, MAY 23, 1845.—We have examined the above account, and find it correct, and have seen the proper vouchers.

WM. W. STONE,
AMOS A. LAWRENCE.

N. B. The donation of Rev. Gerrish Barrett has been added to the fund given by Mr. Tucker.

SUBSCRIPTIONS AND DONATIONS,

For the Year ending May 23, 1845.

Albany, N. Y.
Pilsbury, Amos 25 00

Andover, Mass.
Woods, Leonard 25 00

Boston, Mass.
Abbott, George W. 2 00
A Friend, Mrs. A. 2 00
Aiken, Silas 2 00
Almy, Patterson, & Co. 10 00
Ammidon, Homes 2 00
Amory, Charles 20 00
Amory, William 5 00
Andrews, Henry 5 00
Annual Subscribers, by
  M. Latham, Coll. 160 00
  Do. do. 22 00
Appleton, Nathan 20 00
Appleton, Samuel 30 00
Appleton, William 25 00
Austin, S., Jr. 5 00
Baker, E 5 00
Balch, Joseph 5 00
Ballard, Joseph 5 00
Ballister, Joseph 2 00
Barnard, Charles 5 00
Bartol, C. A. 10 00
B. A. E., Cash 5 00
Bent, Ann 2 00
Bigelow, George T. 5 00
B. J., Cash 5 00
Blake, Charles 1 00
Blake, James 2 00
Boardman, W. H. 5 00
Bond, George W. 2 00
Booth, G. H. 2 00
Bowditch, N. I. 10 00
Bradford, John 3 00
Brimmer, E. 10 00
Broadhead, D. D. 5 00
Brooks, Edward 10 00
Brooks, Peter C. 20 00
Brooks, Peter C., Jr. 20 00
Bullard, W. S. 2 00
Bumstead, John 5 00
Bumstead, Josiah 20 00
Burgess, Benj., & Sons, 5 00
Burrage, I. C. 1 00
Cabot, Samuel 20 00
Callender, George 2 00
Carey, T. G. 5 00
Chadwick, Ebenezer 20 00
Chamberlain, N. B. 5 00
Chapman, Jonathan 10 00
Chickering, J. 5 00
Clapp, James 2 00
Cordis, Thomas 5 00
Cotton, Joseph 10 00

Curtis, Samuel 1 00
Dalton, Peter R. 10 00
Daniel & Co. 2 00
Darracott, George 2 00
Davis, Thomas A. 5 00
Deane, Charles 3 00
Dexter, George M. 10 00
D. J. J. 10 00
Dorr, Samuel 10 00
Eaton, John 2 00
Edmands. J. W. 10 00
Eliot, Samuel A. 50 00
Faxon, George N. 2 00
Fay, F. B 5 00
Fearing, A. C. 2 00
Fisher, Freeman 2 00
Flint, Waldo 5 00
F., R. B. 10 00
French, Jonathan 5 00
Friend 1 00
Friend 25
Friend, Cash 1 00
Friend, (E. W. H.) 1 00
Gassett, Henry 5 00
Gilbert, Jno. & Co. 3 00
Grant & Daniell 10 00
Gray, Francis C. 30 00
Gray, F. T. 2 00
Gray, Horace 20 00
Gray, John C. 20 00
Gray, William 2 00
Greene, Benjamin D. 5 00
Greenleaf. S. 2 00
Gridley, William 2 00
Hall, Andrew T. 3 00
Hall, Henry 3 00
Hall, J. P. 2 00
Hallet, George 5 00
Hallet, J. H. 2 00
Hardy, Alpheus 2 00
Harris, James 3 00
Hawes, Gray, & Co. 5 00
Hayward, George 5 00
Hicks, James H. 2 00
Hobart, Albert 2 00
Homans, Jno. 5 00
Homer, George J. 5 00
Hooper, S. 10 00
Horton, H. J. 3 00
Howe, George 10 00
Howe, S. G. 2 00
Hurd, J. 5 00
Inches, Henderson 2 00
Inches, Henderson, Jr. 2 00
Inches, Misses 10 00
Ingersoll, James 5 00
Iron Company, South
  Boston 5 00
Jackson, Charles 20 00

Jackson, Patrick T. 20 00
Jarves, Deming 10 00
Jellison, Z. 1 00
Johnson, James 5 00
Jones, A. P. 20 00
Jones, H. H. 2 00
Kimball, Daniel 2 00
Kimball, Jewett, & Co. 10 00
Kimball, Jno. 2 00
Knott, James, & Son 2 00
Lambert, William G. 2 00
Lane, Lamson, & Co. 5 00
Lawrence, A. A. 50 00
Lawrence, Abbott, 100 00
Lawrence, Amos 100 00
Lawrence, James 10 00
Lawrence, William 100 00
Lee, Henry, Jr. 2 00
Lee, Thomas 20 00
Lincoln, W. S. 2 00
Little & Brown 5 00
Littlehale, T. S. 5 00
Livermore, Isaac, & Co. 3 00
Lloyd, Mrs. 10 00
Lobdell, T. J. 2 00
Lodge, J. E. 2 00
Lothrop. S. K. 2 00
Lowell, F. C. 10 00
Lowell, John A. 20 00
Lyman, Theodore, Jr. 100 00
Mason, William P. 5 00
Mayer, P. I. 2 00
McBurney, Charles 2 00
McIntire, E. P. 1 00
Merriam, S. P. 1 00
Mills, Charles H. 10 00
Mills, James K. 5 00
Morse, R. M. 1 00
Osgood, J. P. 2 00
Otis, Harrison G. 10 00
Paige, James 5 00
Paine, R. S. 2 00
Parker, James 10 00
Parkman, Francis 5 00
Payson, S. R. 2 00
Perkins, Thomas H. 25 00
Peters, Ed. D 5 00
Phipps, S. & Co. 5 00
Pray, Isaac C. 5 00
Prescott, William 20 00
Putnam, Allen 3 00
Q. T. 1 00
Quincy, J., Jr. 10 00
Reed, Benjamin T. 5 00
Reynolds, W. B. 5 00
Rice, I. S. 5 00
Rice & Thaxter 5 00
Richards, Reuben 2 00
Robbins, Ed. H. 5 00

Rogers, Henry B.	10 00	Wilkinson, A.	2 00	Rodman, Wm. R.	20 00
Rogers, J. G.	2 00	Williams, J. D.	30 00	Rotch, W. J.	2 00
Rogers, J. H.	2 00	Williams, John	5 00	R. W., Jr.	10 00
Rollins, William	5 00	Williams, Moses	3 00		
Ropes, William	10 00	Willis, Nathaniel	10 00	*Peterboro', N. Y.*	
Russell, N. P.	10 00	Winslow, Thomas S.,		Smith, Gerrit	15 00
Sargeant, Bodwell	2 00	by B. P. Winslow,			
Seaver, Benjamin	2 00	Executor. Residue of		*Phillipston, Mass.*	
Shaw & Blake	5 00	$1,000 Legacy	24 75	Chickering, Rev. Joseph, a Legacy	50 00
Shaw, Robert G.	30 00	Wolcott, J H.	10 00		
Shorey, John	2 00	Wyman, Edward	2 00		
Sigourney, Henry	10 00			*Providence, R. I.*	
Simpson, M. S.	5 00	*Cambridge, Mass.*		Burgess, Thomas M.	5 00
Skinner, Francis	10 00	Carpenter, Mrs. D.	5 00	Goddard, W. G.	10 00
Smith & Sumner	3 00	Farrar, John	3 00	Hallet, G. W.	5 00
Sprague, Phineas	5 00	Norton, Andrews	10 00	Hutchins, S.	2 00
Stanton, H. B., for Reports	2 50	Pomeroy, William	10 00	Ives, Hope	15 00
		Sparks, Jared	10 00	Ives, Moses B.	10 00
Steele, Robert	1 00			Ives, R. H.	10 00
Stoddard, Charles	5 00	*Dayton, Ohio.*		Manton, Amasa	10 00
Stone, W. W.	25 00	Blair, Thomas	2 91	Pope, W. G.	3 00
Storer, R. B.	2 00			Smith, J. Y.	5 00
Sullivan, Richard	10 00	*Fall River.*		Waterman, Resolved	2 00
Sumner, Charles	5 00	Westall, John	1 00	Wayland, Francis	20 00
S. W. D.	5 00				
Tappan, Lewis W.	2 00	*Milton, Mass.*		*Reading, Mass.*	
Ticknor, George	10 00	Savings Bank, Boston,		Damon, John, a Legacy	50 00
Timmins. Henry	5 00	Interest on Deposit			
Towne. W. B.	1 00	from Mr. Tucker's		Interest on the same	4 50
Trott, George	5 00	Legacy,	4 00		
Upham, Appleton, & Co.	10 00	Tucker, Nathaniel, Dividend on New England Bank Stock Fund, from his Legacy	27 00	*Somerville.*	
				Bell, Luther V.	50 00
Wales, T. B.	10 00				
Walley, S H.	10 00			*Springfield, N. Y.*	
Warren, Charles H.	5 00			Barrett, Gerrish, from sundry Subscribers	38 07
Warren, George W.	5 00	Do. do.	30 00	Barrett, Gerrish, from sundry Subscribers	38 07
Warren, J. C.	10 00				
Welch, Francis	3 00	*New Bedford, Mass.*		Barrett, Rev. Gerrish	100 00
Weld, William F.	2 00	Cash, a Friend	5 00	Do. do.	10 00
Wells, E. M. P.	25 00	Coffin, Timothy	2 00		
Wells, John	10 00	Coggeshall, J. M.	5 00	*Watertown, Mass.*	
Wetmore, Thomas	10 00	Congdon, James B.	5 00	Cushing, I. S.	20 00
Whiston, F. C.	2 00	Green, D. R.	5 00	Greene, I. S. Copley	10 00
White, B. C.	3 00	Greene, Thomas A.	5 00		
White, C. A.	5 00	Grinnell, Joseph	10 00	*Windsor, Conn.*	
White, F. E.	2 00	Howland, George	20 00	Hooker, Ed. S.	3 25
Whitney, Paul	5 00	Morgan, C. W.	10 00		
Whiton, James	2 00	Parker, John Avery	10 00	*Worcester, Mass.*	
Whittemore, George	2 00	Robeson, Andrew	10 00	Foster, A. D.	10 00
Wigglesworth, Thomas	5 00	Rodman, Benjamin	5 00	Salisbury, Stephen	30 00
Wilder, M. P.	5 00	Rodman, Elizabeth	17 00	Waldo, Daniel	100 00
Wilkins, Carter, & Co.	10 00	Rodman, Samuel	10 00	Waldo, Miss	100 00
Wilkins, Charles	5 00	Rodman, S. W.	5 00		

APPENDIX.

SIXTH ANNUAL REPORT OF THE WARDEN OF THE RHODE ISLAND STATE PRISON.

To the Honorable General Assembly of the State of Rhode Island, October Session, A. D. 1844.

THE undersigned, warden of the State Prison, and keeper of the County Jail in the county of Providence, respectfully submits the following statement of "receipts and expenditures" of said establishments, together with a table showing the "circumstances of each convict in the State Prison," during the year ending September 30, 1844, as by law required.

He would further state, that he has heretofore circumscribed his annual report within the requisitions of law relating to the annual accounts and statistics of the Prison, without, however, deeming himself to be interdicted from the course pursued by the officers of similar establishments elsewhere, in presenting to the inspectors, or to the Assembly, as occasion may require, the results of their observations; with a view to a full understanding of the system which they are called upon to administer, and to all the improvements which time and experience may suggest. The undersigned will therefore take this opportunity of considering, without unnecessary prolixity, several subjects connected with the mode of imprisonment here adopted, by way of a general answer to questions not unfrequently asked, and entitled to a reply from an officer whose position and duties should enable him, if faithful to his trust, to give the information required, in a plain and satisfactory manner.

The inquiry is frequently made, "How does the present system succeed, in comparison with that which, in its main feature of labor in strictly solitary confinement, has been discontinued?" It is well known that this Prison was constructed and established upon that plan, and that the principle of strict seclusion has been given up for reasons deemed imperative. By an act of the General Assembly of this state, passed at the January session, 1843, the inspectors of the State Prison were vested with full power and authority to cause the prisoners then under sentence, or who might thereafter be sentenced to said Prison, "to be enlarged of their confinement, by permitting such prisoners to perform labor in the corridor of said Prison; by permitting more than one person to remain in the cell, or a nurse to be with them in case of sickness; by admitting them to the yard of the prison in the day-time; by admitting such communications to and from their friends, and among themselves, and to receive such books and articles as might be necessary, under such rules and regulations as said inspectors might establish, and furnish to the warden, from time to time, consistent with the safe-keeping of said prisoners." The first of these provisions was immediately carried into effect, by causing the prisoners to perform their labor upon a platform erected in the corridor of the Prison. Subsequently, a convenient workshop has been erected for the purpose; and the prisoners are assembled together on the Sabbath for religious exercises.

Does the result justify the change? is the question. The undersigned is impelled by several reasons, in addition to that already suggested, to make a public reply to it. The change was, from a sense of duty, by him respectfully urged upon those having the authority to advise its adoption; and after a careful observation, extending through a period of more than four years, of the injurious and alarming effects of solitary imprisonment upon the mental and physical condition of those who are the subjects of it. It has been recently suggested by a foreign writer of distinction, that the system of solitary imprisonment in this state failed through the mismanagement of those charged with the duty of carrying it into effect—an imputation which shifts the radical fault of the system itself upon the administration of it, and which may be deemed worthy of notice and refutation. Further, the undersigned believes it to be due to the cause of general humanity, that all mistakes of the penal code, so soon as discovered, should be so freely and distinctly explained, that there may be no danger of their repetition, here or abroad; and that the amendment of them may be carried to the account of "public justice, which, at the present day, has been disrobed of the purely vindictive character formerly associated with it; lays the hand of reluctant severity even on its most deserving victims; avoids all unusual, unnecessary, and cruel inflictions; and looks not only to the security and protection of society, but to the welfare of the prisoner; regarding, in the spirit of Christian benevolence, every crime, however great, as a still greater misfortune, both to the offender and to the state."

In these remarks, I am very far from designing to reflect on the intention and object of any, who were instrumental in devising and establishing this Prison upon the plan of solitary labor; joining as I did with the great majority, who required its erection, by their votes. The plan was generally approved, and widely sanctioned, at home and abroad. The "old jail" system, of herding together, within a narrow compass, prisoners of every age and degree, with its attendant consequences of moral and physical pollution and degradation, was condemned by all; and public opinion, impelled by the prevailing theory of the day, as approbated by the most enlightened philanthropists of this and other countries, very naturally oscillated to the other extreme, and demanded the experiment of entire seclusion of the offender, with wholesome labor, and with the exertion of such moral means as should afford to him the hope of amendment and restoration, (when the limits of the law should permit,) as a purified and reclaimed member of society.

But the system, thus founded in the most honorable and humane intentions, had the inherent and incurable defect of being in opposition to the laws of the physical nature of its subjects, which no human laws can change. Under the old plan of promiscuously herding together by day and night, the prisoner was debased and brutalized; under the new, he is, in too many instances, carried through "a slow, corroding process," to the derangement, or destruction, both of body and mind. This tendency of the solitary system, it is true, was predicted, upon natural principles, by some eminent opponents, whose benevolent sagacity forewarned, though ineffectually, the friends of Prison reform of the result which they might expect; but experience was necessary to exhibit it, and at an expense which it is painful to contemplate.

"The errors of philanthropy are among the most injurious and difficult to avert, as they are associated with good motives, and supported by the zeal of honest men."

It is to one of these, and to its correction, that I have, for the reasons given, now solicited a portion of your attention.

Before proceeding to particulars, I would make the additional remark, that, though the number of prisoners here confined has been small in comparison with those in the Prisons in some other and larger states, no better opportunity was ever afforded to observe, with care and in detail, all the effects of imprisonment on the convicts than that which has been here presented.

Commencing as I did with but three prisoners, and having continued for six years, with an increase of about ten prisoners in each year, I have been enabled to become particularly acquainted with each individual upon his admission, and minutely to notice every change that took place during his confinement.

That the failure of the system of labor in solitary confinement, in the Rhode Island State Prison, was not fairly attributable to the defect of its administration, appears at once from a statement of the mode and regulations of imprisonment here, which were the same as those adopted in older establishments elsewhere. The Prison was erected at a large expense, and is well and substantially built, to answer the purpose designed. The cells, being intended for constant habitation and workshops, were made large on that account, being, in the lower ranges, eight feet broad, fifteen feet deep, and eight feet high. From the second range, about three feet in depth are taken off by the corridors; but from the pitch of the roof, the upper cells are higher, and contain about the same number of cubic feet as the others. Each cell has a pine floor; is sufficiently lighted for the performance of any mechanical labor, with two squares of glass, each 14 inches by 5; is furnished with an abundant supply of pure water, and is warmed in cold weather with hot water circulated through iron pipes. The prisoner is comfortably clad, and sleeps in a wooden bunk, on a pallet and pillow of straw, (unless through sickness or infirmity a feather bed be allowed,) with such quantity of bedding as he may desire. The labor required was, as now, from fifteen minutes after sunrise to one hour before sunset, with two intermissions of half an hour each, for meals, from the 20th of March to the 20th of September; and during the rest of the year, from fifteen minutes after sunrise to 8 o'clock in the evening, with the same intermissions; the use of a light for one hour being also allowed after the close of the evening work.

Suitable medical advice and attendance were also furnished. Proper persons were licensed as moral and religious teachers, who visited the prisoners, principally on Sundays, for the purpose of instruction; and preaching on Sundays was occasionally had in the corridor, the doors of the cells being opened as far as they could be without permitting the prisoners to see or communicate with each other. The Bible, books of prayer, tracts, and several other works of a moral nature, were also furnished to them, together with writing materials on Sundays. Communication in any form, with any person, was, as now, prohibited, excepting with the inspectors, warden, and other officers of the Prison, the physician and moral instructors; and no prisoner, in any case, was permitted to leave his cell, except once in three months, for bathing, and in case of sickness, under the prescription of the physician, for exercise, not exceeding fifteen minutes a day, in the corridor. Corporal punishment was excluded by law from the Prison, until shortly before the solitary system was mitigated; and the only penalties inflicted were the deprivation of food, water, furniture, and bedding, for a longer or shorter time, in cases of refractory conduct, as the occasion might require. No partiality was shown among the prisoners from regard to their previous position in the world. Then, as now, the strict rule of this Prison was to treat all, in all respects, precisely alike, with indispensable exceptions only in cases of sickness and infirmity. The whole system was carried into effect under the constant supervision and frequent visitation of a board of inspectors, having strong confidence in its superiority, and responsible to the legislative body for the discharge of their duties. Before entering upon the duties of his office, the warden visited several Prisons in other states, upon the plan about to be carried into effect here, to possess himself in detail, and from observation, of the best modes of procedure, in order to an exact conformity with the most approved models. Before a change was made in the original plan of the Prison, by order of the legislature, an inquiry was instituted, in that body, into the operation and result; and no complaint or suggestion was made that the original plan had not been properly and completely carried into effect, or had failed from any departure or innovation, authorized or unauthorized, on the part of its administrators. In addition to this, on inquiring for the model of solitary imprisonment, which our censor, Dr. Julius, of Berlin, holds up for imitation, and for non-conformity with which his strictures have been elicited, it is found to be the "New Model Prison," situated near the Caledonia Asylum, in the suburbs of London, which was put in operation four years after this, and in which the prisoners are permitted to assemble for religious worship on Sundays, disguised in hoods, and sitting in separate boxes, and also to take the benefit of air, sunshine, and exercise, in separate yards provided for that purpose, with "shelters or covered ways," that they may not even lose the privilege of going out in inclement weather. It certainly betrays a lapse of memory, or a confusion of ideas, in our learned friend and visitor, to discover an identity in the American system of close confinement, as any where practised, with the very distinct system of the London Prison referred to, which appears to go even beyond the Auburn system, in allowing exercise and diversion out of doors.

I submit, therefore, to your honorable body, upon this brief and incontrovertible statement of facts, that the punishment of solitary imprisonment was administered here in its ordinary and most approved mode, and proceed to exhibit its consequences, and what I deem to be their physiological causes.

Among the small number of prisoners at the onset, the bad effects of solitary imprisonment upon the mind were very apparent, not leading me, however, to consider them as arising from the peculiar confinement and discipline to which they were subjected. Like others, I attributed these effects to the prevalence of bad practices, according to a common notion among the medical attendants of similar establishments. In my capacity of keeper of the County Jail, beside debtors, persons accused and convicted, and occasionally madmen, dangerous to go at large, I had frequently under my observation, on commitment by the magistrates of the city of Providence, vagrants of the most wretched description, who were seized with that species of derangement called *delirium tremens*, arising from the sudden deprivation of an accustomed excessive stimulus of the brain by ardent spirit. In observing these cases, I was forcibly struck with the similarity of the symptoms in those who had become deranged in the *State Prison*, after a confinement of from six to eighteen months in solitude, to those manifested in the Jail in patients who became such after a confinement of but a few days, and undoubtedly from the abstraction of their accustomed excitement by drink. The appearance of similar effects, arising from apparently dissimilar causes, led me to an investigation of the subject, for the purpose, if possible, of ascertaining if such were the fact. From the uniformity of the symptoms of derangement, which made their appearance in a large number of the convicts in the State Prison, and were strongly developed in *one-sixth part* of all who were there committed during a term of about four years, and all placed in the same condition, and under the same discipline, I was satisfied that all were affected by one and the same cause ; and being forcibly impressed with the identity of their derangement with that exhibited in the Jail, arising from the abstraction of alcoholic stimulus, I at length was satisfied that the same general explanation extended to all the cases, though in one class of them no ardent spirit had ever been used to excess ; or, if so used, had been entirely abstained from from six to eighteen months. In both classes of cases, I have come to the conclusion, that the derangement was produced by the abstraction of an accustomed stimulus to the brain, either natural, and requisite to a healthy action, or unnatural, and adapted to the supply of a morbid and injurious appetite, and thus necessary, by a bad habit, to the ordinary mental and physical action of the system. Persons who have never been deprived even of a small portion of what may be called their *natural stimulus*, for any considerable length of time, are little aware of its salutary and indispensable influence. Every moment of our lives brings us under its action, through the external senses, in ten thousand various forms. The succession of day and night, the changing seasons through which we are constantly passing, are all in continual action upon the springs of life. The momentary and everchanging objects which present themselves to the eye, the continual and rapid variety of sounds which fall upon the ear, and, in short, the perpetual succession of phenomena, which address themselves to the senses, are all, in a state of personal liberty, and except in the periodical intermissions of sleep, constantly operating upon the brain, and supplying it with that normal stimulus so necessary to the production of moral, physical, and intellectual health. In fact, all the external senses are but so many avenues, through which new impulses to the system are continually flowing; all which, including also social intercourse, combine in their operations, and give a perpetual impulse to the human system. Now, suddenly abstract from a man these influences, to which he has been so long accustomed; shut him up, with but scanty resources of his own to keep the powers of his mind in action, in a solitary cell, where he must pass the same unvarying round, from week to week, with hope depressed, with no subjects for reflection but those which give him pain to review, in the scenes of his former life; after a few days, with no new impressions made upon his senses, where even the sound of his own hammer is lost upon his ear, and one unvarying sameness relaxes the attention and concentration of his mind, and it will not be thought strange, that, through the consequent debility and irritability of its organ, the mind should wander and become impaired; in short, that the prisoner should have the " horrors," and that too from the same cause that produces the disease in the man whose system has become accustomed to other and greater stimulus than his, and has had that unnatural but habitual stimulus suddenly withdrawn. Is not the brain, as a physical organ, subject to the same laws that govern all other parts of the system? and may it not become paralyzed or deranged for want of action, as well as from exhaustion of excitability by over-action?

Perhaps it would be advisable to draw the parallel more specifically between the two conditions of derangement to which I have alluded. If a man have safely passed through an attack of delirium tremens, arising from the abstraction of his accustomed alcoholic stimulus, he will never be liable to another attack so long as he abstains from that stimulus. The same is true, so far as my observation extends, of the prisoner who has safely passed through the same ordeal in the abstraction of his accustomed stimulus to the senses, such as has been described; and he will spend the remainder of his days, so long as he shall remain in prison without any interval of liberty, though for years in solitude, and never be subject to a like attack. But the consequences may be irreparable, and he may be very much reduced in the scale of being ; without energy, or capacity for action, and unfit to be restored to society; his animal propensities invariably gaining the ascendency over his moral and intellectual faculties, inasmuch as the ordinary stimulus necessary for the former has not been abstracted to so great an extent.

Again, let the long-accustomed stimulus of alcohol be gradually withdrawn from those, who, in consequence of a depraved condition of the body, would otherwise be the subjects of delirium, yet such is the flexibility of the human system, such its power, gradually, within certain limits, to accommodate itself to changes of condition without sustaining material injury, that it may be done with impunity. The same is true, and has been repeatedly exemplified under my observation, in regard to the effects produced by the abstraction of the natural stimulus of the brain in solitary imprisonment ; and, without a single exception, those who have suffered the greatest deterioration from solitude, are men who possessed the smallest portion of intellect, who depended almost wholly upon external influences to keep their brain in action, and who had their accustomed and necessary resources suddenly and almost entirely abstracted. But those who are blessed with better intellects, and who are consequently supplied with a stock of internal resources, upon which to sustain themselves, have been enabled gradually to let themselves down, and have become accommodated to their new and inferior condition, without, or with less perceptible injury.

Again, when the accustomed excessive use of ardent spirits is suddenly suspended, and symptoms of delirium tremens ensue, nothing is better adapted to relieve the patient than the administration of his usual stimulus. The same is true in relation to that derangement produced by solitary imprisonment, in support of which, and more clearly still to show the identity of the two conditions of derangement under consideration, I shall now adduce a few cases of the latter, assuming that those of the former class, as well as the treatment of them, are too well known to require a description at that time.

CASES.

Prisoner No. 6, white, aged 28 years, was sentenced to separate imprisonment for four years. His health was somewhat impaired ; but he was of temperate habits, possessed of ordinary intellect, but uncultivated, with large perceptive faculties, a nervous-sanguine temperament, and a good flow of spirits. He had passed a roving life, without regular employment. He showed symptoms of derangement about the twelfth month of his confinement. The principal feature of his derangement was a constant dread and fear of some imaginary danger. In this state of mind he attempted to commit suicide, to avoid being flogged to death, which he was sure would soon be done, though at that time corporal punishment was not allowed in the Prison. He was continued in solitude during the remainder of his sentence, and was discharged from Prison almost an idiot. As no one knew his name or home, and he was not in a suitable condition to be at large, he was placed in the County Jail for safe-keeping. At this time, every indication in his appearance was, that he would never again be restored in the slightest degree. Being harmless, he was placed in one of the rooms appropriated to debtors, where, to my surprise, after associating with them for several months, he seemed to regain some glimpses of memory, which apparently had been lost for nearly three years. He is now in the Lunatic Asylum at Concord, New Hampshire, in the hope of the restoration of his faculties; but with what success, time has not disclosed.

A similar condition of imbecility, I think, would often be conse-quent upon the excessive use, or the sudden abstraction, of ardent spirits, were it not for the fact, that, in extreme cases, the physical powers sink with the intellectual, and death overtakes the victim. But according to my observations, where a long and excessive use of ardent spirit has been indulged in, although the animal functions may survive the shock of its abstraction, the moral and intellectual facul-ties never regain their original integrity. The same remark will, in my judgment, apply with equal truth to the individual whose system has received any considerable or long-continued derangement, by the abstraction of his natural and accustomed stimulus in solitary con-finement.

Prisoner No. 8, white, aged 40 years, was sentenced for five years; a man of temperate habits and good health, of inferior intellect, with strong passions, and a considerable share of cunning. His tempera-ment was bilious-sanguine, and very much disposed to mirthfulness. He could neither read nor write, and was very ignorant, except of the expedients to gain a dishonest livelihood; his occupation irregular. He became deranged about the tenth month of his confinement. Symptoms of delirium tremens were in his case more completely developed than in the preceding. I have found him in the greatest state of terror and alarm, in consequence of his seeing some one at his window, with a long pike, for the purpose of killing him. Under this impression, I have seen him crouched in some corner of his cell, where he could not be reached from the window, his whole frame in a state of tremor and agitation, indicating the greatest fear. Under this fear and excitement, he also attempted suicide. This state of delusion continued about six months, when he gradually recovered his composure, with the mental faculties much reduced. He re-mained four years in solitary confinement, at which time the system was abolished. But so great was his aversion to leaving his cell for labor, that he was allowed to continue there during the remainder of his time.

Prisoner No. 20, white, aged 32, was sentenced for twenty months. His constitution was impaired by intemperate habits. His mental faculties were feeble and uncultivated; his occupation that of a sailor; no marked indication of temperament, and an even but moderate flow of spirits. He exhibited symptoms of derangement about the twelfth month of confinement, which increased until most of the symptoms of delirium tremens were fully developed, such as tremor of the hands, tongue, and voice, profuse perspiration, a delusion of the senses, and great fear of personal injury from false causes, leading him to arm himself with whatever was in his possession, and give battle to his imaginary enemy with the greatest desperation. He continued in this situation to the expiration of his sentence, having once attempted suicide. After being discharged, his recovery was rapid, and in a few weeks he was apparently restored to a sound state of mind.

Prisoner No. 40, white, aged 28 years, of strong constitution, good health, and of temperate habits, was sentenced for two years. His natural abilities were fair; he was barely able to read, but had never learned to write. His temperament was bilious-sanguine, and of an ordinary cheerful disposition. He showed symptoms of derangement, with a tendency to commit suicide, about the tenth month of confine-. ment, soon exhibiting several well-marked symptoms of delirium tremens. When under great apparent fear and excitement, he related to me a plot he had heard formed in the Prison-yard for taking his life; that he had also seen one of the conspirators at his window, with a gun, for the purpose of shooting him, and that he had saved his life by lying on the floor immediately under the window, where the gun could not be brought to bear upon him ; afterwards, that they resorted to suffocation, by burning sulphur at his ventilator, and that he barely saved his life by applying his face to the window, where he could breathe the external air. At this time, the law relating to the Prison had been so far altered as to allow two or more prisoners to remain in a cell. Accordingly, another prisoner was allowed to be with him, which alone appeared to be the cause of his recovery, after a few weeks, when, at his own request, he was left alone in his cell, where he in a short time relapsed and exhibited all his former symptoms. The company of a convict was again allowed him, as before; and in about four weeks he was restored, without afterwards relapsing into his former condition, though his companion was removed, as before.

Of the *forty* prisoners committed while the strictly solitary system was in operation, ten, or one fourth of the whole number, (two of whom were blacks,) manifested decided symptoms of derangement; seven so much so, as to unfit them for labor for a longer or shorter period, and five were discharged insane, two of whom recovered, and three now remain unrestored to a sound state of mind.

Of the *nineteen* committed since the system was abandoned, three only,—two whites and a black,—have shown symptoms of derangement. One of them is No. 20, whose case has been described, who was recommitted in about twelve months after his discharge, and who relapsed into his former condition about the fourth month of confinement. One other, a black, was so much deranged as to disqualify him for labor, his health at the same time being much impaired, though good when committed. He died of dropsy of the chest, in the tenth month of his imprisonment, and in the sixth week of his being so far deranged as to unfit him for labor. The third is in tolerably good health, and is not disqualified for work, though laboring under constant anxiety, depicted in his countenance, from the hallucination that he is visited by tempters, whispering in his ear the suggestion to commit some criminal act. He showed symptoms of derangement about the sixth month of confinement.

I would here remark, from all the observations that I have been able to make, that but few men, and those strongly constituted, can be subjected to the discipline of solitary imprisonment, as it was here established, without becoming, sooner or later, through its depressing effects, more or less debilitated in some of their physical and mental operations; and I have not the least doubt, that under this, as well as under other systems of imprisonment, hundreds of convicts have been most inhumanly punished, for the innocent exhibition of some eccentricities of conduct during the trying period of their imprisonment, when, upon every principle of humanity, they should have been treated with more than ordinary kindness and compassion. Effects somewhat similar to the above are often, in a greater or less degree, produced by the stagnation of the active powers, after retirement from a long and energetic business life. The individual having secured a competency for the body, without having laid up any internal resources, finds himself sinking under this new state of mental inertia. Upon the withdrawal of the accustomed stimulus of business, nothing is left to keep up the healthy action of the brain, and melancholy, and oftentimes suicide, is the result, and from a cause similar to that which operates in the production of delirium tremens.

Similar effects are not produced upon the mind upon retiring from literary labors and pursuits; and the reason is evident. The literary man carries with him, in his retirement, a store of food for thought and reflection; and although his activity may be diminished, there yet remains sufficient stimulus to support the brain under its somewhat altered circumstances, until it becomes adapted to them. The minds of literary men, however, sometimes become deranged under circumstances analogous to that form of delirium tremens arising directly from the excessive stimulus of ardent spirits. In both cases, the excitability of the brain, from excessive action, becomes exhausted; and in both cases, the worst form of paralysis of that organ is the consequence. In some diseases, also, especially in the malignant form of typhus fever, where there is a sudden loss of the vital powers, a species of delirium ensues, very much resembling delirium tremens, and from which the patient is restored only by the use of the most powerful stimulants.

Upon a review of facts like those I have now detailed, it is impossible for me to hesitate in condemning the penal system of solitary confinement. Were it preferable in an economical point of view, — and the case is widely the reverse, — we could not hesitate in deciding the question between economy and humanity.

" Political society has the undoubted right to vindicate its laws, by assigning to the violation of them such penalties as the public safety and welfare may require, and such as do not conflict with the paramount injunctions of the divine Lawgiver." " It is, as I believe, the right of society to take the life of an offender, if necessary; but not to take his mind, or to subject him to any process of infliction of which mental derangement shall be an ordinary, and not an unusual and unexpected result. There is no pretence of necessity for any system that operates in this way. There are others more safe, practicable, and beneficial." " The legitimate objects for which judicial punishments are inflicted by the political state, are to administer retributive justice to the offender, to secure society against a repetition of his offence, and to deter others from imitating his example. The first object is accomplished by death, imprisonment, or other infliction upon the offender ; the second, by the same means, and, still better, by his reformation ; and both the second and the last, by exhibiting a sufficient counterbalance of evil to weigh down any amount of pleasure or gain which may tempt him or others to do the like. And the amount of pain which society can inflict, is that which is strictly necessary in its own defence. All beyond this partakes of the crime committed, rather than of the justice which seeks to punish it ; is ' cruel and unusual,' and is at war with the sound principles of government and the dictates of humanity."

The improved physiology of the present day, without denying the possibility of an insane mind, according to the popular form of speech, recognizes no such phenomenon, in the present state of existence, without a proximate bodily cause ; though the remote causes may be bodily, or mental, or both. And as the causes of derangement in solitary confinement, both proximate and remote, appear so uniformly to be of a physical nature, and so fully adequate to the effects produced, I do not deem it necessary to dwell on any other than that which it has been my endeavor to exhibit, and which, if it have received any attention from others, has not been estimated as its importance requires.

Without dwelling on the greater expensiveness of the solitary plan, its effects on general health, its failure to deter from crime, (according to the promise held out,) and various other objections, I would remark, that the advantage claimed for it, of greater calmness of demeanor and easier submission to the rules of the place, on the part of the solitary prisoner, has not been realized here. On the contrary, solitude has been found to produce restless irritability, and a peevishness of disposition, impatient of the unnatural restraint imposed on the reluctant body and mind, difficult to be dealt with ; while, in the performance of social labor, in silence, the men have been better subject to control, and have required less frequent exertions of authority than before. When shut up in the cells, they exercised, under the cravings of the social instinct, which walls and chains cannot repress, every contrivance that ingenuity could suggest, by means of the window, and the pipes passing through the cells, to hold some communication with each other ; and they were more frequently successful than would have been supposed possible. While, on the other hand, when the strict seclusion of the cell was done away, and the senses of the prisoners were once more opened to a portion of their accustomed impressions, and the social nature had been partially relieved, by permitting company without conversation, a very marked change came over the prisoners, and they manifested most clearly to the observer, by their greater cheerfulness, alacrity in labor, and prompter compliance with orders, that their condition was much improved, and that they were sensible of it.

In the year preceding the discontinuance of solitary imprisonment, there was an average loss from sickness of twenty-five per cent. upon the labor of the convicts. During the past year, under the system of social labor, the loss, from the same cause, has been about six per cent. The necessity and amount of punishments for disobedience and violations of rules have diminished in about the same proportion. It should be added, however, that corporal punishment has been introduced under the new system, and no doubt has operated to deter from offences, although it has been administered to two prisoners only, in extreme cases.

Another supposed advantage of the solitary plan—that of affording secrecy and seclusion to the prisoner, so that he may go forth into the world again without being recognized, and perhaps threatened or tempted by his associates — is, in practice, wholly illusory. For no man passes into Prison without an open trial, and the knowledge of friends and enemies ; and no man can expect to pass out again without being remembered. A hope of concealing the imprisonment, as the basis of reformation and a new character, is almost sure to be defeated ; and I believe that " experience fully warrants the assertion, that the prospect of thorough and lasting reform is the best where the offence is atoned for on the spot where it was committed, and before its witnesses, by honest exertions, and a life of integrity."

Without seeking a controversy with the officers of other Prisons, I feel, nevertheless, free to say, after an attentive examination of their reports, setting forth the great amount of derangement which prevails under the system of strict solitude, and more especially the reports of the Eastern Penitentiary, at Philadelphia, which was taken as our model, that, in my opinion, the main, prevailing cause of derangement in those prisons has been overlooked ; and that the cases as described have been erroneously attributed to the prevalent practice of masturbation.

It is at the same time asserted, that the very worst and most hopeless form of derangement, arising from this source, viz., dementia, the condition of being demented, and prostrated in body and mind, is frequently curable, and the cases are reported. We read also of *acute* dementia, (*acute* depression, or decay of the faculties!—a phrase which sounds somewhat strangely to an old-fashioned practitioner,) of "erotic enervation," of hypochondria, hallucination, and "*deviltry*," among the list of causes ; from the description of which, I believe them to amount, in the whole, (excepting the *last*, which is not precisely intelligible in this region,) to *enervation of the brain*, the organ of the mind, through the abstraction of the greater portion of its appropriate and external stimulus. At all events, I shall be satisfied if I have said any thing to recall attention to this important subject, and to the closer investigation of the phenomena. If I am in error in this matter, I shall be more happy to be corrected than to detect the errors of others. If I am right, the boasted system of solitude may lose something of popularity, where it is still retained, and humanity will be the gainer.

While it will be seen from the statistics of this Prison, before presented, that the proportion of deranged has fallen from twenty-five per cent., under the solitary system, to *ten* per cent. of new cases, under the present, of solitude by night, with labor in company by day, there is room for improvement, until this opprobrium shall, if possible, be removed, by reducing this deplorable evil to its smallest possible compass. This, of course, will be an object of solicitude with all concerned in the management of the Prison.

In attending to the habits and dispositions of prisoners, it has been a question with me how far they would be benefited by intercourse or communication with friends on the outside. In some prisons, occasional visits are allowed ; in others open letters are permitted to pass to and fro ; and in some, temperance newspapers are circulated. In this Prison, a stricter rule prevails, and no visitors, except those authorized by law, and except in extreme cases of sickness or otherwise, are permitted to see and converse with the prisoners. Without intending to interfere in this or other matters resting in the province of the inspectors, I may be allowed to say, that while there are some who may be almost said to be fortunate in being rescued from the base and contaminating associations with which they have been mixed up, and brought to this place, the case is different with others, who have virtuous, sympathizing friends ; and there is a chord in the heart of the most erring, which can be touched by the hand of kindness, with an unfailing response. In looking over the writing-books which are furnished to the prisoners on Sundays, I have been occasionally struck with the home feeling manifested, and the yearning of prisoners after the better things that have been lost in the pursuits for which they had incurred the penalty of the laws.

It is worthy to be considered whether a proper communication from abroad of the good influences of friends may not sometimes become an important element in the recovery of prisoners to a purpose of amendment, from which they will not so easily be swayed by their former temptations, on returning to the world.

Among the great variety of topics which press upon my attention, there are two popular errors relating to imprisonment, upon which I will offer a few remarks. One is, that the greater the severity practised toward a prisoner, the greater his punishment. It is very common, when improvements in Prisons are suggested, for the greater comfort of the inmates, to hear the observation, that they ought to suffer, and the more the better ; that the way of the transgressor is hard ; and that the only way to benefit him is to make a deep and lasting impression of wholesome severity upon body and mind. It is true that pain is the portion of the prisoner for his offences, and that he must suffer, and deeply suffer, to be benefited. But there is a limit which cannot be passed without defeating the ends of the law, in retribution, public security, and personal reformation, and perverting justice into cruelty without an object.

Says an American writer, " It ought to be impressed on lawgivers, and on all who are called upon to administer penal justice, in any of its modes, that it is possible, and indeed too common, by excess of severity, *to sink the prisoner below the capacity of being punished at all*, in wearing out the vigor and sensibility of body or mind, or both." " Let those who, without due reflection, approve of the utmost harshness and severity to prisoners, that they may be made to feel and reflect, consider but for one moment what must be endured in a State Prison, even where administered under the least stringent regulations; upon the total seclusion of the prisoner from friends, and from the external world, and from the knowledge of what is passing in it, for months and years; upon the suppression of the social nature, and the sufferings of the mind even in the most hardened,—and he will dismiss, at once, an opinion which wars with the superior sentiments of humanity."

The second error, allied to the first, is, that this harshness and severity are necessary to prevent prisoners from repeating their offences, or committing others, and being brought back again to confinement. The very reverse of this statement is the truth. "Words of kindness have subdued hearts in Prison that were callous to bolts and bars." "The only hope of reforming a man in Prison, and preventing his being brought back again, after his discharge, is in appealing to his intellect and moral nature; in dispossessing him of his revenge, if he have any, against his prosecutors; in reconciling him to the justice of his sentence, and to the labor and deprivations to which he is subjected, as being necessary, and tending to his own good; in treating him like a man, who, though fallen, is not lost; in raising up his self-respect, enlightening his ignorance, awakening his conscience; in making him feel that he is not an outcast, and that there are those who ' care for his soul,' and would be glad to see him renovated and restored to his place in society; in governing him with firmness, but with as little severity as possible, and in showing him as much kindness, in every respect, as discipline will permit." With all these means, accompanied by religious instruction, " the expectation of reform in Prison should not be too high, for reformation in the shade, where there is no temptation, like the virtue of hermits and monks, is endangered by exposure to the light; and too frequently will not bear the contact of the world;" and, further, " although in those who have committed what may be called crimes of excitement, there is often no deep-rooted depravity, yet the mass of convicts are those who are so broken down in moral character, as to be past recovery by any agency less potent than the special grace of God." " Hard usage will make a man very desirous to get out of Prison, but it will not prevent him from committing the crime that will send him back. And here lies the error of the advocates of severity. Conscience being seared, desire ascendant, temptation strong, judgment weak and easily deluded by false hopes of concealment or impunity, the old offender is very apt to repeat his crime, at the first opportunity, notwithstanding the recollection of all that he may have endured in the very severest form of imprisonment. Where the greatest severity is practised, will be found the greatest number of recommitments."

The prisoners now committed here possess as fair natural abilities as the average of the community; most of them can read and write. A large majority of the convicts were addicted to the use of ardent spirit. All the cases of murder, — three in number, — and also all the cases of manslaughter, were instigated by "the demon of the distillery."

Of the *fifty-nine* prisoners committed here, *three* have been committed a *second* time, but *none* a *third*.

As appears by the physician's report, the general state of health in the Prison has been good for the year. One cause of the disproportionate tendency to affections of the lungs in inmates of State Prisons, is found in the general disuse of the voice, and consequent debilitation of the lungs, through the indispensable rule of continued silence. Reading aloud, rehearsing and singing in their cells, should be encouraged among prisoners, as a means of counteracting this evil.

There are some other topics, connected with those already adverted to, which time and the space now occupied will require me to defer to some other opportunity.

All which is respectfully submitted, by

THO'S CLEVELAND, M. D.,

Warden of the Rhode Island State Prison.

PROVIDENCE, *October* 30, 1844.

KUNST DER WELT

DIE AUSSEREUROPÄISCHEN KULTUREN

IHRE GESCHICHTLICHEN, SOZIOLOGISCHEN
UND RELIGIÖSEN GRUNDLAGEN

EINE BUCHFOLGE IN 4 SERIEN ZU 4 BÄNDEN

Serie 4

JAPAN

BURMA, KOREA, TIBET

DIE FRÜHEN STEPPENVÖLKER

KUNST DES ISLAM

DIE FRÜHEN STEPPENVÖLKER

DER EURASIATISCHE TIERSTIL
ENTSTEHUNG UND SOZIALER HINTERGRUND

VON KARL JETTMAR

SCHWEIZER DRUCK- UND VERLAGSHAUS AG ZÜRICH

LIZENZAUSGABE FÜR DIE NEUE SCHWEIZER BIBLIOTHEK
© 1964 HOLLE VERLAG GMBH · BADEN-BADEN

I. ENTDECKUNG DER FRÜHEN STEPPENKUNST

Es ist schade, daß keiner der großen russischen Historienmaler die Szene dargestellt hat, die sich am 29. Oktober 1715 in St. Pieterburg, der neugegründeten Hauptstadt, abspielte: Peter dem Großen, dem Zaren aller Reußen, war ein Sohn geboren worden, und die Großen des Reiches strömten herbei, der Zarin Katharina Glückwünsche und Geschenke zu überbringen. Nikita Demidov, Sohn eines leibeigenen Schmieds, aufgestiegen zum reichsten Unternehmer in den Erzschürfen des Urals, vermochte die eindrucksvollste Gabe vor ihr auszubreiten: hunderttausend Rubel in klingender Münze und eine Sammlung von Kunstwerken aus purem Gold. Man wußte von ihrer Herkunft nur, daß sie aus den Grabhügeln Sibiriens stammten, in ABB. SEITE 6 denen fleißige russische Plünderer zur Erbitterung der abergläubischen Eingeborenen schon seit Jahren nach Schätzen wühlten.

Man bestaunte nicht nur den goldenen Glanz – auch die prachtvoll ausgeführten Tierkörper, die das immer wieder abgewandelte Thema der Schmuckstücke bildeten, fanden in dieser Welt barocken Überschwangs allgemeine Bewunderung. Vor allem bei den bis zu handgroßen Platten, die die Hauptgruppe des Schatzes ausmachten, verband sich gekonnte Wiedergabe der natürlichen Formen mit reicher Einlegearbeit in buntem Stein. Besonders Tierkämpfe von wilder Dramatik und doch gebändigter Spannung gefielen den Menschen des 18. Jahrhunderts. Da wand sich eine Schlange um einen Eber wie um einen anderen Laokoon, ein Adler mit geschwungenen Flügeln schlug einen zottigen Yak.

Entscheidend war, daß Peter der Große selbst die Herrlichkeiten zu Gesicht bekam. In ihm lebte ein unbändiger Sammel- und Forschungsdrang. Sein kategorischer Befehl, alle menschlichen Mißgeburten des Riesenreichs in Spiritus zu stecken und abzuliefern, hat bekanntlich seiner neugegründeten Akademie der Wissenschaften die ungeheuerlichste Sammlung von Monstrositäten verschafft, die auf der Welt existiert, eine Orgie des Grauens. Analog verfuhr er hier: Strenge Weisungen ergingen an den Gubernator nach Sibirien, von nun an derartige Funde für die Krone zu sammeln – einschließlich aller sonstigen Kuriositäten, die der Boden hergab, Tier-, Fisch- und Vogelknochen. Wenig später erließ er einen Ukas, der einen förmlich Denkmalschutz anstrebte, Jahrhunderte bevor es in weniger despotisch regierten Staaten zu ähnlichen Einrichtungen kam.

Angesichts der Disziplin, die in Peters Reich herrschte, konnte der Erfolg gar nicht ausbleiben. Bereits zwei Monate später traf die erste Sendung aus Tobolsk ein: zehn Gegenstände vom Charakter des Demidovgeschenks, die wie dieses dem frischgegründeten Raritätenkabinett zugewiesen wurden. Der Gouverneur, Fürst Gagarin, hatte sich beeilt aufzukaufen, was gerade auf dem Markt war und sonst wohl in den Schmelztiegel gewandert wäre. Noch im gleichen Jahr brachte er dann die großartigste Lieferung zusammen – fünfundfünfzig große und zwanzig kleine Gegenstände im Gesamtgewicht von fast vierundzwanzig Kilogramm. Man darf sich dazu vorstellen, daß der um die Gunst seines Herrn besorgte Beamte die Raubgräberei in

Goldplatte des sibirischen Schatzes, den Kampf dreier Raubtiere um eine Beute darstellend. Das Stück gehört zum ältesten Bestand der Eremitage, Leningrad. *Gewicht 517 Gramm*

6

Kupferstich aus dem Werk von Witsen »Noord en Oost Tartarye«, Amsterdam 1785, Stücke einer verlorenen Sammlung wiedergebend. *Vgl. S. 8*

ABB. SEITE 7

noch größerem Rahmen betrieb, als bisher schon üblich war. Vielleicht hatte er auch eine Expedition in noch unberührte Gebiete vorgeschickt. Jedenfalls war damals der große Kehraus. Etwa um die gleiche Zeit erhielt der holländische Gelehrte Nikolas Cornelius Witsen von Freunden vierzig Stück zugeschickt, alle in schwerem Gold, nachdem eine frühere Sendung Seeräubern zum Opfer gefallen war. Diese mehr oder minder illegalen Lieferungen erfolgten offenbar auf Grund von Verbindungen, die Witsen während seines sibirischen Aufenthalts einige Jahre vorher angeknüpft hatte. Leider endete auch die zweite Lieferung durch die Pietätlosigkeit der Erben im Schmelztiegel. Immerhin sind als Illustrationen zu Witsens Werk ausgezeichnete Stiche angefertigt worden.

Noch im 18. Jahrhundert indes versiegte der Goldstrom, ohne daß sich das Rätsel um die Zugehörigkeit des Fundguts irgendwie gelöst hätte. Der einzige Hinweis bestand in der Angabe, im gleichen Zusammenhang seien auch Münzen römischer Imperatoren ans Tageslicht gekommen.

Die Bedeutung dieser Funde und ihres »Tierstils« – um den Ausdruck erstmalig zu gebrauchen, der sich in der Wissenschaft seit Jahrzehnten durchgesetzt hat – tritt noch weit schärfer hervor, wenn wir bedenken,

Tiger verschleppt zwei Kühe ins Dickicht

Die Beine der Kühe

Tiger

Blatt = Dickicht

Fig. 1 – Beispiele für die von Ryndin herausgearbeiteten erzählenden Muster der Kirgisen. (Nach Tokarev 1958)

8

daß die bildende Kunst aller modernen Nomadenvölker der asiatischen Steppen vom Ornament beherrscht wird. Bei den Kazachen z. B. ist es, wie Basenov vor kurzem formuliert hat, das grundlegende und einzige Motiv der bildenden Kunst.

Die Ornamentsysteme der Steppe beruhen auf der überreichen Kombination weniger Grundelemente von meist hoher Abstraktion. Dort, wo Tiere gemeint sind, wird nur als karges Symbol der Schwung des Gehörns oder vielleicht die Rundung eines Hufs wiedergegeben. Das gilt selbst dann, wenn eine religiöse Bedeutung mitschwingt. Nur die eigene Aussage macht es klar, daß einst die Mittelfelder der berühmten turkmenischen Teppiche die Totemtiere jener Sippenverbände wiedergeben, denen die Herstellerinnen angehörten. Mehr als dreitausend kirgisische Muster beruhen auf der Kombination von hundertdreiundsiebzig »Vokabeln«. Lesen können wir sie erst durch die – umstrittenen – Forschungen von Ryndin. So ist es bezeichnend, daß ein Autor wie Glück, der die »Weltgeltung der Türken in der Kunst« hervorheben will, mit der Ausbreitung einer abstrakten Schmuckform wie der geometrischen Ranke argumentiert hat.

FIG. I

Es bleibt unklar, ob die Steppenornamentik ihr Entstehen Anregungen von außen verdankt. Man hat dagegen angeführt, die Applika-

Jurte an zwei Quellen

Zwei Hunde kämpfen um Knochen

Quelle

Hund

Scherengitter als Symbol der Jurte

Knochen

9

Elfenbeinschnitzerei der Ipiutak-Kultur aus Nordwest-Alaska, junges Walroß darstellend. Man hat hier an Einflüsse des skythischen Tierstils gedacht. *Museum of Natural History, New York.*

Vgl. S. 11

tionstechnik in dem angestammten Material der Hirten, in Leder und Filz, führe notwendig zu einer abstrakten Spiral- und Volutenornamentik. Sicher ist jedenfalls, daß sie immer wieder die Einflüsse benachbarter Kulturen in sich aufgenommen hat. Vor allem hat der Nahe Osten auf dem Weg über Iran und Außer-Iran tief auf sie eingewirkt, konkurrierend mit der uralten Strahlungskraft Chinas. Ältestes Erbe innerasiatischer Bauernvölker wirkt nach. Nicht ursprünglichem Schöpfertum begegnen wir hier, sondern den gestauten Stiltrümmern einer langen Vergangenheit. Es ist kein Zufall, daß man die Ornamentik der Steppen als Quelle für ihre wechselvolle Stammesgeschichte zu nutzen versucht.

Bezieht man nun die übrigen Kunstkreise Asiens in die Betrachtung ein, so stellt sich heraus, daß nur im äußersten Nordosten, an der

Beringstraße, ein dem Tierstil der Steppen vergleichbares Zentrum realistischer Tierauffassung besteht. Das Material ist dort meist Knochen. Er wird von den Männern zu Rundskulpturen gestaltet oder mit Gravierungen geschmückt. Überall stößt man auf jenes Erfassen des Tieres und seiner Bewegungen, hinter dem man den Blick des Jägers, das Erbe vieler Generationen spürt. Dabei sind es gerade die seßhaften Gruppen im Küstenbereich, Tschuktschen, Korjaken, Eskimo, von denen wir die reichsten Proben künstlerischer Begabung kennen. Die Ren-Nomaden des Inneren treten völlig zurück.

Nahe scheint auch die Kunst des europäischen Jungpaläolithikums zu stehen. Sie blühte bei Jägergruppen, die nur durch eine extreme Beobachtung des Tiers existieren konnten. Auch sie waren seßhaft und lebten in großen wirtschaftlich eng verbundenen Gemeinschaften.

Der Unterschied zwischen Jägern und modernen Nomaden ließe sich psychologisch erklären: Die heute zur Seßhaftigkeit übergehenden Nomadenvölker der Steppe hatten trotz aller Liebe des Reiters zu seinem Pferd nicht das gleiche, sich zu fast sexueller Spannung steigernde Verhältnis zum Tier. Ihnen fehlte die Verwurzelung, das Grübeln während langer Polarnächte in unterirdischen Behausungen. Ihr Kunstgewerbe blieb den Frauen und abhängigen Meistern überlassen. Ausdruck ihres ausgreifenden Lebensgefühls ist das Epos.

Was heißt das nun für unseren Tierstil? Ist er trotz seiner Heimat in den Steppen noch die Schöpfung von Jägern? Stammt er von »Hyperboräern«, die, das Erbe ihres Jägertums im Blute tragend, aus der Taiga hervorbrachen, um den Steppenraum zu beherrschen? Die Deutung vieler Cervidendarstellungen der frühen Nomadenkunst als Rentiere hat diese Vermutung genährt. Gelehrte von einem so subtilen Einfühlungsvermögen wie der Russe Borovka oder der Engländer Minns haben sie vertreten.

Oder sind es Einflüsse einer übermächtigen, raffinierten Hochkultur, die hier grandiose Primitivität vortäuschen?

Gibt es doch noch einen anderen geistigen Boden, auf dem solche Werke entstehen? Für eine solche Möglichkeit könnte das ornamentale System der Fischervölker im Amurbecken sprechen. Es verwendet in Spiralen und Kurven aufgelöste Tiersilhouetten und ist deshalb unlängst als Ableger der Steppenkunst bezeichnet worden.

Fig. 2 – Tierdarstellungen der Amurvölker (Oltschen und Giljaken). (Nach Ivanov 1954)

Aber wenn dem so wäre, warum treffen wir nicht noch mehr und deutlichere Ableger im Steppenraum selbst? Was trennt die Nomaden der letzten Jahrhunderte von ihren Vorgängern?

So formieren sich hier Probleme, denen wir uns am Ende des Buches stellen müssen. Zuvor aber müssen wir die Provinzen des Tierstils kennenlernen, so wie sie allmählich vor den Augen der Wissenschaft aufgetaucht sind, im Bereiche des gesamten Steppengürtels von Europa bis Ostasien. Freilich können wir nicht überall mit der gleichen Ausführlichkeit vorgehen. Funde, die in den letzten Jahren gemacht wurden oder an Bedeutung gewonnen haben, müssen breiter dargestellt werden. Dafür kann der erdrückende Reichtum, den der lang und intensiv erforschte Boden Südrußlands geliefert hat, besonders kurz behandelt werden. Ihm und der gleichzeitigen griechischen Kolonialkunst soll ein eigener Band der Reihe »Die Kulturen des Abendlandes« gewidmet werden.

Auch die Auswahl der Farbtafeln ist ungewollt subjektiv. Der Verlag erhielt keine Vorlagen für jene Stücke, die in der Eremitage oder im Historischen Museum in Moskau aufbewahrt sind. Das ist schade, es wäre sonst die überwältigende Leistung sowjetischer Ausgräber noch sichtbarer in Erscheinung getreten.

Der Verlag sah sich daher zum Einsatz einer Methode gezwungen, die bereits in Werken von Talbot-Rice, Ghirshman, sowie in einem von Piggot herausgegebenen Prachtband zur Anwendung kam. Der in Mainz wirkende Maler Heinz Prüstel hat die Stücke der Eremitage nach Schwarzweißphotos farbig rekonstruiert. Es ist zu hoffen, daß dieser Notbehelf, der in einem Fall (an der Leningrader Jagdplatte im Werke Ghirshmans) zur Vergoldung aller bunten Einlagen führte, in Zukunft durch eine zunehmende Liberalisierung zwischen Ost und West überflüssig gemacht wird.

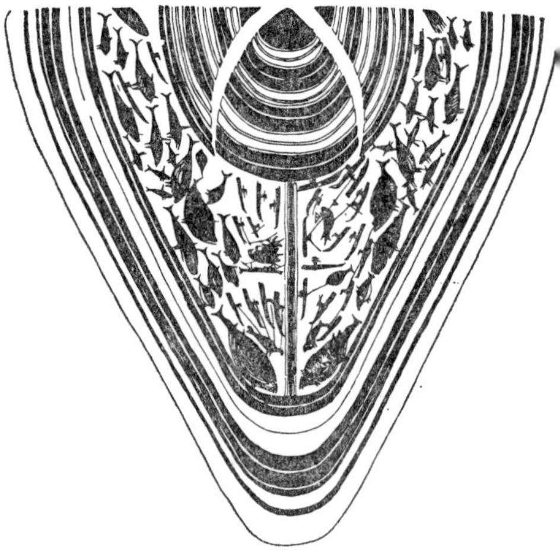

Fig. 3 – Fischfang und Seesaugerjagd. Realistische Darstellung auf einem Augenschirm der Aleuten (von oben gesehen). (Nach Ivanov 1954)

II. DAS PONTISCHE SKYTHIEN

Wir beginnen mit unserem Überblick in Südrußland, denn hier konnte die Blüteperiode des Dekorationssystems, das wir eben kennengelernt haben, zeitlich fixiert und einem bestimmten Volk zugewiesen werden – den Skythen. So wurde es auch üblich, selbst über diesen Raum hinaus von einem »skythischen Tierstil« zu sprechen, bis an die Grenzen Chinas!

Hier wurde ferner der gesamte wirtschaftliche, soziale und politische Hintergrund der künstlerischen Entwicklung aufgerollt. Diese für die Wissenschaft einmalig günstige Situation verdanken wir der Tatsache, daß die Skythen mit griechischen Städten an den Küsten des Schwarzen Meeres in enger Symbiose lebten. Die meisten davon waren von ionischen Kolonisten begründet worden. Sie übernahmen die Aufgabe, die herrschende Bevölkerungsschicht des Inlands mit den typischen Exportprodukten des Mutterlands zu beliefern, also kunstgewerblichen Erzeugnissen, vor allem aber Wein. Galten doch die Skythen der ganzen Antike als gewaltige Zecher, die das sonst übliche Mischen gründlich verachteten. Die Kolonialstädte besaßen darüber hinaus eine umfangreiche eigene Produktion, die sich dem Geschmack der barbarischen Kunden anzupassen wußte. Als Gegenleistung lieferten diese Getreide und Holz, aber auch Sklaven und Pelze, die aus der Tiefe des osteuropäischen Raumes stammten. Es wird sogar von einer Handelsstraße berichtet, die in die sagenhafte Ferne der östlichen Steppe führte.

Griechische Kolonialstädte

Im Binnenhandel spielten die Flüsse eine entscheidende Rolle. Deshalb lagen wichtige Emporien an ihren Mündungen: Tyras am Dnjestr, Tanais am Don. Olbia, das bedeutendste Zentrum, beherrschte gleichzeitig Bug- und Dnjeprmündung. Andere Städte säumten die Küsten der fruchtbaren Krim. Die dichteste Ballung läßt sich an den beiden gegenüberliegenden Halbinseln Kertsch und Taman feststellen, wo Panticapaeum die älteste und wichtigste Kolonie war.

Handel und Ackerbau

Alle Städte haben in ihrem Weichbild intensiv Ackerbau getrieben. Rund um den Bosporus von Kertsch aber wurde die einheimische Bevölkerung hellenisiert, ihre Fürsten trugen bald griechische Namen. Dieses kompliziertere Gewebe rief nach einem strafferen Zusammenschluß als es die Städte mit ihrem Hegemonie- und Bündnissystem

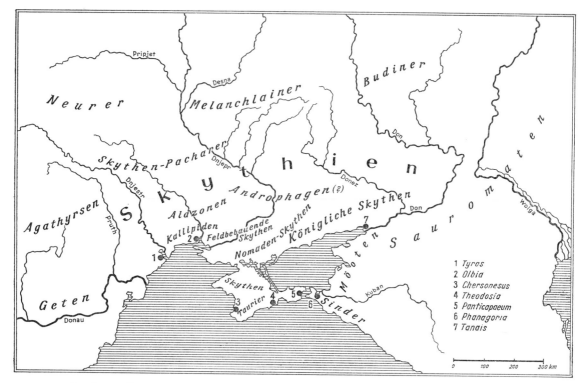

In den antiken Quellen erwähnte Völkerschaften und wichtigste Kolonialstädte im pontischen Skythien. (Nach Očerki Ist. SSSR.)

Bosporanisches Reich darstellten. Es kam daher von Panticapaeum ausgehend zur Gründung eines Staates, an dessen Spitze bereits in der zweiten Hälfte des 5. Jahrhunderts v. Chr. eine einheimische Dynastie trat. Sie herrschte über ein blühendes Reich, das erst in den Wirren des 2. Jahrhunderts v. Chr. seine Bedeutung und Selbständigkeit verlor.

Was die Kolonisten über ihre Partner erfuhren, ist über viele antike Schriftsteller auf uns gekommen, allerdings stark mit Legenden durchsetzt. Die vorhandenen Texte sind mit bewunderungswürdiger Gründlichkeit noch während des 19. Jahrhunderts gesammelt worden, am Vorabend der großen Revolution hat sie Rostovcev kritisch untersucht und mit den Ergebnissen der Archäologie verglichen. Noch immer tauchen im Verlauf der Grabungen in den Städten neue Inschriften auf.

Völkerkarte Skythiens So erfahren wir, daß man den gesamten Bereich zwischen Donaumündung und Don »Skythien« nannte, in diesem Raum aber eine

14

ganze Reihe von Völkern unterschied. Unter ihnen läßt sich wieder eine skythische Kerngruppe herausschälen. Das Namensmaterial verrät, daß sie iranisch gesprochen hat. Sie ist von Nachbarn umgeben, die sich zum Teil der skythischen Lebensweise angeschlossen hatten, zum Teil aber als völlig fremd empfunden wurden, von Agathyrsen, Neurern, Androphagen, Melanchlainern und Budinern. Wahrscheinlich handelt es sich um Thraker, Slawen, vielleicht auch Finnen. Nur bei den östlich von den Skythen sitzenden Sauromaten wird ausdrücklich vermerkt, sie hätten eine ähnliche (d. h. iranische) Sprache. Innerhalb der Skythen unterschied man Bauern – sie nahmen den Westen ein – und Nomaden, östlich des Dnjepr, darunter war die eigentliche Führungsgruppe, der »Königliche Stamm«. Von ihm heißt es, er habe alle anderen Skythen als seine Sklaven betrachtet. Eine eigentümliche Bevölkerung finden wir dann noch auf der Krim, jene düsteren Taurier, die alle Schiffbrüchigen ihrer Großen Göttin opferten. Iphigenie galt dem Euripides als ihre Priesterin, von Herodot wird sie mit der Göttin selbst identifiziert. Östlich vom Asowschen Meer lebten Sinder und Mäoten.

Die Nomadenskythen haben immer wieder das Staunen der antiken *Nomadentum* Autoren erregt: sie pflügen nicht und sie säen nicht. Unstet ziehen sie mit ihren großen Herden von Ort zu Ort, immer auf der Suche nach neuen Weidegründen. Deshalb kennen sie keine festen Häuser, sondern leben in Wagen. Ihre Nahrung sind Fleisch und Milch, auch Pferdemilch, denn von den Stutenmelkern weiß schon Homer. Die Männer verbringen ihre Tage im Sattel, wie verwachsen mit ihrem Tier. Die griechische Vorstellung vom Kentauren, dem Pferdemenschen, hat hier ihren Ursprung genommen.

Die skythische Tracht ist von den Kunsthandwerkern der Schwarz- *Tracht* meerstädte wiederholt dargestellt worden: der Baschlyk, die weiche, den ganzen Schädel umhüllende Mütze, das kurze gegürtete Wams und die »Reithosen«. Die Füße stecken in weichen Lederstiefeln. Da- FIG. 4 mals gab es noch keine Steigbügel (einmal, in einer Szene, die das Zureiten darstellt, sehen wir Lederschlaufen), und der Sattel war kaum mehr als eine Decke. Deshalb wurde ein großer Teil der Waffen am Gürtel befestigt, so der Goryt (ein Köcher, der auch den kurzen Reflexbogen aufnahm) und der Akinakes, das Kurzschwert. Außerdem trug man die Streitaxt oder eine leichte Lanze. Öfters werden kleine Schilde dargestellt. Nur Anführer besaßen offenbar Helme und Brustpanzer.

Die Kampftaktik der Skythen war wie die Kleidung ganz auf Beweg- *Kampfesweise* lichkeit abgestellt. Bereits Herodot sagt, niemand könne ihnen entrinnen, noch sie fassen, wenn sie sich nicht selbst zum Kampfe stellen wollen. Nach blitzschnellem Scheinangriff warfen sie ihr Pferd herum, um dann fliehend nach rückwärts zu schießen.

Kimmerier als Vorläufer der Skythen

Vor den Skythen sollen die Kimmerier die Herren der Pontischen Steppen gewesen sein. Ihre Existenz wird durch zahlreiche Ortsnamen und sagenhafte Berichte bestätigt, die den Schwerpunkt auf der Halbinsel Kertsch haben. Es heißt, sie seien vor dem Ansturm der übermächtigen Skythen am Ostufer des Schwarzen Meeres entlang nach Süden entkommen, ihre Verfolger hätten sich dann um die ganze Breite des Kaukasus »geirrt« und ihren Weg längs des Kaspisees genommen. So seien beide Völker in Vorderasien eingebrochen, wo die Skythen achtundzwanzig Jahre lang geherrscht hätten.

Die Anwesenheit beider Völker in den alten Kulturzentren des Südens wird tatsächlich von vielen orientalischen Quellen bestätigt, einschließlich der Bibel. Allerdings wirken die Kimmerier keineswegs als Flüchtlinge.

Kriegszüge der Kimmerier und Skythen in Vorderasien 8. und 7. Jh. v. Chr.

Im vorderen Osten hatten sich in dieser Zeit Urartu und Assyrien zu Militärmächten von bisher ungekannter Härte entwickelt. Sie strebten nach totaler Herrschaft, was vor allem die Assyrer durch Vernichtungskriege und Verschleppungen zu erreichen trachteten. Andererseits aber verteidigten sie die alte Ökumene erbittert gegen Invasionen aus dem Norden. Dabei setzten sie unbedenklich Barbaren gegen

Fig. 4 – Diese Genreszenen (im Original etwa 5,5 cm hoch) bildeten den Schmuck einer Elektronvase, die im Kurgan von Kul Oba bei Kertsch gefunden wurde. Wir sehen die Behandlung eines schmerzenden Zahnes und das Versorgen einer Fußverletzung. Mit seltener Deutlichkeit hat der griechische Kunsthandwerker des 4. Jhs. v. Chr. hier Bekleidung und Rassentyp dargestellt; die Skythen waren durchaus europid. Sehr gut erkennbar auch der Goryt. (Nach Minns 1913.) Vgl. S. 15

Barbaren ein. Sie füllten ihre eigenen Armeen mit nördlichen Söldner-
verbänden auf, ohne freilich deren Ausschreitungen hintanhalten
zu können. Kimmerier und Skythen waren nur eine Gruppe unter
solchen gefährlichen Verbündeten, allerdings eine besonders aktive.
Im Jahre 714 v.Chr. brachten die Kimmerier Urartu an den Rand des
Untergangs, etwas später traten sie neben Urartu in eine Koalition
ein, die Assyrien bedrohte. Asarhaddon sicherte sich seinerseits die
Hilfe der Skythen, er gab ihrem Anführer Bartatua seine Tochter zur
Frau. Auch später noch kämpften die Kimmerier an der Seite Urartus.
Sie wurden schließlich nach Kleinasien abgedrängt, wo sie auf Unter-
stützung von Verbänden rechnen konnten, die von Thrakien her über
den Hellespont heranrückten. Es gelang den Barbaren, Sardes zu
nehmen. Erst durch das Eingreifen Assyriens ging diese Position wieder
verloren. Die Skythen operierten noch eine Weile weiter. Sie entlaste-
ten die Assyrer durch einen entscheidenden Sieg über die Meder, die
zusammen mit anderen iranischen Stämmen von Nordosten her vor-
drangen. Dies gab ihnen die Möglichkeit zu Plünderungszügen, die
bis an die Grenze Ägyptens führten. Biblische Texte spiegeln die
Schrecken des Skythensturms lebhaft wider. Später wechselten sie
noch einmal die Front. Unter der Führung der Meder beteiligten sie
sich an der Vernichtung der assyrischen Macht, die mit der Plünderung und Zerstörung von Ninive ihren Abschluß fand.

Es ist verständlich, daß es die erste Sorge der konsolidierten medischen *Vertreibung durch*
Großmacht war, sich derartiger Verbündeter eilig zu entledigen. Der *die Meder*
Bericht, der Mederkönig Kyaxares habe die skythischen Anführer bei
einem Trinkgelage umgebracht, klingt völlig überzeugend. Auf ähnliche Weise entledigte man sich noch vor hundertfünfzig Jahren in
Ägypten der Mamelucken. Es ist auch durchaus wahrscheinlich, daß
nach solchen Katastrophen skythische Verbände ihr Tätigkeitsfeld
wieder nach Südrußland zurückverlegten.

Die Kimmerier verschwinden nunmehr aus den Quellen, sie ver-
schwimmen immer mehr in einer mythischen Vergangenheit. Nicht
so die Skythen: um das Jahr 514 v. Chr. unternahm der Achämenide *Skythenfeldzug*
Darius I., König der Perser, die inzwischen die stammverwandten *des Darius*
Meder abgelöst hatten, einen Feldzug gegen sie. In einem riesigen
Umgehungsmanöver überschritt er den Hellespont und stieß dann von
Thrakien aus in den Rücken des Feindes. Trotzdem scheiterte das
Unternehmen an der Weite des Raumes und an jener Strategie, die
dann durch zwei Jahrtausende hindurch die Überlegenheit der Step-
penvölker gegenüber ihren seßhaften Nachbarn ausmachte. Nur mit

Mühe vermochte Darius nach langer vergeblicher Verfolgung des schemenhaft zurückweichenden Feindes wieder die rettende Brücke über den Ister zu erreichen. Herodot hat diesen Feldzug in gewaltiger dichterischer Steigerung beschrieben.

Der Vorstoß wurde nicht wiederholt, weil von nun ab die Perser ihre Anstrengungen auf die Eroberung Griechenlands konzentrierten. Die Bedrohung beider Völker durch einen gemeinsamen Feind mag aber ein günstiges Klima für den kulturellen Kontakt geschaffen haben.

Die Skythen erfreuten sich nun für längere Zeit einer gesicherten Machtposition, die sie zu verschiedenen Vorstößen gegen ihre thrakischen Nachbarn benützten. Allerdings kam es auch zu dynastischen Verbindungen, etwa zum Königshaus der mächtigen Odrysen.

Macht und Reichtum hielten auch während des 4. Jahrhunderts v. Chr.

an, dabei spielte der Erlös von Getreideexporten eine immer größere Rolle. Neue Flächen der Krim wurden dem Ackerbau erschlossen. Allerdings machte sich schon der Druck sarmatischer Stämme bemerkbar, die inzwischen den Don überschritten hatten.

Als Gegenschlag gegen eine solche Unterhöhlung ist vielleicht der Versuch des Königs Atheas zu verstehen, das Skythenreich politisch straffer

zu organisieren. Berühmt ist sein Krieg gegen die thrakischen Triballer. Diese Kämpfe führten zur Bildung skythischen Kolonialbodens westlich der Donaumündung, in der heutigen Dobrudscha. Im hohen Alter aber verlor Atheas gegen einen gewaltigeren Gegenspieler, Philipp von Makedonien, Schlacht und Leben.

Nach der Katastrophe verlagerte sich der Schwerpunkt der skythischen Staatsbildung immer stärker auf die Krim. Nur das Mündungsgebiet des Dnjepr blieb noch unter direkter Kontrolle. Die westliche Steppe ging an die thrakischen Geten, der Osten an die Sarmaten verloren, die von da ab die Weidegründe der königlichen Skythen beherrschten. Kein Wunder, daß die Skythen nun versuchten, wenigstens die griechischen Städte unmittelbar in ihre Macht zu bringen. Damit wollte man den einträglichen Zwischenhandel an sich ziehen. Das gelang wiederholt, sogar das starke Olbia wurde vorübergehend eine Stadt der Skythen. Ihr König Skilurus ließ hier Münzen schlagen, die den Wohnwagen der Nomaden zeigen, auf der Kehrseite aber Hermes und Demeter, die Schützer von Handel und Ackerbau. Selbst das bosporanische Reich geriet in den Bannkreis solcher Politik, so daß die Städte sich schließlich an Mithridates um Hilfe wandten, der sofort bereit war, die Chance zur Ausweitung seines pontischen Königreichs wahrzunehmen. Seine Feldherren, die sich aller Finten und Hilfs-

Fig. 5 – Feldzeichen eines skythischen Anführers aus dem Alexandropol-Kurgan, die »Große Göttin« darstellend. 3.Jh.v.Chr.Bronze. Vgl. unten. (Nach Tolstoi-Kondakov 1889)

mittel der hellenistischen Kriegskunst bedienten, schlugen die Skythen zu Lande – und zu Wasser. Jene besaßen nämlich in der Spätzeit eine eigene Flotte, die, mit Griechen bemannt, die Getreidetransporte gegen Seeräuber beschützen sollte. Wenig später standen die Skythen in dem allerdings vergeblichen Versuch, die Ausweitung der römischen Macht im Schwarzmeerraum zu verhindern, auf seiten des Mithridates. Das siegreiche Rom begnügte sich zunächst mit der Errichtung von Schutzstaaten. Ansätze zu einer aktiveren Politik in der Zeit Kaiser Neros wurden aus innenpolitischen Gründen wieder aufgegeben. Wie Inschriften zeigen, bestand der Skythenstaat auch noch im 2. und 3.Jahrhundert n.Chr. weiter, sich gelegentlich zum Angriff gegen die Städte aufraffend. Erst dann verlieren sich die Spuren im Andrängen neuer Völkerwellen.

So übersehen wir das Schicksal des skythischen Volkes und seiner Staatsbildung im Verlauf von fast tausend Jahren. Es ist klar, daß sich Religion und Brauchtum inzwischen wesentlich verändert haben müssen. Unsere Hauptquellen stammen freilich aus einer sehr frühen Phase – Herodot schrieb ja noch im 5.Jahrhundert v.Chr. Er berichtet, daß an der Spitze des Pantheons eine weibliche Gottheit stand, Tabiti, die der Hestia gleichgesetzt wurde, vermutlich weil man das Herdfeuer als ihr Symbol und Heiligtum ansah. Neben ihr gab es andere weibliche Gestalten; eine schlangenfüßige Erdgöttin wurde als Stammmutter angesehen. Einer weiteren Göttin dienten offenbar verweiblichte Männer, Priester mit gewandeltem Geschlecht, was den Vergleich mit altorientalischen Kultpraktiken nahelegt.

Papaios wurde Zeus gleichgesetzt, Herakles unter seinem griechischen Namen verehrt. Es gab weder Tempel noch Altäre. Nur der Gott des

Religion des 5.Jhs. v. Chr.

Gottheiten
FIG. 5

Krieges verkörperte sich in einem eisernen Schwert, das man auf der Spitze eines künstlichen Hügels unter blutigen Opfern anbetete.

Kriegerische Bräuche Das Kriegsbrauchtum der Skythen war von barbarischer Frömmigkeit erfüllt, die das Interesse Herodots erweckt hat (IV. Buch, Kp. 64–66): »Wenn ein Skythe seinen ersten Feind erlegt, trinkt er von dessen Blut. Die Köpfe aller, die er in der Schlacht tötet, bringt er dem König. Wenn er einen Kopf bringt, erhält er seinen Beuteanteil, sonst nicht.

Skalpieren Sie ziehen den Schädeln die Haut ab, indem sie rings um die Ohren einen Schnitt machen, dann die Haare fassen und den Kopf herausschütteln. Mit einer Ochsenrippe wird das Fleisch abgeschabt, dann die Haut mit der Hand gegerbt und wenn sie weich ist, als Handtuch gebraucht. Der Reiter bindet die Haut an den Zügel seines Pferdes und prahlt damit. Wer die meisten hat, gilt für den tapfersten Helden. Vielfach macht man sogar Kleider aus diesen Kopfhäuten. Sie werden zusammengenäht wie die Hirtenpelze.

Viele häuten auch die rechte Hand ihrer gefallenen Feinde ab mitsamt den Fingernägeln. Sie machen Deckel für ihre Köcher daraus. Die Menschenhaut ist fest und glänzend, weißer und glänzender als fast alle anderen Häute. Manche häuten die ganze Leiche ab, spannen die Haut auf Holz und führen sie auf ihrem Pferde mit. So merkwürdige Gebräuche haben sie.

Schädelbecher Aus den Schädeln selber aber, nicht von allen Erschlagenen, sondern nur von den grimmigsten Feinden, machen sie Trinkschalen. Die Teile unterhalb der Augenbrauen werden abgesägt und der Schädel gereinigt. Wer arm ist, legt dann bloß außen ein Stück Rindsfell herum; der Reiche vergoldet außerdem das Innere des Schädels, und dann trinkt er daraus. Das tun sie sogar mit den Schädeln ihrer Angehörigen, wenn sie mit ihnen verfeindet waren und wenn einer den anderen vor dem Gericht des Königs besiegt hat. Kommt dann ein angesehener Gast zu diesem Sieger, so stellt er ihm die Schädel hin und erzählt von seinen feindseligen Verwandten, deren er Herr geworden sei. Das gilt für heldenhaft und vornehm.

Einmal in jedem Jahre läßt der Häuptling jedes Gaues im Mischkrug Wein bereiten, und alle Männer, die einen Feind erlegt haben, trinken davon. Die, welche keinen erlegt haben, dürfen nicht mittrinken und sitzen abseits, ohne daß man sie beachtet. Das ist für den Skythen die größte Schande. Alle, die eine ganze Menge Feinde erschlagen haben, bekommen gar zwei Becher und trinken aus beiden zugleich.«

Diese Angaben, die immer das höchste Interesse der Ethnographen erregt haben, weil sie Übereinstimmungen mit dem Kriegsbrauchtum vieler Völker erkennen lassen – man spricht dort von »Trophäenjagd«, »Skalpieren« und »Schädelbechern« – lassen im übrigen erkennen, daß der skythische Reiterkrieger zunächst noch nicht in ein System starrer, feudaler Abhängigkeit eingezwängt war. Wie bei den Indianerstämmen Nordamerikas konnte er durch persönliche Heldentaten zu Ruhm und Ehre gelangen.

Nur in scheinbarem Gegensatz dazu steht die absolute Macht des *Göttlicher Ursprung* skythischen Königs (auch moderne, sehr freiheitsliebende Nomaden- *des Herrscherhauses* verbände haben eine absolute Spitze). Ja, die Dynastie durfte sich sogar göttlicher Abstammung rühmen: Herakles soll sie nach einer Legende durch seine Verbindung mit der schlangenfüßigen Göttin begründet haben.

Das Charisma der königlichen Stellung findet in dem von Herodot eingehend beschriebenen Totenritual seinen Niederschlag. Es kennt an düsterer Großartigkeit kaum seinesgleichen in der antiken Welt (IV. Buch, Kp. 71–72):

»Die Grabstätten der Könige befinden sich in der Landschaft Gerrhos, *Totenritual der Könige* in die der Borysthenes als schiffbarer Strom hineinfließt. Wenn der König gestorben ist, wird dort eine große viereckige Grube in die Erde gegraben. Ist sie fertig, so hebt man die Leiche auf einen Wagen. Der Leib ist vorher mit Wachs überzogen worden, der Bauch geöffnet und gereinigt, mit gestoßenem Safran, mit Räucherwerk, Eppich- und Dillsamen gefüllt und wieder zugenäht worden. Die Leiche wird nun von Stamm zu Stamm geführt. Jeder Stamm, zu dem sie gelangt, tut dasselbe, was die königlichen Skythen zuerst tun: jeder schneidet ein Stück von seinen Ohren ab, schert seine Haare, macht einen Schnitt rund um den Arm, ritzt Stirn und Nase und sticht einen Pfeil durch die linke Hand. Dann geht es zum nächsten Stamm, und der vorhergehende gibt der Leiche das Geleit. Endlich nachdem alle anderen Stämme durchwandert sind, gelangen sie nach Gerrhos zu dem fernsten Stamm und zu der Grube. Die Leiche wird darin auf eine Streu gebettet, zu beiden Seiten der Leiche werden Lanzen in den Boden gesteckt, Stangen darüber gelegt und ein Dach aus Flechtwerk hergestellt. Man tötet eines seiner Weiber, seinen Weinschenken, seinen Koch, Pferdeknecht, Leibdiener, Boten, ferner seine Pferde, die Erstlinge alles anderen Viehs und begräbt sie in dem weiten Raum der Grube, der noch leer ist; ebenso auch goldene Schalen, denn Silber- und Erzgeräte nehmen die Skythen dazu nicht. Darauf türmen sie einen großen Grabhügel auf und suchen ihn so gewaltig wie möglich zu machen.

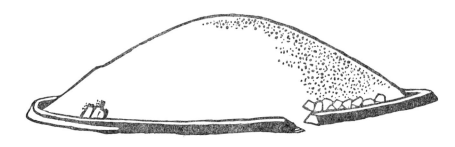

Fig. 6 – Ansicht des Alexandropol-Kurgans (Höhe 21 m) vor Beginn der Ausgrabungen – Nach Tolstoj-Kondakov 1899.) Vgl. S. 23

Ein Jahr später wird die Trauerfeier wiederholt. Die besten von der Dienerschaft des Königs, die noch am Leben sind – das sind eingeborene Skythen; jeder, den der König beruft, wird sein Diener, gekaufte Sklaven kennt man nicht –, werden erdrosselt, fünfzig an der Zahl, ebenso die fünfzig schönsten Pferde. Die Eingeweide werden herausgenommen, die Bauchhöhle gereinigt, mit Spreu gefüllt und wieder zugenäht. Dann wird die Hälfte eines Radreifens an zwei Stangen befestigt, mit der Rundung nach unten, und die andere Hälfte an zwei andere Stangen; in der Weise wird eine ganze Anzahl von Geräten hergestellt. Auf je zwei davon wird nun ein Pferd gehoben, nachdem durch seinen Leib der Länge nach bis zum Halse eine dicke Stange getrieben worden ist; es ruhen die Schultern auf dem einen Reifen, der Bauch an den Hinterbeinen auf dem hinteren Reifen. Vorder- und Hinterbeine schweben in der Luft. Sie legen den Pferden auch Zaum und Gebiß an, ziehen den Zaum aber nach vorn und binden ihn an einen Pflock. Alle fünfzig erdrosselten Jünglinge werden dann auf die Pferde gesetzt, und zwar in der Weise, daß der Leichnam senkrecht, längs des Rückgrats bis zum Halse, mit einer Stange durchbohrt wird, deren unteres hervorstehendes Ende in ein Loch jener waagrechten Stange, die durch das Pferd geht, gesteckt wird. Diese Reiter werden im Kreise um das Grabmal aufgestellt, und dann geht man wieder von dannen.«

Mit ähnlicher Ausführlichkeit handelt Herodot vom Begräbnis der einfachen Leute, von Wahrsagern und Schwurzeremonien. Manche Angaben haben durch zentralasiatische Funde eine plötzliche Bestätigung erhalten, wie wir noch sehen werden.

Verlauf der Grabungen Die antiken Quellen, auf die wir uns bisher stützten, erwähnen mit keiner Silbe eine eigene skythische Kunst. Dieses Problem tauchte vielmehr erst auf, als die Wiedereroberung der Ukraine durch das Zarentum die Möglichkeit zu Grabungen in den überall majestätisch aufragenden Grabhügeln bot, allerdings zu Grabungen, die sich von der FIG. 6 Tätigkeit der Plünderer nur dadurch unterschieden, daß sie staatlich sanktioniert waren und die besten Stücke an die kaiserlichen Sammlungen abgeführt wurden, während sich die geringeren in viele kleinere Museen und Kollektionen zerstreuten.

Den Auftakt machte 1763 der Litoj-Kurgan; darin wurde der herr- *Litoj-Kurgan 1763* liche Melgunov-Schatz gefunden – so benannt nach dem General, der die Öffnung durchführen ließ. Wenn das Interesse weiterhin rege blieb, lag das freilich vor allem an den vielen unverkennbar von griechischen Künstlern gestalteten Beigaben. Daneben erschienen eigenartige Metallarbeiten, die Tiere als Dekorationsmotiv verwendeten, immer wieder Tiere, zunächst als barbarische Auswüchse, nur die Verwendung edlen Materials sicherte auch ihnen eine gnädige Aufnahme. Die skythische Kunst gelangte gewissermaßen an der Hand ihrer griechischen Gefährtin ins Allerheiligste der Archäologie.

Immerhin, unter diesem Aspekt grub man mit erstaunlichem Eifer nach weiteren Altertümern. Französische Adelige, Emigranten der Revolution, und Deutsche wirkten mit. Die Gründung von Lokal- *Lokalmuseen 1805–1826* museen gibt einen Maßstab für das wachsende Interesse: 1805 in Nikolaev, 1811 in Theodosia, 1825 in Odessa und 1826 in Kertsch. Allmählich war klar geworden, daß der barbarische Rest auf Rechnung der Skythen, dieses alten Herrenvolkes gesetzt werden mußte. Seit 1866 versuchte man, in den großen Grabhügelfunden Herodots Beschreibung ihrer Totengebräuche wieder zu erkennen. Mit Handelsverbindungen und Kriegszügen dieses Volkes konnte man auch die Entdeckung ähnlicher Schätze in weit entfernten Gebieten erklären, in Zentralasien oder auf der Balkanhalbinsel. Als gar ein Fund in Vettersfelde in der Mark Brandenburg auftauchte, wirkte das wie ein Appell an die deutsche Gelehrsamkeit. Einer der klarsten und kühnsten Köpfe, der klassische Archäologe Furtwängler, erkannte, daß die *Furtwängler erkennt* eigenartige Stilisierung der Tiere, die den Körper eines Fisches buch- *Problematik des Tierstils* stäblich beleben, nicht einfach als Degenerationserscheinung abgetan werden dürfe. Sicher, die ausführenden Goldschmiede waren griechischer Nationalität, aber sie hatten dem Geschmack ihrer Auftraggeber dienen müssen. Wo aber lagen nun die Wurzeln dieser Tendenz, des »Tierstils«, wie man bald angesichts der Vorliebe für Tiermotive sagte? Furtwängler verwies auf die herbe Strenge der frühen ionischen Kunst, die einen reichen Schatz orientalischer Muster in sich aufgenommen hat.

Archäologische Kommission ab 1859

In Südrußland hatte sich seit der Gründung der archäologischen Kommission in St. Petersburg 1859 die Ausgrabungstätigkeit immer weiter ausgedehnt und systematische Formen angenommen. Das größte Finderglück bewies der überaus rührige, aber auch rücksichtslose und nicht immer korrekte Veselovskij, der bis 1917 am Werk war. Allmählich bekam man eine Übersicht über die wichtigsten Gruppen der Hügelgräber, der »Kurgane«. Eine Ballung von Nekropolen liegt

Wichtigste Kurgangruppen

beiderseits des Dnjepr-Unterlaufs, genau nördlich der Krim, eine weitere südlich und südöstlich von Kiew. Die Dnjepr-Gruppe dürfte zum Kern der skythischen Stämme gehören, ebenso die Grabanlagen im Ostteil der Krim. Andere kennt man im Dnjestr- und Buggebiet, im Karpatenbogen und in Wolhynien. Östlich von Kiew, im Raume von Poltawa, ist ein weiteres Zentrum. Gräber, die besonders intensiv den Kultureinfluß der Städte aufwiesen, fand man auf der Halbinsel Taman. Zunächst wollte man nicht recht wahrhaben, daß die Grabanlagen auch in Gebieten vorkommen, die gar nicht dem skythischen Territorium angehören; im Kubangebiet z. B. saßen Sinder und Mäoten. Dabei hat man gerade dort, in den Kurganen von Ul, die Massenbeigabe von Pferden festgestellt. In regelmäßiger Ordnung lagen die Skelette von mehreren hundert Tieren um die königliche Bestattung.

Certomlyk

Um eine Vorstellung von dem Reichtum, der sich da offenbarte, zu geben, sei hier der Čertomlyk-Kurgan im unteren Dnjepr-Gebiet geschildert: unter einer mächtigen Aufschüttung mit steinernem Sockel öffnete sich ein Schacht, an dessen Ecken Kammern in den Boden vorgetrieben waren. Durch eine davon öffnete sich der Weg in ein großes unterirdisches Gemach, in dessen Wänden kaschierte Nischen als Verstecke dienten. Die königliche Beisetzung, die sich einmal in dieser Kammer befand, war bereits ausgeraubt. Unversehrt waren nur große Bronzekessel geblieben, in denen Tierknochen lagen, außerdem das, was noch in den Wänden steckte. Besonders bemerkenswert sind eine Goldphiale, ein goldener Gorytbeschlag mit mythologischen Szenen griechischer Arbeit, sowie Schwerter, bei denen ebenfalls Griff und Scheide mit Goldblech überzogen waren. In der Kammer, durch die der Gang in die Hauptbestattung führte, waren die Königin (oder die Konkubine) des Herrschers und ein bewaffneter Diener beigesetzt worden. Das Skelett der Frau lag auf den Resten eines hölzernen Katafalks und war mit goldenen Plättchen übersät, die einst die Säume des Kopftuchs bedeckten. Außerdem fand man den üblichen Schmuck,

Goldkamm aus dem Solocha-Kurgan. 4.Jh. v. Chr. *Eremitage, Leningrad*. Auch hier hat die Hand des griechischen Künstlers ethnographische Details festgehalten, so die Verwendung importierter, griechischer Panzer und Helme. *Vgl. S. 26*

also Ringe, Armreifen, Perlen usf. Daneben stand die berühmt gewordene Silberamphore, die an der Schulter jenen Fries trägt, der Skythen beim Zureiten von Pferden darstellt. Ein silbernes Becken und weitere Amphoren befanden sich in ihrer Nähe. In der benachbarten Kammer lagen die Skelette des Waffenträgers und eines Dieners. Ihnen hatte man kostbare Waffen und Goldschmuck mitgegeben. An den Wänden der beiden übrigen Kammern hingen offenbar Kleider, von denen aber auch nur der goldene Zierat erhalten geblieben war. Hier sah man auch vier Prunkhauben für Frauen, geschmückt mit durchbrochenem Goldblech und mit Anhängern, weitere Waffen und zahlreiche Amphoren, die wahrscheinlich mit Wein und Öl gefüllt gewesen waren. An dem Zugang in eine dieser Kammern ruhte das Skelett eines Dieners, in einer anderen ein Hundeskelett, noch an der Kette. Die Aufschüttung des Kurgans enthielt – neben dem Dromos – noch ein besonderes Pferdegrab, das in drei Abteilungen elf Tiere barg. Vier trugen Schirrungs- und Sattelschmuck aus Gold, ebenso viele aus Silber und der Rest aus Bronze. Auch die Stallburschen hatte man mitbestattet.

Bei einem derartigen Reichtum der Königsgräber (es handelt sich ja um keinen Sonderfall) ist es kein Wunder, daß man die Friedhöfe der breiten Bevölkerung nicht systematisch erfaßte. Sie blieben vielmehr jenen Ausgräbern vorbehalten, deren Mittel beschränkt waren.

Als erstes Resultat gewann man aus der unerhörten Fülle die Erkenntnis, daß der gesamte, von Skythen dominierte – wenn auch keineswegs zu einem Staat zusammengefaßte – Raum bis in die Waldsteppe und ins Kaukasusvorland eine Kunstprovinz mit gemeinsamen Entwicklungstendenzen bildete. Nomadische Lebensart ohne Bindung an Haus und Einrichtung scheint auch für die Seßhaften vorbildlich gewesen zu sein, denn überall dienen die künstlerischen Äußerungen primär dem unmittelbaren Schmuck der Person. Die reiche Ausgestaltung der Pferdeschirrung paßt ins Bild. Unpersönliches Kultgerät hat man nicht entdeckt; Herodot hat ja das Fehlen von Tempeln ausdrücklich vermerkt. Wie man Zelt und Wohnwagen dekorierte und einrichtete, ist, abgesehen von einigen Wandgemälden in reichen Nekropolen der Kolonialstädte, erst durch zentralasiatische Funde klar geworden. Der Gepflogenheit der Nomaden entspricht es, daß diese Gebrauchskunst oft von zugewanderten Handwerkern ausgeführt wurde, von Vorderasiaten, Griechen, vielleicht auch Thrakern. Daß ihre soziale Stellung nicht ganz ungünstig war, hat sich bestätigt, als man in der Nähe der skythischen Königskurgane am Dnjepr eine ganze Siedlung von Schmieden ausgrub. Man hat darin zahlreiche Amphoren gefunden, die von dem Weinkonsum der Meister künden. Es handelte sich um keine schlechten griechischen Provenienzen.

Entscheidend ist nun, daß überall Tierbilder das Hauptmotiv der Dekoration bilden. Nicht alle gehören der einheimischen Fauna an. Es handelt sich auch keineswegs um die wirtschaftlich wichtigsten Haustiere. Es liegt vielmehr eine merkwürdige Selektion vor. Manche Bildgedanken stammen sicher aus dem Vorderen Orient wie z. B. der Löwe, bei anderen, etwa beim Eber, vermutet man griechische Herkunft.

Auch die Anordnung der Elemente zueinander gehorcht traditionsreichen Prinzipien. Da finden wir zunächst einmal die »zoomorphe Junktur«, d. h. die freie Kombination von Teilen, die verschiedenen Tierbildern entnommen sind. Sie hat im Nahen Osten eine lange Vor-

Kompositionsprinzipien

Brust- oder Schildschmuck in Form eines Panthers aus dem Kelermes-Kurgan. Beginn des 6. Jhs. v. Chr. *Einlagen aus farbiger Glaspaste und Bernstein. Etwa halbe natürliche Größe. Eremitage, Leningrad.* Wir finden hier die zoomorphe Junktur, wobei Tatzen und Schweif aus Rolltieren bestehen. Da man auch das scharfe Absetzen der Flächen beobachten kann, ist dieses Stück sehr häufig als repräsentativ für den skythischen Tierstil abgebildet worden. *Vgl. S. 28*

27

Fig. 7 – Knochenplatten (etwa 16 cm lang) und Riemenschmuck (etwa 4 cm lang) aus den Zabotin-Kurganen. Älteste Phase des Tierstils: die dargestellten Tiere entstammen der heimischen Fauna, aber ihre Pose ahmt syrohurritische und iranische (Sialk B) Vorbilder nach. Das Zeichen im Zentrum der Figur rechts wird als Sonnensymbol gedeutet. Vgl. S. 30

ABB. SEITE 27

geschichte. Bei manchen so entstandenen Mischwesen, etwa Löwen- und Adlergreifen, ist es recht gut möglich, den Weg in die Steppen zu verfolgen. Auch die Inversion, die Verdrehung des Hinterleibs, um hundertachtzig Grad hat man aus dem Orient ableiten wollen. Sie kommt schon auf kretischen Siegeln vor. Nicht allzuschwer ist es, für Tierkreuze und Tierwirbel südliche Vorbilder zu finden. Neuerdings behauptet man sogar, die charakteristische Pose skythischer Hirsche oder Steinböcke mit unter den Leib gezogenen Beinen stamme aus der syrohurritischen Kunst. Die an eine Fesselung erinnernde Stellung drücke hier das Darbieten des Opfertieres aus. Die durchaus dekorativ gebrauchten Tierkampfszenen, die sehr oft den Überfall einer Raub- katze auf einen Cerviden zum Thema haben, schließen an gängige Traditionen des Südens an. Vermutlich ostasiatischer Herkunft ist das Schließen des Tierkörpers zum Ring, es entsteht das Rolltier.

Schrägschnitt Wenn man sich diese Liste betrachtet, so wird es fast unverständlich, daß doch manche dieser Schöpfungen des pontischen Raums den Stempel unverwischbarer Eigenart tragen. Solche Stücke wirken nicht modelliert, sondern in scharfen Graten werden schräge, durch gespannte Kurven begrenzte Flächen gegeneinander abgesetzt. Es herrscht eine raffinierte Beschränkung auf wenige Motive, und diese werden wieder auf ihr Wesentliches reduziert. Offenbar geht es um die Spannung, um die potentielle Fähigkeit zur Bewegung, nicht um die Bewegung selbst. Die Tierkörper wirken wie Sprungfedern, die Ge- lenke sind betont, alles, was Gier oder Macht ausdrücken kann – so der Rachen der Raubkatze, die Hauer des Ebers, das Geweih des Hirsches –, wird hervorgehoben.

Fig. 8 – Stangenbekrönung (Feldzeichen?) aus dem Kurgan bei Ul, Kubangebiet. Um 500 v. Chr. Bronze, etwa 28 cm hoch. Eremitage, Leningrad. Die strenge Form der Frühzeit ist hier deutlich bewahrt. Man hat die sehr hohe Abstraktion, den kleinen Vogelkopf, der aus dem Halse des Steinbocks herauswächst, und das apotrophäische Auge als Beleg für das jüngere Datum herangezogen. Vgl. S. 30

Man hat manche Eigentümlichkeit dieser Gruppe, die doch den spezifisch skythischen, von eigenen Meistern gefertigten Anteil darstellt, durch eine technische Tradition erklären wollen. Ein Gegeneinander schräger Flächen entsteht, wo Holz oder vor allem Knochen das Material bilden. Mit dem Messer erzielt man Kerbschnitt, wenn man sich auf lineare Elemente beschränkt, oder Schrägschnitt, wenn man zügig und in Kurven arbeitet. Auch manche der unnatürlichen Posen könnten durch das Material erklärt werden. Man wollte eben den Tierkörper in die begrenzte Fläche einer Knochenplatte einpassen. Die Eigentümlichkeiten einer älteren Welt scheinen fortzuleben, selbst bei Umsetzung in wesensfremden Stoff, in Gold oder Bronze.

Ableitung aus Material und Technik

Andere Merkmale versucht man spirituell auf urzeitliches Erbe zurückzuführen. Man nimmt an, jedes Tierelement sei als Symbol aufgefaßt worden, mit Kraft aufgeladen, Segen um sich verströmend. Diese Kraftträger habe man summiert und potenziert, zum Heil und Schutz des Kriegers. Tatsächlich kommt ja bei manchen Naturvölkern eine Überbetonung, etwa der Gelenke, vor. Übersteigerung will magische Wirkung vermehren.

Geistiger Hintergrund

Dieses Prinzip scheint auf die von Griechen gefertigten Stücke überzugreifen. Auch dort sind traditionsreiche Tiermotive zum Teil hochkulturlicher Herkunft im Sinne eines Naturvolks gebraucht, das in einer magisch bestimmten Welt lebt, sie allmählich verläßt.

Diese Formel bot sich an, um die Entwicklungsgeschichte des Tierstils im südrussischen Raum verständlich zu machen.

29

Fig. 9 – Gürtelschnalle aus Žurovka, Dnjepr-Gebiet. Bronzeguß des 5.Jhs. Eremitage, Leningrad. Vielleicht nach einem griechischen Vorbild sind hier zwei Köpfe mit den Unterkiefern aneinandergesetzt. Man spürt eine Verflachung, die sich gegen Ende des 5.Jhs. noch stärker äußert. Vgl. unten

Ablauf der Tierstilentwicklung

FIG. 7

In der Frühstufe, die dem Ende des 7.Jahrhunderts v.Chr. angehört und ihren repräsentativen Ausdruck in den Žabotin-Kurganen findet, sind neben den magisch kräftigen Tierbildern auch noch Heilszeichen anderer Art vertreten. Es ist wenig griechischer, wohl aber vorderasiatischer Einfluß feststellbar.

ABB. SEITE 27

FIG. 12

Die Hochstufe, die mit den Kurganen des frühen 6.Jahrhunderts erreicht wird (Kelermes, Litoj, etwas später Kostromskaja), zeigt vorderasiatischen Einfluß schon durch das Auftreten von Einlegearbeiten mit bunten Steinen. Trotzdem wird nun der symbolische Wert der Tierform am schärfsten empfunden, gerade deshalb genügen wenige, grandios stilisierte Tierkörper – ein Cervide, Raubvögel, ein kleines Raubtier, Steinbock und orientalischer Greif bilden das gesamte Repertoire. Im späten 6. und im 5. Jahrhundert v. Chr. kann diese Einheit nicht gehalten werden. Das verhindert schon die zunehmende Verwendung griechischer Künstler. Hier spürt man eine leise Degeneration, dort wieder ein Zurückgreifen auf älteste Tendenzen. Vielleicht will man

FIG. 8 UND 9

einen anderen Weg zum Erzielen magischer Wirkung beschreiten und führt deshalb die Tierkampfszene ein. Auch die Inversion wird häufiger gebraucht. Von den zahlreichen berühmten Nekropolen, die dieses Stadium verkörpern, seien hier nur die von Žurovka, Ul, Elthegen und der »Goldene Kurgan« bei Simferopol genannt.

Im 4.Jahrhundert v.Chr. verlieren die Tierdarstellungen zunehmend

FIG. 10 UND 11

an Plastik. Es bleiben einfache Linien wie schon einmal in ältester Zeit, oder es entsteht ein üppiges Rankenelement. Dieses Stadium wird z.B.

FIG. 5

durch Čertomlyk, Solocha und den Hauptbestand von Kul Oba verkörpert.

In ihrer letzten Phase zeigt die skythische Kunst einerseits höchste Stilisierung, andererseits aber einen fast plumpen Realismus. Wir dürfen ihn auch auf Rechnung mittelasiatischer Einflüsse setzen, deren Vermittler wohl die siegreich vordringenden Sarmaten waren.

Fig. 10 – Tierwirbel aus Silber, Schmuckplatte für die Pferdeschirrung.
Aus dem Krasnokutsk-Kurgan. 4. Jh. v. Chr. Vgl. S. 30

Beim Herausarbeiten dieses chronologischen Schemas – denn nur darum handelt es sich – haben Gelehrte aus vielen Nationen zusammengewirkt. Der Engländer Minns schuf mit seinem Monumentalwerk: »Scythians and Greeks« die erste, bis heute verwendbare Zusammenfassung. Der Russe Rostovcev veröffentlichte ein brillant geschriebenes Übersichtswerk, der Lette Ginters erarbeitete die erste Monographie über eine skythische Waffe – das Schwert. Wesentlich blieb die Mitarbeit von Deutschen. In den zwanziger und dreißiger Jahren beherrschte noch eine Generation das Feld, die den Problemen des Ostraums aufgeschlossen war. Neben Ebert, dessen Bedeutung von Jahr zu Jahr klarer hervortritt, ist Schefold zu nennen. Dieser legte 1938 den konsequentesten Datierungsversuch vor, auf den wir uns im wesentlichen gestützt haben. Schefold ging grundsätzlich bei der Datierung der Kurgane von den Beigaben griechischer Herkunft aus. Seine Position ist wiederholt angefochten worden, mit dem Argument, gleichzeitige Deponierung bedeute noch keineswegs ein gleiches Herstellungsdatum, schließt aber in der Praxis keine allzu großen Fehlerquellen ein.

Die verantwortlichen Forscher

Das geistige Ringen um den Tierstil war inzwischen nicht ohne Fernwirkung geblieben. Aber während im Westen höchstens der Jugendstil interessante Impulse erhielt und in seiner ornamentalen Grundhaltung

Skythismus

Fig. 11 – Stirnplatte einer Pferdeschirrung aus Bronze aus dem Kuban-Gebiet. 4. Jh. v. Chr. Eremitage, Leningrad. Ein extremes Beispiel für die flächigen und doch rankenhaften Auflösungsformen der Spätzeit. Vgl. S. 30

bestätigt wurde, haben radikale Träumer des frühsowjetischen Rußland sich mit den Skythen identifiziert. Man sah in ihnen die großen
Gegenspieler Europas und der Hellenen und fand bei ihnen den eigenen
grenzenlosen »Maximalismus«, die gepriesene Unversöhnlichkeit des
Geistes wieder. Es entstand eine geistige Strömung, die sich »Skythismus« nannte, nach einem berühmt gewordenen Gedicht Alexander
Bloks, in dem die Verse enthalten sind:

> »Millionen ihr, wir – Menge, Menge, Menge!
> Versucht, ob wir zu kämpfen taugen!
> Ja, Skythen, Asiaten wir!
> Mit gierigen geschlitzten Augen!«

Man kümmerte sich dabei wenig um die Tatsache, daß die von den
Griechen abgebildeten Skythen durchaus europid aussehen, fast wie
russische Bauern. Nur der große Arzt Hippokrates hebt ihre körper-
liche Eigenart hervor, so daß man an einen mongoliden Typus denken
möchte: die Funde haben seine Aussage nicht bestätigt.

Tragische
Forscherschicksale

Neben dieser Aufwallung mutet der Beitrag sowjetischer Gelehrter
zwischen den beiden Weltkriegen eher bescheiden an. Die wichtigsten
Leistungen stammen vielleicht von dem Wolgadeutschen Rau, der die
Datierung der Pfeilspitzen zu einem geschlossenen System ausbaute,
und von Borovka, dessen künstlerische Analysen sich durch hohe Ein-
fühlungsgabe auszeichnen. Beider Lebenswerk endet abrupt. Rau ver-
zweifelte im Elend jener Jahre und verübte Selbstmord, Borovka geriet
in eine der Säuberungswellen.

Kampf gegen
Rostovcevs Thesen

Bei ihren linientreueren Kollegen wurde ein großer Teil der Arbeitskraft von ideologisch gefärbten Angriffen wider die Thesen Rostovcevs
absorbiert. Dieser größte russische Fachmann war schon als Emigrant
verdächtig, seine Zentralthese, die Skythen seien bereits im Vollbesitz
des Tierstils als nomadische Eroberer aus dem Osten aufgetaucht, um
die mutterrechtlichen Bauern Südrußlands zu überschichten, erschien
als Inbegriff bourgeoiser Überheblichkeit. N. Ja. Marr, Sohn eines schot-
tischen Seemanns und einer Kaukasierin, der damals als Vorkämpfer
der proletarischen Wissenschaft galt, hatte eine andere Erklärung an-
zubieten. Marr glaubte – als Sprachwissenschaftler – zeigen zu können,
daß große Völker niemals en bloc wandern. Wenn man trotzdem in
einem Gebiet plötzlich eine neue Sprachgruppe antrifft, so ist das nur
die Folge einer Umstrukturierung, hinter der die soziale, gesetzmäßig
verlaufende Entwicklung steht. Diese anregende, aber zweifellos über-
spannte These wurde Ende der zwanziger Jahre zur allgemeinen

Autochthoniewahn

Richtschnur erhoben. Die sowjetische Archäologie bekam damit den

Auftrag, die Bodenbeständigkeit der Skythen in Südrußland zu beweisen. Das lähmte die freie Forschung, abgesehen davon, daß die Nöte der Zeit nur geringe Mittel für Grabungen übrigließen und die Publikation auf schlechtestem Papier mit fast unbrauchbaren Abbildungen erfolgen mußte.

Erst in den Jahren nach dem Zweiten Weltkrieg rissen die Sowjetforscher wieder die Führung an sich. Man sah jetzt, daß der Autochthoniewahn auch seine guten Seiten gehabt hatte. Um ihm zu dienen, hatte man das Studium der Keramik und des Gebrauchsgeräts ungemein vertieft. Auch arme Gräber wurden sorgfältig erfaßt.

Aufschwung der russischen Archäologie nach 1945

Vor allem aber hatte man sich für die Siedlungen interessiert. So stellte man fest, daß es auch im Kerngebiet der pontischen Skythen entgegen dem Bericht Herodots Wallburgen gab, die von der Viehzucht treibenden Bevölkerung zumindest während des Winters bewohnt wurden. Eine davon, die riesige Kamenskoje Gorodišče, diente offenbar – auf einer Fläche von zwölf Quadratkilometern – den skythischen Großkönigen als Residenz. Sie liegt in unmittelbarer Nähe reicher Kurgane.

Siedlungsgrabungen

Die neue Breitenarbeit gestattete es, in Südrußland an Hand von Totenritual und Keramik mehrere, offenbar stammesmäßig verschiedene Komplexe zu unterscheiden. Man versucht jetzt, die Namen auf sie anzuwenden, die bei Herodot überliefert sind. Neuerlich zeigt sich, daß der Tierstil über die skythisch sprechende Bevölkerung hinausgriff. Auch Stämme slawischer oder thrakischer Herkunft müssen ihn getragen haben.

Ethnogeographie

Für die Masse der Steppen- und Waldsteppenbevölkerung kann man eine Entstehung aus den örtlichen Kulturen der Bronzezeit nachweisen. Selbst die Steppen am unteren Dnjepr, wo nach Herodot das Kerngebiet der königlichen Skythen lag, haben keine kompakte Invasion erlebt. Wohl aber läßt sich eine über Jahrhunderte zerdehnte ethnische Trift aus dem Wolgaraum gegen Westen feststellen. So müssen Kimmerier und Skythen längst Nachbarn gewesen sein. Vielleicht waren sie zwei Stammeskonföderationen, die sich innerhalb desselben Volkes gebildet hatten.

Keine Völkerwanderung – aber plötzliches Auftreten des Tierstils

Negativ verlief das weitere Suchen nach lokalen Vorläufern des Tierstils. Die geringen Indizien, die schon Ebert zusammentragen konnte, wurden trotz aller sowjetischen Bemühungen nur unwesentlich vermehrt. Bronzezeitliche Tierdarstellungen im pontischen Raum blieben eine Seltenheit. Dann, gegen Ende des 7. Jahrhunderts v. Chr., tritt uns plötzlich der Tierstil der Žabotin-Phase entgegen, und zwar in

33

einer faszinierenden Koppelung. Die Bewaffnung entspricht unvermittelt dem von uns oben geschilderten Standard – Goryt, Akinakes, Streitaxt, kurze Lanze. Eine ähnliche Einheitlichkeit in neuen Formen beobachtet man in der Pferdeschirrung. Der plötzliche Übergang zu dieser »skythischen Trias« im 7. Jahrhundert v. Chr. spielt sich in einer Zeit ab, in der Kimmerier und Skythen längst im Nahen Osten operieren. Sie müssen also auch in ihrer Heimat festumschriebene Komplexe gebildet haben.

Man fragt sich natürlich, was den plötzlichen Wandel in Ausrüstung und Kunst ausgelöst hat. Nach dem augenblicklichen Stand unserer Kenntnisse sind drei Lösungen denkbar:

1. Skythische Streifscharen, die im Vorderen Orient operierten, lernten dort nicht nur eine bessere Ausrüstung, sondern auch neue Schmuckformen kennen. Da man sich aber in der Heimat ionischer Werkstätten bediente, kam es – unter Einbeziehung eines recht geringen eigenen Erbes – nicht zu einer einfachen Übernahme, sondern zu einer neuen, griechisch bestimmten Lösung. Sie war so überzeugend, daß sie sich rasch durchsetzte und weithin übernommen wurde.

Diese These ist von Ebert, der sich niemals der Einwanderungskonzeption anschloß, bereits in ihren Grundzügen formuliert worden. Nach dem Zweiten Weltkrieg hat Grakov sie verfochten.

2. Die entscheidenden Ansätze zum Tierstil könnten aber auch schon von über den Kaukasus zurückflutenden Scharen mitgebracht worden sein – vielleicht verschleppte man einfach die Kunsthandwerker. Ionische Meister lösten sie erst allmählich ab.

Die zweite These hat in den letzten Jahren Auftrieb bekommen, als in Persisch-Kurdistan, zunächst im Rahmen eines geschlossenen Schatzes Tierstilobjekte auftauchten, deren Zusammenhang mit den südrussischen unbestreitbar ist. Sie gehören jedenfalls einem erstaunlich frühen

Fig. 12 – Tierfiguren auf dem Goldblech, das den Schaft der Eisenaxt aus dem Kelermes-Kurgan umgibt. Eremitage, Leningrad. Diese orientalische, vielleicht urartäische Arbeit,

Zeithorizont an. Man überlegte daher, ob nicht die Tierstilkunst in ihrer Gesamtheit ein Ableger der vorderasiatischen Entwicklung sei.

Ein repräsentativer Vertreter dieser Auffassung ist Sulimirski. Er meint, eine skythische Abteilung habe sich nach dem Überschreiten des Kaukasus in Aserbeidschan niedergelassen, und dort ein völlig transkaukasisch-vorderasiatisches Kulturgepräge angenommen. Als sie dann, nach größten militärischen Erfolgen, von den Medern schließlich doch zum Abzug gezwungen wurde, habe sie alle in Südrußland zurückgebliebenen Stammverwandten unterjocht. Sie sei zum königlichen Stamm aufgestiegen. Dessen ausgreifende Herrschaft spiegle sich in der Verbreitung des mitgebrachten Tierstils.

Die weitere Komplikation wäre freilich, nur einen Umweg über Iran und Kaukasien anzunehmen, aber eine mittelasiatische oder südsibirische Urheimat. Diese Variante der zweiten Möglichkeit wird durch genaue Motivuntersuchungen nahegelegt, die sowjetische Forscher neuerdings in immer größerer Zahl durchführen. Eine davon will beweisen, daß das »Leitmotiv« der skythischen Kunst, der Hirsch mit untergeschlagenen Beinen und zurückgelegtem Geweih, mittelasiatischen Ursprungs sei. Die Bewahrung der Ausgangsform im Heimatgebiet erkläre nun, führt Člonova weiter aus, das scheinbare Zurückgreifen des 5. Jahrhunderts auf älteste Tendenzen. In Wirklichkeit liege ein neuer Impuls aus dem Osten vor.

3. Die dritte Möglichkeit besteht in der Annahme, es habe von Anfang an, seit dem 7., ja 8. Jahrhundert v. Chr., ein direkter Kontakt mit Zentralasien bestanden (es ist dabei nicht nötig, eine massive Völkerwanderung zu postulieren). So seien östliche Anregungen rezipiert worden, die schließlich zum Tierstil führten. Als Argument könnten die frühesten gegossenen Bronzekessel Südrußlands dienen. Sie sind fast sicher sibirischer Her-

die ins Kuban-Gebiet verschleppt wurde, enthält ein reiches Repertoire, von dem nur ein Teil später zu den Standardmotiven der skythischen Kunst zählt. Vgl. S. 30

kunft, gehen letzten Endes auf die chinesische Metallurgie zurück und tauchen in einer noch völlig unskythischen Formenwelt auf.

Diese Probleme sind heute nicht lösbar, man kann sie nicht einmal behandeln, ohne eine Darstellung der östlichen Problematik voranzustellen. Wir heben uns also den Punkt bis zum Schlußkapitel auf.

Zierscheibe, als Pektorale oder auch als Teil der Pferdeschirrung gedeutet. Griechische Arbeit, unter Verwendung orientalischer Motive. Vettersfelde, 6. Jh. v. Chr. *Gold, Höhe 17 cm. Museum für Vor- und Frühgeschichte, Berlin. Vgl. S. 37*

III. SKYTHISCHE FUNDE IN MITTELEUROPA

1882 stieß man in Vettersfelde in Brandenburg auf die komplette Ausrüstung eines skythischen Anführers: mehrere große Stücke waren aus Gold. Sie zeigten reichen Tierstildekor, allerdings war hier deutlich ein griechischer Künstler im Auftrag eines barbarischen Herrn am Werke gewesen. Furtwängler – wir erwähnten bereits seine Bearbeitung des Hortes, der auch noch zahlreiche kleinere Kostbarkeiten enthielt – äußerte die Vermutung, er sei von einer Skythenschar versteckt worden, die vor dem Angriff des Darius bis in die Tiefe des mitteleuropäischen Raums zurückgewichen sei.

Fund von Vettersfelde <small>ABB. SEITE 36, 38, 39</small>

Später erschien eine Absetzbewegung von so enormen Ausmaßen – man hatte wohl an die Kriege gegen Napoleon oder Karl XII. gedacht – denn doch unglaubwürdig. Man nahm eher an, die Stücke hätten dem Anführer eines Raubzugs gehört, und dafür gab es manchen Anhaltspunkt. Man wußte ja, daß die Skythen plündernd bis an die Grenzen Ägyptens gelangten. Da man weiter der Ansicht war, die Skythen hätten in Südrußland als nomadische Eroberer über friedliche Bauern geherrscht, stand man auch noch vor der Frage, ob sich dieses Spiel nicht in Mitteleuropa außerhalb des Lichtkreises der schriftlichen Quellen wiederholt hatte. War es auch hier zu Ansiedlung und Reichsgründung gekommen?

Eine solche Möglichkeit gewann an Bedeutung, als man bemerkte, daß sich einschlägige Funde in bestimmten Gebieten zu konzentrieren begannen. Waffen und Schmuck skythischer Art vermehrten sich auf-

Einbruchshorizont im 6. und 5. Jh. v. Chr.

Fig. 13 – Goldhirsch von Zöldhalompuszta. Vermutlich Schildschmuck. 5. Jh. v. Chr. Gesamtbreite 23 cm. Ungarisches Historisches Museum, Budapest

FIG. 13, 14 fällig in Mittelungarn, dann wieder in Siebenbürgen und Zentral-
bulgarien. Sie stehen im Rahmen von annähernd gleichzeitigen und –
nach südrussischen Verhältnissen gemessen – sehr frühen Fundgruppen.
Die Datierung verweist immer wieder ins 6. und 5. Jahrhundert v. Chr.
Manches könnte sogar noch dem 7. Jahrhundert angehören. Neben
einigen Stücken, die man für pontischen Import halten könnte, findet
man viele lokale Weiterbildungen pontischer Typen, offenkundig
durch den ererbten Geschmack mitbestimmt.

Fettichs Deutung Fettich hat die schönsten Einzelstücke abgebildet und vorbildlich
analysiert. Er wendet sich dabei gegen die Auffassung, das Auftreten
der Skythen sei hier nur eine Episode gewesen, man müsse vielmehr
mit einer massiven Landnahme rechnen. Schließlich sei allerdings die
Herrenschicht in der breiten Bevölkerung aufgegangen, ein Schicksal, das östliche Nomaden schon einmal zuvor im ungarländischen
Raum erlitten hatten. Auch andere Forscher rechneten mit beträcht-
lichen historischen Auswirkungen, vor allem habe die sog. Lausitzer
Kultur viel unter skythischen Vorstößen zu leiden gehabt.

Kritik durch Sowjetische Archäologen haben diese Konzeption kritisiert. Wie überall
Sowjetforscher bemühte man sich, eine weniger militante Auffassung durchzusetzen.

Goldfisch, als Schildzierart oder als Stirnplatte der Schirrung gedeutet. Vettersfelde, 6. Jh.
v. Chr. *Länge 41 cm. Museum für Vor- und Frühgeschichte, Berlin. Vgl. S. 37*

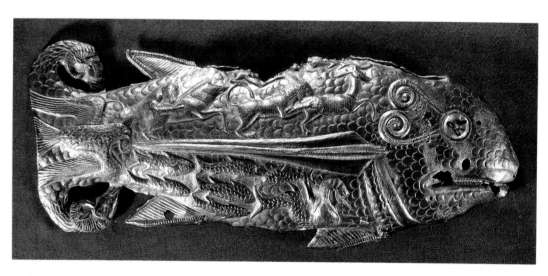

Man wies deshalb darauf hin, daß auch der skythische Kernraum, den wir sicher in den Steppen am Dnjepr zu suchen haben, von Stämmen umgeben war, die zwar kulturell von den Skythen abhängig, aber keineswegs ihre Untertanen waren. Skythische Lebensweise und Kunst erwiesen sich offenbar als äußerst attraktiv, selbst die aktive und abwehrbereite Ananinokultur in der Tiefe der mittelrussischen Waldsteppe orientierte sich nach diesem Leitbild. Haben wir es nicht auch in Mitteleuropa mit solchen Strahlungen zu tun? Dafür spricht, daß die Einflüsse oft aus der Waldsteppe zu stammen scheinen, etwa aus Podolien und dem mittleren Dnjeprgebiet, wo keine Skythen, sondern höchstens eine skythisierte Bevölkerung hauste. Handelsverbindungen und Kulturübernahmen jeder Art bieten sich daher als Erklärung an, aber nicht die Aufrichtung einer riesigen Herrschaft.

Handelsverbindungen, nicht Eroberung

Selbst die sowjetischen Autoren schließen indessen nicht aus, daß ge-

Goldenes Beschlagblech griechischer Arbeit, es bedeckte den oberen Teil der Akinakesscheibe von Vettersfelde. 6. Jh. v. Chr. *Länge 19 cm. Museum für Vor- und Frühgeschichte, Berlin.*

Fig. 14 – Preßmodel aus Bronze, massiver Guß. Fund aus Gartschinovo, Nordostbulgarien. Größte Länge 35 cm. 6.Jh. v. Chr. Seinerzeit im Museum Schumen

legentlich die Skythen persönlich in ihren Strahlungsgebieten erschienen, um herzhaft zu rauben, und sicher wußten sich die Einheimischen, meist thrakische Stämme, ihrer Haut zu wehren. Manches mag also als Trophäe in den Besitz der eingesessenen Krieger gelangt sein. Diese Art von Verbindungen wurden erst unterbrochen, als keltische Einflüsse die Übermacht gewannen. Nur in Bulgarien traf man auf fürst-

Thrakische Fürstengräber

liche Beisetzungen aus dem 4. und 3.Jahrhundert v.Chr., die in Ritual und Beigaben an die Königskurgane des unteren Dnjeprgebiets erinnern. Das erklärt sich durch die engen, durch Heirat gefestigten Beziehungen zwischen der skythischen und der thrakischen Oberschicht. Auch wenn sie sich bekämpften, gehorchten die Herren hier wie dort dem gleichen Kodex. Man stand in lebhaftem Wettbewerb, und damit mag zusammenhängen, daß es in Thrakien standesgemäß wurde, ebenfalls Meister griechischer Herkunft oder zumindest Ausbildung zu engagieren. Der berühmte Schatz von Panagjürischte gehört in einen solchen Zusammenhang. Frau Mancevič glaubt sogar, daß die im Kul-Oba-Kurgan gefundenen Silbergefäße nicht am Bosporus, sondern im metallreichen Thrakien geschaffen wurden. Regelrechte Wanderungen bleiben daneben in begrenztem Rahmen, vom Kolonialboden in der Dobrudscha haben wir schon gehört. Hier in Klein-Skythien blieb das Volkstum bewahrt, auch als die Steppen längst den Sarmaten zugefallen waren.

In der gegenwärtigen Forschungsphase bemüht man sich zu zeigen, daß die Bedeutung der Skythen für die Geschichte Mittel- und Osteuropas nicht übertrieben werden darf, wahrscheinlich ist man dabei schon zu weit gegangen.

IV. SKYTHISCHES IN KAUKASIEN

Die Ebenen nördlich vom Kaukasus, die Einzugsgebiete von Kuban und Terek, gehören ganz selbstverständlich zum Bereich des skythischen Tierstils, obgleich die nomadische oder auch bäuerische Bevölkerung hier eigene Sprachen hatte und vielleicht ältere »kimmerische« Traditionen bewahrte. Die Stämme in den Hochtälern zu beiden Seiten der Hauptkette aber führten ein Dasein, das ganz anderen Regeln gehorchte und von älteren Traditionen bestimmt wurde. Die reiche Aufkammerung ihres Lebensraums wirkte isolierend. Ihre Unabhängigkeit vermochten sie gegen äußere Feinde durch Ausweichen in die Berge zu behaupten. Andererseits waren sie den Hochkulturzentren der Alten Welt relativ nahe. Händler und Kriegerscharen, die auf den Paßstraßen vorüberzogen, sorgten ständig für Anregungen.

Lokalkulturen der Bronzezeit

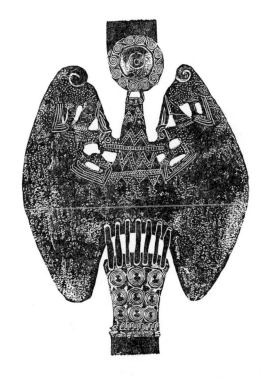

Fig. 15 – Rekonstruktion der Gürtelgarnitur aus dem Gräberfeld Isti-su im Nordostkaukasus. Breite des Mittelteils 19 cm. (Nach Artamonova-Poltavceva, 1950.) Das Stück besteht aus einem runden, mit S-Spiralen verziertem Buckel mit Öse (oben), dem eigentlichen, an beiden Seiten lappenartig verbreiterten Haken, dessen vorderer Teil in die Oberkörper phantastischer Tiere umgestaltet ist, sowie dem mit Warzen verzierten Übergangsstück zum (verlorenen) Lederriemen. Die Verbindung zwischen Haken und Übergangsstück wird durch Ringe hergestellt. Obwohl diese Garnitur schon »skythischer« Zeit angehört (5.bis6.Jh.v.Chr.),ist die phantastische, zu Übertreibungen neigende Grundhaltung der nordkaukasischen Bronzezeit lebendig geblieben. Offenbar liegt das orientalische Schema »Gottheit zwischen den Tieren« zugrunde.

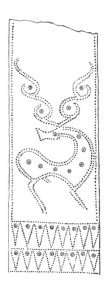

Fig. 16 – Tierzeichnung auf einem Gürtel aus Dušeti, Nord-kaukasus. Weißliches Metall, etwa 8 cm breit. Eremitage, Leningrad. (Nach Artamonova-Poltavceva 1950.) Auch an diesem späten (skythenzeitlichen) Stück ist deutlich, daß die autochthone nordkaukasische Kunst anderen Stilgesetzen ge-horcht als die skythische.

Diese Konstellation erklärt vielleicht, warum sich während der Bronze-zeit Metallgerät und Schmuck zu oft phantastisch übersteigerten For-men entwickelten. Es bildeten sich Lokalkulturen, in denen Beile, Gürtelschließen und Nadeln zu Würdezeichen ausgestaltet wurden, mit reichem Dekor und luxurierenden, manchmal geradezu grotesken Umrissen. Dabei fanden Tierformen, Menschenfiguren und Frucht-barkeitssymbole reiche Verwendung. Ihre religiöse Bedeutung läßt sich nur erraten.

Mit ergiebigen Erzlagern hinter sich fanden die kaukasischen Bronze-gießer einen weiten Abnehmerkreis. Vermutlich haben sie die Formen der Trensen entwickelt, die im 8. und 7.Jahrhundert v.Chr. zwischen Bug und Don gebräuchlich waren. Damit stehen wir aber in der neuralgischen Periode vor der Ausbreitung des eigentlichen Tierstils und müssen uns fragen, ob diese künstlerische Tendenz in den Tier-plastiken Kaukasiens einen bequemen Anknüpfungspunkt fand. Im Kaukasus gibt es reichlich Hirsche und Hirschdarstellungen, man könnte vermuten, die Skythen hätten ihre Vorliebe für ein solches Motiv von hier übernommen.

Nun sind aber die Tierzeichnungen dieses Raumes oft von konvexen Bögen begrenzt. Die kleinen Plastiken zeigen Durchbruchsarbeit, so daß die Körper zu Schellen werden, fast nur mehr aus Stegen bestehen. Solche Eigentümlichkeiten finden wir in Südrußland nur ausnahms-weise – z. B. an sog. Standartenbekrönungen. Es besteht kein eindeu-tiger genetischer Zusammenhang. Wohl aber gibt es viele Entlehnun-

Einflüsse Nordkauka-siens (Koban-Kultur) in den Steppen

FIG. 16

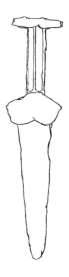

Fig. 17 – Eiserner Dolch von typischer Akinakes-Form, aus dem Gräberfeld von Dvani (Georgien). 7. bis 6.Jh. v.Chr. Länge 30 cm. (Nach Makalatija 1949)

Fig. 18 – Pfeilspitze aus dem Gräberfeld von Dvani (Geor-gien). Bronze, etwa 3,5 cm. (Nach Makalatija 1949.) Auch hier liegt eine eindeutig skythische Form vor.

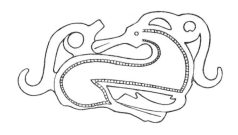

Fig. 19 – Gürtelschließe aus den sogenannten Brunnengräbern von Koban. 11 cm lang. (Nach Hančar 1931.) Das Stück erinnert zwar in seiner schwungvollen Linienführung an Fig. 16, aber es weist mit dem zurückgewendeten Kopf und den unter den Leib geschlagenen Läufen auch typisch skythische Merkmale auf, die einen Verschmelzungsprozeß belegen.

gen, vor allem den Export fertigen Geräts. Bronzegefäße kaukasischer Form mit Tierhenkeln waren offenbar weithin beliebt. Andererseits trifft man bis nach Transkaukasien Gräber, die skythische Waffen und skythischen Schmuck enthalten. Es ist, als seien manche Stämme mit Kriegern durchsetzt gewesen, die sich ihre mächtigen Nachbarn zum Vorbild nahmen. Eine Konzentration der Funde von Steppencharakter besteht an den Paßstraßen (Friedhöfe von Dvani und Samtavro im Zentralgebiet, Mingečaur in Aserbeidschan). Zwei Wege laufen über die Hauptkette, zwei umgehen sie im Osten und Westen.

Nekropolen mit »skythischen« Gräbern bis Transkaukasien

FIG. 17, 18

Die Erklärung dieses Fundbildes ist nicht schwierig: wir hörten ja von der skythischen Macht in den pontischen Steppen und daß zuerst kimmerische, dann skythische Scharen den Kaukasus überschritten, um in die Geschicke des Vorderen Orients einzugreifen. Sie müssen strategische Stützpunkte gehabt haben, in denen ihr Name noch nach Jahrhunderten weiterlebte. Die Tatsache, daß im Georgischen noch heute der Held als »Gimir«, d. h. als Kimmerier bezeichnet wird, mag andeuten, welche Rolle den nördlichen Abenteurern zukam.

Am intensivsten war der Kontakt in frühskythischer Zeit. Später kam es zur Konsolidierung lokaler Herrschaften, achämenidische und hellenistische Einflüsse überwogen.

Im Norden der Hauptkette beobachten wir einen Verschmelzungsprozeß. Dort werden offenbar Motive aus der Steppe von den Gießerwerkstätten übernommen, weitergebildet und dem einheimischen Geschmack angeglichen.

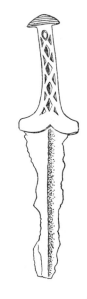

Fig. 20 – Kaukasischer Dolch. Berlin, Museum für Vor- und Frühgeschichte. Der Griff schließt sich zwar um die Klinge wie ein Akinakes-Griff, die durchbrochene Arbeit und der Knauf zeigen aber eigenständige, bis in die »kimmerische« Bronzezeit zurückgreifende Tradition.

43

Um Christi Geburt setzt dann eine neuerliche Überfremdung ein. Diesmal sind es Sarmaten, die in die Berge vordringen, auch weit außerhalb Ossetiens, wo sich ihre – iranische – Sprache bis heute erhalten hat. Sie bringen aber bereits eine Kunst mit, die den uns gesetzten Rahmen überschreitet, wenn sie auch einige alte, ja älteste Traditionen weiterführt.

V. DIE ANANINO-KULTUR IN OSTRUSSLAND

Einflüsse der Steppenreiter, ihrer Lebensweise und Kunst drangen weit nach Nordosteuropa und Sibirien vor. Vermittler war ein Volk, dessen Schwerpunkt nördlich und nordöstlich von Kasan an den Flüssen Vetluga, Vjatka, Kama und Belaja lag. Man hat versucht, es mit einem der von Herodot genannten Namen zu belegen.

Verbreitungsgebiet

Ausgrabungen setzten hier früh ein, bereits um die Mitte des 19. Jahrhunderts. Das Gräberfeld von Ananino lieferte das Bild einer eigenwilligen kriegerischen Kultur. Bereits zehn Jahre später vermochte man sie einigermaßen richtig zu datieren. Die Forschungen rissen nicht ab, denn die dort ansässigen reichen Unternehmer und Kaufmannsfamilien interessierten sich für die Vergangenheit. Das nahe Kasan war ein bedeutendes wissenschaftliches Zentrum. So bemerkte man bald die kulturellen Verbindungen Ananinos nach dem Süden. Freilich wurden die zugehörigen Wallburgen zunächst einer anderen Phase zugewiesen. Sie zeichneten sich durch eine ungewöhnliche Menge an Knochenfunden aus.

Um die Jahrhundertwende beschäftigten sich die besten Köpfe der russischen Archäologie mit dem angewachsenen Material. Schließlich schrieb Tallgren eine Zusammenfassung von geradezu unheimlicher Perfektion. Er übersah die gesamte Literatur, hatte Funde studiert, die in staatlichen und privaten Sammlungen lagen, und besaß Grabungserfahrung. So kam er zu einer Datierung der »Ananino-Kultur«, die sich im wesentlichen bis heute gehalten hat: ins 7. bis zum 3. Jahrhundert v. Chr. Natürlich kannte er die genauen Grenzen der Fundgruppe noch nicht, auch über Wirtschaft, Sozialorganisation und Religion mußte er manche Antwort schuldig bleiben. Es bestand auch noch keine Klarheit über die anthropologische Zusammensetzung der Bevölkerung.

Tallgrens Leistung

FIG. 21

An diesen Punkten hakte die sowjetische Forschung – die die Überlegenheit des Finnen Tallgren immer mit einer gewissen Erbitterung zur Kenntnis genommen hatte – in den nächsten Jahrzehnten ein. Das war nicht weiter schwierig, denn Schmidt, Smirnov, Efimenko und Zbrueva konnten sich auf eine Unzahl neuer und besserer Grabungen stützen, zu denen konsequent angesetzte und straff geführte Expeditionen ausgezogen waren. Efimenko erwies sich in der Auswertung als

Sowjetische Gelehrte

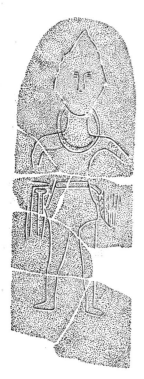

Fig. 21 – Steinerne Grabplatte aus der Nekropole von Ananino, mit der Darstellung eines Kriegers. Deutlich ist der Halsreif erkennbar, Dolch und Bogenfutteral sind nach skythischem Vorbild am Gürtel befestigt. Der Umriß links vom Dolch soll wohl den Pickel wiedergeben. Das Fehlen des Bartes wird mit dem mongoliden Einschlag der Ananino-Bevölkerung erklärt.

geistvoller Einzelgänger; die Resultate der drei anderen Gelehrten aber harmonieren so gut, daß wir ein geschlossenes, relativ unproblematisches Bild erhalten:

Die Siedlungen der Ananino-Leute lagen an Flußläufen. Sie waren so eng – die Ausmaße betrugen höchstens 60 × 150 m –, daß sie nur von einigen Dutzend Menschen bewohnt gewesen sein konnten. Meist waren sie mit Wall und Graben umgeben, in anderen Fällen schließt man auf eine Umgürtung mit Pallisaden. Viehzucht und Feldbau, aber auch Jagd und Fischfang lieferten den Lebensunterhalt.

Enorme Bedeutung besaß der Handel. Offenbar fanden die für den Export geradezu serienmäßig hergestellten Bronzen in der Tiefe der osteuropäischen Wälder einen aufnahmefreudigen Markt. Tüllenbeile, die an der Kama gegossen wurden, fand man bis nach Finnland und Skandinavien hinein. Selbst nach Westsibirien wurden sie exportiert. Die ersten Eisengegenstände verbreiteten sich vermutlich durch das gleiche Handelsnetz. Man kann sich vorstellen, daß dafür Pelze eingetauscht wurden, die in den pontischen Steppen dankbare Abnehmer fanden. Sicher wurden noch andere Produkte über so große Entfernungen ausgetauscht, zum Beispiel Bernstein. Da die Ananino-Leute selbst Sklaven hielten, mögen sie auch Menschenhandel getrieben haben.

Die Erhaltung solcher Verbindungslinien setzte eine entwickelte Kriegstechnik und eine überlegene Organisation voraus. Sie mußte zu einer sozialen Staffelung führen. Diese Vermutung läßt sich bei genauem Studium der Friedhöfe bestätigen. Sie lagen an den Flüssen, die offenbar in den Vorstellungen vom Jenseits eine entscheidende Rolle spielten. Bei den meist ausgestreckt liegenden Skeletten fand man, sorgfältig abgestuft, Beigaben. Den Anführern hatte man reichen Bronzeschmuck und, offenbar als Würdezeichen, figural geschmückte Streitpickel mitgegeben. Deutlich tritt daneben die große Gruppe der

Fig. 22 – Daß man das skythische Bogenfutteral trug, zeigt nicht nur die Grabplatte, sondern auch eine Bronzeminiatur. Abbildungen nach Zbrueva 1952

Fig. 23a und b – Kurzschwert (Akinakes) skythischer Form und Dolch, dessen Ausgestaltung nach Westsibirien weist. (Lugovsker Gräberfeld und Ananino, nach Zbrueva 1952)

freien Krieger hervor. Unterschiede der Bewaffnung mögen nicht nur mit Besitzunterschieden, sondern auch mit dem Lebensalter zusammenhängen. Andere Männergräber sind ohne alle Beigaben – ein Indiz für die bereits erwähnte Sklaverei. Ähnlich gegliedert sind die Frauengräber. Seltsame, wohl nur im Kultgebrauch erklärbare Beigaben bei manchen weiblichen Skeletten verraten, daß es Priesterinnen oder Schamaninnen gab.

In Männergräbern fand man überzählige Schädel. Vielleicht stammen sie von Menschenopfern, die im Totenritual dargebracht wurden, vielleicht aber handelte es sich um erworbene Kopftrophäen – wie bei den Skythen.

Diese Vermutung liegt nahe, weil die Bewaffnung ebenfalls viele skythische Züge aufweist. Man trug das Bogenfutteral und das Kurzschwert. So ist es nicht weiter erstaunlich, daß wir auch hier wieder dem Tierstil begegnen.

Freilich sind die Voraussetzungen hier völlig anders als im Süden. Wir haben allen Grund zu der Annahme, daß bereits im zweiten Jahrtausend, während der Bronzezeit, eine Schnitzkunst bestand, die Tiere realistisch darzustellen wußte. Die besten Zeugnisse lieferten die Hoch-

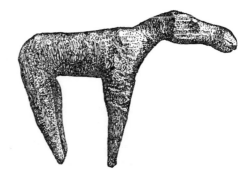

Fig. 24a und b – Schnitzarbeiten aus uralischen Mooren. Kultlöffel und Opfertrog. (Nach Eding 1940)

47

Fig. 25 – Schmuckblech mit Treibarbeit nach kaukasischem Vorbild. (Lugovsker Gräberfeld, nach Zbrueva 1952)

Fig. 26 – Bronzeknopf aus Ananino mit typischem Muster der frühesten noch nicht den Tierstil kennenden Reiterkrieger. (Nach Zbrueva 1952)

FIG. 25

moore des angrenzenden Urals: Als Opfergaben versenkt sind hier prachtvolle Stücke erhalten geblieben, etwa ein hölzerner Trog in Gestalt eines Elchs, von dem man annimmt, er sei zur Aufnahme des Blutes der im Ritus geschlachteten Tiere verwendet worden. Auch Holzlöffel, die die Gestalt von Schwimmvögeln haben, hält man für Kultgegenstände. Die künstlerische Vollendung der Plastiken kontrastiert seltsam mit den groben Konturen von Menschenfiguren, die man als Götterstatuen deutet.

Am Übergang zur Ananino-Kultur treten merkwürdigerweise kaukasische Einflüsse auf. Ihre Vermittler waren vielleicht heimkehrende Streifscharen, die den Wasserweg benützten (Wolga und Kaspi), um in die beuteverheißenden Kämpfe des Südens einzugreifen. Die Ananino-Leute machen durchaus den Eindruck, den man von solchen »Wikingern« der frühen Eisenzeit erwarten darf.

Diese Konstellation gäbe allerbeste Chancen für die These, der »skythische« Tierstil sei in Wirklichkeit hier, im Bereich der Waldsteppe, aus dem Zusammentreffen von nördlicher Schnitztradition und südlichen Anregungen aus Hochkulturen entstanden.

Nun hat die saubere Analyse Tallgrens derartigen Vermutungen ein für allemal den Boden entzogen. Ein Teil der Tierstilobjekte ist einfach aus dem Süden importiert, sei es durch Handel, sei es als Kriegsbeute.

Tierstil vom Skythischen abhängig

Fig. 27a und b – Befestigungshaken in Form eines Pferdekopfes und Schmuckblech in Raubvogelgestalt (Bronze). Realistische und hochstilisierte Stücke stehen in der Ananinokunst nebeneinander. Blech 27b hat Gegenstück in Ostkazachstan. Ananino und Zuevsker Gräberfeld. (Nach Zbrueva 1952)

48

Anderes aber ist an Ort und Stelle gefertigt worden nach Mustern, die man bei den Steppenbewohnern entlehnte. Dagegen setzten sich immer wieder der eigene Geschmack, vor allem aber die eigene religiöse Vorstellungswelt durch. Sehr beliebt wurden Greif und »Rolltier«, die Tierkampfszene hingegen wurde rundweg abgelehnt. Es schoben sich die einheimischen Tiere in den Vordergrund – Bär und Elch. Wenn sie jetzt zum Schmuck von Kämmen, Spinnwirteln und Messern verwendet wurden, so war das vermutlich der Einfluß des Südens: die Freude am Dekorieren ersetzte allmählich den magischen Gebrauch. Die Ausführung hingegen blieb realistisch. Darin erkannte man mit Recht ein Nachwirken der einheimischen Handwerkstradition.

Allmählich lernt man sogar die verschiedenen Verbindungswege zu den Steppen unterscheiden. Man sieht, daß neben den Skythen die sarmatischen Stämme mit der Ananino-Bevölkerung in Kontakt standen.

Das bedeutet nun sicher keine ethnische Verwandtschaft. Wohl aber basierten die weiten Handelsverbindungen der Waldzone vermutlich auf alten sprachlichen Übereinstimmungen, sie hängen mit der Konsolidierung der finno-ugrischen Sprachfamilie zusammen. Solche Verwandtschaften mögen ihrerseits wieder dazu beigetragen haben, daß sich eine Handelsstraße entwickelte, die in der Waldsteppe nach Osten führte. Aus den Wäldern des Ostens mögen dann jene mongoliden Zuwanderer gekommen sein, die den Ananino-Leuten hohe Backenknochen und eine flachere Nase vererbten, wie sowjetische Anthropologen jetzt bei dem Studium des Schädelmaterials konstatierten.

Überall in den Waldsteppen entstanden damals Wallburgen. Man hat den Eindruck, als hätten sich die Bewohner des Nordens zu einer Art Abwehrfront gegen die Überfälle der Nomaden zusammengeschlossen.

Abwehrfront der Waldsteppe

Fig. 28 – Streitaxt aus Elabuga mit besonders reichem, wohl religiös bedeutsamem Tierstilschmuck. Sicher Würdezeichen eines Anführers. Eigentliche Waffe der nördlichen Abwehrfront bis zum Jenissei war der Pickel. (Nach Zbrueva 1952)

49

VI. DIE EXPANSION DER SARMATEN

Von Herodot werden »Sauromaten« als östliche Nachbarn der Skythen erwähnt. Sie sitzen jenseits des Don, also nach der Vorstellung der Antike bereits in Asien, und treten unter den Verbündeten auf, die sich dem Eroberungsfeldzug des Darius entgegenstellen.

Amazonenlegende Die Legende erzählt, sie seien aus einer Verbindung der unverheirateten Mannschaft der Skythen mit den Amazonen entstanden. Diese kriegerischen Frauen seien zuvor von griechischen Helden besiegt und auf Schiffen verschleppt worden, hätten sich aber befreit, ihre Wachmannschaft ins Meer geworfen und seien schließlich an der Küste der Mäotis gelandet. Dort raubten sie sich Pferde und lebten fortan von Plünderungszügen – bis es eben den jungen Kriegern gelang, die Herzen der spröden Schönen zu gewinnen, und sich ein neues Volk bildete. Aber die sauromatischen Frauen zögen immer hoch zu Roß auf die Jagd und in den Krieg, eingedenk ihrer Stammütter. Erst nach der Tötung eines Feindes durften sie heiraten – was manche von ihnen zur Ehelosigkeit verdammte. Das sauromatische Idiom sei dem Skythischen ähnlich, es sei nur durch den Einfluß der Amazonen verdorben worden.

Sauromaten = Sarmaten In diesem Bericht steckt zweifellos ein wahrer Kern: Die Sauromaten, die in den späteren Quellen als Sarmaten bezeichnet werden, waren wie die Skythen ein iranisches Volk. Das läßt sich aus dem in antiken Quellen erhaltenen Namensmaterial deutlich ablesen und findet schließlich auch noch seine Bestätigung darin, daß die Osseten im Kaukasus als späte Nachkommen dieses Volkes der gleichen Sprachgruppe angehören.

Eroberung Südrußlands Wir haben schon von seiner Bewegung nach dem Westen um die Wende des 5. zum 4. Jahrhundert v. Chr. vernommen, die im 3. und 2. Jahrhundert gewaltige Ausmaße annimmt. Ein großer Teil der pontischen Steppen wurde dabei verwüstet, die Skythen konnten sich schließlich nur in Klein-Skythien, an der Dnjeprmündung und auf der Krim behaupten. Gleichzeitig läßt sich eine Aufsplitterung der vordringenden Scharen in Stammesverbände erkennen: Die Jazygen bildeten die Speerspitze gegen Westen, gefolgt von den Roxolanen. Aorser und Siraken schwenkten nach Südwesten ein, so daß sie schließlich an verschiedenen Stellen in den Kaukasus eindrangen. Im

Die Namen der Stämme, ihre Schicksale

50

Phalere (Schmuckplatte für das Pferdegeschirr) von der Schwarzmeerküste. Etwa 2. Jh. v. Chr.
Silber, mit Goldblech überzogen. Cabinet des Médailles, Paris. Vgl. S. 58

Kerngebiet aber formierten sich die Alanen als mächtigster Verband. Teile von ihnen gelangten während der Völkerwanderungszeit bis nach Spanien und Nordafrika, ein Rest hielt sich dann noch jahrhundertelang in Südrußland. Die Osseten leiten sich vor allem von dieser Gruppe ab.

Das Erbe der Skythen traten viele Völker an. Teile des Pontikums wurden zuerst von Thrakern, später von keltischen und germanischen Stämmen besetzt. Die Sarmaten aber, die manches von ihren Nachbarn übernahmen, z. B. die Fibeltracht, blieben bis zur Bildung des Gotenreichs das herrschende Element. Dadurch kamen sie mehrfach

Kämpfe mit Rom mit den Römern in Konflikt. Deren Weltreich hatte einerseits die Donaugrenze gegen eine sarmatisch-germanische Koalition zu schützen, andererseits garantierte sie durch militärische Stützpunkte die Unabhängigkeit der letzten griechischen Kolonialstädte. Selbst im Kaukasus mußte die »Front« gehalten werden. So ist es zu erklären, daß wir bei römischen und hellenistischen Historikern zahlreiche Angaben finden, wenn sie auch über das innere Leben dieses permanenten Gegners nicht allzuviel aussagen. Die vorherrschende Wirtschaftsform blieb zweifellos das Hirtennomadentum. Die Stammesorganisation scheint über alle Wechselfälle der Geschichte erhalten geblieben zu sein. Es lassen sich kriegerische Gefolgschaften erkennen, die sich zu einer Adelsschicht konsolidierten.

Man erklärt oft die erstaunliche Expansion durch eine neue überlegene Bewaffnung: Langschwert und lange Lanze erlaubten in Verbindung

Fig. 29 – Steinernes Altartischchen aus Ljubimovka mit Tierstildekor. 28 cm breit. (Nach Grakov 1928)

Flakon mit Tierstildekor aus dem Chochlač-Kurgan (sog. Schatz von Novočerkask) 1. Jh. v. Chr. *Höhe 9 cm. Original in der Eremitage, Leningrad. Photographie nach einer Galvanoplastik im Victoria and Albert-Museum, London. Vgl. S. 58*

mit einer körperdeckenden Panzerung den Übergang zur Stoßtaktik. *Gepanzerte Reiter*
Die Übereinstimmung mit den Parthern liegt auf der Hand und wird durch antike Darstellungen, zum Beispiel die Reliefs der Trajanssäule, bestätigt.

Eine Zeitlang wollte man den Sarmaten alle späten skythischen Kurgane zuschreiben – ein Irrtum, der allerdings schon von Tolstoj und Kondakov berichtigt wurde. Die Aufdeckung sarmatischer Gräberfelder in ihrem Kerngebiet östlich des Don erfolgte erstaunlich spät, erst nach 1900. Der russische Gelehrte Gorodcov, nicht genial, aber mit ungeheurem Fleiß begabt und reich an Wissen, schuf die Basis, die entscheidende Leistung vollbrachte dann Rostovcev. Besonders in den späten zwanziger Jahren unterzog man die Nekropolen des Wolga- *Einsetzen archäologischer Forschungen* gebiets einer sauberen, konsequenten Grabungstätigkeit, so daß am Vorabend des Zweiten Weltkriegs zwischen Don und Wolga sechshundert Gräber dieser Phase zur Auswertung zur Verfügung standen. Seit dem Zweiten Weltkrieg hat sich die Intensität der Feldforschung ins Ungeheuerliche gesteigert. Die Stalingrad- und die Wolga/Don-Expedition nahmen sich vor allem jener Territorien an, die bei der Anlage von Staubecken zur Überflutung vorgesehen waren.

Rostovcevs Theorie

Diesen riesigen Bestand verwendete man auch hier zu einem frontalen Angriff gegen die Position Rostovcevs. Jener hatte behauptet, Sauromaten und Sarmaten seien zwei völlig verschiedene Völker. Die Sauromaten hielt er für ein mutterrechtliches Bauernvolk, die Sarmaten für eine aus dem Osten anrollende Welle iranischer Nomaden, die die Sauromaten überlagerten und dabei den kaum veränderten Namen erbten. Wir haben erwähnt, woher die Abneigung der Sowjetforscher gegen die These Rostovcevs stammt: aus Ressentiments und der Ideologie der dreißiger Jahre. Das besagt jedoch nichts gegen die sachliche Berechtigung. Den sowjetischen Forschern gelang der unbestrittene Nachweis, daß im Wolgagebiet und am Südfuß des Urals

Widerlegung durch die sowjetischen Forscher

seit der Spätbronzezeit eine Siedlungskontinuität besteht. Es läßt sich dort auch keine massive Einwanderung nachweisen, Sauromaten und Sarmaten müssen daher wohl das gleiche Volk gewesen sein, erwachsen auf der Basis der bronzezeitlichen Balkengräber- und der Andronovo-Kultur.

Man kann auch nicht von einer Beschränkung der »mutterrechtlichen« Tendenzen auf die sauromatische Periode sprechen: noch in späteren Jahrhunderten hat man weibliche Gräber mit Waffen ausgestattet. In den Zentralkurganen mancher Nekropolen wurden reiche Frauenbestattungen gefunden. Daß dem schönen Geschlecht

Fig. 30 – Pfeilspitze aus den Zigolevsker Kurganen. (Nach Smirnov 1961)

Fig. 31 – Schwert der sauromatischen Phase aus Novaja Bogdanovka mit reichem Tierstildekor. Länge 42 cm. (Nach Smirnov 1961)

auch die Priesterwürde zufallen konnte, wird durch die Beigabe steinerner Altartischchen (im Uralgebiet) wahrscheinlich.

FIG. 29

Viel Mühe und Scharfsinn wurden aufgewendet, um eine zeitliche Gliederung des Grabinventars zu gewinnen. Paul Rau kam zu der in ihren Grundzügen bis heute gültigen Klassifikation. Sein »Blumenfeld-Stadium« (nach einem wolgadeutschen Dorf benannt) wird heute als »sauromatische Stufe« bezeichnet, sie gehört in das 6. bis 4. Jahrhundert v. Chr. Es folgen die »frühsarmatische« (4. bis 2. Jahrhundert v. Chr.), darauf die »mittelsarmatische« (1. Jahrhundert v. Chr. bis 2. Jahrhundert n. Chr.) und schließlich noch die »spätsarmatische« Stufe (2. bis 4. Jahrhundert n. Chr.).

Das chronologische System von Rau

ABB. SEITE 59

Durch das sauromatische Gebiet verlief eine deutliche Grenze: den Stämmen an der unteren Wolga stehen jene südlich des Urals gegenüber. In beiden Bereichen setzt aber die typische Reiterbewaffnung gleichzeitig und mit jenen Formen ein, die auch für Südrußland charakteristisch sind. Manche stammen aus dem gemeinsamen Bestand der Steppenvölker, etwa zweiflügelige Pfeilspitzen, andere aus dem Vorderen Orient. Auch die Einwirkung mittelasiatischer Vorbilder ist nicht auszuschließen. Die Umstellung muß sich um die Wende vom 7. zum 6. Jahrhundert v. Chr. schlagartig vollzogen haben. Allerdings löst sich die Verbindung mit den Skythen sehr rasch. So bevorzugt man zum Beispiel längere Schwerter als in den pontischen Steppen.

FIG. 30

FIG. 31

In der frühsarmatischen Stufe bildet die Prochorovka-Kultur in den Steppen südlich vom Ural ein äußerst aktives Zentrum. Mittelasiatische Einflüsse machen sich geltend, die vermutlich von Zuwanderergruppen ausgingen. Damit mag das Auftreten neuer Bestattungsriten zusammenhängen. Im Schädelmaterial ist jedenfalls eine größere Variationsbreite zu bemerken.

Prochorovka-Kultur

Vielleicht als Reaktion darauf zeigt sich in der mittelsarmatischen Stufe eine zunehmende Uniformierung der Bewaffnung. Die Knäufe der eisernen Langschwerter nehmen Ring- oder Sichelform an. Siedlungen fehlen in der Weite der Steppe so gut wie völlig – ein Hinweis auf Nomadentum.

In der spätsarmatischen Phase wird auch das Grabritual einheitlich. Fast alle Schädel sind durch Einbinden in frühester Kindheit deformiert. Den Forschern fiel bald auf, daß es Schwierigkeiten machte, die Helme dieser Zeit aufzusetzen. Wichtig wird der Gebrauch des komplexen Bogens, dessen Enden durch Knochenplatten verstärkt sind. Offenbar ist er von östlichen Zuwanderern mitgebracht worden,

Schädeldeformation

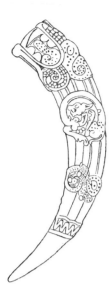

Fig. 32 – Dekor eines Eberhauers; zur Schirrung gehörend. Aus einem Kurgan beim Dorf Blumenfeld (Samara). Etwa 16 cm lang. Die Eigentümlichkeiten der sauromatischen Phase treten hier klar hervor. (Nach Grakov 1928)

deren Spuren man übrigens auch im spätsarmatischen Schädelmaterial feststellt. Neben den bisherigen, rein europiden Typen – die Sarmaten waren blond, wie die antiken Schriftsteller berichten – finden wir jetzt mongolide, mit flacher Augenpartie.

Als der Ablauf im sarmatischen Kernraum geklärt war, fiel es natürlich sehr viel leichter, die Schicksale in den Kolonialgebieten prähistorisch zu erfassen. Allerdings sind die Sowjetforscher mit den bisherigen Resultaten noch keineswegs zufrieden.

In der ganzen Weite des pontischen Raumes gab es bis vor wenigen Jahren nur zweihundert eindeutig sarmatische Gräber. Manchmal findet man typische Grabformen des Ausgangsgebietes wieder, z. B. rechteckige Schächte, in deren Diagonale das gestreckte Skelett liegt. Die soziale Differenzierung ist größer als in der Heimat. Die Gefäßformen bewahren lokale Traditionen älterer Jahrhunderte, ein deutlicher Hinweis darauf, daß die Grundbevölkerung wenigstens stellenweise unter sarmatischer Herrschaft weiterlebt. Besser erforscht ist die sarmatische Expansion im Mündungsgebiet der Donau und am Kuban. Die Sarmaten sind dort zum Ackerbau übergegangen, sie haben Wallburgen angelegt und eine intensive Gewerbetätigkeit entfaltet, so daß sie auch die Stämme des Hinterlandes beliefern konnten.

Es zeichnen sich jetzt die Umrisse eines sarmatischen Vorstoßes nach Südosten, in die Tiefe Mittelasiens ab. Er ist wohl aber kaum so weitreichend und entscheidend gewesen wie manche Gelehrte vermuteten, die von einer »sarmatischen Phase« im Leben der Steppenvölker sprachen.

Seit Minns und Rostovcev ihre klassischen Werke über die Steppenkunst schrieben, ist es üblich geworden, der skythischen Variante des Tierstils – mit Monochromie und Schrägschnitt – eine spätere, sarmatische entgegenzusetzen. Sie ersetzt den Verlust an Prägnanz durch ein neues koloristisches Prinzip. Polychromie wird nun durch die Verwendung von Champlevé und Cloisonné erzielt. Man kombiniert Glasflüsse und bunte Steine mit dem edlen Metall. Sehr oft finden wir auch durchbrochene Arbeit, gelegentlich kommt es zu einer völligen Auflösung ins Ornament. In anderen Fällen treffen wir dagegen rea-

Sarmaten im Schwarzmeergebiet

Sarmatischer Tierstil: Polychromie, Modellierung, durchbrochene Arbeit

listisch modellierte Reliefs. Jedoch die Sicherheit in den Proportionen schwindet.

Rostovcev hat in einer bestechenden Vision diesen jüngeren Tierstil gedeutet, ihn in die allgemeine Entwicklung eingeordnet. Er geht davon aus, daß in Südrußland bereits in einer früheren Phase bunte Einlegearbeiten auftauchten – in Kelermes im 6. Jahrhundert v. Chr. Polychromie, so schließt er, gehört also zum Grundbestand des Tierstils, übernommen aus dem assyrisch-persischen Bereich. In Südrußland sei diese Tendenz freilich sehr bald dem griechischen Stilgefühl erlegen. Im Inneren Asiens aber habe sie sich gehalten – wie man mit den prachtvollen Stücken des Oxusschatzes beweisen könne.

Dieser stark iranisch gefärbte, in Innerasien konservierte Tierstil sei dann um Christi Geburt in einer Entwicklungshöhe, die durch die Goldplatten aus dem Schatz Peters des Großen belegt wird, von den Sarmaten nach Südrußland mitgebracht worden. Zu der Zeit war der griechische Geschmack selbst unsicher geworden und leistete keinen Widerstand mehr. Der politische Niedergang der Skythen hatte die Werkstätten ihrer treuesten Abnehmer beraubt. Frühe parthische Einflüsse machten sich geltend. So kam die Polychromie nun endlich zum Sieg. Sie verband sich in interessanten Mischungen mit den Schmuckformen des Hellenismus und blieb schließlich bis in die völkerwanderungszeitliche Kunst lebendig.

Die sowjetischen Archäologen haben dieser Hypothese keinen Entwurf von ähnlicher Brillanz entgegenzusetzen. Sie blieben in Ursprungsfragen verstrickt. Das Interesse am rein ästhetischen Ablauf lag ihnen fern, das Fehlen neuer Aussagen dazu wurde vor wenigen Jahren ausdrücklich vermerkt. Immerhin sind manche Auswirkungen des neuen Chronologiesystems unübersehbar. Auch die Altaigrabungen, mit denen wir uns noch beschäftigen werden, lassen den Sachverhalt in neuem Licht erscheinen.

Zunächst einmal wurde klar, daß der Tierstil während der sauro- matischen Stufe mit denselben, typisch skythischen Waffen- und

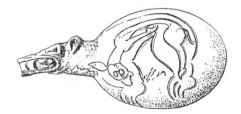

Fig. 33 – Fast noch deutlicher ist die monumentale Geschlossenheit des protoskythischen Tierstils bei diesem Knochenlöffel aus Biče-Obá (bei Orenburg). Griechischer Einfluß fehlt hier völlig. Länge 12 cm. (Nach Grakov 1928)

FIG. 32, 33 Schirrungsformen vergesellschaftet ist wie anderswo. Er bildet auch eine Trias. Der Komplex muß sich sehr rasch, schon zu Beginn des 6. Jahrhunderts v. Chr., durchgesetzt haben, zunächst bei den Reiterkriegern, die ihn ja wohl auch von irgendeinem Feldzug mitgebracht hatten.

Der Frauenschmuck gehorcht (nach Grakov) zunächst noch anderen Prinzipien. Von griechischen Einflüssen ist hier weit und breit nichts zu spüren. Andererseits fehlt jede Andeutung von Polychromie. Am Ural beobachtet man eine engere Beziehung zum südsibirischen Formenkreis, während der Wolgaraum nach Westen tendiert.

Rasche Degeneration
FIG. 34 In den folgenden Jahrhunderten scheint sich dieses von der breiten Schicht der Krieger getragene Kunstwollen zu verflüchtigen. Die Waffen zeigen immer klarer und stereotyper werdende Zweckformen. Die Scheidenbeschläge aus Goldblech (Prochorovka, Buerova Mogila) tragen abstrakte Muster.

Neuauftreten in veränderter sozialer Funktion Gegen Ende der mittelsarmatischen Zeit tritt neuerlich Tierstil auf, jedoch in einem ganz anderen Zusammenhang. Er kommt in reichen Gräbern von Männern und Frauen vor und konzentriert sich auf bestimmte Schmuckgegenstände aus edlem Metall, etwa Halsreifen. Repräsentativ dafür sind die Goldschmiedearbeiten aus dem Chochlač-
ABB. SEITE 53 Kurgan, der sogenannte Schatz von Novočerkask. Er enthält neben einem kleinen Fläschchen und mehreren Etuis prachtvolle Diademe, von denen eins mit hellenistischen Gemmen geschmückt ist; den oberen Rand bekrönen Hirsche geradezu altskythischer Form zwischen ganz atypischen Bäumen.

Begrenzte Bedeutung Dieser späte Tierstil ist mit Polychromie gekoppelt. Aber er bildet nur eine Tendenz unter vielen anderen. Aufnähblättchen für die Kleidung sind nun rein geometrisch geformt. Bei manchen Stücken fällt jener
ABB. SEITE 51 etwas schwerfällige Realismus auf, der in der sasanidischen Kunst so viel statische Würde ausdrücken muß.

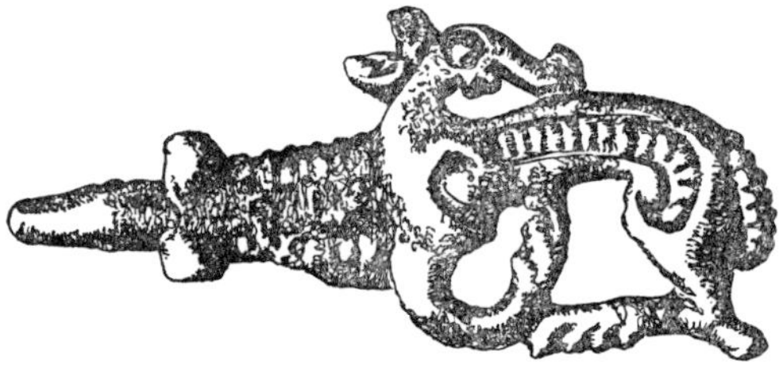

Fig. 34 – Gürtelhaken aus Mastjugino, etwa 9 cm lang. Dieses Stück, dem 4. Jh. v. Chr. angehörend, gehört schon in die Übergangszeit zur frühsarmatischen Periode, die Formen des Tierstils sind abgewandelt, wenig prägnant. (Nach Grakov 1928)

Pseudoschnalle, wurde im Katalog der Iranischen Ausstellung (1961/62) als Luristan-Bronze angeführt. Tatsächlich handelt es sich um ein sarmatisches, vielleicht bereits in der Antike, vielleicht aber auch erst durch den modernen Kunsthandel verschlepptes Stück, repräsentativ für eine dem letzten Jahrhundert v. Chr. angehörende Gruppe. *Vgl. S. 55*

Rostovcev hat zweifellos die Bedeutung des Tierstils in diesem komplizierten Konzert zu stark betont. Darum war er auch so bereit, den vergoldeten, mit bunten Steinen besetzten Silbergürtel von Maikop für echt zu halten. Der wild zupackende Greif, der ihm enthusiastische Äußerungen entlockte, und das so realistisch erliegende Pferd sind jedoch nicht Schöpfungen eines Meisters aus dem 2. Jahrhundert v. Chr., sondern wurden von einem außerordentlich geschickten und geschäftstüchtigen Juwelier aus Odessa gefertigt, dem man die Bilder sibirischer Goldplatten in dem Prachtwerk von Tolstoj und Kondakov als Unterlage zur Verfügung gestellt hatte. Damals, um 1910, datierte

Silbergürtel von Maikop – eine Fälschung

59

man die Vorbilder, die hier zusammengebraut wurden, noch in die hellenistische Zeit. Der Goldschmied hat infolgedessen auch hellenistische
Merkmale eingearbeitet, und die haben die Gelehrten dann wieder
erfreut als Bestätigung für ihre Datierung verwendet. Übrigens stammen die von Salmony publizierten Bleiplatten aus dem gleichen
Laden in Odessa.

Trotzdem braucht die These, die Kombination von Tierstil und
Polychromie sei östlicher Herkunft, nicht falsch zu sein. Wie wir später
sehen werden, war tatsächlich eine solche Kombination in Zentralasien und Südsibirien dauernd vorhanden. Allerdings liegen die besten
Schöpfungen dieser Art – und dazu gehören manche der »sibirischen
Goldplatten« – in einer älteren Phase. Nur in einigen Rückzugsgebieten hielt sich die Tradition lange genug, um bereits mannigfaltig
modifiziert das Sarmatentum zu beeinflussen.

VII. DIE MINUSSINSK-BRONZEN

Noch lange nach der Zeit, in der Jermak der Kosak den Bann gebrochen und den Ural überschritten hatte, verlief die russische Expansion in der Waldsteppe, wobei sie verblüffend rasch die Küste des Pazifik erreichte. Von jener Zone aus konnte man die unendlichen Wälder kontrollieren, in deren Tiefe die Eingeborenen der Pelztierjagd nachgingen – nicht ganz freiwillig, sondern um die ihnen aufgezwungene Kopfsteuer zahlen zu können. Dort fand auch der russische Bauer den besten Boden und ein vertrautes Klima.

Die Steppe selbst blieb vorläufig in der Hand freier, mächtiger Nomadenvölker. Im Osten wurden sie allmählich der Mandschu-Dynastie dienstbar. Jene konservierte sie geradezu kunstvoll in der alten Ordnung, um stets ein Reservoir ungebrochener, schlagkräftiger Barbaren zur Verfügung zu haben. Im Westen aber blieben sie frei bis ins 19. Jahrhundert, erst dann entschloß sich der Zar zu einem imperialistischen Vorstoß nach dem Süden, teils aus Handelsinteressen und teils wohl auch, um den Reichtümern Indiens näherzukommen.

Nur ein abgesplittertes Stück Steppenraum kam frühzeitig unter die Kontrolle der zaristischen Verwaltung. Es ist der Kessel von Minussinsk, das durch viele malerische Erhebungen gegliederte Land zu beiden Seiten des mittleren Jenissei. Es ist von Höhenrücken umgeben, die die Taiga bedeckte, der wilde, wegarme sibirische Urwald. Im Süden und Südosten ragen die Höhen des Sajan empor, den Westen riegelt der Kusnezker Alatau ab, nur an seinen nördlichen Ausläufern vorbei führt ein bequemer Durchgang in die westliche Waldsteppe. Im Nordosten, hinter einer Barriere, die vom Jenissei durchbrochen wird, schließt sich noch eine zweite Steppeninsel an, das kleinere Becken von Krasnojarsk und Kansk. *Geographische Situation*

Hier wollen wir unseren Bericht beginnen, denn hier setzte die Forschung konzentriert ein – warum, das ist leicht zu verstehen.

Minussinsk ist schon von Castrén ein »Riesenkirchhof« genannt worden. Gero von Merhart hat in seinen sibirischen Erinnerungen eine Beschreibung hinterlassen, die es um ihrer Bildhaftigkeit willen verdient, an dieser Stelle zitiert zu werden: *»Riesenkirchhof«*

»Könnte man angeben, wie viele Kurgane auf jedem Quadratkilometer

Fig. 35 – Markierung von Nekropolen verschiedener Zeitstellung durch Steinreihen in der Abakan-Steppe. Nach einer Abbildung aus dem Werk Tolstoj-Kondakov 1890.

der kahlen Steppe stehen, so wäre gewiß einige Anschaulichkeit gewonnen. Aber die Kurgane des Kreises Minussinsk hat noch kein Sterblicher gezählt, und wenn jemals der märchenhafte Tag aufgehen sollte, an dem ein Inventar der dortigen Bodenaltertümer abgeschlossen wird, dann muß dasselbe doch schweigen über die zahllosen Gräber, die seit der Besiedlung des Landes durch seßhafte Bauern vom Boden getilgt wurden. Man kommt einem solchen Wunderding, wie es die Gräbersteppe am Jenissei ist, mit kalten Zahlen nicht bei. Aber steigen wir auf einen der Berge, um deren felsigen Fuß der große Strom rauscht, auf deren Hängen das Edelweiß aus dünnem Steppengras leuchtet und von deren Scheitel der Blick ungehemmt bis zum kahlen Scheitel des Borus, des nächsten Hochberges im Sajan, bis zum ferne dunkelnden Wall des Kusnezker Alatau und bis zu den flachen Wellen der nördlichen Steppe schweift, durchforschen wir die Hänge und Senken und Täler, die Hügel und Flächen, die um uns und unter uns in fremdartiger, starrer und doch so schöner Ruhe liegen. Da, uns zu Füßen, in einsamer hochgelegener Wanne unseres Berges ein erstes Grabfeld, Hügel an Hügel in regelloser Menge, jeder umstellt mit verwitterten Steinen, mit dünnen, aber breiten und hohen Platten von oft grotesker Form, wie sie gerade der Zufall des Brechens ergab; manche sind hingesunken, manche zersprungen und zerfallen, die Mehrzahl aber ragt noch frei empor, und ihre Masse drängt sich in diesem Tal des Todes wie eine versteinerte Herde abenteuerlicher rotdunkler Tiere. Wir suchen das Gewirr zu teilen, zu zählen – es sind mehr denn hundert Hügel auf dem einen engen Fleck, keiner wohl weniger als zehn Geviertmeter bedeckend, viele um ein Mehrfaches größer. Und dort, tiefer am Fuße des Berges ein, zwei, drei solcher Grabfelder in kurzem Abstand, weiter draußen am Ufer ein russisches Dorf und wieder Kurgane, weithin verstreut über das Flachland.«

Die Forschungsgeschichte ist nicht weniger phantastisch als der äußere Charakter der Landschaft. Das Vorspiel lieferte – wie überall in Sibirien – die Raubgräberei. Sie gehörte zu den Begleiterscheinungen russischer Landnahme und hat im Laufe von Generationen eine erstaunliche Perfektion erreicht. Die »Bugrovišči« vererbten ihr durchaus angesehenes Gewerbe vom Vater auf den Sohn. Sie wußten, welchen Plan die oberirdischen Steinzäune und welchen Umfang die Hügel aufweisen mußten, um eine reiche Ausbeute an Gold zu gewährleisten. Sie berechneten genau, wohin der Schacht zielen mußte, um auf die Schmucksachen zu stoßen. Kein Wunder, daß es damals einen regulären Marktpreis für sibirisches Raubgold gab.

Die unvermeidlichen Raubgräber

Daneben lieferte auch der Boden zwischen den Gräbern, wenn er einmal unter den Pflug genommen worden war, eine Unmenge von Bronzen. Dolche, Messer, Beile, Knöpfe und Anhängsel brachten die ackernden Bauern vom Feld. Es wurde üblich, sie den »Tschuden« zuzuschreiben, einem sagenhaften Volk der Vorzeit.

Die zweite Quelle, nämlich die Zufallsfunde, versiegte auch dann nicht, als die goldfündigen Gräber erschöpft waren. Sie lieferte vielmehr im Laufe der Zeit den Löwenanteil von vierzigtausend bekannten Minussinskbronzen.

Zufallsfunde

Wahrscheinlich wäre auch jene Ausbeute sang- und klanglos in den Schmelztiegel gewandert, hätte sich nicht mittlerweile die Wissenschaft für das Wunderland interessiert. Man glaubte, hier auf die bronzezeitliche Kultur der noch ungeteilten ural-altaischen Völkerfamilie gestoßen zu sein, auf das Strahlungszentrum für das nördliche Eurasien. Daher strebten Museumsleiter auf der ganzen Welt danach, sich eine Probe des Segens zu sichern. Washington, London, Oxford, Paris, Berlin, Wien, Budapest, Oslo, Helsinki, Stockholm besorgten sich für gute Rubel einen Anteil. Ein größerer Posten wurde vor einigen Jahren in den Beständen des Hamburger Völkerkundemuseums wiederentdeckt. Trotzdem blieb noch genug für russische Sammlungen, vor allem für die Lokalmuseen von Minussinsk, Krasnojarsk, Tomsk und Irkutsk.

40000 Minussinskbronzen in den Museen der Welt

Vor solcher Diaspora aber liefen die Bronzen zunächst einmal gewinnbringend durch die Hand vieler kleiner Aufkäufer und Agenten. Ein

Sammlung Tovostin

Beispiel mag genügen: Der Kupferschmied Ivan Petrowitsch Tovostin arbeitete seit 1879 in einem kleinen Dörfchen der Umgebung, dann in der Stadt Minussinsk selbst. Von den Einheimischen, Russen wie Tataren, erhielt er öfter Bronzegegenstände mit dem Auftrag, sie in Samoware oder kleine Schmucksachen umzugießen. Nach einer Weile begann er, solche Dinge zu kaufen, und zwar zunächst für Rechnung des Goldsuchers Kuznecov (der im übrigen archäologische Arbeiten schrieb). Zwei Jahre später machte er sich selbständig und veranstaltete förmliche Einkaufsreisen, bei denen er gedruckte Flugzettel mit seinen sensationellen Preisangeboten verteilen ließ. Sie bewegten sich zwischen zehn und fünfzehn Kopeken das Stück. Seine Erwerbungen verkaufte er dann an Touristen, Beamte und Offiziere, wobei er für ein schönes Exemplar bis zu zwanzig Rubel verlangte. Heute würde man sagen, er stieg ganz groß in das Souvenir-Geschäft ein. Es wurde damals Mode, als Erinnerung an die ferne Steppeninsel einen Dolch oder ein großes Messer mitzubringen, sie paßten so gut als Brieföffner auf den Schreibtisch. Auswärtige Kundschaft kam hinzu. Das Historische Museum Kiew allein ließ sich achthundert Stück anhängen, geringen Werts, wie Tovostin später äußerte. Immerhin wurde er schließlich selbst vom Sammeleifer angesteckt. Er schaffte Unikate beiseite und verkaufte, als er sich in fortgeschrittenem Alter vom Geschäft zurückzog, seine Privatkollektion nach Helsinki, wo sie von Tallgren prächtig bearbeitet und publiziert seinen Namen verewigte.

Adrianovs Schicksal Parallel zu solcher Sammeltätigkeit, deren Ergebnisse übrigens auch in Rußland veröffentlicht und ausgewertet wurden, verliefen nur ganz wenige Grabungen mit wissenschaftlichem Ehrgeiz. Die interessantesten führte ab 1887 Alexander Adrianov durch. Er war noch ein blutiger Anfänger (wie er selbst schreibt), als er, den Spaten in der einen Hand, einen archäologischen Leitfaden in der anderen, auf mumifizierte Leichen stieß, auf deren Gesichtern Gipsmasken lagen. Jahrzehnte später sollte er als Revolutionär deportiert werden und gelangte – offenbar durch ein Entgegenkommen der zaristischen Justiz – wieder ins Minussinskgebiet, wo er seine Grabungen fortsetzte. 1918 schloß sich Adrianov jedoch trotz seiner revolutionären Vergangenheit der Koltschakarmee an – und wurde dafür 1920 in Tomsk als Konterrevolutionär erschossen.

Merhart als *Kriegsgefangener* Ein gnädig-ungnädiges Schicksal verschlug auch den österreichischen Prähistoriker und nachmaligen deutschen Universitätsprofessor Gero von Merhart während des Ersten Weltkrieges in diesen Raum. Zuerst saß er in einem Gefangenenlager, dann beschäftigte man ihn in jener etwas freieren Periode, die dem Sturz des Zarenregimes folgte, am Museum Krasnojarsk, und er wußte dieses Privileg trotz nagenden Hungers und ohne jegliche Hilfsmittel mit eisernem Fleiß zu nutzen. Ja, er zögerte seine Entlassung aus der Kriegsgefangenschaft freiwillig um ein halbes Jahr hinaus. Das Buch, das er auf Grund seiner Studien und Grabungen schrieb, zeigt sein erbittertes Ringen um die Materie.

Dennoch war weder Merhart noch Tallgren, dem größten unter den finnischen Forschern, der große Wurf gelungen, nämlich die Bewältigung des ungeheuren Materials durch ein chronologisches System. Das glückte vielmehr erst dem russischen Archäologen Teplouchov an Hand eines fast lächerlich simplen Merkmals. Er brachte nämlich die oberirdischen Kennzeichen der Gräber – Steinzäune, Hügel – in eine typologische Reihe. Sein System, von der frühen Kupferzeit bis weit nach Christi Geburt reichend, bildete den Schlüssel zur Urgeschichte ganz Sibiriens.

Teplouchovs Leistung, sein Ende

Aber Teplouchovs Werk wurde jäh unterbrochen. Er verschwand in einer der großen Säuberungswellen der Stalin-Ära – und harrt auch heute noch seiner posthumen Rehabilitation. Seltsamerweise fiel sein bester westlicher Interpret, der junge Amerikaner Gaul, ebenfalls einer Tragödie zum Opfer, die ganz in den Stil dieser ereignisreichen Forschungsgeschichte paßt: Während des Zweiten Weltkriegs wurde er seiner Sprachkenntnisse wegen dazu ausersehen, als Verbindungsmann über tschechoslowakischem Gebiet mit dem Fallschirm abzuspringen. Er wurde gefaßt und erschossen.

Gaul: noch eine Tragödie

Erst mit Kiselev bewegt sich die Forschung wieder in normalen, ruhigen Bahnen. Nach fleißigen Grabungen, auch im Altai und Sajan, konnte er 1949 eine umfassende Darstellung der Urgeschichte Südsibiriens vorlegen. Sie breitet ein unerhörtes Material vor uns aus und bemüht sich außerdem, nicht mehr die oberflächliche Kennzeichnung der Gräber, sondern vor allem Keramik und Metallgerät als Basis der Chronologie zu verwenden. Leider wurde sie in einer Zeit niedergeschrieben, in der die sowjetische Archäologie stark vom Geiste N. Ja. Marrs durchdrungen war, und ist daher nicht frei von Schematismus.

Kiselevs Übersichtswerk

Was sonst noch erschienen ist, bleibt interessantes Detail, so die Untersuchungen an den gefundenen Schädeln. Nur die Arbeit von Kyzlasov, die der Zeit um Christi Geburt gewidmet ist, erhebt sich über dieses Niveau. Erst in allerjüngster Zeit legen mehrere Autoren – z. B. Členova – wieder scharfsinnige, kritische Untersuchungen vor. Dabei sieht man, daß die Datierungen Kiselevs nicht ausschlaggebend sind. Von großem Wert sind die Untersuchungen des Anthropologen Alekseev, die die etwas zu schematischen Resultate des älteren Debec korrigieren.

Karasuk-Kultur Seit Kiselev nehmen wir an, daß Tierdarstellungen im Minussinskgebiet eher eine Rolle gespielt haben als irgendwo sonst im Steppenraum, nämlich bereits im Rahmen der Karasuk-Kultur.

Es ist sicher, daß man damals Ackerbau trieb. Dafür sprechen umfangreiche Kanalanlagen, die in diese Periode datiert werden können. Dennoch sind keine Siedlungen gefunden worden.

Man ist also auf die Gräberfelder angewiesen. Die Toten ruhen in sehr flach angelegten und natürlich geplünderten Steinkisten, manchmal unter einer geringen Aufschüttung, jedenfalls aber von Zäunen aus hochkant gestellten Steinplatten umgeben, die sich in sauberen Rechtecken aneinanderschließen. Bei den in Rückenlage ausgestreckten Skeletten fand man Schmuckstücke und Aufnähplättchen der Kleidung, alles aus Bronze. Von Speisebeigaben zeugen Tierknochen und Rundbodengefäße, vermutlich gehörten auch die mit-

FIG. 37 gefundenen Messer zum Tafelgerät.

Es ist ganz klar, daß der Typenbestand größer gewesen sein muß, als das Bestattungsritual verrät, die Frage ist nur, welche Ergänzung aus der Fülle der Streufunde darf man sich erlauben? Kiselev reiht hier resolut alle Formen ein, die man in den Perioden mit einem »entgegenkommenderen« Bestattungsritual nicht unterbringen kann, die aber nebenbei die Brücke zwischen der älteren Bronzezeit und der Eisenzeit bilden. So ergibt sich ein ziemlich komplettes Bild der Bewaffnung, die Streitpickel, Dolche und relativ einfache Pfeilspitzen umfaßt. Das Tüllenbeil bildete das wichtigste Gerät.

Tierplastiken als Auch die Dekoration mit kleinen Tierplastiken wurde zunächst auf
Dekor diesem Umweg postuliert. Eine Gruppe von Messern mit Tierkopfknauf stimmt überdies durch die Formgebung von Griff und Schneide mit dem aus den Gräbern bekannten Bestand überein. Erst nach der Aufstellung der Hypothese ergab dann ein freundlicher Grabfund die Bestätigung.

Das Auftreten zumindest des Tierdekors in einer spätbronzezeitlichen Steppenkultur ist natürlich für unsere Problematik von höchster Bedeutung. Vielleicht stehen wir hier überhaupt an der Wurzel des Tierstils? Mit welcher Zeitstellung müssen wir denn zunächst einmal rechnen?

Kiselev blieb nicht bei seinen ersten Feststellungen stehen, seine Hypothese führt weiter. Er glaubt durch Vergleiche fast des gesamten Metallinventars zeigen zu können, daß Karasuk von einem metallurgischen Zentrum erster Ordnung abhängig war, das sich um die Mitte des zweiten Jahrtausends v.Chr. in Nordchina gebildet hatte. Wir kennen es durch die Ausgrabungen von An-yang, der späteren Hauptstadt der Shang-Dynastie (etwa 1500–1027 v.Chr.). Verbindungsglieder seien durch die Ordosbronzen – Zufallsfunde im nordchinesischen Grenzgebiet, mit denen wir uns noch beschäftigen müssen – sowie einzelne Bronzen in der Mongolei ausreichend gegeben. Da der Anthropologe Debec soeben erklärt hatte, das Schädelmaterial der Karasuk-Periode sei sinid, nicht europid wie das der vorhergehenden Phase, nahm Kiselev einfach an, es habe eine Wanderung vom

Fig. 36-38 – Diese Messer, obgleich über die ganze Breite Eurasiens verteilt, gehören in einen typologischen Verband, bezeichnen einen – allerdings breiten – Zeithorizont! Vgl.S. 68

Fig. 36 – Großes Messer mit Tierkopfgriff aus An-yang. (Nach Karlgren 1945)

Fig. 37 – Messer mit Tierkopfgriff aus einem Grabfund bei Abakan, Karasuk-Kultur, Minussinskgebiet. (Nach Jettmar 1950) Vgl.S. 66

Fig. 38 – Bronzemesser aus Seima, Mittelrußland. Zwei stehende Pferde bilden den Griffabschluß. Gesamtlänge fast 40 cm. (Nach Tallgren 1938)

Ordosgebiet bis nach Minussinsk gegeben. Da die Shang dem Brauch huldigten, Kriegsgefangene aus Nachbargebieten in großer Zahl bei der Bestattung ihrer Könige zu opfern, braucht man nicht lange nach einem Motiv zu suchen. Im übrigen seien die Träger der Karasuk-Kultur bereits Halbnomaden gewesen, in deren Wirtschaft die Schafzucht eine große Rolle spielte. Das erkläre auch die häufige Verwendung des Widderkopfs als künstlerisches Motiv.

Diese Hypothese ist bereits von Kühn geahnt worden. Der Sinologe Karlgren hat ebenfalls ihre Konsequenz gesehen, nämlich die Möglichkeit, den gesamten Tierstil der Steppen von China abzuleiten. Der Verfasser dieses Buches hat einiges zu ihrer Verbreitung beigetragen. Leider war sie zu einfach.

Bodenständige Typen Man weiß inzwischen, daß der überwiegende Teil der Metalltypen einheimischer Herkunft ist. Die sogenannten Knickmesser stammen zum Beispiel von jenen merkwürdigen Kupferdolchen des frühen zweiten Jahrtausends v.Chr. ab, die man in Südsibirien unter stumpfem Winkel in einen Knochengriff steckte. In China treten sie viel später auf, offenbar als Entlehnung.

Vor allem aber erwies sich die Zusammensetzung der Minussinsk-bevölkerung in der fraglichen Periode als hoffnungslos kompliziert. Es kommt ein höchst altertümlicher, primitiv-europider Typus vor, der in der unmittelbar vorhergehenden Periode schon verschwunden

FIG. 36 BIS 38 schien. Vielleicht gehörte das Knickmesser zur Ausrüstung dieser Leute. Vorherrschend aber waren verhältnismäßig grazile Brachykephale mit leisen mongoliden Anklängen. Sie entsprechen am ehesten der modernen Pamir-Ferghana-Rasse, die unter heutigen Tadschiken oder Uzbeken zu finden ist. Alekseev hält das für ein Indiz, man habe mit einer Einwanderung aus Zentralasien, etwa aus dem Tarimbecken, aber nicht aus dem Ordosraum zu rechnen. Dort seien in dieser Periode vielmehr breitgesichtige Mongolide zu erwarten, Vorfahren der heutigen Mongolen oder Türken.

Karasuk: keine einheitliche Fazies Das geht nun wieder zu weit. In jener Zeit ist das Auftreten von Europiden auch an den Grenzen Chinas selbst ins Auge zu fassen. Von der Beziehung Ordos–Minussinsk bleibt genügend aufrecht, daß man mindestens mit einer Komponente aus dem chinesischen Grenzraum rechnen muß. Die Richtung der Verbindung wird auch durch immer neu auftauchende Streufunde über die Zentral- und Nordmongolei bestätigt.

Auch in bezug auf die Datierung ist man vorsichtiger geworden. Kiselev, der zunächst einmal kühn Karasuk zwischen 1300–800 v.Chr.

ansetzte, akzeptierte viel zu hohe Daten für An-yang und übersah das chinesische Vergleichsmaterial noch nicht ausreichend. Heute würde man in manchen Fällen eher an eine Entlehnung im Laufe der frühen Chou-Zeit denken. Soeben versucht man, Karasuk in mehrere Kulturareale aufzulösen.

Die folgende Periode – Kiselev hat sie nach einem wichtigen Fundplatz »Tagar-Kultur« getauft – hängt eng mit Karasuk zusammen, zum Beispiel hinsichtlich des Grabrituals, das sich kontinuierlich weiterentwickelt. Daneben wirkt es jedoch merkwürdig, daß mit Beginn der Tagar-Zeit ein gründlicher Wandel des vorherrschenden anthropologischen Typs eintritt. Wir finden großgesichtige Europide wie in der Kupfer- und frühen Bronzezeit. Als Erklärung wird in Erwägung gezogen, daß eine zu Beginn der Karasuk-Phase verdrängte Altbevölkerung aus den Wäldern wieder zurückkehrte und die Oberhand gewann. Vielleicht blieb aber diese Altbevölkerung überhaupt immer im Lande und ging nur zu einem anderen, nicht faßbaren Beisetzungsritual über – etwa der oberirdischen Aussetzung. Erst nach Ablösung der temporären Oberschicht bekam sie die Möglichkeit, deren kostspieliges Totenritual zu übernehmen. Es ist übrigens interessant, daß die Hügel nachweislich erst nach der Aufrichtung des Steinzauns aufgeschüttet wurden. Offenbar zerfiel die Beisetzung in mehrere Abschnitte, die jeweils mit bestimmten Festen verbunden waren. Wir werden uns dessen noch bei der Besprechung der Altaikunst erinnern.

Die Männer wurden mit ihrem persönlichen Schmuck und mit ihren Waffen beigesetzt. So finden wir jetzt Dolche und Messer, Streitpickel, Pfeilspitzen und geschweifte Bronzestäbe, die vermutlich die Verstärkung von Bogen bildeten. Interessanterweise sind selbst die Frauen nicht nur mit ihrem Schmuck, sondern gelegentlich auch mit Waffen beigesetzt worden.

Die Gräber enthielten keinerlei Bestandteile von Pferdeschirrung, obwohl unter den Streufunden genügend Trensen vorhanden sind, die

Tagar-Kultur

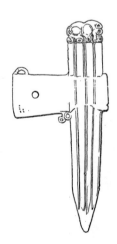

Fig. 40 – Bronzener Streitpickel altertümlicher Form. Nacken mit stehender Tierfigur. Länge etwa 20 cm. Staatliches Historisches Museum, Moskau. (Nach Salmony 1954)

69

Miniaturmesser und Dolchscheide. Vermutlich Tagar II. *Etwa natürliche Größe.*
Museum für Völkerkunde, Hamburg. Vgl. S. 73

beweisen, daß wir es auch hier mit Reiterkriegern zu tun haben. Die Nahrung wurde wie im Pontikum in großen gegossenen Bronzekesseln zubereitet, deren Urbilder übrigens, wie man der Gestaltung der Griffe entnimmt, in China entwickelt wurden.

Reiterkrieger
FIG. 39

Unmittelbar an die Skythen erinnern auch Stangenbekrönungen, die in manchen Männergräbern, offenbar bei verdienten Kriegern, gefunden wurden. Sie sind stets mit Tierplastiken geschmückt. Auch als Schmuck der übrigen Gegenstände treten Tiermotive auf.

Teplouchov, der nur von dem Ergebnis seiner eigenen Grabungen ausging, hatte alle diese Darstellungen in der zweiten und dritten Phase der Minussinsker Kurgan-Kultur untergebracht, das heißt, er setzte sie in die zweite Hälfte des ersten Jahrtausends v.Chr. Danach war natürlich ihre Ableitung kein Problem, sie mochten auf allerhand Umwegen und deshalb entsprechend modifiziert aus dem pontischen Raum übernommen worden sein. Kiselev, der sich hier auf seinem eigensten Gebiet bewegt, hat das zu widerlegen versucht und eine andere Anordnung des Materials vorgeschlagen.

Der Formenschatz der ersten Phase ist nach Kiselev nicht sehr groß. Auf den Messern, die die scharfe Gliederung der Karasuk-Zeit vermissen lassen, sind die Knäufe zu Tierköpfen umgestaltet. An derselben Stelle begegnet uns auch das stehende Tier, eine kleine Bären- oder Eberplastik mit stark gesenkter Schnauze und verschmolzenen Fußpaaren, so daß sie einen Doppelbogen bildet. Vor allem auf den Stangenbekrönungen treten – zunächst recht plumpe – Plastiken von Steinböcken und Ebern mit übersteigerter Muskulatur auf. Das vierte Hauptmotiv bildet ein völlig zum Kreis geschlossenes Raubtier. Es ist von Anfang an schematisch. Nicht nur Augen und Nüstern, sondern auch Tatzen werden als Ringe wiedergegeben, eine Eigentümlichkeit, die ebenfalls bei anderen Tierdarstellungen auffällt. Verhältnismäßig häufig sind Vogelköpfchen. Manchmal erscheinen sie fast auf eine Spirallocke reduziert, manchmal aber bestehen sie aus mehreren Elementen, darunter einem zur Volute vereinfachten Schnabel. Unmittelbar aus diesen Darstellungen lassen sich wieder Bilder von Vogelgreifen entwickeln.

Erste Phase, Tierstil noch »unfertig«

Kiselev hebt nun hervor, daß es sich um zwei Motivgruppen verschiedener Herkunft handelt. Die erste (Tierkopfknauf und stehendes Tier, Bock, Bär bzw. Eber) kann ohne besondere Schwierigkeiten aus der Karasuk-Kultur abgeleitet werden. Die zweite Gruppe (Rolltier, Raubvogelkopf, ringförmige Tatzen) fehlt im Karasuk-Bestand. Dafür tritt sie in den ältesten skythischen Kurganen Südrußlands auf. Da

Karasuk-Erbe, aber auch Einflüsse aus innerasiatischem Zentrum

71

nun wenig später, im 5. Jahrhundert v. Chr., Karasukelemente – etwa das stehende Tier – auch im Pontikum vorkommen, zieht Kiselev daraus die Konsequenz, man habe eben mit zwei Entstehungszentren des Tierstils zu rechnen: einem südrussischen und einem sibirischen. Diese hätten sich bereits in einer frühen Entwicklungsstufe gegenseitig bereichert. Die Basis ihrer Verbindung sei das gleichmäßig erreichte Entwicklungsstadium, der Übergang zur nomadischen Viehzucht. Nun schrieb Kiselev in einer Zeit, in der man in der Sowjetunion ganz im Banne Marrs überall lokale Wurzeln suchte (und fand), daher ging er einfach über die Tatsache hinweg, daß es im pontischen Raum keine der Karasuk-Kultur analoge Vorstufe des Tierstils gibt. Es wäre die Erklärung viel wahrscheinlicher, daß ein bisher unbekanntes Gebiet die spezifischen Elemente der späteren skythischen Kunst einerseits Südrußland vermittelte, wo noch keine Voraussetzungen gegeben waren, andererseits aber Südsibirien, wo es bereits einheimische Ansätze gab. Vielleicht stammt auch die für beide Teile gleich typische Bewaffnung mit dem Kurzschwert aus demselben Gebiet?

Auf keinerlei Schwierigkeiten stößt hingegen die Vorstellung, sibirische Motive seien nach Südrußland entlehnt worden. Ein solcher Weg ist für eine Waffe, nämlich den Streitpickel, und für die Bronzekessel, vermutlich auch für einzelne Messerformen belegt.

Die Zusammenhänge mit Ananino sind allerdings noch wesentlich enger. Das mag sich zum Teil durch einen alten Handelsweg am Rand der Wälder entlang erklären, vor allem aber durch eine Interessengemeinschaft der Waldsteppenbewohner gegenüber den beweglichen Stämmen des Südens. Sie bildeten gewissermaßen eine Abwehrfront, was sich z. B. in der Anlage von Wallburgen spiegelt. Jene des Minussinskgebietes haben keine Kulturschicht und wurden wahrscheinlich nur in Kriegszeiten benutzt.

Bei den Stämmen der nördlichen Peripherie veränderte sich die Sozialorganisation wohl nur ganz allmählich. Deshalb fehlen dort in der ersten Phase der Tagar-Kultur die fürstlichen Gräber, die schon das älteste Skythien kennt, auch die Ausstattung von Frauengräbern mit Waffen erklärt man als altertümliches Relikt. Vermutlich lebte man in Sippenverbänden. Zeichen, die man auf manchen Bronzen fand, werden als Eigentumsmarken gedeutet. Gelegentlich enthielt ein Schatzfund mehrerer derartiger Symbole. Man glaubt, daß man es mit den Vorräten von Gießern zu tun hat, die bereits für einen größeren Markt arbeiteten.

Zweite Phase Das nächste Stadium, angeblich vom Ende des 5. bis zum Beginn des

2.Jahrhunderts v.Chr. reichend, zeigt nicht nur das Auftreten pro-
noncierter sozialer Unterschiede, sondern auch bedeutsame Ein-
brüche im Ritual. Andererseits laufen manche typologische Serien
weiter.

Die Toten werden nun in riesigen Kurganen beigesetzt, deren Holz-   *Kollektivgräber*
kammern dauernd zugänglich blieben. Man hat in ihnen laufend
bestattet, und zwar offenbar nach vorheriger Aussetzung. Nur so ist es
nämlich möglich, daß man die Knochen bereits sortiert deponierte,
zum Beispiel alle Schädel auf einem Haufen. Nun fand man in mehreren Fällen die Züge des Gesichts mit Lehm übermodelliert, so daß   *Totenmasken und*
eigenartige Porträtmasken entstanden. Statt richtiger Waffen und   *Miniaturen*
Geräte verwendete man jetzt Miniaturen aus Bronze, anfangs noch in   ABB. SEITE 70

Bronze, Hirsch mit untergeschlagenen Läufen. Typus I nach Člena; tritt erst im 5. Jahrhundert v.Chr. auf (Tagar II), vermutlich Einfluß des gleichen innerasiatischen Zentrums,
von dem die pontischen Darstellungen des frühen 6. Jahrhunderts abhängig sind. *Etwa Original-*
größe. Museum für Völkerkunde, Hamburg. Vgl. S. 74

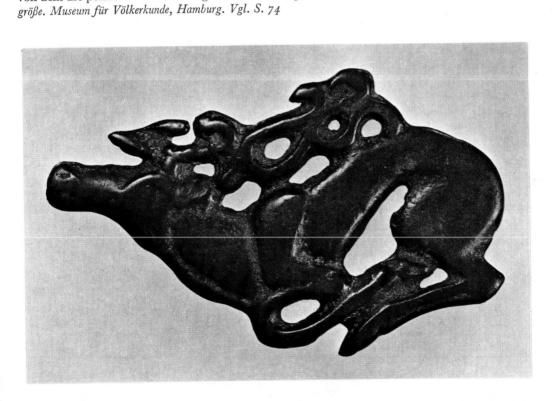

den richtigen Proportionen, später kam es offenbar auch darauf nicht mehr an.

War der Kurgan hinreichend belegt – oft mit mehr als hundert Toten –, dann ließ man die Innenausstattung in Flammen aufgehen, wobei sich die Anlage in einen Meiler verwandelte. Der enge Schacht erlaubte keinen ausreichenden Luftzutritt, das nur verkohlte Holz blieb ausgezeichnet erhalten. Auch die Masken sind durch diesen Brennvorgang der Zerstörung entgangen.

Raubgräber, die auf solche Beinhäuser stießen, mögen dann zur Entstehung jener Sage beigetragen haben, die uns Merhart erzählt: »Vor langer, langer Zeit«, so heißt es bei ihm, »geschah es, daß Bäume zu wachsen begannen, wie sie vorher niemals gesehen worden waren, Birkenbäume mit weißen Stämmen. Im Volk aber lief eine Weissagung um, es werde ein weißer Zar kommen, dessen Macht man nicht widerstehen könne. Da beschlossen sie, zu sterben, ehe sie unterworfen würden; bauten hölzerne Häuser tief im Boden, häuften gewaltige Erdhügel darüber und verbargen sich, als die Zeit gekommen, in diesen selbsterrichteten Gräbern. Feuer setzten sie an die stützenden Balken, und die nachwuchtende Erdlast schied sie für ewig von der Sonne, die sie nur in Freiheit sehen gewollt.«

Fürstengräber In ganz wenigen Fällen traf man unter denselben riesigen, bis zu zehn Meter hohen Aufschüttungen nur Einzelgräber. Offenbar handelte es sich um Fürsten, aufgestiegen aus der Masse des Volkes, die sich nun die Arbeitskraft großer Verbände dienstbar machen konnten. In den Zugangsschächten solcher Anlagen fand man ärmlich ausgestattete Skelette, vielleicht von mitbestatteten Sklaven.

Auch in dieser mittleren Phase der Tagar-Kultur kann das Bild durch zahlreiche Streufunde ergänzt werden. Sie gehören den gleichen Typen *Eisen* an wie die Miniaturen, bestehen aber zum großen Teil aus Eisen. Der künstlerische Schmuck verrät immer noch das Weiterleben von Motiven der Karasuk-Zeit. Sie verlieren aber an Realistik und Ausdruckskraft. Deutlich ist das an den Bocksfiguren erkennbar, die den seitlichen Griff medaillenförmiger Spiegel bilden. Zur Karasuk-Erbschaft gehören ferner Doppeljoche mit Tierkopfenden. Sie dienten wieder der Verstärkung komplexer Bögen.

ABB. SEITE 73 Dafür treten weitere im »skythischen« Bereich verbreitete Motive auf, z. B. der Hirsch mit den untergeschlagenen Füßen, seltsamerweise mit Details der Zeichnung, die in Südrußland nur dem frühen 6. Jahrhundert v. Chr. angehören. Raubtierköpfe zeigen die im Wolgagebiet so häufige gewaltsame Übersteigerung.

Ein einziges Mal hat man in einem solchen Grab Reste einer viereckigen Platte gefunden, die als Gürtelschließe diente. Kiselev benützt dieses winzige Indiz zu der wohl trotzdem richtigen Vermutung, ein großer Teil der sibirischen Goldplatten sei eben in dieser Phase entstanden. Wir werden uns mit dem Problem noch auseinandersetzen müssen, aber erst nachdem wir alle möglichen Anknüpfungspunkte kennengelernt haben. Was wir unter den Zufallsfunden an analogen Darstellungen beobachten, ist nicht sehr eindrucksvoll, vielleicht weil die besten Stücke in Edelmetall ausgeführt waren und eben darum eingeschmolzen wurden. Diese Platten zeigen jedenfalls die üblichen Tierkämpfe.

Kiselev unterläßt es, auf eine Gruppe von Messern einzugehen, die nicht mit Tierfiguren, sondern mit Spiralranken verziert sind. Dennoch macht einerseits die Form, andererseits aber das verwendete Material, nämlich Bronze, die Datierung in die Mittelphase notwendig. Es ist bei den einzelnen Stücken sehr schwer zu entscheiden, ob der Dekor von Anfang an abstrakt gemeint war oder eine Pflanze das Vorbild geliefert hat. In manchen Fällen könnte sogar ein Tierkörper in extremer Stilisierung vorliegen.

Strzygowski glaubte es hier mit der eigentümlichen Weiterentwicklung einer Spiralornamentik zu tun zu haben, er sprach daher von der »geometrischen Ranke«. Tallgren meinte hingegen, die Weinranke als letztes Vorbild erkennen zu können, die auf dem Umweg über Zentralasien aus der griechischen Kunst übernommen wurde. Eine ähnliche Strömung sei im Europa des 4. Jahrhunderts v. Chr. festzustellen, ihre Auswirkungen seien für die keltische Kunst entscheidend gewesen. Das bedeutet natürlich eine gewisse Bereitschaft zur Spätdatierung.

Geometrische Ranke

Alle diese Eigentümlichkeiten im Gepräge der zweiten Phase haben Kiselev nicht gehindert, sie als direkte Fortsetzung, an Ort und Stelle entstanden, aufzufassen.

Spuren einer Invasion

Neuerdings wird das so radikal bezweifelt, daß selbst die Verwendung des gleichen Etiketts fragwürdig erscheint. ČlENOVA schreibt, zu Beginn des 5. Jahrhunderts müßte man im Minussinskbecken mit Zuwanderern rechnen, die aus ihrer mittelasiatischen Heimat nicht nur neue Waffen, sondern auch bestimmte Motive brachten, vor allem den kauernden Hirsch – ihr Stammessymbol. (Man könnte hier ergänzen: auch die Spiral- und Volutenornamentik.) Vielleicht habe es sich um Saken gehandelt, die sich nach dem Feldzug Darius' I. nach dem Norden absetzten. In ihrer Heimat müßten wir eine langsamere

Fragment einer Gürtelplatte mit Darstellung eines äsenden Tieres, und Zierstück unbekannter Verwendung. Beide Objekte weisen Beziehungen zu späten Ordosbronzen auf und gehören in die zweite Hälfte der Tagar-Kultur. *Originalgröße. Museum für Völkerkunde, Hamburg. Vgl. Abb. Seite 161*

Stilentwicklung annehmen als im Schwarzmeergebiet – was nicht unwahrscheinlich ist.

Die neue Hypothese ist nicht nur faszinierend, sie ist ernstzunehmen. Wir werden noch hören, was sie für das Verständnis der Grabkonstruktion zu leisten vermag.

Nebenbei wäre Teplouchov glänzend gerechtfertigt – der »echte« Tierstil wäre doch im Minussinskgebiet spät – und er hätte seltsame, noch nicht ausgegorene Vorläufer.

Die folgende Phase, angeblich vom Beginn des 2. Jahrhunderts v. Chr. bis ins 1. Jahrhundert v. Chr. hineinreichend, wird als Ausklang der Tagar-Kultur, als Übergangsphase bezeichnet. Sie ist im eigentlichen Minussinskgebiet nur dürftig vertreten. Ihr Schwerpunkt liegt im Norden, im Raum um Krasnojarsk. Man ging dazu über, den Toten vor seiner Einlieferung in die Kammer der Riesenkurgane zu verbrennen. Das Maskenbrauchtum wird konsequent weiterentwickelt. Sozialunterschiede lassen sich nun auch in den Kollektivgräbern erkennen, Eisen dient jetzt zur Herstellung von Miniaturen. Tierformen werden relativ selten verwendet und erweisen sich als wenig charakteristisch. *Dritte Phase*

Brandbestattung

Im Süden folgt inzwischen die Taštyk-Kultur, die bis ins 6. Jahrhundert n. Chr. reicht. Nach der Meinung der Forscher, vor allem Kyzlasovs, wurde auch sie durch den Einbruch eines Steppenvolkes aus Südosten ausgelöst. Dieser Zustrom findet allerdings in dem heute studierten Schädelmaterial nur geringen Niederschlag, offenbar weil die Zuwanderer ihre Toten fast ausschließlich verbrannten. Sie ließen sich östlich vom Jenissei nieder, wo die »jurtenförmigen Kollektivkurgane« auf sie zurückgehen. *Taštyk-Kultur*

Ostgruppe: Zuwanderer

Die alte Bevölkerung konzentrierte sich hingegen westlich vom Jenissei, wo sich auch die äußere Form der Kurgane, nämlich ein Pyramidenstumpf, nicht veränderte. *Westgruppe: Autochthone*

Ebenso gehörten Flachgräber mit Einzelbestattungen, die in der gleichen Zeit angelegt wurden, offenbar zum alteingesessenen Bevölkerungselement. Hier entfaltete sich, wie die Funde von Oglachty zeigen, das alte Ritual zu den seltsamsten Blüten. Man mumifizierte die Toten, gab ihnen Masken mit und legte schließlich auch noch eine fast mannsgroße Puppe mit ins Grab, die vielleicht eine Zeitlang – wie wir auf Grund moderner Parallelen vermuten – von der Witwe als Trauerbehelf umhegt worden war. Immer noch war es üblich, Miniaturen von Waffen und Gebrauchsgegenständen beizugeben. *Grabritual* FIG. 41

Man nimmt sicher mit Recht an, daß die letzte Invasion der Steppenbevölkerung durch die Reichsgründung der Hsiung-nu ausgelöst worden war, eines Volkes, mit dessen archäologischen Denkmälern wir uns noch beschäftigen müssen. Es herrschte während seiner höchsten Machtentfaltung auch über das Minussinskgebiet und setzte hier einen kriegsgefangenen chinesischen General als Statthalter ein. Die erbittertsten Kämpfe der Hsiung-nu richteten sich ja gegen China, das mehrfach zu hohen Tributzahlungen gezwungen wurde.

Herrschaft der Hsiung-nu

So ist es kein Wunder, daß Seidenstoffe chinesischer Herkunft auch im Minussinskgebiet auftauchten. Reste von Zeremonialschirmen verraten, daß man sich neuer Würdezeichen bediente.

Wie uns eine allmähliche Angleichung des Bestattungsrituals verrät, verschmolzen Zuwanderer und Altbevölkerung zu einer neuen ethnischen Einheit. In ihrer Kunst spielte die Tierdarstellung noch lange eine erhebliche Rolle, sogar unter Beibehaltung einzelner Motive, etwa des Greifenkopfs oder des stehenden Ebers.

Tierbilder als Kultbehelfe

Gerade diese Darstellungsgruppe ist jedoch jeder Realistik entkleidet. Meist finden wir Silhouetten ohne jeden ästhetischen Anspruch. Wesentlicher noch ist der Wandel der Funktion. Es handelt sich nach der vernünftigen Deutung Kyzlasovs um Amulette. So erklärt man nämlich einen aus einem Astragalus hergestellten Greifenkopf oder zwei gekreuzte Pferdeköpfchen, die sehr häufig vorkommen. Einen höchst seltsamen kleinen Bronzevogel, nämlich eine Gans mit beweglichem Unterkiefer, hat man als Zauberbehelf aufgefaßt. Sicher ist jedenfalls, daß man das Tierbild hier nicht mehr ornamental verwendet hat. Es war Sinnträger und Kultbehelf.

Fig. 41 – Totenmasken der frühen Taštyk-Zeit. Die linke, aus Ujbat, zeigt deutlich den mongoliden Typ der zentralasiatischen Eindringlinge. Deutlich sind Bemalungsspuren erkennbar, vielleicht Tätowierung wiedergebend. Umzeichnungen nach Kiselev 1949. Vgl. S. 77

Auf der anderen Seite kannte die Taštyk-Kultur eine realistische Großplastik. Die Totenmasken der Spätzeit wurden durch eine Verlängerung bis auf die Brust zu regelrechten Büsten ausgestaltet. Es muß auch ganze Menschenfiguren gegeben haben, von denen allerdings nur mehr die in Holz ausgeführten Teile, nämlich Kopf und Hände, erhalten geblieben sind.

Vor allem aber gab es ausgezeichnet proportionierte Statuen von Tieren: Pferden oder auch einem Renpärchen. Sie wurden offenbar als Reittiere, stellvertretend, also wieder in kultischer Funktion, ins Grab gelegt. Es liegt außerordentlich nahe, an einen Zusammenhang mit den Grabplastiken zu denken, die im China der Han-Zeit zur regulären Totenausstattung der Vornehmen gehörten.

Einen religiösen Hintergrund vermutet man bei Steinstatuen liegender Widder. Von ihnen wieder kennt man Nachbildungen in Form kleiner Bronzen. Andere ähnlich ausgeführte Güsse zeigen liegende Rehe.

Aber diese interessante Kunst kann man wohl nicht mehr unter den Begriff eines Tierstils einordnen. Jener scheint hier endgültig und unter Verzicht auf künstlerische Qualität im Magischen zu enden.

VIII. SKYTHENZEITLICHE GRÄBER IM ALTAI

Südwestlich vom Minussinskkessel, im Herzen Zentralasiens, liegt das
Altai-Gebirge, dessen höchster Gipfel, die Belucha, bis zur majestä-
tischen Höhe von 4503 Metern aufragt. In seinem sowjetischen Teil –
die zu China und zur Mongolischen Volksrepublik gehörenden sind
archäologisch so gut wie unerforscht – wurden im Laufe der letzten
Jahrzehnte Funde gemacht, die heute den Stolz der Eremitage bilden,
die wichtigste neue Quelle für das Kulturgepräge der frühen Nomaden.
Wieso diese Schlüsselposition ausgerechnet einem Gebirgsraum zu-
kommen kann, wird leichter verständlich, wenn wir rekapitulieren,
was auch aus späteren Jahrhunderten über die Besiedlungsmöglichkeiten bekannt ist.

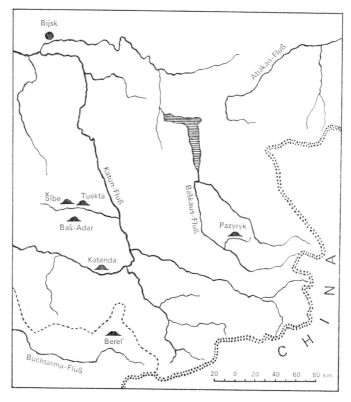

Lageskizze der wichtigsten Nekropolen im Altai. (Nach Rudenko 1960)

Sicherlich hat der Mensch als Jäger seit jeher die überaus reichen Wildbestände genutzt – davon erzählen schon endpaläolithische Stationen. Der Ackerbau, der in diesem Raum seit dem frühen zweiten Jahrtausend v.Chr. einsetzt, blieb jedoch auf die offenen Landschaften am Nordfuß des Gebirges beschränkt. Weit reichere Möglichkeiten bieten sich der Viehzucht. Man kann die Hochweiden im Inneren des Gebirges von den Agrarsiedlungen des Vorlands aus als Almen nutzen, oder es kann sich unter Verzicht auf Ackerbau eine Art von vertikalem Nomadismus entwickeln, so wie heute bei den Kirgisen des Tienschan.

Besiedlungsmöglichkeiten

Wichtig ist, daß die Viehzüchter ihre Hochweiden auf jeden Fall nur im Sommer aufsuchen konnten. Wenn man trotzdem hier bestattete – und wir finden gerade die reichsten Gräber in dieser Zone –, so muß wohl die Vorstellung mitspielen, hier sei die eigentliche Heimat und jedenfalls die letzte Zuflucht des Volkes. Tatsächlich ist von Türken und Mongolen bekannt, daß die Heiligtümer ihrer Sippenverbände in den Bergen lagen, auf den Hochweiden, auf denen sie sich nach Katastrophen – etwa den Überfällen stärkerer Nachbarn – wieder zusammenfinden konnten.

Gehen wir nun zur Forschungsgeschichte über, so stellen wir zunächst einmal fest, daß hier offenbar die »Burgrovišči«, die professionellen Raubgräber der frühen russischen Kolonialzeit, nicht auf ihre Rechnung kamen. Obgleich die meist deutschen Mitglieder der kaiserlichen Sibirienexpeditionen hier viele archäologische Denkmäler entdeckten, stammt offenbar die Masse der Goldfunde entweder aus den westlich angrenzenden Steppen oder aber aus dem Minussinskgebiet.

Archäologische Erforschung

Das lag nicht nur an der Unzugänglichkeit. Die traurige Erklärung der an sich erfreulichen Tatsache ist vielmehr erst jetzt durchschaut worden: die größten und reichsten Kurgane wurden noch im Altertum selbst ausgeraubt!

Beraubung schon im Altertum

Vermutlich lag das daran, daß es im Altai eine »pluralistische« Gesellschaft gab – um den modernen soziologischen Terminus zu gebrauchen. Unter der Herrschaft von »Vertikalnomaden« lebten Ackerbauer am Gebirgsfuß und vermutlich auch Jäger oder schon Renzüchter im Gebirge. Diese Gruppen hielt keinerlei Pietät davon zurück, bei jeder Schwächung oder temporären Abwesenheit ihrer nomadischen Herren soviel Gräber auszuplündern, wie nur irgend möglich.

Deshalb besteht auch die herrliche Sammlung, die der Ingenieur Florov, dem der gesamte Bergbau des Altais unterstand, in den Jahren 1793 bis 1830 anlegte, fast ausschließlich aus Holz-, Knochen- und Bronze-

Sammlung Florov

FIG. 42

Fig. 42 – Kopf eines Tigers. Teil der Pferdeschirrung. Holz, 7,5 cm Durchmesser. Slg. Florov, Eremitage, Leningrad.

gegenständen. Sie gelangten auf Umwegen in die staatlichen Sammlungen, die besten Stücke in die Eremitage.

Radloffs Grabungen Grabungen mit wissenschaftlichen Zielen ließ im Jahre 1856 der junge Wilhelm Radloff durchführen, der als Lehrer in Barnaul tätig war. Dieser aus Berlin stammende Gelehrte, der sich im Laufe vieler Jahrzehnte zum Nestor der russischen Turkologie entwickeln sollte, öffnete in den Hochtälern des Südaltai zwei riesige Kurgane. Unter den Aufschüttungen stieß er auf Schächte, die einst zweifellos reiche, aber eben längst ausgeraubte Bestattungen enthielten. Wie in den skythischen Gräbern Südrußlands hatte man den Toten zahlreiche Pferde mitgegeben, teilweise geschirrt. Es waren seltsamerweise eine Reihe von Gegenständen aus vergänglichem Material erhalten geblieben. Im Katanda-Kurgan lagen die Skelette noch auf hölzernen Bahren, die frei in der intakten, aus Baumstämmen zusammengefügten Grabkammer standen. Die Kleidungsstücke kann man noch heute im Historischen Museum in Moskau bewundern. Merkwürdig genug lagen sie zu einem Bündel zusammengerollt über den mächtigen Pfosten der Zimmerung versteckt – offenbar hatte ein Grabräuber einen Teil der Beute verborgen und war an der geplanten Nachlese verhindert worden.

Natürlich war sich Radloff über die ganze Tragweite seiner Funde nicht im klaren. Er übersah weder ihre kulturgeschichtliche Einordnung – sie enthielten interessante Tierstilobjekte –, noch den Mechanismus der Erhaltungsbedingungen. Die Folge war, daß sich keine systematischen Grabungen anschlossen.

In den nächsten Jahrzehnten begnügte man sich vielmehr mit dem Sammeln von Oberflächenfunden, die in den lokalen Museen landeten, und mit der Besichtigung zahlreicher Tagbaue. Nur gelegentlich griff ein Liebhaber zum Spaten.

Knapp vor dem Ersten Weltkrieg dehnt der uns aus dem Minussinsk-gebiet bekannte Adrianov nach verschiedenen Erkundungsvorstößen das Feld seines Forscherdranges bis in die südlichen Täler des Hochaltai aus. Er öffnete meist kleinere, nicht frostkonservierte, aber säuberlich ausgeraubte Gräber. Ganz unerwartet stieß er dann in einem Steinkreis auf einen kleinen Hort aus Bronzen und Goldblechen mit Tierstildarstellungen. Möglicherweise hatte auch hier ein Räuber einen Teil seiner Beute versteckt. *Adrianov*

In der sowjetischen Periode änderte sich dann das Bild erstaunlich rasch. Kaum waren die Bandenkämpfe und gegenseitigen Erschießungen vorbei, da wurde auch schon vom Leningrader Staatlichen Museum für Ethnographie eine »Altaische Expedition« gegründet, die 1924 ihre Tätigkeit aufnahm. Ihr Leiter war S. I. Rudenko, der sich bereits durch Grabungen im Sarmatengebiet und durch folkloristische Studien unter den Baschkiren seine Sporen verdient hatte. Er zeichnete sich durch Hingabe und Organisationstalent aus. *Altaische Expedition 1924*

Sein fähigster Mitarbeiter, ihm vielleicht noch durch Originalität und kühlen Blick überlegen, war M. P. Grjaznov. Die fast unvermeidliche Folge war, daß es zwischen den beiden Differenzen gab, die offenbar bis zum heutigen Tag weiterwirken, obwohl doch inzwischen jeder von ihnen auf ein Ehrfurcht gebietendes Lebenswerk zurückblicken kann. Noch vor kurzem hat Rudenko den Begleittext Grjaznovs zu einem Tafelband mit erfrischender, durch keinerlei Altersweisheit gebrochener Grobheit besprochen, Grjaznov mit jugendlichem Temperament reagiert. Daß die beiden Gelehrten bei dieser Lage der Dinge ständig abweichende Datierungen produzieren, ist eine zwar für den Studierenden im Augenblick verwirrende, aber vermutlich durchaus fruchtbare Konsequenz.

Dabei erlitten die beiden Kämpen offenbar ein gemeinsames Schicksal: sie gerieten in die Tschistkas, die Säuberungsaktion der Stalin-Periode. Grjaznov wurde 1936 von Tallgren unter den ihres Amtes Enthobenen gemeldet, Rudenko soll – nach gänzlich unverbürgten Berichten – mehrfache Deportierungen nur deshalb überstanden haben, weil seine Kenntnisse der Vermessungstechnik nicht nur bei archäologischen Ausgrabungen, sondern auch bei den Erdarbeiten der Arbeitslager stets willkommen waren. *Schicksale Rudenkos und Grjaznovs*

Mit dieser Situation dürfte es zusammenhängen, daß die Arbeiten der »Altaischen Expedition« 1929 abgeschlossen wurden, obwohl man damals bereits auf ungeheuerliche Erfolge zurückblicken konnte und jede Aussicht auf Fortsetzung derselben gegeben war. Man hatte zwei Kurgane mit Frostkonservierung geöffnet. Vor allem der I. Pazyryk-Kurgan mit seinen gut erhaltenen Pferdekadavern, die von den Sowjets stolz auf der Weltausstellung 1936 in Paris gezeigt wurden, liefert eine erstklassige Situation.

Zu dem Zeitpunkt war die Initiative aber längst auf andere, vermutlich weniger von dem Geruche einer bürgerlichen Vergangenheit umwitterte Forscher übergegangen. Die meisten von ihnen beschäftigten sich, schon nach Maßgabe der sehr sparsam bemessenen Mittel, mit kleineren Kurganen und Siedlungsresten im Vorland (Sergeev, Markov, Černikov). Das war auch notwendig, um den allgemeinen Hintergrund zu klären, vor dem die offenbar für Fürsten angelegten Riesenkurgane stehen.

Altai-Sajan-Expedition unter Kiselev

Nur die Altai-Sajan-Expedition unter Kiselev, der gewissermaßen das Erbe Rudenkos antrat, hatte noch die Möglichkeit, sich auch an umfangreichere Objekte heranzuwagen, allerdings ohne je auf die ersehnte Eislinse zu stoßen. Dafür fand man eine von den Plünderern übersehene, ungestörte Frauenbeisetzung.

Knapp vor dem Zweiten Weltkrieg schlossen sich die Eremitage und das Archäologische Institut der Akademie der Wissenschaften zu einer Aktion zusammen, in deren Dienst der bedeutende Forscher Sosnovskij stand. 1939 erscheint Grjaznov wieder mit einer überaus erfolgreichen Grabung.

Rudenkos Wiederkehr, seine Grabungen

Nach dem Zweiten Weltkrieg standen anscheinend zum ersten Male wirklich großzügige Mittel zur Verfügung. Seltsamerweise erhielt weder Kiselev, der allerdings an einem Übersichtswerk über die gesamte Archäologie Südsibiriens arbeitete, noch Grjaznov, dessen Übersichtswerk über den Altai 1941 den Kriegsereignissen zum Opfer gefallen war, sondern der aus der Versenkung auftauchende Rudenko die einzigartige Chance, die Grabungen an der Pazyryk-Gruppe fortzusetzen. Schon der II. Pazyryk-Kurgan stellte alles bisherige in den Schatten, er wurde nur vom V. Kurgan derselben Gruppe noch einmal erreicht. Rudenko veröffentlichte laufend interessante Berichte über seine Tätigkeit, so zum Beispiel über die Ergebnisse, die im II. Kurgan während eines Sommers erzielt werden konnten. In der kurzen Frist hatte man die Eislinse nur teilweise auftauen können, der Rest wartete noch auf die Behandlung mit heißem Wasser. Ausgerechnet dieser

Zwischenbericht hat die stärkste Popularität erlangt, er, und nicht die Gesamtdarstellung, wurde ins Deutsche übersetzt.

Nach Abschluß der Pazyrykgrabungen wandte sich Rudenko trotz gelegentlicher kritischer Äußerungen seiner Kollegen, vom Strom des Erfolgs getragen, ähnlichen Nekropolen mit gleichen Erhaltungsbedingungen zu. Noch einmal bewährte sich sein Entdeckerglück an Tuékta und Bašadar. Endlich kamen auch moderne Untersuchungsverfahren zur Anwendung; Radiokarbon- und Baumringmethode lieferten Unterlagen zur absoluten, bzw. relativen Datierung. *Moderne Methoden*

Wenn Grjaznov in der gleichen Zeit auch an äußerem Erfolg zurückstehen mußte, so kompensierte er das durch die Aufstellung von Hypothesen, die fast allgemein akzeptiert wurden – nur nicht von Rudenko – und durch Grabungen im Voraltai, die zwar nur ein sehr durchschnittliches Material, aber dafür eine solide Schichtenfolge lieferten. Seit einiger Zeit laufende Grabungen Černikovs westlich des Altais sollen an anderer Stelle berücksichtigt werden. Ausreichend publizieren konnte dieser Forscher allerdings nur jenes Material, das einer älteren Periode – noch vor dem Auftreten der frühen Nomaden – zugehörte. Ebenso erfreulich ist, daß man alte, halbvergessene Grabungen (etwa die Sergeevs) vorlegt. *Grabungen im Vorland*

Die geringe Einigkeit, die wir hinsichtlich der Datierung und allgemeinen Einschätzung gerade der wichtigsten Denkmäler des Altais antreffen werden, läßt eine möglichst vorsichtige Form der Annäherung an diese ungelösten Probleme geraten erscheinen. Wir besprechen deshalb zunächst die Domäne Grjaznovs, die Waldsteppe am Ob, das sogenannte Altai-Vorland. Er hat die Funde, unter denen zum ersten Male Denkmäler des Tierstils auftauchten, auf Grund eigener und älterer Grabungen, die er mehr oder minder der Vergessenheit entriß, unter dem Begriff einer Bol'šaja-Rečka-Kultur zusammengefaßt. Diese datiert er ins 7. Jahrhundert v. Chr. bis 1. Jahrhundert n. Chr. Ihre Träger waren sicher keine Nomaden. Es gibt feste Siedlungen, an denen Grjaznov wichtige stratigraphische Beobachtungen anstellen konnte. Feldbau und Viehzucht bildeten die wirtschaftliche Basis, von Fischfang und Jagd ergänzt. Im Gegensatz zu der vorausgehenden Phase finden sich in den Gräbern auch mongolide Schädel, was durch eine Zuwanderung aus den benachbarten Wäldern erklärt wird. *Bol'šaja-Rečka-Kultur (7.Jh. v.Chr. bis 1.Jh. n.Chr.)*

Schon die erste Phase der Bol'šaja-Rečka-Kultur enthält Anzeichen für eine intensive Verwendung des Pferdes. Es gibt Trensenknebel, die auf weite Beziehungen, bis nach Osteuropa, hindeuten. Man kannte hier noch kein Eisen, die Formen der Bronzen erinnern an jene des FIG. 43

FIG. 44, 45

Fig. 43 – Trensenknebel aus Bronze westlicher Form. Aus den Ausgrabungen Grjaznovs beim Dorf Bol'šaja Rečka am Ob. Vgl. S. 85

Fig. 44 – Bronzemesser gleicher Provenienz wie Fig. 43. Vgl. S. 85

Fig. 45 – Bronzeobjekt, wohl zum Schmuck eines Gürtels gehörend und in der Form an Ordosbronzen erinnernd. Herkunft wie Fig. 43. Vgl. S. 85

Minussinskgebiets. Manche Typen finden sich interessanterweise unter den Ordosbronzen wieder. Unbestreitbar bestand ein intensiver Kontakt mit den Bewohnern der benachbarten Steppen.

Übergang zum Reiterkriegertum

Als negative Folge eben dieses Kontakts erklärt Grjaznov den ungewöhnlich armseligen Charakter der Funde, die der zweiten, der Biisker Phase – vom 5. bis 3. Jahrhundert v. Chr. – angehören. Die seßhaften Bewohner der Waldsteppe seien von ihren nomadischen Nachbarn ständig überfallen und ausgeplündert worden. Tatsächlich kennt man Siedlungen mit Spuren gewaltsamer Zerstörung: in dem Gelenkskopf eines menschlichen Skeletts steckte eine bronzene Pfeilspitze vom Steppentyp. Die Werkstatt eines Bronzegießers enthielt die Trümmer zahlreicher Gußformen aus Ton. Erstmalig tritt an einzelnen Objekten Tierstildekor auf, z. B. an einem Trensenknebel.

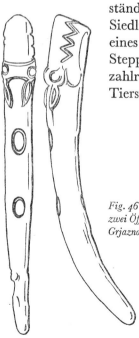

Fig. 46 – Trensenknebel späterer Form (enthält nur noch zwei Öffnungen für den Backenriemen). Aus den Grabungen Grjaznovs am Ob. (Biisker Phase)

Fig. 47 – Gelenkskopf eines menschlichen Knochens, in dem eine Pfeilspitze skythischer Form steckt. Wird von Grjaznov als Zeichen für Kämpfe zwischen den Bewohnern der Waldsteppe und den Nomaden des Südens aufgefaßt.

Fig. 48 – Bronzemesser von der Buchtarma (Altai-Gebiet). Der Knauf zeigt Kopf und Vorderpranken eines Bären (?). Halbe Größe des Originals. Aus den Kurganen bei Solonečnaja Belka, Grabung Adrianovs. Vgl. unten

Erst in der letzten, der Berezovsker Phase (2.Jahrhundert v.Chr. bis 1.Jahrhundert n.Chr.) setzt sich das Eisen endgültig durch. Man beobachtet eine leichte wirtschaftliche Erholung. Grjaznov erklärt hierzu, es sei nun ein festes Tributverhältnis zu den Nomaden hergestellt worden. Die großen, auch zur Unterbringung des Viehs geeigneten Erdhäuser weichen oberirdischen Behausungen.

Wenn wir uns nun dem Hochaltai zuwenden, so finden wir auch hier zunächst ein durchaus noch überschaubares Material, das von den Fachleuten relativ einmütig beurteilt wird. Jene Gräber, in denen bereits Pferdeschirrungen vorkommen, die aber noch kein Eisen enthalten, faßt man zu der Majemir-Phase zusammen, die man analog dem ersten Stadium der Bol'šaja-Rečka-Kultur ins 7.–6.Jahrhundert v.Chr. datiert. Sie enthält aber im Gegensatz zum Vorland bereits Objekte, die man zweifelsfrei dem Tierstil zurechnen kann. Da ja nur ein Rest des ursprünglichen Grabinventars den Raubgräbern entgangen ist, so müssen wir uns mit einigen »Rolltieren« aus Goldblech begnügen, die einst Holzschnitzereien bedeckten, einem Bronzemesser mit Tierkopfknauf und einem Aufnähblech in Form eines Vogelkopfes. Deshalb ist man über jeden Streufund froh, den man als Ergänzung heranziehen kann. Sicher gehört ein runder Bronzespiegel mit erhabe-

Hochaltai

Majemir-Phase

Karger Tierstil

FIG. 48
FIG. 49
FIG. 50

Fig. 49 – Schmuckkopf aus Bronze, mit Goldfolie überzogen. Aus dem sogenannten Schatz der Majemirischen Steppe (Altai). Ungefähr halbe Größe des Originals. Grabung Adrianovs. Vgl. oben

Fig. 50 – Rückseite eines Bronzespiegels archaischer Form. Zufallsfund aus dem Altai. Ungefähr halbe Größe des Originals. Eremitage, Leningrad. Vgl. oben

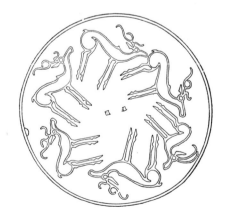

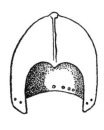

Fig. 51 – Gegossener Bronzehelm frühskythischer Form aus dem Altai. Es handelt sich wohl um eine Gestaltung nach einem Vorbild in anderem Material (Leder). Ähnliche glockenartige Helme wurden auch in China verwendet. Zufallsfund. Eremitage, Leningrad.

nem Rand in diese Phase, dessen Rückseite sechs prachtvoll stilisierte Hirsche zeigt. Bemerkenswert ist auch ein gegossener Bronzehelm. Er gehört zu einem Typ, der vielleicht im Kubangebiet beheimatet war, aber Beziehungen bis nach Ostasien aufweist. Das Fehlen gleichzeitiger fester Siedlungen ist natürlich als Indiz für eine beweglichere Lebensweise gewertet worden.

Pazyryk-Phase   Ein wenig später, sofort nach dem Auftreten des Eisens, setzen die frostkonservierten Kurgane ein. Allein die ältere Gruppe von ihnen – sie mag in groben Zügen der Biisker Phase im Vorland entsprechen – besteht aus acht gewaltigen, gut untersuchten Hügelgräbern, um die sich zahlreiche mittlere und kleine scharen. Es ist unmöglich, das Material in seiner Gesamtheit vorzuführen.

Um aber nicht durch die Schematik, die jeder Übersicht anhaftet, und vorzeitige Analyse das Erlebnis des Wunders zu zerstören, das die Ausgräber überwältigte und das noch heute den Besucher der Eremitage berührt, so soll wenigstens ein Kurgan mit der ganzen verwirrenden Fülle seines Inhalts nun ausgebreitet werden.

II. Pazyryk-Kurgan   Der zweite Kurgan von Pazyryk gehört zu einer Nekropole, die fünf Großkurgane und zahlreiche kleinere in zwei parallelen Ketten angeordnet enthält. Er liegt in ca. 1500 Meter Höhe im Ostaltai in dem früheren Bett eines Gletschers. Geöffnet wurde er, wie erwähnt, von Rudenko im Sommer 1947 und 1948.

Grabanlage   Den Hügel, 36 Meter im Durchmesser und fast 4 Meter hoch, deckt eine Steinkappe. Eine kraterförmige Vertiefung im Zentrum ist durch die Tätigkeit der Raubgräber entstanden. Eine Steinreihe zieht sich von ihr in gerader Richtung nach Osten. Die Aufschüttung unter der Kappe ist aus Lehm und Steinen gemischt. Man stieß darin auf Holzschaufeln und hölzerne Keile, also Baumaterial, das man beim Zuschütten in die Grube geworfen hatte, auch auf ein massives Scheibenrad aus Holz von dreißig Zentimeter Durchmesser, das vielleicht bei der Überführung des Sarges gebraucht worden war.

Darunter öffnete sich ein Schacht von 7,1 × 7,8 Meter Weite und 4 Meter Tiefe. Seinen Boden bedeckte eine Steinschicht, darauf lag Erde, darüber ein Balkenboden. Auf dem stand die Grabkammer in

FIG. 52   Form von zwei ineinander geschachtelten Blockhütten. Der Raum darin maß 3,65 × 4,9 Meter bei 1,5 Meter Höhe. Die Decke der inneren wie der äußeren Kammer war mit Birkenrinde und Strauchwerk belegt, zwischen den Wänden blieben an drei Seiten zwei bis drei Handbreit frei. Ein Stützgerüst aus 35 Zentimeter dicken Stämmen, drei an der Nord-, drei an der Südseite, die durch Querträger verbunden waren, trug die Last von neun Balkenlagen. An der nördlichen Grubenwand hatte man Platz für die beigegebenen Pferde ausgespart, die obersten drei Lagen deckten auch diese.

Die unvermeidlichen Raubgräber freilich hatte diese Panzerung nicht beeindruckt, sie hatten sich senkrecht durch sämtliche Balkenlagen bis in die Kammer hinunter durchgehackt.

Die Pferdebestattung steckte im Eis, dürfte aber, da sie gleichsam auf einer höheren Stufe lag, wiederholt aufgetaut gewesen sein, daher waren die Kadaver stark verwest und von den Balkenschichten zerdrückt. Man konnte jedoch feststellen, daß alle sieben Tiere, die in einer Reihe mit dem Kopf nach Osten auf der rechten oder linken Seite hintereinander lagen, durch den Schlag einer Streitaxt von rhombischem Querschnitt in die Stirn getötet worden waren. Nach dem erhalten gebliebenen Haar waren sie alle von dunkler Farbe, die Mähnen waren gestutzt, die Schwänze teilweise geflochten und kunstvoll eingedreht.

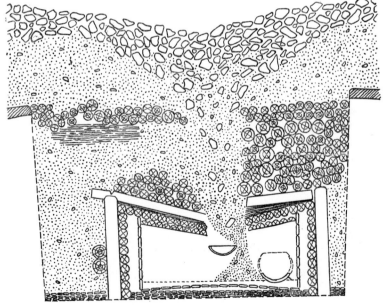

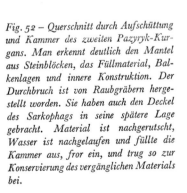

Fig. 52 – Querschnitt durch Aufschüttung und Kammer des zweiten Pazyryk-Kurgans. Man erkennt deutlich den Mantel aus Steinblöcken, das Füllmaterial, Balkenlagen und innere Konstruktion. Der Durchbruch ist von Raubgräbern hergestellt worden. Sie haben auch den Deckel des Sarkophags in seine spätere Lage gebracht. Material ist nachgerutscht, Wasser ist nachgelaufen und füllte die Kammer aus, fror ein, und trug so zur Konservierung des vergänglichen Materials bei.

Vier Pferde hatten Trensenknebel aus Holz, schön geschnitzt, die Enden zu Tierköpfen ausgestaltet – Raubkatze, Gans, Schaf und Steinbock – und mit Zinn- und Goldfolien überzogen. Ein Pferd mit schlichten Hornpsalien trug dafür eine prachtvolle Stirnplatte aus Hirschhorn. Sie zeigt zwei heraldisch angeordnete Gänse im Rachen eines gehörnten, langohrigen Raubtiers. Jede Hälfte für sich bietet eine geschlossene Komposition: der halbe Raubtierkopf wirkt wie eine Seitenansicht. Das Stück zeigt Spuren von gelber und roter Bemalung.

ABB. SEITE 91 Knopfförmige Hirschhornplatten sind mit stilisierten Lotosblüten geschmückt und ebenfalls rot und gelb bemalt, sie saßen offenbar auf den Riemenkreuzungen dieser Garnitur.

Zu dem holzgeschnitzten Geschirr, dessen Psalien in Raubtierköpfen endeten, gehörten kleine Platten, auf denen Plastiken katzenartiger Raubtiere liegen, ebenfalls mit Blattgold überzogen.

FIG. 57 Zwei der Pferde trugen einen maskenartigen Kopfschmuck aus Filz und Leder, leider sehr schlecht erhalten. Einer stellte vermutlich einen Steinbock dar, der von einem Vogel angefallen wird.

Die Sättel bestanden aus Filzdecken und Lederpolstern, sie waren durch Holzbögen versteift. Vielfarbige Filzapplikationen, wohl nur für den Trauerzug angefertigt, prangten auf den Satteldecken. Wir sehen einen Greif, einen Elch oder auch eine Tierkampfszene: einen Leoparden, der einen Elch angreift. Selbst die Sattelbögen hatte man mit Leder beklebt und mit Zinn- und Goldfolie überzogen. Nur einmal treffen wir auf eine Ergänzung durch Brust- und Schwanzriemen. Rückwärts hingen mit Holzkugeln beschwerte Lederstreifen herab, in die Haarquasten eingesetzt waren.

Fig. 53–56 – Trensenknebel bzw. Trensenfragmente aus dem zweiten Pazyryk-Kurgan, repräsentativ für die vier besonders prunkvollen Schirrungen. Holz mit Metallfolie überzogen. Die Darstellungen vereinigen Realistik mit kühner Stilisierung.

Stirnplatte und Besatzstücke eines Pferdegeschirrs aus dem II. Pazyryk-Kurgan. *Horn, geschnitzt und bemalt. Etwas verkleinert. Eremitage, Leningrad. Vgl. S. 90*

Fig. 58 – Ende eines Peitschenstiels, eine der seltenen Pferdedarstellungen von außergewöhnlicher Ausdruckskraft.

FIG. 58

Bei den Pferden lagen kleine Schilde aus parallelen Stäben, genau so wie sie von den griechischen Meistern der pontischen Städte dargestellt wurden. Eine der Pelztaschen enthielt Käse. Die besonders schöne Schnitzarbeit an einem stark zerstörten Peitschenstiel zeigt ein fliehendes Pferd, das von einer Raubkatze, deren Leib sich spiralig um den Stock windet, überfallen wird.

Die Kammer

In der Grabkammer bedeckte eine etwa zwölf Zentimeter hohe klare Eisschicht den Boden. Sie hatte sich bereits vor der Beraubung allmählich aus Kondenswasser gebildet, inzwischen waren empfindliche Substanzen, wie die Speisebeigaben, bereits verwest. Den ganzen übrigen Raum erfüllte dann gelbes, trübes Wasser, das durch den Räubergang nachgeströmt war. Es fror so plötzlich ein, daß es den weiteren Auflösungsprozeß für immer unterbrach. So haben selbst die Räuber ihren positiven Beitrag zur Konservierung geleistet.

Boden und Wände der Kammer waren bis zur Höhe von 65 Zenti-

Fig. 59 – Schmuckborte mit bunten Filzapplikationen. Die Motive sind eindeutig vorderasiatischer Herkunft.

92

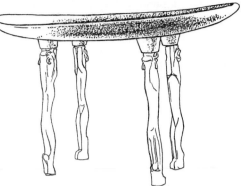

Fig. 60 – Fast in allen Kurganen wurden Tische dieser Art mit schüsselartiger Platte gefunden. Man kann sie durch Herausziehen der Füße »zusammenlegen«, was als Hinweis auf das nomadische Leben der Altai-Bewohner aufgefaßt werden kann. Durchmesser der Platte ca. 60–80 cm, Höhe ca. 30–35 cm.

Fig. 61 – Die Füße solcher Tische, wie Fig. 60 zeigt, sind wieder nach vorderasiatischem Muster als Löwenfiguren ausgestaltet, die eine ungewöhnliche Meisterschaft des Schnitzers verraten.

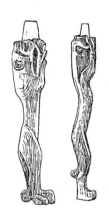

meter mit schwarzem Filz überzogen. Die Schmuckborten aus weißem Filz, über die sich ein Fries aus bunten Lotosblüten zog, gefielen offenbar den Räubern zu gut, sie sind bis auf geringe Reste heruntergerissen. Ebenso erging es den Zierkanten von schmalen »Läufern«.

FIG. 59

An der Südwand stand der Sarkophag, an der Ostwand das Speisegerät und die Musikinstrumente, gegenüber Räuchergefäße mit allem Zubehör, während im Norden, schon außerhalb der Kammer, die Pferde deponiert waren.

Vier kleine Tische mit ovalen, schüsselartig gehöhlten Platten dienten zum Auftragen der Fleischspeisen. Die Räuber hatten die Platten verwendet und schließlich zerstört. Die nur lose eingesteckten Füßchen blieben zumeist in der untersten Eisschicht stecken. Ein Tischchen hatte gedrechselte Beine, zwei weitere ruhten auf gestreckten, überaus eleganten Löwenfiguren. Wieder bemerken wir den Überzug mit Zinn- und Goldfolie, zum Teil auch Bemalung. Unmittelbar daneben

FIG. 60

FIG. 61

Fig. 62 – Handgeschnitztes Holzgefäß auf einem Standring aus Filz. Vgl. S. 94
Fig. 63 – Schöpfer aus Holz mit einem Griff aus Horn in Gestalt eines Tierfußes. Vgl. S. 94
Fig. 64 – Charakteristisch für den Altai der Pazyrykzeit ist diese Vasenform. Sie stammt wohl aus Mittelasien. Vgl. S. 94

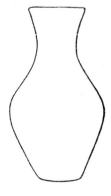

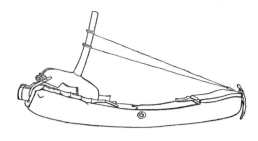

Fig. 65 – Saiteninstrument aus Holz, aus vorhandenen Resten rekonstruiert. Länge ca. 80 cm.

Fig. 66 – Textilmuster aus dem zweiten Pazyryk-Kurgan. Es zeigt die geometrisch-abstrakten Dekorationssysteme, die neben dem Tierstil weiter verwendet werden.

FIG. 64   standen Tongefäße, zwei gleich große und gleich geformte Vasen, einen halben Meter hoch, so wie sie auch in kleineren Kurganen der Pazyrykzeit weit verbreitet sind. Der Bauch der einen war mit zinnüberzogenen Lederapplikationen geschmückt, einem Fries schreitender Hähne, bei der anderen fanden sich Reste von Lotossilhouetten. Zur gleichen Garnitur gehören Holzgefäße, mit seitlich gekrümmter

FIG. 63   Messerklinge geschnitzt. Eines hat das Aussehen eines Schöpfers mit rundem Boden und leicht nach außen gewölbtem Rand. Der geknickte Griff trägt ein Endstück aus Horn, das in einen Pferdefuß ausläuft.

FIG. 62   Das zweite Holzgefäß hat nur eine kurze, senkrechte Griffleiste. Zu diesen Rundbodengefäßen gehörten Standringe aus dickem schwarzem Filz, die mit dünnem Filz von schwarzer oder roter Farbe überzogen und mit Wollfäden vernäht waren. Es fand sich sogar der Rest eines Teppichs mit solchen Filzringen, doch dann stand ausgerechnet ein Flachbodengefäß in einem solchen Untersatz. Ein Eisenmesser mit goldverziertem flachem Griff, das unmittelbar neben diesen Dingen gefunden wurde, gehörte wohl ebenfalls zum Tafelgerät; nicht weit davon lag die zugehörige Holzscheide.

Von den Musikinstrumenten nimmt Rudenko an, sie seien im Kult verwendet worden, aber möglicherweise dienten sie zur Tafelmusik. Eines davon ist eine kleine Trommel aus Hornplatten von sanfter Sanduhrform. Über die Nähte sind Goldlamellen geklebt, die mit einem Schnurornament verziert sind. Dicht daneben lagen zwei Resonanzkörper, die aus massiven Blöcken des gleichen Stammes herausgeschnitten waren. Möglicherweise handelte es sich um ein Doppelinstrument, eine Art Leier. Der Verwendungszweck eines Hammers aus Hirschhorn bleibt unklar, da er für einen Trommelschlägel reichlich massiv gewesen wäre.

Der Sarkophag, sein Inhalt   An der Südwand stand der Sarkophag, ein mächtiger Einbaum von mehr als vier Meter Länge. An den Schmalseiten ist er mit massiven

Fig. 67 – Ledersilhouetten von Rentieren, die den Sarkophag schmückten. Gesamtlänge ca. 80 cm. Vgl. S. 95

Ösen ausgestattet, die vielleicht zum Transport oder zum Hinablassen in die Kammer gedient hatten. Die mit Birkenrinde verkleidete Vorderseite schmückten Lederapplikationen, zwei hintereinander schreitende Rentiere. Der Einbaum war mit einer doppelten Lage schwarzen Filzes ausgekleidet, den Boden bedeckte ein Teppich.

FIG. 67

Die Plünderer hatten den Deckel heruntergerissen und an die Westwand geworfen. Da die Leichen festgefroren waren, mußten die Räuber die Vorderwand zerschlagen, erst dann konnten sie die beiden Toten – wie wir noch hören werden, Mann und Frau – herauszerren. Trotzdem enthielt der Einbaum noch verschiedenes, möglicherweise auch Dinge, die eigentlich gar nicht hineingehörten.

Ein hölzernes »Kissen« mit Lederüberzug hatte wohl als Kopfstütze für einen Toten gedient.

Eine lederne Tasche mit Tragriemen, die oben durch einen Stab versteift war, der in zwei Löwenköpfe auslief, gehörte offenbar zur Aus-

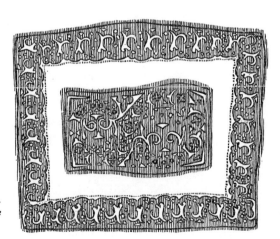

Fig. 68 – Lederbehälter in Form einer »Wandtasche«, d. h. das in der Mitte aufgesetzte Stück ist an der oberen Seite offen. Vgl. S. 96

Fig. 69 – Rückseite eines Spiegels mit Handgriff westlicher Form. Er diente als Anhaltspunkt, um die Pazyrykgruppe in eine spätere sarmatische Phase einzuordnen; eine Auffassung, die von der Forschung heute wieder aufgegeben ist. Vgl. S. 96

Fig. 70 – Die Konstruktion dieses Ohrrings weist Übereinstimmung mit ähnlichen Stücken auf, die sich in dem Schatz Peters d. Gr. befinden. Vgl. S. 98

stattung der Frau – das erklärt den sehr persönlichen Inhalt. Als man sie aufgetaut hatte, kam zuerst ein flaches Lederfutteral zutage. Es bestand aus einem größeren Lederfleck, auf dem ein kleinerer an drei Seiten aufgenäht war. Rand und aufgenähter Teil sind mit Applikationen, einer reichen Komposition aus Lotosornamenten, geschmückt. Das Mittelfeld nimmt eine S-Spirale ein. Die im Tierstil so beliebte Inversion ist hier ins Pflanzliche übertragen. Ähnlich dekoriert ist ein ledernes Fläschchen. Als nächstes Stück erschien ein aparter kleiner Behälter, eine Halbkugel aus Leder, auf einer runden Lederscheibe aufgenäht. Die Öffnung am Scheitelpunkt war mit einem gewölbten Deckel verschlossen. Ein Flammenmuster schmückte die Basis, Dreiblätter den Deckel, der mit Goldlamellen benäht war. Der Inhalt bestand aus Coriander, der im Altertum nicht nur als Gewürz, sondern auch als Heil- und Zaubermittel diente, offenbar ein Import aus dem Süden.

FIG. 69 Natürlich gehörte auch ein Spiegel griechischer Form zur Ausstattung. Er bestand aus zwei miteinander verklammerten Silberplatten, von denen die vordere in einem Griff aus Rinderhorn steckte. Zwischen Mittelbuckel und Randwulst der stark profilierten Rückenplatte war ein Netz feinster Linien eingeritzt.

Bei einer Eisengabel mit divergierenden Spitzen versagte bisher jede Deutung, da der Gegenstand kaum als Eßgerät gedient haben konnte.

FIG. 68 (margin, left of first paragraph)

96

Hirschfigur unbekannter Verwendung. Vielleicht Teil eines Diadems. *Holz, geschnitzt, Geweih aus Leder, früher mit Metallfolie überzogen. Höhe mit Geweih 14 cm. Eremitage, Leningrad. Vgl. S. 98*

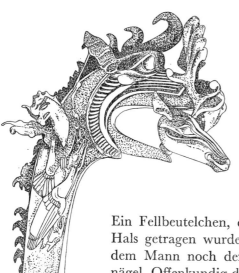

Fig. 71 – Greifenkopf in mythischer Komposition. Möglicherweise handelt es sich um ein Feldzeichen. Höhe ca. 30 cm. Vgl. S. 99

Ein Fellbeutelchen, das ersichtlich an einem Lederstreifen um den Hals getragen wurde, enthielt schwarze Haare, die offenbar weder dem Mann noch der Frau gehörten, sowie abgeschnittene Fingernägel. Offenkundig diente es als Amulett.

Andere Gegenstände auf dem Grunde des Sarges mögen aus einer Tasche herausgefallen sein oder zur Kleidung der Toten gehört haben, so das Fragment eines Hornkamms. Ferner lag dort ein zerbrochener Ohrring, dessen Gegenstück dann in einer Hautfalte am Hals der Frau entdeckt wurde. Beide waren offenbar mit bunten Steinen geschmückt gewesen, auch Perlen aus Knochen und Karneol fand man im Sarge, am Boden der Kammer, ja selbst im Raubgräbergang.

Unter der Kopfstütze lag ein Diadem. Über einem schmalen, mit Leder überzogenen Wollband stolzierte eine ganze Hahnenprozession. Die Tiere sind aus besonders dickem Leder geschnitzt und mit ihren gespaltenen Füßen aufgesteckt. Von dem Band baumeln Streifchen aus Zobelfell herab, die einstmals einen Schmuckbesatz trugen. Außerdem verbargen sich unter der Kopfstütze noch einige holzgeschnitzte Figuren, alle mit Zinn- oder Goldfolie überzogen. Wieder waren Flügel, Hörner oder Ohren aus Leder. Ein kleiner Hirsch (oder Schaufelelch)? mit phantastisch ausladendem Geweih steht auf einer kleinen gerillten Kugel. Sie hat einen Zapfen, muß also irgendwo eingesteckt gewesen sein. Nach den Lederresten zu schließen, waren offenbar sechs ähnliche Hirschfiguren vorhanden gewesen. Dicht dabei lagen noch zwei Greife mit kurzen Flügeln und mächtigen Stirnkämmen, sowie das mit Gold überzogene Köpfchen eines gehörnten Löwengreifen. Rudenko vermutete, daß alle diese Tiere zu einem Diadem zusammengehörten, es handelt sich aber um Fragmente eines Halsreifens.

Eine andere eigenartige Skulptur unbekannter Verwendung fand sich

FIG. 70

ABB. SEITE 97

FIG. 72

ebenfalls im Sarkophag: der Kopf eines Greifen, der in seinem geöffneten Maul einen Hirschkopf vor sich herträgt. Die Seitenflächen
der Plastik sind mit Reliefs bedeckt. Sie zeigen wiederum einen Greifen,
der eine Gans in den Klauen hält. Die Köpfe dieser Greifenfiguren
ragen aus der Fläche heraus. Sie sind separat geschnitzt und eingesteckt. Ohren und Kamm sind aus starkem Leder geschnitten, das
gesamte Werk war einst mit Blattgold überzogen.

FIG. 71

Die gleiche Komposition begegnet uns noch einmal außerhalb des
Sarkophags, allerdings in ganz anderer Ausführung. Ein Lederriemen
läßt die Vermutung aufkommen, das Bild sei irgendwo angebunden
gewesen. Hier verwandeln sich die Enden des Hirschgeweihs in Vogelköpfe. Ohne Zweifel besaß die merkwürdige Motivkombination
(Hirschkopf im Maule des Greifen) einen religiösen oder heraldischen
Sinn.

Die Toten selbst fand man am Boden, auf der primären Eisschicht:
einen Mann und eine Frau, die die Räuber zerhackt und zerstückelt
hatten, um leichter den kostbaren Schmuck abziehen zu können. Darum war auch kein einziges Kleidungsstück heil geblieben. Das größte
erhaltene Stück ist ein langer Mantel aus Eichhörnchenfellen mit der
Haarseite nach innen. Er hat außerordentlich lange und so enge
Ärmel, daß es unmöglich wäre, die Arme hindurchzustecken. Offenkundig wurde er wie der medisch-persische Kandys als Umhang getragen. Außen überziehen ihn parallele Nähte aus starken Sehnen, was
ihm einerseits große Festigkeit, andererseits eine eigenartige Musterung
verleiht. Lederapplikationen an prominenten Stellen geben Hahnen-
kämme wieder, in die goldüberzogene Kupferblättchen eingesetzt sind.
Die Kanten sind mit Pferdefell verbrämt.

Die Toten
und ihre Kleidung

FIG. 73

*Fig. 72 – Rekonstruktion des Halsreifens; die Tierfiguren der Vorderseite aus Holz, mit Metallfolie überzogen. Es handelt
sich um ein besonders schönes Stück, das sich nur mit einigen Reifen des sibirischen Goldschatzes in Leningrad vergleichen läßt.*

Fig. 73 – *Ärmel eines Prunkmantels, dessen Dekor aus verschiedenen Materialien, unter anderem auch Metall, besteht. Tierstilmotive und abstrakte Ornamentik treten nebeneinander auf. Vgl. S. 99*

Ein offenbar als Ergänzung dienender Brustlatz ist aus dem gleichen Material in derselben Technik angefertigt. Den Besatz bilden Zobel- und Otterfell. Hingegen bleibt die Verwendung eines Pelzstreifens unklar, der mit buntem Leder und durchbrochenen Rhomben aus Goldblech geschmückt war. Auch von einem Männerhemd von außerordentlicher Länge und Breite, dessen Ärmel gegen das Handgelenk eng zusammenlaufen, ist die Rede. Reste von mindestens drei verschiedenen Gürteln ließen sich identifizieren. Sie waren aus ziemlich dünnem Leder, aber so dicht mit Sehnenfäden benäht, daß sie wie Stoffgürtel aussahen. Zinnfolie diente als Verstärkung. Der erste war schmucklos. Aufgenähte Lederriemen, mit Gold überzogen, bildeten auf dem zweiten eine prachtvolle geometrische Ranke, wie sie von Minussinskbronzen bekannt ist. Daneben wirkte das Ornament des dritten Gürtels statisch: er war durch Auflagen in Form liegender Rhomben geschmückt, zwischen denen Zinn und Goldblech eingefügt waren. Da, wo Riemen abzweigen, sind rechteckige, aus Silber gegossene Schmuckplatten aufgesetzt, die einen Steinbock mit zurückgewendetem Kopf zeigen, der von einem Löwen überfallen wird. Die Belebung des Tierkörpers durch Punkt- und Bogenmuster sowie das Sparrenornament, das über den Nacken des Löwen läuft, lassen Rudenko an assyrische Darstellungen denken.

FIG. 75

Im Besitz der Frau fanden sich zwei Paare kostbarer Stiefel, aus vielerlei Material kunstvoll aufgebaut. Auch die Sohlen sind verziert. In dem einen Fall handelt es sich um ein kurvilineares, an Pflanzenformen erinnerndes Muster. Weit komplizierter noch ist das zweite Paar. Die Ledersohlen, auch hier flach und ohne Absatz, umgab ein

Fig. 74 – *Sorgfältig übernähter und mit Metallfolie geschmückter Gürtel. Besonders gutes Beispiel für die Verwendung der geometrischen Ranke im frühen Altai.*

Fig. 75 – *Solche Silberplatten verstärkten den Gürtel an der Abzweigungs-stelle der Tragriemen für die Bewaffnung. Das achämenidische Erbe ist hier deutlich erkennbar. Vgl. S. 100*

Fig. 76 – *Dekorationsschema der Fußbekleidung. Man sieht von schräg oben auf den Rist. Tiermotive sind hier mit einer überreichen kurvi-linearen Ornamentik verbunden. Vgl. unten*

doppelter Rahmen in Wollstickerei. Drei Rhomben waren auf die Sohle gestickt, der größte unter dem Ballen, ein kleinerer unter der Ferse und ein ganz kleiner in der Mitte. Die beiden größeren sind noch netzartig untergliedert, in der Mitte eines jeden Feldes saß ein Pyritkristall, insgesamt zweiundvierzig Stück pro Sohle (Pyrit muß als Nebenprodukt im Bergbau gewonnen worden sein). Das Oberleder schmückten Stickereien und Lederapplikationen in kunstvollen Ranken-ornamenten. Über den Rist lief eine Querborte, mit kleinen goldenen Schwimmvögeln besetzt. Noch reicher dekoriert waren die darüber FIG. 76 aufsteigenden, rückwärts geschlitzten Schäfte, auf denen wieder das Lotosmotiv vorherrscht. Hier sind auch kleine Glasperlen als Besatz verwendet. Es ist klar, daß solche prachtvollen Sohlen nur zur Geltung kommen konnten, wenn man mit untergeschlagenen Füßen saß.

Zu jedem Stiefelpaar gehörten Socken aus Filz, einmal in einem Stück, einmal mit eingesetzter Sohle. Die rückwärtige Naht verlief etwas seit-lich von der Ferse, offenbar um Druckstellen zu vermeiden.

Über die Kammer verstreut fanden sich verschiedene Schmuckplätt-chen mit figuralen Darstellungen, von denen man leider nicht weiß, wo sie angebracht waren. Darunter fallen getriebene Kupferbleche mit Goldüberzug auf. Einmal sehen wir zwei heraldisch gegenübergestellte Böcke mit Nackenkämmen, ein anderes Mal in der gleichen Pose zwei

FIG. 77 Adlergreife. Eine kleine Pferdeplastik, die als Anhänger diente, ist in Bronze gegossen und zusätzlich mit dem Meißel bearbeitet. Hingegen war die schöne realistische Darstellung eines Elchs aus Leder. Neben der Sargwand fand man noch einen Streifen dicken Leders, den eine »Hahnenprozession« schmückte. Kleine Plättchen, die Greife in assyrisch anmutender Pose darstellten, waren vermutlich zum Schmuck der Kleidung bestimmt. Andere Fragmente zeigten heraldisch angeordnete Tierkörper.

FIG. 78 Nun zu den Leichen selbst, die durch Mumifizierung und Einfrieren erstaunlich gut erhalten geblieben sind.

Die Frau war ungefähr vierzig Jahre alt, groß und kräftig, mit zierlichen Händen und Füßen, von zweifellos europidem Typ. Das Haar ist abrasiert, vermutlich in Zusammenhang mit der Trepanation. Vielleicht gehört der Zopf, der in einem Futteral steckend in der Kammer gefunden wurde und aus schwarzem, weichem, welligem Haar besteht, zu ihr. Bis auf eine Zahnfistel zeigte sie keinerlei krank-

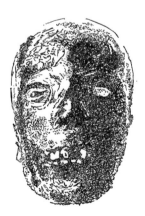

hafte Veränderungen, auch keine Spuren eines gewaltsamen Todes – vielleicht verwendete man vor der Mitbestattung Gift wie im Alten Orient.

»Einschneidend« waren allerdings die im Zusammenhang mit der Mumifizierung vorgenommenen Veränderungen. Die Kopfhaut wurde auf dem rechten Scheitelbein zurückgeklappt, dann der Schädel aufgestemmt, das Gehirn entnommen und der Hohlraum mit irgendeiner pflanzlichen Substanz ausgefüllt. Das Knochenstück setzte man säuberlich wieder ein und vernähte die Kopfhaut mit Pferdehaar. Ähnlich verfuhr man mit dem Bauch: er wurde vom Xiphoid bis zur Symphyse aufgeschnitten, die Eingeweide entfernt und durch pflanzliches Material ersetzt. Darauf nähte man ihn sorgfältig wieder zu.

Merkwürdigerweise zogen sich ähnliche Schnitte vom Gesäß bis zu den Oberschenkeln. Hier hat man Muskelsubstanz entnommen und durch Füllmaterial ersetzt. Das sieht wenig nach einer mumifizierenden Maßnahme aus. Da Herodot (IV, 26) von den zentralasiatischen Issedonen – also mindestens Nachbarn der Altai-Leute – berichtet, sie hätten ihre toten Väter im Rahmen des Leichenmahles verzehrt, so liegt der Verdacht nahe, daß hier Endokannibalismus vorliegt – ein Kommunionsritus während der Bestattungsfeierlichkeit.

Verletzungen am Schädel scheinen von den Beilhieben der Grabräuber herzurühren. Kopf, Hände und Füße waren abgehackt, sogar Finger von der Hand getrennt.

Der Mann war, als er starb, etwa sechzig Jahre alt, äußerst kräftig gebaut, dabei ein typischer Mongolider mit breiten Backenknochen. Leider ist seine Mumie nicht so gut erhalten, abgesehen von den Beschädigungen durch die Grabräuber. Es wurde ihm aber offenbar schon zu Lebzeiten übel mitgespielt. Im rechten Scheitelbein befanden

vertretenen Typ an. Der Mann erinnert an den heutigen Typ der Tungusen; man nimmt an, es handelt sich um einen Eindringling, der zu höchstem Rang aufstieg. Vgl. S. 102

Fig. 79 – Anordnung der Tätowierung am männlichen Körper. Offenbar sind nur jene Körperteile geschmückt, die nicht von Kleidung bedeckt wurden. Vgl. S. 105

Fig. 80 – Besonders gut erhalten ist die Tätowierung der rechten Schulter und des rechten Arms. Die Komposition ist von erstaunlicher Freiheit und Sicherheit. Vgl. S. 105

sich zwei, im linken eine ovale Öffnung, anscheinend von einem Streitpickel herrührend. Man kann nicht sagen, ob er durch diese Schläge die entscheidende Verwundung erhielt, oder ob man ihm damit nur endgültig den Garaus machte. Da sie aus verschiedenen Richtungen kamen, wird eher die erste Deutung zutreffen. Jedenfalls war der Alte im Kampf gefallen.

Anschließend wurde er skalpiert. Man führte einen Schnitt von Ohr zu Ohr und zog die Kopfhaut herunter. Nach der Rückeroberung des Toten mußte man den Schaden für die Beisetzung ausbessern. Man setzte einen falschen Skalp auf die freie Stelle und nähte ihn energisch mit Pferdehaar fest.

Im übrigen wurde der Körper ähnlich behandelt wie der der Frau. Man trepanierte den Schädel und öffnete den Bauch, um die leicht verwesbaren Eingeweide zu ersetzen. An den Schenkeln ist zwar keine Entnahme von Muskelfleisch zu beobachten, wohl aber kleine Einschnitte. Vielleicht dienten sie zum Tränken mit Konservierungsflüssigkeit. Frappierend ist der falsche Bart, der dem Toten über das rasierte Kinn gebunden war. Er bestand aus Pferdehaar, das fransenartig von einem Riemen herunterhing, und war so intensiv geschwärzt worden, daß die Farbe noch in ganzen Klümpchen darin hing.

Tätowierungen Das allermerkwürdigste aber waren die Tätowierungen, die die Extremitäten sowie Teile der Brust und des Rückens bedeckten. Sie müssen

Fig. 82 – Fabeltier, das neben einer besonders eleganten Linienführung die charakteristische Inversion zeigt. Vgl. unten

Fig. 81 – Detail aus Tätowierung Fig. 80

vorgenommen worden sein (unter Verwendung von Ruß), als das Individuum noch wesentlich jünger, jedenfalls aber erheblich schlanker gewesen war. Leider sind große Hautflächen so schlecht erhalten, daß sich die Muster nicht mehr genau erkennen lassen. Die besten Partien – Arme und rechter Unterschenkel – zeigen einen prachtvollen und phantastischen Tierstil. Der Verfertiger mußte ein ungewöhnlicher Künstler gewesen sein. Kühn reihte er Komposition an Komposition. Eine ausgeprägte Vorliebe hegte er für die Inversion.

FIG. 79 BIS 82

An der Westwand der Kammer stieß man (neben einigen Figuren aus Holz und Leder und verschiedenen kleinen Perlen) abermals auf einen Spiegel. Er war aus Bronze und steckte in einem Futteral aus Leopardenfell, mit kleinen Perlchen geschmückt.

Weitaus die wichtigste Entdeckung jedoch bildete ein Bronzekessel mit schmalem Fuß und zwei seitlichen Henkeln, die mit Birkenrinde überzogen waren. Das Gefäß hatte man über einer Schicht von schwarzem Filz bis zum Rand mit großen Steinen angefüllt. Dazwischen fand man, teilweise angekohlt, Samen einer wilden Hanfart. Da Hanf ein starkes Narkotikum enthält, stellte dieser Bronzekessel zweifellos ein Räuchergefäß zur Erzeugung narkotischer Dämpfe dar. Darüber stand ein eigenartiges Gerüst, ein Sechsfuß aus Stäbchen. An einem davon hing eine Lederflasche, die mit Applikationen im Tierstil dekoriert war und in der sich wiederum Hanfsamen (Cannabis sativa L., und

Inhalationsgeräte für Haschisch

FIG. 83

Fig. 83 und 84 – Metallgefäße, die bei der Rauschgift-Inhalation verwendet wurden. Größte Breite ca. 30 cm.

zwar von der Form C. ruderalis Janisch, offenbar eine Wildform) befand. Zu Sechsfuß und Räucherbecken gehörte ein lederner Überwurf, der an den Kanten und im Mittelfeld mit den Darstellungen geflügelter Löwengreifen geschmückt war, die sich auf Elche stürzten; leider war er stark beschädigt. Wir haben es hier mit einem regelrechten Inhalationsapparat zu tun.

In der Ecke, gegen den Sarkophag zu, fand man noch Lederreste mit Spuren eines Lacküberzugs, kupferne Schmuckplättchen in Form einander heraldisch gegenübergestellter Tiere, ein Stück eines Halsreifens mit geschnitzten Greifenköpfen und ein Lederfleckchen, das an den Ecken benäht war (ein Amulett?).

FIG. 84 Ein vierfüßiges Steintischchen, das offenbar zur Darbringung eines Brandopfers diente, entspricht dem »tragbaren Altar« des Sarmatengebietes. Daneben kamen noch verschiedene Kleidungsreste und Fragmente eines schmalen, mit Metallteilen besetzten Ledergürtels zum Vorschein.

In der anderen Ecke fand man einen zweiten Sechsfuß, mit Birkenrinde überzogen und darunter eine weitere bronzene Räucherpfanne quadratischer Form, die auf vier Füßen stand und ebenfalls mit Steinen und Hanfsamen angefüllt war. An einer Seitenwand wies sie einen kurzen Griff auf, an den drei übrigen Aufhängeösen.

Es bedarf wohl kaum einer Erwähnung, daß sich mit solchen Funden die Verheißung des »Tierstils« erstmalig erfüllte. Man hatte immer mit einem verlorengegangenen Kunstgewerbe in vergänglichem Material gerechnet: hier lag es vor. –

I. Pazyryk-Kurgan Der erste Kurgan von Pazyryk, von dem wir schon erzählten, daß er fast zwanzig Jahre früher von Grjaznov und Rudenko ausgegraben wurde, weist einen noch größeren Durchmesser der Aufschüttung und

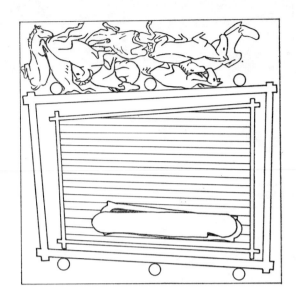

Fig. 85 – Blick in den Schacht des ersten Pazyryk-Kurgans. Deutlich sichtbar sind die ineinandergestellten Kammern mit ihrer Stützkonstruktion und daneben die übereinander geschichteten Pferdekadaver. Der Sarkophag ist bereits geöffnet. Vgl. unten

Fig. 86 – Schmuck der Pferdeschirrung in Palmettenform. Geringfügig verkleinert. I. Pazyryk-Kurgan. Vgl. S. 108

genau die gleiche Planung auf. Es war womöglich noch gründlicher ausgeraubt. So fand man keine Leiche mehr. Der Tote ist wohl zwecks besserer Inspektion an die Oberfläche geholt worden. Überhaupt scheint eine sofortige Sichtung der Beute stattgefunden zu haben: in den Erdmassen, die in den Schacht der Raubgräber nachgerutscht waren, fand man allerhand Fragmente des Inventars, offenbar als wertlos weggeworfen. Der abgebrochene Stiel eines Tüllenbeils scheint aber ein Werkzeug der Räuber, nicht der Kurganerbauer gewesen zu sein.

Der in der Kammer zurückgebliebene Baumsarg ist leidlich erhalten, FIG. 85 er war mit Lederapplikationen geschmückt, die spiegelbildlich gegenübergestellte Hähne zeigen. Ein Rest der Wandbespannung zeigt einen Fries aus Löwenköpfen. Zum allgemeinen Erstaunen erwiesen sich die beigegebenen Pferde als unangetastet, obwohl die Räuber genau über deren Lage unterrichtet waren. Sie waren dabeigewesen, ein Loch in die schützende Wand der Kammer zu hacken, hatten aber den Versuch plötzlich aufgegeben.

Die Pferdekadaver sind zwar durch den Druck der darüberliegenden *Zehn Pferde* Erd- und Steinmassen deformiert, aber recht gut konserviert. Es han- *beigegeben* delte sich um zehn Wallache, die sorgfältige Pflege und eine längere FIG. 87 Züchtungstradition verraten, wenn sie auch keineswegs fremder, mittelasiatischer Herkunft sein müssen, wie man lange behauptete. Auch die

Fig. 87 – Die beiden Tiere, die die Pferdeprozession im Totengeleit anführten, waren besonders reich geschmückt. Die Sättel zeigen empfindliche, nur für den Totenbrauch geschaffene Applikationen. Ein Kopfschmuck ist so ausgestaltet, daß einige Forscher vermuteten, das Pferd sei als Ren verkleidet worden. Daher auch die Bezeichnung des Kopfschmucks als Maske. Man schloß auf eine frühere Rentierzucht der Altaibewohner. Heute verbietet die Fülle der bereits bekannten Kombinationen eine solche Deutung. Rekonstruktion Grjaznovs. Vgl. S. 107

wiederholt zitierte Nachricht, man habe bei der Untersuchung des Mageninhalts der Kadaver eine Fütterung mit Getreide festgestellt, hat sich als Märchen erwiesen. Alle zehn Schirrungen sind erhalten, sie gehören dem bereits aus Pazyryk II bekannten Typ an und werden durch Sättel mit nur niedrigen Bögen ergänzt. Ihr Schmuck, meist Schnitzarbeiten, die mit Goldfolie überzogen sind, umfaßt herrlichste Werke des Tierstils. Einzelne Garnituren (die fünfte und siebente) weisen daneben einen hohen Prozentsatz abstrakter Formen auf, die man als hochstilisierte pflanzliche Motive deutet. Ungewöhnlich ist

FIG. 88, 89

FIG. 86

Tierkampfszenen als Schmuck der Satteldecken. Filzapplikationen, rekonstruiert. Aus dem ersten Pazyryk-Kurgan. Sie stellen den Angriff von Löwengreif (oben) und Adlergreif auf Steinböcke dar. Bei dem oberen Stück ist der vorderasiatische Einfluß besonders spürbar. *(Nach Sunceva) Vgl. S. 110*

Fig. 88 – Behangstück für die Riemen der Pferdeschirrung in Form eines Archarkopfes. Ca. 12 cm hoch. Vgl. S. 108

Fig. 89 – Trensenknebel in Hirschgestalt. Halbe Größe des Originals. Vgl. S. 108

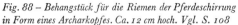

FIG. 90
ABB. SEITE 109

die Verwendung menschlicher Masken als Behang. Die Sättel waren wohl nur für die Beisetzungsfeierlichkeiten mit vielfarbigen Filzapplikationen geschmückt, einige davon zeigen Tierkämpfe, wobei vorderasiatische Vorbilder deutlich zu erkennen sind. Auch hier begegnet uns wieder der sonst im Altai selten abgebildete Hahn. Die beiden besten Pferde tragen Mähnenfutterale sowie die uns bereits bekannten »Masken«, allerdings völlig anderer Konstruktion. Viel Kopfzerbrechen machte den Forschern die Tatsache, daß alle Pferde Ohreinschnitte aufwiesen, so wie sie heute noch in Zentralasien als Eigentumsmarkierungen verwendet werden. Sie sind bei jedem Tier anders, was man zunächst damit erklärte, es handle sich um bei verschiedenen Gelegenheiten erbeutete Tiere.

In dem Füllmaterial des Grabschachts wurden noch ein Rinderjoch und Trümmer eines Wagens gefunden. Offenbar pflegten die Erbauer zerstörtes oder überflüssiges Gerät mit in die Grube zu werfen.

III. Pazyryk-Kurgan

Der dritte Pazyryk-Kurgan weist etwa die gleichen äußeren Maße auf wie der zweite, seine Innenausstattung, nach demselben Prinzip auf-

Fig. 90 – Behangstücke der Pferdeschirrung in Gestalt menschlicher Köpfe. Leicht verkleinert. Während das linke Stück einem westlichen Vorbild entspricht, kann das rechte als Wiedergabe des örtlichen anthropologischen Typs aufgefaßt werden. Vgl. oben

gebaut, war trotz umfangreicher Eislinse stark zerstört. Auch hier
enthielt wieder das Füllmaterial die Reste eines Wagens.
Der Baumsarg war leer, die Räuber hatten den Toten herausgezerrt.
Er trug eine Haube mit Zinnenkrone. Das Haschischritual wird durch
die Reste eines Sechsfußes belegt. Außerdem wurden 24 Pfeilschäfte
gefunden, mit eigenartigen Spiral- und Volutenmustern bemalt. Die
zugehörigen Spitzen fehlen.
Vierzehn Pferde geleiteten diesen Mann ins Grab, fünf davon noch
mit bronzenen Gebissen. Von den Schirrungen ist genügend erhalten,
um wieder die gleiche Mischung von Tierstil und schematischen pflanzlichen Mustern erkennen zu lassen. Fragmente von »Pferdemasken«
passen in das bereits gewohnte Bild, ebenso die eigenartigen Stäbchen-
schilde. Ungewöhnlich ist hingegen, daß man bei den Pferden auch
einen Filzrock entdeckte. Vielleicht die künstlerisch interessantesten
Stücke sind nierenförmige Holzplatten, deren Reliefs auf rotgefärbtem
Grund Elchköpfe zeigen, von frei schwingenden Kurven umgrenzt und
doch prachtvoll in ihren Proportionen erfaßt.

FIG. 91

FIG. 92

Vierzehn Pferde

FIG. 93

Fig. 92 – Ornamente, die zum Schmuck der Pfeilschäfte dienen.
Vgl. oben

Fig. 93 – Schmuckplatte aus Knochen für den Sattelbogen mit der
Darstellung von Elchköpfen. Breite 14 cm. Vgl. oben

Fig. 94 – Wolfsfigur mit typischer Inversion des Hinterteils, als Besatzstück der Pferdeschirrung verwendet. Breite ca. 8 cm. Aus dem IV. Pazyryk-Kurgan. Vgl. unten

Von chinesischem Einfluß zeugt der Fund eines gemusterten Stücks Seide, sowie das Auftreten von Lack.

IV. Pazyryk-Kurgan Der vierte Pazyryk-Kurgan barg unter einer wesentlich kleineren Aufschüttung in normaler Tiefe eine Kammer vom üblichen Format. Sie war durch das Gewicht darüber angehäufter Felsblöcke eingedrückt worden. In ihr standen zwei Baumsärge, der eine enthielt das Skelett eines Mannes, der andere das einer Frau. Im Raum waren Reste des übrigen Inventars verstreut, Bruchstücke von Tischchen, hölzerne Kopfstützen, Stäbchen von zwei Inhaliergeräten. Dieser Kurgan war wieder mit vierzehn Pferden ausgestattet gewesen. Zu deren eisernen

FIG. 94 Gebissen gehörten zum Teil schöngeschnitzte Holzknebel, auch vom Schmuck der Schirrungsriemen ist einiges erhalten geblieben. Eine Peitsche wurde ebenfalls gefunden.

V. Pazyryk-Kurgan Der fünfte Pazyryk-Kurgan wies die übliche Konstruktion auf, er war ausgeraubt, obwohl man zur Füllung des Schachts unter der kraterförmigen Aufschüttung von ungewöhnlicher Höhe (und normalem

Fig. 95 – Rekonstruktionsversuch eines Wandteppichs aus Filz. Dargestellt ist der Kampf zweier Fabelwesen. Die Linienführung weicht von der im Altai üblichen ab. Chinesische und mittelasiatische Vorbilder werden erkennbar. Die Medaillons auf dem Körper der Sphinx lassen sich vielleicht durch thrako-kimmerische Einflüsse erklären. (Nach T. Talbot-Rice.) Vgl. S. 114

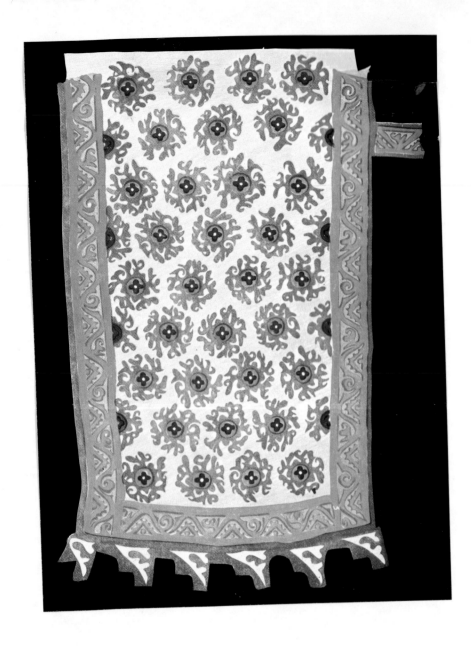

Ornament auf der Schabracke des fünften Pazyryk-Kurgans. Filzapplikation. *Eremitage, Leningrad.*
Vgl. S. 116

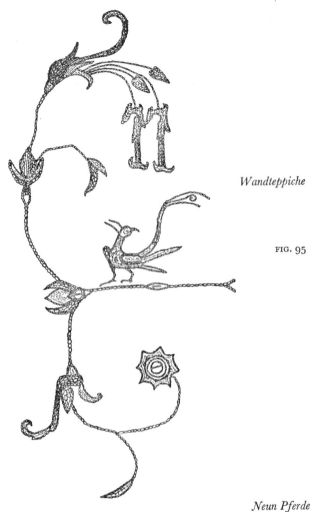

Durchmesser) Felsbrocken von fast drei Tonnen Gewicht verwendet hatte.

In dem Baumsarg ruhten diesmal zwei Tote, ein Mann und eine Frau. Ihre Leichen waren, wenn auch übel zugerichtet, noch vorhanden. Man erkennt deutlich die Mumifizierung. Vom sonstigen Inhalt der Kammer ist vor allem das Fragment eines Wandteppichs aus Filz bemerkenswert. Als man ihn restauriert hatte, zeigte es sich, daß er den Kampf einer geweihgekrönten Sphinx mit einem Phantasievogel darstellt, den man wohl auf chinesische Vorbilder zurückführen muß. Erstaunlich ist ferner eine topfartige Kopfbedeckung aus Holz, an der ein steilaufgerichteter Zopf befestigt ist. Der Rest der Ausstattung (eine kleine, einseitig bespannte Trommel, Reste eines Sechsfußes, mehrere Tischchen) bleibt im Rahmen des beim zweiten Kurgan beobachteten Rituals. An verschiedenen Seiten der Kammer, also ungewöhnlich gelagert, entdeckte man neun Pferde mit eisernen Trensen, für deren Ausstattung man enttäuschend wenig Phantasie aufgewendet hatte. Vier Garnituren sind völlig gleich, ihr einziges Schmuckmotiv ist das Kugelsegment. Auch zwei weitere Schirrungen bevorzugen glatte Linien, nur der Rest wird vom Formengut des Tierstils beherrscht. Ein Pferd wird durch »Maske« und Mähnenfutteral hervorgehoben. Fünf tragen Scha-

Wandteppiche

FIG. 95

Neun Pferde

Fig. 96 – Seidenstickerei. Chinesische Arbeit, die zum Schmuck einer Satteldecke verwendet wurde. Dargestellt sind Fasanen auf einem Blütenzweig. Vgl. S. 116

Rekonstruktion der immer wiederkehrenden Szene auf dem Wandteppich aus dem fünften Pazyryk-Kurgan. Er spielte zweifellos im Totenritual eine wichtige Rolle. Vielleicht gehörte er zum Zelt, in dem die Leiche während der Herrichtung des Kurgans deponiert wurde. *Filz. Format des ganzen Teppichs 4,5 × 6,5 m. Eremitage, Leningrad.*

Fig. 97 – Rekonstruktion eines vierrädrigen Wagens. Vermutlich wurde dieses Gefährt nur für das Trauerzeremoniell gebaut, denn die Vorderachse ist starr; das würde auch erklären, daß das Gefährt zerlegbar konstruiert wurde. Möglicherweise ahmt es ein chinesisches Vorbild nach. Vgl. unten

ABB. SEITE 113

FIG. 96
FIG. 97, 100

bracken aus Filz, eine davon ist mit einem Gewebe vorderasiatischer Herkunft besetzt, ebenso der dazugehörige Brustgurt. Eine andere Satteldecke ist mit weißer Seide überzogen, die eine Stickerei chinesischer Provenienz zeigt. Im Rahmen der Pferdebestattung entdeckte man nun einen zierlichen vierrädrigen Wagen ohne jede Metall-

Fig. 98 – Schnitzarbeiten auf Sarg und Sargdeckel des zweiten Bašadar-Kurgans. Länge des ganzen Sarges 3,10 m. Vgl. S. 119

Fig. 100 – *Schwanendarstellung als Applikation für die Filzbespannung des Wagens Fig. 97 bestimmt. Die Eleganz der Linienführung deutet auf ein chinesisches Vorbild. Vgl. S. 116*

Fig. 99 – Greifendarstellung von einem Medaillon des Teppichs Abb. S. 118

bestandteil, für dessen Aufbau eine Filzbespannung vorgesehen ist, die mit Hochreliefs von Schwänen geschmückt war. Auch Reste von der Kuppel eines Zelts wurden gefunden, ferner ein riesiger Filzteppich. Er ist in zwei Friese gegliedert, die immer wieder die gleiche Szene zeigen, einen Reiter vor einer thronenden Gestalt, die einen stark stilisierten Baum hält. Die Kleidung der dargestellten Personen stimmt nicht mit jener überein, die man aus den in den verschiedenen Kurganen erhaltenen Resten rekonstruieren würde. Außerhalb der Grabkammer lag auch ein Knüpfteppich im Format von etwa 2 × 2 Metern. Er weist 36 Knoten pro Quadratzentimeter auf, man kann also von mittelfeiner Arbeit sprechen. Sein in 24 Quadrate eingeteiltes Mittelfeld wird von zwei umlaufenden Friesen umgeben, die wieder von Schmuckstreifen flankiert werden. Der innere Fries zeigt eine Prozession aus mißverstandenen Damhirschen, der äußere Reiter, aufgesessen oder ihr Pferd neben sich führend. Der innerste und äußerste Schmuckstreifen bauen sich aus zahlreichen Quadraten auf, in die Greife eingeschrieben sind.

Mit dieser kurzen Beschreibung können wir uns hier begnügen, da wir noch bei der analytischen Behandlung des Materials an diesen Punkt zurückkommen werden.

Filzteppich
ABB. SEITE 115

Knüpfteppich
ABB. SEITE 118
FIG. 103

FIG. 99

Ausschnitt aus dem Knüpfteppich des fünften Pazyryk-Kurgans. Die Gestalt des Reiters, der das Pferd führt, erinnert auffällig an Tributbringergestalten der Reliefs in Persepolis. Die völlig unorganische Reitergestalt ist wahrscheinlich eine ungeschickte Weiterentwicklung des Pferdeführermotivs. *Format des ganzen Teppichs 1,90 × 2 m. Eremitage, Leningrad. Vgl. Fig. 103*

Nachdem Rudenko die Ausgrabung von Pazyryk abgeschlossen hatte
(drei kleinere Kurgane haben wir noch an anderer Stelle zu erwähnen),
wandte er sich den Großkurganen von Bašadar zu, einer Nekropole,
die 180 Kilometer weiter westlich an einem Nebenfluß des Katun
liegt. Hier hatte man nämlich eine scheinbar ungestörte Aufschüttung
entdeckt, was sofort die Hoffnung weckte, man könnte endlich auch
auf Goldplatten stoßen, ebenbürtig jenen der sibirischen Kollektion.
Trotzdem erwies sich der riesige Kurgan Bašadar II (58 Meter Durchmesser, 2,70 Meter Höhe) als säuberlich ausgeplündert. Die Kammer
in der ungewöhnlichen Tiefe von über sechs Metern unter dem Erd-
niveau war niedrig und von recht einfacher Konstruktion. Sie hat nur
eine einfache Wand, die Enden der verwendeten Stämme stehen weit
über. An der Nordwand lagen vierzehn Pferde, durch die Tätigkeit
der Raubgräber arg beschädigt. In der Kammer standen ursprünglich zwei Särge, der eine enthielt den einbalsamierten Körper eines
Mannes, der andere den einer Frau. Dieser, mehr in der Mitte der
Kammer aufgestellt, hatte in der niedrigen Kammer die Räuber be-
hindert, als sie sich an den Sarkophag des Mannes heranmachen wollten. Sie hatten ihn daher halb in den Schacht hinaufgezogen und
schließlich mit der grausam zerstückelten Mumie der Frau wieder in
die Kammer zurückgeworfen. Auch den Deckel des Männersarkophags
hatte man hochstemmen müssen.

Am Sarkophag der Frau, infolge der rohen Behandlung nur äußerst
mäßig erhalten, war nur der Deckel mit Spirallocken in orangeroter
Farbe bemalt. Der Sarkophag des Mannes war hingegen reich geschnitzt. Der Deckel, von dem ein Teil abgesplittert, aber leicht zu
rekonstruieren ist, zeigt eine Prozession von vier Tigern, die über zwei
Eber, zwei Elche (ohne Geweih, also wohl weibliche Tiere) und drei
Widder hinwegschreiten. Auf der Südseite des Sarges marschieren
nochmals vier Tiger, nur der letzte steigt dabei auf einen Elch. Vielleicht ist die Darstellung nicht vollendet worden. Es handelt sich um
ein ausgezeichnetes Werk, an dem sich spezifische Unterschiede zu
der in Pazyryk herrschenden Richtung des Tierstils erkennen lassen.
Das Fell des Tigers ist durch geflammte Linien wiedergegeben, die
Körper der übrigen Tiere sind mit einem System von Voluten und
Spirallocken gefüllt. In der Kammer hatten die Räuber die Filzbespannung der Wände abgerissen, die Bronzenägel aber kaum beachtet.
Offenbar war der Metallhunger hier wesentlich geringer als weiter
östlich. Es wurde sogar beobachtet, daß sie von einem Bronzegegen-
stand nur das Blattgold ablösten und das Grundmaterial verschmäh-

ten. Viel größeres Interesse weckten Textilien und Pelze. Trotzdem sind zwei verschiedene Fußbekleidungen erkennbar geblieben: ein Männerstiefel davon hat einen kompliziert geschnittenen Fußteil und einen hohen Schaft aus Fellmosaik. Rechteckchen von wenigen Quadratzentimeter Größe sind in mühseliger Arbeit aneinandergesetzt. In der gleichen Technik hergestellte Kleidungsstücke werden noch Jahrhunderte später von den Hunnen berichtet. Die antike Nachricht scheint Gottfried Keller angeregt zu haben, wenn er in den »Sieben Legenden« Ritter Maus, den »Zahllosen«, sich in einem Mantel aus zahllosen Mäusefellchen der Madonna zum Kampf stellen läßt.

Was sonst noch an winzigen Fragmenten von Textilien gefunden wurde, genügt, um eine erstaunliche Vielfalt an Webtechniken zu belegen. An dem Dekor von Lederstücken bewundern wir den Schwung der Linienführung, auch einzelne Platten in Bronze und Horn sind erhalten geblieben. Wie in Pazyryk II fand man Reste eines Saiteninstruments; Stäbchen eines Zelts verraten die Haschischgarnitur. Hirsch- und Schafsknochen stammen von den mitgegebenen Fleischspeisen. Käse ist nachgewiesen. Tongefäße dienten zur Aufnahme flüssiger Nahrung.

Vierzehn Pferde Die vierzehn Pferde wurden gesattelt und geschirrt deponiert. Die Schirrungen sind stark zerstört, trotzdem lassen sich erhebliche Unterschiede in der Zusammensetzung der einzelnen Garnituren erkennen. Fünf Tiere trugen noch bronzene Trensen, ein Pferd hatte offenbar eine »Maske« mit mächtigen Widderhörnern. Sein Riemenzeug war mit goldüberzogenen Bronzeanhängern geschmückt, die wieder ein vegetabilisches Ornament bilden. Den Sattel schmückten Holzplatten, FIG. 102 die in prachtvoll monumentaler Strenge und Geschlossenheit Adler darstellen. Die Peitsche war mit ausgesucht schönen Tierdarstellungen

Fig. 102 – Stilisierte Vorderansicht eines Adlers, Holzschnitzerei zum Schmuck eines Sattelbogens. Breite ca. 20 cm. Vgl. oben

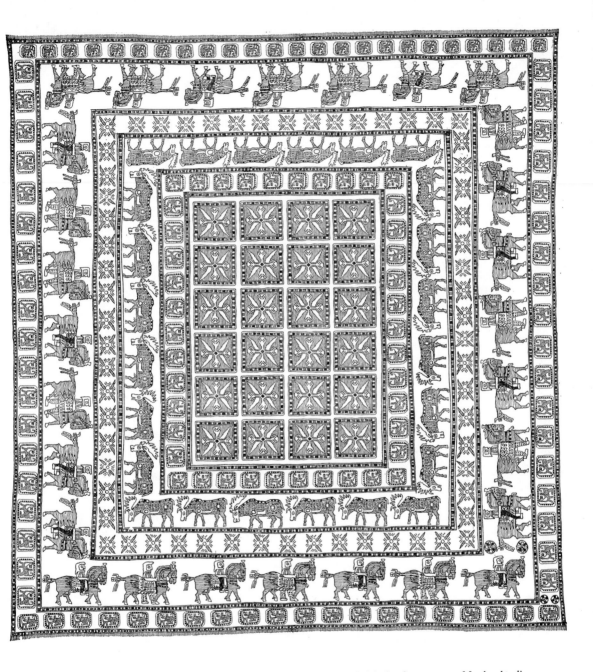

Fig. 103 – Kompositionsschema des Knüpfteppichs aus dem V. Pazyryk-Kurgan. Originalgröße 1,90 × 2 m. Man beachte die Anfangsmarkierungen rechts unten, die wohl den Schluß zulassen, daß es sich hier um einen Spielteppich handelt. (Nach Rudenko 1962.) Vgl. Seite 118

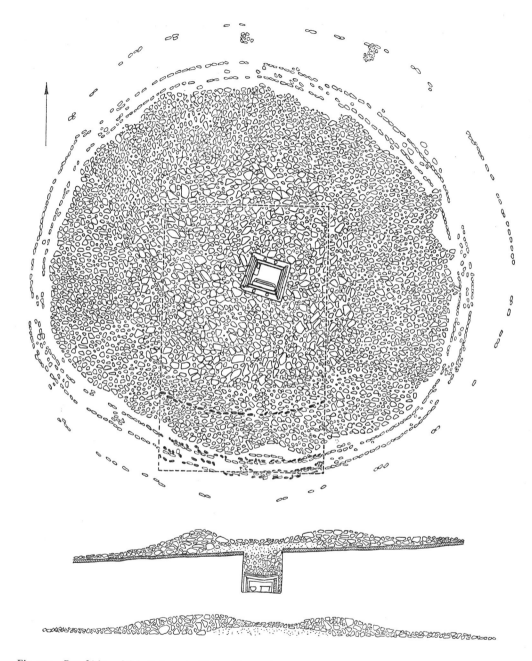

Fig. 104 – Draufsicht und Schnitt des ersten Tuëkta-Kurgans in verschiedenen Profilen. Hier sind deutlich die Steinkreise zu erkennen, die ursprünglich den Bestattungsort markierten, und später nur teilweise von der Aufschüttung überdeckt wurden. Vgl. S. 123

beschnitzt. Große Filzbehänge in Gestalt von Raubtierköpfen dienten zum Schmuck der Sättel. Bei der Herstellung eines der Sättel wurde ein Teppichfragment von ungewöhnlicher Feinheit verwendet (70 Knoten auf den Quadratzentimeter). Das schöne Stück aus Pazyryk V, das eine Weile als ältester Knüpfteppich der Welt galt, ist damit eigentlich entthront.

Weiterer Knüpfteppich

Da der Bašadar-I-Kurgan vermutlich mit Recht erst der nächsten Zeitstufe zugerechnet wird, so schließen hier die beiden großen Tuëkta-Kurgane an, die sich Rudenko wenige Jahre später in einer riesigen, nahe gelegenen Nekropole (mit 197 Hügeln) als Ziel gesetzt hatte.

I. Tuëkta-Kurgan

Tuëkta I gehört mit einem Aufschüttungsdurchmesser von 68 Metern und 4 Meter Höhe zu den größten Anlagen seiner Art. In einem Schacht von über sieben Meter Tiefe stand die geräumige doppelwandige Kammer.

FIG. 104

Trotz des Fehlens äußerer Grabungsspuren war auch sie reichlich ausgeplündert, ja man entdeckte in dem Füllmaterial des Schachts noch die Steigbäume der Räuber. Der Boden der Kammer war an einer Stelle angekohlt. Dort hatten sie Feuer gemacht, vielleicht zum Auftauen der bereits einfrierenden Gegenstände.

Es handelte sich um die Bestattung eines Mannes. Sein ausgezeichnet erhaltener Sarkophag war mit Spirallocken und Tigersilhouetten aus Birkenrinde dekoriert. Die Standardausrüstung bezeugen Tischchen und Gefäße, sowie Reste der Räuchergarnitur. Auch die Kleidung des Mannes kann in großen Zügen festgehalten werden. Von der Bewaffnung wieder sind Pfeilschäfte, eine Dolchscheide – deren Zwinge im Tierstil dekoriert ist –, sowie Fragmente eines eisernen Schwerts übriggeblieben. Vermutlich hatten es die Räuber nur darum nicht entwendet, weil es vor der Mitgabe zerbrochen worden war.

Die acht Pferde blieben ohne jede Schirrung. Dafür entdeckte man weit mehr Garnituren – mindestens achtzehn Sättel und zwanzig Psalienpaare – zwischen den Doppelwänden der Kammer. Offenbar wurden sie durch eine größere Anzahl von Masken ergänzt, denn man stellte acht zugehörige Hörnerpaare aus Holz verschiedenen Formats fest. Silhouetten aus Leder und Birkenrinde schmückten die Sättel; sowohl beim abstrakten Ornament wie bei den Tierdarstellungen ist die gleiche Freude an Spirale und Volute zu beobachten. Unter dem geschnitzten Zubehör der Schirrung ist eine runde Stirnplatte von hohem künstlerischen Interesse, deren Mittelbuckel zwei Adlergreifen in prachtvollem Schwung umschließen.

Acht Pferde

FIG. 105

ABB. SEITE 124

Zu den Eigentümlichkeiten des Kurgans gehörte, daß in der Kammer

Geschnitzte Stirnplatte eines Zaumzeuges aus dem I. Tuekta-Kurgan. *Durchmesser 12 cm. Eremitage, Leningrad. Vgl. S. 123*

ein erstaunlich gut erhaltener Tisch von fast zwei Meter Länge stand. FIG. 106 Er ist ohne jeden Schmuck und erinnert stark an einen Operationstisch. Man nimmt deshalb an, das Möbel habe zum Einbalsamieren der Leichen gedient, man habe sich seiner durch die Beigabe ins Grab entledigen wollen. Auf dem Tisch stand allerdings eine große Schüssel mit kurzen Füßen. Angesichts der Beraubung weiß man natürlich nicht, ob das ihr ursprünglicher Platz war.

Der Kurgan Tuèkta II ist nur halb so groß wie sein unmittelbarer *II. Tuekta-Kurgan* Nachbar. Da er dessen Aufschüttung an einer Stelle überdeckt, muß er später errichtet sein. Er ist auf dieselbe geheimnisvolle Weise beraubt worden. Die Kammer hat nur eine einfache Wand, sie ist durch eine Stützkonstruktion in der üblichen massiven Ausführung geschützt.

Der Baumsarg, der mit der Darstellung einer Hirschprozession geschmückt war, enthielt die Leiche einer Frau. Von ihrem Schmuck und ihrer reichen Lederkleidung sind nur kümmerliche Reste erhalten geblieben. Ebenso sind die acht Pferde von den Räubern einer eingehenden Untersuchung unterzogen worden. Das Blattgold wurde fast durchgehend von ihnen mitgenommen.

Im Vergleich mit diesen Großkurganen haben andere bescheidenere *Einfache* Grabanlagen, z. B. Aragol, verhältnismäßig wenig von künstlerischem *Beisetzungen* Interesse zu bieten. Ihnen fehlt nämlich jene Ausdehnung der Steinkappe, die die Voraussetzung für die Eiskonservierung bildet. Dabei sind sie mit gleicher Gründlichkeit ausgeraubt worden. Sie haben deshalb vor allem für den Gelehrten Interesse, der den sozialen Hintergrund der mächtigen Kurgane einbeziehen will. Allerdings erforderten auch die einfacheren Anlagen, die wir mit Sicherheit in dieser Periode unterbringen können, noch einen recht beachtlichen Arbeitsaufwand. Man hat unter einer – zwar flachen – Steinkappe eine Grube von Mannstiefe ausgehoben, in der man eine Kiste aus Baumstämmen, allerdings oft nur aus einem einzigen Balkenkranz bestehend, aufstellte. Darin wurde der Tote in möglichst reicher Kleidung mit Speise-

Fig. 105 – In Leder geschnittene Silhouette für den Schmuck eines Sattels, einen geweihtragenden Tiger darstellend. Aus Tuèkta I. Der Anteil des Kurvenstils tritt hier besonders deutlich hervor. Vgl. S. 123

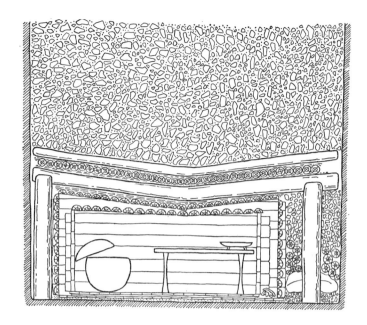

Fig. 106 – Längsschnitt durch die Kammer des ersten Tuĕkta-Kurgans. Vgl. S. 125

beigaben und gegebenenfalls auch Waffen beigesetzt. Den Verschlag deckte man sorgfältig ab. An der Nordseite kommt das Reitpferd zu liegen, offenbar auch bei Frauen. Wo Reste eines Dekors beobachtet wurden, gehorchte er den gleichen Prinzipien wie in den großen Kurganen. Es besteht kein grundsätzlicher Unterschied zu jenen Gräbern des Vorlands, die zu Viehzüchtern – nicht aber den gleichfalls anwesenden Ackerbauern – gehörten.

Gräber mittleren Reichtums Nun gibt es freilich Gräber, die durch Anlage und Reichtum der Ausstattung über diesem Niveau stehen. Die Aufschüttung ist bei ihnen größer, die Kiste wird zur Kammer und steht in erheblicher Tiefe, sie wird bereits durch Balkenlagen, die allerdings bisweilen nur auf Trockenmauern ruhen, vor dem Druck der Erdmassen geschützt. Geschirrte Pferde sind mitgegeben.

Hier müssen drei in Pazyryk geöffnete Gräber eingereiht werden: die Kurgane Pazyryk VI–VIII. Einer davon, die Beisetzung einer Frau, ergab neben Lackresten einen zerbrochenen chinesischen Spiegel.

FIG. 107
Techniken Relativ einfach und überaus dankbar ist es, dieses riesige Material zum Ausgangspunkt für ein Studium der verschiedenen handwerklichen Techniken zu machen. So weiß man zum Beispiel durch die ausgedehnten Blockkonstruktionen, daß den Altai-Stämmen ausge-

Fig. 107 – Fragment eines Bronzespiegels chinesischer Herkunft. Sechster Pazyryk-Kurgan. Durchmesser 12 cm. Vgl. S. 126

zeichnete Zimmerleute zur Verfügung standen, die die verschiedensten Formen von Verzapfungen beherrschten. Mit dem kleinen querschneidigen Tüllenbeil vollbrachte man wahre Wunderwerke. Da die Russen selbst Meister dieses Handwerks sind, braucht man sich nicht weiter zu wundern, daß ihre Gelehrten diesen Bereich besonders intensiv erforscht haben.

Gut studiert sind auch die Textilien. Die Altai-Bewohner beherrschten praktisch alle heute bekannten Techniken mit Einschluß des Gobelins und des echten Knüpfteppichs.

Sehr häufig wurde Leder zu Zwecken verwendet, die uns überraschen, etwa für vollplastische Schnitzwerke oder in Kombination mit Metallfolien (Gold, Zinn). Selbst Keramik wurde damit dekoriert.

Im übrigen darf man von den Bewohnern des Altais keine hochstehende Töpferei erwarten. Ihr Formengut dürfte zum Teil aus Mittelasien abzuleiten sein.

Trotz des Interesses der Raubgräber am Metall genügen die verbliebenen Reste, um festzustellen, daß die Goldgegenstände etwa 20 Prozent Silber enthalten. Das entspricht den natürlichen Vorkommen des Altais. Auch das Kupfer, das 0,1 Prozent Silber enthält, stammt unmittelbar aus dem Altai. Nur die Räuchergefäße bestehen

Herkunft des Metalls

127

aus einer Bronze, die ungewöhnliche Zusätze aufweist, was sie wohl als Importstücke entlarvt.

Wirtschaftsweise Mit Sicherheit festzustellen sind auch noch die elementaren Gegebenheiten des Wirtschaftsbetriebs. Pferd und Schaf müssen eine überragende Rolle gespielt haben. Man hat auch Rinder gezüchtet und als Zugtiere verwendet. Fleisch und Milchprodukte sind als Speisebeigaben mehrfach belegt. Zweifellos wurden die Hochtäler als Almen für das Vieh genutzt, im Winter hielt man sich in den Niederungen auf. Daß man dort in Blockhäusern hauste, ließe sich auf Grund der exzellenten Beherrschung der Holzbearbeitung vermuten. Fest steht auch eine erhebliche Bedeutung der Jagd. Man verfügte über ein erstaunlich reiches Sortiment von Pelzen. Neben Gold mögen sie ein wesentliches Exportgut dargestellt haben.

Kriegswesen Unbestreitbar dürfte ferner sein, daß die »Früchte des Krieges« eine große Rolle im Haushalt der Altai-Bevölkerung spielten. Krieg bildete ja überhaupt die »nationale Industrie« der zentralasiatischen Reiterkrieger. Nicht alles, was wir mittels stilistischer Analyse oder schon durch das Material als Fremdgut erkennen, muß aus regulärem Handel *Raubgut* stammen. Einiges mag Raubgut oder Tribut gewesen, anderes von Reisläufern an fernen Höfen erworben sein. Rudenko hat seinerzeit den kühnen Verdacht geäußert, der im II. Pazyryk-Kurgan beigesetzte Mann habe im Heere der Achämeniden gedient.

Bewaffnung Die Bewaffnung ist erstaunlich standardisiert, sie entspricht ziemlich genau jener, die wir bei den pontischen Skythen kennenlernten. Die hier gefundenen leichten Schilde aus Stäbchen sind dort von griechischen Künstlern abgebildet worden. Auch hier wurden Bogen und Pfeile im Goryt am Oberschenkel getragen, das Kurzschwert entspricht dem Akinakes. Nur der Streitpickel dürfte eine asiatische Spezialität darstellen, die allerdings in den Wäldern Osteuropas und gelegentlich sogar bei den Skythen Anklang fand. Die in der Schirrung festzustellenden Unterschiede lassen sich leicht durch die Anpassung an eine gebirgige Umwelt erklären. Man brauchte hier Brust- und Schwanzriemen sowie höhere Sattelbögen.

Wir haben keine Ahnung, ob die Hirse, die man in Tuekta I fand, aus eigener Ernte stammte oder aus dem Tribut seßhafter Nachbarn. Strittig ist auch, wie sich der Vertikalnomadismus der Altai-Leute konkret auswirkte, ob man nicht lieber von Halbnomaden oder Transhumantes sprechen soll. Grjaznov meint, daß sich im Frühjahr die kompakten Sippenverbände von den stabilen Wintersiedlungen in die Berge vorschoben, Rudenko ist überzeugt, daß sich nur reiche Stammesmitglieder mit großen Herden in Bewegung setzten. Rudenko benutzt das zu einer wahren Philippika gegen den von Grjaznov geprägten Begriff der »frühen Nomaden«. Weder »früh« noch »Nomaden«, lautet seine These, über deren Berechtigung wir uns später den Kopf zerbrechen müssen.

Einig ist man sich nur insofern, als man ein ausgeprägtes Privateigentum annimmt. Damit aber stehen wir vor einer der fundamentalen Fragen, nämlich nach der Sozialordnung im Altai. *Sozialordnung*

Fest steht zunächst einmal, daß kein Anzeichen für eine höhere staatliche Organisation vorhanden ist, es ist daher irreführend, mit vorderasiatischen oder chinesischen Nekropolen zu vergleichen, in denen vergöttlichte Könige inmitten ihres Hofstaates ruhen. Selbst die größten Kurgane liegen inmitten von Ketten kleinerer Hügel, unter denen weniger bedeutende Sippenmitglieder bestattet sind. Auch zwischen der Planung der »reichen« und der »armen« Gräber besteht kein prinzipieller Unterschied. Die sogenannte »Kammer« ist aus dem schlichten Balkenkranz erwachsen. Das erklärt, warum sogar die Andeutung einer Tür fehlt und warum man sich oft mit einer äußerst unpraktischen Höhe des Innenraums begnügte. Die Grabräuber hätten ein Lied davon singen können. Man darf daher nicht mit jenen »Grabhäusern« vergleichen, die im gleichzeitigen China belegt sind. *Kein religiös fundiertes Königtum pontischer Art*

In den Großkurganen sind vielmehr Anführer bestattet, die sich mit ihrer Verwandtschaft eben aus der Masse des Volkes lösten, gestützt auf ihren erworbenen oder ererbten Reichtum und getragen vom Kriegsglück, vermutlich auch Organisationsgabe und Beredsamkeit.

Wie war nun ihre Verwandtschaft organisiert? Natürlich liegt es nahe, an *patriarchalisch* geführte Sippenverbände zu denken, allerdings muß man im Auge behalten, daß für das alte Zentralasien eine hohe, unabhängige Stellung der Frau ausdrücklich belegt ist. Der Perserkönig Kyrus verlor gegen eine Königin der Massageten Schlacht und Leben. *Patriarchalisch geführte Sippenverbände*

In den Kurganen sind jedenfalls die Frauen nicht schlechter ausgestattet als die Männer. Auch sie konnten durch die Beigabe von Reitpferden geehrt werden. Ob die in mehreren Kurganen neben den Männern gefundenen Frauen wirklich gewaltsam getötete und mitbestattete Konkubinen waren, wie man sich orientalisch-phantasievoll vorstellte, ist eher zweifelhaft. Die völlig ebenbürtige Behandlung spricht dagegen, die nachgewiesene Mumifizierung erlaubte ja auch eine Doppelbestattung von Personen, die zu verschiedenen Zeiten gestorben waren. *Hohe Stellung der Frau*

Um den Kern der freien Sippenverbände, die ihre Anführer in den großen Kurganen bestatteten, mögen sich freilich noch mancherlei abhängige Gruppen gelagert haben, die wir (vielleicht infolge oberirdischer Bestattung) niemals fassen werden. In diesen Kreisen sind die Grabräuber zu suchen. Vielleicht hatten sie in den Erzschürfen die Erfahrungen gesammelt, die ihnen bei der Anlage der Schächte zustatten kamen. Deren Tiefe, die bis zu zehn Meter erreicht (es mußte ja auch die Aufschüttung durchstoßen werden), wäre dann nicht mehr so erstaunlich. Sie mögen auch die Lieferanten des kostbaren Pelzwerks gewesen sein.

Auffällig ist die große Zahl der mitgegebenen Reitpferde. Grjaznov erklärt kühn, es handele sich um Tributgaben der von den Verstorbenen abhängigen Clans. Vierzehn Pferde entsprächen eben der Huldigung von vierzehn Einheiten. Da man diese wie bei vielen späteren Nomadenvölkern rituell in zwei Flügel aufgeteilt hatte, gingen auch deren Symbole, dargestellt durch die Masken der Pferde, ins Grab. Wenn wir wie in Pazyryk II sieben Pferde antreffen, dann haben wir eben nur den Anführer des einen Flügels vor uns. So fänden auch die völlig unterschiedlichen Ohrenmarken in Pazyryk I eine plausible Erklärung. Leider ist sie nicht unbedingt stichhaltig. Es sind bei den Pferden deutliche Qualitätsunterschiede feststellbar, und das ließe sich kaum mit ihrer Eigenschaft als Huldigungsgabe vereinbaren. Außerdem fand man schließlich im II. Pazyryk-Kurgan mehr als nur eine Maske.

Rudenko hat nun, von einem anderen Punkt ausgehend, eine Überlegung angestellt, die vermutlich zur Lösung auch dieses Rätsels führt. Wir haben gehört, daß der I. Tuëkta-Kurgan trotz unversehrter Steinkappe beraubt worden ist. Auf die Spuren der Raubgräber stieß man erst in der Füllung des Schachts. Sie waren genau dort in die Tiefe gestoßen, wo sich ihnen die wenigsten Felsbrocken in den Weg legten. Hier entdeckte man noch ihre Leitern. Nach dem Ergebnis der dendrochronologischen Untersuchung sind die dazu verwendeten, noch mit Aststümpfen versehenen Bäumchen nicht später gefällt worden als die Stämme der Grabkammer. In der Tiefe herrschte dann die übliche Verwüstung, im Niveau der Erdoberfläche aber waren alle Spuren sorgfältig verwischt.

Bei der Erklärung dieses Bildes entwickelte Rudenko beachtliche Fähigkeiten als Amateurdetektiv. Er nimmt an, daß die Grabräuber Gelegenheit hatten, die Anlage des Grabes genau zu beobachten, vielleicht waren sie selbst dazu »dienstverpflichtet«. So kannten sie die schwächste Stelle. Die Anlage fand nun in zwei Etappen statt, vielleicht, weil die kurze Sommerzeit nicht ausreichte, vielleicht aber, weil man den mit den Totenfesten verbundenen Aufwand an Schlachtvieh über einen längeren Zeitraum verteilen wollte. Während die Trauergemeinde sich aber mit den Herden im Vorland aufhielt, sahen die Untertanen, die eigentlichen Bewohner der Hochregion, ihre Stunde gekommen. Sie räumten aus, was soeben mit viel Mühe und Feierlichkeit vergraben worden war.

Später wurde dann von den ahnungslosen Nomaden über dem geplünderten Grab der Hügel aufgeworfen, was eine Erdbewegung von etwa 6000 Kubikmetern erforderte. Rudenko nimmt mit Recht an, daß dieser ungeheure Arbeitseinsatz nicht etwa von Sklaven geleistet wurde, sondern von der zusammenströmenden Mitbevölkerung, die an dem grandiosen Leichenmahl teilnehmen durfte. Rudenko berichtet vergleichsweise (und fast träumerisch), er habe noch am 21.–23. September 1927 die Trauerfeier für einen am 25. März des gleichen Jahres verstorbenen reichen Kazachen miterlebt. Damals wurde in fünfzehn Filzzelten bewirtet, ganze Aule stellten sich ein. Vier Pferde, sechs Ochsen und fünfundzwanzig Schafe waren geschlachtet worden, fünfundzwanzig weitere Schafe wurden noch von der Verwandtschaft gestiftet. Überall strotzten die Schüsseln von Fleisch, dampfte die fette Brühe. Nur die früher üblichen Wettkämpfe mußten ausfallen, schon schickten sich die Organe des Sowjetstaates an, diesem rückständigen Wohlleben ein Ende zu bereiten.

Von anderen Völkern – Kafiren, Nagas – weiß man nun, daß die Errichtung von Denkmälern aus gewaltigen Steinen, sogenannte Megalithen, sehr oft mit solchen Totenfeiern zusammenhängt. In ihnen dokumentiert sich die überschäumende Kraft der feiernden Gemeinde. Sie verewigen den Ruhm des Toten, aber auch den seiner weiterlebenden Sippe. Oft glaubt man, der Verdienst käme dem Toten im Jenseits zugute, sichere ihm dort ein standesgemäßes Fortleben oder auch ein höheres Maß an Unsterblichkeit.

Tatsächlich scheinen auch in der Kultur unserer Kurganerbauer Steinsetzungen eine große Rolle gespielt zu haben. Erst jetzt beachtet man, daß es im Umkreis der Kurgane Zäune aus aufgestellten Menhiren gibt, von denen manche eine Länge von mehreren hundert Metern erreichen. Steinkreise umgeben nicht nur die Anlagen, sie wurden auch unter den Aufschüttungen gefunden. Offenbar markierten sie die Zwischenphasen des Rituals. Pferdeknochen unter Steinschüttungen erklärt man als Reste der Festmahlzeiten.

Zweifellos steht der brennende Ehrgeiz von Sippenverbänden, die

Nachträgliche Aufschüttung des Hügels

Totenfeiern

Megalithisches Brauchtum als Regulativ

131

in Freiheit und Reichtum nebeneinanderlebten, hinter dieser herrlichen Verschwendung. Aber dieser Ehrgeiz ist in Bahnen abgeleitet, die mit regelmäßigen Stationen versehen, nicht den gemeinsamen Rahmen sprengen müssen. Der angehäufte Reichtum verströmt bei deren Erreichung in die Feste. So werden Mittel, die zur Bildung einer Gefolgschaft und damit zur Vorherrschaft führen könnten, den Bedürftigen dienstbar gemacht.

Ausdruckswert Stämme, die sich einem so gewaltigen Regulativ unterwerfen, pflegen meist auch den Krieg, wenigstens unter Angehörigen des gleichen Volkstums, durch strenge Spielregeln zu zähmen. Heldentum wird wichtiger als der bloße Sieg, die sinnfällige Trophäe erstrebenswerter als die Vernichtung des Gegners.

Wieder fügt sich das Material in das Bild: wenn wir von den pontischen Skythen durch Herodots Bericht erfuhren, daß es rituelle Ehrungen verdienter Krieger gab, daß der Skalp als Siegeszeichen hochgeschätzt wurde, so begegnet uns jetzt im II. Pazyryk-Kurgan ein Toter, an dem dieses grausige Ritual vollzogen wurde.

Wenn es aber die Tendenz zu gestuften Symbolen des Prestiges gab, dann werden plötzlich die vielen, dem Toten mitgegebenen Pferde verständlich: sie sind Ausdruck der erreichten Stellung, Zeichen seiner Würde. Wahrscheinlich führte man sie paarweise im Trauerzug, wobei die kostbarsten Tiere durch einen Schmuck hervorgehoben, den wir jetzt ungenau als Maske bezeichnen, den Anfang machten.

Kunsthandwerk schafft Prestigesymbole Es ist klar, daß die Betonung des sinnfälligen Ausdrucks von Erfolg die Basis für ein erhöhtes Schmuckbedürfnis bildete. Hinzu trat offensichtlich, daß künstlerische Arbeit an sich hochgeschätzt wurde. Von dem Personenkreis, aus dessen Händen die Schöpfungen der Altai-Kunst stammen, wissen wir wenig genug. Es kann sich jedoch kaum um eine Schicht fremder Herkunft gehandelt haben, die jenen griechischen Handwerkern entsprach, die im Dienste der pontischen Skythen standen. Viel wahrscheinlicher ist, daß es in den einzelnen Sippen Männer gab, die es in der Behandlung einzelner Werkstoffe, vielleicht auch mehrerer, zu besonderer Meisterschaft gebracht hatten und denen daraus Ansehen und Ehre erwuchs. Wir müssen an Verhältnisse denken, wie sie in der Südseekunst der Entdeckungszeit belegt sind. Ähnlich muß es in der Wikingerzeit gewesen sein, damals hieß »Schmied« *Meister noch nicht deklassiert* der kunstfertige Mann schlechthin. Ob solche Meister dann unter dem Schutz mächtiger Anführer lebten und sich ganz deren Dienst widmeten, wissen wir nicht. Wir dürfen vermuten, daß viele nur über ein beschränktes Repertoire an Dekorationsmustern verfügten, manches hatten sie im Laufe ihrer Tätigkeit übernommen, anderes ererbt. Als sicher darf man einen sehr hohen Anteil männlicher Arbeit annehmen, und damit ist bereits ein entscheidender Unterschied zum Kunstgewerbe der modernen zentralasiatischen Völker gegeben. Jene kennen ein traditionelles Haushandwerk, das von den Frauen getragen wird, oder die Kunst des Bazars, die sich jedem anbietet. Nur in beschränktem Umfang – wie bei den Kirgisen – hat sich etwas Vergleichbares erhalten. Dort konnten wir ja auch von einer Vielfalt erzählender Muster berichten.

Vermutlich muß man von dieser sozialen Basis her verstehen, was Grjaznov an Grundsätzlichem über die Altai-Kunst ausgesagt hat. Er stellt eine verblüffende Vielfalt von künstlerischen Gattungen fest: Plastik und Relief, lineare Zeichnung und Silhouette kommen nebeneinander zu ihrem Recht und werden auf die spannendste Weise kombiniert. Dabei werden die verschiedensten Stoffe analog behandelt und ihre Möglichkeiten nur extrem ausgeschöpft. Andererseits wird das Material förmlich überfordert, zum Beispiel beim Schnitzen in dickem Leder.

Eine echte Plastik gelingt am ehesten dort, wo als Grundform ein Stab zur Verfügung stand. Man setzt ihn in die Figur eines ausgestreckten Tieres um, wie z. B. bei den Peitschenstielen und den Tischfüßen. Die meisten Plastiken lassen sich als zwei Reliefplatten auffassen, die in eine Ebene geklappt, eine symmetrische Figur ergeben würden. Die beiden Prinzipien – Stab und Relief – werden kombiniert: dann ragt aus einer Platte senkrecht ein Kopf heraus.

Die Reliefs sind immer streng frontal, mit Hilfe des sogenannten Schrägschnitts in eleganten Kurven hergestellt. Trotzdem entsteht der Eindruck höchster Dynamik, weil in der Draufsicht konzipierte Details um neunzig oder hundertachtzig Grad gedreht werden können – man spricht von Torsion bzw. Inversion. Immer fehlt daher die Basis.

Die zweite Grundform scheint die Silhouette zu sein. Mit dem Relief verbindet sie die Bevorzugung der frontalen oder streng seitlichen Ansicht. Silhouetten liegen eigentlich auch dort vor, wo mit mehreren Farben gearbeitet wird. Diese haben keinerlei Beziehung zur Realität. Es gibt keine Zwischentöne.

Grjaznov macht weiter aufmerksam, daß sich die Eleganz der Komposition auf das einzelne Dekorationsobjekt beschränkt. In der Anordnung bemerkt man eine gewisse Schwerfälligkeit. In langen Reihen hängen die prachtvollen gold- und zinnüberzogenen Platten an den Riemen der Schirrung, ohne Rhythmus, ohne nennenswerte Steige-

rung. Es fehlt jenes Über-sich-Hinausweisen, das die jungpaläolithische
Kunst kennzeichnete. Man hat das bisher übersehen, da ja immer nur
das kleine Objekt außerhalb seines Zusammenhangs vorlag.

Um so erstaunlicher ist, daß im einzelnen die Proportionen so klug
eingehalten oder noch klüger verschoben werden. Daran hängt die
berühmte Realistik der Tierbilder.

Sollte man darauf einen Reim machen, so müßte man wohl von einer
subjektiven Kunst sprechen. Nicht das letzte Resultat, die Anwendung,
in der die Details untergehen, sondern das einzelne Objekt, wie es aus
der Hand des Künstlers kommt, entscheidet. Das ergänzt sich mit den
Interessen des Auftraggebers, er wünscht ja nur, Verdienste zu sammeln, und behängt sich mit Kunstwerken wie mit Trophäen. Man
versteht den ästhetischen Genuß, den der moderne Sammler emp-
findet: er lernt nur mehr das Fragment kennen – auf das es eigentlich
ankam. Auch der Gegensatz zu der späteren Machtkunst der Noma-
denreiche ist offensichtlich, die mit simplen, stereotypen Grundformen
ungeheure Wirkung erreichte.

Dieser hellsichtigen Analyse Grjaznovs, die wir nur in einzelnen Punkten weiterführen mußten, kann Rudenko nur die vertrauten Formeln
vom Tierstil entgegensetzen. Sein Verdienst liegt in einer breiten Darstellung der Motivik, wobei das Resultat bereits in Andeutungen
Grjaznovs vorweggenommen wird. Man unterscheidet:

Aufzählung der Motive durch Rudenko

1. Einfache geometrische Körper, Kegel, Kugel etc., aufsteigend bis
zum Torsionsstab.

2. Eine Spiral- und Volutenornamentik. Ihre Lieblingsfigur ist die
Spirallocke, häufig auch der Wirbel.

3. Motive, die Pflanzenformen schematisch wiedergeben, Palmette,
Blüte, Lotos, geometrische Ranke.

4. Schematische Wiedergaben tierischer Attribute (Widderhorn,
Hirschgeweih, Eberhauer, Raubtierkralle).

5. Reale Tierbilder oder deren Teile – die Spannweite ist ungeheuer.
Belegt sind Fische, Vögel, Cervide (Ren, Edelhirsch, Damwild, Elch),
auch Antilope, Wildschaf, Bergziege, Wildschwein, sehr selten der
Hase. Häufig sind Raubtiere: Wolf, Tiger, Löwe, Schneeleopard. Von
den Raubvögeln ist der Adler der wichtigste. Haustiere fehlen dafür
fast ganz, nur Hahn und vor allem Pferd werden den Wildtieren ebenbürtig eingestuft.

6. Es gibt eine ganze Reihe von Tierkombinationen, also Fabeltieren,
die man zum Teil unter der Bezeichnung »Löwen-« oder »Adlergreif«
zusammenfassen kann.

7. Eine sehr geringe Rolle spielt der Mensch. Es gibt stilisierte Menschenköpfe, einzelne bekleidete Gestalten und Tiermenschen.

8. Vor allem die Tierbilder werden zu größeren Kompositionen zusammengefaßt: als Fries, in heraldischer Anordnung, yang-yinartig sich zum Kreise schließend. Überaus wichtig aber sind Kampfszenen, wobei sich meistens ein Raubtier auf einen Paarhufer stürzt. Szenen, in denen Menschen auftreten, scheinen hingegen einem völlig anderen Stilgefühl zu gehorchen.

Die Frage, die sich hier nun unmittelbar anschließt, richtet sich auf die Entwicklung, die hinter diesen Motivgruppen stehen mag. Welche Herkunft haben sie? In welcher Reihenfolge traten sie in Erscheinung? Welcher Zeitraum stand für einen solchen Ablauf zu Verfügung? *Herkunft der Motive*

Bei einem sehr hohen Prozentsatz steht die fremde Herkunft fest. So ist klar, daß Lotosblüten nicht im Altai erträumt werden konnten, auch das Palmettenmuster ist aus dem Vorderen Orient übernommen. Vorderasiatischer Herkunft ist nicht nur die Idee der Tierkampfszene an sich, auch bestimmte Tierbilder sind entlehnt: Löwe und Damhirsch kommen ja im Umkreis des Altais gar nicht vor. Auch der Hahn, der in der Mythologie der Iranier eine so hohe Rolle spielt, dürfte den Altai nur als Symbol erreicht haben. Die gesamte Gruppe der Fabeltiere geht auf die schöpferische Phantasie des Nahen Ostens zurück, wenn sie auch bei ihrer Einbürgerung viele nördliche Attribute, zum Beispiel das Rengeweih, erhalten hat.

Selbst die großen Szenen, die auf dem Filzteppich des V. Pazyryk-Kurgans abgebildet sind, sind wohl mit ihrem religiösen Kontext zumindest aus Mittelasien übernommen. Den besten Beweis liefert die Tatsache, daß sowohl die Kleidung der dargestellten Personen als auch der Mähnenschnitt des Pferdes nicht mit dem übereinstimmt, was man im Altai tatsächlich beobachten kann. Im Wandbehang des V. Kurgans von Pazyryk ist außerdem chinesischer Einfluß greifbar. Es ist die Frage, wieweit er dem spiegelbildlichen Aufbau mancher Schmuckplatten zugrundeliegt.

Schwieriger ist das Problem, in welchem Verhältnis Tierbild und Spiralornamentik zueinander stehen. Forscher, die gewissermaßen der klassischen Phase der Tierstilforschung treu geblieben sind, haben ein einfaches Reihungsprinzip an der Hand. Hat doch Schefold seinerzeit erklärt, alle Tiermotive würden im Laufe der Stilentwicklung immer naturferner und unkenntlicher, um sich schließlich in ornamentalisierte Zeichen zu verwandeln. Da nun zweifellos die Voluten denselben Schwung aufweisen, den auch die Tierbilder haben, so liegt es nahe, *Chronologische Reihung* sie als deren ornamentalisierte Überreste zu deuten. Weil Pazyryk bereits einen erheblichen Prozentsatz derartiger abstrakter Linienspiele enthält, datierte man es spät, die neuentdeckten Kurgane von Tuėkta und Bašadar mit einem noch höheren Anteil müßten also noch jünger sein. E. Dittrich hat diese Anordnung durch Vergleiche mit Altchina zu untermauern versucht.

Trotzdem ist die traditionelle Auffassung hier nicht überzeugend. Bašadar II müßte nach seinen abstrakten Mustern als spät eingeordnet werden, die realistischen Tierschnitzereien hingegen sprechen für ein frühes Datum. Der greise Minns noch verglich sie begeistert mit Kelermes, ja mit Ziwiye. Das läßt sich nur verstehen, wenn man annimmt, daß danach keine zeitliche Stufung möglich ist, wenn Tierstil und Spiralornamentik im Altai von Anfang an nebeneinander bestanden. Die Vertreter der Frühdatierung von Bašadar II (und damit der Tuėkta-Kurgane) können sich heute auf naturwissenschaftliche Untersuchungen berufen, die man nach amerikanischem Vorbild an den wohlerhaltenen Stämmen der Grabbauten durchführte. Da ist einmal *Dendrochronologie* die Dendrochronologie, d. h. der Vergleich der Baumringfolgen. Sie *als Gegenprobe* genießt einen guten Ruf, liefert aber nur relative Daten. Mit ihrer Hilfe kann man im wesentlichen zwei Horizonte unterscheiden. Zwischen den am besten untersuchten Kurganen des ersten Horizonts (Bašadar II, Tuėkta I und II) und den frühesten Großkurganen des zweiten Horizonts, Pazyryk I und II, liegen etwa hundertdreißig Jahre. Sieben Jahre später wurde dann Pazyryk IV errichtet, dreißig Jahre nach diesem Pazyryk III. Zwischen ihm und dem fünften Kurgan liegen dann noch einmal elf Jahre, so daß die Serie des zweiten Horizonts in einem halben Jahrhundert Platz hat.

Radiokarbondaten Die absolute Datierung mit Hilfe der Radiokarbonmethode, d. h. nach dem Zerfallsgrad des nur in lebender Substanz gespeicherten Kohlenstoffs C_{14}, ergab für Bašadar II und Tuėkta I 520 v. Chr. als Mittelwert, für Pazyryk II 390 v. Chr., das heißt, es taucht noch einmal die Differenz von 130 Jahren auf, eine fast zu schöne Bestätigung. Rudenko stellt sich mit Elan hinter diese Daten, die Kurgane seien wirklich im 6. bis 4. Jahrhundert v. Chr. angelegt. Grjaznov hingegen drückt resolut diese Zeitangaben um ein Jahrhundert, wozu er auch bei der enormen Fehlergrenze der Radiokarbonmethode in diesem Fall (durchschnittlich ± 130 Jahre) völlig berechtigt ist. Im übrigen gründet er seine Reduktion auf typologische Übereinstimmungen, zum Beispiel mit südrussischen Trensen und Pfeilspitzen. Mit seltener Einmütigkeit stehen beide Forscher gegen die Spätdatierer, die die wichtigsten Kurgane in jene Zeit rücken wollten, als schon die Hsiung-nu den Steppenraum beherrschten.

Sicher ist jedenfalls, daß die Spiralornamentik selbständig ist und im Steppenraum ihre lange Vorgeschichte hat. Grjaznov betont, daß es schon zu Beginn des ersten Jahrtausends v. Chr. im Keramik-Dekor der Andronovo-Kultur Mäandermuster gab. Es handle sich um eine Spiralornamentik, die durch das verwendete Instrument, den Kamm-stempel, in gerade Linien zerlegt worden sei. Im übrigen begegneten wir ihr bereits in der Majemir-Phase des Altais. Mit einem Spiral- und Volutenstil im südlichen Steppenraum dürfte zusammenhängen, daß man im fernen Seistan Schirrungsteile fand, die ähnliche Muster FIG. 140 tragen, vielleicht sogar, daß Darius die Holzsäulen einer in Persepolis errichteten Halle um 500 v. Chr. mit fortlaufenden Spiralmustern be-malen ließ. –

In unserer Übersicht haben wir mehrfach auf Gegenstände hinge- *Importgüter* wiesen, die sich schon durch das verwendete Material als Importgüter erkennen lassen. In erster Linie sind das natürlich die Seiden. Ihre chinesische Herkunft ist unbezweifelbar und wird noch durch die stilistischen Eigentümlichkeiten der Muster unterstrichen. Importgut aus dem achämenidischen Bereich läßt sich hingegen nur aus dem Inhalt der Darstellung diagnostizieren. Frauen stehen betend vor einem Opferaltar, dessen Form auf den Persepolisreliefs und auf Siegel-zylindern wiederkehrt. Es liegt nahe, diese Gegenstände für eine Datie-rung zu verwenden, wobei man leider feststellt, daß das chinesische Vergleichsmaterial selbst nur recht fragwürdig datiert ist.

Lubo-Lesinčenko geht deshalb jetzt den umgekehrten Weg. Die west-lichen Verbindungen stützen hingegen die Datierung in achämenidi-sche Zeit.

Interessant an den Importen ist die ungleichmäßige Streuung in Raum und Zeit, die man übrigens auch bei der rein künstlerischen Beeinflussung feststellen kann. Das bedeutet zunächst einmal, daß die verschiedenen Sippenverbände, die ihre Toten im Hochaltai bestatte-ten, selbständig waren, daß sie nicht alle die gleichen auswärtigen Ver- *Kulturverbindungen* bindungen und Berührungspunkte aufwiesen. Tuékta und Bašadar haben offenbar mehr mit dem wesentlichen Mittelasien zu tun, etwa Choresm. In der Pazyryk-Nekropole ist das erst für den spätesten Kurgan, Pazyryk V, typisch. Dieser hat auch schlagartig reiches chine-sisches Importgut. Es ist, als wäre eine Tür nach dem Osten geöffnet worden, vielleicht durch irgendwelche kriegerischen Ereignisse. –

Es war schon auf Grund der älteren Funde klar, daß die Altai-Bevölkerung Merkmale der beiden großen Rassenkreise in sich vereinigte, so wie viele moderne Turkvölker. Die letzten Untersuchungen zeigen, daß dieser mongolide Anteil unerwartet groß war und früh einsetzt. Man denkt heute an Zuwanderer aus der Nordmongolei. Ihnen standen in dem sich noch kaum abschließenden Steppenadel alle Aufstiegsmöglichkeiten offen. Tatsächlich sieht der im II. Pazyryk-Kurgan beerdigte Anführer wie ein Tunguse aus. Man hat ihm vielleicht einen falschen Bart verliehen, um ihn dem Bild einheimischer Würdenträger anzugleichen. Die mitbestattete Frau ist völlig europid.

Trotzdem haben wir noch keine Ahnung, welche Sprache damals im Altai gesprochen wurde. War es ein iranischer Dialekt? Haben wir mit einem prototürkischen Idiom der östlichen Zuwanderer zu rechnen? Jede Möglichkeit ist offen.

Religion

Will man nun dem Material auch noch Aussagen über die religiöse Sphäre abringen, so ist zunächst einmal auf Grund des Bestattungsrituals klar, daß man sich das Jenseits nicht allzu verschieden von der irdischen Existenz vorgestellt hat – mit erheblichen Standesunterschieden, wobei man die Position des Toten zu beeinflussen hoffte. Als Mittel zur Erhaltung der Unsterblichkeit faßte man sicher auch die an allen Toten vorgenommene Einbalsamierung auf. Freilich bemerken wir noch eine ganz andere Funktion, nämlich die Bewahrung der Leiche über die langwierige Errichtung der Grabkonstruktion hinaus. Bei näherer Betrachtung enthüllt sich die Mumifizierung als eine komplizierte und variantenreiche Operation. Jedenfalls öffnete man Hirnschädel und Bauchhöhle, um die am leichtesten in Verwesung übergehenden Substanzen zu entfernen. Auf die übrigen Körperpartien ließ man durch Einschnitte eine konservierende Flüssigkeit einwirken. Oft entfernte man auch ganze Muskelpakete, so daß im Extremfall (Pazyryk V) nur das mit Haut überzogene Skelett zurückblieb. Es liegt nahe, an den in Zentralasien weit verbreiteten Volksglauben zu erinnern, die Wiederauferstehung komme aus Haut und Knochen.

Andere Fragen ergeben sich durch den Fund der Räuchergarnituren. Verwendete man Haschisch als reines Genußmittel? Viel eher möchte man annehmen, es habe zu einer religiösen Zeremonie gedient wie bei den pontischen Skythen, wo es allerdings in einem kollektiven Ritual seinen Platz fand. Haben wir hier eine Vorstufe des Schamanismus vorliegen, der sich dann der Trance geradezu virtuos bediente, sie gewissermaßen als psychotherapeutisches Hilfsmittel verwendete? Vermutlich ja. Die Ekstase ist noch nicht Vorrecht eines religiösen Spezialisten geworden, der den Funktionären der militärischen und politischen Skala Widerpart hält.

Eine sehr eigenartige Beobachtung gelang Wiesner am Knüpfteppich des V. Pazyryk-Kurgans. An drei von den umlaufenden Friesen stellte er Anfangsmarkierungen fest, so wie bei den Plänen unserer Würfelspiele. Daraus schloß er auf eine analoge Verwendung. Nun bietet sich aber jeder Spielplan als Weltbild dar, er öffnet dem Irrationalen die Tür, daher kann man ihn als Hilfsmittel bei einem Kultakt, vor allem für eine Prophezeiung gebrauchen. An eine solche Verwendung ist wohl hier zu denken. Das legen auch die seltsamen, bedeutungsvollen Zahlenverhältnisse in der Bildanordnung nahe. Interessanterweise sind auf dem Teppich Damhirsche dargestellt, die es im Altai gar nicht gab. Die Heimat dieser Tiere ist Kleinasien – das eigentliche Zentrum kultischen Brettspiels.

Ein Divinationsbehelf

Wer waren nun die Gottheiten, deren Willen man hier erkunden wollte? Es gilt als ausgemacht, daß auf dem Filzteppich des V. Kurgans eine weibliche Gottheit abgebildet ist. Da die gleiche Szene auch im pontischen Raum dargestellt wurde, sieht man in ihr jene weitverbreitete Gestalt, die im medisch-persischen Raum Anahita heißt.

Daß die Tierbilder keine Gottheiten höheren Ranges darstellen, ist bereits durch die ornamentale Verwendung klar. Es wäre aber denkbar, daß sie irgendwelchen Kraft- und Segensbringern entsprechen. Dafür ist die reiche Tätowierung des Mannes im II. Kurgan als Beleg angeführt worden. Grjaznov glaubt, daß bestimmte Tiere den Schichten des Kosmos, oberen und unteren Welten zugeordnet waren. Das würde interessante Aspekte sowohl für den eben erwähnten Teppich als auch für bestimmte Kompositionen eröffnen, etwa den im Maul eines Fabeltiers getragenen Hirschkopf. –

In unserer Zusammenstellung haben wir nun eine ganze Reihe von Großkurganen nicht berücksichtigt: Berel' und Katanda, die Radloff eine erste Ahnung von den archäologischen Wundern des Altais vermittelten, Šibe und Bašadar I. Diese Grabanlagen hält man nämlich für jünger, Grjaznov ordnete sie in seine »Šibinsker Phase« ein.

Šibinsker Phase Šibe-Kurgan

Der Šibe-Kurgan hat erhebliche Ausmaße: 45 Meter Durchmesser bei zwei Meter Höhe. Sein großer, sieben Meter tiefer Schacht birgt auf dem Grund die nun schon bekannte Kammer mit doppelter Wand, an ihrer Nordseite lagen vierzehn Pferde, über ihr erhob sich die übliche Stütz- und Schutzkonstruktion, mit dreizehn Lagen von Baumstämmen. Zwei Tote, ein Mann und ein Kind, waren ursprünglich in einem Baumsarg beigesetzt. Man hatte sie einer äußerst gründlichen

Mumifizierung unterzogen, selbst die Muskeln waren fast völlig entfernt und durch pflanzliche Füllmasse ersetzt worden.

In der Kammer wurden viele goldbedeckte Aufnähblättchen gefunden, teilweise von ganz einfacher Form. Reste von Eisengegenständen zeigten Tauschierung in Gold. Auch von einer Lackschale ist die Rede. Bei den Pferdebestattungen wurden Gegenstände im Tierstil entdeckt, zum Beispiel Psalien.

Bei einem Vergleich mit den Angaben der vorhergehenden Phase sieht man keinen wirklichen Unterschied im Ritual. Besonders frappant sind die Übereinstimmungen mit Pazyryk V, dem wohl jüngsten Denkmal des späteren Pazyryk-Horizonts. Hier tritt auch eine ähnlich radikale Einbalsamierung auf.

Nur durch das massenhafte Vorhandensein betont schlicht geformter Aufnähblättchen entsteht eine gewisse Diskrepanz. Man fragt sich, ob das als Berechtigung zum Abgrenzen einer eigenen Phase genügen soll und findet zunächst nur eine Erklärung aus dem Lauf der Forschungsgeschichte: Pazyryk I und Šibe wurden fast gleichzeitig entdeckt, zur selben Zeit wurde auch Noin Ula bekannt. Damals lag es nahe, Šibe als Zwischenglied zwischen diesen beiden Extremen aufzufassen. Man wußte ja noch nicht, daß man auch in der Pazyryk-Gruppe noch auf chinesische Importe stoßen würde.

Kurgane:
Berel', Katanda,
Bašadar I

Allerdings weisen nun andere Hügelgräber deutlichere Unterschiede auf. Berel' hat zum Beispiel viele Pferde, aber fast die Hälfte entbehrt der Schirrung. Katanda enthält keinen Baumsarg mehr, sondern nur hölzerne Bahren. Bašadar I hat eine verhältnismäßig kleine Kammer, an deren Südseite ein Köcher gefunden wurde. Die Mumifizierung erfolgte hier auf eine höchst eigenartige Weise: man hat die Markknochen angebohrt, um sie mit einer Flüssigkeit zu tränken. Andere Kurgane wie Jakonur weisen dann keine Steinkappe mehr auf. Ihre Keramik ist deutlich unterschieden, mit größerer Sorgfalt hergestellt. Rudenko, diesmal nicht ohne Grund, ist nur bereit, diese letzte Gruppe mit reiner Erdaufschüttung als Spätstufe abzutrennen. Das Gros der Archäologen folgt aber doch Grjaznovs schöner und guteingeführter Gliederung. Viele kleinere Kurgane werden hierher gerechnet:

Späteste Kurgane:
Kuraj, Jakonur,
Karakol', Kurota

Kuraj, Jakonur, Karakol', Kurota. Objektiv gesehen dürfte die Zeit nach Pazyryk V eben bei den verschiedenen Stämmen durch ein allmähliches Zerflattern des Rituals gekennzeichnet sein. Qualität der Ausstattung wird durch Quantität ersetzt, zum Beispiel bei den Pferden. Der achämenidische Einfluß schwindet, chinesisches Importgut steht weiterhin zur Verfügung.

Keine künstlerische Einzelleistung dieser späten Phase hat auch nur annähernd die gleiche Beachtung gefunden wie die Gegenstände aus den Pazyryk-Kurganen, wenn wir vielleicht von dem Gewand aus dem Katanda-Kurgan absehen, das im Historischen Museum in Moskau ausgestellt ist. Das hängt nicht nur an den dürftigen Publikationen, sondern auch an einer gewissen Reduktion des Tierstils. An seine Stelle tritt vor allem in den sogenannten Erdkurganen der Besatz mit goldüberzogenen Blättchen einfacherer Form.

Zerflattern von Ritual und Tierstil

Man hat den abstrakten Dekor, der in Tuékta und Bašadar II vorkommt, als Anfang von diesem Ende aufgefaßt, das ist vermutlich nicht richtig. Die schildförmigen Bleche der Spätzeit treten niemals in den frühen Kurganen auf. Es ist nicht nötig, sie aus einer Spiral- oder Volutenornamentik abzuleiten. Was dann in den spätesten Kurganen mit Erdkappe an Wirbelmustern begegnet, das ist wahrscheinlich nicht ein direktes Fortwirken dieses Stilprinzips, sondern durch chinesischen Einfluß entstanden.

Die Datierung, bisher noch nicht durch naturwissenschaftliche Methoden gestützt, ist fragwürdig. Pazyryk V, nur fünfzig Jahre nach Pazyryk I errichtet, erlaubt wohl, statt des von Grjaznov genannten späten Beginns (2. Jahrhundert v. Chr.) bis ins 3. Jahrhundert zu gehen. Ob man mit einer Dauer bis in nachchristliche Zeit rechnen muß, ist ebenso fraglich. Rudenko hat sich strikt dagegen verwahrt.

Absolute Datierung der Šibinsker Phase 3. bis 1. Jh. v. Chr.

Meine im Jahre 1952 entgegen manchen sowjetischen Darstellungen aufgestellte Behauptung, daß sich an diese Phase keine konsequente Fortsetzung schließt, hat sich bewährt. Die nächsten Gräber im Hochaltai sind um viele Jahrhunderte jünger, sie zeigen höchstens einen Abglanz des Tierstils. Vielleicht räumten die Sippen der Herrenbevölkerung den Hochaltai, vielleicht gingen sie auch nur zu einem anderen Bestattungsritual über. Die weitere Entwicklung des Tierstils muß jedenfalls an anderem Material untersucht werden.

Hiatus

IX. DIE HSIUNG-NU IN TRANSBAIKALIEN UND DER NORDMONGOLEI

Forschungsgeschichte Es ist sinnvoll, hier unmittelbar den Raum nördlich der Gobi, Transbaikalien und die Nordmongolei anzuschließen. Er bildete lange Zeit eine Domäne der russischen Forschung. (Erst in allerjüngster Zeit treten mongolische Archäologen, nach sowjetischem Muster geschult, hervor.) Schon während des 18. Jahrhunderts hat man Gräber und andere archäologische Reste beschrieben. Im 19. Jahrhundert erfolgten zahlreiche Ausgrabungen durch Liebhaber und örtliche Museen. Das Hauptinteresse zogen aber natürlich jene weit jüngeren Denkmäler auf sich, zu denen die mit Recht berühmten türkischen Runen-Inschriften gehörten. Das gilt auch für die Orchon-Expedition der Kaiserlich-Russischen Akademie der Wissenschaften.

Schlagartig änderte sich die Situation, als Kozlov, der Führer der mongolisch-tibetischen Expedition 1924 von Funden erfuhr, die der Ingenieur Ballod schon im Sommer 1912 in den Bergen von Noin Ula, nördlich von Ulan Bator, gemacht hatte. Unterstützt von bedeutenden Forschern wie Borovka und Teplouchov deckte er Grabanlagen auf, deren Bau einen enormen Arbeitsaufwand erfordert haben mußte. Am Grunde der bis zu acht Meter tiefen Schächte fanden sich noch trotz der üblichen Ausplünderung kostbare Textilien aus der Zeit um Christi Geburt, teils chinesischer, teils westlicher Herkunft. Auch das sonstige Inventar enthält viele chinesische Importe. So setzte sich bereits damals die Meinung durch, man sei hier auf Fürstengräber der Hsiung-nu gestoßen, jenes mächtigen Volkes, von dessen Kämpfen mit China die Quellen der Han-Zeit immer wieder berichten.

Die Resultate dieser Grabungen wurden zunächst nur höchst fragmentarisch publiziert, zu viele Mitglieder der Expedition fielen der Säuberung anheim. Immerhin war der knappe Bericht Camilla Trevers wenigstens gut illustriert. Heute liegt ein systematisches Werk aus der Feder des unermüdlichen S. I. Rudenko vor – leider mit miserablen Abbildungen.

Trotz dürftigster Berichterstattung waren die Ergebnisse sensationell genug, daß man in der Mongolei weitergrub, allerdings wieder, ohne die Resultate zu veröffentlichen. Günstiger stand es in der Sowjetunion, wo Sosnovskij nicht nur ein Gräberfeld, sondern auch Siedlungen des gleichen Volkes untersuchte, das die Großkurgane angelegt

Das Kerngebiet des alten Hsiung-nu-Reiches wird heute von Mongolen bewohnt. Lange Zeit Träger eines Weltreiches, verloren sie durch die geschickte Politik der in China herrschenden Mandschu-Dynastie sehr an politischer Bedeutung. Buddhistische Klöster absorbierten den Bevölkerungsüberschuß. Trotzdem gelingen auch heute noch Aufnahmen, die das Leben der Steppenkrieger heraufbeschwören. Die Reiter führen an langen Stangen Fangschlingen mit sich.

hatte. Die Grabungen gingen auch nach seinem Tode weiter, neuerlich in ziemlicher Diskretion. Erst über die allerletzten Forschungen in der Mongolei, an denen sich nun auch Einheimische beteiligten, haben wir Berichte, sowohl mongolische als auch russische. Trotzdem bietet sich ein halbwegs geschlossenes Bild nur vom sowjetischen Territorium aus.

Plattengräberkultur ca. 800 bis 150 v. Chr.

In der Waldsteppe südöstlich vom Baikalsee, vor allem an der Selenga, lassen sich zwei Fundgruppen unterscheiden. Die erste, ihrem Charakter nach bronzezeitlich, besteht ausschließlich aus Friedhöfen. Die einzelnen Gräber von ziemlich uniformer Größe tragen oberirdisch Markierungen aus Steinplatten und Steinschüttungen, daher der Name »Plattengräberkultur«. Fast das gesamte Inventar ist geraubt. Der kümmerliche Rest verrät, daß man ähnliche Waffen und Geräte verwendete wie in den Nomadenkulturen des Westens. Unter den Bronzen gibt es einige verschliffene, fast unkenntliche Tierplastiken. Bestimmte Typen entstammen einer östlichen, an der gewaltigen Metallurgie Chinas orientierten Tradition. Eisen bleibt eine Seltenheit. Die wenigen erhaltenen Schädel verraten, daß die Erbauer der Plattengräber mongolid waren, ähnlich den heutigen Tungusen; sicher waren sie mit den Bewohnern der benachbarten Waldgebiete verwandt. Da man keine Siedlungen kennt, aber in den Gräbern die Knochen von Pferden, Rindern und Schafen gefunden hat, hält man die Leute für Nomaden – Reiternomaden, wie der Fund von Schirrungsteilen nahelegt.

Bereits Reiternomaden

In der Spätzeit wird die äußere Markierung der Gräber reicher an Varianten. Man glaubt, daß die Plattengräberkultur von ca. 800 v. Chr. bis zur Mitte des 2. Jahrhunderts v. Chr. bestand.

Ablösung durch Hsiung-nu

Sie wird von einer Kulturgruppe abgelöst, die sich nicht nur durch ein anderes Bestattungsritual, sondern vor allem durch den Reichtum an chinesischen Importgütern auszeichnet, die die Datierung in die Han-Zeit ermöglichen. Aus schriftlichen Dokumenten wird klar, daß man es hier ebenso wie bei den analogen Denkmälern der Nordmongolei mit den archäologischen Spuren der Hsiung-nu zu tun hat.

Wie wir aus chinesischen Quellen wissen, machten sich in der ereignisreichen Geschichte der chinesischen Lehnsstaaten, die vom 8. Jahrhundert v. Chr. an nur mehr sehr oberflächlich durch die nominell herrschende Chou-Dynastie zusammengehalten wurden, häufig nicht-chinesische Nachbarstämme im Nordwesten unangenehm bemerkbar. Auch künstlerisch ist ihr Einfluß nicht zu übersehen. Unter ihnen treten gegen Ende der Chou-Dynastie die Yüe-chi hervor, ein Nomadenvolk von offenbar westlicher Herkunft.

Politische Geschichte

Im Laufe des 3. Jahrhunderts v. Chr. änderte sich die Situation radikal. China wurde durch die Machtpolitik einer kurzlebigen Dynastie politisch geeinigt, ebenso aber auch die Nomaden des Nordwestens: Maotun gründete das Steppenreich der Hsiung-nu. Später hat man ihnen eine lange Vorgeschichte angedichtet und sie mit dem Schicksal älterer chinesischer Dynastien in Verbindung gebracht. Noch heute behaupten sowjetische Autoren, der Name trete schon im 8. Jahrhundert v. Chr. auf. Tatsache ist indessen nur der jähe, gewaltsame Aufstieg – wie bei vielen Steppenvölkern. Ihre eigentliche Herkunft bleibt uns noch verborgen.

An der Wende zum 2. Jahrhundert v. Chr. folgte in China die stabilere Han-Dynastie, aber auch die Hsiung-nu verzeichneten Erfolge. Sie drängten die Yüe-chi nach Westen und preßten sogar den Han eine Zeitlang Tribute ab. In den sich anschließenden Kriegen, die sich über Jahrzehnte zogen, zeigte sich jedoch das hochorganisierte und über außerordentliche Menschenreserven verfügende China überlegen. Es lernte aus der Kampftaktik seiner Nachbarn und verband sie mit einer besseren Strategie. Allmählich ging die Stellung der Hsiung-nu am Südrand der Gobi verloren, selbst die solide Machtbasis nördlich des Wüstengürtels blieb nicht von feindlichen Vorstößen verschont. China sicherte sich die Kontrolle über das Tarimbecken und damit den Handelsweg nach dem Westen, die berühmte »Seidenstraße«. Neue Gruppierungen unter der Führung noch unverbrauchter Stämme zeichneten sich unter den Nomaden ab. Trotz wiederholter Siege wurde schließlich ein großer Teil der wohl recht heterogenen Bevölkerung des Hsiung-nu-Reiches nach dem Westen abgedrängt, man vermutet, daß sich aus solchen Emigranten das Hunnenvolk aufbaut, das in Europa die Völkerwanderung auslöste.

Erst nach dem Untergang der zweiten Han-Dynastie, der auch das Ende einer starken Zentralmacht bedeutete, begann sich das Blatt wieder zu wenden. Teile der aufgesplitterten Hsiung-nu nisteten sich in Nordchina ein, ihre Führer gründeten chinesische Dynastien.

Dieses auf chinesischen Quellen beruhende Bild wird durch die Funde recht eigenartig verschoben. In Transbaikalien, heute auch in der Mongolei, entdeckte man Wallburgen der Hsiung-nu-Zeit. Sie dienten wohl als Stützpunkte im Kampf gegen aufsässige Waldstämme. Die am besten untersuchte ist jedenfalls von Feinden bald nach der Errichtung zerstört und niedergebrannt worden. Ihre Bewohner hatten feste Häuser, offenbar nach chinesischem Vorbild, gebaut. Sie betrieben nicht nur Ackerbau, wie uns Funde von Pflugscharen verraten, sondern widmeten sich auch dem Töpferhandwerk und der militärisch so wichtigen Schmiedekunst. All das ergäbe ein höchst merkwürdiges Bild von Reiternomaden. Wahrscheinlich aber waren die Bewohner dieser Stützpunkte ganz einfach Chinesen, Kriegsgefangene oder Überläufer.

Wallburg in Transbaikalien, an der Ivolga

Die erwähnten »Waldstämme« mögen sich zum großen Teil aus der von den Hsiung-nu verdrängten Steppen- und Waldsteppenbevölkerung zusammengesetzt haben. Der sowjetische Archäologe Okladnikov fand typische Plattengräber weit im Norden, in einer kleinen Steppeninsel inmitten der Taiga Zisbaikaliens.

Gräberfelder der Hsiung-nu

Die Gräber verraten eine scharfe soziale Staffelung. Der einfachste Typus ist oberirdisch nur an einem Steinkreis zu erkennen, der Tote liegt auf einer Steinpackung, nur selten in einem Blockbau geborgen. Vornehmere Leute erhielten einen quadratischen Steinzaun, wenn sie nicht unter flachen Erdhügeln begraben wurden. Später wurde der längliche Blockbau obligatorisch, er ist am Kopfende etwas verbreitert. Gelegentlich finden sich leicht eingezogene Längsseiten. Das ergibt die gleiche Figur, die schon unter den oberirdischen Grabmarkierungen der Plattengräberkultur auffällt. Dem Toten gab man Speisen ins Grab mit, verschiedenes Gerät, Waffen und Pferdegeschirr. Statt der früher üblichen Pferde werden nur mehr deren Schädel deponiert, und

Chinesischer Import

zwar bis zu vier Stück. Seidenstoffe, Jade und Spiegelfragmente chinesischer Herkunft verraten uns, welche Rolle chinesisches Handwerk auch für breitere Schichten der Bevölkerung spielte. In dem Grab eines Anführers entdeckte man ein Kupfersiegel mit chinesischer Inschrift, wohl ein Amtszeichen. Vielleicht noch typischer für die eingetretene Sinisierung ist das Vorkommen von Eßstäbchen. Ein typisches Nomadengerät bilden hingegen Bronzekessel, von denen in Gräbern allerdings nur – pars pro toto – Bruchstücke gefunden wurden. Verstärkungsplatten verraten den Gebrauch des Reflexbogens, der furchtbaren Waffe der Steppenkrieger.

Indigenes Kunstgewerbe

Was man daneben an Produkten eigener künstlerischer Gestaltung antrifft, ist kümmerlich. Da sind zwei kleine Pferdestatuen und mit Goldblech überzogene Bronzeplatten. Greifenköpfchen werden zu chinesischen Wolkenmustern mißbraucht. Alles ist merkwürdig verschliffen, ohne Kraft und Intensität. Nur das frühe Gräberfeld von Derestruj (2.–1.Jahrhundert v.Chr.) ergab zwei durchbrochene Bronzeplatten mit Tierkampfszenen, eine Schnalle in Form eines Büffel-

FIG. 108

kopfs, ja sogar ein Goldblech, das den Angriff eines Greifen auf ein Schaf zeigt. Um so mehr konzentrierten sich alle Erwartungen auf die

Fürstengräber von Noin Ula

Großkurgane in den Bergen von Noin Ula. Sie liegen in etwa 1500 Meter Höhe über dem Meer und sind durch relativ niedrige Aufschüttungen in Form eines Pyramidenstumpfs zu erkennen. Darunter öffnet sich ein Schacht von oft erstaunlicher Tiefe (bis zu 10 Meter), auf dessen Grund die hölzerne Grabkammer steht. Sie ist im Osten, Süden

Fig. 108 – Goldblech mit Tierkampfszene aus dem Derestruj-Gräberfeld. Größte Breite etwa 10 cm. Vgl. S.146

und Westen doppelwandig mit einem Zwischenraum und genau nach den Himmelsrichtungen orientiert. Die Ähnlichkeit mit den Fürstengräbern im Altai springt sofort in die Augen. Für den heutigen Betrachter wird sie noch verstärkt, da auch hier das Zusammenspiel von Frostkonservierung und Beraubung fast nur den vergänglichen Teil des Grabinventars bewahrt hat. Allerdings sind die Gräber so tief, daß die Kammer noch unter der Eislinse liegt. Sie war meist vollständig mit Grundwasser angefüllt. Aber gerade deshalb haben sich die Textilien in erstaunlicher Frische erhalten.

Bei näherer Betrachtung bemerkt man allerdings erhebliche Unterschiede. Die Aufschüttung besteht nur aus Erde (und bedeckt bis zu 1200 Quadratmeter Fläche). Sie ist mit einem Gitter aus Steinreihen überzogen. Vor allem aber zeigt ein allmählich schmäler werdender Wall nach Norden, unter welchem eine schräge Rampe bis in die Tiefe des Schachts führt. In dem Schüttmaterial des Schachts entdeckte man Tierknochen, wohl Reste eines Totenmahls. *Grabkonstruktion*

Die Kammer, ohne den im Altai üblichen Panzer von Baumstämmen, nur durch ihre erstaunlich tiefe Lage geschützt, ist in ihrer Konstruktion fast zart zu nennen. Meist hat man beiderseits gut geglättete Bohlen verwendet und mit Stoff überspannt. Auch der Sarg ist kein Einbaum, sondern aus kunstvoll verzapften Brettern hergestellt. Man vermutet die Arbeit chinesischer Handwerker.

Es fanden sich Überreste von Wagen chinesischer Konstruktion, auch Pferdeschädel, aber es fehlt jeder Hinweis auf die eindrucksvolle Pferdeprozession der Altaileute mit ihren Masken und reichen Schirrungen. Was man an Sätteln und Zaumzeug gefunden hat, reichte gerade für den »persönlichen Bedarf« des Toten. Rudenko glaubt auch, Tragsättel erkennen zu können, aber das bleibt vorläufig unbewiesen. *Wagen, aber keine Massenbeigabe von Pferden*

Ein vergleichbares Massenaufgebot wurde nur an dicken Frauenzöpfen veranstaltet. In einem Grab wurden fünfundachtzig Stück ge- *Frauenzöpfe*

147

Weidende Kamelherde in den Steppen der Mongolischen Volksrepublik. Die äußeren Lebensbedingungen haben sich im Laufe der Jahrtausende nur geringfügig geändert, was die Forscher zunächst zu der leichtfertigen Vermutung verleitet hat, auch die Sozialformen seien gleich geblieben. Das »baktrische« zwei-

höckerige Kamel besaß bei den zentralasiatischen Nomaden große wirtschaftliche Bedeutung, dennoch (oder vielleicht deshalb) blieben Darstellungen im Bereich des Tierstils vereinzelt. Ausnahmen im Schatz Peters des Großen. Man vergleiche auch die sarmatische Platte Seite 59. *Photo Burda*

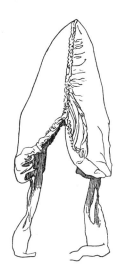

Fig. 109 – Mütze aus ehemals purpurrotem Seidenstoff, verstärkt mit Filz und Birkenrinde-Einlagen aus dem sechsten Kurgan von Noin Ula. Höhe 34 cm. Vgl. S. 151

funden, säuberlich in Futterale gesteckt. Rudenko stellt sich vor, daß der komplette Harem in dieser Form seinem Herrn symbolisch nachfolgte. Die Damen durften wohl am Leben bleiben, waren aber gewissermaßen für das nächste Leben bereits vergeben. Ein derartiges Brauchtum ist bekanntlich im iranischen Raum belegt, wo selbst noch Kinder aus einer späteren Verbindung der Frau dem ersten Gatten zugeschrieben werden. Daß die Haare auf zwei verschiedene Arten geflochten wurden, erklärt Rudenko mit der Abstammung der Frauen aus zwei verschiedenen ethnischen Gruppen, vielleicht aus zwei Phratrien.

Würdezeichen Als Würdezeichen diente – genau nach chinesischem Muster – ein Schirm, dessen Beschläge wieder chinesische Arbeit vermuten lassen. Einen ähnlichen Zweck mögen die häufig auftauchenden Fahnen erfüllt haben, zweizipflige, mit Dreiecken besetzte Streifen, die vielleicht an bronzenen Stangenbekrönungen befestigt waren. Jadestücke mögen als Amtssymbole gedient haben.

Hausgerät Erstaunlich reichhaltig ist das Hausgerät. Wir finden Tischchen, Teppiche, Kessel, viele Lackschalen chinesischer Herkunft und daneben ein urtümlich anmutendes Feuerzeug, bestehend aus einem Brettchen und einem Drillbohrer, schließlich eine Geldkatze. Magische Bedeutung hatte sicher die Beigabe von Haarbüscheln und Finger-

Amulette nägeln, sei es, daß man in ihnen Amulette sah oder daß man sie fremdem Zauber entziehen wollte. Auch die chinesischen Spiegel, von denen immer nur Fragmente gefunden wurden, dienten vermutlich nicht für die Schönheitspflege, sondern wanderten um ihrer Zauberkraft wil-

Waffen len mit ins Grab. Als Waffen finden sich Reflexbogen von anderthalb Meter Länge. Metallstäbe deutet Rudenko – wenig überzeugend – als Keulen. Bronzeplatten sollen als Armschienen gedient haben, nicht als Stirnplatten für Pferde, wie man früher annahm.

In den Gräbern sind nur ganz verstreut Menschenknochen, vor allem Gelenksköpfe, gefunden worden. Es ist keineswegs klar, ob sie von der Hauptbestattung stammen und wie weit sich die Leiche unter den merkwürdigen Bedingungen in der Tiefe zersetzte. Rudenko schweigt sich über dieses Kapitel aus. Möglicherweise haben die Räuber die

Fig. 110 – Fragment eines dunkelroten Woll-
stoffs. Die in braunen und gelblichen Tönen ausgeführte Stickerei zeigt einen Männerkopf, der an
die Porträts der Kushana-Könige erinnert. Vermutlich handelt es sich auch um einen Import aus
dem westlichen Mittelasien. Noin Ula, Tumulus
No. XXV. Etwa 14×20 cm. Vgl. S. 153

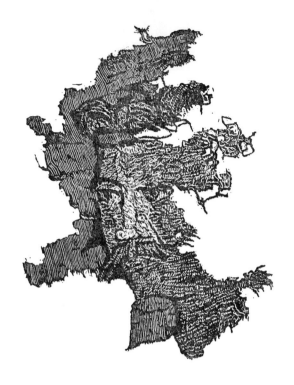

Toten absichtlich zerstückelt und Leichenteile an die Oberfläche ge-
zerrt, die Plünderung wäre dann als magischer Akt mit politischem
Hintergrund aufzufassen. Aus chinesischen Nachrichten wissen wir,
daß die Gräber der Hsiung-nu-Herrscher in Zeiten des Niedergangs
von feindlichen Nachbarn bewußt zerstört wurden.

Manchmal geradezu grotesk zerrissene Fetzen von Textilien, dann
wieder relativ gut erhaltene Kleidungsstücke, kleine, offenbar übersehene Schmuckplatten aus Gold, Bronze und Silber, Reste verschiedener Schachteln und Kassetten vervollständigen das Inventar.

Zusammenfassend können wir sagen, daß wir es zweifellos mit der
Bestattung von Hochadeligen des Hsiung-nu-Reiches, vielleicht sogar
mit den Gräbern der obersten Herrscher, der Shan-Yü, zu tun haben.
Für ihre Bedürfnisse wurden weitgehend die Dienste chinesischer
Handwerker herangezogen. Geschenke des chinesischen Hofes, ver-
schleierte Tribute – heute würden wir von Entwicklungshilfe sprechen
– lieferten einen großen Teil des verwendeten Materials. Die hier und
im Gräberfeld Il'movaja pad' gefundenen Textilien, speziell Seidenstoffe, die man nun endlich zusammenfassend bearbeitet hat, liefern

*Textilien,
besonders Seide*

FIG. 109

151

Rundes Silberblech mit Treibarbeit, ein Yak zwischen zwei Nadelbäumen, über zwei Reihen von kleinen Kuppen stehend. VI. Kurgan von Noin Ula. *14 cm Durchmesser. Vgl. S.153*

einen wertvollen Beitrag zur Geschichte des Kunstgewerbes in der Han-Zeit. Wir bewundern das für diese Phase so typische elegante Linienspiel.

Chinesischer Herkunft ist der zum Schmuck vieler Gegenstände verwendete Lack, vor allem aber finden sich importierte Lackschalen. Eine davon trägt eine gut lesbare Inschrift, die es erlaubt, den Kurgan VI in die ersten Jahrzehnte nach Christi Geburt einzuordnen. Damit ist wohl ein Mittelwert für die ganze Nekropole gegeben. Aber auch bei den Metallarbeiten, vor allem größeren Bronzegefäßen, und bei der feineren Keramik dürfte es sich um Importe oder, wahrscheinlicher noch, um die Arbeit verschleppter Handwerker handeln. *Datierung ins 1. Jahrhundert n. Chr.*

Eine Gruppe von Wollgeweben zeigt hingegen Darstellungen hellenistischen Gepräges, so wie sie zum Beispiel in Kertsch gefunden wurden. Man könnte annehmen, daß es sich um Stücke handelt, die auf der »Seidenstraße« nach Osten wanderten und von den Hsiung-nu in jenen glücklichen Zeiten, in denen sie die Kontrolle über den Handelsweg ausübten, »abgezweigt« worden waren. Es ist jedoch nicht unbedingt sicher, daß man immer eine so weit westliche Herkunft annehmen muß. Aus dem Kurgan XXV stammen ausgezeichnete Stickereien. Sie zeigen Männerköpfe mit Schnurrbärten, die in Gesichtsschnitt und Ausdruck an die Königsporträts der Kushanazeit erinnern. Auch in zwei Reitern hinter ihren edlen Rossen will man Iranier erkennen können. Rudenko glaubt jedenfalls, daß derartige Textilien aus dem hellenistisch beeinflußten Mittelasien stammen, vielleicht sind sie auch von Handwerkern geschaffen, die man an den Fürstenhof der Hsiung-nu geholt hatte. *Einfluß der Seidenstraße*

FIG. 110

Die Edelmetallgegenstände, die wir ja nur als kümmerlichen Rest des früheren Bestandes betrachten können, zeigen kaum Merkmale des Tierstils. Da gibt es unter den mit Granulation geschmückten Goldsachen einen kleinen Rinderkopf, ein weiterer Tierkopf weist Einlagen aus edlen Steinen auf. Vor allem aber haben wir es mit Treibarbeiten zu tun. Die bedeutendsten sind zwei Silberbleche, die einen Yak auf angedeuteten Bergkuppen vor Bäumen zeigen, umrahmt von einem Schnurornament. Ein ähnliches Stück zeigt einen Hirsch. Anzuschließen ist noch ein Rollzylinder aus Knochen, der einen geflügelten Wolf zeigt. Bei keinem Stück kann chinesische Arbeit sicher ausgeschlossen werden. Bergsymbole und Baumdarstellungen sind jedenfalls dem Tierstil fremd. *Kaum echter Tierstil in Metall*

ABB. SEITE 152

Trotzdem hat man viel über die Tierkampfszenen der Noin-Ula-Kurgane geschrieben, der Tierstil der Hsiung-nu mußte sich manche

Applikation auf einem Filzteppich aus dem VI. Kurgan von
Noin Ula. Ein Fabeltier mit dem Körper eines Vielfraß überfällt

einen Elch. Höhe der Zone, an derem unteren Rand ein Überzug aus chinesischer Seide erkennbar ist, etwa 25 cm. *Vgl. S. 156*

tiefsinnige, aus innerer Schau erwachsene Deutung gefallen lassen. Die nicht allzu breite Basis solcher Betrachtungen sind Applikationen, die man auf zwei Teppichen fand. Weitaus besser erhalten und publiziert ist davon das große Exemplar (2,60 × 1,95 Meter), das einst den Boden der Vorkammer im VI. Kurgan bedeckte.

Ein Filzteppich mit Tierkampfszenen

Dieser Filzteppich hat ein Mittelfeld aus vierundzwanzig fortlaufenden Bandspiralen, deren Zwischenräume Zungenvoluten füllen. Um das einfarbige, nur gesteppte Zentrum zieht sich außerhalb einer grob gemusterten Bordüre ein Fries, in dem Baumsymbole mit Tierkampfszenen abwechseln. Eine Szene zeigt jeweils einen Yak, der gegen ein zubeißendes Fabeltier stößt. Es hat einen Tigerkörper und eine Mähne; Geweih und Schwanz laufen in Vogelköpfe aus. Die nächste Szene stellt dann meist einen Vielfraß mit Vogelflügeln und Vogelschwanz dar, der einen fliehenden Cerviden, wahrscheinlich einen Elch, überfällt. Auf den Körpern sind – vermutlich chinesisch beeinflußte – Kurvenornamente zu sehen.

Jüngere, modifizierte Form des Tierstils

Trotz erheblicher dynamischer Realistik sind einige entscheidende Veränderungen gegenüber der Kunst der großen Altai-Kurgane zu bemerken. Das strenge Prinzip, entweder Frontalbild oder aber Seitenansicht zu geben, eventuell beide unter rechtem Winkel zu kombinieren, ist hier aufgegeben worden. Man könnte sogar eine gewisse perspektivische Einstellung vermuten. Nicht mehr die Spannung vor der Bewegung, sondern diese selbst wird dargestellt. Es fehlt die Füllung

ABB. SEITE 154, 155

großer Flächen mit Motiven vorderasiatischer Herkunft (Punkt-, Beistrichmuster), es fehlen die Spiralwirbel. Dafür besteht eine Tendenz zur Verwendung konzentrischer Kreisbogen, als hätte man mit einem Stichel gearbeitet. Das Prinzip der Silhouette ist verschwunden, zur Charakterisierung des Körperteils werden Farbunterschiede verwendet. Man merkt bei genauerer Betrachtung, daß sich manche dieser Eigentümlichkeiten auf den wenigen Stücken von Derestruj wiederfinden, vor allem auf dem Goldblech, das den Angriff eines Greifen auf ein Bergschaf zeigt.

Die beste Bestätigung, daß hier wirklich eine jüngere Phase des Tierstils vorliegt, liefert der Vergleich mit den bisher wenig beachteten jüngeren Altai-Kurganen der Šibe-Phase. Der Kumurtuk-Kurgan im Altai enthält z. B. noch einen Bronzedolch altertümlicher Form, aber daneben eine Platte, die bei der Darstellung von Greifenköpfen die gleichen Parallelschwünge zeigt. Ähnliche Details werden wir auch an den sibirischen Goldplatten wiederfinden.

Vielleicht ist es kein Zufall, daß solche Motive in dem ärmlicheren,

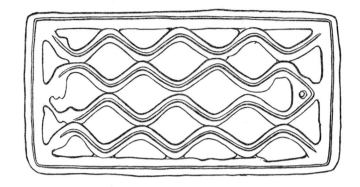

hinterwäldlerischen Derestruj noch in Metall, in Noin Ula aber nur mehr auf den Filzteppichen auftreten (die von den konservativeren Frauen hergestellt wurden). Die Metallurgen bevorzugten bereits eine andere Stilrichtung, wie sie in den getriebenen Silberplatten faßbar wird. Damit würde klar, warum in vielen Kurganen nur so wenige Objekte im Tierstil entdeckt wurden.

Noch eine andere Überlegung wäre hier möglich. Der Filzteppich hat in seinem Aufbau (Friese um ein Mittelfeld aus vierundzwanzig gleichen Figuren) eine vage Ähnlichkeit mit dem Knüpfteppich des V. Pazyryk-Kurgans. Vielleicht hat auch er einen rituellen Hintergrund. Dann wäre es durchaus plausibel, daß auf einem religiös bedeutsamen Stück Symbole verwendet wurden, die einer bereits im täglichen Gebrauch überholten – oder auch nur tabuierten – Formtradition angehörten.

Jedenfalls ist es kaum ratsam, für die Blütezeit des Hsiung-nu-Reiches noch ein allgemeines »Vorherrschen« der Tierstilkunst anzunehmen. Vermutlich fehlten bereits die sozialen Voraussetzungen. Die reichen Importe und die Verwendung chinesischer Handwerker ließen allmählich die eigene Kunst zurücktreten. Aber auch das Interesse hatte sich verlagert. Die Herrschaft des agonalen Prinzips war gebrochen, hier treffen wir nicht mehr freie, gleichberechtigte Sippen, die nach Ruhm und Unsterblichkeit streben und sich selbst in ihrer Kunst verherrlichen, sondern Untertanen eines Großreichs, dessen Herrscher zwar durch einen unüberbrückbaren religiösen Abstand vom Volk getrennt wird, dessen Organisation aber viel vom Nachbarland übernommen hatte, wo damals, seit der Tsin-Dynastie, ein rationales, geradezu macchiavellistisches Prinzip dominierte.

Man hat in den europäischen Hunnen die ersten Träger einer Macht-

kunst sehen wollen. Diesbezüglich waren sie nur die gelehrigen Schüler
ihrer fernöstlichen Vorläufer. Das Prinzip des Tierstils mag damals
bereits ein Überbleibsel gewesen sein, hereinragend aus einer anderen
Welt. Im Hsiung-nu-Reich hielt sich noch der rituelle Gebrauch von
Motiven, die in der vorhergehenden Periode frei übernommen oder
geschaffen, verändert oder aufgelöst worden waren.

X. DIE ORDOSBRONZEN

Inzwischen haben wir genügend über die Mongolei und ihre Grenz-
gebiete erfahren, um uns an die Ordosbronzen heranzuwagen können.
Diese berühmt gewordenen Bronzen, von denen heute nur mehr ein
kleiner Rest unverkauft bei den Händlern liegt – die meisten sind längst
in Museen und Privatsammlungen gelandet – sind stumme Denkmäler
eines archäologischen Skandals erster Ordnung. Die Ursache ist in
dem gutentwickelten chinesischen Antiquitätenhandel, dem Fehlen
einer effektiven Staatskontrolle und vor allem in der Tatsache zu
suchen, daß sich nach dem Ersten Weltkrieg Tierstilobjektive allgemein lebhafter Beachtung erfreuten. Als daher in den Steppen nördlich der Großen Mauer einschlägige Bronzen gefunden wurden, mel-
deten sich sofort Interessenten – im Gegensatz zur Vorkriegszeit. Damals waren die wenigen Stücke, die in der Ausstellung des Burlington-
Clubs auftauchten, noch ohne Echo geblieben. Jetzt aber tätigte das
Britische Museum erste Käufe. Der Durchbruch erfolgte dann in Paris
durch eine Ausstellung im Musée Cernuschi. Die Preise zogen an, das
Angebot an Oberflächenfunden genügte nicht mehr, so beeilten sich
Raubgräber, der Nachfrage nach besten Kräften gerecht zu werden.
Wieweit sich auch Fälscher an der Konjunktur beteiligten, ist noch
nicht restlos untersucht.

Begreiflicherweise wurde der unermüdliche Leiter der Ostasiatischen
Sammlungen in Stockholm, J.G.Andersson, der damals fast im Allein-
gang die chinesische Urgeschichte vorantrieb, auf den neuen Fund-
bestand aufmerksam. Er erwarb eine reiche, aber natürlich völlig

*Auftauchen und
Schicksal der
Ordosbronzen*

ABB. SEITE 161

*Fig. 112 – Ordosbronze phantastischer Form: Reitender Affe. Museum für
Völkerkunde, Wien. Slg. Exner. (Nach Bleichsteiner 1939.) Vgl. S. 160*

undokumentierte Kollektion und publizierte sie in prächtig illustrierten Artikeln, deren Titel durchaus geeignet waren, das Interesse der Mäzene – die er zur Fortsetzung seiner Sisyphusarbeit brauchte – zu wecken. Dem »Weg über die Steppen« folgte die »Jagdmagie im Tierstil«. Minns hatte das zweifelhafte Glück, für die Gruppe, die man bis dahin nach der Provinz Sui-yüan bezeichnete oder beziehungsvoll

Ordos: ursprünglich Mongolenstamm im Hoang-ho-Bogen

»sino-sibirisch« nannte, einen zugkräftigen Namen zu finden: »Ordosbronzen«. Ordos heißt das Steppenland zwischen dem nach Norden ausgreifenden Bogen des Hoang-ho und der Großen Mauer. Andere Gelehrte verwiesen auf geheimnisvolle Zusammenhänge mit der Hallstattkultur. Nicht bestreiten ließen sich merkwürdig diffuse Fäden zu praktisch allen Tierstilprovinzen.

Häufigste Typen

Und immer noch strömten Bronzen auf den Markt, folgten dem Geruch des Geldes nach New York, nach Paris – wo sie sich zu herrlichen Verkaufskollektionen der Händler Loo und Wannieck speicherten – und verzweigten sich schließlich in Dutzende größerer und kleinerer Privatsammlungen, darunter so berühmte wie Stoclet und David-Weill. Manche gelangten direkt oder im Erbgang in Museen. Allmählich gewöhnte man sich an ihre Typen. Es gab da Messer, Dolche,

ABB. SEITE 162

Äxte und Tüllenbeile, Zaumzeug, Gürtelhaken, Stangenbekrönungen, Hohlplastiken von Tieren unbekannter Verwendung, vor allem aber Beschlagstücke, Anhänger, Platten und Plättchen. Überall kehrte das Tierbild wieder, manchmal ernst und großartig wie im pontischen Raum und im Altai, manchmal aber fast spielerisch verformt und kombiniert. Da gibt es Raubtiere mit abnehmbarem oder überhaupt nicht passendem Kopf – einen Wolf mit dem friedlichen Gesicht eines Widders –, aber auch hocherotische Szenen, daneben viel Verwasche-

FIG. 112

nes, Unklares, Dekadentes. Menschenfiguren spielen eine erhebliche Rolle. Insgesamt hat man eine Spannweite des Möglichen vor sich, wie sie bei keiner anderen Tierstilprovinz gegeben ist.

Eine Beruhigung trat erst ein, als die kriegerischen Ereignisse der dreißiger Jahre, das Vordringen der Japaner in Nordchina, dem Aus-

---

Repräsentative Auswahl von Schmuckplatten aus dem Ordos-Raum. Das untere Stück findet seine Parallelen im Schatze Peters des Großen, der Yak (oben links) steht den Darstellungen aus Noin Ula nahe; das Stück mit den zwei äsenden Equiden gehört zu dem abgebildeten Gürtelplattenfragment (Abb. Seite 76) aus Minussinsk. Doch die perspektivische Darstellung eines Widders (oben, rechts) überschreitet den üblichen Variationsbereich des Tierstils. *British Museum, London*

Völlig in den Steppenbereich
gehört jedoch diese Standarten-
bekrönung *(etwas verkleinert),*
British Museum, London Vgl. S. 160

verkauf ein Ende setzten. Welcher Schaden inzwischen angerichtet
worden war, läßt sich daraus entnehmen, daß nicht ein einziger
geschlossener Fundkomplex vorlag. Nur der schwedische Forscher
Arne versuchte, nach den Aussagen von Bauern zwei Grabinventare
zu rekonstruieren. Trotz der Nähe chinesischer Zentren fand sich auf
keinem Stück eine Inschrift. Es blieb also allein der Weg der Analyse
und des Vergleichs.

Ringen um Datierung Viele Gelehrte – darunter Minns – unterschieden in groben Zügen
und Zuordnung zwei Gruppen. Eine sei chinesisch, jedoch in Form und Dekor von

Fig. 113 – Dieser Streitpickel ist in seinem Dekor chinesisch, aber seine Form verweist ihn in den Steppenraum. Die umgekehrte Kombination ist viel häufiger. Länge 20 cm. Museum für Völkerkunde, München. Vgl. unten

einem fremden Element beeinflußt. Die andere nannte man »barbarisch«. Einzelne Typen erinnern so sehr an Schöpfungen des skythischen Tierstils, daß man glaubte, eine Datierung in die letzten Jahrhunderte vor Christus rechtfertigen zu können.

Danach schien die ethnische Zuordnung ziemlich leicht. Die chinesischen Geschichtswerke, die von den tödlichen Kämpfen der beiden Han-Dynastien mit den Hsiung-nu erzählten, waren gut publiziert. Gerade hatten die Funde von Noin Ula den Gelehrten dieses Volk interessant gemacht. Es hatte auch südlich der Gobi über die Ordos-Steppe geherrscht. Warum sollte es nicht Träger jener merkwürdigen Gießerkunst gewesen sein?

Eine solche Überzeugung war übrigens geeignet, den Handelswert der Bronzen weiter zu steigern. Nur gelegentlich wunderte man sich, daß sich die europäischen Hunnen, die man ja für Nachfahren der Hsiung-nu hielt, in bezug auf Tierstil als völlige Versager herausstellten. Aber schließlich war es ein langer, abenteuerlicher Weg von Noin Ula bis zu den Katalaunischen Feldern, da mochte manches verloren gegangen sein.

Noch 1962 schrieb Rudenko ein Buch über Noin Ula, das völlig in dieser Tradition steht. Er macht gewissermaßen eine Anleihe bei den Ordosbronzen, um den in der Nordmongolei und in Transbaikalien nur dürftig vertretenen Tierstil doch noch für die Hsiung-nu reklamieren zu können.

Neuere Grabungen unter dem kommunistischen Regime in Nordchina stützen tatsächlich eine solche Verbindung. Es sind jetzt am Südrand der Gobi Gräberfelder der Han-Zeit entdeckt worden, die in ihrem Charakter nicht chinesisch sind. Sie dürften also den Hsiung-nu zuzuschreiben sein, um so mehr, als in der Nähe auch eine Wallburg entdeckt wurde, ähnlich den Anlagen nördlich der Gobi. Und im Zusammenhang damit fand man durchbrochene Bronzeplatten mit Tierdarstellungen, so wie man sie bisher nur von Oberflächenfunden kannte. Allerdings sind zumindest die in sowjetischen Publikationen abgebildeten Stücke nicht sehr eindrucksvoll, sondern eher unklar, verschwommen.

Wie mir M. v. Dewall liebenswürdigerweise mitteilte, sind freilich in-

Neue Grabungen

Fig. 114 – Ordosmesser mit Tierkopf-Abschluß. Ende des 2. Jahrtausends v. Chr. Länge 18 cm. (Nach Loehr 1951)

zwischen repräsentativere Funde gemacht worden in Gräbern, deren sonstiges Inventar ebenfalls in die Han-Zeit gehört, ja noch später sein könnte. Auch innerhalb des geschlossen chinesischen Kulturgebiets konnte man einige fremde Komplexe mit Ordosbronzen beobachten – wieder mit der Han-Zeit als Datierungsschwerpunkt. Es ist jedoch

die Frage, ob damit das Problem der Ordosbronzen gelöst ist, ob es nicht sehr viel kompliziertere Aspekte enthält. Sind es alle Ordosbronzen, die in diesen späten Grabverbänden vorkommen? Bei den vielen Bronzemessern und Dolchen z.B., die Loehr abgebildet hat, ist das durchaus fraglich. Schon eine Verwendung dieses Metalls in so später Zeit ist nicht wahrscheinlich, es sei denn als Schmuckform oder im kultischen Gebrauch. Tatsächlich erwähnt Dewall an einer Stelle ein Eisenmesser im hanzeitlichen Fund.

Gerade für massive Messer (mit deutlicher Gliederung in Schneide und Griff sowie Schellen- oder Tierkopfabschluß) ist eine solche Zeitstellung auf Grund von Verbindungen einerseits über Südsibirien bis nach Turbino und Seima in Ostrußland, andererseits aber zu An-yang schon mehrfach behauptet worden. In An-yang, dem Zentrum des Shang-Reiches, kommen sie, wie Dewall ausführt, mit Vorliebe als Beigaben in den Wagenkriegerbestattungen vor, die einer kleinen Gruppe von Adeligen in der unmittelbaren Umgebung des Hofes entsprachen.

Da nun der Komplex zweifellos dem ausgehenden zweiten Jahrtausend v. Chr. angehört, so könnte das bedeuten, daß man eine chronologisch ganz anders gelagerte Untergruppe der Ordosbronzen ausscheiden muß, eine Frühphase mit strengen Formen. Aber schon sie kennt, wie wir erwähnten, das Tier als Schmuck.

Welche Konsequenz dies für die Geschichte des Tierstils haben könnte, ist zuerst H. Kühn aufgefallen. Karlgren hat fast widerwillig die unausweichliche Folgerung gezogen und die Möglichkeit ausgesprochen, durch den zeitlichen Vorsprung könne man den gesamten Tierstil der Steppen aus der Shang-Kunst ableiten. Er sei langsam nach Westen weitergesickert, um 500 Jahre später den Pontus zu erreichen. Für die Auffassung Karlgrens spricht, daß die Bedeutung des nord-

Das obere Stück weist prachtvolle Modellierung auf, das untere ist flach und schematisch. Dennoch muß es sich nicht um ein Degenerationsprodukt handeln. Es bestehen Beziehungen zu den großen Rundplatten im Schatz Peters des Großen. Chou-Zeit. *Etwas verkleinert. British Museum, London.*

chinesischen Raums als metallurgisches Zentrum im Laufe der letzten Jahre durch chinesische Grabungen immer stärker hervorgetreten ist. Durch Inschriften gut datierte Nekropolen zeigen uns, daß China nicht nur vom Westen empfangen hat. Auf unbekannten Wegen hat es Europa das Tüllenbeil und die sogenannten Kreuzknöpfe des Hallstattraumes gegeben, so daß man sich fast nicht mehr wundert, daß man in einem Fürstengrab in Deutschland, bei der Heuneburg, echte Seide gefunden hat.

Ein wichtiges Indiz für die These Karlgrens bildet das bereits erwähnte Auftauchen sinider Schädel in den Gräbern der Karasuk-Kultur im Minussinskgebiet. Hier konnten wir auch bei den Metallformen auf eine Abhängigkeit von Ostasien hinweisen. Damals war der chinesische Grenzraum sicher mit Völkern durchsetzt, die Schafe züchteten, vermutlich Vorfahren der tibetischen Nomadenstämme. Man hat vermutet, daß eine solche Gruppe nach dem Jenissei abgedrängt wurde.

Chouzeitliche Gruppe

Andere Indizien sprachen für die Datierung einer weiteren Untergruppe in die letzten Jahrhunderte der Chouzeit. Rudenko hat bei seiner Behandlung der Ordosbronzen fast beiläufig mitgeteilt, es gäbe

ABB. SEITE 3 Tigerdarstellungen, deren Fell ein ähnliches Flammenmuster zeigt wie die Tiger in der »Prozession« auf dem Sargdeckel des zweiten Bašadar-Kurgans. Der aber gehörte nach unserem Urteil in das 5. Jahrhundert v. Chr., Rudenko selbst verwies ihn gar ins 6. Jahrhundert. Es ließen sich weitere Anhaltspunkte solcher Art beibringen. So gibt es Ordosplaketten, deren westliche Verwandte pontische Kunstwerke des 5. Jahrhunderts v. Chr. sind. Bei der Bearbeitung der interessanten, leider in den Kriegswirren verlorengegangenen Sammlung von der Heydt hat der Wiener Gelehrte Griessmaier bereits auf solche Stücke hingewiesen.

Als Einwand gegen die Annahme dieser chouzeitlichen Gruppe könnte man allerdings anführen, daß Dewall eine vorhanzeitliche Kulturprovinz erwähnt, die die Verzierung mit Tierkörpern und Tiergruppen kennt, die sich jedoch von »typischen« Ordosbronzen unterscheidet. Allerdings betrifft sie nur den Ostteil des in Frage stehenden Raums.

Hanzeit und später

Selbst innerhalb der Hanzeit könnte man eine Untergliederung

Die Schmuckplatten können schon infolge ihres symmetrischen Aufbaus, der sich selbst bei der Tierkampfszene (Mitte) bemerkbar macht, in die späte Gruppe eingeordnet werden. Das Auftreten des Yak, der in der Kunst der Hsiung-nu eine große Rolle spielt, bietet eine gute Be-

stätigung (oben). Hinter den Raddarstellungen der untersten Plakette vermutete man buddhistische Einflüsse. *Etwa Originalgröße. British Museum, London. Vgl. S. 168*

treffen. Jene Funde, die dem Material von Derestruj entsprachen, könnten der frühen Hanzeit angehören. Einer späteren Phase werden dann wohl jene Bronzen zuzuschreiben sein, deren Muster nicht für den Altai charakteristisch sind. Es sind dies z. B. Gürtelschnallen mit viereckigem Rahmen und relativ strenger Linienführung, oft ohne eigentliche Tierbilder. Typisch für die Spätzeit dürfte auch eine Vorliebe für Symmetrie und eine eigenartige Verschleifung der Formen sein. Der herrschende Geschmack wurde wohl gerade in der Spätzeit durch chinesische Einflüsse überfremdet, er tendierte bereits in Richtung auf die Ornamentstile der späteren Nomaden.

Vergleich mit Taštyk

Eine große Hilfe für die Einordnung dieser Gruppe ist die inzwischen erfolgte stärkere Erforschung der Taštykkultur im Minussinskgebiet. Sie verwendet das Tierbild in rituellem, aber auch, wie wir gehört haben, in fast spielerisch anmutendem Zusammenhang (mit beweglichem Schnabel etc.). Das könnte die früher erwähnten Statuen mit beweglichem Kopf erklären. Überhaupt hat man häufig das Gefühl,

ABB. SEITE 167

Wolf mit Steinbockgehörn. Mischtiere aus völlig realistischen Einzelelementen treten auch in der Taštyk-Kultur auf, ebenfalls ein Hinweis auf späte Entstehung. *British Museum, London*

es nicht mit Dekorationsstücken, sondern mit Amuletten zu tun zu haben – und auch das paßt zu Taštyk.

Ein anderer Teil der Ordosbronzen mag vielleicht noch später zu datieren sein und somit schon den Nachfolgern der Hsiung-nu zugehören. Zur Anfertigung kleiner Schmuckformen wurde Bronze bis tief in die Eisenzeit hinein verwendet. Wir haben von zentralasiatischen Nomadenstämmen berichtet, wie geschickt sie mit einfachsten Hilfsmitteln zu gießen verstanden, wobei ihnen Viehdung als Heizmaterial diente.

Falls sich die Vermutung, daß sich unter den Ordosbronzen – mindestens – zwei vorhanzeitliche Schichten verbergen, durch geschlossene Fundverbände bestätigt, dann könnte man auch versuchen, ethnische Schichten unter den Herstellern zu unterscheiden.

Die Hsiung-nu erscheinen erst knapp vor ihrer Reichsgründung in den chinesischen Quellen, es ist sehr fraglich, ob sich ihre Vorgeschichte in dem, von China aus gesehen, doch unmittelbar vor der Haustüre liegenden Raum südlich der Gobi abgespielt hat. Es dürften hier andere Stämme gelebt haben – und diese Stämme bewahrten, selbst im Verband des Hsiung-nu-Reiches, den Tierstil besser als die herrschende Schicht.

Landschaft

Wenn wir nun zur Besprechung der neuen und nur oberflächlich er-
forschten Tierstilprovinzen übergehen, so beginnen wir am besten mit
Tuwa. Diese Landschaft, die noch vom Zarismus aus dem chinesischen
Staatsverband losgerissen wurde und eine eigene, eigenartige For-
schungstradition besitzt, gehört heute nach längerem Hin und Her
endgültig zur Sowjetunion. Es handelt sich um ein unzugängliches
Gebiet an den Quellflüssen des Jenissei, sehr stark unterkammert und
von hohen, bewaldeten Gebirgszügen umgeben. Die Nordgrenze bildet
der West-Sajan, er trennt es vom Minussinskbecken. Es stoßen hier auf
engstem Raum die Heimatgebiete von Tiergattungen aneinander,
die man sonst kaum gemeinsam vorstellt: Es gab hier nicht nur Rentiere
und Wildpferde (vielleicht den Kulan), sondern auch den wilden Yak
und das Wildkamel. Man hat hier deshalb ein Ursprungsgebiet der
Viehzucht postuliert. Dabei befinden wir uns nahe der großen Wan-
derstraße zwischen Ost und West, die über die Dsungarische Pforte
verläuft.

Forschungs-
geschichte

Die ersten, höchst effektiven Ausgräber waren auch hier wieder
Adrianov (1915/16) und Teplouchov (1926, 1927 und 1929). Leider
blieb es beiden versagt, ihre Ergebnisse zu veröffentlichen, ein Manko,
das bis heute nicht gutgemacht wurde. Nach einigen isolierten Versuchen und Erkundungsvorstößen grub dann Kyzlasov, der auch das
Material seiner Vorgänger das erste Mal systematisch studierte. Parallel
dazu lief die Bearbeitung des Schädelmaterials durch Debec und später
Alekseev.

Kyzlasov gehörte zu einer Expedition der Moskauer Universität. Er
lieferte nur einen höchst gedrängten Überblick über seine Resultate.
Weit besser veröffentlicht sind Arbeiten der seit 1957 tätigen »Tuwi-
nischen komplexen Expedition des Akademie-Instituts für Ethnographie« unter Führung von Potapov. Man beobachtet allerdings ein
sehr geringes Eingehen auf die Ausführungen von Kyzlasov, und dieser
revanchierte sich darauf mit einer harten Besprechung. Im Endeffekt

Fig. 115 – Bronzemesser aus Tuwa, vielleicht 6.Jh.v.Chr. Streufund. (Nach Kyzlasov 1958)

sind wir dann doch auf seine Ausführungen angewiesen, da das neu ergrabene Material meist späteren Zeitstufen angehört.

Kyzlasov unterscheidet eine Bronzezeit zwischen dem Beginn des zweiten Jahrtausends und dem Ende des 8. Jahrhunderts v. Chr., deren Entwicklung in groben Strichen ähnlich verlief wie im Altai und im Minussinskgebiet. Bemerkenswert ist eine große Anzahl von Erzgruben. Die Zeit vom 7.–3. Jahrhundert v. Chr. faßt er unter dem Begriff einer Ujuk-Kultur zusammen. Ihrer ersten Phase, die bis ins 5. Jahrhundert v. Chr. reicht, kann Kyzlasov nur einen sehr unergiebigen Erdkurgan zuweisen, der eine Kammer aus Stämmen gezimmert enthielt. Auf Grund von auswärtigen Vergleichen können jedoch mehrere Streufunde hier eingereiht werden, darunter ein Messer frühtagarischer Form, dessen Griff mit Hirschbildern verziert und dessen Knauf von einem stehenden Tier bekrönt wird.

Ujuk-Kultur 7. bis 3. Jh. v. Chr.

FIG. 115

Hirschsteine

Besser faßbar ist der Tierstil durch die sogenannten Hirschsteine. Diese Stelen, deren Verbreitungsgebiet vom Altai über Tuwa und die Nordmongolei bis Transbaikalien reicht, standen ursprünglich bei Gräbern. Auf manchen von ihnen, vor allem den ältesten, kann man – in grober Arbeit – einen Gürtel, daran befestigte Waffen sowie Schmuckstücke erkennen, so daß die Deutung als Kriegerfiguren wohl einwandfrei ist. Auf den Seitenflächen sind aber nun, oft schräg übereinander, mehrere Hirschdarstellungen angebracht, und diese Form des Dekors scheint mit der Zeit an Bedeutung zuzunehmen. Die Hirschbilder sind nicht einheitlich. Ein Typus zeigt die Tiere mit gestreckten Beinen wie auf einem aus dem Altai stammenden Spiegel, den wir abgebildet haben (Fig. 50), ein anderer mit untergeschlagenen, parallel zueinander liegenden Extremitäten, also in der üblichen Pose der Minussinskbronzen. Die im südlichen Tuwa beobachtete Form hingegen ist seltsam überzüchtet: mit weit vorgestrecktem Kopf und zwei Geweihästen. Man findet sie einerseits in der östlichen Mongolei und in Transbaikalien wieder, andererseits aber in Ostkazachstan, ferner, und zwar auf Felsbildern, in Fergana und schließlich unter den Bronzen der Spät-Koban-Kultur im Nordkaukasus. Členova, die sich mit Darstellungen von Cerviden in skythischer Zeit beschäftigt hat, meint, diese Verbreitung zeige, daß der Typus ursprünglich von den sakischen Völkern Mittelasiens entwickelt wurde. Wo sie, wenigstens als dünne

Fig. 116 – Hirschstele aus Tuwa. Die am Gürtel befestigten Waffen sind klar zu erkennen. (Nach Kyzlasov 1958)

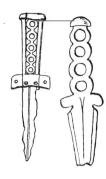

FIG. 117

Fig. 117 – Dolche mit Griffen aus aneinandergereihten Ringen. Links Matra, Ungarn, rechts Tuwa. Streufund. (Nach Kyzlasov)

Varianten des Bestattungsrituals

Oberschicht, herrschten, seien die Gedenkstatuen ihrer Anführer mit diesem Symbol geziert worden, das für das Totemtier des ganzen Volkes stand. Saka soll ja nach einem sowjetischen Linguisten »Hirsch« bedeuten. In diesem Zusammenhang ist interessant, daß wirklich Verbindungen zwischen Tuwa und Osteuropa bestehen. Unter den Zufallsfunden taucht ein Dolch auf, dessen Griff aus nebeneinanderliegenden Ringen aufgebaut ist. Diesen eigentümlichen Zug finden wir in Osteuropa und im Kaukasus wieder.

Die zweite Phase zeichnet sich durch eine erstaunliche Fülle an Bestattungsformen aus, Kyzlasov unterscheidet nicht weniger als sechs. Manche Gräber sind ganz ähnlich denen des gleichzeitigen Minussinskgebietes: man hat den Grabbau vor seiner endgültigen Schließung niedergebrannt und statt der Waffen nur verkleinerte Abbilder mitgegeben.

Auch der Tierstil scheint die gleiche Provenienz zu haben. Andere Anlagen kommen nach den wenigen vorliegenden Berichten auch in der Nordwestmongolei vor. Kyzlasov glaubt, daß solche Gräber von Zuwanderern stammen, die sich jedoch in einen unter einheimischer Führung stehenden Stammesverband eingliedern mußten. Dessen Anführer wurden unter mächtigen Erdkurganen bestattet. Aus ihnen kommen die weitaus meisten Objekte im Tierstildekor. Leider liegen weder Abbildungen noch entsprechende Beschreibungen vor. Andere Gruppen lieferten wesentlich weniger Material. Immerhin sieht man, daß bei den Stämmen, die nach den erbitterten Kämpfen um die Behauptung im Steppenraum Zuflucht in den Tälern des Sajangebirges fanden, verschiedene Stilprinzipien herrschten. Das Schädelmaterial zeigt eine erhebliche Rassenmischung. Neben einem altertümlichen europiden Element herrscht ein mongolides vor, das offenbar nicht aus den Steppen, sondern aus den Waldgebieten des Nordens stammt.

Šurmak-Kultur

In der folgenden Šurmak-Kultur (2. Jahrhundert v. Chr. bis 5. Jahrhundert n. Chr.) bleibt die Vielfalt der Bestattungsrituale bestehen. Im allgemeinen bestehen große Übereinstimmungen mit Taštyk. Sehr deutlich sind Einflüsse der Hsiung-nu, die offenbar längere Zeit hindurch hier herrschten. Um so seltsamer ist es, daß die bekanntgewordenen Schädel zu einem größeren Teil europid sind als die der vorhergehenden Phase. Vielleicht sind unter dem Druck der östlichen Reichsbildung Stämme aus dem Steppenraum, die noch zu diesem Typus gehörten, in den Schutz der Berge ausgewichen. Vom Tierstil wird jetzt nichts mehr berichtet. Offenbar ging seine Rolle – wie im benachbarten Minussinskgebiet – bereits zu Ende.

XII. DIE SAKEN IN MITTELASIEN

Geographischer Aufbau Ein riesiges, für unser Thema zwar äußerst wichtiges, aber nicht besonders ergiebiges Areal haben wir noch zu berücksichtigen: zwischen der Kirgisensteppe und dem Nordrand des Iranischen Plateaus liegen reich gegliederte Landschaften, die man heute in der sowjetischen Literatur als »Mittelasien« zusammenfaßt – um den Begriff »Westturkestan« zu vermeiden. Gewaltige Wüsten dehnen sich hier aus: Karakum, Kyzylkum und Bet-Pak-Dala. Den Ostrand bilden hohe Gebirgsketten, aber dazwischen sind fruchtbare Oasen und lockende Weidegründe eingestreut.

Das hat zur Folge, daß sich die Bevölkerung seit altersher in fleißige Bauern und kriegerische Nomaden gliedert.

Die griechischen Historiker haben uns nicht nur allerhand Namen aus diesem Raum überliefert, sondern auch konkrete Ereignisse und ethnographische Details bewahrt, wobei sie einen großen Teil ihres Wissens von den Persern bezogen. Die Achämeniden kontrollierten während ihrer größten Machtentfaltung das Land bis zum Aralsee, ja bis zum Tienschan. Ihre Königsinschriften bilden heute eine weitere wichtige Quelle. Der Alexanderzug versorgt uns dann mit einem neuen Schub authentischer Nachrichten.

Landschaften und Völker Eine Kette von Oasen zog sich am Rand des Iranischen Plateaus entlang. Hier lagen die Landschaften Hyrkanien, Parthien, Areja, Margiane und Baktrien. Sie beziehen freilich auch jene Gebiete auf dem Plateau mit ein, in denen die Flüsse, die die Oasen speisen, entspringen. Vor dieser Kette liegen exponiert Choresm – am Unterlauf des Amu-Darja, des Oxus der Antike – und Sogdien mit Fergana.

Nomaden muß es auch zwischen den Oasengebieten gegeben haben, die Hauptmasse aber saß nördlich von Sogdien am unteren Syr-Darja (Jaxartes) und an den Nordhängen des Tienschan. Die persischen ABB. SEITE 175 Inschriften nennen sie Saken. Offenbar handelt es sich um eine Sammelbezeichnung, die Griechen brauchten den Begriff »Skythen« oder »Massageten«. Nördlich von den Parthern werden die Daher als Nomaden genannt, von denen man allerdings jetzt feste Siedlungen gefunden haben will. Die ethnographischen Angaben enthalten einige überraschende Momente: man kennt hier keinen Anbau, sondern nur Viehzucht oder – Fischfang. Die Stellung der Frauen ist sehr hoch,

Eine wertvolle Ergänzung zu den antiken Angaben über diesen Raum liefert der Oxusschatz. Ein Wagenmodell aus Gold zeigt, daß man zweirädrige Streit- und Prunkwagen verwendete, auch die Eigentümlichkeiten der Kleidung lassen sich bei den zwei Insassen deutlich erkennen. *Länge 18,8 cm. British Museum, London. Vgl. S. 174*

ähnlich wie bei den Sauromaten. Von einem nördlich anschließenden Volk, den Issedonen, wird darüber hinaus Gemeinbesitz an den Frauen berichtet. Auch die Tötung nutzloser Greise wird erwähnt, ebenso die feierliche Leichenverzehrung durch die nächsten Angehörigen.

Das sind nun alles Eigentümlichkeiten, die nicht ohne weiteres in das übliche Bild indogermanischer Völker hineinpassen. Dennoch gehören nicht nur die seßhaften Völker, sondern offenbar auch der entscheidende Teil der Nomaden zur iranischen Sprachgruppe. Die ältesten Teile des Awesta verraten uns bereits, daß das keineswegs immer ein gutes und friedliches Verhältnis bedeutet hat.

Fig. 118 – Feueraltar aus Bronze, den oberen Rand bekrönen 13 Pantherfiguren. Gesamthöhe 19 cm. Das Stück gehört zu einem 1937 am Issyk-Kul' entdeckten Hort. Es befindet sich heute in der Eremitage, Leningrad. (Nach Bernštam 1952.) Vgl. S. 178

Archäologische Erforschung

Archäologische Forschungen im Oasengürtel des Südens, unter anderem im heutigen Turkmenien, haben eine in große Zeittiefe zurückreichende Agrarkultur vor unserem Blick erstehen lassen. In Choresm hat Tolstov neben alten und ältesten Stationen grandiose Stadtanlagen aufgedeckt, die bereits in der Antike bestanden. Im Osten, der die Gebirgsgebiete einschließt, waren vor allem Expeditionen unter der Leitung Bernštams tätig, der seine Resultate leider in recht schematischer Form vorlegte. In jüngster Zeit haben die Akademien der einzelnen Teilrepubliken eine erstaunliche Ausgrabungstätigkeit entfaltet. Die Übersichtlichkeit leidet jetzt hauptsächlich an der komplizierten Grenzziehung.

Sicher Nomaden zuzuschreiben sind Gräber, die man in großer Zahl am Nordrand des Tienschan und in Semirečien geöffnet hat. In den Berggebieten schieben sie sich weit nach Süden vor, bis in den Altai und Pamir. Man faßt sie unter dem Begriff einer »sakischen Kultur« zusammen – was sogar stimmen dürfte.

Die älteste Phase dieser Kultur wird durch jüngst eröffnete Kurgane im Gebiet von Alma-Ata repräsentiert. Unter einer niedrigen Aufschüttung enthält z. B. ein Kurgan des Gräberfeldes Džuvantobe zwei Gruben. In der einen lag das Pferd, in der anderen der Reiter. Die Männerbeisetzung enthielt nur einen Kamm und ein Messer, beim Pferd fand man Reste der Schirrung, darunter eine Riemenkreuzung

Fig. 119 – Bronzekessel aus Semirečien mit vier Henkeln und drei Füßen, die die Brustpartie von Wildschafen zeigen. Höhe 55 cm. Museum Alma-Ata. (Nach Bernštam 1952.) Vgl. S. 178

Armreifen und Armreifenfragment (Mitte, oben) aus dem Oxusschatz. Starke Unterschiede in der Stilisierung der Tierformen, z. T. ursprünglich mit Zellenschmelz verziert. Der silberne glatte Reifen des unteren Stücks ist moderne Ergänzung. *Durchmesser des größten Ringes (rechts) 8,6 cm. British Museum, London. Vgl. S. 180*

und eine bronzene Trense sehr altertümlicher Form, sowie ein kleines, aus Knochen geschnitztes Pferdeköpfchen. Man entschloß sich zu einer Datierung ins 7.–6. Jahrhundert v. Chr. Spätere Gräber der gleichen Kultur weisen unter der Aufschüttung Gruben auf, deren Wände durch aufgeschichtete Steine verstärkt sind. Die Abdeckung geschieht mit Steinplatten, später durch Balkenlagen. Regelmäßig werden kleine Schalen mit rundem Boden beigegeben, an Waffen fand man Pfeilspitzen und einmal auch einen Dolch in Akinakesform.

Goldenes Greifenfigürchen aus dem Oxusschatz. Vielleicht Schmuck einer Mütze, rückwärts zwei Befestigungsstifte. Zellen zur Aufnahme farbiger Einlagen, der Schwanz des Fabeltieres endet in Form eines Blattes. *Größte Länge nur 6,15 cm. British Museum, London. Vgl. S. 180*

Altartische und Kessel

FIG. 118
FIG. 119

Über »Tierstil« würden wir durch diese Friedhöfe sehr wenig erfahren. Über die Verwendung des Tierbildes geben uns vielmehr Hortfunde Aufschluß. Es handelt sich fast ausschließlich um eigenartige Altartische, die für ein Brandopfer dienten, sowie Kessel, die man vermutlich ebenfalls im Ritus verwendete. Ihr Schmuck besteht in der Regel aus vollplastischen Tiergestalten. Steinböcke oder Ziegen bekrönen

178

den Rand oder schmücken seitlich die Füße. Aber auch Löwengreife und Panther kommen vor.

Das den Tierstil so oft charakterisierende herbe, holzschnittartige Element fehlt völlig. Die Tiere sind plastisch konzipiert. Dafür werden sie manchmal völlig unmotiviert mit S-Spiralen dekoriert, z. B. ein liegender Yak, der sicher zu einem ähnlichen Gegenstand gehörte. Man erinnert sich dabei, daß auch auf dem Kamm von Džuvantobe Spirallocken in Durchbruchsarbeit auftauchen. Es gibt ferner kleine Menschenplastiken, die mit Tieren zu ganzen Szenen zusammengeschlossen sind.

Woher diese im Steppenraum ungewöhnlichen Eigentümlichkeiten abzuleiten sind, lehrt uns der Vergleich mit der Kunst der seßhaften Nachbarvölker, die wir vor allem durch den berühmten Oxusschatz, einen bereits im Jahre 1877 auf baktrischem Boden gemachten Fund, kennen. Er enthält ausgezeichnete realistische Plastiken von Menschen und Tieren, aber auch prachtvolle, hochstilisierte Tierplastiken mit Vertiefungen versehen, die zur Aufnahme von Paste und bunten Steinen dienten. Sie bilden Figuren – Punkt, Komma –, die uns schon aus dem Altai gut bekannt sind, aber hier sehr viel regelmäßiger angewendet werden. Wieder treffen wir auf Fabeltiere, hinter denen altorientalische Vorbilder stehen. *Oxusschatz*

ABB. SEITE 177, 178

Vergleicht man damit die Reliefs von Persepolis und zahlreiche Funde, die man neuerdings auf dem Iranischen Plateau gemacht hat, so wird klar, daß der Oxusschatz den Übergang zu einer ausgedehnten wichtigen Kunstprovinz markiert. Sie umfaßt das Achämenidenreich, hat sich aber wohl schon unter der Herrschaft der Meder aus vielen Elementen synkretistisch aufgebaut. Ihre Nähe zur Steppenkunst wird uns noch beschäftigen, es sei nur vorweggenommen, daß wir es mit dem nächsten Verwandten des Tierstils zu tun haben. Freilich fehlt hier das Spontane, die Lebendigkeit der Nomadenschöpfungen, überall spürt man den mächtigen Auftraggeber durch, der glatte, ästhetisch vollkommene Lösungen verlangt. *Übergänge zur Kunst des iranischen Hochlands*

Die Kulturbeziehungen der sakischen Stämme führen aber nicht nur nach dem Süden. Schon die Tatsache, daß als Werkstoff für die Opfertische und -kessel nicht nur Bronze gewählt wurde, sondern auch Gußeisen, ist vielsagend. Gußeisen ist in China – und fast nur in China – seit vorchristlicher Zeit bekannt, in Europa wird es erst rund zwei Jahrtausende später wichtig. Auch formale Berührungen liegen vor. Neuerdings hat Maenchen-Helfen nachgewiesen, daß chinesische Bronzen deutlich mittelasiatische Einflüsse zeigen, auch jene Muskelzeich- *Chinesischer Einfluß: Gußeisen*

179

Fig. 120 – Bronzeschnalle, Bestandteil der Schirrung.
Aus dem Kurgan Ujgarak 8. Größte Breite etwa 12 cm.
(Nach Tolstov 1962)

nungen, wie wir sie im Oxusschatz so deutlich und regelmäßig beobachten. Die Tiergestalten bedeuten vielleicht generell eine magische Abschirmung. Aus dieser Konzeption, zum Schutz des Gefäßinhalts, mag der Tierhenkel entstanden sein, der später fast im ganzen Steppenraum zu finden ist.

Nekropolen am Syr-Darja

Näher an die bekannten Ausprägungen des Tierstils reicht eine Dekorationsweise, die man jetzt besonders im Syr-Darja-Gebiet, östlich des Aralsees, festgestellt hat. Es handelt sich um vertraute Grundmotive, etwa um das schematische Greifenköpfchen, sie werden aber hier dicht

FIG. 120

aneinandergereiht und bedecken das Stück fast schuppenartig. Aus Streufunden kennen wir schon lange ähnlich dekorierte Objekte, z. B. einen Trensenknebel. Die Friedhöfe, in deren Nähe man jetzt solche Stücke entdeckt hat, verraten eine außerordentlich interessante Differenzierung des Bestattungsrituals. Man baute stabile kreisrunde Sockel, die nur wenige Kammern einschließen und von außen fast an Türme des Schweigens erinnern. Darauf hat man offenbar Hütten oder Pavillons errichtet, in denen man die Toten mit ihren Beigaben verbrannte. Auch unter den Kurganen fand man die Grundrisse solcher niedergebrannter Totenhäuser. Daneben dürfte es Anlagen gegeben haben, in denen nur die Aussetzung der unverbrannten Leiche stattfand. Tolstov hat versucht, die ganze Breite der Überschneidungen darzustellen. Er vermutet, daß die Rituale zunächst einmal verschiedenen sakischen Stämmen eigen waren. Erinnerungen an solche Bestattungsformen sind wieder ins zoroastrische Schrifttum eingegangen. Vermutlich stellt das berühmte Wandgemälde von Pendžikent die Verbrennung im Pavillon dar. Die Aussetzung zum Geierfraß in offenen Türmen war offenbar höchstens für Teile Mittelasiens charakteristisch.

VI. Besšatyr-Kurgan

Von allergrößtem Interesse ist ferner der VI. Besšatyr-Kurgan, den

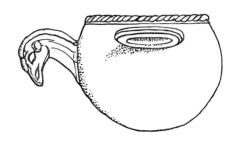

man 180 Kilometer östlich von Alma-Ata entdeckt hat. Er enthält eine hölzerne Kammer, die an Größe den Anlagen von Pazyryk nicht nachsteht, sie ist aber nicht in den gewachsenen Boden eingelassen und völlig anders konstruiert. Nur durch die enorme Trockenheit blieb sie erhalten, freilich mit erschreckender Gründlichkeit ausgeraubt. Darunter, im gewachsenen Boden, hat man merkwürdige Katakomben entdeckt, die vielleicht den Kammern in den Verbrennungssockeln entsprechen. Immerhin erhalten wir einigermaßen eine Ahnung, welche Reichtümer uns hier durch Plünderung verlorengegangen sind.

Es wurde bereits erwähnt, daß sich sakische Nekropolen weit nach dem Süden verstreut finden. Offenkundig schoben sich die Nomaden von Hochweide zu Hochweide vor, ähnlich den heutigen Kirgisen. Eine Eigentümlichkeit der Gräberfelder ist, daß die in Ketten angelegten Kurganaufschüttungen zu einem langen Wall verschmelzen.

In Fergana, das auch schon während der vorangegangenen Periode eine aus den Steppen stammende Bevölkerungsgruppe aufgewiesen hatte, verschmolz die Nomadenkultur mit der einer Agrarbevölkerung, die außerordentlich altertümliche Züge bewahrt hatte, vielleicht sogar noch eine vorindogermanische Sprache redete.

Selbst in den Hochtälern des Ostpamir gibt es »sakische« Gräber. Sie gehören zum Teil einer späten Zeit, den Jahrhunderten um Christi Geburt, an. Zu diesen späten Funden gehört ein höchst eigenartiges Bronzegefäß mit einem angesetzten Tierkopf. Dazu gibt es überraschenderweise ein genaues Gegenstück südlich der Karakorum-Kette, in der heutigen Gilgit-Agency. Litvinskij ist der Meinung, er habe einen Beleg für den sakischen Einbruch nach Nordwestindien entdeckt: dieser habe sich über die Pässe vollzogen.

Der Pamir enthält aber auch altertümlichere Nomadengräber. In

Nomadengräber im Pamir

FIG. 121

Fig. 122 – Bronze eines springenden Steinbocks. Die gegossene Platte hat an der Rückseite eine Öse und bildete den Schmuck eines Bogenfutterals. Breite etwa 6 cm. Kurgan No. 10 im Gräberfeld Pamirskaja I. (Nach Bernštam 1952)

FIG. 122

Sarmatische
Expansion

ABB. SEITE 183

einem war die Grube durch die gewaltigen Hörner von Wildschafen wie gegen dämonische Einflüsse abgeschlossen. Neben dem Toten lagen Bestandteile der Pferdeschirrung. Die Trense, von Steigbügelform, spricht für eine außerordentlich frühe Zeitstellung – fast noch in vorskythische Zeit. Das wird von eigenartigen Riemenkreuzungen »thrako-kimmerischer Form« unterstrichen. Gegossener Bronzeschmuck zeigt das Tierbild: Steinbock und Bär. Gerade die Bärenfigur ist dem »stehenden Tier« des Minussinskgebiets sehr nahe. Auch dem Steinbock ist das schwere, gedrungene Gepräge der südsibirischen Bronzegüsse eigen. Man könnte fast annehmen, es sei eine Gruppe aus dem Norden hierher verschlagen worden.

In den Jahrhunderten nach Christi Geburt treten in sehr großen Teilen Mittelasiens von Kurganen überdeckte Nischengräber auf, in denen europide oder auch mongolide Tote mit deformierten Schädeln ruhen. Man findet sie selbst in Oasen, wo man bisher überhaupt keine Gräber antraf, die seßhafte Bevölkerung also vermutlich ihre Toten aussetzte. Man nimmt an, daß es sich um eine Herrschaftsüberlagerung des ganzen Raumes durch Sarmaten aus dem Wolgagebiet handelt, die allerdings östliche Zuwanderer in sich aufgenommen hatten. Die Tierformen in der Kunst dieser Periode sind sarmatoid. Bei den Gefäßen bleibt der Tierhenkel konsequent erhalten.

Goldenes Armband mit skythischen Motiven. Ein analoges Exemplar befindet sich im Römisch-Germanischen Museum in Köln. Vermutlich handelt es sich trotz der recht altertümlichen Ausführung der Löwenkörper um ein spätes Stück, es könnte einem Anführer jener Nomadenkrieger gehört haben, die im 2. Jahrhundert v. Chr. über Baktrien nach Nordwestindien einbrachen. *Durchmesser 7 cm. Peshawar-Museum, Pakistan. Vgl. S. 182*

Jetzt, am Ende unseres Weges durch die Steppen, bei dem Erfassen der neuen und problemreichen Tierstilprovinzen, müssen wir nach Nord- und Ostkazachstan zurückkehren, dorthin, wo die Tätigkeit der Raubgräber einsetzte.

Vorstöße der
Raubgräber
Die russischen Bauern, die, vom Ural kommend, sich am Ischim-Fluß niederließen, sollen als erste diesem Gewerbe nachgegangen sein, das allerdings nicht weniger gefährlich war als die Goldsuche im Indianerland. Denn die Steppen, in denen die runden Erdhügel lockten, unterstanden keineswegs der Macht des Zaren. Sie bildeten noch lange Zeit Weideplätze von Kazachen und Kalmücken, den Todfeinden der russischen Kolonisten.

Aber wen schreckte das schon, wenn er in einem solchen Kurgan fünf, sechs oder gar sieben Pfund Silber und Gold erbeuten konnte, wie dies der Deutsche Messerschmidt am 25. März 1721 in seinem Tagebuch vermerkt. Man schloß sich also in den Städten wie Tobolsk oder Tomsk zu Expeditionen zusammen. Zwei- bis dreihundert Mann brachen in die Steppe auf, im Frühjahr, solange die Schlittenfähre noch gut war. Bei einer Kette uneröffneter Kurgane zerstreuten sich die Arbeitsgruppen, aber nur bis in Sichtweite, und jeder behielt sein Gewehr bei der Hand. Zu oft waren Einzelgänger ermordet worden.

Manchmal hatte man auch Pech und fand nur Bronzen und verrottetes Eisen. Meist aber lohnte sich die Ausbeute – so sehr, daß viele Schmuckstücke dieser Zeit aus Gräbergold geschmiedet sind. Es hatte bei den Juwelieren seinen festen Preis. Freilich war es notwendig, immer weiter nach Osten vorzurücken und kühner in die Steppe vorzudringen, bis zu zwanzig Tagereisen weit.

Wahrscheinlich wäre der ganze Goldsegen ohne das Dazwischentreten Peters des Großen spurlos versickert. All die goldenen und silbernen Gefäße, Idole, Ketten, Hals- und Armringe, Gürtelplatten und Schnallen wären sang- und klanglos im Schmelztiegel gelandet. Selbst die prachtvolle Kollektion, die sich Peters Vertrauter und Freund, der Holländer Witsen, im Jahre 1716 schicken ließ, erlitt ja schließlich das gleiche Schicksal.

So aber wurde der Zar unter Umständen, die wir um ihrer Dramatik willen in der Einleitung zu diesem Buch erzählt haben, auf die rätselhaften Objekte aus den »tatarischen« Gräbern aufmerksam. Das Resultat seines Sammeleifers bildet jene herrliche Kollektion, die bereits 1726 zweihundertfünzig Objekte aus Gold im Gewicht von insgesamt 74 Pfund umfaßte. Damals bestand sie aus dem Demidov-Geschenk und den Lieferungen der sibirischen Gouverneure Gagarin und Čerkasskij. Der Deutsche Müller hat auf seiner Expedition nach Sibirien noch einige Stücke erwerben können, aber das war nur mehr eine Nachlese. Der Goldrausch hatte plötzlich durch die Erschöpfung aller erreichbaren Gräberfelder ein Ende gefunden. Nur ganz Unentwegte wagten sich noch weiter in die Steppe hinein, in Richtung auf

Schmuckplatte, paarig vorhanden, ein Stück als Pseudoschnalle verwendbar. Überfall eines Löwengreifen auf ein bereits zusammengebrochenes Pferd. Datierung ins 4. Jh. v. Chr. *Breite etwa 12 cm, Gewicht des Paares 307 g. Eremitage, Leningrad. Vgl. S. 197*

die Dsungarei. Das war so gefährlich, daß 1764 ein ausdrückliches Verbot erlassen werden mußte.

Seit 1726 befanden sich die Gegenstände in der neugegründeten Kunstkammer, 1859 wurden sie der Eremitage übergeben. Dort sind heute noch die schönsten Stücke in einer der beiden Goldschatzkammern ausgestellt. Wenn man diesen Raum betritt – nach längerem Umherirren in dem Labyrinth dieses ungeheuerlichen Museums (der Weg durch alle Säle würde einen Fußmarsch von 35 Kilometern erfordern), dann gerät man wie von selbst in jene feierliche Stimmung, die der rätselhaften Pracht angemessen ist.

Inventare,
Datierungsversuche

Selbstverständlich hat man im Laufe von zweieinhalb Jahrhunderten eine ganze Reihe von Inventaren angefertigt, so daß man den Weg der einzelnen Objekte recht gut verfolgen kann. Hinsichtlich der Publikation scheint jedoch ein Unstern zu walten. Das erste Projekt eines illustrierten Kataloges blieb ein Torso, da ein Teil der bereits gestochenen Platten beim Brand der Kunstkammer 1747 zugrunde ging. Die Werke von Linas und Tolstoj-Kondakov im 19. Jahrhundert enthalten nur eine Auswahl. Der 1904 abgeschlossene Katalog von Kieseritzky blieb ungedruckt, vielleicht weil er in deutscher Sprache verfaßt war. Von großer Wichtigkeit wurden die Arbeiten Spicyns im Jahre 1901 und 1906, die bereits einen vielbeachteten Datierungsversuch enthalten. Seitdem riß das Interesse nicht mehr ab, ja es hat sich in den Jahren nach dem Zweiten Weltkrieg verstärkt. Fettich sind einige interessante Beobachtungen gelungen, Salmony einige eher problematische Datierungen. Roes, Haskins und Dittrich haben weitere Überlegungen hinzugefügt.

Gesamtpublikation
von 1962

1962 ist im Rahmen einer umfassenden Bestandsaufnahme aller archäologischen Denkmäler in der UdSSR die längst fällige Gesamtpublikation erschienen. Da inzwischen klar geworden war, daß die Altai-Kurgane den Schlüssel zur Datierung enthalten, hat man dem Ausgräber eben dieser Kurgane die überaus ehrenvolle Aufgabe zugedacht, den Text zu verfassen.

Hoffentlich bleibt diese Edition nicht die letzte. Denn die Farbtafeln sind geradezu erschütternd schlecht und stehen in eklatantem Gegensatz zu den erstaunlichen technischen Fähigkeiten des russischen Volkes, die man bei Raketenstarts immer wieder bewundert. Vor allem aber stellt man bei näherer Betrachtung fest, daß es sich gar nicht um eine echte Gesamtpublikation handelt. Rudenko hat jene Objekte ausgeschieden, die, obgleich sibirischer Herkunft, »aus dem Komplex der grundlegenden Sammlung herausfallen«. Darunter befinden sich

Schmuckplatte aus dickem Goldblech in Gestalt einer eingerollten Raubkatze. Die Zellen dienten zur Aufnahme bunter Einlagen. *Größter Durchmesser
fast 11 cm, Gewicht 221 g. Eremitage, Leningrad. Vgl. S. 188, 195*

ein Rhyton aus achämenidischer Zeit und die Gruppe der sogenannten baktrischen Objekte. Aufgenommen sind hingegen später gemachte
Funde, die aber sicher aus »gleichzeitigen und analogen« Gräbern
stammen.

Die wichtigste – und gewichtigste – Gruppe bilden die Goldplatten, *Goldplatten*
die ein Gewicht von einem halben Kilo erreichen. Sie waren offenbar ABB. SEITE 188
im Grab stets paarig vorhanden und gehören spiegelbildlich zusammen. Selbstverständlich sind nicht mehr alle Garnituren komplett,
kurioserweise ist ein fehlendes Stück von Witsen abgebildet worden.
Es gehörte also zu seiner ins Ausland geschmuggelten Kollektion.
Manche Platten sind rechteckig oder rund, andere haben den Umriß
eines liegenden »B«, wieder andere gleichen einem Rundbogen mit

ABB. SEITE 187

anschließender Schulter. Alle sind durchbrochen gearbeitet. Manche Paare sind sicher Gürtelverschlüsse gewesen. Die hohen Bogenplatten kommen für eine solche Verwendung sicher nicht in Frage. Rudenko nimmt deshalb an, daß sie über der Brust angebracht den Schmuck von Prunkmänteln bildeten. Fettich hat die geistvolle Vermutung geäußert, daß die meisten Goldplatten, typologisch gesehen, als Weiterbildungen der zum selbständigen Ornament gewordenen Riementragösen skythischer Schwertscheiden aufzufassen sind.

Neben einem herrlichen Rolltier, das das Thema einer kreisrunden Platte bildet, finden wir als Hauptmotiv Tierkampfszenen. Wie man bei einem derartig zusammengewürfelten Material nur erwarten kann, lassen sich dabei, abgesehen von erheblichen Differenzen in der künstlerischen Qualität, deutliche Gruppen erkennen.

Die zahlenmäßig stärkste findet ihre Parallelen in den von Rudenko

Goldplatte (paarig vorhanden) zeigt den Kampf eines »mythischen« Wolfs mit einem Tiger. Auf der Rückseite Gewebeabdruck. Stifte zur Befestigung, aber keine Ösen. *Etwa 16 cm lang, Gewicht 526 g. Eremitage, Leningrad. Vgl. S. 187, 197*

ausgegrabenen Altai-Kurganen. Vermutlich enthielten diese auch ähnliche Stücke, sei es aus massivem Gold, sei es aus Holz, mit Goldfolie überzogen.

Ähnlichkeit zu Motiven der Tätowierung im Altai

Eine andere zeigt in wundervoller Modellierung Kompositionen mit ungewöhnlichen Tieren. Wir sehen einen Yak oder auch eine Riesenschlange.

ABB. SEITE 203

Eine dritte Gruppe zeichnet sich durch strenge Symmetrie aus. Die nächsten Parallelen würde man unter den Ordosbronzen finden, mit denen sie auch der »chinesisch« anmutende Bau der Drachenköpfe verbindet.

ABB. SEITE 161, 200

Eine weitere Gruppe hat man »anekdotisch« genannt. Sie läßt sich nicht mehr unter dem Begriff des Tierstils einordnen. Wir sehen zu unserem Erstaunen eine Jagdszene in waldigem Gelände, dann wieder zwei sitzende Personen unter einem Baum, die einen liegenden, vielleicht verwundeten Mann zu bewachen scheinen. Daneben warten zwei Pferde. Hier ist nun Grjaznov eine meisterhafte Beobachtung gelungen. In einem kleinen Artikel stellt er fest, daß die Kopfbedeckung der einen Person mit jenem seltsamen hölzernen Helm identisch sein muß, den die im V. Pazyryk-Kurgan beigesetzte Frau trug. Auf einem Kegelstumpf hat man eine hohe Spitze befestigt, an die der Zopf der Frau angebunden ist. Man denkt daran, daß im gleichen Kurgan ein großer Wandteppich aus Filz gefunden wurde, der ebenfalls szenische Darstellungen trägt. Der Reiter auf diesem Teppich zeigt übrigens eine Tracht und das Pferd einen charakteristischen Mähnenschnitt, die im Altai nicht üblich waren.

Anekdotische Platten
ABB. SEITE 237
FIG. 123, 126

Fig. 123 – Goldplatte (Gegenstück vorhanden) mit Rastszene (oder Totenklage?). Auf der Rückseite zwei Ösen. Etwa 16 cm lang. Eremitage, Leningrad

189

Vielleicht war gerade in diesem Kurgan eine Fürstin mitbestattet, die aus einem Volk stammte, zu dessen »Lokalkultur« die Anfertigung von figurenreichen, erzählenden Kompositionen gehörte, weil es engeren Kontakt zu Völkern hatte, die seßhaft waren und Wandgemälde anfertigten. Dieses Volk könnte auch das chinesische Importgut vermittelt haben, das gerade in Pazyryk V auftaucht. Es käme auch in Frage, wenn man nach den Herstellern der naturalistisch-anekdotischen Goldplatten sucht.

Wir dürfen freilich nie aus dem Auge verlieren, daß wir nur einen Ausschnitt aus jener ungeheuerlichen Fülle von Schöpfungen kennen, die es einst gegeben haben muß und die in den Schmelztiegel wanderte. So bildet ein Kupferstich in dem Werke Witsens zwei Gürtelplatten ab, deren Raubtierfiguren sich durch scharfgratige, kurvenreiche Formen auszeichnen. Zweifellos stehen diese Stücke für eine weitere Gruppe.

Sehr häufig sind bunte Einlegearbeiten. Man verwendete farbige Pasten, Türkise, Korallen und vor allem Bernstein. Förmlich übersät ist eine runde Platte, die einen Hirsch zeigt, der zum Kreis zusammengeschlossen, von Tierkampfszenen umgeben wird. Sie stellen katzenartige Raubtiere im Angriff auf einen Eber dar.

ABB. SEITE 196

Gewebeabdrücke, Rätsel um die Herstellung

Viele Platten weisen eine technisch bedingte Eigentümlichkeit auf, an der man eben lebhaft herumrätselt. Ihre konvexe Rückseite hat eine rauhe Oberfläche, die genau der Struktur eines groben Gewebes entspricht. Meister glaubte, darin die Spuren der Treibarbeit zu erkennen. Das ist ausgeschlossen, schon die Wandstärke verrät, daß die Stücke gegossen sein müssen. Kürzlich gab Jisl einen interessanten Rekonstruktionsversuch des Herstellungsvorgangs: Zuerst habe man auf dem üblichen Weg nach einem holzgeschnitzten Modell eine Matrize angefertigt, dann in diese ein Stück Stoff mit den Umrissen des Gegenstands gelegt und darauf Ton gepreßt. Der Ton sei dann gebrannt zur Patrize geworden, habe aber natürlich die Eindrücke des Gewebes getragen. Auch das kann nach Rudenko nicht stimmen. Die Wandstärke ist ungleichmäßig und größer als der Dicke eines Gewebes entsprechen würde. So entstehen ja auch Plattengewichte von einem halben Kilogramm. Rudenko nimmt deshalb an, man habe beim Formen der Patrize den Raum, der freibleiben sollte, mit Wachs gefüllt, das man mit Stoff abdeckte. Persönlich glaube ich, daß die Abdeckung notwendig war, weil man eben nicht Wachs verwendete (dessen Gebrauch für Nomaden keineswegs selbstverständlich ist), sondern eine andere, weniger geeignete Substanz, vielleicht Ton.

Mützenagraffe, Adlergreif, einen Steinbock schlagend. Das Stück ist aus gepreßten und über-
arbeiteten Goldblechen zusammengesetzt und mit nur teilweise erhaltenen Einlagen aus bunten
Glasflüssen verziert. *Größte Breite etwa 16 cm. Eremitage, Leningrad. Abbildung nach Galvanoplastik
im Victoria and Albert- Museum, London. Vgl. S. 192*

Fig. 124 – Aus Gold gegossene Figur eines liegenden Löwen, dessen Schwanz als Greifenköpfchen endet. Die Zellen nahmen Einlagen aus Bernstein (und Korallen?) auf. Die Plastik (Länge des Originals etwa 4 cm) gehört zu einem massiven, zweigliedrigen Torques (etwa 18 cm Durchmesser, Gewicht 618 g). Eremitage, Leningrad

Schmuckstücke, die einen Onyx im Zentrum einer stark gewölbten Goldfassung aufweisen, die wieder mit Tierkampfszenen bedeckt ist, deutet Rudenko ebenfalls als Kleidungsbesatz.

Hier schließt er auch einen Ring an, auf dessen Peripherie fünf Vogelfiguren aufsitzen.

ABB. SEITE 191 Eine Platte, die in Vorderansicht einen Adlergreif zeigt, der in seinen Fängen einen Steinbock hält, ist schon von Tolstoj und Kondakov als Mützenschmuck von barbarischer Pracht gedeutet worden. Der Greifenkopf sticht scharf aus der Fläche hervor, ganz ähnlich den kombinierten Schnitzarbeiten des Altai-Gebiets.

Halsreifen Zu der nächsten großen Gruppe gehören die Halsreifen. Manchmal haben sie nur die Form eines fast geschlossenen Ringes, oft bestehen sie aus Spiralen, die Enden jedoch sind stets mit Tierkörpern oder -köpfen verziert. Ihre grandiose Ausgestaltung unterliegt den Prinzipien, die wir bei den Goldplatten beobachten konnten.

Andere Halsreifen sind mit Scharnieren versehen, und zwar so, daß zwei ungleich lange Teile entstehen. Das Prinzip der Spirale bleibt meist äußerlich gewahrt. Bei diesem Typ kann man die Ringe vervielfachen und miteinander verbinden, so daß Halskrägen entstehen, die dann weiter umgestaltet werden. Zwischenzonen werden ornamental gefüllt. Der obere Rand kann von mehreren Tierbildern gekrönt werden. Die künstlerisch vollkommensten Stücke sind jedoch FIG. 124 meist einfacher konstruiert. Der figurale Schmuck der Enden wird mit reicher Einlegearbeit versehen.

Armreifen Zu derselben Objektgruppe rechnet Rudenko die Armringe. Auch sie ABB. SEITE 177 bestehen meist aus Drahtspiralen. Gelegentlich wird der Tierkopf am Ende durch eine ganze Komposition ersetzt, die den Angriff eines Raubtiers auf einen Hirsch zeigt. Ungewöhnlich ist ein hoher, durchbrochen gegossener Armreif, dessen Fläche in drei umlaufende Zonen gegliedert ist, die sämtlich Tierkämpfe aufnehmen. Es werden die Angriffe von Wölfen auf ein Pferd und auf Wildschafe dargestellt. Tierbilder schmücken auch die Abschlußleisten der offenen Enden.

Fingerringe Äußerst reich an Varianten sind die Fingerringe. Nur einer, dessen Vorderseite das Bild einer kauernden Wildziege zeigt, ist im Stück gegossen – der nationalen Technik entsprach offenbar auch der Tierstil. Die anderen tragen in ihren Fassungen bunte Steine oder Pasten, einmal auch eine Perle oder aber Platten mit und ohne Dekor. Hier hat man reichlich Granulation und Pseudogranulation verwendet, also Techniken, die uns bisher nicht begegneten. Ein offener Ring ist bezeichnenderweise mit einer Lotospalmette verziert, die vorderasiatischer Herkunft sein muß.

Sehr reich ist die Auswahl an Ohrgehängen, die offenbar von Frauen an beiden Ohren getragen wurden, von Männern aber nur an einem – eine Eigentümlichkeit, die sich bis in die moderne Volkskunde Mitteleuropas verfolgen läßt. Manche Stücke müssen als Amulett verwendet worden sein, denn wir finden auch einmal als Anhänger einen menschlichen Zahn an einem einfachen Kettchen hängend. Ein solches Stück ist auch von Witsen abgebildet worden. Ein andermal finden wir, ebenfalls an einer Kette, nur einen einfachen Doppelhaken, dann wieder ein Köpfchen oder granulationsverzierte Goldperlen. Andere Exemplare haben mehr derartiger Kettchen, es werden Zwischenglieder eingeschoben. Bei wieder anderen sehen wir Trichter, Ringe und goldene Beeren. Schildchen kommen vor, die mit farbiger Paste gefüllt sind, Perlen aus bunten Steinen und kleine Flügelchen treten hinzu. Bei einem besonders reichen Typ wird der untere Teil des Flügels hufeisenförmig verbreitert und kann verschiedene Schmuckformen tragen.

Ohrgehänge

FIG. 70

Der Schatz enthält noch zahlreiche Kleinigkeiten mehr, an denen sich Filigran, Granulation, Gravierung und Cloisonné nachweisen lassen. Manches mag ebenfalls zu Ohrgehängen gehört haben. Hübsch sind Miniaturgefäße; Rudenko überlegt, ob sie zur Aufnahme aromatischer Substanzen oder gar für Pfeilgift gedient haben.

Sonstige Kleinigkeiten

Von einer kleinen, aber künstlerisch hochwertigen Gruppe vermutet Rudenko, sie habe zum Schmuck der Pferdeschirrung gedient. Wir finden Knöpfe, die vermutlich die Riemenkreuzungen bedeckten, und Nachbildungen von Eberhauern in Gold. Hier dominieren sinngemäß massiver Guß und Tierstil. Die zarteren Techniken des persönlichen Schmucks treten zurück.

Schirrungsschmuck

Goldene Anhängsel sind so schwer, daß Rudenko erklärt, sie hätten zum Sattel gehört, obgleich man Gegenstücke aus Holz, nur mit Goldblech überzogen, in den Altai-Kurganen an den Gürteln gefunden hat. Außerhalb dieser großen Gruppen steht ein sehr schönes Pferdeköpfchen, das vielleicht den Abschluß eines Wetzsteins bildete, ein Messergriff, der einst mit reichen Einlegearbeiten verziert war, und vor allem

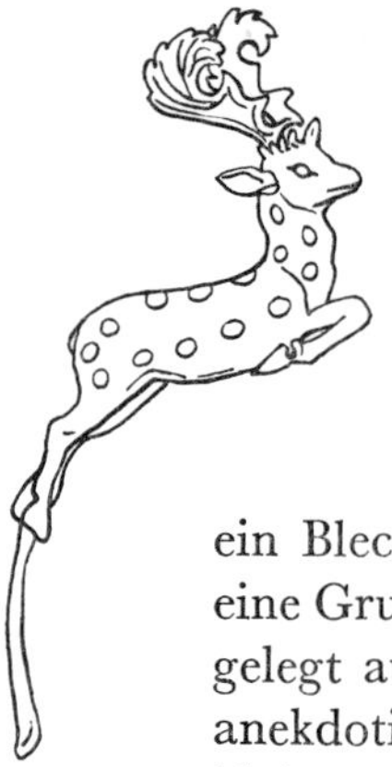

Fig. 125 – Diese naturalistische Plastik eines Damhirsches (Silber, die Flecken des Fells und die Hufe vergoldet) bildete vielleicht den Griff eines Gefäßes (Breite der Figur etwa 8 cm, Gewicht 222 g). Sie gehört zu den wenigen Stücken der sibirischen Kollektion mit genauer Herkunftsangabe. Das Stück wurde von Soldaten am Buchtarma-Fluß ausgegraben, Müller erwarb es dann von Kapitän Bašmakov. Eremitage, Leningrad

ein Blechbeschlag, der einen vierkantigen Stab schmückte. Er zeigt eine Gruppe berittener Krieger, die offenbar Gefallene über den Sattel gelegt aus der Schlacht heimbringen. Das Stück entspricht also den anekdotischen Goldplatten. Unbekannt ist die Verwendung einiger kleiner, recht realistisch ausgeführter Tierplastiken.

Goldschale

Eine schöne Schale mit zylindrischem Hals, waagerecht geripptem Körper und tiergestaltigen Griffen wird von Rudenko ziemlich eingehend behandelt. Er erklärt das Stück für einen Import aus dem Achämenidenreich. Um so weniger versteht man, daß er uns andere Stücke vorenthält, bei denen er die gleiche Herkunft vermutet. –

Datierungsproblem

Der Zugang zum Verständnis der Welt, der diese schier unglaublichen Wunder der Goldschmiedekunst entstammen, wird durch das Datierungsproblem ungemein erschwert.

So lange man sich mit der Auffassung beruhigte, der Tierstil sei aus einer Barbarisierung ionischen Formenguts entstanden, mußte man natürlich annehmen, in Sibirien entstandene Ableger seien erheblich jünger. Auf den Tafeln Witsens sind Münzen römischer Kaiser, z. B. Gordians und Neros abgebildet, das schien die schönste Bestätigung zu sein.

Eine andere, weniger äußerliche Datierungsmöglichkeit erschloß sich, als man eine spätere, polychrome Phase des Tierstils zu unterscheiden begann.

Vergleich mit Kubanfunden

Die Goldplatten weisen reiche Einlegearbeit auf, sie zeigen oft ein phantastisches Linienspiel, ja es lassen sich einige direkte Formparallelen zu Funden aus dem Kubangebiet (Novočerkask) konstatieren. Was lag also näher, als sie ebenfalls in die sarmatische Phase einzureihen? Wir haben bereits gehört, daß ein geschickter Fälscher auf Grund dieser Vermutung weitere Kubanfunde rekonstruierte, die dann als Bestätigung der herrschenden Theorie dienten.

Nun gehört zu der Theorie des sarmatischen Tierstils auch die Vermutung, altskythische Formen hätten in Zentralasien weitergelebt, hier seien Einflüsse der vorderasiatischen Cloisonné-Technik seit langem wirksam. Man könnte also postulieren, daß die Platten entstanden, lange bevor sich der polychrome Stil in Südrußland auswirkte.

Dies wurde aktuell, als die Altai-Grabungen neu begannen und sich ihre Frühdatierung durchsetzte. Hier fand man nämlich weitere Parallelen zu vielen berühmten Stücken des Goldschatzes, aufs engste gekoppelt mit Motiven, deren achämenidische Herkunft unzweifelhaft ist. Rudenko war verständlicherweise auf diesen Aspekt seiner Grabungen besonders stolz. Bereits nach der Entdeckung der tätowierten Leiche erklärte er, das Rätsel des sibirischen Goldes sei endlich gelöst. Von diesem Standpunkt ging er natürlich aus, als ihm die wissenschaftliche Bearbeitung des Schatzes in der Eremitage übertragen wurde. *Parallelen im Altai*

Nach Rudenko sind beide Komplexe durch eine ähnliche Vielfalt künstlerischer Tendenzen gekennzeichnet. Naturalistische Stücke stehen neben phantastischen, ständig wechselt der Grad der Stilisierung. Der Motivschatz umfaßt realistisch beobachtete Tiere ebensogut wie Menschen oder Fabeltiere. Auch in der Behandlung der Details bestehen fortlaufend Übereinstimmungen. Hier wie dort tritt technisch bedingt Schrägschnitt in Erscheinung. Das Fell wird durch geflammte Grate, die Mähne aber durch Schuppen wiedergegeben. Schnauze, Ohren, Pranken werden genormt, wie durch Siegel dargestellt und wieder in der gleichen Richtung variiert. Auf den Muskelpartien der Tiere werden zur Belebung Muster angebracht, am häufigsten Einlagen von Punkt-, Komma- oder Bohnenform. Konturen, die den Schwung der Figur ausmachen, werden durch ein Band kurzer Schraffen hervorgehoben. Wünscht der Künstler, Flächen gegeneinander abzusetzen, so erreicht er das entweder durch eine schlichte Punktierung oder aber durch den Einsatz von Zellenschmelz. Selbst Details weisen identische Ausformung auf, etwa der Schwung der Flügel bei den Greifenfiguren. Manche dieser bis ins einzelne gehenden Übereinstimmungen kehren bei Stücken des Oxusschatzes wieder, etwa die Gliederung großer Körperflächen durch Zellenschmelz. *Vergleich der künstlerischen Prinzipien: Altai – sibirisches Gold*

Da inzwischen in der Altaikunst Zeitstufen erkennbar sind, muß Ähnliches auch bei der sibirischen Kollektion möglich sein, besonders, wenn man gleichzeitig Kontrollvergleiche zum Oxusschatz, zu skythischen und sarmatischen Altertümern anstellt. Diesen Weg versucht Rudenko zu gehen, wobei er sich laufend mit seinen Vorgängern Fettich und Salmony auseinandersetzt. *Zeitliche Gliederung des Schatzes nach Rudenko*

Rudenko glaubt, daß eine schwere goldene Brustplatte in Gestalt eines Rolltiers noch zum beginnenden 6. Jahrhundert gehört. Vergleichs- *6. Jahrhundert v. Chr.*\
ABB. SEITE 187

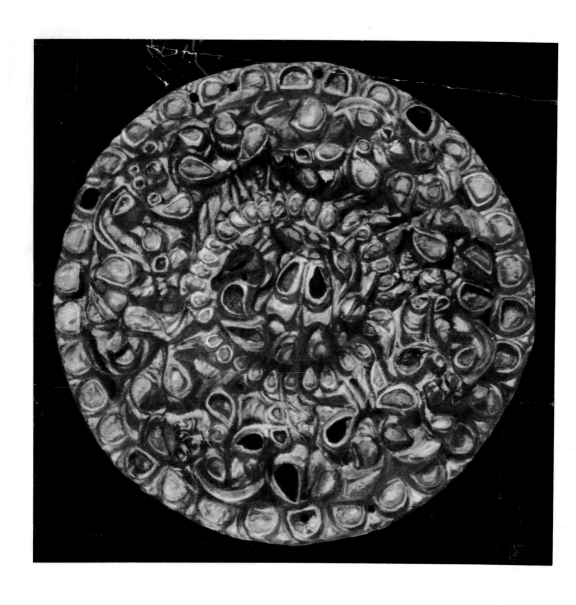

Diese Goldplatte bildete wohl ebenfalls den Schmuck eines Prunkgewandes. (Gegenstück vorhanden.) Die Tierdarstellungen weisen reiche Einlagen aus Türkisen auf, die Tieraugen sind aus schwarzem Stein (oder Paste). *Durchmesser etwa 12 cm. Eremitage, Leningrad. Vgl. S. 190, 197*

196

stücke sind die Rolltiere, die Tatzen und Schwanz des berühmten ABB. SEITE 27
Panthers von Kelermes bilden, sowie eine Bronze der Majemirkultur.
Der Mitte des 6. Jahrhunderts v. Chr. schreibt er dann jene Tierkampf-
platten zu, bei denen das Fell durch geflammte Grate, die Mähne ABB. SEITE 188
aber durch Schuppen wiedergegeben werden. Diese Eigentümlichkeiten treten nämlich bereits im Kurgan Bašadar II auf.
Dem 5. Jahrhundert v. Chr. soll die herrliche runde Platte mit ihren *5. Jahrhundert v. Chr.*
reichen Einlegearbeiten angehören, deren Zentrum einen zusammen- ABB. SEITE 196
gerollten Hirsch zeigt. Als Datierungsschlüssel betrachtet er die Ausgestaltung der Nüstern. In dasselbe Jahrhundert setzt er Stücke, die
sich durch eine gewisse formale Glätte und die häufige Verwendung
der Füllmotive – Punkt, Komma, Bohne – an Stücke des Oxusschatzes
anschließen lassen. Hier reiht er aus starkem Golddraht gefertigte
Arm- und Halsreifen, die bereits erwähnten Anhängsel, sowie einen
sehr schönen Goldknopf ein, der den Überfall eines Raubtiers auf
einen Elch zeigt. Ebenso betrachtet er Scharnierhalsreifen und die
achämenidisch anmutende Goldschale. Er zögert auch nicht, jene
Fingerringe und Ohrgehänge so früh anzusetzen, die sich durch ruhi-
gere Formen auszeichnen.
An die Wende vom 5. zum 4. Jahrhundert oder vielleicht schon ins *5./4. Jahrhundert*
4. Jahrhundert verweist Rudenko auf Grund altaischer Parallelen *v. Chr.*
jene um ihrer Eleganz willen immer wieder abgebildete Platte, die
den Angriff eines Löwengreifen auf ein Pferd darstellt, ferner die ABB. SEITE 185
unruhige, in einen rechteckigen Rahmen gesetzte Szene, die den Kampf
dreier Tiere darstellt, und ein gegossenes Armband mit drei Tier-
kampfzonen. Der Vergleich mit dem Oxusschatz veranlaßt ihn weiter,
die allerschönsten, reich mit Zellenschmelz verzierten Halsreifen noch
in diese Übergangzeit einzuordnen, ebenso die berühmte Mützen-
attache, obgleich Roes den gezackten Kamm des Greifenkopfes erst
in der griechischen Kunst des 4. Jahrhunderts v. Chr. wiederfindet.
Das besage nichts, erklärt Rudenko, es handele sich eben um ein
orientalisches Element, das erst allmählich vom Westen übernommen
wird. Trotz der Einwände anderer Forscher setzt er jene naturalistisch-
anekdotische Platte, die eine Jagd darstellt, so früh an, auch das Blech,
das die Einbringung der Gefallenen wiedergibt. Daß auf der Jagdplatte eine Befestigung des Schwerts zu beobachten ist, die sich von
der skythischen unterscheidet, stört ihn nicht. Maenchen-Helfen hat
ja auch wirklich darin eine Eigentümlichkeit erkannt, die für Stämme
im südlichen Mittelasien charakteristisch war.
Der Umfang dieser Zwischengruppe (5./4. Jahrhundert v. Chr.) muß

freilich als Ausdruck einer gewissen Unsicherheit Rudenkos verstanden werden – es bleibt für das eigentliche 4. Jahrhundert v. Chr. nicht mehr viel übrig, höchstens jene Platten, die in rechteckigem Rahmen symmetrische Darstellungen zeigen, auf Grund sehr vager Beziehungen zu den Pazyryk-Kurganen. Auch Halsreifen in Kragenform, die noch verhältnismäßig einfache Endfiguren aufweisen, sollen diesem Zeitraum angehören.

Gedränge herrscht dann wieder in einer Übergangsgruppe zum 3. Jahrhundert. Damals sollen alle jene Platten entstanden sein, die verschliffene oder thematisch ungewöhnliche Darstellungen enthalten. So wird z. B. einmal der Kampf von Kamelen gegen ein doppelköpfiges Tier dargestellt, das die Vorderkörper von zwei Wölfen vereinigt. Ein Ungeheuer, das auf einem Wolfsleib ein Geweih trägt, das wieder in Greifenköpfchen ausläuft, soll hier einzureihen sein, auch jene recht-

eckigen, plumpen Platten, die einen Wolf im Kampf mit einer Schlange darstellen, ferner die naturalistisch-anekdotische Platte, die die Betreuung oder Beklagung eines Verwundeten unter einem Baume darstellt. Die nur von Witsen abgebildeten scharfgratigen Gürtelplatten sollen hier einzuordnen sein. Parallelen zu sarmatischen Kunstwerken führen zur Einbeziehung einiger Halsreifen.

Dem 3. oder schon dem 2. Jahrhundert soll dann jene überaus schwungvolle Platte zufallen, die den Überfall einer Schlange auf einen Wolf zeigt. Die sonst so schematischen Einlegearbeiten sind hier völlig in die Komposition einbezogen. In der gleichen Endgruppe erscheint eine Greifendarstellung, deren Beziehungen zum sarmatischen Raum nicht zu verkennen sind.

Insgesamt bedeutet dieser Datierungsversuch, daß der Schatz Peters des Großen dem 5. bis 3. Jahrhundert v. Chr. zugewiesen wird, mit einigen Grenzüberschreitungen nach beiden Seiten.

Es fällt auf, daß Rudenko die zweifellos bestehenden Übereinstimmungen zu transbaikalischen und mongolischen Funden der Hsiung-nu-Zeit nicht als Indiz heranzieht. Nicht einmal die 1844 in Verchne-Udinsk gefundene Goldplatte, die nicht nur durch ihre Motivik, sondern schon durch ihre Umrisse einzureihen ist, erscheint ihm als Fixpunkt. Andere haben solche Versuche unternommen.

Soeben trachtete E. Dittrich, nun umgekehrt von Osten her zu einer zeitlichen Klärung zu kommen. Sie will im Goldschatz Stilkreise unterscheiden, von denen zwei den Stufen der Altaikunst entsprechen (aber mit Pazyryk vor Bašadar!). Zwei andere aber werden von ihr »im nordmongolisch-baikalischen Gebiet lokalisiert«, die ältere in

»Noin Ula und Umgebung« wird durch polychrome Kompositionen und die Anwendung bestimmter Kunstgriffe (Dreiviertelprofil der überschnittenen Tierleiber) gekennzeichnet, die spätere mongolisch-baikalische Derestruj-Gruppe kennt auch Kompositionen aus drei und mehr Tieren. Diese beiden östlichen Stilkreise sollen ein Stratum gewissermaßen umgeben, das sich quer durch den Steppenraum legt und dem der Schatz von Novočerkask angehören soll.

In Wirklichkeit dürfte Derestruj erheblich älter sein, als hier vermutet wird. Es brechen die Hsiung-nu-Gräberfelder in Transbaikalien frühzeitig ab, so wie ja auch die Festungen dem Angriff barbarischer Nachbarn erliegen. Dafür ist Noin Ula jünger, bereits in nachchristliche Zeit zu datieren.

Gegenargumente

Vor allem aber handelt es sich bei den Hsiung-nu um die Erstarrung und Konservierung bestimmter Motive im magischen Gebrauch. Wir haben zeigen können, daß der Hauptstrom der künstlerischen Entwicklung bereits längst in eine andere Richtung geht. Auch in Derestruj sind ja nur mehr degenerierte Abkömmlinge der alten Pracht gefunden worden. Gerade diese Stücke sprechen dafür, daß die Blütezeit der Tierdarstellungen vorbei war.

Eine andere Richtung hat der Auflösungsvorgang im Ordosgebiet genommen – hier erfolgt eine Entartung ins Spielerische, vielleicht ins Amulett.

So bleibt die Gliederung Rudenkos vorläufig brauchbarer. Sie ist zumindest konsequent. Wenn er die mongolisch-baikalischen Funde aus den datierenden Vergleichen ausschließt, so nur deshalb, weil er in ihnen verspätete Ausstrahlungen sieht. Bronzeplatten aus dem Minussinskgebiet betrachtet er als Zwischenglieder.

Nicht überzeugend ist freilich, daß er selbst die rechteckigen Platten mit symmetrischen Darstellungen nicht aus dem Osten ableiten will. Hier mag wirklich ein Zentrum im chinesischen Grenzraum beteiligt gewesen sein – aber es lag weiter südlich und war vermutlich älter als die Machtballung der Hsiung-nu.

Aber begrenzte östliche Einflüsse

ABB. SEITE 200

Immerhin machen solche östlichen Vergleichsstücke keine massive Reduktion der Daten Rudenkos notwendig. Wenn man etwas aus dem Schatz mit Sicherheit in die spätere Herrschaftsperiode der Hsiung-nu einreiht, dann eine kleine unscheinbare Schnalle, die keinerlei Tierdarstellungen, sondern nur ein rechteckiges Gitterwerk zeigt.

Wohl aber könnte man einwenden, daß die bisher als Ausgangspunkt verwendeten Datierungen Rudenkos zu hoch gegriffen sind. Wir haben bereits gesehen, daß er die Altai-Funde bis hundert Jahre früher an-

Fettichs Datierungen
bis heute überlegen.
Schwerpunkt im
4. und 3. Jahrhundert
v. Chr.

Ethnische Zuordnung
fraglich

setzt, als der Stilvergleich erfordern würde. Korrigiert man dies, dann sinken selbstverständlich auch die Daten für den Schatz Peters des Großen, der Schwerpunkt verlagert sich ins 4. und 3. Jahrhundert v. Chr. Die vernünftige, nüchterne Betrachtung Fettichs kommt zu ihrem Recht.

Wissen wir damit nun, wer die Hersteller der Goldsachen waren?

Herodot erwähnt eine Reihe von Völkern östlich der Sarmaten. Von ihnen kämen z. B. die Argippäer und die Arimaspen hier in Frage, eventuell die Issedonen, während man die »goldgrabenden Greife«, eine rein sagenhafte Bezeichnung, mit den Altai-Bewohnern identifi-

Goldene Schmuckplatte, reich mit Einlagen aus bunter Paste versehen. (Gegenstück vorhanden, durch einen Haken zur Pseudoschnalle ausgestaltet.) Die Darstellung – zwei Schlangendrachen mit Capridenköpfen zu Seiten eines »Lebensbaums« – ist schon von Borovka mit Schöpfungen der chinesischen Kunst verglichen worden. *Etwa 15 cm breit, Gewicht 353 g. Eremitage, Leningrad.*
Vgl. S. 189, 199

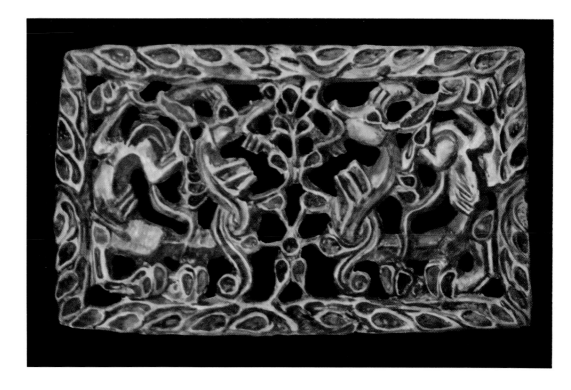

ziert hat. Wahrscheinlich waren die Hersteller der Hauptkomplexe keine Saken, denn deren »Totemtier« war der Hirsch, der, wie wir gesehen haben, als Motiv nur eine geringe Rolle spielt.

Aber leider sind das alles leere Namen. So wendet man sich schließlich wieder hilfesuchend an die Archäologie, um feststellen zu müssen, daß auch sie für Nord- und Zentralkazachstan, die in erster Linie interessanten Räume, wenig zu bieten hat.

1956 beschrieb Grjaznov eine bisher kaum beachtete Gruppe von Grabanlagen von Nordkazachstan, nämlich Kurgane, von denen zangenförmig Steinwalle auseinanderlaufen, was ihnen den anschaulichen Namen »Kurgane mit Schnurrbart« verschafft hat. Er stellte fest, daß sie der skythischen Phase angehören. Im gleichen Jahr begann auch die kazachische Akademie der Wissenschaften mit der Herausgabe einer Serie, die regelmäßig die Berichte der »hauseigenen« Archäologen abdruckt. So wissen wir heute, daß gleichzeitig auch weniger auffallende Anlagen errichtet wurden. Offenbar lebten hier nebeneinander zwei größere Stämme. In welchem Verhältnis zueinander sie standen, wissen wir nicht. *Kurgane in Nordkazachstan*

Wichtig ist, daß auch moderne Streufunde immer wieder die Herrschaft des Tierstils in diesem Raum bestätigen. Wir sehen wohlfundierte Beziehungen zu den Sarmaten im Westen, aber auch zum Altai und Jenisseigebiet. Ein schönes Unikat ist ein Streitpickel, dessen Nacken mit einer Widderplastik geschmückt ist. Das goldene Köpfchen einer Saiga-Antilope mit lyraförmigem Gehörn gleicht genau einem Kunstwerk, das durch die Stiche im Werke Witsens bekannt ist. Bronzetrensen gleichen jenen der Majemirkultur im Altai. Ein Bronzedolch ist mit Voluten und fortlaufenden Spiralen geschmückt. Grjaznov findet Parallelen einerseits in Uzbekistan, andererseits in der Ananino-Kultur. *Tierstil hier belegt*

Auf Grund der gegenwärtigen archäologischen Situation und der alten Angaben, man habe Vorstöße von bis zu zwanzig Tagereisen unternommen, fragt man sich freilich, ob die Raubgräber nicht auch im Gebiet um den Zajsansee, im heutigen Ostkazachstan, operiert haben. Hier sind jedenfalls in jüngster Zeit mächtige Gräberfelder entdeckt worden, die den letzten Jahrhunderten vor Christus angehören. Regionale Unterschiede im Ritual verraten, daß auch hier mehrere Stämme nebeneinander existiert haben müssen. Neben den regulären Bestattungen der freien Nomaden gibt es auch Riesenkurgane – in der Regel säuberlich ausgeraubt. Eine Gruppe, Čilikty, soll den skythischen Großkurganen Südrußlands erstaunlich ähnlich sein. *Gräberfelder in Ostkazachstan*

Trotz aller Zerstörungen hat man hier in Gräbern, die noch dem 6. Jahrhundert v. Chr. angehören, mehrere Goldgegenstände gefunden, Figuren eingerollter Panther, Hirsche und dünne Bleche, die holzgeschnitzte Eberreliefs überzogen.

FIG. 126

Wir befinden uns jetzt unmittelbar vor der Dsungarischen Pforte. Wer hier seine Weidegründe besaß, war geradezu prädestiniert, Verbindungen nach allen Richtungen hin aufrechtzuerhalten. Die Vermutung liegt nahe, daß die Goldplatten mit besonders ausgeprägten östlichen Beziehungen hier gefunden worden sind, ebenso wie jene, die deutliche Übereinstimmungen mit Mittelasien aufweisen. Hier mögen auch frühzeitig mongolisch aussehende Menschen zugewandert sein, wie man sie auf der naturalistisch-anekdotischen Platte mit der Bewachungsszene erkannt haben will. Die Masse der Bewohner war hingegen europid, die Schädel verraten, daß überall noch die Nachkommen der Andronovo-Bevölkerung vorherrschten.

Mehrere Stämme als Hersteller

Jedenfalls muß man als Hintergrund für den gesamten Schatz ein recht komplexes ethnisches Gefüge annehmen, eine Vielzahl von Stämmen, die wohl immer namenlos bleiben werden.

Man hat nun allerdings behauptet, das besage für den Gang der

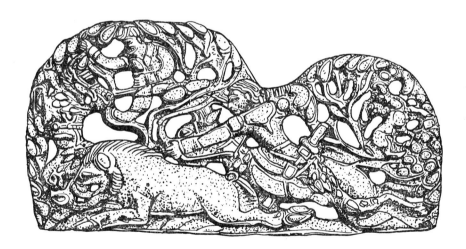

Fig. 126 – Anekdotische Goldplatte (Gegenstück vorhanden) mit Einlagen aus Bernstein und Koralle. Augen aus schwarzem Glas oder Stein. Basisbreite etwa 19 cm, Gewicht 464 g. Berittener Jäger in bewaldeter Berglandschaft. Im Zentrum die Erlegung eines Ebers, links oben ein Mann in einer Baumkrone, der aber sein Pferd festhält, rechts ein offenbar gehetzter Steinbock. Am Verfolger des Ebers beobachtet man eine Trageweise des Schwertes (seitliche Öse an der Scheide), die im südlichen Mittelasien üblich war und von hier nach Ost und West (mit den Kushanas auch nach Indien) ausstrahlte. Eremitage, Leningrad

kunstgeschichtlichen Entwicklung nicht allzuviel. Die Zeitströmungen hätten sich immer sehr gleichmäßig und rigoros durchgesetzt. Konkretes Material spricht dagegen. Wir haben schon bei der Besprechung des Minussinsk-Gebiets gehört, daß in der zweiten Stufe der Tagar-Kultur die Darstellung des Hirsches mit Eigentümlichkeiten durchsetzt ist, die im pontischen Raum längst überholt waren. Man muß also in verschiedenen Gebieten das Überkommene mit wechselnder Zähigkeit bewahrt haben. Nur so läßt sich auch jenes Retardationsproblem erklären, das wir den »Sarmatischen Tierstil« nennen.

Goldplatte mit Darstellung eines Kampfes zwischen Wolf und Riesenschlange. Die vorgesehenen bunten Einlagen fehlen. Rückseite mit Gewebeabdruck und Spuren einer (auch hier erkennbaren) Reparatur. Dorn und Schlitz machen die Platte zu einer Pseudoschnalle, diese Merkmale fehlen dem erhaltenen Gegenstück. So lange und schmale Plattenpaare könnten doch als Gürtelschnallen gedient haben. *Länge 16 cm, Gewicht 222,7 g. Eremitage, Leningrad. Vgl. S. 198*

Da man geneigt war, den Tierstil als eine Fortentwicklung der aus dem Paläolithikum herüberreichenden Jägerkunst aufzufassen und in ihm die künstlerische Kulmination der barbarischen Welt zu sehen, lag es nahe, ihm ein langes Nachwirken einzuräumen. Eine Bereitschaft zur Übernahme seiner Anregungen schien überall gegeben zu sein, wo ein dämonisches Lebensgefühl die Auslieferung an das Schicksal bejahte und dunkel-verstrickt nach Ausdruck drängte. Fettich, der seine Lebensarbeit mit wirklicher Leidenschaft dieser barbarischen Welt neben den Hochkulturen gewidmet hat, formulierte:
»Unter allen Barbarenvölkern sind beginnend mit dem VII.Jahrhundert vor Christi vom Gesichtspunkte der Kleinplastik die Bewohner Südrußlands, die Skythen iranischer Herkunft, die bedeutendsten. Ihre aus verschiedenen barbarischen und klassischen Elementen bestehende Kunst übte in jeder Hinsicht großen Einfluß auf diejenige der umwohnenden Barbarenvölker aus. An verschiedenen Orten entwickelten sich aus den skythischen Grundformen immer wieder neue und neue Animalstile, die nur insofern miteinander übereinstimmen, als bei allen die charakteristischen Eigenschaften der Barbarenkunst in Erscheinung treten: Abweichung vom Naturalismus, resp. geometrische Differenzierung der in der Natur sich findenden Formen oder Vorliebe für vollkommen phantastische Komposition.«

Nachleben in Europa Es fällt auf, daß man diese Zusammenhänge vor allem an europäischem
Germanische Material zeigte. Die altgermanische Tierornamentik ist als zwar recht
Tierornamentik westlicher, aber durchaus legitimer Sproß des skythischen Tierstils angesehen worden. Auch ihr sogenannter »zweiter Stil« wurde trotz erheblicher chronologischer und territorialer Abstände auf die antike Kultur Südrußlands zurückgeführt. Brøndsted, Fettich und viele andere haben zusammengespielt, um das Netz dieser geheimnisvollen östlichen Beziehungen auszudeuten.

Es ist verständlich, daß man die Hunnen, die man ja bezichtigt hat, in einer »von mythischen Bildern erfüllten Welt« gelebt zu haben, gerne als Hauptträger der Tierornamentik gesehen hätte. Ihre Einwanderungssage, die von der Verfolgung eines Hirsches erzählt, wurde in diesem Sinn interpretiert. Tierstilbronzen unterschiedlicher Provenienz mußten als Medium dienen, um ihre Mentalität dem arglosen

Leser nahezubringen. Als es nicht mehr zu übersehen war, daß man sich dabei nur auf ein sehr geringes Material stützen konnte (Tierdarstellungen sind in der hunnischen Kunst Europas ausgesprochen selten), wurde als Ausweg behauptet, das gepunzte Schuppenmuster hunnischer Schmuckbleche gäbe eigentlich die Fiederung eines Raubvogels wieder.

Weit leichter hätte man es diesbezüglich mit der sogenannten spät- *Martinovka-Kultur* hunnischen Metallkunst. Fettich schreibt die Martinovka-Kultur den hunnischen Stämmen zu, die sich ins Dnjepr-Gebiet zurückgezogen hatten. In ihrem kunstgewerblichen Schaffen unterscheidet er eine Komponente, die er schlankweg neoskythisch nennt. Als dann die Avaren im Jahre 568 n.Chr. ins Karpathenbecken einbrachen, haben sie nach Fettich ethnische Elemente aufgenommen, die die Traditionen der Martinovka-Kultur trugen. So sei es zu erklären, daß der in der ABB. SEITE 205 zweiten Hälfte der Avarenzeit auftretende Bronzeguß die neoskythi-

Riemenschmuck mit Greifendarstellung aus dem avarischen Raum. *Slg. Göbl, Wien. Vgl. oben*

Fig. 127 – Gegossene Bronzeplatte mit zoomorpher Junktur. Noch sehr stark vom Tierstil der Steppen beeinflußt (trotz vermutlich recht späten Datums). Bronzeplatte am Jenissei-Kanal gefunden bei Mündung des Jazeva-Flusses. Slg. der Universität Tomsk. (Nach Spicyn 1906)

Avaren sche Stilrichtung »im kulturgeschichtlichen Gesamtbild des frühen Mittelalters« grandios vertritt. Was in der Fachliteratur »Keszthely-Kultur« genannt wurde, das sei im wesentlichen mit diesem neuen Aufblühen der alten Tradition identisch.

Andere Bearbeiter des skythischen Kulturraums haben sich bemüht, diese Fäden weiter und weiter zu verfolgen. T. T. Rice spürt skythische Einflüsse auf angelsächsischen Steinstelen des 11. Jahrhunderts auf. Sie nimmt eine breite Streuung von Nomadenelementen in der slawischen Volkskunst an, ja selbst ein litauisches Bauernhandtuch des 19. Jahrhunderts liefert Vergleichsmaterial.

Je populärer das Niveau der Darstellung gewählt ist, desto weitere Ausstrahlungen werden angenommen. Selbst große Teile der mittelalterlichen Buchmalerei hat man zitiert.

So ist es nicht zu verwundern, daß bei vielen Fachleuten Bedenken gegen eine solche spätskythische Expansion geltend gemacht wurden. Immer wieder hat man eingewendet, daß auch spätrömische oder byzantinische Einflüsse zu ähnlichen Resultaten führen konnten. Auch

Fig. 128 – Wildgans, vermutlich spätes realistisches Stück. Gebiet von Vologda. (Bronzeguß, Gans nach Spicyn 1906)

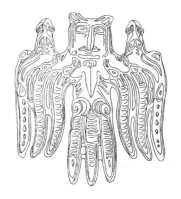

Fig. 129 – Fabelwesen mit den Umrissen eines Vogels und menschlichen Gesichtszügen. Es ist sicher, daß hier eine wichtige religiöse Konzeption dargestellt werden soll. (Eremitage, Kungursker Kollektion, nach Spicyn 1906)

Parallelentstehungen aus einer verwandten geistigen Haltung heraus wurden angenommen.

Es ist in diesem Zusammenhang interessant, sich die Situation in den Weiten des asiatischen Großraums vor Augen zu führen. Auch dort ist das Weiterleben des Tierstils bis in die Gegenwart oder nahe Vergangenheit behauptet worden.

Roerich, selbst aus einer Künstlerfamilie stammend, fand den Tierstil unter den Nomadenstämmen Nordtibets wieder.

Okladnikov erkannte letzte Nachwirkungen im Dekor von jakutischen Sattelbögen.

Vor kurzem behauptete Lopatin das Weiterleben des Tierstils unter den Tungusen des Amurlandes. Die Kunst der Golden, im 5. Jahrhundert von den Altaiern beeinflußt, gehörte zum Tierstilbereich. Noch heute enthalte sie ein modifiziertes Survival der »klassischen« Ausprägung.

Ähnliches Fortwirken wie in Europa will man – wie Fettich selbst ausführte – in Korea und Japan festgestellt haben.   ABB. SEITE 208

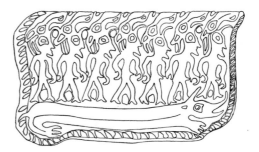

Fig. 130 – Platte »mythologischen« Inhalts, mit typischer Reihung. Auch hier fehlen Tierattribute nicht. Unter den Füßen eine riesige Echse. (Peškova, nach Spicyn 1906)

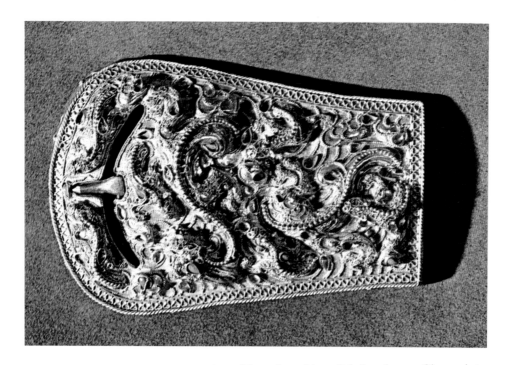

Diese Gürtelschnalle aus Lo-lang (Korea), 1. bis 2. Jahrhundert n. Chr., zeigt deutlich *einen* Weg des Eindringens derartiger Tendenzen. Sie gehörte wohl einem chinesischen Offizier, dessen Ausrüstung unter dem Einfluß der traditionellen Gegner in den Steppen stand. Tiermotive aus den Steppen vereinigen sich hier harmonisch mit einem typisch chinesischen Dekor, dessen Techniken (Filigran und Granulation) allerdings aus dem Okzident stammen. *Gold und Türkise. Nationalmuseum von Korea, Seoul. Vgl. S. 207*

Das beste – und auch am sorgfältigsten untersuchte – Bild eines solchen Nachlebens liefern die Wälder und Tundren beiderseits des Urals, vor allem die berühmte, reiche Landschaft Perm. Hier sind schon während des 19.Jahrhunderts auffällige Funde gemacht worden, die man zunächst ohne jede zeitliche Gliederung unter dem Begriff eines »permisch-skythischen Ornamentstils« einordnete. Es handelte sich meistens um kleine Bronzeplatten, die in gegossener Arbeit realistisch oder auch phantastisch ausgeführte Tiere oder seltener Menschen wiedergeben. Sehr häufig sind Fabelwesen, auch kompliziert ausgeführte Szenen kommen vor. Um ihre Bedeutung und Verwendung zu enträtseln, ging man vom modernen Volksglauben und Brauch der

Permisch-skythischer Ornamentstil

208

ugrischen Stämme aus, die ja einst ganz oder teilweise westlich vom Ural lebten. Jene verwendeten ähnliche Stücke zum Schmuck der Kleidung, als Votivgaben oder aber zum Behang von Götterbildern. Eine durchgehende Verwendung in der Schamanentracht, an die man in einer romantischen Forschungsphase dachte (daher »schamanistische Bronzen«), ist jedoch nicht wahrscheinlich.

FIG. 127, 130

Allmählich begann man, den historischen Ablauf zu übersehen, in dem diese eigenartigen Stücke entstanden sind.

Durch seinen Erzreichtum ist das Gebiet von Perm schon während der Bronzezeit Einbruchsraum gewesen. Die hier entstehende Metallurgie nahm Anregungen aus weit entfernten Gebieten auf (etwa aus dem Kaukasus) und gab sie bis tief in die Waldzone weiter.

Auf dieser Basis entwickelte sich in einem Raum, der auch Perm einschloß, die uns bereits bekannte Ananino-Kultur, die wir schon als Umschlagstelle skythischer Motive und Ideen für Nordosteuropa und Westsibirien kennengelernt haben. Unter südlichem Einfluß wurde damals das Tierbild, das in der Vergangenheit ganz der kultischen Sphäre angehörte, in die Gebrauchskunst übernommen – was allerdings das Mitwirken magischer Vorstellungen nicht ausschließt.

In der Zeit sarmatischer Vorherrschaft über die Steppen entstand dann in konsequenter Weiterentwicklung die Pjanobor-Kultur, die bis ins 5. Jahrhundert n. Chr. hineinreicht. Entscheidend für sie wurde, daß damals unter dem Druck der Reitervölker der Schwerpunkt weiter nach dem Norden verlegt werden mußte. Man trennte sich gewissermaßen von dem großen Fluß der Entwicklung, um ein überaus reiches, den bisherigen Bestand variierendes Eigenleben zu führen.

Pjanobor-Kultur

Unter dieser Formel läßt sich auch die künstlerische Entwicklung verstehen. Manche, skythischer Zeit entstammende Motive wurden nun immer neu und in immer größerer Freiheit abgewandelt und kombiniert, menschliche Gestalten und Gesichter traten hinzu. Neben einzelnen realistischen Tierbildern, bei denen man Verwendung im Rahmen der Jagdmagie vermutet, begegnen uns Mischwesen mit tierischen und menschlichen Attributen. Sie könnten die Götter und Heroen darstellen, von denen die Überlieferungen der Ugrier erzählen. Reihung oder symmetrischer Aufbau werden fast zur Regel. Die plastische Ausformung wird reduziert, manchmal entsteht der Eindruck eines Geflechts. Besonders typisch ist ein Vogel mit ausgespannten Flügeln, der ein menschliches Gesicht vor der Brust trägt. Verständlicherweise spielen die Tiere der Wälder – etwa der Bär – eine hervorragende Rolle. Eine ganz ähnliche, das Althergebrachte variierende Entwicklung

FIG. 130

FIG. 129

Fig. 131 – Diese aus Perm stammende Silberschüssel wurde analog den sibirischen Exemplaren im Kult verwendet, sie ist auch gleicher Herkunft und wurde sekundär mit Tierfiguren und tanzenden Gestalten verziert. Die spitzen Köpfe zeigen, daß Geister dargestellt sind. (Sludka, Slg. Stroganov. Nach Spicyn, Fig. 11)

zeichnet sich an der Pečora und im Ob-Gebiet ab. Dort hat man Gerät aus der Steppe begierig gesammelt, es im Kult gebraucht und schließlich an jahrhundertealten Opferplätzen verwahrt. Die seltsame Folge dieser archivarischen Tendenz ist, daß sich hier der Archäologe ungewöhnlichen Datierungsschwierigkeiten ausgesetzt sieht. Die Auffassungen über die Zeitstellung der westsibirischen Kulturen klaffen um Jahrhunderte auseinander.

FIG. 131 In Perm schließt die bis ins 9. Jahrhundert n. Chr. reichende Lomatovo-Kultur an. Ihre Schatzfunde enthalten byzantinischen und sasanidischen Import, dessen Vermittler nomadische Stämme waren. Künstlerisch ist dies eine Zeit allmählichen Verfalls. Im 10. und 11. Jahrhundert sind nur mehr einige Typen übriggeblieben, die sich dafür durch besondere Realistik auszeichnen. Manche Traditionen reichen weiter bis zum Einsetzen der russischen Kolonisation.

Auch jenseits des Urals hat man mit ähnlicher Treue bewahrt. Sasanidische Silbergefäße wurden hier als religiöse Symbole in großer Zahl gehortet, bis sie schließlich in die Eremitage gelangten. Gerade dieses eindrucksvolle und unbezweifelbare Beispiel aber bestätigt, was auch schon die anderen andeuteten: die besten Belege haben wir offenbar nicht im Steppenraum selbst, sondern in exzentrischen Rückzugsgebieten. Im Kerngebiet sind wir auf ganz wenige, immer wieder ab-

FIG. 132 gebildete und zitierte Funde beschränkt, etwa den Sattelbogen von Kudyrge im Altai (4. Jahrhundert n. Chr.), der in einer gravierten Jagdszene sogar die Inversion des Tierkörpers zeigt.

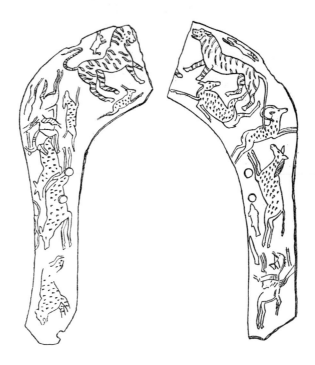

Fig. 132 – Zeichnungen auf dem Sattelbogen von Kudyrge, Altai

Man könnte nun fast annehmen, daß diese Dürftigkeit der bekannten Nachwirkungen im Steppenraum darin gründet, daß das Thema noch nicht den adäquaten Bearbeiter gefunden hat. Es liegen eben noch keine Stilanalysen vor, die sich mit denen der skandinavischen, deutschen und ungarischen Forscher vergleichen lassen. Es ist gewissermaßen der Blick nicht geschult, ganz andere Probleme stehen im Vordergrund.

Die Vermutung wird fast zur Gewißheit, wenn man bedenkt, daß es Fettich sofort möglich war, aus russischen Grabungen asiatisches Vergleichsmaterial zu dem von ihm beschriebenen europäischen Nachleben des Tierstils vorzulegen. In seiner Arbeit »Bronzeguß und Nomadenkunst« hat er diesem Aspekt ein langes und überaus anregendes Kapitel gewidmet.

Trotzdem hat es nicht den Anschein, als sei es nur der fehlende Blick für größere Zusammenhänge, der da die sowjetischen Forscher hindert, sich an der in Europa üblichen allgemeinen Jagd nach überlebenden Tierstilmotiven zu beteiligen. Vermutlich fehlt ihnen auch jene gewisse »Nomadenromantik«, die sich gerade in der Enge Europas und bei ungarischen Forschern deutscher Abstammung entwickeln konnte.

ABB. SEITE 212

Schildbuckel von Herpály (Ungarn). Die Form ist germanisch, die Dekoration dieses zu einer reinen Prunkausstattung, nicht für den kriegerischen Gebrauch bestimmten Stückes ist sarmatisch. Etwa 1. Jahrhundert n.Chr. *Bronze, vergoldet. Original im Ungarischen Nationalmuseum, Budapest, Photographie nach einer Galvanoplastik im Victoria and Albert-Museum, London. Vgl. S. 211*

Vielleicht spürten die sowjetischen Gelehrten stärker die Unterschiede, weil ihnen das grandiose Schaffen der frühen Nomaden tägliches Arbeitsfeld war. Sie kannten auch die modernen Turkvölker und ihre Kunst, hatten also den Bruch zur Gegenwart ständig vor Augen.

Extrem in dieser Richtung ist Grjaznov, dessen intellektuelle Ehrlichkeit wir bei so vielen Gelegenheiten festgestellt haben. Er betont, daß die Kunst der frühen Nomaden eine große und einmalige Blüte darstellt.

Gemäßigter ist die Position Rudenkos. Er sieht die Verbindungen, die vom Kunstgewerbe der großen Altai-Kurgane bis in das moderne Kunstschaffen der Völker dieses Raumes führt, aber er betont vor allem jene Linien, die neben dem eigentlichen Tierdekor herlaufen. Die schon in Pazyryk auftretenden pflanzlichen und abstrakten Muster sind zukunftsträchtig.

Das bedeutet jedenfalls, daß man trotz mancher Reminiszenzen keine Entwicklung vorliegen hat, die sich mit der der germanischen Tierornamentik auch nur entfernt vergleichen ließe. Schon die hunnische Kunst war anders. Seit wir sie durch Alföldi und Werner klarer fassen können, wissen wir, daß sie von einem abstrakten Prinzip beherrscht wurde. Dieses Prinzip und die sogenannte geometrische Ranke blieben auch für alle Zukunft entscheidend, nicht Überlebsel des Tierstils.

Man kann nun fragen, was diese Umwertung, diese Verschiebung der Akzente ausgelöst hat.

Der Hintergrund des Wandels läßt sich nur erfassen, wenn man weiß, worauf es in der frühen Nomadenkunst selbst ankam und ihre ethnischen und sozialen Hintergründe kennt. Wir haben bereits manche Indizien erhalten und müssen uns dem Problem im Schlußkapitel noch einmal stellen.

XV. DIE ENTSTEHUNG VON REITERKRIEGERTUM UND TIERSTIL

Bei der Planung dieses Bandes ging man von der durch zahlreiche Übersichtswerke genährten Vorstellung aus, die Kunst im eurasiatischen Steppenraum bilde während der letzten Jahrhunderte vor Christi Geburt ein einheitliches Phänomen.

Das hat sich an unserem Material bewährt. Als gemeinsames Charakteristikum stellte sich überall ein Repertoire von – teilweise komplexen – Tiermotiven heraus, die in einer spezifischen Weise ornamental gebraucht werden, was man gemeiniglich »Tierstil« nennt. Ferner hat sich *Die Träger:* die alte These bestätigt, daß die Träger dieses Stils Reitervölker ge- *Reiternomaden* wesen sind, deren Lebensbasis die nomadische Viehzucht war. Wo er tiefer in die Waldsteppe hineinreicht, läßt sich das durch eine Beeinflussung von seiten der Nomaden erklären. Auch die gewaltigen Kurgane in den Hochtälern des Altai und die Gräber im Tienschan und Pamir sprengen das Bild nicht. Noch vor kurzem wurden während des Sommers die Hochweiden von den Steppenbewohnern genutzt.

Störender ist die Lücke an Tierstilfunden zwischen Aral und Kaspi, aber man könnte sich auf die außerordentlich ungünstigen Erhaltungsbedingungen und die geringe Durchforschung dieses Raumes berufen. Für das Tarimbecken, das ebenfalls aus dem allgemeinen Bild heraus- fällt, finden wir viel einfacher eine Erklärung. Chinesische Berichte der Han-Zeit erwähnen dort Oasenbewohner, und durch extreme Trocken- heit begünstigte Funde haben dies bestätigt: Getreide und Getreidebrei FIG. 133 gehörten zu den wichtigsten Beigaben der Toten, so daß der vorwiegend agrarische Charakter der Bevölkerung keinem Zweifel unterliegt.

Ungelöste Probleme Ungeklärt blieb in mehr als einem Kapitel die Herkunftsfrage. Das Einsetzen des Tierstils in einem einheitlichen Zeithorizont weist einer- seits auf genetischen Zusammenhang zwischen den verschiedenen »Provinzen«, macht es aber andererseits höchst schwierig, das erste Diffusionszentrum zu finden.

Ungeklärt blieb auch, warum die frühe Nomadenkunst ausgerechnet die Darstellung von Raubtieren und Wild bevorzugt und die in der Wirtschaft des Nomaden wichtigsten Tiere fast vermeidet. Ein notwendiger Zusammenhang zwischen dem Nomadismus und gerade diesem Sujet ist jedenfalls wenig überzeugend, wenn wir bedenken, daß spätere Perioden ganz andere Ausdrucksmittel gefunden haben.

Fig. 133 – Trockenmumie einer alten Frau, aus einem von Sven Hedin geöffneten Grab im Delta des Qum-Darya. Wir erhalten durch derartige Funde eine Vorstellung vom physischen und kulturellen Charakter der nichtnomadischen Bevölkerung des Tarimbeckens, die offenbar sehr lange Traditionen der Bronzezeit beibehielt. (Nach Bergman 1939)

Es ist verlockend, zuletzt doch noch eine Lösung dieser Probleme zu versuchen, indem man die Stilentwicklung des Steppenraums vor einem breiteren Hintergrund betrachtet, auch die Nachbarkulturen einbezieht und sich vor allem über den historischen Weg Rechenschaft gibt, der zu dem kulturellen Gleichgewicht der skythischen Zeit geführt hat. Sowjetische Grabungen der letzten Jahre liefern neue, noch kaum ausgenutzte Grundlagen. Aber auch sie erlauben nur den Aufbau einer Hypothese – analog jenen Skizzen, die schon so viele andere versucht haben. Der Leser darf nie vergessen, auf wie schwankendem Grund sich ein solcher Vorstoß vollzieht.

Die vom Autor vertretene Hypothese

Wir haben davon auszugehen, daß die frühe und mittlere Bronzezeit bis etwa 1200 v.Chr. im Steppenraum eine Zeit relativer Ruhe gewesen sein muß. Die umfangreichen Grabungen, die sowjetische Gelehrte in der Waldsteppe angestellt haben, haben jedenfalls in keinem Punkt die Existenz von Reiternomaden verraten, die auch nur annähernd die spätere Expansionskraft erreichten. Die dynamischen Zentren lagen weiter im Süden, etwa im heutigen Turkmenien, wo sich eben die rinderzüchtenden Stämme zusammengeballt hatten, deren Einbruch nach Indien sich aus den Vedischen Texten erschließen läßt.

Eine Voraussetzung: Bronzezeitliche Bauernkulturen in der westlichen Steppenzone

Nördlich des 40. Breitengrads, in einem ungeheuren Streifen, der von Südrußland bis an die Dsungarische Pforte zieht, herrschte Ackerbau vor. Wo sich ihm auch nur einigermaßen günstige Bedingungen boten, gab es feste Siedlungen. Ihre Bewohner, die einem altertümlichen europiden Typ angehörten, lebten nicht nur von Hirse- und Weizenbau, sondern auch von Viehzucht. Das Pferd diente vor allem als Nahrungsquelle: in den Gräbern sind Pferderippen gefunden worden, vermutlich die Reste der beigegebenen »Kotelettes«. Außerdem wurden die Stuten gemolken, was bereits Homer bekannt war.

An Hand der materiellen Kultur läßt sich in dem riesigen Raum eine gewisse Untergliederung beobachten: im Westen spricht man von einer »Balkengräberkultur«, im Einzugsgebiet des Uralflusses beginnt dann

Balkengräberleute im Westen – Andronovo-Kultur

die »Andronovo-Kultur«, an deren Südrand sich wieder einige Untergruppen von erheblicher Eigenart feststellen lassen.

Wahrscheinlich basierte die gesamte Wirtschaft bei engster Zusammenarbeit der Dorfschaft auf einer genauen Arbeitsteilung der Geschlechter. Die Männer, vielleicht auch nur die unverheiratete Jungmannschaft, zogen mit dem Vieh auf die Weiden, während die Frauen den Acker bestellten. Die Andronovo-Kultur ist der umfangreichste homogene bronzezeitliche Komplex auf dem Gebiet der heutigen UdSSR – das erklärt sich vermutlich durch dieses System: die Männer mit ihren Herden erkundeten immer neue Gebiete, die später dauernd besiedelt werden konnten. Durch den Kontakt der einzelnen Hirtengruppen untereinander verbreiteten sich Neuerungen der Kultur rasch und gleichmäßig. Es muß auch einen Fernhandel gegeben haben, der zum Beispiel das Zinn, das im Altai gewonnen wurde, bis nach Europa vermittelte. Allerdings besaßen die Steppenbauern noch keine ernsthaften Feinde. Ältere Bevölkerungsgruppen mit stärker jägerischer Wirtschaft mögen in die Gebirge zurückgewichen sein.

Keine Reiternomaden

Nur östlich der Dsungarei begann ein anderes Kulturgebiet, das wir mühsam aus den Oberflächenfunden der Gobi zu rekonstruieren trachten. Vermutlich handelte es sich um mongolide Viehzüchter und Jäger. Erosion hat die meisten Stationen unwiederbringlich zerstört. Immerhin lassen sich Anregungen der chinesischen Agrarkultur feststellen. Ein expansives Reiterkriegertum ist auch dort nicht zu finden.

Siedlungskontinuität

Im Westen macht die Kontinuität des anthropologischen Typs in frühen und späten Gräbern klar, daß der größte Teil der nachmaligen Nomadenbevölkerung von diesen alten, relativ friedlichen Steppenbauern abstammte, auch jene Völker iranischer Zunge, die wir als die mächtigsten kennengelernt haben, die Saken jenseits des Jaxartes und die pontischen Skythen. Es muß sich also ein endogener Wandel der Wirtschaftsweise und Lebensform vollzogen haben, nicht etwa eine Neubesiedlung. Grjaznov, dessen Beobachtungsgabe und scharfsinniges Kombinationsvermögen uns bereits mehrfach geholfen hat, glaubt, den Übergang zum Nomadentum an einer Stelle, nämlich bei den Stämmen des Altai-Vorlands, geradezu in flagranti fassen zu können, und zwar mit der unvermeidlichen Konsequenz der Ausplünderung und Bedrückung jener Bevölkerungsteile, die den Wandel nicht rechtzeitig mitmachen konnten oder wollten.

Grjaznovs Hypothese

Er führt aus, die wirtschaftliche Entwicklung in den Steppen habe den Aufbau von immer komplizierter gebauten wirtschaftlichen Einheiten, aber auch weiter ausgreifende Zusammenschlüsse gefordert. Zunächst bestanden nur verstreute kleine Siedlungen, in deren Umkreis es genügend Weiden gab, um die wenigen Rinder zu halten, die man als Milch- und Fleischlieferanten sowie als Zugtiere brauchte. Allmählich züchtete man dann auch noch anderes Vieh, vor allem Schafe und Pferde, was in Kombination mit dem Ackerbau eine größere Anzahl von Hilfskräften erforderte. Man wirtschaftete daher in größeren Verbänden, deren Leiter bereits erhebliche Machtbefugnisse brauchten. Dieses Stadium, das zu Beginn des ersten Jahrtausends v. Chr. erreicht war, spiegelt sich in jenen Siedlungen der späten Andronovo-Kultur, in denen man halbunterirdische Häuser und wahrscheinlich auch Ställe fand, bei deren Ausschachtung bis zu 300 Kubikmeter Erde bewegt werden mußten. Die Häuptlinge jener Siedlungen ruhen in großen und reich ausgestatteten Kurganen. Die Wirtschaft gewann bereits eine deutliche Tendenz zu größerer Beweglichkeit, zum Halbnomadismus.

Vorstufe

Von dieser Form sei dann ein ziemlich plötzlicher Übergang zur extensiven Bewirtschaftung weiteren Steppenbodens erfolgt. Er verlief so rasant, daß die archäologischen Quellen nur den fertigen Vollzug registrieren. Man brauchte lediglich die festen Siedlungen aufzugeben und den Herden in die Tiefe der Steppe hinein zu folgen. Allerdings sei in diesem Augenblick erstmalig eine Gesamtaufteilung aller vorhandenen Weiden nötig geworden. Sie verlief nach dem Recht des Stärkeren, wobei die viel intensiver gewordene Pferdezucht erstmalig einen Masseneinsatz von Reitern gestattete.

Plötzlicher Übergang zum Nomadentum

Reiterkrieger

Da es nun nötig war, die gesamte Bevölkerung beweglich zu machen, übersiedelten selbst Frauen und Kinder in die Wohnwagen, schwerfällige Gefährte, die weiterhin von Rindern gezogen wurden. So stand bald jene Lebensform fertig da, die Herodot von seinen Gewährsleuten beschrieben wurde. Sie breitete sich rasch aus – in einer Art von Kettenreaktion.

Man wird diesem Modell neidlos Anschaulichkeit und Konsequenz zugestehen müssen. Es hat die Tatsache für sich, daß man in der Neuen Welt zweimal – in den Prärien Nordamerikas wie in den Pampas des Südens – einen verwandten Ablauf beobachtet hat: nach der Einführung des Pferdes haben die Indianer in verblüffend kurzer Zeit die Steppe erobert und sind zu neuen Wirtschaftssystemen übergegangen. In den Prärien wurde der Ackerbau plötzlich reduziert, man verlegte sich auf kollektive Büffeljagd.

Analoge Abläufe in der Neuen Welt

Aber gerade dieser Vergleich zeigt, daß wir dem Schema Grjaznovs –

das in der Sowjetunion so weitgehend akzeptiert wurde, daß die ganze folgende Periode offiziell »Zeit der frühen Nomaden« heißt (nur Rudenko lehnt es rundweg ab) – mit Skepsis entgegentreten müssen. Der soziale und wirtschaftliche Umschwung hätte sich in der Neuen Welt nicht so rasch und so radikal vollzogen, wenn es sich nicht um eine Auseinandersetzungsphase von wahrhaft globalem Maßstab gehandelt hätte, die letzten Endes durch die geistige Entwicklung Europas und die sich daran knüpfende koloniale Expansion ausgelöst worden war.

Es hat den Anschein, daß der Übergang der Steppenbevölkerung zum Nomadentum im Rahmen einer ähnlichen Störungszone erfolgt ist.

Klar dokumentiert ist ein Unruhehorizont in Europa. Man spricht hier (mit Wiesner) von einem »Zeitalter der großen Wanderung« und datiert den frühesten Abschnitt zwischen 1250 bis 1100 v. Chr. Damals machten Fremdvölker balkanischer Herkunft zu Wasser und zu Lande den gesamten östlichen Mittelmeerraum unsicher. Die Philister haben die Ägäis durchzogen und Ägypten bedroht, Palästina trägt ihren Namen. Andere Vorstöße richteten sich gegen Kleinasien: das hethitische Reich ist ihnen zum Opfer gefallen, Eneter, Myser und Phryger haben sich dort niedergelassen. Auch die erst später in den Quellen auftauchenden Armenier gehören in diese Bewegung.

Ein ähnlicher Vorgang hat die ethnische Situation Irans verändert.

Während früher die bedrohlichen Gegner der Hochkulturen in den angrenzenden Gebirgsketten saßen, etwa die Kassiten im Zagros, treten jetzt neue Unruhestifter auf, die ihren Schwerpunkt in der Tiefe des Iranischen Plateaus haben. Ghirshman hat in Sialk eine Burg und einen Friedhof ausgegraben, die von ihnen zeugen. Vermutlich haben wir es bereits mit den Vorfahren der iranischen Meder und Perser zu tun.

Möglicherweise bleibt auch Ostasien von solchen Gästen nicht verschont. Schon bei der Machtergreifung der Chou-Dynastie mögen fremde Elemente mitgewirkt haben. Noch wahrscheinlicher ist dies bei den Barbareneinfällen, die im Jahre 770 v. Chr. die Verlegung der Chou-Hauptstadt nach dem Osten erzwingen.

Man hat natürlich gefragt, was hinter dieser ungeheuerlichen Dynamik stecken mag und hat zunächst einmal festgestellt, daß die Stoßkraft der Neuankömmlinge zumindest in Iran, vermutlich aber auch in Europa nicht mehr auf dem Streitwagengeschwader beruhte, einer komplizierten und empfindlichen Waffe, die bisher im Besitz einer hochspezialisierten Adelsschicht gewesen war, sondern auf dem viel gröberen, man

Fig. 134 – Auf einem Rollsiegel von Sialk sind bewaffnete Reiter – Künder einer neuen Zeit – zwischen Fabeltieren dargestellt. Schellen, die wie hier am Hals des Pferdes baumeln, hat man oft gefunden. Sie hatten wohl rituelle Bedeutung. Die Tracht der Reiter ist noch ganz unspezifisch. (Nach Ghirshman 1938/39)

könnte fast sagen »egalitären« Einsatz von Kavallerie. Das Pferd diente nicht mehr als Zugtier, sondern wurde jetzt – allerdings noch ohne Steigbügel und mit einem sehr primitiven Sattel – geritten. *Einsatz von Kavallerie*

Das Reiten erwies sich als überlegen. Nur China war stark genug, um die alte Form trotzdem noch über Jahrhunderte zu konservieren. Die Staaten des Vorderen Orients hingegen übernahmen es, vor allem Urartu und Assyrien, die die Grenzmarken gegen den gefährlichen Nordosten bildeten. Im Laufe des 9. Jahrhunderts v. Chr. entwickelten sie eine eigene Kavallerie. Die Assyrer benutzten sie wenig später für eine regelrechte Vernichtungsstrategie. Sie setzten Reiter zur Verfolgung des geschlagenen Feindes ein und fügten ihm bisher nie gekannte blutige Verluste zu.

Die allmähliche Umrüstung von Streitwagen auf Reitpferde läßt sich in den assyrischen Palastreliefs vom 9. Jahrhundert ab verfolgen. Die berittenen Gegner werden ebenfalls abgebildet. Auch die Tatsache, daß sich die Trensen immer mehr »barbarisieren«, sich Formen annähern, die es im gleichzeitigen Europa gab, spricht für sich. Wir haben ja gehört, daß man immer stärkere Barbarenverbände als Verbündete heranzog. ABB. SEITE 220

Deren Stoßkraft wurde vervielfacht, als die Phryger das bisherige Eisenmonopol der Hethiter gebrochen hatten. Seitdem waren die Randvölker zwischen dem Balkan und der indischen Grenze oft besser in dem neuen Metall ausgerüstet als die alten Großstaaten. Seine Gewinnung war nicht auf wenige Lagerstätten beschränkt, der komplizierte Zinnhandel wurde überflüssig. Es verstärkte sich also die Tendenz zur Massenbewaffnung. *Eiserne Waffen*

Aber wahrscheinlich erfaßt die bisherige Erklärung vom technischen Fortschritt her lediglich einen Ausschnitt der Wirklichkeit. Man wanderte damals nicht nur, weil die Pferde und später das Eisen neue Möglichkeiten erschlossen. Es muß vielmehr eine religiös begründete Bereitschaft zum Auszug in die Ferne bestanden haben. Vielleicht *Religiös begründete Bereitschaft zum Wandern*

Berittene Bogenschützen auf der Flucht vor assyrischen Streitwagen. Einer der Barbaren schießt in der später für die Skythen typischen Weise nach rückwärts, es fehlen aber noch Goryt und Akinakes. Felsrelief aus dem Palast Assurnasirpals II. (883–859 v. Chr.). *British Museum, London. Vgl. S. 219*

erlebten sich damals die Ethnien nach dem Zusammenbruch der frühbronzezeitlichen Adelsherrschaften erstmalig als Volkstümer, im eigenen Recht beruhend und lösbar von Dorf und Gemarkung. Es ist konsequent, daß man damals die Enge des Tempels ablehnte. Es muß eine Unzahl fahrbarer und tragbarer Heiligtümer gegeben haben. Einige sind uns durch glückliche Funde erhalten geblieben (die Sowjetrussin Trever hat sie bearbeitet), andere kann man auf Grund von Modellen rekonstruieren. Daß man das Vogelbild zu ihrem Schmuck verwendet, ist als Symbol unmittelbar verständlich.

Ähnliche Gefährte standen, wie König in scharfsinniger Analyse gezeigt hat, auf den Versammlungsplätzen der Perser, und bei diesem

Volk ist auch die Sozialorganisation erhalten geblieben, die das nötige Zusammenspiel bei jeder Bewegung sicherstellte, die große Klammer über den Sippenverbänden mit ihren Eigeninteressen.

Nach Xenophons Kyropädie waren die freien Perser, die damals allerdings schon eine privilegierte Schicht bildeten, in Altersklassen gegliedert. Im 16. und 17. Lebensjahr wurden die Knaben in die Jungmannschaft übernommen, die unter einem eigenen, gewählten Anführer stand und für sich, gewissermaßen als Vorhut, operieren konnte. Mit 26 Jahren erfolgte die Aufnahme unter die verheirateten, amtsfähigen Männer, die die Hauptmasse des Heeres stellten. Mit 52 Jahren gehörten sie zu den Alten, denen nur mehr richterliche Funktionen vorbehalten waren. Selbst der König unterlag ursprünglich dem Gesetz, er mußte mindestens von seinen militärischen Funktionen zurücktreten.

Persische Altersklassen

An der Realität des Systems und seiner weiten Verbreitung kann nicht gezweifelt werden. Überall tritt es nach dem Unruhehorizont auf. Es bestimmte bei den Chaldern die Gliederung des Heerbanns und das Leben der Könige. Selbst Gottheiten mußten sich ihm einfügen. Die entscheidende Zahl war hier die 28 – damit gelang der Anschluß an den Rhythmus des Mondmonats. Die Spartaner haben es besonders lange bewahrt. Noch wichtiger ist ein Überlebsel in Thessalien, von dem Aristoteles berichtet; hier sind wir in unmittelbarer Nähe des Ausstrahlungszentrums. Ein ganzes Spektrum von Zwischenformen ließe sich noch ermitteln. Es ist die Frage, ob nicht einige Details in der Gründungssage Roms auf eine ähnliche Ordnung deuten. Möglicherweise stehen dahinter jene Kontakte, die den Etruskern den Ruf eintrugen, aus Kleinasien zu stammen. Zweifellos hingen die Steppenvölker mit dieser dynamischen Welt zusammen, auch bei ihnen trat die Sippenverfassung zurück. Ein System von Altersklassen verlieh ihnen die politische und militärische Stoßkraft.

Altersklassen der Steppenvölker

Bei Herodot wird in der Entstehungslegende der Sauromaten eine skythische Jungmannschaft ausdrücklich erwähnt; von den Parnern wissen wir heute, daß sie kein eigenes Volk darstellten, sondern nur die junge Mannschaft der Parther. Der Gemeinbesitz an Frauen, den die griechische Legende innerasiatischen Völkern zuschrieb, war wohl nicht die Eigentümlichkeit ganzer Völker, sondern gehörte vielmehr zu den Gepflogenheiten solcher Verbände. Andere Indizien haben sich in den religiösen Texten iranischer Völker erhalten.

Es ist aber eindeutig, daß im Steppenraum eine Verlagerung des Akzents eintreten mußte. Wo schon bisher die Hirten ein Eigenleben

Fig. 135 – Rechts: bronzener Trensenknebel (Fragment) aus Kjuzeli-gyr in Chorezm; links: Knebel aus St. Sulpice, Schweiz. (Nach Terenožkin 1958)

führten, war es nur konsequent, daß nicht das kompakte Volk wanderte, sondern daß die Jünglinge zu kriegerischen Expeditionen aufbrachen, ähnlich den Banden mancher Stämme in der nordamerikanischen Prärie. Die Altersklasse nahm den Charakter eines Männerbundes an. Wenn man nach Süden zog, stellte man sich in den Dienst der dortigen Großreiche, verbrachte so seine Bewährungsperiode, um schließlich beladen mit Ehre und Beute in das stabilere Dasein der Heimat zurückzukehren. Es entwickelten sich Formen, die den maritimen Unternehmungen der griechischen Sage gleichen, ein durch kultische Formen gefordertes und gebändigtes Reisläufertum.

Unter diesen Gesichtspunkt kann man ohne weiteres einordnen, was wir über die Beteiligung von Kimmeriern und Skythen an den vorderasiatischen Kämpfen wissen. Man hat bemerkt, daß die von Herodot angegebene Aufenthaltsdauer der Skythen im Vorderen Orient annähernd jener Periode entspricht, während der ein Skythe der Altersklasse der Krieger angehörte.

Dabei bestand eine ähnliche Bewegung auch weiter östlich. Es sind z. B. choresmische Söldner im achämenidischen Dienst unter der Besatzungstruppe Ägyptens belegt. Selbst von dem in Pazyryk II beigesetzten Herrn hat man vermutet, er habe am Achämenidenhof gedient. Auf Grund des im Altai belegten Rituals erschien es uns wahrscheinlich, daß es Kriegerverbände gegeben hat, die die Gliederung der Sippen überschnitten.

Auf die Frage, durch welche Mechanik die späteren Nomaden in diese Unruhezone mit ihrer migrationsbereiten Sozialordnung und Religion einbezogen wurden, gibt es seit langem eine scheinbar plausible Ant-

Fig. 136 – Im bronzezeitlichen Europa wurde es üblich, das Spiel der aus Lederriemen geflochtenen Trense durch Knebel aus Geweihstangen zu begrenzen. Dieses System wurde in Metall übersetzt, wobei die Knebel zunächst drei Öffnungen aufwiesen, um den dreigeteilten Backenriemen aufzunehmen – eine Lösung, die bis 500 v.Chr. gültig blieb. Man fand die frühesten Gebisse dieser neuen Art im Friedhof Sialk B. (Nach Ghirshman 1954)

Fig. 137 – Bei frühen Pferdeschirrungen werden sich kreuzende Lederriemen durch Bronzeknöpfe fixiert, die auf der Rückseite vier quadratisch angeordnete Schlaufen aufweisen. Auch dieses Prinzip findet sich repräsentativ in Sialk B. (Nach Ghirshman 1954)

wort. Heine-Geldern, der seinerseits wieder auf älteren Arbeiten fußt, postulierte, ein von Europa ausgehender Vorstoß thrakischer, kaukasischer, selbst germanischer Kräfte habe die friedlichen Steppenbauern aufgescheucht und zur Abwehr mobilisiert. Es habe im 9. und 8. Jahrhundert v. Chr. eine »Völker- und Kulturbewegung« stattgefunden, die aus dem pontischen Raum (daher »pontische Wanderung«) und Nordkaukasien quer durch Innerasien nach Ost- und Südostasien führte. Eine indogermanische Sprache westlicher Prägung, wie sie sich noch zwei Jahrtausende später in Kuča und Qarašahr (Oasen am Nordrand des Tarimbeckens) erhalten hatte, sei durch die Ansiedlung einer Abenteuererschar zu erklären, die damals auf raschen Pferden nach Osten vorstieß. Andere Gruppen, an der chinesischen Grenze abgeschlagen, hätten sich durch Westchina nach Süden durchgekämpft und schließlich in der Dong-son-Kultur Indochinas mit ihren seltsamen reiterlichen Zügen dokumentiert. Geradezu als »Leitfossil« betrachtet Heine-Geldern den sogenannten Tangentenkreis.

Die Hypothese der »pontischen Wanderung«

In seinen früheren Arbeiten ist der Verfasser mehrfach für diese Hypothese eingetreten, für die man tatsächlich Heine-Geldern selbst noch unbekannte Belege finden kann. So will Tolstov eine Keramik osteuropäischer Herkunft im Aralgebiet festgestellt haben. Noch interessanter im Zusammenhang mit einer postulierten Reiterwanderung ist natürlich der Fund eines ganz eindeutig osteuropäischen Trensenknebels im gleichen Gebiet. Auch ein in Tannu Tuwa gefundener Dolch gehört zu einer in Ungarn und im Kaukasus vertretenen Gruppe. Holzkammergräber in Zentralkazachstan (Dyndybei) weisen plötzlich Beziehungen zu den Grabanlagen des östlichen Hallstattkreises auf. Es mehren sich die Anzeichen, daß die Abwanderung der Träger der Karasuk-Kultur bis ins Minussinskbecken durch den gleichen Unruhehorizont verursacht wurde. Vermutlich verließen sie ihr früheres Wohngebiet in der Ordossteppe nicht unter dem Druck der chinesischen Hochkultur, sondern weil sich hier andere Barbaren mit einer stärker militanten Gesittung ausbreiteten. Jedenfalls enthält das Karasukinventar auch einige Indizien für westliche Zusammenhänge.

Zusätzliche Argumente

FIG. 135

FIG. 117

Fig. 138 – Welche Schmuckformen im Heimatgebiet der Kimmerier beliebt waren, zeigt ein Reitergrab in einem Kurgan beim Dorf Zol'noe auf der Krim. Die Knochenplatte mit ihrem Spiral- und Kreisdekor gehört ebenso zur Schirrung wie der runde, durchbrochene Beinknopf, der in der Draufsicht ein Malteserkreuz zeigt (unten). Sehr typisch auch das Muster mit »überschlagenden Wellen« auf einem Knochenzylinder (Mitte). Ende des 8. Jahrhunderts v. Chr. (Nach Ščepinskij 1962)

Trotzdem müssen wir uns heute fragen, ob diese Erklärung ausreicht, ob Osteuropa und der Kaukasus wirklich von so ausschließlicher Bedeutung waren, ob nicht vielmehr Beziehungen zu Völkern des Südens, genauer gesagt zu Iran und Assyrien, die entscheidenden Prozesse auslösten.

Sicher mit der Randzone des Vorderen Orients in Verbindung steht der Wolgaraum. Smirnov gelang der Nachweis, daß unscheinbare Knochengeräte Wangenstücke von Pferdegebissen sind, die man auf Grund ihrer Innenstacheln zu einem im Vorderen Orient weitverbreiteten Formenkreis in Beziehung setzen kann. Ein verhältnismäßig spätes Exemplar können wir mit einer Darstellung auf einem Relief Assurnasirpals II. (883–859 v. Chr.) vergleichen. Möglicherweise waren kleine gebogene Bronzestangen, die eine längliche Öffnung aufweisen, ebenfalls Trensenknebel. Stellt man sie sich mit Lederriemen umwickelt vor, so erhält man eine Form, die auf den assyrischen Palastreliefs dargestellt ist. Die auffälligsten Parallelen ergeben sich allerdings etwas später, zu jenen aus leicht gekrümmten Geweihzacken hergestellten Psalien, die in Assyrien zur Zeit Assurbanipals (668–629 v. Chr.) verwendet wurden.

Es ist die Frage, wie man sich nun technisch einen solchen Kontakt vorstellen soll, bzw. wie man das Fehlen von Funden im Zwischengebiet zu deuten hat. Möglicherweise fuhren abenteuernde Banden die Wolga hinunter und stießen vom Südufer des Kaspisees weiter vor, vollführten also eine Art Seevölkerwanderung en miniature.

Verbindungen zu Sialk B

Eine andere Verbindungslinie führt von den frühesten Reitern auf dem Iranischen Plateau – der Kultur von Sialk B – zu den Vorfahren der Saken nördlich vom Tienschan. Man hat z. B. im Norden Gußformen für eigenartige Absatzbeile gefunden, die man dann tatsächlich in Sialk antraf. Auch die Pfeilspitzen scheinen einem verwandten Typ anzugehören. Die Dreifußkessel und Opfertische können eindeutig von Modellen abgeleitet werden, die unter der Keramik von Sialk B

Fig. 139 – Zoomorphe Fibel aus dem Goldschatz von Michalkovo, Ostgalizien. Die Umrisse des Tieres lassen an Schöpfungen der Koban-Kultur denken, Medaillons beleben die Fläche. Ebenfalls noch 8. Jahrhundert v. Chr. (Nach Gimbutas 1959)

vorkommen. Die Opfertische haben den gleichen durchbrochenen Fußteil. In beiden Gebieten kommen Bronzespiegel vor, die eine flache Griffzunge aufweisen. FIG. 118

Möglicherweise führten diese Fäden noch weit über den Balchaschsee nach Nordosten. Der Verfasser hat versucht, die in der Majemir-Kultur des Altais auftretenden gegabelten Trensenknebel auf assyrischen Reliefs nachzuweisen.

Ebensowenig läßt sich ausschließen, daß es sehr bald auch im Osten des Steppenraums starke Zentren gegeben hat, die ihrerseits nach Westen zurückwirkten. So sind z. B. die Bronzekessel des Minussinskgebiets nach Südrußland exportiert worden und haben dort eine interessante Entwicklung ausgelöst. Sie haben ihrerseits chinesische Vorbilder, nachweisbar an den pilzartigen Auswüchsen der Henkel. Man nahm seinerzeit an, die sogenannten kreuzförmigen Riemendurchlässe der Pferdeschirrung seien von der pontischen Wanderung bis nach Ostasien getragen worden. Jetzt hat man sie in shangzeitlichen Gräbern gefunden, d. h. sie sind in China älter als in Europa. Wir wissen aber nicht, ob sie durch Handel, als Beutegut oder aber durch die Expansion eines östlichen Reitervolkes so weit nach Westen verbreitet worden sind.

Bei dieser Situation ist es nicht mehr aussichtsreich, das Bild durch eine Wirkungskette erklären zu wollen. Man wird sich auf die vorsichtigere Formulierung zurückziehen müssen, der Übergang der Steppenvölker zum Reiternomadismus sei durch den Kontakt mit der gesamten Unruhezone des Südens und Westens ausgelöst oder zumindest mitbestimmt worden. Es handelt sich um einen komplexen Vorgang, den wir niemals in seinen Einzelheiten werden rekonstruieren können, obwohl er sich über eine längere Zeitspanne hinzog. Manche Gebiete wie der Wolgaraum scheinen einen erheblichen Vorsprung gehabt zu haben.

Es ist verständlich, daß in einer solchen Übergangzeit kein künstle-

Mobilisierung der Steppen durch breiten Kontakt mit primärer Unruhezone

Fig. 140 – Dekor eines Metallknopfes, der eine Riemenkreuzung deckte. Nadj-i-Ali, Seistan. Vielleicht 7.Jahrhundert v.Chr. (Nach Ghirshman 1939)

Noch keine einheitliche Steppenkunst

FIG. 138

Tendenzen des 8. Jahrhunderts

FIG. 139

FIG. 140

rischer Stil von imposanter Geschlossenheit und Ausdruckskraft erwartet werden darf. Wir kennen jedenfalls nichts, was an die Schöpfungen heranreicht, die dann im ausgehenden 7. und im 6.Jahrhundert v. Chr. einsetzen. Vorher hat man in den westlichen Steppen Spirale und Volute als wichtigste Dekorationsmotive verwendet, auch runde Medaillons mit einem Balkenkreuz waren außerordentlich beliebt, sie wurden zur Füllung von silhouettenhaft schematisierten Tierbildern verwendet.

Das wenige, das wir über die Kunst der Kimmerier wissen, fügt sich hier ein. Daß andere Stämme ähnliche Schmuckformen verwendeten, verrät der Goldschatz von Michalkovo in Galizien. Die großartigste künstlerische Ausformung solcher Prinzipien erfolgte jedoch bereits außerhalb der Steppen, in der Kultur von Koban.

In Mittelasien war die Situation nicht anders. Vor dem Tierstil treffen wir abstrakte Wirbelmuster. Die frühiranische Station Nadj-i-Ali in Seistan lieferte Bestandteile der Pferdeschirrung, die in einem ausgeprägten Spiralstil verziert sind.

Nordöstlich davon läßt sich eine Zone erkennen, in der man bereits relativ plumpe Tierbilder, die der nordischen Fauna entstammen, wie Bär und Eber, zur Dekoration von Metallgeräten verwendete. Wir sind mit diesem Phänomen bereits bei der Besprechung des Minussinskgebiets konfrontiert worden.

Fig. 141 – Ein Rollsiegel aus Sialk zeigt Tiere, deren Beine unter den Leib gezogen sind. Es könnte also auch diese wichtige »Pose« des Tierstils aus dem Süden entlehnt sein. (Nach Ghirshman 1938/39)

Getriebenes Goldblech. Schatz von Ziwiye, Höhe etwa 16 cm. Teil eines größeren von den Ausgräbern bereits geteilten Stückes. Die Hirsche und Steinböcke in den Feldern weisen frappant skythische Züge auf. Die Ausgestaltung des Netzwerkes entspricht urartäischem Geschmack, wie in Armenien gefundene Bronzegürtel zeigen. *Fragmente im Archäologischen Museum, Teheran. Vgl. S. 229*

In bestimmten Teilen des Steppenraumes scheint man das Winkel-
band als Schmuckmotiv ausgiebig verwendet zu haben, auch in plasti-
scher Umgestaltung.

Die bestechende Lösung, die sich seit dem ausgehenden 7. Jahrhundert
v. Chr. durchsetzt, führt diese Tendenzen nicht einfach weiter. Der
endgültige Tierstil ist, wie wir gesehen haben, sehr viel »kontakt-
stärker«, er verfügt über ein reiches Repertoire von Motiven fremder
Herkunft, die er sich durch eine selbstherrliche Behandlung zu eigen

Greifenköpfchen aus Ziwiye, vielleicht Fassung eines Wetzsteins. *Höhe etwa
7 cm. Archäologisches Museum, Teheran. Vgl. S. 229*

macht. Nur in ganz frühen Denkmälern, etwa den Žabotin-Kurganen, hat man noch die alten abstrakten Zeichen feststellen können – vielleicht weil sie einen sakralen Wert verkörperten.

FIG. 7

Manches an dem neu dazugewonnenen Motivgut mag europäisch sein, anderes sogar chinesisch, die meisten Neuerungen wurden jedenfalls im iranischen Raum übernommen. Sehr oft handelt es sich um uralte vorderasiatische Motive, die von der assyrischen Reichskunst nur weitergegeben wurden.

Einbeziehen iranischer Elemente

Dafür gibt es eine relativ einfache Begründung. In Iran lag das beliebteste und lange Zeit auch das aussichtsreichste Operationsgebiet nördlicher Kriegsexpeditionen. Man strömte von allen Seiten herbei, Kimmerier und Skythen konnten sich hier mit Saken treffen, die in den Steppen am Fuße des Tienschan beheimatet waren. Dazu wurde man mit Anregungen jeder Art geradezu überschüttet. Künstler vieler Völker waren bereit, dem Erfolgreichen beim Schmuck seiner persönlichen Ausrüstung zu dienen.

Unmittelbar greifbar wird diese »Marktsituation« durch den Schatzfund von Ziwiye in Iranisch-Kurdistan, der hier nicht näher analysiert werden muß, weil er von E. Porada in einem anderen Band der Serie ausführlich besprochen wurde. Es mag der Hinweis genügen, daß sein Kern vermutlich aus den zusammengeraubten Besitztümern eines Kriegsherrn bestand, der sich erfolgreich an den Kämpfen zu Beginn des 6. Jahrhunderts v. Chr. beteiligt hatte. So umfaßt der Schatz Arbeiten assyrischer, mannäischer, medischer und skythischer Meister. Besonders frappierend ist das Vorkommen skythischer und assyrischer Motive am gleichen Stück. Offenbar konnte sich ein Künstler mehrerer »Musterbücher« bedienen, auch jenes, das speziell für die nördlichen Barbaren galt. Es läßt sich durchaus die These vertreten, der Tierstil sei in diesem Treibhaus verschiedenster künstlerischer Tendenzen von einer Söldnergruppe in einer Art von Selbstbesinnung, aus dem Bedürfnis nach eigenem Ausdruck heraus, entwickelt und dann rasch von anderen Verbänden in ähnlicher Position übernommen worden.

Schatz von Ziwiye
ABB. SEITE 227, 228, 235

Daß sich hier auf iranischem Boden die endgültige Phase in der Entwicklung des Tierstils abgespielt hat, hat sich bestätigt, seit wir in den letzten Jahren Prunkwaffen und Schmuck der Achämenidenzeit besser kennengelernt haben. Sogar die Gebrauchskunst der medischen Zeit wird allmählich klar. Die grandiose iranische Ausstellung, die in vielen Städten Europas zu sehen war, zeigte ein Material, das dem gleichzeitigen Fundgut der Steppen erstaunlich nahe stand. Man kann geredezu von einem »achämenidischen Tierstil« sprechen. Als Beleg ist

Achämenidischer Tierstil

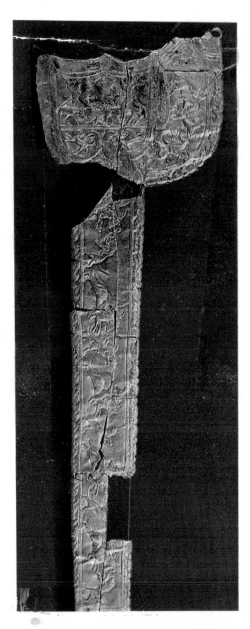

Goldblech, Überzug einer Akinakes-Scheide, ebenfalls Oxus-Schatz. Die dargestellten Kampfszenen entsprechen nicht dem Repertoire der nördlichen Steppenbewohner. *British Museum, London. Vgl. oben*

interessant, daß man Stücke des Oxus-Schatzes abwechselnd für den skythischen Tierstil oder aber für die achämenidische Reichskunst in Anspruch genommen hat. Heute könnte man in der Steppenkunst fast eine barbarisierte Variante der ungleich stabileren achämenidischen sehen – allerdings eine, die dem modernen Geschmack besonders entgegenkommt. Hier wie dort findet man eine reichliche Verwendung des Tierbildes; gewisse Details, etwa die Gestaltung des Mauls oder der Augen, kehren fast unverändert bei beiden wieder, wie wir z. B. bei der Besprechung der Altai-Kunst festgestellt haben.

Wir dürfen nicht vergessen, daß sich auch Bewaffnung und Reitertracht der Steppenvölker auf Normen einspielten, von denen wir annehmen können, daß sie in Iran zumindest ihre letzte Form erhalten hatten. Das gilt z. B. vom Akinakes, dem Kurzschwert, vermutlich auch vom Baschlyk, der Kappe, die nur das Gesicht freiließ. Vielleicht ist überhaupt die skythische Reiterbewaffnung so hoch spezialisiert, weil sie zunächst im Verband anderer Waffengattungen verwendet wurde. Sie setzt Fußtruppen als Gegner voraus.

Die Analyse des gewaltigsten achämenidischen Denkmals, Persepolis, deutet noch auf weitere, sublimere Zusammenhänge. Forschungen der letzten Jahre haben gezeigt, daß diese ungeheure Ballung von Hallen und Korridoren, Stiegenaufgängen und Terrassen, niemals regulär bewohnt worden ist. Godard weist mit Recht darauf hin, daß keine der steinernen Treppen je abgetreten worden ist. Alles bildet nur den ungeheuerlichen Rahmen eines

Armreif aus dem Oxus-Schatz. Die Vertiefungen sind zur Aufnahme verlorener Cloisonné-Einlagen bestimmt. Vermutlich diente das Stück als Herrschaftssymbol oder zeremonielles Geschenk. *Breite 11,5 cm. Victoria and Albert-Museum, London. Vgl. S. 230*

Festes, vermutlich des alten Neujahrsfestes, bei dem sich das Reich in seinem ganzen Glanze spiegelte.

Ghirshman zeigt, daß die Reliefs nur die Bedeutung der einzelnen Räumlichkeiten und Aufgänge illustrieren. Sie erzählen, wie Gesandtschaften von allen Völkern des Reichs einlangten, um Huldigung und Tribut darzubringen. Genau und bewußt unterschieden nach Tracht

und Bewaffnung stiegen sie die Treppen empor, erwiesen dem Groß-
könig die Proskynesis, empfingen seinen Richterspruch, um schließlich
ihre Gaben in den Schatzhäusern zu deponieren. Dieser Ablauf wird
noch sinnvoller, wenn man ihn gegen den Hintergrund der großen
Wanderungsperiode sieht, die damals schon durch die Einrichtung
stabiler Reiche iranischer Nation, des medischen und des persischen,
endgültig zu Ende gegangen war. Es ist, als hätte die grenzenlose
Bewegung, die so lange letzter Ausdruck war, nun ein glückliches Ziel
gefunden, sie ist dienstbar gemacht worden und hat den Charakter
einer Prozession angenommen. Sie endet in einem grandiosen Rahmen
aus Stein, der Ewigkeitswert beansprucht: die frühere Dynamik hat
geradezu megalithischer Statik Platz gemacht.
Die Zerstörung der Anlage durch Alexander den Großen gewinnt von

Wandverkleidung aus farbig glasierten Ziegeln. Die Fabeltiere, die auf dem
Sattelschmuck der Pazyryk-Kurgane dargestellt sind (Abb. S. 91), setzen derartige Vorbilder voraus. Palast des Artaxerxes II. (404–359), in Susa. *Louvre, Paris*

hier aus einen neuen Sinn. Seine Heimat lag nahe einem der alten Unruhezentren, er ist ein Vertreter jener dämonischen Welt. Tatsächlich hat er alle Kräfte wieder freigesetzt, die die Achämeniden durch ihre Kriegszüge in die Steppe zu bannen versuchten.

So ist auch in der achämenidischen Kunst das Motivgut vieler Völker zusammengefügt und in seltsamer Erstarrung konserviert. Die Gesten bleiben wie in der Luft hängen, alles verharrt in äußerster Spannung. *Erstarrende Dynamik findet künstlerischen Ausdruck* Gerade dieses gebändigte Gegeneinander und Nebeneinander muß auf die Steppenvölker größten Eindruck gemacht haben. Es entsprach ihrer Situation. Eine ähnliche Konsolidierung hatte sich in ihrem Dasein vollzogen, wenn auch nicht im Rahmen einer Weltmonarchie. Die extensiven Bewegungen hatten offenbar aufgehört, sie setzen erst nach der Gründung des Hsiung-nu-Reiches wieder ein und werden dann anscheinend von der Dynamik einer anderen Rasse getragen. Dem Ehrgeiz öffneten sich, wie wir an Hand des Altai-Materials zeigen konnten, rituell genormte und gebändigte Aufstiegswege, sie führten zu Ruhm, erst in zweiter Linie zu Macht. Er konnte auch der Ausgestaltung der persönlichen Existenz zugeleitet werden. Nur das erklärt

jenen ungeheuerlichen Reichtum an Erfindung, den wir im Altai kennenlernen.

Man bewältigte erst jetzt das Erlebnis, das im Werden des Reiternomadentums beschlossen lag – und konnte sich aller Mittel bedienen, die der Kontakt mit den Hochkulturen bot.

Beteiligung von Traditionen, die im Steppenraum schon heimisch waren

Wenn wir größten Wert auf die analoge Entwicklung in Iran und Außer-Iran legten, so wollen wir nicht behaupten, die einzige Quelle der Nomadenkunst in den letzten Jahrhunderten vor Christus gezeigt zu haben. Jene älteren Stiltendenzen, die wir erwähnt haben, vor allem die Vorliebe für die Spirale und schwungvolle Volute, wirkten weiter. Es ist ganz deutlich, daß die Vorliebe für Inversion einem solchen urzeitlichen Erbe entstammt – wie bereits Wiesner gesehen hat. Auch der schwerfällige Realismus der Karasuk-Kunst hat weitergewirkt. Möglicherweise ist er durch einzelne Verschiebungen auch im Süden wirksam geworden. Dafür sprechen die erwähnten Funde im Pamir.

FIG. 122

Schrägschnitt aus dem Erbe der Waldsteppe?

Es ist nun die Frage, ob die Tendenz, Tierkörper aus schrägen Flächen mit kurviger Abgrenzung zu bilden (Schrägschnitt), ebenfalls auf ein solches urzeitliches Erbe zurückzuführen ist, oder ob sie einfach durch gewisse technische Voraussetzungen im Nomadengebiet und den Einfluß des Spiralstils erklärt werden muß. Vielleicht hat wirklich eine Gruppe, die in der Waldzone des Urals oder Westsibiriens saß, zusammen mit den Steppenvölkern Reisläufer nach dem Vorderen Orient geschickt. Sie besaß eine überlegene Schnitztradition und stellte deshalb bald die Kunsthandwerker für alle »Expeditionsgruppen«, ähnlich wie sich auch die Achämeniden für bestimmte Künste jeweils der Angehörigen eines oder mehrerer Völker bedienten. Über eine solche Überlegung könnte man die Entstehung eines Tierstilkerns in der nördlichen Waldzone retten – die Diffusion wäre dann von Iran aus, also vom Einsatzgebiet her erfolgt.

Zur Illustration dieses Vorschlags sei erwähnt, daß vor kurzem das Fortleben der in die bewaldete Randzone des Minussinskgebiets abgedrängten Afanasjevo-Bevölkerung, also von Einwanderern des frühen zweiten Jahrtausends v. Chr., nachgewiesen werden konnte. Sie werden plötzlich wieder aktiv und tragen um 700 v. Chr. die früheste Phase der Tagar-Kultur.

Zwischenform des Tierstils in Ostkazachstan?

An sowjetische Arbeiten der letzten Jahre anknüpfend (Členova, Terenožkin), könnte man sogar vermuten, daß in Ostkazachstan am Schnittpunkt südlicher (Spirale, Volute), östlicher (Rolltier), nördlicher (Schnitztradition) und nordöstlicher (Karasuk-Erbe) Einflüsse sich eine Vorstufe des Tierstils bildete. Diese sakische Zwischenform sei schon um die Mitte des 7. Jahrhunderts weithin verschleppt worden (bis in den Kaukasus und nach Südrußland), sie habe aber ihre volle Überzeugungskraft erst n a c h der Begegnung mit dem ästhetischen Erbe Irans erhalten.

Lokales Erbe differenziert

Es liegt nahe, die erheblichen Unterschiede, die von Anfang an zwischen den einzelnen Provinzen der Nomadenkunst bestehen, nicht nur darauf zurückzuführen, daß orientalische Einwirkungen sich je nach der Entfernung von ihrem Einbruchsgebiet verschieden stark auswirkten, vielmehr muß das jeweilige lokale Erbe fast von Anfang an differenzierend gewirkt haben. Im Sarmatengebiet z. B. war das Spiralelement seit jeher schwach vertreten. Um so deutlicher ist es im sakischen Raum Zentralasiens. Auch Richtung und Tempo in der Weiterentwicklung der einzelnen Formen muß örtlich verschieden gewesen sein. Eine spezifische Ausprägung des Hirschmotivs, die sich in Ziwiye äußert (noch 7. Jahrhundert?), dringt im 6. Jahrhundert v. Chr. in den pontischen Raum ein, wo sie rasch der Abwandlung unterliegt. Plötzlich aber treten die alten Formen neu erblüht im Minussinskgebiet auf. Es muß also ein – wohl innerasiatisches – Beharrungszentrum gegeben haben, aus dem die Diffusion nach Südwesten, dann nach Westen, schließlich an den Jenissei erfolgte.

Ist Ostkazachstan auch Beharrungszentrum?

Entwicklung nicht synchron

Damit wird leider die für den Kunsthistoriker so außerordentlich bequeme, noch vor kurzem geäußerte Vorstellung hinfällig, es habe im Steppenraum kurzwellige, aber praktisch generell verbreitete Moden gegeben. So einfach wird uns die Datierung nicht gemacht. Die Weiterentwicklung verlief in den Provinzen nicht synchron.

Vermutlich haben sich ältere, vom Tierstil überholte oder in ihn einbezogene Motivkreise an jenem häuslichen Inventar erhalten, das von konservativeren Frauen hergestellt und benutzt wurde. Davon ist leider meist nur die Keramik erhalten geblieben. Dort, wo wir auch den Rest, der aus vergänglichem Material hergestellt wurde, kennen, staunen wir über die Vielfalt heterogener Dekorationssysteme.

Vielleicht war der Gegensatz zwischen männlichen und weiblichen Schmuckformen bewußt gesetzt, er entsprach der polaren Spannung der auch im Arbeitsprozeß klar getrennten Geschlechter.

Ähnliches kennen wir von modernen Naturvölkern. Das hinderte freilich nicht, daß eine Fürstin oder Priesterin männliche Attribute beanspruchen konnte, und damit den Schmuck der Tierformen.

Bedeutung der Tiermotive?

Erhält man mit dem versuchten Einbau der frühen Nomadenkunst in ein historisches und soziales Modell auch Hinweise zur Bedeutung der wichtigsten Einzelmotive?

Silberschale mit Goldauflagen aus dem Schatz von Ziwiye. *Durchmesser 37,5 cm. Archäologisches Museum, Teheran. Vgl. S. 229*

Wir haben gehört (S. 139), daß der Teppich des V. Pazyryk-Kurgans als Divinationsbehelf diente. Eine analoge Verwendung dieser durch ähnliche Friese gegliederten Schale würde die bisher rätselhaften, an hethitische Hieroglyphen erinnernden Zeichen in der Randzone erklären. Sicher stehen auch die Tierkörper für magische Potenzen.

Gürtelplatte aus dem Ordosgebiet. *Etwa natürliche Größe. British Museum, London.*
Es wird der offenbar nach bestimmten Regeln ablaufende Ringkampf zweier Helden gezeigt.
Grjaznov (1961) weist darauf hin, daß derartige Szenen in den Heldenepen der modernen
Turkvölker häufig geschildert werden. Anhand weiterer Beispiele glaubt er beweisen zu
können, daß diese Epen insgesamt noch in die erste Unruhe-Periode zurückreichen – ins 8. bis
7. Jahrhundert v. Chr. Tierstilentstehung und künstlerische Abrundung der Epen wären
dann analoge Vorgänge.

Die Tierbilder können keine Gottheiten dargestellt haben. Speziell   *Keine Gottheiten*
das pontisch-skythische Pantheon ist durch die Schriftquellen wohl-
bekannt, griechische Künstler haben manche der einheimischen Gottheiten dargestellt. Von den Massageten heißt es, sie hätten die Sonne
angebetet und ihr Pferdeopfer gebracht. Von tiergestaltigen Gottheiten analog jenen der Ägypter ist auch dort nicht die Rede.
Nun gibt es aber in den religiösen Systemen vieler Völker unterhalb
des Pantheons oder einer zentralen Gottesgestalt dämonische Mächte,
die ebenfalls verehrt und gefürchtet werden, an deren Eingreifen bei
bestimmten Gelegenheiten man glaubt. Selbst der Islam hat eine recht
bunte Welt von Geistern und Feen akzeptiert.
So könnte es auch hier sein. Am nächstliegenden wäre der Gedanke,

237

es habe sich um die Darstellung individueller Schutzgeister in Tiergestalt gehandelt, ähnlich jenen, die die Krieger nordamerikanischer Indianerstämme als Jünglinge durch Konzentration und Traumerlebnisse erwerben. Auch die Hilfsgeister der Schamanen treten oft tiergestaltig auf, kämpfen als »Tiermütter«.

In der weiteren Verfolgung dieser Idee gerät man freilich in größte Schwierigkeiten. Im Altai wurde eindeutig festgestellt, daß sich in einer Schirrungsgarnitur oder einer Prunkbekleidung ganz verschiedene Motive kombinierten. Irgendein Sinn ist dabei nicht herauszufinden. (Damit wird es auch schwierig, die Tiere als Wappenfiguren anzusehen.) Man hat sich notdürftig mit der Annahme geholfen, die Toten, die in den Großkurganen ruhen, seien mit den Gaben ihrer Kampfgefährten ausgestattet worden. Aussichtsreicher ist die Vermutung, die Tierbilder hätten eine fast anonyme, magische Potenz besessen. Man habe sie fast ins Unbegrenzte vermehren und speichern wollen, wie die Tibeter ihre Gebete. Vergleichbar wären die aus Fellmosaik bestehenden Kleidungsstücke. Tatsächlich sind im sibirischen Kultgebrauch aus vielen Jagdtrophäen zusammengesetzte Gegenstände bekannt, die die Kraft aller erlegten Tiere enthalten sollen.

Speicherung magischer Kraft

Das würde ein gewisses Herabziehen aus einer erfüllteren religiösen Sphäre bedeuten, und dafür spricht auch der Vergleich mit Iran. Der achämenidische Tierstil diente zweifellos primär dem persönlichen Schmuckbedürfnis. Er wurde möglich, weil Tier und Fabeltier schon einen Teil ihrer früheren Bedeutung verloren hatten, weil die in abstraktere Höhen gerückte Religion ihr Bild zum »Gebrauch« freigab. Analog könnte es hier gewesen sein. Damit läßt sich die Brücke zu Grjaznovs Analyse der Altai-Kunst schlagen, auch er spricht von ihrem subjektiven, eigenartig addierenden Charakter. Eine Riemenkreuzung ist primär die vollendete Schöpfung eines Meisters, sie wird mit ähnlichen Schöpfungen anderer Meister zu einer eher schwerfälligen Garnitur vereinigt. Der Träger behängt sich damit wie mit Trophäen. Das könnte tatsächlich mit einem stereotypen magischen Wert, mit einer fast mechanischen Anordnung von Kraft und Prestige zu verbinden sein. Gerade dadurch wird im einzelnen der individuellen Erfinderkraft freie Bahn gegeben. Auch die griechische Kunst entfaltet sich zum Teil auf Kosten der ursprünglich religiösen Bedeutung. Als Gegenpol gibt es Motivkombinationen, die sicher irgendwelche Mythen voraussetzen, so der im Pazyryk mehrfach auftretende Hirschkopf im Maule eines Fabeltiers.

Aber auch Darstellungen mit mythologischem Hintergrund

FIG. 71

238

Nicht alle diese Mythen müssen einheimischer Herkunft gewesen sein. Wenn man Tiere abbildete, die in den Steppen gar nicht vorkommen (Damhirsch und Riesenschlange), so hat man sie in irgendeinem größeren Zusammenhang übernommen. Der im Altai gefundene Divinationsteppich zeigt deutlich das Einströmen anatolischer Ideen. Auffällig ist ferner, daß gewisse Leitmotive innerhalb des Steppenraums äußerst ungleichmäßig gestreut sind, etwa die Hirschdarstellungen. Die Schwerpunkte liegen in Osteuropa, im Ordosgebiet und von einem bestimmten Zeitpunkt an auch in Südsibirien. Dabei sind die realen Zusammenhänge herüber und hinüber nicht zu bezweifeln. Člen ova hält nun den Hirsch für das Stammestotem der Saken. »Sag« *Hirsch als* bedeute im modernen Ossetisch »Hirsch«. Die Saken hätten sich also *Stammessymbol* »Hirschleute« genannt. Tatsächlich kann man in ihrem Siedlungsgebiet östlich vom Aralsee zwar nur wenige, aber wichtige Hirschdarstellungen nachweisen. In Tuwa gibt es die sogenannten Hirschstelen, die zweifellos Menschen, berühmte Krieger, meinten. Aus demselben Komplex erkläre sich, daß der chinesische Hof von einem innerasiatischen Volk weiße Hirsche (und Wölfe) als Tributzahlung erhielt.

Die Streuung des Hirschbildes über den riesigen Steppenraum, ja bis nach dem heutigen Kurdistan, erklärt Členova durch militante Ausgriffe, vielleicht Herrschaftsbildungen. Andere Völker wie die Sarmaten, die ihre Unabhängigkeit bewahrten, hätten dieses Symbol grundsätzlich abgelehnt. Nach dem politischen Niedergang der Saken sei es fast völlig verschwunden.

Vielleicht ist an diesen Überlegungen etwas Wahres. Aber man wird auch jene komplizierteren Möglichkeiten bedenken müssen, die unsere Sozialanalyse erschloß. Vielleicht hatten sich unter den Jungmann- *Symbol für* schaften Kultverbände gebildet, die den Hirsch als Symbol führten *Kultverbände?* und Beziehungen über weite Strecken aufrechterhielten, ohne daß dies eine Herrschaftsbildung bedeutete.

Das Ende der Tierstilkunst wurde öfters mit der Ablösung der irani- *Ende der Tierstilkunst* schen Führerstellung im Steppenraum durch die Türken und Mongolen in Verbindung gebracht. Die neue Herrenschicht habe nicht nur eine andere künstlerische Begabung, sondern auch andere Traditionen mitgebracht.

Das kann nicht ganz stimmen. Die hochbegabte Altai-Bevölkerung schloß offenkundig bereits starke Elemente östlicher Herkunft ein, vielleicht türkische Einwanderer.

Aus den Schlußfolgerungen dieses Kapitels erhebt sich vielmehr eine

Parthische Münze mit dem Bildnis Phraates III. (70–57 v.Chr.). Die Parther haben noch lange nomadische Symbole – etwa den Bogen – bewahrt. Bezeichnenderweise erhielt sich bei ihnen das Bild des Hirsches als königliches Attribut – was die hier vorliegende Kronenform beweist. *Sammlung Göbl, Wien.*

andere Vermutung: wenn die frühe Nomadenkunst das reife Produkt einer Konsolidierungsphase war, die auf einen Unruhehorizont folgte, in dem man die Tiermotive benachbarter seßhafter Kulturen rezipiert hatte, dann ist es nur konsequent, daß der nächste Unruhehorizont mit der Auflösung des Gleichgewichts auch dem Tierstil die Basis entzog.

Dabei entwickelten die Hauptträger der zweiten Unruhephase – die Hsiung-nu und ihre Rivalen – rasch eine sehr viel straffer organisierte Hierarchie als etwa die Skythen. Von den Türken des 6.Jahrhunderts n.Chr. sind neunundzwanzig Klassen erblicher Würdenträger bezeugt. Dem Ehrgeiz des einzelnen war nicht mehr derselbe Raum gelassen. Es mußten ihm auch nicht mehr so unendlich breite Ausdrucksmöglichkeiten zugebilligt werden. Das Prestige fand seinen vollkommenen Ausdruck in einem minuziösen Trinkzeremoniell. Einer solchen geistigen Haltung war eine »Machtkunst« gemäß – wie Strzygowski richtig gesehen hat. Auch die »künstlerische Umwelt« hatte sich radikal gewandelt. Die benachbarten Hochkulturzentren boten kein realistisches Repertoire von Tierbildern mehr an, im Gegenteil, nach dem Sieg des Islams erfuhr das abstrakte Ornament eine generelle Aufwertung. Noch stärker war der Wandel der inneren, sozialen Bedingungen. Wir haben gehört, daß die Meisterwerke der Altai-Kunst von Leuten hergestellt wurden, die noch kaum aus der Masse des Volkes herausfielen, die noch ihre Rechte als Krieger wahrten wie etwa die »Schmiede« der Wikingerzeit. Bezeichnend ist diesbezüglich ein Fund in Karmir Blur. Man stieß dort innerhalb einer urartäischen Festung auf eine improvisierte Werkstätte. Ein Mann der skythischen Besatzungstruppe hatte gerade aus einer Geweihstange Greifenköpfchen geschnitzt – als die Eroberung durch eine andere skythische Truppe die Idylle unterbrach.

Sozialer Wandel

So etwas wäre einige Jahrhunderte später unmöglich gewesen. Eine zunehmend verfeinerte Arbeitsteilung, auch eine Komplizierung der von den einzelnen Hirten geforderten Aufgaben führten dazu, daß man die Produktion von Waffen und Schmuck an Spezialisten meist fremder Herkunft abschob. Immer wichtiger wurden die Basare der großen Handelsstädte, die an den Peripherien der Steppen entstanden. Die fremde Seide wurde Inbegriff des Reichtums. Ein Steppenherrscher konnte stolz darauf hinweisen, daß sich in seinem riesigen Heere kein Handwerker befand. Kriegsdienst und Hirtenarbeit genügten.

Um so bedeutsamer wurde die Rolle des von Frauen wahrgenommenen Haushandwerks. Man könnte die These aufstellen, die spätere Steppenkunst gerade in ihren eigenwilligsten Schöpfungen – den Teppichen – gehe zwar auf zahllose äußere Anregungen, aber auch auf jene urzeitlichen Motive zurück, die schon vor dem Tierstil existierten und während seiner Blüteperiode von den Frauen bewahrt wurden.

Haushandwerk der Frauen bildet Brücke von der Bronzezeit zum 1. Jahrtausend n. Chr.

Man könnte sagen, das Spiel der geometrischen Ranke, das man als Inbegriff der türkischen Kunst empfand, greife auf jene alte Spiral- und Volutenornamentik zurück.

Wenn es trotzdem in späten Jahrhunderten mehrfach das Wiederaufleben einzelner Tierstilmotive gegeben hat, so entsprach das vermutlich einer konservativen Tendenz der »weißen Knochen«, des Steppenadels, der sich allmählich als geschlossene Klasse etabliert hatte. Rückgriffe auf Stiltrümmer einer bereits sagenhaften Vergangenheit

Tiermotive bleiben als Symbole der Herrenschicht

betonten die Distanz zum gemeinen Volk. Stereotype Wiederholung wurde in Kauf genommen, Verständlichkeit nicht mehr gefordert. Es gehört immer zu dem Anliegen geschlossener Führungsgruppen, Andenken aus der bewegteren Welt zu bewahren, der sie entstammen.

Ähnlich war es im Bestattungsritual. Die Totendenkmäler des Türkenreiches sprechen in ihren großen Inschriften mit archaischen Formeln. Gerade die megalithische Note der Anlagen (die Stelen geben den Toten und die von ihm erschlagenen Feinde wieder) hebt den Herrscher aus der Masse des Volks, den »schwarzen Knochen«, empor.

Selbst die alte hohe Stellung des Handwerkers ist bei der Oberschicht versteinert worden. In Zentralasien hielt sich deshalb lange die Sage vom Schmiedekönig.

Tschingis Chan galt nicht nur als Abkömmling eines Wolfs und einer Hirschkuh, er ist auch in Ausdeutung seines Namens Temudschin als Schmied aufgefaßt worden. So wurde der Welteroberer mit den Vorstellungen jener bereits mythisch gewordenen Vergangenheit umkleidet, in der der Tierstil entstand.

ANHANG

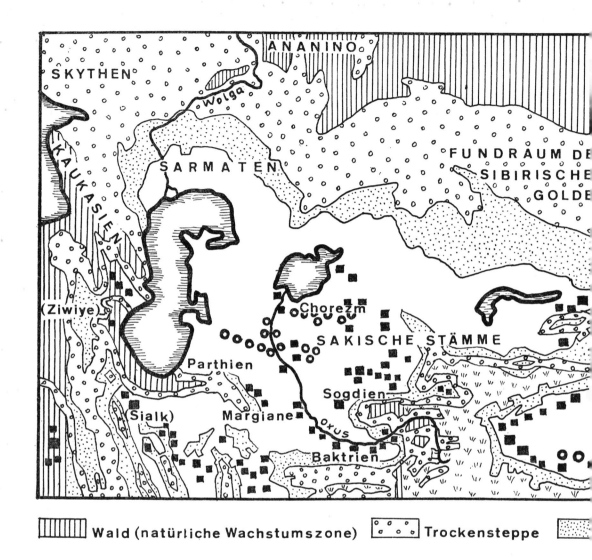

Wald (natürliche Wachstumszone) — Trockensteppe

DER ASIATISCHE STEPPENRAUM

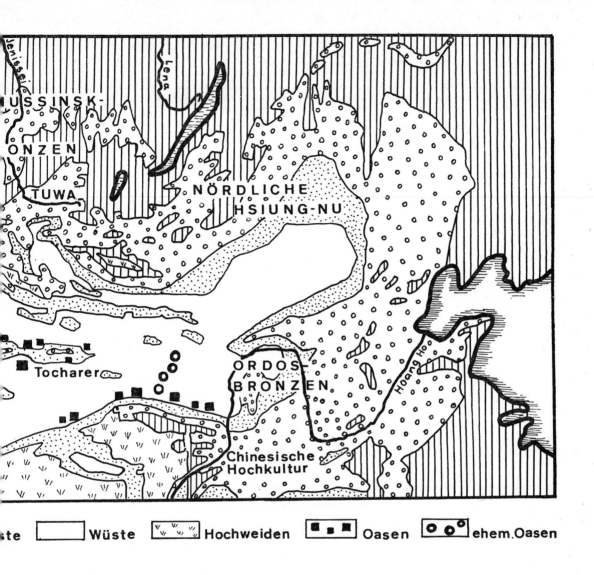

Tierstilprovinzen im asiatischen Teil des Steppenraumes sind mit
Großbuchstaben eingetragen.
Nicht nomadische Völker, Provinzen und Kulturgruppen sind
durch Groß- und Kleinschreibung gekennzeichnet.

	Wichtige Partner der Steppenvölker im Bereich von:		Pontisches Skythien (Kapitel II)	Skythische Funde in Mitteleuropa (Kapitel III)	Kaukasien (Kapitel IV)	Östliches Mittelrußland (Kapitel V)	Wolga Uralst (Kapite
	Iran, Armenien weiteres Vorderasien	China					
900	Assyrische Reichskunst mit reichen Tierdarstellungen Auftreten der Iranier	West-Chou-Reich, Kunst mit ornamentaler Verwendung des Tierstils	Vorherrschaft der Kimmerier Spiral- und Voluten-Ornamentik selten Tierbild	Tierbild gelegentlich verwendet		Kühn stilisierte Tierfiguren im Kultgebrauch	Endstu Balkeng Kultur
800	Mederreich gegründet Assyrien wird unter Sargon III. Großmacht Kimmerier bedrohen Urartu	Barbareneinbrüche Verlegung der Hauptstadt ab 771: Ost-Chou			Kobankultur führend bereits häufig Tiermotive		Endstu Androm Tierdar sehr sel
700	Massives Auftreten der Skythen, Niedergang Assurs, Neubabylonisches Reich Schatz von Ziwiye	Aufstieg der Lehnsstaaten »Tangentenkreis«	Skythenherrschaft Tierstil: Žabotin		Erste Tierstilelemente aus Zentralasien?	Ananino-Kultur Kaukasischer Einfluß	
600	Medisches Großreich 546 Perserreich 514 Skythenzug Darius' I.	Blühen einer Kunst mit reichen Tierdarstellungen	Kelermes: Hochstufe, orientalische, später griechische Einflüsse	Skythische Streifzüge, Landnahme (?) in Mittel-Ungarn, Siebenbürgen, Zentralbulgarien	Eindringen des skythischen Tierstils lokale Ansiedlung von pontischen Skythen	Übernahme des pontisch-skythisch- und sauromatischen Tierstils	Tierstil saurom Phase
500	Expansion nach Mittelasien, Reichskunst auf assyrischem Erbe aufbauend Tierornamentik	ab 481: Chan-Kuo »Streitende Reiche« Huai-Stil	Königliche Kurgane Solocha, Čertomlyk				
400	Niedergang 334 Alexanderzug	Auflösung des Lehns-Systems	Degeneration, Eindringen der Sarmaten Reich des Atheas	Beziehungen zur pontischen Waldsteppe Thrakische Fürstengräber	Mischformen im Nordkaukasus		Frühsar Stufe
300	Seleukidenreich Baktrien und Parthien unabhängig	256 Abdankung des letzten Chou-Herrschers, 221 Einigung unter Ts'in 206 Han-Dynastie	Skythenstaat auf der Krim			Übergang zur Pjanobor-Kultur	Tierstil reduzie
200	Partherreich Baktrien in der Hand von Barbaren	Kämpfe mit den Hsiung-nu		Sarmatische Einflüsse		Tiermotive bleiben weiter wichtig	
100	Weitere Sakeneinbrüche in Ostiran und Indien	Eroberungen im Tarim-Becken Seidenstraße	Zahlreiche sarmatische Funde: »Chochlač-Kurgan«		Sarmatische Besiedlung im Nordkaukasus	erneut sarmatische Einflüsse (siehe Kapitel XIV)	Mittelsa Stufe Tierstil mittelas Einflüss Polychr
0	Im Osten Konsolidierung der Kushana Reichsgründung	9–22 Wang-Mang 24 2. Han-Dynastie					
100	Niedergang der Parther	Abdrängen der Hsiung-nu nach dem Westen					Modell
200							

= Abruptes Einsetzen der Tierornamentik	= Vollausgebildeter Tierstil	= Vorstufen, Degenerationsformen oder geringe Bezeugung des Tierstils

...insk (Kapitel VII)	Hochaltai (Kapitel VIII)	Transbaikalien Nordmongolei (Kapitel IX)	Innere Mongolei Ordosgebiet (Kapitel X)	Tuwa (Kapitel XI)	Mittelasien (Kapitel XII)	Nord- und Ostkazachstan (Kapitel XIII)	
...k-Kultur			Viehzüchter-gruppen mit Karasuk-artigen Kulturen		Oasenbevölkerung und Nomaden ohne Animaldekor	Spätandronovo Keine nennens-werten Tier-darstellungen	900
	Ausläufer der Andronovo-Kultur mit Karasuk-Einflüssen						
...mit ...or de Tiere«			Messer mit Tier-kopfabschluß Nachleben von Einflüssen der Shang				800
...fknauf	Kaum Tierdarstellungen	Plattengräber-Kultur mit					
...Kultur	Majemir-Kultur Begrenzte Anzahl von Tiermotiven	Karasuk-Einflüssen	?	Ujuk-Kultur 1. Phase	Einzelnes Reitergrab mit Tierplastik	Ostkazachstan	700
...eten ...r Tier-						Kurgangruppen Anlage wie im Pontikum	
...gelkopf	Hirschmotive	Tierdekor vereinzelt übernommen	?	Begrenzter Vorrat an Tiermotiven, aber auch Hirsch, Hirsch-Stelen	Nomadengräber im Ostpamir mit Tierstil wie Tagar I	Čilikty, Tierstil voll entwickelt, besonders konservativ	600
					Tierplastiken an Kesseln und Altartischen in Semirečien »Achämenidischer« Tierstil bei Seßhaften		
	Einsetzen der Großkurgane; Pazyryk-Kultur		Ordosbronzen mit reichem Tierstil	2. Phase		Älteste Stücke des sibirischen Goldes (Rolltier)	500
...se der ...Kultur ...der Hirsch ...Motivschatz ...rstils von ...derern aus ...sien ...at?							
		Beziehungen zum Altai und zu Mittelasien	Viele Stämme mit verschiedenen Grabformen		Oxus-Schatz Tierstil im Syr-Darja-Gebiet	Beste Goldplatten mit bunten Einlagen gehören zu Nekro-polen mehrerer Stämme	400
...trische	Pazyryk II (?) Pazyryk V (?)			Mehrere Tierstilvarianten		Spätere Platten zum Teil unter chinesischem Einfluß	300
...ase der ...Kultur	Šibe-Phase	Herrschaft der Hsiung-nu	Herrschaft der Hsiung-nu	Šurmak-Kultur weiterhin viele Lokalgruppen	Sakische Funde im Pamir und im Karakorum, auf dem Weg nach Indien	Späteste Goldobjekte	200
		Derestruj	Auftreten einer abstrakten Ornamentik neben dem Tierstil			Weiterbestehen der Kurgane mit »Schnurbärten«	100
...Kultur	Abwanderung oder Vernichtung der Herrenbevölkerung	Chinesischer Import		Tierbild wie im Taštyk gebraucht			
...der ...tbehelfe ...astik		Fürstengräber von Noin Ula Tierkampfszenen			Nischengräber sarmatischer Zuwanderer		0
...e Motive ...t							100
							200

LITERATURHINWEISE

I. ENTDECKUNG DER FRÜHEN STEPPENKUNST

T. K. Basenov: Ornament Kazachstana v architekture. Alma-Ata 1957

H. Glück: Die Weltstellung der Türken in der Kunst. Wr. Beiträge, II, S. 29ff. 1927

H. Glück: Islamisches Kunstgewerbe, in: Geschichte des Kunstgewerbes aller Zeiten und Völker, Bd. IV (hg. v. H. Th. Bossert), S. 352–431. Berlin-Zürich 1930

H. Glück und E. Diez: Die Kunst des Islam. 2. Aufl. Propyläen-Kunstgeschichte, Bd. V. Berlin 1925

S. V. Ivanov: Realističeskie osnovy iskusstva tunguso-man'žurov. KSIE V, S. 86–90. 1949

S. V. Ivanov: Ornamentika, religioznye predstavlenija i obrjady, svjazannye c amurskoj lodkoj. SE 4–5, S. 62–84. 1935

S. V. Ivanov: Kirgizskij ornament kak ėtnogenetičeskij istočnik. Trudy kirgizskoj archeologo-ėtnografičeskoj ėkspedicii III, S. 59–73. Frunze 1959

I. A. Lopatin: Animal Style among the Tungus on the Amur. Anthropos, Bd. 56, S. 856–868. Fribourg 1961

W. G. Moschkova (übers. v. S. Kuntschik): »Göls« auf turkmenischen Teppichen. Archiv für Völkerkunde, Bd. III, S. 24–43. Wien 1948

J. Strzygowski: Altai-Iran und Völkerwanderung. Leipzig 1917

J. Strzygowski: Asiens bildende Kunst in Stichproben, ihr Wesen und ihre Entwicklung. Augsburg 1930

S. A. Tokarev: Ėtnografija narodov SSSR. Moskau 1958

B. V. Vejmarn: Iskusstvo Srednej Azii. 1940

II. DAS PONTISCHE SKYTHIEN

M. I. Artamonov: Obščestvennyj stroj skifov. Vestnik LGU No. 9, S. 70ff. 1947

A. Bobrinskij: Kurgany i slučajnye archeologičeskie nachodki bliz mestečka Smely. I–III. 1887–1901

G. I. Borovka: Bronzovyi olen' iz Ul'skogo aula. IGAIMK, II. 1922

G. I. Borovka: Kunstgewerbe der Skythen. Bossert, Geschichte des Kunstgewerbes aller Zeiten und Völker, Bd. I, S. 101–157. Berlin 1928 a

G. I. Borovka: Scythian Art. London 1928 b

W. Brandenstein: Die Abstammungssagen der Skythen. Wiener Zeitschrift für die Kunde des Morgenlandes, 52. Bd., H. 1 u. 2, S. 183–211. Wien 1953

D. Carter: The Symbol of the Beast. New York 1957

B. N. i V. I. Chanenko: Drevnosti Pridneprov'ja. 1899 bis 1900

M. Ebert: Südrußland im Altertum. Bonn und Leipzig 1921

N. G. Elagina: O rodoplemennoj strukture skifskogo obščestva po materialam četvertoj knigi Gerodota. SE 3, S. 76–82. 1963

B. V. Farmakovskij: Archaičeskij period v Rossii. MAR 34. 1914

N. Fettich: Die Tierkampfszene in der Nomadenkunst. Recueil d'études dédiées à la mémoire de N. P. Kondakov. Seminarium Kondakovianum, S. 81–92. Prag 1926

M. Gibellino-Krasceninnicowa: Gli Sciti. Rom 1942

B. N. Grakov: Skifi. Kiïv 1947

B. N. Grakov: Očerednye zadači archeologii v izučenii skifo-sarmatskogo perioda. KSIIMK XXXIV, S. 3–6. 1950a

B. N. Grakov: Skifskij Gerakl. KSIIMK XXXIV, S. 7–18. 1950b

B. N. Grakov: Kamenskoe gorodišče na Dnepre. MIA 36. 1954

B. N. Grakov: Skifskie pogrebenija na Nikopol'skom kurgannom pole. MIA 115, S. 56–113. 1962

B. N. Grakov i A. I. Meljukova: Ob ėtničeskich i kul'turnych različijach v stepnych i lesostepnych oblastjach Evropejskoj časti SSR v skifskoe vremja. »Voprosy skifo-sarmatskoj archeologii«, S. 39–93. Moskau 1954

F. Hančar: Die Skythen als Forschungsproblem. Reinecke-Festschrift, S. 67–83. Mainz 1950

A. A. Iessen: K voprosu o pamjatnikach VIII–VII vv do n. ė. na juge Evropejskoj časti SSSR. SA XVIII, S. 49–110. 1953

V. A. Illins'ka: Kurgan Starša Mogili – pam'jatka archaičnoï Skifiï. Archeologija, V. Kiïv 1957

I. V. Jacenko: Skifija VII–V vekov do našej ėry. Trudy GIM, 36. 1959

K. Jettmar: Die Entstehung des skythischen Tierstils. Umschau, 55. Jg., H. 7, S. 203–205. 1955

K. Jettmar: In den Jahren 1955 bis 1962 erschienene Werke zur frühen Nomadenkunst der asiatischen Steppen. Kunstgeschichtliche Anzeigen, N. F., 5. Jg., S. 184–197. Graz/Köln 1961/1962

K. Jettmar: Ausbreitungsweg und sozialer Hintergrund des eurasiatischen Tierstils. MAGW XCII (Hančar-Festschrift), S. 176–191. 1962

A. K. Korovina: K voprosu ob izučenii Semibratnich kurganov. SA 2, S. 174–187. 1957

A. Lappo-Danilevskij i V. Mal'berg: Drevnosti Južnoj Rossii. Kurgan Karagodeuašch. MAR 3. 1894

P. D. Liberov: Mastjuginskie kurgany. SA 3, S. 152 bis 165. 1961

A. P. Mancevič: O skifskich pojasach. SA VII, S. 19–30. Moskau-Leningrad 1941

A. P. Mancevič: Šejnye ubory skifskogo perioda. KSIIMK XXII, S. 68–73. 1948

A. P. Mancevič: K voprosu o torevtike v skifskuju èpochu. VDI 2, S. 196–220. 1949

A. I. Meljukova: Skifskie kurgany Tiraspol'ščiny. MIA 115, S. 114–166. 1962

E. H. Minns: Scythians and Greeks. Cambridge 1913

E. H. Minns: The Scythians and the Northern Nomads. Cambridge Ancient History III. 1925

E. H. Minns: The Art of the Northern Nomads. Proceedings of the British Academy, 28, S. 47 bis 99. London 1945

E. D. Phillips: The Legend of Aristeas: Fact and Fancy in Early Greek Notions of East Russia, Siberia, and Inner Asia. Artibus Asiae, XVIII, 2, S. 161–177. Ascona 1955

E. D. Phillips: A Further Note on Aristeas. Artibus Asiae, XX, 2/3, S. 159–162. Ascona 1957

E. D. Phillips: The Argippaei of Herodotus. Artibus Asiae, XXIII, 2, S. 124–128. Ascona 1960

E. D. Phillips: New Light on the Ancient History of the Eurasian Steppe. American Journal of Archaeology, 61, S. 269–280

N. N. Pogrebova: Grifon v iskusstve Severnogo Pričernomor'ja v èpochu archaiki. KSIIMK XXII, S. 62–67. 1948

N. N. Pogrebova: K voprosu o skifskom zverinom stile. KSIIMK XXXIV, S. 129–141. 1950

E. Pridik: Mel'gunovskij klad 1763 goda. MAR, 31, 1911

B. Rabinovič: O daturovke nekotorych skifskich kurganov Srednego Pridneprov'ja. SA I, S. 79–102. 1936

T. T. Rice: Die Skythen. Ein Steppenvolk an der Zeitwende. Köln 1957

M. Rostovtseff (= Rostovcev): Iranians and Greeks in South Russia. Oxford 1922

M. Rostovtzeff (= Rostovcev): Le centre de l'Asie, la Russie, la Chine et le style animal. Skythika 1 (Seminarium Kondakovianum). Prag 1929a

M. Rostovtzeff (= Rostovcev): The Animal Style in South Russia and China. Princeton 1929b

M. Rostowzew (= Rostovcev): Skythien und der Bosporus, Bd. I. Berlin 1931

A. Salmony: An Unknown Scythian Find in Novocherkassk. ESA X, S. 54–60. Helsinki 1936

A. Salmony: Lead Plates in Odessa. ESA XI, S. 91–102. Helsinki 1937

E. Sarkisyanz: Rußland und der Messianismus des Orients. Tübingen 1955

K. Schefold: Der skythische Tierstil in Südrußland. ESA XII, S. 1–78. Helsinki 1938

K. Schefold: Die skythische Kunst in Südrußland. W. Otto – R. Herbig: Handbuch der Archäologie, 2. 1954

V. V. Šleev: K voprosu o skifskich naveršijach. KSIIMK XXXIV, S. 53–61. 1950

W. Speiser: Vorderasiatische Kunst. Berlin 1952

A. A. Spicyn: Kurgany skifov-pacharej. IAK, S. 87–143. 1918

T. Sulimirski: Scythian Antiquities in Western Asia. Artibus Asiae, XVII, 3–4, S. 282–318. Ascona 1954

T. Sulimirski: Scythian Notes. Palaeologia, IV, 3/4, S. 280–284. 1955

A. M. Tallgren: Zum Ursprungsgebiet des sog. skythischen Tierstils. Acta Archeologica, IV, S. 258–264. Kopenhagen 1933

A. I. Terenožkin: K voprosu ob ètničeskoj prinadležnosti lesostepnych plemen Severnogo Pričernomor'ja v skifskoe vremja. SA XXIV, S. 7–28. 1955

I. I. Tolstoi i N. P. Kondakov: Russkie drevnosti v pamjatnikach iskusstva. Bd. I–III. St. Peterburg 1888–1900

S. N. Zamjatnin: Skifskij mogil'nik »Častye kurgany« pod Voronežem. SA VI, S. 9–50. Moskau-Leningrad 1946

L. Zgusta: Die Personennamen griechischer Städte der nördlichen Schwarzmeerküste. Prag 1955

III. SKYTHISCHE FUNDE IN MITTELEUROPA

V. D. Blavatskij: Frakija i Severnyj Pont. KSIA AN SSSR 89, S. 94–96. 1962

J. Böhm und J. Jankovich: Skythovie na Podkarpatske Rusi Mohilové pohrebište v Kuštanovicich. CARPATICA I. Prag 1936

G. Csallany und M. Párducz: Funde aus der Skythenzeit im Museum zu Szentes. Arch. Êrtesitö 5/6, S. 106–107. 1944/45

N. *Fettich:* La trouvaille Scythe de Zöldhalom-puszta. Archaeologia Hungarica III. Budapest 1928

N. *Fettich:* Der Goldhirsch von Tápiózentmárton. Archeoligai Értesitö XLI. Budapest 1927

N. *Fettich:* Das Tiermotiv der Parierstange des Schwertes von Aldoboly, Siebenbürgen. Prähistorische Zeitschrift XIX, H. 3–4. Berlin 1928

N. *Fettich:* Bestand der skythischen Altertümer Ungarns, in: M. Rostovcev, Skythien und der Bosporus, Bd. I, 2. Teil. Berlin 1931

N. *Fettich:* Der skythische Fund von Gartschinowo. Archaeologia Hungarica XV. Budapest 1934

A. *Furtwängler:* Der Goldfund von Vettersfelde. 43. Winckelmanns Festprogramm. 1883

J. *Hampel:* Scythische Denkmäler in Ungarn. Ethnologische Mitteilungen aus Ungarn, IV. Budapest 1895

M. *Jahn:* Die Skythen in Schlesien. Schlesiens Vorzeit in Bild und Schrift, IX. Breslau 1928

A. I. *Meljukova:* K voprosu o pamjatnikach skifskoj kul'tury na territorii Srednej Evropy. SA XXII, S. 239–253. 1955

J. *Nestor:* Der Stand der Vorgeschichtsforschung in Rumänien. 22. Bericht der Röm.-Germ. Kommission 1932. Frankfurt am Main 1933

M. *Párducz:* Le cimetière Hallstattien de Szentes-Vekerzug. Acta Archaeologica Academiae scientiarum Hungaricae, Bd. II, 1–3, S. 143 bis 169. Budapest 1952

H. *Preidel:* Skythen in Böhmen. Deutsche Heimat IV, S. 340ff. 1928

H. *Preidel:* Der Skytheneinfall in Ostdeutschland und die skythischen Funde aus Böhmen. Altschlesien V. 1934

P. *Reinecke:* Die skythischen Altertümer im mittleren Europa. Zeitschrift für Ethnologie XXVIII. Berlin 1896

M. v. *Roska:* Der Bestand der skythischen Altertümer Siebenbürgens. ESA XI, S. 167–203. Helsinki 1937

J. *Rozen-Pševorskaja:* K voprosu o kel'to-skifskich otnošenijach. SA 3, S. 67–78. 1963

H. *Schmidt:* Skythischer Pferdegeschirrschmuck aus einem Silberdepot unbekannter Herkunft. Prähistorische Zeitschrift 18, S. 1ff. Berlin 1927

T. *Sulimirski:* Scytowie na zachodniem Podolu. Prace Lwowskiego Towarzystwa Prehistorycznego No. 2. Lwów 1936

T. *Sulimirski:* Scythien Antiquities in Central Europe. The Antiquaries Journal No. 1, 2, S. 1–11. 1945

T. *Sulimirski:* Kultura łużycka a Scytowie. Wiadomości Archeologiezne, XVI, S. 76–100. Warschau 1939–1948

IV. SKYTHISCHES IN KAUKASIEN

E. P. *Alekseeva:* Pozdnekobanskaja kul'tura Central'nogo Kavkaza. Učenye zapiski LGU, serija ist. nauk, v. 3. Leningrad 1949

O. A. *Artamonova-Poltavceva:* Kul'tura Severo-Vostočnogo Kavkaza v skifskij period. SA XIV. S. 20–101. 1950

G. M. *Aslanov, R. M. Vaidov i G. I. Ione:* Drevnij Mingečaur. Baku 1959

F. *Hančar:* Einige Gürtelschließen aus dem Kaukasus. ESA VI, S. 146–158. Helsinki 1931

F. *Hančar:* Die Nadelformen des prähistorischen Kaukasusgebietes. ESA VII, S. 113–182. Helsinki 1932

F. *Hančar:* Die Beile aus Koban in der Wiener Sammlung kaukasischer Altertümer. Wiener Prähistorische Zeitschrift XXI, S. 12–44. 1934

F. *Hančar:* Zum Problem des »kaukasischen« Tierstils. Wr. Beiträge, IX, S. 3–34. 1934

F. *Hančar:* Kaukasus – Luristan. Züge kultureller Verwandtschaft des prähistorischen Kaukasusgebietes mit dem Alten Orient. ESA IX, S. 47–112. Helsinki 1934

F. *Hančar:* Probleme des kaukasischen Tierstils. MAGW, LXV, S. 367–385. Wien 1935

A. A. *Iessen:* Severokavkazskie sosudy s izobraženiem olenja. SGAIMK 2. 1931

A. A. *Iessen:* Nekotorye pamjatniki VIII–VII vv. do n. è. na Severnom Kavkaze. Voprosy skifosarmatskoj archeologii, S. 112–131. Moskau 1954

S. M. *Kaziev:* Archeologičeskie raskopki v Mingečaure. Material'naja kul'tura Azerbajdžana. Baku 1949

E. I. *Krupnov:* Drevnjaja istorija Severnogo Kavkaza. Moskau 1960

B. A. *Kuftin:* Archeologičeskie raskopki v Trialeti. Tbilisi 1941

S. J. *Makalatija:* Raskopki Dvanskogo mogil'nika. SA XI, S. 225–240. 1949

B. B. *Piotrovskij:* Archeologija Zakavkaz'ja. Leningrad 1949

B. B. *Piotrovskij i A. A. Iessen:* Mozdokskij mogil'nik. Leningrad 1940

A. M. *Tallgren:* Caucasian Monuments. The Kazbek Treasure. ESA V, S. 109–182. Helsinki 1930

O. G. *Wesendonk:* Archäologisches aus dem Kaukasus. Archäologischer Anzeiger XI. Berlin 1925

V. DIE ANANINOKULTUR IN OSTRUSSLAND

D. N. Éding: Idoly Gorbunovskogo torfjanka. SA IV, S. 133–146. 1937

D. N. Éding: Novye nachodki na Gorbunovskom torfjanke. MIA 1, S. 41–57. 1940

A. P. Smirnov: Očerki drevnej i srednevekovoj istorii narodov srednego Povolž'ja i Prikam'ja. MIA 28. 1952

A. M. Tallgren: L'époque dite d'Ananino dans la Russie orientale. SMYA XXXI. Helsingfors 1919

A. M. Tallgren: Die »altpermische« Pelzwarenperiode an der Pečora. SMYA XI, S. 152–181. 1934

A. V. Zbrueva: Ideologija naselenija Prikam'ja v Anan'inskogo èpochu. TIE, S. 25–54. Moskau-Leningrad 1947

A. V. Zbrueva: Istorija naselenija Prikam'ja v anan'inskuju èpochu. MIA 30. Moskau 1952

VI. DIE EXPANSION DER SARMATEN

M. P. Abramova: Sarmatskaja kul'tura II v. do n. è. – I v. n. è. SA 1, S. 52–71. 1959

M. P. Abramova: Sarmatskie pogrebenija Dona i Ukrainy. SA 1, S. 91–110. 1961

N. V. Anfimov: Meoto-sarmatskij mogil'nik u stanica Ust'-Labinskaja. MIA 23, S. 155–207. 1951

M. Ebert: Südrußland. D. Skythisch-sarmatische Periode. Reallexikon der Vorgeschichte, 13. Bd., S. 52–114. Berlin 1929

N. Fettich: Archäologische Beiträge zur Geschichte der sarmatisch-dakischen Beziehungen. Acta Archaeologica III. Budapest 1953

B. Grakov: Monuments de la culture scythique entre le Volga et les monts Oural. ESA III, S. 25–62. Helsinki 1928

B. Grakov: Deux tombeaux de l'époque scythique aux environs de la ville d'Orenbourg. ESA IV, S. 169–182. Helsinki 1929

B. Grakov: Perežitki matriarchata u sarmatov. VDI 3, S. 100–122. 1947

A. A. Iessen: Tak nazyvaemyj »Majkopskij pojas«. Archeologičeskij sbornik 2, S. 163–177. Leningrad 1961

I. V. Jacenko: Rannee sarmatskoe pogrebenie v bassejne Serengogo Donca. KSIA 89, S. 42–50. 1962

M. I. Maksimova: O date Artjuchovskogo kurgana. SA 3, S. 46–58. 1960

M. G. Moškova: Sarmatskie pamjatniki vostočnych rajonov Orenburgskoj oblasti. KSIA AN SSSR 83, S. 115–126. 1961

M. G. Moškova: Novo-Kumakskij kurgannyj mogil'nik bliz g. Orska. MIA 115, S. 206–241. 1962

M. Párducz: Denkmäler der Sarmatenzeit Ungarns, I–III. Budapest, I. Bd. 1941, II. Bd. 1944 (1947), III. Bd. 1950

P. Rau: Die Hügelgräber römischer Zeit an der unteren Wolga. Mitteilungen des Zentralmuseums der ASR d. Wolgadeutschen, I, 1. Pokrovsk 1927

P. Rau: Prähistorische Ausgrabungen auf der Steppenseite des deutschen Wolgagebietes im Jahre 1926. Mitteilungen des Zentralmuseums der ASR der Wolgadeutschen, II, 1. Pokrosvk 1927

P. Rau: Die Gräber der frühen Eisenzeit im unteren Wolgagebiet. Mitteilungen des Zentralmuseums der ASR d. Wolgadeutschen. Pokrovsk 1929

M. I. Rostovcev: Kurgannyja nachodki Orenburgskoj oblasti èpochi rannjago i pozdnjago Èllinizma. MAR 37. Petrograd 1918

M. I. Rostovcev: Sarmatskija i indoskifskie drevnosti. Recueil d'études dédiées à la mémoire de N. P. Kondakov. Seminarium Kondakovianum, S. 239–258. Prag 1926

M. I. Rostovcev: Sarmatae. Ancient History XI. Cambridge 1936

P. S. Rykov: Suslovskij kurgannyj mogil'nik. Saratov 1947

V. P. Šilov: Kalinovskij kurgannyj mogil'nik. MIA 60, S. 323–523. 1959

I. V. Sinicyn: K materialam po sarmatskoj kul'ture na territorii nižnego Povolž'ja. SA VIII, S. 73–95. 1946

K. F. Smirnov: O pogrebenijach roksolan. VDI 1, S. 213–214. 1948

K. F. Smirnov: Sarmatskie pogrebenija južnogo Priural'ja. KSIIMK XXII, S. 80–86. 1948

K. F. Smirnov: Sarmatskie plemena Severnogo Prikaspija. KSIIMK XXXIV, S. 97–114. 1950

K. F. Smirnov: O nekotorych itogach issledovanija mogil'nikov meotskoj i sarmatskoj kul'tury Prikuban'ja i Dagestana. KSIIMK XXXVII, S. 151–160. 1951

K. F. Smirnov: Itogi i očerednye zadači izučenija sarmatskich plemen i ich kul'tury. SA XVII, S. 133–148. 1953

K. F. Smirnov: Voprosy izučenija sarmatskich plemen i ich kul'tury v sovetskoj archeologii. Voprosy skifo-sarmatskoj archeologii, S. 195 bis 219. Moskau 1954

K. F. Smirnov: Problema proischožden ija rannich sarmatov. SA 3, S. 3–19. 1957

K. F. Smirnov: Meotskij mogil'nik u stanicy Paškovskoj. MIA 64, S. 272–312. 1958

K. F. Smirnov: Vooruženie savromatov. MIA 101. Moskau 1961

A. A. *Spicyn:* Falary Južnoj Rossii. IAK 29. 1909

A. M. *Tallgren:* »Portable Altars«. ESA XI, S. 47 bis 68. Helsinki 1937

M. I. *Vjaz'mitina:* Vivčenija sarmativ na teritorii Ukraïns'koï RSR. Archeologija, VII. Kiïv 1953

VII. DIE MINUSSINSKBRONZEN

V. P. *Alekseev:* Materialy po paleantropologii naselenija Minusinskoj kotloviny vremeni taštykskoj kul'tury. KSIE XX, S. 52–58. 1954

V. P. *Alekseev:* Paleoantropologija Chakassii èpochi železa. Sbornik MAE, XX, S. 238–327. 1961

V. P. *Alekseev:* Paleoantropologija Altae-Sajanskogo nagor'ja èpochi neolita i bronzy. TIE LXXI, S. 107–206. 1961

M. D. *Chlobystina:* Bronzovye noži Minusinskogo kraja i nekotorye voprosy razvitija karasukskoj kul'tury. Leningrad 1962

N. L. *Členova:* Osnovye voprosy proischoždenija tagarskoj kul'tury Južnoj Sibiri. sb. Voprosy istorii Sibiri i Dal'nego Vostoka. Novosibirsk 1961

N. L. *Členova:* Pamjatniki perechodnogo karasuk-tagarskogo vremeni v. Minusinskom kotlovine. SA 3, S. 48–66. 1963

M. A. *Dèvlet:* K voprosu o tagaro-taštykskich vzaimootnošenijach. SA 4, S. 78–83. 1961

V. I. *Fedorov:* Drevnee iskusstvennoe orošenie v rajone Minusinskogo poniženija. MIA 24, S. 137–146. Moskau 1952

J. H. *Gaul:* Observations on the Bronze Age in the Yenisei Valley, Siberia. Papers of the Peabody Mus., XX, S. 149–186. Cambridge Mass. 1943

R. *Ghirshman* bespricht: S. V. Kisselev – Histoire Ancienne de la Sibérie du Sud. Matériaux et recherches archéologiques en U.R.S.S. Artibus Asiae, XIV, 1/2, S. 169–189. Ascona 1951

M. P. *Grjaznov:* Bojarskaja pisanica. Problema istorii, malerial'noj kul'tury 7–8, S. 41–45. Leningrad 1933

M. P. *Grjaznov:* Drevnjaja bronza minusinskich stepej. Trudy otdela istorii pervobytnoj kul'tury, I, S. 237–271. Leningrad 1941

K. *Jettmar:* The Karasuk Culture and Its Southeastern Affinities. BMFEA 22, S. 83–126. Stockholm 1950

S. V. *Kiselev:* Drevnjaja istorija Južnoj Sibiri. 2. Aufl. Moskau 1951

G. v. *Merhart:* Beiträge zur Urgeschichte der Jenissei-Gubernie. SMYA XXXIV, 1, S. 3–46. 1923

G. v. *Merhart:* Bronzezeit am Jenissei. Wien 1926

G. v. *Merhart:* Daljoko. Bilder aus sibirischen Arbeitstagen. Innsbruck o. J.

Ė. *Novgorodova:* Noži karasukskogo vremeni iz Mongolii i Južnoj Sibiri. Mongol'skij archeologičeskij sbornik, S. 11–17. Moskau 1962

S. *Roudenko* (= S. I. *Rudenko*): Les sépultures de l'époque des Kourganes de Minoussinsk. L'Anthropologie XXXIX. Paris 1929

A. *Salmony:* Origin and Age of the »Grazing« Animal. Silver Jubilee Volume of the Zinbun-Kagaku-Kenkyusyo, S. 336–338. Kyoto 1954

A. M. *Tallgren:* Collection Tovostine des antiquités préhistoriques de Minoussinsk. Helsingfors 1917

A. M. *Tallgren:* Trouvailles tombales Sibiriennes en 1889. SMYA XXIX. 1922

A. M. *Tallgren* bespricht Teplouchov – Alte Begräbnisstätten im Minusinsk-Gebiet. Grjaznov – Bronzezeitliche Gräber im westlichen Kasakstan. ESA III, S. 186–188. 1928

S. A. *Teplouchov:* Drevnie pogrebenija v Minusinskom krae. Materialy po ètnografii, III, 2. Leningrad 1927

S. A. *Teplouchov:* Opyt klassifikacii drevnich metalličeskich kul'tur Minusinskogo kraja. Materialy po ètnografii, IV, 2. Leningrad 1929a

S. A. *Teplouchov:* Drevnemetalličeskie kul'tury Minusinskogo kraja. Priroda 6, S. 539–552. 1929

N. G. *Zalkind:* Kraniologičeskie materialy iz taštykskich i tagarskich pogrebenij Bol'sogo Salbykskogo kurgana. Sovetskaja Antropologija 1, S. 57–66. 1959

VIII. SKYTHENZEITLICHE GRÄBER IM ALTAI

V. P. *Alekseev:* Paleoantropologija lesnych plemen Severnogo Altaja. KSIE XXI, S. 63–69. 1954

V. P. *Alekseev:* Paleoantropologija Altaja èpochi železa. Sovetskaja Antropologija 1, S. 45–49. 1958

V. V. *Artem'ev, S. V. Butomo, V. M. Drožžin, E. H. Romanova:* Rezul'taty opredelenija absoljutnogo vozrasta rjada archeologičeskich i geologičeskich obrazcov po radiouglerodu (C^{14}). SA 2, S. 3–11. 1961

G. *Azarpay:* Some Classical and Near Eastern Motives in the Art of Pazyryk. Artibus Asiae, XXII, S. 313–339. 1959

V. I. *Calkin:* K izučeniju lošadej iz kurganov Altaja. MIA 24, S. 147–156. 1952

S. S. *Černikov:* Vostočnyj Kazachstan v èpochu bronzy. MIA 88. 1960

E. *Dittrich:* Das Altai-Gold und China. Zeitschrift der Deutschen Morgenländischen Gesellschaft Bd. 111 (N.F. Bd. 36) Heft 2, 1961, S. 498–511. Wiesbaden 1962

H. Findeisen: Die »Skythen« im Altai vor 2400 Jahren. Kosmos, H. 7, S. 306–311. Juli 1956

A. A. Gavrilova: Raskopki Vtorogo Katandinskogo mogil'nika. SA XXVII, S. 250–268. 1957

M. Grjaznoff(= Grjaznov): Fürstengräber im Altaigebiet. Wiener Prähistorische Zeitschrift, XV, S. 120–123. Wien 1928a

M. P. Grjaznov: Raskopka knjažeskoj mogily na Altae. Čelovek 2–4, S. 217–219. 1928b

M. P. Grjaznov: Pazyrykskoe knjažeskoe progrebenie na Altae. Priroda 11, S. 971–985. 1929

M. P. Grjaznov: Drevnie kul'tury Altaja. Novosibirsk 1930

M. P. Grjaznov: Pazyrykskij kurgan. Moskau-Leningrad 1937

M. P. Grjaznov: Raskopki na Altae. Soobščenija Gos. Ėrmitaža I, S. 17–21. Leningrad 1940

M. P. Grjaznov: Pamjatniki majėmirskogo ėtapa ėpochi rannich kočevnikov. KSIIMK XVIII, S. 9–17. 1947a

M. P. Grjaznov: Raboty Altajskoj ėkspedicii. KSIIMK XXI, S. 77–78. 1947b

M. P. Grjaznov: Pervyj Pazyrykskij kurgan (Gos. Ėrmitaz). Leningrad 1950

M. P. Grjaznov: Kolesnica rannich kočevnikov Altaja. SGE 7, S. 30–32. 1955

M. P. Grjaznov: Vojlok s izobraženiem borby mifičeskich čudovišč iz pjatogo Pazyrykskogo kurgana na Altae. SGE 9, S. 40–42. 1956

M. P. Grjaznov and E. A. Golomshtok: The Pazirik Burial of Altai. The American Journal of Archaeology, XXXVII, 1, S. 30–45. 1933

F. Hančar: The Eurasian Animal Style and the Altai Complex (Cultural historical interpretation with a consideration of the newest Pazyryk discoveries of 1946–1949). Artibus Asiae, XV, 1/2, S. 171–194. 1952

John F. Haskins: Samartian Gold collected by Peter the Great: VII. The Demidov Gift and Conclusions. Artibus Asiae XXII, 1/2, S. 64–78. Ascona 1959

K. Jettmar: The Altai before the Turks. BMFEA, 23, S. 135–223. Stockholm 1951

K. Jettmar: Die Pferdemasken des I. Pazyryk-Kurgans. Veröffentlichungen der Urgeschichtlichen Arbeitsgemeinschaft in der Anthropologischen Gesellschaft in Wien, I. Bd, S. 63–66. Wien 1952

K. Jettmar: Die Fürstengräber der Skythen im Altai. Umschau, Jg. 61, H. 12, S. 368–371. Frankfurt a. M. 1961

K. Jettmar: Zum »Spielteppich« aus dem V. Pazyryk-Kurgan. Central Asiatic Journal, VIII, 1, S. 47–53. 1963

S. V. Kiselev: Sajano-Altajskaja archeologičeskaja ėkspedicija v 1937g. VDI 2, S. 237ff. 1938

S. V. Kiselev: Sajano-Altajskaja archeologičeskaja ėkspedicija v 1938g. VDI 1, S. 252ff. 1939

L. P. Kyzlasov i K. F. Smirnov bespricht S. I. Rudenko – Gornoaltajskie nachodki i skifi. Leningrad-Moskau 1952. SA XIX, S. 328–335. 1954

O. Maenchen-Helfen: Crenelated Mane and Scabbard Slide. Central Asiatic Journal, III, 2, S. 85–138. 1957

P. W. Meister: Ergebnisse der Grabungen im Altai 1939. Ostasiatische Zeitschrift N. F., 18. Jg., S. 62–64. 1942/1943

V. N. Poltorackaja: Mogil'nik Berezovka 1. Archeologičeskij sbornik 3, S. 74–88. Leningrad 1961

V. N. Poltorackaja: Znaki na predmetach iz kurganov ėpochi rannich kočevnikov v gornom Altae. Archeologičeskij sbornik 5, S. 76–90. Leningrad 1962

W. Radloff: Aus Sibirien, Band I und II. Leipzig 1884

M.-Th. Ricard: Quelques observations sur le costume scythique. Studia Antiqua, Antonio Salač Septuagenario Oblata, S. 152–155. Prag 1955

A. Roes: Achaemenid Influence upon Egyptian and Nomad Art. Artibus Asiae, XV, 1/2, S. 18–30. Ascona 1952

S. I. Rudenko: Vtoroj pazyryksij kurgan. Leningrad 1948

S. I. Rudenko: Predvaritel'noe soobščenie o raskopkach v Ulagane 1947g. SA XI, S. 261–270. 1949

S. I. Rudenko: Drevnejšaja »skifskaja« tatuirovka. SE 3, S. 133–143. 1949

S. I. Rudenko: Pjatyj Pazyrykskij kurgan. KSIIMK XXXVII, S. 106–116. 1951

S. I. Rudenko: Gornoaltajskie nachodki i skifi. Moskau-Leningrad 1952

S. I. Rudenko: Bašadarskie kurgany. KSIIMK XLV, S. 30–39. 1952

S. I. Rudenko: Kul'tura naselenija Gornogo Altaja v skifskoe vremja. Moskau 1953

S. I. Rudenko: K voprosu o datirovke i istoriko-kul'turnoj ocenke gornoaltajskich nachodok. SA XXVII, S. 301–306. 1957

S. I. Roudenko (= Rudenko): The Mythological Eagle, the Gryphon, the Winged Lion and Wolf in the Art of Northern Nomads. Artibus Asiae, XXI/2. 1958

S. I. Rudenko: Kul'tura naselenija central'nogo Altaja v skifskoe vremja. Moskau-Leningrad 1960

S. I. Rudenko: Iskusstvo Altaja i Perednej Azii. Moskau 1961

S. I. Rudenko i N. M. Rudenko: Iskusstvo skifov Altaja. Moskau 1949

S. A. Semenov: Obrabotka dereva na drevnem Altae (Po materialam Pazyrykskich kurganov). SA XXVI, S. 204–226. 1956

S. M. Sergeev: O reznych kostjanych ukrašenijach konskoj uzdy iz »skifskogo« kurgana na Altae. SA VIII, S. 289–292. 1946

K. F. Smirnov bespricht: S. I. Rudenko – Gornoaltajskie nachodki i skifi. Moskau-Leningrad 1952. Voprosy istorii, 2, S. 119–122. 1953

K. M. Swoboda: In den Jahren 1950–1955 erschienene Werke zur Kunst Asiens vor dem Islam. Kunstgeschichtliche Anzeigen, N. F., 1. Jg. 1955/56, H. 3/4. Graz-Wien-Köln

A. M. Tallgren: Archaeological Studies in Soviet Russia. ESA X, S. 129–170. Helsinki 1936

A. Umanskij: Pamjatniki kul'tury Altaja. Barnaul 1959

E. S. Vidonova: Katandinskij chalat. Sbornik statej po archeologii SSSR 8, izd. Istorič. Muzeja. Moskau 1938

O. A. Vitt: Lošadi Pazyrykskich kurganov. SA XVI, S. 163–205. 1952

J. Wiesner: Zur Archäologie Sibiriens. Atlantis, XXXI. Jg., 1, S. 44–50. Zürich 1959

I. M. Zamotorin: Otnositel'naja chronologija pazyrykskich kurganov. SA 1, S. 21–30. 1959

M. P. Zavituchina: Mogil'nik vremeni rannich kočevnikov bliz g. Bijska. Archeologičeskij sbornik 3, S. 89–108. Leningrad 1961

IX. DIE HSIUNG-NU IN TRANSBAIKALIEN UND DER NORDMONGOLEI

A. N. Bernštam: Izobraženie byka-jaka na bljachach iz Noin-Ulinskich kurganov. PIDO, 5–6, S. 127–130. 1933

A. N. Bernštam: K voprosu o social'nom stroe vostočnich gunnov. PIDO, 9–10, S. 226–234. 1935

A. N. Bernštam: Gunnskij mogil'nik Noin-Ula i ego istoriko-archeologičeskoe značenie. »Izvestija Akademii Nauk SSSR« Otdelenie obščestvennych nauk, 4. 1937

A. N. Bernštam: Kenkol'skij mogil'nik. Arch. ėkspedicii gos. Ėrmitaza, II. Leningrad 1940a

A. N. Bernštam: Iz istorii gunnov Iv. do n. ė. Sovetskoe vostokovedenie I, S. 51–77. Moskau-Leningrad 1940b

A. N. Bernštam: Očerk istorii gunnov. Leningrad 1951

G. I. Borovka: Kul'turno-istoričeskoe značenie archeologičeskich nachodok ėkspedicii. Kratkie otčety ėkspedicii po issledovaniju Severnoj Mongolii v svjazi s Mongolo-tibetskoj ėkspedicii P. K. Kozlova. AN SSSR. Leningrad 1925

G. Boroffka (= Borovka): Die Funde der Expedition Kozlow in der Mongolei 1924/25. Archäol. Anzeiger, S. 341–368. 1926

G. I. Borovka: Archeologičeskie obsledovanie srednego tečenija r. Toly. Severnaja Mongolija II, S. 43–88. Leningrad 1927

P. P. Chorošich: Olennyj kamen' iz Zabajkal'ja. SA 3, S. 291–292. 1962

A. V. Davydova: Ivolginskoe gorodišče. SA XXV, S. 261–300. 1956

A. V. Davydova i V. P. Šilov: K voprosu o zemledelii u gunnov. VDI 2, S. 193–201. 1953

C. Dorožsurėn: Raskopki mogil chunnu v gorach Noin-ula na reke Chuni-gol (1954–1957gg.). Mongol'skij archeologičeskij sbornik, S. 36–44. Moskau 1962

I. I. Gochman: Materialy po antropologii drevnego naselenija Nizov'ev Selengi. KSIE XX, S. 59 bis 67. 1954

I. I. Gochman: Antropologičeskie materialy iz plitočnych mogil Zabajkal'ja. Sb. MAE, XVIII, S. 428–443. 1958

M. P. Grjaznov: Kinžal s ozera Koto-Kėl'. Izd. Naučn. o-va im. Banzarova. Verchneudinsk 1929

L. N. Gumilev: Chunnu. Moskau 1960

E. Lubo-Lesničenko: Simboličeskoe značenie ornamenta Noin-Ulinskoj tkani MR 1330. SGE XII, S. 50–52. 1957

E. Lubo-Lesničenko: Drevnie Kitajskie šelkovye tkani i vyšivki V v. do n. ė. – III v. n. ė. v sobranii Gosudarstvennogo Ėrmitaža – Katalog. Leningrad 1961

A. P. Okladnikov: Novaja »skifskaja« nachodka na verchnej Lene. SA VIII, S. 285–288. 1946

A. P. Okladnikov: Archeologičeskie issledovanija v Burjat-Mongol'skoj ASSR. KSIIMK XXVII, S. 7–11. 1949

A. P. Okladnikov: Novye dannye po drevnejšej istorii Vnutrennej Mongolii. VDI 4, S. 162–174. 1951a

A. P. Okladnikov: Archeologičeskie issledovanie v Burjat-Mongolii. IAN SIF VIII, 5, S. 440–450. Moskau 1951b

A. P. Okladnikov: Raboty Burjat-mongol'skoj archeologičeskoj ėkspedicii v 1947–1950 godach. KSIIMK XLV, S. 40–47. 1952

A. P. Okladnikov: Jakutija do prisoedinenija k russkomu gosudarstvu. Istorija Jakutskoj ASSR, Moskau-Leningrad 1955

S. I. *Rudenko:* Kul'tura chunnov i Noinulinskie kurgany. Moskau-Leningrad 1962

A. *Salmony:* The Small Finds of Noin-Ula. Parnassus, VIII, 2. 1936

N. *Sêr-Odžav:* Archeologičeskie issledovanija v Mongol'skoj Narodnoj Respublike. Mongol'skij archeologičeskij sbornik S. 5–10. Moskva 1962

G. P. *Sosnovskij:* Nižne-Ivolinskoe gorodišče. PIDO, 7–8, S. 150–156. 1934

G. P. *Sosnovskij:* Dêrestujskij mogil'nik. PIDO, 1–2, S. 168–176. 1935

G. P. *Sosnovskij:* Rannie kočevniki Zabajkal'ja. KSIIMK VIII, S. 36–42. 1940

G. P. *Sosnovskij:* Plitočnye mogily Zabajkal'ja. Tr. Otdela istorii pervobytnoj kul'tury Gos. Êrmitaža, I, S. 273–309. Leningrad 1941

G. P. *Sosnovskij:* Raskopki Il'movoj padi. SA VIII, S. 51–67. 1946

G. P. *Sosnovskij:* O poselenii gunnskoj êpochi v doline r. Čikoja (Zabajkal'e). KSIIMK XIV, S. 35–39. 1947

J. *Tal'ko-Gryncevič:* Materialy k paleoêtnologii Zabajkal'ja. Soobščeno v obščem sobranii Troickosavsko-Kjachtinskogo Otdelenija Priamurskago Otdela RGO 19 dekabrja 1896g. Tomsk 1897

J. *Tal'ko-Gryncevič:* Sudžinskoe doistoričeskie kladbišče v Il'movoj padi. Trudy Troickosavsko-Kjachtinskogo otdelenija RGO, 1/2. 1899

J. *Tal'ko-Gryncevič:* Materialy po paleoêtnologii Zabajkal'ja. Trudy Troickosavsko-Kjachtinskogo otd. RGO, IV/3. 1900

S. A. *Teplouchov:* Raskopki kurganov v gorach Noin-Ula. Kratkie otčety êkspedicii po issledovaniju Severnoj Mongolii v svjazi s Mongolo-tibetskoj êkspediciej P. P. Kozlova. Moskau 1925

C. *Trever:* Excavations in Northern Mongolia (1924–1925). Leningrad 1932

K. V. *Trever:* Nachodki iz raskopok v Mongolii 1924–1925gg. SGAIMK, 9–10. 1931

S. *Umehara:* Studies of Noin-Ula Finds in North Mongolia. The Toyo Bunko Publication Series A, No. 27. Tokyo 1960 (japanisch mit engl. Resumé)

K. V. *Vjatkina:* Archeologičeskie pamjatniki v Mongol'skoj Narodnoj Respublike. SE 1, S. 93–106. 1959

M. V. *Vorob'ev:* Drevnjaja Koreja. Moskau 1961

A. A. *Voskresenskij i N. P. Tichonov:* Technologičeskoe izučenie materialov kurgannych pogrebennij Noin-Uly. IGAIMK XI, 7–9. 1932

J. *Werner:* Ein hunnisches Lager der Han-Zeit in Transbaikalien. Sinica, S. 193–196. 1939

J. *Werner:* Beiträge zur Archäologie des Attila-Reiches. Abhandlungen der Bayerischen Akademie der Wissenschaften. Phil.-Hist. Klasse, N. F., H. 38A, 38B. München 1956

X. DIE ORDOSBRONZEN

J. G. *Andersson:* Der Weg über die Steppen. BMFEA 1. Stockholm 1929

J. G. *Andersson:* Hunting Magic in the Animal Style. BMFEA 4, S. 221–317. Stockholm 1932

J. G. *Andersson:* Selected Ordos Bronzes. BMFEA 5, S. 143ff. Stockholm 1933

J. G. *Andersson:* Researches into the Prehistory of the Chinese. BMFEA 15. Stockholm 1943

T. J. *Arne:* Die Funde von L'uan-ping und Hsüanhua. BMFEA 5, S. 155–175. Stockholm 1933

D. *Carter:* Four Thousand Years of China's Art. New York 1951

Kwang-chih Chang: The Archaeology of Ancient China. New Haven and London 1963

Tê-k'un Chêng: Archaeology in China, Bd. III: Chou China. Cambridge 1963

N. *Egami und S. Mizuno:* Inner Mongolia and the Region of the Great Wall. Archaeologia Orientalis, Ser. B., 1. 1935

V. *Griessmaier:* Sammlung Baron Eduard von der Heydt. Wr. Beiträge. 1936

V. *Griessmaier:* Entwicklungsfragen der Ordos-Kunst. Artibus Asiae, VII, 1–4, S. 122–257. Leipzig 1937

O. *Janse:* Le style du Houai et ses affinités. Revue des Arts Asiatiques, VIII, 3.

O. *Janse:* Notes sur quelques épées anciennes trouvées en Chine. BMFEA 2, S. 67–176. Stockholm 1930

O. *Janse:* Tubes et boutons cruciformes trouvés en Eurasie. BMFEA 4, S. 187–209. Stockhom 1932

L. *Jisl:* Několik nových »ordoských« bronzů a jejich postavení v rámci eurasijského zvěrného styln. Acta Universitatis Carolinae, Philosophica et Historica No. 3/59. Filipúv Sbornik, S. 195–206. Prag 1962

B. *Karlgren:* Ordos und Huai. BMFEA 9. Stockholm 1937

B. *Karlgren:* Huai and Han. BMFEA 13, S. 1–116, 1941

B. *Karlgren:* Some Weapons and Tools of the Yin Dynasty. BMFEA 17, S. 101–144. Stockholm 1945

B. *Karlgren:* Some Bronzes in the Museum of Far Eastern Antiquities Postscript. BMFEA 21, S. 1–22 und 22–25. Stockholm 1949

S. V. *Kiselev:* Mongolija v drevnosti. IAN SIF, IV, 4, S. 355–372. 1947

S. V. *Kiselev:* Neolit i bronzovy vek Kitaja. SA 4, S. 244–266. 1960

H. *Kühn:* Chronologie der Sino-Sibirischen Bronzen. Jahrbuch für prähistorische Kunst XII, S. 162 bis 165. 1937

M. *Loehr:* Weapons and Tools from Anyang and Siberian Analogies. American Journal of Archaeology, LIII, 2, S. 126–144. 1949a

M. *Loehr:* The Earliest Chinese Swords and the Akinakes. Oriental Art, I, 3, S. 132–142. 1949b

M. *Loehr:* Ordos Daggers and Knives. First Part: Daggers. Artibus Asiae, XII, 1–2. Ascona 1949

M. *Loehr:* Ordos Daggers and Knives. Second Part: Knives. Artibus Asiae, XIV, 1–2, S. 77–162. Ascona 1951

M. *Loehr:* Zur Ur- und Vorgeschichte Chinas. Saeculum III, 1, S. 15–55. 1952

O. *Maenchen-Helfen:* Die Träger des Tierstils im Osten. Wr. Beiträge, IX, S. 61 ff. Wien 1935

O. *Maenchen-Helfen:* The Yüeh-chih Problem Reexamined. Journal of the American Oriental Society, 65, S. 71–81. New Haven 1945

O. *Maenchen-Helfen* bespricht F. Altheim – Attila und die Hunnen. Baden-Baden 1951, und H. Homeyer – Attila. Der Hunnenkönig von seinen Zeitgenossen dargestellt. Berlin 1951, in: Gnomon, 24, S. 500–504. 1952

O. J. *Maenchen-Helfen:* The Ethnic Name Hun. Studia Serica Bernhard Karlgren Dedicata, S. 223–238. Copenhagen 1959

P. W. *Meister:* Zur Datierung einer Gruppe von Tierstilbronzen der Nach-Han-Zeit. Ostasiatische Zeitschrift NF, 11. Jg., H. 6, S. 264–265. 1935

E. H. *Minns:* Small Bronzes from Northern Asia. The Antiquaries Journal, X, 1, S. 1–21. London 1930

P. *Pelliot:* Quelques réflexions sur l'art »sibérien« et l'art chinois à propos de bronzes de la collection David-Weill. Documents I. Paris 1929

M. *Rostovtzeff:* Inlaid Bronzes of the Han Dynasty in the Collection of C. T. Loo. Paris-Bruxelles 1927

A. *Salmony:* Die alte Kunst Sibiriens und ihre Beziehungen zu China. Sinica VI, 4. Frankfurt am Main 1931

A. *Salmony:* Der waagrechte Stangenabschluß an der nordchinesischen Grenze und in China. Seminarium Kondakovianum, VI, S. 131–136. Prag 1933

A. *Salmony:* Sino-Siberian Art in the Collection of C. T. Loo. Paris 1933

K. V. *Vasil'ev:* Archeologičeskie issledovanija vo Vnutrennej Mongolii. VDI 3, S. 163–170. 1959

J. *Werner:* Zur Stellung der Ordosbronzen. ESA IX, S. 259–269. 1934

XI. TUWA:

RÜCKZUGSRAUM AN DER WANDERSTRASSE

V. P. *Alekseev:* Očerk paleoantropologii Tuvinskoj avtonomnoj oblasti. TIE XXXIII, S. 374–393. 1956

V. P. *Alekseev:* Paleoantropologija Altae-Sajanskogo nagor'ja èpochi neolita i bronzy. TIE LXXI, S. 107–206. 1961

N. L. *Členova:* Mesto kul'tury Tuvy skifskogo vremeni v rjadu drugich »skifskich« stepnych kul'tur Evrazii. Uč. zap. Tuvinskogo naučno-issledovatel'skogo instituta jazyka istorii i literatury, IX. Kyzyl 1961

N. L. *Členova:* Ob olennych kamnjach Mongolii i Sibiri. Mongol'skij archeologičeskij sbornik, S. 27–35. Moskau 1962

G. F. *Debec:* K paleoantropologii Tuvy. KSIE X, S. 97–111. 1950

A. D. *Grač:* Archeologičeskie issledovanija v zapadnoj Tuve. KSIE XXXIII, S. 19–33. 1955

A. D. *Grač:* Petroglify Tuvy I. SbMAE XVII, S. 385–428. 1957

A. D. *Grač:* Petroglify Tuvy II. SbMAE XVIII, S. 339–384. 1958

L. P. *Kyzlasov:* Ètapy drevnej istorii Tuvy. Vestnik Moskovskogo Universiteta, Istoriko-filologičeskaja serija 4, S. 71–99. 1958

L. P. *Kyzlasov:* Trudy Tuvinskoj kompleksnoj archeologo-ètnografičeskoj èkspedicii In-ta ètnografii AN SSSR, I. Materialy po archeologii i ètnografii zapadnoj Tuvy. Otv. red. L. P. Potapov. Moskau-Leningrad 1960. SÈ 4, S. 225–230. 1961

R. L. *Potapov:* O nekotorych naskal'nych izobraženijach životnych v gorach Tannu-Ola i Mongun-Tajgi. SbMAE XVIII, S. 385–389. 1958

XII. DIE SAKEN IN MITTELASIEN

E. I. *Ageeva i G. I. Pacevič:* Otčet o rabotach Južno-Kazachstanskoj archeologičeskoj èkspedicii 1953 goda. TIIAE, I, S. 33–60. Alma-Ata 1956

K. A. *Akišev:* Otčet o rabote Ilijskoj archeologičeskoj èkspedicii 1954g. TIIAE, I, 1, S. 5–32. Alma-Ata 1956

K. A. *Akišev:* Saki Semireč'ja. TIIAE, 7, S. 204 bis 214. 1959

K. A. *Akišev:* Šestoj Beššatyrskij kurgan. KSIA AN SSSR 91, S. 61–65. Moskau 1962

G. G. Babanskaja: Berkkarinskij mogil'nik. TIIAE
1, S. 189–206. 1956

A. N. Bernštam: Berkkarinskaja prjažka. KSIIMK
XVII, S. 9–11. Moskau-Leningrad 1947

A. N. Bernštam: Osnovnye étapy istorii kul'tury
Semirečja i Tjan'-šanja. SA XI, S. 336–384.
1949

A. N. Bernštam: Istoriko-archeologičeskie očerki
Central'nogo Tjan'-šanja i Pamiro-Alaja. MIA
26. 1952

A. N. Bernštam: Saki Pamira. VDI 1, S. 121–134.
1956

O. M. Dalton: The Treasure of the Oxus (with
Other Examples of Early Oriental Metal-
Work). Second Edition. British Museum
MCMXXVI. London 1926

M. A. Dandamaev: Pochod Darija protiv skifskogo
plemeni Tigrachauda. Kratkie soobščenija
Instituta narodov Azii, 61, S. 175–187. Moskau
1963

N. G. Gorbunova: Kul'tura Fergany v épochu ran-
nego železa. Archeologičeskij Sbornik 5, S. 91
bis 122. Leningrad 1962

K. Jettmar: Archäologische Spuren von Indoger-
manen in Zentralasien. Paideuma, V, 5, S. 236
bis 254. 1952

J. Junge: Saka-Studien. Leipzig 1939

A. K. Kibirov: Archeologičeskie raboty v Central'-
nom Tjan'-Šane 1953–55. Trudy Kirgizskoj
archeologo-étnografičeskom ékspedicii, II,
S. 63–138. Moskau 1959

G. A. Kušaev: Dva tipa kurgannych pogrebennij
pravoberež'ja reki Ili. TIIAE, 1, S. 207–220.
1956

G. A. Kušaev: Rannekočevničeskie kurgany v rajone
gorodišča Baba-Ata. TIIAE, 7, S. 242–247. 1959

E. E. Kuz'mina: Bronzovyj šlem iz Samarkanda.
SA 4, S. 120–126. 1958

B. A. Litvinskij: Saki, kotorye za Sogdom. Trudy
Akademii Nauk Tadžikskoj SSR, Bd. CXX,
S. 91–96. 1960

B. A. Litvinskij: Dachaninskij mogil'nik épochi
bronzy v Zapadnoj Fergane. KSIIMK 80,
S. 47–52. 1960

B. A. Litvinskij: Archaeological Discoveries in the
Eastern Pamirs and the Problem of Contacts
between Central Asia, China and India in
Antiquity. XXV. International Congress of
Orientalists. Papers presented by the USSR
Delegation. Moskau 1960

O. Maenchen-Helfen: A Chinese Bronze with Cen-
tral-Asiatic Motives. BMFEA 30, S. 167–175.
1958

A. G. Maksimova: Predmety épochi rannich kočevnikov v Central'nom muzee Kazachstana (g.
Alta-Ata). TIIAE, I, S. 253–261. Alma-Ata
1956

A. G. Maksimova: Naskal'nye izobraženija uščel'ja
Tamgaly. Vestnik AN Kaz. SSR, 9. Alma-Ata
1958

A. G. Maksimova: Kurgany sakskogo vremeni mogil'-
nika Džuvantove. KSIIMK 80, S. 60–64.
1960

A. M. Mandel'štam: Mogil'nik Aruk-Tau v Biškend-
skoi doline (Južnyi Tadžikistan). KSIIMK 76,
S. 73–82. 1959

A. M. Mandel'štam: K archeologii Karategina.
KSIIMK 80, S. 76–79. 1960

G. S. Martynov: Issykskaja nachodka. KSIIMK 59,
S. 150–156. 1955

V. M. Masson: Pamjatniki kul'tury archaičeskogo
Dachistana i Jugo-Zapadnoj Turkmenii. Trudy
Južno-Turkmenistanskoj archeologičeskoj kompleksnoj ékspedicii, VII, S. 385–457. Aščhabad
1956

V. M. Masson: Drevnezemledel'českaja kul'tura
Margiany. MIA 73. 1959

V. A. Nil'sen: Kyzyl-Kyr. Istorija material'noj kul'-
tury Uzbekistana, 1, S. 60–78. Taškent 1959

O. V. Obel'čenko: Ljavandakskij mogil'nik. Istorija
material'noj kul'tury Uzbekistana, 2, S. 97–176.
Taškent 1961

G. A. Pugačenkova: Grifon v antičnom i sredneveko-
vom iskusstve Srednei Azii. SA 2, S. 70–84. 1959

H. Schoppa: Die Darstellungen der Perser in der
griechischen Kunst bis zum Beginn des Hellenismus. Heidelberg 1933

B. J. Staviskij: Drevnejšie bronzovye izdelija Čača
v Gosudarstvennom Érmitaže. KSIIMK 60,
S. 125–128. 1955

A. Strelkov: Bol'šoj semirečenskij altar'. Sb. S. F.
Ol'denburg. Leningrad 1935

A. M. Tallgren: Turkestan, Bronzezeit. Ebert, Reallexikon XIII, S. 485–486. 1929

S. P. Tolstov: Po drevnim del'tam Oksa i Jaksarta.
Moskau 1962

S, P. Tolstov: Rezul'taty istoriko-archeologičeskich
issledovanij 1961 g. na drevnich ruslach Syr-
Dar'i. SA 4, S. 124–148. 1962

S. P. Tolstov i M. G. Vorob'eva i J. A. Rapoport:
Raboty Chorezmskoj archeologo-étnografičes-
koj ékspedicii v 1957 g. Materialy Chorezmskoj
ékspedicii, 4, S. 3–62. Moskau 1960

M. V. Voevodskij i M. P. Grjaznov: Usun'skie mogil'-
niki na territorii Kirgizkoj SSR (K istorij
usunej). VDI 3, S. 162 ff. 1938

XIII. DAS SIBIRISCHE GOLD,
DIE STEPPEN NORD- UND OSTKAZACHSTANS

E. I. Ageeva i A. G. Maksimova: Otčet Pavlodarskoj ėkspedicii 1955 goda. TIIAE, 7, S. 32–58. 1959

K. A. Akišev: Pamjatniki stariny Severnogo Kazachstana. TIIAE, 7, S. 3–31. 1959

S. S. Černikov: Raboty Vostočno-Kazachstanskoj archeologičeskoj ėkspedicii v 1956 godu. KSIIMK 73, S. 99–106. 1959

S. S. Černikov: K izučenniju drevnej istorii Vostočnogo Kazachstana. KSIIMK 69, S. 12–21. 1957

N. Fettich: Zur Chronologie der sibirischen Goldfunde der Eremitage. Acta Archaeologica (Academiae Scientiarum Hungaricae) T. II, S. 251–268. Budapest 1952

M. P. Grjaznov: Zolotaja bljacha s izobraženiem borby životnych. Sokroviša Ėrmitaža, S. 71–74. Moskau-Leningrad 1949

M. P. Grjaznov: Pamjatniki karasukskogo ėtapa v central'nom Kazachstane. SA XVI, S. 129–162. 1952

M. P. Grjaznov: Severnyj Kazachstan v ėpochu rannich kočevnikov. KSIIMK 61, S. 8–16. 1956

C. Hentze: Beiträge zu den Problemen des eurasischen Tierstils. Ostasiatische Zeitschrift N. F. 6/1, 16. Jg., S. 150–169. 1930

M. K. Kadyrbaev: Pamjatniki rannich kočevnikov Central'nogo Kazachstana. TIIAE, 7, S. 162 bis 203. Alma-Ata 1959

L. P. Kyzlasov i A. Ch. Margulan: Plitočnye ogrady mogil'nika Begazy. KSIIMK XXXII, S. 126 bis 136. Moskau-Leningrad 1950

P. W. Meister: Zur Technik der sibirischen Goldarbeiten. Pantheon XXX, S. 225–227. 1942

A. Salmony: Sarmatian Gold Collected by Peter the Great. I. Introduction, II. The Group with All-over Cloisonné. Gazette des Beaux Arts, Ser. VI, Bd. XXXI, 1, S. 5–14. New York 1947

A. Salmony: Sarmatian Gold Collected by Peter the Great. III. The Early Group with Winged Circle Sockets. Gazette des Beaux Arts, Ser. VI, Bd. XXXIII, 1, S. 321–326. New York und Paris 1948

A. Salmony: Sarmatian Gold Collected by Peter the Great. IV. The Early Sarmatian Group with Embossed Relief. Gazette des Beaux Arts, Ser. VI, Bd. XXXV, 1, S. 5–10. New York und Paris 1949

A. Salmony: Sarmatian Gold Collected by Peter the Great. V. The Middle Sarmatian Group; Embossed Relief and Isolated Inlay Cells. Gazette des Beaux Arts, Ser. VI, Bd. XL, 2, S. 85–92. New York und Paris 1952

A. Spicyn: K voprosu o chronologii zolotych sibirskich bljach s izobraženiem životnych. Zap. Russk. Arch. obščestv. XII. S. Peterburg 1901

A. Spicyn: Sibirskaja kollekcija Kunstkamery. Zap. otd. russkoj i slavjanskoj arch. Russk. Arch. obščestva 8, I, S. 227ff. 1906

A. M. Tallgren: »Portable Altars«, ESA XI, S. 47 bis 68. 1937

XIV. NACHSPIEL

H. Appelgren-Kivalo: Die Grundzüge des permisch-skythischen Ornamentstiles. SMYA, XXVI, 1. 1912

H. Appelgren-Kivalo: Vogelkopf und Hirsch als Ornamentmotive in der Vorzeit Sibiriens. Finnisch-Ugrische Forschungen XII, S. 294ff. 1912

V. N. Černecov bespricht S. I. Rudenko – Kul'tura naselenija Gornogo Altaja v skifskoe vremja. Moskau-Leningrad 1953. SE 2, S. 183–187. 1954

V. N. Černecov: Nižnee Priob'e v I tysjačeletii našej ėry. MIA 58, S. 136–245. 1957

N. Fettich: Das Kunstgewerbe der Avarenzeit in Ungarn. Archeologia Hungarica I. Budapest 1926

N. Fettich: Bronzeguß und Nomadenkunst (mit einem Anhang v. L. Bartucz). Skythika 2. Prag 1929

N. Fettich: Der Schildbuckel von Harpály. Acta Archaeologica, I, S. 221–263. Kopenhagen 1930

N. Fettich: Archäologische Studien zur Geschichte der späthunnischen Metallkunst. Archaeologia Hungarica XXXI. Budapest 1951

V. A. Gorodcov: Podčeremskij klad. SA II, S. 113 bis 150. 1937

B. Laufer: The Decorative Art of the Amur Tribes. Memoirs of the American Museum of Natural History, VII. 1902

N. Mavrodinov: Le trésor protobulgare de Nagy-szentmikloś.

I. N. Roerich: The Animal Style among the Nomad Tribes of Northern Tibet. Seminarium Kondakovianum. Prag 1930

S. I. Rudenko i A. N. Gluchov: Mogil'nik Kudyrge na Altae. Materialy po ėtnografii, III, 2, S. 37–52. Leningrad 1927

B. Salin: Die altgermanische Thierornamentik. Stockholm 1904

C. Schuster: A Survival of the Eurasiatic Animal Style in Modern Alaskan Eskimo Art. Tax: Indian Tribes of Aboriginal America Vol III. Proceedings of the 29th Congress of Americanists. Chicago 1952

H. *Shetelig:* The Origin of the Scandinavian Style of Ornament during the Migration Period. Archaeologia 76. 1927

A. V. *Šmidt:* K voprosu o proischoždenii Permskogo sverinogo stilja. SbMAE, VI, S. 125–164. Leningrad 1927

A. V. *Šmidt (= A. V. Schmidt):* Kačka. Beiträge zur Erforschung der Kulturen Ostrußlands in der Zeit der Völkerwanderung (III.–V.Jh.). ESA I, S. 18–50. Helsinki 1927

A. V. *Šmidt:* Einige Motive der prähistorischen Kunst Transuraliens. Artibus Asiae, III, S.224ff. 1928/9

A. V. *Šmidt:* Oklade iz Podčerema. SGAIMK 11/12, S. 51–55. 1931

A. P. *Smirnov:* Mogil'niki p'janoborskoj kul'tury. KSIIMK XXV, S. 22–32. 1949

A. P. *Smirnov:* Očerki drevnej i srednevekovoj istorii narodov srednego Povolž'ja i Prikam'ja. MIA 28. Moskau 1952

A. A. *Spicyn:* Drevnosti Kamskoj Čudi po kollekcii Teplouchovych. MAR 26. S. Petersburg 1902

A. A. *Spicyn:* Šamanskija izobraženija. Zapiski otd. Russk. i Slavjansk. arch. I. Russk. Arch. Obšč. VIII, 1, S. 29–145, S. Petersburg. 1906

A. M. *Tallgren:* Collection Zaoussailov. Bd. I Helsingfors 1916. Bd. II Helsingfors 1918

A. M. *Tallgren:* Permian Studies. The Genealogy of the Permian Idols. ESA III, S. 63–92. 1928

A. M. *Tallgren:* Zur westsibirischen Gruppe der »schamanistischen« Figuren. Seminarium Kondakovianum, IV. Prag 1931

N. *Toll:* Bronze Plaque from the Collection of Count E. Zichy. ESA IX, S. 270–276. Helsinki 1934

XV. DIE ENTSTEHUNG VON REITERKRIEGERTUM UND TIERSTIL

V. I. *Abaev:* Osetinskij jazyk i fol'klor, 1. Moskau-Leningrad 1949

A. *Alföldi:* Die geistigen Grundlagen des hochasiatischen Tierstiles. Forschungen und Fortschritte, 7. Jg., Nr. 20, S. 278–279. Berlin 1931

A. *Alföldi:* Die theriomorphe Weltbetrachtung in den hochasiatischen Kulturen. Archäologischer Anzeiger 1931, 1/2, S. 394–418 (Sitzungsbericht). 1931

A. *Alföldi:* Königsweihe und Männerbund bei den Achämeniden. Schweiz. Archiv f. Volkskunde, 47, S. 11–16. 1951

I. K. *Anderson:* Ancient Greek Horsemanship. Berkeley und Los Angeles 1961

R. D. *Barnett:* The Treasure of Ziwiye. Iraq XVIII, S. 111–116. 1956

R. *Bleichsteiner:* Zum eurasiatischen Tierstil. Berichte des Asien-Arbeitskreises, 2, S. 9–64. 1939

R. *Bleichsteiner:* Zeremonielle Trinksitten und Raumordnung bei turko-mongolischen Nomaden. Archiv für Völkerkunde, VI/VII, S. 181 bis 208. Wien 1952

S. S. *Černikov:* O termine »rannie kočevniki«. KSIIMK 80, S. 17–21. 1960

M. V. *Christian:* Vorderasiatische Vorläufer des eurasiatischen Tierstils. Wr. Beiträge, XI. 1937

N. L. *Členova:* Skifskij olen'. MIA 115, S. 167–205. 1962

M. v. *Dewall:* Der Gräberverband von Wu-kuants'un/Anyang Oriens Extremus, 7. Jg., H. 2, S. 129–151. 1960

M. v. *Dewall:* Pferd und Wagen als Kulturgut im frühen China. Unveröffentl. Mss. Hamburg 1961

D. N. *Éding:* Reznaja skul'ptura Urala. Trudy GIM X. Moskau 1940

M. *Eliade:* Les Daces et les loups. Numen, VI, 1, S. 15–31. 1959

R. *Ghirshman:* Fouilles de Sialk près de Kashan 1933, 1934, 1937, II. Musée du Louvre – Département des antiquités orientales, série archéologique, V. Paris 1939a

R. *Ghirshman:* Recherches préhistoriques en Afghanistan: Fouilles de Nad-i-Ali dans le Seistan Afghan. Revue des Arts Asiatiques, XIII, 1, S. 10–22. Paris 1939b

R. *Ghirshman:* Notes iraniennes IV – Le trésor de Sakkez, les origines de l'art mède et les bronzes du Luristan. Artibus Asiae, XIII, 3, S. 181–206. Ascona 1950a

R. *Ghirshman:* Masjid-i-Solaiman, Résidencedes premiers Achéménides. Syria XXVII, 3–4, S. 205 bis 220. Paris 1950b

R. *Ghirshman:* Village Perse-achéménide. Mémoires de la Mission Archéologique en Iran, XXXVI, Mission de Susiane. Paris 1954

R. *Ghirshman:* Iran – from the Earliest Times to the Islamic Conquest. Penguin Book. Harmondsworth 1954

R. *Ghirshman:* Notes iraniennes VII – A propos de Persépolis. Artibus Asiae, XX, 4, S. 265–278. Ascona 1957

M. *Gimbutas:* Borodino, Seima and their Contemporaries. Proceedings of the Prehistoric Society for 1956, XXII, No. 9

M. *Gimbutas:* The Treasure of Michalkov. Archaeology, 12, 2, S. 84–87. 1959

A. *Godard:* Le trésor de Ziwiyè. Académie des Inscriptions et des Belles-Lettres. Comptes rendues, S. 168–172. Paris 1949

A. *Godard:* Le trésor de Ziwiyè (Kurdistan). Publications du Service archéologique de l'Iran. Haarlem 1950

A. *Godard:* A propos du trésor de Ziwiyè. Artibus Asiae, XIV, 3, S. 240–245. Ascona 1951

A. *Godard:* L'art de Iran. Paris 1962

V. A. *Gorodcov:* K voprosu o kimmerijskoj kul'ture. Trudy sekcii archeologii RANION II, S. 54 bis 59. 1928

M. P. *Grjaznov:* Nekotorye voprosy istorii složenija i razvitija rannich kočevych obščestv Kazachstana i Južnoj Sibiri. KSIE XXIV, S. 19–29. 1955

M. P. *Grjaznov:* Ètapy razvitija chozjajstva skotovodčeskich plemen Kazachstana i Južnoj Sibiri v èpochu bronzy. KSIE XXVI, S. 21–28. 1957

F. *Hančar:* Roß und Reiter im urgeschichtlichen Kaukasus. IPEK Jg. 1935, S. 49–65. Berlin u. Leipzig 1936

F. *Hančar:* Urgeschichtliche Erkenntnisse zum eurasiatischen Viehzüchternomadentum. Palaeologia, IV, 3/4, S. 264–273. Osaka 1955

F. *Hančar:* Die Kunst der Nomaden. Kleine Weltkunstgeschichte. Stuttgart 1955

F. *Hančar:* Das Pferd in prähistorischer und früher historischer Zeit. Wr. Beiträge, XI. Wien-München 1955

J. *Harmatta:* The Dissolution of the Hun Empire, I. Acta Archaeologica II, S. 277–306. Budapest 1952

K. *Jettmar:* Entstehung des Reiterkriegertums. Handbuch der Weltgeschichte, hg. v. A. Randa, I, Sp. 341–348. Olten 1953

K. *Jettmar:* Zur Wanderungsgeschichte der Iranier. Die Wiener Schule der Völkerkunde, Festschrift zum 25jährigen Bestand, S. 327–348. Wien 1956

K. *Jettmar:* Urgeschichte Innerasiens (Asiatischer Steppengürtel und Sibirien). Abriß der Weltgeschichte – Abriß der Vorgeschichte, S. 150 bis 161. München 1957a

K. *Jettmar* bespricht F. Hančar – Das Pferd in prähistorischer und früher historischer Zeit. Wr. Beiträge, XI, 1955. Central Asiatic Journal III, 2, S. 155–160. Den Haag-Wiesbaden 1957b

H. I. *Kantor:* Oriental Institute Museum Notes No. 11: A Fragment of a Gold Appliqué from Ziviye and Some Remarks on the Artistic Traditions of Armenia and Iran during the Early First Millennium B. C. Journal of Near Eastern Studies XIX, 1, S. 1–14. 1960

S. V. *Kiselev:* Archeologičeskaja poezdka v Mongoliju. KSIIMK XXI, S. 35–38. 1947

S. V. *Kiselev:* Neolit i bronzovyj vek Kitaja. SA 4, S. 244–266. 1960

F. W. *König:* Der falsche Bardija. Dareios der Große und die Lügenkönige. Klotho 4. Wien 1938

F. W. *König:* Die Götterwelt Armeniens zur Zeit der Chalder-Dynastie (9.–7. Jh. v. Chr.). Archiv für Völkerkunde VIII, S. 142–171. Wien 1953

F. W. *König:* Gesellschaftliche Verhältnisse Armeniens zur Zeit der Chalder-Dynastie (9.–7. Jh. v. Chr.). Archiv für Völkerkunde VIII, S. 21 bis 65. Wien 1954

M. N. *Komarova:* Otnosižel'naja chronologija pamjatnikov andronovskoj kul'tury. Archeologičeskij sbornik 5, S. 50–75. Leningrad 1962

E. I. *Krupnov:* Pervye itogi izučenija Vostočnogo Predkavkaza. SA 2, S. 154–173. 1957

E. I. *Krupnov:* Kimmerijcy na Severnom Kavkaze. MIA 68, S. 176–195. 1958

F. *Kussmaul:* Frühe Nomadenkulturen in Innerasien. Tribus, S. 305–360. Stuttgart 1952 und 1953

V. E. *Laričev:* Broncovyj vek Severo-vostočnogo Kitaja. SA 1, S. 3–25. 1961

B. *Laufer:* The Bird-Chariot in China and Europe. Boas Anniversary Volume, S. 410ff. New York 1906

M. *Loehr:* The Stag Image in Scythia and the Far East. Archives of the Chinese Art Society of America IX. 1955

O. *Maenchen-Helfen:* Nachruf für Sir Ellis Hovell Minns, 1874–1953. Man XIII, Article 264. London 1953

J. *Nestor:* Zu den Pferdegeschirrbronzen aus Stillfried a. d. March, N. Ö. Wiener Prähistorische Zeitschrift XXI, S. 108–130. 1934

A. P. *Okladnikov:* Neolit i bronzovyj vek Pribajkal'ja. Istoriko-archeologičeske issledovanie, I und II. MIA 18. Moskau-Leningrad 1950

A. P. *Okladnikov:* Neolit i bronzovyj vek Pribajkal'ja, III (Glazkovskoe vremja). MIA 43. Moskau-Leningrad 1955a

A. P. *Okladnikov:* Peščera Džebel – pamjatnik drevnei kul'tury prikaspijskich plemen Turkmenii. Trudy Južno-Turkmenistanskoj archeologičeskoj kompleksnoj ekspedicii, VII, S. 11–219. Aščabad 1956

A. P. *Okladnikov:* Issledovanija pamjatnikov kamennogo veka Tadžikistana. MIA 66, S. 11–71. 1958

B. B. *Piotrovskij:* Karmir-blur. I. Archeologičeske raskopki v Armenii, 1. Erevan 1950

B. B. Piotrovskij: Skifi i drevnij Vostok. SA XIX, S. 141–158. 1954

B. B. Piotrovskij: Iskustvo Urartu VIII–VI vv do n. è. Leningrad 1962

E. Porada: Alt-Iran. Die Kunst in vorislamischer Zeit. Unter Mitarbeit von R. H. Dyson mit Beiträgen von C. K. Wilkinson. Baden-Baden 1962

A. Salmony: An Ivory Carving from Malta (Siberia) and Its Significance. Artibus Asiae, XI, 4, S. 285–288. Ascona 1948

A. A. Ščepinskij: Pogrebenie načala železnogo veka u Simferopolja. KSIA 12, S. 57–65. Kiev 1962

E. F. Schmidt: The Treasury of Persepolis and Other Discoveries in the Homeland of the Achaemenians. Oriental Institute Communications 21. Chicago 1939

K. F. Smirnov: O pogrebenijach s konjami i truposožženijach èpochi bronzy v Nižnem Povolž'e. SA XXVII, S. 209–221. 1957a

K. F. Smirnov: Archeologičeskie dannye o drevnich vsadnikach Povolžko-Ural'skich stepej. SA 1, S. 46–72. 1961

V. V. Struve: Pochod Darija na sakov-massagetov. IAN SIF, 3, S. 231–250. 1946

T. Sulimirski: Les anciens Archeurs à Cheval. Revue Internationale de l'Histoire Militaire, III, 12, S. 447–461. Paris 1952

A. M. Tallgren: La pontide préscythique après l'introduction des métaux. ESA II. Helsinki 1926

A. I. Terenožkin: Srednee Podneprov'e v načale železnogo veka. SA 2, S. 47–63. 1957

A. I. Terenožkin: Bronzovyj psalij s gorodišča Kjuzeli-gyra v Chorezme. KSIE XXX, S. 34–39. 1958

A. I. Terenožkin: Predskifskij period na dneprovskom Pravoberež'e. Kiev 1961

S. P. Tolstov: Raboty Chorezmskoj archeologo-ètnografičeskoj èkspedicii AN SSSR v 1949–1953gg. Trudy Chorezmskoj archeologo-ètnografičeskoj èkspedicii, II, S. 7–258. Moskau 1958

G. Widengren: Stand und Aufgaben der iranischen Religionsgeschichte. Numen 1/1954, S. 16–83 2/1955, S. 47–134.

G. Widengren: Some Remarks on Riding Costume and Articles of Dress among Iranian Peoples in Antiquity. Arctica, Studia Ethnografica Upsaliensia, XI, S. 228–276. Uppsala 1956

J. Wiesner: Eurasische Kunst in Steppenraum und Waldgebiet. Illustrierte Welt-Kunstgeschichte, hg. von Eugen Th. Rimli/Karl Fischer. Zürich etc. 1959

St. Wikander: Der Arische Männerbund. Lund 1938

H. v. Wissmann: Ursprungsherde und Ausbreitungswege von Pflanzen- und Tierzucht und ihre Abhängigkeit von der Klimageschichte. Erdkunde, Archiv für wissenschaftliche Geographie, XI, 2 und 3, S. 81–94 und 175–193. Bonn 1957

J. A. Zadneprovskij: Drevnezemledel'českaja kul'tura Fergany. MIA 118. 1962

ABKÜRZUNGEN FÜR HÄUFIG ZITIERTE WERKE

BMFEA	Bulletin of the Museum of Far Eastern Antiquities, Stockholm
ESA	Eurasia Septentrionalis Antiqua, Helsinki
GIM	Gosudarstvennyj istoričeskij muzej, Moskva
IAK	Izvestija Archeologičeskoj Komissii, Moskva
IAN SIF	Izvestija Akademii Nauk SSSR, Serija istorii i filosofii, Moskva
IGAIMK	Izvestija Gosudarstvennoj Akademii istorii material'noj kul'tury, Leningrad
IPEK	Jahrbuch für prähistorische und ethnographische Kunst, Berlin
KSIA	Kratkie soobščenija Instituta archeologii, Kiïv
KSIA AN SSSR	Kratkie soobščenija Instituta archeologii Akademii Nauk SSSR, Moskva-Leningrad
KSIE	Kratkie soobščenija Instituta ètnografii, Moskva
KSIIMK	Kratkie soobščenija instituta istorii material'noj kul'tury, Moskva
LGU	Leningradskij gosudarstvennyj universitet
MAGW	Mitteilungen der Anthropologischen Gesellschaft, Wien

MAR	Materialy po archeologii Rossii, Petrograd
MIA	Materialy i issledovanija po archeologii SSSR, Moskva
PIDO	Problemy istorii dokapitalističeskich obščestv, Moskva
RANION	Rossijskaja associacija naučno – issledovatel'skich institutov obščestvennych nauk, Moskva
RGO	Russkoe geografičeskoe obščestvo, Leningrad, Moskva
SA	Sovetskaja archeologija, Moskva
SbMAE	Sbornik muzeja antropologii i ětnografii Akademii Nauk SSSR, Moskva-Leningrad
SE	Sovetskaja ětnografija, Moskva
SGAIMK	Soobščenija Gosudarstvennoj Akademii istorii material'noj kul'tury, Leningrad
SGE	Soobščenija Gosudarstvennogo Ěrmitaža, Leningrad
SMYA	Suomen Muinaismuistoyhdistyksen Aikakauskirja, Helsinki
TIE	Trudy Instituta ětnografii Akademii Nauk SSSR, novaja serija, Moskva
TIIAE	Trudy Instituta istorii, archeologii i ětnografii Akademii Nauk Kazach. SSR, Alma Ata
Umschau	Die Umschau in Wissenschaft und Technik, Frankfurt am Main
VDI	Vestnik drevnej istorii, Moskva
Wr. Beiträge	Wiener Beiträge zur Kunst- und Kulturgeschichte Asiens, Wien

VERZEICHNIS DER FARBTAFELN

VERANTWORTUNG

FARBAUFNAHMEN

KARTEN

TEXTZEICHNUNGEN

Die Zeichnungen wurden angefertigt von H. Prüstel, Mainz

REGISTER

(Die Kursivzahlen beziehen sich auf die Bilder und Bildunterschriften)

INHALTSVERZEICHNIS